marketing

marketing

fourth edition

Paul Baines, Chris Fill,
Sara Rosengren

OXFORD
UNIVERSITY PRESS

Great Clarendon Street, Oxford, OX2 6DP,
United Kingdom

Oxford University Press is a department of the University of Oxford.
It furthers the University's objective of excellence in research, scholarship,
and education by publishing worldwide. Oxford is a registered trade mark of
Oxford University Press in the UK and in certain other countries

© Oxford University Press 2017

The moral rights of the authors have been asserted

Second edition 2011
Third edition 2014

Impression: 1

Published in the United States of America by Oxford University Press
198 Madison Avenue, New York, NY 10016, United States of America

British Library Cataloguing in Publication Data

Data available

Library of Congress Control Number: 2016953952

ISBN 978–0–19–874853–3

Printed in Italy by L.E.G.O. S.p.A.

To Ning, for your constant support and generous love
Paul Baines

To Karen, my loving companion in life
Chris Fill

To Olof, Alma, and Moa—my own dream team
Sara Rosengren

Brief Contents

Detailed Contents

Case Insights

Chapter 1: Aldoraq Water Bottling Plant

Established in 1994 by its founder and owner Khaled A. Almaimani, Aldoraq Water Bottling Plant was one of the first water bottling factories in Madinah, Saudi Arabia. We speak to Abdurahman Almaimani, General Manager, to find out more about how the company seeks to compete with well-known international brands.

Chapter 2: Holdz®

Founded in 2000, Holdz® is an online climbing holds and accessories firm. We speak to its Managing Director, Steve Goodair, to find out more about how the firm meets its customers' needs.

Chapter 3: MESH Planning

How should organizations measure the effectiveness of all touchpoints in interactions with customers, not just marketing communications? We speak to MESH Planning's CEO, Fiona Blades, to find out more.

Chapter 4: Glassolutions Saint-Gobain

How should organizations scan their external environments and what should they do if they identify potential threats and opportunities? We speak to Glassolutions Saint-Gobain's Marketing Director, Michael Butterick, to find out more.

Chapter 5: 3scale

Through its staff and offices in Barcelona and San Francisco, 3scale helps organizations open, manage, and use application programming interfaces (APIs). We speak to Manfred Bortenschlager, API Market Development Director, to find out how the company competes in its marketplace.

Chapter 6: Soberana

When an international beer brand took 10% of the Panamanian beer market, it was time for local brand Soberana to re-evaluate their approach. We talk to the Brand Franchise Manager, Fermin Paus, to find out how they responded.

Chapter 7: Lanson International

Founded in 1760, Champagne Lanson is one of the oldest existing champagne houses in France, making some of the world's finest champagnes. We speak to Paul Beavis, Managing Director, Lanson International, to find out more about how the company looks to further develop its presence in international markets, including the UK.

Chapter 8: Domino's Pizza

How do organizations develop new propositions on a regular basis and remain competitive? We speak to Simon Wallis, Sales and Marketing Director for Domino's Pizza, to find out more.

Chapter 9: Simply Business

Founded in 2005, Simply Business is an online insurance broker. We speak to its Director of Strategy and Pricing, Philip Williams, to find out more about how the company has developed its pricing strategy.

Chapter 10: *The Guardian*

How could an organization realize its objective not only to shift audience perceptions but also to change behaviours? We speak to Agathe Guerrier, Strategy Director at the advertising agency Bartle Bogle Hegarty (BBH), to find out more about the work they undertook for their client *The Guardian*.

Chapter 11: Budweiser Budvar

How should a heritage brand in the Czech Republic design a campaign to reposition itself against competing foreign brands? We speak to Budweiser Budvar's advertising agency account director, Lubos Jahoda, to find out more.

Chapter 12: Spotify

What role does social media play and how should organizations incorporate it into their communication campaigns? We talk to Chug Abramowitz, VP Global Customer Service and Social Media at Spotify, to find out more.

Chapter 13: Aston Martin

The Aston Martin brand, founded in 1913, is synonymous with hand-crafted luxury, peerless beauty, incredible performance, and international motorsport glory. We speak to Simon Sproule, Director of Global Marketing and Communications, to find out how the brand is promoted in China.

Chapter 14: Åhléns

As shopper behaviour is turning increasingly digital, established retailers have to adapt their channel strategies. We talk to Lotta Bjurhult, Business Developer Retail Operations, at Sweden's largest department store chain, Åhléns, to find out what it takes to add an online channel to an existing network of department stores.

Chapter 15: Withers Worldwide

Founded in London in 1896, Withers Worldwide has global revenues of over $200m, 163 partners, employs over 1,000 people, has clients in over 80 countries, and has acted for 42% of the top 100 of the *Sunday Times* Rich List and 20% of the top 100 of the Forbes Rich List. We speak to Laura Boyle, Head of EU Marketing and Business Development, to explore how Withers works to improve the quality of its client relationships.

Chapter 16: Oxford Instruments

How should organizations develop relationships with business partners in international markets? We speak to Lynn Shepherd, Group Director of Communications at Oxford Instruments, to find out more.

Chapter 17: City of London Police

Founded in 1839, the City of London Police (CoLP) police London's 'Square Mile' financial district, with a national responsibility for fraud and economic crime. Because they also police many high profile public events, they also focus on the prevention of terrorism and crime. We speak to Superintendent Helen Isaac to find out how social marketing is used to support law enforcement.

Chapter 18: innocent

How do organizations develop and maintain responsible working practices and attitudes towards the environment and at the same time remain compatible with their customers' values? We speak to Tansy Drake and Dan Germain, Brand Guardian and Head of Brand and Creative at innocent, to find out more.

Author Profiles

Paul Baines is Professor of Political Marketing and Director of the Executive MBA programme at Cranfield University. He is author/co-author of more than a hundred published articles, book chapters, and books on marketing issues. Over the last 20 years, Paul's research has particularly focused on political marketing, public opinion and propaganda. He is a Fellow of the Chartered Institute of Marketing, the Market Research Society (MRS), and the Institute of Directors, and a member of ESOMAR and the Academy of Marketing. Paul's consultancy includes experience working with various government departments on strategic communication research projects as well as many small, medium, and large private enterprises including Glassolutions Saint-Gobain, IBM, 3M, and many more. Paul is Director of Baines Associates Limited.

Chris Fill is Director of Fillassociates, who develop and deliver learning materials related to marketing and corporate communications (see http://www.chrisfill.com). Formerly Principal Lecturer at the University of Portsmouth, Chris now works with a variety of private and not-for-profit organizations including several publishers. He is a Fellow of the Chartered Institute of Marketing, where he was the Senior Examiner responsible for the marketing communications modules and, more recently, the Professional Postgraduate Diploma module Managing Corporate Reputation. In addition to numerous papers published in a range of academic journals, he has written or contributed to over 40 books, including his market leading and internationally recognized textbook, *Marketing Communications,* now in its seventh edition.

Sara Rosengren is Associate Professor of Marketing at Stockholm School of Economics, where she holds the position as Head of Research at the Center for Retailing. She is also a board member of the European Advertising Academy. Sara's research on creative marketing communications has been published in leading academic journals such as the *Journal of Advertising*, the *Journal of Advertising Research*, and the *Journal of Brand Management*. She is especially renowned for her work on advertising equity. Sara is passionate about bridging the gap between marketing academy and practice. She is frequently invited to speak at academic institutions, industry seminars, and company get-togethers, and regularly comments on marketing-related phenomena in the Swedish media.

Acknowledgements

Course textbooks are substantial writing and research projects, resulting from the sweat and toil of many people, not only in design, development, and production, but also in the sales, marketing, and distribution tasks. The production of a textbook is a small component of what is actually an integrated learning and teaching programme including the Online Resource Centre, the book itself, and the various audiovisual components. The fourth edition builds on the work undertaken by many people who have contributed to the development of previous editions, too numerous to re-mention here. Many more people, and some of our previous contributors, kindly also contributed to this fourth edition and its Online Resource Centre. Some of those people are acknowledged below, but there are many others whose contributions should be acknowledged anonymously.

We would like to thank our colleagues and former colleagues at Cranfield University, the Portsmouth Business School, and Stockholm School of Economics for their support and discussions, all of which have in some way made their way into the book in some form. We would like to thank Dr Ning Baines, Birkbeck College, University of London, for contributions to the online resources for the fourth edition.

As with any large textbook project, this work is the result of a co-production between the academic authors and Oxford University Press editors and staff. For the fourth edition, we would like to thank Anthony Hey, our Commissioning Editor, for his support at various stages of the commissioning and development processes. Thanks are also due to Alexandra MacGregor, our Development Editor, and Kate Gilks, our Publishing Editor, particularly for helping us incorporate the comments of the many reviewers, managing the development process so efficiently, and helping to polish the final manuscript. We would like to thank Sal Moore, Production Editor, for her role in shaping the final design of the book and bringing it out on schedule with the help of the designer, Elisabeth Heissler. The media team at Oxford Digital Media, particularly James Tomalin, Sam Cooper, and Matt Greetham, have substantially improved our Online Resource Centre proposition with their great video production work.

Unless our customers, students, and lecturers want to use this book, there's no use in writing and producing it, so we also need to recognize the efforts of the marketing team, Marianne Lightowler, Head of Marketing, and Tristan Jones, Marketing Manager, in developing and implementing the sales and marketing plans for the book.

The original template for the book—going all the way back to the first edition—was developed from six anonymous university lecturer participants of a focus group, who kindly agreed to meet at OUP's offices to discuss what was needed in a new marketing textbook. Our success remains due to the comments they made about what they really wanted in a textbook. For this edition, we have replaced many of the Market Insights, including taking contributions from students, practitioners, and marketing academics.

The authors and publishers would like to thank the following people, for their comments and reviews throughout the process of developing the text and the Online Resource Centre over the last four editions:

David Alcock, *Birmingham City University*, UK
Liz Algar, *University of Essex*, UK
Dr Paolo Antonetti, *Queen Mary University of London*, UK

Malcolm Ash, *Staffordshire University*, UK
Graham Bailey, *University of Chichester*, UK
Dr Nina Belei, *Radboud University*, The Netherlands
Jane Burns, *University College London*, UK
Dr Geraldine Cohen, *Brunel University*, UK
Denise Daniels, *Newcastle University*, UK
Professor John Egan, *Regent's University London*, UK
Dr Fiona Ellis-Chadwick, *Open University Business School*, UK
Dr Margaret Fletcher, *University of Glasgow*, UK
Mike Flynn, *University of Gloucestershire*, UK
Dr Mikael Gidhagen, *Uppsala University*, Sweden
Malcolm Goodman, *Durham University*, UK
Dr Charles Graham, *London South Bank University*, UK
Anne Hampton, *University of Buckingham*, UK
Dr Michael Harker, *University of Strathclyde*, UK
David Harvey, *University of Huddersfield*, UK
Jocelyn Hayes, *University of York*, UK
Mick Hayes, *University of Portsmouth*, UK
Dr Auke Hunneman, *BI Norwegian Business School*, Norway
Dr Elizabeth Jackson, *Newcastle University*, UK
Nigel Jones, *Sheffield Hallam University*, UK
Jaya Kypuram, *University of East London*, UK
Dr Margaret-Anne Lawlor, *Dublin Institute of Technology*, Republic of Ireland
Robert Leonardi, *Södertörns Högskola*, Sweden
Heléne Lundberg, *Mid Sweden University*, Sweden
Dr Nnamdi Madichie, *University of Sharjah*, UAE
Alice Maltby, *University of the West of England*, UK
George Masikunas, *Kingston University*, UK
Dawn McCartie, *Teesside University*, UK
Dr Patrick McCole, *Queen's University Belfast*, Northern Ireland
Tony McGuinness, *Aberystwyth University*, Wales, UK
Richard Meek, *Lancaster University*, UK
Dr Nina Michaelidou, *Loughborough University*, UK
Dr Caroline Miller, *Keele University*, UK
Dr Janice Moorhouse, *University of the West of London*, UK
William Mott, *University of Wolverhampton*, UK
Connie Nolan, *Canterbury Christ Church University*, UK
Pfavai Nyajeka, *University of Hertfordshire*, UK
Wybe Popma, *University of Brighton*, UK
Nicholas Pronger, *Birbeck, University of London*, UK
Professor Andrea Prothero, *University College Dublin*, Republic of Ireland
Chris Richardson, *Aston University*, UK
Neil Richardson, *Leeds Metropolitan University*, UK
Dr Deborah Roberts, *University of Nottingham*, UK
Vicky Roberts, *University of Staffordshire*, UK

Chris Rock, *University of Greenwich*, UK
Irene Roozen, *Katholieke Universiteit Leuven*, Belgium
Professor Michael Saren, *University of Leicester*, UK
Peter Simcock, *Liverpool John Moores University*, UK
Bert Smit, *NHTV Breda University of Applied Sciences*, The Netherlands
Dr Lorna Stevens, *University of Ulster*, UK
Dr Frauke Mattison Thompson, *Kings College London*, UK
Dr Ann Torres, *National University of Ireland Galway*, UK
Professor Paul Trott, *University of Portsmouth*, UK
Dr Prakash Vel, *University of Wollongong*, Dubai, UAE
Peter Waterhouse, *University of Bedfordshire*, UK
Jennie White, *University of Chichester*, UK
Dr Kevan Williams, *University of East Anglia*, UK
Peter Williams, *Leeds Metropolitan University*, UK
Matthew Wood, *University of Brighton*, UK
Professor Helen Woodruffe-Burton, *Northumbria University*, UK

We would particularly like to thank the following lecturers, students, and practitioners who contributed Market Insights to the fourth edition:

Dr Paolo Antonetti, *Queen Mary University of London*, UK
Dr Ning Baines, *Birkbeck, University of London*, UK
Dr Diederich Bakker, *Hanze University of Applied Sciences Groningen*, The Netherlands
Ashwien Bisnajak, formerly *Market Intelligence Manager, Hunkemöller*, The Netherlands (now *Manager Consumer Insights, Coca-Cola Enterprises*, The Netherlands)
Dr Ethel Claffey, *Waterford Institute of Technology*, Republic of Ireland
Dr Jonas Colliander, *Stockholm School of Economics*, Sweden
Dr Denisa Hejlová, *Charles University*, Czech Republic
Will Leach, formerly *VP, BrainJuicer Behavioural Activation Unit*, UK (now *Founder, TriggerPoint*, Dallas, USA)
Dr Frauke Mattison Thompson, *King's College London*, UK
Dr Paul Morrissey, *Waterford Institute of Technology*, Republic of Ireland
Marie O'Dwyer, *Waterford Institute of Technology*, Republic of Ireland
Dr Robert P. Ormrod, *Aarhus University*, Denmark
Anthony Patterson, *University of Liverpool*, UK
Fermin Paus, *Brand Franchise Manager for Soberana*, Panama
Naomi Ramage, then *Music Business Management, Branding, and PR Student at Buckinghamshire New University*, UK
Dr Ian Richardson, *Stockholm University*, Sweden, with support from Maja Magnusson, Cecilia Granström, and Hanna Kretz
Sofie Sagfossen, *PhD Candidate at the Stockholm School of Economics*, Sweden
Leon Savidis, *Business Analyst at Damart*, UK
Dr Sarah Turnbull, *University of Portsmouth*, UK
Karl Wikström, *Planner, TBWA Stockholm*, Sweden

As ever, we have also incorporated a series of practitioner marketing 'problems' within the text. This requires a considerable commitment from practitioners in developing the marketing 'problem' with the authors and filming the 'solution'. We would therefore like to thank the following practitioners who contributed to the new edition for their time, effort, and commitment to this project.

Chug Abramowitz, *VP Global Customer Service and Social Media, Spotify*, Sweden/USA
Abdurahman Almaimani, *General Manager, Aldoraq Water Bottling Plant*, Saudi Arabia
Paul Beavis, *Managing Director, Champagne Lanson UK/International Markets*, UK
Lotta Bjurhult, *Business Developer Retail Operations, Åhléns*, Sweden
Fiona Blades, *CEO MESH Planning*, UK
Manfred Bortenschlager, *API Market Development Director, 3scale.net*, Spain
Laura Boyle, *Head of EU Marketing and Business Development, Withers Worldwide*, UK
Michael Butterick, *Marketing Director, Glassolutions Saint-Gobain*, UK
Tansy Drake, *Brand Guardian, innocent*, UK (now at *Umbrella Collective*)
Steve Goodair, *Managing Director, Holdz®*, UK
Agathe Guerrier, *Strategy Director, Bartle Bogle Hegarty*, UK (now at *Tiny Warrior*)
Lubos Jahoda, *Advertising Agency Account Director, Budweiser Budvar*, Czech Republic
Fermin Paus, *Brand Manager, Soberana*, Panama
Superintendent Helen Isaac, *Community Policing—Uniformed Policing Directorate, City of London Police,* UK
Lynn Shepherd, *Group Director of Communication, Oxford Instruments*, UK (now retired)
Simon Spoule, *Director of Marketing and Communications, Aston Martin Lagonda,* UK
Simon Wallis, *Sales and Marketing Director, Domino's Pizza*, UK
Philip Williams, *Director of Strategy and Pricing, Simply Business*, UK

Many other reviewers who have chosen to remain anonymous contributed considerably to the final proposition. We would like to thank them for taking time out of their busy schedules to comb over various draft chapters of the book. The publishers would be pleased to clear permission with any copyright holders whom we have inadvertently failed, or been unable, to contact.

Preface

Welcome to the fourth edition of *Marketing*. You may be wondering **'Why should I buy this marketing textbook?'** The simple answer is that your marketing lecturers told us you needed a new one! Our first edition was the first truly integrated print and electronic learning package for introductory marketing modules. For this fourth edition, as ever, we've gone further. Before we started writing the fourth edition we consulted marketing lecturers, building on our research for the previous editions, to identify how we might tailor the book and Online Resource Centre to meet your learning needs better. Our aim with the book and the Online Resource Centre is to provide an innovative learning experience, and to pique readers' curiosity to inspire the next generation of marketers to excel in this amazing, exciting, and fast-moving discipline. In our research for the book, we discovered that you needed:

- a greater consideration of how marketing theory links to marketing practice
- the inclusion of a single chapter focused on services marketing
- the inclusion of a single chapter focused on ethics, sustainability, and marketing's impact on society
- an updated digital and social media marketing chapter
- an increased digital presence throughout the book
- the book to contain even more enticing advertising images
- the book to contain even more student-friendly case studies
- the relevant parts of the glossary to be placed at the end of each section rather than at the end of the book
- the book to contain more variety in the format of the Case Insight videos.

As with the first, second, and third editions, the purpose of this package is to bring contemporary marketing perspectives to life for students new to the concept of marketing, and for it to be motivational, creative, applied, and highly relevant to you. We've included brand new international Case Insights including, but not limited to, Aldoraq Water from Saudi Arabia, 3scale.net from Spain, Soberana from Panama, Lanson from France, Spotify from Sweden, and Aston Martin, Withers Worldwide, and the City of London Police from the UK to help illustrate how real-life practitioners tackle marketing problems.

Marketing starts with the fundamentals of marketing from classical marketing perspectives and contrasts these with newer views from the services and societal schools of marketing, helping you to develop your knowledge and understanding of marketing. In the fourth edition, there continues to be extensive coverage of the societal implications of marketing, but importantly we also emphasize how marketing theory operates in practice. This important element means that we have worked harder to relate our Market Insights to the theoretical frameworks, models, and concepts outlined in each chapter. To recognize the importance of the service-dominant logic perspective now so prevalent in marketing, we've re-integrated content on services marketing into one chapter, although there remain throughout the book a large number of Case and Market Insights based on services examples.

On the Online Resource Centre, we also provide you with web-based research activities, abstracts from seminal papers, study guidelines, multiple-choice questions, and a flashcard glossary to help you broaden and reinforce your own learning.

We aim to provide powerful learning insights into marketing theory and practice through a series of 'Insight' features—Case, Market, and Research Insights. *Marketing* is for life, purchased for use on first- and second-year undergraduate marketing programmes, or as reference reading on professional and postgraduate marketing courses, but retained and referred to throughout the course of your marketing or business degree. We sincerely hope you enjoy learning more about marketing! If you have any comments about any of the content in this book, please tweet them to: @DrPaulBaines and add the hashtag, #BainesFill&Rosengren. The more you tweet, the more we learn about what you want from a marketing text.

Who Should Use this Book?

The main audiences for this book are:

- Undergraduate students in universities and colleges of Higher and Further Education, who are taught in English, around the world. The case material and the examples within the text are deliberately global and international in scale so that international students can benefit from the text.

- Postgraduate students on MBA and MSc/MA courses with a strong marketing component will find this text useful for pre-course and background reading, particularly because of the real-life case problems presented at the beginning of each chapter accompanied by audiovisual material presenting the solution available at the Online Resource Centre.

- Professional students studying for marketing qualifications through the Chartered Institute of Marketing, the Direct Marketing Association, and other professional training organisations and trade bodies. The extensive use of examples of marketing practice from around the world make this text relevant for those working in a marketing or commercial environment.

New to this Edition

- Updated with fresh insights from the latest academic and practitioner research.

- Examples of marketing practice looked at through the lens of marketing theories to help you have a deeper understanding of marketing.

- New examples of marketing practice from Europe and around the world.

- Features condensed coverage of services marketing, and coverage of critical perspectives in marketing, all in keeping with market recommendations.

- Downloadable author podcasts summarizing each chapter.

- Additional online learning material, including web links, Internet activities, worksheets, exercises, and further reading, all clearly signposted throughout the textbook.

- Brand new Case Insights and associated audiovisual material featuring well-known companies including Aston Martin, Lanson, and the City of London Police.

How to Use this Textbook

This text seeks to enhance your learning as part of an undergraduate or introductory course in marketing or as pre-reading for your postgraduate or professional course. It can, however, also act as a 'book for life', operating as a reference book for you on matters marketing, particularly during the initial part of your career in marketing and business.

Generally, we only learn what is meaningful to us. Consequently, we have tried to make your learning fun and meaningful by including a multitude of real-life cases. If there is a seminal article associated with a particular concept, try to get hold of it through your university's electronic library resources and read it. Reflect on your own experience if possible around the concepts you are studying. Above all, recognize that you are not on your own in your learning. You have your tutor, your classmates, and us to help you learn more about marketing.

This textbook includes not only explanatory material and examples on the nature of marketing concepts, but also a holistic learning system designed to aid you, as part of your university or professional course, to develop your understanding through reading the text and working with the materials available in the Online Resource Centre. Work through the examples in the text and the review questions; read the seminal articles that have defined a particular sub-discipline in marketing; and use the learning material on the website. This textbook aims to be reader-focused, designed to help you learn marketing for yourself.

As students, we tend to operate either a surface or a deep approach to learning. With the surface approach, we tend to memorize lists of information, whereas with a deep approach, we are actively assimilating, theorizing about, and *understanding* the information. With a surface learning approach, we run into trouble when example problems learnt are presented in different contexts. We may have simply memorized the procedure without understanding the actual problem. Deep approaches to learning are related to better quality educational outcomes and better grades, and the process is more enjoyable. To help you pursue a deep approach to learning, we strongly suggest that you complete the exercises, visit the web links, and conduct the Internet activities and worksheets at the end of each chapter and other activities available at the Online Resource Centre to improve your understanding and your course performance.

Honey and Mumford's Learning Style Questionnaire

Honey and Mumford (1986) developed a learning style questionnaire that divides learners into four categories based on which aspect of Kolb's learning process they perform best at. Completion of the questionnaire, available at a reasonable price as a 40-item questionnaire at http://www.peterhoney.com, provides you with scores on each of the following four categories to allow you to determine your dominant learning style. The four styles are:

1 Activists—where this style is dominant, you learn better through involvement in new experiences through concrete experience. You learn better by doing.

2 Reflectors—where this style is dominant, you are more likely to consider experiences with hindsight and from a variety of perspectives and rationalize these experiences. You learn better by reflecting.

3 Theorists—where this style is dominant, you develop understanding of situations and information by developing an abstract theoretical framework for understanding. You learn better by theorizing.

4 Pragmatists—where this style is dominant, you learn best by understanding what works best in what circumstances in practice. You learn through practice.

Analysis of your learning style will allow you to determine how you learn best at the moment, and give you pointers as to what other approaches to learning you might adopt to balance how you develop. You may already have completed a learning style questionnaire at the beginning of your course and so know which learning styles you need to develop.

We believe most textbooks are designed to particularly develop the theorist learning style. Review-type questions also enhance the reflector learning style. However, in this text, we also aim to develop the pragmatist component of your learning style by providing you with Case Insights, by showing you material in which marketing practitioners discuss real-life problems with which they had to deal. Finally, we ask end of chapter discussion questions which require you to work in teams and on your own, as well as providing Internet activities to complete and web links to visit, to develop your activist learning style.

We aim to enhance your learning by providing an integrated marketing learning system, incorporating the key components that you need to understand the core marketing principles. In this respect, we hope not only that this text and its associated website will facilitate and enhance your learning, making it fun along the way, but that you will find it useful to use this text, and refer back to it, throughout your student and life experiences of marketing.

Learning such an exciting discipline as marketing should be both fun and challenging. We hope that this textbook and its associated resources bring the discipline alive for you and pique your curiosity about how the marketing world works. Good luck with your learning and in your career!

How to Use this Book

This book comes equipped with a range of carefully designed learning features to help you get to grips with marketing and develop the essential knowledge and skills you'll need for your future career.

IDENTIFY & REVIEW *through* Learning Outcomes

Introducing you to every chapter, Learning Outcomes outline the main concepts and themes that will be covered to clearly identify what you can expect to learn. These bullet-pointed lists can also be used to review your learning and effectively plan your revision.

> **Learning Outcomes**
>
> After reading this chapter, you will be able to:
>
> ▶ Define the marketing concept
>
> ▶ Explain how marketing has developed over the twentieth century and into the twenty-first century
>
> ▶ Understand the exchange and marketing mix concepts in marketing

LEARN & EVALUATE *through* Case Insights

Learn from the professionals with real-life case studies from leading marketers at organizations including Aston Martin, innocent, and Spotify. Discover what their businesses aim to do, what their jobs involve, and what kind of challenges they face, before evaluating your own response to tackling their marketing problem. On the Online Resource Centre you can find bespoke video interviews with all these professionals, and gain an insight into how they ultimately resolved their marketing dilemmas.

> 🔍 **Case Insight** 1.1
> **Aldoraq Water Bottling Plant**
>
>
>
> Established in 1994 by its founder and ow[...] Almaimani, Aldoraq Water Bottling Plant v[...] first water bottling factories in Madinah, S[...] speak to Abdurahman Almaimani, Genera[...] out more about how the company seeks t[...] well-known international brands.

ANALYSE & APPLY *through* Market Insights

Contemporary and varied examples from the business world illustrate the concepts discussed in the chapter and prompt you to analyse the marketing practices of a huge range of companies. Theory into Practice boxes will then help you apply the marketing theory to these practical examples, with accompanying questions reinforcing your learning.

> 🫐 **Market Insight** 1.1
> **V&D Goes Bust!**
>
> On New Year's Eve 2015, the Dutch department store Vroom & Dreesman (V&D), owned by US private equity firm Sun Capital, declared itself insolvent after suffering poor sales, a loss of €49m on sales of €604m in 2014, and a year of conflict with unions and landlords. The company was finding it difficult to compete with new competitors and the shift to online purchasing. The company, first established in 1887, had over 10,000 staff and 62 stores across the Netherlands, selling items such as designer clothing and shoes, jewelry, home electric appliances, furniture, china, stationery, books and CDs, and much more. It also owned the La Place restaurant chain in 250 locations. In early 2016,
>
> the future activities of from its financial diffic of up to 70 candidate administrators invited
>
> *Sources:* Anon. (2015a, b
>
>

Research Insight 1.1

To take your learning further, you might wish to read this influential paper.

Borden, N.H. (1964). The concept of the marketing mix. *Journal of Advertising Research*, 4, 2–7.

This easy-to-read early article explains how marketing managers act as 'mixers of ingredients' when devel

RESEARCH & PROGRESS *through* Research Insights

Take your learning further with the key books and journal articles highlighted in Research Insights, to aid your research and progress your understanding of key topics.

Chapter Summary

To consolidate your learning, the key points from this chapter are summarized here.

■ **Define the marketing concept.**

Marketing is the process by which organizations anticipate and satisfy their customers' needs to both parties' benefit. It involves mutual exchange. Over the last 25 years, the marketing concept has changed to recognize the importance of long-term customer relationships to organizations. In addition, most defin of marketing recognize the importance of marketing's impacts on society and the need to curtail these where they are negative.

RECAP & CONSOLIDATE *through* Chapter Summaries

Recap the core themes and ideas of the chapter to consolidate and review your learning in these handy chapter summaries.

Review Questions

1 How do we define the marketing concept?
2 How do the American Marketing Association and the Chartered Institute of Marketing d of marketing differ?
3 How has marketing developed historically?
4 What is the difference between sales and marketing?
5 What is a marketing exchange?

REVIEW & REVISE *through* Review Questions

Stimulating questions at the end of every chapter will review your knowledge and highlight any areas that need further revision ahead of the exam.

Worksheet Summary

To apply the knowledge you have gained from this chapter and test your understanding of marketing theory visit the **Online Resource Centre** and complete Worksheet 1.1.

PRACTICE & UNDERSTAND *through* Worksheet Summaries

These useful summaries signpost to Worksheets available for each chapter on the Online Resource Centre. Visit the Worksheets to put your new marketing knowledge into practice and reinforce your understanding.

Discussion Questions

1 Having read the Case Insight at the beginning of this chapter, how would you advise Aldoraq Wa differentiate itself when competing against local and international brands?

2 Read the section on the marketing mix within the chapter and draw up marketing mixes for the following organizations and their target customers.
A The streaming video company Netflix and its audiences.
B A luxury hotel group and their wealthy clientele.

CHALLENGE & REFLECT *through* Discussion Questions

Develop your analytical and reasoning skills by challenging the theory and reflecting on key issues with these stimulating Discussion Questions designed to create lively debate.

Glossary

advertising a form of non-personal communication, by an identified sponsor, that is transmitted through the use of paid-for media.
aggregated demand demand calculated at the population level rather than at the individual level.
AMA the American Marketing Association is a professional body for marketing professionals

ethnography a subdiscipline derived from anthropology as an approach to research, which emphasizes the collection of data through participant observation of member specific subcultural grouping and observat participation of members of a specific sub grouping.
haul girls women who go shopping for cloth

LOOK UP & CHECK *through* Key Terms and Glossaries

Key Terms are highlighted in blue when they first appear and are collated into Glossaries at the end of each chapter, designed for you to look up terms and check your understanding of essential definitions.

How to Use the Online Resource Centre

www.oxfordtextbooks.co.uk/orc/
baines4e/

The Online Resource Centre is signposted throughout chapters and provides you with access to the following specialized resources:

Student Resources – Free and open-access material available for users of the book.

Case Insight Videos
Watch the book's authors in discussion with the leading marketing practitioners featured in the chapter-opening Case Insights as they expand on the marketing challenges they face and what strategies they use to tackle them. Transcripts of each video are also available.

Worksheets
Task-focused worksheets provide the opportunity to apply and reinforce your understanding of the key marketing frameworks and theories.

Worksheet 1.1: Marketing Principles

Chapter Reference
Chapter 1: Marketing Principles & Society

Overview
This activity introduces you to two frameworks that help us to understand how managers can market their goods and services.

Learning Outcomes
After completing this worksheet you should be able to:
- apply McCarthy's 4P's to a good;
- apply Bitner and Boom's 7P's to a service;
- describe the exchange process;
- discuss the differences and similarities between a good and a service.

Worksheet

Library of Video Links
A bank of links to marketing videos designed to demonstrate key principles and themes in practice.

Chapter 18: Library of video links

Resource Title: The Cooperative
Brand and/or Topic: Cooperative
Resource Description: This is the official channel for the Cooperative Group.
Channel: The Co-operative
Link (URL): http://www.youtube.com/user/TheCooperativeGroup

Resource Title: James Dion: Sustainable Retailing: How Green is Becoming the New Black
Brand and/or Topic: Green Marketing, Retailing
Resource Description: A video with James Dion gives a seminar packed with case studies and examples of retailers large and small who successfully managed to turn their company and stores 'green' and save money by doing it.
Channel: dioncpinc

Author Audio Podcasts
Short audio summaries of each chapter from the authors, to listen to on the go and help you revise.

Multiple-Choice Questions

Test your knowledge of the chapter and receive instant results with these interactive questions. References to page numbers in the book accompany every question to help you navigate to the topics that need further study.

Flashcard Glossary

Learning the jargon associated with the range of topics in marketing can be a challenge, so this online glossary has been designed to help you understand and memorize the key terms in the book.

Employability Guidance and Marketing Career Insights

Listen to students and graduates talk about the skills they've developed at university, and also hear from graduate employment and recruitment specialists about the skills and attributes you'll need to succeed in your job applications and future career.

Internet Activities

Arranged by chapter, these Internet Activities help you develop your knowledge and improve your understanding of the topic through online research.

Research Insights

Follow the links to access the seminal academic papers suggested in the book's Research Insights.

Web Links

Annotated links allow you easy access to up-to-date and reliable marketing-related sites.

Lecturer Resources – For all registered adopters of the book.

VLE Content

To make your teaching more efficient and learning more effective, import all the material available in this Online Resource Centre into your VLE.

PowerPoint Slides

A suite of fully customizable PowerPoint slides for use in lecture presentations accompanies each chapter.

Learning Outcomes

- Define the marketing concept
- Explain how marketing has developed ov
  the twentieth and into the twenty-first cent
- Understand the exchange and marketing
  concepts in marketing
- Describe the three major contexts of

Test Bank

A ready-made interactive testing resource, fully customizable for your teaching and featuring built-in feedback for students, to save you time when creating assessments.

OXFORD
UNIVERSITY PRESS

Chapter 01

1 of 5

Chapter 01 - Question 01
The key focus of the American Marketing Association's (AMA) 2007 definition of marketing is:
- organizational activities
- product components
- Shareholder returns
- Stakeholder value

2 of 5

Chapter 01 - Question 02
The key difference between a customer and a consumer is that:
- A customer purchases a product while a consumer uses a product offering
- A consumer purchases a product and a customer consumes it
- A consumer only exists in B2B marketing contexts

Essay Questions

Provided for each chapter, these stimulating essay questions are accompanied by clear and detailed answer guidance.

Tutorial Activities

Designed for use in seminars and tutorials, and to reinforce practical marketing skills, these activities are directly related to concepts and companies in the book. They offer a range of suggested ideas for easily integrating the book and its resources with your teaching.

Chapter 01

There are five activities available for this chapter. Access the links below to download and view the word documents.

Activity 1.1
Marketing and You

Overview
This activity introduces students to marketing and encourages students to see themselves as a target market be it consumers, customers, purchasers and users, to which products have been marketed.

Learning Outcomes
Students should demonstrate:

- an understanding of the marketing concept;
- awareness of the differing definitions of marketing;
- knowledge of the process of marketing and the differing principles and marketing

Marketing Resource Bank

A suite of interactive and multi-media marketing tools accompanied by detailed teaching notes provide a diverse collection of practical examples to use in your teaching.

Marketing Resource Bank

A suite of marketing tools and video clips accompanied by detailed teaching notes, including examples of viral marketing, online games, and TV advertisements, provides a diverse collection of practical examples to illustrate key theories in each chapter.

Chapter 2: Consumer Buying Behaviour
- MRB 2.1: Optical Illusions (DOC, Size: 170KB)
- MRB 2.2: Cognitive Games (DOC, Size: 170KB)
- MRB 2.3: 41Q's (DOC, Size: 284KB)
- MRB 2.4: Sainsbury 'Celebrity Chef (DOC, Size: 175KB)

Chapter 3: Marketing Research and Customer Insight
- MRB 3.1: From Rio to the Rest of the World (DOC, Size: 172KB)
- MRB 3.2: BrainJuicer; Behavioural Science Approach to Market Research (DOC, Size: 176KB)

Pointers on Answering Discussion Questions

Possible points for inclusion when answering the discussion questions at the end of each chapter of the textbook.

Figures and Tables from the Book

Available for downloading into presentation software or for use in assignments and exam material.

Dashboard

Simple. Informative. Mobile.

Dashboard is a cloud-based online assessment and revision tool. It comes pre-loaded with test questions for students, a homework course if your module leader has adopted Dashboard, and additional resources as listed below. If your lecturer has adopted Dashboard and you have purchased the Dashboard Edition of the book, your standalone access code should be included and will provide instructions on how to sign up for the platform. If you have not purchased the Dashboard Edition or if you have purchased a second-hand copy, you can purchase standalone access online—visit www.oxfordtextbooks.co.uk/dashboard for more information.

SIMPLE: With a highly intuitive design, it will take you less than fifteen minutes to learn and master the system.

MOBILE: You can access Dashboard from every major platform and device connected to the Internet, whether that's a computer, tablet, or smartphone.

INFORMATIVE: Your assignment and assessment results are automatically graded, giving your instructor a clear view of the class's understanding of the course content.

Student Resources

Dashboard offers all the features of the Online Resource Centre, but comes with additional questions to take your learning further.

Lecturer Resources

A preloaded homework course structured around the book is available, supported by a test bank containing additional multiple-choice questions. Your students can follow the preloaded course, or you can customize it, allowing you to add questions from the test bank or from your existing materials to meet your specific teaching needs. Dashboard's Gradebook will automatically grade the homework assignments that you set for your students. The Gradebook also provides heat maps for you to view your students' progress, which helps you to quickly identify areas of the course where your students may need more practice, as well as the areas they are most confident in. This feature helps you focus your teaching time on the areas that matter. The Gradebook also allows you to administer grading schemes, manage checklists, and administer learning objectives and competencies.

Part One
Principles of Marketing

Chapter 1

Marketing Principles and Practice

Learning Outcomes

After reading this chapter, you will be able to:

▶ Define the marketing concept

▶ Explain how marketing has developed over the twentieth century and into the twenty-first century

▶ Understand the exchange and marketing mix concepts in marketing

▶ Describe the three major contexts of marketing application, i.e. consumer goods, business-to-business, and services marketing

▶ Understand the positive contribution marketing makes to society

Case Insight 1.1
Aldoraq Water Bottling Plant

Market Insight 1.1
V&D Goes Bust!

Market Insight 1.2
Servitization at Rolls-Royce

Market Insight 1.3
Harrods: Time for (Thai) Tea

Market Insight 1.4
Google: World-Changing Innovations

Market Insight 1.5
Electrifying Cars

Case Insight 1.1
Aldoraq Water Bottling Plant

Established in 1994 by its founder and owner Khaled A. Almaimani, Aldoraq Water Bottling Plant was one of the first water bottling factories in Madinah, Saudi Arabia. We speak to Abdurahman Almaimani, General Manager, to find out more about how the company seeks to compete with well-known international brands.

Aldoraq, headquartered in Madinah, Saudi Arabia, distributes its natural mineral water products throughout the Kingdom, and particularly in Madinah, Makkah, and Yanbu. It is one of the biggest factories in the Middle East and a member of one of the oldest and largest family-owned businesses in Saudi Arabia. The company produces purified drinking water in different bottle sizes and capacities (from 250ml to 5 gallon containers) and was the first water company in Saudi Arabia to join the International Bottled Water Association (IBWA). The water produced by Aldoraq contains a good percentage of fluoride, is derived from natural water bore-wells and is purified by ozone. In 2015, sales of the company's 250ml, 375ml, and 600ml products were increasing strongly on 2014 sales, but falling slightly in the 2 litre, 1 gallon, 5 litre, and 5 gallon bottle categories. The 5 gallon refill category, however, saw a slight gain.

The future looks bright for bottled water in the Kingdom, with population growth expected at 20% per year until 2019, growing retail infrastructure, and an increasing number of *baqalah* (small independent stores). Aldoraq's customers are mostly hypermarkets, supermarkets, and medium and small stores who distribute or sell bottled water to consumers (restaurants, fast food stores, canteens, hospitals, households, etc.). Other customers include catering companies, hotels, airport retail outlets, and corporate offices. Often such customers are looking for price discounts, longer terms of payment, and even coolers to store the water. Distributors decide to buy bottled drinking water from Aldoraq's factory based on which

products are available in time and can steadily be supplied to customers' volume requirements, terms of deals, and consignments, including beneficial payment terms. Of particular importance to customers is to be able to buy all the products they need from one location. Because there are more than 30 water distributors in Madinah, many customers base their decision on the price they pay.

To promote awareness of our brand, we recommend that customers display our product prominently in their stores, in potential customers' line of sight, and we offer volume discounts to our largest distributors accordingly. In addition, we support our community by giving free water to charities and discounted water to the mosque and other religious places. Nevertheless, more recently, some large hotels and stores have started to purchase only premium water from companies selling international brands, such as Evian, Nestlé, and Aquafina, making it hard for us to compete with them. These big brands are competing by trying to dominate the supply chain system. For example, Aquafina, owned by Pepsico, is pushing its water product alongside other products like Pepsi-Cola. When Aquafina first entered the market, they gave away free samples of water with their Pepsi-Cola product and then pushed customers to buy their Aquafina water brand from them at the same time. Coca-Cola also competed in this way with their water product Arwa.

How should Aldoraq seek to differentiate itself and thereby compete against both local and international brands?

Introduction

How have companies marketed their offerings to you in the past? Consider the last smartphone you bought, the sports teams you follow, the music you stream, and the airlines you've flown on. Why did you decide to purchase these offerings? Each one has been marketed to you to cater for a particular need that you have. Consider how the offering was distributed. What physical and service-based components is it made of? What societal contributions, if any, positive or negative, do these offerings make? Are other versions of these offerings available that meet your needs and the needs of society better? These are some of the questions that marketers should ask themselves when designing, developing, and delivering offerings to the **customer**.

In this chapter, we develop our understanding of marketing principles and marketing's positive impact upon society by defining marketing, comparing and contrasting American, British, and French definitions. (We consider marketing's negative impacts upon society in Chapter 18.) We consider the origins and development of marketing throughout the twentieth and into the twenty-first century. We explore how marketing differs in the consumer (B2C), business-to-business (B2B), and services marketing sectors. The core principles of marketing, incorporating the marketing mix, the principle of marketing exchange, **market orientation**, **relationship marketing**, and **service-dominant logic**, are all considered. This chapter seeks to provide a thorough grounding in the principles of marketing. (Many of these concepts are considered again in detail in later chapters.)

What is Marketing?

Consider your own vast experience of being marketed to throughout your life. So far, you will have been subjected to millions of marketing communications messages, bought hundreds of thousands of offerings, been involved in thousands of customer service telephone or online calls, and visited tens of thousands of shops, supermarkets, and retail outlets (on- and off-line). You're already a pretty experienced customer. Our role here is to explain how professionals do the reverse side of marketing—how they market offerings to customers. Most customers are just like you and will be just as discriminating as you are when buying.

To explain how we go about marketing offerings to customers, we first describe what marketing is. There are numerous definitions, but we present three for easy reference in Table 1.1.

Visit the Online Resource Centre and follow the web links to the CIM and AMA websites to read more about their views on 'What is Marketing?'.

The **CIM** and **AMA** definitions recognize marketing as a 'management process' and an 'activity', although many firms organize marketing as a discrete department rather than as a service across departments (Sheth and Sisodia, 2005). Nike, for example, uses a regional matrix organizational structure, enabling marketing to operate within and across departments, e.g. apparel, footwear (Brenner, 2013). The CIM and AMA definitions both stress the importance of considering the customer, of determining their requirements or needs. The CIM definition refers to customer 'requirements' and the AMA to 'delivering value'. Conversely, our French definition refers to developing an offer of superior **value**. Both the AMA and French definitions refer to an 'offer' and 'offering', recognizing that marketing can be applied equally to the marketing of goods, services, ideas and in the not-for-profit sector.

Table 1.1 Definitions of marketing

Defining institution/author	Definition
The Chartered Institute of Marketing (CIM)	'The management process responsible for identifying, anticipating, and satisfying customer requirements profitably' (CIM, 2015).
The American Marketing Association (AMA)	'Marketing is the activity, set of institutions, and processes for creating communicating, delivering, and exchanging offerings that have value for customers, clients, partners, and society at large' (AMA, 2013).
A French perspective	'Le marketing est la stratégie d'adaptation des organisations à des marchés concurrentiels, pour influencer en leur faveur le comportement des publics dont elles dépendent, par une offre dont la valeur perçue est durablement supérieure à celle des concurrents. Dans le secteur marchand, le rôle du marketing est de créer de la valeur économique pour l'entreprise en créant de la valeur perçue par les clients', which broadly translates as 'Marketing is the strategy of adaptation of organizations to competitive markets in order for them to influence the behaviour of the publics on which they depend, through an offering whose perceived value is durably superior to that of competitors. In the commercial sector, the role of marketing is to create economic value for the company by creating value as perceived by customers.' (Lendrevie and Lévy, 2014).

The CIM definition discusses anticipating/identifying needs and the AMA discusses 'creating … offerings that have value for customers'. Both definitions recognize the need for marketers to undertake marketing research (see Chapter 3) and environmental scanning activity (see Chapter 4) to satisfy customers and, in the long term, to anticipate customers' needs.

The French definition discusses influencing the behaviour of the publics, rather than customers, recognizing the wider remit of marketing in modern society. The challenge, according to the French definition, is to develop an offering that is 'durably superior' to that of the competition. Therefore this definition recognizes explicitly the importance of market segmentation and **positioning** concepts (see Chapter 6 for a detailed treatment of these topics).

The CIM definition presupposes that marketing is a process with a profit motive, although it does not explicitly state whether or not this is for financial profit or for some other form of profit, e.g. of gain in society, as in the case of a charity. The AMA definition is much clearer, arguing that marketing is a process undertaken to benefit 'clients, partners, and society at large'.

What all these definitions display is how the concept of marketing has changed over the years, from transactional concepts like pricing, promotion, and distribution, to relationship concepts such as the importance of customer trust, risk, commitment, and co-creation.

In addition, the nature of the relationships between an organization and its customers, in its offerings and its mission, are different in not-for-profit and for-profit organizations (see Chapter 17). Nevertheless, the broad principles of how marketing is used remain the same. All definitions recognize this widened concept of the wider societal applicability of marketing.

Visit the Online Resource Centre and complete Internet Activity 1.1 to learn more about the professional marketing associations around the world.

What's the Difference Between Customers and Consumers?

What exactly is a customer? And what is the difference between a customer and a **consumer**? The difference is subtle but real. A customer is a buyer, a purchaser, a patron, a client, or a shopper, and therefore someone who buys from a shop, a website, a business or, in the sharing economy, another customer (e.g. Airbnb or eBay).

The difference between a customer and a consumer is that a customer purchases or obtains an offering, but a consumer uses it (or eats it in the case of food).

To illustrate, consider the marketing course you are enrolled on, assuming that you are using this book as an aid to learning on the course. Did you pay your course fees yourself? Or did someone else pay them? If you paid the fees yourself, you are the customer. If someone else paid them, they are the customer, although you make use of, and study for, the degree or course. So you are the consumer in that case.

Another example is Mondelez International's Dairylea Dunkers, a dairy food designed to be a good source of calcium with each pack contributing at least 26% of the daily reference intake of calcium. In this case, the customer is the chief shopper, the mother/father or guardian, and the consumer is the child. Sometimes the customer and consumer can be the same person, e.g. the lady buying cinema tickets for herself and her boyfriend online.

Market Orientation

The concept of market orientation (Kohli and Jaworski, 1990) lies at the heart of marketing. Developing a market orientation is argued to make organizations more profitable in both the long and short-run (Kumar *et al.*, 2011), especially when there is limited competition, unchanging customer wants and needs, fast-paced technological change, and strong economies in operation. In a meta-analysis of market orientation studies, Kirca *et al.* (2005) conclude that market orientation may be imperative for survival in service firms and the source of competitive advantage in manufacturing firms.

But developing a market orientation is not the same as developing a market*ing* orientation. So what's the difference? A company with a marketing orientation would be a company that

Dairylea Dunkers, the moo-vellous snack for children
Source: Reproduced with kind permission of Mondelez International.

recognizes the importance of marketing within the organization, e.g. by appointing a marketing person as chief executive officer (CEO), or as chair of its board of directors (or trustees in the case of a charity), or to the executive team more generally in a limited company or partnership.

Developing a market orientation refers to 'the organization-wide generation of market intelligence pertaining to current and future customer needs, dissemination of the intelligence across the departments, and organization-wide responsiveness to it' (Kohli and Jaworski, 1990). So a market orientation doesn't just involve marketing, it involves all the functions of a company, gathering and responding to market intelligence (i.e. customers' verbalized needs and preferences, data from customer and employee surveys, sales data, and information gleaned informally from discussions with customers and trade partners, from websites, and from social networking sites). Developing a market orientation means developing the following:

- Customer orientation—concerned with creating superior value by continuously developing and redeveloping offerings to meet customer needs. To do so we must measure customer satisfaction on a continuous basis and train front-line service staff accordingly.

- Competitor orientation—requires an organization to develop an understanding of its competitors' short-term strengths and weaknesses and its long-term capabilities and strategies (Slater and Narver, 1994).

- Interfunctional coordination—requires all functions of an organization to work together for long-term profit growth (as shown in Figure 1.1).

Achieving a market orientation so that an organization is internally responsive to changes in the marketplace may take organizations four years or more to develop and requires senior management support, the development of teams to gather the necessary market intelligence data and design appropriate market-based reward systems, and management to implement the recommendations made as a result (Kohli and Jaworski, 1990).

Developing a market orientation within a company is a capability, something that not all companies are able to do. Organizations that manage to develop a market orientation are better at

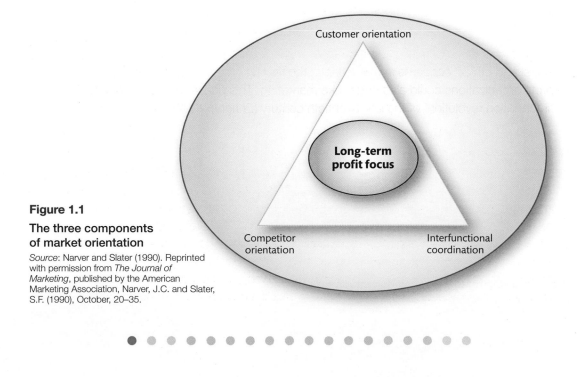

Figure 1.1

The three components of market orientation

Source: Narver and Slater (1990). Reprinted with permission from *The Journal of Marketing*, published by the American Marketing Association, Narver, J.C. and Slater, S.F. (1990), October, 20–35.

market sensing, i.e. understanding the strategic implications of the market for a particular organization, and acting on the information collected through **environmental scanning** exercises. (This topic is covered fully in Chapter 4.) Colgate-Palmolive, the fast-moving consumer goods company, developed a strong market orientation by aligning their company to the task of promoting trade satisfaction, measuring the number of orders delivered on time and the number of orders completed (Day, 1994). Amazingly, up to the year 2000, General Electric (GE)—the American capital, expertise, and infrastructure company—had no substantial marketing organization. Instead, it had been technology driven. To orient GE towards the market, it organized its marketing function into two basic activities: go to market (e.g. segmentation) and commercial essentials (e.g. branding, communications). Then they organized their marketing teams across the company to ensure that they contained a mix of people with different skills, including instigators (who challenge the status quo), innovators (who develop new offerings and processes), integrators (who build bridges across organizational functions and in the marketplace), and implementers (who execute the new ideas). All this was backed with a process custom-designed to evaluate the success of the new approach (Comstock *et al.*, 2010).

A Brief History of Marketing

Marketing as a practice has taken time to evolve as a function in organizations. It can be said to have developed through a four-stage continuum including orientations to production, in the earliest stages with a minimum focus on customers' needs, through to a societal orientation, with a focus not only on customers' needs but also on a wider set of stakeholders' needs at the latter stages of development, as follows.

1 Production period, 1890s–1920s: characterized by a focus in the firm on physical production and supply, where demand exceeded supply, there was little competition, and the range of products was limited. This phase came after the Industrial Revolution.

2 Sales period, 1920s–1950s: characterized by a focus in the firm on personal selling supported by market research and advertising. This phase took place after the First World War.

3 Marketing period, 1950s–1980s: characterized by a more advanced focus in the firm on the customer's needs. This phase came after the Second World War.

4 Societal marketing period, 1980s to present: characterized by a stronger focus on social and ethical concerns in marketing in the firm and a recognition that not-for-profit organizations could also undertake marketing. This phase took place during the 'information revolution' of the late twentieth century (Enright, 2002).

Some marketing historians regard marketing as an invention of the twentieth century (Keith, 1960), while others regard it as a process which evolved over a much longer period of time, without any production era ever having existed at all. Soap firms, for example, were **advertising** in the late nineteenth century in the UK, the USA, and Germany (Fullerton, 1988). The notion that marketing developed from the 1950s is probably wrong, considering that self-service supermarkets operated in America from the 1930s, and products were increasingly developed based on the process of 'consumer engineering', where products were designed and redesigned, using research, to meet customer needs (see Fullerton, 1988). Shaw and Jones (2005: 271) believe that marketing as a concept is at a crossroads in the twenty-first century because it subsumes all social or personal interactions where 'marketing-mix like persuasive communication techniques are used', and question whether the concept has in fact been stretched too far (beyond its commercial origins).

Marketing as a discipline has always developed through the influence of its practitioners, but also through developments in related disciplines, including the areas of industrial economics, psychology, sociology, and anthropology, as follows.

- *Industrial economics influences*—our knowledge of the matching of supply and demand, within industries, owes much to the development of microeconomics. For instance, the economic concepts of perfect competition and the matching of supply and demand underlie the marketing concept, particularly in relation to the concepts of the price at which offerings are sold and the quantity distributed (see Chapter 9) and the nature of business-to-business marketing (see Chapter 16). Theories of income distribution, scale of operation, monopoly, competition, and finance all derive from economics (Bartels, 1951), although the influence of economics over marketing is declining (Howard *et al.*, 1991).

- *Psychological influences*—our knowledge of consumer behaviour derives principally from psychology, especially in the early days, motivation research (see Chapter 3) in relation to consumer attitudes, perceptions, motivations, and information processing (Holden and Holden, 1998), and our understanding of persuasion, consumer personality, and customer satisfaction (Bartels, 1951). Understanding buyer psychology is fundamental to the marketing function. As marketing is about understanding customers' needs, empathy with customers is fundamental.

- *Sociological influences*—knowledge of how groups of people behave derives from sociology, with insights into areas such as how people from similar gender and age groups behave (demographics), how people in different social positions within society behave (class), why we do things in the way that we do (motivation), general ways that groups behave (customs), and culture (Bartels, 1951, 1959). Our understanding of what society thinks as a whole (i.e. public opinion) and how communications pass through opinion leaders (Katz, 1957), and how we influence the way people think and to adopt our perspective, e.g. propaganda research (see Lee, 1945; Doob, 1948), have all informed marketing practice.

- *Anthropological influences*—our debt to **social anthropology** increases more and more as we use qualitative approaches such as **ethnography**, **netnography**, and **observation** in researching consumer behaviour (see Chapter 3), particularly the behaviour of subgroups and cultures (e.g. **tweenagers, haul girls**).

Differences Between Sales and Marketing

When someone is new to marketing, they might ask themselves: what is the difference between selling and marketing? To answer, we can consider the four eras of marketing development outlined above. We see that marketing is an extension from sales. But perhaps a more comprehensive answer is that sales emphasizes the process of 'product push' by creating distribution incentives for both salespeople and customers to make exchanges, whereas marketing is more focused on creating 'product pull', or stoking demand among customers and consumers, and, in marketing, the offering is designed and redesigned through customer insight and co-creation to meet their long-term needs. Marketing activity is geared around understanding and communicating with the customer to help in the design, development, delivery, and determination of the value inherent in the offering, whereas sales is organized principally around enhancing the

---

Table 1.2 Differences between marketing and sales

Marketing	Sales
Tends towards long-term satisfaction of customer needs	Tends towards short-term satisfaction of customer needs; part of the value delivery process as opposed to designing and development of customer value processes
Tends to greater input into customer design of offering (co-creation)	Tends to lesser input into customer design of offering
Tends to high focus on stimulation of demand	Tends to low focus on stimulation of demand; more focused on meeting existing demand

---

distribution and solicitation of the companies' offerings once those offerings have already been designed. Sales departments are mostly concerned with the delivery part of the value creation process. However, sales as a function does and should have inputs to the design phase (through information from sales representatives), the development phase (particularly in test marketing; see Chapter 3), and the determination phase, where salespeople's informal knowledge of customers' needs is critical to the marketing process.

Whereas marketing activities are designed to estimate and stimulate demand, sales activities are designed to promote customer purchase of an offering (AMA, 2015). However, the two functions should be integrated to coexist, rather than clash, in an organization since both functions are important in achieving a market orientation and concomitant improvement in business performance (Le Meunier-Fitzhugh and Piercy, 2011). Table 1.2 provides a summary of the basic differences.

What Do Marketers Do?

To answer this question, the British government worked with relevant stakeholders to map out how the marketing function operates (a role undertaken by the Skills CfA, formerly the Council for Administration). Their consultation indicated that the job covered eight functional areas (see Figure 1.2), each of which is interlinked with stakeholder requirements. These eight areas cover a variety of roles from market intelligence/customer insight generation, to helping develop the customer proposition (see Chapter 8), to managing marketing communications, to developing and using marketing and customer information. An important element, not always undertaken by some firms, is for the marketing function to provide strategic marketing direction for the company. Important operational marketing elements include leading marketing programmes, working with other elements within the organization and outside it, and developing and managing teams, all the while seeking to meet the needs of the marketing function's many and various stakeholders.

Visit the Online Resource Centre and follow the web link to CIM's website outlining the Professional Marketing Standards Framework to learn more about occupational standards for marketing in the UK.

Figure 1.2

A functional map for marketing

Source: The Marketing and Sales Standards Setting Body (2010). Reproduced with the kind permission of Dr Chahid Fourali.

As society constantly changes, so the marketing profession also constantly changes. Marketing's place within the business profession, and society more generally, is often criticized. Whereas doctors, teachers, and judges are generally held in high respect (Worcester *et al.*, 2011: 136), marketing practitioners can sometimes be held in low esteem (Kotler, 2006). Sheth and Sisodia (2006) first suggested that to reform marketing practice and raise its esteem, we need to:

- make marketing a corporate staff function that operates across departments, at a strategic level, like the finance, information technology, legal, and human resource management functions

- ensure that the head of the marketing function has a strategy role and reports directly to the chief executive officer (CEO)

- rename the head of corporate marketing the chief customer officer (CCO)

- provide marketing with capital expenditure budgets in addition to operating expenditure budgets so that the marketing function can make major capital investments (e.g. in CRM projects, big data analytics capability building, or sales and marketing offices in international markets)

- ensure that the marketing function controls branding, key account management, and business development

- ensure that the marketing function manages external suppliers such as research and communications agencies

- set up, within the public limited company, a board-level standing committee, on which senior marketers sit, comparable to audit, compensation, and governance committees.

Interestingly, many of these suggestions still remain true today. More recently, Sheth and Sisodia (2015) have recommended that marketers can reform even further by:

- showing more integrity, gratitude, recognition and humility to, and building real trust with, customers

- building a true dialogue with customers and respecting their privacy

- striving for authenticity by really personalizing customer offerings rather than just appearing to do so

- asking for forgiveness when they commit occasional lapses and treat customers badly

- having the courage to stop over-promising and under-delivering

- showing respect for customers, competitors, and suppliers.

Marketing still has some way to go, not just in its relations with customers but also in terms of the power it wields inside companies. There are still too many major public companies with no marketing representation on their boards. A review of FTSE 350 firms in the UK by the executive search agency Norman Broadbent indicated that only 50 non-executive directors from these companies had a background in marketing (Parsons, 2013). Worse still, 57% of marketing functions within their organizations are divorced from a strategic role and 82% of marketing leaders are dissatisfied with the role and positioning of marketing within their organizations (CIM, 2009). This is unlikely to change unless marketers demonstrate marketing's value more in their organizations. (For a more detailed consideration of how companies structure the marketing function, see Chapter 5.)

This lack of strategic input may arise because marketers are not seen to control all elements of the marketing mix, so often assumed to be under their direct control. For example, marketers do not always control pricing, distribution, product development, and even promotion, given that this is often outsourced to agencies (O'Malley and Patterson, 1998), although it usually exercises influence over all these activities and more. In addition, marketing may not necessarily be organized as a separate department, but the ethos and influence of marketing philosophy may still be apparent and impact upon an organization's decision-making (Harris and Ogbonna, 2003). Marketing is present in all aspects of an organization, since all departments have some role to play with respect to creating, delivering, and satisfying customers. Employees in the research and development (R&D) department designing new products to meet existing customer needs are performing a marketing role. Similarly, members of the procurement department buying components for a new product or service must purchase those components at a specific quality and cost which will meet customer needs. In fact, we can go through all departments of a company, and find that in each department there is a marketing role to be played to some extent. In other words, marketing is distributed throughout the organization, and all employees can be considered as part-time marketers (Gummesson, 1990).

The Principal Principles of Marketing

Despite being studied for around a hundred years, there are few true scientific principles in marketing (Bartels, 1944). By scientific principles, we mean natural rules of law around which a theory can be developed to explain observations (and predict future observations), which cannot be subsequently disproved. Relatively early on in marketing's history, however, Bartels (1951) stated, when discussing whether marketing is an art or science, that only two marketing generalizations exist.

1 As [a consumer's] income increases, the percentage of income spent for food decreases; for rent, fuel, and light remains the same; for clothing remains the same; and for sundries [miscellaneous items] increases (Engels' Law).

2 Two cities attract retail trade from an intermediary city or town in the vicinity of the breaking point (the 50% point) approximately in direct proportion to the populations of the two cities and in inverse proportion to the square of the distance from these two cities to the intermediate town (Reilly's Law of Retail Gravitation).

Clearly, things have changed since Engels produced his 'Law', especially as we now tend to buy our accommodation rather than renting it (although this may change as house prices spiral ever upwards) and food is less expensive than it was 60–70 years ago, so it is debatable as to whether or not the first 'Law' still applies. On the second 'Law', site location specialists for a major supermarket should locate stores near the larger of the major population centres. Again, this might sound obvious as a general principle, but Reilly's Law allows retailers to determine with some degree of precision exactly where that location might be. Nowadays, multiple retail grocers, such as Carrefour in France, Sainsbury's in the UK, Coop in Denmark, Albert Hejn in the Netherlands, and Tesco Lotus in Thailand, use complex mathematical formulae (e.g. algorithms) to determine site location decisions, purchasing land and developing suitable properties in addition to converting existing business premises in suitable locations.

Despite the fact that there are no clear 'laws of marketing', several prominent academics have argued for the need to develop a 'General Theory of Marketing' (Bartels, 1968; Hunt, 1971, 1983). This search continues to the present day but we are no closer to the Holy Grail of a general marketing theory (Hunt, 2013). To move closer towards such a general theory, we need to understand marketing phenomenon more completely, by understanding the following.

■ The behaviour of buyers—why do which buyers purchase what they do, where they do, when they do, and how they do?

■ The behaviour of sellers—why do which sellers price, promote, and distribute what they do, where they do, when they do, and how they do?

■ The institutional framework (e.g. government, society, and so on) around selling/buying—why do which kinds of institutions develop to engage in what kinds of functions or activities to consummate and/or facilitate exchanges, when will these institutions develop, where will they develop, and how will they develop?

■ The consequences for society of buying/selling—why do which kinds of buyers, behaviour of buyers, behaviour of sellers, and institutions have what kinds of consequences on society, when they do, where they do, and how they do (Hunt, 1983)?

The listing indicates how marketing involves a series of highly complex interactions between individuals, organizations, society, and government. We have only a limited understanding of how marketing works in theory and practice. However, although we have no 'laws' of marketing with which to construct a general theory, we can make some law-like generalizations, which do not hold all of the time but hold much of the time in marketing. According to Leone and Shultz (1980), these law-like generalizations are as follows.

- Generalization 1—advertising has a direct and positive influence on total industry (market) sales, i.e. all advertising done at industry level serves to increase sales within that industry.

- Generalization 2—selective advertising has a direct and positive influence on individual company (brand) sales, i.e. advertising undertaken by a company tends to increase the sales of the particular brand for which it was spent.

- Generalization 3—the **elasticity** of selective advertising on company (brand) sales is low (inelastic), i.e. for frequently purchased goods, advertising has only a very limited effect in raising sales.

- Generalization 4—increasing store shelf space (display) has a positive impact on sales of **non-staple** grocery items, such as products bought on impulse (e.g. ice cream, chocolate bars) rather than those that are planned purchases, which are less important but perhaps more luxurious types of goods (e.g. gravy mixes, cooking sauces). For instance, for impulse goods, the more shelf space you give an item, the more likely you are to sell it.

- Generalization 5—distribution, defined by the number of outlets, has a positive influence on company sales (market share), i.e. setting up more retail locations has a positive influence on sales. (For a more detailed consideration of law-like generalizations, see Hanssens, 2009).

As we can see, marketing techniques are still developing in any scientific sense but in the age of the Internet and 'big data' analytics companies are more able to describe—and predict—the behaviour of their consumers, customers, and producers according to some pre-defined formulae. Nevetheless, marketers still have to make use of trial and error, and experimentation and readjustment processes. Gordon and Perrey (2015) argue that we are entering a golden age in marketing, and that advances in data analysis and statistical modelling are increasingly allowing us to measure the returns made on marketing investments and assess and predict customer behaviour more accurately than ever before.

More generally, there are some general concepts that help managers frame their actions as they develop their marketing plans and programmes. These concepts include the concept of

Research Insight 1.1

To take your learning further, you might wish to read this influential paper.

Borden, N.H. (1964). The concept of the marketing mix. *Journal of Advertising Research*, 4, 2–7.

This easy-to-read early article explains how marketing managers act as 'mixers of ingredients' when developing marketing programmes. The marketing mix, popularized as the 4Ps, remains popular today, although the advent of relationship marketing challenged the impersonal notion of marketers as manipulators of marketing policies, and focused more on the need to develop long-term interpersonal relationships with customers.

Visit the **Online Resource Centre** to read the abstract and access the full paper.

exchange in marketing, the marketing mix for products (4Ps) and services (7Ps), market orientation, and **relationship marketing** and **service-dominant logic** for marketing.

Marketing as Exchange

Marketing is a two-way exchange process. It's not solely about the marketing organization doing the work. The customer also inputs—sometimes extensively. Customers specify how we might satisfy their needs, because marketers cannot read their minds. Customers must then pay for the offering. In the mid-1970s, there was an increasing belief that marketing centred on the exchange process between buyers and sellers and associated **supply chain** intermediaries. Exchange relationships were seen to be economic (e.g. a consumer buying groceries) and social (e.g. the service provided by the police on behalf of society paid for by government) (Bagozzi, 1975). This recognition of the underlying exchange relationship within marketing led to the 'broadening' of marketing and the relationship marketing school of marketing (see Chapter 14). There are numerous types of buyer–seller exchanges in marketing. Figure 1.3 illustrates some examples of two-way (**dyadic**) exchanges as follows.

1   In the first exchange type, the exchange takes place between the police who protect the general public from crime and terrorism, and public disorder more generally, and the public who support them, sometimes even through signing petitions to keep police stations in service in a particular locale, and especially through their national and local taxes, depending on the country concerned (see Chapter 16 for a more detailed discussion of the use of marketing by the City of London Police).

2   In the second exchange type, we have a retailer and a customer, say entering a shop (e.g. Albert Hejn—the Dutch supermarket retailer) to purchase groceries, and paying for these with cash or by credit/debit card (see Chapter 14).

3   In the third type of exchange, we have a manufacturer and a retailer. Here, the retailer (e.g. London's Harrods) purchases goods from the manufacturer (e.g. Burberry) through a credit facility (e.g. payment in 30 days), expects any damaged goods to be returnable, and wants the goods delivered in a certain way within a particular time limit. In return, the retailer undertakes to pay a wholesale (i.e. trade discounted) price.

4   In the fourth exchange type, the exchange takes place between a charity and its donors whereby the donors provide funds (by legacy or regular or one-off donation) and the charity makes products and services available to third parties, e.g. Oxfam supporting famine relief in Africa (see Chapter 16).

5   In the fifth exchange type, we have a not-for-profit organization, in this case a theatre, which provides a range of productions designed to entertain and educate its audiences in return for payment.

6   In the sixth type of exchange, we have a manufacturer dealing directly with its customers. An example here would be Dell, the computer manufacturer.

Few marketing exchanges are really this simple. They might involve other individual transactions and multiple combinations. For example, (b) and (c) can be combined to indicate a simple supply chain for, say, an insurance company providing underwriting services to insurance companies selling house insurance policies directly to the general public. Other mechanisms exist in this market of course. Banks and brokers also sell house insurance policies directly to the general

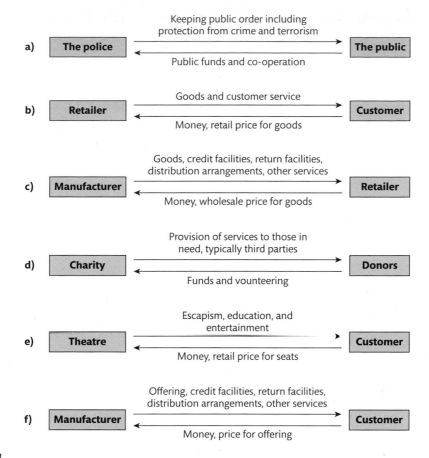

a) **The police** — Keeping public order including protection from crime and terrorism → **The public**
← Public funds and co-operation

b) **Retailer** — Goods and customer service → **Customer**
← Money, retail price for goods

c) **Manufacturer** — Goods, credit facilities, return facilities, distribution arrangements, other services → **Retailer**
← Money, wholesale price for goods

d) **Charity** — Provision of services to those in need, typically third parties → **Donors**
← Funds and vounteering

e) **Theatre** — Escapism, education, and entertainment → **Customer**
← Money, retail price for seats

f) **Manufacturer** — Offering, credit facilities, return facilities, distribution arrangements, other services → **Customer**
← Money, price for offering

Figure 1.3

Examples of marketing exchange processes

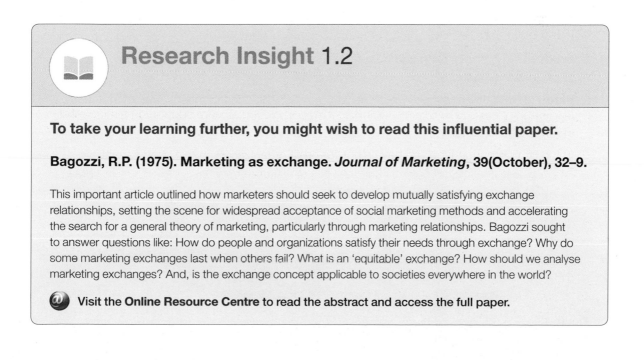

Research Insight 1.2

To take your learning further, you might wish to read this influential paper.

Bagozzi, R.P. (1975). Marketing as exchange. *Journal of Marketing*, 39(October), 32–9.

This important article outlined how marketers should seek to develop mutually satisfying exchange relationships, setting the scene for widespread acceptance of social marketing methods and accelerating the search for a general theory of marketing, particularly through marketing relationships. Bagozzi sought to answer questions like: How do people and organizations satisfy their needs through exchange? Why do some marketing exchanges last when others fail? What is an 'equitable' exchange? How should we analyse marketing exchanges? And, is the exchange concept applicable to societies everywhere in the world?

@ Visit the **Online Resource Centre** to read the abstract and access the full paper.

public. By understanding how exchanges take place between members of the supply chain, we can therefore determine where to add value to the customer experience.

The Marketing Mix and the 4Ps

Neil Borden originally developed the concept of the **marketing mix** in his teaching at Harvard University in the 1950s. His idea was that marketing managers were 'mixers of ingredients'—chefs who concoct a unique marketing recipe to fit the requirements of customers' needs at any particular time. The emphasis was on the creative fashioning of a mix of marketing procedures and policies to produce the profitable enterprise. He composed a 12-item list of elements (with sub-items, not reproduced here), which the manufacturer should consider when developing marketing mix policies and procedures (Borden, 1964):

1 product planning;

2 pricing;

3 branding;

4 channels of distribution;

5 personal selling;

6 advertising;

7 promotions;

8 packaging;

9 display;

10 servicing;

11 physical handling;

12 fact finding and analysis.

This list was simplified and amended by Eugene McCarthy (1960) to the more memorable but rigid 4Ps (see Figure 1.4):

1 **product**—e.g. the offering and how it meets the customer's need, its packaging, and its labelling (see Chapter 8);

2 **place** (distribution channels)—e.g. the way in which the offering meets customers' needs (see Chapter 14);

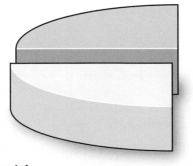

☐ Product
☐ Place
☐ Price
☐ Promotion

Figure 1.4
The 4Ps of the marketing mix

3 **price**—e.g. the cost to the customer, and the cost plus profit to the seller (see Chapter 9);

4 **promotion**—e.g. how the offering's benefits and features are conveyed to the potential buyer (see Chapters 10 and 11).

The intention was to create a simpler framework around which managers could develop their planning. Although there was recognition that all of these elements might be interlinked (e.g. promotion based on the price paid by the consumer), such interplay between these mix components was not taken into account in McCarthy's framework. (See Market Insight 1.1 for an example of why the V&D department store offering in Holland and the marketing mix more generally needs redeveloping.)

Market Insight 1.1
V&D Goes Bust!

On New Year's Eve 2015, the Dutch department store Vroom & Dreesman (V&D), owned by US private equity firm Sun Capital, declared itself insolvent after suffering poor sales, a loss of €49m on sales of €604m in 2014, and a year of conflict with unions and landlords. The company was finding it difficult to compete with new competitors and the shift to online purchasing. The company, first established in 1887, had over 10,000 staff and 62 stores across the Netherlands, selling items such as designer clothing and shoes, jewelry, home electric appliances, furniture, china, stationery, books and CDs, and much more. It also owned the La Place restaurant chain in 250 locations. In early 2016, bankruptcy administrators began trying to find a buyer for parts of the business.

The V&D works council (i.e. the employees) wrote to the bankruptcy administrators, Kees van de Meent and Hanneke de Coninck-Smolders, to request that the owners Sun Capital not be allowed involvement in the future activities of the company, should it emerge from its financial difficulties. However, after suggestions of up to 70 candidate buyers for the business, the administrators invited 10 candidates to submit bids.

Sources: Anon. (2015a, b); Pieters (2015).

Iconic Dutch department store V&D shuts its doors after 128 years of service
Source: iStock.com/Poulssen.

Theory into Practice

This market insight describes how a Dutch department store retailer, aimed firmly at middle-class customers fails after a spell of annual losses which its US owner was no longer prepared to bear. As a result, the company called in the bankruptcy administrators. The market insight demonstrates that not all businesses succeed, even those that have been running with a previously successful model for more than 100 years. The case underlines the importance of staying in touch with customers' needs if a company is to survive in the long term. It also provides an opportunity to understand how marketing strategy can be redesigned using the 4Ps, particularly in relation to multichannel marketing (see Chapter 14).

Market Insight 1.1
continued

Related Topics:

retail marketing, marketing mix; market orientation; multichannel management; distribution.

1 If you were a senior executive at a company which acquired the V&D business from bankruptcy specialists Kees van de Meent and Hanneke de Coninck-Smolders, how would you seek to use the 4Ps to revive the company's marketing to appeal to more consumers? Why might their marketing mix strategy have failed?

2 Why do you think V&D has found it so difficult to alter its business model?

3 What other companies can you think of that need to revive their marketing mixes?

Some commentators have argued that the 4Ps framework is of limited use; however, we include it here because managers continue to use it extensively when devising their marketing plans.

The Extended Marketing Mix

It might seem that what is exchanged in a service context (e.g. purchasing a holiday) is different from a goods context (e.g. buying a car). Therefore by the end of the 1970s it was recognized that the traditional 4Ps approach to marketing planning (see Chapter 5 for a detailed treatment of this topic) based on physical products (e.g. salt, houses, alcoholic drinks) was not particularly useful for either a physical product offering with a strong service component (e.g. tablet computers with extended warranty) or services with little or no physical component (e.g. spa and massage, hairdressing, sports spectatorship) (see Chapter 15.)

Two American scholars (Booms and Bitner, 1981) incorporated a further 3Ps into the marketing mix to reflect the need to market services differently, as follows (see Figure 1.5).

1 Physical evidence—to emphasize that the tangible components of services were strategically important, e.g. potential university students might assess whether or not they want to attend a university and a particular course by requesting a copy of brochures or by visiting the campus to assess the **servicescape** for themselves.

2 Process—to emphasize the importance of the service delivery. When processes are standardized, it is easier to manage customer expectations, e.g. DHL International GmbH, the German international express, transport, and air freight company, is a master at producing a standardized menu of service options, such as track and trace delivery services, which are remarkably consistent around the world.

3 People—to emphasize the importance of customer service personnel, sometimes experts and often professionals interacting with the customer. How they interact with customers, and how

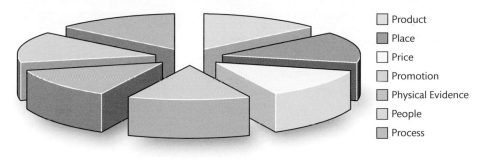

- Product
- Place
- Price
- Promotion
- Physical Evidence
- People
- Process

Figure 1.5
The amended marketing mix for services: the 7Ps

satisfied customers are as a result of their experiences, is of strategic importance. For example, McKinsey & Company prides itself on the quality of its more than 9,000 consultants and its 2,000 research and information specialists as an integral part of its offering (McKinsey, 2016).

Consider how the extended marketing mix is used in the airline industry. For instance, the process component of the services marketing mix has been revolutionized through Internet ticket booking and web check-in services. The traditional middlemen, the travel agencies, have had to radically alter their customer proposition as the major national carriers (e.g. Air France, KLM, British Airways) offer their services directly by Internet to compete with a new class of lower-cost airlines, also offering their services direct to the public via the Internet at substantially lower prices. Many travel agencies put their own services online, customizing their holiday offerings to differentiate their services from the airlines and add value for the customer, offering better deals on insurance, identifying best flight connections, providing advice on best airlines, and offering affiliate hotel deals (Saren, 2006). Two of the top three travel agents are (pureplay) online-only firms, i.e. Expedia (including Trivago, hotels.com, Hotwire) and Priceline (including booking.com). Despite this, a majority of some nationalities continue to book their holidays through traditional travel agents, e.g. Germans and Chinese (Anon., 2014).

The people, process, and physical evidence components of the airline service marketing mix are fundamental in the development of the offering. Of course, airlines do not offer everyone exactly the same level of service. Most airlines offer an economy service, an economy plus service (with slightly more seating space), a business class service (with even more seating space, a better meal, personalized cabin crew service, fast-track service through passport control, and often a limousine service to and from the airport), and a first class service (with personalized menus, luxury transport to and from the airport, and luxurious in-flight seating). Table 1.3 provides a summary of the marketing mix for the airline industry.

Relationship Marketing, Service-Dominant Logic, and Co-Creation

The extended marketing mix was developed after recognition that the 4Ps were inadequate to describe how the marketing of services should be undertaken. But the extended marketing mix also came to be seen as overly transactional and product focused, even for services. The question arose that if marketing was about exchange, shouldn't marketing also be concerned with relationships between those parties that are exchanging value and not just what was exchanged? This was the principal idea behind the development of relationship marketing

Table 1.3 The marketing mix: the airline industry

Marketing aspect	Airline industry
Basic customer need	Safe long- and short-haul transportation, domestic and international.
Target market	Mass consumer market (economy class), the discerning traveller (economy plus), business people (business class), and high-net-worth individuals (first class).
Offering	Typically, differentiated based on class of passenger, with seat size increasing, check-in and boarding times reducing, quality of food increasing, and levels of ancillary services (e.g. limousine service) increasing as we move from economy through business to first class. Some carriers focus on 'no-frills' basic services (e.g. EasyJet, Ryanair, Air Asia).
Price	Substantial difference depending on class of service, type of carrier, and purchasing approach (e.g. via Internet is cheaper).
Principal promotional tools	(1) the Internet (2) press, magazine, and radio advertising, (3) billboards.
Distribution	Increasingly purchased via mobile apps and the Internet, including third-party brokerages such as Expedia as well as, to a lesser degree in many countries, through physical travel agents.
Process	Self-service via mobile phone or Internet or aided by travel agent in retail location. Travel options increasingly customized to the customer's needs, including size of baggage allowance, class of travel, increasing availability of alternative and multicentre locations. Customer and organization use of social media to air and resolve problems now very important.
Physical evidence	Airline loyalty cards and souvenirs, in-flight magazines, in-flight entertainment services, food and snack meals, grooming and toiletry products provided. On some flights, depending on class purchased, suites, bars, and shower facilities are offered.
People	Combination of check-in staff, customer service personnel, baggage handlers, and cabin crew/pilot teams, all of whom interface with the customer or their belongings at different points in the experience.

in the 1990s. The relationship marketing concept spawned further evolution of marketing's conceptual foundations. There was a shift from the need to engage in transactions towards the need to develop long-term customer relationships, including relationships with other stakeholders (Christopher *et al.*, 2002; see Chapter 14) including:

- suppliers;
- potential employees;
- recruiters;

- referral markets—where they exist, e.g. retail banks partly relying on professional services organizations, including estate agents, for mortgage referrals;

- influence markets—e.g. regulatory authorities, politicians, and civil servants (see also Viney and Baines, 2012);

- internal markets, e.g. existing employees.

Hult *et al.* (2011) added shareholders and the local community to this list. For them, the definition of marketing provided by the AMA (see Table 1.1) is inadequate because it fails to consider a wide enough set of stakeholders. The relationship marketing concept was concerned with integrating customer service, quality assurance, and marketing activity (Payne, 1993). Companies employing a relationship marketing approach stressed customer retention over customer acquisition. Customer retention is an important activity in marketing, as research has demonstrated that when a company retains loyal customers it is more likely to be profitable compared with competitors who do not, because customers:

- will increase their purchases over time;

- are cheaper to promote to;

- who are happy with their relationship with a company refer it to others;

- are prepared to pay a (small) price premium if they are loyal (Reichheld and Sasser, 1990).

The idea of developing stronger relationships with existing customers is particularly important in mature industries where markets are saturated, such as utilities and telecommunications, the travel industry, and retail banking, as well as in service-based industries, such as banking and corporate legal services. Retention programmes are developed to focus marketing activity on enhancing customer service satisfaction and rewarding loyalty, building **customer relationship management** (CRM) systems, and undertaking sales promotion activities. Companies have previously been urged to develop long-term interactive relationships (Gummesson, 1987). However, relationship marketing moved the concept away from simply adopting the 4Ps to adopting an **interactive marketing** approach, paying more attention to the customer base rather than being preoccupied with market share (Grönroos, 1994).

More recently, there has been a realization that marketing needed to shift beyond a goods-based paradigm towards a service-dominant logic (Vargo and Lusch, 2004). This new marketing paradigm sees service as *the* fundamental basis of exchange (see Research Insight 1.3). In that sense, for physical goods offerings, the good is simply the distribution mechanism. To understand this concept better, consider the difference between purchasing a music CD from a shop (e.g. HMV) versus streaming a music file from Spotify's subscription service. The knowledge and technologies embedded in the offering by the company to meet the customer's needs are the source of competitive advantage. Because offerings are inherently service-based, customers become co-creators of the service experience. Therefore, in the end, the ultimate value-in-use of the offering is specified by the customer, often after the sale has taken place (see Market Insight 1.2 for an example of how Rolls Royce has transformed its product-service offering through servitization).

According to Prahalad and Ramaswamy (2004a,b), organizations should use co-creation to differentiate their offerings, given that value is tied up inside the customer's experience with the organization. The co-creation experience is about *joint* creation of value, in which customers take part in an active dialogue and co-construct personalized experiences. Therefore organizations

Research Insight 1.3

To take your learning further, you might wish to read this influential paper.

Vargo, S.L. and Lusch, R.F. (2008). Service-dominant logic: continuing the evolution. *Journal of the Academy of Marketing Science*, 36, 1–10.

This article builds on, and updates, the authors' original ground-breaking article (Vargo and Lusch, 2004) which redefined how marketers should think about offerings, arguing that it was necessary to move beyond the idea of tangible versus intangible goods, embedded value and transactions, and other outmoded concepts derived from economics towards the notion of intangible resources and the co-creation of value and relationships. The article asserts that service is the fundamental basis of all exchanges in marketing and that value is always determined by the beneficiary.

Visit the **Online Resource Centre** to read the abstract and access the full paper.

Market Insight 1.2
Servitization at Rolls-Royce

Rolls-Royce is a global provider of integrated power systems and services to the civil and defence aerospace, marine, nuclear, and power systems markets. However, Rolls-Royce plc (which no longer owns the Rolls-Royce motor car brand) has completely redefined itself since the early 1970s when it was nationalized by the then Conservative government after running into financial problems. In 2014, it had underlying revenues of £14.6bn, down 6% on 2013, with an order book of £73.7bn. Product–service revenue ratios in 2014 were 48%/52% in civil aerospace, 39%/61% in defence aerospace, 63%/37% in the marine sector, and 70%/30% in power systems and 37%/63% in the nuclear business. By comparison, after-market sales, as they were then known, were only 20% of the civil aerospace division's revenues in 1981.

Since then, Rolls-Royce has transformed its business model from selling engines and aftercare (to ensure that the engines work properly and are maintained) to selling its customers 'power by the hour', recognizing that it is not in the engine manufacturing business, it is in

the power generation integrated solutions business. In the civil aerospace sector, Rolls-Royce sells its engines with TotalCare®. With TotalCare® a customer enters an overall agreement with Rolls-Royce that provides visibility of cost and a guarantee of product reliability. It

Rolls Royce wins contract to supply IAG with Trent XWB engines and long-term TotalCare® service support
Source: © Airbus S.A.S 2011—photo by e*m company/H. Goussé.

Market Insight 1.2
continued

was first introduced in the 1990s, and charges airline customers based on the total number of hours flown. By collecting data from aircraft engines in flight worldwide on a continuous basis, it maintains those engines better, predicts engine failures, optimizes engine maintenance programmes, and improves future engine design.

Service looks set to become more important than ever with Rolls-Royce's product market opportunities likely to be worth around £1.79tn and the services market opportunities worth £1.38tn between 2012 and 2032.

Sources: Ryals and Rackham (2012); Rolls-Royce (2014); http://www.rolls-royce.com/about/ataglance/.

Theory into Practice

This market insight describes how a major UK manufacturer enhanced its customer offering by shifting from offering a conventional engineering product to an offering based on a product–service mix including a servitized offering, i.e. by offering its product as a service either by selling engines with service contracts, or leasing thrust capacity rather than purely selling an engine.

Related Topics:

product–service mix; servitization; customer needs; customer value.

1 Why do you think Rolls-Royce has been so successful in selling the service concept?

2 Check out the websites of its competitors, Pratt & Whitney and GE. How do their service offerings in their civil aerospace divisions compare with those of Rolls-Royce?

3 Do you think that all manufacturers' products can be servitized?

wishing to enhance customer input to co-creation should map supplier and customer processes to identify how to design their services accordingly (Payne *et al.*, 2008). The process of co-creation therefore potentially shifts value creation from value-in-exchange, at the point of purchase, to value-in-use, after purchase (Grönroos and Voima, 2013). For example, the airplane manufacturer Boeing incorporated feedback from both airline companies and passengers into their Dreamliner plane design before final production (see Chapter 8).

Marketing in Context

Does marketing practice change if we are marketing goods compared with services, and to consumers compared with businesses? To some degree the answer is yes. We've known since the 1960s that services were making important contributions to the US economy (Regan, 1963). Although the product has previously been the focus of marketing practice and theory, it shouldn't continue to be. Figure 1.6 shows clearly how important services are to a wide variety of

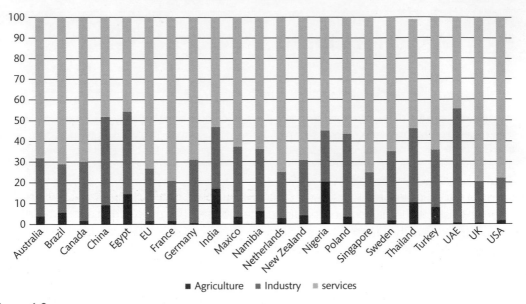

Figure 1.6

Estimated GDP % composition by sector for selected countries (year).

Note: GDP = gross domestic product. All data are estimated for 2014.

Source: Data taken from *CIA World Factbook* (http://www.cia.gov). Reproduced with kind permission of *CIA World Factbook*.

economies around the world, including those in the developed world (e.g. Sweden, Netherlands, UK), the developing world (e.g. Thailand, Brazil), and in the lesser developed countries (e.g. Namibia, Nigeria). Even in China and the United Arab Emirates (UAE), services make up more than 40% of the economy—a substantial contribution.

Marketing techniques need to be adapted to the specific sector in which they are used (Blois, 1974). The context, whether it is industrial (e.g. business-to-business), consumer-based (e.g. retail), or services-based (e.g. business-to-business services like accountancy or business-to-business products like component manufacturers), or not for profit, has an impact on the marketing tools and techniques that we use, although some state that these differences are overplayed and that marketing shares more similarities despite the different contexts (Fern and Brown, 1984; Cova and Salle, 2007). Nevertheless, despite this controversy, whether products are business-to-business or business-to-consumer, they may be either product or service, but all offerings combine some elements of the two. (We discuss the intangible nature of services further in Chapter 15 and not-for-profit marketing in Chapter 17.)

Having identified three unique contexts of marketing—consumer goods, industrial (business-to-business), and services—we briefly discuss how each of these contexts affects how we might undertake marketing activities.

The Consumer Goods Perspective

Bucklin (1963) defined consumer goods as convenience goods (purchased frequently, minimum effort), shopping goods (purchased selectively), or speciality goods (purchased highly selectively). Examples of consumer goods industries include the retail car market, the luxury goods market, and multiple retail groceries. Examples of companies operating in these industries include German car manufacturer Audi, French fashion house Louis Vuitton Moët Hennessey (LVMH), and Unilever, the Anglo-Dutch fast-moving consumer goods company.

The consumer goods perspective has dominated the history of marketing. This perspective gave birth to ideas such as 'marketing mix' and the 4Ps. The consumer goods perspective, borrowing heavily from neoclassical economics, assumes that there are comparatively few suppliers within a particular industry, and that all are rivals for the **aggregated demand** (i.e. demand totalled at population rather than individual level). In fast-moving consumer goods markets (FMCG), the price at which a good is sold is clearly defined. The offering exchanged is tangible (i.e. has physical form) and exchanged between buyer and seller through retail distribution outlets. Consumption takes place at a later point in time, with demand stimulated through the **promotional mix**, i.e. advertising, personal selling, digital and direct marketing, and public relations (see Chapters 10 and 12).

The focus of marketing in this context is on how to facilitate the rapid exchange of goods, the effectiveness of marketing in matching supplier offering to customer demand (e.g. see Market Insight 1.3 on how a British retail institution was slightly adapted for the Thai market), and efficiency in managing the distribution of the product through the supply chain. Of particular importance in this context are the principles and practice of **multichannel marketing** and retailing (see Chapter 14).

Because of the need to stimulate demand from consumers, focus is placed on the importance of advertising (see Chapter 10) to stimulate demand and market research (see Chapter 3) to determine how to develop appropriate consumer products and how they are received by the consumers once launched into the marketplace. Most buying decisions are made by individual customers, but occasionally they are made by several people (e.g. a household including children for a new car, or a friendship group for a particular friend's outfit purchase). Since the advent of the Internet in 1991, digital marketing techniques have greatly increased the amount of information that customers receive, and online procurement approaches now dictate how retailers reorder goods and services from suppliers. (We cover digital and social media marketing in detail in Chapter 12.)

The Services Perspective

The services perspective in marketing was developed around the late 1970s and early 1980s in recognition that the goods-centric marketing approach was ill-suited to the marketing of services. Services marketing thinkers suggested that the intangible performance-dependent nature of services substantially affected the way they should be marketed (Shostack, 1977). There was a focus on the quality of service offered as a result (Grönroos, 1984), as well as a focus on the difference between customer perceptions of actual service quality and their expectations of service quality (Parasuraman *et al.*, 1985).

Some commentators have questioned the use of the product analogy altogether in services marketing (Grönroos, 1998; Vargo and Lusch, 2004). On the debate about whether product and service marketing is different, it is worth noting that services:

- cannot be protected by patent;
- do not make use of packaging;
- lack a physical display;
- cannot be demonstrated in the same way.

Others have argued that there are major similarities (Judd, 1968), including the need to:

- work at full capacity;
- develop trade and service marks;
- use promotional media;

Market Insight 1.3
Harrods: Time for (Thai) Tea

How do companies develop their offerings to meet local consumers' needs in emerging markets? Many global brands sell their offerings using their internationally renowned images, without changing their positioning too significantly when internationalizing. But just how do they pull off this delicate balancing act and still achieve sales success? This was the task facing Boonchai Kongpakpaisarn, the president and CEO of LME, a Thai fashion marketing firm, who brought the quintessential English retail brand, Harrods, to Thailand in late 2013.

Harrods, owner of one of the world's most famous department stores, has been the epitome of English luxury and fashion since its inception in 1849, serving 15m customers per year. In addition to its department store interests it owns Harrods Bank, Harrods Estates, Harrods Aviation, and Air Harrods. The business, employing more than 4000 people and owned by Qatar Holdings, is probably best known for its distinctive green shopping bags, its expansive luxury goods range, and its food hall and tea rooms.

It was in fact Harrods' afternoon tea concept that Kongpakpaisarn considered bringing to Thailand, after visiting the Harrods Tea Room in Ginza, Japan, owned by Mitsubishi Corporation Japan. The idea gained further ground in his mind after he found out that Thais formed one of Harrod's top five overseas customer groups.

Since setting up Harrod's Tea Rooms (with Japan's Mitsubishi Corporation as a partner), he has worked hard to ensure that the Harrods Tea Room concept in Thailand remains true to the English parent, partly by sending his staff to be trained in the UK (rather than getting trainers over from the UK) and by offering English dishes including the Chelsea Set of tea, scones, and clotted cream, the London Metro fish and chips, and even roast beef and Yorkshire pudding. But there is also an adaptation to cater for Thai preferences with dishes containing foie gras and truffles including eggs Benedict foie gras, truffle omelette, and truffle cappuccino soup. Cleverly, Harrods Tea Rooms are located in or near major shopping destinations including in the Siam Paragon and opposite the *Central* department store in Bangkok. Given its apparent popularity, other stores have been planned.

Sources: Anon. (2010); Narataruksa (2014); Pholdhampalit (2014); Ruddick (2014).

Theory into Practice

This market insight describes how a Thai entrepreneur has brought a world-renowned retail brand to the Thai market. It illustrates how a famous foreign international brand can be adapted slightly to cater for local tastes without falling away from the original parent concept.

Related Topics:

market entry method; marketing channels; culture; international marketing; standardization–adaptation; marketing implementation.

1 How important is it that Harrods tea rooms sold a Thai-oriented food range?

2 Would you define the Harrods Tea Room food offering in Thailand as a convenience, shopping, or speciality good?

3 Is the Harrods Tea Room retail offer purely a consumer good? Why do you say this?

- use personal selling techniques;
- use an approach to pricing based on cost and value.

We consider services marketing in more detail in Chapter 14.

The Business-to-Business Perspective

Many marketing textbooks over-emphasize consumer goods marketing, paying inadequate attention to industrial/organizational/business-to-business (B2B) marketing. B2B marketing is different from consumer marketing because the customer focus is a professional buyer within a business rather than an individual per se. B2B marketing requires that marketers deal with more sophisticated customers buying in volume, and often as part of a decision-making unit (with other buyers and technicians), who are trained to buy/procure professionally, and who are rewarded for buying the right propositions at the right price (see Chapter 16).

Much B2B marketing activity revolves around the need to develop strong prospects for a company's offerings, to ensure effective supply chain management operations to develop the market for a B2B offering, and to ensure that it is delivered appropriately. Because buyers typically purchase large volumes of products or complex 'bundles' of services (e.g. customized IT software solutions sold by the German company SAP), tight specifications are usually produced with which suppliers must comply. Buyers try to ensure that they obtain the best supplier possible by offering suppliers a contract to supply for a set period of time through a bidding process.

In public sector markets, the **procurement** process is bound by strict legal guidelines for contracts valued over a set amount. This process creates substantial rivalry, with firms often submitting bids they cannot then fulfil either because they've underpriced themselves, or because they've over-promised what they can deliver; a phenomenon known as the **winner's curse** as the winning company ends up servicing an unprofitable contract (Thaler, 2012).

The emphasis in B2B markets is strongly focused on the development and building of mutually satisfying relationships based on commitment and trust (Morgan and Hunt, 1994) to win the contract in the first instance and then to deliver it to the customer's specifications. Whether or not a firm meets these specifications is in part linked to the **logistics** function (i.e. warehousing, inventory management, delivery) of the firm. Consequently, B2B marketers can create a competitive advantage if they develop a strong linkage between the marketing and logistics functions, developing a strong customer service proposition through (Christopher, 1986):

- cycle time order reduction;
- accurate invoicing procedures;
- reliable delivery;
- effective claims procedures;
- inventory availability;
- good condition of goods/effective service delivery;
- few order size constraints or limited customization of services;
- effective/planned salesperson visits;
- convenient ordering systems/provision of order status information;
- flexible delivery times;
- strong after-sales support.

As indicated earlier, whilst marketing contexts require some degree of adaptation (e.g. marketing an airline seat has differences compared to marketing a jet engine), what connects all these contexts is the need to provide the customer with perceived value regardless of the context. We consider this topic in greater detail in Chapter 9.

Marketing's Positive Impact on Society

So far, we have considered how marketing can be characterized as operating in either the consumer, business-to-business, or services domains. What is common to all these marketing contexts is that the marketer works to satisfy customers. However, more recently, as discussed earlier, there has been a realization that marketing impacts both positively and negatively on society. Let's consider how much the marketing industry contributes positively to society (we consider the negative societal impacts and sustainable marketing considerations in Chapter 18). For example, Wilkie and Moore (1999) describe the complexities of what they call the 'aggregate marketing system'. We can use the example of how marketing brings together the ingredients of an average European 'continental' breakfast. Consider the individual ingredients—for example, coffee or tea, together with Danish pastries, cold cuts of meat, salad and cheese, muesli and cereals, various fruits, the cups/plates and glasses, the oven to cook the pastries, etc. The distributive capacity of the aggregate marketing system is amazing, especially when we consider that there were around 514m people in the EU in 2015, each of whom is brought their own unique mixture of breakfast offerings each morning (see CIA, 2015). Broadly, the aggregate marketing system in most countries works well. We're not all starving and we don't have to ration our food to preserve the amount we eat. Of course, there are parts of certain countries in Africa, North Korea, and parts of China where people are dying of hunger, but these countries often experience imperfections in supply and demand because of political (e.g. war, dictatorship, famine) and environmental (e.g. drought) circumstances. Therefore marketing plays an important role in developing and transforming society (See Research Insight 1.4 and Market Insight 1.4).

Research Insight 1.4

To take your learning further, you might wish to read this influential paper.

Wilkie, W.L. and Moore, E.S. (2011). Expanding our understanding of marketing in society. *Journal of the Academy of Marketing Science*, 40, 53–73.

This article, building on a previous ground-breaking article (Wilkie and Moore, 1999), charts 100 years of marketing thought and the extent to which marketing in society was a key consideration in scholarship during that time. It continues to expand the idea of the 'aggregate marketing system' within society, and maps the field of marketing in society by outlining extant research groups and a research agenda.

Visit the Online Resource Centre to read the abstract and access the full paper.

Market Insight 1.4
Google: World-Changing Innovations

In 1996, Google began life as a research project developing what became their acclaimed search engine and PageRank algorithm. Since those heady early days, Google has completely transformed society—by changing the way we acquire information. Many of Google's other innovations have become part of peoples' daily lives—for example, Google Books, which has digitized millions of books so that people can preview a snippet of their contents prior to making purchase decisions, or Google Maps, which allows people to plan and pursue their travel routes on foot, or by car, bicycle, or public transport wherever they have a mobile Internet connection.

So, what is the company's secret to achieving innovation success? Part of the answer is that Google has been renowned for its policy of giving 20% free time to engineers or developers to work on independent projects; '20% time' projects have included Gmail, Google News, and AdSense. Its corporate principle for innovation is referred to as 'the 8 Pillars of Innovation'. These highlight important ideas for building innovation capacity, such as having a mission, think big but start small, strive for continual innovation, and be willing to fail. But Google's innovation success does not just derive from corporate policy. It is generated from an understanding of what customers and users are thinking. It champions and capitalizes ideas gained from customer insight. Customers or users are deemed as an open source for creativity and inspiration for Google to create something novel.

Google[x], a semi-secret research and development facility, personifies Google's innovation practices. The facility follows in the footsteps of such classic research labs as the Manhattan Project (the US Second World War A-bomb development project) or Bletchley Park (the British code-breaking facility which cracked Nazi Germany's U-boat codes). Its mandate is to invent new technologies or ways to fix anything which presents a significant problem for mankind.

Since its inception in 2010, Google[x] has been home to many avant-garde innovations, including the self-driving car initiative and Internet-connected spectacles, known as Google Glass, among other incredible projects. Apart from the Google[x] lab located in its Googleplex headquarters in Mountain View, Santa Clara, California, Google has also based its innovation labs in other locations, such as New York and Sydney.

In 2014, Google funded a Science, Technology, Engineering, and Maths (STEM) laboratory in an educational venture in Ras Al Khaimah, United Arab Emirates (UAE). The aim of the facility is to give students and teachers training in cutting-edge technologies, including robotics, 3D printing, drone building, and software coding, in areas in which resources are relatively scarce. In 2015, Belfast, Northern Ireland, was selected as the European location for a new innovation lab facility for Google. This facility is designed for collaboration with firms across the UK and Europe based on digital technology. It will generate more than 1,300 jobs for Belfast. Google prides itself on not being a conventional company. In August 2015, Google created a new parent holding company, Alphabet, ostensibly to separate 'moon shot' projects from its day-to-day business.

Sources: Stone (2013); D'Onfro (2015); George (2015); McDonnell (2015); Scott (2015); Tait (2015).

The origin of world changing innovations—the quirky Googleplex in California, USA
Source: © Asif Islam/Shutterstock.

Market Insight 1.4

continued

Theory into Practice

This market insight describes how one of the world's most innovative companies approaches the development of new offerings and how those new offerings impact upon society. A secondary insight from the case is how Google has sought to de-risk the day-to-day business of Google from its inspirational and aspirational world-changing projects by developing a new parent holding company, Alphabet.

Related Topics:

innovation; marketing in society; new product development; marketing organization.

1 Why are the innovations created by companies like Google so important to local communities and society in general?

2 Do futuristic innovations, such as Google Glass or the self-driving car, really help society or do they just generate profit for the developers?

3 What other companies are you aware of that have had a big impact on society? With what offerings?

This market insight was kindly contributed by Dr Ning Baines, Birkbeck, University of London, UK.

Another element of marketing's positive contribution to society is the role it plays in bringing innovations to the marketplace (see Chapter 8 for more details on this). For instance, some of the world's most important inventions have come to us through the aggregate marketing system.

Consider how some of the offerings outlined in Table 1.4 have affected your own life. What would we do without these inventions today? Imagine if the Internet, social media networking, or mobile phones did not exist. We enjoy them because innovative individuals and companies brought these to us. The cardboard carton for storing milk is ubiquitous, but was invented in 1951 in Sweden. Could you imagine ketchup not existing? It was brought to us by Heinz, based on an ancient Chinese recipe for a fish sauce called *ketsiap*!

In each case, the invention outlined has been an extraordinary success. But the aggregate marketing system not only serves to bring consumers those offerings that truly meet their needs, it also serves to stop the failures getting through as well (see Chapter 8). For example, whether or not electric cars become the dominant form of car as opposed to petrol/diesel engine cars depends on the aggregate marketing system and the marketers that exist within it (see Market Insight 1.5). The aggregate marketing system impedes offerings that don't meet consumer needs (for more on the new proposition development process, see Chapter 8).

Table 1.4 Some modern consumer products and their dates of invention

Consumer product	Product attribute	Consumer need	Inventors/pioneers	Year of invention
The chocolate bar	Cocoa-based food	Allowed chocolate to be eaten as opposed to drunk as had traditionally been the case	J.S. Fry & Sons, UK	1847
Ketchup (from the Chinese word *ketsiap*)	A food condiment, derived from the Chinese fish-based sauce *ketsiap*, but adapted for Western taste, using tomatoes	Designed to improve the consumer's enjoyment of their food by improving the taste and reducing the dryness of some foodstuffs	F. & J. Heinz Co., USA	1876
Diesel-fuelled internal combustion engine	An engine with an efficiency of 75% (meaning that 75% of the energy produced was used to power the engine) as opposed to 10% for the steam engines of the day	Enabled independent craftsmen to compete with large industry	Rudolf Diesel, Germany	1892
Breakfast cereals	Cereals which, when milk is added, provide a healthy meal	Quick and easy to prepare foodstuff which was rapidly adopted as a breakfast meal	W.K. Kellogg Foundation, USA	1906
Television	Transmission of moving images	Information, entertainment, and education	Baird Television Development Company, UK/Telefunken, Germany	1929/1932
Carton	Cardboard liquid storage device	Allows liquid foodstuffs to be stored, packaged, and distributed in an environmentally friendly way	TetraPak, Sweden	1951
Seat belt	The three-point seat belt as a safety system in automobiles	Saves people's lives in automobile accidents	Volvo, Sweden	1959

Table 1.4 Some modern consumer products and their dates of invention (continued)

Product	Description	Inventor	Date
Artificial sweeteners	Xylitol, as the sweetener is known, is used to sweeten food products such as sugar-free chewing gum and toothpastes	It sweetens food products without damaging our teeth	Cultor, Finland	1969
Personal computer	Machine allowing users to play electronic games, perform calculations, and write word-processed documents and other applications	Time-saving device simplifying complex writing/arithmetic tasks, offering recreational possibilities, i.e. game-playing	IBM, USA	1980
Mobile phone	A hand-held device for making telephone calls whilst in motion	The ability to stay in telephone contact with others regardless of one's location	NTT, Japan	1979
World Wide Web/web server	A system for linking hypertext documents (i.e. documents linked to other documents) via the Internet; by using a web browser, users can read web pages	Users with access to the Internet can read and share information across large distances	Tim Berners-Lee, UK, & Robert Cailliau, Belgium/ CERN[b], EU	1990
Social networking	A website designed for personal interaction between friends and acquaintances	Provides easy and instantaneous communication between two or more people in multiple locations around the world	Facebook Inc., USA	2004
Needle-free vaccination	A patch-based treatment to prevent the contraction of disease	Allows users to vaccinate without use of needles	ImmunoMatrix LLC, USA	2015

[a]The named companies are not always the inventors per se; they often acquired the patents from the inventor and so were licensed to produce and distribute the invention.

[b] Conseil Européen pour la Recherche Nucléaire.

Sources: Various, including http://www.inventors.about.com and manufacturers' websites.

Market Insight 1.5
Electrifying Cars

The race continues for the production of an all-singing, all-dancing, good-looking electric car which can compete with its diesel/petrol alternatives. It's a small irony then that between 1830 and 1930 the electric car was the dominant product form before the car based on the internal combustion engine (mainly powered by petrol) began to dominate the market. But although silent and pollution-free, the electric car, if it is to regain supremacy, cannot compromise on performance, looks, or handling. Greater public concern and the need for European legislation concerning vehicle fuel emissions to combat global warming have created this stimulus for change. As car drivers are collectively a major user of oil to power their cars, a shift to electric seems obvious, although the drop in oil prices since 2014 has lessened the cost benefits if not the sustainability appeal somewhat.

Although many car companies have now launched electric car models, the Nissan Leaf was the global market leader in 2015, followed by Chevrolet Volt, Toyota Prius, Tesla Model S, and the Mitsubishi Outlander. Other electric cars to enter the market in 2016 include Audi's e-tron quattro, Porsche's Mission E, Hyundai's Ioniq, Citroen's E-Mehari, and General Motor's Bolt SUV. It is estimated that there will be 20m electric vehicles on the road in 2020. Given that the total number of all cars on the planet crossed the 1.2bn mark in 2014, this is still a relatively small proportion of the total cars sold. The business model for electric vehicles is also different from that for conventional petrol/diesel engines. Instead of buying fuel at a station, the purchaser hires the battery and charges up as necessary, either from home or at a charging station. Critical questions for

Porsche's future car, electrifying!
Source: Reproduced with kind permission of Porsche.

potential customers are: Is there a large enough network of recharging stations nearby or is it easy to install the capability to power from home? Will the whole-life costs of an electric vehicle be on a par with/less than the costs of owning a petrol/diesel engine car? Will the electric car perform as well as any hybrid/non-electric vehicle? Will the lower range before recharging be a problem for drivers? Many country's governments are offering incentives to encourage the uptake of electric vehicles. For example, China offers purchase subsidies, Denmark offers exemption from registration and road taxes, Germany offers exemption from road taxes, India offers a price subsidy and reduced excise duty, the Netherlands offers a tax reduction, Sweden offers a tax subsidy, and the US offers a tax credit. Will these incentives, and the benefits of current electric car brands, be enough to tempt people away from their fossil fuel favourites?

Sources: Voelcker (2014); Ayre (2015); Thompson (2015).

Theory into Practice

This market insight describes the process of development of a new product form: the electric car. The fact that the car was originally electric in form but developed from that into a petrol/diesel engine is important, as it illustrates how consumers move from one product form to a different variant once a product standard is improved. The market insight also demonstrates how long it takes for people to move from one product standard to another when an innovation is launched. (See also Chapter 8.)

Market Insight 1.5
continued

Related Topics:

diffusion of innovations; product standards; consumer buying behaviour; technology acceptance; product development.

1 **Will sales of electric cars overtake sales of conventional petrol/diesel cars? When might this be do you think?**

2 **Why do you think Porsche and other luxury car brands have taken so long to develop their own electric car makes?**

3 **Name other well-known offerings which have taken advantage of society's increasingly strong environmental values.**

Therefore it provides a number of benefits to society including the following (Wilkie and Moore, 1999):

- the promotion and delivery of desired offerings;
- the provision of a forum for market learning (we can see what does and what doesn't get through the system);
- the stimulation of market demand;
- the provision of a wide scope of choice of offerings by providing a close/customized fit with consumer needs;
- facilitates purchases (or acquisitions generally, e.g. if no payment is made directly as in the case of public services);
- saves times and promotes efficiency in customer requirement matching;
- brings new offerings, and improvements, to market to meet latent and unserved needs;
- seeks customer satisfaction for repeat purchases.

Visit the Online Resource Centre and complete Internet Activity 1.2 to learn more about how marketing innovation impacts upon society.

However, the aggregate marketing system, or marketing more generally, does not always serve the common good. Marketing is frequently criticized for doing precisely the opposite—for being unethical in nature, manipulative, and creating wants and needs where none previously existed (Packard, 1960). Whilst this chapter has focused on the principles and practice of marketing, and the positive power of marketing in society, there is also a negative impact of marketing on society. This occurs both as a result of unethical marketing practice and because of structural inequalities in the aggregate marketing system. For a detailed critique of the marketing concept, see Chapter 18.

Chapter Summary

To consolidate your learning, the key points from this chapter are summarized here.

■ **Define the marketing concept.**

Marketing is the process by which organizations anticipate and satisfy their customers' needs to both parties' benefit. It involves mutual exchange. Over the last 25 years, the marketing concept has changed to recognize the importance of long-term customer relationships to organizations. In addition, most definitions of marketing recognize the importance of marketing's impacts on society and the need to curtail these where they are negative.

■ **Explain how marketing has developed over the twentieth and into the twenty-first century.**

Whereas some writers have suggested a simple production era, sales era, marketing era development for marketing over the twentieth century, others recognize that marketing has existed in different forms in different countries at different times. Nevertheless, there is increasing recognition that marketing is a more systematic organizational activity, through market research and sophisticated promotional activity, than before. There is also a move towards recognizing the need for companies and organizations to behave responsibly in relation to society.

■ **Understand the exchange and marketing mix concepts in marketing.**

The concept of exchange is important and has been considered by some to be the key to uncovering the elusive 'general theory of marketing'. Empathizing with customers to understand what they want and determining how sellers seek to provide what buyers want is a central concept in marketing. The means by which organizations deploy their marketing programmes is via the marketing mix, which comprises Product (the offering), Place (the distribution mechanism), Price (the value placed on the offering), and Promotion (how the company communicates that value). For services marketing, because of the intangible nature of the service, marketers consider an extra 3Ps, including Physical Evidence (how cues are developed for customers to recognize quality), Process (how the experience is designed to meet customers' needs), and People (the training and development of those delivering the customer experience).

■ **Describe the three major contexts of marketing application, i.e. consumer goods, business-to-business, and services marketing.**

Marketing activity divides into three types, recognizing that marketing activities are designed based on the context in which an organization operates. The consumer goods marketing approach has been dominant, stressing the 4Ps and the marketing mix. Business-to-business marketing focuses on principles of relationship marketing, particularly those required in coordinating supply chain members. Services marketing stresses the intangible nature of an offering, including the need to manage customer expectations levels of service quality and customer experience.

■ **Understand the positive contribution that marketing makes to society.**

The aggregate marketing system delivers to us a wide array of offerings, either directly or indirectly, through business markets, to serve our wants and needs. There is much that is positive about the aggregate marketing system and it has served to improve the standard of living for many people around the world.

Review Questions

1 How do we define the marketing concept?

2 How do the American Marketing Association and the Chartered Institute of Marketing definitions of marketing differ?

3 How has marketing developed historically?

4 What is the difference between sales and marketing?

5 What is a marketing exchange?

6 What is the marketing mix?

7 What is the services marketing mix?

8 What are the three major contexts of marketing application?

9 What is the winner's curse?

10 What positive contributions does marketing make to society?

Worksheet Summary

To apply the knowledge you have gained from this chapter and test your understanding of marketing theory visit the **Online Resource Centre** and complete Worksheet 1.1.

Discussion Questions

1 Having read the Case Insight at the beginning of this chapter, how would you advise Aldoraq Water to differentiate itself when competing against local and international brands?

2 Read the section on the marketing mix within the chapter and draw up marketing mixes for the following organizations and their target customers.

  A The streaming video company Netflix and its audiences.

  B A luxury hotel group and their wealthy clientele.

  C Pharmacies (e.g. Boots UK Ltd., Sweden's Apoteket AB, Holland's Etos B.V.) and their consumers.

  D A company supplying glass to construction companies.

3 Outline simple marketing exchange processes for the following buyer–seller relationships.

  A The relationship between pharmaceutical salespeople and their clients (e.g. medical practitioners, pharmacists, hospitals).

  B The relationship between the fire and rescue service and the public.

  C The relationship between a confectionery manufacturer and multiple retailer grocers.

4 What are the attributes of the offer, and customer needs associated with those attributes, for the following?

  A Bank business accounts (e.g. those offered by Britain's Barclays plc).

  B A university (e.g. Stockholm School of Economics in Sweden) offering places to students on Masters programmes.

    C A Tag Heuer Lady Steel and Rose Gold Quartz Aquaracer design watch for a lady.
    D A company like Withers Worldwide selling legal services to businesses.
    E Watching a boxing match live at Madison Square Garden in New York, USA.

Visit the **Online Resource Centre** and complete the Multiple Choice Questions to assess your knowledge of Chapter 1.

Glossary

advertising a form of non-personal communication, by an identified sponsor, that is transmitted through the use of paid-for media.

aggregated demand demand calculated at the population level rather than at the individual level.

AMA the American Marketing Association is a professional body for marketing professionals and marketing educators based in the USA, operating principally in the USA and Canada.

CIM the Chartered Institute of Marketing is a professional body for marketing professionals based in the UK, with study centres and members around the world.

consumer the user of a product, service, or other form of offering.

customer the person who purchases and pays for (or initially requests and specifies, in the case of a non-financial transaction) a product, service, or other form of offering from a company or organization.

customer relationship management software systems that provide all staff with a complete view of the history and status of each customer.

dyadic essentially means two-way. A commercial relationship that is dyadic is an exchange between two people, typically a buyer and a seller.

elasticity an economic concept associated with the extent to which changes in one variable are related to changes in another. If a price increase in a good causes a decline in volume of sales of that good, we say the good is price elastic and specify by how much. If it causes no change or very little change, we say it is inelastic.

environmental scanning the management process internal to an organization designed to identify external issues, situations, and threats that may impinge on an organization's future and its strategic decision-making.

ethnography a subdiscipline derived from cultural anthropology as an approach to research, which emphasizes the collection of data through participant observation of members of a specific subcultural grouping and observation of participation of members of a specific subcultural grouping.

haul girls women who go shopping for clothes or beauty products and then make a YouTube video showing viewers what they have bought item by item.

interactive marketing is more accurately described as creating a situation or mechanism through which a marketer and a customer (or stakeholders) interact, usually in real time.

logistics the process of transporting the initial components of goods, services, and other forms of offering, and their finished products, from the producer to the customer and then on to the consumer.

market orientation refers to the development of a whole-organization approach to the generation, collection, and dissemination of market intelligence across different departments and the organization's responsiveness to that intelligence.

market sensing an organization's ability to gather, interpret, and act on strategic information from customers and competitors.

marketing mix the list of items a marketing manager should consider when devising plans for marketing products, including product decisions, place (distribution) decisions, pricing decisions, and promotion decisions. Later, the mix was extended to include physical evidence, process, and people decisions to account for the lack of physical nature in service products.

multichannel marketing refers to the use of multiple, usually synchronized, platforms through which to interact with customers in order to communicate with them and distribute an offering.

netnography the branch of ethnography which seeks to analyse Internet users' behaviour.

non-staple in the grocery context, grocery products that are not a main or important food.

observation a research method that requires a researcher to watch, and record, how consumers or employees behave, typically in relation to either purchasing or selling activities.

place or distribution is essentially about how you can place the optimum amount of goods and/or services before the maximum number of members of your target market, at times and locations that optimize the marketing outcome, i.e. sales.

positioning the way that an audience of consumers or buyers perceives a product or service, particularly as a result of the marketing communications process aimed at a target audience.

price the amount the customer has to pay to receive a good or service.

procurement the purchasing (buying) process in a firm or organization.

product anything that is capable of satisfying customer needs.

promotion the use of communications to persuade individuals, groups, or organizations to purchase products and services.

promotional mix the combination of five key communication tools: advertising, sales promotions, public relations, direct marketing, and personal selling.

relationship marketing the development and management of long-term relationships with customers, influencers, referrers, suppliers, recruiters, and employees.

servicescape the physical environment in which a service takes place, e.g. a stadium for a football game.

service-dominant logic (SDL) asserts that organizations, markets, and society are concerned fundamentally with exchange of service, based on the application of knowledge and skills. Therefore it rejects the notion of dualism between goods and services marketing by arguing that all offerings provide a service.

social anthropology the scientific discipline of observing and recording the way humans behave in their different social groupings.

supply chain management the management and coordination of supply-side activities (including planning, sourcing, making, and delivering) from production to consumption in order to enhance customer value.

tweenagers pre-adolescent children, typically taken to be between the ages of 9 and 12, who are hence about to enter their teenage years.

value the regard that something is held to be worth, typically, although not always, in financial terms.

winner's curse terminology associated with the bidding process in commercial markets where a company ends up submitting a bid at a price that is unprofitable or not very profitable just to win the contract.

References

AMA (American Marketing Association) (2013). About AMA: marketing. Retrieve from: https://www.ama.org/AboutAMA/Pages/Definition-of-Marketing.aspx (accessed 27 December 2015).

AMA (2015). Dictionary: sales. Retrieve from: https://www.ama.org/resources/Pages/Dictionary.aspx?dLetter=S (accessed 28 December 2015).

Anon. (2010). History of Harrods department stores. *BBC News*, 8 May. Retrieve from: http://www.bbc.com/news/10103783 (accessed 8 January 2015).

Anon. (2014). Sun, sea and surfing. *The Economist*, 21 June. Retrieve from: http://www.economist.com/news/business/21604598-market-booking-travel-online-rapidly-consolidating-sun-sea-and-surfing (accessed 17 January 2016).

Anon. (2015a). Dutch V&D department store business goes bust. *BBC News*, 31 December. Retrieve from: http://www.bbc.co.uk/news/business-35208209 (accessed 17 January 2016).

Anon. (2015b). V&D on brink of bankruptcy as warm winter hits sales. *DutchNews.nl,* 23 December. Retrieve from: http://www.dutchnews.nl/news/archives/2015/12/vd-on-brink-of-bankruptcy-as-warm-winter-hits-sales/ (accessed 17 January 2016).

Ayre, J. (2015). Electric car demand growing, global market hits 740,000 units. *Clean Technica*, 28 March. Retrieve from: http://cleantechnica.com/2015/03/28/ev-demand-growing-global-market-hits-740000-units/ (accessed 23 January 2016).

Bagozzi, R.P. (1975). Marketing as exchange. *Journal of Marketing*, 3(4), 32–9.

Bartels, R.D.W. (1944). Marketing principles. *Journal of Marketing*, 9(2), 151–8.

Bartels, R.D.W. (1951). Can marketing be a science? *Journal of Marketing*, 15(3), 319–28.

Bartels, R.D.W. (1959). Sociologists and marketologists. *Journal of Marketing*, 24 (2), 37–40.

Bartels, R.D.W. (1968). The general theory of marketing. *Journal of Marketing*, 32(January), 29–33.

Blois, K.J. (1974). The marketing of services: an approach. *European Journal of Marketing*, 8(2), 137–45.

Booms, B.H. and Bitner, M.J. (1981). Marketing strategies and organisation structures for service firms. In: J.H. Donnelly and W.R. George (eds), *Marketing of Services*, Chicago, IL: AMA Proceedings Series, 48.

Borden, N.H. (1964). The concept of the marketing mix. *Journal of Advertising Research*, 4, 2–7.

Brenner, B. (2013). Inside the NIKE matrix. Wirtschafts Universität Wien Case Series, Case 0001/2013. Retrieve from: http://epub.wu.ac.at/3791/1/Nike__WU-CaseSeries.pdf (accessed 28 December 2015).

Bucklin, L.P. (1963). Retail strategy and the classification of consumer goods. *Journal of Marketing*, 27(1), 51–6.

CIA (2015). *The World Factbook—European Union*, Washington, DC: CIA. Retrieve from: https://www.cia.gov/library/publications/the-world-factbook/geos/ee.html (accessed 13 April 2016).

Christopher, M. (1986). Reaching the customer: strategies for marketing and customer service. *Journal of Marketing Management*, 2(1), 63–71.

Christopher, M., Payne, A., and Ballantyne, D. (2002)/ *Relationship Marketing: Creating Stakeholder Value* (2nd edn), Oxford: Butterworth Heinemann.

CIM (Chartered Institute of Marketing) (2009). *In Search of a Strategic Role for Marketing: Leading, Influencing or Supporting*. Cookham: Chartered Institute of Marketing.

CIM (Chartered Institute of Marketing) (2015). Marketing and the 7Ps. Retrieve from: http://www.cim.co.uk/files/7ps.pdf (accessed 27 December 2015).

Comstock, B., Gulati, R., and Liguori, S. (2010). Unleashing the power of marketing. *Harvard Business Review*, October, 90–8.

Cova, B. and Salle, R. (2007). The industrial/consumer marketing dichotomy revisited: a case of outdated justification? *Journal of Business and Industrial Marketing*, 23(1), 3–11.

Day, G.S (1994). The capabilities of market-driven organisations. *Journal of Marketing*, 58(3), 37–52.

D'Onfro, J. (2015). The truth about Google's famous '20% time' policy. *Business Insider UK*, 17 April. Retrieve from: http://uk.businessinsider.com/google-20-percent-time-policy-2015-4?r=US&IR=T (accessed 29 December 2015).

Doob, L.W. (1948). *Public Opinion and Propaganda*. Oxford: Henry Holt.

Enright, M. (2002). Marketing and conflicting dates for its emergence: Hotchkiss, Bartels and the fifties school of alternative accounts. *Journal of Marketing Management*, 18, 445–61.

Fern, E.F. and Brown, J.R. (1984). The industrial/consumer marketing dichotomy: a case of insufficient justification. *Journal of Marketing*, 48(2), 68–77.

Fullerton, R.A. (1988). How modern is modern marketing? Marketing's evolution and the myth of the 'Production Era'. *Journal of Marketing*, 52(January), 108–25.

George, B. (2015). The world's most innovative company. *Huffington Post,* 28 October. Retrieve from: http://www.huffingtonpost.com/bill-george/the-worlds-most-innovativ_b_8406556.html (accessed 28 December 2015).

Gordon, J. and Porroy, J. (2015). The dawn of marketing's new golden age. *McKinsey Quarterly*, February. Retrieve from: http://www.mckinsey.com/insights/marketing_sales/the_dawn_of_marketings_new_golden_age (accessed 17 January 2016).

Grönroos, C. (1984). A service quality model and its marketing implications. *European Journal of Marketing*, 18(4), 36–44.

Grönroos, C. (1994). From marketing mix to relationship marketing: towards a paradigm shift in marketing. *Management Decision*, 32(2), 4–20.

Grönroos, C. (1998). Marketing services: a case of a missing product. *Journal of Business and Industrial Marketing*, 13(4/5), 322–38.

Grönroos, C. and Voima, P. (2013). Critical service logic: making sense of value creation and co-creation. *Journal of the Academy of Marketing Science*, 41(2), 133–50.

Gummesson, E. (1987). The new marketing: developing long term interactive relationships. *Long Range Planning*, 20(4), 10–20.

Gummesson, E. (1990). Marketing orientation revisited: the crucial role of the part-time marketer. *European Journal of Marketing*, 25(2), 60–75.

Hanssens, D.M. (Ed.). (2009). *Empirical Generalizations About Marketing Impact: What We Have Learned from Academic Research*. Cambridge, MA: Marketing Science Institute.

Harris, L.C. and Ogbonna, E. (2003). The organisation of marketing: a study of decentralised, devolved and dispersed marketing activity. *Journal of Management Studies*, 40(2), 483–512.

Holden, A.C. and Holden, L. (1998). Marketing history: illuminating marketing's clandestine subdiscipline. *Psychology and Marketing*, 15(2), 117–23.

Howard, D.G., Savins, D.M., Howell, W., and Ryans, J.K., Jr (1991). The evolution of marketing theory in the United States and Europe. *European Journal of Marketing*, 25(2), 7–16.

Hult, G.T.M., Mena, J.A., Ferrell, O.C., and Ferrell, L. (2011). Stakeholder marketing: a definition and conceptual framework. *AMS Review*, 1, 44–65.

Hunt, S.D. (1971). The morphology of theory and the general theory of marketing. *Journal of Marketing*, 35(April), 65–8.

Hunt, S.D. (1983). General theories and fundamental explananda of marketing. *Journal of Marketing*, 47(4, Fall), 9–17.

Hunt, S. D. (2013). A general theory of business marketing: RA theory, Alderson, the ISBM framework, and the IMP theoretical structure. *Industrial Marketing Management*, 42(3), 283–93.

Judd, R.C. (1968). Similarities and differences in product and service retailing. *Journal of Retailing*, 43(4), 1–9.

Katz, E. (1957). The two-step flow of communication: an up-to-date report on an hypothesis. *Public Opinion Quarterly*, 21(1), 61–78.

Keith, R.J. (1960). The marketing revolution. *Journal of Marketing*, 24(January), 35–8.

Kirca, A.H., Jayachandran, S., and Bearden, W.O. (2005). Market orientation: a meta-analytic review and assessment of its antecedents and impact on performance. *Journal of Marketing*, 69(April), 24–41.

Kohli, A.K. and Jaworski, B.J. (1990). Market orientation: the construct, research propositions and managerial implications. *Journal of Marketing*, 54(April), 1–18.

Kotler, P. (2006). Ethical lapses of marketers. In: J.N. Sheth and R.J. Sisodia (eds), *Does Marketing Need Reform: Fresh Perspectives on the Future*, Armonk, NY: M.E. Sharpe, Chapter 17.

Kumar, V., Jones, E., Venkatesan, R., and Leone, R.P. (2011). Is market orientation a source of sustainable competitive advantage or simply the cost of competing? *Journal of Marketing*, 75(1), 16–30.

Le Meunier-FitzHugh, K. and Piercy, N.F. (2011). Exploring the relationship between market orientation and sales and marketing collaboration. *Journal of Personal Selling and Sales Management*, 31(3), 287–96.

Lee, A.M. (1945). The analysis of propaganda: a clinical summary. *American Journal of Sociology*, 51(2), 126–35.

Lendrevie, J. and Lévy, J. (2014). *Mercator: Tout le Marketing à l'Ère Numérique* (11th edn), Paris: Dunod.

Leone, R.P. and Shultz, R.L. (1980). A study of marketing generalisations. *Journal of Marketing*, 44(Winter), 10–18.

McCarthy, E.J. (1960). *Basic Marketing*. Homewood, IL: Irwin.

McDonnell, F. (2015). New PwC and Google innovation lab will be located in Belfast. *The Irish Times,* 24 November. Retrieve from: http://www.irishtimes.com/business/new-pwc-and-google-innovation-lab-will-be-located-in-belfast-1.2442406 (accessed 28 December 2015).

McKinsey (2016). About us. *McKinsey & Company*. Retrieve from: http://www.mckinsey.com/about_us/who_we_are (accessed 17 January 2016).

Morgan, R.M. and Hunt, S.D. (1994). The commitment–trust theory of relationship marketing. *Journal of Marketing*, 58(3, July), 20–38.

Narataruksa, S. (2014). A cup of joy. *Thailand Tatler*, June, 44–5.

Narver, J.C. and Slater, S.F. (1990). The effect of a market orientation on business profitability. *Journal of Marketing*, 54(4), 20–35.

O'Malley, L. and Patterson, M. (1998). Vanishing point: the mix management paradigm re-viewed. *Journal of Marketing Management*, 14(8), 829–51.

Packard, V.O. (1960). *The Hidden Persuaders*. Harmondsworth: Penguin Books.

Parasuraman, A., Berry, L.L., and Zeithaml, V.A. (1985). A conceptual model of service quality and its implications for further research. *Journal of Marketing*, 49(Fall), 41–50.

Parsons, R. (2013). Companies acting irresponsibly by not letting marketing into c-suite. *Marketing Week*, 27 March. Retrieve from: http://www.marketingweek.co.uk/news/companies-acting-irresponsibly-by-not-letting-marketing-into-c-suite/4006136.article#commentsubmitted (accessed 3 April 2013).

Payne, A. (1993). *The Essence of Services Marketing*. Hemel Hempstead: Prentice-Hall.

Payne, A., Storbacka, K., and Frow, P. (2008). Managing the co-creation of value. *Journal of the Academy of Marketing Science*, 36, 83–96.

Pholdhampalit, K. (2014). Tea with the most elegant of flavours. *The Sunday Nation*, 5 January. Retrieve from: http://www.nationmultimedia.com/sunday/Tea-with-the-most-elegant-of-flavours-30223468.html (accessed 8 January 2015).

Pieters, J. (2015). Dutch department store V&D declared bankrupt: some 10,000 job losses. *NLtimes*, 31 December. Retrieve from: http://www.nltimes.nl/2015/12/31/dutch-dept-store-v-some-10000-job-losses/ (accessed 17 January 2016).

Prahalad, C.K. and Ramaswamy, V. (2004a). Co-creation experiences: the next practice in value creation. *Journal of Interactive Marketing*, 18(3), 5–14.

Prahalad, C.K. and Ramaswamy, V. (2004b). Co-creating unique value with customers, *Strategy and Leadership*, 32(3), 4–9.

Regan, W.J. (1963). The service revolution. *Journal of Marketing*, 27, 57–62.

Reichheld, F.F. and Sasser, W.E., Jr (1990). Zero defections: quality comes to services. *Harvard Business Review*, September–October, 105–11.

Rolls-Royce (2014). *Annual Report 2014*. London: Rolls-Royce plc. Retrieve from: http://ar.rolls-royce.com/2014/ (accessed 18 January 2016).

Ruddick, G. (2014). Harrods pays £118m dividend to Qatar after profits surge. *The Telegraph*, 30 October. Retrieve from: http://www.telegraph.co.uk/finance/newsbysector/retailandconsumer/11198059/Harrods-pays-118m-dividend-to-Qatar-after-surge-in-profitsh.html (accessed 8 January 2015).

Ryals, L. and Rackham, N. (2012). Sales implications of servitization. Presentation to the Key Account Management Best Practice Club, Cranfield School of Management, February. Retrieve from: http://www.som.cranfield.ac.uk/som/dinamic-content/media/Sales%20Implications%20of%20Servitization%20White%20Paper%20Feb%202012%20v2.pdf (accessed 10 April 2013).

Saren, M. (2006). *Marketing Graffiti: The View from the Street*. Oxford: Butterworth Heinemann.

Scott, A. (2015). Google backed lab brings robotics and other technologies to RAK and Northern Emirates. *The National,* 9 April. Retrieve from: http://www.thenational.ae/business/technology/google-backed-lab-brings-robotics-and-other-technologies-to-rak-and-northern-emirates (accessed 28 December 2015).

Shaw, E.H., and Jones, D.B. (2005). A history of schools of marketing thought. *Marketing Theory*, 5(3), 239–81.

Sheth, J.N. and Sisodia, R.J. (2005). A dangerous divergence: marketing and society. *Journal of Public Policy and Marketing*, 24(1), 160–2.

Sheth, J.N. and Sisodia, R.J. (2006). How to reform marketing. In: J.N. Sheth and R.J. Sisodia (eds), *Does Marketing Need Reform: Fresh Perspectives on the Future*. Armonk, NY: M. E. Sharpe, Chapter 20.

Sheth, J.N. and Sisodia, R.S. (2015). *Does Marketing Need Reform? Fresh Perspectives on the Future*. Oxford: Routledge.

Shostack, G.L. (1977). Breaking free from product marketing. *Journal of Marketing*, 41(April), 73–8.

Slater, S.F. and Narver, J.C. (1994). Market orientation, customer value and superior performance. *Business Horizons*, March–April, 22–7.

Stone, B. (2013). Inside Google's secret lab. *Bloomberg Business*, 22 May. Retrieve from: http://www.businessweek.com/printer/articles/118812-inside-googles-secret-lab (accessed 28 December 2015).

Tait, S. (2015). Interview with Google's head of marketing innovation APAC. *Marketing,* 24 September. Retrieve from: https://www.marketingmag.com.au/hubs-c/interview-googles-head-marketing-innovation-apac/ (accessed 28 December 2015).

Thaler, R. (2012). *The Winner's Curse: Paradoxes and Anomalies of Economic Life*. New York: Simon & Schuster.

Thompson, C. (2015). 6 electric cars we can't wait to see in 2016. *Business Insider UK*, 8 December. Retrieve from: http://uk.businessinsider.com/6-electric-cars-we-cant-wait-to-see-in-2016-2015-12 (accessed 23 January 2016).

Vargo, S.L. and Lusch, R.F. (2004). Evolving to a new service dominant logic for marketing. *Journal of Marketing*, 68(January), 1–17.

Vargo, S.L. and Lusch, R.F. (2008). Service-dominant logic: continuing the evolution. *Journal of the Academy of Marketing Science*, 36, 1–10.

Voelcker, J. (2014). 1.2 billion vehicles on world's roads now, 2 billion by 2035: report. *Green Car Reports*, 29 July. Retrieve from: http://www.greencarreports.com/news/1093560_1-2-billion-vehicles-on-worlds-roads-now-2-billion-by-2035-report (accessed 23 January 2016).

Viney, H. and Baines, P. (2012). Engaging government: why it's necessary and how to do it. *European Business Review*, September–October, 9–13.

Wilkie, W.L. and Moore, E.S. (1999). Marketing's contributions to society. *Journal of Marketing*, 63 (Special Issue), 198–218.

Wilkie, W.L., and Moore, E.S. (2011). Expanding our understanding of marketing in society. *Journal of the Academy of Marketing Science*, 40, 53–73.

Worcester, R.M., Mortimore, R., Baines, P., and Gill, M. (2011). *Explaining Cameron's Coalition*. London: Biteback Publishing.

Chapter 2
Consumer Buying Behaviour

Learning Outcomes

After studying this chapter, you will be able to:

▶ Explain the consumer product acquisition process

▶ Explain the processes involved in human perception, learning, and memory in relation to consumer choice

▶ Understand the importance of personality and motivation in consumer behaviour

▶ Describe opinions, attitudes, and values, and how they relate to consumer behaviour

▶ Explain how reference groups influence consumer behaviour

Case Insight 2.1
Holdz®

Market Insight 2.1
Easy Purchasing
at Peugeot in 2015

Market Insight 2.2
Jameson: A Cut Above
the Rest

Market Insight 2.3
Deshopping: When Price
Doesn't Matter

Market Insight 2.4
On Yer Bike!

Market Insight 2.5
The Iftar Market

Case Insight 2.1
Holdz®

Founded in 2000, _Holdz®_ is an online climbing holds and accessories firm. We speak to its Managing Director, Steve Goodair, to find out more about how the firm meets its customers' needs.

Holdz® is a small to medium-sized enterprise specializing in making the polyurethane resin holds that screw onto climbing walls to allow climbers to practise indoors in a safe but natural-looking environment. Our holds are expertly crafted in all shapes and sizes to resemble real rock features, from cracks to crimpz and sloperz to smoothies. We also produce bouldering mats, chalk bags, and clothing.

Typical customers include climbing centres (which simulate climbing on rock faces), bouldering centres (which simulate climbing on large boulders), and serious individual climbers who have built climbing walls in their own houses to allow them to train even harder. Where climbing walls are owned by local councils, they tend to try to buy in volume because they are interested less in the shape of hold they are getting, and more in obtaining a volume discount. I sometimes have to point out to them that I can make holds for low prices but the holds would be so small that they'd be useless! So, we sometimes have to educate our customers about product and typical industry prices. Top route-setters (the people who put the holds on the wall) buy based on the shapes of the holds. This is so that they can make specific climbing route 'problems' requiring climbers to ascend a route in a certain way to different degrees of difficulty from 'easy' through to 'hard' and 'very severe' through to 11 grades of 'extremely severe' (grades 1 to 11). Home wall users tend to buy a pack of holds to get them started, but they also tend to return for more after a few months, for variety and because they have mastered those holds and got stronger.

Because climbers sometimes fall when they ascend difficult routes, we produce heavy duty matting,

which allows climbers to fall more safely and with less likelihood of injury. We have manufactured our matting for 15 years and it has become an industry best-seller. We have such confidence in its quality, that we offer a five year quality guarantee. Overall, we cater for serious climbers, keen on the high product quality that we provide. We have a lot of repeat customers, especially with home walls, and we work hard to look after them. We know they that find holds quite expensive, so we put one or two free holds in with their order as a surprise. Lots of our customers share images of their purchases on social media, a great way of spreading positive word of mouth for us.

To raise awareness of the Holdz® brand, we have in the past sponsored climbing and bouldering competitions, including the International Federation of Sport Climbing World Cup. Whenever they hold a competition, they brand the wall and competitors' vests with sponsors' logos. We engage with our customers mainly by social media, and face to face when we're on the road selling to climbing centres or installing our holds. But we also engage with customers in another unique way. All our products display our logo and climbers subconsciously remember the Holdz® name, and the hold's product type name, when they're hanging onto it for dear life! So, they recall these details when they are looking for the same type of hold when setting their own routes.

In 2006, there were no bouldering centres anywhere in the world. There were only climbing centres with a small bouldering wall. A friend opened the world's first bouldering-only centre in Sheffield and asked us to provide the crash mats. No-one knew how many

Case Insight 2.1
continued

visitors it would receive per day or if a bouldering-only venue would take off but it did. For our crash mats we used foam and PVC (polyvinyl chloride) but the sheer amount of traffic this centre was receiving was phenomenal and it became very popular.

If 150 climbers were doing an average of 30 climbing 'problems' a session, the mats were being hammered 4,500 times per day. Multiply that by a year and that's 1.64m feet-first landings onto the matting. Over time our customers noticed that this force was damaging

the matting as the seams and materials became stressed from the landings requiring its constant replacement. Our customers did not want to continually have to replace the crash matting as this was expensive in materials and labour.

The problem we faced was how could we develop a matting solution for our customers which was both durable and affordable but still allowed us to generate a reasonable profit?

Introduction

What process did you go through when deciding which university course to study? How do you decide which restaurants to go to, or which lipstick to buy? After reading this chapter, you will understand why consumers think and behave as they do. World-class marketers have a profound understanding of customers' needs/wants and behaviour. In this chapter, we explore consumer behaviour (for business-to-business buying behaviour, see Chapter 16). We consider cognitions (thoughts), **perceptions** (how we see things), and learning (how we memorize techniques and knowledge). These are processes that are fundamental in explaining how consumers think and learn about offerings. As consumers, we constantly perceive and learn new things. Learning about offerings is no different from learning about concepts in general. Consider how we find out about the launch of a new offering, e.g. the Fiat Tipo or the BMW PHEV hybrids for its 2, 3, and 7 series vehicles. We don't just know about these offerings intuitively, we learn how they differ from existing petrol-powered cars, their relative benefits and disadvantages in terms of features, the price, and where they are available.

We discuss personality and motivation to illustrate how these psychological concepts affect how we buy. These are important, because offerings are often designed to appeal to particular types of people. Banks target us for personal accounts and investment products based on our personalities and motivations (e.g. how financially risk averse we might be or our attitudes to taking out credit). We also discuss opinions, attitudes, and values to give an understanding of how we are persuaded by **reference groups**, i.e. groups that have an influence over our decision-making. Fast-moving consumer goods companies constantly bombard us with images of celebrity endorsers, who act as our reference groups for a wide variety of offerings. Because marketing comes alive when it is interlinked into the fabric of our social lives, we consider how **social class**, lifecycles, and lifestyles influence consumer behaviour.

Consumer Behaviour: Rational or Emotional?

Consumption rose particularly after the 1950s, as citizens around the world began to prosper in relative peace after the Second World War, and industrial companies turned their attention from producing military equipment and supplies to producing consumer and industrial goods. At this time, consumers were generally thought to act rationally, according to **neoclassical economics** theory, individually maximizing their satisfaction (what economists call **utility**) based on a cost–benefit analysis of price and product scarcity (or availability). The consumer was thought to measure whether or not the functional benefits of an offering outweighed its costs. Such rational purchasing decisions are considered to be based on the offering's physical performance (Udell, 1964).

However, consider an example from the Soviet Union (Russia, pre-1990). In such a strictly regulated planned economy, offerings were design to meet basic functional needs. Nevertheless, consumers sought out televisions produced in certain factories in certain regions or countries because they thought that they were more reliable and produced better pictures. So, even when a country's government attempts to squeeze out human desires, the desire to possess the best of what is available remains.

Nowadays, people are more likely to indulge socio-psychological buying or emotional buying motives. These motives stem from a buyer's social and psychological interpretation of the offering and its performance. Consider our motivations for purchasing particular music tracks, for example. Take the example of 'Uptown Funk' by Mark Ronson. It had nearly 1.4bn hits on YouTube within 15 months of release and was the biggest track of 2015 (Anon., 2016). We are likely to have either bought the iTunes download or accessed it via a streaming service (e.g. Spotify, Apple Music) because of what the music and its associated video represents to us. We buy the music because of how it makes us feel (e.g. excited, elated, happy, amused). We may even have bought it because everyone else was buying it at the time. We did not

Research Insight 2.1

To take your learning further, you might wish to read this influential paper.

Carù, A. and Cova, B. (2003). Revisiting consumption experience: a more humble but complete view of the concept. *Marketing Theory*, 3(2), 267–86.

This highly cited article builds upon, and moves forward, the idea that marketing is based upon consumption experiences developed originally by Holbrook and Hirschman (1982), articulating that marketers should distinguish between consumer experience (experience of the process of consumption) and consumption experience (experience of the usage of the proposition), and between ordinary and extraordinary experiences, and in so doing, recognize that not all marketing experiences need to be perpetually extraordinary.

@ **Visit the Online Resource Centre to read the abstract and access the full paper.**

buy it because it was useful to us, or because it performed some kind of functional purpose, unless of course we are DJs.

 Visit the Online Resource Centre and follow the web link to the Psychology Matters website to learn more about the application and value of psychology in our everyday lives.

Proposition Acquisition

What are consumers thinking when they decide whether or not to buy or, in the case of a not-for-profit consumer, acquire a particular offering? To answer this question, we need to know how offerings move from organizations to consumers. For example, consider luxury brand Hermes' controversial crocodile skin handbags, retailing for US$12,000–223,000 (£8,650–160,825; €11,000–204,000) (Kane, 2015). In a simplified process, the skin is sold by a crocodile farmer to the manufacturer who dries, cures, and tans it, before stitching it and sending it on to the major brand owner who stocks and retails it. At any of these stages, a different supply chain partner could be involved (see Chapter 14).

In the Hermes example, there are transactions between various buyers and sellers as raw materials are transformed into a bag, during the transactions between partners in the supply chain process (what Alderson and Martin (1965) called **transvections**). Understanding transactions and transvections is important because this charts how propositions are developed and move from suppliers through companies to their end-users. Next, we consider the end-user component of the buyer–seller relationship—the perspective of the consumer. (We consider the buyer–seller relationship again in Chapters 15 and 16.)

The consumer proposition acquisition process consists of six distinct stages (see Figure 2.1). The process model is useful because it highlights the importance and distinctiveness of proposition selection and re-evaluation phases in the process. In Figure 2.1, the buying process is iterative, as each stage can lead back to previous stages or move forward to the next stage.

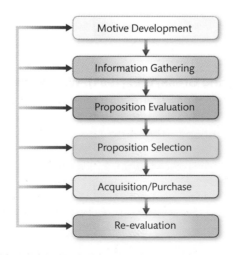

Figure 2.1
The consumer proposition acquisition process

Motive Development

The process begins when we decide that we wish to obtain an offering. This involves the initial recognition that a problem needs solving. To solve the problem, we must first become aware of it. For example, a female consumer decides that she needs to buy a new dress for a party; perhaps she's grown tired of the old one, or she thinks it's out of fashion, or decides to cheer herself up, or buy it for a special occasion (e.g. engagement or hen party), or buy it for a whole host of other reasons.

Information Gathering

In the next stage, we seek alternative ways of solving our problems. Our dress buyer might ask herself where she bought her last dress, how much dresses typically cost, what different retail outlets stock dresses, and where those retailers are located. She might ask herself where she normally buys party dresses (online or offline), what kinds of dresses are in fashion, perhaps which retailers have sales on, which store staff treat her well if she shops in-store, and what the returns policies are of various online and offline retailers. She might consult personal style bloggers online, like the website of Ella Catliff, La Petite Anglaise, which seeks to help readers understand not only what's in and what's not, but how to style products on themselves (Craik, 2015). Alternatively, our party girl might search for ideas of what to wear on Facebook, YouTube, Instagram, and Twitter. Our search for a solution may be active, an **overt search**, or passive. In other words, we are open to ways of solving our problem but we are not actively looking for information to help us (Howard and Sheth, 1969). The search for information may be internal, i.e. we consider what we already know about the problem and the offerings we might buy to solve our problem. Alternatively, it might be external, where we don't know enough

---

📖 Research Insight 2.2

To take your learning further, you might wish to read this influential article.

Sheth, J.N., Newman, B.I., and Gross, B.L. (1991). Why we buy what we buy: a theory of consumption values. *Journal of Business Research*, 22(2), 159–70.

Sheth *et al.*'s highly cited article postulates a theory of how five consumption values drive buyer choice, including functional value (the perceived utility of an alternative choice's performance), social value (the perceived utility of association with the alternative), emotional value (the perceived utility of the affective states, or feelings, aroused by an alternative), epistemic value (the perceived utility of the novelty, curiosity associated with, and knowledge gained from using the alternative), and conditional value (the perceived utility of an alternative resulting from the unique context in which it is used, e.g. cards at Christmas).

@ **Visit the Online Resource Centre to read the abstract and access the full paper.**

about our problem and so we seek advice or supplementary information. At this stage, we build our awareness by increasing our knowledge of both an offering and the competitors making that offering available.

Proposition Evaluation

Once we have all the information necessary to make a decision, we evaluate alternative propositions. But first we must determine the criteria used to rank the various offerings. These might be rational (e.g. based on cost) or irrational (e.g. based on desire or intuition). For example, the dress buyer might ask herself which website or retail outlet is the best value for money and which is the most fashionable. A consumer is said to have an **evoked set** of products in mind when he/she comes to evaluate which particular product, brand, or service he/she wants to solve a particular problem. An evoked set for a party dress buyer might include Zara, H&M, Mango (MNG elsewhere in the world), ASOS, or Net-A-Porter, for instance. The more affluent buyer might visit a department store (e.g. Harrods or Selfridges in the UK), or the websites of DKNY or Gucci, for example. This stage might also be termed the 'consideration' stage.

Proposition Selection

Typically, the offering we eventually select is the one we evaluate as fitting our needs more closely. However, we might select a particular offering away from where we actually buy or acquire it. For example, the party dress buyer may have checked online to make her selection (with the intention of going to the shop to try it on), but when she turned up at the retailer, the dress she wanted was not available, so she decided on an alternative on impulse at the point of purchase. Therefore proposition selection is a separate stage in the proposition acquisition process, distinct from proposition evaluation because there are times when we must re-evaluate what we buy or acquire because what we want is not available, e.g. buying a cinema ticket for one film because the seats for another are sold out.

Acquisition/Purchase

Once selection has taken place, different approaches to purchasing might exist. For example, our dress buyer may make a routine purchase—a dress for work. A routine purchase is a purchase made regularly. Because the purchase is regular we don't get too involved in the decision-making process. We simply buy the offering again that we bought previously unless new circumstances arise. The purchase may be specialized, conducted on a one-off or infrequent basis, e.g. a ball-gown for a ball or formal work event. In this case, we may become much more involved in the decision-making process to ensure that we understand what we are buying and that we are happy that it will satisfy our needs (to look classy perhaps and not cheap). For routine purchases, we might use debit cards or cash, whereas for infrequent purchases we might use a credit or store card. With infrequent purchases, the marketer might ease the pain of payment by offering credit or generous warranties. The lady buying a dress might be intending to purchase the dress, but the store's policy on returns (i.e. whether they allow this or not over what period of time) may have an impact on whether or not she actually buys a dress from that particular shop.

Acquisition also differs by channel and the prevalence of any promotional offers. For example, in the music business, consumers have a choice of whether to purchase music in physical form (CD or even vinyl), download it, or stream it. Whilst digital channels have surpassed physical channels, 46% of the market for music, globally, was still based on physical products (IFPI, 2015). Because the consumer acquires the offering at this stage, it might also be termed the 'conversion' stage.

Re-Evaluation

The theory of **cognitive dissonance** (Festinger, 1957) suggests that we are motivated to re-evaluate our beliefs, attitudes, opinions, or values if the position we hold on them at one time is not the same as the position we held at an earlier period owing to some intervening event, circumstance, or action. This difference in evaluations, termed cognitive dissonance, is psychologically uncomfortable (i.e. it causes anxiety). For example, we may feel foolish or regretful about a purchasing decision (perhaps we spent too much on a night out or on a meal at a slightly too fancy restaurant). Therefore we are motivated to reduce our anxiety by redefining our beliefs, attitudes, opinions, or values to make them consistent with our circumstances (not going to that particular bar as often or to that particular restaurant again). We will also actively avoid situations that might increase our feeling of dissonance.

To reduce dissonance we might try to neutralize it by:

- selectively forgetting information;
- minimizing the importance of an issue, decision, or act;
- selectively exposing ourselves only to new information consonant with our existing view (rather than information which isn't);
- reversing a purchase decision, for instance by taking an offering back or selling it for what it was worth.

The dress buyer might not be happy with her purchase because, although it seemed to fit her in the shop, when she tried it on at home it was too tight or ill-fitting, or it did not flatter her figure as much as she originally thought.

The concept of cognitive dissonance has significant application in marketing. Industrial or consumer purchasers are likely to feel cognitive dissonance if their expectations of proposition performance are not met in reality. This feeling of dissonance may be particularly acute in a high-involvement purchase, e.g. cars, houses, holidays, high-value investment products (see Market Insight 2.1 on Peugeot's 0% interest scheme to minimize customer cognitive dissonance). We are also likely to search out information to reinforce our choice of offering.

On the other hand, if we are happy with our purchase, we might decide to repurchase it, thereby displaying some degree of behavioural loyalty to a particular brand. This stage is termed the loyalty stage. If we really like our purchase we might also encourage others to buy the brand, the so-called advocacy stage. Such advocacy is common in the user-generated content developed online by consumers in relation to everything from films they've watched, to houses they've stayed in (e.g. through Airbnb), to the holidays they've bought (e.g. through Expedia). Evaluating consumer-generated content is an important element of contemporary marketing research (Campbell et al., 2011), sometimes referred to as **'social media listening'**.

HOME　ABOUT　FEATURED IN　BEAUTY　EVENTS　TRAVEL　WHAT I WORE　LINKS

POPULAR

TRAVEL: HYATT REGENCY MAUI RESORT AND SPA

RECENT POSTS

H&M Canada Online Shopping Is Coming!!!

🕐 6 APRIL, 2016　BY 👤 NELIA　💬 5 COMMENTS

It's finally happening! H&M **e-commerce is coming to Canada in 2016, you guys!!!** I can finally stop stalking every item in stores, and order my fave pieces from the comfort of my own couch instead. It's about time. Imagine how much easier shopping those designer collabs is going to be! Obviously, the website will most likely crash from the demand, just like in the US, but at least we now have the option. Are you excited about this? Share your thoughts in the comments.

Photo Credits: H&M

LET'S CONNECT!

f 📷 P 𝕏

SEARCH

Search this website …

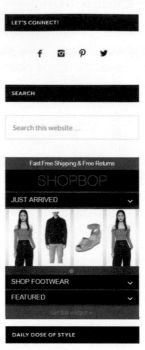

Fast Free Shipping & Free Returns

SHOPBOP

JUST ARRIVED ⌄

SHOP FOOTWEAR ⌄

FEATURED ⌄

DAILY DOSE OF STYLE

Enter your email address to subscribe to Style Blog and receive notifications of new posts by email.

Email Address

SUBSCRIBE

SSENSE

ACNE STUDIOS

SHOP SS16

POPULAR

Consumers often consult sites like Nelia Belkova's Style Blog before making their purchases.
Source: Property of Nelia Belkova.

Market Insight 2.1
Easy Purchasing at Peugeot in 2015

Car manufacturer Peugeot, with its operational headquarters in Sochaux, France, sold 11,563 new cars in Britain, taking a 4.0% share of the market, way behind more popular UK brands such as Ford, Vauxhall, Volkswagen, Audi, BMW, Nissan, and Mercedes-Benz. Market share was down 1.1% over the period from 2009 to 2015. Worldwide, the brand's owner, PSA Peugeot Citroën, saw sales increase by 1.2% in 2015. In Europe, group sales rose by 5.9% to 1,864,000 units. Peugeot made up the bulk of the sales, seeing sales in Europe (particularly the Netherlands, Spain, Italy, and France) increase by 9.4% to 1,086,000 units. The 308 model was in the top three in its small family car segment. The Peugeot brand also saw success in other overseas markets including China (up 6% to 408,000 units), the Middle East and Africa (up 2.3% to 117,000 units), Mexico (up 34%), Chile (up 4%), and India–Pacific, including India, South Korea, and Japan (up 6.5% to 23,800 units).

Given relatively sluggish economic growth, and the low rates of wage inflation in many countries, vehicle manufacturers and dealership sales personnel understand the psychological anxiety car buyers

feel when purchasing new cars, especially after the purchase. The buyer's key consideration is ensuring that they obtain value for money and that they do not feel they have spent their money badly. The problem is particularly acute when customers buy new cars, because new cars are significantly more expensive than second-hand cars.

Considering that cars lose 15–35% of their value in depreciation the moment they leave the showroom, and up to 50% by the third year, we can see why new car buyers feel vulnerable. Of course, there are benefits: new cars look better, incorporate the latest design features, and have reduced maintenance costs.

Car dealers work hard to reinforce the purchase decisions made by new car buyers by sending customers newsletters and offering efficient (or free three-year warranty) after-sales service to ensure that there are no or few maintenance problems. In many cases, new vehicles are sold with free insurance, 0% finance deals, or buy-now-pay-later schemes, all designed to reduce the post-purchase cognitive dissonance car buyers naturally feel after their purchase.

The Peugeot 308: even more attractive when it comes interest-free with free insurance and deposit contribution.

Source: © Dong liu/Shutterstock.

In 2015, Peugeot sweetened the sales with their Just Add Fuel® deal on the 308 model, by offering a time-limited offer of 0% financing over 37 months, 3 years free insurance, and 3 years servicing (including warranty, car tax, and roadside assistance) with only £500 deposit contribution at participating dealers.

But, in the UK in 2016, Skoda, Seat, Nissan, Mazda, Jeep, and Hyundai were all offering 0% finance deals on selected models. The question for Peugeot is: Will the promotion on the 308 help turn the tide of negative sales growth in the UK and result in an increase in market share for Peugeot?

Sources: Mintel (2016); Peugeot (2016).

Market Insight 2.1
continued

Theory into Practice

This market insight describes how a car manufacturer uses sales promotion techniques to help consumers surmount the purchase anxiety they feel about buying a new car in relation to uncertainties such as the cost of maintenance, depreciation, and insurance.

Related Topics:

pricing; cognitive dissonance; sales promotion; post-purchase anxiety; consumer behaviour.

1 What else could Peugeot do to reduce the cognitive dissonance felt by its customers?

2 Do you think that cognitive dissonance would increase or decrease during an economic downturn?

3 Consider a time when you purchased something that left you feeling anxious afterwards. What were you purchasing and why did it make you feel anxious?

Research Insight 2.3

To take your learning further, you might wish to read this influential article.

Cummings, W.H. and Venkatesan, M. (1976). Cognitive dissonance and consumer behavior: a review of the evidence. *Journal of Marketing Research*, 13, 303–8.

A hugely influential development in psychological theory ('dissonance theory') explains how we resolve two sets of inconsistent opinions, attitudes, values, and behaviour, held at two different points, arising after we receive new information forcing us to change our initial position (e.g. on brands purchased). The original theory (Festinger, 1957) proposed that we would change our existing opinions, attitudes, values, and behaviour to the new position to stop us from feeling the psychological discomfort associated with the inconsistent positions we hold. This review article evaluates nearly 20 years of studies to ascertain how dissonance theory explains consumer behaviour, concluding that whilst it seems to explain post-purchase attitude change and repurchase behaviour, it fares less well in explaining selective exposure.

Visit the Online Resource Centre to read the abstract and access the full paper.

In Figure 2.1, the buying process is iterative (i.e. it occurs in steps), particularly at the re-evaluation phase of the acquisition process. This is because the re-evaluation of the offering leads us back to any or all of the previous phases in the proposition acquisition process as a result of experiencing cognitive dissonance. For example, we may have bought a games console (Xbox One) but we are not completely happy with it (e.g. we think that it has poor picture/sound). If it was covered under warranty, this would lead us to the acquisition phase, where a new perfect product should be provided by the retailer. If the product was delivered in perfect working order but we simply didn't enjoy using it, we might go back to the original alternatives we selected (e.g. PS4, Wii U), and pick one of the other alternatives (e.g. one which might offer a larger variety of games). If we are really not sure about which games console to buy after this initial purchase, we might re-evaluate the alternatives we originally selected and then decide. If we really disliked our original purchase, and this shook our belief in what we thought was important in selecting a games console, we might go back to the information-gathering phase to get more of an idea about the offerings available. Finally, if we were extremely disappointed, we might decide that our original motive—the need to play, to relax, and to have fun—can best be solved by purchasing something other than a games console which will still meet the same need (e.g. participation in sport).

Research by the marketing agency Razorfish identified three categories of influencer at different stages of the proposition acquisition process. These include key influencers (with their own blogs and huge numbers of Twitter followers, but who are unlikely to know the consumer), social influencers (people in the consumer's social network, whom they might know personally, commenting in Twitter feeds and on blogs/forums), and known peer influencers (e.g. family members or part of the consumer's 'inner circle'). Of all three types, known peer influencers were the most persuasive (see section on Group Influence later in this chapter), but the three groups were differentially important at different points in the proposition acquisition process. For example, close family and friends exert the most influence at the motive development and information-gathering phases (the 'awareness' phase), YouTube and anonymous peer reviewers exert most influence at the proposition evaluation and selection phases (the 'consideration' phase), and close family and friends exert the most influence in the proposition selection and acquisition phases (the 'action' phase) (Sheldrake, 2011).

Perceptions, Learning, and Memory

Often consumers do not understand the messages marketers convey because they have not received, comprehended, or remembered those messages, or because the messages were unclear. Consumer understanding depends on how effectively the message is transmitted and perceived. In this section, we discuss how messages are perceived and remembered (consideration of how messages are communicated is undertaken in Chapters 6 and 10–12). In any one day, consumers receive thousands of messages.

Consider, for instance, a typical working woman in Paris, France, who might well be awoken by her clock radio, blaring out adverts for *Galeries Lafayette*. While eating her breakfast, she encounters advertisements on her television. She picks up visual advertisements in the *Paris Match* magazine she is reading, say, and when she opens her post, which includes direct mail from charities (e.g. Médecins Sans Frontières) and financial service organizations (BNP Paribas etc.). On her way to the Métro station she might encounter billboards advertising, among other things, L'Oréal for instance. On the Métro, she will probably encounter more visual adverts on the train. When she arrives at work, and after being further bombarded with online ads and sponsored Internet search ads, she has been subjected to hundreds of auditory, visual, and audiovisual advertising messages demanding her attention. When she retires to bed, this could have extended to thousands. If we also consider that consumers are recipients of social and interpersonal messages as well—through word of mouth and social media (e.g. Facebook and Twitter)—we begin to realize how sophisticated human perception, learning, and memory processes must be to attend to, filter, and store so many messages.

Perceptions

The American Marketing Association (AMA, 2016) defines perceptions as follows: 'based on prior attitudes, beliefs, needs, stimulus factors, and situational determinants, individuals perceive objects, events, or people in the world about them. Perception is the cognitive impression that is formed of "reality" which in turn influences the individual's actions and behaviour toward that object'. If we paid attention to all the messages we receive, rather than filtering out those we find meaningful, we would probably become overloaded, just like a computer when it crashes. The process of screening meaningful from non-meaningful information is known as **selective exposure** (Dubois, 2000).

As consumers, we are interested in certain types of offerings that are relevant to us when we receive marketing messages. So, men would not usually be interested in adverts about handbags (as opposed to 'man-bags') unless they wanted to buy one as an anniversary, birthday, or travel gift for a special woman in their lives. Equally, young people are not usually interested in advertising messages for pensions. If you were looking to book a flight, you would become interested in messages from airline companies and travel agents, especially if these include sales promotions. Even washing machine adverts become interesting if your washing machine has broken down! The messages we choose to ignore and forget are removed from our perception, enabling us to process those messages that we wish to consider more effectively. So, we avoid exposure to certain messages and actively seek out others. We may also expose ourselves selectively to particular messages through the media we choose to read (e.g. certain newspapers, magazines, ezines, Facebook pages, Twitter feeds) or watch (e.g. certain terrestrial, cable, satellite, or Internet TV channels). Many people do not read a daily newspaper and therefore will not see press advertisements, although they may see sponsored search ads on websites, or read, respond, and interact with Twitter posts or companies' Facebook pages. Some people do not listen to the radio often or at all. Therefore it is important to determine which **media** channels customers use.

Advertisers label this concept of representing the personal importance a person attaches to a given communication message as **involvement**. This is important because it explains a person's receptivity to communications, and people can therefore be segmented into high, medium, and low involvement groups (Michaelidou and Dibb, 2008). We are interested in consumers' receptivity because we are interested in changing or altering their perceptions of particular offerings. We know, from earlier in the chapter, that offerings can be characterized on the basis of whether consumers use rational or emotional thinking to evaluate their relative appeal. Figure 2.2 illustrates a variety of common products and how they are generally perceived by US consumers (see Ratchford, 1987).

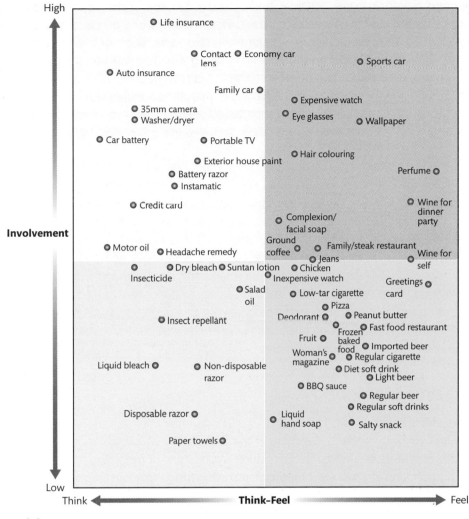

Figure 2.2

Involvement/think–feel dimension plot for common products

Source: Ratchford, B.T. (1987), 'New insights about the FCB grid', *Journal of Advertising Research*, 27(4), 24–38.

We should note that the position for a particular offering is an average of all consumers and may not represent a particular individual's decision-making well. So, for example, the purchase of life insurance is regarded as being in the high involvement/thinking quadrant. The positioning of this type of offering indicates the need for more informative advertising/promotion. An expensive watch, residing in the high involvement/feeling quadrant, suggests a need for emotional advertising. Offerings in the low involvement/thinking quadrant (e.g. liquid bleach) indicate the use of advertising/promotion to create and reinforce habitual buying. Finally, offerings in the low involvement/feeling quadrant, e.g. women's magazines, should be promoted on the basis of personal satisfaction (Ratchford, 1987).

Another way of displaying how people think about particular offerings uses perceptual mapping, a technique used since at least the early 1960s (Mindak, 1961). People view champagne brands differently in the UK, using (brand) personality keywords zesty/mellow and fresh fruit/baked fruit. Lanson is associated with zesty and fresh fruit, whilst Moët et Chandon is associated with mellow and baked fruit (we consider brand differentiation in more detail in Chapters 6 and 13). Organizations deliberately seek to position themselves in the minds of specific target audience groups. To do this properly, they must understand the nature of the group's subculture. However, organizations risk causing offence if they position a brand on particular dimensions which are misperceived, or perceived correctly but negatively. The Irish bookmaker Paddy Power drew 5,525 complaints to the UK's advertising standards watchdog ASA after it offered incentives to bet on the Oscar Pistorius trial, and caused serious offence by trivializing the issues surrounding a murder trial, a woman's death, and disability, using the wording 'It's Oscar time, money back if he walks' (ASA, 2015).

Brands can thrive or die based on how their customers perceive them. Sometimes companies fail to position their offerings appropriately. For example, in 2015, Bud Light ran a campaign that completely 'missed the mark' and was forced to apologize after using inappropriate 'pro-rape' wording as part of its campaign, namely: 'the perfect beer for removing "no" from your vocabulary for the night #upforwhatever' (Richards, 2015). Companies sometimes also need to change how their brands are perceived because they have developed negative associations (see Market Insight 2.2). For example, British supermarket retailer Tesco lost its customers' love after a £263m accounting scandal in 2014 and increasing supplier dissatisfaction with its trading approach, causing the company to report its biggest ever loss of £6.5bn in 2015 (Magee, 2015). Conversely, sometimes organizations position their offerings well, as Toyota did when developing the Lexus brand for the premium car market.

Learning and Memory

How do consumers continually learn about new offerings, their relative performance, and new trends? The answer is by learning. Learning is the process by which we acquire new knowledge and skills, attitudes, and values through study, experience, or modelling others' behaviour. Theories of human learning include **classical conditioning**, **operant conditioning**, and **social learning**.

■ Classical Conditioning—Russian Nobel Laureate, Ivan Pavlov, investigated the digestive and nervous system of dogs, measuring the amount of saliva produced in response to food under certain conditions. He realized that his dog salivated before food was served and set out to ascertain why. By carrying out a series of experiments and manipulating stimuli before the food was presented, he realized that if, for example, he rang a bell before serving food, the dogs would associate the sound of the bell (the conditioned stimulus) with the presentation of food (the unconditioned stimulus) and begin salivating. So, classical conditioning occurs when the unconditioned stimulus becomes associated with the conditioned stimulus. In other words, we learn by associating one thing with another—in this case, the sound of the bell with the arrival of food. This approach to learning is frequently used in marketing, for example: 1) jingles in advertising, e.g. Danone's 'mmm, Danone' sonic logo to indicate the lip-smacking 'goodness' of its offerings; 2) supermarkets include bakery sections to cause consumers to buy more as they associate the smell of warm bread with eating; 3) perfume and aftershave manufacturers (e.g. L'Oréal) place free samples of products in sachets in magazines so that when readers see an advert for a particular brand of perfume/aftershave they associate the image they see with the smell, and so are more likely to purchase the product when they see its image in the future.

Market Insight 2.2
Jameson: A Cut Above the Rest

Jameson Irish Whiskey is the most popular Irish whiskey in the world, with around 60m bottles sold last year globally. Produced at the Jameson Distillery in Middleton, County Cork, it is the flagship whisky of Irish Distillers. Today, it is distributed in 122 countries worldwide and accounts for the largest share of the global Irish whiskey market. It is also the fastest growing international whiskey brand.

The Jameson brand originates from 1780 and as such has a strong brand heritage. It is a high-end premium whiskey brand, and is triple distilled, contributing to its smooth and distinctive taste. The green bottle helps distinguish it from the competition and reinforces its Irish heritage. The brand's motto 'Sine Metu' (without fear, confident, and independent) is clearly indicated on the bottle's label and encapsulates the brand's fearless personality. Jameson Whiskey is viewed as 'a serious whiskey that doesn't take itself too seriously' and knows how to have fun. It has been described as a brand that is serious in the making, but not in the drinking.

Jameson is currently trying to break the age-old notion that whiskey is just for old men by targeting younger men and women aged 25–35. This is

reflected in their use of advertising and social media to connect with this coveted age cohort. Jameson has been heavily involved in sponsorship of film, through its association with the 'Jameson Dublin International Film Festival', 'Jameson First Shot', and 'Jameson Empire Done in 60 Seconds'. Since 2003 they have been title sponsor of the Dublin International Film Festival, which has fast become Ireland's premier feature film festival, playing host to a plethora of Irish and Hollywood stars, from Colin Farrell to Danny DeVito and Richard Dreyfuss.

Each year 130 films are presented over the 11-day festival from all over the globe, many of them Irish premieres. 'Jameson First Shot' is an international competition that offers film-makers the chance to direct their own script with Kevin Spacey mentoring and acting in the lead role. In the past, these actors have included Adrien Brody, Uma Thurman, Willem Dafoe, and Maggie Gyllenhaal. Finally, 'The Jameson Empire Done in 60 Seconds' competition has also raised the profile of the Jameson brand internationally. It challenges up-and-coming film-makers worldwide to script and shoot their own 60 seconds remake of classic movies. These three sponsorship opportunities have helped to promote the Jameson brand's deep heritage within film and allowed it to connect with its target audience in a meaningful way.

The whiskey's popularity among celebrities is well noted, with people such as Lady Gaga and Rihanna extolling its virtues. Lady Gaga has described Jameson as her 'long-term boyfriend', while Rihanna even mentions the brand in her song 'Cheers (Drink to That)'. Such promotion by two of the world's hottest pop stars is an incredible boost for the Jameson brand, which continues to grow in popularity.

Jameson, the most popular Irish whiskey in the world
Source: Image courtesy of Irish Distillers Limited.

Sources: Anon., 2012a; Russell, 2012; Flanagan, 2014; http://www.jamesonfirstshot.com; http://www.thewhiskyexchange.com; www.jamesonwhiskey.com/us/article/jameson-done-in-60-seconds-empire-awards.

Market Insight 2.2
continued

Theory into Practice

This market insight describes how an Irish whiskey distiller has sought to reposition itself from a brand drunk by old men to one drunk by younger people, including women, using Hollywood celebrities, an association with cinema, and sponsorship.

Related Topics:
celebrity endorsement; repositioning; sponsorship.

1 Describe the personality traits of the Jameson Whiskey brand. How have these personality traits been established?

2 How has the brand's association with film impacted on the public's perception of the brand? What is the brand's main motivation for engaging in arts/film sponsorship?

3 Lady Gaga and Rihanna are just two well-known celebrities who have publicly expressed their love for the Jameson Whiskey brand. How do these celebrities exert group influence and contribute to social learning?

This market insight was kindly contributed by Marie O'Dwyer, Waterford Institute of Technology, Republic of Ireland.

- Operant Conditioning—B.F. Skinner (1954) was one of the pioneers of the behaviourist school of learning. He argued that learning was the result of operant conditioning whereby subjects would act on a stimulus from the environment. The resulting behaviour was more likely to occur if this behaviour was reinforced. In other words, operant conditioning is learning through behavioural reinforcement. Skinner termed this 'reinforcement', as the behaviour would occur more readily in connection with a particular stimulus if the required resulting behaviour had been reinforced through punishment or reward. In marketing, consider the typical in-store sales promotion. Perhaps it's a new yoghurt brand offered in a supermarket. If we don't normally eat this brand and we're curious, we might try it because there are no costs in terms of time, effort, or money in having a taste. The sales promotion provides the stimulus, the trial behaviour occurs, and if the yoghurt is liked and the consumer rewarded with a money-off coupon, the behaviour of purchasing that particular yoghurt brand is reinforced (for more on sales promotion, see Chapter 11). Supermarkets reinforce our loyalty by providing reward cards and points for purchasing particular items (e.g. the Nectar card in Britain or the stamps system used by the retailer 7-Eleven in their convenience stores worldwide).

- Social Learning—this theory was proposed by the psychologist Albert Bandura, who suggested that humans are less animalistic than Skinner suggests. Bandura (1977) argued that we can delay gratification and dispense our own rewards or punishment. As a result, we have

Five of the world's most iconic logos

Sources: Google and the Google logo are registered trademarks of Google Inc., used with permission. Used with permission from McDonald's Corporation. © Facebook. © Nike. © LG.

more choice over how to react to stimuli than proposed by Skinner, who felt that we blindly followed our instinctual drives. We can reflect on our own actions and change future behaviour. This led to the idea that humans learn not only from how they respond to situations but also from how other humans respond to situations. Bandura called this modelling. In social learning, we learn by observing others' behaviour. The implications for marketers are profound. For adolescents, role models include parents, athletes, and entertainers, but parents are the most influential (Martin and Bush, 2000). Parents socialize their children into purchasing and consuming the same brands that they buy, actively teaching them consumer skills—materialistic values and consumption attitudes—in their teenage years. Interaction with peers also makes adolescents more aware of different offerings (Moschis and Churchill, 1978). Companies have long recognized the power of peers, particularly in the social media world, encouraging purchasers to leave reviews of products that they have previously bought, 'like' their Facebook pages, and retweet their messages. Research indicates that those who read reviews are twice as likely to select a product compared with those who do not (Senecal and Nantal, 2004).

But what happens once consumers have learnt information? How do they retain it in their memories and what stops them from forgetting such information? Consumers do not necessarily have the same experience, and therefore knowledge, of particular offerings. Knowledge develops with familiarity, repetition of marketing messages, and a consumer's acquisition of product/service information. Marketing messages need to be repeated often as people forget them over time, particularly the specific arguments or message presented. The general substance or conclusion of the message is marginally more likely to be remembered (Bettinghaus and Cody, 1994: 67).

We enhance memorization through the use of symbols, such as corporate identity logos, badges, and signs. Shapes, creatures, and people carry significant meanings, as seen in badges, trademarks, and logos. Airlines around the world have adopted symbols, e.g. the kangaroo of Australian airline Qantas. Well-recognized symbols worldwide include the KFC 'Colonel' symbol, Intel's symbol, Apple's bitten apple logo, Coca-Cola's ubiquitous script logo, and Google's multicoloured script symbol.

Our memories, as a system for storing perceptions, experience, and knowledge, are highly complex (Bettman, 1979). A variety of memorization processes affect consumer choice, including the following.

- Factors affecting **recognition** and **recall**—less frequently used words in advertising are recognized more and recalled less. The information-processing task in transferring data from short-term to long-term memory differs for recognition (2–5 seconds) and recall (5–10 seconds). Under high states of arousal, e.g. where the consumer is subject to time pressure, recognition speeds are increased whereas recall speeds are hindered. In practical terms, the more unique a campaign's message, the better it is recognized but the worse it is recalled.

- The importance of context—memorization is strongly associated with the context of the stimulus, so information available in memory will be inaccessible in the wrong context. For example, vacuum cleaner manufacturers advertising in sports magazines are unlikely to be remembered.

- Form of object coding and storage—we store information in the form it is presented to us, either by object (brand) or dimension (offering attribute), but there is no evidence that one form is organized into memory more quickly or more accurately than the other (Johnson and Russo, 1978).

- Load processing effects—we find it more difficult to process information into our short- and long-term memories when we are presented with a great deal of information at once.

- Input mode effects—short-term recall of sound input is stronger than short-term recall of visual input where the two compete for attention, e.g. in television and YouTube advertising.

- Repetition effects—recall and recognition of marketing messages/information increase the more a consumer is exposed to them, although later exposures add less and less to memory performance.

Evidence suggests that where consumers have little experience or knowledge of an offering, provision of in-store point-of-purchase information is more successful than general advertising (Bettman, 1979). This is why brand manufacturers frequently conduct product trials in-store, offering consumers the opportunity to try the offering without expending time, money, and effort in purchasing it (see Chapter 11 for more on sales promotion). This approach places the brand in the consumer's evoked set, and helps them contextualize the particular product and remember it when they shop next time. Consumer knowledge of offerings can be incomplete and/or inaccurate, as consumers frequently think that they know something about an offering that is not accurate and believe this strongly (Alba and Hutchinson, 2000).

Personality

How and what we buy is also based on our personalities. **Personality** is that aspect of our psyche which determines how we respond to our environment in a relatively stable way over time. There are various theories of personality. Here, we consider three main approaches:

1 the psychoanalytic approach, which stresses self-reported unconscious desires;

2 trait theory, which stresses the classification of personality types;

3 the self-concept approach, which concerns how we perceive ourselves as consumers.

The Psychoanalytic Approach

Sigmund Freud devised a theory of motivation that considered us to be irrational beings. According to Freud (1927), a person's personality is based on their sexual development from infancy to adulthood. Freud stated that an adult's personality is developed according to how well they cope with crises that occur during various development phases in between these age-stages. Freud believed that we are motivated by our subconscious drives, incorporating a system comprising three interrelated components: the id, the ego, and the superego.

- **Id**—this part of our psyche harbours our instinctual drives and urges, a kind of seething mass of needs, which require instant gratification. This aspect corresponds to Kahneman's (2011) **'System 1' thinking**.

- **Ego**—this part of our psyche attempts to find outlets for the urges in our id and acts as a planning centre to determine the opportunities for gratification of our urges. According to Freud, the ego is moderated by the superego. This aspect corresponds to Kahneman's (2011) **'System 2' thinking**.

- **Superego**—this part of our psyche controls how we motivate ourselves to behave to respond to our instincts and urges, so that we do so in a socially acceptable manner and avoid any feelings of guilt or shame. It acts as a social conscience.

(For an excellent illustration of the importance of Freud's thinking in the development of marketing and public relations, see *Century of the Self*, the four-part Adam Curtis documentary originally shown on BBC Television in the UK.)

Psychoanalytic ideas of human personality and development were applied to marketing consumer goods by the public relations specialist Edward Bernays, Freud's nephew, in America, and by many others. The application of psychoanalytic methods and concepts to the understanding of consumer behaviour was known as motivation research (Collins and Montgomery, 1969). This technique, which aimed to understand people's motivations to purchase, was adopted extensively in the 1960s and 1970s using qualitative research to identify subconscious desires (Dichter, 1964; Kotler, 1965). Although the psychoanalytic approach is little used in market research today, it highlighted people's unconscious desires when purchasing goods.

The Trait Approach

This approach to personality categorizes people into different personality types or so-called traits (pronounced 'trays'). Researchers characterize personalities using bipolar scales, including the following traits:

- sociable–timid;
- action-oriented–reflection-oriented;
- stable–nervous;
- serious–frivolous;
- tolerant–suspicious;
- dominant–submissive;
- friendly–hostile;

- hard–sensitive;
- quick–slow;
- masculine–feminine.

Researchers frequently talk about the 'big five' personality dimensions: extraversion (sociable, fun-loving, affectionate, friendly, talkative), openness (original, imaginative, creative, daring), conscientiousness (careful, reliable, well-organized, hard-working), neuroticism (worrying, nervous, highly strung, self-conscious, vulnerable), and agreeableness (soft-hearted, sympathetic, forgiving, acquiescent) (McRae and Costa, 1987). Certain types of personality prefer certain brands; for example, 'conscientious' people prefer 'trusted' brands, extroverts prefer 'sociable' brands. There are also gender differences: neurotic males and conscientious females prefer 'trusted brands' (Mulyanegara et al., 2009). An understanding of personality types therefore helps marketers to segment customer groups using personality dimensions (see Chapter 6).

Various companies use personality as a segmentation criterion; for example, car manufacturers link personality to particular car attributes (e.g. safety features, aesthetics, handling). Makers of running shoes and mobile phones are interested in two personality traits in particular, extraversion and openness to experience, because these traits link to attitudinal and purchase loyalty displayed towards those brands (Matzler et al., 2006).

Visit the Online Resource Centre and complete Internet Activity 2.1, an online quiz, to learn more about your own personality across a number of key personality traits.

Self-Concept Approach

People also buy offerings because of what the brand represents to them and its relation to the buyers' perception of their own self-concept or personality. This relates not only to the proposition itself, but also to values, socially responsible behaviour, and opportunities for networking (Bhattacharya and Sen, 2003), both online and offline. So, we buy brands that resemble how we perceive ourselves, but marketers can also shape customer behaviour by reinforcing particular identities and redefining what it means to have that identity or creating new highly desirable identities (Champniss et al., 2015). In the luxury goods market, buyers typically divide into one of two categories.

1 Those who made their purchases based on product quality, aesthetic design, and excellence of service, motivated by the desire to impress others, their ability to pay high prices, and the ostentatious display of their wealth.

2 Those who bought luxury goods based on what they symbolize; purchasing luxury goods represented an extreme form of the expression of their own values (Dubois and Duquesne, 1993).

Consumers buy products based on self-concept through self-giving behaviour (Mick and DeMoss, 1990). Gift-giving is a common phenomenon, particularly among family, friends, and work colleagues. It is highly symbolic, connoting love (e.g. Valentine's and Mother's/Father's Days), congratulations (e.g. wedding presents), regret (e.g. a card after offending a loved one), and dominance (e.g. clothes bought by a girl for her boyfriend to change his look). Self-giving arises from different motivations, e.g. to reward oneself, to be nice to oneself, to cheer oneself up, to fulfil a need, and to celebrate. There is a link between the purchase of clothing as a self-gift, i.e. a special purchase rather than a typical purchase, and a consumer's self-concept. An extreme example of when people purchase products to build their self-concept, although it tends to work in the short term and damages longer-term self-concept perceptions, occurs in compulsive consumer behaviour (e.g. gambling, excessive drinking). Compulsive shoppers, for example, are motivated in part to change their mood and improve their self-esteem (Furnham, 2014).

 Visit the Online Resource Centre and complete Internet Activity 2.2, to take a test on compulsive shopping and to learn more about the disorder.

Motivation

Abraham Maslow (1943) suggested a hierarchical order of human needs, as outlined in Figure 2.3. According to Maslow, we satisfy lower-order physiological needs first, before safety needs, belongingness needs, esteem needs, and finally the need for self-actualization. There is little research evidence to confirm Maslow's hierarchy, but the concept possesses logical simplicity, making it a useful tool for understanding how we prioritize our own needs and therefore why we might buy what we buy. In contemporary societies, offerings focus on solving consumer needs in the esteem and self-actualization categories, as needs in other categories are already provided for. However, in the poorer parts of sub-Saharan Africa, for example, offerings operate for some citizens at the level of solving safety and belongingness needs. The implications for marketers are that offerings aimed at the mass market in Africa in the self-actualization category (e.g. higher education, long-haul travel) are likely to fail. This does not mean that there are no market segments with this need. There are groups of people in sub-Saharan Africa whose income allows them to enjoy such offerings.

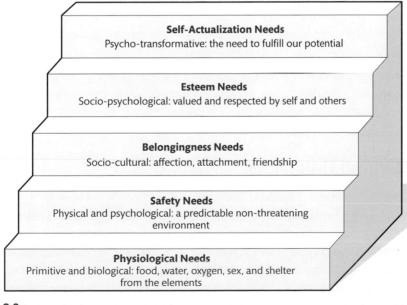

Figure 2.3

Maslow's hierarchy of needs

Source: Adapted from Maslow (1943). This content is in the public domain.

There is still debate about whether consumers are motivated by rational (as outlined by Howard and Sheth (1969)) or irrational motives. Holbrook *et al.* (1986) started to consider irrational motives when they suggested that our wants could be latent, passive, or active, and were related to both intrinsic and extrinsic reasons, as follows:

- latent—needs are hidden, our subject is unaware of his/her need;
- passive—the costs of acquisition exceed, for the moment, the expected satisfaction derived from acquisition;
- active—the subject is both aware of his/her needs and expects perceived benefits to exceed the likely costs of acquisition.

According to Holbrook *et al.* (1986), when our needs are active they can arise either through **habit**, or through the brand selection process, which the authors call **picking**. Picking is the deliberative selection of an offering from among a repertoire of acceptable alternatives, even though the consumer believes the alternatives to be essentially identical in their ability to satisfy his/her needs. It can be motivated by intrinsic or extrinsic evaluations or both. Intrinsic evaluation occurs because a consumer likes a product, perhaps because of anticipated pleasure from using it. Alternatively, an extrinsic evaluation might occur because a friend mentioned that it was a great product. Extrinsic evaluations can also entail explicit cost–benefit analyses. Extrinsic reasons for purchase can be subdivided into five categories.

1 Economic—concerned with expenditure of money, time, and effort in purchasing and consuming an offering. Economists refer to the concept of **price elasticity** of demand to explain how demand is affected when price is increased or decreased.

2 Technical—concerned with the offering's perceived quality of performance in the anticipated usage situation.

3 Social—concerned with the extent to which a purchase will enhance a person's feelings of esteem, personal worth in relation to others (cf. Maslow's hierarchy), and general adherence to group norms and effects (see section on Theory of Planned Behaviour).

4 Legalistic—concerned with what are perceived to be the legitimate demands of others (e.g. buying on behalf of a company, or for a child or spouse).

5 Adaptive—(a form of social learning) concerned with imitating others, seeking expert advice (e.g. from blogs, social networking sites, or industry and consumer magazines), or relying on the reputation of a particular company or brand in cases of uncertain or limited purchasing information.

Theory of Planned Behaviour

Theories of motivation in marketing help us understand why people behave as they do. The theory of planned behaviour explains that behaviour is brought about by our **intention** to act in a certain way. This intention to act is affected by the attitude a subject has towards a particular behaviour, encompassing the degree to which a person has favourable or unfavourable evaluations or appraisals of the behaviour in question. Intention to act is also affected by the subjective norm, which is perceived social pressure to perform or not perform a particular behaviour (see section on Group Influence). Finally, intention to act is affected by perceived behavioural control, referring to the perceived ease or difficulty of performing the behaviour, based on a reflection on past experience and future obstacles. Figure 2.4 provides a graphical illustration.

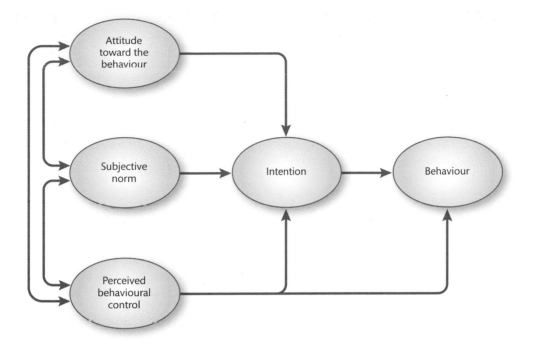

Figure 2.4
Theory of planned behaviour
Source: Azjen (1991).

Public Health England uses a 'disgust' appeal to discourage 'roll-up' smoking
Source: Image courtesy of DARE and Public Health England. Photography by Nick Georghiou.

For example, if we consider cigarette use, we might have different attitudes towards smoking based on our geographical location, e.g. whether we live in France or China versus Britain or New Zealand. We might think we can't give up smoking because we need a cigarette to calm our nerves (maybe we have a stressful job). Equally, we also consider the opinions that significant others have towards smoking cigarettes (e.g. our spouses, children, or friends). If

Research Insight 2.4

To take your learning further, you might wish to read this influential article.

Azjen, I. (1991). The theory of planned behaviour. *Organisational Behaviour and Human Decision Processes*, 50, 179–211.

In this highly cited seminal article, the author outlines how behaviour and behavioural intention to act in a certain way are affected by the attitude the subject has towards a particular behaviour, the subjective norm, and perceived behavioural control. The author developed our understanding of the fact that how humans intend to act may not be how they end up acting in a given situation. Intention, perception of behavioural control, attitude toward the behaviour, and subjective norm all reveal different aspects of the target behaviour and serve as possible directions for attack in attempts to alter particular behaviours, making this a powerful motivational theory in marketing.

@ **Visit the Online Resource Centre to read the abstract and access the full paper.**

we place ourselves in the mind of government (de)marketers, the key elements of the theory of planned behaviour (i.e. attitudes, subjective norms, and perceived behavioural control) can help us understand how to discourage smoking. For example, we could (a) try to alter subjects' attitudes towards smoking, (b) change their views on how others see them as smokers, or (c) change their perceptions of how they perceive their own ability to give up (see Chapter 17 for a wider discussion of social marketing). An advertising campaign called 'Smokefree' from Public Health England, running in late 2015, actively discourages smoking by showing 'disgusting' images of 'rotting' entrails in roll-up cigarettes. The idea is to make people realize that smoking roll-ups is just as dangerous as smoking manufactured cigarettes (Siciliano, 2014). (See also Market Insight 2.2 on deshopping/fraudulent returning.)

The Importance of Social Contexts

Although our own personality and other characteristics impact on how we consider and consume offerings, the opinions, attitudes, and values of others also affect how we consume, as we discovered with the theory of planned behaviour. Our internal perspective is determined not only by our own thoughts and personality structures but also by the input of others. Other people have an effect on our opinions, attitudes, and values, as considered further in the next section.

Opinions, Attitudes, and Values

Opinions are quick responses given to opinion poll questions about current issues or instant responses to questions from friends. They are held with limited conviction because we have often not yet formed or fully developed an underlying attitude on an issue. An opinion might be what we think of the latest advertising campaign for a high profile brand. **Attitudes**, by comparison,

Market Insight 2.3
Deshopping: When Price Doesn't Matter

A growing trend in retailing is when customers purchase an item, use it, and return it for a refund having never had any intention of paying for it. The problem is prevalent among some women when buying clothes. Of course, for deshopping to occur, retailers have to operate lenient returns policies, but many do. Research suggests that nearly 50% of British women may have bought garments and taken them back for a refund after use. This trend, known as **deshopping,** a category of **fraudulent returning** (sometimes also called 'free renting'), may actually have cost US retailers up to $16bn per annum in 2012. The US National Retail Federation (NRF) estimates in 2015 show that retailers expected 3.5% of all returns to be made fraudulently, that 72.6% of NRF's members said that they had experienced deshopping from their customers, and that documented returns fraud actually cost $2.2bn (but this underestimates how much deshopping activity is not picked up).

Given the high cost to retailers (particularly online, since customers cannot try on products beforehand), what should they do about it? Many actually seem reluctant to tackle the problem. A theory of planned behaviour analysis might suggest that retailers should (a) try to alter buyers' attitudes towards deshopping by persuading them that it is socially or morally unacceptable, (b) change customers' views on how others see them as deshoppers (by trying to stigmatize this behaviour), and/or (c) change deshoppers' perceptions of the likelihood that they will get away with this behaviour.

Retail thieves don't look like deshoppers, but they steal like them.
Source: © photomak/Shutterstock.

What other measures have retailers introduced to tackle the problem? Harder measures to counter deshopping include charging a 're-stocking' fee; with a 'clicks and bricks' operation, encouraging in-store only returns, and developing a database of customers who regularly return items (to allow staff to ask more questions to evaluate the legitimacy of the return). For instance, Marks & Spencer has reduced its returns window from 90 to 35 days, introduced dedicated returns desks (away from payment desks), and taken customers' details to check how frequently they have returned items previously. Retailers can also prosecute repeat offenders (assuming that they can compile the evidence needed by the police).

Sources: King *et al.* (2008); Anon. (2012b); King and Balmer (2012); McAvoy (2015).

Theory into Practice

This market insight considers the cost to the retailer of an important problem in retailing—deshopping. The market insight uses a theory of planned behaviour analysis to understand how retailers might deal with the problem as well as considering enforcement measures. The difficulty lies in developing a returns policy which enhances the customers' desire to buy an offering but does not at the same time facilitate retail crime.

Market Insight 2.3
continued

Related Topics:

returns; retail crime; shop-lifting.

1 **How do deshoppers justify their behaviour?**

2 **Have you ever deshopped? If you have, why did you do this? If you have not, do you know anybody who has?**

3 **How can retailers tackle this problem?**

are held with a greater degree of conviction, over a longer duration, and more likely to influence behaviour. **Values** are held even more strongly than attitudes, underpinning our attitudinal and behavioural systems. Values are linked to our conscience, developed through the familial socialization process, through cultures and subcultures, and through our religious influences, and are frequently formed in early childhood (cf. Freud's superego concept from earlier in the chapter).

Opinions are **cognitive**, i.e. based on thoughts. Attitudes are what psychologists term **affective**, i.e. linked to our emotional states. Values are **conative**, i.e. they are linked to our motivations and behaviour. Although we may have a specific attitude towards something, we do not always follow it in terms of our behaviour. In other words, we may want to be more fashionable in our dress sense but we don't bother trying new styles! VALs™ ('values and lifestyles') is a psychographic framework that is used to segment consumers into differing types based on their opinions, attitudes, values, and behaviours. (See Chapter 6 for more on psychographic segmentation.)

Visit the Online Resource Centre and follow the web link to the VALs™ online survey to identify which VALS type you fall into.

Group Influence

Consumers learn through imitation, i.e. social learning. We've learnt, for instance, by observing and copying our parents and friends. As consumers we may consider our opinions, attitudes, values, and behaviour patterns compared with specific reference groups. A reference group is: 'one that the individual tends to use as an anchor point for evaluating his/her own beliefs and attitudes. One may or may not be a member and may or may not aspire to membership in a reference group. It can have great influence on one's values, opinions, attitudes, and behaviour patterns' (AMA, 2016). Group membership can exert a positive effect with the group, i.e. one's individual patterns of behaviour are congruent with the group. For example, die-hard fans of the *Twilight* franchise have had themselves fitted with fang-like teeth (Roderick, 2015). Group membership can also exert a negative effect. Churches, political parties, and trade unions, for example, can be the foci of both positive (congruent) and negative (incongruous) behaviour for their members. If a consumer feels that his/her freedom to choose is being threatened, he/she may react against this intervention. A consumer whose decision alternative is blocked, partially or wholly, can become increasingly motivated to go against that specific decision alternative through rebellious behaviour (Clee and Wicklund, 1980). Such rebellious behaviour might include the creation of **spoof adverts**, poking fun at and caricaturing a brand. Such parodies can seriously damage a brand if they are credible (Sabri and Michel, 2014) and when there is a gap between the image the firm is trying to project and the reality of the firm's actions as experienced by the public (Berthon and Pitt, 2012).

Children who are told that they cannot have particular offerings desire them more as a result (Rummell *et al.,* 2000). For example, the 'tweenage' daughter (aged between 10 and 12 years old) told by her father not to wear make-up may do so, while the rebellious teenage son drinks too much alcohol against his mother's advice. This form of negative group influence occurs because of **psychological reactance**.

Consumers' assumptions about an individual's behaviour, based on identifying group membership, become automated if they are frequently and consistently made (Bargh and Chartrand 1999). This represents a form of social learning. For instance, a Swedish male consumer might purchase Abba-branded herring because this was the brand his parents ate at the breakfast table, whereas a French female beverage consumer might drink Orangina religiously because that is what her parents provided for her as a child. The link between a consumer and a particular reference group depends on how closely the consumer associates with a particular reference group. Where we do associate closely, the attachment to the brand is often assumed. For example, consumers identifying with the motorcycling genre might ride Harley-Davidson bikes because the motorcycle crowd generally buys Harley-Davidson bikes.

Message receipt is also affected by peer group pressure, through word of mouth, online and offline, whether intended or not. Members of groups tend to conform to a group norm, enhancing the self-image of the recipient and increasing the feeling of group identity and belongingness. Therefore consumers may have their own cultures and sub-cultures, which impact on how a particular marketing message may be received. Some marketing messages might incorporate **celebrity endorsement** appeals, e.g. through popular culture role models who have influence over the target consumer group. H&M, the Swedish fashion retailer, has made use of renowned pop artists over the years, including British sports personality David Beckham and American singer Katy Perry, to advertise its brands, particularly to young people. (See Market Insight 2.4 on the power of celebrity endorsement for a sports participation campaign in Ireland.) Marketing campaigns frequently leverage the persuasive power of reference group membership through word-of-mouth campaigns, e.g. when consumers discuss their experiences on Twitter and Facebook. Mars Inc. got itself into hot water in 2012 when it paid various celebrities, including footballer Rio Ferdinand, to endorse its Snickers product as part of its 'You're not you when you're hungry' campaign through Twitter in the UK by sending five tweets, four of which were teasers (i.e. which did not reveal that they were sponsored advertising) and only the final one of which revealed the advertising nature of the communication. Some of these celebrities' followers were upset because they were having products promoted to them through this medium, so they made complaints to the Advertising Standards Authority (ASA) (see Chapter 4). Interestingly, the ASA adjudication, the first of its kind on the use of social media for advertising in the UK, ruled that the tweets were acceptable (Bartnett, 2012).

Word-of-mouth communication is powerful because we trust the opinions of our friends and colleagues. For example, in the beauty and personal care market (Mintel, 2011, 2012)

Market Insight 2.4
On Yer Bike!

In the 1980s, Irishman Sean Kelly was one of the most feared cyclists in the world. He was the first rider to be assigned World Number 1 status when rankings were introduced in 1984 and held this position for a record six years. An astonishing career saw Kelly record 193 professional victories, most notably in the 1988 Vuelta De España. In recent times, the legendary cyclist has become involved in an annual initiative in his home region that has helped revolutionize cycling participation rates in Ireland. The inaugural Sean Kelly Tour of Waterford was held on 19 August 2007, with the principal aim of stimulating interest in cycling as an exercise activity amongst a wide cross-section of society. Kelly himself was one of the 600 enthusiastic participants who took to the scenic roads of County Waterford. The branding of the event, utilizing the name of such a renowned and popular athlete, has been critical in the growth of the Kelly Tour. Innovative public relations, online, and social media campaigns have also inspired growth in participation rates to 6,500 for the 2015 version of the Tour. The event showcases the benefits of cross-agency co-operation in social marketing drives. Waterford Sports Partnership and Waterford County Council operate seamlessly, in tandem with the local cycling community, to provide a varied offering that caters for the serious cyclist, casual participants, and families alike. Support from the central government

Irish Sports Council and commercial sponsor An Post has also been essential in growing the Tour. Indeed, An Post saw the opportunity to complement and replicate the success of the Kelly Tour, by rolling out a series of four other similar events around Ireland. This 'An Post Cycle Series' commenced in 2009 and has also seen considerable incremental year-on-year growth in participation rates. These events have proved to be a significant catalyst in the growth of cycling as an exercise activity. In 2007, there were 5,600 cyclists affiliated to 174 clubs in Ireland. This figure has grown dramatically in the intervening years, with Cycling Ireland reporting a membership in excess of 23,000 people across 398 clubs in 2014; 64% of these are categorized as leisure/non-competitive cyclists, while the proportion of female membership has grown from 8% to 18% in this time period. These figures do not include the growing numbers of recreational cyclists who are not affiliated to a club, a trend that is quite apparent on a daily basis on Irish roads. Government-led initiatives, such as the increased provision of cycle lanes and tax breaks for people purchasing bikes as a means of commuting to work, have complemented the success of the organized mass participation events in raising the popularity of cycling to levels not seen in generations.

Sources: Ipsos MRBI/Irish Sports Council (2013); Cycling Ireland (2014); Kelly (2015).

Theory into Practice

This market insight indicates how two civic organizations worked in partnership to promote (a) cycling participation (particularly to the benefit of Waterford Sports Partnership) and (b) tourism (particularly to the benefit of Waterford County Council), which a cycling event would generate. To generate the kind of mass participation needed for an event of this kind, they engaged a credible sports personality, an Irish champion cyclist.

Related Topics:
social marketing; sports sponsorship; reference groups; celebrity endorsement.

Market Insight 2.4
continued

1 **What are the factors that you deem essential to translate the success of a mass participation event into increased ongoing exercise participation?**

2 **How can non-profit-making events such as this maximize their exposure through the suite of marketing communications channels available to them?**

3 **Discuss examples of how the 'brand name' of iconic sports personalities could be used to support initiatives/interventions that stimulate regular exercise engagement in your country?**

This market insight was kindly contributed by Dr Paul Morrissey, Waterford Institute of Technology, Republic of Ireland.

---

different influences include, in order of importance: the opinions of family and friends; the company/product website; shop assistants; passively reading articles in magazines or newspapers; proactively looking up reviews online or in magazines; actively researching using forums and chatrooms, or by reading about it on Twitter. Men are more likely to gain product updates in a news format and women more likely to visit online stores. Mums are particularly likely to share beauty content. Of those who said something positive about a product online, 45% bought the product based on a vlogger (video blogger) recommendation (Mintel, 2015).

In the next section, we consider how consumer behaviour is affected by social class, lifestyle, and lifecycle.

Social Grade

In marketing, the term 'social grade' refers to a system of classification of consumers based on their socio-economic grouping. **Social grade** was originally developed for the IPA National Readership Survey (NRS) in the 1950s, and was subsequently adopted by JICNARS (the Joint Industry Committee for National Readership Surveys) on its formation in 1968. Social grade is a means of classifying the population by the type of work they do based on the occupation of the chief income earner, i.e. the member of the household with the largest income. NRS Ltd (the successor to JICNARS) provides social grade population estimates, not only for the National Readership Survey, but also for a number of other major industry surveys. These population estimates are obtained from the Survey's interviews with a representative sample of some 36,000 adults every year (see Table 2.1). There is a widely held belief that consumers make purchases based on their socio-economic position within society, and that different social classes have different self-images, social horizons, and consumption goals (Coleman, 1983). Such variations in attitudes, motivations, and value orientations reflect differences in occupational opportunities and demands, childhood socialization patterns, and educational influences, leading consumers to vary in their purchase behaviours across social classes (Williams, 2002).

Table 2.1 Social grading scale

Social grade	Social status	Occupational status	Population estimate, Great Britain, age 15+ (July 2014–June 2015) (%)	Population estimate, Great Britain, age 15+ (July 1984–June 1985) (%)
A	Upper middle class	Higher managerial, administrative, and professional	4	3
B	Middle class	Intermediate managerial, administrative, and professional	23	14
C1	Lower middle class	Supervisory, clerical, and junior managerial, administrative and professional	27	22
C2	Skilled working class	Skilled manual workers	22	29
D	Working class	Semi- and unskilled manual workers	15	18
E	Those at lowest levels of subsistence	State pensioners, casual and lowest grade workers, unemployed with state benefits only	9	14

Source: National Readership Survey. Reproduced with the kind permission of the National Readership Survey.

Lifestyle

Marketers increasingly target consumers on the basis of their lifestyles (see also Chapter 6). The AMA define lifestyle as 'the manner in which the individual copes and deals with his/her psychological and physical environment on a day-to-day basis', 'as a phrase describing the values, attitudes, opinions, and behaviour patterns of the consumer', and 'the manner in which people conduct their lives, including their activities, interests, and opinions' (AMA, 2016). For example, a segmentation of the South Australian wine market reveals the following lifestyle types (Bruwer and Li, 2007).

■ Conservative knowledgeable wine drinkers (19.2% of the population)—more likely to be male (57%), well educated, and well remunerated; this segment drinks wine frequently (particularly red), displaying connoisseur qualities when buying wine.

- Enjoyment-oriented social wine drinkers (16.2% of the population)—more likely to be female and younger; this segment likes white and sparkling wine and has an eye for value for money.
- Basic wine drinkers (23.5% of the population)—a predominantly male segment, as happy drinking beer as wine, depending on what's available.
- Mature time-rich wine drinkers (18.2% of the population)—this older male segment displays connoisseur tendencies and is interested in the provenance of his wine.
- Young professional wine drinkers (22.9% of the population)— predominantly female and employed in the professions; this segment tends to drink red wine, mainly at business functions.

German auto manufacturer, Porsche, has also previously segmented its customers using a lifestyle approach, based on the following clusters (Taylor, 1995).

- 'Top guns'—representing 27% of the market: people who are driven, ambitious, expected to be noticed, and enjoy power and control.
- 'Elitists'—representing 24% of the market: people from the upper classes, often with wealth obtained from inheritance. The car is seen as a car and not an extension of the person's personality.
- 'Proud patrons'—representing 23% of the market: this group of people see the car as a self-reward for their hard work and achievements.
- 'Bon vivants'—representing 17% of the market: this group tend to be thrill-seekers and see the car for its excitement value.
- 'Fantasists—representing 9% of the market: this group see the car as a means of escape and might feel guilty owning one.

Whether or not the customer base for Porsche's automotive offerings still corresponds to the above classification is a moot point as segments can change over time. More recently, a sport vehicle for daily use segment appears to be emerging, comprising women and the younger consumer. For this segment, the Cayenne CUV and the Panamera four-door sport saloon particularly appeals (Zoeller, 2015).

In order to generate clusters of consumers according to different lifestyle types, marketers typically ask consumers questions around their activities, interests, and opinions (AIO). If marketers fit around a consumer's lifestyle, consumers are more likely to benefit from, and appreciate, the proposition offered. (We cover lifestyle segmentation further in Chapter 6.)

Lifestage

Marketers frequently hypothesize that people in certain stages of life purchase and consume similar kinds of offerings. In research undertaken in the USA in the 1960s, Wells and Gubar (1966) determined that there were nine categories of lifecycle stage in a consumer's life, from leaving home to living as a solitary survivor without a spouse. In contemporary society, the lifestage concept needs a degree of readjustment to take into account that fewer people are getting married, and at a later age, than they were in the 1960s, that there are more singles with children, and increasingly there is a move by couples towards cohabiting. (See Chapter 6 for more on current life-stage segmentation approaches.)

Visit the Online Resource Centre and complete Internet Activity 2.3 to learn more about how Volkswagen uses the family lifecycle to communicate its brand values to its target audience.

Most market research agencies routinely measure attitudes and purchasing patterns based on life stage to determine differences among groups. Table 2.2 indicates that there is a difference in the types of offering purchased as a result, with solitary survivors far more likely to purchase funeral plans, nursing home care, and cruise holidays, and bachelors more likely to spend their income on package and long-haul holidays and educational service products, for instance. Diesel, the Italian denim brand, has become the first mainstream clothing retailer to advertise, controversially, on a pornographic website Pornhub (one of the world's top 100 most visited websites), as well as on dating apps Grindr and Tinder, in order to project a young sexy image (Croft, 2016). Tour operators, such as Saga, also target particular demographic groups, specifically the older traveller, typically with more sedate appeals.

Ethnic Groups

In a globalized society, marketers are increasingly interested in how to market offerings to ethnic groups within particular populations. Such groups can be large, with their own specific customs. They can represent an opportunity either to build a niche market or to consolidate an existing market, i.e. by appealing to a new set of consumers in addition to the old. For example, in the USA, the Hispanic population—often immigrants from Mexico—and the Black population together represent a sizeable proportion of the total population. European countries also have sizeable ethnic populations; for example, in France there is a large Black African population and in Germany a large Turkish community. France and Britain both have large Muslim populations. In Sweden, there are large groups of Finns, former Yugoslavs, Iraqis, and Iranians. In Dubai, in the United Arab Emirates, a large community of expatriates exists, particularly from India. These groups within a country represent a potential opportunity for the marketer, if they are sizeable enough to be profitable and have similar needs within the group and different needs from the rest of the population. For example, multicultural consumers spent about $3.4tr in the USA in 2015 and, importantly, ethnic groups behave differently (Gil and Rosenberg, 2015). For example, in the USA, Asian Americans disproportionately purchase organic foods (compared with Whites) and social causes are particularly important to Hispanics. Cui (1997) proposes that in any country where there are ethnic marketing opportunities, a company has four main strategic options as follows.

1 Total standardization—use the existing marketing mix (see Chapter 1) without modification to the ethnic market. This is very difficult to do. Even Coca-Cola, well known for its ardent approach to standardization, adapt their Cola around the world (e.g. by adding pineapple in Indonesia to cater for local tastes).

2 Product adaptation—use the existing marketing mix but adapt the product to the ethnic market in question, e.g. Nestlé sells green tea flavoured KitKats in Thailand.

3 Advertising adaptation—use the current marketing mix but adapt the advertising, particularly the use of foreign languages, to the target ethnic market by promoting the product using different associations that are more resonant with ethnic audiences (e.g. stores in some parts of Finland advertise in Swedish and Finnish to cater for the minority Swedish population, and stores in the USA advertise in Spanish).

4 Ethnic marketing—use a totally new marketing mix, e.g. Bollywood films are aimed at audiences in the Indian sub-continent and in the Indian diaspora around the world, using strong love and ethical themes, and a musical format. (See also Market Insight 2.5.)

Table 2.2 The life-stage concept

Bachelor stage: young single people not living with parents/guardians	Newly married or long-term cohabiting: young, no children	Full nest I: youngest children under 6	Full nest II: youngest children 6 or over	Full nest III: older married couples with dependent children	Empty nest I: older married couples, no children living at home, chief income earner or both in work	Empty nest II: older married couples, no children living at home, chief income earner or both retired	Solitary survivor, in work	Solitary survivor, retired
Few financial burdens	Better off financially since dual wages	Home purchasing at peak	Financial position better	Financial position better still	Home ownership at peak	Drastic cut in household income	Medical needs will depend on age	Same medical needs as other retired group
Fashion opinion leaders	High purchase rate of consumer durables	Low level of savings	Sometimes both parents in work	Both parents more likely to be in work	Most satisfied with savings and financial position	More likely to stay at home		Drastic cut in income
Recreation or ented.				Some children will have part-time jobs	Interested in travel, recreation, self-education			
				High average purchase of consumer durables	More likely to give gifts and make charitable contributions			
					Less interested in new products			
Buy: basic kitchen equipment, basic furniture, cars, package and long-haul holidays, education	**Buy:** cars, refrigerators, package holidays	**Buy:** washer–dryers, TV, baby food and related products, vitamins, toys	**Buy:** larger-sized family food packages, cleaning materials, pianos, child-minding services	**Buy:** better homeware and furniture products, magazines, and non-essential home appliances	**Buy:** luxurious holidays, eating out, home improvements	**Buy:** medical appliances and private healthcare, products which help sleep and digestion	**Buy:** financial, healthcare and retirement plans Meals for one	**Buy:** household staples, cruise holidays, nursing home services, funeral plans

Source: Adapted from Wells and Gubar (1966). Published by American Marketing Association.

Have a Break, Have a Green Tea KitKat!

Source: © Paul Baines.

Market Insight 2.5
The Iftar Market

Each year, around the world, many of the 1.6bn-strong **Ummah** (worldwide community of Muslims) come together to observe the holy month of Ramadan. Ramadan is the celebration of the first revelation of the Qu'ran to the Prophet Muhammad (pbuh), by fasting (no food, drink, sex, or cigarettes) from sunrise to sunset, by giving to charity and doing good deeds for others. Only children, the elderly, travellers, the sick, and breastfeeding or pregnant women are exempt from the daytime fasting. Come sunset, the fast is broken with the communal 'iftar' meal for Sunnis (Shia pray first before any food is consumed). The typical iftar might first comprise dates with water or a yoghurt drink and, after the Mahgrib prayer at sunset, soup, salad, appetizers, and main dishes (with halal meat, rice, and fruit being the staples). Before sunrise, suhoor can be eaten, a typically lighter meal, washed down with a couple of glasses of water.

There were around 2.8m Muslims in the UK in 2011, according to the 2011 Census. Given this relatively large number (about 5% of the population), Ramadan is now the third most important religious event for supermarkets in sales terms, preceded only by Christmas and Easter. Other festivals that supermarkets cater for include Diwali (celebrated by Sikhs, Hindus, and Jains), and Rosh Hashanah and Passover (Jewish New Year and Jewish Spring liberation festival respectively), with Tesco, Sainsbury's, and Waitrose all offering enhanced kosher ranges at this time.

In 2015, Britain's supermarkets enjoyed a Ramadan sales uplift of around £100m. Tesco, Sainsbury's, Asda Walmart, and Morrisons all ran Ramadan promotions and reaped the benefits. Morrisons expected to sell 2m tons of rice and 80,000 boxes of dates, and Tesco expected to turn over £30m from the Ramadan product range.

There are difficulties, however. Both Morrisons and Tesco found themselves in hot water after selling pork products (or in Tesco's case Smokey Bacon Pringles) under Ramadan promotional signage, causing outrage in some quarters. Over-eating after sundown also poses health risks, prompting the NHS to warn against breaking the fast with a feast with dedicated content on the NHS Choices website. In Dubai, in the United Arab Emirates, government officials have also warned against over-buying and wastage (hinting that Ramadan is supposed to be about **ascetic** observance) and provided information screens in retail outlets on good shopping practice habits during Ramadan. Supermarkets have also responded by offering food baskets containing essential items at affordable prices in the period leading up to Ramadan.

Sources: Bingham (2015); Botros (2015); Burman (2015); Duell (2015); Gani (2015); MCB (2015); http://www.nhs.uk/livewell/healthyramadan/Pages/healthyramadanhome.aspx.

Market Insight 2.5
continued

Theory into Practice

This market insight indicates the significant market opportunities that can exist in developing offerings for particular ethnic groups, who demonstrate unique consumption behaviour based around their different **cultural mores**. It also indicates some of the difficulties inherent in targeting a niche market, particularly in getting the offering right for the targeted ethnic group without offending them (and not offending other customers by targeting that ethnic group explicitly, although this is not directly mentioned in this case).

Related Topics:

reference group; multicultural marketing; segmentation; targeting; positioning; international marketing.

1 How would supermarkets decide which stores will offer their Ramadan product ranges?

2 Besides the type of food eaten, and the timing of when the food is eaten, how else might Muslim shopping behaviour differ from that of non-Muslims?

3 Is it appropriate for supermarkets to be targeting Muslims at Ramadan with food and drink offers? Why do you say this?

Chapter Summary

To consolidate your learning, the key points from this chapter are summarized here.

- Explain the consumer product acquisition process.

  Consumer buying behaviour has rational and irrational components, although rational theories tend to dominate the marketing literature. There are a variety of models of consumer buying behaviour, but the consumer product acquisition model is perhaps the simplest to understand, stressing how the consumer goes through six key stages in the product acquisition process, including motive development, information gathering, product evaluation, product selection, acquisition, and re-evaluation.

- Explain the processes involved in human perception, learning, and memory in relation to consumer choice.

  The human perception, learning, and memory processes involved in consumer decision-making are complex. When designing advertising, developing distribution strategies, designing new offerings, and implementing other marketing tactics, marketers should (repeatedly) explain the information associated with these actions to consumers. Such an approach is necessary to encourage consumers to engage with, remember, and learn about different offerings, which in turn influences consumers' buying decisions.

- **Understand the importance of personality and motivation in consumer behaviour.**

  Consumers are motivated differently in their purchasing behaviour depending on their personalities and social identities and, to some extent, how they feel that their personality or social identity fits with particular offerings. Maslow's (1943) seminal work on human needs helps us to understand how we are motivated to satisfy five key human desires. From the theory of planned behaviour (Azjen, 1991), we know that how we intend to behave is not always how we actually behave, because this is affected by our attitudes towards the behaviour in question, a subjective norm (how we think others perceive that behaviour), and our own perceptions of how we can control our behaviour.

- **Describe opinions, attitudes, and values, and how they relate to consumer behaviour.**

  Opinions are relatively unstable positions that people take in relation to an issue or assessment of something. Attitudes are more strongly held and are more likely to be linked to our behaviour. Values are more strongly held still and are linked to our conscience. Marketers are interested in all three because they help us to understand consumers better and to develop marketing approaches, particularly when it comes to positioning and repositioning an offering.

- **Explain how reference groups influence consumer behaviour.**

  Reference groups, including such role models as parents, entertainers, and athletes, have an important socializing influence on consumption behaviour, particularly, but not solely, in adolescence. However, where we live, what social class we come from, what lifestyle we lead, what stage of the lifecycle we are in, and which ethnic group we belong to also have an impact on our behaviour as consumers. Celebrity endorsers are powerful influencers in this regard, particularly when they project a particular lifestyle which others seek to emulate.

Review Questions

1 What is the process consumers go through when buying offerings?
2 What is cognitive dissonance and how does it relate to consumer behaviour?
3 How are the psychological concepts of perception, learning, and memory relevant to understanding consumer choice?
4 How are concepts of personality relevant to understanding consumer behaviour?
5 How are concepts of motivation relevant to understanding consumer behaviour?
6 What is the theory of planned behaviour?
7 What are opinions, attitudes, and values, and how do they relate to consumer behaviour?
8 How do reference groups influence how we behave?
9 What is celebrity endorsement?
10 How does lifestyle and ethnicity influence how we buy?

Worksheet Summary

To apply the knowledge you have gained from this chapter and test your understanding of consumer buying behaviour visit the **Online Resource Centre** and complete Worksheet 2.1.

Discussion Questions

1   Having read Case Insight 2.1 at the beginning of this chapter, how should Holdz™ develop its matting solution for their bouldering centre corporate customers to take account of the considerable volumes of feet-first falls from climbers but still allow Holdz™ to generate a reasonable profit?

2   Describe the purchasing process you used to obtain the following using the consumer product acquisition model shown in Figure 2.1.

   A   chocolate bar (e.g. Snickers or Cadbury's Dairy Milk in the UK, Plopp in Sweden, Droste in the Netherlands);

   B   flight to the Caribbean from your home country;

   C   tablet computer to help you write essays and group work for your marketing course;

   D   dishwasher;

   E   a householder receiving refuse collection services from the local council (paid for indirectly through local council taxes).

3   Use the theory of planned behaviour to explain consumer motivations to pursue the following behaviours:

   A   purchase of a room at Raffles Hotel, Singapore;

   B   a visit to the Abba Museum in Stockholm, Sweden;

   C   voting during an election in France;

   D   sky diving in California, USA.

4   What kinds of celebrity endorsers have you noticed companies using in their advertising to persuade you to adopt the following?

   A   make-up (e.g. L'Oréal, Lancôme);

   B   beer (e.g. Heineken);

   C   beverages (e.g. Coca-Cola or Pepsi);

   D   crisps/potato chips (e.g. Walker's, Popchips).

5   Use PowerPoint to develop a short presentation on ethnic marketing, highlighting some examples of how companies develop different offerings and promote themselves to different ethnic groups.

   Visit the Online Resource Centre and complete the Multiple Choice Questions to assess your knowledge of Chapter 2.

Glossary

affective a psychological term referring to our emotional state of mind. Values are affective because they are linked to our feelings about things.

ascetic self-discipline, self-denial, and abstention from sensual pleasure for religious reasons.

attitudes refers to mental states of individuals that underlie the structuring of perceptions and guide behavioural response.

celebrity endorsement usually famous or respected members of the public, used by advertisers to market specific goods and services because they are perceived to be expert or knowledgeable or because of their ability to display particular attractive qualities.

classical conditioning a theory of learning propounded by Russian physiologist Ivan Pavlov, who carried out a series of experiments with his dogs. He realized that if he rang a bell before serving food, the dogs would automatically associate the sound of the bell (conditioned stimulus) with the presentation of the food (unconditioned stimulus), and begin salivating. Classical conditioning occurs when the unconditioned stimulus becomes associated with the conditioned stimulus.

cognitive a psychological term relating to the action of thinking about something. Our opinions are cognitive. Cognitions are mental structures formed about something in our minds.

cognitive dissonance a psychological theory proposed by Leon Festinger in 1957 which states that we are motivated to re-evaluate our beliefs, attitudes, opinions, or values if the position we hold on them at one point in time does not concur with the position held at an earlier period owing to some intervening event, circumstance, or action.

conative a psychological term relating to our motivations to do something. Attitudes are conative because they are linked to our motivations to do things.

cultural mores the customs and manners of a social group.

deshopping the deliberate purchase of an item where there is an intention to return it for a refund after a single use.

ego a Freudian psychoanalytical concept which denotes that part of our psyche that attempts to find outlets for the urges in our id, moderated by the superego.

evoked set a group of goods, brands, or services for a specific item brought up in a person's mind in a particular purchasing situation and from which he/she makes a decision as to which product, brand, or service to buy.

fraudulent returning the act of defrauding a retail outlet by abusing the return process.

habit a repetitive form of behaviour, often undergone without conscious rational thought in a routine way.

id a Freudian psychoanalytical concept referring to the part of our psyche that harbours our instinctual drives and urges.

intention in the consumer context, this is linked to whether or not we intend/are motivated to purchase a good or service.

involvement the greater the personal importance a person attaches to a given communication message, the more involvement they are said to have with that communication.

media facilities used by companies to convey or deliver messages to target audiences. Media is the plural of medium.

neoclassical economics refers to a meta-theory of economics predicated on delineating supply and demand based on rational individuals or agents each seeking to maximize their individual utility by making choices with a given amount of information.

operant conditioning a learning theory developed by B.F. Skinner, which suggests that when a subject acts on a stimulus from the environment (antecedents), this is more likely to result in a particular behaviour (behaviour) if that behaviour is reinforced (consequence) through reward or punishment.

opinions refer to observable verbal responses given by individuals to an issue or question and are easily affected by current affairs and discussions with significant others.

overt search the point in the buying process when a consumer seeks further information in relation to a product or buying situation, according to the Howard–Sheth model of buyer behaviour.

perception a mental picture in our heads based on existing attitudes, beliefs, needs, stimulus factors, and factors specific to our situation, which governs the way we see objects, events, or people in the world about us. Our perceptions govern our attitudes and behaviour towards whatever we perceive.

personality that aspect of our psyche that determines the way in which we respond to our environment in a relatively stable way over time.

picking in the context of consumer behaviour, this word has a different meaning from the same term used in common parlance. It is the process of deliberative selection of a product or service from among a repertoire of acceptable alternatives, even though the consumer believes the alternatives to be essentially identical in their ability to satisfy his/her need.

price elasticity the percentage change in volume demanded as a proportion of the percentage change in price, usually expressed as a negative number. A score close to zero indicates that a product or service price change has little impact on quantity demanded, whereas a score of –1 indicates that a product or service price change effects an equal percentage quantity change. A value above –1 indicates a disproportionately higher change in quantity demanded as a result of a percentage price change.

psychological reactance when a consumer perceives their freedom to pursue a particular decision alternative is blocked, wholly or partially, they become more motivated to pursue that decision alternative.

recall a measure of advertising effectiveness based on what an individual is able to remember about an ad.

recognition when new images and words presented are compared with existing images and words in memory and a match is found.

reference group a group that an individual uses to form his/her own beliefs and attitudes. A reference group can be positive, in which we align our opinions, attitudes, values, or behaviour with theirs, or negative, in which we are repelled by their behaviour and seek to dissociate our opinions, attitudes, values, and behaviour from theirs.

selective exposure the process associated with how consumers screen out the information that is not considered meaningful or interesting.

social class system of classification of consumers or citizens, based on the socio-economic status of the chief income earner in a household, typically into various subgroupings of middle- and working-class categories.

social grade a system of classification of people based on their socio-economic group, usually based on the household's chief income earner.

social learning social learning theory, advocated by Albert Bandura, suggests that we can learn from observing the experiences of others, and in contrast with operant conditioning we can delay gratification and even administer our own rewards or punishment.

social media listening the process of obtaining and evaluating what is being said about a company, its offerings, or individual employees on social networking sites (e.g. Facebook, Instagram and Twitter).

spoof adverts negative advertising, often but not always generated by amateurs, parodying an original campaign using humour, caricature, and ridicule appeals.

superego a Freudian psychoanalytical concept, which denotes the part of our psyche that controls how we motivate ourselves to respond to our instincts and urges in a socially acceptable manner.

System 1 thinking decision-making cognitive function which is fast, automatic, frequent, emotional, stereotypic, and subconscious as opposed to System 2 thinking (Kahneman, 2011).

System 2 thinking decision-making cognitive function which is slow, effortful, infrequent, logical, calculating, and conscious as opposed to System 1 thinking (Kahneman, 2011).

transvections a term proposed by Alderson and Martin (1965) to denote the relationships (transactions) that occur in the development of a product or service that crosses between company (i.e. product/service) ownership boundaries to produce a finished product or service. We would now consider such cooperation in manufacturing from the perspective of supply chain management as vertical integration or cooperation.

Ummah the worldwide community of Muslims.

utility a measure of satisfaction or happiness obtained from the consumption of a specific

good or a service in economic thought, typically measured as an aggregate.

value the regard that something is held to be worth, typically, although not always, in financial terms.

References

Alba, J.W. and Hutchinson, J.W. (2000). Knowledge calibration: what consumers know and what they think they know. *Journal of Consumer Research*, 27, 123–56.

Alderson, W. and Martin, M.W. (1965). Toward a formal theory of transactions and transvections. *Journal of Marketing Research*, 2(May), 117–27.

AMA (2016). *Dictionary of Marketing Terms*. Retrieve from https://www.ama.org/resources/Pages/Dictionary.aspx? (accessed 22 February 2016).

Anon. (2012a). Jameson renews Dublin film festival sponsorship to 2015. *ShelfLife*, 30 January. Retrieve from: http://www.shelflife.ie/jameson-renews-dublin-film-festival-sponsorship-to-2015/ (accessed 25 February 2016).

Anon. (2012b). Retail fraud: Return to vendor—a dress on loan. *The Economist*, 3 March. Retrieve from: http://www.economist.com/node/21548928 ([accessed 2 July 2016).

Anon. (2016). Mark Ronson's track Uptown Funk was the biggest track of 2015. *The Guardian*, 4 January. Retrieve from: http://www.theguardian.com/music/2016/jan/04/mark-ronson-uptown-funk-biggest-track-2015 (accessed 28 February 2016).

ASA (2015). 2014's most complained about ads. Advertising Standards Authority, 20 February. Retrieve from: https://www.asa.org.uk/News-resources/Media-Centre/2015/2014-most-complained-about-ads.aspx#.Vs97ffmLTIU (accessed 25 February 2016).

Azjen, I. (1991). The theory of planned behaviour. *Organisational Behaviour and Human Decision Processes*, 50, 179–211.

Bandura, A. (1977). *Social Learning Theory*. Englewood Cliffs, NJ: Prentice-Hall.

Bargh, J.A. and Chartrand, T.L. (1999). The unbearable automaticity of being. *American Psychologist*, 57(7, July), 462–79.

Bartnett, E. (2012). Rio Ferdinand Snickers tweets 'acceptable' rules ad watchdog. *The Daily Telegraph*, 7 March. Retrieve from: http://www.telegraph.co.uk/technology/twitter/9126724/Rio-Ferdinand-Snickers-tweets-acceptable-rules-ad-watchdog.html (accessed 22 February 2016).

Berthon, P.R. and Pitt, L. (2012). Brands and burlesque: toward a theory of spoof advertising. *AMS Review*, 2(2–4), 88–98.

Bettinghaus, E.P. and Cody, M.J. (1994), *Persuasive Communication* (5th edn), London: Harcourt Brace.

Bettman, J.R. (1979). Memory factors in consumer choice: a review. *Journal of Marketing*, 43(Spring), 37–53.

Bhattacharya, C.B. and Sen, S. (2003). Consumer–company identification: a framework for understanding consumers' relationships with companies. *Journal of Marketing*, 67(April), 76–88.

Bingham, J. (2015). What is Ramadan and why does it matter? Why Muslims fast, when to fast and what to avoid. *The Telegraph*, 18 June. Retrieve from: http://www.telegraph.co.uk/news/religion/11682139/What-is-Ramadan-and-why-does-it-matter.html (accessed 2 March 2016).

Botros, M. (2015). Stocking up on groceries for Ramadan an 'incorrect approach': official. *Gulf News*, 18 June. Retrieve from: http://gulfnews.com/news/uae/society/stocking-up-on-groceries-for-ramadan-an-incorrect-approach-official-1.1537169 (accessed 2 March 2016).

Bruwer, J. and Li, E. (2007). Wine-related lifestyle (WRL) market segmentation: demographic and behavior factors. *Journal of Wine Research*, 18(1), 19–34.

Burman, J. (2015). More Muslim outrage after supermarket sells pork next to Ramadan sticker. *Express*, 26 June. Retrieve from: http://www.express.co.uk/news/uk/587010/Muslim-Ramadan-pork-Morrisons-Tesco-London (accessed March 2016).

Campbell, C., Pitt, L.F., Parent, M., and Berthon, P. (2011). Tracking back-talk in consumer-generated advertising: an analysis of two interpretative approaches. *Journal of Advertising Research*, 51(1), 224–38.

Carù, A. and Cova, B. (2003). Revisiting consumption experience a more humble but complete view of the concept. *Marketing Theory*, 3(2), 267–86.

Champniss, G., Wilson, H.N., and Macdonald, E. (2015). Why your customers' social identities matter. *Harvard Business Review*, January–February. Retrieve from: https://hbr.org/2015/01/why-your-customers-social-identities-matter (accessed 28 February 2016).

Clee, M.A. and Wicklund, R.A. (1980). Consumer behaviour and psychological reactance. *Journal of Consumer Research*, 6, 389–405.

Coleman, R.P. (1983). The continuing significance of social class to marketing. *Journal of Consumer Research*, 10(3), 265–80.

Collins, L. and Montgomery, C. (1969). The origins of motivational research. *British Journal of Marketing*, 13(2, Summer), 103–13.

Craik, L. (2015). Are personal style bloggers the most powerful people in fashion? *Evening Standard*, 18 February. Retrieve from: http://www.standard.co.uk/fashion/are-personal-style-bloggers-the-most-powerful-people-in-fashion-10053103.html (accessed 25 February 2016).

Croft, C. (2016). Dirty Diesel puts ads for underwear on porn site. *Sunday Times*, 17 January. Retrieve from: http://www.thesundaytimes.co.uk/sto/news/uk_news/article1657225.ece (accessed 1 July 2016).

Cui, G. (1997). Marketing strategies in a multi-ethnic environment. *Journal of Marketing Theory and Practice*, 5(1), 122–35.

Cummings, W.H. and Venkatesan, M. (1976). Cognitive dissonance and consumer behavior: a review of the evidence. *Journal of Marketing Research*, 13, 303–8.

Cycling Ireland (2014). *Cycling Ireland Strategic Plan: A Pathway for Cycling Excellence 2014-2019*. Dublin: Cycling Ireland. Retrieve from: http://www.cyclingireland.ie/downloads/cycling%20ireland%20-%20strategy.pdf (accessed 2 July 2016).

Dichter, E. (1964). *The Handbook of Consumer Motivation: The Psychology of the World of Objects*. London: McGraw-Hill.

Dubois, B. (2000). *Understanding the Consumer: A European Perspective*. London: FT/Prentice Hall.

Dubois, B. and Duquesne, P. (1993). The market for luxury goods: income versus culture. *European Journal of Marketing*, 27(1), 35–44.

Duell, M. (2015). Ramadan boosts Britain's big supermarkets with £100m sales uplift as Muslims prepare lavish sundown meals. *Mail Online*, 23 June. Retrieve from: http://www.dailymail.co.uk/news/article-3135796/Ramadan-boosts-Britain-s-big-supermarkets-100million-sales-uplift-Muslims-prepare-lavish-sundown-meals.html (accessed 2 March 2016).

Festinger, L. (1957). *A Theory of Cognitive Dissonance*. Palo Alto, CA: Stanford University Press.

Flanagan, P. (2014). Rihanna and Lady Gaga help put Irish whiskey in high spirits. *Irish Mirror*, 24 September. Retrieve from: www.irishmirror.ie/news/irish-news/rihanna-lady-gaga-help-put-4317956 (accessed 27 February 2016).

Freud, S. (1927). *The Ego and the Id*. Richmond: Hogarth Press.

Furnham, A. (2014). Compulsive buying. *Psychology Today*, 5 December. Retrieve from: https://www.psychologytoday.com/blog/sideways-view/201412/compulsive-buying (accessed 28 February 2016).

Gani, A. (2015). Muslim population in England and Wales nearly doubles in ten years. *The Guardian*, 11 February. Retrieve from: http://www.theguardian.com/world/2015/feb/11/muslim-population-england-wales-nearly-doubles-10-years (accessed 2 March 2016).

Gil, M. and Rosenberg, S. (2015). The multicultural edge: rising super consumers. Nielsen Company, March. Retrieve from: http://www.nielsen.com/content/dam/corporate/us/en/reports-downloads/2015-reports/the-multicultural-edge-rising-super-consumers-march-2015.pdf (accessed 2 March 2016).

Holbrook, M.B. and Hirschman, E.C. (1982). The experiential aspects of consumption: consumer fantasies, feelings and fun. *Journal of Consumer Research*, 9(September), 132–40.

Holbrook, M.B., Lehmann, D.R., and O'Shaughnessy, J. (1986). Using versus choosing: the relationship of the consumption experience to reasons for purchasing. *European Journal of Marketing*, 20(8), 49–62.

Howard, J.A. and Sheth, J.N. (1969). *The Theory of Buyer Behavior*. New York: John Wiley.

IFPI (2015). IFPI publishes digital music report 2015. IFPI, 14 April. Retrieve from: http://www.ifpi.org/news/Global-digital-music-revenues-match-physical-format-sales-for-first-time (accessed 24 February 2016).

Ipsos MRBI/Irish Sports Council (2013). *The Irish Sports Monitor 2013 Annual Report*. Dublin: Irish Sports Council. Retrieve from: http://www.irishsportscouncil.ie/Research/Irish-Sports-Monitor-Annual-Report-2013/ (accessed 2 July 2016).

Johnson, E.J. and Russo, J.E. (1978). The organisation of product information in memory identified by recall times. In: K. Hunt (ed.), *Advances in Consumer Research*, Vol. 5. Chicago, IL: Association for Consumer Research, 79–86.

Kahneman, D. (2011). *Thinking, Fast and Slow*. London: Penguin.

Kane, C. (2015). Why a $223,000 Hermes Birkin bag might actually be a good investment. *Fortune*, 23 June. Retrieve from: http://fortune.com/2015/06/23/hermes-birkin-investment/ (accessed 28 February 2016).

Kelly, S. (2015). *Hunger: Sean Kelly—The Autobiography*. Hemel Hempstead: Peloton Publishing.

King, T. and Balmer, J. (2012). When the customer isn't right. *HBR Blog Network*, 17 February. Retrieve from: http://blogs.hbr.org/cs/2012/02/when_the_customer_isnt_right.html (accessed 2 July 2016).

King, T., Dennis, C., and Wright, L.T. (2008). Myopia, customer returns and the theory of planned behaviour. *Journal of Marketing Management*, 24(1–2), 185–203.

Kotler, P. (1965). Behavioral models for analyzing buyers. *Journal of Marketing*, 29(October), 37–45.

McAvoy, K. (2015). Fraudulent returns cost retailers $2.2bn. *Spend Matters*, 24 December. Retrieve from: http://spendmatters.com/2015/12/24/fraudulent-returns-cost-retailers-2-2-billion/ (accessed 27 February 2016).

McRae, R.R. and Costa, P.T. (1987). Validation of the five-factor model of personality across instruments and observers. *Journal of Personality and Social Psychology*, 52, 81–90.

Magee, K. (2015). Inside Tesco's new ad strategy. *Campaign*, 16 October. Retrieve from: http://www.campaignlive.co.uk/article/inside-tescos-new-ad-strategy/1368667 (accessed 25 February 2016).

Martin, C.A. and Bush, A.J. (2000). Do role models influence teenagers' purchase intentions and behavior? *Journal of Consumer Marketing*, 17(5), 441–54.

Maslow, A.H. (1943). A theory of motivation. *Psychological Review*, 50, 370–96.

Matzler, K., Bidmon, S., and Grabner-Kräuter, S. (2006). Individual determinants of brand affect: the role of the personality traits of extraversion and openness to experience. *Journal of Product and Brand Management*, 15(7), 427–34.

MCB (2015). British Muslims in numbers. Muslim Council of Great Britain. Retrieve from: http://www.mcb.org.uk/wp-content/uploads/2015/02/MCBCensusReport_2015.pdf (accessed 2 March 2016).

Mick, D.G. and DeMoss, M. (1990). To me from me: a descriptive phenomenology of self-gifts. *Advances in Consumer Research*, 17, 677–82.

Michaelidou, N. and Dibb, S. (2008). Consumer involvement: a new perspective. *Marketing Review*, 8(1), 83–99.

Mindak, W. A. (1961). Fitting the semantic differential to the marketing problem. *Journal of Marketing*, 25(April), 29–33.

Mintel (2011). Men's Grooming and Shaving Products—UK, October 2011. Retrieve from: http://www.mintel.com (accessed 22 February 2016).

Mintel (2012). Social Media: Beauty and Personal Care—UK, April 2012. Retrieve from: http://www.mintel.com (accessed 22 February 2016).

Mintel (2015). Social Media: BPC—UK, June 2015. Retrieve from: http://www.mintel.com (accessed 28 February 2016).

Mintel (2016), Car Review—UK, February 2016. Retrieve from: http://www.mintel.com (accessed 25 February 2016).

Moschis, G.P. and Churchill, G.A., Jr (1978). Consumer socialisation: a theoretical and empirical analysis. *Journal of Marketing Research*, 15(November), 599–609.

Mulyanegara, R.C., Tsarenko, Y., and Anderson, A. (2009). The Big Five and brand personality: investigating the impact of consumer personality on preferences towards particular brand personality. *Journal of Brand Management*, 16(4), 234–47.

Peugeot (2016). News, 12 January. Retrieve from: http://www.peugeot.co.uk/news/psa-peugeot-citroen-worldwide-sales-up-in-2015/ (accessed 25 February 2016).

Ratchford, B.T. (1987). New insights about the FCB grid. *Journal of Advertising Research*, 27(4), 24–38.

Richards, V. (2015). Bud Light apologises for 'pro-rape' advertising campaign. *Independent*, 29 April. Retrieve from: http://www.independent.co.uk/news/world/americas/bud-light-apologises-for-pro-rape-advertising-campaign-10212332.html (accessed 2 July 2016).

Roderick, L. (2015). Cult creation. *The Marketer*, March/April, 30–3.

Rummell, A., Howard, J., Swinton, J.M., and Seymour, D.B. (2000). You can't have that! A study of reactance effects and children's consumer behaviour. *Journal of Marketing Theory and Practice*, 8(1), 38–45.

Russell, M. (2012). Irish Fog: 9 myths about whiskey mogul John Jameson. *Business Insider*, 16 March. Retrieve from: www.businessinsider.com/meet-john-jameson-2012-3?IR=T (accessed 25 February 2016).

Sabri, O. and Michel, G. (2014). When do advertising parodies hurt? The power of humor and credibility in viral spoof advertisements. *Journal of Advertising Research*, 54(2), 233–47.

Senecal, S. and Nantal, J. (2004). The influence of online product recommendations on consumers' online choices. *Journal of Retailing*, 80, 159–69.

Sheldrake, P. (2011). *The Business of Influence: Reframing Marketing and PR for the Digital Age*. Chichester: John Wiley.

Sheth, J.N., Newman, B.I., and Gross, B.L. (1991). Why we buy what we buy: a theory of consumption values. *Journal of Business Research*, 22(2), 159–70.

Siciliano, L. (2014). Watch: Graphic anti-smoking ad shows father rolling and smoking rotting flesh. *The Telegraph*, 29 December. Retrieve from: http://www.telegraph.co.uk/news/health/11315959/Watch-Graphic-anti-smoking-ad-shows-father-rolling-and-smoking-rotting-flesh.html (accessed 28 February 2016).

Skinner, B.F. (1954). The science of learning and the art of teaching. *Harvard Educational Review*, 24, 88–97.

Taylor, A. (1995). Porsche slices up its buyers. *Fortune*, January, 16, 24.

Udell, J.G. (1964). A new approach to consumer motivation. *Journal of Retailing*, Winter, 6–10.

Wells, W.D. and Gubar, G. (1966). Life cycle concept in marketing research. *Journal of Marketing Research*, 3(November), 355–63.

Williams, T.G. (2002). Social class influences on purchase evaluation criteria. *Journal of Consumer Marketing*, 19(3), 249–76.

Zoeller, S. (2015). Target market segment strategy: Porsche. *Stephen Zoeller's Marketing Blog*. 13 November. Retrieve from: http://www.stephenzoeller.com/target-market-segment-strategy-porsche/ (accessed 28 February 2016).

Chapter 3

Marketing Research and Customer Insight

Learning Outcomes

After studying this chapter, you will be able to:

▶ Define the terms market research, marketing research, and customer insight

▶ Describe the customer insight process and the role of marketing research in it

▶ Explain the role of marketing research and list the range of possible research approaches

▶ Define the term big data and describe its role in marketing

▶ Discuss the importance of ethics and the adoption of a code of conduct in marketing research

▶ Note the concept of equivalence in relation to obtaining comparable data

Case Insight 3.1
MESH Planning

Market Insight 3.1
Using Marketing Metrics in a State Monopoly

Market Insight 3.2
CHP System Customer Insight: The Brief

Market Insight 3.3
CHP System Customer Insight: The Proposal

Market Insight 3.4
How Scent Sells Lingerie at Hunkemöller

Market Insight 3.5
Why Ask?

Case Insight 3.1
MESH Planning

How should organizations measure the effectiveness of all touchpoints in interactions with customers, not just marketing communications? We speak to MESH Planning's CEO, Fiona Blades, to find out more.

MESH Planning, an innovative market research agency, was set up in 2006. Fiona Blades had worked previously as an advertising planning director, seeing at first hand how organizations were seldom able to get the data they needed from traditional campaign evaluation, since these were often overly focused on TV advertising. There was also a tendency to believe that, because advertising effectiveness questions were added to **brand health** monitoring, it was advertising that caused changes in brand health, when this is often not the case. In fact, MESH data shows that usage is the most influential **touchpoint** for almost all categories of offering. Results of traditional campaign analysis were always reported well after the campaign, making it too late to make interim changes. MESH Planning's response was to develop a research process to measure touchpoint effectiveness using a process called real-time experience tracking (RET). This focuses on experiences that capture the essence of what brands are made of, not interim measures.

RET fuses a number of different data sources, using traditional survey data as well as analysing experiences quantitatively, and then applying statistical measurements to them and viewing qualitative comments. Because MESH has planners (account planners and media planners) as well as researchers, the output for the client is more recommendation/action focused than findings/research focused.

Clients come to MESH because RET collects people's responses to different touchpoints, including those that they haven't been able to get before (e.g. seeing whether it is TV, online, or retail activity which drives brand consideration). The approach is faster and more cost effective than previous tools such as **market mix modelling**. Beyond marketing campaigns, clients want to understand the impact of retail activity and the path to purchase. MESH clients have reported good results with RET: Energizer executives calculated that the new measures led to a threefold improvement in advertising cost-effectiveness, increasing Energizer's revenue in the razor category by 10% in less than four months; LG Electronics won the coveted POPAI award for retail marketing effectiveness and attributed this to working with MESH; and BSkyB re-evaluated how to spend £150m per annum using RET analytics.

Gatorade, another client, decided to reposition its offering from being in the sports drink category to sports nutrition. Its launch in Mexico included TV advertising, sponsorship, and an innovative channel strategy which used experiential channels such as gyms, fitness centres, and parks.

How could research be designed to determine, if someone experienced an experiential touchpoint, whether having this experience impacted positively on their perceptions of the brand, and specifically on those related to Gatorade's sports nutrition attributes?

Introduction

Most of us take it for granted that great companies make great offerings. But how do companies develop successful offerings? More often than not, companies develop propositions using research programmes designed to identify customers' changing needs. They are based on the knowledge that market research and customer insight can bring. Along with marketing communications, marketing research is a key sub-discipline of marketing practice and a fundamental component of the marketing philosophy.

Contemporary marketing research is very much affected by technology. Digitalization has lead to a proliferation of information and data available to marketers. This shift in availability, often referred to as big data, is currently transforming the market research industry. Traditional market research companies, such as Gallup and A.C. Nielsen, are under pressure from large tech firms (e.g. IBM and Adobe) as well as fast-growing analytic companies (e.g. BrainJuicer and Qualtrics) offering a wide range of tools to track customer behaviours in real time (ESOMAR, 2015).

We begin this chapter by defining the difference between 'marketing research' and 'market research'. Whereas market research is conducted to understand markets—customers, competitors, and industries—marketing research also investigates the impact of marketing strategies and tactics. Marketing research thus subsumes market research. 'Customer insight' refers to actionable knowledge about customers gained through research. We then introduce the different steps that marketers need to go through when conducting research. We also introduce big data, which is increasingly being used to generate insights that lead to strategic marketing decisions. Finally, we consider the challenges of conducting international marketing research.

Definitions of Marketing Research and Customer Insight

Marketing research generates information to provide management with sufficient insight to make informed decisions. It follows the philosophical marketing premise that organizations must understand the motivations, desires, and behaviours of their customers and consumers to survive and thrive. We speak of marketing research, market research, and customer insight, but these terms are not interchangeable, although they are related. In addition, marketing analytics is often used to denote the analytical procedures used to analyse information collected from a range of different sources, often referred to as big data. We outline the definitions of these concepts in Table 3.1.

Market research is work undertaken to determine the structural characteristics of the industry of concern (e.g. demand, market share, market volumes, customer characteristics, and segmentation), whereas marketing research is work undertaken to understand how to make specific marketing strategy decisions (e.g. for pricing, sales forecasting, proposition testing, and promotion research). Marketing research is further characterized by being systematic, meaning that the procedures followed in each step of the research process are methodologically sound, well documented, and, as far as possible, planned in advance (Malhotra, 2010).

Table 3.1 Definitions in marketing research

Term	Originator	Definition
Big data	(Authors)	The systematic gathering and interpretation of high volume, high velocity, and/or high variety information using cost-effective innovative forms of information processing to enable enhanced insight, decision-making, and process automation (adapted from various definitions, e.g. McAfee and Brynjolfsson, 2012; Press, 2014).
Customer insight	Said, Macdonald, Wilson, and Marcos	'Knowledge about the customer that is valuable for the firm' (Said *et al.*, 2015).
Market research	International Chamber of Commerce (ICC)/European Society for Opinion and Market Research (ESOMAR)	'Market research, which includes social and opinion research, is the systematic gathering and interpretation of information about individuals or organizations using the statistical and analytical methods and techniques of the applied social sciences to gain insight or support decision making. The identity of respondents will not be revealed to the user of the information without explicit consent and no sales approach will be made to them as a direct result of their having provided information' (ESOMAR, 2008).
Marketing analytics	American Marketing Association (AMA)	'Marketing analytics involves the discovery and communication of meaningful patterns in data from metrics like traffic, leads, sales, advertising, promotions, web activity, social media, and any other relevant marketing activity or financial data. Marketing analytics can be defined by their use of mathematical distributions, statistical sources, or analytical techniques (e.g., regression) for their construction' (AMA, 2015).
Marketing research	American Marketing Association (AMA)	'Marketing research is the function that links the consumer, customer, and public to the marketer through information—information used to identify and define marketing opportunities and problems; generate, refine, and evaluate marketing actions; monitor marketing performance; and improve understanding of marketing as a process. Marketing research specifies the information required to address these issues, designs the method for collecting information, manages and implements the data collection process, analyses the results, and communicates the findings and their implications' (AMA, 2015).

In contrast, customer insights are generated based on the knowledge gained by different research activities. Information requires transformation to generate insight. Customer insights are thus distinct from customer information as they are an acquired, deeper understanding of customers. Marketing analytics refers to the mathematical and statistical analytical procedures used to distil insights out of high-volume, high-velocity and/or high-variety information, typically denoted as big data. We will discuss this further in the section on big data, but before that we will look at different steps in the insight generation and market research processes, respectively.

Visit the Online Resource Centre and follow the web links to the MRS and ESOMAR to learn more about these professional marketing research associations.

The Customer Insight Process

Understanding customers is at the core of the marketing concept and the basic idea with these systems is that marketing information should be used for timely continuous information to support decision-making. Research is thus a foundational element of marketing practice, but some companies and sectors value it more than others. In 2014, consumer packaged goods (22%), media (15%), and pharmaceutical (12%) companies accounted for almost half of the total demand for market research (ESOMAR, 2015).

Customer insight is typically derived from fusing knowledge generated from a range of sources, including industry reports; sales force data, **competitive intelligence**, CRM data, employee feedback, social media analysis data, and managerial intuition (see also section on Big data below). Barwise and Meehan (2011) distinguishes between high-tech and low-tech sources to generate insights. High-tech sources include quantitative marketing research, customer database analysis and big data. Low-tech sources include qualitative market research, but also casual observations, mystery shoppers, and employee feedback. Typically, both high- and low-tech sources are used to generate insights.

Visit the Online Resource Centre and to learn more about how Colgate-Palmolive, Procter and Gamble, and Wal-Mart combine high and low tech sources in their market research.

A customer insight is of value if it is rare, difficult to imitate, and of potential use to formulate management decisions (Said *et al.*, 2015). Cowan (2008) suggests that for organizations to genuinely make use of insights CEOs/CMOs, researchers, and insight managers need to do the following:

- CEO/CMOs should recognize the importance of supporting the insight process, ask 'helicopter' (i.e. wide-scoping) questions, not try to guess the answers to strategic problems, demand evidence-based answers, and provide the necessary resources.
- Researchers: should view themselves as problem-solvers not reporters, focus on trying to gain a causal understanding, not just describing attitudes, and focus on changing the marketing situation.
- Insight managers should challenge strategy assumptions that the organization is making, challenge the 'obvious' solution since it is often wrong, analyse and combine all existing relevant data, and devote greater resources to extracting insight.

The information obtained through marketing research, competitive intelligence, and internal sources are typically integrated into a marketing information system (MIS). MIS provides a formalized set of procedures for generating, analysing, sorting and distributing information to decision makers on an on-going basis (Malhotra, 2010). The kind of information marketers need includes (Ashill and Jobber, 2001):

- aggregated marketing information in quarterly annual summaries;
- aggregated marketing information around offerings/markets (e.g. sales data);
- analytical information for decision models (e.g. SWOT, segmentation analyses);
- internally focused marketing information (e.g. sales, costs, marketing performance indicators);
- externally focused marketing information (e.g. macro and industry trends);
- historical information (e.g. sales, profitability, market trends);
- future-oriented marketing information (e.g. horizon scanning information);
- quantitative marketing information (e.g. costs, profit, market share, customer satisfaction, **net promoter score**);
- qualitative marketing information (e.g. buyer behaviour, competitor strategy information).

This information could be provided on a continuous and/or an ad hoc basis. Continuous industry trend information is gleaned from industry reports and secondary data sources, whereas ad hoc research typically involves some kind of primary data collection (i.e. data that is collected specifically for that purpose). The main difficulty for the marketing manager is to obtain and customize the marketing information systems (MIS) to fit their company's specific needs, as these change according to industry, and to ensure that the data are input on a timely and continuous basis. Another limitation of MIS is that they tend to have a rigorous structure and as such cannot be easily manipulated to assess different options. Decision support systems (DSS) are integrated systems that allow decision-makers to interact directly with databases and models, allowing them to assess different decisions in terms of a 'what if' analysis (Malhotra, 2010).

Market Insight 3.1
Using Marketing Metrics in a State Monopoly

Systembolaget was the world's first alcohol monopoly and remains the only retailer of alcohol in Sweden. In the past decade they have become a leader in customer satisfaction in the retail industry.

The Swedish Government has given Systembolaget the task of selling alcohol in a responsible manner, thereby contributing to reducing the harmful effects of alcohol in society. In other words, and in contrast with most privately owned companies, the goal is not to make a profit or to sell as much as possible, but rather to reduce the harmful effects of the products they sell. In addition, to be able to keep the monopoly, Systembolaget needs to ensure that the general public supports the monopoly.

Marketing research is an important tool for ensuring that Systembolaget stays true to the task given.

Systembolaget continuously measures customer satisfaction across all of its more than 400 stores. These studies allow them see what kind of shops provide customers with most satisfaction. They can

Market Insight 3.1
continued

also identify the most important drivers of satisfaction. It turns out that the service staff and social responsibility (i.e. reducing the harmful effects of alcohol) are key drivers of satisfaction.

Systembolaget also measures the work satisfaction and motivation of its employees. Since the service staff are an important driver of customer satisfaction, the staff receive training to be able to answer questions related to all products on sale. They are also trained to communicate in a responsible manner with regard to the products.

To track public support, Systembolaget measures support for the existence of a monopoly among the general public. This tracking includes both customers and non-customers of Systembolaget. The tracking shows a high level of support from the general public; four out of five say they would vote to keep it, if there was a referendum today. The level of customer satisfaction also contributes to this support. As long as customers are satisfied, they will support the existence of the monopoly.

Systembolaget cannot use sales to evaluate the appropriateness of its strategy. Therefore the insights gained from customer, employee, and the general public surveys are very important. In fact, guided by market research, some major changes have taken place over the past decade, such as the change of all stores from over-the-counter to self-service and the introduction of home deliveries.

Customer satisfaction is a key metric for Systembolaget
Source: © Magnus Fond.

Theory into Practice

Marketing research generates information to provide management with sufficient insight to make informed decisions. This information can be used to devise new offers, but also to evaluate what is currently being done. In order to use marketing research to assess what is being done, continuity is important as this allows decision-makers to compare key metrics over time and before and after certain changes. For Systembolaget, continuously measuring customer and employee satisfaction as well as public support for the monopoly provides direct feedback on how well they are fulfilling the task given to them by the Swedish Government.

Related Topics:
customer satisfaction; employee satisfaction; customer service; service encounters; retailing.

1 **What functions of a company should be measured?**

2 **Data collection can be expensive. Is it necessary to measure customers, employees, and general opinion?**

3 **How can a company keep up to date even if there Is no competition?**

This market insight was kindly contributed by Sofie Sagfossen, PhD Candidate at the Stockholm School of Economics, Sweden.

Research Insight 3.1

To take your learning further, you might wish to read this influential paper:

Said, E., Macdonald, E.K, Wilson, H.N., and Marcos, J. (2015). How organisations generate and use customer insight. *Journal of Marketing Management*, 31(9–10), 1158–79.

In this article, the authors investigate how organizations generate and use customer insights. Based on case studies of four organizations in different sectors (charity, telecom, training, IT) they develop a framework for insight generation and insight use. The results show that insight generation requires alignment between market research providers, internal insight specialists, and internal insights users. What is more, they highlight the role of insights in aiding interpretation of research results as well as dealing with information overload. This framework provides a starting point for (re)designing processes within and beyond the firm to optimize insight generation and use.

@ Visit the **Online Resource Centre** to read the abstract and access the full paper.

Commissioning Market Research

Much market research is not conducted in house by marketers. When commissioning research, a client determines whether or not he/she wants to commission an agency, a consultant, a field and tabulation (tab) agency, or a data preparation and analysis agency. Typically, a consultant might do a job that does not require extensive fieldwork, a field and tab agency is used when the organization can design its own research but not undertake the data collection, a data preparation and analysis agency when it can both design and collect the data but does not have the expertise to analyse it, and a **full-service agency** when it does not have the expertise to design the research and collect or analyse the data.

Agencies are shortlisted according to some criteria and asked to make a presentation of their services. Visits are made to their premises to check the quality of their staff and facilities, and previous reports are considered to assess the quality of their work. Permission to interview or obtain references from their clients is usually requested. Each agency is evaluated on its ability to undertake work of an acceptable quality at an appropriate price. The criteria used to evaluate an agency's suitability (after proposal submission) includes the following:

- the agency's reputation;
- the agency's perceived expertise;
- whether the study offers value for money;
- the time taken to complete the study;
- the likelihood that the research design will provide insights into the **management problem**.

Shortlisted agencies are given a preliminary outline of the client's needs in a **research brief** and asked to provide proposals on research methodology, timing, and costs. After this, an agency is selected to undertake the work required. In the long term, clients are most satisfied with flexible agencies that avoid rigid research solutions and demonstrate professional knowledge of the industry, have an ability to focus on the management problem and provide solutions, and consistent service quality (Cater and Zabkar, 2009).

The Marketing Research Brief

The research brief is a formal document prepared by a marketer (client) and submitted to the marketing research agency. When marketing research is conducted in-house, the manager requiring the research prepares a brief for the market research manager. The brief outlines a management problem to be investigated (see Market Insight 3.2 for an example). The typical contents of a research brief include the following.

- A background summary—providing a brief introduction and details about the company and its offerings.

- The management problem—a clear statement of why the research is needed and what business decisions depend upon its outcome.

- The marketing research questions—a detailed list of the information necessary to make the decisions outlined.

- The intended scope of the research—the areas to be covered, which industries, type of customer—should be provided. The brief should give an indication of when the information is required and why that date is important (e.g. pricing research required for a sales forecast meeting).

- Tendering procedures—the client organization should outline how agencies are selected as a result of the tendering process. Specific information may be required, such as CVs from agency personnel involved in the study and referee contact addresses. The number of copies of the report required and preferences with regard to layout and format are also outlined.

Market Insight 3.2
CHP System Customer Insight: The Brief

Markus Henneberg is the director of Turbine Generators Limited (TGL), a start-up combined heat and power (CHP) system manufacturing company based in Ipswich. The company has won government funding to develop a prototype CHP system. Having just joined the company, Markus decides that the company should invest in concept testing research to determine the market potential for the CHP offering, which is likely to appeal to both domestic residential customers (who seek to replace their household boilers with a system which is 20% more efficient) and industrial customers (e.g. national house builders who run many homes off one large CHP system and require larger-scale energy efficiency). Markus expects the energy retail sector to see significant turbulence over the next five years. Whilst the CHP market is relatively new, his competitive

Market Insight 3.2

continued

intelligence indicates that several other similar research and development (R&D) projects are being undertaken by rival start-ups and established boiler manufacturers. Accordingly, TGL would like to know whether their concept CHP system is acceptable to its potential industrial and domestic customers, what the likely market potential is for this offering, and what features are important to potential residential and industrial customers. Markus invites proposals from four market research agencies and provides them with the following information concerning TGL's research objectives. Specifically, they would like this research to do the following for both potential residential and industrial customers.

1   Indicate how both sets of potential customers perceive this offering and its expected performance.

2   Determine when/where/how existing boiler/CHP systems (and associated services) are sourced and bought and the price ranges customers are prepared to pay.

3   Compare the TGL prototype CHP product with existing alternative offerings for each market to determine which products customers perceive are best.

4   Determine what customers' decision factors are when choosing a particular supplier.

5   Evaluate the market potential of the two markets and provide an indication of the existing competition.

Markus spends two hours meeting with each of four bidding organizations, briefing them on the background to the company and outlining why he wants to conduct the research requested. Of the four companies who each submit a proposal, Markus is most impressed with the one submitted by Robinson–Bennett International. He decides to meet its Research Director to discuss their proposal.

Source: Market Research Society (MRS). Adapted and reproduced with kind permission.

Theory into Practice

A market research brief typically includes a summary of the company and its offerings, a statement of why the research is needed and what it will be used for. It also includes a detailed list of the information necessary and the intended scope of the research as well as information about important deadlines, and tendering procedures.

Related Topics:

new product development; innovation; marketing environment; B2C/B2B.

1   **Do you think that this brief has clear research objectives? Why do you say this?**

2   **Does the research brief indicate or imply that a specific methodology should be used? If so, which method does it imply?**

3   **What other types of research might be conducted to tackle the given research objectives?**

The Marketing Research Process

There are numerous basic stages that guide a marketing research project (see Figure 3.1). The first, and most crucial, stage involves problem definition and setting the information needs of the decision-makers. The client organization explains the basis of the problem(s) it faces to the market researcher. This might be the need to understand market volumes in a potential new market or the reason for an unexpected sudden increase in uptake of an offering. Problem definition does not always imply that threats face the organization. The initial stage allows the organization to assess its current position, define its information needs, and make informed decisions about its future.

Stage 1. Problem Definition

The first step in a market research project is defining the management problem and writing the research brief. Often, the problem is described in vague terms, as organizations are not always sure what information they require. An example might be Carrefour, the supermarket chain, explaining that sales are not as strong as expected in their Czech Republic stores

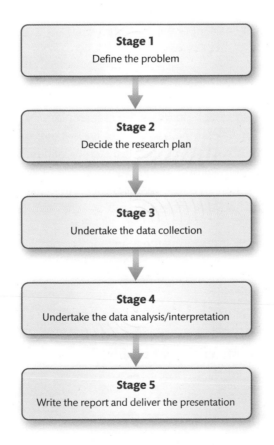

Figure 3.1

Marketing research process

Source: Baines and Chansarkar (2002). © John Wiley & Sons. Reproduced with permission.

Carrefour, the French supermarket chain, operates globally
Source: © PhotoStock10/Shutterstock.

and wondering whether or not this is due to the emergence of a competitor supermarket (see Figure 3.2). The problem description provides the researcher with relatively little depth of understanding of the situation in which the supermarket finds itself, so he/she needs to discuss the problem with the staff commissioning the study to investigate further. This allows the researcher to translate the management problem into a marketing research question. Typically, this question may include a number of sub-questions for further exploration. For example, a marketing research question, and a number of more specific sub-questions, is shown in Figure 3.3.

The marketing research question transforms the management problem into a question while trying to remove any assumptions made by the organization's management. Sometimes the management problem is clear. The organization needs a customer profile, an industry profile,

> **Management problem**
>
> Sales at the new store have not met management expectations, possibly due to the emergence of a new competitor

Figure 3.2
Example of a management problem

MARKETING RESEARCH QUESTION

Why are sales levels not meeting management expectations?

1. Sub-question: Has customer disposable income in the area declined over the last six months?
2. Sub-question: Is a new competitor, Tesco, taking away customers?
3. Sub-question: Are customers tired/bored of the current product range in the existing supermarket?
4. Sub-question: Are customers conducting more of their shopping online?
5. Sub-question: Were management expectations set too high and/or market potential overestimated?

Figure 3.3

Example of a marketing research question

an understanding of buyer behaviour, or to test advertising concepts for its next campaign. The more clearly the commissioning organization defines the management problem, the easier it is to design the research to solve that problem. Once the agency discusses the brief with the client, the agency provides a detailed outline of how they will investigate the problem. This document is called the research proposal. Figure 3.4 briefly outlines a typical marketing **research proposal** and Market Insight 3.3 provides an example.

The basic structure and contents of a typical research proposal should include the following:

▶ **Executive Summary**—a brief summary of the research project including the major outcomes and findings. Rarely more than one page in length. It allows the reader to obtain a summary of the main points of the project without having to read the full report.

▶ **Background to the Research**—an outline of the problem or situation and the issues surrounding this problem. This section demonstrates the researcher's understanding of the management problem.

▶ **Research Objectives**—an outline of the objectives of the research project including the data to be generated and how this will be used to address the management problem.

▶ **Research Design**—a clear non-technical description of the research type adopted and the specific techniques to be used to gather the required information. This will include details of data-collection instruments, sampling procedures, and analytical techniques.

▶ **Personnel Specification**—the details of the people involved in the collection and analysis of the data, providing a named liaison person and outlining the company's credibility in undertaking the work.

▶ **Time Schedule**—an outline of the time requirements with dates for the various stages to completion and presentation of results.

▶ **Costs**—a detailed analysis of the costs involved in the project is usually included for large projects or simply a total cost for the project.

▶ **References**—typically three references are outlined so that a client can be sure that an agency has the requisite capability to do the job in hand.

Figure 3.4

A marketing research proposal outline

Market Insight 3.3
CHP System Customer Insight: The Proposal

Client's Information Needs

The client Turbine Generators Ltd, a start-up company, is looking to exploit new combined heat and power system technologies in residential and industrial markets using natural gas. Its prototype system is 20% more efficient than existing boiler systems in the marketplace, producing savings in energy costs and reductions in carbon emissions. This system is likely to appeal not only to householders replacing existing boiler systems but also to industries aiming to reduce their rising energy costs. Turbine Generators Ltd wishes to understand whether or not its prototype CHP system is acceptable to both residential and industrial customers, what decision factors they rely on when selecting a system of this type, what the price ranges are for comparable systems, how this system compares with existing systems available in the marketplace, and what the market potential for each of the two main markets is.

Research Objectives

The research will answer the following questions.

1 What is the size of the marketplace for combined heat and power systems for (a) residential customers and (b) industrial customers?

2 What channels are used by existing competitors within the residential and industrial marketplaces to distribute CHP/boiler products, and what are those competitors' relative market shares?

3 What criteria do industrial and residential customers use to evaluate the perceived value of different CHP/boiler systems before purchase?

4 How do industrial and residential customers rate TGL's prototype CHP system and those of its competitors in relation to the attributes listed in research question 3? (Attributes are likely to include price, service, performance, warranty, etc.).

5 What is the decision-making process used by (a) industrial customers and (b) residential customers when they seek to purchase a boiler/CHP system (and associated services)?

Research Programme Proposed

Initially, a three-stage research programme is recommended, involving desk research, qualitative research, and quantitative research. We recommend that desk research is carried out initially to map the structure of this market offering for both industrial and residential markets. Qualitative research will be carried out before the quantitative stage to provide a stronger understanding of how potential customers perceive this new offering and the decision-making processes they go through to purchase it. This will provide a stronger understanding of how the samples should be determined in the quantitative research. Finally, quantitative research will be used to provide a stronger understanding of the market potential for the offering and a representative overview of how industrial and residential customers rate the prototype and those of its competitors on various dimensions.

Desk Research Phase

This phase will involve the systematic search of market intelligence databases, industry reports, and industry magazines, together with a trawl of the websites and publicly available company records of the main existing distributors and manufacturers in the CHP/boiler market, including members of the Energy Retail Association. The intention of this research is to pull together a market map of the distribution arrangements within both residential and industrial markets for CHP/boiler products. Therefore the analysis aims to provide answers to the research questions 1 and 2.

Qualitative Research Phase

Sampling

Given the need to cover both industrial and residential markets, we recommend conducting a series of 20 in-depth interviews across a variety of industrial segments (identified in the desk research phase) with industrial customers (five SMEs, five medium-sized companies, five large companies, and five mixed) and a total of 12 discussion groups in different cities across the UK (by male/female in the following cities: London,

Market Insight 3.3
continued

Cardiff, Glasgow, Belfast, Birmingham, and Bristol). In addition to the gender mix, the groups will incorporate a mix of age groups and previous experience of buying a boiler/CHP system. The in-depth interviews with potential industrial customers will be conducted in person at the offices of the interviewee using an interview of approximately 45 minutes duration. The discussion groups will last between 60 and 90 minutes and will be held at a central location within each of the cities listed.

Data Analysis

The qualitative data will be fully transcribed before analysis. All verbatim quotes obtained from in-depth interviews and discussion groups are reviewed for the first set of interviews to ensure that our interviewers are questioning correctly before they proceed further. The analysis will use a thematic analytic approach based on research questions 3, 4, and 5.

Quantitative Research Phase

For this stage, we propose using a computer-assisted web-interviewing methodology (CAWI) for both the industrial and residential customers. CAWI allows us to use complex question routing and skip patterns, and undertake more efficient sample management. We aim to interview approximately 200 industrial interviewees using a judgemental sampling method, identifying appropriate companies and respondents In conjunction with TGL. For the residential customer research, we would aim to purchase six questions on a standard omnibus survey through a subcontracted research agency.

Sampling

In the industrial survey, respondents will be screened to ensure that they are the appropriate person responsible for purchasing CHP or boiler systems for their organization. We expect that this will differ and be dependent on sector, and will include a cross-section of job titles from procurement to technical managers to quantity surveyors. To determine the correct number of interviews to conduct in a given research study, we need to consider several factors, including the

overall objective, requirements for subset analysis, and in this case the overall size of the target universe. Given the diverse customer base and target market, we recommend using an overall sample size of 200 interviews. Using standard industrial classification (SIC) codes and company size, we will draw the sample proportionally to TGL's key intended target markets using a judgemental sampling methodology. In order to facilitate the selection of the sample, we will purchase lists of client companies from Dun & Bradstreet and/or other reputable list providers.

In the residential survey, we will use a subcontracted omnibus survey provider. Respondents will be screened to ensure that they either own or mortgage their own home. The subcontracted agency typically uses a sample size of $c.1,000$ respondents and aims to ensure that the sample is representative of the UK population by questioning panels constructed using a combination of gender, working status, location, age, ethnicity, and socio-economic status. The survey uses a random sampling methodology and weighting to ensure a representative sample.

Data Analysis

On finalization of the fieldwork, collected data will be processed and tabulated. Data are then tested for statistical significance (at the 95% confidence level) where possible. Cluster analysis will be employed to determine whether or not any segments emerge from either the residential or the industrial samples. Multiple regressions will be undertaken to determine the key drivers of both the residential and industrial customers' perceptions of the prototype offering. A Robinson–Bennett International executive will talk through the results and answer any questions. Topline survey results are checked regularly and a response analysis is produced. This regular check allows us to identify errors as quickly as possible. The analysis aims to answer research questions 1, 3, and 4.

Reporting

We will work in partnership with TGL to ensure that the results from the research are actionable. If

Market Insight 3.3
continued

required, the report can be produced in PowerPoint and structured in line with the research objectives to include all aspects of the methodology and sampling. The report will be designed to include charts and tables to best depict the main findings, together with clear and concise commentary. Two copies of the report, with accompanying tables, will be delivered as hard copy to TGL.

Costing and Schedule

Desk research = £5,000
Qualitative in-depth interviews = £10,000
Discussion group interviews = £24,000

CAWI set-up, sample incentives, and project management = £10,000
Omnibus survey = £5,000
Quantitative data analysis = £5,000
Qualitative analysis, data interpretation and reporting = £10,000
Total = £69,000

We suggest that the study is undertaken in the period from November 2013 until the end of February 2014.

Source: The authors wish to thank the Market Research Society for permission to publish this material.

Theory into Practice

After receiving a brief the research company (or in-house research team) transforms the management problem into a research question while trying to remove any assumptions made by the organization's management. Sometimes this requires a lot of thought as management might have formulated the problem very precisely. Having specified the objectives of the research the company then moves on to develop a plan for how to get the information needed. The plan provides a detailed outline of how they will approach the research problem, which is typically referred to as a research proposal.

Related Topics:

new product development; innovation; marketing environment; B2C/B2B.

1 **How does the proposal compare with the brief in Market Insight 3.2?**

2 **Do you think that a postal survey might be a more appropriate way of reaching residential consumers? What other approaches might you select?**

3 **Do you think the research objectives are feasible given the budget requirements? Why do you say this?**

Stage 2. Decide the Research Plan

Once the marketing research question(s) have been decided it is time to develop a research plan. At this stage, the framework for conducting the project is developed. In developing this framework, marketing researchers need to consider what type of research is needed. The market research need can be specified based on objective (exploratory, descriptive, causal research), as well as source (primary versus secondary data), and methodology (qualitative versus quantitative). The research need will have implication for the design of the research plan.

Type of Marketing Research: Objectives

Generally speaking, we define three types of research objectives: exploratory, descriptive, and causal. These categories specify the type of management problem that the research should solve.

1 **Exploratory research** is used when little is known about a particular management problem and it needs to be explored further. Exploratory designs enable the development of hypotheses or in developing new concepts.

2 **Descriptive research** focuses on accurately describing the variables being considered, such as market characteristics or spending patterns, in key customer groups. Examples of descriptive research are consumer profile studies, usage studies, price surveys, attitude surveys, sales analyses, and media research.

3 **Causal research** is used to determine whether one variable causes an effect in another variable. In order to determine causality, experimental or longitudinal studies are needed. Experiments are characterized by the marketing researchers manipulating a specific variable (cause) thought to influence important outcomes (effect), thereby allowing them to carefully test causation. Longitudinal studies, on the other hand, track the effect of a certain variable (cause) over time. Examples of causal research are studies of customer satisfaction and advertising effectiveness, which typically sets out to understand what factors of an offer or an ad impacts on consumer evaluations.

Type of Marketing Research: Source

When conducting research we can either use what is already known or devise research that creates new knowledge. **Primary research** is research conducted for the first time, involving the collection of data for the purpose of a particular project. Secondary data is second-hand data, collected for someone else's purposes. **Secondary research** (also **desk research**) involves gaining access to the results of previous research projects. This method can be a cheaper and more efficient process of data collection. We can do a large amount of secondary research free by visiting a business library or searching the Internet. Other sources of secondary data include the following.

- Government sources, including export databases, government statistical offices, social trend databases, and other resources.
- The Internet, including sources identified using search engines, blogs and microblogs, and discussion groups.
- Company internal records, including information housed in a marketing information/CRM system (see Chapter 14) or published reports. Where no formal marketing information system exists, we would identify sales reports, marketing plans, and research reports commissioned previously.

- Professional bodies and trade associations: these organizations frequently have databases available online for research purposes, which may include industry magazine articles and research reports.

- Market research companies: these organizations frequently undertake research into industry sectors or specific product groups and can be highly specialized. Examples include Mintel, Euromonitor, ICC Keynote, and Google.

We would usually undertake secondary research initially to see whether someone has undertaken similar research previously. For example, if an entertainment company had recently bought a new cinema property and wanted to know who lived in the local area, it could consult secondary data sources to ascertain the characteristics of people living in the area (e.g. gender, age, population size). However, if they wanted to know what film genres customers prefer, they might survey a sample of the population.

Visit the Online Resource Centre and follow the web links to learn more about these market research organizations.

In practice, most research projects involve both secondary and primary research, with the desk research occurring initially to ensure that the company doesn't waste money. Primary research is undertaken to cover the gaps in the company's knowledge once all available secondary data has been evaluated. Once this initial insight is gleaned, we determine whether or not to commission a primary data study. Assuming primary research needs to be undertaken, researchers usually design their research by considering what type of research to employ. Marketing directors should understand what types of study can be conducted because this impacts on the type of information collected, and hence the data they receive to solve their management problem.

Type of Marketing Research: Methodology

At the outset of a research project, we might consider whether to use qualitative research or quantitative research or a combination. **Qualitative research** denotes research methodologies relying on small samples, using open and probing questions that set out to uncover underlying motives and feelings. The data gathered is then interpreted focusing on meanings, and typically is quite hard to replicate. Typically qualitative research is intended to provide insights and understanding of the problem setting and thus it is frequently used in exploratory market research. The main methods for collecting qualitative data are individual interviews, focus groups, and observations.

Quantitative research methods are used to elicit responses to predetermined standardized questions from many respondents. This involves collecting information, quantifying the responses as frequencies or percentages, and analysing them statistically. Quantitative research is thus commonly used in descriptive and causal marketing research, and replication is a highly desirable property of the outcome of such research. Thus quantitative data collection methods are much more structured than qualitative data collection methods. Common methods include different types of surveys (online, offline), face-to-face or telephone interviews, and longitudinal studies.

Table 3.2 summarizes key differences between qualitative and quantitative research methods. Although qualitative research methods are typically characterized as being exploratory and

Table 3.2 Qualitative and quantitative research methods compared

Characteristic	Qualitative	Quantitative
Purpose	Oriented towards discovery and exploration	Oriented towards cause and effect
Procedure	Emerging design, merges data collection and analysis	Predetermined design, separates data collection and analysis
Emphasis	Meaning and interpretation	What can be measured
Role of researcher	Involved, used as a 'research instrument'	Detached, uses standardized research instruments
Unit of analysis	Analyses a holistic system	Analyses specific variables
Size of sample	Involves a small number of respondents, typically less than 30	Involves a large number of respondents, more than 30
Sampling approach	Uses purposively selected samples	Uses probability sampling techniques

quantitative methods as being descriptive or causal, methods are not intrinsically associated with one kind of research purpose or another. The key concern is not which methods are used to generate data, but how they are used and for what purpose. There are also several ways of combining qualitative and quantitative research. What is more, many methods can be used qualitatively or quantitatively depending on purpose. For example, open and participative observations are typically used in qualitative research (e.g. ethnography), whereas structured observations (e.g. mystery shopping) are used in quantitative research. Another example is content or sentiment analysis, which often starts out by qualitatively assessing different exemplars (e.g. ads or comments in social media) and then gradually builds a vast amount of such observations that are analysed quantitatively. For example, user-generated content in social media can be mined for meaning to better understand consumer quality perceptions for different brands without having to ask questions (e.g. Tirunillai and Tellis, 2014).

The client (or in-house research client) may also have specific budget constraints or know which particular approach they intend to adopt. However, the choice primarily depends on the circumstances of the research project and its objectives. If much is known about the management problem based on past research/experience, it may be appropriate to use quantitative research to understand the problem further. If there is little pre-understanding of the management problem, it would be better to explore the problem using qualitative research to gather insights. Globally, 73% of marketing research investment is spent on quantitative research. The share is even higher in Portugal (95%), Finland (92%), and Sweden (92%), whereas it is typically lower in developing countries (ESOMAR, 2015). Industry surveys also indicate that marketers increasingly combine both qualitative and quantitative methods (Murphy, 2015).

Market Insight 3.4
How Scent Sells Lingerie at Hunkemöller

BrainJuicer is an innovative UK-based market research agency
Source: © BrainJuicer.

Behavioural economics explores why people sometimes make irrational decisions and why their behaviour does not follow traditional economic models. It has produced hundreds of fascinating academic case studies, but many businesses find it hard to apply in a way that produces real business advantage.

One exceptional example was when BrainJuicer and lingerie retailer Hunkemöller worked to create and test interventions, based around behavioural economic designs, in Hunkemöller stores in the Netherlands. Why did Hunkemöller want to use behavioural economics? There is a growing body of evidence of the immense importance of context in decision-making. This means that small interventions in the environment can have a small but significant impact on customer behaviour and sales. For instance, in a related study for a separate BrainJuicer client, introducing a brand logo at the point of sale was associated with a 4% increase in purchases for that brand. Context—for example, music, scent, and emotion—plays a huge part in shopper decisions, but shoppers hardly notice some of the most important factors, so researching it can be very difficult. The study explained how using scent in Hunkemöller stores led to a striking gain in average customer value. BrainJuicer began by undertaking a behavioural audit of the retail environments of Hunkemöller stores, and consumers' behaviour within them, in order to design appropriate in-store interventions designed to increase sales. The experiment was designed using an alternating experimental and control store run over

six weeks, alternating week on week, to measure the effect of using scent in stores as a 'prime'—making customers feel happy and romantic before buying their lingerie. Store sales data were used for effectiveness data. This work was supplemented with a short questionnaire when customers exited the store, which was designed to uncover the extent to which they had enjoyed their visit and noticed the intervention (the scent prime).

The experiments showed that in-store scent increased average customer basket value for Hunkemoller by 20%. Hunkemoller would later roll out scent in all new and refurbished stores. The research also helped the company to develop protocols for undertaking behavioural economic research—running audits, creating interventions, and working with a research agency to make the interventions happen and understand how to prime customer emotion and satisfaction. The results of the research offered a strong argument for continuing the experimental hands-on research approach rooted in behavioural science and backed up with traditional data. It's a method pointing to the future of research—away from what customers say and towards what they do.

Hunkemöller use behavioural economics to create and test interventions in their stores
Source: © 360b/Shutterstock.

Sources: Leach and Bisnajak (2013); Goyal (2013); http://www.Hunkemöller.com/en/about-us/corporate-info.html; http://www.brainjuicer.com/html/stream/labs.

Market Insight 3.4
continued

Theory into Practice

Experiments are used when the research problem has to do with understanding cause and effects (causal research). In an experimental study the researcher manipulates different potential causes to understand the resulting effects. For example, when Hunkemöller introduced (manipulated) a logotype (cause), purchases were up 5% (effect). This allowed them to understand causation without having to ask customers about it.

Related Topics:
consumer buying behaviour; shopping experience; retailing.

1 **Why do you think it was necessary to use a behavioural experimental approach?**

2 **Why is it necessary to use a control group in an experiment?**

3 **What other decision-making scenarios can you think of that might use the experimental approach?**

This market insight was kindly contributed by Will Leach, formerly VP, Brainjuicer Behavioural Activation Unit, and Ashwien Bisnajak, formerly Market Intelligence Manager, Hunkemöller.

Designing the Research Project

Once we know what type of research to conduct, we should consider:

- who to question and how (the sampling plan and procedures to be used);
- what methods to use (e.g. discussion groups or an experiment);
- which types of questions are required (open questions for qualitative research or closed questions for a survey);
- how the data should be analysed and interpreted (e.g. what approach to data analysis should be undertaken).

Research methods describe the techniques and procedures to obtain the necessary information. We could use a survey or a series of in-depth interviews. We might use observation to see how consumers purchase goods online or how employees greet consumers when they enter a particular shop, i.e. mystery shopping. We could use consumer panels where respondents record their weekly purchases or their TV viewing habits over a specified time period. Nielsen Homescan is a service where consumers use specially developed barcode readers to record their supermarket purchases in return for points, which are redeemed for household goods. Table 3.3 summarizes the most commonly used qualitative and quantitative methods used by marketers in 2015. As seen in this table, companies increasingly use online methods. According to the 2015 Chief Marketing Officer (CMO) survey, many marketers rely on digital online technology for understanding consumer needs: 40% use online customer surveys, 26% use online customer observations, 19% use online customer experiments, and 6% study the online use of words or pictures by customers to gain insights (Moorman, 2015).

Table 3.3 Top five qualitative and quantitative data collection methods in 2015

Qualitative	Quantitative
1. Focus groups (in person)	1. Online surveys
2. In-depth interviews (in person)	2. Mobile surveys
3. In-depth interview (telephone)	3. Computer-assisted telephone interviews (CATI)
4. In-store/Shopping observations	4. Face-to-face surveys
5. Interviews/Groups using online communities	5. Computer-assisted personal interviews (CAPI)

Source: Murphy (2015).

Research Insight 3.2

To take your learning further, you might wish to read this influential paper.

Kozinets, R.V. (2002). The field behind the screen: using netnography for marketing research in online communities. *Journal of Marketing Research*, **39(1), 61–72.**

In this highly cited pioneering article, the author coins the term 'netnography', an adapted ethnographic method, and outlines the research approach designed to make researching of online communities faster and simpler than standard ethnographic methods and less obtrusive than traditional qualitative approaches.

Visit the **Online Resource Centre** to read the abstract and access the full paper.

Figure 3.5 indicates the key considerations when designing qualitative and quantitative research projects. The design of marketing research projects involves determining how each of these components interrelates with the others. The components comprise the following:

- research objectives;
- sampling method;
- the interviewing method to be used;
- research type and methods undertaken;
- question and questionnaire design;
- data analysis.

When designing research projects, we must first determine the type of approach to use for a given management problem (e.g. exploratory, descriptive, or causal). Then we determine which techniques are most capable of producing the desired data at the least cost and in the minimum time period.

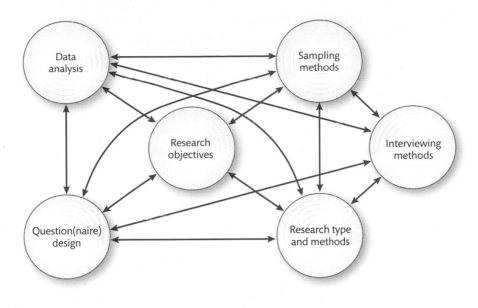

Figure 3.5

The major components of research design

Source: Baines and Chansarkar (2002). © John Wiley & Sons Limited. Reproduced with permission.

To determine whether or not we've got the 'right' data, we must determine its validity (i.e. do the data correctly describe the phenomenon they measure?) and reliability (i.e. would the data be replicated in a future repeat study of the same type?). Generally, certain types of research (e.g. exploratory, descriptive, causal) use certain methods/techniques. For instance, exploratory research studies use qualitative research methods, non-probability sampling methods, and non-statistical data analysis methods. Descriptive research projects often adopt survey interviews using quota or random sampling methods and statistical analysis techniques. Causal researchers use experimental research designs using convenience or **probability sampling** methods and statistical data analysis procedures.

Stage 3. Data Collection and Sampling

This stage involves the conduct of fieldwork and the collection of data. At this stage, we send out questionnaires, or run online focus group sessions, or conduct a netnographic study, depending on the decisions taken in the first design stage of the fieldwork. The procedures undertaken when conducting the fieldwork might relate to how to ask the questions of the respondents—whether this be using the telephone, mail, or in person—and how to select an appropriate sample, how to **pre-code** the answers to a questionnaire (quantitative research), or how to code the answers arising out of open-ended questions (particularly with qualitative research).

The research manager might be concerned about whether or not to conduct the research in-company or commission a field and tab agency. Other issues concern how to ensure high data quality. When market research companies undertake shopping mall intercept interviews, they usually re-contact a proportion of the respondents to check their answers to ensure that the interviews have been conducted properly.

In qualitative research, samples are often selected on a convenience or judgemental basis. In quantitative research, we might use either probability or non-probability methods including the following.

- **Simple random sampling**, where the population elements are accorded a number and a sample is selected by generating random numbers which correspond to the individual population elements.

- **Systematic random sampling**, where population elements are known and the first sample unit is selected using random number generation, but after that each of the succeeding sample units is selected systematically on the basis of an nth number, where n is determined by dividing the population size by the sample size.

- **Stratified random sampling**, where a specific characteristic(s) is used (e.g. gender, age) to design homogeneous subgroups from which a representative sample is drawn.

Non-random methods include the following.

- **Quota sampling**, where criteria like gender, ethnicity, or some other customer characteristic are used to restrict the sample, but the selection of the sample unit is left to the judgement of the researcher.

- **Convenience sampling**, where no such restrictions are placed on the selection of the respondents and anybody can be selected.

- **Snowball sampling**, where respondents are selected from rare populations (e.g. high performance car buyers). Respondents might initially be selected from responses to newspaper adverts and then further respondents are identified using referrals from the initial respondents, thereby 'snowballing' the sample.

With the growth of online market research, the reliance on Internet panels has become increasingly common. Two types of panel are used in online research (Miles, 2004). Access panels, which provide samples for survey-style information, are made up of targets especially invited by email to take part, with a link to a web survey. Proprietary panels, set up or commissioned by a client firm, are usually made up of that company's customers. To encourage survey participation, the researchers use incentives (e.g. a prize draw). However, there are pros and cons associated with undertaking online research (see Table 3.4).

Research Insight 3.3

To take your learning further, you might wish to read the following influential paper:

Evans, J.R. and Mathur, A. (2005). The value of online surveys. *Internet Research*, 15(2), 195–219.

This highly cited paper outlines the strengths and weaknesses of undertaking online research. The article also compares online survey approaches with other survey formats, making it a particularly useful paper for those undertaking online research.

@ **Visit the Online Resource Centre to read the abstract and access the full paper.**

> **Table 3.4 Advantages and disadvantages of online research**

The pros of online research	The cons of online research
1 Clients and analysts can see results compiled in real time	1 Demographic profile of online panels can differ from that of the general population
2 Online surveys save time and money compared with face-to-face interviews	2 If questionnaires take longer than 20 minutes to fill in, quality can suffer and they may be uncompleted
3 Consumers welcome surveys that they can fill in when they want to and often need no incentive to do so	3 Poor recruitment and badly managed panels can damage the data
4 A more relaxed environment leads to better quality, honest, and reasoned responses	4 Technical problems, such as browser incompatibility, can mean that panellists fail to complete the survey
5 Panellist background data allows immediate access to key target audiences unrestricted by geography	5 Programming costs are higher than for offline questionnaires
6 Programming facilitates question order, allowing skipping and randomization of questions more easily	6 Sometimes survey questionnaires can be perceived as junk mail

Source: Miles (2004: 40); Evans and Mathur (2005).

Visit the Online Resource Centre and complete Internet Activity 3.1 to learn more about the Market Research Portal, a useful source of online research resources.

Stage 4. Data Analysis and Interpretation

This stage comprises data input, analysis, and interpretation. How the data are input depends on the type of data collected. Qualitative data, usually alphanumeric (i.e. words and numbers), is often entered into computer software applications (e.g. NVivo) as word-processed documents or as video or sound files for content analysis. Quantitative data analysis uses statistical analysis packages (e.g. **SPSS**). In these cases, data are numeric and entered into spreadsheet packages (e.g. Microsoft Excel) or directly into the statistical computer application. Online questionnaires are useful because the data are automatically entered into a database, saving time and ensuring a higher level of data quality. If **computer-assisted personal interviewing (CAPI)** or **computer-assisted personal telephone (CATI)** methods are used, analysis can occur instantaneously as the interviews are undertaken. **Computer-assisted web interviewing (CAWI)** techniques allow the researcher to read the questions from a computer screen and directly enter the responses of the respondents. CAWI techniques are also commonly applied using the Internet, allowing playback of video and audio files.

Market research methods are used to aid managerial decision-making. Information obtained needs to be valid and reliable, as company resources are deployed on the basis of the information gleaned. **Validity** and **reliability** are important concepts in quantitative market research. They aid researchers in understanding the extent to which the data obtained from the study represent reality and 'truth'. Quantitative research methods rely on the degree to which the data elicited might be reproduced in a later study (i.e. reliability) and the extent to which the data generated are bias free (i.e. valid). Validity is defined as 'a criterion for evaluating measurement scales; it represents the extent to which a scale is a true reflection of the underlying variable or construct it is attempting to measure' (Parasuraman, 1991: 441). One way of measuring validity is the use of the researcher's subjective judgement to ascertain if an instrument is measuring what it is supposed to measure (content validity). For instance, a question asked about job satisfaction does not necessarily infer loyalty to the organization.

Reliability is defined as 'a criterion for evaluating measurement scales; it represents how consistent or stable the ratings generated by a scale are' (Parasuraman, 1991: 443). Reliability is affected by concepts of time, analytical bias, and questioning error. We can also distinguish between two types of reliability, i.e. internal and external reliability (Bryman, 1989). To determine how reliable the data are, we conduct the study again over two or more time periods to evaluate the consistency of the data. This is known as the test–retest method. This measures external reliability. Another method used involves dividing the responses into two random sets and testing both sets independently using **_t_-tests** or **_z_-tests**. This would illustrate internal reliability. The two different sets of results are then correlated. This method is known as split-half reliability testing. These methods are more suited to testing the reliability of rating scales than that of data generated from qualitative research procedures. The results of a quantitative marketing research project are reliable if we conduct a similar research project within a short time period, and the same or similar results are obtained in the second study. For example, if the marketing department of a travel agency chain interviewed 500 of its customers and discovered that 25% were in favour of a particular resort (e.g. a particular Greek island), and then repeated the study the following year and discovered that only 10% of the sample were interested in the same resort, the results of the first study can be said to be unreliable in comparison and the procurement department should not base its purchase of package holidays purely on the previous year's finding.

In qualitative research, concepts of validity and reliability are generally less important, because the data are not used to imply representativeness. Qualitative data are more about the generation of ideas and the formulation of hypotheses. Validity can be assured by sending out transcripts to respondents and/or clients for checking, to ensure that what they have said in in-depth interviews or focus groups was properly reproduced for analysis. When the analyst reads the data from a critical perspective to determine whether or not this fits with their expectations, this constitutes what is termed a **face validity** test. Reliability is often achieved by checking that similar statements are made by the range of respondents, across and within the interview transcripts. Interviewees' transcripts are checked to assess whether or not the same respondent, or other respondents, have made the discussion point. Such detailed content analysis tends to be conducted using computer applications (e.g. NVivo).

Stage 5. Report Preparation and Presentation

The final stage of a research project involves reporting the results and the presentation of the findings of the study to the external or in-house client. The results should be presented free from bias. Marketing research data are of little use unless translated into a format that is meaningful to the manager or client who initially demanded the data. Senior people within the commissioning organization who may or may not have been involved in commissioning the work often attend presentations. Usually, agencies and consultants prepare their reports using a basic pre-written template.

Market and Advertisement Testing

Marketing research reveals attitudes to a campaign, brand, or some other aspect of the exchange process, whereas market testing, by comparison, measures actual behaviour. There is a difference, as attitudes do not always determine action (see Chapter 2). For instance, a consumer may respond very positively to the launch of a new TV set in surveys, but family circumstances or lack of funds may mean the TV is never purchased. Market testing studies use **test markets** to carry out controlled experiments in specific country regions, where specific adverts can be shown, before exposing the 'new feature' (offering, campaign, distribution, etc.) to a full national or even international launch. Another region or the rest of the market may act as the **control group** against which results can be measured. For example, films are often test-screened before release because of the substantial cost of producing the film in the first place.

Marketing research is used to test advertisements, whether these are in print, online, or broadcast via radio or TV. The research company Millward Brown International is renowned for this type of research. A variety of methods are used to test adverts. Typically, quantitative research is undertaken to test customer attitudes before and after exposure to see if the advert has had a positive impact or not. In addition, research occurring after exposure to the ad tests the extent to which audiences can recognize a particular advert (e.g. by showing customers a copy of a TV advert still, a print advert, or a photo online) or recall an advert without being shown a picture (we call this unaided recall). Qualitative research identifies and tests specific themes that might be used in the adverts and to test **storyboards** and **cuts** of adverts (before they are properly produced). More recently, advances in technology allow us to evaluate visual imagery more objectively, without relying on respondents' opinions. For example, technology company 3M offer a service 3M VAS (Visual Attention Service) which allows users to test communications material to see if specific sections of the communication will be noticed and in what order, using algorithms based on sophisticated eye-tracking research. Another approach to proposition and marketing communication testing uses facial coding analysis.

Market Insight 3.5
Why Ask?

Over time, many methods have been developed to test ads, ranging from self-reported assessment of recall, liking, and purchase intent, to sophisticated statistical approaches, referred to as market mix models, to evaluate ex post advertising effects.

The past decade has experienced an explosion of research in neuroscience and the use of multiple neurophysiological methods to study advertising. This growth is due to a combination of technological advances making functional magnetic resonance imaging (fMRI), electroencephalography (EEG), eye tracking, and other neurophysiological tools more accessible and less costly.

A recent study by a group of American researchers developed an experimental protocol to compare how well six commonly used methods predict real-world advertising success in terms of advertising elasticity. The methods used were as follows.

■ Traditional self-reports: capture conscious reactions, typically by asking direct questions related to the ad and brand (e.g. ad liking, brand attitude, and purchase intention)

Market Insight 3.5

continued

- Implicit measures: capture the unconscious reaction, typically by using response latencies (e.g. how long does it take to pair brands with positive and negative words)

- Eye tracking: measures participants' attention when viewing ads (e.g. which information, in what order, and for how long)

- Biometrics: measures the physiological or automatic responses to an external stimulus (e.g. heart rate, breathing, and skin conductance)

- EEG: measures variations in electrical signals of cortical brain regions when viewing ads and brands

- fMRI: localizes and tracks changes in blood oxygenation during cognitive tasks, which can be used as a direct measure of exogenous and endogenous attention.

The findings show that traditional self-reported advertising measures explain the most variance in advertising elasticities. They thus support more than 50 years of advertising research demonstrating that asking questions regarding measures such as purchase intent are, indeed, good predictors of advertising success. But the findings also show that fMRI measures can help explain advertising elasticities beyond these baseline traditional measures. For practitioners, this research proves that current methods are reliable, but that measuring biological reactions rather than relying on asking questions only can give additional insights.

Sources: Stipp (2015); Venkatraman *et al.* (2015).

Theory into Practice

Traditional market research focuses on asking questions. There is, however, often a discrepancy between what consumers say and what they do. This has, in turn, led the marketing research industry to adapt new methodologies that do not rely on consumers' answers to questions, but rather on their actual biological reactions. The study discussed indicates that traditional advertising measures based on asking questions about consumer reactions to ads are, in fact, valid. But it also shows that you can learn more about what advertising works by also adding fMRI.

Related Topics:

advertising effectiveness; marketing communications; consumer reactions; neuromarketing

1 How are implicit measures, eye tracking, biometrics, EEG, and fMRI different from traditional advertising tracking methods?

2 Why could it be important to collect participants' unconscious responses in research on proposition and marketing communication testing?

3 Can you think of other circumstances in which implicit measures, eye tracking, biometrics, EEG, and fMRI analysis would be useful for marketers?

Big Data and Marketing Analytics

Big data is the systematic gathering and interpretation of high volume, high velocity, and/or high variety information using cost-effective innovative forms of information processing to enable enhanced insight, decision-making, and process automation. It thus refers to a more comprehensive set of data than that traditionally used to provide marketing information and customer insights.

The notion of 'big' refers primarily to the volume, velocity, and variety of data used (McAfee and Brynjolfsson, 2012; Erevelles *et al.*, 2016). Volume denotes the sheer amount of information used. As an illustration, Wal-Mart collected more than 2.5 petabytes of data every hour in 2012. A petabyte is one quadrillion bytes, or the equivalent of about 20m filing cabinets' worth of text. Velocity refers to the fact that data is recorded in real time. For example, using location data from cell phones, Google is able to offer up-to-date information about travelling time adjusted for traffic. Variety denotes that big data analytics combines data from several different sources. For example, combining customer databases with social media and mobile data can give a more comprehensive understanding of shopper behaviours than what was possible before.

With increasing digitization of the everyday life of business and consumers, the availability of data is growing rapidly. The different sources employed in big data analysis can be divided into five categories: (1) public data, (2) private data, (3) data exhaust, (4) community data, and (5) self-quantification data (George *et al.*, 2014). Public data refers to information held by governments or local communities (e.g. with regard to incomes, transportation, or energy use) that is accessed under certain restrictions in order to guard individual privacy. Private data refers to data held by private organizations or individuals and which cannot readily be imputed from public sources. Examples are customer database information or browsing behaviours online. 'Data exhaust' refers to data that is passively collected—non-core data with limited or zero value to the original data-collection partner. When individuals adopt and use new technologies (e.g. smartphones), they generate ambient data as by-products of their everyday activities. These data can be recombined with other data sources to create new insights. Another

---

Research Insight 3.4

To take your learning further, you might wish to read this influential paper:

Erevelles, S., Fukawa, N., and Swayne, L. (2016). Big data consumer analytics and the transformation of marketing. *Journal of Business Research*, 69(2), 897–904.

This paper introduces a theoretical framework for when and how big data can lead to sustainable competitive advantage. More specifically, it discusses how three resources—physical, human, and organizational capital—moderate (1) the process of collecting and storing evidence of consumer activity as big data; (2) the process of extracting consumer insight from big data; and (3) the process of utilizing consumer insight to enhance dynamic/adaptive capabilities.

@ Visit the **Online Resource Centre** to read the abstract and access the full paper.

source of data exhaust is information-seeking behaviour, such as online search and call centre calls, which can be used to infer people's needs, desires, or intentions. Community data refers to distilled unstructured data, for example consumer reviews on products or liking in social media, which is combined into dynamic networks that capture social trends. Individuals using technology to quantify their personal actions and behaviours reveal self-quantification data, for example through wristbands which monitor exercise and movement.

Marketing Research and Ethics

Marketing research should be carried out in an objective, unobtrusive, and honest manner. Researchers are also concerned about the public's increasing unwillingness to participate in marketing research and the problem of recruiting suitable interviewers. The apathy among interviewees is probably associated with the growing amount of research conducted, particularly through intrusive telephone interviewing, which is increasing, and door-to-door survey interviewing, which is declining. Marketing research is increasingly conducted online, creating its own set of ethical concerns. For example, how can we verify that someone online is who he or she says they are? Is it acceptable to observe and analyse customer blogs and social networking site conversations? In social media research, ethical problems include the need to be open and transparent when conducting research within communities and anonymizing and paraphrasing comments (since verbatim comments can often be tracked back to a particular user in online research). However, the ethics of conducting social media research are still in development. Consequently, key organizations like ESOMAR and the MRS are still devising clear policies on the topic.

Marketing research neither attempts to induce sales nor attempts to influence customer attitudes, intentions, or behaviours. The MRS key principles are as follows (MRS, 2014: 3).

1 Researchers shall ensure that participation in their activities is based on voluntary informed consent.

2 Researchers shall be straightforward and honest in all their professional and business relationships.

3 Researchers shall be transparent as to the subject and purpose of data collection.

4 Researchers shall respect the confidentiality of information collected in their professional activities.

5 Researchers shall respect the rights and well being of all individuals.

6 Researchers shall ensure that participants are not harmed or adversely affected by their professional activities.

7 Researchers shall balance the needs of individuals, clients, and their professional activities.

8 Researchers shall exercise independent professional judgement in the design, conduct, and reporting of their professional activities.

9 Researchers shall ensure that their professional activities are conducted by persons with appropriate training, qualifications and experience.

10 Researchers shall protect the reputation and integrity of the profession.

The MRS Code of Conduct, based on the ESOMAR Code, is binding on all members of the MRS. Members of the general public are entitled to assurances that no information collected in a research survey will be used to identify them, or be disclosed to a third party without their consent. Data in European countries is also subject to an EU data protection directive. Respondents must be informed of the purpose of the research and the length of time that they will be involved in it. Research findings must also be reported accurately and not used to mislead. In conducting marketing research, researchers have responsibility for themselves, their clients, and their respondents/participants.

The results of research studies should remain confidential unless otherwise agreed by the client and agency, and the agency should provide detailed accounts of the methods employed to carry out the research project where their clients request this.

Visit the Online Resource Centre and complete Internet Activity 3.2 to learn more about the Marketing Research Code of Practice adopted by ESOMAR.

International Marketing Research

Marketing researchers find it challenging to understand how culture operates in international markets and how it affects research design. Complexity in the international business environment makes international marketing research more complex because it affects the research process and design. Key decisions include whether to customize the research to each of the separate countries in a study using differing scales, sampling methods, and sizes, or to try and use a single method for all countries, adopting an international **sampling frame**. In many ways, this debate mirrors the standardization–customization dilemma common in international marketing generally (see Chapter 7).

International researchers try to ensure that comparable data are collected despite differences in sampling frames, technological developments, availability of interviewers, and the acceptability of public questioning. Western approaches to marketing research, data collection, and culture might be inappropriate in some research environments because of variations in economic development and consumption patterns. How comparable are the data related to the consumption of Burger King's offerings collected through personal interviews in the UAE, telephone interviews in France, and shopping mall intercept questionnaires in Sweden? Can an online panel across all countries be used instead? Ensuring comparability of data in research studies of multiple markets is not simple. Concepts could be regarded differently, the same offerings could have different functions, language may be used differently, even within a country, offerings might be measured differently, the sample frames might be different, and finally the data collection methods adopted might differ because of variations in infrastructure. Table 3.5 outlines three types of equivalence: **conceptual equivalence**, **functional equivalence**, and **translation equivalence**. All three types of equivalence impact on the semantics (i.e. meaning) of words used in different countries, e.g. in developing the wording for questionnaires or in focus groups. Getting the language right is important because it affects how respondents perceive the questions and structure their answers.

When designing international research programmes, we need to consider how the meaning of words is different and how the data should be collected. Different cultures have different ways of measuring concepts. They also live their lives differently, meaning that it may be necessary to collect the same or similar data in a different way. Table 3.6 outlines how measurement, sampling, and data collection equivalence impacts on international research.

Table 3.5 Types of semantic equivalence in international marketing research

Type of equivalence	Explanation	Example
Conceptual equivalence	When interpretation of behaviour, or objects, is similar across countries, conceptual equivalence exists.	Conceptual equivalence should be considered when defining the research problem, in wording the questionnaire, and determining the sample unit, e.g. there would be less need to investigate 'brand loyalty' in a country where competition is restricted and product choice is limited.
Functional equivalence	Functional equivalence relates to whether a concept has a similar function in different countries.	Using a bicycle in India, where it might be used for transport to and from work, or France, where it might be used for shopping, is a different concept from purchasing a bike in Norway where it might be used for mountain biking. Functional differences can be determined using focus groups before finalizing the research design by ensuring that the constructs used in the research measure what they are supposed to measure.
Translation equivalence	Translation equivalence is an important aspect of the international research process. Words in some languages have no real equivalents in other languages.	The meaning associated with different words is important in questionnaire design since words can connote a different meaning from that intended when directly translated into another language. To avoid translation errors of these kinds, the researcher can adopt one of the following two methods. 1 Back translation—a translator fluent in the language in which the questionnaire is to be translated is used and then another translator whose native language was the original language is used to translate back again. Differences in wording can be identified and resolved; 2 Parallel translation—a questionnaire is translated using a different translator fluent in the language which the questionnaire is to be translated into, as well as from, until a final version is agreed upon.

As we can see in Table 3.6, achieving comparability of data when conducting international surveys is difficult. Usually, the more countries included in an international study, the more likely it is that errors will be introduced, and that the results and findings will be inaccurate and liable to misinterpretation. International research requires local and international input. Therefore the extent to which one can internationalize certain operations of the research process depends on the objectives of the research.

With international projects, the key decision is to determine how much to centralize and how much to delegate work to local agencies. There is, throughout this process, ample opportunity

Table 3.6 Types of measurement and data collection equivalence

Type of equivalence	Explanation	Example
Measurement equivalence	The extent to which measurement scales are comparable across countries.	Surveys are conducted in the USA using imperial systems of measurement, whilst the metric system is used in Europe. Clothing sizes adopt different measurement systems in Europe, North America, and Southeast Asia. Multi-item scales present challenges for international researchers as dissatisfaction might not be expressed in the same way in one country compared with another. Some cultures are more open in expressing opinions or describing their behaviour than others.
Sampling equivalence	Determining the appropriate sample to question may produce difficulties when conducting international marketing research projects.	The respondent profile for the same survey could vary from country to country, e.g. different classification systems are in existence for censorship of films shown in the cinema in France compared with Britain.
Data collection equivalence	When conducting research studies in different countries, it may be appropriate to adopt different data collection strategies.	Typically, data collection methods include (e)mail, personal (or CAPI), or telephone (or CATI). ▪ Mail or email—used more where literacy or Internet access is high and where the (e)mail system operates efficiently. Sampling frames are compiled from electoral registers, although it is now illegal in some countries to use these lists. European survey respondents can be targeted efficiently and accurately as international sampling frames do exist. ▪ Telephone/CATI—in many countries, telephone penetration may be limited and computer-assisted telephone interviewing software, using random digit dialling, more limited still. ▪ Personal interviews/CAPI—used most widely in European countries favouring the door-to-door and shopping mall intercept variants. Shopping mall intercept interviews are not appropriate in Arab countries where women must not be approached in the street. Here, comparability is achieved using door-to-door interviews. In countries where it is rude to openly disagree with someone (e.g. China), it is best to use in-depth interviews.

for misunderstanding, errors, and lack of cultural sensitivity. To proceed effectively, the central agency should identify a number of trusted local market research providers on a variety of continents. Typically, an international agency will have a network of trusted affiliates who are monitored on a continual basis.

Chapter Summary

To consolidate your learning, the key points from this chapter are summarized here.

■ **Define the terms market research, marketing research, and customer insight.**

Market research is research undertaken about markets (e.g. customers, channels, and competitors), whilst marketing research is research undertaken to understand the efficacy of marketing activities (e.g. pricing, supply chain management policies). Customer insight derives from knowledge about customers, which can be turned into an organizational strength.

■ **Describe the customer insight process and the role of marketing research in it.**

Understanding customers is at the core of the marketing concept and the basic idea with these systems is that marketing information should be used for timely continuous information to support decision-making. Customer insight is typically derived from fusing knowledge generated from a range of sources, including industry reports, sales force data, competitive intelligence, CRM data, employee feedback, social media analysis data, and managerial intuition. A customer insight is of value if it is rare, difficult to imitate, and of potential use in formulating management decisions.

■ **Explain the role of marketing research and list the range of possible research approaches.**

Marketing research plays an important role in the decision-making process and contributes through ad hoc studies as well as continuous data collection, through industry reports, and from secondary data sources, as well as through competitive intelligence either commissioned through agencies or conducted internally with data gathered informally through sales forces, customers, and suppliers. What methodology is used depends on the type of research problem (exploratory, descriptive, causal), availability of data (primary or secondary sources), and the type of insight sought (qualitative or quantitative).

■ **Define the term big data and describe its role in marketing.**

Big data can be defined as the systematic gathering and interpretation of high volume, high velocity, and/or high variety information using cost-effective innovative forms of information processing to enable enhanced insight, decision-making, and process automation Big data thus refers to a more comprehensive set of data than that traditionally used to provide marketing information and customer insights.

■ **Discuss the importance of ethics and the adoption of a code of conduct in marketing research.**

Ethics is an important consideration in marketing research because consumers and customers either provide personal information about themselves or personal information is collected from them. Their privacy needs to be protected through observance of a professional code of ethics and the relevant laws in the country where the research is conducted.

■ **Note the concept of equivalence in relation to obtaining comparable data.**

International market research is complex because of the differences in language, culture, infrastructure, and other factors, which intervene in the data collection process, making it more difficult to obtain comparable equivalent data.

Review Questions

1 How do we define market research?
2 How do we define marketing research?
3 How do we define customer insight?
4 What is big data?
5 What are the different types of research that can be conducted in marketing research?
6 Why is a marketing research code of conduct important?
7 What is a marketing information system and how is it used in the customer insight process?
8 What is the concept of equivalence in relation to obtaining comparable data from different countries?
9 How are the different aspects of the research process affected by differences in equivalence between countries?

Worksheet Summary

To apply the knowledge you have gained from this chapter and test your understanding of marketing research and customer insight visit the **Online Resource Centre** and complete Worksheet 3.1.

Discussion Questions

1 Having read Case Insight 3.1, how would you advise MESH Planning to develop a suitable research proposal for Gatorade to evaluate the effectiveness of their marketing activities? Use the outline proposal in Figure 3.4 to help you design the research.

2 Orange, the telecommunications company, wants to conduct a market research study aimed particularly at discovering what market segments exist across Europe and how customers and potential customers view the Orange brand. Advise them on the following key components.

   A Write a market research question and a number of sub-questions for the study.
   B How would you go about selecting the particular countries in which to conduct the fieldwork?
   C What process would you use when conducting the fieldwork for this multi-country study?

3 What type of research (i.e. causal, descriptive, or exploratory) should be commissioned in the following contexts? Explain why.

   A By the management of the airline Etihad in the United Arab Emirates when it wants to measure passenger satisfaction with the flight experience.
   B By Nintendo when it wants new ideas for online games for a youth audience.
   C By the Spanish fashion retailer Zara when it wants to know what levels of customer service are offered at its flagship stores.

D By Procter & Gamble, makers of Ariel detergent, when it wants to test a new packaging design for six months to see if it is more effective than the existing version. Fifty supermarkets are selected from one key P&G account. In 25 of them the new design is used, and in the other 25 the existing version is used.

4 You've recently won the research contract to evaluate customer satisfaction for Pret a Manger, the food retail chain specializing in sandwiches, soups, and coffee. Your key account manager wants to increase customer satisfaction further using the knowledge gained from the study to identify potential new food offerings. Suggest a suitable research design (hint: you can advise more than one type of study) to:

A Collect information about levels of customer satisfaction.

B Decide what new food offerings customers might like to see.

In addition, your account manager asks you to outline what secondary data you can find in the area, detailing market shares, market structure, and other industry information, identifying specific secondary data sources and reports.

5 The following questions are concerned with international marketing research.

A How should Boeing coordinate international marketing research to determine how to increase sales of its Dreamliner jet in the airline market?

B Why is it difficult to achieve comparability of data across countries?

@ Visit the **Online Resource Centre** and complete the **Multiple Choice Questions** to assess your knowledge of Chapter 3.

Glossary

behavioural economics the study of the psychology of consumer decision-making, particularly seeking to explain irrational decision-making and behaviour.

brand health the overall condition of a brand relative to the context in which it operates.

causal research a technique used to investigate the relational link between two or more variables by manipulating the independent variable(s) to see the effect on the dependent variable(s) and comparing effects with a control group where no such manipulation takes place.

competitive intelligence the organized, professional, systematic collection of information, typically through informal mechanisms, used for the achievement of strategic and tactical organizational goals.

computer-assisted personal interviewing (CAPI) an approach to personal interviewing using a hand-held computer or laptop to display questions and record the respondents' answers.

computer-assisted telephone interviewing (CATI) an approach to telephone interviewing using a laptop or desktop computer to display the questions to the interviewer who reads them out and records the respondent's answers.

computer-assisted web interviewing (CAWI) an approach to online interviewing where the respondent uses a laptop or desktop computer to access questions in a set location to which the respondent must go. Questions are automatically set based on the respondent's answers.

conceptual equivalence the degree to which interpretation of behaviour, or objects, is similar across countries.

control group a sample group used in causal research, which is not subjected to manipulation of some sort. See causal research.

cuts adverts are initially produced in cartoon format, complete with dialogue, before they are produced, filmed, and edited.

descriptive research a research technique used to test and confirm hypotheses developed from a management problem.

desk research a technique used to collect data that has previously been collected for a purpose other than the current research situation. The process is also referred to as secondary research.

exploratory research a research technique used to generate ideas to develop hypotheses based around a management problem.

face validity the use of the researcher's or expert's subjective judgement to determine whether an instrument is measuring what it is designed to measure.

full-service agency an advertising agency that provides its clients with a full range of services, including strategy and planning, designing the advertisements, and buying the media.

functional equivalence relates to whether or not a concept has the same function in different countries.

management problem a statement that outlines a situation faced by an organization requiring further investigation and subsequent organizational action.

marketing research the design, collection, analysis, and interpretation of data collected for the purpose of aiding marketing decision-making.

market mix modelling a research process which uses multiple regression analysis based on customer survey data to ascertain the relative contributions of different promotional techniques on a customer-based dependent variable (e.g. awareness, intention to buy).

net promoter score a system for measuring the loyalty of customer relationships by determining the extent to which customers are prepared to advocate an organization.

pre-code in surveys, in order to speed up data processing, answers to questions are assigned a unique code e.g. male 1, female 2, so that they can easily be analysed.

primary research a technique used to collect data for the first time that has been specifically collected and assembled for the current research problem.

probability sampling a sampling method used where the probability of selection of the sample elements from the population is known. Typical examples include simple random, stratified random, and cluster sampling methods.

qualitative research a type of exploratory research using small samples and unstructured data collection procedures, designed to identify hypotheses, possibly for later testing in quantitative research. The most popular examples include in-depth interviews, focus groups, and projective techniques.

quantitative research research designed to provide responses to pre-determined standardized questions from a large number of respondents involving the statistical analysis of the responses.

reliability the degree to which the data elicited in a study are replicated in a repeat study.

research brief a formal document prepared by the client organization and submitted to either an external market research provider (e.g. a market research agency or consultant) or an internal research provider (e.g. in-house research department) outlining a statement of the management problem and the perceived research needs of the organization.

research proposal a formal document prepared by an agency, consultant, or in-house research manager and submitted to the client to outline what procedures will be used to collect the necessary information, including timescales and costs.

sampling frame a list of population members from which a sample is generated, e.g. telephone directories, membership lists.

secondary research a technique used to collect data that has previously been collected for a purpose other than the current research situation. The process is often referred to as desk research.

SPSS Statistical Package for the Social Sciences, a software package used for statistical analysis marketed by SPSS, a company owned by IBM.

storyboards before advertisements are made, an outline of the story that the advertisement will follow is produced showing key themes, characters, and messages.

test markets regions within a country used to test the effects of the launch of a new product or service, typically using regional advertising to promote the service and pre- and post-advertising market research to measure promotional effectiveness.

touchpoint an occasion when a consumer engages with a brand including those not directly associated with advertising activities.

translation equivalence the degree to which the meaning of one language is represented in another after translation.

t-**test** a statistical test of difference used for small randomly selected samples with a size of less than 30.

validity the ability of a measurement instrument to measure exactly the construct it is attempting to measure.

z-**test** a statistical test of difference used for large randomly selected samples with a size of 30 or more.

References

AMA (2015). Definition of marketing research, American Marketing Association, October. Retrieve from: http://www.marketingpower.com/aboutama/pages/definitionofmarketing.aspx (accessed 28 December 2015).

Ashill, N.J. and Jobber, D. (2001). Defining the information needs of senior marketing executives: an exploratory study. *Qualitative Market Research*, 4(1), 52–60.

Baines, P. and Chansarkar, B. (2002). *Introducing Marketing Research*. Chichester: John Wiley.

Barwise, P. and Meehan, S. (2011). Customer insights that matter. *Journal of Advertising Research*, 51(2), 342–4.

Bryman, A. (1989). *Research Methods and Organization Studies*. London: Unwin Hyman.

Cater, B. and Zabkar, V. (2009). Antecedents and consequences of commitment in marketing research services: the client's perspective. *Industrial Marketing Management*, 38, 785–97.

Cowan, D. (2008). Forum: Creating customer insight. *International Journal of Market Research*, 50(6), 719–29.

ESOMAR (2008). ICC/ESOMAR International Code of Marketing and Social Research Practice. Retrieve from: http://www.esomar.org/uploads/public/knowledge-and-standards/codes-and-guidelines/ESOMAR_ICC-ESOMAR_Code_English.pdf (accessed 28 December 2015).

ESOMAR (2015). *Global Market Research Report 2015: An ESOMAR Industry Report*. Retrieve from: https://www.esomar.org/uploads/public/publications-store/reports/global-market-research-2015/ESOMAR-GMR2015_Preview.pdf (accessed 2 July 2016).

Erevelles, S., Fukawa, N., and Swayne, L. (2016). Big Data consumer analytics and the transformation of marketing. *Journal of Business Research*, 69(2), 897–904.

Evans, J.R. and Mathur, A. (2005). The value of online surveys. *Internet Research*, 15(2), 195–219.

George, G., Haas, M., and Pentland, A. (2014), From the Editors: Big Data and management. *Academy of Management Journal*, 57(2), 321–6.

Goyal, M. (2013). UK-based BrainJuicer finds out how chocolates can boost lingerie sales, *Economic Times of India*, 14 April. Retrieve from: http://media.brainjuicer.com/media/files/The_Economic_Times_India.pdf (accessed 28 May 2013).

Kozinets, R.V. (2002). The field behind the screen: using netnography for marketing research in online communities. *Journal of Marketing Research*, 39(1), 61–72.

Leach, W. and Bisnajak, A. (2013). How scent sells lingerie. Paper presented at the ESOMAR Congress, 22–25 September, Istanbul.

Malhotra, N.K. (2010), *Marketing Research: An Applied Orientation* (6th edn). Upper Saddle River, NJ: Pearson.

McAfee, A. and Brynjolfsson, E (2012). Big data: the management revolution. *Harvard Business Review*, October, 2–9.

Miles, L. (2004). Online, on tap. *Marketing*, 16 June, 39–40.

Moorman, C. (2015). CMO Survey Report: Highlights and Insights. Retrieve from: http://cmosurvey.org/files/2015/09/The_CMO_Survey-Highlights_and_Insights-Aug-2015.pdf (accessed 4 November 2015).

MRS (2014). *Code of Conduct*, Market Research Society. Retrieve from: https://www.mrs.org.uk/pdf/mrs%20code%20of%20conduct%202014.pdf (accessed 28 December 2015).

Murphy, L.F. (2015). The GRIT Report, Greenbook Research Industry Trends Report. Retrieve from: http://www.greenbook.org/pdfs/2015GRIT_WINTER_Q3-4.pdf (accessed 29 January 2016).

Parasuraman, A. (1991), *Marketing Research* (2nd edn), Wokingham: Addison-Wesley, 280–309.

Press, G. (2014). 12 Big Data definitions: what's yours? *Forbes*, 3 September. Retrieve from: http://www.forbes.com/sites/gilpress/2014/09/03/12-big-data-definitions-whats-yours/#6923e9821a97 (accessed 31 January 2016).

Said, E., Macdonald, E.K, Wilson, H.N., and Marcos, J. (2015). How organisations generate and use customer insight. *Journal of Marketing Management*, 31(9–10), 1158–79.

Stipp, H. (2015). Speaker's Box: The evolution of neuromarketing research: from novelty to mainstream. *Journal of Advertising Research*, 55(2), 120–2.

Tirunillai, S. and Tellis, G. (2014). Mining marketing meaning from online chatter: strategic brand analysis of big data using latent Dirichlet allocation. *Journal of Marketing Research*, 51(4), 463–79.

Venkatraman, V., Dimoka, A., Pavlou, P.A., Khoi Vo, Hampton, W., Bollinger, B., *et al.* (2015). Predicting advertising success beyond traditional measures: new insights from neurophysiological methods and market response modeling. *Journal of Marketing Research*, 52(4), 436–52.

Part Two
Marketing Management and Strategy

Chapter 4
The Marketing Environment

Learning Outcomes

After reading this chapter, you will be able to:

▶ Identify and define the three core areas of the marketing environment

▶ Describe the key characteristics associated with the marketing environment

▶ Explain PESTLE analysis and show how it is used to understand the external environment

▶ Explain the environmental scanning process

▶ Analyse the performance environment using the Porter's Five Forces industry analysis model

▶ Analyse an organization's product/service portfolio to aid resource planning

Case Insight 4.1
Glassolutions Saint-Gobain

Market Insight 4.1
For Statoil the Falling Price Means…

Market Insight 4.2
Health Issues Slim Down Product Sales

Market Insight 4.3
L'Oréal Advances Beauty Through Technology

Market Insight 4.4
Ice Cream: Rivalry Hots Up

Case Insight 4.1
Glassolutions Saint-Gobain

How should organizations scan their external environments and what should they do if they identify potential threats and opportunities? We speak to Glassolutions Saint-Gobain's Marketing Director, Michael Butterick, to find out more.

Glassolutions Saint-Gobain operates in all the main sectors of the glass and glazing industry in the UK. This depth of activity is a key differentiator and strength for our business, but it does make the business complex in its scope as a result. Different segments of our markets exhibit growth and contraction at different times as a consequence of a multitude of factors in the marketing environment. The task is to track and anticipate these trends to maximize their profit potential. Therefore we carry out an annual business planning and budgeting process. Key inputs to the process include sales tracking and analysis (e.g. by sector, segment, geographic region), primary market research (including surveys and key account analysis), secondary market research, sales team feedback, key competitor tracking and benchmarking, and contingency planning.

In addition, we prepare a Long-Term Strategic Plan that covers a five-year period and is presented annually to the Saint-Gobain Head Office in Paris. This Long-Term Plan is reviewed periodically throughout the year. The output of our environmental scanning is used to determine business strategy and our strategic and tactical marketing priorities. Some aspects of our operating environment don't change much from year to year, but we are acutely aware that, even in mature industries like ours, the dynamics of markets is not static. We look for changes that present both opportunities and threats to our business. A good example of this is likely changes in legal and regulatory legislation.

Changes in our industry's technical standards, such as the Building Regulations and the Window

Energy Rating scheme, have a major influence on our business. Technical leadership of our industry is one of our key differentiators, and to protect this leadership, we need solutions in place to meet future technical requirements. Government legislation also affects us in ways beyond technical standards. The need to improve the energy efficiency of housing to tackle fuel poverty and reduce carbon emissions has put high performance glass and glazing products high up the agenda. Recent Government initiatives such as the 'Green Deal' and the Energy Company Obligation (ECO) are examples of legislation that have affected our environment and presented new opportunities.

Our environmental scanning process tracked the evolution and development of the Government's policy on the Green Deal and Energy Company Obligation (ECO) funding. We identified that this policy could deliver an opportunity for Glassolutions Saint-Gobain and the wider glass and glazing industry. With such a large and complex initiative it actually absorbed a relatively large proportion of our marketing resources to properly engage with and follow the evolution of the initiative, but we took a conscious decision that the potential impacts, both positive and negative, were simply too great to ignore. As a business, we supported the broad aims of the policy and participated in the consultation processes that the Government organized. But we didn't always agree with the detail of how the initiatives ultimately developed. As the Government's policy on the Green Deal and ECO developed, we realized that the initiative as it was unfolding was

Case Insight 4.1
continued

unlikely to deliver any significant benefit for the glass and glazing industry.

We identified that the processes and legislative framework constructed for the Green Deal and ECO initiatives prevented funding reaching the replacement window industry. This was because the cost of installing modern replacement A-rated energy efficient windows was considered high relative to the carbon savings obtained. The other issue was that replacement windows also deliver consumer benefits in terms of aesthetics, security, and acoustics in addition to the primary benefit of thermal insulation; ECO funding in particular is all about thermal insulation and couldn't be used to support these other benefits.

Therefore our problem was: how could we persuade Government, specifically the Department for Business, Energy & Industrial Strategy, to reconsider how they funded green initiatives in the replacement window industry for the benefit of Government, the industry, and Glassolutions Saint-Gobain?

Introduction

Have you ever wondered how organizations adapt to the changing business environment? How do companies keep up with the many changes that occur in politics, markets, and economics? What processes do they use to try to anticipate changes in technologies? We consider these and other questions in this chapter.

The operating environment for all organizations, whether they be commercial, charitable, governmental, or in the public sector more generally, is never static and seldom entirely predictable, and can therefore profoundly affect a company's course of action. We examine the nature of the marketing environment, determine environment-related issues, and provide a context for developing marketing strategies that are explored in Chapter 5.

Now, consider the degree to which an organization can influence the various environmental forces acting on it. The external environment, for example, consists of political, social, and technological influences, and organizations often have very limited influence on these. The performance environment consists of competitors, suppliers, and indirect service providers who shape the way and extent to which organizations achieve their objectives. Here, organizations have a much stronger level of influence. The internal environment concerns the resources, processes, and policies an organization manages to achieve its goals. These elements can be influenced directly by an organization. Each of these three marketing environments is discussed in this chapter (see Figure 4.1).

By understanding the nature and trends of the elements that make up these three interlocking environments, an organization can assert varying degrees of control, allocate scarce resources more efficiently, and move closer to achieving its goals and overall performance outcomes, in both the short and the longer term.

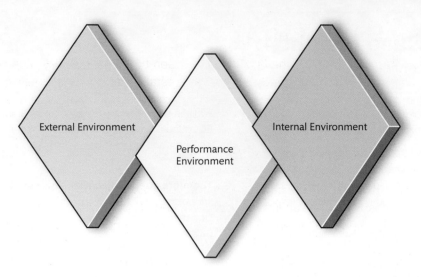

Figure 4.1
The three marketing environments

Understanding the External Environment

The external environment is characterized in two main ways. In the first, the elements do not have an immediate impact on the performance of an organization, although they might do in the longer term. In the second, although the elements can influence an organization, it is not possible to control them. This suggests that the level of risk attached to the external environment is potentially high. To make sense of the external environment, we use the well-known acronym **PESTLE**. This is the easiest and one of the most popular frameworks for examining the external environment. PESTLE stands for the Political, Economic, Socio-cultural, Technological, Legal, and Ecological environments, as shown in Figure 4.2.

Figure 4.2
The external marketing environment

The Political Environment

The political environment relates to the interaction between business, **society**, and **government.** The legal environment, considered later, relates to established laws and regulations associated with consumers and business practices. An understanding of the political environment embraces the conditions that exist before laws are enacted, when they are still being formed, or when they are in dispute. Political environmental analysis is important because companies can detect signals concerning potential legal and regulatory changes in their industries and have a chance to impede, influence, and alter that legislation.

Although the **political environment** is in many ways uncontrollable, there are circumstances when an organization, or an industry coalition, can affect legislation in its own favour. There is increasingly an understanding that business–government relations, properly undertaken, can be a source of **sustainable competitive advantage** (see also Chapter 5). In other words, organizations can outperform other organizations over time if they can manage their relationships with government and regulatory bodies better than their competitors (Hillman *et al.*, 2004; Lawton and Rajwani, 2011). Any understanding of the political environment and the actions taken by constituent firms should also be considered through a legal framework and with an ethical lens. For example, the 2016 agreement between the UK Government and Google over the alleged under-payment of corporation tax may be considered to be legal, but some question the ethics associated with global firms who shift their tax domicile in order to pay minimal rates of corporation tax.

In June 2015, WikiLeaks released a draft of the Trans-Pacific Partnership, which was claimed would boost trade and investment across 40% of the world economy. Amongst other things, this exposure revealed that multinational pharmaceutical companies would have greater information and more control over national decisions about individual country health sectors than before. Dorling (2015) points out that the treaty would threaten Australia's Pharmaceutical Benefits Scheme, and increase the cost of medicines.

Companies, however, can also fall foul of governments if they fail to play by a country's rules and regulations, written and unwritten. For example, when the Oslo-based Nobel Prize Committee awarded the Peace Prize to Chinese dissident civil rights activist, Liu Xiaobo, China switched its preferred trade supply of salmon from Norway to Scotland, increasing its order from 8 tonnes in the first nine months of 2010 to 4,897 tonnes in the same period of 2012 (Anon., 2012a).

Because legislation is such a technical area, few firms have the capability to understand and influence legislation without employing specialists. In such circumstances, special industry lobbyists are hired to represent clients with government decision-makers and regulators, and to provide strategic advice to clients on how to design their strategic communication campaigns. Generally, there are several ways in which marketers might conduct business–government relations in various countries.

- Lobbyist firms, with key industry knowledge, can be engaged either permanently or as needed.
- **Public relations** consultancies (e.g. Weber Shandwick) can be commissioned for their political services, often having members of parliament or others with a high degree of political influence serving as directors and/or advisers, in jurisdictions where this is legal.
- A politician may be paid a fee to give political advice on matters of importance to an organization, where this is legal within that particular jurisdiction and that politician is not serving directly within the government in question on the same portfolio as that on which they are advising.

- An in-house public relations manager might handle government relations directly.

- An industry association might be contacted to lobby on behalf of members (e.g. in the European financial services industry, the Banking Federation of the EU).

- A politician may be invited to join the board of directors, board of trustees, or board of advisers of an organization to aid the company in developing its business–government relations, where this is legal.

Organizations often collaborate in order to influence governments. This can be achieved through industry or trade bodies or by working with other large companies in their industry. For example, EuropaBio is made up of three main segments of the European biotechnology industry: healthcare (Red Biotech), industrial (White Biotech), and agri-food (Green Biotech). Experts from member companies actively participate in working groups and taskforces which cover a wide range of issues and concerns particular to their industry in an attempt to influence key **stakeholders**, including national governments and the European legislature.

The Economic Environment

Companies and organizations must develop an understanding of the economic environment because a country's economic circumstances have an impact on what economists term factor prices within a particular industry, for a particular organization. These factors could include raw materials, labour, building and other capital costs, or any other input to a business. The economic environment of a firm is affected by the following items.

- Wage inflation—annual wage increases in a particular sector will depend on the supply of labour in that sector. Where there is scarcity of supply, wages usually increase (e.g. doctors).

- Price inflation—how much consumers pay for goods and services depends on the rate of supply of those goods and services. If supply is scarce, there is usually an increase in the price of that consumer good or service (e.g. petrol).

- **Gross domestic product (GDP)** per capita—the combined output of goods and services in a particular nation is a useful measure for determining relative wealth between countries when comparisons are calculated per member of the population (GDP per capita at **purchasing power parity**, see next paragraph).

- Income, sales, and corporation taxes—these taxes, typically operating in all countries around the world, usually at different levels, substantially affect how we market different offerings.

- Exchange rates—the relative value of a currency vis-à-vis another currency is an important calculation for those businesses operating in foreign markets or holding financial reserves in other currencies.

- Export quota controls and duties—restrictions are often placed on the amounts (quotas) of goods and services that any particular firm or industry can import into a country, depending on which trading bloc or country a company or firm is exporting to. In addition, countries sometimes charge a form of tax on particular items as well to discourage or encourage imports and to protect their own economies.

When operating in other countries, we should understand how exchange rates and living standards operate. We might also need to understand how prices or labour costs change if we are importing our goods and services, or components of them, from another country, i.e. our factor prices. This is known as the rate of price or wage inflation. Difficulties arise when comparing prices across different countries. Rather than compare costs for individual products through the prevailing exchange rate, economists prefer to calculate prices for a particular basket of goods—a fixed list of common items—and compare the costs in one country with those in another. This is known as the **purchasing power parity exchange rate,** and allows us to compare the relative costs between two countries for a given item.

Organizations usually have little impact on the wider economic environment as they have little control over macroeconomic variables. For example, firms have no control over oil prices, which might affect their business in different ways. The challenge when examining the macroeconomic environment is to foresee changes in the environment and how they might affect the firm's activities. If a computer company in Sweden imports silicon chips from Japan and pays for them in Swedish kronor, but the exchange rate for the yen is rising against the Swedish kronor (in other words, you get more yen per kronor perhaps because of strong Japanese export sales to Europe), then you might decide to source your silicon chips from another country to ensure that your own prices are unaffected.

Similarly, if **inflation** drives consumer prices higher in a particular country, the price of goods might become more expensive, triggering a fall in sales. Typically, during a **recession** consumers tend to purchase fewer goods and increase their savings, and prices fall further as producers try to stimulate demand. However, prices can increase during a recession. It is, therefore, important to understand the wider general economic trends and a firm's marketplace. Surveys of consumer expectations of inflation, forecasts of foreign exchange rates, wage forecasts, and much other financial information are frequently available from government central banks.

Visit the Online Resource Centre and complete Internet Activity 4.1 to learn more about how the contribution of service industries to the UK's national economy has changed over the last 10 years.

Market Insight 4.1
For Statoil the Falling Price Means ...

Norway is one country where the effects of the plunging world price of crude oil have had a wide range of consequences. For years the buoyant Norwegian economy had been built on the energy industry. With the state-run oil and gas company Statoil paying an average annual salary of 1m kroner ($130,000) to its 23,000 employees, the Norwegian energy industry accounted for 15% of the economy, more than half of exports, and 80% of the state's income. Through this the country benefited from generous holiday allowances, the highest sickness benefits in the world, and shorter working hours than elsewhere. In addition,

a massive $860bn reserve was built up during the good years.

All of this changed when the price of a barrel of Brent crude oil started to tumble in 2015 from a steady three-year average of around $110 to below $60. Prices have fallen for several reasons including a glut in world oil supply, partly caused by a slowdown in the Chinese economy, and the nuclear agreement between Iran and the USA, which saw a return of Iranian oil to world markets. The strength of the US dollar has also been cited, all of which are beyond the control of the

Market Insight 4.1
continued

Norwegian government, its oil industry, or any individual company such as Statoil.

The impact of this slide has been wide reaching as competition in the industry intensified. At this price more than half the offshore fields being developed along the Norwegian continental shelf became uneconomical to operate. Oil rig owners could no longer rent out their fleets to drillers at $400,000 or more a day, and the speculatively built new rigs had no users. This contraction has impacted carriers, suppliers, and oil companies, plus the yards servicing the oil and shipping industry. Indeed, the drastic drop in oil prices has had consequences along the supply chain as smaller organizations, such as component part manufacturers, welders, and training organizations shrink to absorb the cutbacks.

At the time of writing over 15,000 workers have been laid off, but more redundancies are expected as the impact spreads to allied sectors such as travel, restaurants, and hotels, which have all been hit. Some oil workers are planning to work abroad, knowing that their remuneration package will be substantially inferior to that experienced in Norway. Other workers have been able to negotiate a temporary four-day work week, and effectively a 15% pay cut, in order for their employers to withstand the changed economic context.

The collapse in the price of oil in 2015 devastated the industry forcing many companies, such as Statoil, to reduce their costs and make thousands of their workers unemployed
Source: Harald Pettersen/Statoil ASA.

The next wave is expected to hit consumer spending as disposable incomes fall and spending on high value and technology products, such as electronic goods, holidays, and cars are hit. In addition, future generations will inevitably suffer as the downward shift in living standards continues to bite.

Sources: Anon. (2015a); Anon. (2015b); Vogdrup-Schmidt (2015); Menton (2015).

Theory into Practice

The fall in the global price of oil can be interpreted through Keynesian economic theory. This focuses on the determination of prices, outputs, and income distributions in markets through demand and supply. This holds that if demand for a particular good or service such as oil falls, that in turn causes the price for oil to fall. There are some situations in which this self-correction is staggered or delayed, leading to high unemployment and dormant factories (oil rigs and processing plant). Intervention through a central institution, such as a government, and banks can vary interest rates to stimulate or depress supply and demand.

The fall in demand for oil and the potential over-supply as Iran re-entered the world market demonstrate how demand and supply interact and the impact this has had on the collapse of the price of oil.

Market Insight 4.1
continued

Related Topics:

each of the PESTLE elements; performance environment; environmental scanning; change theory; marketing relationships.

1 Do you think that Statoil should have foreseen the potential crash in oil prices? If so, what steps could they have taken?

2 To what extent should oil companies seek to protect themselves from external forces?

3 Why should the industry contraction be of concern to the Norwegian Government when it has such huge reserves, sufficient to support all displaced employees?

Visit the **Online Resource Centre** and follow the web link to learn more about how Statoil has managed since the price of oil has fallen.

Research Insight 4.1

To take your learning further, you might wish to read this highly influential paper.

Danciu, V. (2013) The future of marketing: an appropriate response to the environment changes. *Theoretical and Applied Economics*, 20, 5(582), 33–52.

This paper looks at trends within different aspects of the marketing environment. This provides a helpful insight into the complexity and diversity of the various environments within which organizations operate.

Visit the **Online Resource Centre** to read the abstract and access the full paper.

The Socio-Cultural Environment

Lifestyles are constantly changing and, over time, consumers shift their preferences. Companies that fail to recognize changes in the socio-cultural environment and adapt or change their offerings often fail. For example, the new focus on healthy eating and lifestyles has impacted on two major brands in particular, McDonald's and Coca-Cola. After several years of falling sales McDonald's admitted in 2015 that they had failed to keep pace with changing consumer tastes. Their restructuring plan was designed to streamline operations and discard layers of bureaucracy, and as a result save the company $300m in costs.

Coca-Cola have faced a similar issue as volume sales of fizzy drinks fell in the USA for the tenth consecutive year in 2014. Although diversification strategies have taken the brand into juices and bottled water markets, the brand has had to be reframed as a 'treat' and provided in smaller 8-oz bottles (Munshi, 2015). See also Market Insight 4.2.

When considering the socio-cultural environment, firms need to consider the changing nature of households, demographics, lifestyles, and family structures, and changing **values** in society.

Demographics and Lifestyles

Changes in population proportions impact on an organization's marketing activity. In the UK (and some other European countries) immigration from Poland after EU enlargement increased the UK Polish population, with some supermarkets specifically targeting Poles using adverts in Polish and by stocking products such as borscht, meatballs, pickled vegetables, and sauerkraut soup (BBC, 2006). According to the UN Population Division (2012), by 2050 India's population is set to reach around 1.6bn, China's is set to reach 1.3bn, America's is due to reach 400m, and the UK's only 73m. Some countries, such as Japan and Russia, will experience a fall in their populations. These changes will have profound implications for the different consumer and industrial sectors.

In addition, there will also be shifts within the different age groups within different populations. Some countries have a relatively large proportion of people in the 65-year-old-plus age bracket (the 'silver' or 'grey' market, so-called because of the colour of their hair). Some countries and regions, such as many African and Middle Eastern countries, have a comparatively large number of younger citizens. These shifts in population and the relative differences in age structure in different countries give rise to different-sized markets for brand propositions. Clearly, the market for private pensions in Europe is likely to increase as national governments and the EU develop appropriate schemes, which is encouraging for insurance and pension groups. This is just one example, as there are a whole host of offerings that might be targeted at these different groups.

People's lifestyles are also changing. In Europe, there is a trend towards marrying later and a greater tendency to divorce than in previous generations. In some countries, there has been a growth in single-person households. There is a rise of same-sex marriages in industrialized nations, and some countries and states within countries have legitimized these more than others (e.g. Argentina, the countries of Scandinavia, Iceland, the Netherlands, South Africa, and France).

Societal changes, however, need not necessarily be demographic, or lifestyle oriented, to impact marketing. Changes are taking place within society that affect how consumers interact with an organization's marketing activity. Customers are increasingly happy to work with companies and organizations to solve problems. Howe (2006) refers to this phenomenon as **crowdsourcing**. Whitla (2009) suggests that the role and process of crowdsourcing is to identify a task or group of tasks currently conducted in-house, and then release the task(s) to a 'crowd' of outsiders who are invited to perform the task(s) on behalf of the company (for a fee or prize). This invitation might either be truly open to everyone or restricted in some way to ensure that those who respond are only those qualified to undertake the task. This approach can help marketers gain insights into both new product/service development and marketing communications.

Market Insight 4.2
Health Issues Slim Down Product Sales

Sales of store-bought packaged (sliced) bread fell 8% in the UK in 2014, following a series of external influences. The UK's three biggest sliced bread brands, Warburtons, Hovis, and Kingsmill, which account for 60% of packaged bread sales in the UK, collectively lost £121m in bread revenue in 2014. Asda announced that it was losing £500,000 per week in bread sales, or about 5m loaves.

The reasons for this downward shift include increasing awareness of the need for healthy eating, a consumer shift towards higher protein products and lower carbohydrates, and a renewed interest in fresh artisan variants. Television programmes, such as *The Great British Bake Off*, have spurred interest in home baking to the extent that sales of baking trays at Waitrose soared by 881% and those of bakeware increased by 55%, all during one week before the 2015 series started. At the same time, sales of biscuits and cakes have fallen, in part, it is claimed, due to the influence of the *Bake Off* show.

Food and beverage companies, like their fast food counterparts, have faced increasing pressure from governments as obesity rates have increased around the world. National governments have begun to scrutinize their public health policies. Several countries, such as Denmark, Finland, Hungary, and France, have introduced a 'fat tax'. These are added by governments to products with high fat content, such as confectionery (including chocolate), dairy products, and sugary foods and drinks, in a bid to reduce public consumption of high fat foods, the obesity epidemic, and the consequent impact on public health and public healthcare budgets.

The huge success of television programmes such as *The Great British Bake Off* does nothing to encourage healthier eating habits.
Source: © *The Great British Bake Off*/Love Productions & BBC.

A key ethical issue arises if you are CEO of a major food manufacturer: should you seek to circumvent the obesity issue by reducing the fat content in your products (and educating consumers to buy lower calorie options), or ignore the obesity issue, therefore selling the same product (and perhaps lobbying government not to introduce the tax), or pursue some mixture of these approaches?

As part of Tesco's 10-point plan against obesity, they decided that they would no longer sell high sugar drinks targeted at children in the juice category. As a result high sugar drinks such as Ribena, Capri-Sun, and Rubicon fruit juice cartons were delisted and are not available from its stores.

Sources: Green (2000); Barrie (2015); Davidson (2015); Ward (2015); Young (2015).

Theory into Practice

There are a wide range of theories that could be used to interpret the actions of both brand managers and consumers within this scenario. Clearly society has attempted to make consumers aware of the need to eat healthy foods. This can be interpreted through explanatory theory. This holds that the nature of a

problem needs to be communicated, and then a range of variables need to be identified that can be used to influence audiences.

Kurt Lewin (1935) developed a three-stage theory of change. Change theory can be used to understand

Market Insight 4.2
continued

the behavioural change that consumers experience as a result of processing, in this case, societal messages about the dangers of obesity. Lewin argues that change occurs through a three-part process: unfreezing (understanding and searching for new healthier food and so stopping the current behaviour)—change (to new healthier foods)—refreezing (establishing the new behaviour foods as the standard diet).

Related Topics:

the political, socio-cultural, and economic environments; competitive advantage; industry analysis.

1 **What are the advantages and disadvantages to food manufacturers of producing new lower calorie or healthier versions of their existing products?**

2 **To what extent will the UK government's 'sugar tax' impact the sales of high sugar drinks such as Ribena? Explain your reasoning.**

3 **Why do you think that Tesco decided to delist high sugar drinks yet still sell other sugar and high calorie products such as Mars bars?**

The Technological Environment

The emergence of new technologies has affected most businesses. Examples include technologies that impact productivity and business efficiency, such as changes in energy, transportation, information, and communication technologies. New technology also changes the way that companies go to market. For example, companies are now compelled to use a variety of channels. These include mobile-device-based applications as well as traditional websites and physical stores. For example, one unusual app enables shoppers to test whether a melon is ripe. The shopper rests the microphone on a melon, presses a button, and taps the melon, and the app uses an algorithm to determine whether the melon is ready to eat.

Changes in technology particularly affect high technology industries, where firms must decide whether they wish to dominate that market by pushing their own particular technology standards, especially where new technology renders existing standards obsolete. For example, cloud computing and digital music files have taken over from the tape and vinyl record manufacturing industries.

When scanning the technological environment, attention has to be given to research and development (R&D) trends, and the R&D efforts of competitors. Strategies to ascertain these involve regular searches of patent registration, trademarks, and copyright assignations, as well as maintaining a general interest in technological and scientific advances. For example, in the pharmaceutical and chemical industries, companies develop new compounds based on modifications of compounds registered for patents by their competitors; this is referred to as **reverse engineering**.

The reverse engineering principle can be observed in other industries where new propositions are based on competitor offerings, through 'me-too' or imitation marketing strategies. This is often the result of a firm's inability to turn their technological advances into a sustainable competitive advantage (Rao, 2005). As soon as a new offering is introduced, it is quickly copied. To overcome this, firms attempt to introduce a consistent stream of new propositions, and stay as close to the consumer as possible. See Market Insight 4.3 to see how L'Oréal uses technology to help maintain its dominant position in the beauty market.

For most firms, the risk of investing in radical or cutting edge technologies is high as the potential benefits are unsubstantiated. Fear of obsolescence is usually a strong incentive to invest in new technologies (Chandy et al., 2003). Therefore companies have every reason to be concerned about the impact of technological changes on their product and service lifecycles. However, innovation becomes a necessary condition in the strategic marketing decision-making of high technology firms. For less technology-intensive firms, innovation, whether it is process- or product/service-focused, or at least rapid adoption of new offering variants based on competitors' offerings, is still necessary to stay ahead of the competition.

Market Insight 4.3
L'Oréal Advances Beauty Through Technology

The world of beauty and cosmetics has traditionally been based on people physically visiting a store and smelling a perfume or trying a lipstick prior to purchase. Advances in technology are seen by companies such as L'Oréal, the largest company in the beauty sector, as an opportunity to advance their market leadership and, with it, change consumer behaviour.

L'Oréal has used data and analytics to help identify beauty trends early. For example, dip-dyed hair emerged as a search term on Google Trends long before it became a popular trend. As the figures grew, L'Oréal saw an opportunity and created a full product called Préférence Les Ombrés. Recognizing and realizing the potential resulted in €50m euro sales in the first two years.

L'Oréal also launched a beauty app called Makeup Genius. This works by transforming the front-facing camera of an iPhone or iPad into a virtual mirror, enabling users to 'try on' products virtually. The app uses advanced facial mapping technology that has previously only been used in Hollywood and the gaming industry. It is used to overlay products like lipstick and eyeliner onto the user's face. The company is now hoping to bring out versions for hair colour, hair styling, and skincare.

L'Oréal plan to integrate the Makeup Genius technology into bathroom mirrors, giving users access to everyday coaching and advice from beauty professionals in their homes. In addition, there will be improved sensors that will measure lifestyle habits, skin tone, sleeping patterns, stress, activity, pollution, and sun exposure, and combine all this data to offer customers personalized beauty advice.

Vichy and La Roche Posay are L'Oréal brands that focus on products designed for sensitive or problematic skin. These use live chat to help guide consumers on the best products for their skin concerns. These brands also offer online skincare diagnostics, and customers can consult dermatologists on their particular concerns.

L'Oréal have been experimenting with everything that links to Instant Messaging, and are very interested in everything to do with video, like Periscope and Twicer. At the time of writing, the company was also investigating the use of flexible wearable electronics, designed to collect and transmit data from the body, and has also partnered with a bioprinting start-up company called Organovo to look at the potential of 3D-printed skin production to test products for toxicity and efficacy.

Sources: Shayon (2014); Curtis (2015); Scocco (2015); Westcott (2015); http://www.loreal.com.

Market Insight 4.3
continued

Theory into Practice

At a macro level Schumpeter (1934) identified that innovation can be seen as waves that serve to restructure a market, to the advantage of those who grasp discontinuities faster. He termed this as 'creative disruption', which can be used to interpret L'Oréal's focus on technology.

Teece (1986) suggested that imitability and complementary assets represent two important factors that determined the success of an innovation. Imitability concerns the ease with which competitors can copy or duplicate the technology or process underpinning an innovation. Protection in terms of intellectual property rights, procedures, and tacit knowledge can serve to act as barriers.

Complementary assets such as marketing channels, brand name, reputation, and positioning gravitate around and support the core innovation. The interchange between these factors shapes the success of the innovation. So, if L'Oréal's imitability is high (the technology can be accessed by competitors) and its complementary assets are strong, the success of the innovation(s) is likely to be high and profitable.

Finally, the Diffusion of Innovations theory can be used to explain and predict how, why, and at what rate L'Oréal's new ideas and technology will spread through its different markets and cultures.

Related Topics:

the technological and socio-cultural environments; competitive advantage; industry, strategic, and portfolio analysis.

1 To what extent might L'Oréal's use of advanced technology represent a sustainable competitive advantage over its competitors?

2 If the number of consumers who adopt these interactive technologies is relatively small, why should L'Oréal continue with this strategy?

3 If a firm's external environment is uncontrollable, why should they devote resources to monitor it?

The Legal Environment

The legal environment covers every aspect of an organization's business. Laws and regulation on the transparency of pricing, the prevention of restrictive trade practices, product safety, good practice in packaging and labelling, the abuse of a dominant market position, and codes of practice in advertising, to take just a small selection, are enacted in most countries.

Product Safety, Packaging, and Labelling

In the European Union, product safety is covered by the General Product Safety Directive to protect consumer health and safety for both member states within the EU and importers from third-party countries to the EU or their EU agent representatives. Where products pose serious risks to consumer health, the European Commission can take action, imposing fines and criminal sentences for those contravening the Directive. The General Product Safety Directive does not cover food safety; this is subject to another EU Directive, which has established a European Food Safety Authority and a set of regulations covering food safety. Companies operating in these sectors need to keep up with changes in legislation, as failure might jeopardize their business.

In the pharmaceutical industry, regulations govern testing, approval, manufacturing, labelling, and the marketing of drugs. Most countries also place restrictions on the prices that pharmaceutical companies can charge for drugs. In Japan, price regulations are stipulated for individual products. Up until 2014, in the UK, strict controls were placed on the overall profitability of products supplied by a specific company to the National Health Service under the Pharmaceutical Price Regulation Scheme. Since then the scheme has used a value-based pricing mechanism (DH/ABPI, 2012). For more on value-based pricing approaches, see Chapter 9.

Companies that develop cosmetics and fragrances are required to comply with legislative measures designed to protect users. This means that there is a need to ensure that products remain cosmetics and are not reclassified under different regulations, such as those related to medicines, which makes innovation within the cosmetic industry more difficult (Gower, 2005).

Product labelling regulation in the EU tends to relate to the recycling of packaging and waste to ensure that it complies with environmental regulations. In the USA packaging and labelling regulations are more concerned with fair practice and ensuring that packaging does not contain misleading advertising statements. Different countries around the world have different regulations, so importers and exporters should be aware of these rules from the outset.

Codes of Practice in Advertising

Advertising standards differ around the world. In the UK, advertising is self-regulated, i.e. by the advertising industry itself. In other countries, advertising is restricted by legislation. In the UK, advertising is regulated by the Advertising Standards Authority (ASA), which has a mission to apply codes of practice in advertising and uphold advertising standards for consumers, business, and the general public. Such self-regulatory agencies operate in other countries (e.g. the Bureau de Vérification de la Publicité in France, and the Advertising Standards Council in India). In the EU, the European Advertising Standards Alliance oversees both statutory and self-regulatory provision in most European countries and even in non-European countries including Russia, Canada, the USA, New Zealand, and Turkey. See Chapters 10 and 11 for a more general discussion of advertising.

Restrictions on the advertising of alcohol products exist in most parts of the world, In the UK, for broadcast advertising communications, codes of practice exist for both radio and TV, typically with specific regulations for alcohol advertising specifying that claims cannot be made in relation to sexual prowess, fitness or health, courage or strength. In Thailand alcohol products cannot be advertised before 10 p.m. In France, the manufacturers of alcoholic beverages, are obliged to show a government health warning on all advertisements. In the UK, breweries and distillers have voluntarily placed the message 'drink responsibly' in the copy of their adverts for many years.

Government health warnings also apply to tobacco products, and tobacco advertising is now virtually banned in all forms around the world. In most Western countries, consumers are

Tobacco packaging using shock-based images to deter users
Source: © Newspix/REX/Shutterstock.

dissuaded from smoking not only through high taxes placed on tobacco to reduce consumption and public restrictions on where people can smoke (e.g. Sweden, India, Bahrain, Ireland, UK, etc.), but also through legislation banning and restricting advertising and requiring the placing of government health warnings on packages. In some countries, including Canada and Australia, government health warnings provide stark warnings and graphic pictures. In Canada, the size of the health warning was increased to cover 75% of the pack (CTV News, 2012), whilst Australia was the first country to introduce plain packaging for all tobacco brands in late 2012.

The Ecological Environment

The concept of marketing sustainability is now established as increasing numbers of consumers express concern about the impact that companies are having on ecological environments. For example, there is increased demand for 'organic' food, incorporating principles of better welfare for the animals they consume as food products and less interference with the natural processes of growing fruit and vegetables, such as the use of pesticides and chemical fertilizers.

Sustainability issues embrace the sourcing of products from countries with poor and coercive labour policies. Both Nike and Apple have actively changed parts of their supply chain following investigations. Consumers are also keen to ensure that companies and their products are not damaging the environment or causing harm to consumers. This has been accompanied by a rise in the popularity of Fairtrade products.

An important question for marketers concerns the way in which an organization should embrace and incorporate the changing trend in sustainability? To answer this question, Orsato

(2006) suggests that a company can adopt one of the following four different green marketing strategies.

- Eco-efficiency—developing lower costs through organizational processes such as the promotion of resource productivity (e.g. energy efficiency) and better utilization of by-products. This approach should be adopted by firms that need to focus on reducing the cost and environmental impact of their organizational processes. Supermarket chains in Norway and other Scandinavian countries have encouraged recycling for a long time.

- Beyond compliance leadership—the adoption of a differentiation strategy through organizational processes such as certified schemes to demonstrate their ecological credentials or their environmental excellence, for example the adoption of the UN Global Compact principles or other Environmental Management System (EMS) schemes and codes. This approach should be adopted by firms that supply industrial markets, such as car manufacturers.

- Eco-branding—the differentiation of a firm's products or services to promote environmental responsibility. Examples include Duchy Originals, the British Prince of Wales' food brand, the Thai King Bhumipol's Golden Place brand, or the Toyota Prius.

- Environmental cost leadership—through offerings that provide greater environmental benefits at a lower price. This strategy particularly suits firms operating in price and ecologically sensitive markets, such as the packaging and chemical industries.

Whatever the company and industry, ecological trends in marketing look set to stay and further develop as the sustainability debate rages on and companies use it to develop their own competitive strategies. It is important to assess how this movement towards greener and more sustainable marketing is affecting a particular industry to ensure that a company within that industry is not adversely affected by these changes (e.g. by non-compliance with regulatory change such as packaging) or can take advantage of the opportunities (e.g. a haulage company taking advantage of hybrid engine lorries to reduce energy costs).

Information about each of these sub-environments is gathered in order for an assessment to be made about the potential impact on the organization. Organizations need to monitor all PESTLE elements, but some are more important than others. For example, pharmaceutical organizations such as GlaxoSmithKline monitor legal and regulatory developments (e.g. labelling, patents, and testing), the Environment Agency monitors political and ecological changes (e.g. flood plains for housing developments), road haulage companies should watch for changes that impact on transport development (e.g. congestion charging, diesel duty, toll roads), and music distributors should monitor changes in technology and associated social and cultural developments (e.g. downloading trends and cloud computing).

Environmental Scanning

To understand how external environments change, organizations need to put in place methods and processes to inform them of developments. The process of gathering information about a company's external events and relationships, in order to assist top management in its decision-making and the development of its course of action, is referred to as **environmental scanning** (Aguilar, 1967). This is the internal communication of external information about issues that may potentially influence an organization's decision-making process, focusing on the identification of emerging issues, situations, and potential threats in the external environment

(Albright, 2004). Environmental scanning is an important component of the strategic marketing planning process considered in Chapter 5.

We can gather information in environmental scanning exercises using company reports, newspapers, industry reports and magazines, government reports, and marketing intelligence reports (e.g. those published by Datamonitor, Euromonitor, and Mintel).

Visit the Online Resource Centre and follow the web links to learn more about the information and services provided by Datamonitor, Euromonitor, and Mintel.

'Soft' personal sources of information obtained through networking, such as contacts at trade fairs, particularly for competitive, legal, and regulatory information, are also important. Such verbal personal sources of information can be critical in fast-changing environments (May *et al.*, 2000) when reports from government, industry, or specific businesses have yet to be written and disseminated.

Visit the Online Resource Centre and complete Internet Activity 4.2 to learn more about a number of sources that can be useful when conducting a scan of the marketing environment.

The process through which companies scan the marketing environment typically involves three stages (see Figure 4.3). In Stage 1, the focus is principally, but not exclusively, on data gathering. In Stage 2, the focus is principally, but not exclusively, on interpreting the data gathered in a process of environmental interpretation/analysis, and in the final stage, the focus is principally, but not exclusively, on strategy formulation.

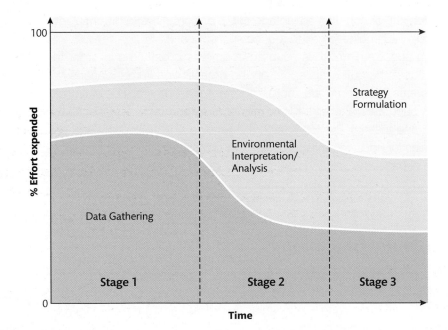

Figure 4.3

The environmental scanning process

Source: Adapted from O'Connell and Zimmerman (1979). Reproduced with the kind permission of *California Management Review*.

During each of the key scanning stages, there is also some activity in each of the other two areas so that each of the three processes dominates a particular stage but is also present at the other stages. Although the process seems relatively straightforward, and simply a matter of collecting the 'right' information, barriers to effective environmental scanning exist because it is difficult to determine what is the 'right' information. In addition, data gathering can be time-consuming. In such cases, the information gathered ceases to provide a useful input to strategic marketing decision-making. In addition, multinational corporations may see opportunities and desire organizational change, and collect the right data to take advantage of those opportunities, but fail to actually undertake such opportunities because of **switching costs** and organizational inertia related to production, sourcing, and other business operations.

Some companies, however, have developed a proactive approach by considering potential future **scenarios** facing their company. For example, in its analysis of the world energy market to 2050, the multinational energy company Shell identifies two possible future energy scenarios based on how governments and companies respond to the energy production and sustainability challenge. In its 'scramble' scenario, there is energy price volatility, no effective carbon pricing, coal and biofuels are emphasized and renewables forced in by legislation, with a patchwork of national standards. In the 'blueprints' scenario, effective carbon pricing is established early, energy efficiency standards are put in place, the transport sector is electrified, and new energy infrastructure develops (Royal Dutch Shell, 2012). These two scenarios help Shell to plan for alternate realities until it becomes clear which one, or neither, of the scenarios is likely to occur.

Scanning and understanding the external environment through the PESTLE framework will reveal different influences and trends within different industries and sectors. Therefore it is important to realize that particular industries will focus on different issues and elements within the framework.

Research Insight 4.2

To take your learning further, you might wish to read this highly influential paper.

Levitt, T. (2004) Marketing myopia. *Harvard Business Review*, July–August (originally published in 1960).

This is, perhaps, the most famous and celebrated article ever written on marketing. It won the author the McKinsey Award. It has twice been reprinted in the *Harvard Business Review*. The central thesis of the article, as true today as it was in 1960, is that companies must monitor change in the external environment and keep abreast of their customers' needs or they risk decline.

@ **Visit the Online Resource Centre to read the abstract and access the full paper.**

Understanding the Performance Environment

The **performance environment**, sometimes called the microenvironment, consists of those organizations that either directly or indirectly influence an organization's operational performance. The performance environment, therefore, encompasses not only competitors but also suppliers and other organizations such as distributors, who all contribute to an industry's value chain. There are three main types.

1 Those companies that compete against the organization in the pursuit of its objectives.

2 Those companies that supply raw materials, goods, and services, and those that add value as distributors, dealers, and retailers further down the marketing channel. These organizations have the potential to influence directly the performance of the organization by adding value through production, assembly, and distribution of products prior to reaching the end-user.

3 Those companies that have the potential to influence *indirectly* the performance of the organization in the pursuit of its objectives. These organizations often supply services such as consultancy or financial services, or are marketing research or communication agencies.

Analysis of the performance environment is undertaken so that organizations can adapt to better positions relative to those of their stakeholders and competitors. These adjustments are made in recognition of emerging trends, as circumstances develop, and/or in anticipation of evolving environmental and performance conditions.

Knowledge about the performance arena allows organizations to choose how and where to operate and compete, given limited resources. Knowledge allows adaption and development in complex and increasingly turbulent markets. Conditions vary from industry to industry. Some are full of potential and growth opportunities, such as cruise holidays, Fairtrade food, and the online travel and gaming industries, whereas others are in decline or at best stagnating, for example high street music stores and camera retailers.

Analysing Industries

An industry is composed of various organizations that market similar offerings. According to Porter (1979), we should review the 'competitive' environment within an industry to identify the major competitive forces, as this helps assess their impact on an organization's present and future competitive positions. Numerous variables help to determine how attractive an industry is and shape the longer-term profitability for the different companies that make up the industry.

Think of industries such as shipbuilding, cars, coal, and steel, where levels of profitability have been weak and unattractive to prospective new entrants. Now think of industries such as high technology, fashion, airlines, and banking, where levels of profitability have traditionally been high. The competitive pressures in all these markets vary quite considerably, but there are enough similarities to establish an analytical framework to gauge the nature and intensity of competition. Porter suggests that competition in an industry is a composite of five main competitive forces. These are the level of threat that new competitors will enter the market, the threat posed by substitute products, and the bargaining power of both buyers and suppliers. These, in turn, affect the fifth force, the intensity of rivalry between the current competitors. Porter called these variables the Five Forces of Competitive Industry Analysis (see Figure 4.4).

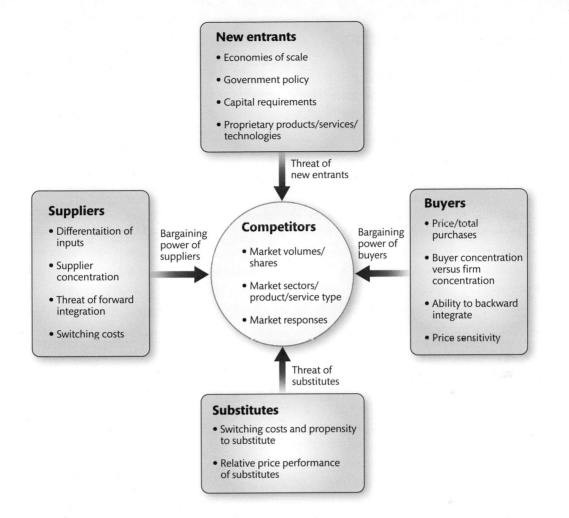

Figure 4.4

Industry analysis: Porter's five forces

Source: Adapted from Porter (1979). Reproduced with the kind permission of Harvard Business School Publishing.

As a general rule, the more intense the rivalry between the industry players, the lower their overall performance. On the other hand, the lower the rivalry the greater will be the performance of the industry players. Porter's model is useful because it exposes the competitive forces in operation in an industry and can lead to an assessment of the strength of each of them. The collective impact determines what competition is like in the market. As a general rule, the stronger the competitive forces the lower the profitability in a market. An organization needs to determine a competitive approach that allows it to influence the industry's competitive rules, protect it from competitive forces as much as possible, and give it a strong position from which to compete.

New Entrants

Industries are seldom static. Companies and brands enter and exit industries all the time. Consider the UK beverage industry; it has witnessed the entrance of energy drink manufacturers such as Red Bull. This company has been competing head on with industry stalwarts

Pepsico, Coca-Cola, and GlaxoSmithKline's Lucozade, the original energy drink in the UK beverage market.

When examining an industry, we should consider whether economies of scale are required for successful performance within it. For instance, motor manufacturing in the UK requires significant investment in plant and machinery. Unfortunately, as British labour costs are high and foreign direct investment incentives (e.g. government development grants) are not as lucrative as they once were, many British-based motor manufacturers have moved to Eastern Europe and the Far East. New entrants may be restricted through government and regulatory policy, or they may be frozen out of an industry because of the capital requirement necessary to set up business. For example, in the oil and gas industry, huge sums of capital are required not only to fund exploration activities but also to fund the extraction and refining operations.

Companies may be locked out because companies within a market are using proprietary offerings or technologies. A good example of this is the pharmaceutical industry where patents protect companies' investments in new medicines. The cost of developing a new medicine in 2014 was around $2.56bn (Edney, 2014). Few companies can afford to compete in a market where the set-up and ongoing R&D costs are so large. One strategic response in the industry has been a wave of mergers and alliances, as pharmaceutical companies attempt to build critical mass in R&D, marketing, and distribution.

Substitutes

In any industry, there are usually substitute offerings that perform the same function or meet similar customer needs. Levitt (1960) warned that many companies fail to recognize the competitive threat from newly developing offerings. He cites the American railroad industry's refusal to see the competitive threat arising from the development of the automobile and airline industries in the transport sector.

Consider the telecommunications sector in the UK. As telecommunications markets continue to converge with the development of broadband Internet services, we see a variety of different companies operating in the same competitive marketspace, e.g. Everything Everywhere (Orange and T-Mobile), BT, Virgin Media, and many others. With the long-standing development of VOIP (voice over Internet protocol)—the Internet telecommunication voice transmission standard—fixed-line telecommunications has become a commodity and firms operating in the area now look to develop value-added services such as video-on-demand, streaming, interactive gaming, and web-conferencing services.

Most countries' fixed-line operators have found it difficult to hold on to their original subscribers, partly because cheaper alternatives are appearing in the market (e.g. cable, Internet, and fusion plans incorporating mobile and fixed lines and TV packages). It takes time for consumers to become aware of new offerings and obtain the necessary information to allow them to make a decision over whether or not to switch. Consumers consider the switching costs associated with such a decision, which, in turn, affects their propensity to substitute the offering for another. They consider the relative price performance of one offering over another. For example, if we wish to travel from Amsterdam to Paris, we can fly from Schiphol airport to Charles de Gaulle airport, take the train, or drive. We would consider the relative price differences (the flight is likely to be the most expensive, but not always) and we would also factor in to this decision how comfortable and convenient these different journeys were hypothetically before we finally make our choice. In analysing our place within an industry, we should consider what alternative offerings exist in the marketplace, which also meet, to a greater or lesser extent, our customers' needs.

Buyers

Companies should ask themselves what percentage of their sales a single buyer represents. This is an important question because if one buying company purchases a large volume of offerings from the supplying company, as car manufacturers do from steel suppliers, it is likely to be able to demand price concessions (price/total purchases) when there are a lot of competing suppliers in the marketplace relative to the proportion of buyers (buyer concentration versus firm concentration). Buyers may also decide to increase their bargaining power through **backward integration**. For instance, a company is said to have integrated backwards when it moves into manufacturing the offerings it previously bought from its suppliers.

Tesco plc—the British multiple retail grocer, operating in 10 markets outside the UK in 2016—also sells financial services including debt and credit services which it previously would have purchased from Visa and MasterCard **merchant** operators. As for many years customers have tended to pay using credit/debit cards rather than cash, Tesco has lowered its transaction costs by setting up its own credit/debit services. Nevertheless, for the other suppliers in a market, it means that they effectively have a new entrant into the market and hence a new competitor.

Another factor impacting on a buyer's bargaining power is how price sensitive a particular company is. Depending on their trading circumstances, some companies might be more price sensitive than other buyers. If such companies are more price sensitive and yet there are a lot of competing suppliers for their business, they are likely to switch supplier rather than be loyal to one supplier. Most companies try to enhance other factors associated with an offering, e.g. after-sales service or product/service customization, to try to reduce a client company's **price sensitivity**. When analysing an industry, we should understand the bargaining power that buyers have with their suppliers as this can impact on the price charged and the volumes sold or total revenue earned.

Suppliers

Any industry analysis should determine how suppliers operate and the extent of their bargaining power. For example, the aircraft manufacturing market consists of a small number of major suppliers, such as Boeing and Airbus, and a large number of customers, namely national airlines and low cost airline companies. The suppliers have the stronger bargaining advantage. Conversely, in the computer gaming industry, there are a large number of suppliers, such as game production companies and game console component manufacturers. The few customers—Sony, Nintendo, and Microsoft—hold the bargaining advantage. We should also consider whether or not the suppliers are providing unique components, products, or services that may enhance their bargaining situation. In some industries, suppliers increase their market dominance by forward integration. For example, a toy manufacturer could set up a retail outlet or ecommerce facility to sell its own products direct to end-users. Forward integration not only allows companies to better control their own supply chains, but also allows them to sell at lower prices, thereby increasing sales and profit from increased retail sales as well. Equally, if companies face high switching, economic, resource, and time costs associated with using another supplier, the supplier has stronger bargaining power with that particular company.

Competitors

To analyse an industry, we must also understand how the companies within that particular market operate. For example, in the UK cosmetic sector, the market-leading cosmetic manufacturers are Avon European Holdings Ltd, Estée Lauder Cosmetics Ltd, L'Oréal (UK) Ltd, Procter & Gamble Ltd, the Unilever Group, and large retailers such as Boots Group plc, The Body Shop International plc, and Superdrug Stores plc. In undertaking a competitor analysis we should outline each company's structure (e.g. details of the main holding company, the individual business unit, any changes in ownership), current and future developments (these can often be gleaned from reading company prospectuses, websites, and industry reports), and the company's latest financial results. We would be interested in calculating the market volumes and shares for each competitor, as market share is a key indicator of company profitability and return on investment (Buzzell *et al.*, 1975).

The importance of understanding competitors cannot be overstated. Noble *et al.* (2002) found that organizations who pay particular attention to their competitors generally perform better than those who do not. To undertake an analysis of a firm's competitors, five key questions must be answered.

- Who are our competitors?
- What are their strengths and weaknesses?
- What are their strategic goals?
- Which strategies are they following?
- How are they likely to respond?

Who Are Our Competitors?

Competitors are those firms who provide offerings that attempt to meet the same market need as our own. There are several ways in which a need might be met, but essentially two approaches can be identified. Firms need to be aware of their direct and indirect competitors. Direct competitors provide similar offerings to the same target market, for example EasyJet, Flybe, and Ryanair. Direct competitors also offer a product in the same category, but target different segments. For example, in addition to major global manufacturers Unilever and Nestlé, emerging niche brands such as Jude's (UK), Ciao Bella (USA), R&R Ice Cream (Europe), and Mengniu Dairy (China) all offer a range of ice creams for different target markets (Hughes Neghaiwi and Geller, 2015). Indirect competitors are those who address the same target market but provide a different offering to satisfy the market need, for example Spotify, Sony, and Apple's iPod.

By understanding who the main competitors are, it becomes possible to make judgements about the nature and intensity of the competition. This also provides a view about how a firm's marketing strategy should evolve. For example, the strategy of a market leader, which identifies little competition, will be different from that of a small firm trying to establish a small market share. The former may try to dominate the whole market, whereas the latter may attack the leader or find a small under-serviced segment, called a **niche market**, and make it their own.

What Are Their Strengths and Weaknesses?

Getting information about a competitor's range of offerings and their sales volumes and values, their profitability, prices, and discount structures, the nature of their relationships with suppliers and distributors, their communications campaigns and special offers, are all important. In some circumstances, getting information about new offerings that are either in development or about to be launched can be critical.

In addition to these marketing elements, however, it is important to obtain information about a whole range of other factors, not just their marketing activities. These factors include their production and manufacturing capabilities, their technical, management, and financial resources, and their processes, distribution channels, and relative success in meeting customer and market needs.

As this information accumulates and is updated over time, we use the information to understand two main issues: first, what a competitor's strengths and weaknesses might be and, second, either to avoid the areas where competitors are strong or to exploit their weaknesses. The overall task is to determine what **competitive advantage** a competitor might have and whether this advantage can be sustained, imitated, or undermined. See Chapter 5 for more information about competitive advantage, and how to analyse an organization's strengths and weaknesses and opportunities and threats.

What Are Their Strategic Goals?

Contrary to popular opinion, profit is not the single overriding strategic goal for most organizations. Firms develop a range of goals, encompassing ambitions such as achieving a certain market share, market leadership, industry recognition for technological prowess or high quality performance, or market reputation for innovation, environmental concern, or ethical trading.

Developing a full understanding of a competitor's strategic goals is not easy and can usually only be inferred from a competitor's actions. Some firms try to recruit senior executives from competitors to get real insight into their strategic intentions. Although this happens quite frequently, it is not an ethical way of operating, and organizations can impose severe legal and financial constraints on employees in terms of who they can work for if they leave and the timescale in which they are not allowed to work in the industry.

Which Strategies Are They Following?

Once a competitor's goals are understood it becomes easier to predict what its marketing strategies are likely to be. These strategies can be considered through two main factors, competitive scope and positioning.

Competitive scope refers to the breadth of the market addressed. Is the competitor attempting to service the whole of a market, particular segments, or a single niche segment? If they are servicing a niche market, one of the key questions to be asked is whether they will want to stay and dominate the niche or are they simply using it as a trial before springboarding into other market segments.

Brands can be **positioned** in markets according to the particular attributes or benefits a brand offers. Cameras might be positioned according to their technical features, whereas cosmetics are often positioned on style and fashion, frequently with campaigns led by brand ambassadors who are considered to personify the brand values. Once this is understood, the marketing mix elements are aligned to support the positioning strategy. Some brands are positioned based on price and a low cost strategy. This approach requires a focus on reducing costs and expenses rather than investing heavily in marketing communications and/or research and development. We consider low-cost strategies later in this chapter.

Visit the Online Resource Centre and complete Internet Activity 4.3 to learn more about the importance of analysing a competitor's strategic activities.

How Are They Likely to Respond?

Understanding the strategies of competitors helps inform whether they are intent on outright attack or defence, and how they might react to particular strategies initiated by others. For example, a price cut might be met with a similar reduction, a larger reduction, or none at all. Changes in the levels of investment in advertising might produce a similar range of responses.

Some market leaders believe that an aggressive response to a challenger's actions is important, otherwise their leadership position might be undermined. There are a range of responses that firms may use, reflecting organizational objectives, leadership styles, industry norms, and new strategies born of new owners.

Suppliers and Distributors

So far, analysis of the performance environment has concentrated on the nature and characteristics of a firm's competitive behaviour. This is important, but Porter also realized that suppliers can influence competition and he built this into his Five Forces model. However, since he published his work there have been several significant supply-side developments, notably the development of outsourcing. Outsourcing concerns the transfer of non-core activities to an external organization that specializes in the activity or operation. For example, transport and delivery services are not core activities for most companies, although they constitute an important part of the value they offer their customers. In Japan, the Hitachi Transport System, a **third-party logistics** (3PL) service, is used by companies as an outsourced provider to transport their goods. Many suppliers, therefore, have become an integral part of a firm's capabilities. Rather than act aggressively they are more likely to be cooperative and work in support of the firm that has outsourced the work to them.

Similar changes have occurred downstream in terms of a manufacturer's marketing channel. Now it is common to find high levels of integration between a manufacturer and their distributors, dealers, and retailers. Account needs to be taken of the strength of these relationships and consideration given to how market performance might be strengthened or weakened by the capabilities of the channel intermediary. Suppliers and distributors have become central to how firms can develop specific competitive advantages. Analysis of the performance environment should incorporate a review of key suppliers and distributors to the firm under analysis.

Research Insight 4.3

To take your learning further, you might wish to read this highly cited and influential book.

Porter, M.E. (1980). *Competitive Strategy: Techniques for Analysing Industries and Competitors.* **New York: Free Press.**

This book expanded Porter's first public presentation of his ideas about industry analysis in a *Harvard Business Review* article the previous year. The central tenet of the book is that industry profitability and performance is a result of the interaction of five forces: supplier power, buyer power, competitive rivalry, the availability of substitutes, and the extent of new competitive entrants into an industry. The Porter's Five Force technique for analysing industries is still used prolifically by marketing and strategy executives today.

Visit the Online Resource Centre to find out more about this book.

Market Insight 4.4
Ice Cream: Rivalry Hots Up

Ice cream, often regarded as an indulgent treat, is a market that was worth £1,115m in the UK in 2015. The market has three main sectors: artisan, impulse, and take-home. Artisan is high quality handmade ice cream, made by small local producers. In the UK this represents less than 20% across all age ranges, but in Italy there are over 30,000 specialist ice cream parlours. The second sector is impulse ice cream, which is heavily branded and made by large multinational companies, and is bought for immediate consumption. It is this sector's performance that is most subject to weather conditions. The third sector is take-home, where 25% of ice cream products are supplied by private label brands. Bought from large retailers, mostly supermarkets, as tubs and multipacks, this sector caters for home consumption.

Within each of these sectors there are sub-sections. For example within the take-home sector there are family, luxury, premium, and super-premium markets. Despite the recession, several manufacturers have been looking for growth within the take-home sector. This is because many consumers have traded up to luxury and/or premium ice cream as a sharing product for social evenings spent at home.

Unilever, the third largest consumer goods company, is the world's largest producer of ice cream. Its leading brands include Magnum, Ben & Jerry's, Cornetto, Carte d'Or, and Solero. The Magnum brand is a core part of Unilever's strategy, and is one of the largest within the European ice cream market. Part of Unilever's strategy involves brand extensions through new flavours.

Nestlé is Unilever's closest competitor. Nestlé's offerings include the Extreme brand, Dreyers, the premium Mövenpick brand, and their Nestlé own brand. Nestle also license the Haagen-Daz super-premium brand, which in the UK generates approximately £50m.

R&R Ice Cream is the largest supplier to the European own-label market, and supplies ice cream brands such as Rolo, Toffee Crisp, and Rowntree's Fruit Pastilles. R&R has made a number of acquisitions, including the Yoomoo brand of frozen yoghurt, and has purchased Italy's leading supplier of ice cream to the own-label sector Eskigal.

Other suppliers within the European ice cream market include Mars and Frederick's Dairies. The latter supplies Cadbury branded ice cream products—examples of which include Creme Egg and Buttons—as well as Vimto and Del Monte ice cream.

In the UK there are four main retailers, which collectively account for over 82% volume share of retail distribution in the ice cream market. The remainder of the retail network is very fragmented, but producers have little bargaining power in the market.

Sources: Thomas (2013); Anon. (2014); Smith (2014); Mintel (2016).

Ben & Jerry's compete by emphasizing their values and concern for the environment
Source: © Keith Homan/Shutterstock.

Market Insight 4.4
continued

Theory into Practice

Porter's Five Forces Model is the framework best suited to analysing markets, in this case the ice cream market. Although the amount of information provided is limited, it should be clear that understanding the way different competitors operate, identifying their brands and strategies, and identifying their goals should lead to a clearer appreciation of the performance environment, and from that how best to proceed.

Related Topics:

marketing strategy; brand management; customer experience; marketing relationships; marketing mix.

1 To what extent do you believe it is sufficiently realistic for executives to assume new roles and to act out strategies that might be adopted by competitors?

2 In a country of your choice, identify any two brands within the ice cream market, visit their websites (and other resources) and determine their relative competitive strengths.

3 Select an ice cream brand and determine how the external and performance environments might influence the success of the brand.

Understanding the Internal Environment

An analysis of the internal environment of an organization is concerned with understanding and evaluating the capabilities and potential of the products, systems, human, marketing, and financial resources. An analysis of an organization's resources should not focus on the relative strength and weakness of a particular resource, but look at the absolute nature of the resource itself. As Thompson (1990) suggests, 'resources are not strong or weak merely because they exist … their value depends upon how they are being managed, controlled and used'. Attention here is given to two main elements, products and finance, through **portfolio analysis**.

Portfolio Analysis

When managing a collection or portfolio of offerings, we should appreciate that understanding the performance of an individual offering can often fail to give appropriate insight. What is really important is an understanding of the relative performance of the offerings. By creating a balance of old, mature, established, growing, and very new offerings, there is a better chance of delivering profits now and at some point in the future, when the current offerings cease to be attractive and profitable. One of the popular methods for assessing the variety of businesses/offerings that

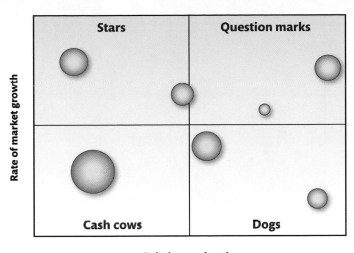

Figure 4.5

The Boston Box

Source: Reprinted from B. Hedley, 'Strategy and the business portfolio', *Long Range Planning*, 10, 1, 12. © 1977, with permission from Elsevier.

an organization has, involves the creation of a two-dimensional graphical picture of the comparative strategic positions. This technique is referred to as a portfolio matrix.

The Boston Consulting Group (BCG) developed the original idea and their matrix—the **Boston Box**, shown in Figure 4.5—is based on two key variables, market growth and relative market share (i.e. market share as a percentage of the share of the product's largest competitor, expressed as a fraction). Thus, a relative share of 0.8 means that the product achieves 80% of the sales of the market leader's sales volume (or value, depending on which measure is used). This is not the strongest competitive position but is not a weak position either. A relative market share of 1 means that the company shares market leadership with a competitor with an equal share. A relative market share of 2 means that the company has twice the market share of the nearest competitor.

In Figure 4.6, the vertical axis refers to the rate of market growth and the horizontal axis refers to an offering's market strength, as measured by relative market share (as described above). The size of the circles represents the sales revenue generated by the product. Relative market share is generally regarded as high when you are the market leader, i.e. the relative market share is 1 or greater. Determining whether or not market growth rate is high or low is more problematic and depends on the type of industry. In some industries, a market growth rate of 5% might be regarded as high, whereas in others this might be 10%. The benchmark between high and low is often taken to be 10%. This lack of clarity on what are regarded definitively as high and low rates of market growth is a key criticism of the approach.

Question marks (also known as 'problem children') are offerings that exist in growing markets but have low market share. As a result there is negative cash flow and they are unprofitable. Stars are most probably market leaders but their growth has to be financed through fairly heavy levels of investment. Cash cows, on the other hand, exist in fairly stable, low growth markets and require little ongoing investment. Their high market share draws both positive cash flows and high levels of profitability. Dogs experience low growth and low market share, and generate negative cash flows. These indicators suggest that many of them are operating in declining markets and they have no real long-term future.

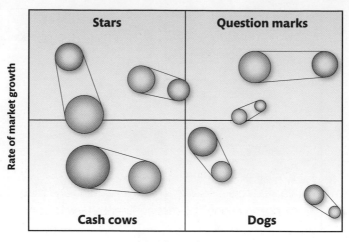

Figure 4.6

Present and future positions in the BCG matrix

Source: Reprinted from B. Hedley, 'Strategy and the business portfolio', *Long Range Planning*, 10, 1, 12. © 1977, with permission from Elsevier.

Divestment however, need not occur just because of low share. For example, when the pharmaceutical firm Merck sold Sirna Therapeutics to Alnylam Pharmaceuticals the sale of the drug delivery subsidiary was announced as enabling Merck to remain consistent with their strategy of reducing their emphasis on platform technologies. Merck's policy is to assess whether particular assets are core to their strategy, whether they provide competitive advantage, and whether they might generate greater value as part of Merck or outside Merck (Zhu, 2014).

From a reverse perspective, in 2009, Coca-Cola bought a £30m stake in innocent drinks, in an attempt to give it access to the smoothie market which, prior to 2008 and the recession, had grown rapidly over the previous 10 years and in which it had no presence whatsoever. By buying a minority 18% stake in innocent, which it increased by 40% to a 58% majority stake in 2010, Coca-Cola bypassed the set-up costs of developing their own 'question mark' smoothie product, thereby gaining a market presence at a relatively modest cost and giving it the option in due course to buy the company outright if it and the innocent management so desire (Reynolds, 2011).

Portfolio analysis is an important analytical tool as it draws attention to the cash flow and investment characteristics of each of a firm's offerings and indicates how financial resources can be manoeuvred to attain optimal strategic performance over the long term. Essentially, excess cash generated by cash cows should be utilized to develop question marks and stars, which are unable to support themselves. This enables stars to become cash cows and self-supporting. Dogs should only be retained as long as they contribute to positive cash flow and do not restrict the use of assets and resources elsewhere in the business. Once they do, they should be divested or ejected from the portfolio.

By plotting all of a company's offerings onto the grid it becomes visually easy to appreciate just how well balanced the portfolio is. An unbalanced portfolio would be one that has too many offerings clustered in one or two quadrants. Where offerings are distributed equally, or at least are not clustered in any one area, and where market shares and cash flows equate with their market position, the portfolio is financially healthy and well balanced. By analysing the portfolio in this way it becomes possible to project possible strategies and their outcomes.

Portfolio Issues

Portfolio analysis is an important guide to strategic development, if only because it forces answers to questions such as the following.

- How fast will the market grow?
- What will be our market share?
- What investment will be required?
- How can a balanced portfolio be created from this point?

The questions posed and the answers generated through use of the Boston box, however, do not alone generate marketing strategies. As with all analytical tools and methodologies, the BCG provides strategic indicators, not solutions. It is management's task to consider information from a variety of sources and then make decisions based on their judgement. The Boston Box has been criticized for providing rigid solutions to product portfolio evaluation when exceptions to the rule might exist, e.g. proposing that 'cash cow' products should not be invested in, when a company may rely solely on its 'cash cow' products to provide profits and not necessarily have new offerings in the pipeline to replace them. Equally, the Boston Box proposes that 'dog' offerings should be divested when, in fact, they may actually be returning a profit to the company.

Finding the necessary and objective data to plot the positions of products or SBUs on the two axes of relative market share and market growth rate can also be problematic. Reliable industry data may not always be available. Finally, it is not always easy to determine what market we are concerned with. For example, if we consider the smoothie market, does this include fruit-based milkshakes, or fruit juices more generally?

Research Insight 4.4

To take your learning further, you might wish to read this influential paper.

Morrison, A. and Wensley, R. (1991). Boxing up or boxing in: a short history of the Boston Consulting Group Share/Growth Matrix. *Journal of Marketing Management*, 7(2), 105–29.

This highly readable and critical article outlines the history of the development of the Boston Box portfolio analysis concept from academic and practitioner perspectives. The article concludes that the concept is useful in strategic planning but that those using it should be aware of its limitations, namely around the scope of the technique, the assumptions it makes, how it defines and classifies markets by share and growth, its failure to consider the political dimensions of strategy development, that there are strategic implementation difficulties of the strategies proposed in real firms, and that the matrix explains what strategy to undertake but not how to do it.

See also:
Kang, W. and Montoya, M. (2014) The impact of product portfolio strategy on financial performance: the roles of product development and market entry decisions. *Journal of Product Innovation Management*, 31(3), 516–34.

Visit the Online Resource Centre to read the abstracts and access the papers in full.

Marketing Audit

As part of the process for developing a marketing strategy it is necessary to make sense of all the information that has been collected. This phase, referred to as the strategic market analysis part of the marketing strategy process, requires a marketing audit to be undertaken. Just as a financial audit considers the financial health of an organization, so the marketing audit considers its marketing health. In particular, it brings together views about the three environments. First, it considers the external opportunities and threats, where management has little or no control. Second, it considers the nature, characteristics, and any changes occurring within the performance environment, where management has partial influence. Third, it reviews the quality and potential of the organization's products, marketing systems, resources, and capabilities as part of the internal environment, where there is full control. The topics normally undertaken as part of the marketing audit are shown in Figure 4.7.

The audit covers the marketing environment, an organization's objectives and strategies, its marketing programmes and performance, plus the organization itself and the relevant marketing systems and procedures. We undertake marketing audits because they bring together critical information, identify weaknesses in order that they can be corrected, and provide a platform to build marketing strategy.

The marketing audit can be undertaken either by an internal team, led by a senior manager, or if a more objective interpretation is desired, an outside consultant can be used. Whoever conducts the audit it should be undertaken on a regular annual basis and be regarded as a positive activity that can feed into marketing strategy. Marketing audits should not be instigated in response to a crisis.

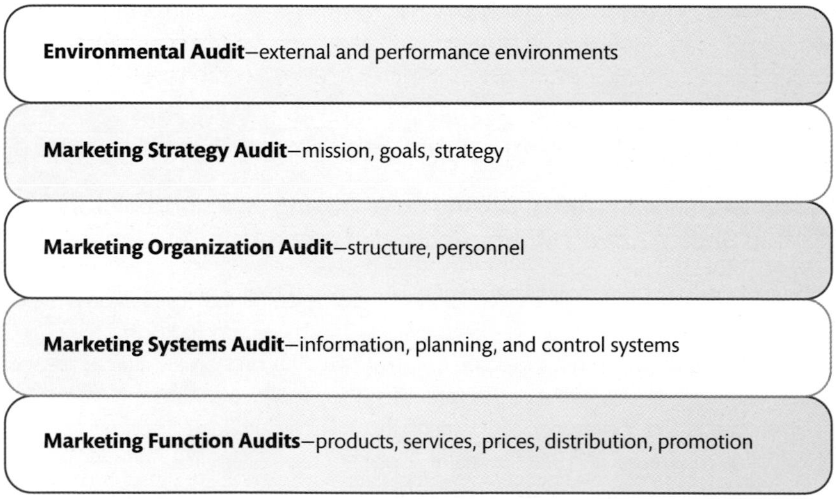

Environmental Audit—external and performance environments

Marketing Strategy Audit—mission, goals, strategy

Marketing Organization Audit—structure, personnel

Marketing Systems Audit—information, planning, and control systems

Marketing Function Audits—products, services, prices, distribution, promotion

Figure 4.7
Dimensions of a marketing audit

⟳ Chapter Summary

To consolidate your learning, the core points from this chapter are summarized here.

■ **Identify and define the three key areas of the marketing environment.**

The marketing environment incorporates the external environment, the performance environment, and the internal environment. The external environment incorporates macro-environmental factors, which are largely uncontrollable and which organizations generally cannot influence. The performance environment incorporates key factors within an industry, impacting on strategic decision-making. The internal environment is controllable and is the principal means, through its resource base, by which an organization influences its strategy.

■ **Describe the key characteristics associated with the marketing environment.**

The external environment consists of the political, social, and technological influences, and organizations have limited influence on these. The performance environment consists of the competitors, suppliers, and indirect service providers, shaping the way organizations achieves their objectives. Here, organizations have more influence. The internal environment concerns the resources, processes, and policies organizations manage to achieve their goals.

■ **Explain PESTLE analysis and show how it is used to understand the external environment.**

We considered the various components of the external marketing environment that may impact on any particular organization using the PESTLE acronym, which includes the following factors: political, economic, socio-cultural, technological, legal, and ecological factors. Some of these factors are more important than others in any particular industry.

■ **Explain the environmental scanning process.**

The environmental scanning process consists of the data-gathering phase, the environmental interpretation/analysis phase, and the strategy formulation phase. The three processes are interlinked, but, over time, more attention is focused on each one more than the others so that at the end of the process, greater effort is expended on using knowledge gleaned from the external and competitive environments to formulate strategy based on changes occurring and identified in the company's environment.

■ **Analyse the performance environment using the Porter's Five Forces industry analysis model.**

The most common technique used to analyse the performance environment is Porter's Five Forces Model of Competitive Analysis. Porter concludes that the more intense the rivalry between the industry players, the lower will be their overall performance. On the other hand, the lower the rivalry the greater will be the performance of the industry players. Porter's Five Forces comprise (1) supplier bargaining power, (2) buyer bargaining power, (3) threat of new entrants, (4) rivalry of competitors, and (5) threat of substitutes.

■ **Analyse an organization's product/service portfolio to aid resource planning.**

An organization's principal resources relate to the portfolio of offerings that it carries and the financial resources at its disposal. We use portfolio analysis, specifically the Boston Box approach, to determine whether different strategic business units or product/service formulations are stars, dogs, question marks, or cash cows; each category of which suggests differing levels of cash flow and resource requirements to develop. It is important to undertake a marketing audit as a preliminary measure to allow proper development of marketing strategy.

? Review Questions

1 Identify the three main marketing environments.
2 How might changes in the political environment affect marketing strategy?
3 How might changes in the economic environment affect marketing strategy?
4 How might changes in the socio-cultural environment affect marketing strategy?
5 How might changes in the technological environment affect marketing strategy?
6 How might changes in the legal environment affect marketing strategy?
7 How might changes in the ecological environment affect marketing strategy?
8 What are the three stages of the environmental scanning process?
9 What are Porter's Five Forces?
10 What is product portfolio analysis and why is it useful?

✎ Worksheet Summary

@ Visit the **Online Resource Centre** and complete Worksheet 4.1. This will help you learn how the PESTLE framework, Five Forces model, and BCG matrix can be used to analyse the marketing environment. It will also help you understand how the internal, external, and performance environments interact.

◢ Discussion Questions

1 Having read the Case Insight at the beginning of this chapter, how would you advise Glassolutions Saint-Gobain to persuade the Government, specifically the Department for Business, Energy & Industrial Strategy, to reconsider how they fund green initiatives in the replacement window industry?

2 Read Market Insight 4.2: Health issues slim down product sales. Search the Internet for further information on the healthy eating debate, obesity, and 'fat taxes', and then answer the following questions.

   A What changes have taken place in the external environment to bring about the introduction of 'fat taxes' in different countries?
   B How should firms such as Warburton's ensure that they keep up to date with trends in consumer lifestyles, government legislation, and competitor new proposition development?
   C What strategies in relation to proposition development and promotion might Ribena adopt to ensure that they do not get delisted by other supermarkets?

3 Undertake an environmental analysis using PESTLE, by surfing the Internet for appropriate information and by using available market research reports, for each of the following markets.

   A The automotive market (e.g. you might be VW, Renault, BMW, Ford, or Toyota).
   B The global multiple retail grocery market (e.g. you might be Walmart, Carrefour, or Tesco).
   C The beer industry (e.g. you might be InBev, Carlsberg, Heineken, Miller Brands, or Budweiser Budvar).

4 Analyse the ecological marketing environment for the cosmetics industry in a country of your choice. Look specifically at socio-cultural patterns and trends in habits, particularly in relation to male versus female grooming. You should surf the Internet for appropriate documents and market intelligence material to help you develop your arguments.

5 Using the data in Table 4.1 identify the relative market shares of the various brands in the UK beer market. Use the market growth rate figure as the difference in total sales between 2009 and 2011. Then draw up a Boston Box to illustrate the product portfolio for each of the key companies and their brands.

Table 4.1 UK beer market

	2012/13		2013/14		2014/15		Change 2012/13–2014/15
	£m	%	£m	%	£m	%	%
Stella Artois (AB InBev)	532	15	522	15	532	15	–
Foster's (Heineken)	509	15	518	15	474	13	−6.9
Carlsberg (incl. Carlsberg Export)	412	12	386	11	359	10	−12.9
Budweiser (AB InBev)	301	9	333	9	336	10	11.6
Carling (Molson Coors)	331	10	340	10	320	9	−3.3
Kronenbourg (Heineken)	114	3	125	4	123	4	7.9
San Miguel (Carlsberg)	93	3	88	2	100	3	7.5
Peroni (SABMiller)	84	2	96	3	99	3	17.9
Beck's (AB InBev)	101	3	98	3	95	3	−5.9
Tennent's (C&C)	88	3	86	2	87	2	−1.1
Others	533	16	607	17	668	19	25.3
Own-label	338	10	338	10	330	9	−2.4
Total	**3,436**	**100**	**3,537**	**100**	**3,523**	**100**	**2.5**

Note: Totals may not add up to 100% because of counting error.
Source: Mintel (2015).

Visit the **Online Resource Centre** and complete the Multiple Choice Questions to assess your knowledge of Chapter 4.

Glossary

backward integration when a company takes over one or more of its suppliers, it is said to be backward integrating. Taking over a buyer is forward integrating.

Boston Box a popular portfolio matrix commonly also referred to as the BCG, developed by the Boston Consulting Group.

competitive advantage achieved when an organization has an edge over its competitors on factors that are important to customers.

competitive scope the breadth of an organization's focus as measured either horizontally (by the range of its target industries, market segments, or geographical regions) or vertically (by the extent to which it is integrated).

crowdsourcing when an organization outsources a function originally undertaken by its employees to a group ('crowd') of people either as an open call or in a more restricted way.

environmental scanning the management process internal to an organization designed to identify external issues, situations, and threats that may impinge on an organization's future and its strategic decision-making.

government the system of organization of a nation state.

gross domestic product (GDP) a measure of the output of a nation, the size of its economy. It is calculated as the market value of all finished goods and services produced in a country during a specified period, typically available annually or quarterly.

inflation when prices rise.

merchant a merchant performs the same functions as an agent, but takes ownership.

niche market a small part of a market segment that has specific and specialized characteristics that make it uneconomic for the leading competitors to enter this segment.

performance environment organizations that directly or indirectly influence an organization's ability to achieve its strategic and operational goals.

PESTLE an acronym used to identify a framework that examines the external environment. PESTLE stands for the Political, Economic, Socio-cultural, Technological, Legal, and Ecological environments.

political environment that part of the macroenvironment concerned with impending and potential legislation and how it may affect a particular firm.

portfolio analysis an assessment of a company's mix of products, services, investments, and other assets in order to optimize the use of resources and to assess its suitability, level of risk, and expected financial return.

positioning the way that an audience of consumers or buyers perceives a product or service, particularly as a result of the marketing communications process aimed at a target audience.

price sensitivity the extent to which a company or consumer increases or lowers their purchase volumes in relation to changes in price. Thus, a customer is price insensitive when unit volumes drop proportionately less than increases in prices.

public relations a non-personal form of communication used by companies to build trust, goodwill, interest, and ultimately relationships with a range of stakeholders.

purchasing power parity an economic theory that seeks to determine the relative value of currencies between countries, so that there is an equivalence of purchasing power.

purchasing power parity exchange rate a measure used to determine relative wealth of the population based on the cost of an identified basket of goods, which allows us to compare the wealth of one population with another.

recession a fall in a country's gross domestic product for two or more successive quarters in any one year.

reverse engineering the process of developing a product from the finished version (e.g. from a competitor's prototype) to its constituent parts rather than the usual approach from components parts to a finished product.

scenarios pictures of the future that show how different outcomes may result from different strategic decisions.

society the customs, habits, and nature of a nation's social system.

stakeholders people with an interest, a 'stake', in the levels of profit an organization achieves, its environmental impact, and its ethical conduct in society.

sustainable competitive advantage when an organization is able to offer a superior product to competitors, which is not easily imitated and enjoys significant market share as a result.

switching costs the psychological, economic, time, and effort-related costs associated with

substituting one product or service for another or changing a supplier from one to another.

third-party logistics a firm that provides part or all of the supply chain management functions for another company. These can include operational services such as warehousing and transportation.

values the standards of behaviour expected of an organization's employees.

References

Aguilar, F.Y. (1967). *Scanning the Business Environment*, New York: Macmillan.

Albright, K.S. (2004). Environmental scanning: radar for success. *Information Management Journal*, May–June, 38–45.

Anon. (2012a). Fish farms: Salmond's salmon. *The Economist*, 1 December, 36.

Anon. (2014). Country Report: ice cream in the United Kingdom, *Euromonitor International*, October. Retrieve from http://www.euromonitor.com/ice-cream-in-the-united-kingdom/report (accessed 11 October 2015).

Anon. (2015). Crude price tumble forces lifestyle changes among oil-rich Norwegians. *Fox News*, 24 February. Retrieve from http://www.foxbusiness.com/markets/2015/02/24/crude-price-tumble-forces-lifestyle-changes-among-oil-rich-norwegians/ (accessed 21 September 2015).

Anon. (2015a). 15,000 jobs cut in the Norwegian oil industry. *Norway Post*, 16 April. Retrieve from: http://www.norwaypost.com/index.php/business/oil-a-gass/30825 (accessed 21 September 2015).

Barrie, J. (2015). Tesco, please don't take away my Ribena! *The Telegraph*, 27 July, Retrieve from: http://www.telegraph.co.uk/foodanddrink/healthyeating/11766006/Tesco-please-dont-take-away-my-Ribena.html (accessed 10 September 2015).

BBC (2006). Supermarkets covet Polish spend, BBC News, 10 September. Retrieve from: http://news.bbc.co.uk/1/hi/business/5332024.stm (accessed 11 April 2010).

Buzzell, R.D., Gale, B.T., and Sultan, R.G.M (1975). Market share—a key to profitability. *Harvard Business Review*, January–February, 97–106.

Chandy, R.K., Prabhu, J.C., and Antia, K.D. (2003). What will the future bring? Dominance, technology expectations and radical innovation. *Journal of Marketing*, 67 (July), 1–18.

CTV News (2012). Larger anti-smoking warnings now on cigarette packs. *CTV News*, 19 June. Retrieve from: http://www.ctvnews.ca/health/larger-anti-smoking-warnings-now-on-cigarette-packs-1.844025 (accessed 6 January 2013).

Curtis, S. (2015). L'Oréal: how technology is transforming beauty. *The Telegraph*, 18 July. Retrieve from: www.telegraph.co.uk/technology/news/11744292/LOreal-How-technology-is-transforming-beauty.html (accessed 10 September 2015).

Danciu, V. (2013). The future of marketing: an appropriate response to the environment changes. *Theoretical and Applied Economics*, 20(5), 33–52.

Davidson, L. (2015). The Great British Bake Off is killing packaged bread. *The Telegraph*, 12 August. Retrieve from: http://www.telegraph.co.uk/finance/newsbysector/retailandconsumer/11799225/The-Great-British-Bake-Off-is-killing-packaged-bread.html (accessed 10 September 2015).

DH/ABPI (2012). Joint DH/ABPI statement on arrangements for pricing branded medicines from 2014. Department of Health/Association of the British Pharmaceutical Industry, 3 August. Retrieve from: http://www.dh.gov.uk/health/2012/08/abpi-dh-statement/ (accessed 5 January 2013).

Dorling, P. (2015). Medicines to cost more and healthcare will suffer, according to WikiLeaks documents. *Sydney Morning Herald*, 10 June. Retrieve from: http://www.smh.com.au/national/medicines-to-cost-more-and-healthcare-will-suffer-according-to-wikileaks-documents-20150610-ghkxp0.html (accessed 8 August 2015).

Edney, A. (2014). Cost to develop a drug more than doubles to $2.56 billion. *Bloomberg*, 18 November. Retrieved from: http://www.bloomberg.com/news/articles/2014-11-18/cost-to-develop-a-drug-more-than-doubles-to-2-56-billion (accessed 9 October 2015).

Gower, I. (ed.) (2005). *Cosmetics and Fragrances Market Report 2005*. London: Keynote.

Green, J. (2000). The role of theory in evidence-based health promotion practice. *Health Education Research*, 15(2), 125–9.

Hillman, A., Keim, G.D., and Schuler, D. (2004). Corporate political activity: a review and research agenda. *Journal of Management*, 30(6), 837–57.

Howe, J. (2006). The rise of crowdsourcing. *Wired*, 14 (6, June). Retrieved from: www.wired.com/wired/archive/14.06/crowds.html (accessed 17 April 2010).

Hughes Neghaiwi, B. and Geller, M. (2015). Changing tastes churn up ice cream industry. *Reuters*, 1 September. Retrieved from: http://www.reuters.com/article/2015/09/01/food-icecream-idUSL5N1134KC20150901 (accessed 9 October 2015).

Lawton, T. and Rajwani, T. (2011). Designing lobbying capabilities: managerial choices in unpredictable environments. *European Business Review*, 23(2), 167–89.

Levitt, T. (1960). Marketing myopia. *Harvard Business Review*, July–August, 45–56.

Lewin, K. (1935). *A Dynamic Theory of Personality*. New York: McGraw-Hill.

May, R.C., Stewart, W.H., Jr, and Sweo, R. (2000). Environmental scanning behaviour in a transitional economy: evidence from Russia. *Academy of Management Journal*, 43(3), 403–27.

Menton, J. (2015) Why are oil prices falling? Here are four reasons crude prices continue to trend lower. *International Business Times*, 16 March, Retrieve from: http://www.ibtimes.com/why-are-oil-prices-falling-here-are-four-reasons-crude-prices-continue-trend-lower-1848742 (accessed 21 September 2015).

Mintel (2015). *Beer—UK*, December 2015. Retrieve from: http://www.mintel.com (accessed 5 January 2012).

Mintel (2016). *Ice Cream and Desserts—UK—2016*. London: Mintel.

Munshi, N. (2015). Changing consumer tastes hurt McDonald's and Coca-Cola. FT.com, 27 May. Retrieve from: http://www.ft.com/cms/s/2/bf189450-ef22-11e4-87dc-00144feab7de.html#axzz3mN4QuLRE (accessed 21 September 2015).

Noble, C.H. , Sinha, R.K. , and Kumar, A. (2002). Market orientation and alternative strategic orientations: a longitudinal assessment of performance implications. *Journal of Marketing*, 66(4), 25–40.

O'Connell, J.J. and Zimmerman, J.W. (1979). Scanning the international environment. *California Management Review*, 22(2), 15–23.

Orsato, R.J. (2006). Competitive environmental strategies: when does it pay to be green?' *California Management Review*, 48(2), 127–43.

Porter, M. (1979). How competitive forces shape strategy. *Harvard Business Review*, March–April.

Porter, M.E. (1980). *Competitive Strategy: Techniques for Analysing Industries and Competitors*. New York: Free Press.

Rao, P.M. (2005). Sustaining competitive advantage in a high-technology environment: a strategic marketing perspective. *Advances in Competitiveness Research*, 13(1), 33–47.

Reynolds, J. (2011). innocent hints at 100% sale to Coca-Cola. *Marketing*, 24 August. Retrieve from: http://www.marketingmagazine.co.uk/news/1086577/innocent-hints-100-sale-Coca-Cola/ (accessed 6 January 2013).

Royal Dutch Shell (2012). Shell energy scenarios to 2050. Retrieve from: http://www.shell.com/global/future-energy/scenarios/2050.html (accessed 5 January 2013).

Schumpeter, J.A. (1934). *The Theory of Economic Development*. Cambridge, MA: Harvard University Press.

Scocco, D. (2015). Innovation zen, Retrieve from: http://innovationzen.com/blog/2006/08/24/innovation-management-theory-part-5/ (accessed 9 October 2015)

Shayon, S. (2014). L'Oréal taps smart tech for Genius Makeup App. Brandchannel, 16 May. Retrieve from: http://brandchannel.com/2014/05/16/loreal-taps-smart-tech-for-genius-makeup-app/ (accessed 10 September 2015).

Smith, S. (2014). The UK ice cream market: what consumers eat and why? *PRNewswire*, 21 January. Retrieve from: http://www.prnewswire.com/news-releases/the-uk-ice-cream-market-what-consumers-eat-and-why-241286941.html (accessed 11 October 2015).

Teece, D.J. (1986). Profiting from technological innovation. *Research Policy*, 15(6), 285–305.

Thomas, J. (2013). Ice cream and desserts market—it keeps raining. *Frozen Food Europe*, 15 February. Retrieve from: http://www.frozenfoodeurope.com/article/markets/ice-cream-and-desserts-market-it-keeps-raining (accessed 11 October 2015).

Thompson, K.M. (1990). *The Employee Revolution: Corporate Internal Marketing*. London: Pitman.

UN Population Division (2012). *World Population Prospects: The 2010 Revision*. Retrieve from: http://esa.un.org/unpd/ppp/Figures-Output/Population/PPP_Total-Population.htm (accessed 5 January 2013).

Vogdrup-Schmidt, L. (2015). Employees accept pay cut to save Norwegian yard. *Shippingwatch*, 26 May. Retrieve from: http://shippingwatch.com/Services/article7734135.ece (accessed 21 September 2015).

Ward, V. (2015). Cake and biscuit sales slowdown as Bake Off fuels boom in home baking. *The Telegraph*, 2 September. Retrieve from: http://www.telegraph.co.uk/culture/tvandradio/great-british-bake-off/11839482/Cake-and-biscuit-sales-slow-down-as-Bake-Off-fuels-boom-in-home-baking.html (accessed 14 October 2015).

Westcott, L. (2015). L'Oréal to start printing 3-D skin with bioengineering company. *Newsweek*, 20 May. Retrieved from: http://www.newsweek.com/loreal-start-printing-3-d-skin-bioengineering-company-334204 (accessed 10 September 2015).

Whitla, P. (2009). Crowdsourcing and its application in marketing activities. *Contemporary Management Research*, 5(1), 15–28.

Young, T. (2015). A fat tax is not the way to fight obesity. *The Telegraph*, 29 July. Retrieved from: http://www.telegraph.co.uk/news/health/news/11770042/A-fat-tax-is-not-the-way-to-fight-obesity.html (accessed 12 October 2015).

Zhu, K. (2014). Top 4 reasons to divest. *Axial*, 12 February. Retrieved from: http://www.axial.net/forum/top-4-reasons-divest/ (accessed 9 October 2015).

Chapter 5
Marketing Strategy

Learning Outcomes

After reading this chapter, you will be able to:

▶ Describe the strategic planning process and explain the key influences that shape marketing strategy

▶ Analyse current conditions, and formulate marketing strategies

▶ Explain the different types of strategic marketing goals and associated growth strategies

▶ Describe the concepts associated with strategic market action

▶ Appreciate the main issues associated with strategy implementation, including the principles of marketing metrics

▶ Explain the key elements of a marketing plan

Case Insight 5.1
3scale

Through its staff and offices in Barcelona and San Francisco, 3scale helps organizations open, manage, and use application programming interfaces (APIs). We speak to Manfred Bortenschlager, API Market Development Director, to find out how the company competes in its marketplace.

Steven Willmott and Martin Tantow founded 3scale in 2007, convinced that the world would become web enabled with APIs (application programming interfaces) as a critical digital infrastructure requirement. The initial 3scale product focused on an API marketplace, providing a matchmaking service between API providers and API consumers. The company quickly shifted to a more powerful business model—providing management capabilities for API providers. Now, 3scale sells an API management product based on monthly subscriptions with different price plans, starting with a free plan in its basic form (freemium, also known as the Software-as-a-Service, SaaS model). This model is successful because it perfectly serves customers' needs for flexibility and scale. Today, 3scale powers the APIs for close to 700 organizations.

Application programming interfaces are a software technology which provide organizations with a novel and effective way of distributing and leveraging digital assets. APIs represent gateways to an organization's data or services (i.e. digital assets), which can be programmed and accessed by software increasing automation, scalability, and efficiency. As an analogy, APIs can be seen as an automatic door to a building with a security mechanism (like a pass code or a chip card). Digital transformation and digital strategies are based on APIs. The 3scale API management product provides the essential security, visibility, and control, so that organizations can define and measure their strategies when using APIs. In terms of value chain and customer requirements, our service uses a B2B2C (business to business to customer) model as follows: API provider (owning and providing digital assets)

serves a developer (developing and distributing web or mobile apps) who serves the end-user (the final consumer of the apps, and APIs).

The most important customer requirements from the developer's perspective are, first, the value of the data or service that the API provides access to (the more unique, the higher the value), and, second, simplicity of access to the API. The most important customer requirements from an end-consumer's perspective are added value to an application via additional functionality. This is often achieved via so-called 'API mashups', where a developer combines the APIs of various API providers to create something new for the end-consumer. Other requirements are 'user experience', which includes ease of use, clarity, consistency, and speed.

3scale operates in a very fast moving industry. To be successful, customer focus is essential. We need to constantly adapt our offering in terms of product features and the pricing model. To achieve that we need to integrate engineering, marketing, and sales processes, and be able to react to change quicker than our competitors. We differentiate between 'self-service' and 'enterprise' customers. Self-service customers adopt the 3scale offer almost without any human interaction, whereas customers on enterprise plans get 24/7 phone support and/or higher guaranteed product reliability. 3scale has three main competitive differentiators.

1   The 3scale product is modular and uses cloud technologies in a unique way. Based on the customer's requirements, they can choose to host

Case Insight 5.1
continued

some of the product modules in 'the cloud' and some on their own IT infrastructure. This gives unmatched availability, scalability, and flexibility.

2   3scale offers the shortest time to value in the market, achieved via a comprehensive self-service model and detailed documentation. Customers can adopt 3scale very quickly and leverage the benefits of APIs instantly.

3   The freemium subscription model is fair and transparent with very competitive pricing. Customers appreciate the low barrier of entry and the subscription model is easy to understand, with no surprises.

One complex problem was that Amazon Web Services (AWS)—based around cloud technologies—launched the Amazon API Gateway product. This was perceived by many observers in the API management market to be a potential threat. With its size and financial resources, the expectation was that it could have a substantial impact on existing players in the market.

The question was: what strategy should we develop to circumvent this competitive threat?

Introduction

Have you ever thought about how organizations organize themselves so that they can make sales, achieve profits, and keep their stakeholders satisfied? This does not happen accidentally. A great deal of thought, discussion, planning, and action needs to occur, which involves getting answers to questions such as which markets the organization should be operating in, what resources are necessary to be successful in these markets, who are the key competitors and what strategies are they using, how can we develop and sustain a competitive advantage, and what is happening in the world that might affect our organization? Indeed, these are some of the key questions facing 3scale in Case Insight 5.1, and you may notice that they refer to issues that represent the strategic context in which organizations operate. These contextual issues can be considered in terms of four main elements, namely (1) the organization (and its resources, skills, and capabilities), (2) the target customers, (3) the firm's competitors, and (4) the wider environment. These are set out in Figure 5.1.

For example, Samsung's strategic context is shaped by its communications expertise and leading-edge technology skills, customers who expect a stream of added value communication-related products, and its main competitor, Apple. In addition, the wider environment is becoming politically more sensitive to climate change issues, terrorism, social change, the repercussions of the economic crisis, and surges in technological development. By understanding and managing these four elements, we can develop a coherent strategic marketing plan through which offerings have a greater chance of success than if no analysis or planning is undertaken. For marketing strategy to be developed successfully, it is necessary to understand an organization's strategic context and to then formulate and fit the strategy to complement the strategic context. Many organizations articulate their strategic context and their intended performance in the markets they target in terms of a framework that defines their vision, mission, values, organizational goals, and organizational strategy.

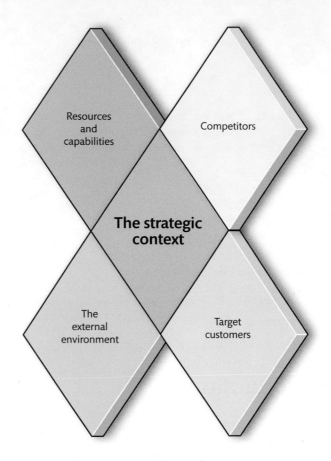

Figure 5.1
The four elements of the strategic context

The **vision** sets out an organization's future. It is a statement about what an organization wants to become, giving shape and direction to an organization's future. A vision should stretch an organization in terms of its current position and performance, yet also help employees feel involved and motivated to want to be part of the organization's future. According to their website, Samsung Electronics' vision for the current decade is to 'Inspire the World, Create the Future'. As part of this vision, Samsung plans to drive $400bn in revenue and become one of the world's top five brands by 2020.

The **mission** represents what the organization wishes to achieve long term. It should be a broad statement of intention, setting out an organization's purpose and direction. It should be oriented to particular markets and customers. A mission applies to all parts of an organization, binding its many elements together. Above all else, however, the mission should provide a reference point for its managers and employees to make decisions concerning which opportunities to pursue and which to ignore. It should aid investment and development decision-making. Table 5.1 gives examples of different mission statements.

Mission statements are sometimes prepared as a public relations exercise or are so generic that they fail to provide sufficient guidelines or inspiration. Some are not realistic and should be avoided. For example, to expect an airport such as Adelaide or Hong Kong to become the largest airport in the world is infeasible. Good mission statements are market, not product, oriented. For example, the product-oriented approach 'we make and sell lorries and trucks' is too general and runs the risk of becoming outdated and redundant. By focusing on the needs of the customers,

Table 5.1 A selection of mission statements

Organization	Mission statement
Tesco	To create value for customers to earn their lifetime loyalty.
Coca-Cola	▪ To refresh the world ▪ To inspire moments of optimism and happiness ▪ To create value and make a difference
SAS	We provide Best Value for Time and Money to Nordic Travellers whatever the purpose of their journey.
Oxfam	Oxfam works with others to overcome poverty and suffering
IBM	We strive to lead in the invention, development, and manufacture of the industry's most advanced information technologies, including computer systems, software, storage systems, and microelectronics. We translate these advanced technologies into value for our customers through our professional solutions, services, and consulting businesses worldwide.
JCB	Our mission is to grow our company by providing innovative, strong, high performance products and solutions to meet our global customers' needs. We will support our world-class products by providing superior customer care. Our care extends to the environment and the community. We want to help build a better future for our children, where hard work and dedication are given their just reward.

the mission can be more realistic and have a much longer lifespan. So, 'we transport your products quickly and safely to your customers', or 'logistical solutions for your company', provides a market approach to the mission statement. Amazon.com does not per se sell books, Kindles, and DVDs (product approach); much better to say that Amazon.com 'strives to be Earth's most customer-centric company where people can find and discover virtually everything they want to buy online'. Similarly, Haier, the leading Chinese manufacturer, do not just make home appliances, 'they make lives more convenient and comfortable through innovative appliances'.

Visit the Online Resource Centre and complete Internet Activity 5.1 to learn more about the use of mission and vision statements by different organizations and their implications for marketing activities.

An organization's **values** must coincide with its vision and mission, because they define how people should behave with each other in the organization and help shape how the goals will be achieved. Organizational values define the acceptable interpersonal and operating standards of behaviour. They govern and guide the behaviour of individuals within the organization. Organizations that identify and develop a clear, concise, and shared meaning of values and beliefs shape the organizational culture and provide strategic direction.

Organizational values are important because they can help to guide and constrain not only behaviour but also the recruitment and selection decisions. Without them, individuals tend to pursue behaviours that are in line with their own individual value systems, which may lead to inappropriate behaviours and a failure to achieve the overall goals. However, values per se do not drive a business. As Williams (2010) informs us, they drive the people within the business. For values to be of value and have meaning, they must be internalized within the organization.

Market Insight 5.1
Values Matter

IKEA has claimed for many years that their values have affected the way they work. 'These values are as important at an IKEA store in Ireland as they are in a photo studio in Sweden or a distribution centre in China'.

Humbleness and willpower

We respect each other, our customers and our suppliers. Using our willpower means we get things done.

Leadership by example

Our managers try to set a good example, and expect the same of IKEA co-workers.

Daring to be different

We question old solutions and, if we have a better idea, we are willing to change.

Togetherness and enthusiasm

Together, we have the power to solve seemingly insoluble problems. We do it all the time.

Cost-consciousness

Low prices are impossible without low costs, so we proudly achieve good results with small resources.

Constant desire for renewal

Change is good. We know that adapting to customer demands with innovative solutions saves money and contributes to a better everyday life at home.

Accept and delegate responsibility

We promote co-workers with potential and stimulate them to surpass their expectations. Sure, people make mistakes. But they learn from them!

However, few organizations set out how their values are derived. IBM is an exception. In an open statement Samuel J. Palmisano, Chairman, President, and Chief Executive Officer, recalls the way in which IBM's current values originated. He refers to the importance and time spent thinking, debating, and determining IBM's fundamentals. He states that in a time of great change, IBM needed to affirm reasons for being, for setting out how the company is different to others and what should drive individual employee behaviour. He says, 'Importantly, we needed to find a way to engage everyone in the company and get them to speak up on these important issues. Given the realities of a smart, global, independent-minded, 21st-century workforce like ours, I don't believe something as vital and personal as values could be dictated from the top.'

Samuel J. Palmisano, IBM's Chairman, President and Chief Executive Officer, has worked openly to develop an inclusive culture based on agreed values.
Source: Gage Skidmore/ Wikimedia Commons/ CC-BY-SA-3.0.

Market Insight 5.1
continued

So, for a three-day period, all 319,000 IBMers around the world were invited to engage in an open 'values jam' on the global intranet. Following much open debate, honesty, and involvement the employees determined the following values.

- Dedication to every client's success.

- Innovation that matters, for our company and for the world.

- Trust and personal responsibility in all relationships.

The statement concludes with 'To me, it's also just common sense. In today's world, where everyone is so interconnected and interdependent, it is simply essential that we work for each other's success. If we're going to solve the biggest, thorniest and most widespread problems in business and society, we have to innovate in ways that truly matter. And we have to do all this by taking personal responsibility for all of our relationships—with clients, colleagues, partners, investors and the public at large. This is IBM's mission as an enterprise, and a goal toward which we hope to work with many others, in our industry and beyond.'

Sources: Based on http://www.ikea.com/; http://www.ibm.com/ibm/values/us/.

Theory into Practice

The IBM example supports the generally accepted ideas that an organization's values should be about what an organization wants to become, by giving shape and direction to its future. IBM's vision, and the process by which it was achieved, demonstrates the importance not only of stretching itself in terms of its performance, but also of involving employees and embracing them so that they are motivated to want to be part of IBM's future.

Notice also how IBM's values complement its vision and mission. By defining how all employees should behave and the importance of relationships within the organization, IBM has helped to shape how their goals can be accomplished.

Related Topics:
mission statements; corporate strategy; SWOT.

1 How do these two sets of values differ?

2 What might be the impact on employees of seven rather than three sets of values?

3 Find a third set of values, this time from a not-for-profit organization, and compare these with those of IKEA or IBM.

Organizational goals at the strategic level represent what should be achieved—the outcomes of the organization's various activities. These may be articulated in terms of profit, market share, share value, return on investment, or numbers of customers served. In some cases, the long term may not be a viable period and a short-term focus is absolutely essential. For example, should an organization's financial position become precarious it may be necessary to focus on short-term cash strategies to remain solvent and so remove any threat arising from a takeover or administrators being called in prior to bankruptcy.

Organization or **corporate strategy** is the means by which organizational resources are matched with the needs of the organization's operations environment. Corporate strategy involves bringing together human resources, logistics, production, operations, marketing, IT, and the financial parts of an organization into a coherent strategic plan that supports, reinforces, and accomplishes the organization's goals in the most effective and efficient way. In this chapter, we are concerned with the make-up of marketing strategy and how it should support and reinforce corporate strategy.

In some very large organizations the planning process is made complicated and difficult because the organization operates in significantly different markets. In these cases the organization creates **strategic business units** or SBUs. Each SBU assumes the role of a separate company and creates its own strategies and plans to achieve its corporate goals. So, the Indian company Tata operates through seven SBUs, namely Information Technology and Communications, Engineering, Materials, Services, Energy, Consumer Products, and Chemicals. Each of these Tata companies operates independently. Royal Philips Electronics use four SBUs: Domestic Appliances and Personal Care, Lighting, Medical Systems, and Consumer Electronics. All of these represent significantly different markets, each with their own characteristics, customer needs, and competitors.

According to McDonald (2002: 37), a global guru of marketing planning, the strategic marketing planning process consists of a series of logical steps to be worked through to arrive at a marketing plan. These steps can be aggregated into four phases. The first phase is concerned with setting the right mission and corporate goals. The second involves reviewing the current situation or context in which the organization is operating. The third phase is used to formulate strategy, and the final phase considers the allocation of resources necessary to implement and monitor the plan.

A broad level, the strategic marketing planning process is as follows.

- At the corporate level the organization sets out its overall vision, mission, and values.

- Measurable corporate goals are established that apply to the whole organization.

- A series of analyses and audits are undertaken to understand the external situation in which the organization intends to operate and the resources available to be used.

- Strategies are formulated and probable outcomes estimated.

- Depending on the size of the organization, the range of businesses (SBUs) and/or offerings is determined, and resources are allocated to help and support each one.

- Each business and/or offering then develops detailed functional and competitive strategies and plans, such as a marketing strategy and plan.

- The plan is implemented and the results measured and used to feed into the next planning cycle.

Marketing strategy and planning should support and contribute to the overall company strategy. However, it should also be understood that marketing strategy and planning can occur at the business, offering, or market level (see Figure 5.2).

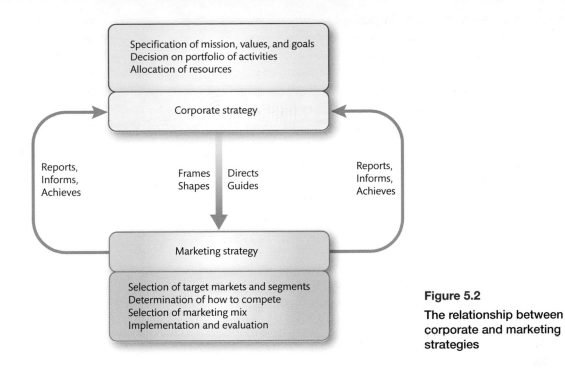

Figure 5.2

The relationship between corporate and marketing strategies

Research Insight 5.1

To take your learning further, you might wish to read this influential paper.

Mintzberg, H. (1987). The strategy concept: Five Ps for strategy. *California Management Review*, 30(1), 11–26.

Mintzberg's paper made an important contribution because it argued that strategy should not be regarded as a linear sequential planning process. He shows that strategy can also be interpreted as a plan, ploy, pattern, perspective, and position.

Visit the Online Resource Centre to read the abstract and access the full paper.

Strategic Marketing Planning—Activities

The development of a strategic marketing plan is a complex and involved process. It does not occur in linear logical steps as implied earlier, but certain key aspects can be identified. These aspects concern three broad activities that are necessary when considering the development of marketing strategy and will form the framework through which we examine this topic (see Figure 5.3).

Figure 5.3 shows that it is necessary to first develop knowledge and understanding of the marketplace, referred to here as **strategic market analysis**. Secondly, it is necessary to determine what the marketing strategy should achieve, i.e. what are the strategic marketing

Figure 5.3
**Three key activities of marketing
strategy development**

goals that need to be accomplished? The third decision area concerns how the goals are to be achieved. This relates directly to strategic market action, i.e. how the strategies should be developed as plans and how these plans should be implemented. These three activities form the basis of this chapter and are considered next.

Strategic Market Analysis

The starting point of the marketing strategy process is the development of knowledge and understanding about the target market(s) identified as part of the corporate strategy. Different people in the organization have varying levels of market knowledge and expertise, some of it accurate and up to date, but some out of date and inaccurate. It is therefore crucial that all people involved in the strategy process are well informed with accurate, pertinent, and up-to-date information.

In Chapter 4 we saw how PESTLE and environmental scanning processes can be used to understand and make sense of the external environment. We considered Porter's (1985) Five Forces model to understand industry dynamics and how firms should compete strategically if they are to be successful in the performance environment. We also learned about the key elements necessary to appreciate our competitors' actions and intentions. In addition we had insight into the importance of understanding the internal environment and how a firm's resources need to complement the external and performance environments. The task now is to assimilate this information, to bring it together in a form that can be easily understood.

SWOT Analysis

Perhaps the most common analytical tool is **SWOT analysis**. SWOT stands for Strengths, Weaknesses, Opportunities, and Threats. It is a series of checklists derived from the marketing audit and PESTLE analysis, and is presented as internal strengths and weaknesses, and external opportunities or threats. Strengths and weaknesses relate to the internal resources and capabilities of the organization, as perceived by customers (Piercy, 2002).

■ A strength is something an organization is good at doing or something that gives it particular credibility and market advantage.

■ A weakness is something an organization lacks or performs in an inferior way in comparison with others.

Opportunities and threats are externally oriented issues that can potentially influence the performance of an organization or offering. Information about these elements is generated through PESTLE analysis.

- An opportunity is the potential to advance the organization by the development and satisfaction of an unfulfilled market need.
- A threat is something that at some time in the future may destabilize and/or reduce the potential performance of the organization.

SWOT analysis is used to determine an organization's strategic position. It highlights the need for a strategy to produce a strong fit between the internal capability (strengths and weaknesses) and the external situation (opportunities and threats). SWOT helps to sort through the information generated in the audit, to identify the key issues, and prompts thought about converting weaknesses into strengths and threats into opportunities, i.e. generating conversion strategies. For example, some companies have developed and run call centres for their own internal use, but saw opportunities to use their strength to run call centres for other companies. For example, a few years ago, one major computer company only used its call centre during the day. An opportunity was spotted to run the call centre at night, routing calls for a nationwide pizza company.

In inexperienced hands, SWOT often leads to long lists of items. Although the SWOT process may lead to the generation of these lists, the analyst should be attempting to identify the key strengths and weaknesses and the key opportunities and threats. These key elements should impact on strategy; if they don't, they should not be in the analysis. A strength is not a strength if it does not have strategic implications and is not a strength in relation to competitors.

Once the three or four elements of each part of the SWOT matrix have been derived then a number of pertinent questions need to be asked.

1 Does the organization do something far better than its rivals? If it does, this is known as a competitive advantage (distinctive competence, differential advantage), and can lead to a competitive edge.

2 Which of the organization's weaknesses does our strategy need to correct and is it competitively vulnerable?

3 Which opportunities can be pursued and are there the necessary resources and capabilities to exploit them?

4 Which strategies are necessary to defend against the key threats?

Figure 5.4 depicts a SWOT grid for a small digital media agency. The outcome of a successful SWOT analysis is a series of decisions that help develop and formulate strategy and goals. Note that there are no more than four items in any one category, not a whole list of ten or so items. It is important to prioritize and make a judgement about what is really key. The actions that follow the identification of key issues should be based around matching opportunities with strengths and weaknesses with threats. In this example, it may be possible to diversify into professional services, a **niche market** (an opportunity), using particular contractors who have knowledge and relevant expertise (a strength).

Weaknesses need to be addressed, not avoided. Some can be converted into strengths, others into opportunities. In this example, entering the professional services market would probably increase the number of customers and enable premium rates to be earned.

Strengths	Weaknesses
Quick to respond to changes in the marketing environment	Too much work from a few clients and at non-premium rates
Flat management encourages fast decision-making	Few project management skills
Use of contractors enables flexibility—lowers employment costs/finance and improves customers' perception of expertise	High office and finance costs Low customer base
Opportunities	Threats
Emerging markets such as professional services (e.g. dentists, lawyers, surveyors)	Larger media houses buying business
New distribution channels	Speed of technological advances
Tax incentives to encourage eCommerce	Contractors have low levels of loyalty

Figure 5.4

A SWOT analysis for a small digital media agency

Threats need to be nullified. For example, by building relationships with key contractors (suppliers) and selected larger media houses, these threats might be dissipated, and even developed into strengths.

Visit the Online Resource Centre and complete Internet Activity 5.2 to learn more about the use of SWOT analysis.

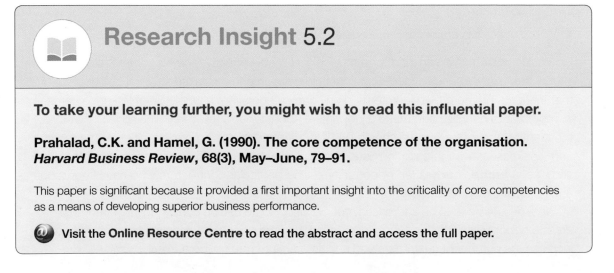

Research Insight 5.2

To take your learning further, you might wish to read this influential paper.

Prahalad, C.K. and Hamel, G. (1990). The core competence of the organisation. *Harvard Business Review*, 68(3), May–June, 79–91.

This paper is significant because it provided a first important insight into the criticality of core competencies as a means of developing superior business performance.

Visit the Online Resource Centre to read the abstract and access the full paper.

Strategic Marketing Goals

The purpose of strategic market analysis is to help managers understand the nature of an industry, the way firms behave competitively within the industry, and how competition is generally undertaken. From this information it becomes easier to determine exactly what the marketing strategy should actually achieve, i.e. what the strategic marketing goals should be.

There are several types of strategic objective but four main ones are considered here. These are niche, hold, harvest, and divest goals, and they are considered briefly. However, the section that follows considers a further objective, namely growth (see Figure 5.5).

Niche objectives are often the most suitable when firms operate in a market dominated by a major competitor and financial resources are limited. A niche can either be a small segment or even a small part of a segment. Niche markets arise because it is not economic for the leading competitors to enter this segment because these customers have special needs and the leading firm does not want to devote resources in this way. To be successful in niche markets, it is important to have a strongly differentiated product offering, supported by a high level of service. The Australian Government identified several niche markets when exploring the development of its tourism business. It identified sports, cycling seniors, culture and the arts, backpackers, health, people with disabilities, caravanning and camping, food, wine, and agri-tourism as potential niche markets.

Hold objectives are concerned with defence. They are designed to prevent and fend off attack from aggressive competitors. Market leaders are the most likely to adopt a holding strategy as they are prone to attack from new entrants and their closest rivals as they strive for the most market share. Market leadership is important as it generally drives positive cash flows, confers privileges such as strong bargaining positions with suppliers, and enhances image and reputation. Holding strategies can take a number of forms, varying from 'doing nothing', in order to maintain market equilibrium, to implementing a counter-offensive defence, to withdrawing from a market completely.

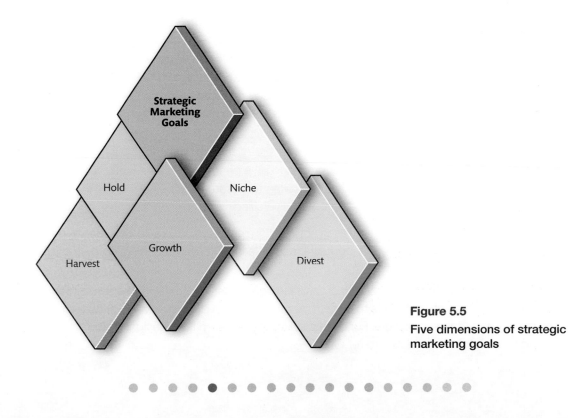

Figure 5.5

Five dimensions of strategic marketing goals

Australian tourism has been developed around the identification of niche markets
Source: © James Fisher/Tourism Australia.

Harvesting objectives are often employed in mature markets as firms/offerings enter a decline phase. The goal is to maximize short-term profits and stimulate a positive cash flow. By stripping out marketing communications and research and development (R&D) it becomes possible to generate cash for use elsewhere. These funds generate new offerings, support 'stars', or turn 'question marks' into 'dogs' (see Chapter 4).

Divest objectives are sometimes necessary when offerings continue to incur losses and generate negative cash flows. Divestment can follow on naturally from a harvesting strategy. Typically, low share offerings in declining markets are prime candidates to be divested. Divestment may be actioned by selling off the offering should a suitable buyer be available, or simply withdrawing from the market. For example, Procter & Gamble (P&G) divested the Sunny Delight orange drink brand, General Motors sold off Saab to sports car manufacturer Spyker, and Ford sold off Jaguar to the Indian company Tata. In 2014 Johnson & Johnson divested its Ortho Clinical Diagnostics unit, which makes blood-screening equipment and laboratory blood tests, to the Carlyle Group.

Growth

The vast majority of organizations consider growth to be a primary objective. However, there are different forms of growth and care needs to be taken to ensure that the right growth goals are selected. Growth can be intensive, integrated, or diversified.

- **Intensive** growth refers to concentrating activities on markets and/or offerings that are familiar. By increasing market share or introducing new offerings to an established market, growth is achieved by intensifying activities.

- **Integrative** growth occurs where an organization continues to work with the same offerings and the same markets but starts to perform some of the activities in the value chain that were previously undertaken by others. For example, Benetton moved from designing and manufacturing their clothing products into retailing.

	Present Products	New Products
Present Markets	Market Penetration	Product Development
New Markets	Market Development	Diversification

Figure 5.6
Ansoff's matrix
Source: Adapted from Ansoff (1957).

- Growth through **diversification** refers to developments outside the current chain of value-adding activities. This type of growth brings new value chain activities because the firm is operating with new offerings and in new markets.

The idea that growth is allied to product–market relationships is important, and Ansoff (1957) proposed that organizations should first consider whether new or established products are to be delivered in new or established markets. His product–market matrix (Figure 5.6), otherwise known as Ansoff's matrix, is an important first step in deciding what the marketing strategy should be. The product–market matrix is examined further in Chapter 7.

A strategy employed by several large corporations targets new or adapted products at extremely poor people in underdeveloped countries. Referred to as 'bottom-of-the-pyramid' (BoP) strategies (Prahalad, 2004), the approach requires firms to offer products at extremely low prices to the poorest individuals. By managing an extremely low cost base, low margins can be generated. Respectable profits can be achieved, however, because of the huge sales volumes. For example, Bangladesh is regarded as an attractive market as it has a population of over 163m. Unilever sold its Wheel brand detergent to low-income consumers in India using this strategy (Payaud, 2014).

Genuine BoP marketing strategies are considered to involve three main elements. First, they are directed at the very poor and feature both affordability and availability. Second, they have a consumer orientation featuring adaptability and consumer education. Third, they are considered to be both fair and inclusive growth, so that local communities are able to participate in all stages of the value chain. See Market Insight 5.2 for examples of this strategy.

Market Insight 5.2
Targetting the Bottom of the Pyramid

Nestlé's strategy involves developing a wide range of popularly positioned products (PPPs) for low income consumers around the world. PPPs include culinary products, beverages, and dairy and confectionery products sold under a number of major global brands, including Maggi, Nido, and Nescafé. One such PPP, developed in 2009, comprises high quality food products that provide nutritional value to low income consumers. These products are sold at an affordable price and in appropriate formats to address the needs of some 3bn lower income consumers worldwide. PPPs may be fortified with micronutrients that help to address the deficiencies (iron, zinc, iodine, and vitamin A) that are most prevalent among lower income consumers. For example, to help address iodine deficiency, Nestlé developed iodine-enriched Maggi products (bouillons, seasonings, and noodles) using iodized salt.

PPPs are manufactured in single-serve packs which meet the need of consumers for both affordability and convenience. Single-serves are adapted to on-the-go consumption, which is very popular.

In Cameroon, consumers prefer to buy Nido, a powdered milk, in 26-gram single-serves because the quantity corresponds exactly to what is needed for a glass of milk. This avoids over-consumption and waste. Single-serves are also convenient because

Market Insight 5.2
continued

they avoid problems linked to conservation such as humidity, pests, and a lack of refrigeration. Products are manufactured locally using local perishable agricultural raw materials produced through Nestlé-trained local subcontractors. Cooking caravans travelling through the villages are used to inform consumers about the product benefits and how they should be used.

P&G's Children's Safe Drinking Water Program (CSDW) provides water purification packets on a not-for-profit basis. In partnership with CARE, PSI, and World Vision, the programme supplies more than 5bn litres of purified drinking water to more than 65 countries. P&G announced that it would provide 2bn litres of clean drinking water every year by distributing 200m P&G water purification packets every year in the developing world (Procter & Gamble Report, 2012). P&G's overall marketing strategy however, involves distributing their international brands to BoP markets, with pack sizes adapted to complement local purchasing power. This indicates that, unlike Danone who are involved with

food products, P&G are not so concerned with the environment or the inclusion of local communities in procurement, production, or distribution processes.

Sources: Payaud (2014); http://www.csdw.org/csdw/index.shtml; http://www.nestlenido.com/#aboutnido.

P&G's Children's Safe Drinking Water Program provides water purification packets on a not-for-profit basis.
Source: Photo courtesy of Procter & Gamble.

Theory into Practice

The PPPs can be considered in the light of the three main elements that are considered to constitute BoP strategies. First it is clear that PPPs are directed at the very poor (affordability and availability) and that they are consumer oriented, as they are adaptable and help to

inform or educate consumers. Evidence that the third element is present—that they are considered to be both fair and inclusive so that local communities are able to participate in all stages of the value chain—is not entirely clear as this element is not always fully implemented.

Related Topics:

mission and values; strategic analysis; strategic goals; competitive advantage; generic strategies.

1 **Apply the elements that identify BoP products to P&G's CSDW programme.**

2 **Why do you believe P&G and Nestlé are involved with BoP strategies?**

3 **Find another example of a BoP strategy.**

Strategic Market Action

The final set of marketing strategy activities concerns the identification of the most appropriate way of achieving the goals and putting the plan into action—the implementation phase.

There is no proven formula or tool kit that managers can use simply because of the many internal and external environmental factors. Managers draw upon experience to know which strategies are more likely to be successful than others. Next, we consider ideas about competitive advantage, generic strategies, competitive positioning, strategic intent, and marketing planning and implementation (see Figure 5.7).

Competitive Advantage

According to Hoffman (2000: 6), **competitive advantage** is 'the prolonged benefit of implementing some unique value-creating strategy not simultaneously being implemented by any current or potential competitors along with the inability to duplicate the benefits of this strategy'. In other words, sustainable competitive advantage (SCA) is achieved when an organization has a significant and sustainable edge over its competitors when attracting buyers. Advantage can also be secured by coping with the competitive forces better than its rivals. Advantage can be developed in many different ways. Some organizations have an advantage simply because they are the best-known organization or brand in the market. Some achieve it by producing the best-quality offering or having attributes that other offerings do not have. For example, some pharmaceutical brands have an advantage while patent protection exists. As soon as the patent expires and competitors can produce generic versions of the drug, the advantage is lost. Some organizations have the lowest price, whereas others provide the best support and service in the industry. Whatever the advantage, the superiority has to be sustainable through time.

According to Porter (1985), the conditions necessary for the achievement of SCA are as follows.

1 The customer consistently perceives a positive difference between the offerings provided by a company and its competitors.

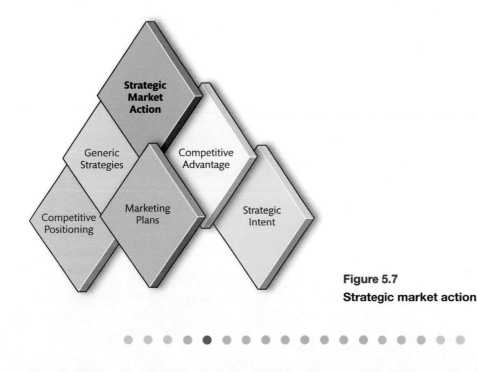

Figure 5.7
Strategic market action

Research Insight 5.3

To take your learning further, you might wish to read this influential paper.

Day, G.S. and Wensley, R. (1988). Assessing advantage: a framework for diagnosing competitive superiority. *Journal of Marketing*, 52(2), April, 1–20.

As the title suggests this paper considers a framework for identifying competitive advantage. It achieves this by first considering the elements of competitive advantage and then brings together both competitor- and customer-focused elements in order to identify 'points of superiority'.

Visit the Online Resource Centre to read the abstract and access the full paper.

2 The perceived difference results from the company's relatively greater capability.

3 The perceived difference persists for a reasonable period of time. SCA is only durable as long as it is not easily imitated.

Generic Strategies

If the importance of achieving a competitive advantage is accepted as a crucial aspect of a successful marketing strategy, then it is necessary to understand how strategies can lead to the development of sustainable competitive advantages. Porter (1985) proposed that there are two essential routes to achieving above average performance. These are to become the lowest cost producer or to differentiate the offering until it is of superior value to the customer. These strategies can be implemented in either broad (mass) or narrow (focused) markets. Porter suggested that these give rise to three generic strategies: overall cost leadership, differentiation, and focus strategies.

Cost leadership does not mean a lower price, although lower prices are often used to attract customers. By having the lowest cost structure, an organization can offer standard offerings at acceptable levels of quality, yet still generate above average profit margins. If attacked by a competitor using lower prices, the low cost leader has a far bigger cushion than its competitors. Charging a lower price than rivals is not the critical point. The competitive advantage is derived from *how* the organization exploits its cost/price ratio. By reinvesting the profit, for example by improving product quality, investing more in product development, or building extra capacity, long-run superiority is more likely to be achieved.

A **differentiation** strategy requires that all value chain activities are geared to the creation of offerings that are valued by, and which satisfy, the needs of particular broad segments. By identifying particular customer groups, where each group has a discrete set of needs, a product can be differentiated from its competitors. The fashion brand Zara differentiated itself by reformulating its value chain so that it became the fastest high street brand to design, produce, distribute, and make fashion clothing available in its shops.

Customers are sometimes prepared to pay a higher price, a price premium, for offerings that deliver superior or extra value. For example, the Starbucks coffee brand is strongly differentiated

Waitrose seeks to differentiate itself from other supermarkets in various ways, including the exterior appearance of its stores
Source: © Education Images/Getty.

and valued, as consumers are willing to pay higher prices to enjoy the Starbucks experience. However, differentiation can be achieved by low prices, as evidenced through the success of low cost airlines, such as the UK's Ryanair and easyJet.

Offerings can be differentiated using a variety of criteria; indeed, each element of the marketing mix is capable of providing the means for successful long-term differentiation. Differentiation can lead to greater levels of brand loyalty. For example, in contrast to low cost ASDA, Waitrose provides a strongly differentiated supermarket service.

Focus strategies are used by organizations to seek gaps in broad market segments or find gaps in competitors' ranges. In other words, focus strategies help to seek out unfulfilled market needs. The focused operator then concentrates all value chain activities on a narrow range of offerings. Focus strategies can be oriented to being the lowest cost producer for the particular segment or offering a differentiated offering for which the narrow target segment is willing to pay a higher price. This means that there are two options for a company wishing to follow a focus strategy. One is low cost and the other is differentiation, but both occur within a particular narrow segment. The difference between a broad differentiator and a focused differentiator is that the former bases its strategy on attributes valued across a number of markets, whereas the latter seeks to meet the needs of particular segments within a market.

Porter argues that, to achieve competitive advantage, organizations must achieve one of these three generic strategies. He argues that to fail to be strategically explicit results in organizations being 'stuck in the middle'. This means that they achieve below average returns and have no competitive advantage. It has been observed, however, that some organizations have been able to pursue low cost and differentiated strategies simultaneously. For example, an organization that develops a large market share through differentiation and by creating very strong brands or through technological innovation may well also become the cost leader.

Competitive Positioning

Having collected industry information, analysed competitors, and considered our resources, perhaps the single most important aspect of developing marketing strategy is to decide how to compete in selected target markets. A key decision that arises is: what position do we want in the market?

The position that a product adopts in a market is a general reflection of its market share. Four positions can be identified: market leader, market challenger, market follower, and market nicher, and each has particular characteristics, as set out in Table 5.2.

There are two main reasons for understanding the competitive positions adopted by companies. The first is to understand the way various firms are positioned in the market, and from that

Table 5.2 Types of market position

	Characteristics	Prime strategies
Market leader	The market leader has the single largest share of the market. Market leadership is important as it is these offerings and brands that can shape the nature of competition in the market, set out standards relating to price, quality, speed of innovation, and communications, as well as influencing the key distribution channels.	Attack the market: create new uses, users, or increase frequency of use. Defend the position: regular innovation, larger ranges, price cutting and discounts, increased promotion.
Market challengers	Products that aspire to the leadership position are referred to as market challengers. These may be positioned as number two, three, or even four in the market. They actively seek market share and use aggressive strategies to take share from all of their rivals.	Attack the market leader: use pricing, new product attributes, sharp increase in advertising spend. Attack rivals: special offers and limited editions, offer superior competitive advantages. Maintain status quo.
Market followers	These firms have low market shares and do not have the resources to be serious competitors. They pose no threat to the market leader or challengers and often adopt me-too strategies when the market leader takes an initiative.	Avoid hostile attacks on rivals. Copy the market leader and provide good quality products that are well differentiated. Focus on differentiation and profits, not market share.
Market nichers	Nichers are specialists. They select small segments within target markets that larger companies fail to exploit. They develop specialized marketing mixes designed to meet the needs of their customers.	Provide high level of specialization: geographic, proposition, service, customer group. Provide tight fit between market needs and the organization's resources.

they can understand where the company is currently positioned and decide where it wants to be positioned. This shapes the nature and quantity of the resources required and the strategies to be pursued. Some of these strategies are set out in Table 5.2.

Market Insight 5.3
Strategies to Span the Skies

Lower fuel prices and an improving economic environment, were partly responsible for the near 6% growth in airline passenger traffic in 2014 and for the predictions of continued growth in the period up to 2020. China and the Middle East have experienced the greatest growth, followed by Europe, North America, and then the Asia–Pacific region (excluding China) and Latin America.

Growth in the air travel market means that airlines have to make strategic decisions about how to grow their businesses. Airlines can grow by adding more frequencies and nonstop markets to their networks, but this can lead to a fragmentation of their existing networks. The other approach is to increase airplane capacity and/or size. The evidence indicates that most of the air travel growth has been met by an increase in new nonstop markets (airport pairs) and by growth of frequency.

Airlines need to make decisions about the type of aircraft that they wish to use, and this decision reflects the business model the airline decides to pursue. Low cost carriers (LCCs) represent a fast-growing business segment. Norwegian, Southwest, easyJet, Ryanair, and Jetstar are typical low cost carriers. Often referred to as 'no-frills' airlines, they have evolved through strategies which provide customers with low seat prices, but fees for other services such as baggage and food. This model has been referred to as 'pay-for-everything-extra-but-a-seat model'. These carriers generally operate from secondary airports and use a single type of aircraft to increase utilization rates. For example, Southwest's entire fleet consists of Boeing 737 aircraft. LCCs rely on direct marketing, offer a single-class product, do not provide in-flight meals, and do not offer frequent flyer programmes, all of which help to keep employment costs low.

Norwegian is the third-largest low cost airline in Europe and introduces new aircraft to its fleet on a regular basis. This is because new aircraft consume less fuel and require less maintenance, which in turn

enables Norwegian to offer low fares. New aircraft offer improved environmental credentials and are more comfortable than their predecessors.

LCCs compete with mainstream, or legacy, airlines who offer a tiered range of seating products, in-flight meals and entertainment, airport lounges, and frequent flyer programmes, all at varying premium fares dependent on seat location.

What might have been a clear separation between the offerings of these two types of carrier has started to become more obscure. Legacy carriers have been uncomfortable with the growth of LCCs, and both Delta and British Airways have recently introduced a new type of fare which is only applied to routes that compete with low cost carriers. Referred to as a 'budget' or 'basic economy' fare, these tickets carry no refunds, upgrades, or complimentary pre-boarding and there is a much reduced number of perks that a frequent flyer might experience.

Sources: Martin (2015); Anon. (2014); Uszynski (2013); http://www.norwegian.com.

Norwegian is the third-largest low cost airline in Europe. Part of its strategy is to introduce new aircraft on a regular basis.
Source: © DyziO/Shutterstock.

Market Insight 5.3
continued

Theory into Practice

Many early ideas about competitive marketing strategies have developed from the military and are based on approaches to warfare. Two main approaches can be identified, based on two classical works on military strategy, Sun Tzu's *The Art of War* and Clausewitz's *On War*. Fundamentally, these are **attack strategies** and on **defence strategies**. Within each there are variations; for example, flanking, pre-emptive, bypass, and contraction strategies. For more information, see Macdonald and Neupert (2005).

The growth of LCCs such as Ryanair and easyJet have been based upon flanking attacks on legacy carriers, such as British Airways and Delta. BA served broad markets with a highly differentiated service and ignored the low cost no-frills niche segment. Ryanair, and other LCCs, spotted the flanking opportunity and have established themselves in the relatively new market.

Related Topics:
strategic analysis; strategic goals; competitive advantage; generic strategies.

1 **How might the attack and defence strategies be used to interpret the emergence of 'basic economy' fares by certain legacy carriers?**

2 **If you were marketing director at Norwegian, how would you establish a competitive advantage?**

3 **Which types of growth strategy might legacy carriers pursue?**

@ Visit the **Online Resource Centre** and access Internet Activity 5.3 to learn more about business planning in the airline market.

www.bplans.com/airline_business_plan/executive_summary_fc.php

Networks, Cooperation, and Relationships

Ideas about strategy have developed from those based on competition through attack and defence strategies, considered in Market Insight 5.3. An alternative perspective is to consider ways in which customer value can be increased through cooperation. By working cooperatively with other companies and their brands, relationships evolve. These in turn provide strong opportunities to add value through the differentiation of brands and considerable competitive advantage.

In order to develop collaborative inter-organizational relationships it is necessary to consider an organization's whole system, or network, of stakeholder relationships. This is because networks hold together partly through 'an elaborate pattern of interdependence and reciprocity' (Achrol, 1997: 61). Indeed, it is the network of relationships that provides the context within which exchange behaviours occur.

Cooperative relationships within these networks benefit participants through shared knowledge about offerings, markets, and competitors, can lead to improvements in product and brand performance, and help to develop stronger market positions, enabling the more efficient use of resources (Harbison and Pekar, 1998). This all adds up to a unique form of differentiation that can be of significant value to customers. For example, Cisco have a Strategic Ecosystem Group, which is responsible for collaborating with partner firms such as Ericsson, Inspur (China), and Apple. The common goal is to collaborate and build next generation offerings together, before taking them to market through Cisco's channels (Dix, 2016).

At the corporate level, cooperative relationships, sometimes referred to as alliances, can be considered as a spectrum. At one end, cooperation is based around simple transactions. At the other end, cooperation can be formally established through a stand-alone organization where both parties share ownership.

Outsourcing and renewable purchasing agreements are relatively short-term cooperative arrangements. Information sharing can be seen through agreements to distribute offerings, licensing and technological collaboration represents resource and asset sharing, while cooperation based on share ownership is normally seen in mergers and acquisition activity, which has a long-term perspective. In 2012, telecommunications leaders T-Mobile and Orange developed a jointly owned company, Everything Everywhere or EE. The company combined the skills and resources of both parent organizations, particularly in network architecture and branding.

The detail concerning these various arrangements is not the focus of the strategy. What lies behind the concept of cooperation is the competitive advantage that can be developed. In particular, competitors are usually unable to determine how performance is achieved through these alliances, and even if they can, it is exceedingly difficult to replicate as they do not have the necessary or complementary resources and do not have the same history of investments. All organizations in a cooperative arrangement, sometimes called a network alliance, have an advantage over their rival organizations outside an alliance. However, not all alliances and mergers are successful; indeed a large number of them fail. For example, the merger between Daimler and Chrysler in 1998 proved troublesome immediately because of the clash of cultures and values between the German and US organizations. In 2007 the merger was dissolved when it was decided that both entities would be more profitable separated rather than continue as a paired unit.

At a marketing level, alliances can be developed through key distributors and retailers to control the distribution channel. Relationships with prominent or geographically important dealers provide opportunities for exclusive distribution to reach target markets. Relationships can also be developed with strategically important customers. These customers are referred to as key accounts, and a large number of resources are often channelled into developing and supporting these accounts (see Chapter 12). In many markets, there is little difference between offerings, so organizations try to differentiate themselves based on the services they provide their customers both before and after a purchase has been made. Relationships between customer and supplier can be strengthened through the provision of services, as the service is perceived to offer added value.

Relationships can also be developed with consumers. Marketing strategies designed to retain customers often use loyalty schemes and customer retention programmes. These are supported by database management and marketing facilities. Relationships can also develop through branding. Some consumers develop a strong affinity with a brand to the extent that they want to share their relationship with others and talk openly (word-of-mouth communication) about their positive brand experiences. Relationships with suppliers are important simply because competitive advantages can be developed through cost reduction, speed to market, and product differentiation.

Marketing strategy should be founded on developing customer value and this can be achieved through a strategy based on building cooperative relationships with a network of suppliers, customers, distributors, and other strategically relevant stakeholders. The centrality of cooperation and relationships within marketing has become an important concept for both organizations and marketing academics. Marketing has evolved from ideas that are based solely around the 4Ps (see Chapter 1). Now marketers think and act in terms of the different types of relationships that an organization has and try to find ways of improving the right relationships with the right customers. This is referred to as relationship marketing (see Chapters 1 and 15).

Platform Strategies

The network approach not only supports the idea of collaboration and relationship development, but its principles underpin the basis on which contemporary competitive activity is beginning to be undertaken.

Ideas about conventional strategy have been based around a linear value chain approach which considers successive supplier/distributor participants adding value as a product moves along a chain to be consumed by end-user customers. van Alstyne *et al*. (2016) refer to this as a **pipeline** effect.

Today, firms such as Apple combine the pipeline approach with a new **platform strategy**. For example, the iPhone and its operating system enable two sets of participants to be connected, creating a two-sided market. So, app developers and app users both generate value through the iPhone platform. The value generated increases as the number of developers and users increases. This is referred to as 'network effects', a central tenet of platform strategy (van Alstyne *et al*., 2016).

Companies such as Airbnb, Uber, and Alibaba all operate through platforms, and a key characteristic is their lack of ownership of any physical assets. Their use of information technology and vast amounts of data has meant that their platforms have been built quickly and relatively inexpensively. They have also disrupted the competitive landscape within their respective industries.

Platform businesses bring together producers and consumers to drive high-value exchanges. Their source of value and their competitive advantage is rooted in both information and data, and the interactions that the platform generates. So, as the number of Uber platform participants has increased, so has the value that Uber has delivered to both sides of their market. It becomes easier for drivers to find fares and for consumers to get rides. For more information about pipeline and platform strategies we encourage readers to see Research Insight 5.4.

Research Insight 5.4

To take your learning further, you might wish to read this influential paper.

van Alstyne, M.W., Parker, G.G., and Choudary, S.P. (2016). Pipelines, platforms, and the new rules of strategy. *Harvard Business Review*, April.

These authors have considered the way in which platform strategies work and compared them with pipeline or more traditional interpretations of strategy. All readers interested in marketing strategy should read this and the emerging raft of papers about changes in strategy.

Visit the **Online Resource Centre** to read the abstract and access the full paper.

Implementation

For ease of explanation, the marketing planning process has been depicted as a linear sequential series of management activities. This certainly helps to simplify understanding about how strategy can be developed and it also serves to show how various activities link together. However, strategy development and planning, whether it be at corporate, business, or functional level, is not linear, does not evolve in preset ways, and is not always subject to a regular pre-determined pattern of evolution. Indeed, politics, finance, and interpersonal conflicts all shape the nature of an organization's marketing strategy. As Browne and Cuddihy (2011) point out, many have argued that there is a need for innovation, flexibility, and creativity for effective marketing planning and strategy making, particularly in the current turbulent times.

Marketing implementation is a fundamental process in marketing because it is the action phase of the strategic marketing process. Whereas many of the concepts in this text help us to design marketing programmes, the implementation phase is about actually doing it. In reality, then, it is the most exciting part of marketing because it is the least predictable.

The implementation of any marketing plan, however, is far from straightforward due in part to the large number of variables. Four elements that impact on the implementation of most strategic marketing plans can be identified, as depicted in Figure 5.8.

The Structure and Type of Marketing Function

The structure and type of marketing function used by an organization can influence the degree to which the implementation process is successful. How we organize ourselves to undertake the task of marketing has an impact on how effective we are.

A marketing department can be structured in many ways, but the internal alignment with the sales department, how brands are managed, and how the reporting lines involve the SBU and corporate headquarters, accompanied with varying levels of bureaucracy, can be influential.

A major problem concerns the increasing complexity associated with contemporary brand management. Mitchell (2012) refers to globalization, the growing importance of customer

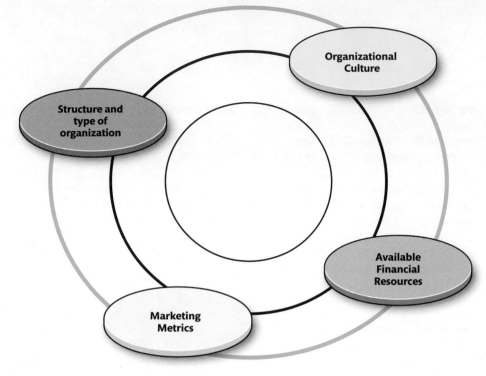

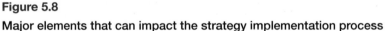

Figure 5.8

Major elements that can impact the strategy implementation process

experience, the significance of retailer power, the role of **category management**, and the recent surge in the use and influence of social media as factors that have redefined the nature of a brand manager's job. Managing increasing amounts of information, projects, and content have added layers of complexity and responsibility.

Organizational Culture

The structural issue needs to be considered alongside the degree to which a marketing orientation prevails across an organization. Marketing is present in all aspects of an organization, as all departments have some role to play with respect to creating, delivering, and satisfying customers. For example, employees in the R&D department designing new offerings for poorly met existing customer needs are performing a marketing role. Similarly, members of the procurement department buying components for a new offering must purchase components of specific quality and at a certain cost that will meet customer needs. In fact, we can go through all the departments of a company and find that there is a marketing role to be played in each. In other words, marketing should be distributed throughout an organization and all employees should be considered as part-time marketers (Gummesson, 1990). Marketing is not something that only people in the marketing department undertake.

Apart from the need to have a customer orientation, the extent to which the prevailing organizational culture is innovative is also regarded as important (Menon and Varadarajan, 1992). An atmosphere which promotes creativity, innovative behaviour, and a willingness to take risks can have a positive impact on employee commitment (see Market Insight 5.4).

Market Insight 5.4
Empowering Employees—Strategically

Red Hat, the global leader in the provision of open-source software, recently changed their approach to strategy development. Teams were formed around an initial set of priorities and, through the use of wikis and other online tools, made these 'open' so that any Red Hat employee could respond with ideas and suggestions. After five months of idea generation the best ideas were shaped into nine strategic priorities. New teams were formed, with the task of identifying one or two of the most important strategic initiatives. They were also empowered to implement the plans without further approvals.

Today, Red Hat updates and evaluates strategy on an ongoing basis, as employees input ideas and initiatives on a continuous basis. Red Hat have placed the responsibility for planning and execution with the same people who do the work, and this has led to improved responsiveness to new opportunities or shifts in the market.

Hindustan Unilever Limited (HUL) is India's largest consumer products company. It is a household name and market leader in various categories including detergents, tea, and soaps.

A strategy to become more customer oriented was launched at HUL's Mumbai headquarters. One of the initiatives, called 'Consumer Shoes', involved displaying all feedback concerning a cross-section of HUL's diverse product portfolio. No matter how harsh, or even savage, the comments were, they were all put up on a wall for everyone to see. Also on the wall are pictures of various types of footwear.

Staff commented on how the packaging of the toothpaste brand Fire-Freeze, a variant of Closeup, was not very good. Another observed that an ice cream competitor, Mother Dairy, had better flavours than HUL's own Kwality Walls brand.

However, unlike most feedback systems which channel customer comments, these were comments posted by HUL's employees. The strategy is for the 'Consumer Shoes wall' to empower brand teams to respond to the comments and to develop an action plan. The company admit that they used to think that interaction with customers was something that only marketing and sales should do, but now they realize that everyone in the company needs to regard consumers as their primary stakeholders.

HUL are also considering utilizing employees within the proposition development process. For example, HUL's Beauty & Wellness business includes 125 Lakme salons and about 20 Ayush therapy centres. In an effort to eradicate mistakes before consumers find them, HUL gave its employees big discounts to encourage them to try new versions of their Lakme beauty salons before they are launched.

Sources: Pinto (2011); Balakrishnan (2012); Gast and Zanini (2012); Bruzzese (2015) https://agriandfoodtidbits.wordpress.com/tag/foodampbeverages/.

Theory into Practice

Both the Red Hat and HUL examples demonstrate the role and strategic importance of actively involving employees in the strategy process. There are numerous theories regarding employee engagement, most based on Kahn's (1990) paper in which he affirms that when individuals are engaged they bring their cognitive, emotional, and physical elements to the performance of their work role. In addition there are theories about job satisfaction, organizational commitment, and job involvement plus well-known theories such as the psychological contract and even Maslow's hierarchy of needs.

These examples demonstrate the importance of organizational culture and the need for a customer orientation throughout the organization, in particular the role of an innovative atmosphere within which to participate in the strategy process.

Market Insight 5.4
continued

Related Topics:
mission; values; strategic goals; strategy process.

1 Which is of greater value, consumer or employee feedback? Justify your answer.

2 What might be the disadvantages for HUL of using their employees to comment on the Lakme salons?

3 Why do so many companies continue with the annual strategy review process?

The manner and involvement of top management in supporting the implementation process is also significant. Research shows that it is critically important that the process of marketing strategy planning occurs within a suitably positive culture. By engaging key decision-makers such as marketing managers, and in some cases all employees, in the various phases of the marketing planning process, the viability of the chosen strategy options is considerably enhanced (Ramaseshan *et al.*, 2013) and as a result senior management is more likely to achieve above average performance outcomes.

A final element concerns the level of freedom, or autonomy, that managers have to make meaningful decisions and independently adjust behaviours. Managers without suitable autonomy may waste critical managerial resources or fail to respond to competitors' actions. As the level of perceived job autonomy is positively associated with the level of perceived organizational commitment (Moon, 2000) the implementation of a marketing plan may be jeopardized if managers do not feel empowered to make changes independently of senior management.

The Available Financial Resources

The amount of financial support allocated to brands can often be contentious and lead to considerable internal political strife. This reflects constituency-based theory, which emphasizes that internal functions, such as marketing and others, are always striving for the resources that they feel are necessary to satisfy their goals (Anderson, 1982). Once the aggregate amount is determined, however, managers should devise a marketing budget indicating how much is to be spent on marketing activities and when. Yet, there are no hard and fast rules on how much should be allocated to marketing spend. A generally held view is that many companies lack a formal and appropriate budgeting process. When marketing budgets are properly determined, they are based on preset tasks, numerical and timed goals, and of course sales forecasts. These should be produced in association with support from the finance department of an organization.

A marketing budget may be between 1% and 10% of sales revenues (excluding salaries), but exactly how much is spent on marketing activities is dependent on the particular industry, each firm, and the overall economic climate. For example, McKinsey & Co. report that following

Research Insight 5.5

To take your learning further, you might wish to read this influential paper.

Ramaseshan, B., Ishak, A., and Kingshott, R.P.J. (2013). Interactive effects of marketing strategy formulation and implementation upon firm performance. *Journal of Marketing Management*, **29 (11–12), 1224–50.**

This paper looks at the issues and the role of marketing managers' commitment and involvement in implementing marketing strategies. The authors show how the commitment of marketing managers' towards strategy implementation has a significant positive impact on organizational performance. Innovative culture, top management support, and job autonomy were considered to be the key antecedents of managers' commitment.

@ Visit the **Online Resource Centre** to read the abstract and access the full paper.

a recession successful companies were found to have invested over 9% more in marketing than their competitors. In addition to this, Kehrer (2015) claims that companies that maintain or even increase their marketing spend during an economic downturn are very likely to recover faster than their competitors when the economy recovers. However, empirical work by Srinivasan *et al.* (2011) suggests that investment in both R&D and advertising during a recession should be based on the actual conditions facing the firm.

Marketing Metrics

The implementation of any marketing plan is incomplete without methods to control and evaluate its performance. It is vitally important to monitor the results of the programme as it unfolds, not just when it is completed. Therefore measures need to be stated in the plan about how the results of the plan will be recorded and disseminated throughout the team. Recording the performance of the marketing plan against targets enables managers to make adjustments if it does not perform as expected, possibly because of unforeseen market events.

The marketing budgeting process is a political process whereby scarce resources are allocated within a company. Clearly, where a department can demonstrate the effectiveness of the resources it has previously used, the more likely it is to receive an increase in the budget for the next year. Over the last 15 years or so, we have seen the rise in importance of measuring marketing effectiveness. The controls used to measure the effectiveness of the implementation process are referred to as **marketing metrics**.

There is increased recognition of the need to determine efficiency and effectiveness in organizational marketing efforts. In the past, marketing control has been achieved through the annual marketing plan, through analysis of company profitability, some measure of efficiency (e.g. number of employees as a proportion of revenue or in retailing, net profit per square foot/metre of retail space), or in terms of market share or some other strategic measure. But in the past these measures have been focused towards financial or human resource measures. More recently,

Figure 5.9
Key marketing performance metrics

there has been a considerable shift in thinking towards the need for customer-based measurements (Kaplan and Norton, 1992). There has been a move towards setting **key performance indicators**, towards which companies measure their progress in order to determine whether or not they have improved or maintained their performance over a given period of time.

Research indicates that British companies are now using a variety of strategic marketing metrics as key performance indicators (KPIs) in marketing. The selection and use of KPIs depends on their relevance to what is being measured; however, KPIs should be selected in the context of strategic plans and associated higher level goals (Lamont, 2012). Scottish Power uses software that enables it to keep track of the factors that underpin its main objective, which is customer retention. These factors include the proficiency with which customer issues are resolved, and the provision of alternative interaction channels.

An organization's strategic goals should always be used to guide the way metrics are interpreted. For example, Lamont (2012) refers to Scottish Power who asked their call centre agents to offer additional services such as boiler care. As a result call time increased by 8–10%, a metric that had to be seen in terms of their retention plan rather than a drop in their agents' productivity.

We now discuss the benefits and limitations of ten key marketing performance metrics (see Figure 5.9).

Profit/Profitability

Unsurprisingly, profit and profitability is the main key performance measure, where profit is broadly how much cash there is left in the business when expenses are subtracted from revenues generated. This approach indicates the 'bottom line'. It represents what is left over either for distribution to the shareholders of the business, whether that be a private or public business, or for reinvestment in the business.

However, the problem with profit/profitability is that its link with marketing activity is not always clear. The process required to determine the link requires considerable input from the finance department to measure the contributions individual offerings make towards the overall profit levels of a business. Therefore it can be difficult to determine whether the marketing activity itself has led to improved levels of profitability or some other factor was responsible, e.g. the collapse of a competitor. Finally, we might have a very profitable business operating in the short term, e.g. with customers buying more of a low value overpriced offering, but in the long term customers would defect and leave the business.

Sales

Sales value or volume is a key performance measure, where sales value is determined by measuring how many units of an offering are sold and multiplying by the average unit price and sales volume is calculated by determining how many units of an offering have been sold. The benefit of using this metric is that sales values and volumes can be measured directly against individual offerings. Sales values and volumes are easier to determine and require limited input from the finance department, unlike the determination of profit/profitability. Sales values and volumes may be linked to geographical sales territories, and so when sales fall in a particular territory, and efforts have been made to increase sales, it is relatively easy to determine whether or not those efforts have been successful.

The use of sales volumes as a marketing metric is more problematic because with high-volume turnover products, particularly in brokerages where companies sell other companies' offerings, the profit may actually be disproportionately low. In such a situation, it would be wiser to measure profit/profitability, where the data are available. However, sales values may also hide the fact that an offering is being sold at unprofitable levels. Rewarding a sales force for selling large quantities of an offering at an unprofitable level is a recipe for disaster—the long-term decline of a company.

Gross Margin

Frequently, companies measure their performance based on the gross profit margins they can achieve in a particular industry. For example, the gross profit margin for supermarkets in the UK is around 5–8%, whereas in the USA gross profit margins are considerably lower at around 2–5%. However, supermarkets generally operate on very high volume sales. Therefore they can afford to operate on low gross profit margins. For example, some restaurants operate a 200–300% gross margin on their wine. When gross margins for one company are compared with those of other companies in the industry, where the data are available (e.g. for publicly quoted companies), companies can determine whether or not they need to reduce their costs or increase their prices.

The problem with using gross margins as a marketing metric is that they do not always provide an indication of how much the customer is actually willing to pay. For example, smoothie manufacturers (e.g. innocent) generally operate higher gross margins (because they charge higher prices) than manufacturers in the fruit juice category (e.g. Del Monte, Minute Maid). However, if the smoothie manufacturers had set their initial prices based on typical fruit juice margins, they would never have been as successful as they have, especially when we consider that innocent achieved sales revenue of around £100m in its first 10 years.

Awareness

Nearly eight in ten respondents mentioned (brand) awareness as an important marketing metric. However, although a customer may be aware of a brand, it does not mean they will buy that brand. Correspondingly, (brand) awareness is not a particularly good measure for determining the effectiveness of marketing activity, particularly in the short term, as it may take time for the increased awareness to lead to increases in sales, if it does at all.

However, (brand) awareness is a very useful metric for determining whether your marketing communications activity is entering customer consciousness. The more a target market recognizes a brand, the more likely they are to become purchasers of it. Nevertheless, building awareness may not necessarily build sales. As consumers we can become aware of a brand, but not particularly like it, and therefore not buy it. Brands can be marketed heavily but not achieve success; examples include Strand cigarettes, Ford Edsel, and Tesco Fresh and Easy in the USA. Awareness does not necessarily lead to purchase.

Market Share

One of the principal measures of market performance, the measurement of market share, is enshrined in many marketing strategy models such as the Boston Consulting Group's growth share matrix (see Chapter 4). Measuring market share is useful for determining a company's performance within the marketplace, particularly when measured relative to the market leader, because it gives an indication of how competitive a company is. Cadbury's, the confectionery company, use this metric in conjunction with other marketing metrics such as brand awareness and advertising spend (Ambler, 2000).

A company's (company A) market share is determined by measuring that company's sales revenues, incorporating the sales of all companies within the industry including company A, as a proportion of total industry sales revenues as follows:

$$\text{market share}_{(\text{company A, \%})} = \frac{\text{sales revenue}_{(\text{company A, £})}}{\text{total industry sales revenue (£)}} \times 100$$

Relative market share is determined by measuring the market share of company A against the market share of the market leader, or the nearest competitor (if company A is the market leader), as follows:

$$\text{relative market share}_{(\text{company A, \%})} = \frac{\text{market share}_{(\text{company A, \%})}}{\text{market share}_{(\text{market leader, \%})}}$$

If company A is the market leader, relative market share is a value greater than one unit. Nevertheless, a company's market share, as determined by the value of the sales, does not necessarily point to a profitable company. Many a company has started a price war (see Chapter 9) in order to try to steal market share from a competitor, only to find prices fall generally in the industry, which inevitably leads to a decline in their own profitability.

Number of New Products

Most companies pride themselves on their capacity to innovate. In many industries, innovating new offerings is vital for the prosperity of the industry. For example, pharmaceutical companies manage a pipeline of new drug compounds at various stages in the process of new proposition development.

When they do finally develop a drug, they quickly patent it to protect their multibillion dollar investments and to ensure that they can reap the financial rewards from the drug's development.

In 2006, pipeline problems occurred for global pharmaceutical manufacturers AstraZeneca and GlaxoSmithKline, when various high profile compounds failed at the clinical trial stage, sending their share prices lower as a result (Griffiths, 2006). 3M (formerly the Minnesota Manufacturing and Mining Corporation), the company behind the Post-it note, among other innovations, uses the proportion of sales attributable to new products as one of its marketing metrics (Ambler, 2000).

Nevertheless, simply developing new offerings without measuring or predicting their impact on the sales of existing offerings can be problematic, as the new offering can cannibalize the existing sales without adding any new business. In addition, this strategy may cause customer confusion as customers try to determine what they want from a variety of offers.

Mobile telephone companies quickly learned in the late 1990s and early 2000s that many consumers wanted a monthly charge service offering a limited range of telephone call packages, which included text message bundles and set levels of call time, or a pay-as-you-go plan with more limited options. What they didn't want was lots of different-priced telephone handset offers with many different call packages, offering different call charges for different times. Consumers wanted price transparency.

Relative Price

The price of a company's offerings can be indicative of how much they are valued in the marketplace. **Relative price** is determined by measuring the price of company A's offering against the price of the market leading company, or the nearest competitor (if company A is the market leader) as follows:

$$\text{relative price}_{\text{(company A's offering, unit)}} = \frac{\text{price}_{\text{(company A's offering, £)}}}{\text{price}_{\text{(market leader's offering/nearest competitor, £)}}}$$

If company A is the market leader, relative price is a value greater than one unit.

There is increasing recognition that a company that can charge a price premium vis-à-vis its competitors has a competitive advantage over them. One approach to measuring brand equity actually uses relative price premiums (Ailawadi *et al.*, 2003).

The problem with measuring marketing effectiveness using relative price only is that a company may only obtain a proportion of the total revenue possible in a marketplace if the price it charges is too high. In other words, a higher relative price may lead to a smaller market share if customers do not value your offering more than the competitors' offerings.

Customer Satisfaction

Many companies operate on the principle of satisfying their customers. Companies in the travel and leisure industry (e.g. Hilton Hotels, TUI, and Hawaiian Airlines) work hard to satisfy their customers and to ensure an enjoyable experience. In the past, this meant measuring service quality levels (see Chapter 15) to determine whether companies were providing the level of quality of service that customers expected. In some industries, customer satisfaction is notoriously low, but customers perceive the costs of switching their business to other providers to be too high. Retail banking services are a good example here as customers are reluctant to switch banks even when they are dissatisfied (Keaveney, 1995). Energy companies such as ScottishPower measure the proportion of their customers who leave and switch supplier. This is referred to as 'churn rate' in the industry. Churn rate is a measure of disaffected customers as a proportion of new customers. Ironically, customer service is so poor at ScottishPower—it received over twice as many complaints as its closest rival—that it was named as the worst in the energy business (Budworth, 2015).

Some companies attempt to go beyond simply satisfying customers, and empower their employees to provide a high level of individual and personal help for customers. For example, staff at the Ritz-Carlton hotels are authorized to spend up to $2,000 so that they can resolve a customer's problem without having to refer to a manager (Hanselman, 2012).

Nevertheless, businesses may spend too much time and effort serving customers who are neither profitable nor offer the most profit potential in the future. Generating high levels of customer satisfaction or delight may ultimately reduce shareholder value because the costs involved produce lower levels of profitability. In other words, the extra costs of improving customer satisfaction from 95% to 99.5% of customers may not be worth it.

Customer Advocacy

According to Reichheld (2003), successful firms create exceptional growth by nurturing loyal customers. They invest huge amounts of time and effort in measuring customer satisfaction. However, most of the indices they have previously employed are complex, produce unclear results, and do not connect to profits or growth. The net promoter score (NPS) was developed based on measuring how likely it is that a customer would recommend a firm to a friend or a colleague. The more promoters a company can gain, the bigger its growth, since the inclination to promote relates to a strong degree of loyalty and growth (Reichheld, 2003). The NPS is calculated based on the ratio of promoters to detractors. Based on their responses on a 0–10 rating scale, customers are then categorized into the following groups:

i) promoters—those who are rated extremely likely to recommend (9–10 rating).

ii) passively satisfied—those who are rated likely to recommend (7–8 rating).

iii) detractors—those who are extremely unlikely to recommend (0–6 rating).

The percentage of detractors is subtracted from the percentage of promoters to produce the NPS. Companies that earn an NPS greater than 75% enjoy very strong customer loyalty. By plotting a firm's NPS against the company's revenue growth rate, Reichheld (2003) found that in industries such as the airline or car rental industries there was a strong relationship between net promoter scores and a company's revenue growth rate. The advantages claimed for the NPS can be summarized as follows.

i) Having the highest NPS in a business sector gives rise to growth rates of, on average, 2.5 times higher than those of competitors.

ii) Each 12-point escalation in NPS relates to a doubling of the growth rate of a firm.

iii) Using other metrics together with NPS provides no further predictive advantage. (Reichheld claims that NPS is the only metric that is needed!)

However, the NPS approach has drawn some key criticisms. Keiningham *et al.* (2008) claimed that the results of the original study yielded different and contrasting results and that a single-metric approach does not outperform dual- or multi-metric models.

Distribution/Availability

The extent to which an offering is distributed within the marketplace can be an important marketing metric. For example, a Hollywood blockbuster film studio will want to ensure maximum take-up of its motion pictures through many cinemas, as the more cinemas the film is shown in, the higher the box office takings will be. In other businesses, the quantity of locations within which a product is sold matter less than the quality of those locations. For example, the premium mobile phone brand, Vertu, is sold through specialist retail outlets only, such as Selfridges and Harrods in London, Paragon in Singapore, Brusco Gioielli in Rome, and Vertu branded shops in such countries as Russia and Lebanon. Cosmetics companies (e.g. French cosmetics giant L'Oréal) distribute their new offerings initially through speciality cosmetics outlets and prestigious department stores, before stocking the products in supermarkets and other department stores later in the campaign.

In a wide range of diverse industry sectors, distribution is critical so that customers can readily purchase a company's offerings. For this reason, companies set up sophisticated systems to link their customers' purchasing needs with their own purchasing and distribution needs. Airline yield management systems, for example, reconcile customer pricing information with live seat availability, taking into account customers' price elasticities (see Chapter 9), in order to maximize total sales revenues. Measures of distribution and offering availability are critical in this and many other industries.

The use of KPIs varies considerably but research by Mintz and Currim (2013) indicates that a manager's use of KPIs is driven by a group of variables that describe the context in which the manager operates. They refer to 'firm strategy, metric orientation, type of marketing mix decision, firm and environmental characteristics' (Mintz and Currim, 2013: 32). They also find that use of metrics is positively associated with marketing mix performance. In particular, that there is positive association between the use of marketing metrics and the performance of the marketing mix.

Research Insight 5.6

To take your learning further, you might wish to read this influential paper.

Kaplan, R.S. and Norton, D. P. (1992). The balanced scorecard: measures that drive performance. *Harvard Business Review*, January–February, 71–9.

This much-quoted seminal article outlined how companies should move beyond financial measures of performance to measures of performance incorporating financial, internal, innovation, and learning, and customer perspectives, seeking to answer questions such as: How do we look to shareholders? What must we excel at? Can we continue to improve and create value? And how do customers see us? The paper sparked a revolution in company performance measurement practice.

Visit the **Online Resource Centre** to read the abstract and access the full paper.

Managing and Controlling Marketing Programmes

There is increasing debate about how we measure the performance of marketing programmes to control them better. Traditionally companies try to maximize marketing effectiveness. That is, they measure market share growth, revenue growth, and market position, and marketing efficiency. The last of these is a measure of sales and marketing expenses as a proportion of gross revenue. There is some evidence that companies that succeed on one dimension, i.e. either marketing efficiency or effectiveness, succeed less on the other (Vorhies and Morgan, 2003). This makes sense because, to be effective at marketing, we have to spend more on marketing activity, which makes us marketing inefficient! Firms that can be both marketing effective and marketing efficient probably do so by changing the 'rules of the game'. They do not spend on high cost activities like advertising to achieve effectiveness; instead they consider new and innovative approaches, which make customers pay more attention.

One problem is that whilst marketers often consider strategy *formulation* to be problematic, they do not see strategy *implementation* as an issue. Managers frequently assume that implementation follows strategy as a sequential process. In fact, the two processes are often interlinked and run in parallel (Piercy, 1998). In other words, marketing strategy may be, and is, formulated on the basis of implementation considerations in the same way that implementation decisions are based on strategy formulation decisions.

In Figure 5.10, we can measure how effective and efficient our strategy has been by using the metrics for efficiency and effectiveness outlined earlier. Where we consider that marketing implementation has been efficient, but marketing strategy has not been effective, we should reformulate strategy as key performance indicators have not been met, otherwise we are likely to reduce shareholder value in the longer term. This situation means that we have spent marketing

Figure 5.10

The marketing strategy–implementation matrix (KPIs, key performance indicators)

Sources: Adapted from Bonoma (1984) and McDonald (1985).

resources well in achieving what we set out as our strategy, but we employed the wrong strategy for what we wanted to do. The control imperative is to intervene quickly to reformulate the marketing strategy.

The dream situation is that we operate an efficient implementation plan and an effective marketing strategy. In this situation, we prosper. There is no control imperative except to maintain a watching brief to see how competition might react, as this may force us to rethink our strategy.

Where implementation of an ineffective marketing strategy plan is inefficient we are likely to face rapid ruin! We are spending scarce resources badly on doing the wrong things. The control imperative requires a fundamental rethink of what we are doing and how we are doing it.

Finally, where we are operating an effective marketing strategy, but implementing it inefficiently, the control imperative is to reconsider how we implement marketing programmes. Although this situation may not be disastrous in the short term, where competition is adopting a more efficient approach, it could lead to mergers, sales, or takeovers in highly competitive industry sectors.

Marketing Planning

We have considered the key activities associated with the strategic marketing planning process, essentially one of analysis, goals, and action. For organizations to be able to develop, implement, and control these activities at the offering and brand level, marketing plans are derived. This final section considers the characteristics of the marketing planning process, identifies the key activities, and considers some of the issues associated with the process.

Marketing planning is a sequential process involving a series of activities leading to the setting of marketing objectives and the formulation of plans for achieving them (McDonald, 2002: 27). A marketing plan is the key output from the overall strategic marketing planning process. It details a company's or brand's intended marketing activity. Marketing plans can be developed for periods of one year, two to five years, and anything up to 25 years. Too many organizations, however, regard marketing plans as a development of the annual round of setting sales targets that are then extrapolated into quasi-marketing plans. This is incorrect as it fails to account for the marketplace, customer needs, and resources. The strategic appraisal and evaluation phase of the planning process should be undertaken first. This covers a three to five year period and provides a strategic insight into the markets, the competitors, and the organization's resources that shapes the direction and nature of the way the firm has decided to compete. Once agreed, this should be updated on an annual basis and modified to meet changing internal and external conditions. Only once the strategic marketing plan has been developed should detailed operational or functional marketing plans, covering a one-year period, be developed (McDonald, 2002). This makes marketing planning a continuous process, not something undertaken once a year or, worse, when a product is launched.

A marketing plan designed to support a particular offering consists of a series of activities that should be undertaken sequentially. These are presented in Table 5.3.

Many of the corporate level goals and strategies and internal and external environmental analyses that are established within the strategic marketing planning process can be replicated within each of the marketing plans written for individual products, product lines, markets, or even SBUs. As a general rule, only detail concerning offerings, competitors, and related support resources need change prior to the formulation of individual marketing mixes and their implementation within functional level marketing plans.

Table 5.3 Key activities within a marketing plan

Activity	Explanation
Executive summary	Brief one-page summary of key points and outcomes.
Overall objectives	Reference should be made to the organization's overall mission and corporate goals, the elements that underpin the strategy.
Product/market background	A short summary of the product and/or market to clarify understanding about target markets, sales history, market trends, main competitors, and the organization's own product portfolio.
Marketing analysis	This provides insight into the market, the customers, and the competition. It should consider segment needs, current strategies, and key financial data. The marketing audit and SWOT analysis are used to support this section.
Marketing strategies	This section should be used to state the market(s) to be targeted, the basis on which the firm will compete, the competitive advantages to be used, and the way in which the product is to be positioned in the market.
Marketing goals	Here, the desired outcomes of the strategy should be expressed in terms of the volume of expected sales, the value of sales and market share gains, levels of product awareness, availability, profitability, and customer satisfaction.
Marketing programmes	A marketing mix for each target market segment has to be developed along with a specification of who is responsible for the various activities and actions and the resources that are to be made available.
Implementation	This section sets out: ▪ the way in which the marketing plan is to be controlled and evaluated ▪ the financial scope of the plan ▪ the operational implications in terms of human resources, R&D, and system and process needs.
Supporting documentation	Marketing plans should contain relevant supporting documentation, too bulky to be included in the plan itself but necessary for reference and detail, e.g. the full PESTLE and SWOT analyses, marketing research data, and other market reports and information plus key correspondence.

The strategic marketing planning process starts with a consideration of the organization's goals and resources and an analysis of the market and environmental context in which the organization seeks to achieve its goals. It culminates in a detailed plan which, when implemented, is measured to determine how well the organization performs against the marketing plan.

Chapter Summary

To consolidate your learning, the key points from this chapter are summarized here.

- **Describe the strategic planning process and explain the key influences that shape marketing strategy.**

  The strategic planning process commences at the corporate level, where the organization sets out its overall mission, purpose, and values. These are then converted into measurable goals that apply to the whole organization. Then, depending upon the size of the organization, the range of businesses (SBUs) and/or offerings is determined and resources allocated to help and support each one. Each business and/or offering has detailed functional and competitive strategies and plans, such as a marketing strategy and plan, developed around them.

  There are three key influences on marketing strategy. These are strategic market analysis, which is concerned with developing knowledge and understanding about the marketplace, strategic marketing goals, which are about what the strategy is intended to achieve, and strategic market action, which is about how the strategies are to be implemented.

- **Analyse current conditions, and formulate marketing strategies.**

  SWOT analysis is used to determine an overall view of the strategic position and highlights the need for a strategy to produce a strong fit between the internal capability (strengths and weaknesses) and the external situation (opportunities and threats). SWOT analysis serves to identify the key issues and then prompts thought about converting weaknesses into strengths and threats into opportunities.

- **Explain the different types of strategic marketing goals and associated growth strategies.**

  There are several types of strategic objective but the four main ones are niche, hold, harvest, and divest goals. However, the vast majority of organizations consider growth to be a primary objective. Although there are different ways of classifying growth, intensive, integrated, or diversified are generally accepted as the main forms.

- **Describe the concepts associated with strategic market action.**

  Strategic market action is concerned with ways of implementing marketing strategies. Various concepts and frameworks have been proposed, and, of these, we considered ideas about competitive advantage, generic strategies, and competitive positioning.

- **Appreciate the main issues associated with strategy implementation, including the principles of marketing metrics.**

  The implementation of most strategic marketing plans involves four main issues. These are: the structure and type of marketing function, organizational culture, financial resources, and marketing metrics or the controls used to measure the effectiveness of the implementation process.

  Many companies now use various marketing metrics to monitor performance. These include metrics in the following areas: profit/profitability; sales, value, and volume; gross margin; awareness; market share; number of new products; relative price; number of customer complaints; consumer satisfaction; customer advocacy; distribution/availability; total number of customers; marketing spend; perceived quality/esteem; loyalty/retention; and relative perceived quality.

- **Explain the key elements of a marketing plan.**

  The key elements associated with the structure of a marketing plan are: overall objectives; product/market background; market analysis; marketing strategy and goals; marketing programmes; implementation, evaluation, and control. Although depicted as a linear process, many organizations do not follow this process, or do not include all these elements, or undertake many of these elements simultaneously.

? Review Questions

1 What is the difference between vision and mission?

2 Identify the four elements that make up the strategic context?

3 What are the key elements of the strategic planning process?

4 How might understanding a firm's competitors help to develop marketing strategy?

5 Identify the key characteristics of SWOT analysis. What actions should be taken once the SWOT grid is prepared?

6 What is the difference between intensive and diversified growth?

7 How does Porter argue that firms can differentiate themselves in one of two main ways? What are they and how do they work?

8 Name four elements that might influence strategy implementation.

9 What are the main marketing metrics?

10 List the core parts of a marketing plan?

✎ Worksheet Summary

@ To apply the knowledge you have gained from this chapter and test your understanding of marketing strategy visit the **Online Resource Centre** and complete Worksheet 5.1.

⚡ Discussion Questions

1 Having read Case Insight 5.1, how would you advise 3scale with regard to Amazon's entry into the market?

2 Find three examples of mission statements and associated organizational goals. Then, using these examples, discuss the value of formulating a mission statement and the benefits that are likely to arise from setting organizational-level goals.

3 If the external environment is uncontrollable, and markets are changing their shape and characteristics increasingly quickly, there seems little point in developing a strategic marketing plan. Discuss the value of formulating marketing strategies and plans in the light of these comments.

4 After a successful period of 20 years trading, a bicycle manufacturer noticed that their sales, rather than increasing at a steady rate, were starting to decline. The company, Rapid Cycles, produced a range of bicycles to suit various segments and distributed them mainly through independent cycle shops. In recent years, however, the number of low cost cycles entering the country had increased, with many distributed through supermarkets and national retail chains. The managing director of Rapid Cycles feels that he cannot compete with these low cost imports and asks for your opinion about what should be done. Discuss the situation facing Rapid Cycles and make recommendations regarding their marketing strategy.

5 Explain which marketing metric(s) might be used in the following circumstances:

   A A newly themed Irish pub with a marketing objective to give customers the best pub experience in the immediate area in the first year of its operation.

   B A large health and fitness organization wanting to expand its chain of gymnasiums to other countries across Europe within a five-year timescale.

   C The manufacturers of a designer cosmetic, such as the Gucci Pour Homme II, wishing to determine how well distributed their product is.

   D A pharmaceutical company wishing to find out whether its new asthma product will be better received in the marketplace in the next 12 months compared with competing brands and if it can hold its price premium.

@ **Visit the Online Resource Centre and complete the Multiple Choice Questions to assess your knowledge of Chapter 5.**

Glossary

attack strategies derived from military origins, these strategies seek to achieve growth objectives.

category management the management of a discrete group of similar or related products whereby each category is run as a mini-business within a retailing or ourchasing context.

competitive advantage achieved when an organization has an edge over its competitors on factors that are important to customers.

corporate strategy the means by which the resources of the organization are matched with the needs of the environment in which the organization decides to operate.

cost leadership a strategy involving the production of goods and services for a broad market segment, at a cost lower than all other competitors.

defence strategies derived from military origins, these strategies need to be deployed quickly and save time when faced with frontal or flanking attacks.

differentiation a strategy through which an organization offers products and services to broad particular customer groups, who perceive the offering to be significantly different from, and superior to, those of its competitors.

diversification a strategy that requires organizations to grow outside their current range of activities. This type of growth brings new value chain activities because the firm is operating with new products and in new markets.

divest a strategic objective that involves selling or killing off a product when products continue to incur losses and generate negative cash flows.

focus strategy a strategy based on developing gaps in broad market segments or gaps in competitors' product ranges.

harvesting a strategic objective based on maximizing short-term profits and stimulating positive cash flow. Often used in mature markets as firms/products enter a decline phase.

hold a strategic objective based on defending against attacks from aggressive competitors.

integrative a growth strategy based on working with the same products and the same markets but starting to perform some of the activities in the value chain that were previously undertaken by others.

intensive a growth strategy that requires an organization to concentrate its activities on markets or products that are familiar.

key performance indicators a set of quantifiable measures used to determine and compare an organization's achievements in terms of meeting its strategic and operational goals.

marketing metrics a measure or set of measures that senior marketers use to assess the performance of their marketing strategies and programmes.

mission a statement that sets out an organization's long-term intentions, describing its purpose and direction.

niche market a small part of a market segment that has specific and specialized characteristics that make it uneconomic for the leading competitors to enter this segment.

organizational goals the outcomes of the organization's various activities, often expressed as market share, share value, return on investment, or numbers of customers served.

pipeline a linear approach to value creation through a chain of interelated organizations.

platform strategy an approach which enables organizations to connect their business with a host, in order to build products and services on top of it, and co-create value. Sometimes referred to as 'plug and play', platforms are developing through digital environments.

relative price denotes the price of company A's product/service as a proportion of the price of a comparable product/service of typically the market leading company (B), or its nearest competitor (where A is the market leader).

strategic business unit an organizational unit which, for planning purposes, is sufficiently large to exercise control over the principal strategic factors affecting its performance. Typically abbreviated to SBU, these might incorporate an entire brand and/or its sub-components, or a country region, or some other discrete unit of an organization.

strategic market analysis the starting point of the marketing strategy process, involving analysis of three main types of environment: the external environment, the performance environment, and the internal environment.

SWOT analysis a methodology used by organizations to understand their strategic position. It involves analysis of an organization's strengths, weaknesses, opportunities, and threats.

values the standards of behaviour expected of an organization's employees.

vision how an organization sees its future and what it wants to become.

References

Achrol, R.S. (1997). Changes in the theory of interorganisational relations in marketing: toward a network paradigm. *Journal of the Academy of Marketing Science*, 25(1), 56–71.

Ailawadi, K., Lehmann, D.R., and Neslin, S.A. (2003). Revenue premium as an outcome measure of brand equity. *Journal of Marketing,* 67(October), 1–17.

Ambler, T. (2000). Marketing metrics. *Business Strategy Review*, 11(2), 59–66.

Anderson, P.F. (1982). Marketing, strategic planning and the theory of the firm. *Journal of Marketing*, 46, 15–26.

Anon. (2014) Current market outlook, Boeing. Retrieve from: http://www.boeing.com/resources/boeingdotcom/commercial/about-our-market/assets/downloads/Boeing_Current_Market_Outlook_2015.pdf (accessed 14 August 2015).

Ansoff, I.H. (1957). Strategies for diversification. *Harvard Business Review*, 35(2), 113–24.

Balakrishnan, R. (2012). How Hindustan Unilever is making every employee a marketer. *Economic Times*, 18 July. Retrieve from: http://articles.economictimes.indiatimes. com/2012-07-18/news/32730917_1_hemant-bakshi-hul-employees-feedback (accessed 27 July 2012).

Bonoma, T.V. (1984). Making your marketing strategy work. *Harvard Business Review*, March–April, 69–76.

Browne, S. and Cuddihy, L. (2011). Questioning the currency of marketing planning today. *Irish Marketing Review*, 21(1-2), 49–57.

Bruzzese, A. (2015). Red Hat's CEO: how to scale engagement as business grows, *Fast Track*, 13 July. Retrieve from: http://quickbase.intuit.com/blog/2015/07/13/red-hats-ceo-how-to-scale-engagement-as-business-grows/ (accessed 7 August 2015).

Budworth, D. (2015). Scottish Power tops complaints league. *The Times*, 5 June. retrieve from: www.thetimes.co.uk/tto/money/article4461915.ece (accessed 11 August 2015).

Day, G.S. and Wensley, R. (1988). Assessing advantage: a framework for diagnosing competitive superiority. *Journal of Marketing*, 52(2), April, 1–20.

Dix, J. (2016). Inside the strategy team at Cisco. *Network World*, 15 February. Retrieve from: http://www. networkworld.com/article/3033153/lan-wan/inside-the-strategy-team-at-cisco.html (accessed 22 March 2016).

Gast, A. and Zanini, M. (2012). The social side of strategy. *McKinsey Quarterly*, May. Retrieve from: www. mckinseyquarterly.com/Strategy/Strategy_in_Practice/ The_social_side_of_strategy_2965 (accessed 1 February 2013).

Griffiths, K. (2006). Pharmaceuticals: UK drug giants hit by pipeline problems. *Daily Telegraph*, 27 October, 3.

Gummesson, E. (1990). Marketing orientation revisited: the crucial role of the part-time marketer. *European Journal of Marketing*, 25(2), 60–75.

Hanselman, A. (2012), Joshie the Giraffe—a remarkable story about customer delight! *Social Media Today*, 18 May. Retrieve from: http://socialmediatoday.com/ andyhanselman/552313/joshie-giraffe-remarkable-story-about-customer-delight (accessed 10 February 2013).

Harbison, J.R. and Pekar, P. (1998). *Smart Alliances: A Practical Guide to Repeatable Success*. San Francisco, CA: Jossey-Bass.

Hoffman, N.P. (2000). An examination of the sustainable competitive advantage concept: past, present, and future. *Academy of Marketing Science Review*, 4. Retrieve from: http://www.amsreview.org/articles/ hoffman04-2000.pdf (accessed 30 January 2013).

Kahn, W.A. (1990). Psychological conditions of personal engagement and disengagement at work. *Academy of Management Journal*, 33(4), 692–724.

Kaplan, R.S. and Norton, D.P. (1992). The balanced scorecard: measures that drive performance. *Harvard Business Review*, January–February, 71–9.

Keaveney, S.M. (1995). Customer switching behavior in service industries: an exploratory study. *Journal of Marketing*, 59(April), 71–82.

Keiningham, T.L., Aksoy, L., Cooil, B., and Andreassen, T.W. (2008). Linking customer loyalty to growth. *Sloan Management Review*, 49(4), 50–7.

Kehrer, D. (2015) Precision attribution fuels marketing effectiveness. *Admap*, February, 22–4.

Lamont, J. (2012). Targeting KPIs for better business performance. *KM World*, 21(8), 12–13.

Martin, G. (2015). When legacy airlines degrade themselves with budget fares. *Skift*, 27 April. Retrieved from: skift. com/2015/04/27/when-legacy-airlines-degrade-themselves-with-budget-fares/ (accessed 27 April 2015).

Macdonald, J.B. and Neupert, K.E. (2005). Applying Sun Tzu's terrain and ground to the study of marketing strategy. *Journal of Strategic Marketing* 13(December), 293–304.

McDonald, M. (1985). Marketing planning and Britain's disoriented directions. *Journal of Marketing Management*, 1, 21–5.

McDonald, M. (2002). *Marketing Plans and How to Make Them* (5th edn). Oxford: Butterworth Heinemann.

Menon, A. and Varadarajan, P.R. (1992). A model of marketing knowledge use within firms. *Journal of Marketing*, 56, 53–71.

Mintz, O. and Currim, I.S. (2013). What drives managerial use of marketing and financial metrics and does metric use affect performance of marketing mix activities? *Journal of Marketing*, 77 (March), 17–40.

Mintzberg, H. (1987. The strategy concept: Five Ps for strategy. *California Management Review*, 30(1), 11–26.

Mitchell, A. (2012). Brand managers: then and now. *Marketing*, 23 May, 28–30.

Moon, M. J. (2000) Organizational commitment revisited in new public management: motivation, organizational culture, sector, and managerial level. *Public Performance & Management Review*, 24, 177–94.

Prahalad, C.K. (2004). *Fortune at the Bottom of the Pyramid: Eradicating Poverty Through Profits*. Upper Saddle River, NJ: Pearson Education.

Prahalad, C.K. and Hamel, G. (1990). The core competence of the organisation. *Harvard Business Review*, 68(3), May–June, 79–91.

Payaud, M.A. (2014). Marketing strategies at the bottom of the pyramid: examples from Nestle, Danone, and Procter & Gamble. *Global Business and Organizational Excellence,* January–February, 51–63.

Piercy, N. (1998). Marketing implementation: the implications of marketing paradigm weakness for the strategy execution process. *Journal of the Academy of Marketing Science*, 26(3), 222–36.

Piercy, N. (2002). *Market-Led Strategic Change: Transforming the Process of Going to Market*. Oxford: Butterworth Heinemann.

Pinto, V.S. (2011). HUL to push Lakme salons, new products. *Business Standard*, 19 February. Retrieve from: http://www.business-standard.com/india/news/hul-to-push-lakme-salons-new-products/425759/ (accessed 30 January 2013).

Porter, M.E. (1985). *The Competitive Advantage: Creating and Sustaining Superior Performance*. New York: Free Press.

Ramaseshan, B., Ishak, A., and Kingshott, R.P.J. (2013). Interactive effects of marketing strategy formulation and implementation upon firm performance. *Journal of Marketing Management*, 29(11–12), 1224–50.

Reichheld, F.F. (2003). The one number you need to grow. *Harvard Business Review*, 81(12), 47–54.

Srinivasan, R., Lilien, G.L., and Sridhar, S. (2011). Should firms spend more on research and development and advertising during recessions? *Journal of Marketing*, 49(75), 49–65.

Uszynski, R. (2013) Southwest Airlines Marketing Strategy, *ISSUU*. Retrieved from: http://issuu.com/rainelleu/docs/ southwest_airlines/3?e = 6172574/1804712 (accessed 14 August 2015).

van Alstyne, M.W., Parker, G.G., and Choudary, S.P. (2016) Pipelines, platforms, and the new rules of strategy.

Harvard Business Review, April. Retrieve from: https://hbr.org/2016/04/pipelines-platforms-and-the-new-rules-of-strategy?cm_sp = Article-_-Links-_-Top%20of%20Page%20Recirculation (accessed 24 March 2016).

Vorhies, D.W. and Morgan, N.A. (2003). A configuration theory assessment of marketing organisation fit with business strategy and its relationship with marketing performance. *Journal of Marketing*, 67(January), 100–15.

Williams, R. (2010). What do corporate values really mean? *Psychology Today*, 7 February. Retrieve from: http://www.psychologytoday.com/blog/wired-success/201002/what-do-corporate-values-really-mean (accessed 6 July 2016).

Chapter 6

Market Segmentation and Positioning

Learning Outcomes

After studying this chapter, you will be able to:

▶ Describe the principles of market segmentation and the STP process

▶ List the characteristics and differences between market segmentation and product differentiation

▶ Explain consumer and business-to-business market segmentation

▶ Describe different targeting strategies

▶ Discuss the concept of positioning

▶ Consider how the use of perceptual maps can assist in the positioning process

Case Insight 6.1
Soberana

Market Insight 6.1
Differentiating Medical Devices

Market Insight 6.2
Segmenting Facebook Users

Market Insight 6.3
Recapturing Lost B2B Customers

Market Insight 6.4
Positioning Premium Beer

Market Insight 6.5
Exploring C–D maps for Strategic Positioning

Case Insight 6.1
Soberana

When an international beer brand took 10% of the Panamanian beer market, it was time for local brand Soberana to re-evaluate their approach. We talk to the Brand Franchise Manager, Fermin Paus, to find out how they responded.

Beer is an integral part of the Panamanian culture, mainly because of its tropical location and weather. Panama is surrounded by the Caribbean Sea and Pacific Ocean, and the temperature is above 25°C every day, all year. Not surprisingly, therefore, it has the highest beer consumption in Latin America, and in 2013 it had the greatest consumption per capita with 71 litres, ranking it 22nd in the world's beer consumption index.

Historically, the market has had two main players that compete with national and international brands and have more than 90% of the total volume: Cerveceria Nacional (part of the ABI/SabMiller group) and us, Cervecerias Baru Panama (part of the Heineken group). The rest of the market is dominated by international brands managed by trading companies. Because of its high per capita intake, market expansion opportunities are limited and slow. This means that the main growth strategies for beer players are about gaining market share at the expense of their competitors.

In 2010, Cerveceria Nacional introduced Miller Lite, after becoming the only operation outside the USA to produce and sell the brand locally. The entrance of this brand accelerated a latent consumer trend. Consumers had been shifting their flavour preferences from traditional lager beers to soft/light options and Miller Lite matched those new preferences perfectly. Consumers were changing their behaviour, and looked for beers that enabled them to extend their drinking time (more beers in more time) yet not make themselves ill or inebriated. Beers with both low alcohol and bitterness, and with a softer taste matched this

Soberana is a soft lager sold in the Panamanian market
Source: Reproduced with kind permission of Soberana.

requirement. Miller Lite was positioned as an upper mainstream option, and priced a few cents above local brands.

The intrinsic product attributes and the pricing strategy, together with an American legacy, which is an important aspirational consumption driver for Panamanians, transformed Miller Lite into one of the most important players in the market. The brand grew strongly and achieved more than 10% market share. This new segment of soft/light beers now accounts for more than 70% of the Panamanian beer market.

Case Insight 6.1
continued

At the time of Miller's growth we had two local brands in the market, PANAMA and Soberana. The former was the company's main national focus, while the latter was mainly distributed in the central region of the country and was generally neglected in that it lacked a marketing strategy or supporting resources. These brands have different flavour profiles; PANAMA is a regular lager, while Soberana is a soft lager beer.

Soberana was launched in 1969 and its name, which means sovereign in English, refers to a historic Panamanian moment. In the 1960s Panama started claiming its sovereignty over territories that were in hands of the USA, which had entered the country at the beginning of the 20th century to finish the construction of the Panama Canal.

As Soberana was distributed mainly in the central region, its market was limited to just 25% of the population. Its price strategy, a few cents below mainstream brands, and promotional/functional messages in the brand communications supported a value positioning. The brand was mostly consumed by adults over 45 years old. This had a negative effect on the brand equity indicators and image perception. By 2011, Soberana had the lowest equity indicators in the market and a strong negative image perception. Accordingly, Soberana was not differentiated in any particular way, and was not perceived to be an aspirational brand.

By the end of 2011, Miller Lite was sourcing volume from all the national brands and was the only brand in the market capitalizing on this new consumer trend.

Our problem, therefore, was how to respond to the changing market needs and challenge Miller Lite's increasingly dominant market leader position.

Introduction

Have you ever wondered how we decide to target certain market segments with our marketing activities? Think about fashion retailers for a moment: How do they identify which people to communicate with about their new ranges? Do they base it on where you live, your age, your gender, your media usage, or something else? In this chapter, we consider how organizations decide on which segments of a market to concentrate their efforts. This process is known as **market segmentation** and is an integral part of marketing strategy (see Chapter 5). After first defining market segmentation, we explore the differences between market segmentation and **product differentiation** to clarify the underlying principles of segmentation. We consider consumer and **business-to-business** market segmentation in detail.

The STP Process

The method by which whole markets are subdivided into different segments is referred to as segmentation, targeting, and positioning. This is normally referred to as the **STP process** (see Figure 6.1).

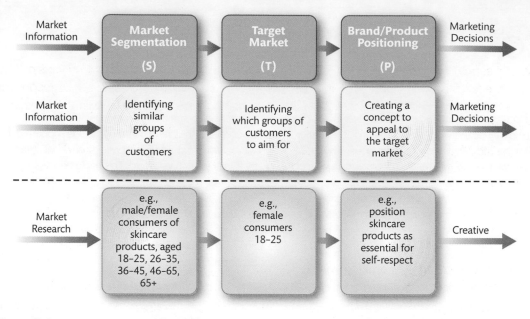

Figure 6.1
The STP Process

Marketers use the STP process in order to identify who, out of all their potential customers, they should focus on, i.e. identify the most attractive and accessible groups of customers or segments. They also use STP to identify new products and service opportunities, to develop suitable positioning and **communication** strategies, and to allocate scarce resources to support key marketing goals.

Organizations commission segmentation research in order to revise their marketing strategy, investigate a declining brand, launch a new offering, or restructure their pricing policies. When operating in highly dynamic environments, segmentation research should be conducted at regular intervals to identify changes in the marketplace. The key benefits of the STP process include the following.

■ Enhancing a company's competitive position, providing direction and focus for marketing strategies, including targeted advertising, new proposition development, and brand differentiation. For example, Coca-Cola identified that Diet Coke was seen as 'feminine' by male consumers. Therefore the company developed Coke Zero, targeted at the health-conscious male segment of the soft drinks market.

■ Examining and identifying market growth opportunities through identification of new customers, growth segments, or proposition uses. For example, fashion brand Burberry was once perceived as frumpy and even considered as gangwear. Now it is chic and in demand around the world.

■ Effective and efficient matching of company resources to targeted market segments, promising greater return on marketing investment (ROMI). For example, ASDA Wal-Mart use data-informed segmentation strategies to target direct marketing messages (online and offline) and rewards to customers offering long-term value to the company.

The Concept of Market Segmentation

Market segmentation is the division of a mass market into distinct and identifiable groups or segments, each of which have common characteristics and needs, and display similar responses to marketing actions. For example, Lee (2013) identifies four main segments in the consumer photography market.

- The **slow photography** segment consists of consumers who share the pleasure associated with the creation and capture of an image, as much as the photo itself. They like photography and the capture of a high quality image is integral to the activity.

- The **fast photography** segment involves the speedy creation and consumption of images. Most of the images are used for immediate communication, very often through social media to be shared with friends and family. Mobile devices are a key device for this segment.

- The **casual photography** segment capture occasional photos for memory-keeping purposes. These people rarely take photos and can be categorised as snapshot photographers.

- The **intelligent photography** segment is characterized by people who wish to blend high quality images with the need for social and memory-keeping purposes. They enjoy using innovate techniques and new devices.

A selfie is an example of Lee's fast photography segment
Source: © Vladimir Gjorgiev/Shutterstock.

Market segmentation was first defined as 'a condition of growth when core markets have already been developed on a generalized basis to the point where additional promotional expenditures are yielding diminishing returns' (Smith, 1956). It forms an important foundation for successful marketing strategies and activities (Wind, 1978).

The purpose of market segmentation is to ensure that elements of the marketing mix, namely price, distribution, products, and promotion (and people, process, and physical evidence for service offerings), meet the needs of different customer groups. As companies have finite resources, it is not feasible to produce all the required offerings for all the people all of the time—you can't be all things to all people. The best we can do is provide selected offerings for selected groups of people most of the time. This enables the most effective use of an organization's scarce resources.

Market segmentation is related to product differentiation as follows.

- A product differentiation strategy involves highlighting a product's attributes and features in order to emphasize the differences and distinguish it from competitors and other product offerings.

- A market segmentation strategy requires a focus on particular segments or groups of customers who share similar needs or characteristics.

In fashion retailing, for example, if you adapt your clothing range so that your skirts are more colourful, use lighter fabrics, and have a very short hemline, this styling might appeal to younger women. This is product differentiation—a focus on the product offering. Alternatively, if you target older women, you might need to change the styling of your skirts by using darker heavier fabrics, with a longer hemline. This is market segmentation with a focus on market segments (see Market Insight 6.1).

Market Insight 6.1
Differentiating Medical Devices

The medical device market is segmented in many ways, but products are differentiated to meet broad customer needs. Four categories of products and services can be distinguished.

- **Premium differentiated** Innovative products and services, which drive premium prices, are usually differentiated by efficacy, outcomes, or care delivery. These are often supported by heavy selling and servicing models.

- **Premium undifferentiated** These products and services are not clinically distinguishable from competitors' offerings. They are offered by many premium companies, whose success is based on established customer relationships or strong branding.

- **Value** These products and services are designed to meet 'good enough' standards for product quality, efficacy, safety, and service standards. These customers are happy to trade off innovation, quality, and service in return for a price which can be 20–40% lower than that for premium products.

- **Basic** These rudimentary products and services compete purely on price and are often used where providers only wish to supply a basic service. This is a large, yet competitive, sector where margins and opportunities are limited.

Source: Llewellyn *et al*. (2015).

Market Insight 6.1
continued

Theory into Practice

Theoretically, product differentiation is primarily concerned with managing supply, whereas segmentation is primarily concerned with managing demand. Where product differentiation is successful monopolistic competition occurs.

Firms that develop a portfolio of products and distinguish them through their key attributes are effectively practising product differentiation. They are influencing supply in order to manage demand. Therefore, a manufacturer in the medical devices market might develop a range of products based on functionality which is different (superior) to its competitors.

In contrast, the same firm might choose to segment the market's customers based on a range of factors, and then develop medical devices to suit the needs of particular segment(s). This is market segmentation, and is rooted in the idea of managing demand in order to influence supply.

A theoretical issue that arises from this is: does product differentiation lead to segmentation? In Market Insight 6.1, the value category might lead to identifying a group of customers who prefer value products and services and this in turn might lead to segmenting this group based on a range of needs or benefits.

Related Topics:

economic theories of competition (monopolistic, oligopolistic, perfect, and imperfect); value; competitive advantage.

1 Should product differentiation be regarded as an alternative to market segmentation strategies?

2 What process should companies follow in the medical device market in order to adopt a market segmentation approach?

3 Under what circumstances should market segmentation be used rather than product differentiation?

Market segmentation was proposed as an alternative development strategy in markets with few competitors selling an identical product—imperfectly competitive markets. Where there are many competitors selling identical products, market segmentation and product differentiation can produce similar results because competitors imitate each other's strategic approaches faster, and product differentiation approaches meet market segment needs more closely. Because consumers exhibit a wider range of tastes and have greater disposable income, marketers increasingly design offerings around consumer demand (market segments) rather than around their own production needs (product differentiation). See Figure 6.2.

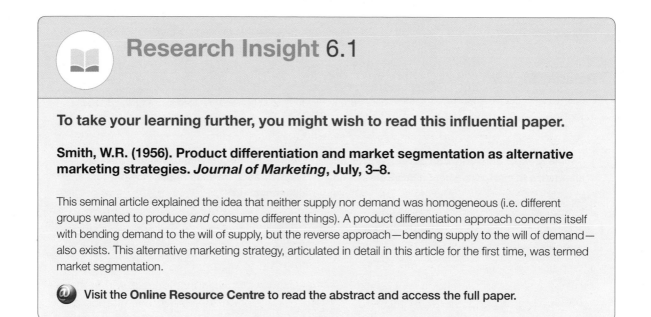

Figure 6.2

The difference between market segmentation and product differentiation

---

Research Insight 6.1

To take your learning further, you might wish to read this influential paper.

Smith, W.R. (1956). Product differentiation and market segmentation as alternative marketing strategies. *Journal of Marketing*, July, 3–8.

This seminal article explained the idea that neither supply nor demand was homogeneous (i.e. different groups wanted to produce *and* consume different things). A product differentiation approach concerns itself with bending demand to the will of supply, but the reverse approach—bending supply to the will of demand—also exists. This alternative marketing strategy, articulated in detail in this article for the first time, was termed market segmentation.

@ Visit the Online Resource Centre to read the abstract and access the full paper.

The Process of Market Segmentation

To aid market segmentation, there are two main approaches. The first adopts the view that markets consist of customers that are similar. The task is to identify groups that share particular differences. This is the **breakdown method**. The second approach considers markets to consist of customers that are different. The task is to find similarities. This is known as the **build-up method** (Griffith and Pol, 1994).

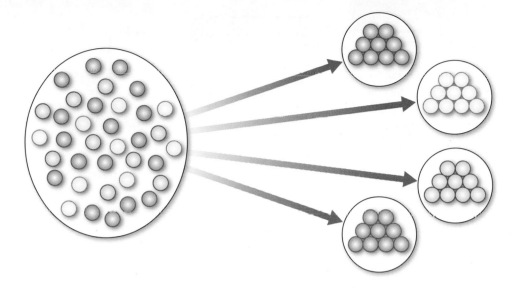

Figure 6.3
Segment heterogeneity and member homogeneity

The breakdown approach is the most established method for segmenting consumer markets. The build-up approach seeks to move from the individual level where all customers are different, to a more general level of analysis based on the identification of similarities (Freytag and Clarke, 2001). The build-up method is customer oriented, seeking to determine common customer needs. The aim of both methods is to identify market segments where identifiable differences exist between segments—segment heterogeneity—but similarities exist between members within each segment—member homogeneity (see Figure 6.3).

In **business markets**, segmentation should reflect the relationship needs of the organizations involved. However, problems remain concerning the practical application and implementation of B2B **segmentation**. Managers report frequently that the analytical processes are reasonably clear, but it is unclear how they should choose and evaluate the various market segments (Naudé and Cheng, 2003). Segmentation theory has developed in an era when a transactional goods-centric approach to marketing was predominant rather than the service-dominant logic existing today. Under the transactional approach, resources are allocated to achieve designated marketing mix goals. However, customers within various segments have changing needs, and therefore those customers may change their segment membership (Freytag and Clarke, 2001). Consequently, market segmentation programmes should use current customer data.

Market Segmentation in Consumer Markets

To segment consumer markets, we use market information based around key customer-, product-, or situation-related criteria. These are classified as segmentation bases and include profile criteria (e.g. who are my market and where are they?), behavioural criteria (e.g. where, when, and how does my market behave?), and psychological criteria (e.g. why does my market behave

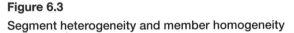

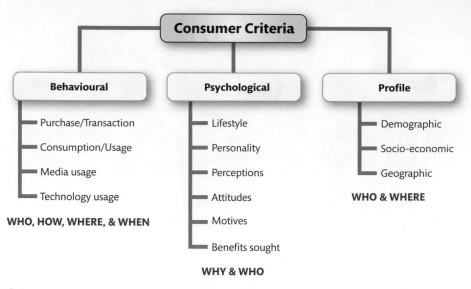

Figure 6.4

Segmentation criteria for consumer markets

that way?) (see Figure 6.4). A fourth segmentation criterion is contact data, a customer's name and full contact details beyond their postcode (e.g. postal address, email, mobile and home telephone numbers). Contact data are useful for tactical-level marketing activities, e.g. direct and digital marketing (see Chapters 11 and 12).

Table 6.1 illustrates the key characteristics associated with each of the main approaches to consumer market segmentation.

When selecting different segmentation bases, the trade-off between data acquisition costs and the ability of the data to predict customer choice behaviour should be considered. Demographic and **geodemographic** data are relatively easy to measure and obtain; however, these bases suffer from low levels of accuracy in predicting consumer behaviour (see Figure 6.5). In contrast, behavioural data (e.g. **product usage**, purchase history, and media usage), although more costly to acquire, provide a more accurate means of predicting future behaviour. For example, the brand of toothpaste you purchased previously is more likely to be the brand of toothpaste you purchase in future. However, customer choices are also influenced by susceptibility to marketing communications.

Profile Criteria

One way of segmenting consumer markets is to use profile criteria to determine who consumers are and where they are located. To do this, we use demographic methods (e.g. age, gender, race), socio-economics (e.g. determined by social class or income levels) and **geographic** location (e.g. using postcodes). For example, a utility company might segment households on geographical area to assess regional brand penetration, or an insurance company might segment the market based on age, employment, income, and asset net worth to identify attractive market segments for a new investment portfolio. These are all examples of segmentation based on profile criteria.

Table 6.1 Segmentation criteria

Base type	Segmentation criteria	Explanation
Profile	Demographic	Key variables concern age, sex, occupation, level of education, religion, social class, and income characteristics
	Lifestage	Based on the principle that people need different offerings at different stages in their lives (e.g. childhood, adulthood, young couples, retired)
	Geographic	The needs of potential customers in one geographic area are often different from those in another area, due to climate, custom, or tradition.
	Geodemographic	There is a relationship between the type of housing and location that people live in and their purchasing behaviours.
Psychological	Psychographic (lifestyles)	By analysing consumers' activities, interests, and opinions, we can understand individual lifestyles and patterns of behaviour affecting their buying behaviour and decision-making processes. We can also identify similar offering and/or media usage patterns.
	Benefits sought	The motivations customers derive from their purchases provide an insight into the benefits they seek from the use of an offering.
Behavioural	Purchase/transaction	Data about customer purchases and transactions provides scope for analysing who buys what, when, and how often, how much they spend, and through what transactional channel they purchase.
	Product usage	Segments can be derived on the basis of customer usage of the offering, brand, or product category. This may be in the form of usage frequency, time of usage, or usage situations.
	Media usage	What media channels are used, by whom, when, where, and for how long provides useful insights into the reach potential for certain market segments through differing media channels, and also insight into their media lifestyle.

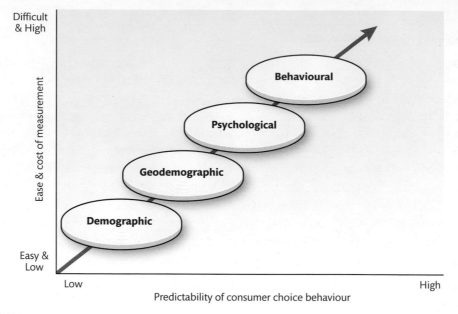

Figure 6.5

Considerations for segmentation criteria accessibility and use

Source: From Shimp. *Integrated Marketing Communications in Advertising and Promotion®, International Edition*, 7e. © 2007 South-Western, a part of Cengage Learning, Inc. Reproduced with permission.

Demographic

Demographic variables relate to age, gender, family size and lifecycle, generation (e.g. baby boomers, Generation Y), income, occupation, education, ethnicity, nationality, religion, and social class. They indicate the profile of a consumer and are useful in media planning (see Chapter 11).

Age is a common way of segmenting consumer markets (e.g. children are targeted for confectionery and toys because their needs and tastes are different from older people). For example, Yoplait Dairy Crest (YDC) launched Petits Filous Plus probiotic yogurt drinks to extend the brand and increase its appeal among 4- to 9-year-olds and their parents.

Gender differences have also spawned a raft of offerings targeted at women. For example, beauty and fragrance offerings (e.g. Clinique, Chanel), magazines (e.g. *Cosmopolitan*, *Heat*), hair care (e.g. Pantene, Clairol), and clothes (e.g. H&M, New Look). Offerings targeted at men include magazines (e.g. *GQ*) and beverages (e.g. Carlsberg, Coke Zero). Some brands develop offerings targeted at both men and women, e.g. fragrances (e.g. Calvin Klein) and watches (e.g. Rolex).

Income or socio-economic status is an important demographic variable because it determines whether or not a consumer can afford an offering (see Chapter 2). This comprises information about a consumer's personal income, household income, employment status, disposable income, and asset net worth. Many companies target high net worth individuals (e.g. Rolls-Royce, NetJets, Vertu) offering high end exclusive offerings. However, targeting low income earners can also be profitable. German discount supermarkets (e.g. Aldi) make a good profit by targeting low income segments. Major supermarket groups like Carrefour and Tesco use an understanding of customer socio-economics to develop their own-label offerings. For example, Tesco Finest is developed for market segments with high disposable income, in contrast with Tesco Value which is marketed to the price-conscious low income segment.

Lifecycle

Lifestage analysis posits that people have varying amounts of disposable income and different needs at different times in their lives. For example, adolescents need different offerings from single 26-year-olds, who need different offerings compared with a 26-year-old married person with young children. Major supermarkets (e.g. ASDA Wal-Mart, Tesco) have all invested in the development of offerings targeted at singles with high disposable incomes and busy lifestyles by offering 'meal for one' ranges, which compare with 'family value' and 'multipacks' targeted at families. As families grow and children leave home, the needs of parents change and their disposable income increases. Certain types of holiday (e.g. Thomas Cook's package holidays) and automobiles (e.g. people carriers) become more attractive to people in the lifestage when they have children. A modern lifecycle classification (i.e. Target Group Index (TGI)) classifies 12–13 lifestage groups based on age, marital status, household composition, and children (e.g if they have children and the child's age) (see Table 6.2). (See also Chapter 2 for a historical example of lifestage segmentation).

@ **Visit the Online Resource Centre** and follow the web link to Kantar Media to learn more about the TGI.

Table 6.2 BMRB-TGI lifestage segmentation groups

Lifestage group	Demographic description
Fledglings	15–34, not married and have no son or daughter; living with own parents
Flown the nest	15–34, not married, do not live with relations
Nest builders	15–34, married, do not live with son/daughter
Mid-life independents	35–54, not married, do not live with relations
Unconstrained couples	35–54, married, do not live with son/daughter
Playschool parents	Live with son/daughter and youngest child 0–4
Primary school parents	Live with son/daughter and youngest child 5–9
Secondary school parents	Live with son/daughter and youngest child 10–15
Hotel parents	Live with son/daughter and have no child 0–15
Senior sole decision-makers	55, not married and live alone
Empty nesters	55, married, and do not live with son/daughter
Non-standard families	Not married, live with relations, do not live with son/daughter, and do not live with parents if 15–34
Unclassified	Not in any group

Source: Reproduced with the kind permission of Kantar Media.

Geographics

This approach is useful when there are clear locational differences in tastes, consumption, and preferences. For example, whereas the British celebrate Christmas with turkey dishes, Swedes often eat fish and many Germans opt for goose. These consumption patterns provide an indication of preferences according to differing geographical regions. Markets can be considered by country or region, size of city or town, postcode, or population density such as urban, suburban, or rural. It is often said that American beer drinkers prefer lighter beers compared with their UK counterparts, whereas German beer drinkers prefer a much stronger drink. In contrast, Australians prefer colder more carbonated beer than drinkers in the UK or the USA.

In addition to proposition selection and consumption, geographical segmentation is important for retail location, advertising and media selection, and recruitment. For example, recruitment to the armed forces draws people with similar demographic attributes from a variety of geographic areas. Low cost formats might be used for retail outlets in low income regions. Direct sales operations (e.g. catalogue sales) can use census information to develop better customer segmentation and predictive models. Interestingly, book publishers have long segmented based on geographical markets, frequently charging consumers in developing countries much less for a book than those in the developed world and trying to enforce a non-import policy so that these cheaper books do not enter Western markets. A recent case in the USA, however, may hinder publishers' abilities to enforce the import ban, meaning that they will no longer be able to offer developing world segments the much cheaper prices that they have previously enjoyed (Esposito, 2013).

Geodemographics

Geodemographics is a natural outcome when combining demographic and geographic variables. The marriage of geographics and **demographics** has become an indispensable market analysis tool, as it can lead to a rich mixture of who lives where. Two of the best known UK geodemographic systems are ACORN and MOSAIC.

Visit the Online Resource Centre and complete Internet Activity 6.1 to learn more about how we use databases compiled with geodemographic data to profile market segments effectively.

Developed by the British market research group CACI, ACORN (A Classification of Residential Neighbourhoods) demonstrates how postcode areas are broken down into six categories, 18 groups, and 62 types. The categories include the following groups:

i) affluent achievers

ii) rising prosperity

iii) comfortable communities

iv) financially stretched

v) urban adversity

vi) not private households

ACORN is a geodemographic tool used to identify the UK population and its demand for a variety of offerings to assist marketers so that they can determine where to locate operations, field sales forces, retail outlets, and so on. ACORN can also be used to determine where to plan marketing communications and social media marketing campaigns.

Visit the Online Resource Centre and follow the web link to CACI to learn more about the ACORN system.

MOSAIC is a similar geodemographic segmentation system, developed by Experian and marketed globally. The system is based on the classification of 155 person types aggregated into 67 household types and 15 groups to create a three-tier classification that can be used at the individual, household, or postcode level.

Visit the Online Resource Centre and follow the web link to Experian to learn more about the MOSAIC system.

Psychological Criteria

Psychological criteria used for segmenting consumer markets include the types of **benefits sought** by customers from brands in their consumption choices, attitudes, and perceptions (e.g. feelings about fast cars) and **psychographics** or the lifestyles of customers (e.g. extrovert, fashion conscious, high achiever).

Benefits Sought

The benefits sought approach is based on the principle that we should provide customers with exactly what they want, based on the benefits they derive from use (Haley, 1968). This might sound obvious, but consider what are the real benefits, both rational and irrational (see Chapter 2), for the different offerings that people buy, such as mobile phones and sunglasses. Major airlines often segment on the basis of the benefits passengers seek from transport by differentiating between the first class passenger (given extra luxury benefits in their travel experience), the business class passenger (who gets some of the luxury of the first class passenger), and the economy class passenger (who gets none of the luxury of the experience but enjoys the same flight). Morrissey and Baines (2011) segmented the Irish youth sports participation market based on the benefits that young people seek in sport participation, creating the following four segments.

1 The enthusiast—members exercise principally for enjoyment and fitness (strength/ endurance and nimbleness) and tend to be regular exercisers.

2 The social competitor—members, who tend to be regular exercisers, male, and relatively young, exercise principally for interpersonal and affiliation motives. Interpersonal motives reflect individuals driven by the competitive and challenging aspects of exercise, in addition to peer recognition. Affiliation motives indicate a desire for social interaction and building of friendship through exercise.

3 The healthy looker—members exercise principally for aesthetic and health motives and tend to be females and non-regular exercisers.

4 The reluctant exerciser—members, who tend to be female and non-regular exercisers, exhibit below average motivation for all motivational constructs, with interpersonal and enjoyment motives being substantially below average.

Psychographics

Psychographic approaches rely on the analysis of consumers' activities, interests, and opinions to understand consumers' individual lifestyles and behaviour patterns. Psychographic segmentation includes understanding the values that are important to different customer types.

A traditional form of lifestyle segmentation is AIO, based on customers' Activities, Interests, and Opinions. Taylor Nelson Sofres (TNS) developed a UK Lifestyle Typology based on lifestyles and classified the following lifestyle categories: belonger, survivor, experimentalist, conspicuous consumer, social resistor, self-explorer, and aimless.

International Harvester (IH) undertook value-based segmentation to discover why farmers consistently rated John Deere (JD) equipment, their arch competitor, as 'more reliable'. IH had invested heavily to minimize breakdowns, but JD continued to lead the reliability rankings. Surveys about repair problems revealed it was the downtime caused by breakdowns that most affected farmers because of the days of lost productivity waiting for repairs. JD's customers perceived reliability to be much less of a problem because of JD's extensive service-oriented dealer network that stocked spare parts and offered temporary tractors, which served to get a farmer working again quickly. JD was serving a different segment of farmers, those driven by the value of a total service solution, which JD complemented well (Anon., 2013).

See Market Insight 6.2 which considers the motivations people have for using Facebook.

Behavioural Criteria

Product-related methods of segmenting consumer proposition markets include using behavioural methods (e.g. product usage, purchase, and ownership) as bases for segmentation. Observing consumers as they use offerings or consume services can be an important source of ideas for new uses or proposition design and development. Furthermore, new markets for existing offerings can be signalled, as well as appropriate communication themes for promotion. Purchase, ownership, and usage are three very different behavioural constructs that can be used to aid consumer market segmentation.

Usage

A company may segment a market based on how often a customer uses its offerings, categorizing these into high, medium, and low users. This allows the development of service specifications or marketing mixes for each user group. For example, a coach operating company might target heavy users of public transport differently to heavy users of private vehicles. Consumer usage of offerings can be investigated from three perspectives.

1 Social interaction perspective—symbolic aspects of usage and the social meanings attached to the consumption of socially conspicuous offerings such as a car or house are considered (Belk et al., 1982; Solomon, 1983). For example, Greenpeace launched a television campaign targeting owners of four-wheel drive cars highlighting the environmental social stigma of their car purchase.

2 Experiential consumption perspective—emotional and sensory experiences are considered as a result of usage, especially emotions such as satisfaction, fantasies, feelings, and fun (Holbrook and Hirschman, 1982). For example, Oxo gravy campaigns have emphasized how usage of Oxo brings families together and expressed family values such as love, sharing, and spending time together.

3 Functional utilization perspective—the functional usage of products and their attributes in different situations is considered (Srivastava et al., 1978; McAlister and Pessemier, 1982). For example, how and when cameras are used, how often, and in what contexts.

Market Insight 6.2
Segmenting Facebook Users

As the use of social networks has become a core means of communication for many people, finding a way to segment users effectively has become increasingly important. It is clear, however, that an insight into the different segments of network users would be of great assistance to marketing practitioners.

Early social network segmentation approaches were based on usage behaviour. A typical study identified five consumer segments based on levels of brand engagement, word-of-mouth referral behaviour, and purchase intention, derived from their exposure to social network marketing activities. Facebook's own segmentation tool enables ads to be targeted at audiences based on certain traits and interests, including geographic region, gender, age, the brands followed, and their social network connections.

Unfortunately, this approach fails to uncover the reasons why people use social networks. People are motivated to subscribe to these networks for a variety of reasons, but four main needs can be identified: socializing, entertainment, self-status seeking, and information seeking.

Research based on these motivations has identified four Facebook segments.

(1) **Devotees** This segment accesses Facebook with high frequency and for long periods of time. Their goal is to socialize with friends, find entertainment, seek status, and gather information. Typically, this segment is more likely to contain individuals under 30 years of age.

(2) **Agnostics** This segment uses Facebook less frequently and for shorter periods of time than other users. They have the least motivation to use Facebook, but when they do their focus is primarily social.

(3) **Socializers** These people are light users and use Facebook in short bursts to satisfy socializing and entertainment needs.

Four segments of Facebook users have been identified.
Source: © JaysonPhotography/Shutterstock.

(4) **Finders** This segment comprises moderate to heavy users of Facebook. Their primary use is to gather information, whilst socializing and entertainment are of secondary importance. Finders tend to be females rather than males.

This segmentation typology is not rigid as people can migrate across groups. For example, enthusiasts can become non-enthusiasts if Facebook strategies do not meet their needs.

These findings suggest that, among other things, communications directed at Socializers should provide an instant reward because of their infrequent use of Facebook. Marketing activities directed at Finders should emphasize the information-gathering element. For Devotees, marketers should deliver content that is high in terms of sociability, entertainment, and status value and carries high-quality information.

Understanding that not everyone uses or wishes to use Facebook and other social networks is important in order not to waste marketing resources.

Sources: Park *et al.* (2009); Shao *et al.* (2015); Sornoso (2015).

Market Insight 6.2
continued

Theory into Practice

The hierarchy of needs theory developed by Maslow (1943) states that people are motivated to achieve certain needs. He classified these as physiological, safety, love, (and esteem), and self-actualization. Using this framework, the use of social media might be attributed to a need for love and esteem, and in some case self-actualization.

This interpretation might be seen as a little too generalized, so use of usage and gratifications theory (U&G) might be more appropriate as this is an established approach to understanding how individuals use media.

The theory was originally applied to the mass media, but is now considered to be a valid theoretical model appropriate for application in a social media context. It is based on the notion that individuals are motivated to engage with media in order to satisfy why and how people actively seek out specific media to satisfy specific needs. It is an audience-centred approach which can be interpreted as not 'What does media do to people?', but rather 'What do people do with media?'.

As people's motivations to use Facebook differ, understanding these motivations is considered to be an effective basis for segmentation. The underlying principle is that motivations are derived from social, cognitive, and psychological needs. It has been established by several researchers that there are four main motivations (for using social media).

- **Socializing**—network members seek emotional support, a sense of belonging and friendship.

- **Entertainment**—individuals seek the experiential and entertainment value offered through participation with others through the Internet.

- **Self-status seeking**—participation in social networking has been shown to have a positive influence on a user's sense of identity and to enhance their self-status.

- **Information seeking**—members perceive the richness of information sought through social networks because of the trust in and objectivity offered by their contacts.

Related Topics:

competitive advantage; trust and commitment.

1 **How might rival social networks develop alternative segments if the research indicates that there only four main motivations for people to use them?**

2 **Why might Facebook be interested in understanding the different user motivations?**

3 **Find two different online communities and make a list of the motivations people might have to join them? What are the similarities and how might this lead to identifying effective segments?**

Service providers often segment markets based on their customers' purchase behaviour. This might involve segmentation by loyalty to the service provider, or length of relationship, or some other mechanism.

Transaction and Purchase

The development of electronic technologies, such as electronic point of sale (EPOS) systems, standardized product codes, radiofrequency identification (RFID) systems, quick response (QR) codes, and integrated purchasing systems (e.g. web, in-store, telephone) has facilitated a rapid growth in the collection of consumer purchase and transactional data. For example, browsing and purchase data allows Amazon to make recommendations of offerings that are more likely to appeal to consumers. EPOS systems allow retailers to track who buys what, when, for how much, in what quantities, and with what incentives (e.g. sales promotions). Companies have the ability to monitor purchase patterns in various geographical regions, at different times or seasons of the year, for various offerings, and increasingly for differing market segments. Social media can also be analysed to track what people are saying once they have purchased and used particular offerings.

Transactional and purchase information is very useful for marketers to assess who are their most profitable customers. By analysing the recency, frequency, and monetary value of purchases (RFM), marketers can identify their most profitable market segments. Customers who purchase most recently, frequently, and spend the most would be classified as profitable customers. Transactional data are records of behaviours and provide some insight into purchasing trends. Online, we can track from where someone is accessing our website. For example, if someone is coming to us from a price comparison website, they are probably price sensitive, but if they arrive from a product review website, they have probably already decided what they want and so are less price sensitive (Stiving, 2012).

The executional segmentation category focuses on how individual customers are treated. One approach is through 'triggers', such as commercially significant occurrences on a customer's account. A late payment fee might indicate that a customer's needs have changed, or a customer who has just taken out cash via a credit card might need credit and be a target for a loan. The trigger information typically needs to be combined with an assessment of the customer's credit status to ascertain whether a loan would be an appropriate offer for a customer who has just been charged a late payment fee, or an overdraft extension. Barclays also considers 'events' on customer accounts, for example when a customer's insurance requires renewal, or a mortgage comes to an end, or when moving house, getting married, and having children. Barclays focuses on executional segmentation by modelling customer responses to customer action prompts (CAPs). This is referred to as 'propensity modelling'. The approach combines transactional data from current accounts and credit cards with external data sources to provide a picture of customers' lifestyles, lifestages, and finances. The fused data allows the development of propensity models which predict customers' likelihood of responding to particular promotional offers.

Media Usage

The logic of segmenting markets by frequency of readership, viewership, or patronage of **media vehicles** is well-established. For example, heavy and light magazine readers might respond differently to ads with different creative appeals (Urban, 1976). Segmenting users on their media usage frequency can provide insights into whether or not a publisher attracts and retains consumers who are more or less responsive to an advertiser's communication. This information

Research Insight 6.2

To take your learning further, you might wish to read this influential paper.

Beane, T.P. and Ennis, D.M. (1987). Market segmentation: a review. *European Journal of Marketing*, 32(5), 20–42.

This article provides a useful insight into the main bases for market segmentation and the strengths and weaknesses of the key statistical methods we use to analyse customer data to develop segmentation models. The authors suggest that there are many ways of segmenting a market and it is important to exercise creativity when doing so.

@ Visit the **Online Resource Centre** to read the abstract and access the full paper.

provides input when evaluating the efficiency and effectiveness of media. Furthermore, differences in frequency may lead to differences in response to repeated passive ad exposures, competing ads of other sponsors, and prior ad exposure.

Frequency of media usage has been the predominant measure of media usage experience. However, Olney *et al.* (1991) and Holbrook and Gardner (1993) have identified viewing time as an important dependent variable in a model of advertising effects. On media websites, users might be segmented by either their visit frequency or their dwell time (how long they spend on a site) among other variables.

Segmentation in Business Markets

Business-to-business market segmentation is the identification of 'a group of present or potential customers with some common characteristic which is relevant in explaining (and predicting) their response to a supplier's marketing stimuli' (Wind and Cardozo, 1974). There are two main groups of interrelated variables used to segment business-to-business markets (see Table 6.3). The first involves organizational characteristics, such as **organizational size** and location, sometimes referred to as **firmographics**. Those seeking to segment might start with these variables. The second group is based on the characteristics surrounding the decision-making process. Those organizations seeking to establish and develop customer relationships would normally expect to start with these variables.

Organizational Characteristics

These factors concern the buying organizations that make up a business market. There are a number of criteria that can be used to cluster organizations, including size, geography, market served, value, location, **industry type**, usage rate, and **purchase situation**. We discuss the main three categories used below (see Figure 6.6).

Table 6.3 Segmentation bases used in business markets

Base type	Segmentation base	Explanation
Organizational characteristics	Organizational size	Grouping organizations by relative size (MNCs, international, large, SMEs) enables the identification of design, delivery, usage rates or order size, and other purchasing characteristics
	Geographic location	Often the needs of potential customers in geographic areas are different from each other
	Industry type (SIC codes)	Standard industrial classifications (SICs) are used to identify and categorize industries and businesses
Customer characteristics	Decision-making unit (DMU) structure	Attitudes, policies, and purchasing strategies allow organizations to be clustered
	Choice criteria	The types of offerings bought and the specifications companies use when selecting and ordering offerings form the basis for clustering customers and segmenting business markets
	Purchase situation	Segmenting buyers by how a company structures its purchasing procedures, the type of buying situation, and whether buyers are in an early or late stage in the purchase decision process

Note: MNC = multinational corporation; SMEs = small and medium-sized enterprises.

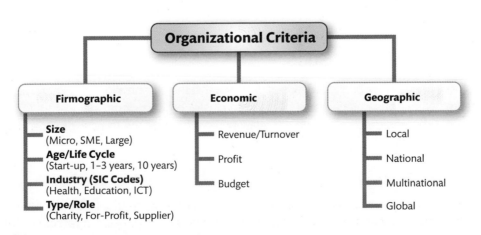

Figure 6.6

Segmentation by organizational characteristics

Organizational Size

By segmenting organizations by size, we can identify particular buying requirements. Large organizations may have particular delivery or design needs based on volume demand; for example, supermarkets such as France's Carrefour and Britain's Tesco pride themselves on purchasing goods in sufficiently large quantities to enable them to offer them at a cheaper price. The size of the organization often impacts on the usage rates of an offering, so organizational size is linked to whether an organization is a heavy, medium, or low buyer of a company's offerings.

Geographical Location

Geotargeting is one of the more common methods used to segment business-to-business markets, and is often used by new or small organizations attempting to establish themselves. This approach is useful because it allows sales territories to be drawn around particular locations that salespersons can service easily (e.g. Scotland, Scandinavia, Western Europe, the Mediterranean). Alternatively, sales territories may be based on specific regions within a country; for example, in Eastern Europe they may be based on individual nations (i.e. Poland, Czech Republic, Romania, and Hungary). However, this approach becomes less useful as the Internet cuts across geographic distribution channels (see Chapters 11, 12, and 14).

SIC Codes

Standard Industrial Classification (SIC) codes are used to understand market size. They are easily accessible and standardized across most Western countries (e.g. the UK, Europe, and the USA). However, some marketers have argued that SIC codes contain categories too broad to be useful. Consequently, SIC codes have received limited application, although they do provide 'some preliminary indication of the industrial segments in [a] market' (Naudé and Cheng, 2003). More commonly, companies sometimes segment B2B markets using industry types (so-called 'verticals'). For example, a law firm might segment its customers into financial services, utilities, transport, and retailing, among others.

 Visit the Online Resource Centre and complete Internet Activity 6.2 to learn more about how we use SIC codes to segment business markets.

Customer Characteristics

These factors concern the characteristics of buyers within the organizations that make up a business market. Numerous criteria could be used to cluster organizations, including by decision-making unit, by purchasing strategies, by relationship type, attitude to risk, **choice criteria**, and purchase situation.

Decision-Making Unit

An organization's decision-making unit may have specific requirements that influence purchase decisions in a particular market, e.g. policy factors, purchasing strategies, the level of importance attached to these types of purchases, or attitudes towards vendors and risk. These characteristics can be used to segregate groups of organizations for particular marketing programmes. Segmentation might be based on the closeness and level of inter-dependence existing between organizations. Organizational attitudes towards risk and the degree to which an organization is willing to experiment through the acquisition of new industrial offerings varies. The starting point of any business-to-business segmentation is a good database or customer relationship management system. It should contain customer addresses, contact details, and detailed purchase and transactional history. Ideally, it will also include the details of those buyers present in the customer company's **decision-making unit structure**.

Market Insight 6.3
Recapturing Lost B2B Customers

Customer churn for firms such as FedEx, UPS, and XPO in the logistics industry can reach 20–25%. Customers switch suppliers for a variety of reasons, but some of the more common ones concern core service failures, dissatisfactory service encounters, price, inconvenience in terms of time, location, or delays, poor response to service failure, competition, ethical problems, and involuntary switching. It is important, therefore, for all firms to understand these switch/defection behaviours in order to reduce their incidence, retrieve lost customers, and so lower their long-run costs.

Segmenting B2B markets based on customers who have been lost is not necessarily the same as segmentation to find new customers. One of the reasons for this is that 'lost customers' leave a portfolio of transactions that can be used by the sales force to leverage a return. Research suggests that five distinct segments of lost customers can be identified and actioned.

■ **Bought away customers**—often very price oriented, these customers are attracted by competitive prices. A decision to regain this segment needs to take into account how easy and profitable it will be to retain them in the light of their price vulnerability.

■ **Pulled away customers**—this segment is characterized by buyers seeking better overall value who will collaborate with suppliers to achieve higher benefits and/or lower costs.

Therefore the solution to winning back these 'lost customers' is to co-develop value propositions that are unique and sustainable.

■ **Unintentionally pushed away customers**—these customers leave because they perceive that they have been mistreated or neglected. An apology is required, but where there have been service/product failures, service recovery and re-acquisition may include compensation, reimbursement, and discounts. In severe cases, often when mistakes have been repeated, customers can only be retrieved after personnel changes in either or both the buying and sales centres.

■ **Moved away customers**—this segment is characterized by customers who no longer need or value in the product/service offerings. They might have moved physically or to different markets that the selling company cannot serve. Although lost for good, a positive ending to the relationship is regarded as important to secure referrals and helpful word of mouth.

■ **Intentionally pushed away customers**—These problematic or unprofitable customers are deliberately let go as the selling company no longer wants their business. Allowing them to build relationships with competitors should be matched by a positive dissolution to help maintain a strong reputation and brand image.

Source: Keaveney (1995); Lopes *et al*. (2001); Liu *et al*. (2015).

Market Insight 6.3
continued

Theory into Practice

The process of segmenting customers who leave their suppliers is an important part of the relationship management process, of which sales management is an integral part. Segmentation within a relationship context requires identification of the characteristics of lost customers which enables categorization of defection patterns. Sales people are in a stronger position to understand customers' reasons for leaving and to then reduce the level of customer churn and retrieve some 'lost customers'.

Relationship management theory, therefore, is a key underpinning approach to understanding this aspect of segmentation analysis. Relational factors are important antecedents to positive outcomes and this indicates that trust, commitment, satisfaction, and other dimensions are essential elements for the development of long-run quality relationships between buyers and sellers.

Predicting, or at least anticipating and successfully managing a relationship's ending, is commercially important and the 'exit, voice, and loyalty' (EVL) framework devised by Hirschman (1974) provides a means of interpreting this process.

Related Topics:

customer lifecycle; loyalty; collaboration; customer lifetime value.

1 Discuss the view that if retrieving lost customers is costly, and then keeping them is problematic, there is little point in segmenting and actively trying to get them back.

2 To what extent is a high churn rate a function of poor customer management?

3 Using a different industry, try to determine how companies try to retain customers.

Choice Criteria

Business markets can be segmented on the basis of the specifications of offerings that they choose. For example, an accountancy practice may segment its clients by those that seek 'compliance'-type accounting offerings such as audits and tax submission work, companies that require management accounting services, and companies that require a complex mix of both. A computer manufacturer might segment the business market for computers by those requiring computers with strong graphical capabilities (e.g. educational establishments, publishing houses) and those requiring computers with strong processing capabilities (e.g. scientific establishments). Companies do not necessarily need to target multiple segments, however. They might simply target a single segment, as RM, an IT technological solutions provider, has done successfully in the UK education market.

Purchase Situation

Companies sometimes seek to segment the market on the basis of how organizations buy. Three questions associated with segmentation by purchase situation should be considered.

1 What is the structure of the buying organization's purchasing procedures? Centralized, decentralized, flexible, or inflexible?

2 What type of buying situation is present? New task (i.e. buying for the first time), modified rebuy (i.e. not buying for the first time, but buying something with different specifications from previously), or straight rebuy (i.e. buying the same thing again)?

3 What stage in the purchase decision process have target organizations reached? Are they buyers in early or late stages and are they experienced or new?

For example, a large global consulting and IT services company like Infosys from India might segment the market for IT project management services into public and private sectors. The focus might then be on fulfilling large government contracts that are put out to tender, where a group of selected buyers are offered the opportunity to bid for an exclusive franchise to deliver agreed services for a defined period of time.

Typically in segmenting business markets, a service provider can use a mix of macro- and micro-industrial market segmentation approaches by defining the customers a company wants to target using a macro-approach, such as standard industrial classification or geographic region, and then further segmenting using the choice criteria for which they select a company. In other words, multi-stage market segmentation approaches are often adopted.

Target Markets

The second important part of the STP process is to determine which of the segments uncovered should be targeted and made the focus of a comprehensive marketing programme. Ultimately, managerial discretion and judgement determines which markets are selected and exploited. Kotler (1984) suggested that the DAMP acronym, should be applied for market segmentation to be effective. That is all segments must be:

- **D**istinct—is each segment clearly different from other segments? If so, different marketing mixes, will be necessary.

- **A**ccessible—can buyers be reached through appropriate promotional programmes and distribution channels?

- **M**easurable—is the segment easy to identify and measure?

- **P**rofitable—is the segment sufficiently large to provide a stream of constant future revenues and profits?

Another approach to evaluating market segments uses a rating approach for different segment attractiveness factors, such as market growth, segment profitability, segment size, competitive intensity within the segment, and the cyclical nature of the industry (e.g. whether or not the business is seasonal, such as retailing). Each of these segment attractiveness factors is rated on a scale of 0–10 and loosely categorized in the high, medium, or low columns, based on either set criteria or subjective criteria, depending on the availability of market and customer data and the approach adopted by the managers undertaking the segmentation programme (see Table 6.4).

Table 6.4 Examples of segment attractiveness factors

Segment attractiveness factors	Rating		
	High (10–7)	Medium (6–4)	Low (3–0)
Growth	>2.5%	2.5–2.0%	<2.0%
Profitability	>15%	10–15%	<10%
Size	>£5m	£1m–£5m	£1m
Competitive intensity	Low	Medium	High
Cyclicality	Low	Medium	High

Source: McDonald and Dunbar (2004). Reproduced with permission.

Other examples of segment attractiveness factors might include segment stability (i.e. stability of the segment's needs over time) and mission fit (i.e. the extent to which dealing with a particular segment fits the mission of your company). Once the attractiveness factors have been determined, the importance of each factor can be weighed and each segment rated on each factor. This generates a segment attractiveness evaluation matrix (see Table 6.5).

Decisions need to be made about whether a single offering is made available to a range of segments, or a range of offerings to multiple segments or a single segment, or whether one

Table 6.5 Example of a segment attractiveness evaluation matrix

Segment attractiveness factors	Weight	Segment 1		Segment 2		Segment 3	
		Score	Total	Score	Total	Score	Total
Growth	25	6	1.5	5	1.25	10	2.5
Profitability	25	9	2.25	4	1.0	8	2.0
Size	15	6	0.9	5	0.9	7	1.05
Competitive intensity	15	5	0.75	6	0.9	6	0.9
Cyclicality	20	2.5	0.5	8	1.6	5	1
Total	100		5.9		5.65		7.45

Source: McDonald and Dunbar (2004). Reproduced with permission.

offering should be presented to a single segment. Whatever the decision, a marketing mix strategy should be developed to meet segment needs, which reflects the organization's capabilities and competitive strengths. Key questions around the development of the marketing mix include: How can the segment(s) be reached with appropriate communications? What is the media consumption pattern of the target audience? Where can they gain access to our offerings to purchase them? Does the offering need to be adapted for different segments and should it be priced the same or differently for all segments?

Targeting Approaches

Once segments are identified, an organization selects its preferred approach to targeting. Four differing approaches can be used (see Figure 6.7).

- The **undifferentiated approach**—where there is no delineation between market segments and the market is viewed as one mass market with one marketing strategy for the entire market. Although expensive, this approach is used for markets where there is limited or no segment differentiation (e.g. housing offered by local authorities).

- The **differentiated targeting approach**—where there are several market segments to target, each being attractive to the marketing organization. To exploit them, a marketing strategy is developed for each segment. For example, HP has developed its product range and marketing strategy to target the following user segments of computing equipment: home office users; small and medium-sized businesses, large businesses, and health, education, and government departments. A disadvantage of this approach is the loss of economies of scale because of the resources required to meet the needs of multiple market segments.

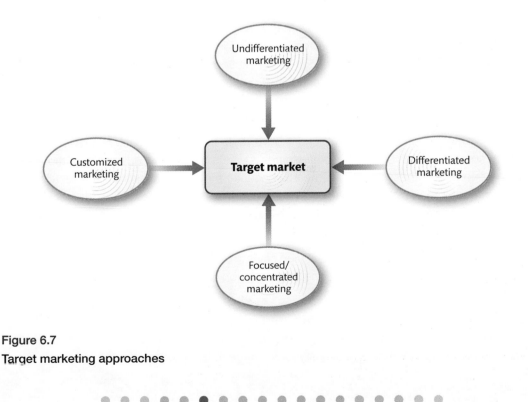

Figure 6.7
Target marketing approaches

- A **concentrated marketing strategy (niche marketing strategy)**—where there are just a few market segments. This approach is adopted by firms with limited resources to fund their marketing strategy, or who adopt a very exclusive strategy in the market. The UK's Co-operative Bank targets consumers interested in a bank with ethical lending and investment credentials. This approach is used frequently by small to medium-sized and micro-sized organizations with limited resources (e.g. an electrician may focus on local residences).

- A **customized targeting strategy**—where marketing strategy is developed for each customer rather than each segment. This approach predominates in B2B markets (e.g. marketing research or advertising services) or consumer markets with high value, highly customized products (e.g. purchase of a custom-made car). For example, a manufacturer of industrial electronics for assembly lines might target and customize its offering differently for Nissan, Unilever, and SCA, given the differing requirements in assembly line processes for the manufacture of automobiles, foodstuffs, and hygiene products (e.g. hand-dryers).

Segmentation Limitations

Whilst market segmentation is a useful process for organizations to divide customers into distinct groups, it has been criticized for the following reasons.

- The process approximates offerings to the needs of customer groups, rather than individuals. Therefore there is a chance that customers' needs are not fully met. However, **customer relationship marketing** (CRM) processes and software allow companies to develop customized approaches for individual customers. Integrating CRM processes and segmentation schemes can therefore require considerable extra planning.

- There is insufficient consideration of how market segmentation is linked to competitive advantage (Hunt and Arnett, 2004). The product differentiation concept is linked to the need to develop competing offerings, but market segmentation does not stress the need to segment on the basis of differentiating the offering from competitors. This angle should be integrated into the segmentation scheme if the scheme is to be more effective.

- It is unclear how valuable segmentation is to managers. Suitable processes/models to measure the market segmentation effectiveness have yet to be developed. It has been argued that much money spent on segmentation schemes is wasted, partly because organizations don't spend enough on these studies and partly because they don't assimilate the results of the study into the organization's strategy development processes (Incite, 2009). Market segmentation is, therefore, an organizational capability and some organizations are better at it than others (Poenaru and Baines, 2011).

Dibb *et al.* (2001) suggested that segmentation plans in business-to-business markets frequently fail because businesses fail to overcome segmentation implementation barriers including the following.

- Infrastructure barriers—culture, structure, and the availability of resources prevent the segmentation process from ever starting, e.g. there may be a lack of financial resource or political will to collect the market data necessary for a segmentation programme.

Research Insight 6.3

To take your learning further, you might wish to read this influential paper.

Hellwig, K. Morhart, F., Girardin, F., and Hauser, M. (2015). Exploring different types of sharing: a proposed segmentation of the market for 'sharing' businesses, *Psychology & Marketing*, **32(9), 891–906.**

This paper reports research which identified segments based on an individual's approach to sharing. The consumers in this representative sample of 1121 Swiss-Germans and Germans were grouped into four potential clusters of sharing consumers—sharing idealists, sharing opponents, sharing pragmatists, and sharing normatives—based on a set of trait-related, motivational, and perceived socio-economic variables.

Ⓐ   **Visit the Online Resource Centre to read the abstract and access the full paper.**

- Process issues—lack of experience, guidance, and expertise can hamper how segmentation is undertaken and managed. Typically, market research agencies and in-house market research teams use market and customer insight data and statistical software packages to undertake this task. However, because the different statistical methods provide different results, care must be taken in determining which method to use and how to interpret these results when they are produced.

- Implementation barriers—once a new segmentation model is determined, how do organizations move towards a new segmentation model? This may require a move away from a business model based on offerings (e.g. engine sizes for fleet buyers), to one based on customer needs.

Positioning

Having segmented the market, determined the size and potential of market segments, and selected specific target markets, the third part of the STP process is to position a brand within the target market(s). **Positioning** is the means by which offerings are differentiated from one another to give customers a reason to buy. It encompasses two fundamental elements. The first concerns the attributes, the functionality, and the capability that a brand offers (e.g. a car's engine specification, design, and carbon emissions). The second positioning element concerns the way in which a brand is communicated and how customers perceive the brand relative to competing brands. This element of communication is important as it is not what you do to an offering that is important, but 'what you do to the mind of a prospect' (Ries and Trout, 1972) that determines how a brand obtains its market positioning (see Market Insight 6.4).

Market Insight 6.4
Positioning Premium Beer

The history of the Belgian beer brand Leffe can be traced back to 1240. Its current success, however, can be credited to its positioning and association with contemporary food and lifestyles, rather than its taste and historic values associated with traditional brewing and ingredients.

Despite its super-premium price the brand has experienced strong growth in France, nearly doubling its market share between 2008 and 2013. This growth has been achieved by associating the brand as an 'aperitif', a time when social interaction occurs before a meal, normally associated with wine. The brand was positioned as the ideal first drink of the evening, particularly when accompanied by traditional foods like dry-cured ham and cheese.

The bottle uses foil wrapping around the neck, similar to champagne, reinforcing the premium cue. Rather than use conventional media, Leffe uses an online newsletter called *Leffervescense*. In addition to featuring its own products, the newsletter is used to introduce readers to celebrity chefs and artisanal food producers. Heineken in the USA have now followed this path by aligning itself with hand-crafted products that 'embody Heineken's aspirational and metropolitan essence'.

In Italy, Peroni is priced below the average for mass-market brands. Nastro Azzuro is Peroni's upmarket brand offering; it is premium priced and does not carry the Peroni name. When the owners SABMiller launched Peroni in the UK, they recoupled the names and positioned Peroni Nastro Azzuro against its Italian origins. Research identified the target audience as confident, socially mobile, 25–34 year old status seekers, who were optimistic about the future and their ability to control it. They were referred to as 'modern sophisticates'. Using conventional media the brand was associated with 'the Golden Age of Italy'. TV advertising used stereotypical images of Italy, sixties nostalgia, and premium brand cues such as flying boats, carefree lifestyle, and powerboats.

Source: Hollis (2014a); Hollis (2014b); http://www.brandunion.com.

Theory into Practice

The way in which individuals perceive, organize and interpret stimuli is a reflection of their past experiences and the classifications used to understand the different situations each individual encounters every day. Consumers attempt to evaluate a product's attributes using the physical cues of taste, smell, size, and shape. Sometimes, as with the beer market, no difference can be distinguished, so the consumer has to make a judgement on factors other than the physical characteristics of the product, and this means branding, and this means positioning.

Positioning concerns the presentation of products and services through a particular mental frame. There are several levels or frames against which a brand can be positioned, and premium branding is one of these frames. For the UK market, Peroni chose to position against a romanticized Italian lifestyle frame. Leffe's frame was a particular consumption scenario—one that is credible and relevant.

We know that successful positioning requires that all elements associated with a brand complement and reinforce one another. By associating the brand as an upmarket and different aperitif, Leffe sought ways to reinforce this perception. This was accomplished through the choice of packaging, messaging, media, and association with artisan foods and chefs. The space in people's minds that Leffe created, and then filled, enabled the brand to be positioned with

Market Insight 6.4
continued

a degree of competitive advantage as other brands would find it difficult to position against Leffe using the same criteria. This is because competitors attempting to invade this perceptual space would not been seen as credible or relevant, as Leffe already owned that frame.

Related Topics:

branding; perception; audience information processing; competitive strategy; communication theory.

1 **Identify two other ways in which these two beer brands could be positioned.**

2 **What problems might arise when positioning museums and other cultural attractions?**

3 **Choose a market (e.g. fashion, hair care, air travel) and determine how any three brands in that market are positioned. Are they successful?**

Positioning concerns an offering's attributes and design: how the offering is communicated, and the way these elements are fused together in customers' minds. It is not the offering (physical or otherwise) that is important for positioning, nor just the communication that leads to successful positioning. For example, claims (through communication) that a shampoo will remove dandruff will be rejected if the offering fails to deliver. Positioning, therefore, is about how customers judge an offering's value relative to competitors, its ability to deliver against the promises made, and the potential customers have to derive value from the offering. To develop a sustainable position, we must understand the market in which the offering is competing.

At a simple level, the positioning process begins during the target market selection process. Key to this process is identifying those attributes considered to be important by consumers. For a car manufacturer, these attributes may be tangible (e.g. the gearbox, transmission system, seating, and interior design) and intangible (e.g. the reputation, prestige, and allure that a brand generates). By understanding what customers consider to be the ideal standard that each attribute needs to attain and how they rate the attributes of each brand in relation to the ideal level, and each other, it becomes possible to see how a brand's attributes can be adapted and communicated to become more competitive.

Perceptual Mapping

Understanding the complexity associated with the different attributes and brands can be made easier by developing a visual representation of each market. These are known as perceptual maps. The 'maps' are used to determine how various brands are perceived according to the key attributes that customers value. This is important because position-ing is a two-way process by which organizations seek to impose attribute perceptions onto customers and customers assimilate those perceptions, modify them, or reject them entirely. **Perceptual mapping**, therefore, allows a geometric comparison of how competing prod-ucts are perceived (Sinclair and Stalling, 1990). Typically, the closer offerings/brands are clustered together on a perceptual map, the greater the competition. The further apart the positions, the greater the opportunity for new brands to enter the market. For example, in the non-vintage champagne market there are numerous brands competing with each other across differing attributes. Figure 6.8 shows the positioning of key champagne brands in the non-vintage market. Here the positions are based on attributes relating to the type of fruit used and the taste. It can be seen that leading brands Lanson, Bollinger, and Moët et Chandon occupy distinct positions in their 'own' quadrants. See Case Insight 7.1 for more information about Lanson International, a leading champagne house.

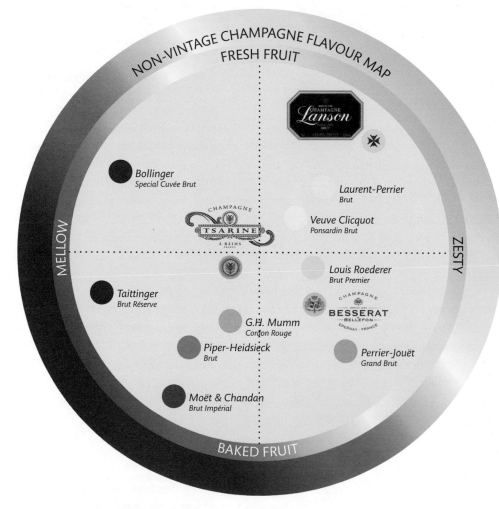

Figure 6.8

Perceptual map for non-vintage champagne

Source: Reproduced with kind permission of Lanson International UK Ltd.

Perceptual mapping data reveal strengths and weaknesses that can assist strategic decisions about how to differentiate on the attributes that matter to customers the most.

C–D Maps

One of the issues associated with these conventional approaches to positioning is that brand performance cannot be incorporated and is measured separately to positioning in most organizations. In response to this challenge Dawar and Bagga (2015) have developed the centrality–distinctiveness (C–D) map, which incorporates performance dimensions.

Centrality is concerned with the extent to which a brand, such as Coca-Cola in soft drinks and McDonald's in fast food, are most representative of their type or category. They serve as reference points by which others in the category are understood.

Distinctiveness refers to a brand's individuality and the extent to which it is positioned away from the direct competition of popular central brands. The authors refer to Tesla in cars and Corona in beer as good examples of brands with strong distinctiveness scores.

Figure 6.9 depicts the four quadrants that a C–D Map represents.

- **Aspirational brands** are highly differentiated and have wide appeal. Examples of cars include Mercedes and BMW, and for beer Guinness and Heineken. It is quite common for highly distinctive brands to command higher prices than brands that score low on this dimension.

- **Mainstream brands** tend to be the first that come to mind when consumers think of the category. Their wide appeal and popularity is countered by their low distinctiveness, which in turn tends to reduce their capacity to command a premium price. Ford and Chevrolet for cars and Miller and Busch for beer are good examples.

- **Unconventional brands** have unique distinctive characteristics that separate them from traditional products in the category. Cars such as Tesla, Mini, and the Smart car, and beers such as Leffe and Peroni can be considered as unconventional.

- **Peripheral brands** are seldom recalled by consumers as first choice and have little to distinguish them. Examples include Kia and Mitsubishi for cars and Old Milwaukee for beer. It follows that they have to carry low prices yet they can still be successful.

See Market Insight 6.5 for an example of how C–D Maps can be used.

The Centrality-Distinctiveness Map

The C-D map links consumers' perceptions about brands with their business performance. Brands are positioned in quadrants according to how customers score them on two universal dimensions: **centrality** and **distinctiveness.** Each quadrant carries strategic implications for sales, pricing, risk, and profitability. The distribution of brands across the map offers insights about competitive opportunities and threats.

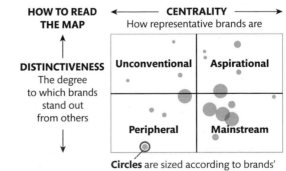

Figure 6.9

A C–D map

Source: Used with the kind permission of HBR.

Market Insight 6.5
Exploring C–D Maps for Strategic Positioning

When considering the C–D maps for the US beer and car markets, research shows quite clearly that the higher a brand scores on centrality, the greater is its sales volume. This indicates that improving a brand's centrality should be a key strategic goal for many brands. Cars such as Toyota and beer brands such as Budweiser were considered to be the most central brands with the largest sales volumes. In terms of price, however, increased centrality leads to a fall in prices as competition intensifies. In direct contrast, research indicates that the higher a brand's distinctiveness the lower will be its sales volume, for both cars and beer. However, these brands can charge a higher price, as demonstrated by Porsche and Guinness.

The C–D maps shown in Figure 6.10 depict brands in the US car and beer markets. Their positions across the four quadrants indicate the strategies followed and possible directions in the future, based upon both positioning and performance.

The underlying strategic imperative is that sales volumes tend to increase, and prices fall as a brand becomes increasingly central. In contrast sales volumes tend to fall as distinctiveness increases, yet these brands can also increase prices.

C–D MAPS FOR CARS AND BEER
To create C–D maps, the researchers surveyed adults across the U.S. about their perceptions of

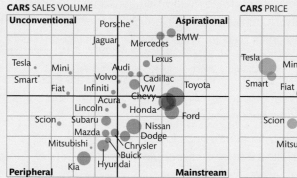

Notes: Brands are at the parent level. Cars are passenger only.

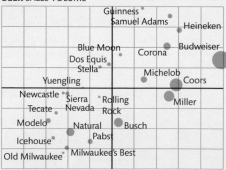

Source: Dawar and Bagga (2015)

© HBR.ORG

Figure 6.10
C–D maps for cars and beer
Source: Used with the kind permission of HBR.

Market Insight 6.5
continued

30 car brands and 23 beer brands, asking them to rank the brands, on a 0–10 scale, on **centrality** and **distinctiveness**. Sales volume tends to increase with centrality, and prices tend to fall. The more distinctive a brand is, the lower the sales volume and higher the price. Many brands succeed by being both central and distinctive (BMW and Guinness, for example), while others compete by being neither (Kia and Old Milwaukee). Firms can use a C–D map to identify positioning opportunities and unexpected threats.

Source: Dawar and Bagga (2015).

Theory into Practice

Positioning maps, sometimes referred to as perceptual, brand, or spatial maps, are important techniques for measuring and evaluating consumer perceptions of a range of offerings in a market. These maps are developed according to consumers' views (perceptions) for ranking a variety of similar offerings based on specific attributes and features. Having determined the positions of competing brands on a perceptual map, individual firms can develop strategies to move and occupy a different, seemingly stronger, competitive position. Indeed, these maps have been an important tool for marketers not only for their diagnostic capabilities, but also for their ability to visually portray the competitive marketplace.

C–D maps represent a development of positioning maps, as these combine performance criteria.

Related Topics:

competitive strategy; consumer perception.

1 **To what extent do C–D maps represent a major advance in technique and marketing insight?**

2 **If C–D maps encompass brand performance, in what circumstances might perceptual maps have an effective role to play in strategy development?**

3 **Select a market (other than cars and beer) and develop an outline C–D map based on your perceptions.**

Research Insight 6.4

To take your learning further, you might wish to read this influential paper.

Dawar, N. and Bagga, C.K. (2015). A better way to map brand strategy, *Harvard Business Review*, June. Retrieve from: https://hbr.org/2015/06/a-better-way-to-map-brand-strategy (accessed 6 November 2015).

Business performance metrics such as pricing and sales are excluded from conventional perceptual mapping tools. In this article a new type of map is presented, one that links a brand's position to competitors according to its perceived 'centrality' (how representative it is of the company) and 'distinctiveness' (how much it stands out from other brands) with its business performance along a given metric.

Visit the **Online Resource Centre** to read the paper and watch a video to learn more about C–D maps.

Positioning and Repositioning

Understanding brand positioning helps marketers to improve a brand's performance through modification of the marketing communications used to support a brand. Through marketing communications, especially advertising, information can be conveyed about each attribute in order to adjust customers' brand perceptions. Marketing communications can be used to position brands either functionally or expressively (symbolically) (see Table 6.6). Functionally positioned brands emphasize features and benefits, whereas expressive brands emphasize the ego, social, and hedonic satisfactions a brand brings (see Chapter 2). Both approaches make a promise: for example, for hair care, the promise is to deliver cleaner, shinier, and healthier hair (functional) or hair we are confident wearing because we want to be admired, or because it is important that we feel more self-assured (expressive). Different positioning approaches are likely to be more successful than others with particular offerings. For example, in the compact car market, Fuchs and Diamantopoulos (2010) found that direct benefit positioning (based on functional aspects) is likely to be more effective than indirect benefit positioning (based on experiential/symbolic dimensions), and that expressive positioning is more effective than functional approaches. User positioning can also provide a sound alternative to benefit positioning.

Technology, customer tastes, and competitors' new offerings are reasons why markets might change. For example, Disney acquired Lucasfilm in 2012 with a plan to launch the seventh *Star Wars* film in 2015 and others beyond. To be successful, however, Disney needed to reposition and target the new films at the generation which grew up with the *Clone Wars* cartoon and *Lego Star Wars* characters rather than those who watched the original trilogy in the late 1970s and 1980s (Garrahan, 2012). Thus, if the brand positioning adopted is strong, if the brand was the first to claim the position, and the position is continually reinforced with clear simple messages, there may be little need to alter the position originally adopted. Marketers should be alert and prepared to reposition their brands as the relative positions occupied by brands, in the minds of customers, will be challenged on a frequent basis, especially by competing offerings. Repositioning is often difficult

Table 6.6 Proposition positioning strategies

Position	Strategy	Explanation
Functional	Product features	Brand positioned on the basis of attributes, features, or benefits relative to the competition, e.g. Volvos are safe; Red Bull provides energy.
	Price quality	Price can be a strong communicator of quality. John Lewis Partnership (the UK department store) uses the tagline 'never knowingly undersold' to indicate how it will match competitors' prices on the same items to ensure its customers always get good value.
	Use	By informing when or how an offering can be used, we create a mental position in buyers' minds, e.g. Kellogg's reposition their offerings to be consumed throughout the day, not just at breakfast (e.g. Special K).
Expressive	User	By identifying the target user, messages can be communicated clearly to the right audience. Flora margarine was initially for men and then it became 'for all the family'. Some hotels position themselves as places for weekend breaks, leisure centres, conference centres, or all three.
	Benefit	Positions can be established by proclaiming the benefits that usage confers on consumers. The benefit of using Sensodyne toothpaste is that it alleviates the pain associated with sensitive teeth.
	Heritage	Heritage and tradition are sometimes used to symbolize quality, experience, and knowledge. Kronenbourg 1664, 'Established since 1803', and the use of coats of arms by many universities are designed to convey heritage to build long-term trust.

to accomplish because of the entrenched perceptions and attitudes held by customers towards brands and the cost of the vast (media) resources required to make these changes.

Repositioning revolves around an offering and the way it is communicated. It should be noted, however, that repositioning carries a number of risks. These include alienating the current customer base, inaccurate forecasting and rejection by the new audience, and of course competitors closing opportunities or seizing the position vacated. Repositioning also incurs substantial costs, both internally through planning and managerial time, and externally through communication with both distributors and customers to inform them about the new position. The following four ways outline how to approach repositioning, depending on the individual situation facing a brand. In some cases, a brand might need to be adapted before relaunch.

1 **Change the tangible attributes and then communicate the new proposition to** *the same market*. UBS, the financial services firm whose reputation was shattered following an estimated $2bn loss due to insider trading, spent four years transforming itself internally before relaunching and repositioning as a wealth management company (Rooney, 2015). Berger Paints India repositioned its products following the acquisition of the Sherwin Williams decorative paints business. The goal was to avoid competition within

Research Insight 6.5

To take your learning further, you might wish to read this influential book.

Ries, A. and Trout, J. (2006). *Positioning: The Battle for your Mind*. **London: McGraw-Hill Professional.**

Al Ries and Jack Trout's book, originally published in 1981, remains the bible of advertising strategy. They define 'positioning' not as what you do to an offering to make it acceptable to potential customers, but what you do to the mind of the prospect. Positioning requires an outside-in rather than an inside-out thinking approach.

@ **Visit the Online Resource Centre to read more about this book.**

the group and this was achieved through a dual-brand strategy. By removing some of the lower-end products, Sherwin Williams was repositioned within a different price bracket.

2 **Change the way a proposition is communicated to the original market**. The Norwegian oil and gas company, Statoil Hydro was repositioned globally as Statoil by communications agency Hill & Knowlton Strategies, raising its profile in key markets across Europe including the UK.

3 **Change the target market and deliver the same proposition**. On some occasions, repositioning can be achieved through marketing communications alone, but targeted at a new market. For example, the soft drink Orangina repositioned as a premium adult drink, targeting those who remember it from childhood French holidays.

4 **Change both the proposition (attributes) and the target market**. Xerox have repositioned themselves from being a document company to a diversified business services company, running call centres and processing insurance claims and even toll payments (Carone, 2013).

Chapter Summary

To consolidate your learning, the key points from this chapter are summarized here.

■ **Describe the principles of market segmentation and the STP process.**

Whole markets are subdivided into different segments through the STP process. STP refers to the three activities—segmentation, targeting, and positioning—that should be undertaken sequentially if segmentation is to be successful. Market segmentation is the division of a market into different groups of customers with distinctly similar needs and offering requirements. The second part of the STP process determines which segments should be targeted with a comprehensive marketing mix programme. The third part of the STP process is to position a brand within the target market(s).

■ **List the characteristics and differences between market segmentation and product differentiation.**

Market segmentation is related to product differentiation. Given an increasing proliferation of tastes, marketers have sought to design offerings around consumer demand (market segmentation) more than around their own production needs (product differentiation).

■ **Explain consumer and business-to-business market segmentation.**

Data, based on differing consumer, user, organizational, and market characteristics, are used to segment a market. These characteristics differ for consumer (B2C) and business (B2B) contexts. To segment consumer goods and service markets, market information based on certain key customer-, product-, or situation-related criteria (variables) is used. These are classified as segmentation bases and include profile, behavioural, and psychological criteria. To segment business markets, two main groups of interrelated variables are used: organizational characteristics and buyer characteristics.

■ **Describe different targeting strategies.**

Once identified, the organization selects its target marketing approach. Four different approaches exist: (1) undifferentiated, (2) differentiated, (3) concentrated or niche, and (4) customized target marketing.

■ **Discuss the concept of positioning.**

Positioning provides the means by which offerings can be differentiated from one another and gives customers reasons to buy. It encompasses physical attributes, the way in which a brand is communicated, and how customers perceive the brand relative to competing brands.

■ **Consider how the use of perceptual maps can assist in the positioning process.**

Perceptual maps are used in the positioning process to illustrate differing attributes of a selection of brands. They also illustrate existing levels of differentiation between brands, how our brand and competing brands are perceived in the marketplace, how a market operates, and strengths and weaknesses that can assist with making strategic decisions about how to differentiate the attributes that matter to customers in order to compete more effectively in the market. C–D maps enable brand performance to be incorporated into the strategy positioning process.

Review Questions

1 Define market segmentation and explain the STP process.

2 What is the difference between market segmentation and product differentiation?

3 Identify four different ways in which markets can be segmented.

4 How do market segmentation bases differ in business-to-business and consumer markets?

5 How can market segmentation bases be evaluated when target marketing?

6 What are the different approaches to selecting target markets?

7 Describe the principle of positioning and why it should be undertaken.

8 What are perceptual maps and what can they reveal?

9 Explain three ways in which brands can be positioned.

10 Make a list of four reasons why organizations need to reposition brands.

Worksheet Summary

Visit the **Online Resource Centre** and complete Worksheet 6.1. This will aid in learning about the STP process used to develop who to market to and in what way, while differentiating from the competition.

Discussion Questions

1 Having read Case Insight 6.1, how would you advise Soberana to respond to the changing consumer tastes and the challenge of Miller Lite in Panama?

2 In a group with other colleagues from your seminar/tutor group, discuss answers to the following questions.

A Using the information in Table 6.7 on the champagne market, and a suitable calculator, determine which segments have the greatest potential profit.

B What other data do we need to determine the size of the market (market potential)?

Table 6.7 The champagne and sparkling wine market by segment

Social class	Enthusiasts (%) AP = £20 F = 5/year	Sparkling sceptics (%) AP = £10, F = 3/year	Price driven (%) AP = £8.50, F = 3/year	Uneducated (%) AP = £15 F = 2/year
AB (n = 8m)	25	31	30	14
C1 (n = 14m)	23	23	32	21
C2 (n = 8m)	27	26	33	14
DE (n = 10m)	20	26	40	14

AP = average price, n = population size, F = number of bottles purchased per year (all data hypothetical); % segment sizes per socio-economic group and segment descriptions only from Mintel (2012).

---

3 Discuss which market segmentation bases might be most applicable to:

A A fashion retailer segmenting the market for womenswear.

B A commercial radio station specializing in dance music and celebrity news/gossip.

C A Belgian chocolate manufacturer supplying multiple retail grocers and confectionery shops across Europe (e.g. Godiva).

D The Absolut Company, headquartered in Sweden, supplying high quality vodka around the world.

E Rakbank in Dubai, United Arab Emirates, when segmenting the market for its credit card.

4 Write a one-sentence description of the attributes and benefits that are attractive to target consumers for an offering with which you are particularly familiar (e.g. Apple in the computer category or Samsung in the mobile phone category), using the statement provided. Explain how these attributes and benefits are different from those of competitors. Your positioning statement might be as follows:

[Product A] provides [target consumers] with [one or two salient product attributes]. This distinguishes it from [one or two groups of competing product offerings] that offer [attributes/benefits of the competing products].

A Briefly describe the target market segment. This should summarize the defining characteristics of the segment (e.g. demographic, psychographic, geographic, or behavioural).

B Briefly explain your reasons for believing that the attributes/benefits of your positioning statement are important for your target segment. Draw a perceptual map that summarizes your understanding of the market and shows the relative positions of the most important competing products.

@ Visit the **Online Resource Centre** and complete the Multiple Choice Questions to assess your knowledge of Chapter 6.

Glossary

benefits sought by understanding the motivations customers derive from their purchases it is possible to have an insight into the benefits they seek from product use.

breakdown method the view that the market is considered to consist of customers who are essentially the same, so the task is to identify groups that share particular differences.

build-up method considers a market to consist of customers that are all different, so here the task is to find similarities.

business markets characterized by organizations that consume products and services for use within the manufacture/production of other products or for use in their daily operations.

business-to-business activities undertaken by one company which are directed at another.

choice criteria the principal dimensions on which we select a particular product or service. For a hairdresser, this might be price, location, range of services, level of expertise, friendliness, and so on.

communication the sharing of meaning created through the transmission of information.

concentrated marketing strategy (niche marketing strategy) recognizes that there are segments in the market. However, a concentrated strategy is implemented by focusing on just one, two, or a few market segments.

customer relationship marketing all marketing activities and strategies used to retain customers. This is achieved by providing customers with relationship-enhancing products and/or services that are perceived to be of value and superior to those offered by a competitor.

customized targeting strategy a marketing strategy is developed for each customer as opposed to each market segment.

decision-making unit structure the attitudes, policies, and purchasing strategies used by organizations provide the means by which organizations can be clustered.

demographics key variables concerning age, sex, occupation, level of education, religion, and social class, many of which determine a potential buyer's ability to purchase a product or service.

differentiated targeting approach recognizes that there are several market segments to target, each being attractive to the marketing organization. To exploit market segments, a marketing strategy is developed for each segment.

firmographics an approach to segmentation of business-to-business markets using criteria such as company size, geography, standard industrial classification (SIC) codes, and other company-oriented classification data.

geodemographic this approach to segmentation presumes that there is a relationship between the type of housing and location that people live in and their purchasing behaviours.

industry type (SIC codes) standard industrial classifications (SICs) are codes used to identify and categorize all types of industry and businesses.

lifestage analysis is based on the principle that people need different products and services at different stages in their lives (e.g. childhood, adulthood, young couples, retired, etc.).

market segmentation the division of customer markets into groups of customers with distinctly similar needs.

media vehicle an individual medium used to carry advertising messages.

organizational size grouping organizations by their relative size (MNCs, international, large, SMEs) enables the identification of design, delivery, usage rates, or order size and other purchasing characteristics.

perceptual mapping a diagram, typically two-dimensional, of 'image space' derived from attitudinal market research data which displays the differences in perceptions that customers, consumers, or the general public have of different products/services or brands in general.

positioning the way that an audience of consumers or buyers perceives a product or service, particularly as a result of the marketing communications process aimed at a target audience.

product differentiation when companies produce offerings that are different from competing firms.

product usage segments are derived from analysing markets on the basis of their usage of the product offering, brand, or product category. This may be in the form of usage frequency, time of usage, and usage situations.

psychographic (lifestyles) analysing consumers' activities, interests, and opinions, we can understand individual lifestyles and patterns of behaviour, which in turn affect their buying behaviour and decision-making processes. On this basis, we can also identify similar product and/or media usage patterns.

purchase situation this approach segments organizational buyers on the way in which a buying company structures its purchasing procedures, the type of buying situation, and whether buyers are in an early or late stage in the purchase decision process.

STP process the method by which whole markets are subdivided into different segments for targeting and positioning.

undifferentiated approach there is no delineation between market segments, and instead the market is viewed as one mass market with one marketing strategy for the entire market.

References

Anon. (2013). Berger to reposition Sherwin Williams brand. *Chemical Business,* October, 27(10), 60.

Beane, T.P. and Ennis, D.M. (1987). Market segmentation: a review. *European Journal of Marketing*, 32(5), 20–42.

Belk, R.W., Bahn, K.D., and Mayer, R.N. (1982). Developmental recognition of consumption symbolism. *Journal of Consumer Research*, 9(June), 4–17.

Carone, C. (2013). Xerox's brand repositioning challenge. *Ad Age*, 12 March. Retrieve from: http://adage.com/article/cmo-strategy/xerox-s-brand-repositioning-challenge/240285/ (accessed 4 May 2013).

Dawar, N. and Bagga, C.K. (2015). A better way to map brand strategy. *Harvard Business Review*, June. Retrieve from: https://hbr.org/2015/06/a-better-way-to-map-brand-strategy (accessed 6 November 2015).

Dibb, S., Simkin, L., Pride, W.M., and Ferrell, D.C. (2001). *Marketing Concepts and Strategies*. Boston, MA: Houghton Mifflin.

Esposito, J. (2013). The fall and rise of market segmentation. *The Scholarly Kitchen*, 22 March. Retrieve from: http://scholarlykitchen.sspnet.org/2013/03/22/the-fall-and-rise-of-market-segmentation/ (accessed 29 April 2013).

Freytag, P.V. and Clarke, A.H. (2001). Business to business segmentation. *Industrial Marketing Management*, 30(6, August), 473–86

Fuchs, C. and Diamantopoulos, A. (2010). Evaluating the effectiveness of brand-positioning strategies from a consumer perspective. *European Journal of Marketing*, 44(11/12), 1763–86.

Garrahan, M. (2012). Disney grabs a galaxy of opportunity. *Financial Times*, 1 November, 19.

Griffith, R.L. and Pol, L.A. (1994). Segmenting industrial markets. *Industrial Marketing Management*, 23, 39–46.

Haley, R.I. (1968). Benefit segmentation: a decision-oriented research tool. *Journal of Marketing*, 32, 30–5.

Hellwig, K., Morhart, F., Girardin, F., and Hauser, M. (2015). Exploring different types of sharing: a proposed segmentation of the market for 'sharing' businesses. *Psychology & Marketing*, 32(9), 891–906.

Hirschman, A.O. (1974). Exit, voice, and loyalty: further reflections and a survey of recent contributions. *Social Science Information*, 13(7), 7–26.

Holbrook, M.B. and Gardner, M.P. (1993). An approach to investigating the emotional determinants of consumption durations: why do people consume what they consume for as long as they consume it? *Journal of Consumer Psychology*, 2(2), 123–42.

Holbrook, M.B. and Hirschman, E.C. (1982). The experiential aspects of consumer behaviour: consumer fantasies, feelings and fun. *Journal of Consumer Research*, 9(September), 132–40.

Hollis, N. (2014a). How Peroni uses images of Italy's 'Golden Age' to justify a price premium. *Millward Brown Blog*, 7 July. Retrieve from: http://www.millwardbrown.com/global-navigation/blogs/post/mb-blog/2014/07/07/how-peroni-uses-images-of-italy-s-golden-age-to-justify-a-price-premium (accessed 11 November 2015).

Hollis, N. (2014b). Beer brand Leffe taps into contemporary food trends to grow. *Millward Brown Blog*, 5 November. Retrieve from: http://www.millwardbrown.com/global-navigation/blogs/post/mb-blog/2014/11/05/beer-brand-leffe-taps-into-contemporary-food-trends-to-grow#sthash.eR1mDL3G.dpuf (accessed 11 November 2015).

Hunt, S.D. and Arnett, D.B. (2004). Market segmentation strategy, competitive advantage and public policy: grounding segmentation strategy in resource-advantage theory. *Australasian Marketing Journal*, 12(1), 7–25.

Incite (2009). Anything but business as usual. *Incite Segmentation Newsletter*, Spring. Retrieve from: http://www.incite.ws/segmentation_web/VISION%20-%20Anything%20but%20business%20as%20usual.pdf (accessed 28 April 2013).

Keaveney, S.M. (1995). Customer switching behavior in service industries: an exploratory study. *Journal of Marketing*, 59(April), 71–82.

Kotler, P. (1984). *Marketing Management*. Upper Saddle River, NJ: Prentice Hall.

Lee, E. (2013) A new market segmentation for capture-enabled devices. *InfoTrends*, 23 September. Retrieve from: http://blog.infotrends.com/?p = 12447 (accessed 17 February 2016).

Liu, A., Leach, M., and Chugh, R. (2015) A sales process framework to regain B2B customers. *Journal of Business & Industrial Marketing*, 30(8), 906–14.

Llewellyn, C., Podpolny, D., and Zerbi, C. (2015). Capturing the new 'value' segment in medical devices. *McKinsey Insights*, January. Retrieve from: http://www.mckinsey.com/insights/health_systems_and_services/capturing_the_new_value_segment_in_medical_devices (accessed 29 October 2015).

Lopes, L., Alves, H., and Brito, C. (2001). Lost customers: determinants and process of relationship dissolution. Presented at: 40th EMAC Conference, Ljubljana, Slovenia, 24–27 May. Retrieve from: https://bibliotecadigital.ipb.pt/bitstream/10198/6257/4/Lost%20customers_EMAC2011.pdf (accessed 1 November 2015).

McAlister, L., and Pessemier, E. (1982). Variety seeking behaviour: an interdisciplinary review. *Journal of Consumer Research*, 9(December), 311–22.

McDonald, M., and Dunbar, I. (2004), *Market Segmentation: How to Do It, How to Profit from It*, Oxford: Elsevier.

Maslow, A. H. (1943), A theory of human motivation, *Psychological Review*, 50(4), 370–96.

Mintel (2012), *Champagne and Sparkling Wine—UK—July 2012*, Retrieve from www.mintel.com, accessed 23 April 2013.

Morrissey, P. and Baines, P. (2011). Segmenting exercise participants by surface level participation motivation. Presented at: Australian and New Zealand Marketing Academy Conference, Perth, Australia, 28–30 November.

Naudé, P. and Cheng, L. (2003). Choosing between potential friends: market segmentation in a small company. Presented at: 19th IMP Conference, Lugano, Switzerland. Retrieve from: http://www.impgroup.org/conferences.php (accessed December 2007).

Olney, T.J., Holbrook, M.B., and Batra, R. (1991). Consumer response to advertising: the effects of ad content, emotions, and attitude toward the ad on viewing time. *Journal of Consumer Research*, 17(March), 440–53.

Park, N., Kee, K.F., and Valenzuela. S. (2009). Being immersed in social networking environment: Facebook groups, uses and gratifications, and social outcomes'. *CyberPsychology & Behavior*, 12(6), 729–33.

Poenaru, A. and Baines, P. (2011). An organizational capability model of market segmentation. Presented at: Australian and New Zealand Marketing Academy Conference, Perth, Australia, 28–30 November.

Ries, A. and Trout, J. (1972). The positioning era cometh. *Advertising Age*, 17(24, April), 35–8.

Ries, A. and Trout, J. (2006). *Positioning: The Battle for your Mind*. London: McGraw-Hill Professional.

Rooney, L. (2015). UBS unveils major brand overhaul, *Forbes.com*, 1 September. Retrieve from: http://web.b.ebscohost.com/ehost/detail/detail?vid = 6&sid = 49c728c8-b54f-4b4e-8e1e-30afe33a7cdb%40sessionmgr115&hid = 123&bdata = JnNpdGU9ZWhvc3QtbGl2ZQ%3d%3d#AN = 109219931&db = bch (accessed 9 November 2015).

Shao, W., Ross, M., and Grace, D. (2015). Developing a motivation-based segmentation typology of Facebook users. *Marketing Intelligence & Planning,* 33(7), 1071–86.

Sinclair, S.A. and Stalling, E.C. (1990). Perceptual mapping: a tool for industrial marketing. A case study. *Journal of Business and Industrial Marketing*, 5(1), 55–65.

Smith, W.R. (1956). Product differentiation and market segmentation as alternative marketing strategies. *Journal of Marketing*, July, 3–8.

Solomon, M.R. (1983). The role of products as social stimuli: a symbolic interactionism perspective. *Journal of Consumer Research*, 10(December), 319–29.

Sornoso, E. (2015). How to build custom Facebook audiences for marketing and advertising. *Search Engine Journal*, 9 February. Retrieve from: http://www.searchenginejournal.com/build-custom-facebook-audiences-marketing-advertising/124251/ (accessed 29 October 2015).

Srivastava, R.K., Shocker, A.D., and Day, G.S. (1978). An exploratory study of the influences of usage situations on perceptions of product markets. Presented at the Advances in Consumer Research Conference, Chicago, IL.

Stiving, M. (2012). Brilliant price segmentation—an example. *Pragmatic Pricing*, 4 May. Retrieve from: http://pragmaticpricing.com/2012/05/04/brilliant-price-segmentation-an-example/ (accessed 4 May 2013).

Urban, C. (1976). Correlates of magazine readership. *Journal of Advertising Research*, 19(3, June), 7–12.

Wind, Y. (1978). Issues and advances in segmentation research. *Journal of Marketing Research*, 15(August), 317–37.

Wind, Y. and Cardozo, R.N. (1974). Industrial market segmentation. *Industrial Marketing Management*, 3(March), 155–66.

Chapter 7
International Market Development

Learning Outcomes

After studying this chapter you should be able to:

▶ Define international market development as a market growth strategy

▶ List the different forms of international marketing strategy

▶ Identify the key drivers for international market development

▶ Describe the criteria used to identify and select international markets

▶ Discuss how environmental factors influence the choice of international marketing strategy decisions

▶ Explore various international market entry methods

Case Insight 7.1
Lanson International

Market Insight 7.1
Primark Heads Stateside

Market Insight 7.2
Ad-apt in São Paulo?

Market Insight 7.3
LEGO: To Translate or Localize?

Market Insight 7.4
Milking Trust in China

Market Insight 7.5
Fast Food Franchising: Still Appetizing?

Case Insight 7.1
Lanson International

Founded in 1760, Champagne Lanson is one of the oldest existing champagne houses in France, making some of the world's finest champagnes. We speak to Paul Beavis, Managing Director, Lanson International, to find out more about how the company looks to further develop its presence in international markets, including the UK.

Lanson currently works in over 30 countries around the world and this has been developed over a number of years, driven by the increase in demand for champagne in the UK, which started over 15 years ago. Generally, we believe a company should look at international markets when its appetite for growth exceeds the current in-market capacity. Obviously general economic market conditions apply and these need to be considered before we enter any new markets. For us a key success factor for successfully entering a new market is having data, data, and more data! Having the absolute facts about your markets is essential—it's a case of examination (of the market), diagnosis (of the entry method, what channels to use, and how to promote our brand), and prescription (of the operational approach).

Before we enter a market, we look at the current shape and size of the markets today, but also (and this is seldom easy) we try to forecast how the category will be shaped in the next 3–5 years. One key trend that we can see in the global economy today is a concentration of spending power across and within certain markets. In order to tap into those segments, internationalization has to be a core part of our strategy for the future. So, we evaluate a potential market's economic conditions, searching for market data not just about current volumes but more about consumer trends, the knowledge gap (what do we know versus what don't we know about their attitudes and behaviour), other drinks categories such as spirits, and growth in wine consumption generally.

All of this insight primarily helps us to plan our route-to-market strategy. This also involves ascertaining more generally what strategy we should deploy in terms of our market positioning—whether we use a subsidiary brand model or a distributor/agency model, and considering the financial implications of each of these.

Part of the problem in the UK is that as categories become more mature, as the UK is now, there is a real need to be able to explain why your brand is essential in the marketplace. The hardest question any business should ask itself is: What is my true competitive advantage?

In the UK market, champagne (with sales of £141.3m in 2014) has generally seen strong competition from sparkling wine brands, particularly Prosecco (with sales of £181.8m in 2014) and especially in the off-licence trade, but Lanson enjoys the position of being the No.1 rosé brand and the No.2 non-vintage champagne brand. Meanwhile, Spanish Cava has seen a recent decline in sales. Lanson was therefore faced with a couple of key questions in relation to its international market development strategy:

How should a French brand like Lanson seek to differentiate itself in a category which is dominated, in the UK, by a competitor focus on 'advertising' and the colour of the label?

Once we had achieved success in the UK, how might we replicate this success in other international markets?

Introduction

Have you ever considered where the products you purchase and consume are produced or manufactured? Have a look at the food products in your kitchen or the clothes in your wardrobe. Are they from the UK, Scandinavia, China, or Asia? We now consume more products, read more information, and travel to more overseas countries than ever before.

In the light of the increasing internationalization of world markets, increased foreign trade, changes in technology, and the economic impact of foreign markets, **international marketing** is essential for the survival of many organizations. Even organizations that only compete in domestic markets are affected, as they increasingly compete with foreign organizations. An understanding of international business, marketing, and globalization is essential for marketing in the twenty-first century.

This chapter explores the issues that marketers should consider when developing effective international marketing strategies and policies. This includes international market development, the criteria used to select attractive international markets, the forces in international markets that shape our activities, and the different methods for international market entry, as well as the impact of country of origin effects.

Types of International Organization

Before we consider the strategies and issues associated with international marketing, consideration should be given to understanding the different types of organization that operate in international markets. There are several typologies, particularly from the work of Keegan (1989), Bartlett and Ghoshal (1991), and de Mooij (1994). Their view is that organizations can be regarded as national, international, multinational, global, or transnational (see Table 7.1), each of which has different strategic orientations towards customers and their markets.

Organizations operate domestically using a marketing mix designed to meet the needs of the home market. This usually means offering a standardized proposition. Some domestic organizations evolve into international organizations as they win 'overseas' business. The first step is to use their domestically oriented marketing mix, and at a later stage adapt it to the needs of the new 'overseas' market.

This adaptation phase signals the emergence of a multinational strategy and corresponding type of organization. These organizations regard the world in which they operate as comprising discrete regions, with each requiring its own marketing mix. Each country/area reports to a world head office and performance is geared to meet financial targets.

As growth occurs and more regions are brought into an organization's scope, so it transforms into a global enterprise. Global organizations are characterized by strategies founded on an understanding that the similarities across country/area markets, not the differences between them, are important. Customers are seen as part of a single global picture; therefore a standardized marketing mix is preferred. All decision-making is centralized.

Transnational organizations develop out of global enterprises. These are relatively sophisticated companies which establish operations in many countries around the world based on

Table 7.1 Types of international organization

Type of organization	Explanation
National organizations	These organizations operate within domestic borders. The marketing policy is to serve customers with a single marketing mix. In multiple retail grocery, examples include Jumbo (the Netherlands), Morrisons (UK), and Axfood AB (Sweden), which owns the Willys and Hemköp retail outlets.
International organizations	These organizations see their overseas operations as attachments to a central domestic organization. The marketing policy is to serve customers domestically and offer these same marketing mixes in other countries (e.g. Burger King).
Multinational organizations	These organizations see their overseas activities as a portfolio of independent businesses. The policy is to serve customers with customized country marketing mixes (e.g. Royal Dutch Shell).
Global organizations	These organizations regard their overseas activities as feeders or delivery tubes for a unified global market. The policy is to serve the global market with a standardized marketing mix (e.g. Nike).
Transnational organizations	These organizations regard their overseas activities as a complex process of coordination and cooperation. Decision-making is shared. The policy is to serve global business environments using flexible global resources to formulate different global marketing mixes. For example, ArcelorMittal, Vodafone and Nestlé all hold over 90% of their assets abroad (Anon., 2012).

Sources: Adapted from Bartlett and Ghoshal (1991) and de Mooij (1994).

wholly or partially owned subsidiaries. The headquarters is the hub of the operations, based in one country, but managing the operations across all other countries. Transnational companies seek to serve global customers by developing efficient operations. These are based on utilizing technologies to generate synergies through the 'creation, accumulation, transferring and sharing of knowledge that exists in different locations' (de Pablos 2006: 556).

Organizations need to be flexible and adapt to changing market conditions. As domestic markets stagnate, and technology and communication opportunities develop, opportunities come and go. In addition, organizations seek efficiency and flexibility with regard to their use of materials and resources. The use of strategic alliances and outsourcing arrangements complements this goal, and network-based organizations spanning the globe emerge. Li & Fung, based out of Hong Kong, is a case example of a multinational consumer goods design, development, sourcing, and logistics company, providing a global supply chain capability to many high street brands.

Understanding these different types of international organization is important, not just from a structural perspective but also for the formulation and implementation of business and marketing strategies. Next, we explore ways in which organizations develop their operations, the decisions they make, and the factors and issues influencing their decision-making.

International Market Development: A Growth Strategy

Marketing strategy is about matching market opportunities to an organization's resources (what it can do) and its objectives (what management wants it to achieve). Successful strategies begin with the identification of attractive market opportunities using Ansoff's matrix (see Figure 7.1; also Chapter 5). This matrix is also referred to as the product–market matrix. It provides a useful way of considering the relationship between strategic direction and market opportunities (see Chapter 5 for a detailed consideration). This matrix provides four broad strategic options available to organizations, depending on whether the product and/or the market are considered to be new to or existing in an organization.

The matrix illustrates, implicitly, that risk increases the further the strategy moves away from known positions—an existing product and/or an existing market. Product development (a new proposition) and market development (a new market) typically involve greater risk than market penetration (existing offering and existing market). Diversification, a new offering in a new market, carries the greatest risk of all. Although four types of opportunity are presented, some organizations pursue more than one type simultaneously. Here, we pay specific attention to the strategy of 'market development' from an international perspective.

A market development strategy involves increasing sales by selling existing offerings in new markets, either by gaining new customers domestically or by entering new markets internationally. The goal is to sell more of the same things to different people. We might target different geographical markets at home and/or abroad, or target different segments, perhaps a different behavioural profile from our existing customers. For example, Ryanair's airline offering was first marketed at those seeking low cost travel but has recently been aimed, with some service enhancements (e.g. priority boarding, seat choice), at business travellers. Another example is the use of military equipment, repurposed for consumer purposes (e.g. the Hummer, from the American Motor Corporation was originally based on the High Mobility Multipurpose Wheeled Vehicle (HMMWV) or Humvee, built for the US military). We have also seen chains such as Gregg's, a British baker, expanding into new geographical locations domestically by targeting new audiences through differing retail outlets in motorway service stations, and Dixons, the British electrical group, set up Dixons Travel, an airport retail chain. These are all examples of developing new markets domestically for an existing offering.

Entering a new international market with an existing offering represents a high risk strategy. To build brand awareness and minimize risk, organizations often rely on the reputation of their brands in domestic markets. For example, Aston Martin's foray into the Chinese market is a good example of international market development (see Chapter 13).

	Present Products	**New Products**
Present Markets	Market Penetration	Product Development
New Markets	Market Development	Diversification

Figure 7.1

Ansoff's matrix

Source: Adapted from Ansoff (1957).

Table 7.2 Key differences between domestic and international marketing

Domestic marketing	International marketing
Native language	Many languages
Dominant culture	Multicultural
Research relatively straightforward	Research is complex
Relatively stable environment	Frequently unstable environment
Single currency	Exchange rate problems
Business conventions understood	Conventions diverse and unclear

Source: Fill (2009).

Major large organizations, such as Pepsico, Mercedes Benz, and Huawei, use their reputation earned in well-established domestic and international markets to gain early entry in rapidly developing markets. A key decision is whether to pursue new audiences in the domestic market or enter new international markets. Some of the main differences between domestic and international marketing include language, culture, complexity of research and decision-making, market knowledge, and marketing environment stability (see Table 7.2). For example, international markets are often seen as more unstable than domestic markets because of their sensitivity to fluctuations in currency rates, immigration patterns, and political and trade relations. Furthermore, development in international markets requires a relatively high degree of investment by an organization and a greater understanding of the changing nature of world markets.

International Market Development

Entering international markets is a key market development strategy for organizational growth and has been a feature of civilizations for thousands of years, ever since the first 'money'—based on metal objects—changed hands in commercial transactions around 5000 BC (Bellis, 2015). However, in the last two centuries international trade has grown enormously in scale and complexity. With this growth, different approaches to international market development have developed.

Some firms take an ad hoc approach to international marketing, only responding to customer export requests on a reactive basis. Others, such as H&M and BMW, develop an international marketing strategy proactively, to complement their domestic strategy. In the UK, for example, the Royal Mint is the world's leading exporter of circulating coin-based currency with 15% of the available market (Anon., 2015a). However, for some, international market development is their only marketing strategy and their domestic operations are considered of minor importance. Standard Chartered, a company formed as a result of the merger of two banks founded in London in the 1850s, has over 90,000 staff in 71 countries. Much of its business comes from international markets; only 6.7% of its business now comes from Europe (Standard Chartered, 2014). Regardless, the approach selected should depend on the resources available, the industry, and the type of offering. For example, some offerings, such as smartphones, airplane manufacture, and tourism, are international by nature. The high degree of investment in research and product development in these industries necessitates a move into international markets as domestic markets may not provide sufficient sales and profit.

A seminal study by Johanson and Vahlne (1977) determined that companies tend to build up their commitment to international operations as they gain more knowledge about that market, and gain increased confidence in their operations as their activities in that country are increased. Previously, researchers at Uppsala University in Sweden (Johanson and Wiedersheim-Paul,1975) had identified that most firms followed a four-stage process of internationalization, starting with serving the domestic market, then penetrating foreign markets by exporting, then developing sales offices in the foreign market, and then developing foreign production facilities. This model has been criticized, however, as some firms have developed an international business orientation from inception (known as **born global** firms). For example, Chetty and Campbell-Hunt (2004) found a cluster of New Zealand firms that display this tendency, principally because they cannot survive in the relatively small market that New Zealand represents. They identified significant differences in how born global firms operate compared with those who internationalize traditionally as outlined in Table 7.3.

Table 7.3 Key differences between traditional and born global approaches to internationalization

Internationalization attributes	Traditional internationalization view	Born global view
Home market	Domestic market developed first	Domestic market irrelevant as often too small
Previous internationalization experience	None expected	Founder likely to have extensive experience in relevant international markets
Extent of internationalization	Foreign markets developed sequentially	Many foreign markets developed simultaneously
Psychic distance	Markets entered in order of psychic distance	Psychic distance irrelevant
Learning to internationalize	Markets entered at a pace of learning about new markets	Learning occurs rapidly because of superior internationalization knowledge
Firm strategy	Not central to motivation to internationalize	Realization of competition requires rapid internationalization
Use of information and communication technologies	Not central to internationalization	Enabler of global market reach (e.g. the Internet, social media) and learning
Networks of business partners	Used in early stages and replaced as internal resources developed	Rapid development of global reach requires comprehensive network of partners
Time to internationalize	Not crucial to firm success, slow	Crucial to firm success, rapid

Source: Adapted from Chetty and Campbell-Hunt (2004).

Research Insight 7.1

To take your learning further, you might wish to read this influential paper.

Chetty, S. and Campbell-Hunt, C. (2004). A strategic approach to internationalization: a traditional versus a 'born-global' approach. *Journal of International Marketing*, **12(1), 57–81.**

Based on research undertaken amongst New Zealand firms, this article critiques the notion that there is a standard approach to internationalizing a brand and that some brands, rather than launching from domestic markets, have to target international marketing from the organization's inception.

Visit the **Online Resource Centre** to read the abstract and access the full paper.

The EPRG classification (Perlmutter 1969) specifies four strategic orientations to international market development: **ethnocentric**, **polycentric**, **regional**, and **geocentric** (see Figure 7.2). The first two of these assume a localized approach. An ethnocentric approach views the domestic market (home market) as the most important, with foreign markets seen not to be a serious threat. With a polycentric approach, each overseas market is seen as a separate domestic market and the organization seeks to position itself as local to that country. In some

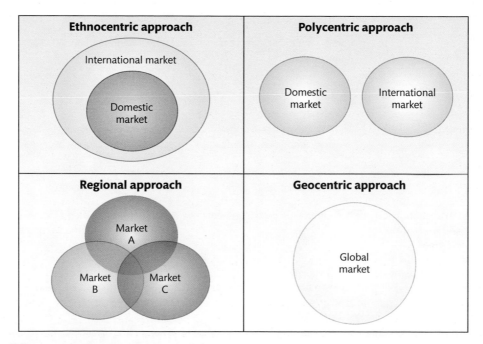

Figure 7.2
EPRG strategic orientations for international marketing

instances, each market has its own manufacturing and marketing operations, with only a limited overlap.

The last two approaches adopt a standardized approach. A regional approach groups countries together, usually on a geographical basis (e.g. Europe or Europe, Middle East, and Asia (EMEA)), and provides for the specific needs of consumers within those countries. In this instance, national boundaries are respected, but do not have the same importance as cultural differences. A geocentric approach assumes that the world is a single global market, with the organization targeting global segments (e.g. high net worth individuals) and global opportunities to rationalize communications, production, and product development.

Lynch (1994) categorizes a company's strategic nature based on the size of its geographic operations using five categories as follows.

- Local scale—organizations operating within national and local boundaries with little opportunity or desire to trade internationally (e.g. the local hairdresser or the body repair garage working mainly for insurance companies).

- National scale—organizations focusing on the domestic market, but which find opportunities from foreign markets based on ad hoc customer enquiries.

- Regional scale—organizations focusing on specific regions within a regional trading bloc (e.g. Europe or **Mercosur**) as opposed to operating throughout that trading bloc (e.g. all five full members of Mercosur rather than just, say, Paraguay) and gain experience of operating abroad on a smaller scale. For example, Norwegian and Swedish organizations have a long tradition of trade relations with other Scandinavian countries as a first experience of cross-national trade.

- European scale—with increasing changes in the European Union and the rise in the number of member states, many organizations have turned their attention to marketing throughout Europe. Some argue that Europe is, in fact, one geographic market with a number of segments that transcend national boundaries, especially as some of the risks of international trade have been reduced or eliminated (e.g. currency, with the introduction of the euro). However, some will remain forever (e.g. language, culture, infrastructure), requiring differing investment in communications, product, and channel development.

- World scale—these organizations have a strong European base, but now operate in a range of different world markets through direct investment or joint venture, or on an exporting basis. For example, P&G, Shell, AstraZeneca, and Danone derive a significant portion of sales from outside Europe. One example is Primark, a leading Irish clothing retailer striving for world-scale operations through its market expansions into the USA (see Market Insight 7.1).

Market Insight 7.1
Primark Heads Stateside

Primark is a fast-growing Irish retailer, operating 306 stores in 11 countries, owned by Associated British Foods, the proprietor of such well-known brands as Allinsons, Twinings, Ovaltine, Patak's, Jordan, and Ryvita, among many others. Primark started life as Penneys in Dublin in 1969 (and now has 36 stores in Ireland) but has quickly grown from its domestic base by launching stores around the world. The company relatively quickly set up in the UK in 1973 (which now has 168 stores), Spain in 2006 (where it now has

Market Insight 7.1
continued

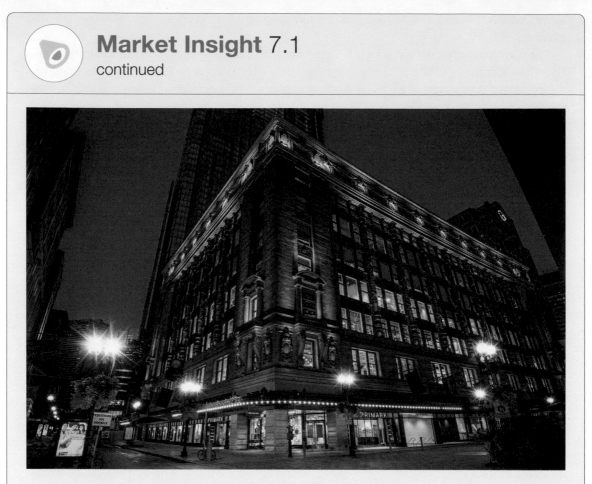

Two countries divided by a common language: can the Irish retailer conquer the USA?
Source: © Lou Jones www.fotojones.com.

41 stores), the Netherlands in 2008 (where it has 13 stores), Portugal (9 stores), Germany (20 stores), and Belgium (4 stores) in 2009, Austria (4 stores) in 2012, France (8 stores) in 2013, and America (2 stores) in 2015. In 2016, the company opened its first store in Italy, in Arese Milan.

Primark has enjoyed rapid growth between 2009 and 2014, with sales rising a cool 140%. Its strategy of selling good quality clothing at very cheap prices seems to be a hit everywhere. The company works hard to maintain its low cost leadership through lean supply chain management practices, limited marketing spend, and high volume procurement. City analysts at UBS reckoned the company was worth up to £19bn in 2014.

Whilst the European launches seem an obvious next step, the US launch seems risky. Such a move pits the company directly against strong brands such as Ross, T.J.Maxx, Marshalls, Old Navy, Forever 21, Gap, and H&M. What's more Gap is having a particularly tough time, announcing that it intended to close a quarter of all its stores in North America in 2015. Naysayers might also cite Tesco's failure in the US market after it launched Fresh & Easy in California, costing it £1.2bn. According to a Barclay's survey, more than half of British retailers think the US is the hardest market to enter, behind China in second place, despite sharing the same language. One reason cited for retail market entry failure in the US is considering the US to be a homogeneous market, rather than a patchwork quilt of different states with different customer attitudes and behaviours. Typically, on the first day of a new store opening, customers mob the store, grabbing everything they can find. The question is: Will the Americans feel the same 'Primania' as their European counterparts?

Sources: Morris (2013); Shawcross (2014); Anon. (2015b); ABF (nd).

Market Insight 7.1
continued

Theory into Practice

This market insight describes how a retailer is developing its international markets. Primark appears to be following the traditional internationalization approach whereby it develops an international position once it has developed its own domestic market (Ireland and, particularly, the UK). However, the US market is often regarded as a very different market from the UK, because customer practice and the culture are significantly different.

Related Topics:

market selection; market entry method; psychic distance; psychological proximity; foreign direct investment; culture.

1 Using Perlmutter's (1969) strategic orientation classification (EPRG), how would you classify the scale of Primark's operations?

2 Why do you think Primark have decided on entering the US market? (Hint: Consider what market selection criteria they used.)

3 What do Primark need to do to succeed in the US market where other European retailers have failed?

International Competitive Strategy

When entering international markets, the key competitive decision to make is to what extent should the firm standardize or adapt its marketing strategy. According to Zou and Cavusgil (2002), a firm should adapt its promotional efforts only when it needs to, to respond to customer needs, media usage, or advertising regulation. In an analysis of the rise of global competition, Hout *et al.* (1982) suggest that, strategically, an organization can adopt different degrees of adaptation to markets based on a local/global, a multi-domestic, or a global competitive approach to their international marketing strategy (see Figure 7.3).

Figure 7.3
The spectrum of competitive strategies

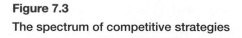

Research Insight 7.2

To take your learning further, you might wish to read this influential paper.

Zou, S. and Cavusgil, S.T. (2002). The GMS: a broad conceptualization of global marketing strategy performance and its effect on firm performance. *Journal of Marketing*, 66(October), 40–56.

This article discusses three separate perspectives of global marketing strategy (GMS) considerations including degree of standardization, configuration-coordination, and degree of integration, and shows how a consideration of these can link to firm performance.

@ Visit the Online Resource Centre to read the abstract and access the full paper.

Multi-Domestic Competitive Strategy

With a **multi-domestic competitive strategy**, organizations pursue separate marketing strategies in each foreign market and consider how to compete on the basis of each market. This can also be referred to as an **adaptive orientation** because organizations adapt their operations, procurement, and market research/insight generation to a particular country, and develop a strategy for that specific market (see also Chapter 4). Consequently, cultural, legal, language, communication, and geographical differences in each market are accounted for. The Malaysian group Gentings have therefore adapted their London Chinatown offering to include baccarat to appeal to wealthy Chinese tourists (Blitz, 2014). In the fashion business, for example, there are key differences in style between the USA, France, Italy, the UK, and China, particularly in terms of 'street style' and those who are perceived to be influential bloggers and fashion designers. In any company, a central headquarters might coordinate financial controls, research and development activities, and marketing policies worldwide, but strategy and operations are often decentralized. Each subsidiary is considered to be a profit centre and expected to contribute earnings and growth consistent with market opportunity, with competition on a market-by-market basis (Hout *et al.*, 1982). See also Market Insight 7.2 for an understanding of how advertising might need to be adapted when operating in different regions.

Global Competitive Strategy

Globalization refers to the process by which all that we experience in life is becoming standardized world-wide through the free flow of goods and services, people, capital, and information (Sirgy *et al.*, 2007). Globalization is accompanied by the increasing consolidation of organizations within various industries, including pharmaceuticals, financial services, and airlines.

The importance and significance of global trade was first identified by Levitt, who stated that 'the global cooperation operates with resolute constancy—at low relative cost—as if the entire world

Market Insight 7.2
Ad-apt in São Paulo?

When companies internationalize they face many strategic questions, such as: Where shall we go? How shall we internationalize? Which parts of our marketing strategy should we adapt to the local market, and which can we standardize across all of our markets? Whilst many of these decisions are not directly visible to the consumer, one aspect most consumers will be in direct contact with is advertising. Almost all companies, from Coca-Cola to Google, from the clothes industry to the food industry, adapt their advertising strategies to the local markets in which they operate. Take Snickers, for example: the world's biggest chocolate bar produced a truly global brand idea with the slogan: 'You're not you when you're hungry', but then adapted their advertisements to feature local celebrities and symbolism to make the advertisement relevant to the target market in which the individual ad was shown. Similarly, IKEA sells an almost identical lifestyle across the globe, but adapts its advertising to local markets.

Photos of their famous catalogue are adjusted to reflect the cultural values of the local target audience. But what do you do when you have identified a great new potential market and you find out that in it, you're not allowed to advertise? No, really!!

In 2007, the world's seventh largest, and Brazil's most important, city São Paulo became the first city in the world to put into effect a radical near-complete ban on outdoor advertising. São Paulo introduced 'Lei Cidade Limpa', or the Clean City Law. Citing that the city needed to combat various forms of pollution, the then mayor said: 'We decided that we should start combating pollution with the most conspicuous sector—visual pollution'. The new law outlaws the use of all outdoor advertisements, including billboards, transit, and front-of-store advertisements. Even pamphleteering in public spaces has been made illegal. Imagine a city of 11 million inhabitants stripped of all its advertising!

São Paulo consumers breathe easily after the advertising ban but advertisers choke!
Source: © Bloomberg/Getty.

Market Insight 7.2
continued

Clearly not everyone was in full support. The new law raised great concern among local and global businesses. How would they convey their advertising messages to their customers? They argued that the advertising ban would entail a revenue loss of $133 million at 2007 prices. Consumers even argued that the loss of advertising billboards would take away from São Paulo's identity and they would lose the appeal of being a world metropolis. Imagine London without Piccadilly Circus's neon billboards (or the neon billboards in Times Square in New York), or the red buses without the ads for the latest movies criss-crossing London.

Yet, despite the initial uproar, the ad ban has been a success: with more than 70% approval from the city's residents. And it seems that the movement to ban ads in cities is catching on, In 2009 Chennai in India banned billboards, as did several US states, followed by Grenoble in 2014 (which banned all street advertising). The difficulty though is that cities earn significant revenues from their partnerships with advertising companies. Even São Paolo has seen some of its advertising return, though in a much more organized fashion. Nevertheless, the question still arises: How do you advertise if the city pulls your ambient advertising space and what do you lose by shifting to alternative advertising forms?

Sources: Douglas and Wind (1987); Harris (2007); Mahdawi (2015).

Theory into Practice

This market insight describes how companies entering the Brazilian market, and specifically the city of São Paolo (and by extension other cities where advertising is restricted or banned), need to identify new ways to communicate with their customers. The example shows that companies should never take for granted how they can best communicate with their customers. It also shows that the regulatory and marketing environments need to be assessed before a market is selected and the entry method is developed.

Related Topics:

standardization–adaptation; market entry; culture; regulatory environment; marketing environment; marketing communications; advertising.

1 As a result of the ban, do you think São Paulo has become an unattractive market for international and global brands?

2 What kind of creative new advertising strategies might these companies use to overcome their inability to engage in outdoor advertising? Which advertising channels become more important?

3 Would you advise these companies to use adapted or standardized advertising campaigns in this particular market?

This market insight was kindly contributed by Dr Frauke Mattison Thompson, King's College London, UK.

(or major regions of it) were a single entity; it sells the same things in the same way everywhere' (Levitt, 1983: 92–3). However, there have also been detractors from this argument, who argue that whilst it was appropriate to operate a global competitive approach to business, the key to success is to customize the offering, adapting it to local needs (Quelch and Hoff, 1986). This debate is still ongoing.

A global competitive strategy represents a **standardized approach**. This requires that organizations see the world as one large (global) market and that they sell the same propositions in the same way throughout the world, ignoring local, regional, and national differences. Standardization assumes that global cultures are converging, and that any cultural differences are superficial (Wind and Perlmutter, 1973; Levitt, 1983; Douglas and Douglas, 1987). The attractions of the standardization approach include improved operational efficiencies, enhanced customer preference, increased competitive leverage, and, importantly, substantial cost reductions (Herbig and Day, 1993). Objectors to this approach argue that cultural, legal, and national differences inhibit trade, especially when an organization assumes that differences are superficial. They argue that there might be genuine **psychic difference**—a difference in perceptions between the people of the two countries (domestic and foreign markets)—in how they perceive or use a particular offering (Evans, 2010). For example, when Carlsberg launched Somersby Cider into the Swiss market, it used a novel approach even though the brand was on sale in 35 countries already. It recruited an online consumer panel to co-create a brand awareness campaign, and then sent each member a crate of 24 bottles, and 2,000 bottles to friends of the panel members, and asked them all to have a party and take pictures and post them online. This approach raised awareness of the brand from 6% to 20% the day before the formal product launch took place (Anon., 2015c). Communication is one of the biggest barriers to effective international marketing and is heightened when the standardization approach is used. One outcome is that advertising messages can be badly phrased or misinterpreted (see Table 7.5).

One way of evaluating the extent of psychic distance between home and target markets is to formally analyse them using the CAGE acronym (Ghemawat, 2001). This requires that the marketer consider a possible target market against a home market on the dimensions of culture (e.g. languages, religion, social norms), administration (e.g. government policies, colonial ties), geography (e.g. physical remoteness, size of country, climate differences), and the economy (e.g. differences in consumer incomes, cost of labour).

An effective global competitive strategy comprises two elements. The first is **selective contestability**, the ability to contest successfully in any international market an organization chooses to compete in. It is based on the core marketing principles of segmentation, targeting, and positioning (STP; see Chapter 6). This requires that generic markets are divided into meaningful sub-markets or segments, that the most attractive of these are then selected, and that the offering is, consequently, positioned appropriately. This process lies at the very heart of any competitive strategy, irrespective of whether or not the organization is competing in a regional, national, or global market. The second element is **global capability**. This concerns an organization's ability to bring its entire worldwide resources to bear on any competitive situation, irrespective of location. A global brand goes far beyond an organization's physical presence in differing national markets, reflecting the existence of a global image. This universal recognition distinguishes an organization pursuing a focused strategy in numerous national markets. Examples include global players such as Apple (consumer electronics), Microsoft (software), Intercontinental Hotel Group (hotels), and Spar (convenience stores).

It is worth pointing out that not everyone believes globalization to be a good thing. As a consequence, an anti-globalization movement has developed to compete directly with the legitimacy and power of multinational corporations. In particular, anti-globalization protesters argue that multinationals abuse labour, particularly in developing countries, fail to pay sufficient taxes, sandblast out cultural differences with standardized products, and trample on individual liberty. (We discuss some of these issues further in Chapter 18.)

 Visit the Online Resource Centre and complete Internet Activity 7.1 to learn more about how companies like KFC use a 'glocal' approach by acting globally, but adapting to local differences.

Research Insight 7.3

To take your learning further, you might wish to read this influential paper.

Levitt, T. (1983). The globalisation of markets. *Harvard Business Review*, May–June, 92–102.

This article is seminal, cited frequently, and despite its age remains remarkably relevant today. Levitt draws attention to the prevalence of global markets, considers the reasons for their development, and considers why and how organizations should offer globally standardized products that are advanced, functional, reliable, and low-priced.

Visit the **Online Resource Centre** to read the abstract and access the full paper.

Drivers of International Market Development

Although international marketing is now ubiquitous, it is worth considering how it became so commonplace. Key drivers for globalization are set out in Figure 7.4. The most common are the following.

- Historical accident—unplanned events trigger international market development. In1941, during the Second World War, Coca-Cola leader Robert Woodruff wanted to distribute a bottle of Coke to anyone in uniform anywhere in the world for 5 cents. To do so, he set up a special group of 'technical observers' to manage 64 bottling plants, producing 5 bn bottles of Coke to servicemen and women around the world (Mooney, 2008). As a result, a wider range of people tasted the drink and an opportunity arose for Coca-Cola to build the brand through a new distribution strategy. This is said to be one of the main reasons behind the growth of Coca-Cola's international marketing operations.

- Excess stock—with over-production or insufficient sales, excess stock can build up. With limited opportunities for sales in domestic markets, organizations seek out international sales

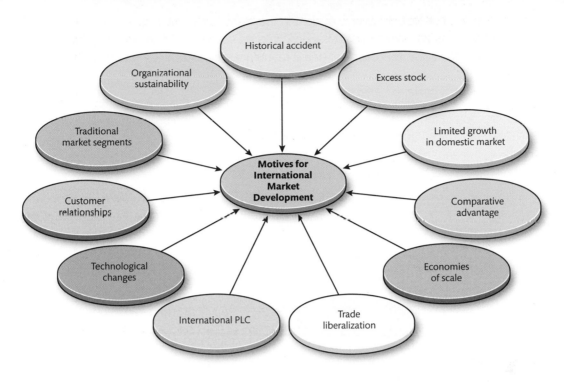

Figure 7.4
Motives for international market development

opportunities to remove excess stock. When the product is sold at a lower price in the foreign market than is charged in the domestic market, this is called dumping. Such an approach does not constitute a long-term entry strategy.

- Limited growth in domestic markets—one way to avoid domestic competition when growth is limited in home markets is to enter international markets. For example, given the strong competition in the home markets of the USA and Europe, in 2015 AB InBev announced a merger after its offer of a cool $104 bn for SAB-Miller was accepted by shareholders. The strategic rationale is that the deal will give AB InBev brands access to growing markets in Africa and Latin America (where it is not presently strong) and the combined entity will control a third of the world beer market (Colley, 2015).

- Comparative advantage—some regions/countries develop core competencies and reputations for producing certain offerings, raw resources, or work skills. This presents an opportunity to develop **comparative advantage**. For example, champagne is produced by 15,800 winegrowers and 300 champagne houses in the Champagne region of France, exporting about 307m bottles in 2014 (Anon., 2014). Certain countries offer differential labour costs and specialized skills, for example, China and manufacturing, or India and service process outsourcing (e.g. call centres). This presents an advantage not only in labour and operating costs but, for some industries, savings in transport and manufacturing costs.

- Economies of scale—for some offerings the cost of development and production can be high. To achieve an effective return on investment high volume production runs are necessary, and this requires large world markets. Examples include smartphones and aircraft manufacture.

A high degree of standardization is evident in the manufacture of aircraft, such as the frame wings, and engine, with superficial changes such as seating spacing and arrangements tailored for local markets. This enables aircraft manufacturers to achieve global **economies of scale**.

- Trade liberalization—with regional trade bloc creation (e.g. the European Union (EU); the North American Free Trade Agreement (NAFTA); the Association of Southeast Asian Nations (ASEAN) Free Trade Area Agreement) and the reduction of barriers to trade worldwide, many organizations engage in global competition with international firms in domestic markets, and domestic organizations are increasingly moving abroad to compete overseas.

- International product lifecycle—the internationalization process occurs when an offering reaches different stages of its lifecycle in different countries. For example, Royal Enfield, a British motorcycle producer, ceased production in Britain in 1970 but continued production in in India (where it granted a local partner a license in 1955). The company now seeks to become the global leader in mid-sized motorcycles after investing Rs 500 crore ($80m) in a new factory and technology centre (Agence France-Presse, 2015).

- Technological changes—advances in electronic communications (e.g. the Internet) have enabled international trade. Online channels are increasingly being used to sell into new markets because of open access and low costs. Changes in the technological infrastructure have provided small and medium-sized enterprises (SMEs) with a way of increasing exports with low entry costs.

- Customer relationships—as organizations move abroad, international marketing activities affect the whole supply chain, from end-users, through intermediaries, to producers and raw material suppliers. For example, as Toyota enters new foreign markets, its product components also change and suppliers will need to match the requirements of its new manufacturing and assembly production process. This is also true for service-based industries. However, the difference is that there will be an increasing need to locate an organization's services much closer to the customer, either through branch offices or through subsidiaries placed strategically throughout a number of foreign markets. Withers Worldwide, a leading corporate legal services firm, has 18 offices in 10 countries.

- Transnational market segments—the growth in groups of people with similar needs but who inhabit different countries, called transnational market segments, occurs because of migration, such as Chinese working in Singapore, similarities in demographics (e.g. **Generation Y**), or similarities in lifestyles (e.g. homosexuals). From a conceptual perspective, a truly global organization should segment markets based on similar characteristics, even across national borders as country of residence/birth is less relevant with increasing migration.

- Organizational sustainability—the broader the range of markets served, the less likely it is that failure in one market will result in overall organizational decline. Different markets are always at different stages of development and competitive intensity. An international market portfolio provides an organization with an increased chance of organizational sustainability. For example, McDonald's, the fast-food restaurant operator, has not suffered a strong decline in its overall reputation worldwide, despite food scandals in China and Japan (Martin and Fujikawa, 2015).

However, whatever the motivation for international market development, a planned approach considerably increases the chances for success. Once international market entry has been decided as an organizational growth strategy, certain decisions have to be made to increase the chances of success. These include determining which foreign markets to pursue, which methods are the most suitable for entering new markets, and which strategy to adopt to appeal to the desired needs of foreign markets.

International Market Selection

The selection of international markets should be based on a consideration of a potential market's overall attractiveness, itself based on a number of factors including market size and growth as the two most important among the following:

1 **Market size and growth rate** Market size refers to the number of current and potential customers. Market size can also be measured in terms of the sales value that these customers represent. Using these figures alone can be misleading, however, as some regions increase in attractiveness and others decline. Whilst the three major world markets were once what Ohmae (1982, 1985) called the Triad—Europe, America, and Japan—rapid growth is increasingly observed in Pacific Rim countries (China, Singapore, South Korea, and Taiwan), the BRIC group (Brazil, Russia, India, and China), and the MINT countries (Malaysia, Indonesia, Nigeria and Turkey), whilst growth in Western markets is anaemic. Although disposable income in these countries is unevenly distributed, the overall increasing prosperity of their populations has created demand for Western luxury brands to signal individual success and increasing personal wealth. Brands such as Burberry, Hershey, Apple, and IKEA have experienced considerable growth in recent years, whilst brands like Prada, Nestlé and Rolls-Royce have fared less well (Doland, 2015).

2 **Market access** Accessibility refers to the extent that customers can be contacted with marketing communications and can obtain an offering through distribution and sales outlets. Media availability, industry infrastructure, channel networks, and local cultural norms all potentially limit or hinder market access. For example, in many countries former state telecommunications still maintain widespread (monopoly) market control. This results in few openings for foreign brands to enter these markets, despite there being few legal issues or import difficulties. Some countries also impose high tariffs to protect local industry.

3 **Geographical proximity** The physical distance between a potential market and the domestic market can have a direct impact on resource requirements. For example, trade between Brazil and the UK requires more resourcing than trade between Sweden and Norway.

4 **Psychological proximity** This refers to the perceived cultural and societal similarities between countries. Earlier, we discussed psychic difference, the difference in perceptions between what people think about an offering in a domestic market and how that same offering is perceived in a foreign market. These two concepts can be seen as existing at opposite ends of a perceptual similarity/difference spectrum. For example, some see greater cultural similarity between the UK and Australia than between the UK and the Netherlands. A related concept was developed by Dutch management theorist Geert Hofstede, who argued that people from different countries displayed different mental programming, which affected their outlook and how they interrelated with people (see Market Insight 7.3 for more on this topic).

Market Insight 7.3
LEGO: To Translate or Localize?

LEGO®, the Danish manufacturer of plastic building bricks, is a global toy company, with revenues of DKr 28.6bn (€3.8bn). The company's website provides product-related content targeted at the company's core consumer segment: 5- to 12-year old builders, and their grandparents and parents, who typically make the purchases. The company is also expanding in emerging markets, having opened offices in Malaysia, Turkey, and China. The physical product, the plastic brick, is identical around the world; the 20 + languages that are used on the LEGO website are not. So how does LEGO deal with being present in a global range of markets. Does LEGO translate the content into the local language, is the content localized, or both?

The global reach of the Internet has led LEGO to develop language-specific websites for each of its major markets. However, the challenge for marketers is to take both translation and localization into consideration as these issues are not the same. Translating text on LEGO's website is straightforward; localizing the website for each of the major markets is a completely different story as it demands an in-depth knowledge of consumer attitudes and preferences in the individual country, together with an appreciation of cultural differences.

Many of LEGO's target consumers live outside the UK and USA and cannot understand English; not only this, but the young consumers do not necessarily share LEGO's European cultural origins. Therefore, the marketing challenge for LEGO is to make sure that the company website is translated *and* localized in a way that respects these cultural differences. Translation of product descriptions is straightforward but there

are constraints on the ability of LEGO to localize their website—the global standardization of the physical product, the LEGO sets, places limits on the content that can be provided. So how can LEGO provide localized content for a globally standardized product?

Surprisingly, apart from the translated product descriptions, much of the content on the LEGO website is not actually localized. Content is developed from the outset to be seen by young consumers around the world and is structured around videos of the LEGO products with sound effects rather than language. These videos showcase each of the products in an appropriate setting so that LEGO's global audience can see the different functions of the products, such as opening doors, working propellers, and so on. Other content that does not need translating are games based on LEGO products with pictorial instructions, and short animated sequences.

Where localization is apparent is in country-specific marketing campaigns. Here, translation is not necessarily a factor, as there are even differences between the two largest English-speaking markets, the USA and the UK. The two markets use the same language, so no translation is necessary, but consumer preferences for different product themes and unique holiday traditions make localization a key marketing consideration. The marketing challenge that LEGO faces is to identify which elements of their online marketing need to be translated, and which elements need to be localized. Translation is not the same as localization.

Sources: Anderson (2014); Anon. (2015d); http://www.lego.com/en-gb/.

Theory into Practice

This market insight illustrates that to adapt to cultural differences, organizations use three internal processes (Mughan, 1993). The first is empathy, i.e. they try to recognize a situation from the customer's perspective and adapt their behaviour accordingly. The second is to provide cultural training, particularly for employees working directly with distributors or customers. The third is to recruit direct from the local labour

market—the quickest route. Successful international organizations tend to have a diverse representation of nationalities in their senior management teams. The insight also illustrates the difficulties inherent in determining the extent to which a company should standardize or adapt its offerings into new markets. This task is made particularly difficult when, like LEGO, the company operates in a large number of countries.

Market Insight 7.3
continued

Related Topics:

standardization–adaptation; culture; language; marketing communications; digital marketing.

1 Go to the LEGO® website and change the country by clicking on the flag icon. Choose a country with a different language. Which content is translated, and which is localized? Why do you think that this is the case?

2 Now find the 'products' page and change the country to the Chinese LEGO® website. What do you see?

3 Now compare the UK and the US websites. What happens to the content that you see?

This market insight was kindly contributed by Dr Robert P. Ormrod, Aarhus University, Denmark.

Research Insight 7.4

To take your learning further, you might wish to read this influential paper.

Hofstede, G. (1983). The cultural relativity of organizational practices and theories. *Journal of International Business Studies*, 14(2), 75–89.

This seminal and very highly cited article built on Hofstede's previous work (Hofstede, 1980), which outlined that people from different cultures differed in terms of how they are 'mentally programmed', and therefore think and respond, on the basis of four dimensions: power distance, uncertainty avoidance, individualism–collectivism, and masculinity–femininity. This work specifically rejected the notion that management was homogenizing around the world and that one perspective (e.g. that of the USA) could be applied everywhere.

Visit the **Online Resource Centre** to read the abstract and access the full paper.

5 **Established competitors** When competition is intense, foreign market entrants will be received less favourably. For example, this might potentially result in price competition or in entrants finding it difficult to obtain distribution agreements with supply chain partners.

6 ***Entry costs*** These can vary greatly between markets and strategies. For example, physical distribution costs can be extremely high in a country such as the USA or India where the distances between production plants and consumers can be immense. In other countries, distances might be comparably short, but marketing channels and supply chains are long and complex or lack the infrastructure to support them. For example, the healthcare infrastructure in various sub-Sahara African countries differs greatly from that in more established European countries such as Britain and Sweden.

> **Table 7.4** International market screening questions

Factor	Questions to consider
Market	▪ What is the level of market growth/decline? ▪ What is the market potential? ▪ What distribution channels exist, if any?
Proposition fit	▪ Is there a market opportunity for this offering? ▪ Is there demand or interest in an offering of this type? ▪ Will the offering require adaptation to fit into the market?
Competition	▪ Are the existing competitors, if any, in this market national and international in nature? ▪ How aggressive is the competition? ▪ What degree of power do existing competitors exercise in this market? ▪ What barriers to entry currently exist? ▪ How might the competition respond to our market entry?
Market entry	▪ What entry methods are most attractive for us to enter this market? ▪ What will market entry cost us? ▪ How might local partners support us in entering the market? ▪ How similar are the foreign culture, values, and attitudes when compared with our domestic market?
Resources	▪ How much do we need to invest to enter this market? ▪ What will the mix of local and expatriate staff be in entering this market? ▪ What development do we need to undertake to allow us to enter this market? Examples might include acculturation, language training, export development skills. ▪ Can we rely on existing marketing channels for market entry or do we need to develop new ones?
Trade barriers	▪ What legal or regulatory factors could influence our market entry or operational approach? ▪ Will import tariffs or quotas be imposed on us? ▪ Can we repatriate any profits generated out of the country or are there restrictions on this? ▪ Are there any constraints on foreign organizations operating in this market, e.g. in terms of allowing foreign majority ownership structures of local firms? ▪ Will different product/manufacturing standards apply in this market?

7 **Profit potential** This refers to the number of potential customers and the profit margin that the group can generate in that market. Even though per unit profit margins might be small, a country with a large potential market might still be attractive for the overall profit generated. For example, Indonesia and Pakistan might each offer large potential profits. Powerful buying groups, low per capita income, and strong competition are all factors that can reduce profit margins.

International market selection requires good market intelligence about the market environment and marketing opportunities. In reality, market screening can be random, driven by customer enquiries or market demand for an offering or knowledge gained through media or social networks. Visits to the potential markets are also required for further insights and first-hand market knowledge, and to aid the development of networks and relationships. Questions that are useful for international market screening are detailed in Table 7.4.

International Marketing Environment

It is important to understand the marketing environments of intended foreign markets in order to assess and select foreign markets properly. Frequently, however, firms looking to go to market internationally pay insufficient attention to aspects of the global marketing environment, including socio-cultural, economic, legal/institutional, and political developments (Young, 2001).

Social Factors

Differences in society, values, and demography can all affect the acceptability and therefore uptake, of an offering in international markets. In some countries, such as the UK, Sweden, and Canada, there are increasing numbers of new mothers returning to work, placing more reliance on grandparents, nannies, and childminders for childcare responsibilities. This contrasts with the composition of other markets and the greater level of cross-generation households, as found in China and Japan, where grandparents are a central part of the family unit and reside in the family household. Interestingly, because of house price increases in the UK, there is also an increasing trend of multigenerational living (Davidson, 2013). Migration and the associated movement of social values can also influence social factors. In Canada, for example, immigration accounts for around 66% of Canada's population growth (Martel, 2015). An awareness of these changes and transient social structures and values is imperative.

Cultural Factors

Culture is important in international market development strategy because it concerns the beliefs, norms, and values that guide the behaviour of groups of potential customers and other stakeholders. It comprises language, education, religion, lifestyle, taboos, and norms. Culture affects how people define their wants and needs through consumption and how they interact with each other. For example, Unilever controls 27% of global ice cream sales, but markets them differently to countries according to cultural norms. For example, portion sizes are different and there is more distribution through scoop shops in some countries compared with others (Askew, 2015). In Italy, Unilever acquired GROM to gain a foothold in the premium gelato market in addition to selling its usual brands, Carte d'Or, Algida (also sold as Walls), Cucciolone, Cornetto, and Max (Watrous, 2015). Nevertheless, sometimes there are cultural behaviour changes. In France, for example, although French shoppers have tended to buy their bread as baguettes on a daily basis, they are now increasingly buying sliced bread, such as that sold by Barilla, an Italian food group (Anon., 2015e).

Culture influences the way we interact with each other. For example, following the movement of many call centre jobs to India, some have been transferred back to the UK. Clearly, for organizations serious about international marketing, cultural sensitivity is paramount. Business conduct differs throughout the world based around the following.

- Time—including attitudes towards punctuality, sanctity of deadlines, time to make someone's acquaintance, and length of discussion time. According to Lewis (2014), Anglo-Saxons and Norrhern Europeans believe time is scarce, have a linear view of time (that it progresses from past, through present into future), focus on individual tasks, and are particularly concerned with keeping schedules and punctuality. In contrast, Southern Europeans (e.g. Spanish, Italians) and Arabs work in multi-active time, undertaking numerous tasks at the same time, where schedules are of lesser importance. Priority is given instead to the relationship significance of a meeting. Finally, in the Far East, time is seen as cyclical, i.e. there is greater reflection on relationships over the long term than in the present, but in China, for example, there is usually great respect, and humility, for others' schedules and time.

- Business cards—including when and how to offer, whether to translate them or not, who gives them first, and how they should be received. For example, in China, the card should be proffered with both hands. In India, one should use the right hand to give and receive business cards. In Japan, business cards are exchanged with great ceremony, in contrast with the UK and elsewhere in Europe where there is no ceremony (Kwintessential, nd).

- Business gifts—including whether or not they are acceptable, what value of gift is reasonable, and whether or not they should be opened in the view of the giver. In some markets, corporate gift giving and receiving is appropriate. The extra-territorial reach of the UK Bribery Act makes giving and receiving gifts for UK businesses a real concern—see Chapter 18 for more on this topic (Institute of Business Ethics, 2012).

- Dress codes—including what should be worn for what business occasions and the relative degree of formality. Whether or not to wear a suit and tie to a meeting differs by country (e.g. wearing ties to a meeting is less common in Scandinavia than in the UK).

- Entertainment—including what type and formality of occasion are acceptable, table manners and etiquette, what type of cuisine should be served, where the event should be held, and what cultural/religious codes should be observed or are taboo. For example, in Japan, seating for business entertaining is likely to be arranged by rank.

- Body language—including greetings (e.g. whether to shake hands, kiss, wai, or bow), facial and hand gestures and their meaning, the acceptability of physical proximity, touching, and different forms of posture (Mead, 1990). McDonald's take careful note of the Thai wai greeting by having a Ronald McDonald statue greeting customers with a wai at each of their restaurants.

Language is particularly important when considering foreign market entry as sellers will often need to use a customer's own language. However, English is increasingly becoming the **lingua franca** (i.e. a common language between non-native speakers). Language issues also arise for the way brand names, slogans and taglines, and product packaging might be used. In French-speaking Quebec in Canada, a region which is hypersensitive to the use of French language in place of English, KFC is known as PFK (Poulet Frit Kentucky). This is despite the fact that in France it is known as KFC. In several Spanish-speaking areas of the USA, KFC is known as PFK (Pollo Frito Kentucky). The implication is that all forms of marketing communications should be translated to ensure correct interpretation and meaning. If communication is to be in Arabic, there needs to be consideration of whether or not to use local dialects such as Maghreb or Gulf Arabic. We should also consider the target audience. If the audience is business personnel, the vocabulary, grammar, and punctuation ought to reflect this. If the audience is informal or young, then a relaxed language style might be used. Getting the language style right for the target audience is important, as failures can be devastating (see Table 7.5).

Table 7.5 Examples of international brand blunders

Brand/Company	Brand launch location	Misinterpretation
American Dairy Association	Mexico and other Hispanophone countries	The company launched its 'Got milk?' campaign into Spanish-speaking countries which translated as 'Are you lactating?'
Colgate	France	Introduced toothpaste called 'Cue', which is the name of a pornographic magazine
Ford Pinto	Brazil	In Brazilian Portuguese, 'pinto' means 'tiny male genitals'
Honda	Sweden	Honda was originally going to launch its Honda Fit brand, strong in Asia, into European markets as Fitta but realized this word connoted female genitalia in Swedish and quickly changed the name to Jazz despite having already printed its brochures with the erroneous term
Mercedes Benz	China	Mercedes Benz entered the market with the brand 'Bensi' which means 'rush to die' in Chinese
Nike	USA (and globally)	Nike had to recall 38,000 pairs of basketball trainers after a logo meant to look like fire was instead interpreted as the Arabic script for 'Allah'
Panos	Russia	This Belgian goods company decided to promote its range of sandwiches using the brand name 'Panos', not realizing that this translated into diarrhoea in Russian.
Umbro	UK	The British sporting goods company called a new brand of its trainers 'Zyklon' but received large numbers of complaints as this was the name of the gas used to kill millions of people in Nazi concentration camps in the Second World War
Vicks	Germany	The German translation of the brand name as 'Ficks' connotes 'sexual penetration'

Sources: Carscoops (2007); Fromowitz (2013); James (2014); My French Communication Agency (nd).

Consumption Attitudes

Customer perceptions of a product or a company's country of origin can influence the way customers react (see Market Insight 7.4). To reduce the risk of such adverse perceptions, organizations sometimes enter markets with consumption attitudes similar to those in the domestic market (i.e. where the psychic distance is lower). Examples include organizations exporting from Spain to Mexico, Ireland to the UK, New Zealand to Australia, and Sweden to Norway. Entering such markets lowers the risk, as organizations can learn and develop knowledge before entering and research consumption attitudes more easily.

Market Insight 7.4
Milking Trust in China

Branded products and services can be found in every sector of the economy. The most prominent are in consumer markets, where Coca-Cola, Nike, and Gillette take pride of place in any brand ranking list. Not so in China. According to Interbrand's *Best China Brands Report* not one consumer brand makes it into the Top 10. There, local Internet megabrand Tencent tops the charts, with banks taking up seven of the next nine niches.

The question for fast-moving consumer goods is: Are brands relevant for consumer choice in the world's second-largest consumer economy? In principle, brands help consumers identify their preferred products and reduce risk. Brands also indicate product quality and origin. 'Made in China' is not yet a tag associated with high quality by many Western consumers, and even their Chinese counterparts distrust some locally produced and branded goods. Such consumer concern was exacerbated when at least six infants died and thousands more were injured by tainted baby milk powder in 2008. Sales of locally made baby formula duly came to a near standstill, with demand for Western-made formulas rising to unprecedented heights. With the aid of overseas personal shoppers, or *daigous*, many Chinese parents have been purchasing their milk powder directly from European or American supermarket shelves. In 2014, this helped milk powder become the second-largest category of overseas goods to be purchased online by Chinese shoppers. Foreign milk powder brands are actually available in Chinese supermarkets, but the branding landscape of this product category is cluttered and confusing. Over 30 different brands are on offer and many supermarkets carry at least five non-Chinese milk powder brands. But supermarket prices are higher than those online and Chinese customers tend to distrust those imported products that are readily available from local supermarkets.

The true significance of branding to purchase decisions could not be more evident than in the milk powder category in China. Trust, quality, and country of origin are all important to concerned parents and the consumer motivation of risk avoidance has helped Western milk powder brands become a household item for many young Chinese families.

Sources: Interbrand (2014); Zhang (2015).

Theory into Practice

This market insight explains how a local milk scandal has changed Chinese consumers' perceptions of local brands. As a result, they now no longer trust Chinese brands and favour Western ones instead. The insight demonstrates how country of origin perceptions can both positively and negatively influence consumer preferences. A secondary learning from this insight is how it demonstrates the long-term damage to reputation that a crisis can cause.

Market Insight 7.4
continued

Related Topics:

country of origin; consumer trust; branding; consumer preferences.

1 **Do you see ways for Chinese milk powder brands to regain trust among Chinese customers?**

2 **Should Western manufacturers of baby milk powder further exploit the worries of Chinese consumers?**

3 **In which other product categories do you think the 'country of origin effect' could**

also play a significant role for Chinese consumers?

This market insight was kindly contributed by Dr Diederich Bakker, Hanze University of Applied Sciences Groningen, The Netherlands.

Technological Factors

The technological capability and rate of development in a country can have significant implications for how marketers communicate, new proposition development, and the overall success of a market entry strategy. In many international markets, new technology can change the way an organization goes to market (Sclater, 2005), for example through e- or m-commerce. Nevertheless, in some developing markets, lower level technologies like radio remain the principal channel for marketing communications, as TV diffusion is limited. In other countries (e.g. Nigeria), smartphone usage exceeds fixed-line Internet penetration. Therefore it is important to profile the penetration levels of different communication technologies and the supporting infrastructure when entering foreign markets.

Many customer needs and wants are constrained by the prevailing technological infrastructure. For example, whether gas or electricity is used for cooking depends on that country's energy mix and infrastructure. The type of telephone used depends on the telecommunication and economic infrastructure. Wireless telephony penetration frequently exceeds wireline (landline) penetration in developing countries. However, the needs and usage of mobile phones in developing markets differs considerably from that in mature markets. Nokia, the Finnish mobile phone manufacturer, looked for practical design features to make mobile handsets for people living in developing countries, such as India, more relevant, and despite declining sales in Western markets have managed to increase their sales in developing countries. They learned that in hot countries, where many roads are unpaved, features such as dustproof keypads are important and of value to customers.

Economic Factors

Market potential can be affected by many different local and international economic factors. Factors that should be considered when entering a new market include basic information about per capita disposable income, consumption patterns, and unemployment trends. Typical economic measures to help assess a particular country's market potential include:

- measures of per capita income
- ownership rates of durables (e.g. smartphone penetration)
- **consumer price indices (CPIs)**
- unemployment rates
- **gross national product (GNP)**
- market and population sizes
- currency exchange rates.

When assessing a market's attractiveness, these and other measures can usually be acquired from a number of sources, including business libraries, the online resource centres of professional bodies, and market intelligence/research databases.

Political and Legal Factors

Political and legal factors might also hinder or enable international marketing opportunities. For example, governments often offer subsidies and other forms of assistance to particular organizations when entering foreign markets by, for example, setting up and covering the cost of overseas trips. The UK government, in a bid to stimulate export, developed an advertising campaign around how it supports businesses looking to export.

Some governments hinder exporters by placing taxes and tariffs on certain companies and goods to deter prospective importers and protect domestic industries. Measures invoked by governments to protect their domestic industries include the following:

- quotas—used to limit the amount of goods allowed into a country;
- duties—special taxes on imports, which seek to disadvantage the importer's pricing strategy;
- non-tariff barriers—these include legislation designed so that importers have to adapt their offerings, which is often expensive, before the item is legally saleable in the host country.

Governments also try to alleviate unemployment and stimulate economic activity. As such, many countries encourage foreign investment by providing tax concessions and support of various kinds to persuade international organizations to set up their manufacturing units, or service units, in depressed areas. For example, both China (e.g. the Shanghai Free Trade Zone) and the UAE (e.g. Dubai Gold and Diamond Park) have set up trade zones within their territories with favourable tax incentives to attract foreign direct investment.

Political issues can cause difficulties for international marketers, sometimes causing withdrawal from a market, such as Google's experience in China when it withdrew to Hong Kong after the Chinese insisted on the application of mandatory censorship filters to its search engine product. In some countries, a government regime change may have little effect on commercial life, but in others the change can be profound, as in Romania after the execution of former dictator Nicolai Ceausescu in 1989 and the fall of Communism. Sometimes governments restrict foreign investment and ownership by setting up strict market entry conditions. This might involve working with a local organization as the majority shareholder and/or owner. Other restrictions

"Our expert Government adviser helped us get a handle on exporting"

Smruti Sriram, CEO of Supreme Creations

Businesses looking to export can work with an expert International Trade Adviser. To discover how Supreme Creations benefited from Government support and how you can too, visit **greatbusiness.gov.uk/exporting**

BUSINESS IS GREAT BRITAIN

The British Government helped Supreme Creations, the world's largest ethical manufacturer of reusable bags, eco-packaging, and giveaways, to export its wares

Source: Courtesy of BIS/UKTi.

include employment laws, health and safety regulations, financial laws, patent protection regulation, data protection requirements, and electronic transactions legislation.

Visit the Online Resource Centre and complete Internet Activity 7.2 to learn more about how the international strategies of firms such as Starbucks, Apple, Google, and Primark stand up to pressures on taxation, supply and ethics.

Market Entry Selection Criteria

There are several ways in which organizations can enter foreign markets. This decision is complex and depends on the company's objectives, its type of offering, and factors associated with the target country. Six criteria to consider when selecting the market entry method (Paliwoda 1993) are presented in Figure 7.5. The importance of each depends on the organization's international marketing objectives.

1 **Speed and timing** Some foreign market entry methods take months, whereas others can be executed immediately. Therefore the organization should ascertain how quickly it wishes to enter a target market.

2 **Costs** Different methods require different levels of investment: consequently, the costs and benefits of each method should be considered carefully.

3 **Flexibility** Some methods provide organizations with different levels of flexibility over their activities in a new market and future development opportunities. For example, some methods (e.g. foreign direct investment) might require long-term contractual agreements or financial commitments.

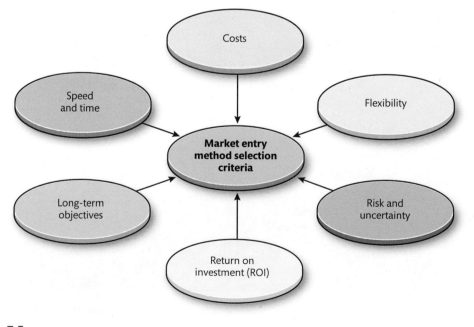

Figure 7.5
Criteria when selecting market entry methods

4 **Risk and uncertainty** Numerous risk factors are involved with entry into new and foreign markets. Some entry methods allow for a reduction of risk and uncertainty. These include joint ventures and direct foreign investment. The latter might ease political pressure, e.g. reducing barriers to entry, including tariffs and import quotas. However, these methods also require a larger degree of financial investment than indirect exporting or licensing.

5 **Return on investment (ROI)** The ROI needs to be considered with the first and second criteria (speed and timing, and costs). Some organizations look for a fast ROI through their market entry strategies, and thus the speed and timing of market entry is crucial to ensure a quick return on the investment. For example, it may take years to build a factory in a foreign market, and thus it is more suitable to develop a partnership with an existing local manufacturer who can provide this resource, thus increasing the speed of ROI.

6 **Long-term objectives** An organization needs to review what it wants to achieve in the long term from its entry into a new foreign market, as some market entry methods will provide more flexibility and leverage for long-term opportunities than others.

Market Entry Methods

There are several approaches that an organization can adopt when entering international markets. Each offers a level of risk commensurate with the potential rewards on offer through that entry method (see Figure 7.6). The higher the risk, the higher the possible rate of return. An organization's willingness and ability to commit the appropriate managerial, financial, and operational resources is crucial to realizing the potential rewards.

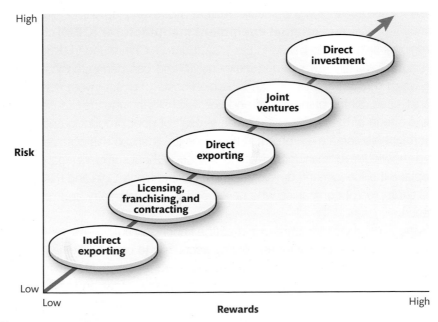

Figure 7.6
Market entry methods

Some organizations use a mixture of methods, depending upon the importance of each international project. Nissan changed from indirect exporting to direct investment when it established a UK manufacturing base in the 1980s. Despite a relatively small share of the UK market at the time, the development of the European Single Market offered the potential of huge ongoing rewards. The Lanson case at the beginning of the chapter highlights how the company uses different market entry methods in different markets, sometimes using distributors and at other times developing an overseas office (e.g. North America).

The entry method selected should fit the type of offering and the nature of the competition. For example, some offerings, such as fast food restaurants and coffee houses, tend towards franchising. Others, including textiles and car components, use offshore manufacturing. Regional products, such as wine, cheese, chocolate, and luxury food items, are typically exported directly, or indirectly via distributors/agents.

Indirect Exporting

Indirect exporting is when production and manufacture occur in the domestic market but an intermediary is employed to sell the offering into the foreign market. For example, New Cambridge and Hands-On are two agencies in Thailand which act on behalf of numerous British universities.

An exporting manufacturer seeks to benefit from an intermediary's knowledge, its contacts and business networks, and its experience in the target market. This reduces the producer's risk, but the size of the producer's potential rewards is reduced to compensate the intermediary. This approach is a good way for SMEs with limited resources to test a target market.

Licensing, Franchising, and Contracting

When making the decision to manufacture abroad, firms consider entry approaches including licensing, franchising, and/or contracting. **Licensing** occurs when an organization (the licensor) grants another (the licensee) the right to manufacture goods, use patents or particular processes, or exploit trademarks in a particular market. For example, ARM Holdings licenses its microprocessor technology to **original equipment manufacturer (OEM)** companies worldwide, with regional sales teams based in the USA, Europe, China, Japan, Korea, Taiwan, and India. Licensing is relatively low risk and inexpensive, and can generate income from foreign markets by avoiding high import tariffs and the high costs of direct investment. However, this method offers limited control of the brand, and possible risks include the licensee damaging the reputation and image of the licensor's name as a result of poor product quality and ineffective marketing. It might also create a problem in that once the licensee has obtained the necessary expertise and knowledge for manufacture of the offering, without sufficient legal protection it may be able to replace the licensor and develop its own offering. Coca-Cola and Pilkington Glass are both famous examples of companies who have used this market entry approach to develop a global presence.

Franchising is used when the brand owner (the franchisor) authorizes another organization (the franchisee) to produce or market an offering according to certain criteria laid down by the franchisor in return for fees and/or royalties. Therefore Franchising is a way for a company to both leverage income from its brand (as licensees pay franchise fees and royalties) and extend the brand's market coverage. The most successful franchise operations are household names, including KFC, SUBWAY®, McDonald's, and Inter IKEA systems (the owner of the IKEA trademarks) (see Market Insight 7.5).

Market Insight 7.5
Fast Food Franchising: Still Appetizing?

Franchising is used by a variety of organizations to expand internationally. Some companies in the fast food sector anchor their growth around franchising. For example, Subway, founded in the USA in 1965, has 44,422 restaurants operating in more than 111 countries worldwide.

As with most franchise operations each Subway franchise owner is responsible for paying an initial franchise fee. However, they are also required to find suitable store locations, take care of the leasehold improvements and equipment, hire employees and operate restaurants, and pay an 8% royalty to the company plus a separate fee for advertising.

Subway identifies two main types of location for their retail outlets. A traditional restaurant is to be found in high streets and shopping centres. A non-traditional restaurant is located in airports, hospitals, bus and rail stations, or other sites.

Costs vary in relation to the size and type of the restaurant. A lower cost restaurant might require fewer leasehold improvements, less seating, and less equipment expenditure. Moderate and higher cost restaurants might require extensive interior renovations, extensive seating, and additional equipment. In the USA, Subway suggests that the costs vary from $114,800 to $258,300 for restaurants in traditional locations and $84,300 to $200,100 for those in non-traditional locations. There is also an initial upfront one-off franchise fee for the first restaurant of around $15,000 and $7,500 per restaurant thereafter.

All franchise operations experience difficulties at some time. For example, Yum! Brands, who own KFC, Pizza Hut, and Taco Bell, uses franchising and licensing as its primary growth route into most countries. In China, they have adopted a direct investment strategy and own most of their 6,867 restaurants (by the third quarter of 2015), with 568 franchisees. When Yum! started operations in China, rather than import US managers, it employed people from other Asian economies such as Singapore, Hong Kong, and Malaysia. Yum! partnered with the state-owned enterprises and established its own distribution centres at a time when the country's transport infrastructure was poor. KFC's menu changes regularly and is explicitly Chinese, with delicacies such as rice congee with pickles, egg custard tarts, and tree fungus salad on offer. In the same way Chinese Pizza Huts reflect local tastes with squid, shrimp, and pineapple pizza on offer at the spacious low lit, yet pricey, restaurants. Nevertheless, despite the sheer size of the Chinese market with its 1.3bn population, Yum! announced it was to spin off the Chinese operation to become a separately traded company in the latter part of 2016, paying its American parent a percentage of sales. Part of the problem has been a series of food scandals in 2014 and the question of whether or not the Chinese still enjoy the novelty of eating in Western-style restaurants.

Sources: Burkitt (2013); Frean (2015); Kaiman (2013); http://www.subway.co.uk/business/franchise/facts_and_history.aspx; http://www.subwaydevelopmentgroup.com/faq.html; http://www.yum.com/investors/restcounts.asp.

Theory into Practice

This market insight describes how fast food retailers tend to use a mixture of franchising, licensing, and foreign direct investment when developing their retail outlets abroad. The Subway example demonstrates the considerable costs of purchasing and setting up a franchise, but this is often more than recouped by the significant amount of business that comes the franchisor's way as a result of having the reputation and expertise of a strong brand behind them. The second example of Yum! brands in China shows how even an initially successful operation with a huge market potential can end up in difficulties. As a result, Yum! is seeking to minimize the financial risk to the parent brand by spinning out its Chinese division.

Market Insight 7.5
continued

Related Topics:

market entry method; franchising; licensing; psychic distance; financial risk; culture.

1 Given its product offering, why do you think that Subway has been so successful in so many different countries?

2 Why do you think Yum! has decided to sell off its Chinese operations?

3 Why do you think Yum! favoured owning its own outlets (foreign direct investment strategy) rather than a franchising strategy?

The main benefits of franchising are managerial and financial. Financially, a firm can achieve rapid growth in market coverage, with the franchisee bearing the most risk through their investment in capital assets, such as equipment and premises, working capital, and other operating costs. However, the effectiveness of this form of market entry method relies on the strength of the franchisor–franchisee relationship, the commitment of the franchisee, the resources and support provided by the franchisor, and market interest in the franchise brand. Burger King, owned by Restaurant Brands International, is established in more than 100 countries, with 350,000 team members (employees) serving more than 11m customers per day and thereby earning more than $17bn in annual sales in 2014. Since 2011, it has set up 350+ new restaurants in Brazil, 275+ in Turkey, 300+ in Russia and 325+ in China (RBI, 2015).

Contracting refers to situations where a manufacturer contracts an organization in a foreign market to manufacture or assemble a product in that market. This approach avoids the costs involved in the physical distribution and supply chain issues associated with producing the offering in the home market and selling it overseas. Unlike licensing, contractors have control over all marketing activities. This method is also flexible as it avoids problems of currency fluctuations, import barriers, and the high costs and knowledge required for international distribution.

Visit the Online Resource Centre and complete Internet Activity 7.3 to learn more about how Yum! brands uses franchising to develop its Pizza Hut, KFC, and Taco Bell brands

Direct Exporting

Direct exporting requires that the manufacturing organization itself distributes the offering direct to customers in foreign markets. Here, the organization treats its international customers in the same way as its domestic market customers. It takes responsibility for finding and selecting customers, agents, and distributors, and directly supporting their efforts. The direct exporting approach can be time consuming and expensive. However, it gives manufacturers more control and profits than is possible when using intermediaries. Further advantages include direct access to market intelligence and the building of a clear presence in the market. For example, Spain is the world's largest exporter of wine by volume where it is exported, particularly to France where it is frequently resold as French wine (Burgen, 2015). Bulldog, a British brand of male grooming products, launches into overseas markets (e.g. Sweden, South Korea) by developing relationships with key retailers (Hurley, 2015).

Joint Ventures

When a foreign organization and a domestic organization join forces, either by buying into each other or by establishing a separate jointly owned enterprise, a **joint venture** is created. By working together, the participant organizations have enough resources to develop or enter a foreign market. For example, one partner might have the finance, and the other the know-how. Sometimes a joint venture is the only way an organization can enter into or gain a foothold in a foreign market, for example because of legislation. Joint ventures tend to have a limited lifespan as the needs of each party alter and develop over time. They work best in sectors where there is a high degree of local adaptation to the market. Factors that contribute to a successful joint venture partnership include the following:

- ensuring an appropriate balance of power
- developing strong communication channels between the partners at several points of contact and levels
- developing a mechanism for conflict resolution (e.g. before an issue goes to court)
- clarity of agreed inputs and divisions of benefits
- jointly defined goals and parameters
- compatibility in how the two partners operate and their strategic vision
- equal commitment from both partners
- complementary skills for mutual benefit.

Direct Investment

Direct investment or foreign manufacture involves some form of manufacturing or production in the target country. Advantages include a commitment to the local market, fast availability of parts, and market detection of changes in the local environment. The extent of direct investment can range from the assembly of parts through to R&D-led innovation. Another means of market entry through direct investment is the acquisition or takeover of an organization in the foreign market. Nevertheless, it is very important to monitor how effective an overseas investment is over time. Sometimes it is necessary to exit from an investment. Tesco's exit from its US supermarket business Fresh & Easy in late 2012 was painful as it had not made any profits. By 2015, Tesco was also seeking a buyer for its South Korean business Homeplus in order to partially pay off its debt mountain of £21.7bn (Jung-A *et al.*, 2015).

Chapter Summary

To consolidate your learning, the key points from this chapter are summarized here.

■ **Define international market development as a market growth strategy.**

Given the increasing internationalization of world markets, increased foreign trade, and international travel, international marketing is frequently a core activity for many organizations. A market development strategy involves increasing sales by selling existing offerings in new markets, either by targeting new audiences domestically or entering new markets internationally. International market development is growing in importance because of changes in the economic, social, and political landscape. The main considerations are the degree of risk and adjustment an organization is willing to undertake and the identification of potential opportunities within foreign markets.

■ **List the different forms of international marketing strategy.**

When entering international markets, a key competitive decision is whether the approach should be to standardize or adapt the marketing strategy. Organizations can adopt a local/global, multi-domestic, or global competitive international marketing strategy. The decision is based on the type of offering, the attitudes of the organization, and the resources available for market entry.

■ **Identify the key drivers for international market development.**

Many factors motivate an organization to develop markets in international markets. These include historical accident, the need to move excess stock, limited growth in domestic markets, comparative advantages, economies of scale, trade liberalization, technological changes, customer relationships, the development of transnational market segments through immigration, and organizational sustainability.

■ **Describe the criteria used to identify and select international markets.**

Assessing market attractiveness is very important as different markets have varying levels of attractiveness. Markets may be chosen according to various criteria including market accessibility, market and population size, geographic proximity, psychological proximity/psychic distance, level and quality of competition already in the market, cost of entering the market, and the market's profit potential.

■ **Discuss how environmental factors influence the choice of international marketing strategy decisions.**

The analysis of environmental forces can help to identify which countries or regions should be given priority and which market entry strategy would be best suited to that country/region. Factors to consider include social, cultural, and consumption attitudes, and technological, economic, political, and legal factors.

■ **Explore various international market entry methods.**

The decision regarding which method to use to enter a foreign market is based on six main factors: speed and timing, costs and the required levels of investment, flexibility, risk and uncertainty, expected return on investment (ROI), and the long-term objectives. Once reviewed, organizations use one or more of the following methods of entry: indirect exporting; licensing, franchising; contracting; direct exporting; joint ventures; direct investment.

? Review Questions

1 What factors influence international market development strategies?

2 Identify the key differences between multi-domestic and global competitive strategies.

3 What criteria should an organization use to assess the attractiveness of a foreign market?

4 Outline the main environmental factors that impact international marketing.

5 What methods can an organization use to enter a foreign market?

6 What criteria should be considered when selecting an entry method to an international market?

7 When would an organization standardize rather than adapt its offering/promotional approach?

8 What are the key differences between indirect and direct exporting?

9 Identify the benefits of using franchises in international marketing.

10 What key success factors are associated with international joint ventures?

✎ Worksheet Summary

@ To apply the knowledge you have gained from this chapter and test your understanding of international market development visit the **Online Resource Centre** and complete Worksheet 7.1.

⚡ Discussion Questions

1 Having read Case Insight 7.1, how would you advise Lanson International to further differentiate itself in its category in the UK market? How would you also advise Lanson to develop its international markets?

2 What are the main criteria a company should consider when deciding to enter a new international market?

3 Which of the following factors would have the greatest impact on a fashion retailer's assessment of the attractiveness of a foreign market: political, legal, social–cultural, or technological? Why?

4 Identify the key issues that an Asian low cost airline should consider when expanding into new international markets?

5 Marketed heavily on their country of origin brand image, what impact do you think joint ventures with domestic vineyards or direct investment would have on the perception of wine brands in a foreign market?

6 Take note of the country of manufacture, assembly, and origin of five of your recent purchases. Which countries and regions are represented? What impact do you think the political and legal environment has had on their importation?

@ Visit the **Online Resource Centre** and complete the Multiple Choice Questions to assess your knowledge of Chapter 7.

Glossary

adaptative orientation a firm believes that each country should be approached separately as a different market, buying or conducting market research into the particular country and developing specific market strategy for that particular market.

born global firms which develop an international orientation to their business immediately without proceeding to develop an offering in their domestic market first.

comparative advantage the ability to produce goods and/or services at a lower opportunity cost than other firms or individuals.

consumer price indices (CPIs) A measure of the current prices of a basket of goods in a particular country, usually expressed in US dollars in **purchasing power parity** terms.

contracting where a manufacturer contracts an organization in a foreign market to manufacture or assemble the product in that foreign market.

culture the values, beliefs, ideas, customs, actions, and symbols that are learned and shared by people within particular societies.

direct exporting the manufacturing firm itself distributes its product offering direct to customers in foreign markets.

direct investment or foreign manufacture, some form of manufacture or production in the foreign or host country is sometimes necessary.

economies of scale the reduction in cost of each additional unit as production increases and operational efficiencies are realized.

ethnocentric approach views the domestic market (home market) as the most important, and overseas markets as inferior with foreign imports not seen as representing a serious threat.

franchising a contractual vertical marketing system in which a franchisor licenses a franchisee to produce or market goods or services to certain criteria laid down by the franchisor in return for fees and/or royalties.

Generation Y People born in the 1980s and 1990s, regarded as being familiar with digital technologies.

geocentric approach sees the world as a single market—global—with the organization looking for global segments (e.g. ageing market) and global opportunities to rationalize communications, production, and product development.

global capability the willingness and capability to operate anywhere in the world with a direct result in global brand recognition.

globalization refers to increasing global connectivity, integration, and interdependence in the economic, social, technological, cultural, political, and ecological spheres.

gross national product (GNP) total domestic and foreign added value claimed by residents of a state.

indirect exporting production and manufacture of the product offering occurs in the domestic market and involves the services of other companies (intermediaries) to sell the product in the foreign market.

international marketing marketing activity that crosses national boundaries.

joint venture two organizations come together to create a jointly owned third company. This is an example of cooperative as opposed to competitive operations in international marketing.

licensing a commercial process whereby the trademark of an established brand is used by another organization over a defined period of time in a defined area, in return for a fee, to develop another brand.

lingua franca a bridge, or third language—language between two communicators of different nationalities, speaking two other languages.

Mercosur Mercado Común del Sur is a regional Latin American trading bloc designed to promote free trade, and the movement of people and currency. Its full members are Argentina, Bolivia, Brazil, Paraguay, Uruguay, and Venezuela. Its associate members are Chile, Peru, Colombia, and Ecuador.

multi-domestic competitive strategy where an organization pursues a separate marketing strategy in each of its foreign markets while viewing the competitive challenge independently from market to market.

original equipment manufacturer a manufacturer who sells another company's product, service, or technology, often as a component of an integrated offering, under its own name and brand.

polycentric approach each overseas market is seen as a separate domestic market, and each country is seen as a separate entity, and the firm seeks to be seen as a local firm within that country.

psychic difference the perceptual difference that exists between how people in a home market view an offering versus a foreign market based around culture, language, religion, politics, economics, and other country distinctions.

purchasing power parity an approach used to compare the relative values of currencies from different countries.

regional approach grouping countries together, usually on a geographical basis (e.g. Europe), and providing for the specific needs of consumers within those countries.

selective contestability the ability to disaggregate generic markets into meaningful submarkets or segments, select those most attractive, and position the product offering appropriately.

standardized approach a firm operates as if the world were one large market (global market), ignoring regional and national differences, selling the same products and services the same way throughout the world.

▌▌ References

ABF (nd). Our grocery brands. Associated British Foods. Retrieve from: http://www.abf.co.uk/about_us/our_group/our_grocery_brands (accessed 25 October 2015).

Agence France-Presse (2015). India's legendary Royal Enfield motorcycle to expand production. *The Guardian*, 18 February. Retrieve from: http://www.theguardian.com/world/2015/feb/18/indias-legendary-royal-enfield-motorcycle-to-expand-production-to-uk (accessed 10 November 2015).

Anderson, E. (2014). Rebuilding Lego, brick by brick. *The Times*, 7 December, 7.

Anon. (2012). Biggest transnational companies. *The Economist*, 10 July. Retrieve from: http://www.economist.com/blogs/graphicdetail/2012/07/focus-1 (accessed 24 March 2016).

Anon. (2014). Key market statistics 2014. Champagne.fr. Retrieve from: http://www.champagne.fr/en/champagne-economy/key-market-statistics (accessed 10 November 2015).

Anon. (2015a). The Royal Mint: coining it. *The Economist*, 21 February, 26.

Anon. (2015b).Faster, cheaper fashion. *The Economist*, 5 September, 63.

Anon. (2015c). Support for cider drinking. *Impact*, April, 14.

Anon. (2015d). So everything is awesome at Lego, just as the song says. *The Times*, 26 February, 47.

Anon. (2015e). Bread in France: forget the baguette. *The Economist*, 27 June, 34.

Ansoff, H.I. (1957). Strategies of diversification. *Harvard Business Review*, 25(5), 113–25.

Askew, K. (2015). Analysis: Unilever's plan to grow global ice cream sales margins. *Just-Food*, 31 July. Retrieve from: http://www.just-food.com/analysis/unilevers-plan-to-grow-global-ice-cream-sales-margins_id130732.aspx (accessed 27 October 2015).

Bartlett, C. and Ghoshal, S. (1991). *Managing Across Borders: The Transnational Solution*. Cambridge, MA: Harvard Business School Press.

Bellis, M. (2015). The history of money. About.com. Retrieve from: http://inventors.about.com/od/mstartinventions/a/money.htm (accessed 11 November 2015).

Blitz, R. (2014). The bet on Chinese gamblers. *The Financial Times*, 29 May. Retrieve from: http://www.ft.com/cms/s/0/50070822-e284-11e3-89fd-00144feabdc0.html (accessed 15 November 2015).

Burgen, S. (2015). Spain becomes the world's biggest wine exporter in 2014. *The Guardian*, 6 March. Retrieve from: http://www.theguardian.com/world/2015/mar/06/spain-worlds-biggest-wine-exporter-2014-bulk-sales-spainish-wine (accessed 22 November 2015).

Burkitt, L. (2013). China spreads chicken blame. *Wall Street Journal*, 25 January. Retrieve from: http://online.wsj.com/article/SB10001424127887323539804578263450081445528.html (accessed 19 November 2015).

Carscoops (2007). Why Honda didn't call the Fit-Jazz by its intended name. Carscoops.com, 21 September. Retrieve from: http://www.carscoops.com/2007/09/why-honda-didnt-call-fit-jazz-by-its.html (accessed 21 November 2015).

Chetty, S. and Campbell-Hunt, C. (2004). A strategic approach to internationalization: a traditional versus a 'born global' approach. *Journal of International Marketing*, 12(1), 57–81.

Colley, J. (2015). Why beer drinkers lose in the SABMiller-ABInBev merger. *Fortune*, 15 October. Retrieve from: http://fortune.com/2015/10/15/sabmiller-ab-inbev-merger-beer-drinkers-lose/ (accessed 10 October 2015).

de Mooij, M. (1994). *Advertising Worldwide*. Hemel Hempstead: Prentice Hall.

de Pablos, P.O. (2006). Transnational corporations and strategic challenges: an analysis of knowledge flows and competitive advantage. *Learning Organization*, 13, 544–59.

Davidson, M. (2013). Generation game: the return of the extended family home. *The Telegraph*, 9 May. Retrieve from: http://www.telegraph.co.uk/finance/property/buying-selling-moving/10046242/Generation-game-the-return-of-the-extended-family-home.html (accessed 19 November 2015).

Doland, A. (2015). Defying tough times, these four foreign brands are successful in China. *Advertising Age*, 29 June. Retrieve from: http://adage.com/article/global-news/foreign-brands-successful-china/299242/ (accessed 15 November 2015).

Douglas, S. and Douglas, Y.W. (1987). The myth of globalisation. *Columbia Journal of World Business*, Winter, 19–29.

Douglas, S.P. and Wind, Y. (1987). The myth of globalization. *Columbia Journal of World Business*, 22(4), 19–29.

Evans, J. (2010). *Marketing Aspects of Psychic Distance*. Chichester: John Wiley, 6.

Fill, C. (2009), *Marketing Communications: Interactivity, Communities, and Content* (5th edn), Harlow: Prentice Hall.

Frean, A. (2015). Fast-food giant says China is not as yummy as it was. *The Times*, 21 October, 42.

Fromowitz, M. (2013). Cultural blunders: brands gone wrong. *Campaign*, 7 October. Retrieve from: http://www.campaignasia.com/BlogEntry/359532,Cultural + blunders + Brands + gone + wrong.aspx (accessed 21 November 2015).

Ghemawat, P. (2001). Distance still matters. *Harvard Business Review*, 79(8), 137–47.

James, G. (2014). 20 epic fails in global branding. Inc.com, 29 October. Retrieve from: http://www.inc.com/geoffrey-james/the-20-worst-brand-translations-of-all-time.html (accessed 21 November 2015).

Harris, D.E. (2007). Sao Paolo: a city without ads. *Adbusters*, 3 August. Retrieve from: https://www.adbusters.org/magazine/73/Sao_Paulo_A_City_Without_Ads.html (accessed 25 October 2015).

Herbig, P.A. and Day, K. (1993). Managerial implications of the North American Free Trade Agreement. *International Marketing Review*, 10, 15–35.

Hofstede, G. (1980). Motivation, leadership, and organization: do American theories apply abroad? *Organizational Dynamics*, 9(1), 42–63.

Hofstede, G. (1983). The cultural relativity of organizational practices and theories. *Journal of International Business Studies*, 14(2), 75–89.

Hout, T., Porter, M. E., and Rudden, E. (1982). How global organizations win out! *Harvard Business Review*, September–October, 98–108.

Hurley, J. (2015). Why success abroad needn't be a shaggy dog story. *The Times*, 31 August, 42–3.

Institute of Business Ethics (2012). The ethics of gifts & hospitality. *Business Ethics Briefing*, Issue 29 (November), 1. Retrieve from: https://www.ibe.org.uk/userassets/briefings/ibe_briefing_29_ethics_of_gifts_&_hospitality.pdf (accessed 24 March 2016).

Interbrand (2014). Interbrand Releases Best China Brands Report 2014, Shanghai. Retrieved from: http://interbrand.com/newsroom/interbrand-releases-2014-best-china-brands-report/ (accessed November 2015).

Johanson, J. and Wiedersheim-Paul, F. (1975). The internationalization of the firm: four Swedish cases. *Journal of Management Studies*, 12(3), 305–22.

Johanson, J. and Vahlne, J.E. (1977). The internationalization process of the firm: a model of knowledge development and increasing foreign market commitments. *Journal of International Business Studies*, 8(1), 23–32.

Jung-A, S., Mundy, S., and Sender, H. (2015). Tesco nears the $6bn deal with MBK to offload South Korea unit. *Financial Times*, 3 September, 19.

Kaiman, J. (2013). China's fast-food pioneer struggles to keep customers saying 'YUM!'. *The Guardian*, 4 January. Retrieve from: http://www.guardian.co.uk/world/2013/jan/04/china-fast-food-pioneer (accessed 19 November 2015).

Keegan, W.J. (1989). *Global Marketing Management*. Englewood Cliffs, NJ: Prentice Hall.

Kwintessential (nd). Business card etiquette. Retrieve from: http://www.kwintessential.co.uk/cultural-services/articles/business-card-etiquette.html (accessed 24 March 2016).

Levitt, T. (1983). The globalization of markets. *Harvard Business Review*, May–June, 92–102.

Lewis, R. (2014). How different cultures understand time. *Business Insider*, 1 June. Retrieve from: http://www.businessinsider.com/how-different-cultures-understand-time-2014-5?IR = T (accessed 24 March 2016).

Lynch, R. (1994). *European Business Strategies: The European and Global Strategies of Europe's Top Organizations*. London: Kogan Page.

Mahdawi, A. (2015). Can cities kick ads? Inside the global movement to ban urban billboards. *The Guardian*, 12 August. Retrieve from: http://www.theguardian.com/cities/2015/aug/11/can-cities-kick-ads-ban-urban-billboards (accessed 25 October 2015).

Martel, L. (2015). Population growth: migratory increase overtakes natural increase. *Statistics Canada*,

18 November. Retrieve from: http://www.statcan.gc.ca/pub/11-630-x/11-630-x2014001-eng.htm (accessed 19 November 2015).

Martin, A. and Fujikawa, M. (2015). Food scandals push McDonald's Japan into loss. *Wall Street Journal*, 5 February. Retrieve from: http://www.wsj.com/articles/food-scandals-push-mcdonalds-japan-into-loss-1423121899 (accessed 15 November 2015).

Mead, R. (1990). *Cross-Cultural Management Communication*. New York: John Wiley.

Mooney, P. (2008). Coke and the US troops. Coca-Cola Company, 11 November. Retrieve from: http://www.coca-colacompany.com/stories/2008/11/coke-and-the-us/ (accessed 10 November 2015).

Morris, R. (2013). Fresh & Easy failure: can UK firms make it in the US? *BBC News*, 17 April. Retrieve from: http://www.bbc.co.uk/news/business-22168463 (accessed 25 October 2015).

Mughan, T. (1993). Culture as an asset in international business. In: Preston, J. (ed.), *International Business: Texts and Cases*. London: Pitman, 78–86.

My French Communication Agency (nd). Top 10 cultural and linguistic blunders in international advertising. Retrieve from: http://www.my-french-communication-agency.com/top-10-cultural-linguistic-blunders-international-advertising/ (accessed 21 November 2015).

Ohmae, K. (1985). *Triad Power*. London: Macmillan.

Ohmae, K. (1992). *The Borderless World: Power and Strategy in the Interlinked Economy*. London: Fontana.

Paliwoda, S. (1993). *International Marketing* (2nd edn). Oxford: Butterworth Heinemann.

Perlmutter, H.V. (1969). The tortuous evolution of the multinational corporation. *Columbia Journal of World Business*, January–February, 9–18.

Quelch, J.A. and Hoff, E. J. (1986). Customising global marketing. *Harvard Business Review*, May–June, 59–68.

RBI (2015). Earnings conference call—third quarter 2014. Restaurant Brands International Investor

Relations Presentation, 27 October. Retrieve from: http://investor.rbi.com/en/investor-information/legacy-filings/burger-king.aspx?sc_lang = en&Category = earnings-release&Subcategory = *&Date = 01/01/2014&DateEnds = 31/12/2014 (accessed 22 November 2015).

Sclater, I. (2005). The digital dimension. *The Marketer,* May, 22–3.

Shawcross, J. (2014). The rise and rise of Primark. *Aol Money*, 23 March. Retrieve from: http://money.aol.co.uk/2014/03/23/the-rise-and-rise-of-primark/ (accessed 25 October 2015).

Sirgy, M., Lee, D.-J., Miller, C., Littlefield, J., and Atay, E. (2007). The impact of imports and exports on a country's quality of life. *Social Indicators Research*, 83, 245–81.

Standard Chartered (2014). Annual Report 2014. Retrieve from: https://www.sc.com/annual-report/2014/ (accessed 25 October 2015).

Watrous, M. (2015). Unilever acquires Italian gelato business. *Food Business News*, 10 February. Retrieve from: http://www.foodbusinessnews.net/articles/news_home/Business_News/2015/10/Unilever_acquires_Italian_gela.aspx?ID = %7B1D32187D-03D3-4D41-B938-E8BFCC35A13E%7D&cck = 1 (accessed 27 October 2015).

Wind Y. and Perlmutter, H.V. (1973). Guidelines for developing international marketing strategies. *Journal of Marketing*, 37(April), 14–23.

Young, S. (2001) What do researchers know about the global business environment? *International Marketing Review*, 18, 120–9.

Zhang, Y. (2015). Down times for many daigou amid crackdown by customs. *Global Times*, 22 October. Retrieve from: www.globaltimes.cn/content/948382.shtml (accessed 11 November 2015).

Zou, S. and Cavusgil, S.T. (2002). The GMS: a broad conceptualization of global marketing strategy performance and its effect on firm performance. *Journal of Marketing*, 66(October), 40–56.

Part Three
Managing Marketing Programmes

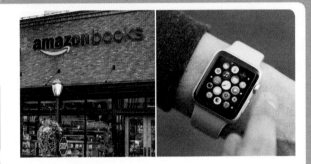

Part Three
Managing Marketing Programmes

Chapter 8
New Proposition Development and Innovation

Learning Outcomes

After studying this chapter you should be able to:

▶ Explain the different levels of a proposition

▶ Identify and describe the various types of product propositions and explain particular concepts relating to the management of products, including the product lifecycle

▶ Explain the relationship between product and service offerings and describe the product–service spectrum

▶ Explore the processes and issues associated with innovating new propositions

▶ Describe how new propositions are adopted by markets

Case Insight 8.1
Domino's Pizza

Market Insight 8.1
Cuba's Cohiba—Communist or Capitalist?

Market Insight 8.2
Battle of the Superjumbos

Market Insight 8.3
Online Fashion PLC

Market Insight 8.4
When a Product Is a Service

Market Insight 8.5
Streaming Wars: Apple versus Spotify

Case Insight 8.1
Domino's Pizza

How do organizations develop new propositions on a regular basis and remain competitive? We speak to Simon Wallis, Sales & Marketing Director for Domino's Pizza, to find out more.

Our expertise and passion for delivering hot fresh pizzas has earned us numerous awards and the loyalty of millions of pizza lovers around the world. Our mission is to be the favourite pizza delivery company in the world and we have set out several priorities to enable us to achieve this goal. One of these priorities is to 'deliver consistently high quality food on time' and another is to 'innovate in ways that matter to our team members and customers'. Speed and service are central elements that impact all parts of our business.

To satisfy these goals the development of new products that are valued by our customers is really important, yet it can be problematic and a constant challenge. For example, the environment in which we operate has changed in many ways in recent years. The economic downturn has served to flatten sales for everyone in the market. This has resulted from new consumer spending habits, a heightened interest in obesity and healthy eating issues, and new entrants who have brought fresh ideas, such as the surge of interest in Mexican products and restaurants. In addition to these external issues, new product development impacts a wide range of functions within the company and our franchises, such as finance, operations, and logistics, as well as marketing.

Our response to these internal and external issues has been to work closely with our customers and franchisees in order to review not only the quality of our pizzas and menu choice, but also to develop and introduce new products that exceed customer expectations. Ideas for new products come from a variety of sources. These include customers, suppliers, internal sources, and our Marketing Advisory Council, which consists of selective franchisees.

Appropriate ideas are then filtered across five main evaluative criteria: the franchisees, financial tests to ensure the proposition is viable, operations, and various new product development requirements including strategy, competitors, taste, and packaging. Ideas that get through these filters are developed into prospective products, which are then subject to test marketing which includes hall tests and in-store trials. Those with suitable feedback receive investment funding and are developed prior to a full market launch.

One of the problems facing Domino's Pizza is to find ways to balance the increased costs and longer operational times associated with new ingredients and products with the central tenets of service and speed on which the business is founded.

Introduction

A Samsung smartphone, a train journey from Calgary to Vancouver on the Rocky Mountaineer Train, a cappuccino at Costa Coffee in Stockholm, the Singapore *Straits Times* newspaper, a copy of the Brazilian magazine *Claudia*, a haircut in Hawaii, and a manicure in Manila are all commercial propositions or offerings. But do they all completely meet their customers' needs? By stating this, we are suggesting that offerings are only ever approximate solutions to customers' needs. No-one can ever completely design a proposition to meet everyone's needs all of the time. The term 'proposition' includes the tangible and intangible attributes related not just to physical goods but also to services, ideas, people, places, experiences, and even a mix of these various elements. Anything that can be offered for use and consumption, in exchange for money or some other form of value, is referred to as a **proposition** or offering. We occasionally use the term product as well, although this has goods-centric connotations.

A bar of soap, a Rimmel lipstick, or a Vega factory conveyor belt are all tangible products. **Tangibility** therefore refers to an item's ability to be touched and whether it can be stored. By comparison a ferry trip from Wellington to Picton in New Zealand or a visit to the hairdresser Toni & Guy cannot be touched and are incapable of being stored. These are intangible products (i.e. services). Interestingly, however, there has been an increasing shift, particularly in the business-to-business world, of servitizing products (i.e. making products into services). We discuss this intriguing marketing phenomenon in more detail later in this chapter.

Soap is a purely tangible good, whereas a financial services product, such as a pension or savings account, is a pure service. They lie at opposite ends of a spectrum (see Figure 8.1). In between the pure good and the pure service lie a host of goods–services combinations. Many products have intangible components; for example, computers are sold with warranties and cars are sold on finance deals with 0% interest. These intangible aspects are often called product intangibles. Indeed, many organizations have developed the intangible service element of their offering to help differentiate themselves in the marketplace.

This spectrum of product–service combinations incorporates strategies designed to increase the value offered to customers through improved services. However, developing the service element to provide a point of differentiation is not always a successful strategy, as it can attract price competition. As prices fall, offerings can become commoditized and customers may find it difficult to understand the value offered by competing firms. To avoid this, some organizations develop a third approach based around improving customer experience.

The customer experience strategy is not based on either the tangible or intangible attributes of brands, but refers to the memories and fantasies that individuals retain or imagine as a result of their interaction with an offering (Tynan and McKechnie, 2009). Memories of experiences related to product usage, events, visits, or activities are internalized, unlike products and services which are generally external to each person. Indeed, the idea that people consume emotions has long

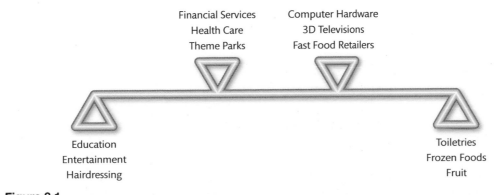

Figure 8.1

A spectrum of proposition combinations

been recognized as an important and influential aspect of the marketing discipline (Holbrook and Hirschman, 1982). The memories and fantasies concept is best illustrated through the activities of theme and leisure parks. For more information on customer experiences, see Chapter 15.

In this chapter, we consider the nature of propositions, before exploring issues associated with their innovation and development. We start with a consideration of the principal characteristics associated with products, and then discuss the notion of how all products are essentially services (i.e. service dominant logic). The second part of the chapter examines ideas and processes related to the development of new propositions in general.

Product Levels

When people buy propositions they are not just buying the simple functional aspect that a product offers; there are other complexities involved in the purchase. For example, the taste of coffee granules is an important benefit arising from the purchase of a jar of instant coffee. However, in addition to this core benefit, people are also attracted to the packaging, the price, the strength of the coffee, and some of the psychosocial associations that we have learnt about a brand. The Cafédirect brand, for instance, seeks to help people understand its ties with the Fairtrade movement and so provide some customers a level of psychosocial satisfaction through their contribution. To understand these different elements and benefits, we refer to three different proposition forms: the core, the embodied, and the augmented forms (see Figure 8.2).

- The core proposition consists of the real core benefit or service. This may be a functional benefit in terms of what the offering will enable you to do, or it may be an emotional benefit in terms of how the product or service will make you feel. Cars provide transportation and a means of self-expression. Cameras make memories by recording a scene, person, or object through the use of digital processes or, originally, film.

- The embodied proposition consists of the physical good or delivered service which provides the expected benefit. It consists of many factors, for example the features and capabilities,

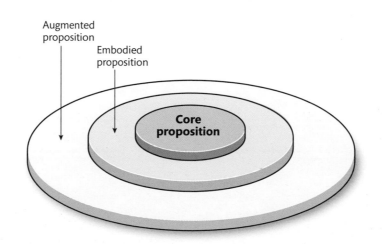

Figure 8.2
The three proposition forms

the durability, the design, the packaging, and the brand name. Cars are supplied with different styles, engines, seats, colours, and boot space, and digital cameras are offered with a variety of picture qualities, screen sizes, pixels, zoom and telephoto features, editing, and relay facilities.

- The augmented proposition consists of the embodied offering plus all those other factors that are necessary to support the purchase and any post-purchase activities, for example credit and finance, training, delivery, installation, guarantees, and the overall perception of customer service.

When these levels are brought together it is hoped that they will provide customers with a reason to buy and keep buying. Each individual combination or bundle of benefits constitutes added value and serves to differentiate, for example, one sports car from another sports car, or one disposable camera from another. Marketing strategies need to be designed around the actual and augmented propositions, as it is through these that competition occurs and people are able to understand how one disposable camera differs from another.

Understanding what a brand is to its customers and how they experience the brand is vitally important. Pepsi's battle with Coca-Cola during the 1960s and 1970s saw it gradually reduce Coke's dominant market share. Famously, the battle culminated in 1985 when Coke abandoned its original recipe and introduced New Coke, a sweeter formulation designed to attract Pepsi's young market. Coke's customers boycotted New Coke, there was public outrage, and Pepsi temporarily became market leader. New Coke was soon dropped, and the original was brought back and relaunched as Classic Cola, re-establishing its credentials and retrieving the No.1 spot. The problem was that Coke had not appreciated the value that the proposition as a whole represented to its primary customers. Customers were therefore consuming more than just the drink itself. The sum of the core, embodied, and augmented propositions, encapsulated as the brand Coca-Cola, drew passion from its customers and was overlooked by the market researchers when searching for a means to arrest Pepsi's progress. See Market Insight 8.1 for a product levels discussion in relation to Cuban cigar brand Cohiba.

Market Insight 8.1
Cuba's Cohiba — Communist or Capitalist?

The Cohiba cigar, made by Habanos S.A (50% owned by Imperial Tobacco plc), is the Cuban nation's most famous export. Legend has it that it was created by Che Guevara (then Minister of Industry) at the request of Fidel Castro. It is named after the Taino Indian word for the blend of leaves smoked by the island's early inhabitants. The product's distinctive flavour derives from the blend of leaves selected from fields in the Vuelta Abajo region and a special fermentation process. The brand is known for its distinctive black and yellow design. The cigar was first rolled in 1966.

Folklore suggests that once the Cuban President, Fidel Castro, was informed about the brand by his security guards, he became an advocate, and was frequently photographed smoking or holding the cigar.

The famous El Laguito factory produced the Cohiba cigars and distribution was closely controlled as they were exclusively for Castro and his friends. The cigar's reputation grew, mainly because of the photographic associations with Castro and because they were used as diplomatic gifts for foreign dignitaries.

Market Insight 8.1
continued

In 1982, the Cohiba was distributed internationally on a limited basis via Cubatabaco—the state tobacco marketing bureau—but was banned from sale in the USA because of the embargo on Cuban products (which ended in 2015, although some restrictions are maintained). Despite this, the illicit nature of the brand contributed to its popularity and a strong black market emerged. The brand is imbued with an association with luxury and extravagance. At first there were three product forms: the Panetela, the Corona Especial, and the Lancero. In 1989, three new ones were added: the Robusto, the Exquisito, and the Espléndido. These six are now referred to as Cohiba's classic line. In 1992, the Siglo (meaning century) I, II, III, IV, and V were launched. The most recent addition, in 2012, was the Cohiba Piramides Extra. These cigars are regarded as some of the finest and most popular cigars in the world. In a brand survey conducted by Bain & Company in the UK, the percentage of people who rated the brand highly (7–10 on a 10-point scale) less those who rated it lower (0–6), reached 57%, higher than Rolex, Audi, and HTC.

Despite the increasing social intolerance of smoking in many parts of the world, the Cohiba cigar still stands out as a product of desire, to the point of becoming as fashionable as designer shoes and handbags. Although sales in Western countries have declined, especially in Spain, its most important market, sales in many parts of Asia, especially China, have grown considerably. The Cohiba is a simple cigar, yet it has become a luxury item, with some priced at around £40 to £50 each.

Cohiba: first rolled by Che Guevara and smoked by Fidel Castro, as legend has it.
Source: iStock.com/FrankvandenBergh.

A brand born of communism and revolution is now valued by capitalists and entrepreneurs alike.

Sources: Osborn (2011); Anon. (2012a); Anon (2012b).

Theory into Practice

This market insight describes how a product developed in a highly restricted market economy, that of Cuba, came to be perceived as one of the world's finest cigar brands. We can consider the core proposition to be the benefits derived from smoking (we will not consider the health risks at this point, although they clearly exist as smoking kills users), which include initial stimulation followed by a sense of relaxation (therefore tobacco has biphasic chemical properties). The embodied proposition consists of the sweet distinctive taste, the packaging, the user's association with the Cohiba brand name, and the design of the cigar itself. The augmented proposition relates to the process of obtaining the Cohiba cigar, its availability, often through exclusive physical retail outlets such as airport duty free shops and specialist tobacconists (e.g. C Gars in London, Cigarrummet in Stockholm, or La Casa del Habano in The Hague) and specialist online tobacco stores.

Market Insight 8.1
continued

Related Topics:
product levels; branding; country of origin effect; international marketing.

1 **How do you think the product's origins have affected perceptions of the brand?**

2 **How might the Cohiba product and brand be further developed?**

3 **How do you think the US removal of trade barriers with Cuba and the lifting of sanctions in 2015 will affect perceptions of the brand in the US? (Hint: think of the possible impact on price and how this might impact on supply).**

The development of the web, social media, and other digital technologies have impacted on the nature of the offering and the benefits accruing from using it. This has opened opportunities for organizations to redefine their core and actual propositions, often by supplementing them with 'information' about the offering, e.g. providing white papers or games designed to engage website visitors with the brand. Another approach has been to transform current offerings into digital offerings, e.g. Netflix with video downloads as opposed to DVDs or Blu-ray. A further approach is to change the bundle of offerings, sometimes achieved by presenting an online catalogue that offers a wider array than the offline catalogue.

There are a number of ways in which **digital value** can help augment the proposition (Chaffey *et al.*, 2009). This can be done by coordinating activities to engage the customer through an increasingly digital purchase journey, harnessing content to empower the consumer to build their own identity, recognizing the need to think like a multimedia publisher, and plotting how to gather and use the increasing amount of digital data available (Edelman, 2010). For example, many companies provide evidence of the awards they have won, whereas others parade testimonials, case studies, white papers, endorsements, and customer comments, all as part of a **content marketing** strategy. These are designed to provide credibility, reduce risk, and enable people to engage with or purchase a brand. The key contribution of the Internet, in this context, is that it offers digital value to customers, sometimes as a supplement and sometimes as a complete alternative to the conventional established core offering.

It is important at this stage to point out that most of the costs associated with the development of a new proposition are the result of the design of the proposition. In other words, getting the design of a proposition wrong at the beginning of the new proposition development process can be very costly. There has long been recognition of the importance of joint working between marketing and research and development (R&D) (Hise *et al.*, 1990) (see Research Insight 8.1). Importantly, though, there is also increasing recognition not only of the importance of collaboration between the marketing function and research and development teams, but also of customer input to the design and development of new products (see Market Insight 8.2).

Visit the Online Resource Centre and complete Internet Activity 8.1 to learn more about how HSBC approaches new product development.

Market Insight 8.2
Battle of the Superjumbos

In the global aerospace industry for large wide-bodied passenger planes, two companies (a duopoly) battle it out in a perpetual war for customers. But they have completely different visions of what their customers want. Boeing predicted that people would want to fly directly to a wide and growing range of destinations and developed the 787 Dreamliner, whilst Airbus predicted that people would want to fly from one major hub airport to another (e.g. London Heathrow to Singapore or Dubai) and developed the A380. Accordingly, the two companies developed completely different planes. The largest Airbus A380 could seat up to 840 passengers and had a range of 15,000km whilst the Dreamliner had an initial seat capacity of 250 (now up to 323) and a range of 15,200km. Importantly, though, the Dreamliner has lower fuel costs with a higher fuel efficiency (0.12 to 0.05km/litre).

Boeing spent around 8 years developing the 787 Dreamliner product at a reputed cost of $32bn. It finally entered service in 2010, but analysts believe that it will not recoup its investment until 2019 or after the first 1,000 planes have been sold. Each plane sells at around $225m (for the 787-8 version). Customers were involved at various levels of the development process. Major airlines (e.g. All Nippon Airways) were involved in the design and specification, major suppliers from around the world had input to plane design and production (e.g. Rolls-Royce, Saab, Mitsubishi,

KAL-ASD), and even passengers could input their views through a dedicated website. When the first plane was delivered, it was three years late. By late 2015, Boeing had cumulative orders for 1,142 787s, of which it had delivered 354.

In contrast, the cost to Airbus of developing the A380, over 10 years, was reputedly around $25bn, somewhat cheaper than Boeing, and they delivered the first plane to Singapore Airlines in 2007, two years late. It used four teams of designers, one from each of its partners: France's Aérospatiale, Deutsche Aerospace, British Aerospace, and Spain's CASA. Each plane sells at a cool $414m and uses a double-decker design. Airbus has forecast that the market for very large planes between 2007 and 2033 will be around 1,230. By late 2015, it had cumulative orders for 317 A380s of which 176 had been delivered.

In the battle for the world's most popular superjumbo, Boeing appears to be winning, given the size of the order book (by volume and total revenue). Its bet on the popularity of point-to-point routes also appears to have been correct. But given the size of Airbus's order book, it is also doing very nicely. With the world's major airports becoming increasingly congested, might airlines shift to buying the bigger A380s rather than buying more 787s?

Sources: Anon. (2007); Ausick (2014, 2015); Armitage (2015); http://www.airbus.com/company/market/orders-deliveries/; http://www.boeing.com/commercial/#/orders-deliveries.

Theory into Practice

This market insight describes rival product development for the two major companies operating in the duopolistic global aerospace market. It highlights how the two companies developed opposing ambitious visions of the future of the aerospace market and developed their products, the A380 (Airbus) and the 787 (Boeing), accordingly. Boeing co-created the design of their product using

input from suppliers, airlines, and even passengers. Airbus initially consulted with airlines and developed their product from its supplier partner owners. The case highlights the difficulties of, and risks associated with, managing large aerospace development projects, especially given that both companies' products were delivered late (and billions of dollars over budget).

Market Insight 8.2
continued

Related Topics:

new product development; co-creation; product design; time to market.

1 Why do you think it took so long for both companies to develop their rival propositions?

2 What customer needs did they incorporate into the design of their propositions?

3 What might the next generation of plane look like in 2034?

Research Insight 8.1

To take your learning further, you might wish to read this influential paper.

Hise, R.T., O'Neal, L., Parasuraman, A., and McNeal, J.U. (1990). Marketing/R&D interaction in new product development: implications for new product success rates. *Journal of Product Innovation Management*, 7(2), 142–55.

This paper explains the importance of the interaction between marketing and research and development (R&D) in new product development. The authors report results of their analysis of the NPD procedures of 252 large manufacturing companies, concluding that joint working between marketing and R&D during the design stage of new products is a key factor in explaining NPD success.

Visit the **Online Resource Centre** to read the abstract and access the full paper.

Classifying Products

There are two main ways of classifying products—as consumer products and as business-to-business products. Consumers buy products to satisfy personal and family needs, and industrial and business products buy either as a part of the business operations or to make other products for resale. Some offerings, such as light bulbs and toilet tissue, are bought by both consumers and businesses.

Consumer Products

The first way of classifying consumer products is to consider them in terms of their durability. Durable goods, such as bicycles, music players, and refrigerators, can be used repeatedly and provide benefits each time they are used. Non-durable goods, such as yoghurt and newspapers, have a limited duration and are often only used once. Services are intangible propositions and cannot be stored (see Chapter 15 for more on this topic).

Durable goods often require the purchaser to have high levels of involvement in the purchase decision. There is a high perceived risk in these decisions and so consumers can spend time, care, and energy searching, formulating, and making the 'right' decision. As a result, marketers should seek to understand these patterns of behaviour, provide and make accessible sufficient amounts of appropriate information, and ensure that there is the right type of service and support necessary to meet the needs of the target market.

Non-durable goods, typically food and grocery items, reflect low levels of involvement and buyers are seldom concerned with which particular product they buy. Risk is seen to be low and so there is little or no need to shop around for the best possible price. Buyers may buy on availability, price, habit, or brand experience.

A deeper and more meaningful way of classifying consumer products is to consider how and where consumers buy them. In Chapter 2, we considered how consumers make purchases. In particular, we looked at **extensive problem-solving, limited problem-solving**, and **routinized response behaviour**. Classifying products according to the behaviour consumers demonstrate when buying them enables marketing managers to develop more suitable and appropriate marketing strategies. Four main behavioural categories have been established: **convenience products**, **shopping products**, **speciality products**, and unsought products.

Convenience products are non-durable and are bought because the consumer does not want to put very much effort, if any, into the buying decision. Routinized response behaviour corresponds most closely to convenience products as they are bought frequently and are inexpensive. Most decisions in this category are made habitually, and if the usual brand is unavailable an alternative brand is selected, or none at all if it is seen to be too inconvenient to visit another store.

Convenience products can be subdivided into three further categories. These are staples, impulse, and emergency products (see Table 8.1). All of these types of convenience product indicate that different marketing strategies might be required to make each work. However, one element common to all is distribution. If the product is not available when an emergency arises, or when a consumer is waiting to pay or walking around the supermarket, then a sale cannot be made. Pricing is also important, as customers know the expected price of convenience items and may well switch brands if price exceeds that of the competition.

Shopping products are not bought as frequently as convenience products, and as a result consumers do not always have sufficient up-to-date information to make a buying decision. The purchase of shopping products such as furniture, electrical appliances, jewellery, and mobile phones requires some search for information, if only to find out about the latest features. Consumers give time and effort to planning these purchases, if only because the level of risk is more substantial than that associated with convenience products. They will visit several stores and use the Internet and word-of-mouth communications for price comparisons, product information, and the experience of other customers. Not surprisingly, levels of brand loyalty are quite low, as consumers switch brands to get the level of functionality and overall value they need.

Table 8.1 Categories of convenience products

Type of convenience product	Explanation
Staple products	Staples are available almost everywhere. They include groceries (e.g. bread, milk, soft drinks, and breakfast cereals) and also petrol. They are bought frequently and habitually. In France, the daily purchase of a baguette still constitutes an important social habit.
Impulse products	These are offerings that consumers had not planned to buy but are persuaded to pick up, particularly when they see **point-of-sale** advertising materials. Typically, these items are located close to tills in supermarkets (the point of sale) so that customers waiting to be served are attracted to them. Chewing gum, chocolate bars, and magazines are typical impulse purchases, unlike a bottle of milk or petrol which is typically planned.
Emergency products	Bought as and when necessary; buyers are more intent on buying a solution than obtaining the right quality or image-related offering. So, purchase of a bandage when someone is cut or injured, finding a locksmith when your house key stops working, or, in a business-to-business context, purchasing new plant and machinery when the old machinery stops working suddenly.

The marketing strategies followed by manufacturers, and to some extent retailers, need to accommodate the characteristics of limited problem solving. Shopping products do not require the mass distribution strategies associated with convenience products. Here, a selective distribution strategy is required as, although the volume of purchases is lower and margins are higher, consumers often want the specialist advice offered by knowledgeable expert retailers.

Speciality products represent high risk, are very expensive, and are bought infrequently, often only once, and correspond to extended problem-solving. People plan these purchases carefully, search intensively for information on the offering, and are often only concerned with a particular brand and in finding a way of gaining access to an outlet that can supply it. It is possible to find speciality products in many areas, e.g. limited edition sports equipment (Big Bertha golf clubs), rare paintings and artwork (Monet, Picasso), watches (Omega), writing instruments (Montblanc), haute couture (Christian Dior), and certain restaurants and multi-destination holidays (Hayes & Jarvis). All have unique characteristics, which for buyers means that there are no substitute offerings available or worth considering.

Marketing strategies to support speciality products focus strongly on a very limited number of distribution outlets, and advertising that seeks to establish the brand name and values. The few retailers appointed to carry the item require detailed training and support so that the buyer experiences high levels of customer service and associated prestige throughout the entire purchase process.

Montblanc, a speciality product
Source: Courtesy of Montblanc.

Unsought products refer to a group of offerings that people do not normally anticipate buying, or indeed want to buy. Very often, consumers have little knowledge or awareness of the brands in the marketplace and are only motivated to find out about them when a specific need arises. Examples include car windscreens cracking (Autoglass®) and funerals (Co-operative Funeral Care). In a similar way, life insurance was once sold through heavy pressurized door-to-door selling as people did not see the need to buy it. That has changed with legislation, but double-glazing (e.g. Everest) and timeshare holiday salespeople still have a reputation for selling their offerings in this way.

Business Products

Unlike some consumer products, bought for personal and psychological rewards, business propositions are generally bought on a rational basis to meet organizational goals. These are either used to enable the organization to function smoothly or they form an integral part of the products, processes, and services supplied by the organization for resale. In the same way as consumer products are classified according to how customers use them, business propositions are classified according to how organizational customers use them. The six main categories are as follows.

- Equipment goods cover two main areas concerning the everyday operations of the organization: **capital equipment goods** and **accessory equipment goods**. Capital equipment goods are buildings, heavy plant, and factory equipment required to build or assemble products. They also include major government schemes to build hospitals, motorways, and bridges. Whatever their nature, they require substantial investment, are subject to long planning processes, are often one-off purchases designed to be used for a considerable period of time, and require the involvement of a number of different people and groups in the procurement process. Accessory equipment goods should support the key operational processes and activities of the organization. Typically, they are photocopiers, computers, stationery, and office furniture. These items cost less than capital equipment goods, are not expected to last as long as capital equipment goods, and are often portable rather than fixed. Whereas a poor capital equipment purchase may put the entire organization at risk, a poor accessory purchase frustrates and slows down activities but is unlikely to threaten the existence of the organization.

- Raw materials are the basic materials used to produce finished goods. Minerals, chemicals, timber, and food staples, such as grain, vegetables, fruit, meat, and fish, are extracted, grown, or farmed as necessary and transported to organizations that process them into finished or semi-finished products. They are bought in large quantities, and buyers often negotiate heavily on price. However, these buying decisions can also be influenced by non-product factors such as length of relationship, speed of delivery, service quality, and credit facilities.

- Semi-finished goods are raw materials that have been converted into a temporary state. For example, iron ore is converted into metal sheets that can be used by car and aircraft manufacturers, washing machines, and building contractors.

- **Maintenance, repair, and operating (MRO)** goods: these are products, other than raw materials, that are necessary to ensure that the organization continues to function. Maintenance and repair goods such as nuts and bolts, light bulbs, and cleaning supplies are used to maintain the capital and accessory equipment goods. Operating supplies are not directly involved in the production of finished goods nor are they a constituent part, but oil for lubricating machinery and office stationery (including flash drives and paperclips) are all necessary to keep the organization functioning.

- Component parts: these are finished complete parts bought from other organizations. These components are then incorporated directly into the finished product. So, for example, Ford will buy in finished headlight assemblies and mount them directly into their Ford Mustang, Vignale, or Transit models as appropriate.

- Business services are intangible services used to enhance the operational aspects of organizations. Most commonly, these concern management consultancy, finance, and accounting, including auditing, legal, marketing research, information systems, and marketing communications.

Product Range, Line, and Mix

To meet the needs of a number of different target markets, most organizations offer a variety of **products** and **services**. Although some offer an assortment based on an individual core product, it is rare that an organization offers a single product, although there are examples including Crocs Inc. (footwear), Bogdahn International GmbH (Flexi dog leashes), and WD-40 Company Inc. (lubricant). Consumer organizations, such as Gillette, offer a range of shaving products for men; industrial organizations, such as Oliver Valves, offer a range of valves for the offshore and onshore petrochemical, gas, and power generation industries. To make sense of,

Table 8.2 Product Terms In Relation to Samsung

Product term	Explanation
Product item	A distinct single product within a product line. Samsung's Galaxy S6 edge + is a product item.
Product line	A group of closely related products—related through technical, marketing, or user considerations. For example, all three Galaxy S6 phones offered by Samsung constitute a product line.
Product mix	The total number of product lines offered by an organization. At Samsung, this would mean all the mobile devices, televisions, print solutions, domestic appliances, cameras, and accessories they offer, as well as business-to-business products including microchips, semiconductors, and flash memory and hard drive devices.
Product line length	The number of products available in a product line: the three products available within the Samsung Galaxy S6 range (S6, S6 edge, S6 edge +).
Product line depth	The number of variations available within a product line. For example, in the USA, the Samsung Galaxy S6 edge + has three trim colours (black, silver and on selected models white pearl), four network providers, and two types of memory capacity (32GB and 64GB). The total product line depth is 16.
Product mix width	The number of product lines within a product mix.

and understand, the relationships that one set of products have with another, a variety of terms have emerged. Table 8.2 sets out these different terms using Samsung Electronics Co. Ltd, the South Korean conglomerate, as an example.

Visit the Online Resource Centre and complete Internet Activity 8.2 to learn more about the terminology relating to a product range.

Product Lifecycles

Underpinning the product lifecycle (PLC) concept is the belief that offerings move through a sequential predetermined pattern of development similar to the biological path that life forms follow. This pathway, known as the **product lifecycle**, consists of five distinct stages, namely development, introduction, growth, maturity, and decline. Sales and profits rise and fall across the various lifestages of the product, as shown in Figure 8.3.

Products move through an overall cycle which consists of different stages. Speed of movement through the stages will vary, but each product has a limited lifespan. Although the life of a product can be extended in many ways, such as introducing new ways of using the product,

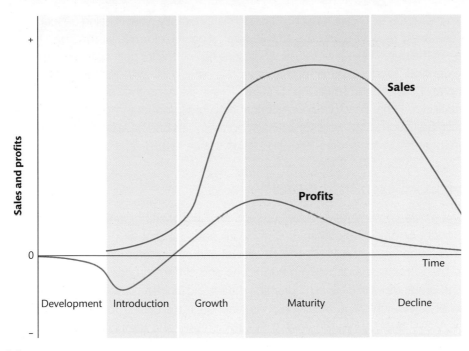

Figure 8.3
The product lifecycle

finding new users, and developing new attributes, the majority of products have a finite period during which management needs to maximize their returns on the investment made. In Sweden, mobile phones have an overall lifespan of 9–12 months, so it is important to extend the sales period, especially through maturity. Apple and others do this through 'appstores'. The firm offers existing iPhone customers the possibility of purchasing additional applications and games (Leistén and Nilsson, 2009). There is some evidence (from Germany) that electronic goods manufacturers are deliberately shortening product lifecycles, thereby adding **built-in obsolescence** (Ala-Kurikka, 2015).

Just as the nature and expectations of customer groups differ by stage, so do the competitive conditions. This means that different marketing strategies, relating to the offering and its distribution, pricing, and promotion, need to be deployed at particular times so as to maximize financial returns.

The product lifecycle concept does not apply to all offerings in the same way. For example, some offerings reach the end of the introduction stage and then die as it becomes clear that there is no market to sustain them. Some products follow the path into decline and then hang around sustained by heavy advertising and sales promotions, or they are recycled back into the growth stage by repositioning activities. Some products grow very quickly and then fade away rapidly. Fashion products are pertinent examples here, with Zara changing its product range on average every 3 weeks (Saren, 2006).

The brands of many fast-moving consumer goods (FMCGs) are sustained through a supermarket listing. Terminating a listed brand, and losing the shelf space to a competitor, is difficult to accept simply because getting the listing in the first place is so difficult and because of the need to recoup the substantial investment put into the brand since its conception. Supermarkets often delist an underperforming brand unless the brand owner presents a suitable variant capable of replacing the ailing brand (Clark, 2009).

When discussing the PLC care must be taken to clarify exactly what is being described. The PLC concept can apply to a product class (computers), a product form (a laptop), or a brand (Sony). The shape of the curve varies, with product classes having the longest cycle as the mature stage is often extended. Product forms tend to comply most closely with the traditional cycle shape, whereas brand cycles tend to be the shortest. This is because they are subject to competitive forces and sudden change. So, whereas hatchback cars (product form) enjoyed a long period of success, brands such as the Ford Escort had shorter cycles and have been replaced by cars that have more contemporary designs and features, in this case the Ford Focus.

Is the PLC Concept Useful?

The PLC is a well-known and popular concept, and is a useful means of explaining the broad path a product or brand has taken. It also clearly sets out that no product, service, or brand lasts forever. In principle, the PLC concept allows marketing managers to adapt strategies and tactics to meet the needs of evolving conditions and circumstances. In this sense, it is clear, simple, and predictable. However, in practice the PLC is of limited use. For example, one problem is identifying which stage an offering has reached in the cycle. Some brands do not follow the classical S-shaped curve (Figure 8.3), but rise steeply and then fall away immediately after sales reach a crest. These shapes reflect a consumer fad when rapid obsolescence occurs, or there is a craze for a particular piece of merchandise, typified by fashion clothing, skateboards, and toys. Another possible product lifecycle form is when demand for a brand is rejuvenated. An example, is Ford's redevelopment of the Ford Mustang, now on sale in Europe as well as in the USA (see Figure 8.4). Other examples include Swiss watchmakers redefining their products as a status good rather than a timepiece, for example the Rolex and Omega brands (Anon., 2014). So great care is required when using the PLC, as its role in commerce and when developing strategy is weak, but it is helpful generally as a way of explaining how brands develop (see Market Insight 8.3). Historical sales data do not help managers to identify when an offering moves from one stage to another. This means that it is difficult to forecast sales, and hence determine the future shape of the PLC curve.

The PLC model works reasonably well when the environment is relatively stable and not subject to dynamic swings or short-lived customer preferences. However, contemporary marketing managers are not concerned where their brand is within the product lifecycle; there are many

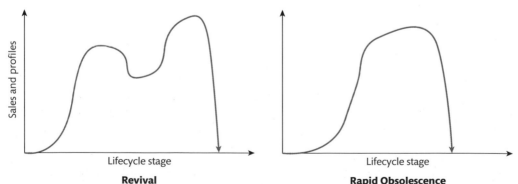

Figure 8.4
Types of Product Lifecycle Form

other more meaningful ways and metrics for understanding the competitive strength and development of a brand (e.g. benchmarking). The PLC concept has also been criticized for giving managers tunnel vision, as they assume that a brand follows a pre-ordained advance along the curve when in fact a product can fail at any stage (Moon, 2005).

Market Insight 8.3
Online Fashion PLC

Firms such as Germany's Zalando, a cross-platform **pureplay** online fashion brand operating in more than 14 countries, and ASOS, the UK's market leader in online fashion retailing, dominate the European e-commerce fashion market. ASOS has online stores in the UK, USA, France, Germany, Italy, Spain, Australia, and Russia, but delivers to 240 countries. Both companies have thousands of product items on their websites and can introduce hundreds of new items each week. Zalando even offer free shipping and returns.

Understanding the principles underpinning the lifecycle can help these firms work out the length of each item's sales period, manage the stocking requirements, and plan for the introduction of new ranges. For example, in the world of online fashion, the following cycle might be evident.

- Introduction—a new skirt is presented online, given lots of visibility, and is linked directly through newsletters and social media sites and also from the homepage. Some fashion leaders adopt the new skirt, while digital influencers (such as fashion bloggers) who have been alerted previously to the launch are given access to more detailed information and, in some cases, samples.

- Growth—offline articles, online placements, and word of mouth help sales to grow. Stock management becomes critical as it is essential not to disappoint customers.

- Maturity—competition becomes intense and it is necessary to remind audiences about the offering online. More stock may be required to ensure continuity of supply. For example, a dress from the previous summer collection may still be selling well. At some point during this stage, the firm may cut the price to clear remaining stock. Sales provide an opportunity to make space in the warehouse for new offerings.

- Decline—the skirt becomes unfashionable and is replaced by a new design.

Each of these specific stages of development has different characteristics, requiring different business and marketing approaches. This, in turn, has led to the development of software systems and applications that are geared to manage the individual characteristics of each stage. Importantly, ASOS also operates in the southern hemisphere where seasons are opposite to the UK, allowing the company to sell its products continuously. Product lifecycle management (PLM) systems are used to deal with online catalogues, design collaboration (enabling geographically dispersed employees to work on designs together), style information (an item's sales history), and various facilities designed to integrate order tracking, invoicing, and operations activities.

Sources: Pukhtina (2013); Perks (2014).

Theory into Practice

This market insight describes how the product lifecycle concept operates in an online fashion retailing environment with specific reference to two firms which dominate the European market. The insight also shows how the Internet channel has allowed fashion companies to develop very high revenues and customer bases in a relatively short period of time.

Market Insight 8.3
continued

Related Topics:

fashion retailing; international marketing; multichannel marketing.

1 How might, for example, ASOS's marketing activities change as it moves into the mature stage?

2 Use a search engine to find the leading online fashion company in Australia, Canada, and another country of your choice. What do all these companies have in common?

3 How might customers' needs change over the next five years?

ASOS plc: not out of fashion anytime soon
Source: © Bloomberg/Getty.

Service-Dominant Logic

Some researchers believe that products alone are not capable of meeting all of a customer's needs (Grönroos, 2009), particularly in business markets. For business customers to derive value from a product they need to use it and that often requires a level of integration or coordination with a supplier's processes and systems. This, it is argued, resembles more of the characteristics of a service than a core product offering. There is recognition that satisfying a customers' needs is inherently a service, i.e. selling bottled water as a physical product is really the offering of a thirst quenching service. Marketing should be considered a customer management process. This entails not only proposing how an offering might be of value to customers, but enabling and supporting them to create the value they require through their use of the product.

This notion of all propositions really embodying a service is referred to as the **service-dominant logic** (SDL) approach, and was first proposed by Vargo and Lusch (2004) (see also Chapter 1). The traditional marketing management approach can be considered as product-dominant logic. So, if products alone are insufficient to meet customer needs, it is better to consider services as a more realistic means of understanding how marketing works (see Research Insight 8.2).

In more recent work, Vargo and Lusch (2016) update their original thinking to develop 11 foundational premises (FP1-11) about the essentially service-based nature of marketing.

FP2—Indirect exchange masks the fundamental basis of exchange.

FP3—Goods are distribution mechanisms for service provision.

FP4—Operant resources (i.e. knowledge and skills) are the fundamental source of strategic benefit.

FP5—All economies are service economies.

FP6—Value is co-created by multiple actors (e.g. organizations), always including the beneficiary.

FP7—Actors (i.e. organizations) cannot deliver value but can participate in the creation and offering of value propositions.

FP8—A service-centred view is inherently beneficiary oriented and relational.

FP9—All social and economic actors (e.g. organizations) are resource integrators.

FP10—Value is always uniquely and phenomenologically determined by the beneficiary.

Research Insight 8.2

To take your learning further, you might wish to read this influential paper.

Vargo, S.L. and Lusch, R.F. (2004). Evolving to a new dominant logic for marketing. *Journal of Marketing*, 68 (1, January), 1–17.

This paper introduces the ideas concerning service-dominant logic. It sets out the conceptual underpinning of the approach by tracking back and considering previous major marketing approaches, outlining eight foundational premises concerning how the proposition in marketing is inherently a service, and that this requires a reconsideration of how marketing should be undertaken.

Visit the **Online Resource Centre** to read the abstract and access the full paper.

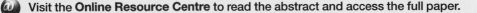

FP11—Value co-creation is coordinated through actor-generated (e.g. organization-generated) institutions and institutional arrangements.

The service-dominant logic concept has been criticized for being of little practical use to marketers (O'Shaughnessy and O'Shaughnessy, 2009) but it has generated important discussions about how organizations and their customers work together to co-create new propositions and that, regardless of the physical embodiment of those propositions, they are inherently a service offering. We turn to how new propositions are developed in the next section.

Developing Propositions for Products and Services

In this section we examine the principles and approaches used to innovate and develop new propositions for both products and services.

Developing New Product Propositions

One of the key points that the product lifecycle concept tells us is that products do not last forever; their usefulness diminishes at some point, and eventually nearly all come to an end and die. There are many reasons for this cycle: technology changes quickly so products are developed and adopted faster; lifecycles are shortening, and so new products are required faster than before. In addition to this, global competition means that if an organization is to compete successfully and survive it needs to continually offer superior value to its customers. Therefore a key management task is to control the organization's range or portfolio of products, and to anticipate when one product will become tired and new ones will be necessary to sustain the organization and help it to grow.

The term 'new products' can be misleading. This is because there is a range of newness, relevant to both the organization and to customers. Some new products might be totally new to both the organization and the market; for example, the Dyson vacuum cleaner, with its dual cyclone technology, revolutionized the market previously dominated by suction-based vacuum cleaners. However, some new products might only be minor adaptations that have no real impact on a market other than offering an interesting new feature (e.g. new colours, flavours, and pack sizes).

Unfortunately, 'new' propositions do not appear at the click of one's fingers. They have to be considered, planned, developed, and carefully introduced to the market. In order to ensure a stream of new propositions, organizations have the following three main options.

- Buy in finished products from other suppliers, perhaps from other parts of the world, or license the use of other products for specific periods of time (e.g. Samsung does this by licensing its processor technology).

- Develop products through collaboration with suppliers or even competitors, for example. as Sony tried to do, but failed, with Ericsson in the mobile phone business (see Parnell, 2012).

- Develop new products internally, often through R&D departments or by adapting current products through minor design and engineering changes (e.g. as Dyson did with its vacuum cleaner).

Whatever the preferred route, they all necessitate a procedure or development pattern through which they are brought to the market. It would be wrong to suggest that there should be a uniform process (Ozer, 2003), as there are many approaches to new product development and also the procedures adopted by an organization reflect its attitude to risk, its culture, its strategy, the product and market, and, above all else, its approach to the development of customer relationships.

The success rate of new products is consistently poor. No more than one in ten new consumer products succeed. According to Drucker (1985), there are three main reasons for this.

1   No market exists for the product, e.g. the famous electric car, the Sinclair C5, launched in 1985 in the UK and swiftly withdrawn nine months later when the company folded (Roberts, 2015).

2   There is a market need but the product fails to meet customer requirements, e.g. Frito-Lay's WOW! fat-free crisps, made with olestra, launched in the USA in 1998 but caused gastrointestinal problems in consumers and were quietly withdrawn in 2004 (Glass, 2012).

3   The product's ability to meet the market need, although satisfactory, is not adequately communicated to the target market, e.g. Buckler, a very low alcohol beer in the Dutch market in the 1980s (Institute of Brilliant Failures, nd).

Successful new propositions are developed partly by understanding customer needs and competitors, and partly by developing the technology to meet the identified needs. For example, when an Asian entrant to the US market for medical devices and capital equipment quickly established itself, it was thought that their lower prices were the main reason for their success. However, when a major manufacturer reviewed their own proposition they also analysed customer needs and the nature of the competition. The results showed that the US manufacturer's products were perceived to lag slightly behind its competitor on several critical attributes that mattered more to customers than had previously been thought. The competitor's product also cost less to manufacture, and the competitor had considerable room to lower its costs further. The US manufacturer's response was to close the cost gap by generating ideas that bridged 80% of the cost disadvantage. This was achieved without compromising features that users valued (Narayanan *et al.*, 2012).

The development of new propositions is a complex and high risk task, so organizations usually adopt a procedural approach. The procedure consists of several phases (stages and gates) that enable progress to be monitored, test trials to be conducted, and the results analysed before there is any commitment to the market. The most common new product development process (NPDP) is set out in Figure 8.5.

The NPDP presented here should be considered as a generalization. Actions can overlap or even occur out of sequence depending on the speed, complexity, and number of people or organizations involved in the NPDP. Apart from some minor issues, the process is the same when developing new products for both consumer and business markets. The process is generally perceived to be linear (but is not required to be such) in that new proposition development occurs only after managers are satisfied with progress of the development project at each stage. Therefore there is a go-no–go decision at each stage (i.e. a gate). This process is often referred to as a stage–gate model.

Visit the Online Resource Centre and follow the web link to the Product Development and Management Association (PDMA) to learn more about the professional development, information, collaboration, and promotion of new product development and management.

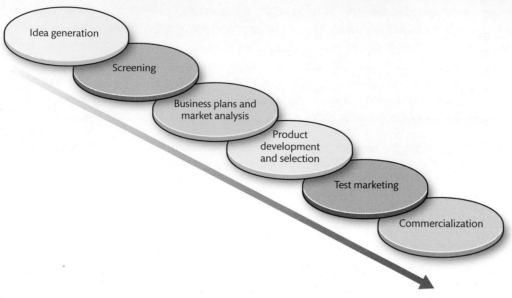

Figure 8.5
Stages in the new product development process

Idea Generation

Ideas can be generated through customers, competitors (through website and sales litera-ture analysis), market research data (such as reports), social media analyses, R&D, customer service employees, the sales force, project development teams, and secondary data sources such as sales records. What this means is that organizations should foster a corporate culture that encourages creativity and supports people when they bring forward new ideas for product enhancements and other improvements. 3M famously allow their engineers and scientists to spend 15% of their time pursuing projects of their own choice and 30% of a division's revenue must come from products developed in the previous four years. Over the years, the company has introduced such pioneering products as the Post-it note, Scotch tape, and the first elec-tronic stethoscope with Bluetooth technology. To encourage resourcefulness in the company, 3M allow employees to bid for seed capital to form their own venture teams, and allow engineers and scientists to obtain the same level of prestige and compensation as corporate management (Govindarajan and Srinivas, 2013).

 **Visit the Online Resource Centre** and complete Internet Activity 8.3 to learn more about how two leading FMCG companies approach the new product development process.

Screening

All ideas need to be assessed so that only those that meet predetermined criteria are advanced. Key criteria include the fit between the proposed new idea and the overall corporate strategy and objectives. Another consideration involves the views of customers, determined using concept testing. Other approaches consider how the market will react to the idea and what effort the organization will need to make if the offering is to be brought to market successfully. Whatever approaches are used, screening must be a separate activity to the idea generation stage. If it is not, creativity might be impaired.

Business Planning and Market Analysis

The development of a business plan is crucial, simply because it will indicate the potential and relative profitability of the product. To prepare the plan, important information about the size, shape, and dynamics of the market should be determined. The resultant profitability forecasts will be significant in determining how and when the product will be developed, if at all.

Product Development and Selection

In many organizations, several product ideas are considered simultaneously. It is management's task to select those that have commercial potential and are in the best interests of the organization and its longer-term strategy, goals, and use of resources. There is a trade-off between the need to test and reduce risk, and the need to go to market and drive income to get a return on the investment committed to the new proposition. This phase is expensive, so only a limited number of projects are allowed to proceed into development. Prototypes and test versions are developed for those projects that are selected for further development. These are then subjected to functional performance tests, design revisions, manufacturing requirements analysis, distribution analysis, and a multitude of other testing procedures.

Test Marketing

Before committing a new product to a market, most organizations decide to test market the finished product. By piloting and testing the product under controlled real-market conditions, many of the genuine issues as perceived by customers can be raised and resolved while minimizing any damage or risk to the organization and the brand. **Test marketing** can be undertaken using a particular geographical region or specific number of customer locations. The intention is to evaluate the product and the whole marketing programme under real working conditions. Test marketing (or field trials) enables the product and marketing plan to be refined or adapted in the light of market reaction, but before release to the whole market. British supermarket group Sainsbury's has built a central London lab, and hired 500 specialists, in order to test new ways of shopping, especially on mobile apps, given that customers' lives have changed and they have become more 'promiscuous shoppers' (Anon., 2015a). It is vital for organizations to set up a system to measure the success or failure of new product development. Criteria for measuring success and failure include, but are not limited to, measures based on customer acceptance, financial performance, and product and firm level considerations (Griffin and Page, 1993).

- Customer acceptance measures:
  - customer acceptance
  - customer satisfaction
  - net revenue goals
  - net market share goals
  - net unit sales goals.
- Financial performance measures:
  - break-even period
  - margin goals
  - profitability goals
  - IRR (internal rate of return)/ROI (return on investment).

- Product level measures:
  - development cost
  - launched on time
  - product performance level
  - net quality guidelines
  - speed to market.
- Firm level measurements:
  - percentage of sales attained as a proportion of new products/services.

See Chapter 3 for more information about test marketing.

Commercialization

To commercialize a new product a launch plan is required. This considers the needs of **distributors**, end-user customers, marketing communication agencies, and other relevant stakeholders. The objective is to schedule all those activities that are required to make the launch successful. These include communications (to inform audiences of the product's capabilities and to position and persuade potential customers), training, and product support for all customer-facing employees.

Any perceived rigidity in this formal process should be disregarded. Many new offerings come to market via rather different routes, at different speeds, and at different levels of preparation.

Developing New Service Propositions

So far, the focus has been on the processes associated with developing new products, without reference to services. This is partly because researchers have paid much more attention to the development issues with products. This has altered in recent years as many Western economies have become increasingly service oriented.

Möller *et al*. (2008) have developed ideas based on the logic that value creation is key to the development of innovative service offerings and concepts. They distinguish three service innovation strategies:

1 established services within competitive markets;

2 incremental service innovation targeting value-added propositions;

3 radical service innovation which aims to produce completely novel offerings.

Established services with a relatively stable value creation process are often generated under intense competition to improve operational efficiency. Dell is cited as a manufacturing business based on a simple concept, specifically selling computer systems directly to customers (rather than through retailers or other middlemen). Dell's market leadership is the result of a constant focus on delivering positive product and service experiences to customers.

Incremental service innovation describes a value creation strategy in which services are developed to provide extra value. Working together, the service provider and the client can produce more effective solutions. The prime example is Google which, in addition to providing Internet search services for individual consumers, provides search services for corporate clients including advertisers, content publishers, and site managers. Google continually develops new service applications based on its back-end technology and the use of linked PCs that respond immediately to each query. Google's innovation has resulted in faster response times, greater scalability, and lower costs. But Google also has a vast constellation of innovation projects including a spin-off company to investigate extending the human lifespan (Calico), Google's driverless car, Google Fiber, Chromecast, and many more.

Radical service innovation is concerned with value creation generated through novel or unusual service concepts. This requires new technologies, offerings, or business concepts, and involves radical system-wide changes in existing value systems. MySQL, the world's leading open-source database software producer, uses this approach. By making the source code of the software freely available to everybody, the software is available to everyone to use and/or modify. However, all derivative works must be made available to the original developers. As a result, MySQL have been able to increase the number of users and developers, and subsequently offer their clients improved levels of service. This has led to increased financial performance.

Enhancing Products Through Service Development

It is helpful to view proposition innovation in the light of the product–service spectrum introduced at the start of this chapter. Services do not always need to be seen purely as an extension or add-on to a product offering; they can also be a way of creating value opportunities for clients. Shelton (2009) considers service innovation in the context of four stages of solution management maturity. The early stages of innovation maturity are characterized by a product focus with a relatively small amount of services used only to augment and complement the products. The mature stages are characterized by much higher levels of service, some integrated with the products to provide solutions for customer problems.

- Stage 1—in this stage, services are used as aftersales product support (e.g. parts and repair services). Service innovation is framed around maintaining the product and ensuring that customers are satisfied with their product purchase. As a result, customers typically view the service and product business as distinct entities.

- Stage 2—this stage is characterized by aftersales services designed to complement the core product. Here, services should improve customer satisfaction with existing products, should increase loyalty, and may generate additional purchases. Shelton (2009) refers to Hewlett Packard's 'PC Tune-Up' which, for a fee, provides a set of diagnostics to assess and manage customers.

- Stage 3—at this stage, the portfolio includes a full line of services and products designed to provide a clearly differentiated offering aimed at solving clients' lifecycle problems. Shelton (2009) refers to Motorola's 'Total Network Care' (TNC) which provides end-to-end support services for wireless networks. Although the service organization is often consolidated into one identifiable business, products are still core to the company. End-user customers see no major perceived boundaries between products and services.

- Stage 4—at this, the highest end of innovation maturity, firms seek to integrate the services dimension as part of their total offer. Known as 'servitization', this involves the provision of an integrated bundle of product–service solutions for the entire lifecycle of their customers, 'from cradle to grave'. These solutions are developed collaboratively with clients and therefore require a deep understanding of the customer's overall business. These firms, often market leaders, generate innovative solutions through buyer–seller collaborative processes. Solutions are developed that are of mutual value. See Market Insight 8.4 for an example of servitization.

Market Insight 8.4
When a Product Is a Service

Some organizations offer products and services as an integrated bundle, where the services are an integral part of the core product. This is referred to as 'servitization' and enables customers to create the value they require rather than be dependent on suppliers. Examples of servitization can be seen in many sectors, but manufacturers have been prominent in developing this form of strategy.

In the world of office products, Xerox offers 'Managed Print Services' where risks are borne by the manufacturer and customers pay fees on a per use basis over several years. The product therefore shifts from printing equipment to 'document solutions'. In automotive, Michelin moved from selling tyres to business customers to selling kilometres when it launched Michelin Fleet Solutions in 2000, leasing tyres to fleet buyers like TNT, Geodis, and Schenker. Results were initially poor between 2000 and 2003 but improved after a concerted effort to redevelop the business model, with both revenues and operating margins increasing thereafter. Caterpillar, the world's largest manufacturer of mining and construction equipment, has also servitized its products, which range from tractors to gas turbines, by offering services designed to offer its customers the capacity to move rock and earth rather than simply selling them construction equipment.

In transport systems, the Otis Elevator Company—the world's leading supplier of lifts, escalators, and moving walkways (Trav-O-Lators®)—offers a variety of services including the EMS Panorama™ system, which allows customers to monitor, control, and gather information from escalators and lifts, and Otis Elite™ service, which provides early and accurate diagnostics in case of equipment failure (like a lift getting stuck), minimal lift repair times, passenger reassurance, proactive communication with the equipment owner over the repairs taking place, and customized lift operation (e.g. restricting access to certain floors).

The question therefore arises: With propositions like these, why sell them as just products?

Sources: Renault *et al.* (2010, 2012); Baines and Lightfoot (2013); Baines (2014); http://www.innovation-portal.info/wp-content/uploads/Deep-dive-Servitization.pdf; www.otis.com.

Theory into Practice

This market insight describes how manufacturers can transform their products, and therefore the customer value derived from them, by either turning their products into services or enhancing their products by adding substantial service components to create a totally unique proposition.

Related Topics:

service-dominant logic; product levels; product design; customer value; services marketing; relationship marketing.

1 **Is servitization really a glorified service contract? What do you think is the real value of this approach?**

2 **Do you think servitization could be undertaken by manufacturers who do not produce high technology products?**

3 **What are the disadvantages of developing a servitized proposition?**

Servitization strategies have been used to create value in a number of different industries. Robinson *et al.* (2002) report their use in the chemical industry, where price-led strategies tend to dominate in a commodity context. What is noticeable is that where commodity chemical firms have implemented servitization, one of the more prominent uses has been to help build relationships and reduce both the attitudinal and physical distance between partner organizations.

 Visit the Online Resource Centre and complete Internet Activity 8.4 to learn more about how two leading service-based organizations approach the service development process.

Service Development

As the distinctions between what is a product and what is a service blur, it could be argued that the traditional distinction between product development and service development is becoming increasingly artificial (Papastathopoulou and Hultink, 2012). Managers responsible for new service development should establish a system that incorporates a formal procedure for generating and evaluating new service ideas, a drawing board approach for identifying and designing the necessary service elements and processes, testing of new services with customers and with frontline staff to eliminate potential failure points, and a documented launch plan to ensure the proper marketing of new services (de Brentani, 1991). This process is not dissimilar to the stage–gate model outlined in Figure 8.5.

An organization developing services should have processes which become more formal as the project progresses over time, have well-established idea-screening processes in place to determine which new ideas will be given the go-ahead by senior management, and have a system in place to ensure that the staff are well trained and committed to selling the new service (Edgett, 1994). Services should be designed to ensure that it is easy for customers to be involved in the development of the new service, and actively contribute to the service design process. This customer involvement is often a critical success factor in the development of successful new services, perhaps even more so than in new product development projects, because of the enhanced nature of the customer–producer interaction (see Research Insight 8.3, and Chapter 12 for more on the simultaneous production/consumption of services and their marketing implications).

Some services undergo **beta testing**, where a version of the service is made available to customers and any imperfections are identified and removed before the final version of the service is launched. Software developers have made use of this approach extensively, as have music streaming companies such as Google, with Google Music Key and even, allegedly, Apple with Apple Music for Android (Chenze, 2015). See also Market Insight 8.5.

Service development researchers point to the need for organizations, if they are to improve the effectiveness of their service development processes, to:

- leverage their employees' skills, resources and experiences in the new service development process;
- develop more customer-oriented services;
- undertake an interdisciplinary approach to service development, bringing together marketing, operations and innovation staff (Papastathopoulou and Hultink, 2012).

Market Insight 8.5
Streaming Wars: Apple versus Spotify

In June 2015, Apple revealed that it would offer a 'revolutionary' new music streaming service based on the music streaming service it had acquired after purchasing Beats, with a target of acquiring 100m paying subscribers. Obtaining such a user base might be achievable if 20% of their 500m or so iTunes users worldwide connect to the subscription service. But whilst Apple's music download service iTunes and their music storage and play device, the iPod, were innovative in 2001, another company had beaten them to the streaming market. Spotify, a Swedish company using a **freemium** business model, already had 20m paying subscribers and 55m users on its free ad-supported service, and has largely displaced iTunes in the desktop and smartphone distribution channels. Spotify was the music streaming market leader in 2015, with modest long-term ambitions of achieving 40m paying subscribers, although the company is unprofitable, having lost nearly $200m in 2014.

Yet the music streaming market is attractive, with 40m paying subscribers worldwide and growing by about 50% each year. The question arises: What new features will Apple bring to the music streaming party? Apple has stated that it will differentiate its service by generating playlists chosen by people rather than algorithms, offer a superior music search process, and provide a 24-hour radio station (Beats One), but it will not offer a free ad-supported service.

Apple are therefore seeking to cream off Spotify's most lucrative customers—the quarter of Spotify users who pay to subscribe represent three-quarters of the company's revenues. And their approach might just work as artists such as Taylor Swift (who removed herself from Spotify) are fed up with the pittance

Spotify pioneered free music streaming but faces competition from Apple
Source: Courtesy of Spotify.

(around $0.007 per stream) that they receive when their tracks are played over the free ad-supported service (though they receive considerably more from the subscription service).

Taking the potential challenge from the world's largest brand seriously, Spotify raised $500m, presumably to help it further develop its own music streaming service. But Apple are not the only competition. Google has been beta testing its Music Key service, which will shift YouTube to a freemium business model like Spotify's. And Apple has tried to enter the market before when it launched, unsuccessfully, its Beats Music service in 2014. Google had also previously launched a service in 2011 which failed—Google Play Music All Access. This is clearly a hard market to crack, not least because, until recently, music customers were happier to download music illegally and risk criminal prosecution than pay for it. What is clear is that now that customers are shifting back to paying for their music, the battle for market leadership will intensify.

Sources: Anon. (2015b); Sexton (2015); Witt (2015).

Theory into Practice

This market insight describes how music distributors are competing to offer music streaming services. It illustrates how Spotify stole a march on Apple's iTunes service by developing a technologically superior approach to music distribution (streaming versus digital downloading). The case also illustrates the difficulties inherent in designing and offering a new service when technological standards and business models are still in flux.

Market Insight 8.5
continued

Related Topics:

service design; technological generations; diffusion of innovation; customer value; beta testing.

1 Why do you think Apple has come so late to the music streaming market?

2 What does Spotify need to do to retain its market leadership?

3 How do you think music distribution might develop in the future? What service developments might take place?

Research Insight 8.3

To take your learning further, you might wish to read this influential paper.

Edvardsson, B., Kristensson, P., Magnusson, P., and Sundström, E. (2012). Customer integration within service development: a review of methods and an analysis of in situ and ex situ contributions. *Technovation*, 32(7), 419–29.

This interesting paper outlines how customer feedback can be integrated into new service development. It develops a framework for categorizing customer integration methods based on whether the data are obtained in situ or ex situ and in-context or ex-context, creating four types of customer informant: the *correspondent* (in-situ/in-context, reporting live from the situation); the *reflective practitioner* (ex-situ/in-context, reporting from 'the armchair'); the *tester* (in-situ, ex-context, reporting from 'virtual heaven'); the *dreamer* (ex-situ/ex-context, the creative generating wild and imaginative ideas). The article explains how it is insufficient to follow customer requirements in new service development, nor should companies try to lead customers; rather they should work with them to co-create new service propositions.

@ **Visit the Online Resource Centre to read the abstract and access the full paper.**

The Process of Adoption

The process by which individuals accept and use new propositions is referred to as adoption (Rogers, 1983). The different stages in the **process of adoption** are sequential and are characterized by the different factors that are involved at each stage (e.g. the media used by each individual). The process starts with people gaining awareness of a proposition as it moves

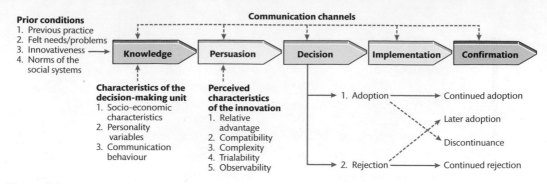

Figure 8.6

Stages in the innovation decision process of adoption

Source: Reprinted with the permission of Free Press, a Division of Simon & Schuster, Inc., from *Diffusion of Innovations, fifth edition*, by Everett M. Rogers. © 1995, 2003 Everett M. Rogers. Copyright © 1962, 1971, 1983 Free Press, a Division of Simon & Schuster, Inc. All rights reserved.

through various stages of adoption before a purchase is eventually made. Figure 8.6 sets out the various stages in the process of adoption.

In the knowledge stage, consumers become aware of the new proposition. They have little information and have yet to develop any particular attitudes towards the product. Indeed, at this stage consumers are not interested in finding out any more information.

The persuasion stage is characterized by consumers becoming aware that the innovation may be of use in solving a potential problem. Consumers become sufficiently motivated to find out more about the proposition's characteristics, including its features, price, and availability.

In the decision stage, individuals develop an attitude toward the proposition and reach a decision about whether the innovation will meet their needs. If this is positive they will experiment with the innovation.

During the implementation stage, the innovation is tried for the first time. Sales promotions often use samples to allow individuals to test the product without any undue risk. Individuals accept or reject an innovation on the basis of their experience of the trial. Consider, for example, the way that supermarkets or duty-free airport retailers use sampling to encourage people to try new food and drink products. The final confirmation stage is signalled when an individual successfully purchases the proposition on a regular basis without the help of the sales promotion or other incentives.

The model in Figure 8.6 assumes that the adoption stages occur in a predictable sequence, but this is not always the case. Rejection of the innovation can occur at any point, even during implementation and the very early phases of the confirmation stage. Generally, mass communications are more effective in the earlier phases of the adoption process for propositions that buyers are actively interested in, and more interpersonal forms are more appropriate in later stages, especially implementation and confirmation.

Diffusion Theory

Consumers may have both functional and emotional motives when purchasing, but customers adopt new propositions differently. Their different attitudes to risk, and their level of education, experience, and needs, mean that different groups of customers adopt new propositions at

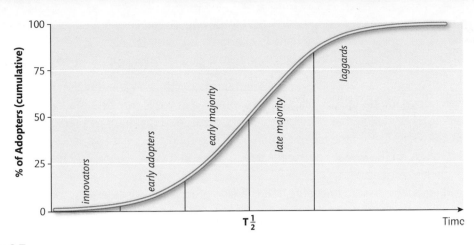

Figure 8.7

The process of diffusion

varying speeds. The rate at which a market adopts an innovation is referred to as the **process of diffusion** (Rogers, 1962). According to Rogers, there are five categories of adopters, as shown in Figure 8.7.

- **Innovators**—this group, which constitutes 2.5% of the buying population, is important because they have to kick-start the adoption process. These people like new ideas, and are often well educated, young, confident, and financially strong. They are more likely to take risks associated with new propositions. Being an innovator in one category, such as buying a new smartphone, does not mean that a person will be an innovator in another category, such as registering for a Global MBA programme. Innovative attitudes and behaviour can be specific to just one or two areas of interest.

- **Early adopters**—this group, 13.5% of the market, is characterized by a high percentage of opinion leaders. These people are very important for speeding up the adoption process. Consequently, marketing communications need to be targeted at these people who, in turn, will stimulate word-of-mouth communications to spread information. Although early adopters prefer to let innovators take all the risks, they enjoy being at the leading edge of innovation, tend to be younger than any other group, and above average in education. Other than innovators, this group reads more publications and consults more salespeople than all others.

- **Early majority**—this group, which forms 34% of the market, is more risk averse than the previous two groups. Individuals require reassurance that the offering works and has been proved in the market. They are above average in terms of age, education, social status, and income. Unlike the early adopters, they tend to wait for prices to fall, prefer more informal sources of information, and are often prompted into purchase by other people who have already purchased.

- **Late majority**—a similar size to the previous group (34%), the late majority are sceptical of new ideas and only adopt new offerings because of social or economic factors. They read few publications and are below average in education, social status, and income.

- **Laggards**—this group of people, 16% of the buying population, are suspicious of all new ideas and their opinions are very hard to change. Laggards have the lowest income, social status, and education of all the groups, and take a long time to adopt an innovation, if at all.

According to Gatignon and Robertson (1985), the rate of diffusion is a function of the speed at which sales occur, the pattern of diffusion as expressed in the shape of the curve, and the size of the market. This means that diffusion does not occur at a constant or predictable speed; it may be fast or slow. One of the tasks of marketing communications is to speed up the process so that the return on the investment necessary to develop the innovation is achieved as quickly and as efficiently as possible.

Marketing managers need to ensure that diffusion groups are considered when attempting to understand and predict the diffusion process for innovations. It is likely that a promotional campaign targeted at innovators and the early majority, and geared to stimulating word-of-mouth communications, will be more successful as a result (see Research Insight 8.4).

Research Insight 8.4

To take your learning further, you might wish to read this influential paper.

Peres, R., Muller, E., and Mahajan, V. (2010). Innovation diffusion and new product growth models: a critical review and research directions. *International Journal of Research in Marketing*, **27(2), 91–106.**

This paper usefully explains that diffusion of new propositions is far more complex and multifaceted than past work assumed because consumers are exposed to a greater range of influences, including word-of-mouth communications, network externalities, and social signalling. The authors discuss how social networking sites are altering the diffusion process (because of online **influentials** and the presence of online social hubs), how network effects impact upon diffusion (with slow initial growth in diffusion followed by a surge in demand, especially with high technology products as consumers wait and see if a particular technology standard takes off), and, importantly, turning points in diffusion, such as take-offs (when adoption increases exponentially, often as prices are reduced and consumer uncertainty is reduced) and saddles (when demand dips temporarily and increases again, for example as a result of technological changes or macro-economic events). Technological generations (where an upgraded proposition is introduced) also impact on diffusion, not least because they encourage existing users to shift to the new proposition, and may also encourage non-users to leapfrog to the new technological standard without having bought the previous incarnation.

@ Visit the **Online Resource Centre** to read the abstract and access the full paper.

Chapter Summary

To consolidate your learning, the key points from this chapter are summarized here.

■ **Explain the different levels of a proposition.**

A proposition encompasses all the tangible and intangible attributes related not just to physical goods but also to services, ideas, people, places, experiences, and even a mix of these various elements. Anything that can be offered for use and consumption, in exchange for money or some other form of value, is referred to as a proposition. Unlike products, services are considered to be processes. Propositions encompass three levels: the core proposition consisting of the real core benefit or service (e.g. bottled water is thirst quenching); the embodied proposition consisting of the physical good or delivered service which provides the expected benefit (e.g. the packaging); the augmented proposition consisting of the embodied offering plus all those other factors that are necessary to support the purchase and any post-purchase activities (e.g. the exclusivity associated with Voss bottled water and its Norwegian heritage).

■ **Identify and describe the various types of product propositions and explain particular concepts relating to the management of products, including the product lifecycle.**

Consumer and business products are classified in different ways, but both classifications are related to the way customers use them. Consumer products are bought to satisfy personal and family needs, and industrial and business products are bought either as a part of the business's operations or to make other products for resale. To meet the needs of different target markets, most organizations offer a range of products and services which are grouped together in terms of product lines and product mix. Products are thought to move through a sequential pattern of development, referred to as the product lifecycle. It consists of five distinct stages: development, birth, growth, maturity, and decline. Each stage of the cycle represents a different set of market circumstances and customer expectations that need to be met with different strategies.

■ **Explain the relationship between product and service offerings and describe the product–service spectrum.**

A service is any act or performance offered by one party to another that is essentially intangible. Consumption of the service does not result in any transfer of ownership, even though the service process may be attached to a physical product. There is a spectrum of product–service combinations. At one extreme, there are pure products with no services, such as grocery products. At the other end of the spectrum are pure services where there is no tangible product support, such as education and dentistry. In between, there is a mixture of product–service arrangements. The product–service spectrum recognizes that many products combine physical goods with a service element.

■ **Explore the processes and issues associated with innovating new propositions.**

The development of new propositions is complex and high risk, so organizations usually adopt a procedural approach. The procedure consists of several phases that enable progress to be monitored, test trials to be conducted, and the results analysed before there is any commitment to the market. The development of new services follows a similar staged process, whereby additional services are added to a core product until a point is reached where the service and the core product are integrated into a bundled offering. This is known as servitization.

■ **Describe how new propositions are adopted by markets.**

The processes of adoption and diffusion explain the way in which individuals adopt new propositions and the rate at which a market adopts an innovation. The process by which individuals accept and use new propositions is referred to as adoption (Rogers, 1983). The different stages in the adoption process are sequential and are characterized by the different factors that are involved at each stage. The rate at which a market adopts an innovation differs according to an individual's propensity for risk, and is referred to as the process of diffusion (Rogers, 1962).

❓ Review Questions

1 Draw the spectrum of product–service combinations and briefly explain its main characteristics.
2 Identify the three levels that make up a proposition.
3 Describe the three types of convenience good and find examples to illustrate each one.
4 What are the six types of business product?
5 What is the product lifecycle and what key characteristics make up each of its stages?
6 How do the essential characteristics of services affect the marketing of services?
7 What are the main stages associated with the development of new product propositions?
8 What is servitization?
9 Name four companies that have used the servitization approach and explain how.
10 Why is a knowledge about the process of adoption useful to marketers?

✏️ Worksheet Summary

@ To apply the knowledge you have gained from this chapter and test your understanding of innovation and new proposition development visit the **Online Resource Centre** and complete Worksheet 8.1.

⚡ Discussion Questions

1 Having read Case Insight 8.1, how should Domino's Pizza maintain their values of speed and service when faced with increased costs/operational times associated with the launch of new propositions?

2 Consider how the different types of consumer offering impact on how those responsible market these offerings.

3 Working in small groups, select a professional service and a consumer service organization and consider and compare the extent to which they overcome the marketing problems associated with intangibility and variability.

4 Prepare a brief report in which you explain the nature of the product lifecycle for a grocery brand of your choice. Consider how it might be used to improve your brand's marketing activities, and from this highlight any difficulties that might arise when using the product lifecycle to develop strategies.

5 Discuss the view that it is not worth the huge investment necessary to develop new propositions, when it is just as easy to copy those of the market leader.

Glossary

accessory equipment goods support the key operational processes and activities of the organization.

beta testing occurs when software is made available on a website to allow users to test the functionality of the service after it has gone through a development phase and prior to any modification before full commercialization.

built-in obsolescence when a manufacturer develops a product so that it deliberately requires replacement in order to enhance sales and/or profitability.

capital equipment goods buildings, heavy plant, and factory equipment necessary to build or assemble products.

content marketing the marketing process for the creation and dissemination of narrative (non-product) content to attract and engage a specific target audience to encourage a particular marketing action (e.g. sales).

convenience products non-durable goods or services, often bought with little pre-purchase thought or consideration.

digital value the means by which digital processes and systems can be used to provide customers with enhanced product and service value.

distributors organizations that buy goods and services, often from a limited range of manufacturers, and normally sell them to retailers or resellers.

durable goods goods bought infrequently, which are used repeatedly and involve a reasonably high level of consumer risk.

early adopters a group of people in the process of diffusion who enjoy being at the leading edge of innovation and buy into new products at an early stage.

early majority a group of people in the process of diffusion who require reassurance that a product works and has been proven in the market before they are prepared to buy it.

extensive problem-solving occurs when consumers give a great deal of attention and care to a purchase decision where there is no previous or similar product purchase experience.

freemium A business model incorporating the offer of a free basic service together with a paid-for enhanced service.

influentials People who have the ability to persuade others to think, believe, or behave in a certain way.

innovators a group of people in the process of diffusion who like new ideas, and are most likely to take risks associated with new products.

laggards a group of people in the process of diffusion who are suspicious of all new ideas and whose opinions are very hard to change.

late majority a group of people in the process of diffusion who are sceptical of new ideas and only adopt new products because of social or economic factors.

limited problem-solving occurs when consumers have some product and purchase familiarity.

maintenance, repair, and operating (MRO) products, other than raw materials, that are necessary to ensure that the organization is able to continue functioning. Often referred to as consumables.

non-durable goods low-priced products that are bought frequently, used just once, and incur low levels of purchase risk.

point of sale time and place at which a sales transaction takes place.

process of adoption the process through which individuals accept and use new products. The different stages in the adoption process are sequential and are characterized by the different factors that are involved at each stage.

process of diffusion the rate at which a market adopts an innovation. According to Rogers (1962), there are five categories of adopters: innovators, early adopters, early majority, late majority, and laggards.

product anything that is capable of satisfying customer needs.

product lifecycle the pathway a product assumes over its lifetime. There are said to be five main stages: development, introduction, growth, maturity, and decline.

proposition a product or service that represents a promise made to customers and stakeholders.

pureplay A company that focuses exclusively on one offering or operates only on the Internet.

routinized response behaviour a form of purchase behaviour which occurs when consumers have suitable product and purchase experience and they perceive low risk.

service any act or performance offered by one party to another that is essentially intangible and where consumption does not result in any transfer of ownership.

service-dominant logic (SDL) asserts that organizations, markets, and society are concerned fundamentally with exchange of service based on the application of knowledge and skills. Therefore it rejects the notion of dualism between goods and services marketing by arguing that all offerings provide a service.

servitization an integrated bundle of products and services where the services are an integral part of the core product.

shopping product a type of consumer product that is bought relatively infrequently and requires consumers to update their knowledge prior to purchase.

speciality products these are bought very infrequently, are very expensive, and represent very high risk.

tangibility possessing the characteristics of something that is physical, i.e. it can be touched. As a result, it has form. When products are tangible they have physical presence.

test marketing a stage in the new product development process, undertaken when a new product is tested with a sample of customers or is launched in a specified geographical area, to judge customers' reactions prior to a national launch.

▌▌ References

Ala-Kurikka, S. (2015). Lifespan of consumer electronics is getting shorter, study finds. *The Guardian*, 3 March. Retrieve from: http://www.theguardian.com/environment/2015/mar/03/lifespan-of-consumer-electronics-is-getting-shorter-study-finds (accessed 20 December 2015).

Anon. (2007). Dreamliner hit by six-month delay. *BBC News*, 11 October. Retrieve from: http://news.bbc.co.uk/1/hi/business/7038294.stm (accessed 23 December 2015).

Anon. (2012a). Champions of design: Cohiba. *Marketing*, 15 August, 22.

Anon. (2012b). Cohiba among most recommended brands. Imperial Tobacco, 26 January. Retrieve from: http://www.imperial-tobacco.co.uk/index.asp?page = 78&newscategory = 25&newsid = 1363 (accessed 13 December 2015).

Anon. (2014). Schumpeter: second wind. *The Economist*, 14 June, 76.

Anon. (2015a). Sainsbury's trials connected kitchens to understand 'promiscuous' shoppers. *Marketing*, June, 13.

Anon. (2015b). The music business. *The Economist*, 13 June, 76.

Armitage, J. (2015). How Airbus' bet on big went awry. *The Independent*, 15 August, 49.

Ausick, P. (2014). Will more seats help the Airbus A380 pay back its development cost? 24/7 *Wall St*, 24 September.

Retrieve from: http://247wallst.com/aerospace-defense/2014/09/24/will-more-seats-help-the-airbus-a380-pay-back-its-development-cost/ (accessed 23 December 2015).

Ausick, P. (2015). What does Boeing 787 Dreamliner cost? 24/7 *Wall St*, 26 July. Retrieve from: http://247wallst.com/aerospace-defense/2015/07/26/what-does-boeing-787-dreamliner-cost/ (accessed 23 December 2015).

Baines, T., and Lightfoot, H. (2013). *Made to Serve: How Manufacturers Can Compete Through Servitization and Product Service Systems*. Chichester: John Wiley.

Baines, T. (2014). Bringing production and service together. *The Sunday Times*, 27 January. Retrieve from: http://raconteur.net/business/bringing-production-and-service-together (accessed 23 December 2015).

Chaffey, D., Mayer, R., Johnston, K., and Ellis-Chadwick, F. (2009). *Internet Marketing* (4th edn), Harlow: FT/Prentice Hall.

Chenze, E. (2015). Apple Music for Android Beta invites to start rolling out soon. *Techweez*, 29 September. Retrieve from: http://www.techweez.com/2015/09/29/apple-music-android-beta-betabound/ (accessed 24 December 2015).

Clark, N. (2009). Knowing when to swing the axe. *Marketing*, February, 30–1.

de Brentani, U. (1991). Success factors in developing new business services. *European Journal of Marketing*, 25(2), 33–59.

Drucker, P.F. (1985). The discipline of innovation. *Harvard Business Review*, 63(May–June), 67–72.

Edelman, D.C. (2010). Four ways to get more value from digital marketing. *McKinsey Quarterly*, March. Retrieve from: http://www.mckinsey.com/business-functions/marketing-and-sales/our-insights/four-ways-to-get-more-value-from-digital-marketing (accessed 23 March 2016).

Edgett, S. (1994). The traits of successful new service development. *Journal of Services Marketing*, 8(3), 40–9.

Edvardsson, B., Kristensson, P., Magnusson, P., and Sundström, E. (2012). Customer integration within service development: a review of methods and an analysis of in situ and ex situ contributions. *Technovation*, 32(7), 419–29.

Gatignon, H. and Robertson, T.S. (1985). A propositional inventory for new diffusion research. *Journal of Consumer Research* 11(March), 849–67.

Glass S. (2012). What were they thinking? The chips that sent us to the loo. *Fast Company*, 17 January. Retrieve from: http://www.fastcompany.com/1809002/what-were-they-thinking-chips-sent-us-running-loo (accessed 23 December 2015).

Govindarajan, V. and Srinivas, S. (2013). The innovation mindset in action: 3M Corporation. *Harvard Business Review*, 6 August. Retrieve from: https://hbr.org/2013/08/the-innovation-mindset-in-acti-3 (accessed 22 December 2015).

Grönroos, C. (2009). Marketing as promise management: regaining customer management for marketing. *Journal of Business and Industrial Marketing*, 24(5/6), 351–9.

Griffin, A. and Page, A.L. (1993). An interim report on measuring product development success and failure. *Journal of Product Innovation Management*, 10(4), 291–308.

Hise, R.T., O'Neal, L., Parasuraman, A., and McNeal, J.U. (1990). Marketing/R&D interaction in new product development: implications for new product success rates. *Journal of Product Innovation Management*, 7(2), 142–55.

Holbrook, M.B. and Hirschman, E.C. (1982). The experiential aspects of consumption: consumer fantasies, feelings, and fun. *Journal of Consumer Research*, 9(2), 132–40.

Institute of Brilliant Failures (nd). Buckler beer on the Dutch market. Institute of Brilliant Failures. Retrieve from: http://www.briljantemislukkingen.nl/en/2012/02/buckler-beer-on-the-dutch-market/ (accessed 23 December 2015).

Leistén, J. and Nilsson, M. (2009). Crossing the chasm: launching and re-launching in the Swedish mobile phone industry. Bachelors Dissertation, Jönköping International Business School. Retrieve from: http://hj.diva-portal.org/smash/record.jsf?pid = diva2:158025 (accessed 13 December 2015).

Möller, K.; Rajala, R., and Westerlund, M. (2008). Service innovation myopia? A new recipe for client/provider value creation. *California Management Review*, 50(3), 31–48.

Moon, Y. (2005). Break free from the product life cycle. *Harvard Business Review*, 83(5), 86–94.

Narayanan, A., Padhi, A., and Williams, J. (2012). Designing products for value. *McKinsey Quarterly*, October. Retrieve from: http://www.mckinsey.com/insights/innovation/designing_products_for_value (accessed 13 December 2015).

Osborn, A. (2011). World's biggest cigar festival opens in Havana. *The Telegraph*, 24 February. Retrieve from: http://www.telegraph.co.uk/journalists/andrew-osborn/8345341/Worlds-biggest-cigar-festival-opens-in-Havana.html (accessed 13 December 2015).

O'Shaughnessy, J. and O'Shaughnessy, N.J. (2009). The service-dominant perspective: a backward step? *European Journal of Marketing*, 43(5/6), 784–93.

Ozer, M. (2003). Process implications of the use of the internet in new product development: a conceptual analysis. *Industrial Marketing Management*, 32(6), 517–30.

Papastathopoulou, P. and Hultink, E.J. (2012). New service development: an analysis of 27 years of research. *Journal of Product Innovation Management*, 29(5), 705–14.

Parnell, B.-A.(2012). Offical: Sony and Ericsson are divorced. *The Register*, 16 February. Retrieve from: http://www.theregister.co.uk/2012/02/16/sony_ericsson_divorce_final/ (accessed 23 December 2015).

Peres, R., Muller, E., and Mahajan, V. (2010). Innovation diffusion and new product growth models: a critical review and research directions. *International Journal of Research in Marketing*, 27(2), 91–106

Perks, R. (2014). Online fashion retailing—what's next? *Mintel*, 10 March. Retrieve from: http://www.mintel.com/blog/retail-market-news/online-fashion-retailing-whats-next-2 (accessed 20 December 2015).

Pukhtina, T. (2013). Zalando—marketing at its best! *Fashion Marketing Secrets*, 26 August. Retrieve from: http://fashionmarketingsecrets.com/2013/08/26/zalando-marketing-at-its-best/ (accessed 21 December 2015).

Renault, C., Dalsace, F., and Ulaga, W. (2010). Michelin Fleet Solutions: from selling tyres to selling kilometres—teaching note. The Case Centre, Case 510-103-8. Retrieve from: http://www.thecasecentre.org (accessed 23 December 2015).

Renault, C., Dalsace, F., and Ulaga, W. (2012). Michelin Fleet Solutions: from selling tyres to selling kilometres. The Case Centre, Case 510-103-1. Retrieve from: http://www.thecasecentre.org (accessed 23 December 2015).

Roberts, G. (2015). Sinclair C5: Sir Clive Sinclair's one seat wonder celebrates 30 years since its launch. *Mirror*, 5 January. Retrieve from: http://www.mirror.co.uk/news/uk-news/sinclair-c5-sir-clive-sinclairs-4920067 (accessed 23 December 2015).

Robinson, T., Clarke-Hill, C.M., and Clarkson, R. (2002). Differentiation through service: a perspective from the commodity chemicals sector. *Service Industries Journal*, 22(3), 149–66.

Rogers, E.M. (1962). *Diffusion of Innovations*. New York: Free Press.

Rogers, E.M. (1983). *Diffusion of Innovations* (3rd edn). New York: Free Press.

Saren, M. (2006). *Marketing Graffiti: The View from the Street*. Oxford: Butterworth Heinemann.

Sexton, P. (2015). And now the streaming screaming starts as Apple declares war on Spotify. *The Sunday Times*, 14 June, 3.

Shelton, R. (2009). Integrating product and service innovation. *Research Technology Management*, 52(3), 38–44.

Tynan, C. and McKechnie, S (2009). Experience marketing: a review and reassessment. *Journal of Marketing Management*, 25(5/6), 501–17.

Vargo, S.L. and Lusch, R.F. (2004). Evolving to a new dominant logic for marketing. *Journal of Marketing*, 68(1), 1–17

Vargo, S.L. and Lusch, R.F. (2016). Institutions and axioms: an extension and update of service-dominant logic. *Journal of the Academy of Marketing Science*, 44(1), 5–23.

Witt, S. (2015). Kicking and streaming. *Financial Times*, 13–14 June, 1–2.

Chapter 9
Price and Customer Value Decisions

John Lewis

stripe

Learning Outcomes

After studying this chapter, you will be able to:

▶ Explain the concept of price elasticity of demand

▶ Define price, and understand its relationship with costs, quality, and value

▶ Describe how customers perceive price

▶ Understand pricing strategies and how to price new offerings

▶ Explain cost-, competitor-, demand-, and value-oriented approaches to pricing

▶ Explain how pricing operates in the business-to-business setting

Case Insight 9.1
Simply Business

Market Insight 9.1
Sugar Tax: Paying Sweetly?

Market Insight 9.2
Price Discount Illusions

Market Insight 9.3
Yielding More at BA

Market Insight 9.4
John Lewis: Still Never Knowingly Undersold?

Market Insight 9.5
Stripe: Revolutionizing Online Payments

Case Insight 9.1
Simply Business

Founded in 2005, Simply Business is an online insurance broker. We speak to its Director of Strategy and Pricing, Philip Williams, to find out more about how the company has developed its pricing strategy.

Simply Business has grown from a team of six in a room near Tower Bridge in London to one of the UK's largest small to medium-sized enterprises (SME) insurance provider. It provides cover for about 360,000 small businesses in the UK for liability insurance lines (employers' liability, professional indemnity, public/ products liability) in addition to specialty landlord insurance. Its simple and fast online quote process allows customers to receive quotes and buy from a range of different insurance companies simultaneously, providing an instantly comparable, and ordered, panel of prices.

We are proud of our technological capability, seeing ourselves as a tech business first and foremost which happens to operate as an insurance brokerage. Our main competitors in the online SME insurance market include Hiscox, Direct Line for Business, AXA, and Towergate, but our market is constantly developing. The online market has grown by about 20% year on year. Of the 5.8m businesses in the UK, 5.1m are classified as SME, but businesses usually buy their insurance through local high street brokers. This is changing, especially at the microbusiness end, as customers get used to comparing and buying their personal insurance online. Four large price comparison websites have grown in the UK to dominate personal insurance (Compare the Market, Money Supermarket, GoCompare, and Confused.com). Whilst price comparison for home and motor insurance is now well established, the comparison sites have not ventured into the less homogeneous and smaller SME insurance market. Simply Business moved into this vacuum and formed strategic partnerships with two of the large

aggregators (Money Supermarket and GoCompare) to develop a **white-labelled product** price comparison portal.

Since a management buy-out in 2013, we have continued to grow revenues by around 25% year on year. We have won numerous awards including, in 2015 and 2016, the number one spot in the 'Sunday Times Best Company to Work for' awards. To develop our unique proposition, we felt that we needed to extend our control over the value chain. Therefore, not only do we provide a platform for customers to compare business insurance rates, but we have also obtained delegated authority from our panel of around 20 insurance providers to bind policies on their behalf. So, we handle all customer interactions, including payment, and have agreement to handle all but the largest claims without the need for the insurers to become involved.

The traditional approach to setting prices in the business insurance market has been to use the cost-plus method. Insurers set a risk rate for each customer based on the details provided by the customer within a proposal form (e.g. postcode, turnover, number of staff). A base cost is determined using these details, before adding additional loads for expenses, reinsurance, and broker commission. Broker commission is typically negotiated between each broker and insurer on a broker by broker basis. Those brokers able to provide higher volumes of business, or those who can provide superior quality clients (through unique selection processes or route to market), are most able to negotiate higher levels of commission.

Case Insight 9.1

continued

Whilst this strategy and business model is straightforward, for us at Simply Business it was based on two negatives as far as customer value was concerned. A price comparison using the standard methodology would show customers an unfair picture, with business insurance prices with lower costs before commission appearing below prices with higher costs (as a result of a higher negotiated commission level). From a customer viewpoint, we knew it would be difficult to justify to our customers why our commission received from different insurers should be different. Secondly, control of customer volumes is difficult to manage as any commission change must be negotiated with a supplier. This is easily manageable in an offline environment, but more difficult in an online world with significantly increased volumes and increased customer price sensitivity driven by ease and access to competition. So, we used our scale to negotiate a flexible commission structure with our insurance providers. This has allowed Simply Business to move to a demand-oriented pricing approach and standardize commissions on quotes, presenting a fair comparison to customers with no incentive for Simply Business to sell one product over another. This transparent approach reflects our brand, which focuses on honesty and simplicity.

One extra difficulty is that all prices quoted for customers are generated specifically for that individual or business and tailored to their requirements, and different customers have different price sensitivities. We wanted to respond to some customers' requirements for price discounts but it would be too onerous to negotiate with each of our suppliers for each quotation. We also knew that we could not afford to discount all our customers' policies across the board.

Therefore the question that arose was: How could we develop a system which offered tailored policies, including discounts, to those customers who were more price sensitive?

Introduction

When did you last buy something that you thought was really expensive? Was it worth the price you paid? Did you wonder if others would think it was expensive too? Exactly when is a price expensive and when is it not? How do companies set prices? What procedures do they use? Since price wars are self-defeating, why do companies start them or respond to them in the first place? These are just some of the questions we set out to consider in this chapter.

Our understanding of pricing and costing has developed from accounting practice. Economics has also contributed to our understanding of pricing through models of supply and demand, operating at an aggregate level (i.e. across all customers in an industry). Psychology contributes greatly to our understanding of customers' perceptions of prices. Marketing as a field integrates all of these components to provide a better understanding of how the firm sets price to achieve higher profits and maintain satisfied customers. Pricing is the most difficult aspect of the marketing mix to comprehend because an offering's price is linked to the cost of the many different **components** that make up a particular proposition. The marketing manager rarely controls costs and prices of a particular offering, and usually refers to the accounting and finance department, or the marketing/financial controller, to set prices.

In this chapter, we provide insight into how customers respond to price changes, what economists call **price elasticity** of demand, which is an indication of the value they perceive in a particular price. We define price, quality, costs, and value, and outline the relationship between them. We provide insights into how customers perceive and learn about prices, a necessary step prior to evaluating them and their fairness, which impacts on customers' willingness to pay. We describe the four main approaches to pricing based on evaluating costs and adding a margin, copying competitors' prices, basing prices on demand, and pricing according to perceived customer value. We also consider the two principal means by which to price a new proposition, based on skim and market penetration pricing. Finally, we consider what pricing tactics are used in the business-to-business setting.

Price Elasticity of Demand

This concept was first developed in the field of economics but it is a very useful concept in marketing. Price elasticity of demand provides us with an understanding of how demand shifts with changes in price. Such information is useful, but the data needed to determine price elasticities requires detailed research of price and quantity changes over time. Price elasticity is affected by both brand and category characteristics, as well as by general economic conditions, including such factors as time, product category, brand (manufacturer versus own-label), stage of product lifecycle, country, household disposable income, and inflation rates (Bijmolt et al., 2005).

In some categories, for example cigarettes as opposed to washing powder, changes in price (whether positive or negative) lead to smaller changes in demand. For instance, a 10% increase in cigarette prices might only lead to a 2% decrease in quantity sold. Conversely, a 10% increase in washing powder prices might lead to a 20% decrease in sales. In this case, we say that washing powder is the more price-elastic offering. We define price elasticity as the percentage change in quantity demanded as a proportion of the percentage change in price. Mathematically, this is displayed as follows:

Price elasticity of demand =

$$\eta \text{ (pronounced } eta\text{)} = \frac{\text{Percentage change in quantity demanded}}{\text{Percentage change in price}} \quad (1)$$

When the price of an offering rises/falls the quantity demanded falls/rises. When the percentage change in price is positive (negative), the percentage change in quantity demanded is negative (positive). Consequently, the price elasticity of demand is always negative. The price elasticity of demand for most marketed goods is somewhere between −9 and −1. In a meta-analysis of a set of 1851 price elasticities, based on 81 studies, the average price elasticity was found to be −2.62 (Bijmolt et al., 2005). In other words, for these goods (including consumer durables and other types of products), a 10% increase in price would produce an average 26.2% decrease in quantity demanded. This is an average across offerings. Individual products and services can vary greatly from this average. Generally, we can refer to three main extremes of price elasticity. These are as follows.

1 Unit price elasticity of demand ($\eta = -1$). In this case, a 10% increase (decrease) in price produces a 10% decrease (increase) in quantity demanded.

2 Zero price elasticity of demand ($\eta = 0$). In this situation, any change in price, either positive or negative, has absolutely no or an infinitesimal impact on quantity sold. Such a situation is highly unlikely ever to occur.

3 Infinite price elasticity of demand ($\eta = \infty$). In this case, changes in quantity sold have no or an infinitesimal impact on price. This situation is also highly unlikely to occur.

Governments use price elasticity data to determine which offerings to tax (see Market Insight 9.1). For example, petrol (gasoline) and tobacco have tended to be taxed because increases in prices resulting from tax increases have a lesser impact on quantity supplied compared with other offerings. According to research conducted in the USA, typical price elasticities range from –1 to –5 for grocery products, from –1.5 to –3.0 for consumer durables, from 0.2 to 0.7 for innovative pharmaceutical products, from –2.0 to –100.0 for standard industrial products, from –0.3 to –2.0 for specialty industrial products, from –0.7 to –1.5 for luxury cars and from –1.5 to –3.0 for normal cars, from –1.0 to –5.0 for airline services, from –0.7 to –1.0 for rail services, and from –0.3 to –1.0 for standard telecommunication services (Dolan and Simon, 1997). Marketing managers should seek to understand whether their offerings are price elastic or inelastic because this allows them to predict how price changes will affect the total quantity supplied in the market.

Market Insight 9.1
Sugar Tax: Paying Sweetly?

In the March 2016 Budget, UK Chancellor of the Exchequer George Osborne introduced a sugar tax on fizzy drinks. The idea is to introduce the tax in order to reduce the consumption of sugar, which is thought to be a leading cause of obesity and related diseases (e.g. heart disease, diabetes), costing the National Health Service (NHS) up to £27bn per year. The Government believes the tax will raise £520m in its first year of introduction in 2018, much of which is ring-fenced for spending on sport in schools. The government plans two tax rates: (1) drinks with high sugar content, e.g. the 330ml Coke, with a price of around 68p in supermarkets in 2016, will attract 8p extra tax in 2018; (2) drinks with lower sugar content, e.g. the 330ml Coca-Cola Life, also around 68p in supermarkets in 2016, will be taxed at 6p in 2018. The Government's intention, taking account of inflation, appears to be to add about 10% to the price of high sugar drinks and about 7.5% to the low sugar versions.

A previous study of the price elasticity of demand in the USA between 1938 and 2007 has indicated that a 10% increase in the price of soft drinks should reduce consumption by 8–10%. A study in Britain in the early 1990s indicated that soft drinks had a price elasticity of demand of –0.935 and an associated **advertising elasticity** of 0.015. This indicates that if there had been a 10% increase in price in Britain in the 1990s, there would have been a 9.4% decrease in demand, and that if there had been a 10% increase in advertising expenditures, there would have been a 0.2% increase in demand. However, the Government is far more worried about the impact of end-of-aisle display and price discounting on the consumption of sugary drinks than about broadcast advertising, since the former have a higher influence than the imposition of a tax, increasing consumption by up to 50% and 22%, respectively.

When Mexico, the country with the highest obesity rate in the world, introduced a sugar tax in 2014, the 10% tax reduced sales of fizzy drinks by 12% (a price elasticity of demand of –1.2). Norway, Finland, Hungary, and France have all also imposed sugar taxes and seen declines in sugar consumption as a result. However, in 2013, Denmark abandoned its plan for a tax on sugar after a similar tax on fat was unsuccessful. The drinks industry has also fought back, impeding sugar taxes in some American states and in Slovenia. When France imposed a sugar tax in 2012, the evidence indicated that retailers passed on nearly all of the tax to consumers. However, in Britain this is not a forgone conclusion.

Market Insight 9.1
continued

Manufacturers might decide to swallow the tax and maintain their prices at existing levels. If they do, they would lower their profit margins, but consumption is unlikely to be affected. If they could reduce their cost structures at the same time, they might even be able to completely mitigate the effects of the tax. An alternative strategy would be to develop new lower sugar offerings which attract less tax but do not compromise on taste. Either way, given the difficult market for soft drink manufacturers in Britain, neither option hits a sweet spot.

Sources: Anon. (2015a); Anon. (2016a); Andreyeva *et al.* (2010); Colchero *et al.* (2015); Donnelly (2016); Duffy (1999); Lavin and Timpson (2013); PHE (2015).

Theory into Practice

This case illustrates the scenario facing drinks manufacturers when Britain introduces a sugar tax in 2018. The case focuses around the major decision that these companies will need to make. Should they pass on the tax to consumers or should they absorb the tax and allow their profit margins to be reduced? The answer partly lies in an understanding of how British consumers respond to potential price changes (i.e. their price elasticity of demand). It is likely, however, that a 10% tax increase would result in a decrease in demand of around 10%.

Related Topics:

pricing; cost-plus pricing; price elasticity of demand; advertising elasticity of demand; price perception.

1 **What decision would you make if you were the CEO of Coca-Cola in the UK?**

2 **What other data might help you make a decision? Why do you say this?**

3 **To offset the likely drop in demand when the tax is imposed, do you think it would make sense to advertise more? Why do you say this?**

The Concept of Pricing and Cost

Pricing

Pricing is a complex component of the marketing mix. The term **price** has come to encompass the following meanings: 'the amount of money expected, required, or given in payment for something; an unwelcome experience or action undergone or done as a condition of achieving an objective; decide the amount required as payment for something offered for sale; and discover or establish the price of something for sale' (Oxford Dictionaries, 2016). In marketing terms, we consider price as the amount the customer has to pay or exchange to receive an offering. For example, when purchasing a Burger King cheeseburger meal for children (incorporating the burger, small apple fries, Tropicana drink, and toy), the price exchanged for the meal might be, say, $3.59

in the USA or £3.99 in the UK. The kid's cheeseburger combo in Pakistan comprises the burger, fries, and a drink for 345 rupees. The £3.99 element is the price—the assigned numerical monetary worth of the kid's cheeseburger meal in the UK. However, the notion of pricing an offering is often confused with a number of other key marketing concepts, particularly cost and value.

 Visit the Online Resource Centre and follow the web link to the Professional Pricing Society (PPS) to learn more about pricing and the pricing profession.

Proposition Costs

To price properly, we need to know what the offering costs us to make, produce, or buy. Cost represents the total money, time, and resources sacrificed to produce or acquire an offering. For example, the costs incurred to produce the Burger King kid's cheeseburger meal includes the cost of heat and light in the restaurant, advertising and sales promotion costs, costs of rent or of the mortgage interest accrued from owning the restaurant, management and staffing costs, and the franchise fees paid to Burger King's central headquarters to cover training, management, and marketing. There are costs associated with the distribution of the product components to and from farms and other catering suppliers to the restaurants. There are the costs to acquire and maintain computer and purchasing systems, and the costs of the packaging, bags, and any extras like the BK® crown and other gifts and toys.

Typically, a firm determines what their fixed costs are, and what their variable costs are, for each proposition. These items vary for individual industries. Table 9.1 provides a general indication of what is included. Fixed costs do not vary according to the number of units of goods made or services sold, and are independent of sales volume. In a Burger King restaurant, fixed costs are the cost of heating and lighting, rent, and staffing costs. In contrast, variable costs depend on the number of units of goods made or services sold. For example, with the production of Burger King cheeseburger meals, when sales and demand decrease, fewer raw goods such as cheeseburger ingredients, product packaging, and novelty items such as toys are required, so less spending on raw materials is necessary. Conversely, when sales increase, more raw materials are used and spending rises.

Table 9.1 Examples of fixed and variable costs

Fixed costs	Variable costs
Manufacturing plant and equipment	Equipment servicing costs
Office buildings	Energy costs
Cars and other vehicles	Mileage allowances
Salaries	Overtime and bonus payments
Professional service fees (e.g. legal, architectural)	Professional services fees (e.g. legal) in a business with a strong regulatory regime (e.g. pharmaceuticals)

The Relationship Between Pricing and Proposition Costs

The relationship between price and costs is important because costs should be substantially less than the price assigned to a proposition, otherwise the firm will not sell sufficient units to obtain sufficient revenues to cover costs and make long-term profits (see equations (2) and (3)):

$$\text{Total revenue} = \text{volume sold} \times \text{unit price} \tag{2}$$

$$\text{Profit} = \text{total revenue} - \text{total costs} \tag{3}$$

The price at which a proposition is set is important because increases in price have a disproportionately positive effect on profits and decreases in price have a disproportionately negative effect on profits. For example, in one study (Baker *et al.*, 2010: 5), it was identified that:

- a 1% improvement in price achieves an 8.7% improvement in operating profit;
- a 1% improvement in variable costs achieves only a 5.9% improvement in operating profit;
- a 1% improvement in volume sales achieves a 2.8% improvement in operating profit;
- a 1% improvement in fixed costs achieves only a 1.8% improvement in operating profits.

Until recently, organizations have had fairly rudimentary methods of assessing the effectiveness of their pricing decisions, but changes in computing power and the availability of data now allows companies to simulate thousands of 'what if' pricing scenarios to predict likely demand and profit levels (Michard, 2016). Therefore, whenever possible, we should aim to increase prices. However, deciding how to price a proposition is complex, and customers seldom want to pay more. Consider Burger King again. A firm like Burger King might well have 100 products on any one restaurant menu (including meals, individual burgers, ice creams, drinks, salads, their **secret menus,** etc.) in any one country. If we bear in mind that different countries have different menus to incorporate local tastes (e.g. the 480¥ Premium Kuro Burger® in Japan, where the product is served in a black bun, and the Fisher Royale® available in Turkey for £16.50 and available throughout much of the Middle East as Hammour Royale®), we can envisage that, worldwide, Burger King must have an enormous menu of products, despite the appearance of standardization. But how do we cost and price each individual product? The first step is to determine costs but, in any one restaurant, how do we allocate fixed costs such as heat and light, rent and tax, to each of the individual offerings sold? Once we've allocated the fixed costs, we need to determine variable costs for each offering. Once we've allocated fixed costs and determined the variable costs associated with an offering, we set its initial price. But costs of components, such as heat and light, and other costs change constantly. How do we determine whether we need to change our prices on an item after we've set them because of changes in component costs? After all, we can't keep changing prices every time a component cost changes. So, at what point do we change a product offering's price?

To increase the accuracy of the cost data, we need to spend more time collecting and analysing it. Determining costs is an exercise where we trade off accuracy with the benefits and costs of data collection, storage, and processing (Babad and Balachandran, 1993). Determining costs and prices is more difficult when organizations are split into separate profit centres selling on to other divisions within the same company, especially when these adopt inefficient **transfer pricing** mechanisms (Ward, 1993). For example, Airbus, the airline company owned by EADS

(European Aeronautic Defence and Space Company), assembles its planes using parts made in several European countries. When these parts are made by the respective divisions, they are sold on using a transfer pricing process to the main holding company which assembles the plane from its component parts.

But it's not just costs that matter; we might observe changes in demand for our offerings, as customers' desires change. In setting pricing levels, we should also consider customers' price perceptions.

Customer Perceptions of Price, Quality, and Value

Marketers are concerned with how individuals react to the way offerings are priced, questioning how consumers perceive prices and why they perceive them as they do. Here, we consider individual perceptions of proposition quality and value, and their relationship to customer response to prices.

Proposition Quality

Quality is important in setting proposition pricing levels. Quality is defined as 'the standard of something as measured against other things of a similar kind; the degree of excellence of something; a distinctive attribute or characteristic possessed by someone or something' (Oxford Dictionaries, 2016). In this context, the quality of goods and services relates to standards to which that offering performs as a need-satisfier. For example, a very high quality car (e.g. the Aston Martin DB11 or the Porsche Panamera) will satisfy both our aesthetic needs for aerodynamic beauty and our ego and functional needs for high performance road-handling, speed, and power. But quality is not a single standard in an offering. It encompasses many standards as there are many levels at which our needs might or might not be satisfied.

Quality is multifaceted (i.e. different functional and non-functional needs) and multilayered (i.e. degrees of satisfaction). Because each person has their own definition of quality, we prefer to talk of 'perceived quality'. For example, some might be very dissatisfied, and some highly satisfied, even with the same offering.

The Relationship between Quality and Pricing Levels

There is an assumption that as price increases, so does quality, and that in general price reflects quality. However, research has demonstrated that there is only a weak relationship between price and perceived quality, although this is category-dependent (Gerstner, 1985). For example, 'snob' consumers in the fashion clothing and perfume sectors (see Amaldoss and Jain, 2005; Yeoman and McMahon-Beattie, 2006) assume that higher prices reflect higher quality garments and fragrances. The idea that price indicates quality (**perceived quality**) assumes that prices are objectively determined by market forces. In truth, people within firms set prices, often dispassionately, to try to obtain the maximum profit possible. Various studies to determine whether or not price bears a relation to quality found that a general price–perceived quality relationship does not exist (Gerstner, 1985; Zeithaml, 1988), except for wine and perfume (Zeithaml, 1988). Völckner and Hofmann (2007) conducted a meta-analysis of studies investigating the price–perceived quality relationship published between 1989 and 2006, and found that the price effect on perceived quality had decreased. Interestingly, they also found that the price–quality relationship is stronger in studies that investigate higher priced products and use samples from European countries, but is weaker for services, durable goods, and respondents who are familiar with the offering.

However, a study designed to understand the relationship between price and quality when price information is available online (Boyle and Lathrop, 2009) found that US consumers believe that higher prices correspond to higher quality for **consumer durables** (e.g. cars, televisions), but are less likely to perceive this with non-durables (e.g. foodstuffs).

The Relationship between Perceived Value, Product Quality, and Pricing Levels

Value is defined as 'the regard that something is held to deserve; importance, worth, or usefulness of something; principles or standards of behaviour; one's judgement of what is important in life; the numerical amount denoted by an algebraic term; a magnitude, quantity, or number' (Oxford Dictionaries, 2016). There are differing views on how it should be calculated. In marketing terms, value refers to the quality of what we get for what we pay. It is often expressed by the following equation:

$$\text{Value} = \frac{\text{quality}}{\text{price}} = \text{quality rating per unit of currency} \tag{4}$$

A related version of this equation replaces quality with 'benefits', i.e. those benefits obtained from buying an offering, and price with 'costs'. This approach to quantifying value indicates that to increase a customer's perception of the value of an offering, we must either lower the price or increase the quality (and this can be hard to measure). Note that, mathematically, the equation only works when we pay something, i.e. more than 0p (otherwise we divide by zero which is mathematically undefined). So this equation could not be used to determine the value we place on an item we are given (even though this item might have some residual value and could potentially be resold on eBay or Amazon Exchange for instance). This example also illustrates the difference between inherent value (what you could get for it if it was resold) and value in exchange (what you are prepared to pay for it). Therefore in some ways the intuitive definition in equation (1) is a simplistic conception of value. It also suffers from the fact that quality is not always well defined. Is it a rating or is quality the customer's perceived reference price for the offering given its benefits? If this is the case, then any calculated figure for 'value' greater than 1 indicates a good deal, less than 1 a bad deal, and equal to 1 a satisfactory deal.

This brings us to the following equation suggested by Leszinski and Marn (1997: equation (3)), consultants at McKinsey, to calculate the value to the customer:

$$\text{Value} = \text{perceived benefits} - \text{perceived price} \tag{5}$$

In this equation, the customer perceives positive value if the perceived benefits (a proxy for quality) outweigh the price paid for those benefits. Usefully, if the price paid is zero (an item is given away), the value to the customer is the value of the perceived benefits (which makes sense), and if there are no benefits, the value is the negative value of the price paid. When the benefits of an offering are reduced, the value is also seen to be reduced if customers notice the difference in offerings. An example of this occurred when Cadbury reduced the number of chocolate fingers in its traditional pack from 24, weighing 125g, to 22, weighing 114g, with an increase in price from around £1.19 in 2014 to around £1.43 in 2015 (Hayward, 2015), changing the cost of each chocolate finger from 4.96p to 6.5p (for a marginally lighter chocolate finger at 5.18g compared with 5.21g). In our view then, equation (5) is the best way to express the relationship between price and value.

Influences on Customer Price Perceptions

A Framework for Price Perception Formation

How we perceive prices as customers can be summarized in a theoretical framework (see Figure 9.1). Here, price perceptions are based on a variety of antecedents. Once we see a price, we make a judgement. This judgement is a newly formed price perception which affects our willingness to pay, which in turn affects our purchase behaviour. Price perceptions are affected by prior beliefs, prior knowledge of reference prices, prior experiences with the offering or brand under consideration, price consciousness (i.e. how aware we are of prices), our own price sensitivities (how much extra we are prepared to pay for something), customer characteristics, and cultural factors. We compare the price we see with internal reference prices (price knowledge gained from experience) and external reference prices (what others tell us prices should be, perhaps through price comparison websites). **Reference prices** are price bands against which

---

Research Insight 9.1

To take your learning further, you might wish to read this influential paper.

Völckner, F. and Hofmann, J. (2007). The price–perceived quality relationship: a meta-analytic review and assessment of its determinants. *Marketing Letters*, 18(3), 181–96.

This article uses a meta-analytic approach to evaluate various studies performed between 1989 and 2006 to provide evidence that there is an increasingly weakening relationship between price and perceived quality.

Visit the **Online Resource Centre** to read the abstract and access the full paper.

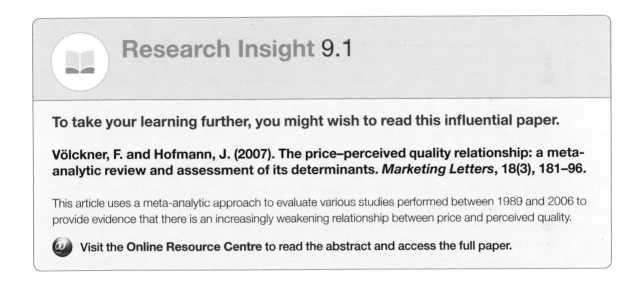

Antecedents	Price Perception	Willingness to Pay	Purchase Behaviour
• Prior beliefs • Prior reference prices • Prior experiences • Price conciousness • Price sensitivity • Cultural factors • Consumer's characteristics	Influenced by: • Reference prices • Quality perception • Brand awareness • Brand loyalty • Product familiarity • Assymetries of information	Influenced by: • Perception of price fairness • Latitude of price acceptance • Magnitude of purchase • Frequency of purchase • Price presentation • Advertising	Influenced by: • Purchase intention • Contextual factors • Consumer promotons • Perceptions of store quality • Online versus offline stores

A cyclical process

Figure 9.1

A framework for price perception formation

Source: Mendoza and Baines (2012).

customers judge the purchase price of offerings. Reference prices can be viewed as predictive price expectations based on prior experience with those offerings or gained through word of mouth.

Price perception formation is influenced by exposure to reference prices (internal and external), quality perceptions, brand awareness, brand loyalty, product familiarity, memory of prices (paid previously and seen previously), and asymmetries of information (the extent to which the customer does not know various factors about the offerings). Price perceptions affect customers' willingness to pay. Willingness to pay is influenced by perceptions of the fairness of prices set, latitude of price acceptance (customers appear willing to accept a price within a range of prices, suggesting a 'price zone of tolerance'), magnitude (absolute price) and frequency of purchase, price presentation (how prices are presented might produce different levels of willingness to pay), and advertising.

Actual purchase behaviour is influenced by purchase intention, contextual factors (e.g. store format, location, timing, and out-of-stock situations), promotions (e.g. in-store and external promotions), perceptions of store quality, and whether or not the customer is online or in-store, partly because it is much easier to comparison shop online than it is in-store. However, price perception formation is a dynamic process. In other words, the framework indicates that once the purchase behaviour occurs, there is a recalibration of the customer's price perception because new purchase experiences and new information provide the stimulus for that recalibration. Therefore the process is cyclical. Next, we consider key elements within the price perception process: willingness to pay, price consciousness, and pricing cues.

Willingness to Pay

In an online consumer survey of price perceptions in the US (Sheth *et al.*, 2006), around half of the respondents (53%) had strongly negative perceptions of the price of replacement razor cartridges and prescription drugs, and a quarter of respondents (27%) regarded airline pricing negatively. This indicates that we memorize certain prices for some items, and when companies deviate from those prices we perceive them as unfair. A key question is: Why do some consumers see one proposition's price as fair and others don't? If we are to price an offering according to customer needs, we should understand which customers think a particular price is a fair price to pay, or what they expect to pay, or what they think others would pay. For example, Superdrug in the UK was forced to review its 'sexist' pricing after an investigation by *The Times* revealed that women were being charged more than men on certain offerings such as razors. In some retailers, the gender price surplus that women were expected to pay for similar products was 37% more (Hipwell and Ellson, 2016).

Price Consciousness

In addition to deciding whether a price is fair or what customers expect to pay, we also need to know whether customers are conscious of prices in a particular category. Most people do not have a good knowledge of prices. Think of your parents or a friend significantly older than you. Do they know the monthly subscription price for streaming music tracks? Do you know the price of a good quality dining table or £200,000 worth of life insurance cover? As an industrial buyer, how much should you pay for the installation and servicing of a new HR system, say Oracle's PeopleSoft application, designed to keep records for 5,000 staff? These examples indicate that our price experience contributes to what we know about reference prices. Our experience is limited to previous actual or considered purchases. There are certain groups of grocery items that supermarket shoppers are more likely to know, and it is these items that supermarkets frequently discount, and advertise, to attract shoppers, rather than other lesser known items, where prices may be raised. Items including bread, milk, and baked beans are discounted because shoppers assume that if these items are discounted, other items must be discounted. So, if people do not know the reference prices of particular offerings, how can they determine their fairness? In the UK, supermarkets are under increasing pressure to pay farmers more for their produce, since many supermarket chains have been selling it at less than the price they were paying the farmers and the public have increasingly seen this as unfair (Neville, 2015).

Pricing Cues

Estimating reference prices is subject to seasonality for some items including flowers, fruit, and vegetables (particularly exotic varieties like orchids from Thailand or tulips from Holland), quality and size of items are not universal across companies' offerings, product designs vary over time, and customers might not purchase some offerings frequently (Anderson and Simester, 2003).

Instead, when customers assess prices, they estimate value using **pricing cues** because they do not always know the true cost and price of the item that they are purchasing. These pricing cues include sale signs, odd-number pricing, the purchase context, and price bundling and rebates.

- **Sale signs** act as cues, indicating the availability of a bargain. This seduces the customer to purchase, suggesting to the buyer that an item is desirable and may not be available if it's not bought quickly enough. The sale sign uses scarcity as a persuasive device because the scarcer we perceive an offering to be, the more we want it (Cialdini, 1993), sometimes regardless of whether we need it.

- **Odd-number pricing** Another pricing cue is the use of odd-number endings—prices that end in nine. Have you ever wondered why the Nintendo Wii U you bought was, say, $299, or £229, or SEK2,999? Why not simply round it up to $300, £230, or SEK3,000? According to Anderson and Simester (2003), raising the price of a woman's dress in a national mail order catalogue from $34 to $39 increased demand by 33%, but demand remained unchanged when the price was raised to $44! The question is why did the increase in demand take place when there was a higher price? It is unlikely that demand would have increased if the item was priced at $38. The reason is that we perceive the first price as relative to a reference price of £30 (which is £34 rounded down to the nearest unit of ten) and more expensive, whereas the second price of $39 we perceive as cheaper than a reference price of $40 (which we rounded up to the nearest ten). (See Market Insight 9.2.)

- **Purchase context** Our perception of risk is greater if we are continually reminded of it than if we consider it only at the point of purchase. For example, gyms use the technique of charging a monthly fee, even though they often demand a one-year membership agreement, for precisely this reason. In fact, a monthly price (instead of an annual, semi-annual, or quarterly charge) drives a higher level of gym attendance as customers are more regularly reminded of their purchase. So, the way you set your price does not just influence demand, it also drives consumption (Gourville and Soman, 2002). Research on **price anchoring** shows that if we are exposed to higher priced items first, our reference prices are anchored at the higher level, whereas if we are exposed to lower prices, they are anchored at the lower level (Smith and Nagle, 1995). Therefore it makes sense to redesign catalogues to include more expensive items in the earlier pages (Nunes and Boatwright, 2001) or in an online store to show the most

Market Insight 9.2
Price Discount Illusions

Consider a situation where you are in an airport duty-free environment. Let's assume that the several outlets are all selling high quality Belgian chocolates. In two different stores, you are offered different promotional offers. In both outlets, the original price of, say, the Godiva Gold Collection Box of 14 chocolates is £15.99 for 165g. Your choice of promotional offers is 25% extra free in one shop versus 25% off the price in another. Which shop is selling the better offer or is this just the same offer? Make your choice now before reading on.

Now consider that you are browsing the website of ASOS, the British online fashion and beauty store. You are looking to buy a particular branded jacket. Let's say it's a Parka London jacket. Its original price was £285. However, you remember that it has been discounted twice, first by 20% and then by a further 25%. Let's assume that for some reason you cannot see the final price. Would you prefer to take this double discount deal or one where the jacket was discounted once by 40%? Make your choice now before reading on.

If we revisit the Godiva chocolate offer, the 25% extra free means we get 206g for £15.99, which is equivalent to 7.75p per gram. The 25% discount means that we get 165g for £11.99, which is equivalent to 7.27p per gram. So the better deal is the price discount, and price discounting by 25% is not the same as offering 25% extra free.

On the jacket offer, given that the original price was £285, a 20% first discount followed by a further 25% discount would mean a final price of £171. A one-off discount of 40% would mean a final price of £171. In other words, the two discounts are the same.

Sources: Chen *et al.* (2012); http://www.godivachocolates.co.uk/gifts; http://www.asos.com.

Theory into Practice

This market insight describes how difficult it is to perceive the value in different prices and how apparently similar offers can be different and apparently different offers be the same. Marketers frequently use the psychology of consumer price perception when price setting.

Related Topics:

perception; sales promotion; consumer behaviour; reference pricing; willingness to pay.

1 Did you get both answers correct? If you did your arithmetic is excellent and you need not worry again about misreading prices. If not, how will this knowledge affect your shopping behaviour?

2 When was the last time you bought a discounted offering? What did you buy and why?

3 What offerings are most frequently discounted and what offerings are seldom discounted?

expensive items on a page first by default (though the customer should be able to sort them afterwards as desired). Location also has an impact on price perceptions. For example, we will pay more for a can of Coca-Cola from a hotel mini-bar than from the hotel bar or a supermarket, indicating the context-specific nature of price perception.

Research Insight 9.2

To take your learning further, you might wish to read this influential paper.

Gourville, J. and Soman, D. (2002). Pricing and the psychology of consumption. *Harvard Business Review*, 80(9), 90–6.

This is a useful article summarizing how marketing managers should consider not only the price at which customers are likely to purchase an offering but how the way that price is set also affects consumption. This article suggests that marketers might counter-intuitively want to draw customers' attention to the price paid so that they can achieve greater value in using the offering and generate a longer-term impact on customer retention. The article has strong implications for organizations selling subscriptions and memberships.

Visit the Online Resource Centre to read the abstract and access the full paper.

Visit the Online Resource Centre and complete Internet Activity 9.1 to learn more about the impact that the purchase context (e.g. time of day, week, online versus telephone booking, etc.) has on the pricing of budget airline services.

Price Bundling and Rebates

Marketers highlight their prices to customers by bundling other products and services into an offering to make the price look more reasonable. For example, magazines frequently bundle gifts in with the magazine to make it appear more attractive; this is called **pure price bundling**. Sunday newspapers (in Britain, France, Thailand, Sweden) often contain numerous supplements (e.g. fashion, entertainment, property) to make the newspaper appear greater value for money. New cars are sold with three years' warranty on parts so customers know that they won't have to pay for any repairs within the warranty period. Fast food restaurants have meal deal offers where you can buy a burger, fries, and a drink at a cheaper price than buying all the items individually (so-called **mixed price bundling**). Price bundling does not always mean that the company needs to give the customer other items. We might simply be offered a rebate, i.e. given money back. Credit card companies offer cashback schemes on money spent on their credit cards as a proportion of the total amount spent (e.g. Amex Platinum offers 5% introductory cashback and then 1.25% cashback on purchases thereafter with an annual fee).

Pricing Strategies and Objectives

Companies set their pricing strategy based around what their pricing objectives are. The four main pricing strategies are as follows.

1. Premium pricing—which focuses on pricing an offering to indicate its distinctiveness in the marketplace, e.g. Aston Martin prices the DB11 in this way at around £150,000 (see Chapter 13).

2. Penetration pricing—where the price is set low relative to the competition to gain market share. Amazon has adopted this approach to build its now substantial customer base. This strategy is frequently used for new proposition launches (see next section).

3. Economy pricing—where the prices are set at a bare minimum to attract price-sensitive customers. Supermarkets often use this approach with their everyday low pricing approach (e.g. Walmart in the USA, Aldi all over Europe, and Jumbo in the Netherlands).

4. Price skimming—where the price is initially set high and then lowered in sequential steps. Apple iPhone adopted this strategy, for example. This strategy is frequently used for the launch of new offerings (see next section).

Companies' pricing objectives may relate to other objectives, e.g. to maximize profit, or to achieve a satisfactory level of profits or sales, or achieve a particular return on investment. Companies may price to generate cash flow, offering discounts for quick payment. A firm's pricing objectives could be marketing based, e.g. pricing to achieve a particular market share (so-called market penetration pricing) or to position the brand so that it is perceived to be of a certain quality. Sometimes companies price their propositions simply to survive, e.g. pricing to discourage new competitors from entering the market by lowering prices to maintain sales volumes when competitors lower their prices. Alternatively, a company might price to avoid price wars, maintaining prices at levels similar to its competitors—so-called competitor-oriented pricing. Finally, a company may price to achieve certain social goals (e.g. a pharmaceutical company pricing a drug to ensure maximum reach in a highly disease afflicted country). The important consideration is whether or not the pricing objective is reasonable and measurable. Often, companies pursue different pricing objectives simultaneously, and some pricing objectives may be incompatible with each other. For example, pricing to increase cash flow by offering quick payment discounts is not compatible with maximizing profitability. However, it is compatible with obtaining a satisfactory profitability, as long as the discounts offered are not greater than the cost of the offerings sold.

Launch Pricing

When launching new offerings, organizations tend to adopt one of two classic pricing strategies (both outlined above). With the first approach, they charge an initially high price and reduce the price over time, recouping the cost of the research and development (R&D) investment from sales to the group of customers who are prepared to pay the higher price (hence 'price skimming' the market). In the second approach, they charge a lower price in the hope of generating a large volume of sales and recouping their R&D investment that way (hence 'penetration pricing'). Figure 9.2 shows both market penetration and market skimming price strategies and their hypothetical impact on quantity demanded (Q1 and Q2, respectively). For any given demand curve, the market skimming price offers a higher unit price than the market penetration price. The actual amount sold at each of these unit prices depends on the price elasticity of demand, and a more inelastic demand curve would give greater revenue from a market skimming price than a market penetration price as the quantity sold would not be very different between the two prices. On average, the market skimming price is likely to yield a lower quantity of offerings sold than the market penetration price.

Skim pricing is a fairly standard approach for high technology offerings or those offerings that require substantial R&D investment initially (e.g. games consoles and prescription

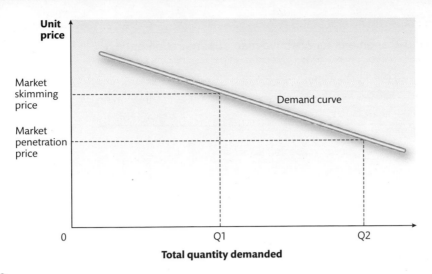

Figure 9.2

Launch pricing strategies

Source: Adapted from Burnett (2002). Reproduced with the kind permission of the author, John Burnett.

pharmaceuticals). For example, Microsoft dropped the price for its Xbox One machine, bringing the official base price to $299 in 2016, having opened with a launch price of $500 (Thier, 2016). The skim pricing approach is particularly appropriate under certain conditions (Dean, 1950; Doyle, 2000). These conditions are shown in Table 9.2.

The market penetration pricing approach is used for fast-moving consumer goods and consumer durables, where the new offering introduced is not demonstrably different from existing formulations. So, if a car manufacturer introduced a new coupé, relatively similar to its previous model, which had no new features and was not significantly better than competing models, it might use the market penetration pricing strategy. Items aimed at capturing price-sensitive customers might use this approach. Nissan stated that they will use this pricing approach with the launch of the Datsun Redi GO model in India in 2016, which will be priced at between ₹2.5 lakh and ₹4 lakh (Anon., 2015b). In a recessionary environment, customers are particularly sensitive to the value they receive when purchasing consumer or business-to-business offerings (see Research Insight 9.4). The penetration approach is more effective under the specific conditions (Dean, 1950; Doyle, 2000) outlined in more detail in Table 9.3.

Table 9.2 Conditions for effective skim pricing

1 When companies need to recover their R&D investment quickly

2 When demand is likely to be price inelastic

3 Where there is an unknown elasticity of demand since it is safer to offer a higher price and then lower it, than offer a lower price and try to increase it

4 Where there are high barriers to entry within the market

5 Where there are few economies of scale or experience

6 Where product lifecycles are expected to be short

> **Table 9.3 Conditions for effective market penetration pricing**
>
> 1 Where there is a strong threat of competition
> 2 When the offering is likely to exhibit a high price elasticity of demand in the short term
> 3 Where there are substantial savings to be made from volume production
> 4 Where there are low barriers to entry
> 5 Where product lifecycles are expected to be long
> 6 Where there are economies of scale and experience to take advantage of

Research Insight 9.3

To take your learning further, you might wish to read this useful paper.

van Heerde, H.J., Gijsenberg, M.J., Dekimpe, M.G., and Steenkamp, J-B.E.M. (2013). Price and advertising effectiveness over the business cycle. *Journal of Marketing Research*, **50(2), 177–93.**

This article considers whether or not marketing activity (specifically pricing and advertising) is affected by the economic cycle (e.g. expanding economy versus contracting economy). The authors estimate short- and long-term advertising and price elasticities for 150 brands across 36 consumer packaged goods categories, using 18 years of monthly UK data from 1993 to 2010. They conclude that during economic contractions consumers are less responsive to advertising and react more strongly to price reductions. Generally, the authors suggest reallocation of marketing expenditure from advertising to price discounting, but only if the firm's objective is to maintain sales (as opposed to profit maximization). There are differential effects for categories and even brands within categories, e.g. advertising elasticity is high (i.e. more advertising creates more sales) during a contraction for food brands but not for beverages. For premium mass brands, advertising during a recession can lead to greater willingness to pay and reductions in price sensitivity (i.e. people will pay more). Interestingly, the authors also find that consumer packaged goods firms tend to do less well in an expanding economy as consumers shift spending to out-of-home spending but return to in-home spending during a contraction.

@ Visit the **Online Resource Centre** to read the abstract and access the full paper.

Pricing Approaches

Price setting depends on various factors, including how price affects demand, how sales revenue is linked to price, how cost is linked to price, and how investment costs are linked to price (Doyle, 2000). Price setting also depends on how sales revenue relates to price. Raising prices tends to increase revenue up to a point, but then further increases in unit price produce declining increases in revenue. The relationship between price and sales revenue follows a bell curve (see Figure 9.3).

Costs vary with price in a linear fashion as higher prices reduce volume sales, producing lower total costs (see Figure 9.4). Third, investment costs, including both **working capital** and **fixed capital** (cost of plant and machinery etc.), also affect prices, with lower prices tending to require higher sales volume targets to be set with correspondingly higher levels of investment. Investments are made at fixed intervals (e.g. on six-monthly cycles), with investment costs dropping compared with price increases (and sales volumes decreases). The relationship between investment and price looks like a downward staircase (see Figure 9.5).

Broadly, there are four types of underlying pricing approaches:

1 the cost-oriented approach (i.e. prices set based on costs);

2 the demand-oriented approach (i.e. prices set based on price sensitivity and demand);

3 the competitor-oriented approach (i.e. prices set based on competitors' prices);

4 the value-oriented approach (i.e. prices based on what customers believe to offer value).

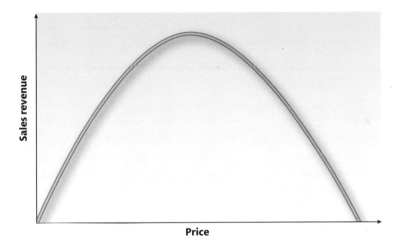

Figure 9.3
How price relates to sales revenue

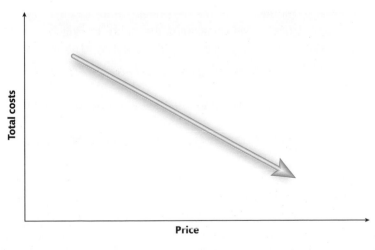

Figure 9.4
How price relates to total costs

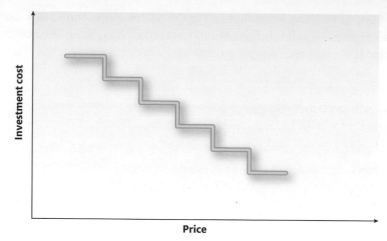

Figure 9.5

How price relates to investment costs

When setting prices, an organization might use a combination of these. For example, identifying the costs and trying to work out potential demand before setting a price is a common approach. We consider each of these pricing approaches in more detail next.

The Cost-Oriented Approach

This approach advances the idea that the most important element of pricing is the cost of the component resources that constitute the offering. It can be used for services, in a business-to-business context, or in a product context. Therefore the marketer sells output at the highest price possible, regardless of the buyer's preferences or costs. If that price is high enough compared with the seller's costs, the firm earns a profit and survives. If not, either the seller finds a way of increasing the price or lowering costs or both, or they don't survive (Lockley, 1949). The cost-oriented approach considers the total costs of a proposition in the pricing equation but does not take into account non-cost factors, e.g. brand image, degree of prestige in ownership, or effort expended.

One approach to determining price is using mark-up pricing, often used in the retail sector. This method operates on the basis of a set percentage mark-up. When used, the cost-oriented method leads to the use of list prices, with single prices set for all customers. We simply add a mark-up to the cost of X% and this constitutes the price. In British supermarket retailing, the mark-up is around 6–8%, but in American supermarket retailing it is often around 4% or less. Mark-ups on wine served in restaurants are typically between 200% and 300%. The cost-oriented approach requires us first to determine the price we set that just covers our costs. This is known as break-even pricing. It represents the point at which our total costs and our total revenues are exactly equal.

To exemplify the concept of mark-up pricing further, we use the example of a computer company selling high quality laptop computers costing £1,000 per unit to manufacture. Suppose that the computer company uses the mark-up pricing method, adding 66.7%. The final price set is given by

$$\text{Sales price (£)} = (\text{mark-up}^* \times \text{cost}) + \text{cost} = (0.67 \times 1{,}000) + 1{,}000 = £1{,}670 \qquad (6)$$

Note that mark-up is expressed as a decimal between 0 and 1 (divide mark-up percentage by 100 to get a mark-up figure).

It is important to note that the gross profit margin (i.e. the proportion of the revenue which is profit) is not the same as the mark-up percentage (which is a proportion of cost). The gross profit margin in the preceding example is given by

$$\text{Gross margin (\%)} = (\text{mark-up/sales price}) \times 100 = (670/1{,}670) \times 100 = 40.11\% \quad (7)$$

If we consider that in a supply chain there is typically more than one customer interaction, as we move along the supply chain, each partner takes their share, adding to the costs and the final selling price. A toy (e.g. a teddy bear) bought by a UK importer from a Chinese toy manufacturer based in Hong Kong, typically free on board (which means all costs after shipping are borne by the importer), brought to Britain, warehoused, stored, financed, and eventually sold at £5.90 (in cases of 12), may well have cost around £4.50 to that importer. The eventual retail price would probably be around the £10 retail price point, i.e. £9.99. The mark-up (MU) here for the retailer is expressed by

$$\text{MU(\%)} = [(\text{sales price/cost}) - 1] \times 100 = [(£9.99/£5.90) - 1] \times 100 = 69\% \quad (8)$$

The mark-up for the importer is much lower at 31% = [(£5.90/£4.50) − 1] × 100. However, the importer may well buy a container of the teddy bears, comprising say 4,800 individual bears (400 boxes, each containing 12 units), and sell these over the three months between September and November for the Christmas retail season. The retailer, by contrast, may sell only six boxes of 12 during the period October to December, so the retailer has to make a higher profit on a smaller volume with a wider range of items to give the customer some choice.

The cost-oriented approach does mean that we have to use a mark-up pricing approach. In some industries, prices are based on fixed formulae, set with a supplier's costs in mind. For example, in the ethical prescription pharmaceutical industry in France, Italy, and Spain government-fixed formulae have tended to dictate prices with limited scope for pharmaceutical manufacturers to negotiate, whereas in the UK and Germany the tradition has been for the country's national health authorities not to fix individual product prices but to set an overall level of profitability with which the pharmaceutical manufacturer must agree, based on a submission of their costs (Attridge, 2003). In the UK, however, there is increasing recognition that the current pharmaceutical pricing system, the Pharmaceutical Price Regulation Scheme (PPRS), is inadequate for containing costs and incentivizing innovation (Latif, 2013).

The Demand-Oriented Approach

With the demand approach to pricing, the firm sets prices according to how much customers will pay. This approach is prevalent in marketing services, but again could be used in business-to-business or consumer marketing contexts. Airline companies frequently operate this approach, with customers paying different amounts for seats with varying levels of service attached. Most airline companies operate three types of cabin service. Emirates, for instance, offers First Class, Business Class, and Economy with varying benefits according to the price paid based on the seat pitch (and availability as a bed), the entertainment package, the quality of the meal options, availability and quality of airport lounges, transportation to and from the airport, the in-flight service offered, and the experience through immigration and security. Other benefits at Emirates are available through membership and loyalty schemes, including premier access through immigration lanes, instant seat upgrades, and priority seats. This has four tiers of membership, blue, silver, gold, and platinum, depending on the number of miles a passenger has flown. Low cost carriers in Europe, such as Ryanair, Norwegian, EasyJet, and Germanwings, tend to operate

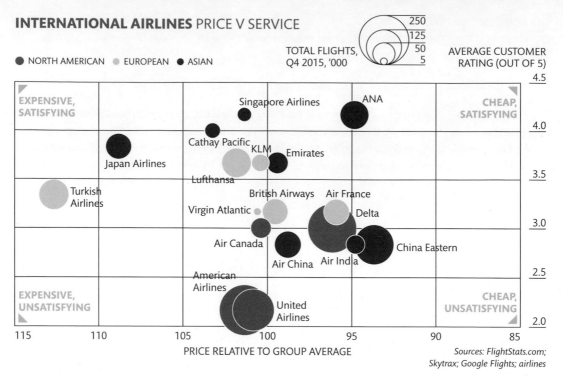

Figure 9.6

International airlines: price versus service

Source: From *1843* magazine © 2016 The Economist Newspaper Limited. All rights reserved.

fairly sophisticated yield management approaches via online booking systems. These set prices to ensure that planes operate at full capacity by charging increasing amounts as the purchase date gets closer to the travel date, flying on particular days of the week, and managing the price at which different service classes are sold (see Market Insight 9.3). Tickets are usually priced cheaply initially to increase demand (and generally priced substantially less than the legacy airline carriers such as British Airways, SAS, or Air France). There is a general perception among passengers that Asian airlines offer the best service for the price charged, with European airlines perceived as not particularly satisfying and US airlines as very unsatisfying, as illustrated in Figure 9.6 (Anon., 2016b).

Market Insight 9.3
Yielding More at BA

Yield management is a special case of the use of differential pricing (i.e. charging different prices for different segments) with the management of supply and demand (i.e. prices increase as the time to fly draws nearer) to maximize income. To explain, consider the reason why British Airways (BA) might have introduced a new service level, the BA World Traveller Plus class,

around the year 2000. The new service was pitched between economy and business class for a group of customers who wanted a better service than economy but were not prepared to pay business class prices.

But would introducing a new service such as World Traveller Plus be profitable? Consider a BA service

Market Insight 9.3
continued

from London Heathrow to Bangkok using the Boeing 747-400 ER plane, which carried 416 passengers. The World Traveller Plus service offered better seating arrangements (just slightly less space than business class) and better entertainment compared with economy class. Before introducing the World Traveller Plus class, the aeroplane's three-class seating arrangements had 23 people in first class (with a 61 inch seat pitch), 80 people in business (with a 39 inch seat pitch), and 313 in economy (with a 31 inch seat pitch). By 2016, BA's business class offered 6ft fully flat beds and first class offered 6ft 6 inch beds, so things have changed a bit since 2000. With a three-class seating arrangement, with first class prices set at, say, £7,000 in the year 2000 for a seat from London Heathrow to Bangkok return, business class at £4,000 return, and economy set at £800 return, the revenue obtained by BA on a full flight at 100% capacity is outlined in Table 9.4.

However, if BA offer a fourth class, between economy and business class, priced at £1,400, they can increase their profits. This is possible because seat pitches can be changed and classes reconfigured in a short period of time. If BA kept the 23 first class seats, and the 80 business class seats as before, but cordoned off 67 economy seats to make World Traveller Plus seats (increasing seat pitch from 31 inches to 35 inches) and kept the remaining 236 seats in economy class with the usual seat pitch, the revenue generated on a full flight at 100% capacity would be as outlined in Table 9.5, which shows that the change in configuration yields an extra £45,800. This configuration assumes that the airline can sell 67 seats at £1,400 on the basis of an increase in leg-room and a slight change in the entertainment offering.

In theory, there is nothing to stop BA from installing a fifth or even a 50th class. Each change could increase

Table 9.4 Revenue obtained from three-class seating arrangement

Class	Price and seat details	Revenue obtained
First	23 seats @ £7,000	£161,000
Business	80 seats @ £4,000	£320,000
Economy	313 seats @ £600	£187,800
Total revenue		**£668,800**

Table 9.5 Revenue obtained from four-class seating arrangement

Class	Price and seat details	Revenue obtained
First	23 seats @ £7,000	£161,000
Business	80 seats @ £4,000	£320,000
World Traveller Plus	67 seats @ £1,400	£93,800

Market Insight 9.3

continued

Class	Price and seat details	Revenue obtained
Economy 233 seats @ £600		£139,800
Total revenue		**£714,600**
Increase in revenue with extra class		£714,600 – £668,800 = £45,800

revenue further. In an ideal world, BA could customize services to passengers on the basis of exactly what they wanted and are prepared to pay for, but this is not realistic because of aeroplane configuration and maintenance constraints. Customers can now state how much they will pay for flights on Priceline.com and Hotwire.com, but they must pay upfront and cannot name the carrier or exact time of travel.

Sources: Brennan *et al.* (2008); Dennis (2012).

Theory into Practice

In this example, BA used a demand pricing approach to take advantage of a principle economists call **consumer surplus**. This is the difference in price between what a customer is willing to pay and what is actually paid, with the latter being less than the former. This can also be expressed as follows:

Consumer surplus = price willing to pay – price actually paid   (9)

BA realized that some customers were prepared to pay more for an enhanced service. This market insight considered yield management for an airline service, but differential pricing approaches (and online booking using the principle of prices paid in early booking being less expensive than later booking) can be adopted for many services, including hotel rooms, cinema/theatre bookings, even corporate legal services (in theory), and many more. In principle, therefore, yield management provides the customer with greater flexibility in when to book a service and the type of service to book and gives the service provider a means of maximizing the sales of their services, increasing services capacity (i.e. reduce services inventory), and increasing revenues.

Related Topics:

market segmentation; product differentiation; inventory management; pricing.

1 **Why do you think people are prepared to pay more when they book airline seats late?**

2 **Do you think customers in, say, business class would be unhappy if they knew that a passenger they were sitting next to had paid less than they had for the same seat? Why do you say this?**

3 **Do you think that an upmarket chain of hair salons could use a yield management system to book customers for different classes of stylist (e.g. stylist, senior stylist, style director, manager)?**

Companies operating a demand pricing policy should be wary of overcharging their customers, particularly where customers' requests are urgent. Examples include emergency purchases such as funeral services. When companies do set charges that are perceived to be unfair, they are liable to claims of **price gouging**. For example, in 2015, Turing Pharmaceuticals, under former CEO Martin Shkreli, raised the price of anti-infection drug Daraprim by 5,555% from $13.50 to $750 (Crow, 2015), although later reduced the price for hospitals by 50% after a media backlash (Constantinides and Rahman, 2015). In another example, the UK Competition and Markets Authority accused drug giant Pfizer and its supply chain partner Flynn Pharma of 'excessive and unfair' prices when Pfizer raised the price of anticonvulsant drug phenytoin sodium (used to treat seizures) by between 8 and 17 times when selling the drug on to Flynn Pharma, who then sold it on to Britain's National Health Service (NHS) for 25–27 times the original price charged by Pfizer. The drug had originally cost the NHS £2.3m, which jumped to £30–40m in 2013 and 2014 (Anon., 2015c).

The Competitor-Oriented Approach

Companies can also set prices based on competitors' prices, the so-called 'going rate', sometimes known as 'me-too' pricing. This approach is used in business-to-business, services and consumer marketing contexts. The advantage here is that when your prices are lower than those of the competition, customers are more likely to purchase from you, provided that they know your prices are lower.

Price guarantee schemes like the one outlined in Market Insight 9.4 seek to provide customers with the peace of mind of knowing that the price paid is competitive. In reality, such schemes are expensive to operate, requiring continuous monitoring of the full range of competitors' prices and a strong focus on cost control. However, it is worth considering that adopting a competitor-oriented pricing strategy can lead to price wars.

Market Insight 9.4
John Lewis: Still Never Knowingly Undersold?

The leading British department store John Lewis Partnership owns 32 department stores, 12 John Lewis at Home stores, 346 Waitrose supermarkets, a production unit, shops at St Pancras train station and at London Heathrow Terminal 2, and a farm, and operates the e-commerce site Johnlewis.com. In 2014, it celebrated its 150th birthday. With around 91,500 staff, John Lewis saw gross sales of just over £11bn in 2016. What is unique about John Lewis is that it operates through a constitution where the company is owned by its employees and has as its mission the 'happiness of its members'. Despite the economic doldrums, the company's Christmas trading statement for 2016 indicated great success at the tills with like-for-like sales up 5.1% on the previous year, and a 21.4% rise in online revenues.

But John Lewis Partnership also differs in another unique way from its competitors. It offers a policy of price matching and refunds if customers can find the same product cheaper at another retailer, made possible by its social enterprise nature and the fact that it does not seek to purely maximize short-term profits. Its policy, named 'Never Knowingly Undersold' has been available since 1925, perhaps the longest-running price promotion in British retailing. Things changed in 2011, when it changed the policy to match prices offered by other physical store retailers who were also online. John Lewis does occasionally come under flack, with some customers looking for a refund when they have identified something sold cheaper elsewhere but have not been refunded because, according to John Lewis, the product is not exactly the same. Often this

Market Insight 9.4
continued

John Lewis's famous price promotion
Source: Courtesy of John Lewis. © David Gill Photography.

has been the result of the fact that John Lewis offers different warranty terms. The question now for most customers is will they continue to perceive this price promotion as fair or will they not care about the price difference because the quality of the offering is so good?

Sources: Brignall (2011); Benady (2015); Anon. (2016c); http://www.johnlewispartnership.co.uk/about.html.

Theory into Practice

In this example, we outline the difficulties that a highly popular British department store encounters in running a price guarantee scheme. Nevertheless, John Lewis carefully balance selling quality items with the price guarantee that if those items are available cheaper elsewhere (i.e. the exact same product with the same warranty terms), they will refund the difference. However, most customers have such trust in the brand that they would be satisfied knowing that John Lewis always intends to match its prices to competitors' offers and so may not even compare the prices at all.

Related Topics:

discounting; price guarantee; price promotions; retailing.

1 Do you think the cost of collecting the competitor pricing data is justified for this promotion commercially? Why do you say that?

2 What other data does John Lewis need to determine how customers perceive competing prices from different retailers?

3 Is it ethical to offer a price guarantee scheme with strict conditions before paying out a claim? Why do you say this?

Research Insight 9.4

To take your learning further, you might wish to read this influential paper.

Reinemoeller, P. (2014). How to win a price war. *Sloan Management Review*, 55(3), 15–17.

This article, based on a study of Albert Hejn in the Netherlands, explains that companies can win price wars by leveraging five strategic capabilities, including (1) the ability to affirm the need for a price war, (2) the ability to carefully select an appropriate battlefield using advanced analytics capabilities, (3) the ability to pick a single target competitor, (4) staying under the radar (by targeting former customers rather than explicitly poaching new customers), and (5) the ability to align revenues with reformed cost structures.

@ **Visit the Online Resource Centre** to read the abstract and access the full paper.

@ **Visit the Online Resource Centre** and complete Internet Activity 9.2 to learn more about how John Lewis bring the 'Never Knowingly Undersold' promise to life in their advertising.

Price wars occur when competitors' pricing policies are almost exclusively focused on competitors rather than customers, when price is pushed downwards, and when pricing results in interactions between competitors that lead to unsustainable prices. For example, in 2003 when Dutch supermarket retailer Albert Hejn slashed its prices in response to competition from Aldi and Lidl, the resulting battle saw an 8.2% reduction in food prices, costing Dutch supermarkets €900m (£700m) and 30,000 jobs in a single year (van Heerde *et al.*, 2008; Blackhurst, 2014), although by 2005, after the price war had ended, Albert Hejn managed to regain lost market share to become market leader again (Reinemoeller, 2014).

In a review of more than 1,000 examples, researchers found that price wars could be averted if companies responded to market-based, firm-based, product-based, and consumer-based early warning signals (van Heerde *et al.*, 2008). So, some firms under certain circumstances within certain industries are more susceptible to price wars than others (see Table 9.6).

Table 9.6 Circumstances under which price wars are more or less likely to occur

Circumstances under which price wars are more likely to occur

1. As market entry occurs and an entrant gains, or is expected to gain, a sizeable market position
2. When an industry possesses excess production capacity—this stimulates the intensity of the price war
3. When markets have marginal or negative growth prospects
4. Where market power within an industry is highly concentrated
5. Where barriers to exit are greater (meaning that it's difficult to leave an industry, e.g. because of high investment costs)

Circumstances under which price wars are more likely to occur

6   Where financial conditions of at least one firm in the industry worsen or as a firm approaches bankruptcy

7   Where the offering concerned is of strategic importance to the company

8   When an offering is more like a commodity and so does not command a price premium

9   When firms introduce very similar offerings to one another

10   When there is little brand loyalty in evidence from customers

11   When customers are more highly price sensitive—this also increases the intensity of the price war

Circumstances under which price wars are less likely to occur:

1   One or more firms have established a reputation for strong and tough responses to past price wars

2   Where markets have intermediate levels of market power concentration (so neither suppliers nor buyers are dominant in a market)

Calculating and anticipating competitor response is important when setting prices and responding to competitors' price cuts. We should analyse consumer responses when a competitor starts to cut prices, but if purchase behaviour changes only modestly or temporarily, other marketing mix elements (e.g. promotion, distribution, or product differentiation) may be more likely to win back customers (van Heerde *et al.*, 2008).

We do not always have to respond to a price war with a price cut. Instead, we might promote increased service quality (Rust *et al.*, 2000) or customer value improvements more generally.

The Value-Oriented Approach

Even in the consumer durables category (e.g. furniture, **white goods**, carpets), where we might expect customers to be less price sensitive, firms practise pricing approaches with customers' considerations in mind (Foxall, 1972). We term this the value-oriented approach to pricing, because prices are set on the basis of buyers' perceptions of specific product/service attribute values rather than on costs or competitors' prices. This approach can be used in business-to-business, services, and consumer contexts.

We no longer live in an era where offerings are priced at what people can afford, because people are generally much wealthier now than they were 30 or more years ago. Resources are more plentiful and consumers have much of what they need. So, they are more interested in obtaining value from the offerings they buy. With value-based pricing, the pricing process begins with the customer, determining what value they derive from the offering and then determining price, rather than the opposite approach used in cost-oriented pricing, where costs are determined first and then the price is set.

In value-based pricing, deciding what is of value to the customer is determined using customer research. The result may be that the company does not necessarily offer a cheaper price. In fact, it could mean a higher-priced offering. If that offering was to represent true value to the customer, they must feel that it has more benefits than equivalent offerings. A recent study of 1, 812 pricing professionals demonstrated that a value-based pricing strategy is positively linked to firm performance, whereas a cost-based approach is not (Liozu and Hinterhuber, 2013). A good example of a brand using this approach is L'Oréal, which has for a long time advertised its products using spokesmodels, e.g. South Korean model Soo-Joo Park, British pop sensation and television personality Cheryl Fernandez-Versini, Chinese model Xiao Wen Ju, Dutch model Lara Stone, and Hollywood actress Naomi Watts, among many others, on the basis that we should use their products 'because we're worth it'.

Research indicates that brands that generate revenues over and above those obtained by an own-label or generic version of the offering also generate revenue premiums, which acts as a useful measure of **brand equity** (Ailawadi et al., 2003). Brand equity is important, because it contributes to company valuations when they are sold, acquired, or merged. Companies increasingly focus on generating price premiums. Nevertheless, a price premium is useless if it's perceived to be unfair. When setting value-based prices, it is important to consider the following.

1 What is the market strategy for the segment? What does the supplier want to accomplish?

2 What is the differential value that customers are likely to perceive? (That is, the value between this offering and the next best alternative, assuming that the differential value can be verified with the customer's own data.)

3 What is the price of the next best alternative?

4 What is the cost of the supplier's offering?

5 What pricing tactics will be used initially (e.g. price discounting)?

6 What is the customer's expectation of a 'fair' price? (Anderson et al., 2010). (See Market Insight 9.2.)

Pricing Management

In the information era, marketing information systems (MkIS), database technologies, and Internet-enabled technologies have changed how companies make pricing decisions. Pricing strategies such as 'real-time' or 'dynamic' pricing have increasingly developed in both B2C and B2B markets, sometimes through online price comparison sites, online auctions, and companies' own websites, because prices can be changed easily. For example, Amazon updates its price list every 10 minutes based on constant data analysis (Anon., 2016d). Dynamic pricing even allows changes at the customer level (Grewal et al., 2011).

Visit the Online Resource Centre and follow the web links to http://www.Kelkoo.co.uk, http://www.PriceRunner.se, http://www.touelsexprix.com, http://www.beslist.nl, http://www.preissuchmaschine.de/, all examples of online price comparison decision aids in different European countries.

Comparison sites have developed large customer databases covering all types of offerings including complex services such as gas and electricity supply, insurance, mobile phone packages, and travel, as well as standard offerings like cars and breakdown cover. Marketers are working in an increasingly price-transparent environment, and they should recognize that pricing is a capability that some companies are better at than others. Those companies that are excellent at pricing manage their costs and price complexity well, and offer sustainability and innovation in pricing approaches (Hinterhuber and Liozu, 2012). Online retailers are increasingly recognizing that it's not just the price that matters but how easy it is to pay online, because a more efficient payment process can lead to more time shopping (see Market Insight 9.5).

Market Insight 9.5
Stripe: Revolutionizing Online Payments

Fintech (financial technology), start-ups, and scaling companies are identified as key drivers in the international financial services sector. One example of this is a start-up called Stripe, recently valued at a cool $5bn. Stripe was founded in 2011 by two Irish brothers, Patrick and John Collison, to simplify the online payments process. Until recently, the payment sector for the credit card and banking industry was based on 1980s business models where the costs of inefficiencies were passed on to merchants and small businesses.

Stripe, frequently considered a rival to PayPal, provides processing services for online and mobile transactions. Essentially, the company provides a suite of APIs (application programming interfaces) which allow businesses to integrate payment processing technologies into mobile apps and services, thereby facilitating credit card payments, bank transfers, and bitcoin transactions. One of Stripe's unique selling points is that it makes the digital payment process via smartphones and websites 'so pain-free it's practically invisible', without the need for integration with third-party payment service providers such as PayPal. This seamless experience entices customers to stay longer on a merchant's website while also reducing the time taken to make a payment. As a result, this encourages customer retention.

Recently, Stripe has revised its service to facilitate payments in over 130 currencies, thereby massively extending its market reach. In addition, Stripe's latest service 'Stripe Connect' provides a service that allows merchants to change their business models (such as their pricing strategy or their target market) at any time, which is a key requirement for today's fluid,

stripe

Simple logo, pain-free payment transactions
Source: Courtesy of Stripe.

rapidly changing business environment. For example, transportation companies are often required to quickly pivot to address regulatory changes in the markets in which they operate, or companies might want to quickly grow a market share in a new sector following which they can adapt their business model once their position as a leading provider is established.

The Stripe payment model is similar to its competitors, such as PayPal, but Stripe charges a flat rate in each country of operation. For example, in Europe for every successful charge on a credit card, it costs 1.4% + 25c or 2.9% + 25c for cards from non-European countries. This amount decreases based on volume. In addition, although PayPal follows the same basic fee structure and boasts of providing payment for transactions faster than Stripe (within one business day), their pricing includes a number of service fees on top of their flat rate. Stripe presents another competitive advantage in terms of data portability meaning that, unlike its competitors, Stripe facilitates the migration of customer credit card data in a secure and PCI (Payment Card Industry) compliant manner.

Sources: Newenham (2014); Perez (2015); Quittner (2015); TSO (2015); https://stripe.com/ie/pricing.

Theory into Practice

This market insight shows how an Irish company achieved exponential growth by revolutionizing the online payments process. By offering a flat-rate per credit card transaction, as opposed to monthly fees,

Stripe made it easy, particularly for small businesses, to develop an online payments facility and process payments from many countries (since Stripe charges only a modest exchange rate). Paypal, Stripe's

Market Insight 9.5
continued

major rival, has since acquired Braintree, a payment processing company using a similar business model to Stripe. The market insight therefore illustrates both

the importance of having a clear pricing strategy and how an easy payment process can generate greater amounts of business for an organization

Related Topics:

pricing; online retailing (see also Case Insight 5.1 on 3scale.net).

1 **If a company is considering Stripe versus PayPal, what might drive their final decision? (Hint: do a search of both companies' payment approaches on the web).**

2 **What approach to pricing is Stripe using at present? In your answer, describe how Stripe uses marketing cues to persuade customers**

that *their rates* are good value compared with those of their competitors.

3 **As a consumer, if you are making a payment online, what pricing tactics, if any, influence your decision to stay longer on a merchant's website?**

This market insight was kindly contributed by Dr Ethel Claffey, Waterford Institute of Technology, Ireland

Pricing Tactics

In reality, when setting prices, an organization trades off the different approaches by considering all the following factors:

- Competition—how much are competitors charging for similar offerings?
- Cost—how much do the individual components that make up our offering cost?
- Demand—how much of this product or service will we sell at what price?
- Value—what components of the offering does the customer value and how much are they prepared to pay for them?

Although we outline four main pricing approaches, there are in fact many different possible pricing tactics within these approaches that could be used including the following.

- List pricing—where a single price is set for an offering, e.g. hotels charge what they call 'rack rates' for hotel conferencing facilities, combining residential accommodation for a set number of delegates with daytime accommodation for a conference room, refreshments, and lunch.
- Loss-leader pricing—where the price is set at a level lower than the actual cost incurred to produce it. This approach is often used in supermarkets on popular price-sensitive items (e.g. best-selling novels) to entice customers in store. The loss incurred is made up by increasing the prices of other less price-sensitive items or absorbed as a short-term promotional cost.

- Promotional pricing—companies temporarily reduce their prices below the standard price to raise brand awareness and encourage trial. Such approaches incorporate the use of loss leaders, sales discounts, cash rebates, low interest financing (e.g. car manufacturers frequently offer 0% interest-free financing deals), and other price-based promotional incentives. For example, in late 2015, French hypermarket chain Leclerc advertised and offered Epson printers at a price of €44.99, down from €54.99, for a fixed 10-day period, with the tagline *'Chez E. Leclerc, vous savez que vous achetez moins cher'* (translating to 'At E. Leclerc, you know you are buying cheaper').

- Segmentation pricing—setting prices for different groups of customers, e.g. Unilever's ice cream is offered as various different ice cream products at differing levels of quality and price ranging from super-premium (e.g. Ben & Jerry's ice cream available in cinemas) to economy offerings (e.g. standard ice cream available in supermarkets). Economists call this approach **price discrimination**.

- Customer-centric pricing—Cross and Dixit (2005) suggest that companies can take advantage of customer segments by measuring their value perceptions, measuring the value created, and designing a unique bundle of products and services to cater to the value requirements of each segment, and continually assessing the impact this has on company profitability, taking advantage of up-selling (e.g. offering a customer a more expensive offering in the same category) and cross-selling (e.g. selling other different offerings to the same customer).

- Pay-what-you-want pricing—this approach to pricing, used by street music artists, allows customers to pay whatever they want. It has also occasionally been used in publishing, for example music publishing, when Radiohead released their album *In Rainbows* in 2007 (Anon., 2012), and book/game publishing by Humble Bundle, which allows customers to also donate part of their fee to a charity (Baddeley, 2015). Under certain circumstances, customers may pay more using this scheme than if companies set the price (Kim *et al*., 2009), although others have argued that it only works for promotions and is in the long run a 'dangerous pricing technique' (Leatherdale, 2015) offering 'slim pickings' (Harford, 2013). It tends to work best where an offering has a low marginal cost, when there is a fair-minded consumer, where an offering could be sold at a wide range of prices, in a competitive marketplace, and where there is a strong relationship between buyer and seller (Shan, 2015).

Business-to-Business Pricing

Business-to-business markets sell offerings to other businesses. They differ from consumer markets because buyers are professionally trained procurement executives, often with qualifications from professional institutes (e.g. the Chartered Institute of Purchasing and Supply in the UK, the Australian Association of Procurement and Contract Management in Australia, or SILF, the Swedish Purchasing and Logistic Association. Their function is often highly technical, even for apparently simple offerings. For example, to produce a pen, a manufacturer might buy the pens in Italy, packaging and printing from China, refills from Germany, and the final product assembly in Bulgaria.

In the business-to-business context, the discussion of price takes place between the buyer and the seller in an atmosphere where both are trying to make the best commercial decision for their organizations. The seller wants to maximize profit (by getting a high price), and the buyer wants to procure at a low price to lower costs and maximize their profits. Their task is to resolve their mutual needs in a win–win situation. From the seller's perspective, there are numerous pricing tactics that can be adopted including the following.

- Geographical pricing—prices are based on customer location (e.g. pharmaceutical companies sell their prescription drugs at different prices in different countries). This might include FOB (free on board) factory prices where the price represents the cost of the goods and the buyer must pay for all transport costs incurred. FOB destination pricing is where the manufacturer agrees to cover the cost of shipping to the destination, but not transport costs incurred on arrival at the port (air or sea).

- Negotiated pricing—prices set according to specific agreements between a company and its clients or customers (e.g. professional services such as architectural or structural engineering). This approach occurs where a sale is complex and consultative, although sales representatives should not concede on price too quickly before properly understanding a client's needs (Rackham, 2001).

- Discount pricing—companies reduce the price on the basis that a customer commits to buying a large volume of that offering now or in the future, or is prepared to pay for it quickly. Large retailers work on the discount principle when buying for their stores. Their mighty procurement budgets and long experience ensure that they buy at cheaper prices from their suppliers and so lower their costs. Note that when price is discounted, we disproportionately reduce the operating profit (Baker *et al.*, 2010).

- Value-in-use pricing—this approach focuses attention on customer perceptions of the attributes of offerings and away from cost-oriented approaches. It prices offerings based on what the customer is prepared to pay for individual benefits received from that proposition, so the company must first ascertain what benefit components the customer perceives to be important, quantify those benefit values, determine the price equivalence of value, rate competitive and alternative products to provide a benchmark for price determination, quantify the value in use (i.e. the value in using our product vis-à-vis our competitors), and only then is the price actually fixed (see Christopher (1982) for a detailed discussion). This approach is particularly used for industrial propositions.

- Relationship pricing—this approach seeks to understand customers' needs before pricing the offering around those needs to generate a long-term relationship. This means offering excellent financial terms, credit or more lenient time periods for payment, or discounts based on future sales revenue or the risk involved in the purchase.

- Pay-what-you-want pricing—this approach allows customers to pay whatever they want for an offering. For example, the legal services firm, CMS Cameron McKenna has offered this pricing approach to its corporate clients (Hollander, 2010).

- Transfer pricing—this occurs in large organizations where considerable internal dealing between different company divisions occurs, often across national boundaries. Prices may be set at commercial rates, on the basis of negotiated prices between divisions, or using a cost-based approach, depending on whether the division is a cost or profit centre. Internal dealings can sometimes mean that the final offering is overpriced for a given customer. Airbus Industries, the European aircraft manufacturer owned by parent company EADS (European Aeronautic Defence and Space Company), adopts this approach when constructing its planes built from components made in different countries.

- Economic value to the customer (EVC) pricing—with this approach, a company prices an offering according to its perceived value by the purchasing organization (i.e. total profit generated less the costs paid), typically through a comparison with a reference or market-leading offering, taking into consideration not only the actual purchase price of the offering but also the start-up and post-purchase costs to give an overall indication of how much better its pricing structure is compared with that of a competitor. The final price is then set based on a negotiation between the buyer and seller over the difference in value and how likely this value is to be achieved. This kind of pricing approach might be used by a large consultancy solutions company such as IBM when it sells its system solutions.

- Tendering and bid pricing—with this approach, organizations invite other organizations to bid for the right to deliver a particular job or task (a tender) and to name their own price. This approach is used heavily by public sector organizations. The difficulty arises in that organizations don't always provide a budgetary range to allow bidders an idea of what price would be accepted. The manager should know the profitability of his/her bid when determining the price, and aim to discover the winning bidder's name and price on lost jobs where possible (Walker, 1967). Ross (1984) argues that it is often better not to ask 'What price will it take to win this order?' but 'Do we want this order, given the price our competitors are likely to quote?'. Where the winning bidder obtains an unprofitable contract that he/she is duty bound to deliver because their bid price was set so low, this is known as the **winner's curse**.

Chapter Summary

To consolidate your learning, the key points from this chapter are summarized here.

- **Explain the concept of price elasticity of demand.**

  Price elasticity of demand allows us to determine how the quantity of an offering relates to the price at which it is offered. Inelastic propositions are defined as such because increases/decreases in price produce relatively smaller decreases/increases in sales volumes, whereas elastic offerings have larger similar effects. Understanding price elasticity helps us devise demand-oriented pricing mechanisms.

- **Define price, and understand its relationship with costs, quality, and value.**

  Price, costs, quality, and value are all interrelated. Price is what an offering is sold for and cost is what it is bought for. When value is added to a proposition the price that can be obtained exceeds the cost. Price and cost are often confused, and are assumed erroneously to be the same thing. They are not. Quality is a measure of how well an offering satisfies the need it is designed to cater for. Value is best described either as a function of the quality of an offering as a proportion of the price paid or the perceived benefits less the perceived price.

- **Describe how customers perceive price.**

  Understanding how customers and consumers perceive pricing helps when setting prices. Customers have an idea of reference prices based on what they ought to pay for an offering, what others would pay, or what they would like to pay. Their knowledge of actual prices is limited to well-known and frequently bought and advertised offerings. Consequently, customers tend to rely on price cues such as odd-number pricing, sale signs, the purchase context, and price bundles when deciding whether or not value exists in a particular proposition.

■ **Understand pricing strategies and how to price new offerings.**

There are four main pricing strategies including premium pricing (pricing an offering to indicate its distinctiveness in the marketplace), penetration pricing (pricing low relative to the competition to gain market share), economy pricing (pricing at the bare minimum to attract price-sensitive customers), and price skimming (setting the price high initially, and then lowering it in sequential steps). The two classic approaches to pricing new offerings are market skimming and market penetration pricing. The former is favoured when a company needs to recover its R&D investment quickly, when customers are price-insensitive or of unknown price sensitivity, when product lifecycles are short (see Chapter 8), and when barriers to entry to competitors are high. The latter is favoured when these conditions do not exist.

■ **Explain cost-, competitor-, demand-, and value-oriented approaches to pricing.**

There are a variety of different pricing policies that can be used depending on whether we are pricing a consumer, service, or industrial offering. They tend to be cost-oriented (based on what we paid for it and what mark-up we intend to add), competitor-oriented (the so-called going rate or based on what price competitors sell an offering at), demand-oriented (based on how much of an offering can be sold at what price), or value-oriented (what attributes of the offering are of benefit to the customer and what will they pay for them).

■ **Explain how pricing operates in the business-to-business setting.**

A variety of pricing tactics are used in the business-to-business setting, including geographical, negotiated, discount, value-in-use, relationship, pay-what-you-want, transfer, economic value to the customer, and bid pricing. Business-to-business pricing differs in that buyers are frequently expert in purchasing for their organizations. They are likely to pay particular attention to the value that they derive from the offering.

Review Questions

1. Define price, cost, quality, and value and how they relate to each other.
2. Explain the concept of price elasticity of demand, giving examples of offerings that are both price elastic and price inelastic.
3. What are pricing cues?
4. How does odd number pricing work?
5. What are the four main pricing strategies?
6. When might you use price skimming as a pricing approach?
7. When might you use penetration pricing?
8. Name four business-to-business pricing tactics.
9. Under what circumstances does the pay-what-you-want pricing approach work best?
10. How does pricing operate in tender and bidding processes?

Worksheet Summary

To apply the knowledge you have gained from this chapter and test your understanding of price decisions visit the **Online Resource Centre** and complete Worksheet 9.1.

Discussion Questions

1 Having read Case Insight 9.1, how would you advise Simply Business to develop a pricing system which offers tailored policies, including discounts, to those customers who are more price sensitive?

2 A range of scenarios are presented in which you are given some information on the price context. What pricing policy would you use when setting the price in the following situation (state the assumptions under which you are working when you decide on each one)?

   A The owner of a newly refurbished themed Irish pub in a central city location (e.g. Amsterdam or Oslo) wants to set the prices for his range of beers with the objective of attracting a new customer base.

   B The product manager at American car maker Ford wants to set the price range for the Ford Mustang in the UK launched in Summer 2016 (http://www.ford.co.uk/Cars/newmustang).

   C You are the manager at a well-known large legal services firm (e.g. Bird & Bird) in Denmark, and your client, from a €20m turnover medium-sized import–export company, commissions work in relation to a recent company acquisition. What further information would you require in order to price such work and what pricing approaches could you offer?

3 How would you go about determining the price sensitivity of your customers if you were a cinema marketing manager and you wanted your cinemas to operate at full capacity throughout the week, including matinée and late (after 10 p.m.) seats, and not just at weekends and in the evenings?

4 Identify an entrepreneur or shop owner that you know. Ask them how they set their prices for the propositions that they sell? What pricing tactics do you think they use?

5 Research and examine the prices of five different items in two different supermarkets (where possible selling similar or identical products and pack sizes in each to allow comparison). What are the average prices for each of the items and how does each supermarket compare with the other?

@   Visit the **Online Resource Centre** and complete the **Multiple Choice Questions** to assess your knowledge of Chapter 9.

Glossary

advertising elasticity measure of how responsive the demand for offerings is in relation to changes in advertising expenditure (i.e. how effective an advertising campaign is in generating new sales).

brand equity the revenues generated from consumers' perception of the brand rather than from the product itself.

components part of something larger (e.g. an engine as part of a car, or the casing, ink, and packaging as parts of a pen).

consumer durables manufactured consumer products that are relatively long-lasting (e.g. cars or computers) as opposed to non-durables (e.g. foodstuffs).

consumer surplus the difference between the price a customer is willing to pay and what they actually pay.

fixed capital the cost of plant, equipment, and machinery owned by a business.

mixed price bundling when a product or service is offered together with another typically complementary product or service, which is also available separately, in order to make the original product or service seem more attractive (e.g. a mobile phone package with text messages and international call packages included in the price).

perceived quality a relative subjective measure. We use the term perceived quality because there is no truly objective absolute measure of product or service quality.

price the amount the customer has to pay to receive a good or service.

price anchoring a cognitive bias whereby humans have a tendency to rely heavily on information first offered rather than that collected later.

price discrimination occurs where the price of a good or service is set differently for certain groups of people.

price elasticity the percentage change in volume demanded as a proportion of the percentage change in price, usually expressed as a negative number. A score close to zero indicates that a product or service price change has little impact on quantity demanded, whereas a score of −1 indicates that a product or service price change effects an equal percentage quantity change. A value above −1 indicates a disproportionately higher change in quantity demanded as a result of a percentage price change.

price gouging occurs when a seller sets the price of a good or service at a level far higher than is considered reasonable.

pricing cues proxy measures used by customers to estimate the reference price of a product or service. Examples include quality, styling, packaging, sale signs, and odd-number endings.

pure price bundling when a product or service is offered together with another typically complementary product or service, which is not available separately, in order to make the original product or service seem more attractive (e.g. a CD with a music magazine).

reference price the price band against which customers judge the purchase price of goods and services in their own minds.

secret menus —many fast food outlets have menus that are not displayed but can be requested, e.g. Burger King offer a mustard Whopper® and Frings (fries with onion rings), among numerous other items.

transfer pricing typically occurs in large organizations and represents the pricing approach used when one unit of a company sells to another unit within the same company.

value the regard that something is held to be worth, typically, although not always, in financial terms.

white goods large electrical goods used in residences, typically but not necessarily white in colour (e.g. refrigerators, washing machines).

white-labelled product an offering developed by one organization which other organizations rebrand and market as if were their own.

winner's curse terminology associated with the bidding process in commercial markets where a company ends up submitting a bid at a price that is unprofitable or not very profitable just to win the contract.

working capital in accounting terms, this represents a company's short-term financial efficiency and is the difference between its current assets (what it owns) and its current liabilities (what it owes).

References

Ailawadi, K., Lehmann, D.R., and Neslin, S.A. (2003). Revenue premium as a outcome measure of brand equity. *Journal of Marketing*, 67(October), 1–17.

Amaldoss, W. and Jain, S. (2005). Pricing of conspicuous goods: a competitive analysis of social effects. *Journal of Marketing Research*, 42(February), 30–42.

Anderson, E. and Simester, D. (2003). Mind your pricing cues. *Harvard Business Review*, September, 96–103.

Anderson, J.C., Wouters, M., and van Rossum, W. (2010). Why the highest price isn't the best price. *Sloan Management Review*, 51(2), 69–76.

Andreyeva, T., Long, M.W., and Brownell, K.D. (2010). The impact of food prices on consumption: a systematic review of research on the price elasticity of demand for food. *American Journal of Public Health*, 100(2), 216–22.

Anon. (2012). Paying what you want: conscience versus commerce. *The Economist*, 5 May. Retrieve from: http://www.economist.com/node/21554218 (accessed 5 April 2016).

Anon. (2015a). Stopping slurping: tax on fizzy drinks seem to work as intended. *The Economist*, 28 November. Retrieve from: http://www.economist.com/news/finance-and-economics/21679259-taxes-fizzy-drinks-seem-work-intended-stopping-slurping (accessed 21 March 2016).

Anon. (2015b). Upcoming cars in India: new hatchbacks under ₹4 Lakh. *carandbike*, 3 December. Retrieve from: http://auto.ndtv.com/news/upcoming-cars-in-india-new-hatchbacks-under-rs-4-lakh-720235 (accessed 20 March 2016).

Anon. (2015c). Viagra giant 'stiffed NHS'. *The Sun*, 7 August, 55.

Anon. (2016a). A tax on sugar: pricier pop. *The Economist*, 19 March. Retrieve from: http://www.economist.com/news/britain/21694993-levy-drinks-may-change-recipes-not-waistlines-britain-gets-new-tax-sugary-drinks (accessed 21 March 2013).

Anon. (2016b). International airlines: price vs service. *The Economist 1843*, April/May, 141.

Anon. (2016c). John Lewis hails strong Christmas trading. *Sky News*, 6 January. Retrieve from: http://news.sky.com/story/1617537/john-lewis-hails-strong-christmas-trading (accessed 19 March 2016).

Anon. (2016d). Flexible figures. *The Economist*, 30 January, 64.

Attridge, J. (2003). A single European market for pharmaceuticals. Could less regulation and more negotiation be the answer?' *European Business Journal*, 15(3), 122–43.

Babad, Y.M. and Balachandran, B.V. (1993). Cost driver optimisation in activity-based costing. *Accounting Review*, 68(3), 563–75.

Baddeley, A. (2015). When 'pay what you want' means 'don't pay at all'. *The Guardian*, 26 April. Retrieve from: http://www.theguardian.com/books/2015/apr/26/when-pay-what-want-means-dont-pay-online-bookshop (accessed 20 March 2016).

Baker, W.L., Marn, M.V., and Zawada, C.C. (2010). *The Price Advantage* (2nd edn). Hoboken, NJ: John Wiley.

Benady, A. (2015). Peter Cross: never knowingly undersold. *PR Week*, 19 April. Retrieve from: http://www.prweek.com/article/1341269/peter-cross-knowingly-oversold (accessed 19 March 2016).

Bijmolt, T.H.A., van Heerde, H.J., and Pieters, R.G.M. (2005). New empirical generalisations on the determinants of price elasticity. *Journal of Marketing Research*, 42, 141–56.

Blackhurst, C. (2014). Check out the Dutch for supermarket price wars. *Evening Standard*, 2 October, 47.

Boyle, P.J. and Lathrop, E.S. (2009). Are consumers' perceptions of price–quality relationships well-calibrated? *International Journal of Consumer Studies*, 33, 58–63.

Brennan, R., Baines, P., Garneau, P., and Vos, L. (2008). *Contemporary Strategic Marketing* (2nd edn). Basingstoke: Palgrave Press, 196–9.

Brignall, M. (2011). John Lewis Partnership: never knowingly undersold? *Guardian*, 5 February. Retrieve from: http://www.guardian.co.uk/money/2011/feb/05/john-lewis-never-knowingly-undersold (accessed 18 March 2016).

Burnett, J. (2002). *Core Concepts in Marketing*. Chichester: John Wiley.

Chen, H., Marmorstein, H., Tsiros, M., and Rao, R.R. (2012). When more is less: the impact of base value neglect on consumer preferences for bonus packs over price discounts. *Journal of Marketing*, 76(4), 64–77.

Cialdini, R.B. (1993). *Influence: The Psychology of Persuasion*. New York: Quill William Morrow.

Christopher, M. (1982). Value-in-use pricing. *European Journal of Marketing*, 16(5), 35–46.

Colchero, M.A., Salgado, J.C., Unar-Munguía, M., Hernández-Ávila, M., and Rivera-Dommarco, J.A. (2015). Price elasticity of the demand for sugar sweetened beverages and soft drinks in Mexico. *Economics & Human Biology*, 19, 129–37.

Constantinides, A. and Rahman, K. (2015). Pharmaceutical entrepreneur who jacked up AIDS pill price by 5000% says he should have charged even more. *Mail Online*, 5 December. Retrieve from: http://www.dailymail.co.uk/news/article-3347441/Martin-Shkreli-said-raised-price-Daraprim-more.html (accessed 13 March 2016).

Cross, R.G. and Dixit, A. (2005). Customer-centric pricing: the surprising secret for profitability. *Business Horizons*, 48, 483–91.

Crow, D. (2015). A provocateur in the pharma wars. *Financial Times*, 26–27 September, 3.

Dean, J. (1950). Pricing policies for new products. *Harvard Business Review*, November, 45–53.

Dennis, N.P.S. (2012). *Developments in Airline Pricing and Revenue Management. Proceedings of the European Transport Conference*, 8–10 October, Retrieve from: http://abstracts.aetransport.org/paper/index/id/4051/confid/18 (accessed 14 March 2016).

Dolan, R.J. and Simon, H. (1997). *Power Pricing: How Managing Price Transforms The Bottom Line*. New York: Free Press.

Donnelly, L. (2016). Sugar tax in Mexico cuts sales of sugary drinks by 12 per cent. *The Telegraph*, 6 January. Retrieve from: http://www.telegraph.co.uk/news/health/news/12085408/Children-aged-five-eating-own-weight-in-sugar-every-year.html (accessed 21 March 2016).

Doyle, P. (2000). *Value-Based Marketing: Marketing Strategies for Corporate Growth and Shareholder Value*. Chichester: John Wiley.

Duffy, M. (1999). The influence of advertising on the pattern of food consumption in the UK. *International Journal of Advertising*, 18(2), 131–68.

Foxall, G. (1972). A descriptive theory of pricing for marketing. *European Journal of Marketing*, 6(3), 190–4.

Gerstner, E. (1985). Do higher prices signal higher quality. *Journal of Marketing Research*, 22(2), 209–15.

Gourville, J. and Soman, D. (2002). Pricing and the psychology of consumption. *Harvard Business Review*, 80(9), 90–6.

Grewal, D., Ailawadi, K.L., Gauri, D., Hall, K., Kopalle, P., and Robertson, J. R. (2011). Innovations in retail pricing and promotions. *Journal of Retailing*, 87(S1), S43–52.

Harford, T. (2013). Pay-what-you-want pricing: play tag with price tags. *Financial Times*, 16 August. Retrieve from:

http://www.ft.com/cms/s/2/fd79cc8e-0467-11e3-a8d6-00144feab7de.html (accessed 20 March 2016).

Hayward, S. (2015). So this is what Cadbury thinks of biscuit lovers. *Sunday Mirror*, 12 April, 24.

Hinterhuber, A. and Liozu, S. (2012). Is it time to rethink your pricing strategy? *Sloan Management Review*, 53(4), 76.

Hipwell, D. and Ellson, A. (2016). Superdrug takes razor to sexist pricing. *The Times*, 5 February, 21.

Hollander, G. (2010). Camerons invites legal clients to pay what they want for legal work. *The Lawyer*, 5 August. Retrieve from: http://www.thelawyer.com/camerons-invites-clients-to-pay-what-they-want-for-legal-work/1005236.article (accessed 19 March 2016).

Kim, J-Y., Natter, M., and Spann, M. (2009). Pay what you want: a new participatory pricing mechanism. *Journal of Marketing*, 73(1), 44–58.

Latif, A. (2013). Value based pricing. *The Lancet: Policy Matters*, 16 August. Retrieve from: http://ukpolicymatters.thelancet.com/value-based-pricing/ (accessed 14 March 2016).

Leatherdale, D. (2015). Do pay-what-you-want pricing strategies work? *BBC News*, 22 July. Retrieve from: http://www.bbc.co.uk/news/uk-england-33609867 (accessed 20 March 2016).

Lavin, R. and Timpson, H. (2013). *Exploring the Acceptability of a Tax on Sugar-Sweetened Beverages: Brief Evidence Review*. Centre for Public Health, Liverpool John Moores University. Retrieve from: http://www.cph.org.uk/wp-content/uploads/2013/11/SSB-Evidence-Review_Apr-2013-2.pdf (accessed 21 March 2016).

Leszinski, R. and Marn, M.V. (1997). Setting value, not price. *McKinsey Quarterly*, February. Retrieve from: http://www.mckinsey.com/business-functions/marketing-and-sales/our-insights/setting-value-not-price (accessed 14 March 2016).

Liozu, S.M. and Hinterhuber, A. (2013). Pricing orientation, pricing capabilities, and firm performance. *Management Decision*, 51(3), 594–614.

Lockley, L.C. (1949). Theories of pricing in marketing. *Journal of Marketing*, 13(3), 364–7.

Mendoza, J. and Baines, P. (2012). Towards a consumer price perception formation framework: a systematic review. *Proceedings of the Australia and New Zealand Marketing Academy Conference*. Retrieve from: http://pandora.nla.gov.au/pan/25410/20140311-1105/anzmac.org/conference/2012/papers/173ANZMACFINAL.pdf (accessed 19 March 2016).

Michard, Q. (2016). Why brands should be using data analytics to inform pricing strategy. *Impact*, 8(January), 68–9.

Newenham, P. (2014). Irish founded payments start-up Stripe now valued at $3.5bn. *Irish Times*, 2 December. Retrieve from: http://www.irishtimes.com/business/technology/irish-founded-payments-start-up-stripe-now-valued-at-3-5-billion-1.2023112 (accessed 19 March 2016).

Neville, S. (2015). Supermarkets surrender to farmers after milk price protest. *The Independent*, 15 August, 46.

Nunes, J.C. and Boatwright, P. (2001). Pricey encounters. *Harvard Business Review*, July–August, 18–19.

Oxford Dictionaries (2016). 'Price', 'Value', 'Quality'. Retrieve from: http://oxforddictionaries.com/definition/english/price?q = price; http://oxforddictionaries.com/definition/english/quality?q = quality; http://oxforddictionaries.com/definition/english/value?q = value (accessed 19 March 2016).

Perez, S. (2015). Stripe's new product helps marketplaces go global more quickly. Techcrunch.com, 23 March. Retrieve from: http://techcrunch.com/2015/03/23/stripes-new-product-helps-marketplaces-go-global-more-quickly/#.uxlor18:sOTB (accessed 19 March 2016).

PHE (2015). *Sugar Reduction: The Evidence for Action*. October. London: Public Health England. Retrieve from: https://www.gov.uk/government/uploads/system/uploads/attachment_data/file/470179/Sugar_reduction_The_evidence_for_action.pdf (accessed 21 March 2016).

Quittner, J. (2015). The twentysomething brothers behind a $3.6bn payments company. Inc.com, 22 April. Retrieve from: http://www.inc.com/jeremy-quittner/2015-30-under-30-stripe.html (accessed 19 March 2016).

Rackham, N. (2001). Winning the price war. *Sales and Marketing Management*, 253(11, November), 26.

Reinemoeller, P. (2014). How to win a price war. *Sloan Management Review*, 55(3), 15–17.

Ross, E.B. (1984). Making money with proactive pricing. *Harvard Business Review*, November–December, 145–55.

Rust, R.T., Danaher, P.J., and Varki, S. (2000). Using service quality data for competitive marketing decisions. *International Journal of Service Industry Management*, 11(5), 438–69.

Shan, C. (2015). Where can the 'pay-what-you-want' model succeed? *Quora*, 2 June. Retrieve from: https://www.quora.com/Where-can-the-pay-what-you-want-model-succeed (accessed 20 March 2016).

Sheth, J.N., Sisodia, R.S., and Barbulescu, A. (2006). The image of marketing. In: J. N. Sheth and R.S. Sisodia (eds), *Does Marketing Need Reform*. New York: M.E. Sharpe, 26–36.

Smith, G.E. and Nagle, T.T. (1995). Frames of reference and buyer's perceptions of value. *California Management Review*, 38(1), 98–116.

Thier, D. (2016). Microsoft just dropped the Xbox One price again. *Forbes/Tech*, 18 March. Retrieve from: http://www.forbes.com/sites/davidthier/2016/03/18/microsoft-just-dropped-the-xbox-one-price-again/#3527d83920f1 (accessed 20 March 2016).

TSO (2015). *IFS 2020: A Strategy for Ireland's International Financial Services Sector 2015-2020*. Retrieve from: http://www.finance.gov.ie/sites/default/files/IFS2020.pdf (accessed 19 March 2016).

van Heerde, H.J., Gijsbrechts, E., and Pauwels, K. (2008). Winners and losers in a major price war. *Journal of Marketing Research*, 45(5), 499–518.

van Heerde, H.J., Gijsenberg, M.J., Dekimpe, M.G., and Steenkamp, J-B.E.M. (2013). Price and advertising effectiveness over the business cycle. *Journal of Marketing Research*, 50(2) 177–93.

Völckner, F. and Hofmann, J. (2007). The price-perceived quality relationship: a meta-analytic review and assessment of its determinants. *Marketing Letters*, 18(3), 181–96.

Walker, A. W. (1967). How to price industrial products. *Harvard Business Review*, September–October, 125–32.

Ward, K. (1993). Gaining a marketing advantage through the strategic use of transfer pricing. *Journal of Marketing Management*, 9, 245–53.

Yeoman, I. and McMahon-Beattie, U. (2006). Luxury markets and premium pricing. *Journal of Revenue and Pricing Management*, 4(4), 319–28.

Zeithaml, V.A. (1988). Consumer perceptions of price, quality and value: a means–end model and synthesis of evidence. *Journal of Marketing*, 52(July), 2–22.

Chapter 10
Principles of Marketing Communications

Learning Outcomes

After studying this chapter you should be able to:

▶ Define and describe the nature, purpose, and scope of marketing communications

▶ Explain three models of communication and describe how personal influences can enhance the effectiveness of marketing communication activities

▶ Understand the models used to explain how marketing communications and advertising work

▶ Understand the role of marketing communications in marketing

▶ Describe the different steps in the strategic marketing communications planning process

▶ Describe what culture is and explain how it can impact on the use of marketing communications

Case Insight 10.1
The Guardian

Market Insight 10.1
On the Watch for a New Kind of Watch

Market Insight 10.2
The Biggest Influencer on YouTube

Market Insight 10.3
Reinventing Advertising for the Digital Age

Market Insight 10.4
Advertising, Arabic Style

Case Insight 10.1
The Guardian

How could an organization realize their objective not only to shift audience perceptions but also to change behaviours? We speak to Agathe Guerrier, Strategy Director at the advertising agency Bartle Bogle Hegarty (BBH), to find out more about the work they undertook for their client *The Guardian*.

The Guardian is a truly impartial media organization that is rooted in the principles of independent journalism. The Scott Trust was set up to protect this independence, and to this day *The Guardian*'s sole purpose remains the pursuit of the truth. This philosophy shapes the way they communicate: 'Facts are sacred, but comment is free'.

The Guardian is made by Progressives, for Progressives. A Progressive is a curious and connected individual who welcomes change as a positive force. Progressives are not defined by income, age, or any other demographic data.

Today's *Guardian* is defined by its open operating system (OOS). By encouraging participation and debate, by welcoming contributions and challenges, they seek to provide the broadest and most comprehensive view of the world. Openness means that they don't put their content behind a pay wall—a radical stance in today's media landscape. It also means that they don't believe journalists to be the only voices of authority, or to be able to complete the entire editorial process on their own—instead, what they do is initiate the creation of content, and then invite bloggers, contributors, readers, and commentators to enrich and evolve it.

The Guardian uses marketing communications in order to support the key drivers of their commercial strategy. The first of these is to drive newspaper sales which, although in structural decline, still represent nearly half of *The Guardian*'s revenues. Therefore it is strategically crucial that they defend them in a competitive marketplace.

A second driver concerns the digital reach of the brand via our desktop and mobile products. As a media brand their reach is a key driver of digital advertising revenue. Marketing and communications aim to grow their UK and international reach.

The third driver is digital engagement. Known, active, and engaged users of their digital products are more valuable than anonymous and disengaged visitors. To this end, a strand of the marketing and communications strategy is dedicated to increasing digital engagement—registrations, participation, time spent, and frequency.

However, *The Guardian* has had to face certain problems. The first concerns their potential audience of Progressives. It was known from brand health tracking that they weren't aware of how much *The Guardian* had changed (mainly the Open philosophy), and they scored low on image items such as 'modern', 'innovative', and 'dynamic'.

Secondly, from their trade audience (advertisers and media agencies), they knew that they were struggling with the perception of being a worthy, left-wing, pedantic, and niche newspaper brand.

In terms of direct competition, most of the traditional newspaper sector was actually suffering from a similar fate. The real threat was from the new entrants in the knowledge sector, those of the digital age—Twitter, TED, YouTube—that are really redefining people's attitudes and behaviours when it comes to seeking, consuming, and understanding news content.

For a long time there has been little investment in the brand, with marketing spend focused on tactical campaigns such as promoting a certain supplement or feature. The challenge now was to find a way of changing perceptions of *The Guardian* (as a dusty

Case Insight 10.1
continued

left-wing newspaper brand) amongst a large potential audience of digitally connected, inquisitive news readers. They wanted this audience to realize that *The Guardian* had evolved and was now a radically innovative leader of the digital age.

Therefore the problem was not only how to go about shifting perceptions, but also to change behaviours by driving a larger online audience to the desktop product.

Introduction

Have you ever wondered how organizations such as *The Guardian* manage to communicate effectively with so many different people and organizations? Well, this is the first of two chapters that explain how this can be accomplished through the use of marketing communications. This chapter introduces and explains what marketing communications is and how it can be planned. The following chapter considers the configuration of the marketing communications mix.

Marketing communications is about developing messages that can be understood and acted on by target audiences. The purpose of this chapter is to introduce some of the fundamental ideas and concepts associated with such communications. To achieve this, the chapter commences with a definition of marketing communications. We then proceed by discussing the scope and functions of marketing communications. The latter includes a consideration of communications theory. This is important because it provides a basis on which to appreciate the different ways in which marketing communications are used. Communications theory specifies the scope of the subject and provides a framework within which to appreciate the various communications activities undertaken by organizations. We then present principles by which marketing messages are communicated and consider how marketing communications might work. The chapter concludes with an overview of what culture is and how it can impact on marketing communications.

This chapter is intended to help you understand some of the fundamental ideas associated with planned marketing communications. It sets out the broad scope of marketing communications and enables you to appreciate the diversity of this fascinating subject. The tools and media used by marketing communications are an important aspect of this topic, and Chapter 11 is devoted to a fuller examination of each of them.

Defining Marketing Communications

Marketing communications can be defined as a management process through which an organization attempts to engage with its various audiences. By conveying messages that are of significant value, audiences are encouraged to offer attitudinal and behavioural responses (Fill, 2013).

There are three main aspects associated with this definition: engagement, audiences, and responses.

- Engagement—what are the audiences' communications needs and is it possible to engage with them on their terms using one-way, two-way, or dialogic communications?

- Audiences—which specific audience(s) do we need to communicate with and what are their various behaviour and information-processing needs?

- Responses—what are the desired outcomes of the communication process? Are they based on changes in perception, values, and beliefs, or are changes in behaviour required?

Engagement deals with the way that communication influences its audiences (see section on 'How marketing communication works'). What to expect in terms of engagement is largely dependent on the decisions made with regard to the target audience and target responses for different marketing communication activities (see the section on 'Planning marketing communication').

The Scope of Marketing Communications

As discussed in Chapter 1, promotion is one of the Ps of the marketing mix, and is responsible for the communication of the proposition to the target market. Marketing communications is a more contemporary term for promotion. It is used to communicate elements of an organization's offerings to target audiences. The offer might refer to a product, a service, or the organization itself as it tries to build its reputation.

Marketing communications can be considered from a number of perspectives. Although it is an activity used by organizations with varying degrees of sophistication, it is mainly concerned with the way in which audiences are encouraged to perceive an organization and/or its offerings. Therefore it should be regarded as an audience-centred activity. Fundamentally, marketing communications comprises three elements: (1) a set of tools, (2) the media, and (3) messages. The five common tools are advertising, sales promotion, personal selling, direct marketing, and public relations. In addition, a range of media, such as TV, radio, press, and the Internet, are used to convey messages to target audiences (these are covered in more detail in Chapter 11).

Still, these tools, media, and messages are not the only sources of information for consumers. There is also implicit and important communication through the other elements of the marketing mix (e.g. a high price is symbolic of high quality) as well as unplanned or unintended experiences (empty stock shelves or accidents) in relation to the offer.

Figure 10.1 (Hughes and Fill, 2007) highlights the breadth and complexity of managing marketing communications. Our focus in this chapter will be on planned marketing communications (Duncan and Moriarty, 1998). This component is really important because it has the potential not only to present offers in the best possible way, but also to influence people's expectations about both product and service experiences. See Market Insight 10.1 for an example of marketing communications, which draws on a range of media.

🅐 **Visit the Online Resource Centre** and follow the web link to the European Association of Communication Agencies (EACA) to learn more about advertising, media, and sales promotion activities across Europe.

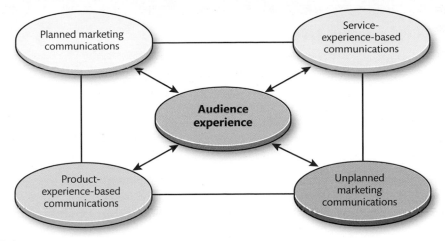

Figure 10.1

The scope of marketing communications

Source: Hughes and Fill (2007). Adapted with the kind permission of Emerald Group Publishing Limited and Westburn Publishers.

Market Insight 10.1
On the Watch for a New Kind of Watch

In September 2014 Apple CEO Tim Cook announced the company's first original product since the introduction of the iPad in 2010—the Apple Watch. With this product, Apple step into a new territory for the company. In the words of Cook: 'We've never sold anything as a company that people could try on before'.

Marketing communications played a large role in the launch of the Apple Watch

Source: © Anna Hoychuk/Shutterstock.

Market Insight 10.1
continued

The watch had been much awaited and the news of its arrival spread quickly. The announcement was followed by a long period of anticipation, as the watch did not become available to consumers until late April 2015.

Throughout this period Apple shared information about the product and its design on their website as well as in different interactions with the press. For example, it was highlighted that the watch would come in three different forms: the Apple Watch Sport in polished or black stainless steel, the standard Apple Watch in grey or silver anodized aluminum, and the luxury Watch Edition, available in rose or yellow. Consumers were told that prices would start at $349 with luxury watches priced around $10,000. Information about pre-orders

and availability at Apple stores (to which initial sales were restricted) was shared on- and offline.

To conquer the marketplace, Apple also launched its advertising campaign for the release with a 12-page insert in the March issue of *Vogue*. This outlet was selected based on the insight that in order to succeed, the Apple Watch must have an appeal not only as a gadget, but also as a fashion statement.

Apple does not share data about sales for specific products, but states that 2015 sales of the Apple Watch were up against the company's internal forecasts. According to estimates the Apple Watch accounted for at least 50% of all smart watch sales in 2015.

Sources: Williams (2014); Moynihan (2015); Pierce (2015)

Theory into practice

Although the 4Ps of marketing all convey important information about a product or service on offer, marketing communications typically refers to planned communication ('promotion').

Marketing communications played a large role in the launch of the Apple Watch. The design ('product'), the pricing ('price'), and the distribution ('place') all conveyed information about the intended positioning of the new product, but the public announcement of the watch by Cook, the way information about the product,

price, and place of the coming launch was shared, as well as the advertising campaign used to support the launch are examples of marketing communications.

The type of media used in marketing communication can be categorized as paid for, owned, and earned media (POEM) (see Chapter 11). The event could be considered part of a strategy to gain earned media, the sharing of information was mainly through Apple's own media, and the advertising campaign an example of bought media.

Related Topics:

new product development; pricing; distribution; advertising.

1 **How successful would you say that the launch was? What role would you attribute to marketing communications in it?**

2 **In what way do design, pricing, and distribution influence perceptions of the Apple Watch?**

3 **Why did Apple choose *Vogue* as an important media vehicle for the launch?**

How Marketing Communications Works

Ideas about how advertising, then promotion, and now marketing communications works have been a constant source of investigation, endeavour, and conceptual speculation. To suggest that a firm conclusion has been reached would be misleading and untrue. However, particular ideas have stood out and have played a more influential role in shaping our ideas about this fascinating topic. Some of these are presented here. Before considering the specific theories about how *marketing* communication works we will, however, take a closer look at communication theory. This is important as it provides a foundation on which to base our understanding of marketing communications.

Communication Theory

Communication theory is important as it helps explain how and why certain marketing communication activities take place. Communication is the process by which individuals share meaning. Therefore it is necessary for participants to be able to interpret the meanings embedded in the messages they receive, and then, as far as the sender is concerned, be able to respond coherently. The act of responding is important, as it completes an episode in the communication process. Communication that travels only from the sender to the receiver is essentially a one-way process and the full communication process remains incomplete. This form of communication is shown in Figure 10.2.

When Marabou display their chocolate bars on a poster in the Stockholm metro, the person standing on the platform can read it, understand it, and may even be entertained by it. However, the person does not have any immediate opportunity to respond to the ad in such a way that

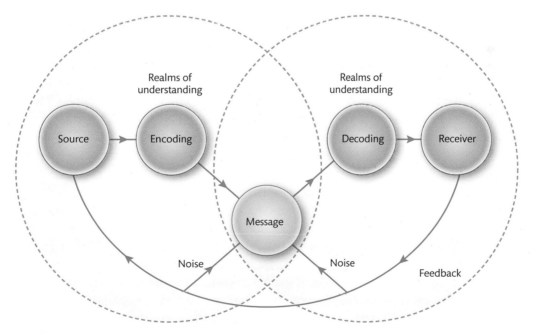

Figure 10.2

A linear model of communications

Sources: Based on Schramm (1955); Shannon and Weaver (1962).

Marabou can hear, understand, and act on their comments and feelings. When that same ad is presented on a website or a sales promotion representative offers that same person a chunk of Marabou milk chocolate when they are shopping in a supermarket, there are opportunities to hear, record, and even respond to the comments that the person makes. This form of communication travels from a sender (Marabou) to a receiver (the person in the supermarket) and back again to Marabou. It is referred to as a two-way communication and represents a complete communication episode.

Visit the Online Resource Centre and follow the web link to the International Association of Business Communicators (IABC), a business network which aims to improve marketing communications effectiveness among communication professionals.

These basic models form the basis of this introduction to communication theory. It is important that those involved in managing and delivering marketing communications understand these processes and the associated complexities. Through knowledge and understanding of the communication process, they are more likely to achieve their objective of sharing meaning with each member of their target audience. This not only helps create opportunities to interact with their audiences, but also encourages some people to develop a dialogue, the richest and most meaningful form of communication.

Understanding the way communication works provides a foundation on which we can better understand not only the way that marketing communications works, but also how it can be used effectively by organizations. Three main models or interpretations of how communication works are considered here: the linear model, the two-way model, and the interactive model of communication.

The Linear Model of Communication

The linear model of communication, first developed by Wilbur Schramm (1955), is regarded as the basic model of mass communications. The key components of this model are set out in Figure 10.2.

The model can be broken down into a number of phases, each of which has distinct characteristics. The linear model emphasizes that each phase occurs in a particular sequence, a linear progression, which, according to Theodorson and Theodorson (1969), enables the 'transmission of information, ideas, attitudes, or emotion from one person or group to another (or others), primarily through symbols'. The model and its components are straightforward, but it is the quality of the linkages between the various elements in the process that determines whether the communication will be successful.

The source is an individual or organization, which identifies a problem requiring transmission of a message. The source of a message is an important factor in the communication process. First, the source must identify the right problem and, second, a **receiver** who perceives a source to lack conviction, authority, trust, or expertise is not likely to believe the messages sent by that source.

Encoding is the process by which the source selects a combination of appropriate words, pictures, symbols, and music to represent the message to be transmitted. The various bits are 'packed' in such a way that they can be unpacked and understood. The goal is to create a message that is capable of being easily comprehended by the receiver.

Once encoded, the message must be put into a form that is capable of transmission. It may be oral or written, verbal or non-verbal, in a symbolic form or in a sign. The channel is the means by which the message is transmitted from the source to the receiver. These channels may be personal or non-personal. The former involves face-to-face contact and **word-of-mouth** communications, which can be extremely influential. Non-personal channels are characterized by mass media advertising, which can reach large audiences. Ads placed in newspapers such as *The Guardian* are typical of this approach. Whatever the format chosen, the source must be sure that what is being put into the message is what they want to be decoded by the receiver.

Once the receiver, an individual or organization, has seen, heard, smelt, or read the message, they decode it. In effect, they are 'unpacking' the various components of the message, starting to make sense of it and give it meaning. The more clearly the message is encoded the easier it is to 'unpack' and comprehend what the source intended to convey when they constructed the message. Therefore **decoding** is that part of the communication process where receivers give meaning to a message.

Once the message is understood, receivers provide a set of reactions referred to as a response. These reactions may vary from an emotional response based on a set of feelings and thoughts about the message to a behavioural or action response.

Feedback is another part of the response process. It is important to know not just that the message has been received, but also that it has been correctly decoded and the right meaning attributed. However, although feedback is an essential aspect of a successful communication event, feedback through mass media channels is generally difficult to obtain, mainly because of the inherent time delay involved in the feedback process. However, feedback through **personal selling** can be instantaneous, through explicit means such as questioning, raising objections, or signing an order form. For the mass media advertiser, the process can be vague and prone to misinterpretation. If a suitable feedback system is not in place, the source will be unaware that the communication has been unsuccessful and is liable to continue wasting resources. This represents inefficient and ineffective marketing communications.

Noise is concerned with influences that distort information and, in turn, make it difficult for the receiver to correctly decode and interpret the message as intended by the source. So, if a telephone rings, or someone rustles sweet papers during a sensitive part of a film screened in a cinema, the receiver is distracted from the message.

Research Insight 10.1

To take your learning further, you might wish to read this influential paper.

Friestad, M. and Wright, P. (1994). The persuasion knowledge model: how people cope with persuasion attempts. *Journal of Consumer Research*, 21(1), 1–31.

This paper provides a useful framework for the 'realms of understanding' surrounding marketing communications. More specifically, it discusses how consumer understanding of what marketers are trying to achieve ('persuasion knowledge') influences their reactions to different types of marketing communications. The insights offered in this paper have proved very useful in understanding reactions to new forms of marketing communications, such as blog sponsorships and branded content.

Visit the **Online Resource Centre** to read the abstract and access the full paper.

The final component in the linear model concerns the 'realm of understanding'. This is an important element in the communication process because it recognizes that successful communications are more likely to be achieved if the source and the receiver understand each other. This understanding concerns attitudes, perceptions, behaviour, and experience—the values of both parties to the communication process. Effective communication is more likely when there is some common ground—a realm of understanding between the source and receiver.

One of the problems associated with the linear model of communication is that it ignores the impact that other people can have on the communication process. People are not passive; they actively use information, and the views and actions of other people can impact on the way information is sent, received, processed, and given meaning. One of the other difficulties with the linear model is that it is based on communication through mass media.

This model was developed at a time when first radio and then TV, with only a few channels, were the only media available. Today there are hundreds of TV channels, and audiences use the Internet, mobile phones, and an increasing array of digital equipment to manage their work, leisure, and entertainment. Increasing numbers of people engage with interactive-based communications and, in some circumstances, such as online gaming, organizations and individuals can be involved in real dialogue. Therefore the linear model is no longer entirely appropriate.

The Two-Step Model of Communication

One interpretation of the linear model is that it is a one-step explanation. Information is directed and shot at prospective audiences, rather like a bullet being propelled from a gun. However, we know that people can have a significant impact on the communication process and the **two-step model**, sometimes referred to as the influencer model, goes some way to reflecting their influence (see Figure 10.3).

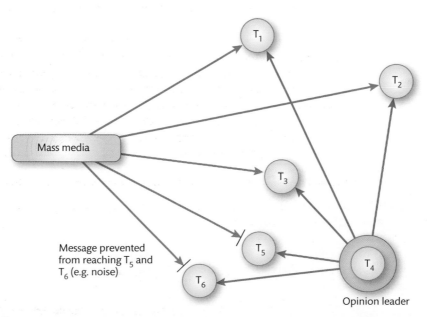

Figure 10.3

The two-step model of communications

Source: Marketing Communications (6th edn) Fill, C. (2013). Reproduced with the kind permission of Pearson Education Limited. © Pearson Education Limited 2013.

The two-step model compensates for the linear or one-step model because it recognizes the importance of personal influences when informing and persuading audiences to think or behave in particular ways. This model depicts information flowing via various media channels to particular types of people to whom other members of the audience refer for information and guidance. There are two main types of influencer. The first is referred to as an **opinion leader** and the other is an **opinion former**. The first is just an ordinary person who has a heightened interest in a particular topic. The second is involved professionally in the topic of interest. These are discussed in more detail later in this chapter, but they both have enormous potential to influence audiences. This may be because messages from personal influencers provide reinforcement and message credibility, or because this is the only way of reaching the end-user audience.

The Interaction Model of Communications

This model is similar to the two-step model but it has one important difference. In this interpretation, the parties are seen to interact among themselves and communication flows among all the members in what is regarded as a communication network (see Figure 10.4). Mass media are not the only source of the communication.

Unlike the linear model, in which messages flow from the source to the receiver, through a channel, the **interaction model** recognizes that messages can flow through various channels and that people can influence the direction and impact of a message. It is not necessarily one-way but interactive communication that typifies much of contemporary communications. In Case Insight 10.1, at the beginning of this chapter, the desire of *The Guardian* to be open requires the use of social media to encourage audience participation. The interaction among different people,

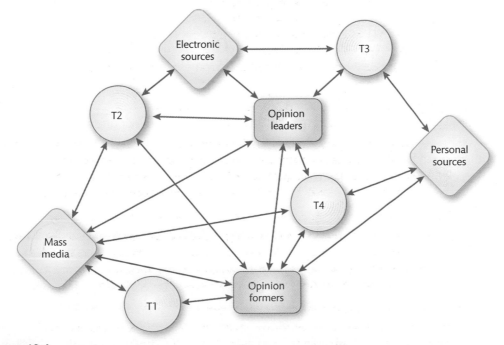

Figure 10.4

An interaction model

sometimes only referring to *The Guardian* indirectly, is a good demonstration of the interaction model in practice.

Interaction is an integral part of the communication process. Think of a conversation with a friend: the face-to-face, oral-based, and visual-based communication enables both of you to consider what the other is saying, and to react in whatever way is appropriate. Mass communication does not facilitate this interactional element, and therefore the linear model might be regarded as an incomplete form of the pure communication process.

Interaction is about actions that lead to a response, and much attention is now given to the interaction that occurs between people. However, care needs to be taken because the content associated with an interactional event might be based on an argument, a statement of opinion, or a mere casual social encounter. What is important here is interaction that leads to mutual understanding. This type of interaction concerns 'relationship specific knowledge' (Ballantyne, 2004). That is, the interaction is about information that is relevant to both parties. Once this is established, increased levels of trust develop between the participants so that eventually a dialogue emerges between communication partners. Therefore interactivity is a prelude to dialogue, the highest or purest form of communication.

Dialogue occurs through reasoning, which requires both listening and adaptation skills. Dialogue is concerned with the development of knowledge that is specific to the parties involved and is referred to as 'learning together' (Ballantyne, 2004: 119). The development of digital technologies has been instrumental in enabling organizations to provide increased interaction opportunities with their customers and other audiences. Think of the number of times when watching TV that you are prompted to press the red button to get more information. For example, many news programmes now encourage viewers to tweet, phone, or email comments, opinions, and pictures about particular issues. This is an attempt to get audiences to express their views about a subject and in doing so promote access to and interaction with the programme. Whereas at one time interaction only really occurred through personal selling, it is now possible to interact, and so build mutual understanding with consumers, through the Internet and other digital technologies. Indeed, Hoffman and Novak (1996) claim that interactivity between people is now supplemented by interactivity between machines. This means that the interaction, or indeed dialogue, that previously occurred through machines can now occur with the equipment facilitating the communication.

Personal Influencers

As mentioned earlier, two main types of personal influencer can be recognized: opinion leaders and opinion formers. In addition, social media has led word of mouth among regular consumers to become even more influential. These different types of personal influencers are now discussed in turn (see also Market Insight 10.2).

Opinion Leaders

Studies of American voting and purchase behaviour by Katz and Lazarsfeld (1955) led them to conclude that some individuals were more predisposed to receiving information and then reprocessing it to influence others. They found that these individuals had the capacity to be more persuasive than information received directly from the mass media. They called these people opinion leaders, and one of their defining characteristics is that they belong to the same peer group as the people they influence—they are not distant or removed.

It has been reported in subsequent research that opinion leaders have a greater exposure to relevant media, and as a result have more knowledge/familiarity and involvement with a certain

Market Insight 10.2
The Biggest Influencer on YouTube

In April 2010 Felix Kjellberg, then a 21-year old Swedish engineering student, created a new account on YouTube. For some time he had been posting videos of himself playing video games on YouTube, but having forgotten the password to the initial account he was forced to set up a new one: PewDiePie. Little did he know that this account was going to change his life.

Kjellberg's videos turned out to be very popular. In fact, Kjellberg's foul-mouthed videos have absolutely dominated YouTube over the past years. Many attribute his success to the attention he pays to his fans. Kjellberg spends a lot of time talking about them, answering their questions in the YouTube comments section, and forming a community of 'bros'.

In 2011 he dropped out of university to be able to devote more time to his YouTube channel, and in 2012 it had over a million subscribers. Since then,

Kjellberg has broken numerous records on YouTube. For example, his PewDiePie channel grew from 12m subscribers in August 2013 to more than 20m in January 2014. In September 2015, PewDiePie was the world's largest independent YouTube channel with 10.1bn total views and 39.3m total subscribers. By January 2016 the channel had more than 11bn views and close to 42m subscribers.

In 2015, it was reported that Kjellberg had made approximately US$7.4m (SEK36.7m) on his YouTube channel in 2014. Although the figure is staggering in itself, putting it in relation to his popularity clearly highlights why many YouTubers turn to sponsorships for funding. In fact, given the size of his channel at that time, this means that he made about 20.6 cents per subscriber that year.

Sources: Rosengren (2012); Tamburro (2014); Kosoff and Jacobs (2015)

Theory into practice

The two-step model of communications recognizes the importance of personal influences when informing and persuading audiences to think or behave in particular ways. There are two main types of influencers. An opinion leader is an ordinary person who has a heightened interest in a particular topic. An opinion

former is involved professionally in the topic of interest. Many YouTubers start out small. After a while, as their following increases, they become important opinion leaders. Those who become really big, such as Kjellsson/PewDiePie then move on to become opinion formers.

Related Topics:

social media; digital marketing; user-generated content.

1 At what stage would you say that Kjellberg moved from an opinion leader to an opinion former? Is it possible to say?

2 Visit the PewDiePie YouTube channel. To what extent is Kjellberg's communication with his followers based on interaction and dialogue?

3 Visit the PewDiePie YouTube channel. What opportunities does it offer to marketers?

category of offering than others. Non-leaders, or **opinion followers**, turn to opinion leaders for advice and information about offerings they are interested in. Opinion leaders are also more gregarious and self-confident than non-leaders, and are more confident of their role as an influencer (Chan and Misra, 1990). Therefore it is not surprising that many marketing communication strategies are targeted at influencing opinion leaders as they will, in turn, influence others. For example, *Vogue* magazine has an 'Influencer Network', a panel of 1,000 women. These influencers provide feedback on a range of issues, including new offerings, upcoming fashion collections, and ad creatives. They are encouraged to talk about particular offerings on their social networks, raising awareness of them and of *Vogue* itself (Moses, 2011).

This approach has been used to convey specific information and help educate large target audiences through TV and radio programmes. For example, TV programmes such as *Coronation Street*, *Eastenders*, and *Emmerdale*, and radio programmes such as *The Archers* (UK soaps), have been used as opinion leadership vehicles to bring to attention and open up debates about many controversial social issues, such as contraception, abortion, drug use and abuse, and serious illness and mental health concerns.

Opinion Formers

The other main type of independent personal influencer is the opinion former. They are not part of the same peer group as the people they influence. Their defining characteristic is that they exert personal influence because of their profession, authority, education, or status associated with the object of the communication process. They provide information and advice as part of the formal expertise they are perceived to hold. For example, shop assistants in music equipment shops are often experienced musicians in their own right. Aspiring musicians seeking to buy their first proper guitar will often consult these perceived 'experts' about guitar brands, styles, models, and associated equipment such as amplifiers. In the same way, doctors carry such conviction that they can influence the rate at which medicines are consumed. Drug manufacturers, such as GlaxoSmithKline and Pfizer, often launch new drugs by enlisting the support of eminent professors, consultants, or doctors who are recognized by others in the profession as experts. These opinion formers are invited to lead symposia and associated events, and in so doing build credibility and activity around the new proposition.

Organizations target their marketing communications at opinion leaders and formers to penetrate the market more quickly than relying on communicating directly with the target audience. However, in addition to these forms of influence, reference needs to be made to spokespersons. There are some potential problems that advertisers need to be aware of when considering the use of celebrities. First, does the celebrity fit the image of the brand, and will the celebrity be acceptable to the target audience now and in the long run? If the lifestyle of the celebrity changes, what impact will the changes have on the target audience and their attitude towards the brand? For example, the well-publicized allegations about the bad behaviour of the supermodel Kate Moss led to the loss of several sponsorship and brand endorsement contracts (e.g. H&M and Burberry), although it is alleged that her overall income actually increased as a result of the negative publicity and sales through her Topshop brand soared.

The second problem concerns the impact that the celebrity makes relative to the brand. There is a danger that the receiver remembers the celebrity but not the message or the brand. The celebrity becomes the hero, rather than the proposition being advertised.

All of the models of communication discussed have a role to play in marketing communications. Mass media communication in the form of broadcast TV and radio is still used by organizations to reach large audiences. Two-way and interaction forms of communication are used to reach smaller, specific target audiences and to enable a range of people to contribute to the process. Interaction and dialogue are higher levels of communication and are increasingly used to generate personal communication with individual customers. The skill for marketing practitioners is to know when to move from one-way, to two-way, to interactive, and then dialogue-based marketing communications.

Word of Mouth

This type of communication does not involve any payment for media because communication is freely given through word-of-mouth conversation. Word-of-mouth communication is 'interpersonal communication regarding products or services where the receiver regards the communicator as impartial' (Stokes and Lomax, 2002).

Personal influence within the communication process is important. This is because customers perceive word-of-mouth recommendations as objective and unbiased. In comparison with advertising messages, word-of-mouth communications are more robust (Berkman and Gilson, 1986). Word-of-mouth messages are used either as information inputs prior to purchase or as a support and reinforcement of their own purchasing decisions.

People like to talk about their product (service) experiences. The main stimulus for behaviour is that the offering in question gave them either particular pleasure or particular displeasure. These motivations to discuss experiences vary between individuals and with the intensity of the motivation at any one particular moment. One hotel gave away teddy bears to guests on the basis that the guests would be happy to talk about their stay at the hotel, with the teddy bear acting as a prompt to provoke or induce conversation.

For every single positive comment there are ten negative comments. For this reason, word-of-mouth communication was once seen as negative, unplanned, and having a corrosive effect on a brand's overall communications. Today, organizations actively manage word-of-mouth communications to generate positive comments and as a way of differentiating themselves in the market. Viral marketing or 'word of mouse' communication is an electronic version of the spoken endorsement of an offering. Often using humorous messages, games, video clips, and screen savers, information can be targeted at key individuals who then voluntarily pass the message to friends and colleagues and in so doing bestow, endorse, and provide the message with much valued credibility. Both online and offline word of mouth is becoming increasingly important for marketing communications to have its desired impact (Keller and Fay, 2012).

For organizations such as *The Guardian*, who target communications at Progressives, it is important to direct messages at those individuals who are predisposed to such discussion, as it is likely that they will propel word-of-mouth recommendations. Therefore the target is not necessarily the target market, but opinion leaders within target markets—individuals who are most likely to volunteer their positive opinions about the offering, and who, potentially, have some influence over people in their peer group.

Visit the Online Resource Centre and complete Internet Activity 10.1 to learn more about the importance of word of mouth in contemporary advertising.

Marketing Communication Theory

As mentioned earlier there is no coherent theory or model explaining how marketing communications or advertising works. The first important idea about how advertising works was based on how the personal selling process works. Developed by Strong (1925), the **AIDA** model has

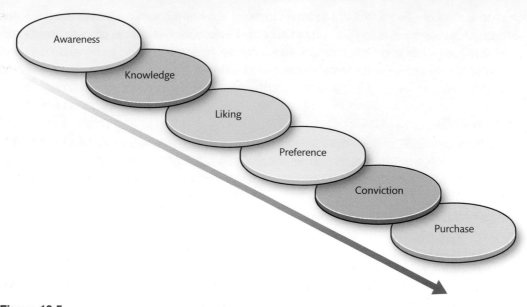

Figure 10.5
Stages in the hierarchy of effects model

become extremely well known and is used by many practitioners. AIDA refers to the need first to create awareness, secondly to generate interest, and then to drive desire, from which action (a sale) emerges. As a broad interpretation of the sales process this is generally correct, but it fails to provide insight into the depths of how advertising works. Thirty-six years later, Lavidge and Steiner (1961) presented a model based on what is referred to as the **hierarchy of effects** approach. Similar in nature to AIDA, it assumes that a prospect must pass through a series of steps for a purchase to be made. It is assumed, correctly, that advertising cannot generate an immediate sale because there are a series of thought processes that need to be fulfilled prior to action. These steps are represented in Figure 10.5.

Research Insight 10.2

To take your learning further, you might wish to read this influential paper.

Duncan, T. and Moriarty, S. (1998). A communication-based marketing model for managing relationships. *Journal of Marketing*, **62(April), 1–13.**

This is one of the most important academic papers in the field of marketing communications. It is important because it led the transition from a functional perspective of integrated marketing communications to one that emphasized its role within relationship marketing.

Visit the **Online Resource Centre** to read the abstract and access the full paper.

These models have become known as hierarchy of effects (HoE) models, simply because the effects (on audiences) are thought to occur in a top-down sequence. Some of the attractions of these HoE models and frameworks are that they are straightforward, simple, easy to understand, and, if creating advertising materials, provide a helpful broad template on which to develop and evaluate campaigns.

Although attractive, this sequential approach has several drawbacks. People do not always process information, nor do they always purchase offerings following a series of sequential steps. This logical progression is not reflected in reality when, for example, an impulse purchase is followed by an emotional feeling towards a brand. There are also questions about what actually constitutes adequate levels of awareness, comprehension, and conviction. How can it be known which stage the majority of the target audience has reached at any one point in time, and is this purchase sequence applicable to all consumers for all purchases?

The Strong and Weak Theories of Advertising

So, if advertising cannot be assumed to work in just one particular way, what other explanations exist? Of the various models put forward, two stand out. These are the strong (Jones, 1991) and the weak (Ehrenberg, 1974) theories of advertising.

The Strong Theory of Advertising

According to Jones (1991), advertising has a strong effect as it can persuade people to buy an offering that they have not previously purchased. Advertising can also generate long-run purchase behaviour. Under the **strong theory**, advertising is believed to be capable of increasing sales for a brand and for the **product class**. These upward shifts are achieved through the use of manipulative and psychological techniques, which are deployed against largely passive consumers who, possibly because of apathy, are either generally incapable of processing information intelligently or have little or no motivation to become involved.

This interpretation is a persuasion view and corresponds very well to the HoE models referred to earlier. Persuasion occurs by moving buyers towards a purchase by easing them through a series of steps, prompted by timely and suitable promotional messages. It seems that this approach correlates closely with new offerings where new buying behaviours are required.

The strong theory has close affiliation with an advertising style that is proposition oriented, where features and benefits are outlined clearly for audiences, and pack shots are considered important.

The Weak Theory of Advertising

Contrary to the strong perspective, is the view that a consumer's brand choices are driven by purchasing habit rather than by exposure to promotional messages. One of the more prominent researchers in this area was Ehrenberg (1974), who believed that advertising represents a weak force. He believed that advertising has little impact on persuading consumers to buy offerings, mainly because consumers are active, not passive, information processors.

Ehrenberg proposed that the **ATR** (awareness–trial–reinforcement) framework is a more appropriate interpretation of how advertising works. Both Jones and Ehrenberg agree that awareness is required before any purchase can be made, although the elapsed time between awareness and action may be very short or very long. Out of the mass of people exposed to a message, a few will be sufficiently intrigued to want to try an offering (trial)—the next phase.

Reinforcement follows to maintain awareness and provide reassurance to help customers repeat the pattern of thinking and behaviour. Advertising's role is to breed brand familiarity and identification (Ehrenberg, 1997).

According to the **weak theory**, advertising is employed as a defence, to retain customers and to increase brand usage. Advertising is used to reinforce existing attitudes, not necessarily to drastically change them. This means that when people say that they 'are not influenced by advertising' they are, in the main, correct.

Both the strong and weak theories of advertising are important because they are equally right and equally wrong. The answer to the question 'How does advertising work?' lies somewhere between the two, and is dependent on the context. For advertising to work, involvement is likely to be high and so here the strong theory is the most applicable. However, the vast majority of product purchase decisions generate low involvement, and so decision-making is likely to be driven by habit. Here, advertising's role is to maintain a brand's awareness with the purchase cycle, so the weak theory is most applicable.

Visit the Online Resource Centre and complete Internet Activity 10.2 to learn more about the strong and weak theories of advertising.

A Composite Approach

Most of the frameworks presented so far have their roots in advertising. If we are to establish a model that explains how marketing communications works, a different perspective is required—one that draws on the key parts of all the models. This is possible as the three key components of the attitude construct lie within these different models. Attitudes have been regarded as an important aspect of marketing communications activities, and advertising is thought to be capable of influencing the development of positive attitudes towards brands (see also Chapter 2).

The three stages of attitude formation are that we learn something (cognitive or learning component), feel something (an affective or emotional component), and then act on our attitudes (behavioural or conative component). So, in many situations we learn something, feel something towards a brand, and then proceed to buy or not to buy. These stages are set out in Figure 10.6.

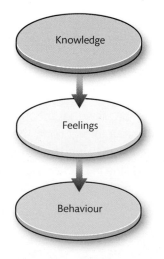

Figure 10.6
Attitude construct—linear

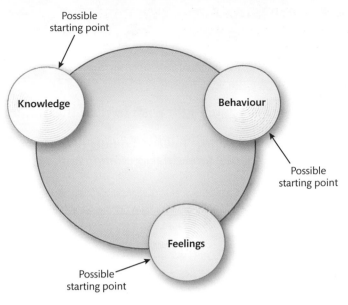

Figure 10.7
Attitude construct—circular

The HoE models and the strong theory contain this sequential approach of learn, feel, do. However, we do not always pass through this particular sequence, and the weak theory puts greater emphasis on familiarity and reminding (awareness) than the other components. So, if we look at Figure 10.7, we can see that these components have been worked into a circular format. This means that, when using marketing communications, it is not necessary to follow each component sequentially. The focus can be on what the audience requires, and this might be on the learning, feeling, or doing components, as determined by the audience. In other words, for marketing communications to be audience centred, we should develop campaigns based on the overriding need of the audience at any one time, based on their need to learn, feel, or behave in particular ways.

Learn

Where learning is the priority, the overall goal should be to inform or educate the target audience. If the offering is new, it will be important to make the target audience aware of the offering's existence and to inform them of the brand's key attributes and benefits. This is a common use for advertising as it has the capacity to reach both large and targeted audiences. Other than making them aware of the offering's existence, other tasks include showing the target audience how a brand is superior to competitive offerings, perhaps demonstrating how an offering works and educating the audience about when and in what circumstances the brand should be used.

Feel

Once the audience is aware of a brand and knows something about how it might be useful to them, it is important that they develop a positive attitude towards the brand. This can be achieved by presenting the brand with a set of emotional values that it is thought will appeal and be of interest to the audience. These values need to be repeated in subsequent communications to reinforce the brand attitudes.

Research Insight 10.3

To take your learning further, you might wish to read this influential paper.

Gilliland, D.I. and Johnston, W.J. (1997). Toward a model of business-to-business marketing communications effects. *Industrial Marketing Management*, 26, 15–29.

An interesting paper that is based around a model that is designed to address how marketing communications works in a business-to-business environment. The authors introduce a number of important concepts and issues that relate to the subject in different ways.

Visit the **Online Resource Centre** to read the abstract and access the full paper.

Marketing communications should be used to involve and immerse people in a brand. So, for example, advertising or brand placement within films and music videos will help show how it fits in with a desirable set of values and lifestyles. Use of suitable music, characters that reflect the values of either the current target audience or an aspirational group, a tone of voice, colours, and images all help to create a particular emotional disposition and understanding about what the brand represents or stands for. For some people, advertising only works at an emotional level and the cognitive approach is irrelevant.

Do

Most organizations find that, to be successful, they need to use a much broader set of tools, and that the goal is to change the behaviour of the target audience. This behavioural change may be about getting people to buy the brand, but it may often be about motivating them to visit a website, call for a brochure, fill in an application form, or just encouraging them to visit a shop and sample the brand free of payment and any other risk. This behavioural change is also referred to as a 'call to action'.

When the accent is on using marketing communications to drive behaviour and action, **direct-response advertising** can be effective. It is said that 40% of TV ads have a telephone number or website address. However, sales promotion, direct marketing, and personal selling are particularly effective at influencing behaviour and calling the audience to act.

The Role of Marketing Communications in Marketing

Marketing communications are used to achieve one of two principal goals. The first concerns the development of brand values (i.e., feelings, emotions, and beliefs about a brand or organization). Brand communication seeks to make us think positively about a brand, and helps us to remember and develop positive brand attitudes in the hope that when we are ready to buy that type of offering again, we will buy brand X because we feel positively about it. *The Guardian* knew that they had to use marketing communications to change the perception that some people had of the newspaper.

The alternative and more contemporary goal is to use communications to make us behave in particular ways. Rather than spend lots of money developing worthy and positive attitudes towards brands, the view of many today is that we should use this money to encourage people to behave differently. This might be through buying the offering, or driving people to a website, requesting a brochure, or making a telephone call. This is called behaviour change and is driven by using messages that provide audiences with a reason to act, or what is referred to as a **call-to-action**. *The Guardian* had to use marketing communications to increase the number and frequency of visitors to their website—in other words, a change of behaviour.

So, on the one hand, communications can be used to develop brand feelings and, on the other, to change or manage the behaviour of the target audience. These are not mutually exclusive; for example, many TV advertisements are referred to as direct-response ads because they not only attempt to create brand values but also carry a website address, telephone number, or details of a special offer (sales promotion). In other words, the two goals are mixed in a hybrid approach.

The success of marketing communication depends on the extent to which messages engage their audiences. These audiences can be seen to fall into three main groups.

1 Customers—these may be consumers or end-user organizations.

2 Channel members—each organization is part of a network of other organizations such as suppliers, retailers, wholesalers, value-added resellers, distributors, and other retailers who join together, often freely, to make the offering available to end-users.

3 General stakeholders—organizations and people who either influence or are influenced by the organization. These may be shareholders, the financial community, trade unions, employees, the local community, or others.

Therefore marketing communications involves not just customers but also a range of other stakeholders. It can be used to reach consumers as well as business audiences.

Marketing Communications Tasks

Digitalization has had a large impact on marketing communications. Over the past decade there have been some sizeable changes to the way the marketing communications industry is structured, not just in the UK but across the globe. One of the most important of these has been the emergence of a number of powerful and dominant industry groups, such as WPP and News Corporation, whose business interests span cross-media ownership, content development, and delivery. The changing industry structure is a response to several variables, particularly developments in technology, the configuration of the communications mix and media used by organizations, and the way in which client-side managers are expected to operate. These changes mean that marketing communication in general, and advertising in particular, is in constant flux (see Market Insight 10.3 and Chapters 11 and 12).

Despite these constant changes the task of marketing communications has remained the same. Fundamentally, marketing communications can be used to engage audiences by

Table 10.1 The DRIP tasks for marketing communications

Marketing communication tasks	Explanation
To differentiate	In many markets, there is little to separate brands (e.g. mineral water, coffee, printers). In these cases, it is the images created by marketing communications that help *differentiate* one brand from another and position them so that consumers develop positive attitudes and make purchasing decisions.
To reinforce	Communications may be used to *remind* people of a need they might have or of the benefits of past transactions with a view to convincing them that they should enter into a similar exchange. In addition, it is possible to provide *reassurance* or comfort either immediately prior to an exchange or, more commonly, post purchase. This is important as it helps to retain current customers and improve profitability. This approach to business is much more cost effective than constantly striving to lure new customers.
To inform	One of the most common uses of marketing communications is to *inform* and make potential customers aware of the features and benefits of an organization's offering. In addition, marketing communications can be used to educate audiences, to show them how to use an offering or what to do in particular situations.
To persuade	Communication may attempt to *persuade* current and potential customers of the desirability of entering into an exchange relationship.

undertaking one of four main tasks, referred to by Fill (2002) as the **DRIP** model. In no particular order, communications can be used to differentiate brands and organizations, to reinforce brand memories and expectations, to inform (i.e. to make aware or educate audiences), and finally to persuade them to do things or to behave in particular ways. See Table 10.1 for an explanation of each of these tasks.

Visit the Online Resource Centre and complete Internet Activity 10.3 to learn more about the way the fashion house Burberry uses marketing communications.

These tasks are not mutually exclusive; indeed, campaigns might be designed to target two or three of them. For example, the launch of a new brand will require that audiences be informed, made aware of its existence, and enabled to understand how it is different from competitor brands. A brand that is well established might try to reach lapsed customers by reminding them of the key features and benefits and offering them an incentive (persuasion) to buy again. For example, M&S's website Style and Living is a digital magazine designed to showcase what is new in Marks & Spencer's stores and give fashion and style advice. However, it only features offerings available at M&S. The website is an integral part of the company's communication mix and is used, among many other activities, to engage customers with the brand and drive readers into the store to shop.

On the Style & Living website M&S offers fashion and style advice
Source: Courtesy of Marks and Spencer.

Market Insight 10.3
Reinventing Advertising for the Digital Age

The digital age hit advertising like a wrecking ball. It smashed existing power structures and empowered ordinary people to create their own mass communication. It also broke the consumer decision journey into pieces, leaving advertisers to figure out how the new reality fitted together. Here are three important changes shaping the future of advertising.

1. **The zero moment of truth** The first effect of the digital age was the end of control. Brands can no longer control what is being said about them, and in what order or form it reaches the masses. People have the power to universally share and access actual experiences of a brand, influencing the choices of people just starting their own decision journey. The experience of initial users moves 'upstream' to affect future users. Google dubbed this the ZMOT (zero moment of truth). This phenomenon is most clearly illustrated by Yelp reviews, where real customer experience trumps restaurant reviews and own promotions. A quick smartphone search is now the starting point for many brand experiences, and the bridge between initial need and final decision.

2. **The attention economy** The second effect of the digital age was to make it increasingly difficult to buy attention. The media landscape grew more user-centric, putting pressure on brands to earn attention—to engage rather than interrupt. A successful campaign now goes beyond bought media, and straight into the news and your personal newsfeed. Increasingly, that means that the new aim of advertising is to create either fame or friendship: in the first case to make the brand a celebrity that creates a big splash (see Chapter 12, Market Insight 12.4), or in the second case to make the brand become a 'friend', providing relevant updates in social media (H&M on Instagram is a good example). The brand needs to have a social role, which makes it earn attention—again and again—and builds salience and preference over time.

3. **The brand purpose** The third effect is a shift from communication to action—from message to mission, and from talk to walk. It's no longer enough for a brand to claim a benefit—it needs to prove and believably act on it. This creates a need to find a

Market Insight 10.3

continued

Real customer experiences are important to consider in marketing communications
Source: © Gil C/Shutterstock.

clear purpose—a brand mission, ideal, or theme that the brand can put into practice in all contact points—and serves as a platform for innovation and relationship building. This is a property shared by many great brands, but well exemplified by Red Bull's mission to uplift mind and body—'to give you wings'—put into practice through numerous sponsorships, bold stunts, and of course the product itself.

These key changes mark the end of the age of interruption, and the beginning of an age of disruption—for the people, by the people—where smartphones act as decision guides, entertainment centres, and voting booths, all rolled into one. The new advertising model is being built right now, with advertisers looking for new ways to create experiences that are emotional, relevant, and shareable, and will launch brands to fame, familiarity, and (hopefully) fortune.

Theory into Practice

Fundamentally, marketing communications is used to engage audiences. It does so by undertaking one of four main tasks: differentiating, reinforcing, informing, and persuading (DRIP). However, the context in which marketing communications does this has changed dramatically in the past decade. Thus, marketers must constantly update the tools, media, and messages used to achieve engagement.

Market Insight 10.3

continued

Related Topics:

consumer decision-making; digital marketing; mobile marketing; user-generated content; content marketing.

1 **Do you agree with the changes described in this insight?**

2 **How does each of the three changes impact marketing communication?**

3 **What examples have you seen of marketing communications that seem to have been developed with each of the three changes in mind?**

This market insight was kindly contributed by Karl Wikström, Planner, TBWA Stockholm, Sweden.

Marketing Communications Planning

Management's task is to formulate and implement a communication strategy that blends the right mix of tools and media to deliver the right messages in the right place, at the right time, for the right audience. Strategically, the main decisions have to do with defining the appropriate target audience and setting the right objectives. To accomplish this, there are inevitably a series of issues that need to be addressed before decisions can be made. These issues embrace a range of activities, such as developing strategy in the light of both audience and brand characteristics, agreeing communication objectives, and then formulating, implementing, and evaluating marketing communication strategies and plans, many of which need to be integrated—an important topic itself in contemporary marketing communications. Developing the right message and the configuration of the right mix of tools and media are more tactical decisions and will be covered in greater detail in Chapter 11.

To understand what a marketing communications plan should achieve, it is helpful to appreciate the principal tasks facing marketing communications managers.

- Who should receive the messages?
- What should the messages say?
- What image of the organization/brand are receivers expected to retain?
- How much is to be spent establishing this new image?
- How are the messages to be delivered?
- What actions should the receivers take?
- How do we control the whole process once implemented?
- What was achieved?

For many reasons, planning is an essential management activity and, if planned marketing communications are to be developed in an orderly and efficient way, the use of a suitable framework is necessary. A framework for integrated marketing communications plans is presented in Figure 10.8.

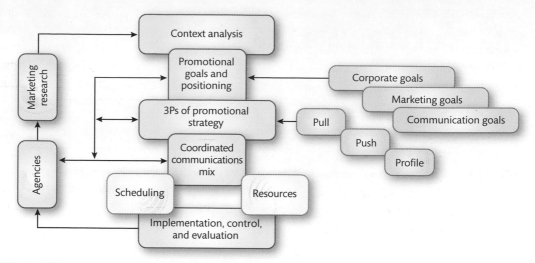

Figure 10.8

The marketing communications planning framework

Source: *Marketing Communications* (6th edn) Fill, C. (2013). Reproduced with the kind permission of Pearson Education Limited. © Pearson Education Limited 2013.

The marketing communications planning framework (MCPF) provides a visual guide to what needs to be achieved and brings together the various elements in a logical sequence of activities. As with all hierarchical planning models, each level of decision-making is built on information generated at a previous level in the model. Another advantage of using the MCPF is that it provides a suitable checklist of activities that need to be considered. The MCPF represents a sequence of decisions that marketing managers undertake when preparing, implementing, and evaluating communication strategies and plans. This framework reflects a deliberate or planned approach to strategic marketing communications.

In practice marketing communications planning is not always developed as a linear process as depicted in this framework. Indeed, many marketing communications decisions are made outside any recognizable framework, as some organizations approach the process as an integrative and sometimes spontaneous activity. However, the MCPF approach presented here is intended to highlight the tasks to be achieved, the way in which they relate to one another, and the order in which they should be accomplished.

Elements of the MCPF

A marketing communications plan should be developed for each level of communications activity, from strategy to individual tactical aspects of a campaign. The difference between them is the level of detail that is included.

Context Analysis

The marketing plan is the bedrock of context analysis (CA). This will already have been prepared and contains important information about the target segments, business and marketing goals, competitors, and the timescales in which the goals are to be achieved. The CA needs to elaborate and build on this information to provide the detail so that the plan can be developed and justified.

The first and vital step is to analyse the context in which marketing communications activities are to occur. Unlike a situation analysis used in general planning models, context analysis should be communications oriented and use the marketing plan as a foundation. There are four main components of the communications context analysis: customer, business, internal, and external contexts.

Understanding the customer context requires information and market research data about the target audiences specified in the marketing plan. Here, detailed information about their needs, perceptions, motivation, attitudes, and decision-making characteristics relative to the proposition category (or issue) is necessary. In addition, information about the media and the people they use for information about the category needs to be determined.

Understanding the business or marketing context, and the marketing communications environment in particular, is also important as these influence what has to be achieved. If the marketing strategy specifies growth through market penetration, then not only will messages need to reflect this goal but it will also be important to understand how competitors are communicating with the target audience and which media they are using to do this.

Analysis of the internal context is undertaken to determine the resource capability with respect to supporting marketing communications. Three principal areas need to be reviewed:

- people resources (are people, including agencies, with suitable marketing communications skills available?);
- financial resources (how much is available to invest in marketing communications?);
- technological resources (are the right systems and processes available to support marketing communications?).

The final area to be reviewed is the wider external context. Similar to the areas considered during the strategic analysis, emphasis is placed on the political, economic, societal, ecological, and technological conditions. However, the impact on marketing communications needs to be emphasized. For example, if economic conditions become tough, people have lower levels of disposable income. Sales promotions, promotional offers, and extended credit terms become more attractive in this context.

Context analysis provides the rationale for the rest of the plan. It is from the CA that the marketing objectives (from the marketing plan) and the marketing communications objectives are derived. The type, form, and style of the message are rooted in the characteristics of the target audience, and the media selected to convey messages should be based on the nature of the tasks, the media preferences and habits of the audience, and the resources available.

Marketing Communications Objectives

Having performed a context analysis, the next step is to define marketing communication objectives. Many organizations assume that their marketing communications goals are the same as their sales targets. This is incorrect because there are so many elements contributing to sales, such as competitor pricing, product attributes, and distributor policies, that making marketing communications solely responsible for sales is naive and unrealistic. Ideally, marketing communications objectives should consist of three main elements: corporate, marketing, and communications objectives:

- Corporate objectives are derived from the business or marketing plan. They refer to the mission and the business area that the organization believes it should be in.
- Marketing objectives are derived from the marketing plan and are sales oriented. These might be market share, sales revenues, volumes, return on investment (ROI), and other profitability indicators.

- Communications objectives are derived from the context analysis and refer to levels of awareness, perception, comprehension/knowledge, attitudes, and overall degree of preference for a brand. The choice of communications goal depends on the tasks that need to be accomplished.

These three elements constitute the overall set of marketing communications objectives. They should be set out in **SMART** terminology, i.e. each should be specific, measurable, achievable, realistic, and timed. Thus, at this point in the planning process, the brand's positioning intentions are developed and these should be related to the market, the customers, or a product dimension (see also Chapter 6). The justification for this will have been identified in the context analysis.

Marketing Communications Strategy

The marketing communications strategy is derived from the objectives and context analysis. There are three types of strategy: pull for the end-user markets, push for the trade and channel intermediaries, and profile designed to reach all significant stakeholders. The DRIP roles of marketing communications can be used to elaborate the relevant strategy to be pursued. For example, if a new brand is being launched, the first task will be to inform and differentiate the brand for members of the trade before using a pull strategy to inform and differentiate the brand for the target end-user customers. For example, the UK retailer John Lewis has developed a reputation for a series of highly emotional and well-executed campaigns in the lead-up to Christmas. In the 2015 campaign, the TV ads used a little-known Norwegian artist named Aurora to cover Oasis's *Half the World Away*. The song subsequently made its way on to the official UK chart.

An organization wishing to signal a change of strategy and/or a change of name following a merger or acquisition may choose to use a profile strategy, and the primary task will be to inform about the name change. An organization experiencing declining sales may choose to remind customers of a need or it may choose to improve sales through persuasion.

A traditional pull strategy in the grocery sector used to be based on delivering mass media advertising supported by below-the-line communications, most notably sales promotions delivered in-store and through direct mail and email to registered customers (e.g. Tesco Clubcard customers). The decision to use a pull strategy should be supported by a core message that will try to differentiate (position), remind or reassure, inform, or persuade the audience to think, feel, or behave in a particular way. This approach can be interpreted as a pull/remind or pull/position communication strategy, as this describes the audience and direction of the strategy and also clarifies what the strategy seeks to achieve.

A push strategy should be treated in a similar way. The need to consider the core message is paramount as it conveys information about the essence of the strategy. Push/inform, push/position, or push/key accounts/discount might be examples of possible terminology.

Although these three strategies are represented here as individual entities, they are often used as a 'cluster'. For example, the launch of a new toothpaste brand will involve a push strategy to get the product on the shelves of the key supermarkets and independent retailers. The strategy would be to gain retailer acceptance of the new brand and to position it for them as a profitable new brand. The goal is to get the toothpaste on the retailers' shelves. To achieve this, personal selling supported by trade sales promotions will be the main marketing communications tools. A push strategy alone would be insufficient to persuade a retailer to stock a new brand. The promise of a pull strategy aimed at creating brand awareness and customer excitement needs to be created, accompanied by appropriate public relations activities and any initial sales promotions necessary to motivate consumers to change their brand of toothpaste. The next step is to create particular brand associations and thereby position the brand in the minds of the target consumer audience. Messages may be primarily informational or emotional, but will endeavour to convey a brand promise. This may be accompanied or followed by the use of incentives to encourage consumers to trial the product. To support the brand, carelines and a website, as well as a buyer reference point, will need to be put in place to provide credibility.

Communications Method

This part of the plan includes a number of activities. A creative or message needs to be developed for each specified target audience in the strategy. This should be based on the positioning requirements and will often be developed by an outside communications agency. Simultaneously, it is necessary to formulate the right mix of communication tools to reach each particular audience. In addition, the right media mix needs to be determined, both online and offline. Again, media experts will most probably undertake this task. Here, integration is regarded as an important feature of the communication mix. This is covered more in detail in Chapter 11.

The Schedule

The next step is to schedule the way in which the campaign is to be delivered. Events and activities should be scheduled according to the goals and the strategic thrust. So, if it is necessary to communicate with the trade prior to a public launch, those activities tied into the push strategy should be scheduled prior to those calculated to support the pull strategy. Similarly, if awareness is a goal, then, funds permitting, it may be best first to use TV and poster ads offline plus banners and search engine ads online before using sales promotions (unless sampling is used), direct marketing, point of purchase, and personal selling.

Resources

The resources necessary to support the plan need to be determined. These refer not only to the financial issues but also to the quality of available marketing expertise. This means that the right sort of marketing knowledge may not be present internally and may have to be recruited. For example, if a customer relationship management system (CRM) initiative is being launched, it will be important to have people with knowledge and skills related to running CRM programmes. With regard to external skills, it is necessary that the current communications agencies are capable of delivering the creative and media plan. This is an important part of the plan, which is often avoided or forgotten about. Software project planning tools, simple spreadsheets, or Gantt charts can be used not only to schedule the campaign but also to chart the resources relating to the actual and budgeted costs of using the selected tools and media.

Control and Evaluation

Once launched, campaigns should be monitored. This is to ensure that if there is any major deviation from the plan, opportunities exist to get back on track as soon as possible. In addition, all marketing communications plans should be evaluated. There are numerous methods of evaluating the individual performance of the tools and the media used, but perhaps the most important measures concern the achievement of the communication objectives.

Feedback

The marketing communications planning process is completed when **feedback** is provided. Not only should information regarding the overall outcome of a campaign be considered, but so should individual aspects of the activity. For example, the performance of the individual tools used within the campaign, whether sufficient resources were invested, the appropriateness of the strategy in the first place, whether any problems were encountered during implementation, and the relative ease with which the objectives were accomplished are aspects that need to be fed back to all internal and external parties associated with the planning process.

This feedback is vitally important because it provides information for the context analysis that anchors the next campaign. Information fed back in a formal and systematic manner constitutes an opportunity for organizations to learn from their previous campaign activities, a point often overlooked and neglected.

Cultural Aspects of Marketing Communications

Marketing communications has the potential to influence more than just customers. Indeed, a wide range of other stakeholders, such as suppliers, employees, religious and faith groups, trade unions, and local communities, can be targeted.

The tools, media, and messages used by organizations influence, and are influenced by, the culture and environment in which they operate. Culture and related belief systems are significant factors in the way organizations choose to communicate in the different areas and regions in which they operate. For example, communications based on the strong theory of advertising are observed more frequently in North America, whereas examples of the weak theory are quite prevalent in Europe.

In this final part of the chapter, consideration is given to some of the cultural issues associated with marketing communications (see Market Insight 10.4 for an example).

Market Insight 10.4
Advertising, Arabic Style

Cultural values are an important consideration for brands in the Middle East, especially when advertising to Muslim consumers. While each country has its own guidelines to regulate advertising messages and prevent offensive products and services from being promoted, brands need to take cultural values into consideration when developing advertising for Muslim consumers across the region.

In many Middle Eastern countries advertising alcohol or gambling is forbidden, and there are other cultural taboos that brands need to be aware of. In Saudi Arabia, for example, women must wear black if they are shown outside the house, and showing dogs in the house or pigs in any advertising is not allowed.

Shaking hands or serving food with your left hand is also considered a cultural taboo, and so advertising must be sensitive to this.

Culture dictates that any form of marketing communications should be respectful of the Islamic faith and show respect for women and the elderly. Advertising messages should be fair and truthful, and hence avoid being critical of competitive brands.

Heritage is also seen to be an important part of Middle East culture. Many brands choose to reflect cultural aspects in their advertising campaigns and draw heavily on the cultural heritage of the country in their communications strategy. It is not unusual

Market Insight 10.4
continued

for advertising in the Gulf States to include images of traditional sailing vessels (dhows) or camels to represent their trading heritage. Arabic language and calligraphy are other devices used by brands to show an appreciation of cultural heritage.

Family plays a central role in Middle Eastern culture, and the family is often a focus of advertising. In 2014 PepsiCo ran a campaign in the Middle East called Ramadan Reunions, which was based on getting families together for the month of Ramadan. As Ramadan is traditionally seen as a month of gatherings, this emotional campaign sought to reunite families

and draws on the importance of family bonds among Muslim consumers. Similarly, in 2014 Johnson's Baby developed a campaign called Grandparents Frame, which distributed digital picture frames to grandparents in the Middle East, allowing them to receive images of their grandchildren living abroad. The campaign demonstrates the importance of family in the Middle East and highlights how powerful marketing communications can be when it taps into the cultural values of the consumer.

Sources: Otterman (2007); Traboulsi and Guidère (2009); Anon. (2014a); Anon. (2014b)

Theory into Practice

Given that marketing communications is an audience-centred activity, it is important to keep in mind that audiences are part of a cultural context, which will influence how they interpret the messages used. When working with marketing communications on a global

scale, marketers must bear in mind how both legal and cultural requirements differ. As highlighted in this market insight both PepsiCo and Johnson & Johnson have adjusted their advertising in the region to align with these requirements.

Related Topics:

consumer decision-making; international marketing; culture; advertising.

1 **What cultural values are most important for marketers to consider in your country?**

2 **What would be the key holidays for advertisers to consider in your country?**

3 **What role do older people typically play in advertising in your country?**

This market insight was kindly contributed by Dr Sarah Turnbull, University of Portsmouth, UK.

Culture

Culture refers to the values, beliefs, ideas, customs, actions, and symbols that are learnt by members of particular societies. Marketing communications should be an audience-centred activity, whether those audiences are located domestically or anywhere around the globe. Therefore, as there are so many international, regional, and local communities, each with cultural variances, so the development of marketing communications for these audiences must be based on a sound understanding of their culture.

> **Table 10.2 Characteristics of culture**
>
> | Cultural characteristic | Explanation |
> | --- | --- |
> | Learned | Culture is not innate or instinctual, otherwise everyone would behave in the same way. Human beings across the world do not behave uniformly or predictably, and they learn values and behaviours that are shared with common groups. Therefore different cultures exist and there are boundaries within cultures, framing behaviours and lifestyles. |
> | Interrelated | There are deep connections between different elements within a culture. Therefore family, religion, business/work, and social status are interlinked. |
> | Shared | Cultural values are passed through family, religion, education, and the media. This progression of values enables culture to be passed from generation to generation. This is important as it provides consistency, stability, and direction for social behaviour and beliefs. |

Source: *Global Marketing: A Decision-Oriented Approach* (4th edn), Hollensen, S. (2007). Pearson Education Limited.

Culture is important because it provides individuals within a society with a sense of identity and an understanding of what is deemed to be acceptable behaviour. According to Hollensen (2007), it is commonly agreed that culture has three key characteristics: culture is learned, inter-related, and shared. See Table 10.2 for a fuller account of these variables.

These boundaries between cultures are not fixed or rigid, as this would suggest that cultures are static. Instead they evolve and change as members of a society adjust to new technologies, government policies, changing values, and demographic changes, to mention but a few

Research Insight 10.4

To take your learning further, you might wish to read this influential paper.

Harris, G. (1996). International advertising: developmental and implementational issues. *Journal of Marketing Management*, **12(6), 551–60.**

This paper considers the international advertising practices of several major advertisers (multinationals), and explores the extent to which they attempt to standardize their advertising across the countries in which they have a presence. The conclusion that no one organization adopts full standardization was important at the time of publication, and paved the way for the subsequent stream of research in this field.

Visit the **Online Resource Centre** to read the abstract and access the full paper.

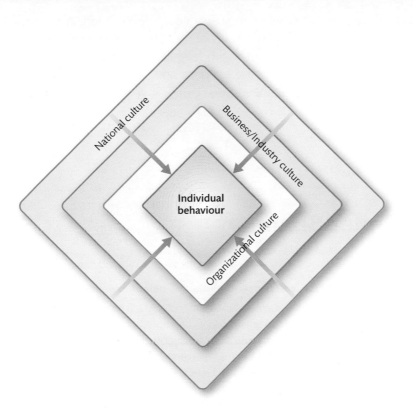

Figure 10.9

Layers of culture

Source: *Global Marketing*: *A Decision-Oriented Approach* (5th edn), Hollensen, S. (2010). Pearson Education Limited.

dynamic variables. Unsurprisingly, therefore, brands and symbols used to represent brands have different meanings as they are interpreted in the light of the prevailing culture.

Culture consists of various layers. Hollensen (2010) refers to a nest of cultures, with one inside another, a structure that is similar to a 'Russian doll' (Figure 10.9). Here, it can be imagined that a buyer in one country and a seller in another are faced with several layers of culture, all interrelated and all influencing an individual's behaviour.

- National culture—sets out the cultural concepts and the legislative framework governing the way business is undertaken.

- Industry/business culture—particular business sectors adopt a way of doing business within a competitive framework. The shipping business, for example, will have its own way of conducting itself based on its own heritage. As a result, all participants know what is expected and understand the rules of the game.

- Organizational culture—not only does an organization have an overall culture but the various subcultures also have a system of shared values, beliefs, meanings, and behaviours.

- Individual behaviour—each individual is affected by, and learns from, the various cultural levels.

Marketing communications, at both a formal and informal level, needs to assimilate these different levels to ensure that an individual's behaviour is understood and the decision-making processes and procedures within which they operate are appreciated. In many markets, there is little to separate brands (e.g. mineral water, coffee, printers). In these cases, it is the images created by marketing communications that help differentiate one brand from another and position them so that consumers develop positive attitudes and make purchasing decisions. The way in which different societies perceive these same brands is a reflection of the cultural drivers that frame people's perceptions.

⟳ Chapter Summary

To consolidate your learning, the key points from this chapter are summarized here.

■ **Describe the nature, purpose, and scope of marketing communications.**

Marketing communications is a management process through which an organization attempts to engage with its various audiences. Marketing communications, or promotion as it was originally called, is one of the 4Ps of the marketing mix. It is used to communicate an organization's offer relating to products, services, or the overall organization. In broad terms this management activity consists of several components. There are the communications experienced by audiences relating to their use of products and the consumption of services. There are also communications arising from unplanned or unintended experiences, and there are planned marketing communications.

■ **Explain the three models of communication and describe how personal influences can enhance the effectiveness of marketing communication activities.**

The linear or one-way model of communication is the traditional mass media interpretation of how communication works. The two-way model incorporates the influence of other people in the communication process, whereas the interactional model explains how communication flows not just between sender and receiver but throughout a network of people. Interaction is about actions that lead to a response and, most importantly in an age of interactive communication, interactivity is a prelude to dialogue, the highest or purest form of communication.

■ **Understand the models used to explain how marketing communications and advertising work.**

These models have evolved from sequential approaches such as AIDA and the HoE models. A circular model of the attitude construct helps understanding of the tasks of marketing communication, namely to inform audiences, to create feelings and a value associated with offerings, and to drive behaviour.

■ **Understand the role of marketing communications in marketing.**

The role of marketing communications is to engage audiences, and there are four main tasks that it can be used to complete. These tasks are summarized as DRIP, i.e. to differentiate, reinforce, inform, or persuade audiences to behave in particular ways. Several of these tasks can be undertaken simultaneously within a campaign.

■ **Describe the different steps in the strategic marketing communications planning process.**

Management's task is to formulate and implement a communication strategy that blends the right mix of tools and media to deliver the right messages in the right place, at the right time, for the right audience. The marketing communications planning framework (MCPF) identifies the following key steps in this process: context analysis, marketing communications objectives, marketing communications strategy, communications method, scheduling, resources, control and evaluation, and feedback.

■ **Describe what culture is and explain how it can impact on the use of marketing communications.**

Culture refers to the values, beliefs, ideas, customs, actions, and symbols that are learned by members of particular societies. Culture is important because it provides individuals within a society with a sense of identity and an understanding of what is deemed to be acceptable behaviour. Culture is learnt, the elements are interrelated, and culture is shared among members of a society or group. Organizations that practice marketing communications in international environments have to be fully aware of the cultural dimensions associated with each of their markets. In addition, they need to consider whether it is better to adopt a standardized approach and use the same unmodified campaigns across all markets, or adapt campaigns to meet the needs of local markets.

Review Questions

1 What role does marketing communication ('promotion') play in the marketing mix?

2 What is the linear model of communication and each of its main elements?

3 Make brief notes outlining the meaning of interaction and how dialogue can develop.

4 What are the main differences between opinion leaders and opinion formers?

5 What is a hierarchy of effects model?

6 What are the strong and weak theories of advertising?

7 Why is the circular interpretation of the attitude construct better than the linear form?

8 Explain the key role of marketing communications and find examples to illustrate the meaning of each element in the DRIP framework.

9 What is the relation between corporate objectives, marketing objectives, and communications objectives?

10 Hollensen (2010) argues that culture is made up of three elements and four layers. Name them.

Worksheet Summary

To apply the knowledge you have gained from this chapter and test your understanding of marketing communications visit the **Online Resource Centre** and complete Worksheet 10.1.

Discussion Questions

1 Having read Case Insight 10.1, how would you advise the marketing team at *The Guardian* to use marketing communications to change the perceptions and behaviour of Progressive newspaper readers?

2 Consider the key market exchange characteristics that will favour the use of linear or one-way communication and then repeat the exercise with respect to interactional communication. Discuss the differences and find examples to illustrate these conditions.

3 Day Birger et Mikkelsen is a leading Danish fashion retailer, providing a range of fashion clothing for young people aged 18–35. As a marketing assistant you have just returned from a conference at which

the role of personal influencers was highlighted. You now wish to convey your new knowledge to your manager. Prepare a brief report in which you explain the nature of opinion leaders and opinion formers as well as consumer word of mouth in general and discuss how they might be used by Day Birger et Mikkelsen to improve their marketing communications. Using at least three examples, make it clear who you think would make good opinion formers for Day Birger et Mikkelsen.

4 Discuss the extent to which marketing communications should be used by organizations to persuade audiences to buy their offerings.

5 To what extent should organizations operating an advertising standardization policy consider the culture of the countries they are operating in?

@ Visit the **Online Resource Centre** and complete the **Multiple Choice Questions** to assess your knowledge of Chapter 10.

Glossary

AIDA a hierarchy of effects or sequential model used to explain how advertising works. AIDA stands for awareness, interest, desire, and action (a sale).

ATR a framework developed by Ehrenberg to explain how advertising works. ATR stands for awareness–trial–reinforcement.

call-to-action a part of a marketing communication message that explicitly requests that the receiver act in a particular way.

decoding that part of the communication process in which receivers unpack the various components of the message, and begin to make sense and give the message meaning.

dialogue the development of knowledge that occurs when all parties to a communication event listen, adapt, and reason with one another about a specific topic.

direct-response advertising advertisements that contain mechanisms such as telephone numbers, website addresses, email addresses, and snail mail addresses. These are designed to encourage viewers to respond immediately to the ads. Most commonly used on television and known as DRTV.

DRIP the four primary tasks marketing communications can be expected to accomplish: differentiate, reinforce, inform, and persuade.

encoding a part of the communication process when the sender selects a combination of appropriate words, pictures, symbols, and music to represent a message to be transmitted.

feedback a part of the communication process referring to the responses offered by receivers.

hierarchy of effects (HoE) general sequential models used to explain how advertising works. Popular in the 1960s–1980s, these models provided a template that encouraged the development and use of communication objectives.

interaction model the flow of communication messages that leads to mutual understanding about a specific topic.

noise influences that distort information in the communication process and, in turn, make it difficult for the receiver to decode and interpret a message correctly.

opinion followers people who turn to opinion leaders and formers for advice and information about products and services they are interested in purchasing or using.

opinion formers people who exert personal influence because of their profession, authority, education, or status associated with the object of the communication process. They are not part of the same peer group as the people they influence.

opinion leaders people who are predisposed to receiving information and then reprocessing it in order to influence others. They belong to the same peer group as the people they influence; they are not distant or removed.

personal selling the use of interpersonal communications with the aim of encouraging people to purchase particular products and services, for personal gain and reward.

product class a broad category referring to various types of related products, e.g. cat food, shampoo, or cars.

receivers individuals or organizations who have seen, heard, smelt, or read a message.

SMART an approach used to write effective objectives. SMART stands for specific, measurable, achievable, realistic, and timed.

strong theory a persuasion-based theory designed to explain how advertising works.

two-step model a communication model that reflects a receiver's response to a message.

weak theory a view that suggests advertising is a weak force and works by reminding people of preferred brands.

word of mouth a form of communication founded on interpersonal messages regarding products or services sought or consumed. The receiver regards the communicator as impartial and credible as they are not attempting to sell products or services.

References

Anon. (2014a). JOHNSON's Baby Grandparents Frame (2014) Impact BBDO website. Retrieve from: http://impactbbdo.com/#!&pageid = 0&subsection = 9&itemid – 27 (accessed 20 November 2015).

Anon. (2014b). PepsiCo Ramadan Reunions. Impact BBDO website. Retrieve from: http://impactbbdo.com/#!&pageid = 0&subsection = 9&itemid = 51 (accessed 20 November 2015).

Ballantyne, D. (2004). Dialogue and its role in the development of relationship specific knowledge. *Journal of Business and Industrial Marketing*, 19(2), 114–23.

Berkman, H. and Gilson, C. (1986). *Consumer Behavior: Concepts and Strategies*. Boston, MA: Kent Publishing.

Chan, K.K. and Misra, S. (1990). Characteristics of the opinion leader: a new dimension. *Journal of Advertising*, 19(3), 53–60.

Duncan, T. and Moriarty, S. (1998). A communication-based marketing model for managing relationships. *Journal of Marketing*, 62(April), 1–13.

Ehrenberg, A. S. C. (1974). Repetitive advertising and the consumer. *Journal of Advertising Research*, 14(April), 25–34

Ehrenberg, A.S.C. (1997). How do consumers come to buy a new brand?' *Admap*, March, 20–4.

Fill, C. (2002), *Marketing Communications: Contexts, Strategies and Applications* (3rd edn). Harlow: FT/Prentice Hall.

Fill, C. (2013), *Marketing Communications: Brands, Experiences and Participation* (6th edn). Harlow: FT/Prentice Hall.

Friestad, M. and Wright, P. (1994). The persuasion knowledge model: how people cope with persuasion attempts. *Journal of Consumer Research*, 21(1), 1–31.

Gilliland, D.I. and Johnston, W.J. (1997). Toward a model of business-to-business marketing communications effects. *Industrial Marketing Management*, 26, 15–29.

Harris, G. (1996). International advertising: developmental and implementational issues. *Journal of Marketing Management*, 12(6), 551–60.

Hoffman, D.L. and Novak, P.T. (1996). Marketing in hyper computer-mediated environments: conceptual foundations. *Journal of Marketing*, 60(July), 50–68.

Hollensen, S. (2010). *Global Marketing: A Decision-Oriented Approach* (5th edn). Harlow: FT/Prentice Hall.

Hughes, G. and Fill, C. (2007). Redefining the nature and format of the marketing communications mix. *Marketing Review*, 7(1), 45–57.

Jones, J.P. (1991). Over-promise and under-delivery. *Marketing and Research Today*, 19(40), 195–203.

Katz, E. and Lazarsfeld, P.F. (1955). *Personal Influence: The Part Played by People in the Flow of Mass Communication*. Glencoe, IL: Free Press.

Keller E. and Fay, B. (2012). Word-of-mouth advocacy: a new key to advertising effectiveness. *Journal of Advertising Research*, 52(4), 459–64.

Kosoff, M. and Jacobs. H. (2015). The 15 most popular YouTubers in the world. *Business Insider* 18 September 2015. Retrieve from: http://uk.businessinsider.com/the-most-popular-youtuber-stars-in-the-world?r = US&IR = T (accessed 24 January 2016).

Lavidge, R.J. and Steiner, G.A. (1961). A model for predictive measurements of advertising effectiveness. *Journal of Marketing*, 25(6), 59–62.

Moses, L. (2011). Vogue casts 1,000 influencers for network. *Adweek*, 52(26), 11 July. Retrieved from: http://www.adweek.com/news/advertising-branding/vogue-casts-1000-influencers-network-133299 (accessed 16 December 2012).

Moynihan, T (2015). Yes, there's a market for that $10,000 Apple Watch. *Wired*, 3 September. Retrieve from: http://www.wired.com/2015/03/yes-theres-market-10000-apple-watch/ (accessed 24 January 2016).

Otterman, S. (2007). Does the veiled look sell? Egyptian advertisers grapple with the hijab. *Arab Media and Society*, Issue 2. Retrieved from: http://www.arabmediasociety.com/?article = 205 (accessed 2 December 2015).

Pierce, D (2015). Iphone killer: the secret history of the Apple watch. *Wired*, May. Retrieved from: http://www.wired.com/2015/04/the-apple-watch/ (accessed 24 January 2016).

Rosengren, L. (2012). Han hoppade av Chalmers—blev heltidskändis på Youtube. IDG.se, 2012-11-1. Retrieved from: http://cio.idg.se/2.1782/1.477094/han-hoppade-av-chalmers—blev-heltidskandis-pa-youtube (accessed 24 January 2016).

Schramm, W. (1955). How communication works. In W. Schramm (ed.), *The Process and Effects of Mass Communications*. Urbana, IL: University of Illinois Press, 3–26.

Shannon, C. and Weaver, W. (1962). *The Mathematical Theory of Communication*. Urbana, IL: University of Illinois Press.

Stokes, D. and Lomax, W. (2002). Taking control of word of mouth marketing: the case of an entrepreneurial hotelier.

Journal of Small Business and Enterprise Development, 9(4), 349–57.

Strong, E.K. (1925). *The Psychology of Selling*. New York: McGraw-Hill.

Tamburro, P. (2014). PewDiePie's $7.4 million salary actually highlights YouTube's low wages. *Crave Online*, 8 July. Retrieved from: http://www.craveonline.com/site/875679-pewdiepies-7-4-million-salary-actually-highlights-youtubes-low-wages#aMwrUeZ4WY2Cv86K.99 (24 January 2016).

Theodorson, S.A. and Theodorson, G.R. (1969). *A Modern Dictionary of Sociology*. New York: Cromwell.

Traboulsi, S. and Guidère, M. (2009). Tell me which country you live in, I'll tell you which ad to broadcast. *The Observers France* 24, 20 July. Retrieve from: http://observers.france24.com/en/20090720-tell-which-country-you-live—tell-you-which-ad-broadcast-saudi-arabia-advertising-rules (accessed 2 December 2015).

Williams, R. (2014). Apple launches iPhone 6, 6 Plus and Apple Watch. *The Telegraph*, 9 September. Retrieved from: http://www.telegraph.co.uk/technology/apple/11086000/Apple-launches-iPhone-6-6-Plus-and-Apple-Watch.html (accessed 24 January 2016).

Chapter 11
Configuring the Marketing Communications Mix

Can I paint the world as it feels, not just as it looks?

In their works, artists leave a legacy that stimulates the mind and challenges existing perceptions. By supporting the visual arts, we offer our clients, our people and our alumni scope for inspiration and new perspectives. This helps make our world work better.

ey.com/uk/arts

VIVE UNA #VIDASOBERANA

SOBERANA

CERVEZA

SOBERANA

Learning Outcomes

After studying this chapter you should be able to:

▶ Describe the role and configuration of the marketing communications mix

▶ Explain the characteristics of each of the primary tools, messages, and media

▶ Set out the criteria that should be used to select the right communications mix

▶ Discuss the changing marketing communications landscape

▶ Consider the principles and issues associated with integrated marketing communications

Case Insight 11.1
Budweiser Budvar

Market Insight 11.1
Variable Mixes

Market Insight 11.2
Adele Teases Out Her Mix for *25*

Market Insight 11.3
Damart Modernizes Its Welcome Programme

Market Insight 11.4
EY Uses Art to Distinguish Itself

Market Insight 11.5
A New Integrated Mix for Soberana

Case Insight 11.1
Budweiser Budvar

How should a heritage brand in the Czech Republic design a campaign to reposition itself against competing foreign brands? We speak to Budweiser Budvar's advertising agency account director, Lubos Jahoda, to find out more.

Budweiser Budvar has a 750 year tradition of brewing beer in the Czech Republic. Although there has been a long-running dispute with other brewers who use the same Budweiser name, one of the current issues facing the Budvar brand concerns the decline in the size of the overall Czech beer market. Since 2009 there has been a shift towards small authentic local breweries. This is because Czechs believe the multinationals (SAB Miller, Heineken, Molson Coors) have destroyed the essence of Czech beer by using inferior ingredients and making what is called 'EuroBeer', a universal beer that has no clear distinguishing taste or character. The big breweries have been trying to resolve the situation through innovation, as a result of which we now see loads of 'radler' beer (flavoured beer) in the market.

Surprisingly, many customers saw Budvar as a 'big brewery team', similar to the big breweries. We have also seen consumers move from away from Budvar towards small local breweries. But, as anyone who has ever visited the brewery knows, Budvar is more authentic than the smallest of breweries, using the same ingredients and production processes as were used 118 years ago. Another problem concerns the way the brand was perceived. Budvar is seen as a very rational beer, a quality beer or 'Czech beer', but there is little emotional connection with the brand.

It was clear that we needed to reposition the Budvar brand, to differentiate it and enable Czech consumers to make an emotional connection with the brand. The question was how best to achieve this.

Research has shown that Czech people are generally more inclined to adopt the line of least resistance in order to avoid problems, and that means agreeing or saying 'yes'. However, many Czech people deeply resent such concessions and do not identify themselves with these types of compromise. This issue of dissent provided us with a pertinent platform on which to reposition the brand. This is because Budvar has repeatedly rejected various pressures. For example, we have refused to dumb down or use substitute ingredients. Budvar has also rejected the idea that we should reduce the maturing time during the brewing process. We have also refused outright to sell our brand name to our competitors, and have also said no to licensing production away from České Budějovice (Budweis).

From this insight we developed the NO campaign, one that is rooted in the Czech psyche, Budvar's foundations, and can be seen in everything Budvar does, from just 'making beer' to fighting for its name and reputation across the world. The campaign had two main aims. First at a product level, it aimed to build the image of Budvar as a quality beer, which was not associated with the multinational brewers. Second, at a brand level, it aimed to build a strong emotional link with consumers.

The question was how should we develop the NO campaign? How should we interpret and communicate the NO message without being negative? Obviously advertising was going to play a central role, but which other disciplines should we use? Which mix of media would be best at delivering the NO campaign to achieve the greatest impact?

Introduction

What 'touchpoints' do you have with your mobile phone provider? Perhaps these might be email, telephone, SMS, Twitter, direct mail items, and/or snail mail for personal communications? What about TV ads, web pages, articles and ads in magazines, posters, and perhaps news items that generate general brand awareness? Organizations use a variety of tools, **media**, and messages to engage their audiences. Collectively, these are referred to as the marketing communications mix—a set of five tools, a variety of media and messages that can be used in various combinations, and different degrees of intensity, to communicate successfully with target audiences.

The five principal marketing communications tools are **advertising**, **sales promotion**, **public relations**, **direct marketing**, and **personal selling**. In addition, the media is used primarily, but not exclusively, to deliver advertising messages to target audiences. Although 'media' refers to any mechanism or device that can carry a message, we refer to paid-for media, processes, and systems that are owned by third parties, such as the News Corporation (who own *The Sun* and *The Sunday Times* newspapers plus the BSkyB TV platform), Condé Nast (who own *Tatler*, *Vanity Fair*, and *Vogue* magazines, among others), Singapore Press Holdings (who own the *Business Times* in Singapore), and Time Warner Inc., a 'leading media and entertainment company, whose businesses include interactive services, cable systems, filmed entertainment, TV networks and publishing'. These organizations rent out time and space to client organizations so that they can send their messages and make content available to engage various audiences. The list of available paid-for media is expanding, but it is possible to identify six key classes. These are broadcast, print, outdoor, in-store, digital, and other (which includes both cinema and ambient media). All of these are explored in this chapter.

On completing this chapter, you should understand the main characteristics associated with the principal tools, messages, and media that make up the mix. Readers should also appreciate that by reconfiguring the mix it is possible to achieve different goals. Finally, through an integrated approach to marketing communications a more efficient and effective outcome can be accomplished.

The Role of the Marketing Communications Mix

The **marketing communications mix** consists of five main tools, four forms of messages or content, and three types of media. These are depicted in Figure 11.1 and each is explored later in this chapter.

Traditionally, organizations were able to use a fairly predictable and stable range of tools and media. Advertising was used to build awareness and brand values, sales promotions were used to stimulate demand, public relations conveyed goodwill messages about organizations, and personal selling was seen as a means of getting orders, particularly in the business-to-business market. However, there have been some major changes in the environment and in the way organizations communicate with their target audiences. Digital technology has given rise to a raft of different media and opportunities for advertisers to reach their audiences. We now have access to hundreds of commercial TV and radio channels. Cinemas show multiple films at

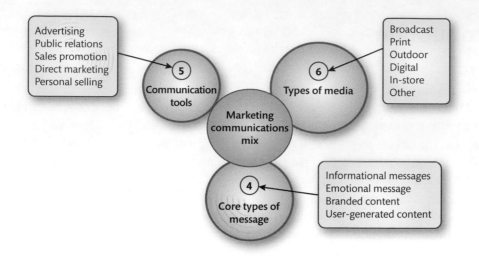

Figure 11.1

The elements of the marketing communications mix

multiplex sites, and the Internet has transformed the way in which we communicate, educate, inform, and entertain ourselves.

This expansion of the media is referred to as **media fragmentation**. At the same time, people have developed a whole host of new ways to spend their leisure time; they are no longer restricted to a few media. This expansion of an audiences' choice of media is referred to as **audience fragmentation**. So, although the range and type of media has expanded, the size of audiences that each medium commands has generally shrunk. In addition, the recent rise in the use of ad-blocking software by consumers has further complicated the task of managing the marketing communications mix.

The Internet enables opportunities to engage consumers at different points in their day and at different stages in their purchase decision-making journeys. Many organizations have found that the principles through which particular tools work offline do not necessarily apply in an interactive environment.

For organizations, one of the key challenges is to find the right mix of tools, messages, and media that enable them to reach and engage with their target audiences effectively and economically. To do this they have had to revise and redevelop their marketing communications mixes. For example, in the 1990s, there was a dramatic rise in the use of direct-response media as direct marketing emerged as a new and powerful tool. Since then the use of the Internet and digital technologies has enabled an increasing variety of interactive forms of communication, where the receiver has far greater responsibility for their part in the communication process and is encouraged to interact with the sender. As a result of these changes, many organizations are redistributing their investments in favour of digital or interactive media (see Chapter 12).

 **Visit the Online Resource Centre** and complete Internet Activity 11.1 to learn more about how Toyota uses an interactive website to inform its target audience about a complex proposition, the Hybrid Synergy Drive.

This has shifted the role of the media. Previously the emphasis of a mix was to enable and persuade customers to buy products and services in the short term. Today, although a short-term focus still prevails for many firms, goals such as developing understanding and preference, reminding and reassuring customers, and building brand value, have become accepted as important aspects of marketing communications. This longer-term brand-building perspective has been shown by Binet and Field (2103) to be a more profitable approach than a short-term direct-response focus on sales.

Market Insight 11.1
Variable Mixes

Benadryl

Hay fever suffers can be affected by different types of grass and tree pollen, at virtually any time of the year. The unpredictability of pollen counts led market-leading brand Benadryl to raise their brand profile within the allergy market through the use of the BENADRYL® Social Pollen Count.

This involved the use of Benadryl's own interactive map and the sponsorship of part of the Met Office site. The goal was to help sufferers fight hay fever. Using daily updates of official Met Office data and encouraging hay fever sufferers to report local pollen levels, Benadryl were able to show other sufferers across the UK what the pollen count was in different areas. They were also able to direct people to nearby stockists of the BENADRYL® product range.

The LEGO Movie

To celebrate the release of *The LEGO Movie* an entire TV ad break made of LEGO, was broadcast on Sunday 9 February 2014 during *Dancing on Ice*. Four recent UK TV ads—for the British Heart Foundation, Confused.com, BT, and Premier Inn, were all re-created, frame by frame and brick by brick, in LEGO.

People were helped to connect to *The LEGO Movie* (not just LEGO) as the ads were separated by five different two-second 'stings'. These featured characters from the movie and *The LEGO Movie* logo. The break ended with a 40-second trailer for the movie. The entire break was also simultaneously released in full on YouTube to ensure that those who missed the ad could see it and catch up with the social media

conversation. The ad was never screened again on television but was used in cinemas before showing *The Lego Movie*.

Volvo Trucks

In order to change drive perceptions and awareness of the launch of a new range of heavy duty Volvo trucks, a viral marketing campaign, featuring a series of live test videos, was produced. Each video showcased different new technical aspects such as their stability (with a tightrope walker), and the reliability and strength of the front towing hooks (hoisting a truck 20 metres above the water in Gothenburg harbour with the Volvo Trucks President standing on the front panel). Others included a video demonstrating the ground clearance (by driving 'over' one of their technicians buried up to his neck in sand) and a truck manoeuvring through tight streets in Pamplona in Spain chased by furious bulls to demonstrate agility and speed.

The final video featured the actor Jean-Claude Van Damme performing a spectacular splits, balanced on the wing mirrors of two reversing Volvo FM trucks. This showcased the precision of the dynamic steering enabling the truck drivers to maintain exactly the same distance apart and speed while travelling in reverse.

The videos were posted on YouTube and Facebook channels, whilst the use of public relations and tailored press information made sure it was distributed online to the news media and bloggers to amplify the story.

Source: Carter (2014); Ridley (2014); Anon (2015a); http://www.benadryl.co.uk/social-pollen-count; http://www.metoffice.gov.uk/health/public/pollen-forecast.

Market Insight 11.1
continued

Theory into Practice

These three campaigns demonstrate different ways of configuring the communications mix. The Benadryl campaign shows how an established consumer brand used sponsorship and interactive media. This campaign actively involved people, and through participation was able to associate itseld with an authoritative and trusted body (the Met Office).

The LEGO Ad Break campaign used television, cinema, and social media, with public relations providing support and credible information for use by news organizations. This is a more traditional approach, although the single use of one large ad break is unusual.

The B2B Volvo Trucks campaign is also unusual as it is convention to use significant print advertising, heavy media relations, and in some cases sponsorship. The use of viral marketing is a recognition that decision-making in this market now involves a variety of stakeholders, including several influencers such as drivers, families, and friends. The campaign conveys factual information about product attributes by engaging emotional executions. It should be noted that the success of the viral content and its amplification across the Internet is due in part to good use of public relations, as well as social media.

Related Topics:

corporate advertising; creativity; word of mouth; opinion leaders and formers.

1 Describe the key elements of the message in each of these campaigns.

2 How do the media used for these campaigns enable messages to reach target audiences?

3 Which of these three campaigns impresses you most? Why?

It is now expected that marketing communications, and the mix of tools, messages and media used, needs to move beyond the product information model and become an integral part of an organization's overall communications and relationship management strategy. Above all else, the marketing communications mix should be utilized as an audience-centred activity.

The pursuit of integrated marketing communications has become popular. An increasing number of organizations are trying to use the mix more efficiently, to coordinate what they say and when they say it, and to develop relationships not just with key customers, but also with key suppliers and other important stakeholders. Today, therefore, an increasing number of organizations are reformulating and integrating the mix to encourage customer retention, not just acquisition.

Selecting the right tools

The principal or primary tools referred to in the previous section subsume other tools such as brand placement, sponsorship, and exhibitions. Although the tools can be seen as independent entities, each with their own skills and attributes, a truly effective mix works when the tools complement each other and work as an interacting unit. One of the challenges facing marketing communications managers is how to extract the full potential from the tools (and other elements) selected. Only by appreciating their characteristics is it really possible to get an insight into how to select the right mix of tools for each communication task.

Advertising

The role of advertising has always been based on the notion of clients renting media time or space in order to place product or brand messages to engage and influence audiences. Unfortunately, many forms of marketing communications are invariably seen by the public as 'advertising', a confusion that embraces public relations and publicity, sponsorship, brand placement, and wider media-based activities.

Advertising was once formally referred to as a 'non-personal form of communication, where a clearly identifiable sponsor pays for a message to be transmitted through media'. There are several issues associated with this definition, and in an attempt to update how advertising is defined Richards and Curran (2002) suggested the following:

> a paid, mediated form of communication from an identifiable source, designed to persuade the receiver to take some action, now or in the future.

Since then the nature of advertising and the different forms of engagement have, of course, evolved with changing technology, economic development, and societal and cultural values. Dahlen and Rosengren (2016) have identified three particular dynamics which they believe need to be incorporated within any contemporary definition of advertising. These are (new) media and formats, (new) 'consumer' behaviours related to advertising, and the extended effects of advertising. See Research Insight 11.1.

Today, it can be argued that advertising is not just about paid media, that it does not always seek to just persuade audiences, and that the source need not be identifiable, nor non-personal.

Research Insight 11.1

Dahlen, M. and Rosengren, S. (2016) If advertising won't die, what will it be? Towards a new definition of advertising. *Journal of Advertising*, 45(3), 334–45.

This paper provides a timely and interesting consideration of the way advertising has been and should be defined, within an academic context. Taking into account a range of issues and developments, the authors propose a new definition that they believe is more fit for purpose.

Visit the **Online Resource Centre** to read the abstract and access the full paper.

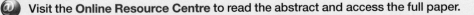

Sales Promotion

Sales promotions offer a direct inducement or an incentive to encourage customers to buy an offering. These inducements can be targeted at consumers, distributors, agents, and members of the sales force. Sales promotions are concerned with offering customers additional value to induce an immediate sale. These sales might well have taken place without the presence of an incentive; it is simply that the inducement brings the time of the sale forward. The key forms of sales promotion are sampling, coupons, deals, premiums, contests and sweepstakes, and, in the trade, various forms of allowance.

Public Relations

Public relations (PR) is used to influence the way an organization is perceived by various groups of stakeholders, such as employees, the public, supplying organizations, and the media. PR does not require the purchase of airtime or space in media vehicles, such as television magazines or online. These types of message are low cost, and are perceived to be extremely credible. PR attempts to co-integrate its own policies with the interests of stakeholders and formulates and executes a programme of action to develop mutual goodwill and understanding.

Different types of PR can be identified but the main approach is referred to as 'media relations' and consists of press releases, conferences, and events. Other forms of PR include lobbying, investor relations, and corporate advertising. Two further activities, sponsorship and crisis communications, are discussed later in this chapter. Through the use of PR, relationships can be developed which, in the long run, are considered to be in the interests of all parties.

Direct Marketing

The primary role of direct marketing is to drive a response and shape the behaviour of the target audience with regard to a brand. This is achieved by sending personalized and customized messages, often requesting a 'call-to-action', designed to provoke a change in the audience's behaviour.

Direct marketing is used to create and sustain a personal and intermediary-free communication with customers, potential customers, and other significant stakeholders. In most cases this is a media-based activity and offers great scope for the collection and utilization of pertinent and measurable data. Some of the principal techniques are direct mail, telemarketing, email, and, increasingly, Internet-based communications such as 'Search'. One of the key benefits of direct marketing is that there is limited communication wastage. The precision associated with target marketing means that messages are sent to, received, processed, and responded to by members of the target audience, and no others. This is unlike advertising, where messages often reach some people who are not targets and are unlikely to be involved with the brand.

Visit the Online Resource Centre and follow the web links to the Federation of European Direct and Interactive Marketing Association (FEDMA) and the Institute of Promotional Marketing (IPM) to learn more about the communication tools of direct marketing and sales promotions.

Personal Selling

Personal selling involves interpersonal communication through which information is provided, positive feelings developed, and behaviour stimulated. Personal selling is an activity undertaken by an individual representing an organization, or collectively in the form of a sales force. It is a highly potent form of communication simply because messages can be adapted to meet the requirements of both parties. Objections can be overcome, information provided in the context of the buyer's environment, and the conviction and power of demonstration can be brought to the buyer when requested.

An overview of each of the tools highlights a number of characteristics that are shared. These are the degree to which a tool and the message conveyed is controllable, the credibility of the message conveyed, the associated costs, the degree to which a target audience is dispersed, and the DRIP task that marketing communications is required to accomplish (see Chapter 10). These five elements can serve as a starting point when selecting the right marketing communications mix, and each is considered in turn.

Table 11.1 provides a summary of the relative strengths of each of the tools of the communications mix against these criteria. However, although depicted individually, the elements of the mix should be regarded as a set of complementary instruments, each potentially stronger when it draws on the potential of the others. The tools are, to a limited extent, partially interchangeable, and in different circumstances different tools should be used to meet different objectives. For example, in a business context, personal selling will be the predominant tool, whereas in a consumer market context, advertising has traditionally reigned supreme.

Table 11.1 The relative strength of the tools of the marketing communication mix

	Advertising	Sales promotion	Public relations	Direct marketing	Personal selling
Level of control	Medium	High	Low	High	Medium
Level of cost	High	Medium	Low	Medium	High
Level of credibility	Low	Medium	High	Medium	Medium
Level of dispersion					
Consumer audiences	Low	Medium	High	High	Medium
B2B audiences	Medium	High	High	Medium	High
Primary DRIP tasks	Differentiating Informing	Persuading	Differentiating Informing	Persuading Reinforcing	Persuading

What is clear is that the nature, configuration, and use of what was once called the promotional mix has changed. No longer can the traditional groupings of tools be assumed to be the most effective forms of communication. The role of the media in the communication process is now much more significant than it was previously. The arrival and development of digital media expands opportunities for people and organizations to converse globally, personally, more speedily, and factually. Word-of-mouth communication also plays a more significant part in contemporary communications, especially as communications-literate consumers are increasingly sceptical of messages conveyed by many organizations.

Market Insight 11.2
Adele Teases Out Her Mix for *25*

When she began her career Adele preferred intimate small venues, and generally avoided headline music festivals or giant arenas. The longer she stayed out of the spotlight, the bigger the mystique surrounding her. As her career blossomed her approach changed, headlining the Glastonbury Festival in 2016 and now undertaking huge arena tours. Despite this she still leads a private life, barely tweets, and restricts the number of interviews she gives, deliberately staying out of the headlines wherever possible.

The launch of Adele's single *Hello* in 2015, which, apart from *Skyfall* for the Bond film, was her first since 2011, was eagerly awaited by her fans. The single represented a significant part of the campaign for the release of her album *25*. The first activity was a 30-second teaser video featuring the introduction to *Hello*, during an ad in *The X Factor* on Sunday 18 October 2015. This ad only featured the lyrics, which were presented on screen as an unidentified singer sang off screen. There was no supporting information—who, what, where, or even when.

The teaser ad was followed by a period of controlled silence, enabling the rumours, gossip, and hearsay to build a momentum of its own, and drive demand. The hush spurred a surge of Adele-based 'media conversations'. There was also a deluge of amateur recordings, made by fans through their smartphones, all posted on social media.

The official video for *Hello* was given to TV stations on 23 October 2015. The ITV show *Good Morning Britain* showed two short clips across the show. The video went on Vevo after the TV broadcast. Adele then did a radio interview with Nick Grimshaw on Radio 1, and

Adele on stage during her *25* tour
Source: © Scott Barbour/Stringer/Getty.

then with Chris Evans on Radio 2, the biggest radio breakfast show in the country. She then gave a print interview with *i-D* magazine.

The *Hello* single was released the following day and, unlike many other album releases, there was an absence of 'instant grats', or drip-fed advance downloads of a handful of songs for those who pre-ordered the album on iTunes.

The release of *Hello* shattered many records. The video had the most views in the first 24 hours on Vevo (ousting Taylor Swift), it had 100m YouTube views within five days (shifting Miley Cyrus to number two), and it was the first song to be downloaded a million times in its first week. *Hello* had the highest number of sales in a week for any tune since 2000. In the UK there were 259,000 downloads in its first week which, when combined with 7.32m streams, gave it a combined chart tally of 333,000.

Sources: Morris (2015); Forde (2015).

Market Insight 11.2
continued

Theory into Practice

The release of Adele's album *25* demonstrates the use of all three elements of the marketing communications mix: tools, messages, and media.

The primary tools used were advertising, public relations, and direct marketing. The messages or content can be considered to be her music plus the Adele personality factor and her associated fame. The media used includes broadcast (TV and radio), print, and digital, including social media. The use of a teaser ad during the biggest music show on British TV appears to have been a deliberate statement about the thrust and path of the entire campaign. Her use of traditional (linear) media (TV, radio, magazines) is not about ignoring the Internet, more a deliberate attempt at integration, as social media took over and amplified messages, regardless of source.

This mix is considered to be reasonably conventional within the music industry. A more contemporary approach is to encourage the artist to flood social media, primarily Twitter, Facebook, and Instagram, with their thoughts, activities, comments, and opinions about a range of topics and issues, regardless of whether or not there is a current campaign. The reasoning for this always-on approach is that there is a fear that silence will lead to a decline in the number of fans, as they would be distracted by other artists. Musicians are seen as advocates for their own music. A substantial social media presence enables artists to reach out and engage with their fans at a personal level which helps them sell concert tickets, merchandise, and music.

Sales of *21* in the UK reached 4.78m copies, with 78.6% on CD. Sales of *19* were 86.9% on CD. Today, most albums would expect a 50% digital and 50% CD split.

Related Topics:
word of mouth; amplification; source credibility.

1 **How significant was the teaser ad in the overall success of the release of the album *25*?**

2 **Why do you think Adele chose not to follow the 'always-on' approach to the release of *25*? Did she miss an opportunity?**

3 **Which other tools and media might be used by musicians when releasing albums?**

Marketing Communications Messages

Our consideration of communication theory in Chapter 10 confirms the importance of sending the right message, one that can be understood and responded to in context. From a receiver's perspective, the process of decoding and giving meaning to messages is affected by the volume and quality of information received, and the judgement they make about the methods and how well the message is communicated. We also know that for messages to be processed successfully, they should reflect a balance between the need for information and the need for pleasure or enjoyment in consuming the message. We can identify four main forms of message content which are not independent entities. These are informational, emotional, user-generated, and branded content.

Informational Messages

Messages can be categorized as either proposition-oriented and rational or customer-oriented and based on feelings and emotions. As a general but not universal guideline, when audiences experience high involvement (see Chapter 2), the emphasis of a message should be on the information content, with the key attributes and the associated benefits emphasized. For example, ad campaigns for charities (e.g. Greenpeace, Oxfam), financial services (Allianz, Banco do Brasil, Aviva), weight loss and supplements (Weightwatchers, Holland & Barrett), and government campaigns for health, tax, and other state services normally make a statement about the product ingredients and deliver a rational reason to behave in a particular way.

Emotional Messages

When audiences experience low involvement, messages should attempt to gain an emotional response. For example, ads for fashion, cosmetics, fast food, and soft drinks often engage audiences through the use of fear, humour, animation, and storytelling. The use of celebrity endorsers and peer-to-peer word of mouth can also amplify these messages.

There are, of course, many situations where both rational and emotional messages are needed by buyers to make purchasing decisions. These include cars, smartphones, dentistry, energy suppliers, and apps, to name a few.

The presentation of messages should reflect the degree to which factual information or emotional content is required for a message to engage an audience, namely command attention and then be processed. There are numerous presentational or executional techniques, and Table 11.2 outlines some of the more commonly used appeals.

Visit the Online Resource Centre and complete Internet Activity 11.2 to learn more about how Bacardi uses product demonstration and a digital media format (.mp3) to inform target audiences how to make a Bacardi Mojito.

User-generated Content

The development of social media has enabled individuals to communicate with organizations, communities, friends, and family. The content of the message can be about brands, experiences, or events, and is developed and shared by individuals. This is referred to as **user-generated content** (UGC) and can be seen in action at, for example, YouTube, Snapchat, Flickr, and Twitter. Kaplan and Haenlein (2010) consider UGC to be all of the ways in which people make use of social media, and it refers to the various forms of media content that are publicly available and created by end-users.

There are three main elements that can be used to identify the presence of UGC. The first is that the content needs to be freely accessible to the public. This means that it should be published either on an open website or on a social networking site accessible to a selected group of people. Second, the material needs to demonstrate creativity, and third, it should

---

Table 11.2 Information and emotional appeals

Information-based messages

Factual	Messages provide rational logical information, and are presented in a straightforward no-frills manner.
Slice of life	Uses people who are similar to the target audience presented in scenes which the target audience can readily associate with and understand. For example, washing powder brands are often presented by stereotypical 'housewives', who are seen discussing the brand in a kitchen.
Demonstration	Brands are presented in a problem-solving context. So, people with headaches are seen to be in pain, but then take brand X which resolves the problem.
Comparative	In this approach, brand X is compared favourably, on two or three main attributes, with a leading competitor.

Emotion-based messages

Fear	Products are shown either to relieve danger or ill-health through usage (e.g. toothpaste), or to dispel the fear of social rejection (e.g. e.g. anti-dandruff shampoos) or discourage behaviour (anti-smoking ads).
Humour	The use of humour can draw attention, stimulate interest, and place audiences in a positive mood.
Animation	Used to reach children and as a way of communicating potentially boring and uninteresting offerings (gas/electricity, insurance) to adults.
Sex	Excellent for getting the attention of the target audience, but unless the offering is related (e.g. perfume, clothing) these ads generally do not work.
Music	Good for getting attention and differentiating between brands.
Fantasy and surrealism	Used increasingly to provide a point of differentiation and brand intrigue (e.g. Cadbury's chocolate, Coca-Cola).

be amateur in nature, in the sense that it has not been created by an agency or professional organization.

Although there have been instances of commercial involvement in UGC, the very nature of this type of content takes the communication initiative away from organizations. As a result, marketers are listening to and observing consumers through UGC. Through this approach, many are finding out the different meanings consumers attribute to brands, which assists brand development and helps to reposition brands.

Some companies invite consumers to offer content (ads), thereby utilizing crowdsourcing (see Chapter 12). For example, each year Doritos run a major user-generated campaign called 'Crash the Super Bowl'. In this competition consumers are encouraged to create and submit an ad for the brand. The top 10 ads are selected by a panel before the public select the winning ad through an online vote.

However, UGC can work against an organization's best interests. For example, following a dramatic fall in the value of an Australian taxi licence after the arrival of Uber, the Victorian Taxi Association launched a social media campaign with a view to rallying customers to support their local cab drivers and share their positive experiences of riding in a taxi. All that the #yourtaxis hashtag did was motivate thousands of seething users to unleash their feelings about poor service and dubious driving. Customers swamped Twitter with stories of overcharging, sexual perversion, and personal hygiene issues, as well as an inability to get from A to B (Ritson, 2015).

Branded Content

Branded content refers to the use of entertainment material which features a single company or brand. The recent growth in the use of branded content rests with a drive to realize the potential that 'owned' media offers. **Branded content** can enable conversations, particularly in social media, and this serves to raise a brand's profile and its credibility.

One of the earliest forms of branded content is customer publishing. Under this model, organizations develop magazines with articles and content considered to be of interest to their customers. The magazine includes references to, even articles and stories about, the sponsoring brand. The development and distribution of these magazines to the brand's customer base is a paid media operation.

Today consumers use a variety of platforms and devices, so there is a need to develop content for use across the web, mobile, email, video, social media, and apps. This provides

Research Insight 11.2

To take your learning further, you might wish to read this influential paper.

Dahl, D.W., Frankenberger, K.D., and Manchanda, R.V. (2003). Does it pay to shock? Reactions to shocking and nonshocking advertising content among university students. *Journal of Advertising Research*, 43(3), 268–81.

This classic paper examines the effectiveness of shock advertising compared with fear and information appeals. They find that shocking content in an advertisement significantly increases attention, benefits memory, and positively influences behaviour. The literature review and consideration of different types of appeal is helpful.

@ Visit the **Online Resource Centre** to read the abstract and access the full paper.

an opportunity to integrate material and allow customers to form a coherent or interconnected experience with a brand. Native advertising, which refers to ads that follow the form, function, and sometimes the context of the host provided that they have social relevance (Norman, 2015), provides an element of integration. Norman argues that fashion and beauty ads in *Glamour* and *Vanity Fair*, and ads from sports equipment manufacturers within related activity-based magazines and websites, represent native advertising. He shows that 'in stream' ads and those used in Twitter, LinkedIn Sponsored Updates, Facebook News Feed, and Buzzfeed are also examples of what constitutes 'native advertising'.

To conclude this section, we briefly note content marketing. This has become a significant digital approach, and is defined by the Content Marketing Institute as:

> a strategic marketing approach focused on creating and distributing valuable, relevant, and consistent content to attract and retain a clearly-defined audience—and, ultimately, to drive profitable customer action.

Key to the principle of content marketing is the creation and dissemination of content that is consistent and that does not overtly attempt to sell products and services. The goal is to provide audiences with valuable information that enhances understanding and knowledge. Content marketing is examined in more detail in Chapter 12.

The Media

Once a client has decided to use a particular message, decisions need to be made about how and when it is conveyed to engage target audiences. There is a huge and expanding range of media available, and making sure that the right mix of media channels is selected is becoming increasingly challenging. Table 11.3 gives a general list of media set out by classification, type, and vehicle. Some media are owned by a client organization; for example, their website or the signage outside a building. However, these media do not enable messages to reach a very large or targeted audience, nor do they allow for specific proposition-oriented messages to be conveyed to particular target audiences. In most circumstances, therefore, client organizations need to use media owned by others and pay a fee for renting the space and time to convey their messages. In the next section we consider the terminology and the role of the media, before we examine digital media, and finally the principles of direct response media.

The development of digital media has had a profound impact on the way client organizations communicate with their audiences. Generally, the trend has been to reduce the amount of traditional media used and increase the amount of digital online and mobile media. For example, major FMCG companies Procter & Gamble and Unilever have reduced the amount they spend on television and increased their digital investments. The main impact of this has been to improve the effectiveness of their campaigns, as the television plus digital media combination drives superior performance compared with using the two media independently (Whitehouse, 2014).

Visit the Online Resource Centre and complete Internet Activity 11.3 to learn more about the differing media that was used for the Ray-Ban 'Neverhide' campaign.

Table 11.3 Summary classification of the main forms of media

Class	Type	Vehicles
Broadcast	TV	*Coronation Street, X Factor*
	Radio	Classic FM, Capital Radio
Print	Newspapers	*Sunday Times, Mirror, Daily Telegraph*
	Magazines:	
	Consumer	*Cosmopolitan, Woman*
	Business	*The Grocer, Plumbing News*
Out-of-home	Billboards	96-, 48-, and 6-sheet
	Street furniture	Adshel
	Transit	Underground stations, airport buildings, taxis, hot-air balloons
Digital media	Internet, social media, auctions, billboards, apps	Websites, email, Facebook, Instagram, Twitter, eBay, Clear Channel, Google Play
In-store	Point of purchase	Bins, signs and displays, gondolas, slatwalls
	Packaging	Coca-Cola contour bottle
Other	Cinema	Pearl & Dean
	Exhibitions and events	Ideal Home, Motor Show
	Product placement	Films, TV, books
	Ambient	Litter bins, golf tees, petrol pumps, washrooms
	Guerilla	Flyposting

An Overview of Each Class of Media

Using the classification presented in Table 11.3 the following section provides a brief description of each class of media.

Broadcast

Advertisers use broadcast media (television and radio) because they can reach mass audiences with their messages at a relatively low cost per target reached. Broadcast media allow advertisers to add visual and/or sound dimensions to their messages. This helps them to demonstrate the benefits of using a particular offering and can bring life and energy to an advertiser's message. Television uses sight, sound, and movement, whereas radio can only use its audio capacity to convey meaning. Both media have the potential to tell stories and to appeal to people's emotions when transmitting a message. These are dimensions that the print media find difficult to achieve effectively within an advertiser's time and cost parameters.

Print

Newspapers and magazines are the two main media in the print media class; others include custom magazines and directories. Print is very effective at delivering messages to target audiences as it allows explanation in a way that is not possible with most other media. This may be in the form of either a picture or a photograph demonstrating how an offering should be used. Alternatively, the written word can be used to argue why an offering should be chosen and detail the advantages and benefits that consumption will provide for the user.

Out-of-home (OOH)

Out-of-home (outdoor) media consist of three main formats: street furniture (such as bus shelters), billboards (which consist primarily of 96-, 48-, and 6-sheet poster sites), and transit (which includes buses, taxis, and the Underground). The key characteristic associated with OOH media is that they are observed by their target audiences at locations away from home, and they are normally used to support messages that are transmitted through primary media, namely broadcast and print. OOH media can therefore be seen as secondary, but important, support media for a complementary and effective media mix.

Digital

Generally, most traditional media provide one-way communications, where information passes from a source to a receiver but there is little opportunity for feedback, let alone interaction. Digital media enable two-way interactive communication, with information flowing back to the source and again to the receiver, as each participant adapts their message to meet the requirements of their audience. For example, banner ads can provoke a click, this takes the receiver to a new website where the source presents new information and the receiver makes choices and responds to questions (e.g. registers at the site), and the source again provides fresh information. Indeed, the identity of the source and receiver becomes blurred in this type of communication.

These interactions are conducted at high speed, low cost, and usually with great clarity. People drive these interactions at a speed that is convenient to them; they are not driven by others. Space (or time) within traditional media is limited, so costs rise as demand for the limited space/time increases. Conversely, as space is unlimited on the Internet, costs per contact fall as more visitors are received.

In-store

There are two main forms of in-store media: point-of-purchase (POP) displays and packaging. Retailers control the former and manufacturers the latter. The primary objective of using in-store media is to get the attention of shoppers and stimulate them to make purchases. The content of messages can be controlled easily by both retailers and manufacturers. In addition, the timing and the exact placement of in-store messages can be equally well controlled. There are a number of POP techniques, but the most frequently used are window displays, floor and wall racks to display merchandise, posters, and information cards, plus counter and checkout displays. Packaging has to protect and preserve products, but it also has a significant communication role and is a means of influencing brand choice decisions.

Other

Two main media can be identified, cinema and ambient. Cinema advertising has all the advantages of television-based messages such as high-quality audio and visual dimensions, which combine to provide high impact. However, the vast majority of cinema visitors are people aged 18–35, so if an advertiser wishes to reach different age group segments, or perhaps a national audience, not only will cinema be inappropriate but the costs will be much higher than those for television. Ambient media are regarded as out-of-home media that fail to fit any of the established outdoor categories.

Ambient media can be classified according to a variety of factors. These include posters (typically found in washrooms), distribution (e.g. ads on tickets and carrier bags), digital media (in the form of video and LCD screens), sponsorships (as in golf holes and petrol pump nozzles), and aerials (in the form of balloons, blimps, and towed banners).

The Changing Role of the Media

The continuing proliferation of the media has led to an increasingly complex media landscape. This makes decisions about which combination of media channels should be used more challenging. It should be recognized however, that digital media has enabled more accurate, more realistic, and faster campaign measurement.

The idea that 'digital' defines a particular media format is redundant as digital technologies can be applied to most classes of media that were identified earlier. For example, digital out-of-home (OOH) technology has become so technologically advanced that digital billboards can be altered in seconds to generate trending messages. In addition, automated (programmatic) media buying enables the display of contextual ads that only display messages that reflect surrounding conditions, such as the temperature or location. Out-of-home can also send push messages directly to the phones of people in the vicinity (Lepitak, 2015).

To reflect these changes, practitioners use a media classification known as POEM, which stands for paid-for, owned, and earned media (see Table 11.4). POEM reflects the increasing scope of contemporary media and the range of media opportunities to engage audiences. POEM assumes that media is not just about paid-for media and embraces all items that can be used to convey brand-oriented messages, regardless of whether a payment is necessary.

> ### Table 11.4 POEM—a classification of the media by source

Type of media		Explanation
P	Paid-for	Advertising traditionally requires that media time and space are rented from a media owner in order to convey messages and reach target audiences. The selection of the media mix is planned, predetermined, and measured in terms of probable size of audience, costs and scheduling.
O	Owned	Organizations have a range of assets that they can use to convey messages to audiences, and through which they can develop conversations. Ownership means that there are no rental costs, as with paid-for media. For example, a brand name or product display on a building, a telephone number or URL on a vehicle, or the use of the company website and its links to other sites do not incur usage fees.
E	Earned	Earned media refers to comments and conversations, both offline and online, in social media, in the news, or through face-to-face communications, about a brand or organization. These comments can be negative or positive, but the media carrying them are diverse and can be referred to as 'unplanned', although many campaigns seek to stimulate strong word-of-mouth communications through earned media.

Source: *Marketing Communications* (7th edn). Fill, C. and Turnbull, S. (2016). Pearson Education Limited. © Pearson Education Limited 2016.

Using Media for Brand Building or Direct Response

For a long time commercial media have been used to convey messages designed to develop consumers' attitudes and feelings towards brands. This is referred to as an attitudinal response and concerns brand building over the longer term. Today, many messages are designed to provoke audiences into responding, either physically, cognitively, or emotionally. This is referred to as a behavioural (direct) response, which concerns activation and is essentially a short-term activity. It follows, therefore, that attitude and behaviourally oriented communications require different media.

Direct-response media are characterized by the provision of a contact mechanism, such as a telephone number or web address, and increasingly through search activities on the Internet. These mechanisms enable receivers to respond to messages. Direct mail, search, telemarketing, and door-to-door activities are the main direct-response media, as they allow more personal, direct, and evaluative means of reaching precisely targeted customers. However, in reality, any type of media can be used, simply by attaching a telephone number, website address, mailing address, or response card. Table 11.5 sets out the main media used within direct-response marketing.

Direct-response media also allow clients the opportunity to measure the volume, frequency, and value of audience responses. This enables them to determine which direct-response media work best, and so helps them become more efficient as well as more effective. Direct-response

Table 11.5 Direct-response (DR) media formats

Types of DR media	Explanation
Digital media	The use of the Internet, email, viral marketing, blogging, and social networking sites now represents the major form of interactive and direct-marketing opportunities. In particular, 'search' enables brands to be reached by audiences who can then be converted into customers.
Telemarketing	The telephone provides interaction, flexibility, immediate feedback, and the opportunity to overcome objections, all within the same communication event. Telemarketing also allows organizations to undertake separate marketing research, which is both highly measurable and accountable in that the effectiveness can be verified continuously and call rates, contacts reached, and the number and quality of positive and negative responses are easily recorded and monitored.
Carelines	Carelines and contact centres enable customers to complain about a product performance and related experiences, seek product-related advice, make suggestions regarding product or packaging development, and comment about an action or development concerning the brand as a whole.
Radio and television	Television has much greater potential than radio as a direct-response mechanism because it can provide a visual dimension. Nearly half of all television ads carry a response mechanism.
Print	There are two main forms of direct-response advertising through the printed media: first, catalogues, and second, magazines and newspapers. Consumer direct print ads sometimes offer an incentive, and are designed explicitly to drive customers to a website where transactions can be completed without reference to retailers, dealers, or other intermediaries.
Door-to-door	Although the content and quality can be controlled in the same way, door-to-door response rates are lower than direct mail because of the lack of a personal address mechanism. Door-to-door can be much cheaper than direct mail as there are no postage charges to be accounted for.

TV (DRTV) is attractive to service providers such as those in financial services, charities, and tourism, but grocery brands are increasingly using this format. The growth in video advertising reflects the involvement of people in their online and mobile activities.

In addition, TV, mobile, and online media are complementary. Consumers often research an offering online only after watching a TV ad. This is known as media meshing, because TV is good at displaying ads and brand building, whereas online advertising is best at search (Berne, 2009) (see also Chapter 12).

Visit the Online Resource Centre and follow the web link to the Radio Advertising Bureau (RAB) to learn more about the role and importance of radio in today's fragmented media landscape.

One aspect that is crucial to the success of a direct-response campaign is not the number of responses but the conversion of leads into sales. This means that the infrastructure to support these activities must be thought through and implemented, otherwise the work and resources invested at the visible level will be wasted if customers cannot get the information they require when they respond.

To conclude this section, we ask an important question: How much of a firm's media budget should be directed towards brand-building activities, and how much should be generating short-term responses? The answer rests with an understanding of the campaign goals and media characteristics. Those media with a broad reach such as TV, radio, out-of-home, and other traditional display media, as well as online display, are best for brand building. Those channels which enable tight targeting, such as search, telemarketing, email, and classified media are more appropriate for short-term selling to narrow audiences. Extensive research by Binet and Field (2013) shows that, on average, a 60/40 brand building/response split appears to maximize efficiency and effectiveness.

Market Insight 11.3
Damart Modernizes Its Welcome Programme

Damart, a French clothing company, operates in the UK, Belgium, Luxembourg, Switzerland, and the USA, and also through partnerships in Australia, Cyprus, and Spain, distributing their products to over 10m customers worldwide.

Damart UK started to update their direct response campaigns targeted at new customers because of a desire to modernize its welcome programme to reflect the changes in recruited customers' preferences. Previously, first-time ordering customers were entered into an intensive welcome campaign. This involved sending them a catalogue every two weeks for a 26-week period. After this, they entered a more traditionally modelled customer mailing plan.

This approach generated a high level of second orders from customers. Unfortunately, it also brought a high level of customer attrition as newly recruited customers requested to be removed from the company's marketing programmes.

It was clear that this method was not appropriate and a new communications approach was needed. So, rather than focus on direct-response campaigns based solely on transactions, a new mix was developed in order to build relationships over the longer term and so realize higher lifetime customer value.

Any fresh approach required a more informed understanding of their new customers, which could then be used to reconfigure the communications mix to influence their subsequent orders. For example, if a customer's first order was placed on the web, they wanted to know the source of their order. Was it an online ad, from a media insert, or an off-the-page magazine ad? Where a new customer can be identified as 'pure web and email', subsequent customer communications can now be channelled through the web via improved personalization in marketing emails.

If a new customer has responded to a heavily discounted offer, analysis can reveal whether a full-price order can be obtained from a main catalogue, or if this customer will have an overall lower lifetime value. If the latter is the case then they can reduce their initial investment in marketing communications.

By driving new customers to order online they can reduce the operational costs associated with processing offline orders and expose forms of cross-selling not available via mail order. It also means they can invest more in web activities, including search.

Market Insight 11.3

continued

Theory into Practice

At one level Damart's move represents a significant strategic marketing shift. The previous approach was largely sales driven and was geared to moving stock. This is an inside-out view, where sales represent the dominant perspective. The shift to a more complex multichannel approach is in part a recognition of the need to put customers first—a marketing orientation. The new communication mix represents an outside-in perspective, which is more likely to bring long-term success.

At another level the change in the configuration of the communication mix at Damart signals a move away from a purely response-based behavioural goal to one that seeks to build brand value over time. This links with the work of Binet and Field (2013) who found that the optimal balance of a communication mix was 60/40. This is 60% of the mix designed to build a brand and 40% geared to driving an immediate response.

Related Topics:

message appeals; budgeting; communications strategy.

1 **To what extent does the shift in the balance of the mix represent a brand nearing maturity rather than any other factor? What role might social media play in developing this brand?**

2 **Should organizations such as Damart be concerned about upsetting or irritating a few customers when a campaign successfully drives sales?**

3 **Visit the site of another fashion retailer and consider whether their mix is configured to drive brand response or build brand associations. What is the reasoning for your judgement?**

This market insight was kindly contributed by Leon Savidis, Business Analyst, Damart

Research Insight 11.3

To take your learning further, you might wish to read this influential paper.

Levy, S. and Gvili, Y. (2015) How credible is e-word of mouth across digital-marketing channels? *Journal of Advertising Research*, 55(1), 95–109.

People share information easily across a variety of digital channels, yet judging the credibility of the message and the source is difficult. The authors of this paper suggest that any evaluation of eWOM messages can stem from three key channel properties: social capital, information richness, and interactivity. Readers are provided with a useful insight into ideas about social capital, eWOM, within a digital media context.

@ **Visit the Online Resource Centre to read the abstract and access the full paper.**

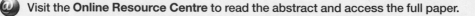

Other Promotional Methods and Approaches

In addition to the primary elements mentioned earlier, there are numerous other instruments used by organizations to reach their audiences. These can be regarded as secondary tools that are used to support the primary mix, although they can be used in their own right as stand-alone methods of communications. Some of these other instruments are briefly considered here.

Sponsorship is normally associated with public relations, but it has strong associations with advertising. Now considered as an important discipline in its own right, sponsorship is regarded as 'a commercial activity whereby one party permits another an opportunity to exploit an association with a target audience in return for funds, services, or resources' (Fill, 2009: 599). Sports, arts, and programme sponsorship are the principal types, designed to generate awareness and brand associations, and to cut through the clutter of commercial messages. Some sponsorship arrangements are being used to actively demonstrate a firm's business credentials. For example, the logistics company DHL sponsor the Red Bull Air Race. In addition to the normal exposure and associations DHL also provide transportation services. So, by moving planes, fuel, and broadcast equipment the brand is able to demonstrate its functional expertise and tell stories about these activities (Anon., 2015b).

Brand placement is also a form of sponsorship and represents a relationship between film/TV producers and managers of brands. Through this arrangement, brand managers are able, for a fee, to present their brands 'naturally' within a film or entertainment event. Such placement is designed to increase brand awareness, develop positive brand attitudes, and possibly lead to purchase activity.

Packaging provides an important form of communication, critical at the point of sale. Packaging can be an integral part of a brand's story. For example, the 'Get Well Soup' campaign by Heinz enabled people to gift a can of soup to someone not feeling well, so reinforcing the brand's nurturing position. Greater customization and personalization of packaging has been enabled through digital printing.

Field marketing is about providing support for the sales force and merchandising personnel. One of the tasks is concerned with getting free samples of a product into the hands of potential customers. Another task is to create an interaction between the brand and a new customer, and yet another is to create a personal and memorable brand experience for potential customers.

Exhibitions are held for both consumer and business markets. Organizations benefit from meeting their current and potential customers, developing relationships, demonstrating products, building industry-wide credibility, placing and taking orders, generating leads, and gathering market information. For customers, exhibitions enable them to meet new or potential suppliers, find out about new offerings and leading-edge brands, and get up to date with market developments. In business markets, exhibitions and trade shows can be an integral element of the marketing communications mix. Meeting friends, customers, suppliers, competitors, and prospective customers is an important sociological and ritualistic event in the communications calendar for many companies.

Viral marketing is a fairly recent development based on the credibility and reach associated with word-of-mouth communications. Porter and Golan (2006: 33) refer to viral marketing in terms of how information is communicated and suggest that it commonly involves the 'unpaid peer-to-peer communication of provocative content originating from an identified sponsor using the Internet to persuade or influence an audience to pass along the content to others'.

Numerous definitions have been proposed, but according to van der Lans *et al.* (2010) viral marketing concerns the mutual sharing and spread of marketing-relevant information, initially distributed deliberately by marketers to stimulate and capitalize on word-of-mouth (WOM) behaviours.

Crisis communications have become increasingly necessary as the incidence of crises has increased. This appears to be due to an increasing number of simple managerial mistakes, incorrect decision-making, technology failures, and uncontrollable events in the external environment. For example, both TalkTalk and AshleyMadison.com have had to communicate with their

---

Market Insight 11.4
EY Uses Art to Distinguish Itself

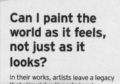

Can I paint the world as it feels, not just as it looks?

In their works, artists leave a legacy that stimulates the mind and challenges existing perceptions. By supporting the visual arts, we offer our clients, our people and our alumni scope for inspiration and new perspectives. This helps make our world work better.

ey.com/uk/arts
#EYArts

The better the question.
The better the answer.
The better the world works.

EY
Building a better working world

Art is an integral element of the company culture at EY.
Source: © 2016 EY LLP.

In an attempt to distinguish itself in a crowded B2B marketplace, professional services firm EY (formerly known as Ernst & Young) has been sponsoring art for over 20 years. They claim that this strategy helps to single them out as both different and interesting.

One of their high profile sponsorships is the EY Tate Arts Partnership, a six-year partnership extending from 2013 to 2019, which so far has resulted in EY sponsoring four exhibitions at Tate Modern, Tate Britain, and many of the Plus Tate partners around the country (with three more to come by 2019). EY's corporate memberships at the British Museum, the National Gallery, the Royal Academy, Tate Liverpool, Tate St Ives, and the V&A, extend the reach of the firm's involvement in art.

EY ensures that its target audience is fully aware of the partnership through a series of multichannel marketing activities. This includes holding many private client events at the galleries, such as early morning tours, receptions, dinners, family art workshops, and evening viewings. The EY name and logo also appear on all materials for the exhibitions, giving the brand huge exposure.

Art is an integral element of the company culture. Apart from its own art collection of over 350 pieces, the firm's arts club, which has nearly 2500 members, organizes social events and trips to places of significant interest. Employees receive art guide training, which can entitle them to act as guides at client events. All employees have complimentary access to the galleries, members' rooms, and internal arts competitions, and there are discounts on events and access to private views.

EY have also sponsored several leading sports events, including the Rugby World Cup, the Ryder Cup, and the Commonwealth Games.
Source: McGreal (2015); http//:www.ey.com.

Market Insight 11.4
continued

Theory into Practice

Sponsorship involves two main parties, a sponsor and a sponsored organization. The success of any sponsorship can be considered in terms of the degree of fit between these two parties. This level of fitness in turn helps determine the relative effectiveness of the relationship, and hence the success of the sponsorship.

Sponsorship can be considered in terms of the use of association. By being seen to be associated with an established, credible, and knowledgeable entity such as Tate, EY can expect to inherit and be seen to share

similar associations. In much the same way Tate seeks to benefit from being seen to be associated with EY.

Sponsorship represents a form of collaborative communication, in the sense that two (or more) parties work together in order that one is enabled to reach the other's audience. These associations are considered to offer mutual value to the parties concerned. Sponsorship can be considered in terms of a network of actors (media agencies, different audiences, event organizers) rather than just the sponsor and sponsored. This expands the realm of interaction and introduces a wider range of issues.

Related Topics:

relationship marketing; network analysis; corporate advertising; emotional intensity.

1 Why might EY focus their sponsorship and their culture on art?

2 What might be the key associations that EY want to make through their involvement with prestigious sports events?

3 How might EY's sponsorship lead to a crisis?

stakeholders and try to restore customer and media confidence following the loss of customer data to computer hackers.

Organizations are encouraged to plan for crisis events so that they can respond quickly using planned communications. Using websites, social media, and mobile technologies, managers of an afflicted organization can post up-to-date information quickly, and through video and news media attempt to reassure communities by explaining events honestly, demonstrating concern, and sympathizing with any affected groups, before explaining what is being done to rectify the situation.

There are many other, largely digital media, methods of communicating with target audiences: mobile communications, SMS, blogging, and podcasting to name a few. These are all considered in Chapter 12.

Research Insight 11.4

To take your learning further, you might wish to read this influential paper.

Athanasopoulou, P. and Sarli, E. (2015) The development of new sponsorship deals as new business-to-business services. *Journal of Business & Industrial Marketing*, 30(5), 552–61.

This paper utilizes a new service development perspective to consider the processes followed by sponsors and sport properties in developing sponsorship deals. Using four case studies involving Premier League football clubs, the paper examines the complex relationship-based business-to-business services and identifies three main phases, namely information collection, proposal preparation and presentation or receipt and analysis, and negotiations and contract signing. The literature review is both relevant and helpful.

Visit the **Online Resource Centre** to read the abstract and access the full paper.

The Changing Marketing Communications Landscape

There have been some major changes to the way the marketing communications industry is structured, not just in the UK but across the globe. One of the most important of these has been the emergence of a number of powerful and dominant industry groups, such as WPP and the News Corporation, whose business interests span cross-media ownership, content development, and delivery. The changing industry structure is a response to several variables, particularly developments in technology, the reconfiguration of the communications mix, and, in particular, the media used by organizations and the way in which client-side managers are expected to operate, that is to drive short-term sales results.

There can be no doubt that technology has had a dramatic impact on the communications industry. As a result, the way organizations configure the communications mix has changed considerably. The sales force was the dominant tool of the mix used by organizations operating in business markets. Many organizations in business-to-business markets have slashed the size of their sales forces, partly to cut costs but also to use technology more efficiently, and allow the sales force to focus on their main activity, namely to build and maintain viable customer relationships. However, their use of digital marketing communications has yet to reach its full potential (Karjaluoto *et al.*, 2015).

Today, the use of sponsorship, direct and event marketing, and online, mobile, and digitally driven interactive media is growing at the expense of offline mass media advertising and sales promotions in consumer markets. In addition, there are multichannel digital opportunities to reach audiences. As a result one strategy has been to build content that can be deployed across different channels. For example, *The Guardian* newspaper's advertising strategies are structured around the distribution of rich content through different channels throughout a working day. In the morning, brief content is moved through mobile channels as commuters use smartphones during their commute to work. At lunchtime, content is switched to desktops when social media is updated, and in the evening, when audiences relax, there is a change to the use of tablets as they can digest richer content.

A key area of change within the media concerns the use of content. Traditionally, content is provided by a client organization, which uses the media to interrupt and transfer its message to its target audience, usually a mass audience. Advancements in digital media and changes in consumer behaviour now enable audiences not only to generate their own content but also to discuss and consider the opinions and attitudes of others. This means that advertisers no longer have control over what is said about their brands, who says it, and when. The rise of online communities and social networking sites, blogging, wikis, and RSS feeds enable users to create content and become more involved with a brand.

Recently there have been substantial changes in the digital media landscape. These include the development of automated ad buying, convergence, and increasing levels of ad avoidance and the use of ad-blockers.

Automation

The automation of the media planning, buying, and selling process is referred to as 'programmatic'. The conventional media planning approach to buying ad space and time involves media planners purchasing TV and radio programmes or space (magazines, newspapers and billboards) on behalf of their clients, whose messages then interrupt the target audiences' reading and viewing activities.

Programmatic is about systems which automatically buy audiences, wherever they appear, according to particular predetermined parameters. A subsection of programmatic is real-time bidding (RTB), an auction dimension. This approach allows advertisers to automatically present ads to specific online or mobile audiences which reflect their browsing behaviour.

Convergence

Convergence refers to a 'bringing together', in this case of media and various technologies. This can be seen in various ways including content served over a number of devices used by consumers, different technologies packaged as one entity (e.g. Sky selling broadband), and new platforms such as television through games consoles.

This movement represents a threat to traditional media owners. For example, newspaper publishers experience declining readership as people get their news at different times of the day from a variety of digital news platforms through various devices. In turn, this can be seen as an opportunity by reformatting content and distributing it across different digital platforms, and so attracting different advertisers.

Digital media owners such as Google, Apple, Facebook, Amazon, and Netflix are all seeking cut-through, some creating new platforms such as Amazon Prime. Others see collaboration as a viable strategy, as demonstrated by the BBC, C4, Five, and BT working together to create YouView.

Ad Avoidance

Finally, the changes in the way ads are presented through the media, and the rise of digital media in particular, has led to an increased use of ad-blockers. This software screens out and prevents the presentation of ads. This raises questions about the longer-term effectiveness of online and mobile advertising, about the role of content in apps, privacy, and the ethics and morality of advertising to audiences who are largely disinclined to engage with advertising. When Apple released iOS 9, the new operating system enabled ad-blocking and deep linking in apps. Part of the motivation was to enable iPhone users to have a cleaner and faster web experience (Gosh, 2015). One of the questions raised by this development, however, is that if mobile advertising becomes ineffective, how will content be paid for in the future?

Integrated Marketing Communications

So far in this chapter we have looked briefly at the five main tools, ideas about how messages should be developed, and how the media landscape is evolving. For these to work most effectively and most efficiently however, it makes sense to integrate them so they work as a unit. In so doing, they will have a greater overall impact. This bringing together is referred to as **integrated marketing communications (IMC)**.

Integrated marketing communications has become a popular approach with both clients and communications agencies. Ideas about IMC originated in the early 1990s. At first, it was regarded as a means of orchestrating the tools of the marketing communications mix, so that audiences perceive a single consistent unified message whenever they have contact with a brand. Duncan and Everett (1993) referred to this new, largely media-oriented approach as *orchestration*, *whole egg*, and *seamless* communication.

IMC can be considered from both a tactical and strategic perspective. The former is well understood and practised, but the latter is less well developed (Kerr and Patti, 2015).

The tactical perspective can be observed in the following levels of integration identified by the Institute of Practitioners in Advertising (IPA).

- **Advertising-led**—campaigns united by 'look and feel'. Referred to as the 'matching luggage' concept, unification is often achieved visually through an icon (celebrity, logo, brand identifier) deployed across all tools and media.

- **Brand-led orchestration**—campaigns built on the tangible brand concept associated with a specific need-state, occasion, tightly defined target audience, or a specific 'point of market entry' upon which to focus the activity and the channel orchestration.

- **Participation-led integration**—campaigns based on the use of digital media designed to integrate brands into people's lives through conversation and brand and audience interaction.

At a strategic level, Luxton *et al*. (2015) consider IMC as part of a firm's overall capability which contributes to brand performance. This is achieved by enabling the development and implementation of IMC campaigns which results in positive brand-related market performance and improved financial outcomes. Kerr and Patti (2015) developed a measure of strategic integration which evaluates organizational proficiency and diagnoses the integration of IMC campaigns. This has yet to be operationalized.

For a period soon after IMC was first considered there were numerous definitions as the concept was explored. Since then, Duncan (2002), Grönroos (2004), Kitchen *et al*. (2004), and Kliatchko (2008) have provided various definitions and valuable insights into IMC. Although there have been fewer definitions advanced in recent years, there is still little conformity about what constitutes and defines IMC (Reinold and Tropp, 2012). In the light of this vagueness the following definition is used:

> IMC can represent both a strategic and tactical approach to the planned management of an organization's communications. IMC requires that organizations coordinate their various strategies, resources and messages in order that they enable meaningful engagement with audiences. The main purposes are to develop a clear positioning and encourage stakeholder relationships that are of mutual value.
>
> (Fill and Turnbull, 2016)

Embedded within this definition are links with both business-level and marketing strategies plus confirmation of the importance of the coherent use of resources and messages. What should also be evident is that IMC can be used to support the development and maintenance of effective relationships, a point made first by Duncan and Moriarty (1998) and then by both Grönroos (2004) and Ballantyne (2004).

One quite common use of an integrated approach can be seen in the use of the tools. For example, rather than use advertising, public relations, sales promotions, personal selling, and direct marketing separately, better to use them in a coordinated manner. So, organizations often use advertising or sales promotion to create awareness, then involve public relations to provoke media comment, and then reinforce these messages through direct marketing or personal selling. The Internet can also be incorporated to encourage comment, interest, and involvement in a brand, yet still convey the same message in a consistent way. Mobile communications are used to reach audiences to reinforce messages and persuade them to behave in particular ways, wherever they are. The evolution of digital media poses problems for IMC and for planning marketing communications activities. Some of these issues concern campaign metrics and measurement, budgeting, brand control, and content development (Winer, 2009).

IMC has emerged for many reasons, but the two main ones concern customers and costs. First, organizations began to realize that their customers are more likely to understand a single message, delivered through various sources, than to try to appreciate a series of different messages transmitted through different tools and a variety of media. Therefore IMC is concerned with harmonizing the messages conveyed, so that audiences perceive a consistent set of meanings within the messages they receive, through all touchpoints. The second reason concerns costs. As organizations seek to lower their costs, it is becoming clear that it is far more cost effective to send a single message, using a limited number of agencies and other resources, than to develop several messages through a number of different agencies.

At first glance, IMC might appear to be a practical and logical development that should benefit all concerned with an organization's marketing communications. However, there are issues concerning the concept, including what should be integrated, over and above the tools, media, and messages. For example, what about the impact of employees on a brand, and other elements of the marketing mix, as well as the structure, systems, processes, and procedures necessary to deliver IMC consistently through time? There is some debate about the nature and contribution IMC can make to an organization, if only because there is a no main theory to underpin the concept (Cornelissen, 2003).

Market Insight 11.5
A New Integrated Mix for Soberana

Soberana's out of home communications in 2015
Source: Courtesy of Soberana.

Soberana's old (left) and new (right) packaging
Source: Courtesy of Soberana.

Soberana is a mainstream beer brand in Panama owned by Cervecerias Baru Panama (part of the Heineken group). The brand was relaunched in 2012, and since then it has experienced incredible growth. It has tripled its volume and share of market in just three years (see Chapter 6, Case Insight 6.1, for more background information).

Soberana needed to be repositioned from a value brand consumed by people over 40 to an aspirational brand in order to appeal to young consumers aged 18–25 and so assure the brand's continued growth.

The creative territory 'Live a Sovereign life' (Vive una Vida Soberana) was developed to give the brand a clear role (*soberana* means sovereign in English). A 'Sovereign Life' suggests a life full of rights and no obligations. We developed more than 50 different rights including the 'the right to be yourself', 'the right to defeat your fears', and 'the right to go out on Mondays'. This creative territory is strongly associated with Soberana's functional benefits, the main one being the low alcohol content which extends drinking time.

The 'Megaphone Man' (MM) character was developed to announce the rights of the 'Sovereign Life'. He is a personification of the brand, a cool young man who remains unknown; you will never see his face. MM was launched at the end of 2015 with a fully integrated campaign plan, including a strong media plan with a teaser phase to introduce the central character.

To create awareness about MM, he first appeared unbranded in more than 15 nationwide TV afternoon/evening shows and stated a different 'right' related to each TV presenter. He appeared in a variety of news, entertainment, sports, and celebrity shows. The media used for the campaign included television, cinema, radio, and print, as well as OOH materials and digital content. Each communication event in the integrated campaign conveyed a different right, customized per media. Having many rights was extremely important because the new creative territory was about living a life full of rights, not a life with only one or two. Research identified the most important rights and these were amplified through different media.

As well as traditional digital formats, the brand also exploited two of the fastest growing platforms, Instagram and Spotify. With the aim of generating relevant social media content, MM declared rights and took selfies with more than 40 celebrities, reaching more than 600,000 users. Moreover, by communicating the right to listen 'to music without interruption'

Market Insight 11.5
continued

Soberana gave away more than 150 Spotify Premium accounts through different online promotions.

In addition, we started using experiential consumer platforms. Surfing is a relevant and aspirational sport for young consumers, so we became the main sponsor of the Panamanian Surf tournament. This has helped associate the brand with a 'cool' lifestyle.

We had previously updated our packaging, which served to reinforce the new positioning. Out went our returnable bottle with a serigraphy logo, and in came a new sleek modern design. This change had an incredibly positive impact on consumers' perceptions of Soberana.

Theory into Practice

The way in which the marketing communications mix is planned and managed directly affects the degree to which a level of integration is achieved. The repositioning of Soberana and the mix used to influence brand perception demonstrates the effective use of various mix elements and the use of planning to achieve particular goals. IMC can be considered at a tactical or strategic level, and based on the information provided the Soberana case appears to be a tactical interpretation. Note how the campaign opened with an attention-getting device which was

then used to build awareness and understanding as conventional media deployed the 'rights' message. Only then was digital media used to build engagement and associations.

There is no unifying IMC theory, but it is clear that the Soberana team planned and managed the repositioning with an integrated approach. They clearly attempted to bring the various elements of the mix together so that one reinforced the other and ultimately brand resonance improved.

Related Topics:

perception; relationship marketing; corporate communication.

1 **Which of the IPA's different levels of integration best interprets Soberana's integrated campaign?**

2 **Identify the key elements of the communication mix used by Soberana. What else might have been included?**

3 **What are the key integrating elements in this campaign?**

This market insight was kindly contributed by Fermin Paus, Brand Franchise Manager for Soberana in Panama.

Although IMC has yet to become an established marketing theory, the original ideas inherent in the overall approach are intuitively appealing and appear to be of value. What is integration to one person may simply be coordination and good practice to another, and until there is a theoretical base on which to build IMC, the term will continue to be misused, misunderstood, and interpreted in a variety of ways.

Research Insight 11.5

To take your learning further, you might wish to read this influential paper.

Ots, M. and Nyilasy, G. (2015). Integrated marketing communications (IMC): Why does it fail? *Journal of Advertising Research*, 55(2), 132–45.

This paper provides an interesting view of IMC implementation as a reason for its failure. The researchers find four aspects of IMC implementation dysfunction: miscommunication, compartmentalization, loss of trust, and decontextualization.

Visit the **Online Resource Centre** to read the abstract and access the full paper.

Chapter Summary

To consolidate your learning, the key points from this chapter are summarized here.

- **Describe the role and configuration of the marketing communications mix.**

  Organizations use the marketing communication mix to convey messages and to engage their various audiences. The mix consists of five tools, four main forms of messages or content, and three forms of media. These elements are mixed and adapted to meet the needs of the target audience and the context in which marketing communications operate. Tools and media are not the same, as the former are methods or techniques, whereas the media are the means by which messages are conveyed to the target audience.

- **Explain the characteristics of each of the primary tools, media and messages.**

  Each of the tools, advertising, sales promotion, public relations, direct marketing and personal selling communicates messages in different ways and achieves different outcomes. Messages are a balance of informational and emotional content. Some content can be branded whilst some can be generated by users. Media can be classified according to whether it is paid, owned or earned. Each medium has a set of characteristics that enable it to convey messages in particular ways to and with target audiences.

- **Set out the criteria that should be used to select the right communications mix.**

  Using a set of criteria can help simplify the complex and difficult process of selecting the right marketing communications mix. There are five key criteria, namely: the degree of control over a message, the credibility of the message conveyed, the costs of using a tool, the degree to which a target audience is dispersed, and the task that marketing communications is required to accomplish.

- **Discuss the changing marketing communications landscape.**

  Advancements in digital media and changes in consumer behaviour now enable audiences to not only generate their own content but also discuss and consider the opinions and attitudes of others. This means that advertisers no longer have control over what is said about their brands, who says it, and when. The rise of online communities and social networking sites, blogging, wikis, and RSS feeds enable users to create content and become more involved with a brand.

Recently there have been substantial changes in the digital media landscape. These include the development of automated ad buying, convergence, and increasing levels of ad avoidance and the use of ad-blockers.

■ **Consider the principles and issues associated with integrated marketing communications.**

Rather than use advertising, public relations, sales promotions, personal selling, and direct marketing separately, integrated marketing communications is concerned with working with these tools (and media) as a coordinated whole. So, organizations often use advertising to create awareness, then involve public relations to provoke media comment, sales promotion to create trial and then reinforce these messages through direct marketing or personal selling to persuade audiences. The Internet can also be incorporated to encourage comment, interest, and involvement in a brand, yet still convey the same message. Mobile communications are used to reach audiences to reinforce messages and persuade audiences to behave in particular ways, wherever they are.

? Review Questions

1. Make brief notes about the nature and role of the marketing communications mix and explain how the configuration has changed.
2. Write a definition for advertising, public relations, and one other tool from the mix. Identify the key differences.
3. Why do organizations like to use direct-response media?
4. How does media fragmentation fragment audiences?
5. What five criteria can be used to select the right mix of communication tools?
6. Make a list of the four main message formats and find an example to illustrate each one.
7. Write brief notes explaining the differences between informational and emotional messages.
8. Write a list that categorizes the media. Find a media vehicle to represent each type of media.
9. To what extent are online, mobile, and digital media likely to replace the use of traditional media?
10. What are the principles of integrated marketing communications?

✎ Worksheet Summary

To apply the knowledge you have gained from this chapter and test your understanding of the marketing communications mix visit the **Online Resource Centre** and complete Worksheet 11.1.

Discussion Questions

1   Having read Case Insight 11.1, how would you advise Budweiser Budvar on how to develop their 'NO' campaign? How should they communicate the 'NO' message without being negative? What promotional tools should they use for the campaign? What mix of media would be best at delivering the 'NO' campaign to achieve the greatest impact?

2   Discuss the view that the changing configuration of the marketing communications mix is a result of changing consumer behaviour rather than any other factor.

3   Select an organization you are familiar with or would like to work for. Visit their website and try to determine their use of the marketing communications tools, messages, and media. How could their mix be improved?

4   Select an organization in the consumer technology industry or one which you would like to work for. Visit their website and look at their ad archive and read the press releases. Determine their approach to marketing communications. Now visit the website for their main competitor and determine their marketing communications. Discuss the similarities and differences.

5   Zylog is based in Denmark and manufactures and distributes a range of consumer electronic equipment. Ennike Christensen, Zylog's new marketing manager, has indicated that she wants to introduce an integrated approach to the firm's marketing communications. However, Zylog does not have any experience of IMC, and their current communications agency, Red Spider, has started to become concerned that it may lose the Zylog account. Discuss the situation facing Zylog and suggest ways in which they might acquire the expertise they need. Then discuss ways in which Red Spider might acquire an IMC capability.

@   Visit the **Online Resource Centre** and complete the Multiple Choice Questions to assess your knowledge of Chapter 11.

Glossary

advertising a form of non-personal communication, by an identified sponsor, that is transmitted through the use of paid-for media.

audience fragmentation the disintegration of large media audiences into many smaller audiences caused by the development of alternative forms of entertainment that people can experience. This means that to reach large numbers of people in a target market, companies need to use a variety of media, not just rely on a few mass media channels.

branded content use of entertainment material delivered through paid or owned media which features a single company or product/service brand.

brand placement the planned and deliberate use of brands within films, television, and other entertainment vehicles with a view to developing awareness and brand values.

crisis communications a part of public relations which is used to protect and defend a brand (individual or organization) when its reputation is damaged or threatened.

direct marketing a marketing communications tool that uses non-personal media to create and sustain a personal and intermediary-free communication with customers, potential customers, and other significant stakeholders. In most cases this is a media-based activity.

direct-response media media that carry advertising messages enabling audiences to respond immediately. Most commonly used in print, banner ads, and on television (known as DRTV).

exhibitions events when groups of sellers meet collectively with the key purpose of attracting buyers.

field marketing a marketing communications activity concerned with providing support for the sales force and merchandising personnel.

integrated marketing communications (IMC) an approach associated with the coordinated development and delivery of a consistent marketing communication message(s) with a target audience.

marketing communications mix a set of five tools, a variety of media, and messages that can be used in various combinations, and with different degrees of intensity, to communicate with specific audiences.

media facilities used by companies to convey or deliver messages to target audiences. Media is the plural of medium.

media fragmentation the splintering of a few mainstream media channels into a multitude of media and channel formats.

packaging protects contents and communicates key rational and emotional information about a brand

personal selling the use of interpersonal communications aimed at encouraging people to make a purchase, for personal gain and reward.

public relations a non-personal form of communication used by companies to build trust, goodwill, interest, and ultimately relationships with a range of stakeholders.

sales promotion a communication tool that adds value to a product or service with the intention of encouraging people to buy now rather than at some point in the future.

sponsorship a marketing communications activity, whereby one party permits another an opportunity to exploit an association with a target audience in return for funds, services, or resources.

user-generated content (UGC) content made publicly available over the Internet which reflects a certain amount of creative effort and is created by users, not professionals.

viral marketing the unpaid peer-to-peer communication of often provocative content originating from an identified sponsor using the Internet to persuade or influence an audience to pass along the content to others.

References

Anon. (2015a) Case study. Volvo trucks live test series: the best of digital marketing. *Best Marketing*. Retrieve from: http://www.best-marketing.eu/case-study-volvo-trucks-live-test-series/ (accessed 17 December 2015).

Anon. (2015b). DHL turns sponsorship into 'active ads'. *Warc*, 10 November. Retrieve from: http://www.warc.com/LatestNews/News/DHL_turns_sponsorship_into_active_ads.news?ID=35692 (accessed 14 November 2015).

Athanasopoulou, P. and Sarli, E. (2015) The development of new sponsorship deals as new business-to-business services. *Journal of Business & Industrial Marketing*, 30(5), 552–61.

Ballantyne, D. (2004). Dialogue and its role in the development of relationship specific knowledge. *Journal of Business & Industrial Marketing*, 19(2), 114–23.

Berne, S. (2009). Four in ten viewers driven online by TV ads. *NewMediaAge*, 19 August. Retrieve from: www.nma.co.uk/four-in-ten-viewers-driven-online-by-tv-ads/ (accessed 6 July 2013).

Binet, L. and Field, P. (2013). *The Long and Short of It*. London: IPA.

Carter, M. (2014). How Volvo trucks pulled off an epic split and a game-changing campaign. *Fast Company*, 18 June. Retrieve from: http://www.fastcocreate.com/3031654/cannes/how-volvo-trucks-pulled-off-an-epic-split-and-a-game-changing-campaign (accessed 17 December 2015).

Cornelissen, J.P. (2003). Change, continuity and progress: the concept of integrated marketing communications and marketing communications practice. *Journal of Strategic Marketing*, 11, 217–34.

Dahl, D.W., Frankenberger, K.D., and Manchanda, R.V. (2003). Does it pay to shock? Reactions to shocking and nonshocking advertising content among university students. *Journal of Advertising Research*, 43(3), 268–81.

Dahlen, M. and Rosengren, S. (2016). If advertising won't die, what will it be? Towards a new definition of advertisin. *Journal of Advertising*, 45(3), 334–45.

Duncan, T. (2002), *IMC: Using Advertising and Promotion to Build Brands*. New York: McGraw-Hill.

Duncan, T. and Everett, S. (1993). Client perceptions of integrated marketing communications. *Journal of Advertising Research*, 3(3), 30–9.

Duncan, T. and Moriarty, S. (1998). A communication-based marketing model for managing relationships. *Journal of Marketing*, 62(April), 1–13.

Fill, C. (2009). *Marketing Communications: Interactivity, Communications and Content* (5th edn). Essex: Prentice Hall.

Fill, C. (2013). *Marketing Communications: Brands, Experience and Participation* (6th edn). Harlow: FT/Prentice Hall.

Fill, C. and Turnbull, S. (2016). *Marketing Communications: Discovery, Creation and Conversations* (7th edn)., Harlow: Pearson Education.

Forde, E. (2015). How Adele owned pop all over again by going back to the 1980s. *The Guardian*, 4 November. Retrieve from: http://www.theguardian.com/music/musicblog/2015/nov/04/adele-25-pop-music-back-to-the-1980s-hello (accessed 12 November 2015).

Gosh, S. (2015) Apple's iOS 9 forces a dramatic rethink for mobile marketing. *Marketing Magazine*, 1 September. Retrieve from: http://www.marketingmagazine.co.uk/article/1362246/apples-ios-9-forces-dramatic-rethink-mobile-marketing (accessed 10 December 2015).

Grönroos, C. (2004). The relationship marketing process: communication, interaction, dialogue, value. *Journal of Business and Industrial Marketing*, 19(2), 99–113.

Kaplan, A.M. and Haenlein, M. (2010). Users of the world, unite! The challenges and opportunities of social media. *Business Horizons*, 53(1), 59–68.

Karjaluoto, H., Mustonen, N., and Ulkuniemi, P. (2015) The role of digital channels in industrial marketing communications. *Journal of Business & Industrial Marketing*, 30(6), 703–10

Kerr, G. and Patti, C. (2015) Strategic IMC: from abstract concept to marketing management tool. *Journal of Marketing Communications*, 21(5), 317–39.

Kitchen, P., Brignell, J., Li, T., and Spickett Jones, G. (2004). The emergence of IMC: a theoretical perspective. *Journal of Advertising Research*, 44, 19–30.

Kliatchko, J. (2008). Revisiting the IMC construct: a revised definition and four pillars. *International Journal of Advertising*, 27(1), 133–60.

Lepitak, S. (2015). It's about the here and now. *The Drum*, 22 June. Retrieve from: http://www.thedrum.com/news/2015/06/22/it-s-about-here-and-now-jean-charles-decaux-transforming-our-cities-digital-out-home (accessed 5 December 2015).

Levy, S. and Gvili, Y. (2015) How credible is e-word of mouth across digital-marketing channels? *Journal of Advertising Research*, 55(1), 95–109.

Luxton S., Reid, M., and Mavondo, F. (2015). Integrated marketing communication capability and brand performance. *Journal of Advertising*, 44(1), 37–46.

McGreal, J. (2015) Campaign of the month: EY, *B2B Marketing*, June. Retrieve from: http://www.b2bmarketing.net/knowledgebank/branding/features/campaign-month-ey, accessed 8 December 2015.

Morris, C. (2015). The amazing marketing machine behind Adele. *Fortune*, 7 November. Retrieve from: http://fortune.com/2015/11/07/adele-hello-marketing-machine/ (accessed 12 November 2015).

Norman, R. (2015) Interaction—2015. *GroupM*. Retrieved from http://www.groupm.com/sites/default/files/extra-files/GroupM_Interaction_January2015.pdf (accessed 11 April 2015).

Ots, M. and Nyilasy, G. (2015). Integrated marketing communications (IMC): Why does it fail? *Journal of Advertising Research*, 55(2), 132–45.

Porter, L. and Golan, G.J. (2006). From subservient chickens to brawny men: a comparison of viral advertising to TV advertising. *Journal of Interactive Advertising*, 6(2), 30–8.

Reinold, T. and Tropp, J. (2012). Integrated marketing communications: how can we measure its effectiveness? *Journal of Marketing Communications*, 18(2), 113–32.

Richards, J.I. and Curran, C.M. (2002). Oracles on 'advertising': searching for a definition. *Journal of Advertising*, 31(2), 63–77.

Ridley, L. (2014). Watch 'groundbreaking' Lego ad break by PHD. *Campaign*, 10 February. Retrieve from: http://www.campaignlive.co.uk/article/watch-groundbreaking-lego-ad-break-phd/1230530#k3XwhqoVTjhwSBkB.99 (accessed 17 December 2015).

Ritson, M. (2015). Postcards from the digitally disrupted. *Marketing Week*, 1 December. Retrieve from: http://www.marketingweek.com/2015/12/01/mark-ritson-postcards-from-the-digitally-disrupted/ (accessed 7 December 2015).

van der Lans, R., van Bruggen, G., Eliashberg, J., and Wierenga, B. (2010). A viral branching model for predicting the spread of electronic word-of-mouth. *Marketing Science*, 29(2), 348–65.

Whitehouse, L. (2014). P&G continue to make big increases in its advertising spend. *CosmeticDesign.com*, 24 July. Retrieve from: http://www.cosmeticsdesign.com/Business-Financial/P-G-continues-to-make-big-increases-in-its-advertising-spend (accessed 21 December 2015).

Winer, R.S. (2009). New communications approaches in marketing: issues and research directions. *Journal of Interactive Marketing*, 23, 108–17.

Chapter 12
Digital and Social Media Marketing

Learning Outcomes

After studying this chapter you should be able to:

▶ Define digital marketing and social media marketing

▶ Explain how digitalization is transforming marketing practice

▶ Discuss key techniques in digital marketing and social media marketing

▶ Review how practitioners measure the effectiveness of social media marketing

▶ Discuss crowdsourcing and explain how it can be harnessed for marketing

Case Insight 12.1
Spotify

Market Insight 12.1
Who's in Charge?

Market Insight 12.2
Play it Forward

Market Insight 12.3
Searching the Amazon

Market Insight 12.4
The Epic Split

Case Insight 12.1
Spotify

What role does social media play and how should organizations incorporate it into their communication campaigns? We talk to Chug Abramowitz, VP Global Customer Service and Social Media at Spotify, to find out more.

Spotify's dream is to make all the world's music available instantly to everyone.

Our streaming service launched in Sweden in 2008 and as of 2015 we were available in 58 markets with more than 75m active users. Of these, over 20m are paid users. Today, Spotify brings you the right music for every moment—on computers, mobiles, tablets, home entertainment systems, cars, gaming consoles, and more.

Social media has been an important part of Spotify's growth in two ways. The marketing team has worked with agencies to create social media campaigns that engage customers and attract them to the Spotify brand, while the customer support team has monitored social media channels and used them as tools to help dissatisfied customers.

Lately, we've noticed that the customer support social media team is more effective than our agencies at customer engagement. The agencies are typically less in tune with what Spotify actually stands for and our tone. And, while customer service is primarily about reacting to customers' concerns and praise, our reactions help to build the Spotify brand.

For example, after solving someone's issues our customer support social team regularly replies by drafting a message in a playlist. Jelena Woehr, a satisfied customer, shared her experience online of a playlist where the titles of the songs spelled out a message 'Jelena/You Are Awesome/Thanks a Lot/For These Words/It Helps Me/Impress/The Management'. The list quickly went viral.

We call these RAKs, which stands for Random Acts of Kindness. This is our way of doing something special for our customers that highlights music and our product in a very Spotify way. Our internal support advisors came up with RAKs, which is why I think they nail our tone of voice so well.

My focus now is to devise a strategy that incorporates the spot-on tone our social media support team has in our marketing campaigns. Most likely, campaigns will continue to be agency created, but they will have to be filtered through the lens of our in-house social media crew. We also need to be better at using what we already have internally, in terms of both our content and our people. At Spotify, we create tons of content and we're not maximizing its value. Why have an agency make content when internal teams are developing materials that espouse Spotify's brand at its core? On top of that, Spotify's employees love music and go to gigs every week. We're missing an engagement opportunity with tremendous potential to show who we are and our entire company's love of music.

It's clear that social media offers so many possibilities, especially to a brand like Spotify that's centred on music, an integral part of most people's life. Social media offers the potential to show a company's passion for what it does, and nobody is fully taking advantage of that yet. There are many brands out there doing interesting things here and there, but no one has been able to put it all together on a consistent basis. We're going to be the ones who do it. And to move forward the first thing we need to figure out is:

Case Insight 12.1

continued

PLAYLIST

James is a Hero
We love you James!
Created by: **@SpotifyCares** · 10 songs, 32 min

▶ PLAY   FOLLOW   (...)

Filter

SONG	ARTIST	📅
Sweet Baby James	James Taylor	2014-10-15
You're Awesome	Adrian B. King	2014-10-15
The World	Empire of the Sun	2014-10-15
Is	Maps & Atlases	2014-10-15
A	Mindy Manley Little	2014-10-15
Better Place	Sevendust	2014-10-15
With You	Linkin Park	2014-10-15
In It	Brandon Bolin	2014-10-15
Stay	Coasts	2014-10-15
Classy	luxury elite	2014-10-15

Another example of Spotify's use of playlists as Random Acts of Kindness (RAK)
Source: Courtesy of Spotify.

How can we combine customer support's great engagement like Random Acts of Kindness with the type of advance planning and scale needed for marketing campaigns?

Introduction

Consider for a moment your own personal use of digital technology and social media. How often do you go online? What device do you use? And what do you use it for? Now consider for a moment how you used digital technology and social media five years ago. How often did you go online? Using what devices? Doing what?

Most likely you will notice that your behaviours have changed rather dramatically in the past five years. Devices such as the iPhone and the iPad, now an integral part of many people's everyday life, were first introduced to the market as recently as 2007 and 2010, respectively. The same is true for many of the services and apps we use. Airbnb (founded in 2008), Spotify (founded in 2006), and Uber (founded in 2009), which have used digital technology to transform how we travel, listen to music, and move around cities, all began their international expansions in the 2010s. Similarly, Instagram was launched in 2010, Snapchat in 2011, and Tinder in 2012.

Today, many of the social interactions and information exchanges in which we engage are facilitated by digital and social media technologies enabled by Internet technology. By June 2015, internet penetration stood at 27.0% in Africa, 38.8% in Asia, 73.5% in Europe, 49.0% in the Middle East, 87.9% in North America, 53.9% in Latin America/Caribbean, and 72.9% in Oceania/Australia (Internet World Stats, 2015). The world's most networked ready economy—a measure of the degree to which economies leverage information and communication technologies for enhanced competitiveness—in 2015 was Singapore, with Finland ranking second and Sweden third. The UK ranked eight, the Netherlands fourth, UAE 30th, China 51st, and India 69th out of 142 countries evaluated, according to a study by INSEAD/World Economic Forum (Dutta *et al.*, 2015). With increasing broadband penetration (increasingly via mobile devices), the adoption of digital and social media marketing techniques is vital. Apps, blogs, microblogs, social networking sites, wikis, and other multimedia sharing services have become commonplace. The technological development is rapidly changing the way that consumers behave and marketers need to adapt accordingly.

As people change how they communicate, the marketing profession has turned to digital and social media marketing to complement, and sometimes replace, traditional marketing channels and activities. However, digitalization is not only altering consumer expectations of their interaction with organizations online; it is changing marketing in all forms.

Digitalization enables a shift in consumer behaviours that transforms expectations and interactions between consumers and marketers beyond the digital touch points being used. Digital and social media affect the very core of marketing, as they can be used to both anticipate and satisfy needs through mutually beneficial exchanges. Whereas digital marketing has typically focused on using digital and social media platforms to communicate (e.g. through search engine marketing and corporate websites) and satisfy needs (e.g. online retailing and digital products), companies are also increasingly turning to them as a tool for market insights (e.g. big data and social media monitoring), meaning that they are also used for understanding needs.

Throughout the rest of this chapter, we will focus on digital marketing and social media marketing as a tool to communicate and interact with consumers. First, we define digital and social media marketing and track their evolution. We will then move on to discuss key areas of digital marketing communications: Internet advertising, search marketing, email marketing, social media marketing, content marketing, and mobile marketing. We then define crowdsourcing and explain how it is used in marketing. Finally, we review some wider considerations in the development of digital marketing strategy.

Digital Marketing

Digital marketing is the management and execution of marketing using digital electronic technologies and channels (e.g. web, email, digital TV, wireless media) and digital data about user/customer characteristics and behaviour. It is an established, and increasingly important, subfield of marketing brought about by advancements in digital media technologies and digital media environments. Digital marketing extends beyond Internet marketing, which is one form of digital marketing specific to the use of Internet-only technologies (e.g. web, email, intranet, extranets), in that it makes use of a range of different electronic technologies and channels such as mobile telephony, digital display advertising, and the Internet of things.

A variety of terms related to digital marketing are used, including e-marketing, Internet marketing, direct marketing, interactive marketing, mobile marketing, and social media marketing among many others. Although these terms are sometimes incorrectly used interchangeably, they each have their own specific meaning (see Table 12.1). Increasingly digital marketing is being used as an umbrella term, whereas the other terms are used to describe specific subsets of digital marketing activities in terms of using certain types of digital technology, such as Internet ('Internet marketing'), social media ('social media marketing'), or mobile ('mobile marketing'), or types of direct ('direct marketing') or interactive ('interactive marketing') communication with consumers. Sometimes social marketing is used as a synonym for social media marketing. This is incorrect, as social marketing is an established term referring to the use of marketing to

Table 12.1 Defining digital marketing terms

Digital marketing	Management and execution of marketing using digital electronic technologies and channels (e.g. web, email, digital TV, wireless media) and digital data about user/customer characteristics and behaviour.
Direct marketing	'A specific form of marketing that attempts to send its communications direct to consumers using addressable media such as post, Internet, email, and telephone and text messaging' (Harris, 2009).
Interactive marketing	Marketing that moves away from a transaction-based effort to a conversation (i.e. two-way dialogue) and can be described as a situation or mechanism through which marketers and customers (e.g. stakeholders) interact, usually in real time. Not all interactive marketing is electronic (e.g. face-to-face sales).
e-marketing	Process of marketing accomplished or facilitated through the use of electronic devices, applications, tools, technologies, platforms, and/or systems. It is not limited to one specific type or category of electronic technology (e.g. Internet, TV), but includes both older analogue and developing digital electronic technologies.
Internet marketing	Process of marketing accomplished or facilitated via the use of Internet technologies (e.g. web, email, intranet, extranet).
Mobile marketing	A set of practices that enable organizations to communicate and engage with their audience in an interactive and relevant manner through and with any mobile device or network (MMA, 2009).
Social marketing	Marketing designed to influence the behaviour of a target audience in which the benefits of the behaviour are intended by the marketer to accrue primarily to the audience or to the society in general and not to the marketer (AMA, 2015)
Social media marketing	A form of digital marketing that describes the use of the social web and social media (e.g. social networks, online communities, blogs, wikis) or any online collaborative technology for marketing activities

influence the behaviour of a target audience in which the benefits of the behaviour are intended by the marketer to accrue primarily to the audience or to society in general and not to the marketer. Social media marketing is increasingly being used by, for example, non-profit and public organizations to achieve such social benefits. Thus the terms are not synonyms.

 Visit the Online Resource Centre and follow the web link to the eMarketer website for a comprehensive source of information on marketing in a digital world.

The world of digital marketing is under continuous change. The Internet has paid a key role in the digitalization of marketing. Over the past couple of years social media and mobile have driven the development. In the coming years virtual reality, wearable technology, and the Internet of things are expected to have a large impact on digital marketing (de Mers, 2015). Before looking more closely at different types of digital marketing activities, we will briefly review the evolution of digital and social media marketing.

Evolution of the Internet

Looking back, important developments in digital marketing include the introduction of the World Wide Web and the proliferation of mobile handsets and interactive digital TV in the 1990s, the increasing popularity of text messaging (SMS) through to the introduction of 3G mobile phone technology, the rapid development and adoption of digital social media in the 2000s, and the shift to 4G mobile phone technology.

Each technological change has impacted on marketing practice. Since the early 1990s, the Internet has evolved from the provision of static information resources to providing greater social interaction to a self-organizing intelligent social web, and digital marketing has evolved with it. In the early days, marketers replicated offline marketing and publishing efforts, often using brochure-ware sites lacking in dynamic content and interactivity, thereby following a traditional 'marketing push' approach (see Chapter 10). Since then the rise of social media has led marketing to evolve away from a hierarchical one-sided mass communication model towards more participatory technologies (e.g. social channels and online communities). These technologies facilitated the practice of user-generated, co-created, and user-shared content with a focus on the active (not passive) user/participant. By facilitating user participation, they contributed to a digital development away from a one-way model of information being 'pushed' to target audiences, to a multichannel and multi-user approach in which web users were empowered to 'pull' down information and/or interact with the organization and content, as well as with each other (consumer-to-consumer). In its current iteration, the web is evolving in terms of its ability to understand the meaning of all the content and participation available online. This means that the web has shifted from the provision of static information resources to providing greater social interaction to a self-organizing intelligent social web.

Taken together this development means that consumers are increasingly reliant on digital tools to guide their behaviours. It also means that consumers are becoming more and more used to determining what information they want, when they want it, and how they want it. The web enables consumer pull (rather than organization push), ever greater customer participation, co-creation of offerings (not just mass production), dialogue, and shared control over the form and content of a brand. This, in turn, is changing how marketers communicate, share information, interact, and create (or produce) an offering. The implications for digital marketing will be discussed further in the following sections.

Evolution of Social Media

Social media has had a significant impact on marketing in the past 15 years. Social media refers to a wide range of online word-of-mouth forums including blogs, company-sponsored discussion boards, and chat rooms, as well as consumer-to-consumer messaging services, consumer product or service rating websites and forums, Internet discussion boards and forums, moblogs (sites containing digital audio, images, movies, or photographs), and social networking websites (Mangold and Faulds 2009). Social media enables individuals and organizations to connect to each other by means of digital devices such as laptops, pads, and smartphones. Whereas social interactions have always been central to human, and thus consumer, behaviour, social media enables those interactions to expand in time and place. It also enables them to be made visible to more people, marketers included.

In 2015, the global average social media penetration was 29%, with North America having the highest penetration at 59%. In Europe just under half of the population has at least one social network account (Western Europe, 47%; Eastern Europe, 46%). Social networking sites have seen massive growth since their inception. In 2014, Iceland (70%) and Norway (64%) had the largest share of monthly active social media users in Europe, followed by Malta and Denmark (both 58%), and Sweden and the UK (both 57%) (Anon., 2015a). In 2015, 72% of Internet users in the UK had a social media profile, compared with 22% in 2007, and four-fifths (81%) of them use social media at least once a day (Ofcom, 2015). Facebook is by far the world's largest social network with over 1,550m users globally (for an overview of the top 10 largest social media networks in 2016, see Table 12.2).

Social media has had a major impact on marketing. In fact, many argue that it has turned marketing practice upside down. Previously held beliefs are no longer valid, and marketers are working on adjusting to these changes. There are two main changes.

The first major change has to do with power. The social media enables users to generate, share, and comment on content at their own discretion (van den Bulte and Wuyts, 2007). Content in social media is **co-created** by consumers rather than (as in traditional offline media) primarily created by media companies and marketers. The proliferation of **user-generated content** (i.e. content made available over the Internet which reflects creative effort and is created outside professional routine and practices (Wunsch-Vincent and Vickery, 2007)), such as **review sites** (e.g. Epinions.com, Tripadvisor.com, and reviews on Amazon.com) and widely shared first-hand feedback about consumer experiences (e.g. through a picture and comment on Instagram), means that consumers have become increasingly influential. Social media allows consumers to share their experiences with each other at their own discretion, making service and product quality assessments widely available, and thereby shifting power from marketers to consumers.

The second shift has to do with *control*. Whereas marketers have traditionally been in charge of the messages they communicate, this is no longer the case. In a social media environment consumers are not only able to create and modify content to pertain to their needs, and share this content with consumers, companies, or third parties, but also have a voice in reacting to product offers and marketing that they do or do not like. As an example, the choice

Table 12.2 Top 10 social media networks in 2016	
Social network	**Users (million)**
Facebook	1,550
WhatsApp	900
QQ	860
Facebook Messenger	800
Qzone	653
WeChat	650
Tumblr	555
Instagram	400
Twitter	320
Baidu Tieba and Skype (tie)	300

Source: Anon. (2016).

of (very thin or objectified) models used by fashion retailers in their advertisements is frequently debated and questioned in social media (recent examples include H&M and American Apparel), forcing the retailers to rethink the way they cast models in all their marketing communications. With social media come higher transparency and less control for marketers in terms of how their communication is received and passed on.

This exemplifies how social digital technologies require a different mindset regarding the role and purpose of marketing (Christodoulides, 2009). The brand manager, who used to be the 'custodian' of the brand, is now the 'host', whose main role is not to control but to facilitate sharing, participation, connectivity, and the co-creation of an offering, regardless of whether that is good or bad (Mitchell, 2001). The changing power and control over communication clearly shows how social media marketing is not about mass marketing, but about facilitating real *conversations* around the organization, the brand, or an individual. To engage in these digital conversations requires trust and transparency, and involves authentic engagement in a real two-way dialogue.

Thus the development of social media marketing is not only impacting on where managers spend their budgets, but is also challenging how they communicate, share information, interact, and create (or produce) an offering. When anybody on the Internet can create, comment on, or share information about what companies, brands, organizations, or people do, what they represent, and how they work, they no longer have power or control over how they are perceived in the marketplace. Marketers increasingly have to find strategies to share such control, be it through the use of hash tags that help co-create meaning around brands and campaigns, or

Market Insight 12.1
Who's in Charge?

In the past 15 years or so, social media has evolved from a debating ground for the initiated few to a conversational arena for the masses. Nowhere is this more evident than when it comes to discussions about purchases, companies, and brands. Customers taking their negative experiences online cause headaches for many marketing executives. Social media conversations, even in a company's own social media channels, are difficult to control, and if they are handled poorly they sometimes tend to spin out of control and become issues in their own right. Moreover, the public nature of social media conversations makes such failings available to everyone for a very long time.

One example is the case of US retailer Target and Mike Melgaard. Mr Melgaard, upon surfing Facebook one night, discovered that Target had removed gender-based labels on its toys. Anticipating outraged reactions from his more conservative American compatriots (with whom he does not agree on this issue) he quickly set up a fake Facebook account called Ask For Help, and included a profile picture similar to that of Target's own bulls-eye logo. Mr Melgaard then began commenting on the many negative posts that were soon piling up on Target's Facebook page, as if he were an actual Target customer service representative. Over the course of 16 hours, Mr Melgaard gave humorous and slightly obnoxious replies to almost 50 posts before his fake account was shut down. One of Mr Melgaard's comments included a response to a negative post which began 'I know this means little to Target, but I am tired of all this political correctness…' Mr Melgaard replied; 'Actually Gary, it means NOTHING to us that you feel this way. Have a great day!'

Target, when queried about the incident, offered a neutral statement that they are committed to customer service for everyone and that Mr Melgaard clearly did not represent the company. A few days later, however, Target quietly endorsed Mr Melgaard's actions by posting a picture of two toy trolls on their Facebook page with the caption 'Remember when trolls were the kings of the world? Woo hoo! They're back and only at Target stores'. The photo generated over 30,000 likes. Mr Melgaard, under his own name this time, commented on the photo saying: 'Target. Seriously You are AWESOME'. That comment alone generated more than 2500 likes.

Source: Colliander and Wien (2013); Nudd (2015a); (Nudd, 2015b).

Theory into Practice

As we have seen, social media has fundamentally changed marketing, with the two key changes being shifts in power and control. The shift in power occurs as social media enables consumer to generate, share, and comment on content at their own discretion. What is more, such consumer-generated content is easily and widely shared, thereby shifting power from marketers to consumers. In terms of control, social media enables consumers to voice any concerns that they have with regard to a brand, its offer, and its marketing. This leaves little room for error. Taken together, this means that marketers have to adapt to a role as a 'host', whose main role is not to control, but to facilitate conversations around the brand, regardless of whether what is being said is good or bad.

In Target's case, the shift in power and control is evident in the behaviours and comments of both Mr Melgaard and the consumers opposing the unisex toy assortment. Target reacts to the conversation as a host clarifying the different roles of consumers taking part. After discussion has gone silent, they also find a way to rejuvenate it by subtly commenting on what has happened.

Related Topics:

digital marketing; social media marketing; co-creation; content marketing; customer service.

Market Insight 12.1

continued

1 Visit Target's website. In your opinion, what segment does Target consider their main target (no pun intended) audience? Among that audience, do you think Target benefited from Mr Melgaard's actions?

2 What do you make of Target's strategy to cope with the situation? Could/should they have done something differently?

3 How do you think Target's decision to quietly endorse Mr Melgaard's actions affected this incident and their core business?

This market insight was kindly contributed by Dr Jonas Colliander, Stockholm School of Economics, Sweden.

by means of viral campaigns which consumers pass on and share with each other. Marketing activities related to social media are discussed further in the sections on Social Media Marketing and Crowdsourcing.

Visit the Online Resource Centre and complete Internet Activity 12.1 to learn more about how EY use Twitter to maintain an ongoing real dialogue with their followers.

How Digitalization is Transforming Marketing

The changing nature of the socio-technical environment means that many marketing executives must reconsider how brand management and marketing activities more generally need to change to suit the digital environment. Not only do digital channels operate differently from traditional ones, but consumer behaviours shaped by them will also affect behaviours in traditional media.

Research Insight 12.1

To take your learning further, you might wish to read this influential paper.

Kozinets, R.V., de Valck, K., Wojnicki, A.C., and Wilner, S.J.S (2010). Networked narratives: understanding word-of-mouth marketing in online communities. *Journal of Marketing*, 74(2), 71–89.

This paper develops a theoretical framework for understanding conversations around brands in social media. Through a qualitative study of social media marketing using bloggers and an extensive review of extant word-of-mouth theory, the article gives insights into how marketers employing social media marketing should plan, target, and leverage social media conversations.

Visit the Online Resource Centre to read the abstract and access the full paper.

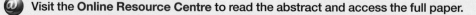

It is also important to remember that digital marketing does not exist in a silo, independent of other marketing principles (e.g. pricing, distribution, or customer service). Integrating digital marketing into marketing research (see Chapter 3), marketing communications plans (see Chapter 11), and channel distribution plans (see Chapter 12) requires detailed consideration if it is to be effective, not least because the digital environment is not simply another channel, but a channel in which consumers often behave differently. Therefore digital marketing should be considered more widely because digital media allows consumers to interact with other consumers, quite often outside the control of the organization around which they might be interacting.

Thus digital technology has the potential to transform marketing at the core. In fact, it is transforming business. According to a study by McKinsey & Co., companies that are integrating digital technology into their business perform significantly better financially than those who are not (Alldredge *et al.*, 2015). The same study identifies the following key characteristics for such digitally advanced companies.

- **Strategy** Ninety per cent of online leaders have digital initiatives fully integrated into their strategic planning process, not as a bolt on. They avoid getting bogged down in over-planning and instead focus on testing the viability of a market, product, or segment in near real time—through limited releases, small campaigns to compare markets, and prototyping with early adopters.

- **Culture** While 84 percent of companies indicate that their culture is risk averse, companies such as Amazon and Google embrace a different mentality: 'We think big and are not afraid to fail'. Instead of waiting for perfection, digital leaders adopt a fail–fast-forward mindset. They push a simple product into the market, gauge interest, collect customer feedback, and iterate. There is an emphasis on failing often and succeeding early.

- **Organization** Leading companies use non-traditional organizational structures, digital talent acquisition, and management to execute their digital vision. Sixty-five per cent of digital leaders have an aggregated digital budget and sufficient budget allocation to scale their digital initiatives.

- **Capabilities** Digital leaders make decisions based on data and build capabilities that connect people, processes, and technology across all channels that engage with consumers. Eighty per cent of digital leaders effectively invest in their digital IT infrastructure to support growth. That means moving beyond model building to implementing processes that can mobilize relevant internal and external resources to take action quickly.

It is thus clear that mastering digital marketing is becoming vital to succeed in the contemporary market place and that doing so means integrating digital technology and media into all corporate activities. For clarity, we shall continue this chapter by discussing digital *marketing communications*. However, it should be noted that, in practice, marketing activities related to understanding consumers (see Chapters 2 and 3) and satisfying their needs (see Chapter 14) are increasingly interrelated and in order to fully reap the benefits of digital and social media marketing they should be managed such that they reinforce each other.

Digital Marketing Communications

Investments in digital marketing communications are growing rapidly. Focus is primarily on communication using Internet-only technologies (e.g. web, email, intranet, extranet), which are accessed using desktops, laptops, mobile devices, and/or tablets, but different types of

Market Insight 12.2
Play it Forward

In November 2015 IKEA launched a new play collection Lattjo, which includes a variety of games, musical instruments, and toys that feature new characters inspired by insects, roots, animals, and vegetation. The mission of the Lattjo collection is to encourage people, both young and old, to play more.

'We know that the world wants and needs more play. In our research we've seen that 50% of all adults want to find their inner child, and that both children and parents want to play more together', says Maria Thörn, Range Manager at Children's IKEA.

This insight is based on thorough research. Overall, IKEA has conducted interviews with nearly 30,000 parents and children from 12 countries. The results clearly show that parents want to spend quality time with their children, but find it difficult to carve out playtime. Over half of the parents surveyed also said that play can include the use of smartphones, tablets, game consoles, and computers. Based on these concerns the Lattjo collection was designed to remove barriers to play and connect online and offline play.

With a long tradition of offering playful experiences for children in their store, the Lattjo collection is the first effort to make children's IKEA digital. In addition to the physical product, the collection includes a 'Play-together-when-apart-app'. Through the app children and adults can enjoy social play even if they are not physically in the same place. All the games depend on collaboration and togetherness. The more people play together, the more togetherness points they get.

The launch of the Lattjo collection is built around more than 25 animated short films created by DreamWorks Studios. These animated stories celebrate and expand the imaginative worlds of the Lattjo characters in playful 2D and stop-motion animation. The video series utilizes DreamWorks Animation's storytelling expertise to bring the collection to life.

'Working with our world-class storytellers, this content series is a celebration of imagination and play that we hope surprises and delights viewers as they meet these characters in the coming months', said Brian Robinson, Global Head of Creative Design and Development at DreamWorks Animation.

Sources: Budds (2015); Madov (2015); Miller (2015).

IKEA's Lattjo collection sets out to inspire young and old to play together
Source: Used with the permission of Inter IKEA Sytems B.V.

Theory into Practice

The growth of digital technologies is not only changing consumer behaviour, it is changing business. Successful marketing in a digital world requires digital marketing to be integrated into marketing research as well as marketing communication and channels distribution plans. However, digital marketing should be considered and adapted more widely than just as a new communication or distribution channel. It can help create new business opportunities and enable new relationships (and thereby insights) with and between consumers.

The launch of Lattjo shows that IKEA has embraced digitization. The physical products are complemented by digital games that encourage social play around them (the app). A digital campaign built around carefully created films complements the in-store launch, and all aspects of the launch are social.

Market Insight 12.2

continued

Related Topics:

digital marketing; social media marketing; content marketing; new product development.

Visit IKEA's website and look for the Lattjo collection. Then visit IKEA's YouTube channel and watch the Lattjo films.

1 How has IKEA adapted its offer to an increasingly digital environment?

2 How has IKEA adapted its offer to an increasingly social environment?

3 What key learning do you think that IKEA will take away from the Lattjo launch? How can this be used in developing other parts of the IKEA offer in the future?

digital displays and tracking devices are also increasingly being used to market products and brands.

Not all digital marketing communications fit with a traditional definition of advertising as paid placements. As consumers are actively searching and sharing information on the Internet, marketers need to make sure that information is easily accessed and shared, meaning that the brand's own online channels and the potential of its content to be passed on is becoming increasingly important. Whereas traditional media are easily divided into formats based on the underlying logic, this is not the case for digital marketing communications. The borders between paid ('advertising') media, earned ('publicity' and 'word of mouth'), and own media (e.g. websites, profiles on social media, emails) are blurry and hard to establish. For example, the IKEA films described in Market Insight 12.2 reached consumers in several ways. They were used in paid placements (e.g. display ads on newspaper websites), made shareable for newspapers, bloggers, and consumers to pass on to their readers/friends (e.g. on social media), and published on IKEA's own channels (e.g. website, YouTube channel). Typically, the different aspects of a digital marketing communication campaign are tightly linked and hard to disentangle.

In the following we will discuss some of the most frequently used digital marketing communication activities in more detail.

Internet Advertising

Internet advertising refers to a form of marketing communication that uses the Internet for the purpose of advertising regardless of what device is being used to access it. Typically it involves marketers paying media owners for carrying their messages on their websites. Payment is impression based (e.g. cost-per-thousand (CPM) pricing), performance based (e.g. cost per click, sale, lead, acquisition, or application), or straight revenue share (e.g. percentage commission paid upon sale). The aim of Internet advertising is to increase website traffic and/or encourage product trial, purchase, and repeat purchase activity (Cheng *et al.*, 2009), and ad format and payment should be adapted accordingly.

A list of different Internet ad formats and their definitions is given in Table 12.3. Internet advertising in the UK totalled £7.194bn in 2014, and in the first six months of 2015 it increased by 13.4% compared with the same period in 2014 (IAB/PwC, 2015a), with much of the growth being driven by mobile, digital video, and social media.

Major considerations when using Internet advertising include the following,

- Cost—Internet adverts are still relatively cheap compared with traditional advertising.
- Timeliness—Internet adverts can be updated at any time with minimal cost.
- Format—Internet adverts are richer, using text, audio, graphics, and animation. In addition, games, entertainment, and promotions can be incorporated.
- Personalization—Internet adverts can be interactive and targeted to specific interest groups and/or individuals.
- Location-based—by using wireless technology and geolocation technology (GPS), Internet advertising can be targeted to consumers wherever they are (e.g. near a restaurant or theatre).
- Intrusive—some Internet advertising formats (e.g. pop-ups) are seen as intrusive and suffer more consumer complaints than other formats.

Recent developments in Internet advertising focus on programmatic buying, in which advertising is planned, analysed and optimized via demand-side software interfaces and algorithms. Recently, there has also been a lot of controversy with regard to online advertising. Firstly, reports of exposure to online advertising have been inflated. This is due to the automated systems used to account for exposure not being able to distinguish actual viewers from automated viewers ('bot traffic'). In fact, it is estimated that in 2014 22.8% of web traffic worldwide came from 'bad bots' (fraudsters and hackers), a little over a third came from 'good bots' (e.g. search indexing), and human traffic only accounted for 40.9%, down from 54.8% in 2013 (Anon., 2015b). Secondly, the use of ad-blocking software (i.e. software that blocks advertising content from appearing on websites) is growing rapidly. In 2015, the share of active ad-block users worldwide was up by 42%, totalling 198m active users (Ingram, 2015).

Visit the Online Resource Centre and follow the web link to the Interactive Advertising Bureau (IAB) to learn more about developments and standards for Internet advertising activities (including those relating to programmatic buying, bot traffic, and ad blocking).

Search Marketing

The growth in digital content available through the web has given rise to a number of interactive decision aids used to help web users locate data, information, and/or an organization's digital objects (e.g. pictures, videos). The main two types of decision aids are a search directory (web directory) and a search engine.

A **search directory** is a human-edited database of information. It lists websites by category and subcategory, with categorization usually based on the whole website rather than one page or a set of keywords. Search directories often allow site owners to submit their site directly for inclusion, and editors review submissions for fitness. Examples of search directories are Yahoo Pages and The Open Directory Project (http://www.dmoz.org). Given its large scope Amazon could also be considered to offer a search directory for shopping.

In contrast, a **search engine** operates algorithmically or uses a mixture of algorithmic and human input to collect, index, store, and retrieve information on the web (e.g. web pages, images,

Table 12.3 Types of Internet advertising format

Ad format	Description	Share of Internet ad investments*
Banner advertising	Advertiser pays an online company for space on one or more of the online company's pages to display a static or linked banner or logo.	16%
Sponsorship	Advertiser pays for custom content and/or experiences, which may or may not include ad elements such as display advertising, brand logos, advertorial, or pre-roll video.	2%
Search	Advertisers pay online companies fees to list and/or link their company site domain name to a specific search word or phrase (includes paid search revenues). Search categories include paid listings, contextual search, paid inclusion, and site optimization.	38% (excluding mobile search)
Lead generation	Advertisers pay fees to online companies that refer qualified potential customers (e.g. auto dealers which pay a fee in exchange for receiving a qualified purchase inquiry online) or provide consumer information (demographic, contact, behavioural) where the consumer opts in to being contacted by a marketer (email, post, telephone, fax). These processes are priced on a performance basis (e.g. cost per action, lead or enquiry), and can include user applications (e.g. for a credit card), surveys, contests (e.g. sweepstakes), or registrations.	4%
Classifieds and auctions	Advertisers pay fees to online companies to list specific products or services (e.g. online job boards and employment listings, real estate listings, automotive listings, auction-based listings, Yellow Pages).	5%
Rich media	Display-related ads that integrate some component of streaming interactivity. Rich media ads often include Flash or Java script, but not content, and can allow users to view and interact with products or services (e.g. scrolling or clicking within the ad opens a multimedia product description, expansion, animation, video, or 'virtual test-drive' within the ad).	3%
Digital video advertising	Advertising that appears before, during, or after digital video content in a video player (i.e. pre-roll, mid-roll, or post-roll video ads). Digital video ads include TV commercials online and can appear in streaming content or in downloadable video. Display-related ads on a page (that are not in a player) which contains video are categorized as rich media ads.	7%

> **Table 12.3** continued

Ad format	Description	Share of Internet ad investments*
Mobile advertising	Advertising tailored to and delivered through wireless mobile devices such as smartphones, feature phones (e.g. lower-end mobile phones capable of accessing mobile content), and media tablets. Typically taking the form of static or rich media display ads, text messaging ads, search ads, or audio/video spots, such advertising generally appears within mobile websites (e.g. websites optimized for viewing on mobile devices), mobile apps, text messaging services (i.e. SMS, MMS), or mobile search results (i.e. 411 listings, directories, mobile-optimized search engines). Mobile advertising formats include search, display (banner ads, digital video, digital audio, sponsorships, and rich media), and other advertising served to mobile devices.	25% (see Table 12.6 for a breakdown)
Digital audio	Refers to partially or entirely advertising supported audio programming available to consumers on a streaming basis, delivered via the wired and mobile Internet.	Not available

*Based on US-ad spend in 2014. Because of rounding the figures might not add up to 100%.
Source: IAB/PwC (2015b).

information, and other types of files), making this information available to users in a manageable and meaningful way in response to a search query. Information is retrieved by a web crawler (also known as a spider), which is an automated web browser that follows every link on the site, analysing how it should be indexed using words extracted from page and file titles, headings, or special fields called meta-tags. The indexed data are then stored in an index database for use in later queries. When a user enters a query into a search engine (typically using keywords), the engine examines its index and provides a listing of the best-matching web pages according to its criteria on search engine result pages (SERPs). There are only a few dominant search engines in the market, with Google leading the global market share rankings with 89%, followed by Yahoo! and Bing, both at 4%, and the Chinese Baidu at just below 1% (Anon., 2015c).

Search engines have evolved significantly over the years. Whereas searches in their early years of Internet focused on keywords, today semantic analysis ensures that they also take into account previous search behaviour and knowledge about the context (e.g. when, where, how, and who) in which the search is being made. An example of contextual adaption is local searches where search results are adapted to the position where the search is undertaken.

Given its central role in consumer online behaviour it is not surprising that search is central to most digital marketing strategies. In 2015, 52% of all Internet advertising investments were in search. Search, often referred to as search engine marketing (SEM), is one of the main forms of Internet advertising, with a UK spend of £3.74bn in 2014 accounting for about 52% of total UK online ad spend (IAB/PwC, 2015a). Its aim is to promote websites by increasing their visibility in SERPs. SEM methods include paid listings, contextual search, paid inclusion, and search optimization.

- **Paid listings**—payments made for clicks on text links that appear at the top or side of search results for specific keywords. The more a marketer pays, the higher the position it gets. Marketers only pay when a user clicks on the text link. Paid listings or **pay per click (PPC)** typically means that the advertisers bid on keywords or phrases relevant to their target market, with sponsored/paid search engine listings to drive traffic to a website. The search engine ranks ads on the basis of a competitive auction and other related criteria (e.g. popularity, quality). Google AdWords, Yahoo! Search Marketing, and Bing Ads are the three largest ad-network operators, with all three operating under a bid-based model.

- **Contextual search** is a form of targeted advertising, with advertisements (e.g. banners, pop-ups) appearing on websites. The advertisements themselves are selected and served by automated systems based on the content displayed to the user. A **contextual advertising** system scans the text of a website for keywords and returns advertisements to the web page based on what the user is viewing. Google AdSense was the first major contextual advertising program. Payments are typically only made for clicks (PPC) on text links that appear in an article based on the context of the content, instead of a user-submitted keyword.

- **Paid inclusion** occurs when a search engine company charges fees related to inclusion of websites in their search index. Some organizations mix paid inclusion with organic listings (e.g. Yahoo!), whereas others do not allow paid inclusion to be listed with organic lists (e.g. Google and Ask.com). Payments are made to guarantee that a marketer's URL is indexed by a search engine (i.e. it isn't paid only for clicks, as in paid listings).

- **Site optimization** occurs when a website's structure and content is improved to maximize its listing in organic search engine results pages using relevant keywords or search phrases. Payments are made to optimize a site in order to improve the site's ranking in SERPs. Increasingly, there is recognition that search engine optimization (SEO) and social media are interlinked. Dunphy (2012) argues that 'every share, like, re-tweet, +1, subscription, and pin means one more endorsement for your website, simultaneously increasing your search creditability. By gaining a massive amount of social shares, you're not just boosting your SEO signals and your site visibility—you're also creating content with value for your customer base'.

All these search marketing methods allow marketers to match users with content according to their interests. Search engines and directories take a different approach, but one thing unites them—search marketing is one of the most cost-effective methods of digital marketing. However, although search is still by far the largest online ad format, it is declining slightly in importance as digital marketers look increasingly to shift budget into mobile and social channels.

Email Marketing

Email is one of the most frequently used digital marketing tools. Email marketing includes 'opt-in' and 'opt-out' mailing lists, email newsletters, and discussion list subscriptions. Given that companies themselves, based on CRM programs and other mailing lists, run many email marketing activities, the lead generation category listed in Table 12.4 only covers parts of all email marketing activities. Email, when used properly, goes beyond simply sending a sales message. It helps to create trust, retain customers, build customer referrals, and generate revenues. What is more, email marketing tends to be appreciated by consumers. For example, 63% of UK office workers reported that they preferred to receive brand communications this way compared with 6% preferring to be reached by social media and 5% by a mobile app (Anon., 2015d).

Market Insight 12.3
Searching the Amazon

Search is a key behaviour online and Google is the go-to place for search. Or is it? In 2015, 44% of US consumers stated that they head directly to Amazon when searching for products, up from 30% in 2012. In comparison, 34% go straight to a search engine such as Google, Yahoo, and Bing.

Whereas Google has done its part in making product discovery and search intuitive, convenient, and seamless, Amazon now seems ready to step in and take over. Almost half of US consumers bypass search engines and other websites in favour of Amazon when on a shopping mission. This means that the search bar is increasingly becoming a key asset in Amazon's user experience.

Enabling search not only allows consumers to find the products they are looking for, it also enables Amazon to collect valuable data on consumer searches and relate them to actual sales. On-site search queries are clear expressions of user intent. Coupled with reviews from the millions of Amazon customers who have left appraisals on the website, the data is invaluable, and Amazon continually leverages it to intelligently promote products across their website.

Amazon's advanced algorithmic recommendation capability accurately predicts intent and suggests products better than any other website. Now, Amazon is using its shopping pattern data to get advantages

offline as well. In November 2015 Amazon opened its first bricks-and-mortar bookstore in Seattle, USA. Seattle was chosen for the first physical bookstore because it's close to Amazon's headquarters and because Seattle is a top market for readers.

In opening a bookstore, Amazon is betting that the vast store of data it generates from shopping patterns on its website will give it advantages in its retail location that other bookstores cannot match, and that using this data to pick titles that will most appeal to Seattle shoppers will allow Amazon to succeed where others have not.

Sources: Greene (2015); Leggatt (2015); B. Johnson (2015).

The assortment in Amazon's physical store has been selected using data on online shopping patterns
Source: © SEA STOCK/Shutterstock.

Theory into Practice

The vast amount of digital content available through the web has given rise to a number of interactive decision aids used to help web users find what they are looking for. The main two decision aids are search directories (web directories) and search engines. Increasingly, search results are adapting semantic analysis in which

they take into account contextual factors (e.g. who is searching, for what, at what time, and using what device) to come up with relevant results. Alongside search giants Google, retailers such as Amazon are also working hard to facilitate search and monetize the data that it generates.

Related Topics:

digital marketing; search marketing; retailing; marketing channels.

Market Insight 12.3

continued

Visit Amazon's website and search for a product that you are interested in.

1 What options for finding the product do you have? How useful is the directory? How useful is the search engine?

2 What type of contextual information does Amazon seem to use to guide the results that are presented?

3 How do the search results you get on Amazon differ from what you would get using Google, Bing, or Yahoo!?

Importantly with email marketing, the communicator only sends the message to those who have agreed to receive messages. Such **permission-based email marketing** is a highly cost-effective form of digital marketing (Waring and Martinez, 2002; Cheng *et al.*, 2009). As a marketing tool, it is easy to use and costs little to send. However, costs can be higher when personalizing messages and where a database must be developed or purchased. Nevertheless, email can reach millions of willing prospects in minutes. Unsolicited emails, which clog email servers and use up much-needed Internet bandwidth, are referred to as **spam**.

In designing a successful email campaign marketers need to think carefully about the target audience and their willingness to receive emails. This means that they should provide a mechanism for list members to opt in or opt out and to choose what type of email offerings they are interested in receiving (e.g. newsletter, discount offers, and specific updates). As far as possible, emails should be personalized. Using an email system that allows tracking and reporting on all elements of the campaign (including opens, clicks, pass along, unsubscribe, and bounce-backs) allows marketers to closely test and monitor different email marketing strategies in terms of when and how often to send them, as well as what to offer, write, and highlight. The insights gained from such data mining exercises can be invaluable. For example, a large-scale study of more than a billion emails over a two-year period showed that people are 38% more likely to click, and 47% more likely to convert, when they are presented with a percent-off rather than a dollar/pound-off offer (O'Brien 2015). According to the same study, short subject lines (6–10 words), visual and personalized messages, and clear calls to action are key to a successful email.

Social Media Marketing

Social media marketing describes the use of the social web and social media (e.g. social networks, online communities, blogs, wikis) or any online collaborative technology for marketing activities (e.g. sales, public relations, research, distribution, customer service). Social media marketing includes both the creation and curation of corporate/brand profiles and content on social media and advertising. Social media advertising (SMA) refers to advertising delivered on social platforms, including social networking and social gaming websites and apps, across all device types.

Marketers are increasingly investing in social networks (e.g. Facebook, LinkedIn, QQ in China), video-sharing sites (e.g. YouTube), image-sharing sites (Flickr, Pinterest), blogging platforms (WordPress), and microblogs (Twitter) for marketing purposes. According to the 2015 Chief Marketing Officer (CMO) survey, 11% of marketing budgets are invested in social media in 2015, and this share is expected to grow to 24% in the next five years (Moorman, 2015). In 2016, the growth rate for social media in Western Europe is expected to be 23% (Anon., 2015e).

As discussed in the section on Evolution of Social Media, social media has changed the way that brand and consumers relate by shifting control and power away from marketers and enabling conversations. However, the social web does not make conversations happen; it just supports them. By understanding how social media supports conversations, businesses can open up interactions with individuals and communities. For example, companies respond to customer care queries and concerns using Twitter and Facebook, share brand-related behind-the-scenes imagery on Instagram and Pinterest, and promote time-limited offers on Snapchat. Examples of marketing activities to stimulate conversations are as follows (Mangold and Faulds, 2009).

- Networking platforms (e.g. Sephora's Beauty Insiders, Nike +).
- Blogs and social media tools to engage customer—because customers like to give feedback on a broad range of issues (see section on Content Marketing).
- Both Internet and traditional promotional tools to engage customers.
- Information on, for example, correct or alternative product usage.
- Exclusivity—because people like to feel special.
- Offerings that are designed from the perspective of consumers' desired self-images and with talking points to make advocacy easier; for example, the US budget airline JetBlue makes leather seats and televisions available to its customers.
- Support for causes that people value.
- Memorable stories—the UK food and beverage company innocent outlines the story of the foundation of the firm on its website. The story has it that three friends set up a stall to sell smoothies at a London music festival. A sign above the stall reads 'Should we give up our jobs to make these smoothies?', and people are asked to throw their empties into one of two bins marked either 'Yes' or 'No', where 'Yes' wins. Needless to say, 'Yes' won.

The important point is real conversation, i.e. authenticity. When EY hired an agency to manage its university/college recruiting presence on Facebook, the results were poor. Only when the organization enlisted a group of interns who were active Facebookers to contribute did the conversation become more authentic and draw more traffic, contributing to the company's rapid rise in *Business Week* magazine's ranking of top firms that college students want to work for (Kane *et al.*, 2009). For a discussion of what content works best on social media, see the section on Content Marketing.

Paid media placements online and offline have been found to be important for getting conversations going (e.g. Niederhoffer *et al.*, 2007; Keller and Fay, 2012). In 2015, marketers invested $23.68bn in paid social media advertising worldwide (Anon., 2015e). This was up 35.5% from 2014. According to the same estimates social media advertising is expected to comprise 16% of all digital ad spending by 2016. In the USA and Canada advertisers will spend more than $50 per social media user, and that outlay is expected to reach $71.37 per user in just two years, a reflection of growing spending against a maturing user base. In Western Europe the equivalent investments are $25.26 in 2015 and $34.40 in 2017. In 2015, 65.5% of all investments in social media worldwide were spent on Facebook. eMarketer estimated that in 2015 the company would make $15.50bn in ad revenues (Anon., 2015e). This can be compared with Twitter, which is expected to take $2.09bn (8.8%) of global social network ad spending and LinkedIn, which will make $900m in advertising.

@ The options available for social media advertising differ between different social media platforms. They are also constantly changing. **Visit the Online Resource Centre** and undertake Internet Activity 12.2 around advertising options on different social media platforms.

Evaluating Social Media

Although marketers agree that social media marketing is key to success in the contemporary market place, many marketers are still struggling in terms of how to evaluate these activities. In 2015, only 15.0% of CMOs were able to prove the impact of those investments quantitatively, 44.5% had a good qualitative sense of the impact, and 41.5% were not yet able to show the impact (Moorman, 2015). This clearly shows that engaging in social communities provides several opportunities for marketers, but it can also be a challenge.

As social media is increasingly used as part of the marketing manager's planning (for both communications and research), there is an increasing need to understand whether what marketers are doing in social media is working or not. Web activity is amazingly measurable, because web users leave traces of their presence and activity on the various sites they visit. However, the process of measuring social media effectiveness requires a detailed sevenfold process (CIM, 2013).

1. Start by looking at measurement metrics (Table 12.4 provides a detailed list of the most frequently used social media measures and how their use has evolved).

2. Review your social media campaign objectives. For example, was your motivation to (i) build traffic on your website, (ii) improve brand perceptions, (iii) deepen relationships with customers, (iv) learn from the community, (v) drive purchase intent, (vi) foster dialogue, (vii) promote advocacy, (viii) facilitate support, or (ix) spur innovation (Murdough, 2009; Owyang and Lovett, 2010).

3. Map your campaign—in this phase the brand owner identifies how the brand is consumed on the web by showing (a) brand-generated content, (b) consumer-generated content, (c) consumer-fortified content (e.g. by showing online locations where consumers can go to distribute content relating to the brand), and (d) exposure to content consumers (e.g. favourable product reviews on websites).

4. Choose the criteria and tools of measurement by (a) determining the criteria for assessing effectiveness and (b) selecting the most appropriate software measurement tools.

5. Establish a benchmark (e.g. by measuring where your company is in relation to some of the metrics in Table 12.4).

6. Undertake the campaign, and then analyse the outcomes and propose changes by comparing the outcomes against your proposal benchmarks to assess the variance between the two. This makes it possible to ascertain what changes are necessary to meet the benchmark targets.

7. Continue to measure on a daily, weekly, monthly, and quarterly basis.

Content Marketing

Content marketing is an approach to marketing communication in which brands create and disseminate content to consumers with the intention that the content generates interest, engages consumers, and influences behaviour (Stephen et al., 2015). Although branded content has

Table 12.4 Social media measures used by marketers

Rank	Measure	Percentage of total respondents	
		2010	2014
1	Hits/visits/page views	48%	60%
2	Number of followers and friends	24%	45%
3	Repeat visits	35%	39%
4	Conversion rates (from visitor to buyer)	25%	31%
5	Buzz indicators (mentions, shares)	16%	24%
6	Sales levels	18%	17%
7	Online products/service ratings	8%	14%
8	Customer acquisition costs	12%	14%
9	Net promoter score	8%	13%
10	Revenue per customer	17%	13%
11	Text analysis ratings	7%	12%
12	Customer retention costs	8%	6%
13	Abandoned shopping carts	4%	6%
14	Profits per customer	9%	6%

Source: Moorman (2014).

been around for more than 100 years (with one of the pioneering examples being the *Guide Michelin*, which included restaurant recommendations to get French car owners to drive more and thus increase their need for Michelin tyres), this marketing activity has accelerated in the digital space.

Most of the digital marketing communication activities discussed so far rely on consumers actively deciding to take part in marketing. For example, search marketing requires consumers to actively click on a link, and social media marketing relies on consumers actively engaging (liking, sharing, co-creating) content created by brands. This means that brands are under increasing pressure to create online content that consumers value. Therefore marketers are paying increasing attention to creating online content that can benefit their target audiences by adapting

Research Insight 12.2

To take your learning further, you might wish to read this influential paper.

Hoffman, D.L. and Fodor, M. (2010). Can you measure the ROI of your social media? *MIT Sloan Management Review*, **52(1), 41–9.**

This article suggests that, rather than considering the organization's investment in social media, what should be considered are the customers' investments, i.e. their motivations to use and continue using an organization's social media resources. The authors argue that the return on investment (ROI) from this perspective stresses more fruitful long-term customer relationships.

Visit the **Online Resource Centre** to read the abstract and access the full paper.

traditional journalism and publishing techniques. These activities are often referred to as content marketing. Although the appropriate definition of content marketing is debated (Neff 2015), there is little doubt that these practices are important for marketers.

Global content marketing investments reached $144.8bn in 2014 and are expected to grow to 313.4bn by 2019. Whereas content marketing investments have traditionally been more common in B2B, growth rates in B2C are expected to be higher than in B2B, making the share of investments between the two balanced at 50/50 by 2019 (PQ Media, 2015). What is more, 90% of marketers state that they use content marketing in some form, and 60% are intending to increase content marketing in the near future (Stephen *et al.*, 2015). In addition, strategies to direct the target audience to the content need to be in place; this is most commonly done via search marketing, promotions, and advertising (Pulizzi and Handley, 2015).

Thus the intention of content marketing is to create content that has value for the receiver (e.g. by being useful, educational, or entertaining in and of itself), thereby pulling the consumer toward the brand. There are numerous ways to create such value. Whereas B2C content marketing typically has focused on entertainment and information and B2B on knowledge and competence (for an overview of the most commonly used content marketing tactics among B2Bs, see Table 12.5), these borders are blurring. For example, Volvo Trucks, which offer heavy trucks to a professional audience, has recently been very successful in a content-centred campaign focusing on entertaining and spectacular online videos (see Market Insight 12.4), and Red Bull has transformed their content operations into a fully fledged media house specializing in high quality coverage of extreme sports (Red Bull Media House). Thus there is plenty of opportunity to provide value in a way that can be mutually beneficial for the brand and the receiver.

Successful content marketing depends on a marketer being able to balance the needs of the brand and the needs of the receiver. Typically, this requires taking contextual aspects, such as the timing and the place (e.g. social media or paid platform) of the communication into account. For example, research shows that for social media branded content to be influential in persuading consumers to engage in desirable ways (e.g. clicking a link, spreading word of mouth), marketers must design content that is *not* highly persuasion oriented. What is more, the social

Rank	Tactic	Use
1	Social media content	92%
2	eNewsletters	83%
3	Articles on own website	81%
4	Blogs	80%
5	In-person events	77%
6	Case studies	77%
7	Videos	76%
8	Illustrations/photos	69%
9	White papers	68%
10	Online presentations	65%

Table 12.5 Top B2B content marketing tactics 2015

Source: Pulizzi and Handley (2015).

media content needs to be adapted to consumer behaviour on the platform being used. For example, on Facebook the most successful content is relevant to the brand, but does not have an advertisement-like tone or a clear message. Thus this content should not use 'hard sell', or even 'soft sell', but rather open up for consumers to make sense of it themselves. This is particularly important when the audience comprises mostly core consumers since they are somewhat less forgiving of and more sensitive to pushy messages (Stephen *et al.*, 2015).

Mobile Marketing

Mobile marketing is the set of practices that enables organizations to communicate and engage interactively with their audiences through any mobile device or network (MMA, 2009). With the added benefits of store-and-send technology giving the option of message storage, mobile marketing is quick, inexpensive, and reaches markets wherever they are, despite limitations in message content.

According to the 2015 Chief Marketing Officer (CMO) survey, marketers invested 6% of their marketing budgets in media in 2015, and expected this share to grow to 16% in the following three years (Moorman, 2015). Investments in mobile are through both paid media (mobile advertising) and the development of own media such as apps. In 2015, mobile comprised about 25% of total Internet advertising and was growing faster than other online format. Since 2010 the compound average growth rate for mobile advertising in the USA has been 110%. Similar

Research Insight 12.3

To take your learning further, you might wish to read this influential paper.

Rosengren, S. and Dahlén, M. (2015). Exploring advertising equity: how a brand's past advertising may affect consumer willingness to approach its future ads. *Journal of Advertising*, **44(1), 1–13.**

This paper investigates what drives consumer willingness to pay attention to advertising. Based on empirical studies of more than 1,700 consumers and 100 brands in more than 12 different product categories it shows how adding value in advertising is vital to succeeding in digital environments where consumers are increasingly in charge of their own media consumption.

Visit the Online Resource Centre to read the abstract and access the full paper.

Market Insight 12.4
The Epic Split

Volvo Truck Live Test Series is a multipart online video series that shows various technical features of Volvo's trucks tested in spectacular and entertaining ways. For example, in the first test video, tightrope walker Faith Dickey is filmed walking across a rope tied between two speeding trucks, and in the most famous film Belgian action hero Jean-Claude Van Damme carries out his signature split between two reversing trucks.

The live test series was initially created to launch a new range of trucks in 2012. This was the company's first major launch in 20 years. Given the changing media landscape they were looking for a new and innovative launch campaign to outsmart the competition. The purpose of the films was to create awareness and pave the way for further marketing in Volvo Trucks' 140 local markets.

Research into truck buyers and the product features of the new trucks revealed two key insights. The first was that truck drivers have strong emotional bonds with their trucks. The second was that many people influence truck-buying decisions—ranging from the driver to his or her family and friends, colleagues and bosses, clients, and the businesses whose products the trucks carry.

These two insights had a significant impact on the nature of the films produced. Emotion plays a key role in conveying the product benefits. What is more, the films appeal to more than one target audience. Experienced truck drivers are amazed by the precision of the driving, while others focus on the spectacular demonstration. The series format was selected to

Volvo Trucks use a broad appeal in their ads to target the many people who influence truck-buying decisions
Source: © Taina Sohlman/Shutterstock.

Market Insight 12.4
continued

ensure longevity and enable the films to be combined with supporting content, including detailed product information about each new truck and the technology innovations behind their features.

In 2015 the campaign was awarded the prize for the most effective ad campaign in the world at the Cannes Lions International Festival of Creativity. Between June 2012 and May 2014, Volvo Trucks' Live Test

films generated more than 100m YouTube views and were shared online nearly 8m times. Overall, the campaign generated 20,000 media reports worldwide. In addition, more than half the truck owners who had seen the films stated that they were more than likely to choose Volvo the next time they bought a truck.

Sources: Berger and Milkman (2012); Carter (2014); Dumenco (2015).

Theory into Practice

Consumers are becoming increasingly used to determining what information they want, when they want it, and how they want it. Therefore marketers have to create online content that consumers voluntarily seek out and pass on ('pull') rather than force their communication on them ('push'). Marketing that creates and disseminates content to consumers in order to generate interest, engage consumers, and influence behaviour is referred to as content marketing. Despite the term 'consumer' being used in the definition, content marketing is most commonly used in B2B marketing tactics with social media content, eNewsletters, and articles on corporate websites being the most common formats.

The Volvo Live Test Series is an example of B2B content marketing. By testing the technical features of the new trucks in spectacular and entertaining ways Volvo Trucks created a pull for its marketing. The films were created to add value both to the primary audience consisting of professional truck owners and secondary audiences consisting of the families and relatives, as well as the customers and colleagues, of these drivers. The need to adapt to different buyer roles is typically important in B2B marketing. The series format also allowed the campaign to last for a long time (films were released between 2012 and 2014 and are still available online) and to be adapted to local marketing needs in different markets.

Related Topics:

digital marketing; content marketing; viral marketing; buying behaviour; B2B.

1 **Why do you think the Van Damme film was so successful?**

2 **How and why were people motivated to access the video on YouTube? How do motivations**

vary between truck owners and other target audiences?

3 **What other viral campaigns have you seen? Were they successful and, if so, why (not)?**

growth rates can be found in Europe. Just as with traditional online advertising, mobile advertising relies on several different ad formats, with display and search advertising being the largest (see Table 12.6).

Table 12.6 Types of mobile advertising format

Ad format	Description	Share of Internet ad investments*
Display advertising	Banner ads, digital video, digital audio, sponsorships, and rich media advertising served to mobile devices.	49%
Search	Advertisers pay fees to online companies to list and/or link their company site domain name to a specific search word or phrase (includes paid search revenues). Search categories include: paid listings, contextual search, paid inclusion, and site optimization.	49%
Other formats	NA	4%

*Based on US ad spend 2014. Because of rounding, the figures might not add up to 100%. NA = not applicable.
Source: IAB/PwC (2015b).

Mobile is the fastest growing online medium. Increasingly, we can access digital technologies, share information, socialize online, and play games on the move. The number of mobile Internet users has grown exponentially as the wireless infrastructure and mobile devices required to support the mobile Internet have evolved. As an illustration, Swedish smartphone usage was 8% of total Internet time in 2011, and by 2015 it had increased to 29%, with 12- to 35-year-olds using their mobiles more than half of the Internet time (Findahl, 2015). According to a study of US mobile users, mobile Internet use is split about equally between mobile apps and web browsers (MillwardBrown Digital, 2015).

Current changes in behaviours clearly show that mobile is taking over more and more of consumer online searches, and that marketers need to consider how to stay relevant and accessible at different stages in the consumer decision process. Increasingly, the use of smartphone apps is becoming the default mechanism for such searches. These apps use a combination of barcode scanning and location-based services to provide relevant information, for example showing only stores near the consumer when she is carrying out a price comparison. Thus these apps are suited to delivering context-specific, and hence more relevant, information to consumers. Mobile search also enables the convergence of online and offline, for example by enabling barcode scanning.

Depending on factors such as context, product category, user experience, and availability of (other) information, consumers' mobile search behaviours focus on different types of information. Daurer *et al.* (2015) investigated consumer searches via an app that enables product searches based on barcodes. The results show that access to more types of information, especially product-related information, reduces search on price information. This suggests that availability of information content can lower price sensitivity in mobile search. They also found that mobile search does not necessarily occur at the point of purchase. Consumers carry out mobile search in many situations other than shopping (e.g. while consuming the product), suggesting that companies need to adapt their marketing beyond the point of

Research Insight 12.4

To take your learning further, you might wish to read this influential paper.

Edelman, D.C. and Singer, M. (2015). Competing on customer journeys. *Harvard Business Review*, 23, 118–29.

This article discusses how digital and mobile technology has changed how consumers research and buy products and how companies need to come up with new tools, processes, and organizational structures to proactively lead digital customers from consideration to purchase and beyond.

@ Visit the **Online Resource Centre** to read the abstract and access the full paper.

purchase. In addition, geographic travel (mobility), the availability of specific types of product information, and contextual factors (e.g. economic surroundings, competition, and weather) influence search intensity.

Location-based marketing has long been expected to be the next big thing in mobile advertising. However, adaptation has been slow and location-based marketing still makes up just a small part of total mobile investments. In part, this may be explained by technological problems which result in location-based assessments having low accuracy. Thus location-based marketing is expected to pick up pace in the next few years as the accuracy of mobile technologies improves (L. Johnson 2014, 2015).

@ Consumers are increasingly searching for information about products through various digital platforms and devices, but is this the case for all products? **Visit the Online Resource Centre** and undertake Internet Activity 12.3 to find out more about online and offline search.

Crowdsourcing

Whilst the previous discussion has concerned social media, technologies, and marketing, and how marketing is increasingly being co-created with consumers, we will now consider how marketers make use of social media to interact and co-create with communities through the technique of crowdsourcing. Crowdsourcing is used increasingly in marketing. Various definitions exist for the term, including the following:

> Crowdsourcing, a term that combines 'crowd' and 'outsourcing', loosely means engaging a large group of people to come up with an idea or solve a problem. Some companies use the process to draw on the knowledge and opinions of a wide body of Internet users to create better products and marketing plans, or solve other problems.
>
> (Vallone, 2011)

Crowdsourcing represents the act of a company or institution taking a function once performed by employees and outsourcing it to an undefined (and generally large) network of people in the form of an open call. This can take the form of peer-production (when the job is performed collaboratively), but is also often undertaken by sole individuals. The crucial prerequisite is the use of the open call format and the large network of potential labourers.

(Howe, 2006: 5)

Crowdsourcing can be used in marketing in different ways, with different requirements for the role of the crowd, the end-goal, how the crowd is remunerated, and the size and diversity of the crowd necessary for the task. However, it is probably most helpful to think of it used in four main categories: the crowdsourcing of (1) routine activities, (2) content, (3) creative activities, and (4) funding (see Table 12.7). One example of the crowdsourcing of routine activities was reCAPTCHA (CAPTCHA stands for Completely Automated Public Turing test to tell Computers and Humans Apart). The initiative for this was to digitize books by supplying websites with CAPTCHA protection from bots attempting to access restricted sites. The CAPTCHA test requires users to retype images of words not recognized by optical character recognition (OCR) machines, and in so doing helps to digitize the Internet archive and the archives of the New York Times. iStockphoto and openstreetmap are good examples of companies which crowdsourced content (see also Table 12.8). Companies which have used crowdsourcing for creative activities include InnoCentive (see also Table 12.8) and Wilogo, which use crowdsourcing mechanisms for research and development projects and to produce

Table 12.7 Forms of crowdsourcing (CS)

Consideration	CS of routine activities	CS of content	CS of creative activities	CS of funds
Role of the crowd	Provision of time, the ability to process information	Provision of content (especially information)	Provision of solutions, ideas, knowledge	Provision of monetary recourses
Goal	Division of labour (integrative)	Division of labour (integrative)	Winner takes all (selective)	Raise money
Remuneration	Micro-payments	Micro-payments or volunteer	Micro- to high payments	Equity/loan/ reward
Size of the crowd	Very important	Very important	Of little importance	Very important
Diversity of the crowd	Not important	Very important	Very important	Not important
Commercial examples	reCAPTCHA	iStockphoto, openstreetmap	InnoCentive, Wilogo	FundedByMe

Source: Burger-Helmchen and Pénin (2011) and the authors.

Table 12.8 Pioneer and recent users of crowdsourcing

Organization	Date (first use)	Details
Pioneer users		
Threadless	2000	Began selling T-shirts with designs developed and rated by its user community, instead of expensive designers, in an ongoing competition process. Winning designers received $2,000 prize money and $500 voucher to spend at Threadless. Submitters of winning slogans received $500 prize money.
iStockphoto	2000	Sells royalty-free stock images, media, and design elements using material sourced online from a crowd of largely amateur artists, designers, and photographers. Contributors receive a percentage of the purchase price when their images are downloaded. A smaller group of contributors screen new applicants and maintain the image database, earning a higher percentage from work downloaded.
InnoCentive	2001	Began life as a spin-off company from US pharmaceutical giant Eli Lilly. InnoCentive works by posting online research and development (R&D) and scientific challenges for its crowd of users to solve. Winning contributors are paid a large financial incentive and InnoCentive takes a fee for hosting the challenge.
More recent users		
LEGO®	2012	Developed its product innovation platform LEGO® Cuusoo, released initially as a beta version, to invite users to submit LEGO product ideas and get them rated by other users. Any idea which receives 10,000 votes is considered by the LEGO product review board for production. If a user's LEGO idea is chosen, the submitting user receives a 1% royalty on total net sales of that product. Initial ideas receiving more than 10,000 votes included the Exo Suit and the Back to the Future™ Time Machine (see Kronsberg, 2012).
Flippin' Burgers	2012	Flippin' Burgers, a gourmet hamburger restaurant in Stockholm, Sweden, has not only been ranked the greatest burger restaurant outside America (Santana, 2014), but also has crowd funding to thank for its existence. Before it opened, Flippin' Burgers was launched on the crowdfunding site fundedbyme.se to test the demand and to gather capital. In two months 178 people donated a combined total of SEK 36,000 based on a promise that they would, sometime in the future, be able to try a hamburger which didn't exist from a restaurant that didn't exist.
McDonald's	2014	Invited its UK consumers to a virtual kitchen where they could help create the perfect burger. Participants were able to build their burger using over 80 ingredients. Fans then voted for the their favourites on the My Burger website. The creators of the top 12 burgers were invited to make their burgers and a judging panel picked the top five which were served in 1,200 McDonald's locations across the UK (Thinkwithgoogle, 2014).
Volvo Cars	2015	Instead of buying expensive ad time during the Superbowl, Volvo decided to hijack the car brands that did. To this end, consumers were given the opportunity to nominate someone they deemed deserving of a Volvo XC60 every time any car spot aired during the live event. All they had to do was tweet using the hashtag #VolvoContest. In four hours, Volvo received 50,000 tweets with the program hashtag (the most of any automotive brand) (Buss, 2015).

logo designs, respectively. When it comes to crowdsourced funding there are several different websites offering this possibility to companies. According to a recent report from one of them, the success of crowd funding campaigns is highly contingent on social media sharing as well as the accuracy and reliability of market assessments and financial forecasts (Lundquist and Gromek, 2015).

Crowdsourcing is becoming increasingly ubiquitous in marketing as organizations seek to use it to reduce their marketing costs, reduce the time required to undertake a particular task, find and use resources (skills, labour, money) that do not exist in-house, obtain information and market intelligence, design new products and services, and design promotional material. One of the key considerations when setting up a crowdsourcing task is how to motivate the crowd to take part. One common rule of thumb suggests that 90% of visitors to the site will consume the content (see the task), 9% will partially engage (read the task, consider taking part or request further information), and 1% will fully engage (e.g. provide a submission). See Table 12.8 for examples of early pioneers and recent users of crowdsourcing in marketing.

Legal and Ethical Considerations

The rise in digital resources, and their increasing use for marketing activities, is accompanied by complications and changes to legislation and regulated business practices. The types of legal, ethical, and regulatory issues that marketers need to consider include the following.

- Jurisdiction—where does digital marketing activity take place? Commercial law is based on transactions within national boundaries, but digital marketing exposes both individual organizations and the community to information, transactions, and social activity outside these boundaries (e.g. EU legislation and Microsoft).

- Ownership—who owns the content we create and share? Copyright law is a national issue, and the copyright laws (what can and cannot be used without the originator's permission) differ from one country to another. Some countries do not have copyright or intellectual property protection, and so ideas, designs, etc. sent to those countries can be taken and used without the agreement of the copyright holder. The value of copyright is also being questioned with the increase in user-generated and co-created content, and the rise of the Creative Commons (CC) free license system.

- Permissions—do we have the right permissions to upload and share content? Privacy legislation is also national or regional, and the right of an individual or organization to use information is subject to this legislation. A new EU-wide **cookies** law, which came into place in 2012 requires companies to make it clear to users when they are saving a cookie onto someone's computer. Although some countries have no privacy legislation, the EU Data Protection Directive has resulted in Europe becoming one of the most highly regulated jurisdictions in the world when it comes to data protection requirements. However, that does not directly govern the activities of organizations founded in the USA (e.g. Microsoft, Facebook).

- Security—how secure are the data and information we share? Information and transaction security and protection from fraud and identity theft is another area of increasing change. Legislation varies from country to country and region to region, with further differences evident in the laws that govern and protect consumer and business interests (e.g. distance selling regulations, consumer protection (e-commerce) regulations).

- Accessibility—does everyone who wants access have access? Disability and discrimination legislation also requires consideration. As more services and marketing information is being shared digitally, the right to access and usability for all becomes an important agenda item for the dissemination of information and services.

Visit the Online Resource Centre and complete Internet Activity 12.4 to learn more about consumer privacy concerns.

Chapter Summary

To consolidate your learning, the key points from this chapter are summarized here.

- **Define digital marketing and social media marketing.**

  Digital marketing is the management and execution of marketing using digital technologies and channels (e.g. web, email, digital TV, Internet) to reach markets in a timely, relevant personal, interactive, and cost-efficient manner. It is related to, but distinct from, e-marketing, direct marketing, and interactive marketing. Social media marketing is a form of digital marketing which uses social networking sites to produce content that users will share and which will in turn create exposure of the brand to customers and thereby increase or reinforce its customer base.

- **Explain how digitalization is transforming marketing practice.**

  The growth of digital technologies is not only changing consumer behaviours, it is changing business. Successful marketing in a digital world requires digital marketing to be integrated into marketing research, products, and services, as well as marketing communication and channel distribution plans. Thus digital marketing should be considered and adapted more widely than just as a new communication or distribution channel. It can help create new business opportunities and enable new relationships (and thereby insights) with and between consumers.

- **Discuss key techniques in digital marketing and social media marketing.**

  Key techniques in digital marketing include Internet advertising, search marketing, email marketing, social media marketing, content marketing, and mobile marketing. Characteristic of digital marketing, especially that through social media, is that marketers need to give up some control and power to consumers. Marketers must share control over their brands with their online users; users will co-create content and generate their own content; customers will develop their own communities which marketers should seek to contribute to rather than usurp. It is about dialogue, conversation, and listening rather than monologue and transmitting.

- **Review how practitioners measure the effectiveness of social media marketing.**

  In order to measure the effectiveness of a social media campaign, marketers should follow a seven-step process: identifying a set of appropriate social media metrics; reviewing the social media campaign objectives; mapping the campaign by highlighting links to brand-generated content, consumer-generated content, consumer-fortified content, and exposure to content(ed) consumers; choosing the criteria and tools of measurement; establishing a benchmark; undertaking the campaign; and measuring it frequently.

■ **Discuss crowdsourcing and explain how online communities can be harnessed for marketing purposes.**

Crowdsourcing is the process of outsourcing a task or group of tasks to a generally large 'crowd' of people. It can be used in marketing to outsource routine activities, obtain content (e.g. Volvo/Twitter campaign), or obtain creative input (e.g. LEGO—new product development). It can also be used as a way to gain access to financial resources (e.g. Flippin' Burger—funding of restaurant).

? Review Questions

1 Define how digital marketing differs from interactive and Internet marketing.
2 How is digitalization transforming marketing practice?
3 Compare and contrast the difference between 'pull' and 'push' approaches to digital marketing.
4 What is social media and how has it changed marketing?
5 What is social media marketing and why do marketers use it?
6 How can you measure the effectiveness of social media marketing?
7 What is content marketing and why do marketers use it?
8 How is the growth of mobile devices (e.g. smartphones) impacting on marketing?
9 What marketing activities can crowdsourcing support?

✎ Worksheet Summary

@ To apply the knowledge you have gained from this chapter and test your understanding of digital and social media marketing visit the **Online Resource Centre** and complete Worksheet 12.1.

Discussion Questions

1 Having read Case Insight 12.1 at the beginning of this chapter, how could Spotify use social media to support its service and build customer loyalty?

2 Do you think that digital resources are redefining marketing?

3 Why are many marketers having difficulties adapting to a situation where they have to share control and power over a brand with consumers?

4 Privacy and ownership of digital information is increasingly challenged. When participating on Facebook I think I control my own data and information, but do I? Discuss.

@ **Visit the Online Resource Centre and complete the Multiple Choice Questions to assess your knowledge of Chapter 12.**

Glossary

co-created content (CCC) is the act of interacting, creating content or applications, by at least two people.

contextual advertising a form of targeted advertising on websites, with advertisements selected and served by automated systems based on the content displayed to the user.

cookie an electronic 'token'—a piece of data or record transmitted by a webserver to a client computer. More simply put, a cookie is a small text file found on your hard drive that allows information about your web activity patterns to be stored in the memory of your browser.

digital marketing the process of marketing accomplished or facilitated through the application of electronic devices, appliances, tools, techniques, technologies, and/or systems.

mobile marketing the set of practices that enable organizations to communicate and engage with their audience in an interactive and relevant manner through any mobile device or network.

paid inclusion can provide a guarantee that the website is included in the search engine's natural listings.

pay per click (PPC) advertising that uses sponsored search engine listings to drive traffic to a website. The advertiser bids for search terms, and the search engine ranks ads based on a competitive auction as well as other factors.

permission-based email marketing (opt-in) opt-in email or permission marketing is a method of advertising by electronic mail wherein the recipient of the advertisement has consented to receive it.

review site a website on which reviews can be posted about people, businesses, products, or services, such as Epinions.com, Tripadvisor.com, and reviews on Amazon.com.

search directory a database of information maintained by human editors. It lists websites by category and subcategory, usually based on the whole website rather than one page or a set of keywords.

search engine operates algorithmically or using a mixture of algorithmic and human input to collect, index, store, and retrieve information on the web and make it available to users in a manageable and meaningful way in response to a search query.

spam unsolicited email, the junk mail of the twenty-first century, which clogs email servers and uses up much needed bandwidth on the Internet.

user-generated content (UGC) content made publicly available over the Internet which reflects a certain amount of creative effort and is created by users not professionals.

References

Alldredge, K., Newaskar, P., and Ungerman, K. (2015). The digital future of consumer-packaged-goods companies. McKinsey Insights. Retrieve from: http://www.mckinsey.com/insights/consumer_and_retail/the_digital_future_of_consumer_packaged_goods_companies (accessed 4 November 2015).

AMA (2015). http://www.marketing-dictionary.org/ama (accessed 25 February 2016).

Anon. (2015a). Statistics and facts about social networks. Retrieve from: http://www.statista.com/topics/1164/social-networks/ (accessed 4 November 2015).

Anon. (2015b). How bothersome is bot traffic? Retrieve from: http://www.emarketer.com/Article/How-Bothersome-Bot-Traffic/1013178?ecid = NL1002#sthash.iOmlm2xU.dpuf (accessed 8 November 2015).

Anon. (2015c). Worldwide market share of leading search engines from January 2010 to July 2015. Retrieve from: http://www.statista.com/statistics/216573/worldwide-market-share-of-search-engines/ (accessed 8 November 2015).

Anon. (2015d). People prefer email for brand outreach in the UK, *E-marketer*. Retrieve from: http://www.emarketer.com/Article/People-Prefer-Email-Brand-Outreach-UK/1013083 (accessed 4 November 2015).

Anon. (2015e). Social network ad spending to hit $23.68 billion worldwide in 2015, *E-marketer*. Retrieve from: http://www.emarketer.com/Article/Social-Network-Ad-Spending-Hit-2368-Billion-Worldwide-2015/1012357#sthash.LKObvSEJ.dpuf (accessed 4 November 2015).

Anon. (2016). Leading social networks worldwide as of January 2016, ranked by number of active users (in millions). Retrieve from: http://www.statista.com/statistics/272014/global-social-networks-ranked-by-number-of-users/ (accessed 22 July 2016).

Berger, J. and Milkman, K.L. (2012). What makes online content viral? *Journal of Marketing Research*, 49(April), 192–205.

Budds, D. (2015). How IKEA is defining the state of play (with a little help from DreamWorks) *FastCo Design*. Retrieve from: http://www.fastcodesign.com/3052589/behind-the-brand/how-ikea-is-defining-the-state-of-play-with-a-little-help-from-dreamworks (accessed 22 July 2016).

Burger-Helmchen, T. and Pénin, J. (2011). Crowdsourcing: définition, enjeux, typologie [trans. Crowdsourcing: definition, stakes, typology]. *Revue Management et Avenir*, 41(January), 254–69.

Buss, D. (2015). Volvo wins its Super Bowl contest: 5 questions with EVP Bodil Eriksson. *Brandchannel*. Retrieve from: http://brandchannel.com/2015/02/03/volvo-wins-its-super-bowl-contest-5-questions-with-evp-bodil-eriksson/ (accessed 4 November 2015).

Carter, M. (2014), How Volvo pulled off an epic and game-changing split. *Fast Company*. Retrieve from: http://www.fastcocreate.com/3031654/cannes/how-volvo-trucks-pulled-off-an-epic-split-and-a-game-changing-campaign (accessed 12 November 2015).

Cheng, J.M.-S., Blankson, C., Wang, E.S.-T., and Chen, L.S.-L. (2009). Consumer attitudes and interactive digital advertising. *International Journal of Advertising*, 28(3), 501–25.

Christodoulides, G. (2009). Branding in the post-internet era. *Marketing Theory*, 9(1), 141–4.

CIM (2013). How to measure the impact of your social media campaign, Chartered Institute of Marketing, Marketing Expert [Forum]. Retrieve from: http://www.cim.co.uk (accessed 17 February 2013).

Colliander, J. and Wien, A. (2013). Trash talk rebuffed. What can we learn from the phenomenon of consumers defending companies criticized in online communities? *European Journal of Marketing*, 47(10), 1733–57.

Daurer, S., Molitor, D., Spann, M., and Manchanda, P. (2015). Consumer search behavior on the mobile internet: an empirical analysis. Marketing Science Institute Working Paper Series 2015, Report No. 15–111. Retrieve from: http://papers.ssrn.com/sol3/papers.cfm?abstract_id=2603242 (accessed 22 July 2016).

de Mers, J. (2015). The top 7 online marketing trends that will dominate 2016. *Forbes*, 29 September. Retrieve from: http://www.forbes.com/sites/jaysondemers/2015/09/29/the-top-7-online-marketing-trends-that-will-dominate-2016/#782466854c04 (accessed 11 November 2015).

Dumenco, S. (2015) Volvo Trucks 'Epic Split' wins again; takes home Creative Effectiveness Grand Prix. *AdAge*. Retrieve from: http://adage.com/article/special-report-cannes-lions/volvo-trucks-live-test-series-epic-split-wins/299177/ (accessed 12 November 2015).

Dunphy, J. (2012). SEO and social media get married. *Econsultancy*, 24 December. Retrieve from: http://econsultancy.com/uk/blog/11406-seo-and-social-media-get-married. (accessed 11 February 2012).

Dutta, S., Geiger, T., and Lanvin, B. (eds) (2015), *The Global Information Technology Report: 2015. ICTs for Inclusive Growth*, World Economic Forum/INSEAD. Retrieve from: http://www3.weforum.org/docs/WEF_GITR2015.pdf (accessed 15 October 2015).

Edelman, D.C. and Singer, M. (2015). Competing on customer journeys. *Harvard Business Review*, 9(11), 88–100.

Findahl, O. (2015). Svenskarna och internet. Retrieve from: https://www.iis.se/docs/SOI2014.pdf (accessed 4 November 2015).

Greene, J (2015). Amazon opening its first real bookstore—at U-Village. *Seattle Times*. Retrieve from: http://www.seattletimes.com/business/amazon/amazon-opens-first-bricks-and-mortar-bookstore-at-u-village/ (accessed 6 November 2015).

Harris, P. (2009). *Penguin Dictionary of Marketing*. London: Penguin Books.

Hoffman, D.L. and Fodor, M. (2010). Can you measure the ROI of your social media? *MIT Sloan Management Review*, 52(1), 41–9.

Howe, J. (2006).The rise of crowdsourcing. *Wired*, 14.06 (June). Retrieve from: http://www.wired.com/wired/archive/14.06/crowds.html (accessed 26 January 2013).

IAB/PwC (2015a). Digital Adspend Study UK. Retrieve from: http://www.iabuk.net/research/library/h1-2015-digital-adspend-results (accessed 4 November 2015).

IAB/PwC (2015b). IAB internet advertising revenue report 2014 full year results. Retrieve from: http://www.iab.com/wp-content/uploads/2015/05/IAB_Internet_Advertising_Revenue_FY_2014.pdf (accessed 4 November 2015).

Ingram, M. (2015). Publishers only have themselves to blame for the ad-blocking apocalypse. *Fortune*, 13 August. Retrieve from: http://fortune.com/2015/08/13/publishers-only-have-themselves-to-blame-for-the-ad-blocking-apocalypse/ (accessed 8 November 2015).

Internet World Stats (2015). Internet usage statistics: the internet big picture. Retrieve from: www.internetworldstats.com/stats.htm (accessed 15 October 2015).

Johnson, B (2015). The evolution of search on Amazon. *Internet Retailer*. Retrieve from: https://www.internetretailer.com/commentary/2015/06/11/evolution-search-amazon (accessed 6 November 2015).

Johnson, L. (2014). Mobile marketers know who you are and where you've been and what you're reading on your phone. *Adweek*, 24 September. Retrieve from: http://www.adweek.com/news/technology/mobile-marketers-know-who-you-are-and-where-youve-been-158491 (accessed 13 November 2015).

Johnson, L. (2015). Are marketers finally getting the hang of location-based mobile ads? *Adweek*, 28 September. Retrieve from: http://www.adweek.com/news/technology/are-marketers-finally-getting-hang-location-based-mobile-ads-167212 (accessed 13 November 2015).

Kane, G.C., Fichman, R.G., Gallaugher, J., and Glaser, J. (2009). Community relations 2.0. *Harvard Business Review*, 87(11), 132–42.

Keller, E. and Fay, B. (2012), 'Word-of-mouth advocacy: a new key to advertising effectiveness. *Journal of Advertising Research*, 52(4), 459–64.

Kronsberg, M. (2012). How Lego's great adventure in geek-sourcing snapped into place and boosted the brand. *Fast Company*, 2 February. Retrieve from: http://www.fastcompany.com/1812959/how-legos-great-adventure-geek-sourcing-snapped-place-and-boosted-brand (accessed 2 February 2013).

Leggatt, H (2015). Amazon the go-to place for consumers to search for products. *BizReport: Search Marketing*: 9 October 9. Retrieve from: http://www.bizreport.com/2015/10/amazon-the-go-to-place-for-consumers-to-search-for-products.html (accessed 6 November 2015).

Lundquist, A. and Gromek, M. (2015). Successful equity crowdfunding campaigns—a Nordic review. Fundedbyme.com. Retrieve from: http://www.slideshare.net/MichalGromek/successful-equity-crowdfunding-campaigns3 (accessed 9 November 2015).

Madov, N. (2015). DreamWorks creates a magical world for IKEA's new line of toys. Retrieve from: http://creativity-online.com/work/ikea-welcome-to-the-world-of-lattjo/43838 (accessed 22 July 2016).

Mangold, W.G. and Faulds, D.J. (2009). Social media: the new hybrid element of the promotion mix. *Business Horizons*, 52, 357–65.

Mitchell, A. (2001). *Right Side Up: Building Brands in the Age of the Organised Consumer*. London: HarperCollinsBusiness.

Miller, M.J. (2015). Play it forward: IKEA taps DreamWorks to bring Lattjo games to life. Retrieve from: http://www.brandchannel.com/2015/10/26/ikea-dreamworks-lattjo-102615/ (accessed 22 July 2016).

MillwardBrown Digital (2015). The new mobile mantra—setting mobile strategies based on insights not intuition. Retrieve from: https://www.millwardbrowndigital.com/mobile-mantra/ (accessed 11 November 2015).

MMA (2009). Buy mobile marketing. Mobile Marketing Association. Retrieve from: http://mmaglobal.com/about/content_category/research/10/341 (accessed 22 July 2016).

Moorman, C. (2014). CMO Survey Report: highlights and insights. Retrieve from: http://cmosurvey.org/files/2014/09/The_CMO_Survey-Highlights_and_Insights-Aug-2014.pdf (accessed 4 November 2015).

Moorman, C. (2015). CMO Survey Report: highlights and insights. Retrieve from: http://cmosurvey.org/files/2015/09/The_CMO_Survey-Highlights_and_Insights-Aug-2015.pdf (accessed 25 February 2016).

Murdough, C. (2009). Social media measurement: it's not impossible. *Journal of Interactive Advertising*, 10(1), 94–9.

Neff, J. (2015). Is it content or is it advertising? *Advertising Age*, 12 October. Retrieve from: http://adage.com/article/ad-age-research/content-advertising/300858/ (accessed 4 November 2015).

Niederhoffer, K., Mooth, R., Wiesenfeld, D., and Gordon, J. (2007). The origin and impact of CPG new-product buzz: emerging trends and implications. *Journal of Advertising Research*, 47(4), 420–6.

Nudd, T (2015a). Man poses as target on Facebook, trolls haters of its gender-neutral move with epic replies. *Adweek*. Retrieve from: http://www.adweek.com/adfreak/man-poses-target-facebook-trolls-haters-its-gender-neutral-move-epic-replies-166364 (accessed 22 July 2016).

Nudd, T (2015b). Target loved the guy who trolled its haters, judging by this genius Facebook post. *Adweek*. Retrieve from: http://www.adweek.com/adfreak/target-loved-guy-who-trolled-its-haters-judging-genius-facebook-post-166408 (accessed 22 July 2016).

O'Brien, M. (2015). How to construct the perfect marketing email. *ClickZ*. Retrieve from: http://www.clickz.com/clickz/news/2431283/how-to-construct-the-perfect-marketing-email (accessed 4 November 2015).

Ofcom (2015). Adults' media use and attitudes: Report 2015. Retrieve from: http://stakeholders.ofcom.org.uk/binaries/research/media-literacy/media-lit-10years/2015_Adults_media_use_and_attitudes_report.pdf (accessed 4 November 2015).

Owyang, J. and Lovett, J. (2010). Social marketing analytics: a new framework for measuring results in social media. Retrieve from: http://www.slideshare.net/jeremiah_owyang/altimeter-report-social-marketing-analytics (accessed 17 February 2013).

PQ Media (2015). Global content marketing forecast 2015–19'. Retrieve from: http://www.pqmedia.com/execsummary/PQMediaGlobalContentMarketingForecast2015-19-EXECSUMM.pdf (accessed 4 November 2015).

Pulizzi, J. and Handley, A. (2015). B2B content marketing: 2015 benchmarks, budgets, and trends. Retrieve from: http://contentmarketinginstitute.com/wp-content/uploads/2014/10/2015_B2B_Research.pdf (accessed 11 November 2015).

Rosengren, S. and Dahlén, M. (2015). Exploring advertising equity: how a brand's past advertising may affect consumer willingness to approach its future ads. *Journal of Advertising*, 44(1), 1–13.

Santana, F. (2014). The 10 greatest burger places outside America. *Daily Meal*, 27 September. Retrieve from: http://www.thedailymeal.com/10-greatest-burger-places-outside-america (accessed 9 November 2015).

Shankar, V. and Balasubramanian, S. (2009). Mobile marketing: synthesis and prognosis. *Journal of Interactive Marketing*, 23(2), 118–29.

Stephen, A.T., Sciandra, M.R., and Inman, J.J. (2015). The effects of content characteristics on consumer engagement with branded social media content on

Facebook. Marketing Science Institute Working Paper Series 2015 Report No. 15-110. Retrieve from: msi.org/reports/the-effects-of-content-characteristics-on-consumer-engagement-with-branded/ (accessed 22 July 2016).

Thinkwithgoogle (2015). My burger. Retrieve from: https://www.thinkwithgoogle.com/campaigns/my-burger-mcdonalds.html (accessed 4 November 2015).

van den Bulte, C., and Wuyts, S. (2007). *Social Networks and Marketing*. Boston, MA: Marketing Science Institute.

Vallone, J. (2011). Crowdsourcing could predict terror strikes, gasoline prices. *Investors' Business Daily*, 29 August, 5.

Waring, T. and Martinez, A. (2002). Ethical customer relationships: a comparative analysis of US and French organisations using permission-based email marketing. *Journal of Database Marketing*, 10(1), 53–70.

Wunsch-Vincent, S. and Vickery, G. (2007), Participative web: user-created content. OECD. Retrieve from: http://www.oecd.org/internet/interneteconomy/38393115.pdf (accessed 4 November 2015).

Chapter 13
Branding Decisions

Learning Outcomes

After studying this chapter you should be able to:

▶ Explain the characteristics and principal types of brands and branding

▶ Discuss ways in which brands work through associations and personalities

▶ Examine how branding has evolved, utilizing relational, and co-creation perspectives

▶ Explain how brands can be built

▶ Describe the principal issues associated with branding in services, B2B, internal, and global contexts

▶ Explore the issues and activities associated with brand equity and demonstrate why branding is important to marketing managers

Case Insight 13.1
Aston Martin

Market Insight 13.1
How to Avoid Damaging a Brand

Market Insight 13.2
Musicians Dying for Success

Market Insight 13.3
The Mashing of Peppa Pig

Market Insight 13.4
B2B Branding...Sintex Is the Name

Case Insight 13.1
Aston Martin

The Aston Martin brand, founded in 1913, is synonymous with hand-crafted luxury, peerless beauty, incredible performance, and international motorsport glory. We speak to Simon Sproule, Director of Global Marketing and Communications, to find out how the brand is promoted in China.

Aston Martin's brand projects: Power. Beauty. Soul. We see this as more than a tagline. It's about the mission for the company. Naturally, these words describe the attributes of our cars, but we bring more than a beautiful car to our customers. As with all products in the luxury market, they are a discretionary purchase and and are bought for a variety of reasons. The common denominator, however, is the emotional connection our cars have with customers and the physical product and values of the company/brand. With an Aston Martin, you join an exclusive club with only 80,000 members (the total number of cars produced in our 103-year history). By contrast, our large mainstream competitors will produce that many cars in three days!

The Aston Martin brand also stands for beautiful hand-crafted cars, evident in every aspect of the product and, for our customers, when they visit the factory in Gaydon, Warwickshire, and see the cars being made. The iconic Hollywood British spy character James Bond has become a brand attribute for Aston Martin through the 50-year association that started with the DB5 in Goldfinger. However, for our customers in new and emerging markets like China, James Bond may not have the same cultural resonance as it does in the UK. For those new customers to Aston Martin, we stand for the best of British style and elegance combined with the power of our V8 and V12 engines. In essence, we are the quintessential British GT car and more. We describe our branding approach as the 'Goldilocks strategy'—getting the balance between exclusivity

and accessibility just right. Although we are selling a luxury product to 1% of the world's population, we have a massive popular following: 6.5m Facebook fans and more than a million fans on Instagram. We need to be constantly mindful that the respect granted to our brand from our fans is an important motivator for our customers buying an Aston Martin. The simplest way to describe this is to be stuck in heavy traffic at a busy intersection. Our customers tell us that they always get let out of a junction … which in the most basic way speaks to the respect and affection people have for our cars. So our brand strategy is to balance the aspirational nature of the company and its products, but at the same time be friendly and accessible to all.

To implement our branding strategy, we combine high technology—we are in the process of implementing Salesforce to run our customer engagement—and a very personal touch. Buying an Aston Martin is not only about the cars, but becoming part of a family where you feel welcomed and valued. Like the majority of auto makers, we operate a franchise business with dealers handling the majority of the sales and service interface. That said, our customers also seek a direct relationship with the 'factory', and we encourage and embrace those relationships. I spend time with customers every week! To convey the brand values to target customers, we are moving towards storytelling driven by content and experiences. We invest relatively little in conventional advertising, preferring to engage our customer and fans with interesting and cool content.

Case Insight 13.1
continued

We want to encourage customers to spend time with us, visit the factory, and attend events and motor races. The most convincing way to sell an Aston Martin is a test drive.

The question for Aston Martin was how should it go about raising brand awareness and brand familiarity in China, an important emerging market?

Introduction

Our world is full of brands; from soap powders and soft drinks to airlines and financial services, even musicians, sports and film stars, buildings, cities and destinations, and social networks. Brands are configured in all shapes, sizes, entities. So, there are a huge variety of branding opportunities and, as Case Insight 13.1 rightly notes, people form associations with brands, but what exactly is a **brand**? How are brands developed? Who really creates them? What exactly is the nature of these relationships? Why are they significant? These are the key questions we explore in this chapter.

Branding is a process by which manufacturers and retailers help customers to differentiate between various offerings. It enables customers to make associations between certain attributes or feelings and a particular brand. If this differentiation can be achieved and sustained, a brand is considered to have a competitive advantage. It is not necessary for people to buy brands to enjoy and understand them. Successful brands create strong, positive, and lasting impressions through their communications, and associated psychological feelings and emotions, not just their functionality through use.

Brand names provide information about content, taste, durability, quality, price, and performance, without requiring the buyer to undertake time-consuming comparison tests with similar offerings or other risk reduction approaches to purchase decisions. In some categories, brands can be developed through the use of messages that are entirely emotional or image based. Many of the products in FMCG sectors, where there is low customer involvement, use communications based largely on imagery, such as Tetley in food and drink, New Look in fashion, and Revlon in cosmetics. Other sectors, such as houses or pharmaceuticals where purchase involvement tends to be higher, require rational information-based messages supported by image-based messages. In other words, a blend of messages may well be required to achieve the objectives and goals of the campaign.

We saw in Chapter 6 that a comprehensive segmentation strategy involves targeting and positioning brands. Positioning is concerned with the processes associated with creating and altering the perceptions consumers have about a firm's products or brands (Crawford, 1985). In other words, brand positioning is not about a brand's physicality, it is about the place the brand occupies in a consumer's mind (Ries and Trout, 1972).

Brand positioning is a strategic activity used to differentiate and distinguish a brand, so that a consumer understands the brand, not just remembers it. As Tudor and Negricea (2012) rightly state, branding and positioning are interrelated. A credible position cannot be sustained without a strong brand, and a brand cannot be developed or preserved without the audience perceiving a justifiable position.

In addition to the largely transactional positioning strategies set out in Chapter 6, some brands attempt to position themselves as relational brands. The aim is to attract relationship oriented buyers—people who, as Crosby (2012: 10) indicates, appreciate and seek 'recognition, appreciation, personalization, customization, exceptional customer service, fairness, reciprocity, information sharing, honesty/trustworthiness, cooperative problem solving and harmonious interactions' with their chosen brands.

To help achieve this, brands need to make relational promises. As examples, Crosby (2012: 10) refers to Nordstrom, BMW, Whole Foods, and American Express, whose promise is 'personalized concierge services and travel consultants to help unlock a world of VIP treatment and benefits'. Of course, successful brand positioning is not a one-time activity. Customer interactions and perceptions can alter as contexts evolve. This can mean that brands need to be repositioned and so different, increasingly relational promises, are developed as personal unique positions are sought out.

Successful brands such as Aston Martin, Airbnb, and Uber represent customer promises and shape their expectations. When expectations and experiences through brand usage match the promise, brand performance is accomplished. Successful brands tend to be innovators and deliver consistently on their promises. This serves to reinforce the positioning and credibility of the promise.

Therefore successful brands capture three core brand elements: promises, positioning and performance. These are depicted at Figure 13.1 as the Three Brand Ps (3BPs). At the core of this concept is communication, which enables a promise to be known (brand awareness), positions the brand correctly (brand attitude), and delivers brand performance (brand response).

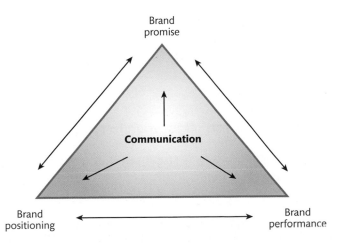

Figure 13.1

The triangulation of the 3 brand Ps

Source: Marketing Communications (7th edn) Fill, C. and Turnball, S. (2016). Reproduced with the kind permission of Pearson Education Limited. © Pearson Education Limited 2016.

What is a Brand?

A brand can be distinguished from its proposition or unbranded commodity counterparts by the perceptions and feelings that consumers have about its attributes and performance. Bottled water, for example, is essentially a commodity, but brands such as Highland Spring, Aqua Falls, and Crystal Clear have all developed their offerings with imagery which serves to enhance customer feelings and emotions about the actual water in the packaging. Ultimately, a brand resides in the mind of the consumer (Achenbaum, 1993).

Brands are products and services that have added value. This value has been deliberately designed and presented to augment a product with values and associations that are recognized by, and are meaningful to, their customers. Although marketing managers have to create, sustain, protect, and develop the identity of the brands for which they are responsible, it is customer perception, the use of the various senses that help fashion images of these brands, and the meaning and value that customers give to the brand that is important. Therefore, both managers and customers are involved in the branding process.

de Chernatony and dall'Olmo Riley (1998) identified 12 types of brand definition, but one of the more common interpretations is that a brand is represented by a name, symbol, words, or mark that identifies and distinguishes a proposition or company from its competitors. However, brands consist of much more than these various elements. As Aaker (2014: 1) remarks, 'far more than a name or a logo it is an organization's promise to a customer to deliver what a brand stands for ... in terms of functional benefits but also emotional, self-expressive and social benefits'. From this, Rossiter (2014) reinforces his view that brand awareness and brand attitude are core branding elements.

Brands have character, even personalities, and in order to develop character it is important to understand that brands are constructed of two main types of attributes: intrinsic and extrinsic.

Research Insight 13.1

To take your learning further, you might wish to read this influential paper.

de Chernatony, L. and dall'Olmo Riley, F. (1998). Defining a brand: beyond the literature with experts' interpretations. *Journal of Marketing Management*, 14(4/5), 417–43.

This paper provides an insight into the different ways a brand can be interpreted. It was published at the end of the twentieth century, and the authors suggest some interesting perspectives that were developed in subsequent years.

@ Visit the **Online Resource Centre** to read the abstract and access the full paper.

Intrinsic attributes refer to the functional characteristics of a proposition, such as its shape, performance, and physical capacity. If any of these intrinsic attributes were changed, this would directly alter the proposition. **Extrinsic attributes** refer to those elements that are not intrinsic and, if changed, do not alter the material functioning and performance of the proposition itself. These include devices such as the brand name, marketing communications, packaging, price, and mechanisms that enable consumers to form associations that give meaning to the brand. Buyers often use the extrinsic attributes to help them distinguish one brand from another, because in certain categories it is difficult for them to make decisions based on the intrinsic attributes alone. For example, many financial companies develop brands because their propositions are very complex and many consumers are reluctant or unable to give the time and effort necessary to understand them. By developing a single brand, firms such as Prudential and Zurich have tried to establish high levels of trust and reliance in their brands, as this can help to reduce customers' perceived risk, and speed up the decision-making process.

Why Brand?

Brands represent opportunities for both consumers and organizations (manufacturers and retailers) to buy and sell products and services easily, more efficiently, and relatively quickly. The benefits are now considered from each perspective. Consumers like brands for the following reasons.

- They assist people to identify their preferred offerings.
- They reduce levels of perceived risk and in doing so improve the quality of the shopping experience.
- They help people to gauge the level of product/service/experience quality.
- They reduce the amount of time spent making proposition-based decisions and, in turn, decrease the time spent shopping.
- They provide psychological reassurance or reward, especially for offerings bought on an occasional basis.
- They inform consumers about the source of an offering (country or company).

Branding helps customers identify the offerings they prefer to use to satisfy their needs and wants. Equally, branding helps them to avoid the brands that they dislike as a result of previous use, or because of other image associations or other psychological reasoning.

Consumers experience a range of perceived risks when buying different offerings. These might be financial risks (Can I afford this?), social risks (What will other people think about me wearing this dress or going to this bar?), or functional risks (Will this smartphone work?). Branding helps to reduce these risks so that buyers can proceed with a purchase without fear or uncertainty. Strong brands encapsulate a range of values that communicate safety and purchase security.

In markets unknown to a buyer or where there is technical complexity (e.g. computing, financial services), consumers use branding to make judgements about the quality of an offering. This, in turn, helps consumers save shopping time and again helps reduce the amount of risk they experience.

Perhaps, above all other factors, branding helps consumers develop relationships based on respect and trust, as exemplified by Aston Martin. Strong brands are normally well trusted, and annual surveys often announce that Apple, British Airways, and Kellogg's are some of the most trusted brands. Similarly, these surveys declare those brands that are least trusted by consumers, and very often these coincide with falling sales and reducing market share. Creating trust is important, as it enables consumers to buy with confidence.

Market Insight 13.1
How to Avoid Damaging a Brand

Some brands have failure thrust on them by competitors, and some thrust it on themselves.

Examples of those thrusting it on themselves are car manufacturers Toyota and the VW group who managed to trash their own reputations through a manufacturing failure. Toyota were guilty of selling cars with defective window switches that could catch fire, leading to the recall of 6.5m cars. VW admitted to the deliberate falsification of the emissions data on a range of diesel vehicles. Their lower than actual CO_2 emissions and engine performance misled authorities and customers alike, leading to huge fines, recall bills for over 11m vehicles, and a discredited reputation.

Some campaigns can damage brands. Mr Kipling claimed for a long time that they 'make exceedingly good cakes'. His warm and comforting claim had become a familiar and reassuring brand call. In the late noughties, however, competition from in-store bakery products led to declining sales. The company's response was to introduce a Mrs Kipling whose character only succeeded in grating on the audience. She was depicted as scathing of her husband's efforts, wishing he was exceedingly good at everything else as he snored next to her in bed. Designed to reflect the customer, the approach backfired, the character was hastily dropped, and Mr Kipling reappeared.

The UK Labour party decided to use a pink campaign minibus for the 2015 General Election in an attempt to entice crucial women voters. Immediately derided as patronizing on social media, the minibus was quickly jettisoned.

The Orange Tango brand built a strong position through some memorable advertising campaigns, outflanking Coca-Cola's Fanta. Britvic, the brand owner, then introduced Apple Tango, which grew well following a great, but unrelated to Tango, launch campaign. Britvic repeated their success with a blackcurrant flavour, again using a different campaign. Whilst sales of the apple and blackcurrant variants grew, sales of Tango fell by over 20% and Fanta seized the chance to become the category leader.

Finally, a failure to check the details can also damage a brand. For example, the original logo designed for the 2020 Tokyo Olympics had to be abandoned when a lawsuit filed against the committee claimed that the logo infringed the copyright of Olivier Debie's

The Labour Party's decision to use a pink campaign bus to engage female voters in the 2015 UK General Election was quickly reversed following scathing comments on social media.
Source: © JUSTIN TALLIS/Stringer/Getty.

Market Insight 13.1

continued

design for the Théâtre de Liège. The Tokyo 2020 Organizing Committee was forced to withdraw the image and to start the whole process of designing and selecting a new logo, but this time with a new committee.

Sources: Burrows (2014); Coleman (2015); Huggler (2015).

Theory into Practice

These examples serve to highlight some of the multidimensional issues and complexities associated with managing brands. The car examples show how a brand is composed of various physical intrinsic attributes which can represent a customer promise. It is also composed of intangible exterior attributes. Failure on an attribute can lead to brand failure.

The Mr Kipling example demonstrates how brand communication can influence brand performance. First, the original Mr Kipling represented a strong brand personality through which audiences were enabled to make appropriate brand associations. Second, the introduction of a Mrs Kipling character led to inappropriate and unwelcome customer perceptions because the warm personality of Mr Kipling had been displaced.

The Labour Party example serves to show that patronizing customers serves no long- or short-term brand goals.

The demise of Orange Tango was caused by a failure to be consistent with a core brand idea.

Finally, the Tokyo Olympics logo fiasco brings to light the legal and financial issues associated with brand management.

Related Topics:

brand personality; associations; building; attributes; relationships.

1 **Consider the reasons why another brand of your choice failed.**

2 **Visit Interbrand's website and their list of the world's top 100 brands. Choose three at random and try to determine what has made them successful.**

3 **To what extent might brand management always be responsible for brand success and failure.**

@ Visit the **Online Resource Centre** and access the branding articles on the **American Marketing** Association's web site.

Many brands are deliberately imbued with human characteristics, to the point that they are identified as having particular personalities. These **brand personalities** might be based around being seen as friendly, approachable, distant, aloof, calculating, honest, fun, or even robust or caring. For example, Timberland is rugged, Victoria's Secret is glamorous, Virgin is associated with youthfulness and rebelliousness, and management consultancies such as PwC seek to be seen as successful, accomplished, and influential. Marketing communications play an important role in communicating the essence of a brand's personality. By developing positive emotional links with a brand, consumers can find reassurance through their brand purchases.

Manufacturers and retailers use brands for the following reasons.

- They can increase the financial valuation of companies.
- They enable premium pricing.
- They help differentiate the proposition from competitive offerings.
- They can deter competitors from entering the market
- They encourage cross-selling to other brands owned by the manufacturer.
- They develop customer trust, loyalty/retention, and repeat-purchase buyer behaviour.
- They assist the development and use of integrated marketing communications.
- Contribute to corporate identity programmes.
- They provide some legal protection.

Branding is an important way for manufacturers to differentiate their brands in crowded market-places. This enables buyers to recognize the brand quickly and make fast unhindered purchase decisions. One of the brand-owner's goals is to create strong brand loyalty to the extent that customers always seek out the brand, and become better prepared to accept cross-product promotions and **brand extensions**.

Perhaps one of the strongest motivations for branding is that it can allow manufacturers to set premium prices. Brands such as Andrex, Stella Artois, and L'Oréal charge a premium price, often around 25–35% higher than the average price in their respective product categories. Premium prices allow brand managers to reinvest in brand development, and in some markets this is important in order to remain competitive. However, it should not be assumed that the establishment of a brand will lead to automatic success. Many brands fail, sometimes because a firm does not invest in a brand at the level required, or because management have not recognized or accepted the need to change, adapt, or reposition their brands as market preferences have moved on.

The greater the number of product-based brands, the greater the motivation for an organization to want to develop a corporate brand. Organizations such as Aviva and Johnson & Johnson use an umbrella branding approach. This requires that they only need to invest heavily in one brand, rather than in each and every product-based brand. This approach is not applicable to all sectors, although in business-to-business markets, where there is product complexity, corporate branding is an effective way of communicating and focusing on a few core brand values.

Visit the Online Resource Centre and complete Internet Activity 13.1 to learn more about how major organizations perceive the importance of branding and their brands.

How Brands Work: Associations and Personalities

The development of successful brands requires customers to be able to make appropriate brand-related associations. Normally these should be based on utilitarian functional issues, as well as on emotions and feelings towards a brand.

Clayton and Heo (2011) refer to brand image, perceived quality, and brand attitude as the main dimensions of **brand associations**, citing work by Aaker (1991), Keller (1993), and Low and Lamb (2000) in this area. Keller (1993) believes that brand associations themselves are made up of the physical and non-physical attributes and benefits aligned with attitudes to create a brand image in the mind of the consumer. Jin and Sung (2011) claim that there is a wealth of empirical evidence to support the claim that people tend to attribute human personality characteristics to non-human entities. The symbolic meanings that brands acquire is called brand personality and is known as the set of human characteristics associated with a brand (Aaker 1997). The development of brand personalities means that marketing managers can position their brands using emotional attributes, and so develop stronger consumer–brand relationships (Ahmad and Thyagaraj, 2014). As Brochado *et al.* (2015) report, to be successful a brand has to have a strong brand personality, and to achieve this it needs to be a core component within brand positioning and differentiation strategies (Valette-Florence and de Barnier, 2013).

These associations and images may sometimes enable consumers to construe a psycho-social meaning associated with a particular brand. The idea that consumers might search for brands with a personality that complements their self-concept is not new, as identified by McCracken (1986) (see Market Insight 13.2 for more information about McCracken's theory). Belk (1988) suggested that brands offer a means of self-expression, whether this is in terms of who they want to be (desired self), who they strive to be (ideal self), or who they think they should be (ought self). Brands, therefore, provide a means for individuals to indicate to others their preferred personality, as they relate to these 'self' concepts.

This emotional and symbolic approach is intended to provide consumers with additional reasons to engage with a brand beyond the normal functional characteristics a brand offers (Keller, 1998), which are so easily copied by competitors. Aaker (1997) developed the **Brand Personality Scale**, which consists of five main dimensions of psychosocial meaning, subsuming 42 personality traits. The dimensions are sincerity (wholesome, honest, down-to-earth), excitement (exciting, imaginative, daring), competence (intelligent, confident), sophistication (charming, glamorous, smooth), and ruggedness (strong, masculine). These are depicted in Figure 13.2.

Aaker's initial research was conducted in the mid-1990s and revealed that, in the USA, MTV was perceived to be best on excitement, CNN on competence, Levi's on ruggedness, Revlon on sophistication, and Campbell's on sincerity. Jin and Sung (2011) believe that a brand can be associated with various demographic characteristics such as gender, age, social class, and lifestyle. They also cite human personality traits and suggest that Hummer and North Face are examples of brands that are associated with ruggedness, Toyota and Dell are regarded as reliable, although recent car recalls might have damaged Toyota's strength on this dimension, Airbnb and Uber are regarded as trendy, and finally Lexus and Ralph Lauren are regarded as sophisticated.

These psychosocial dimensions have subsequently become enshrined as dimensions of brand personality. Aaker developed a five-point framework around these dimensions in order to provide a consistent means of measurement. The framework has been used frequently and cited many times by academics and marketing practitioners. For example, various studies have found that consumers choose brands which reflect their own personality (Linville and Carlston, 1994; Phau and Lau, 2001). They prefer brands that project a personality that is consistent with their self-concepts. As Arora and Stoner (2009: 273) indicate, 'brand

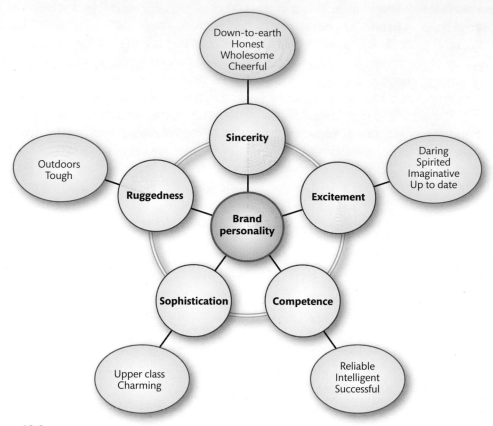

Figure 13.2

Five dimensions of psychosocial meaning

Source: Reprinted with permission from J. Aaker (1997) 'Dimensions of brand personality', *Journal of Marketing Research* 34 (August), 347–56, published by the American Marketing Association.

personality provides a form of identity for consumers that expresses symbolic meaning for themselves and for others'. Brand personality, therefore, can be construed as a means of creating and maintaining consumer loyalty, if only because this aspect is difficult for competitors to copy.

Customers assign a level of trust to the brands they encounter. Preferred brands signify a high level of trust and indicate that the brand promise is delivered. Therefore marketing managers need to ensure that they do not harm or reduce the perceived levels of trust in their brands. Indeed, action should be taken to enhance trust. One way of achieving this is to use labels and logos to represent a brand's values, associations, and source. For example, many brands use the 'footprint' symbol to refer to the amount of carbon dioxide associated within a brand's supply chain. All Apple products are signified, and identified, by the fruit with a bite removed, and UK meat products carry a red tractor symbol. According to the National Farmers Union, the red tractor logo indicates that the meat was produced to exacting standards of food safety, kindness to animals, and environmental protection. This is intended to reassure customers about the origin and quality of the meat.

Brand Names

Choosing a name for a brand is a critical foundation stone because, ideally, it should enable all of the following to be accomplished:

- be easily recalled, spelled, and spoken;
- be strategically consistent with the organization's branding policies;
- be indicative of the offering's major benefits and characteristics;
- be distinctive;
- be meaningful to the customer;
- be capable of registration and protection.

Sometimes social pressure or even a crisis can stimulate a change of name. For example, Philip Morris changed the overall company name to the Altria Group following sustained attacks about its cigarette and tobacco products. Research in Motion (RIM) changed its official name to Blackberry in January 2013, when its share value fell by 90%. Although changing the name alone does not stop the cause of the crisis, it can trigger a change in culture, values, and approach. Brand names need to transfer easily across markets, and to do this successfully it helps if customers can not only pronounce the name but can also recall it unaided. Problems can arise through interpretation. For example, the launch of Puffs tissues in Germany might have been easier if management had known that *Puff* means brothel in German.

One of the reasons that high-profile grocery brands are advertised so frequently is to create brand name awareness, so that when a UK customer thinks of pet food they think of Felix or Winalot, or a Swedish customer thinks of Mjau and Doggy. Names that are difficult to spell or are difficult to pronounce are unlikely to be accepted by customers. Short names such as Lego, Mars, Sony, Flash, or Shell have this strength.

Brand names should have some internal strategic consistency and be compatible with the organization's overall positioning. Ford Transit, Virgin Atlantic, and Cadbury Dairy Milk are names that reflect their parent company's policies that the company name prefixes their product brand names. Some brand names incorporate a combination of words, numbers, or initials. The portable 'sat nav' TomTom GO 510/610 and Canon's EOS 700D DSLR digital camera use names that do not inform about the functionality, but use a combination of words and numbers to reflect the parent company, product line to which they belong, and a hint of their technological content. A brand's functional benefit can also be incorporated within a name as this helps to convey its distinctive qualities. Deodorant brands such as Sure and Right Guard use this approach, although Lynx has relied on imagery plus fragrance and dryness.

Most brands do not have sufficient financial resources to be advertised on TV or in any mainstream media. Therefore it is not possible to convey brand values through imagery and brand advertising. For these brands it is important that the name of the brand reflects the functionality of the offering itself. So, the super adhesive No More Nails, Cling Film, and Snap-on-Tools all convey precisely what they do through their names. For these brands, packaging and merchandising is important in order to communicate with customers in-store.

Increasingly, brands are being developed through the use of social media. This is essentially about people talking, either spontaneously to one another, through blogs, or through formal or informal communities, about brands that they have experienced in some way. The role of brand managers has transposed from that of guardians to that of brand hosts (Christodoulides, 2009), who now listen to these conversations and then adapt their brands accordingly (see Chapter 3). What this suggests is that the control and identity of a brand have moved from the brand owner to the consumer.

 Visit the Online Resource Centre and complete Internet Activity 13.2 to learn more about generating brand names.

Types of Brand

There are three main types of brands: manufacturer, distributor, and generic.

Manufacturer Brands

In many markets, and especially the FMCG sector, retailers are able to influence the way in which a product is displayed and presented to customers. As a result, manufacturers try to create brand recognition and name recall through their marketing communications activities with end-users. The goal is to help customers identify the producer of a particular brand at the point of purchase. For example, Persil, Heinz, Cadbury, and Coca-Cola are strong manufacturers' brands; they are promoted heavily, and customers develop preferences based on performance, experience, communications, and availability. So, when customers are shopping they use the images they have of various manufacturers, combined with their own experience, to seek out their preferred brands. Retailers who choose not to stock certain major **manufacturer brands** run the risk of losing customers.

Distributor (or Own-Label) Brands

The various organizations that make up the marketing channel often choose to create a distinct identity for themselves. The term distributor or own-label brand refers to the identities and images developed by the wholesalers, distributors, dealers, and retailers who make up the marketing channel. Wholesalers, such as Nurdin & Peacock, and retailers, such as Argos, Gap, Sainsbury's, Jeronimo Martens in Portugal, and Plus Retail in the Netherlands, have all created strong brands.

This brand strategy offers many advantages to the manufacturer, who can use excess capacity, and retailers, who can earn a higher margin than they can with manufacturers' branded goods and at the same time develop strong store images. Retailers have the additional cost of promotional initiatives, necessary in the absence of a manufacturer's support. Some manufacturers, such as Kellogg's, refuse to make products for distributors to brand, although others (Cereal Partners) are happy to supply a variety of competitors.

Occasionally, conflict emerges, especially when a **distributor brand** displays characteristics that are very similar to the manufacturer's market leader brand. Coca-Cola defended their brand when it was alleged that the packaging of Sainsbury's new cola drink was too similar to their own established design.

Generic Brands

Generic brands are sold without any promotional materials or any means of identifying the company, with the packaging displaying only information required by law. The only form of identification is the relevant product category, e.g. plain flour. As it is not necessary to pay for promotional support, these brands are sold at prices that are substantially below the price of normal brands. However, although they were briefly successful in the 1990s, their popularity has declined and manufacturers see no reason to produce these 'white carton' products. Only firms in the pharmaceutical sector use this type of brand.

Branding Strategies

An overall branding strategy can provide direction, consistency, and brand integrity within an organization's portfolio of brands. This provides the basis of the brand architecture. There are three core brand strategies: individual, family, and corporate.

Individual Branding

Once referred to as a multibrand policy, individual branding requires that each product offered by an organization is branded independently of all the others. Grocery brands offered by Unilever (e.g. Knorr, Cif, and Dove) and Procter & Gamble (e.g. Fairy, Crest, and Head & Shoulders) typify this approach.

One of the advantages of this approach is that it is easy to target specific segments and to enter new markets with separate names. If a brand fails or becomes subject to negative media attention, the other brands are not likely to be damaged. However, there is a high financial cost as each brand needs to have its own promotional programme and associated support.

Family Branding

Once referred to as a multiproduct brand policy, family branding requires that all the products use the organization's name, either entirely or in part. Microsoft, Heinz, and Kellogg's all incorporate the company name, as it is hoped that customer trust will develop across all brands. Therefore promotional investment need not be as high. This is because there will always be a halo effect across all the brands when one is communicated, and brand experience will stimulate word of mouth following usage. A prime example of this is Google, who have pursued a family brand strategy with Google Adwords, Google Maps, and Google Scholar to name but a few. What is more impressive is that Google's shattering achievements have been accomplished in just 10 years and with minimal advertising spend.

Line family branding is a derivative policy whereby a family branding policy is followed for all products within a single line. Bosch is a technology company operating in the automotive, industry, and home markets. Many of its products are branded Bosch, but they use line branding for their Blaupunkt and Qualcast brands in their car entertainment and garden products divisions.

Corporate Branding

Many retail brands adopt a single umbrella brand, based on the name of the organization. This name is then used at all locations, and is a way of identifying the brand and providing a form of consistent differentiation and a form of recognition, whether on the high street or online. Major supermarkets such as Tesco in the UK, Carrefour in France, and ASDA Wal-Mart use this branding strategy to attract and help retain customers.

Corporate branding strategies are also used extensively in business markets, such as IBM, Cisco, and Caterpillar, and in consumer markets where there is technical complexity, such as financial services. Companies such as HSBC and Prudential adopt a single-name strategy. One of the advantages of this approach is that promotional investments are limited to one brand. However, the risk is similar to family branding, where damage to one offering or operational area can cause problems across the organization. For example, when the BBC experienced editorial problems with their *Newsnight* programme, which resulted in extensive and persistent negative media coverage; not only did the Director-General decide to resign, but questions were asked about declining trust and reputation concerning the whole of the BBC.

Visit the Online Resource Centre and follow the web link to learn more about IBM's corporate brand.

How to Build Brands

The development of successful brands is critical to an organization's success. Keller (2009) believes that this is best accomplished by considering the brand-building process in terms of steps. The first is to enable customers to identify with the brand and help them make associations with a specific product class or customer need. The second is to establish what the brand means by linking various tangible and intangible brand associations. The third step is concerned with encouraging customer responses based around brand-related judgement and feelings. The final step is about fostering an active relationship between customers and the brand.

Figure 13.3 depicts the rational steps on the left-hand side, whereas the emotional counterpart is shown on the right-hand side. In the centre are six blocks which make up a pyramid, echoing these rational and emotional steps. To achieve a successful brand, or brand resonance, Keller argues that a foundation is necessary and that these building blocks need to be developed systematically. Below, we apply the brand pyramid to a shampoo brand to understand the terminology further.

- Brand salience—how easily and often do customers think of the shampoo brand when thinking about hair care brands or when shopping?

- Brand performance—how well do customers believe the shampoo brand cleans and conditions their hair?

- Brand imagery—describes the extrinsic properties of the shampoo (the colour, packaging, product consistency, associations) and the level to which these satisfy customers' psychological or social needs.

- Brand judgements—focus on customers' own personal opinions and evaluations about the shampoo.

- Brand feelings—customers' emotional responses and reactions with respect to the shampoo brand when prompted by communications, by friends, or when washing their hair.

- Brand resonance—the nature of the relationship customers have with the shampoo brand and the extent to which they feel loyal to the brand.

Brand resonance is most likely to result when marketers create proper salience and breadth and depth of awareness. From this position 'points of parity and points of difference' need to be

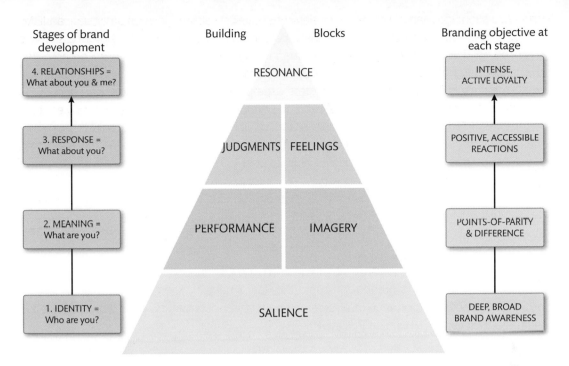

Figure 13.3

Brand pyramid: building blocks

Source: Keller, K.L., 'Building strong brands in a modern marketing communications environment', *Journal of Marketing Communications*, July 2009, Taylor & Francis. Reprinted by permission of the publisher (Taylor & Francis Ltd, http://www.tandf.co.uk/journals).

established, so that positive judgements and feelings can be made that appeal to both the head and the heart respectively.

 Visit the Online Resource Centre and follow the web link to learn more about Keller's Brand Equity model.

Branding Perspectives

So far we have assumed a largely managerial perspective with regard to the concept of brand. However, there are other approaches to understanding brands and what they represent. These draw on sociological, psychological, and socio-cultural interpretations about brands and their consumption. We consider two important perspectives. The first considers relational issues and how people are believed to interact with brands and develop relationships through repeated consumption. The second reflects contemporary issues about co-creation and **customer branding**. This reverses the managerially driven view that brands are just a product of marketers.

Brand Relationships

Although branding has its roots in identification and differentiation, a 'brand-mark is a relational asset whose value to the firm is contingent on past, present and future interactions with various firm stakeholders' (Ballantyne and Aitken, 2007: 366). Fournier (1998) was one of the first researchers to introduce and utilize relationship theory to understand the roles that brands play in the lives of consumers.

Originally relationship marketing was considered to be most relevant in inter-organizational relationships. Here, the management of relationships between buying and selling organizations is considered valid and appropriate, more so than in the relationship between an organization and a consumer. Fournier changed this when she explored ideas about consumers who think about brands as if they were human characters—the personification of brands. She also found that consumers accept attempts by marketers to personalize brands (e.g. through advertising), which suggests interaction and relationship potential. She identified six facets which characterize brand relationship quality. These are love and passion, a connection between the brand and self, a high degree of interdependence, a high level of commitment, intimacy, and a positive evaluation of brand quality.

Fournier believes that it is important to understand consumer–brand relationships, and that by understanding how consumers interact with brands, and the meaning that brands represent to people through consumption, marketing theory and practice can be advanced. She argues that it is necessary to consider the broad context of consumers' lives to understand the role and relationship that brands play in them. In addition, meaningful consumer–brand relationships can be observed when the brand represents the key dimension 'perceived ego significance'. Fournier stresses the importance of understanding what consumers do with brands that adds meaning to their lives (see Market Insight 13.2).

Market Insight 13.2
Musicians Dying for Success

Michael Jackson, Bob Marley, Kurt Cobain, and Ian Curtis are all highly regarded music icons whose lucrative businesses have thrived since their deaths.

Although their reputations might not have been prolonged if fans were not so emotionally affected by news of their deaths, it is the post-death branding activities that have contributed to their brand longevity. The bombardment of new memorabilia merchandise and the release of previously unknown material by marketers and estate holders keen to squeeze every drop of profit appears to have become a regular branding exercise for deceased musicians.

The importance of emotional impact on consumers is understood, and we can see how such exploitation of our intrinsic functions can impact buying decisions through the death of a music artist. For example, the news about Michael Jackson's death in June 2009 spread like wildfire. This was followed by a huge surge in sales of his back catalogue, as well as driving his *Greatest Hits* album to the top of the charts that month.

Once they are dead, the value of a musician's portfolio rises because generally no more new material can be released by the artist and copyright ownership passes on to the next of kin who, if they act quickly, can turn the late artist into a post-death iconic brand. Bob Marley's family were quick to exploit his musical stature, using T-shirts, mugs, and lighters; they even named a cannabis strain after the Rastafarian icon.

Media coverage of Ian Curtis's suicide in 1980 encouraged people to find out more about Joy Division. Their album *Unknown Pleasures*, which had initially struggled to sell, made it in the Top 10 charts and created huge new admiration of and interest in Joy Division in the months following Curtis's death. Years after his death, Joy Division is still a strong influence in the music world, as even today new generations discover their music. The album cover for *Unknown Pleasures* appears on T-shirts, and numerous books regarding his life and death, written by former bandmates and his wife, are widely available. These constant reminders have led consumers to associate Ian's

Market Insight 13.2
continued

The grief felt by Amy Winehouse's fans following her death, was accompanied by a surge of interest in her music
Source: © Dutourdumonde Photography/Shutterstock.

sad story with the band's music, so creating a strong emotional connection. All of this gives the estate owners a rationale to perpetuate the brand through remasters, re-releases, and memorial-related merchandise.

Amy Winehouse's download sales increased to 1.15m in the USA the year following her death, compared with 170,000 downloads earlier that year. Four years later, a documentary commemorating her life and a book

written by her father were released, making $1.5m for the Amy Winehouse Charity Foundation.

Elvis Presley, who died in 1977, also has a powerful iconic image. By 2000 (23 years after death) his estate had earned $32bn from record sales, merchandise, and licensing deals.

Sources: Caulfield (2012); Adebayo (2014); Anon. (2009); Anon. (n.d.).

Theory into Practice

Undoubtedly, ideas about brand relationships can be used to understand the scenario presented in this market insight. One approach would be to use social influence theory which considers the change in behaviour that one person (the musician) causes in another, intentionally or unintentionally. This is due

to the way the changed (grieving) person perceives themselves in relationship to the deceased musician as well as to other people and society in general. Three particular areas of interest in social influence concern conformity, compliance and obedience.

Market Insight 13.2

continued

We propose that McCracken's (1986) meaning transfer theory might play a role in explaining the increased attention associated with deceased musicians. This theory, often used to explain product placement activities, suggests that a celebrity (musician) encodes a unique set of meanings into the product they are endorsing (music), which is then transferred to an individual's intent on capturing some of the desirable meanings. The relative rush to purchase music when a musician dies might, therefore, represent a means of capturing a share of what has become a finite set of desirable meanings.

It is the emotional and symbolic value that is transferred, not the functional value of the music. The successful propagation of music after a musician's death can be attributed to an understanding of the unique values that the musician represented and what they mean to fans.

Related Topics:

brand personality; brand meanings; relationships.

1 **How might the recent deaths of David Bowie and Prince be reflected not just in sales of their music but in other areas of culture and society?**

2 **Using the Internet, find out more about social influence theory and apply the core concept to this scenario.**

3 **Make a list of other brand-related situations in which the termination of the brand has led to increased or delayed sales.**

This market insight was kindly contributed by Naomi Ramage, Music Business Management, Branding and PR student, Buckinghamshire New University.

Perhaps the most important finding of Fournier's research concerns the meaning that consumers attribute to brands, and how this differs from those meanings intended by brand managers. This contribution has been developed in many areas, including business-to-business markets where it is now recognized that both sellers (suppliers) and buyers (their customers) and other stakeholders co-create brand meanings. As Ballantyne and Aitken (2007) state, this indicates that brand meanings are socially constructed.

The increasing use of user-generated content in the form of blogs, tweets, wikis, and social networks now enables consumers to assume a greater role in defining what a brand means to them, something which they now share with their friends, family, and contacts, rather than with the organization itself. This means that both managers and customers are involved in the branding process. The control of brands used to reside with brand owners. Today, this influence has shifted to consumers as they redefine what brands mean to them and how they differentiate among similar offerings and associate certain attributes or feelings and emotions with particular brands.

However, as Bengtsson (2003) argues, there is doubt about whether consumers really want a relationship with brands, or even if they do have a relationship with them. His doubt concerns whether relationship theory is appropriate when examining the way consumers interact with brands.

Research Insight 13.2

To take your learning further, you might wish to read this influential paper.

Fournier, S. (1998). Consumers and their brands: developing relationship theory in consumer research. *Journal of Consumer Research*, 24(4), 343–73.

This paper has already been characterized as a modern classic by Bengtsson (2003), such is its significance and contribution to our understanding of marketing and consumer research. The author discusses the need to incorporate relationship marketing theory with branding and explores the types of relationships people form with brands.

Visit the Online Resource Centre to read the abstract and access the full paper.

---

de Lencastre and Côrte-Real (2010) believe a brand to be a sign and use **semiotics**, the science of signs, as a basis for a model that considers the different components of the relationships among them. They attempt to integrate the multiple facets of the brand concept and define three main brand dimensions: the identity sign itself, the marketing object to which the sign refers, and the market response to the sign. One of the points they make is that brands today are largely regarded as socio-cultural concepts in which relational and community issues replace the former power-based managerial perspective whereby brand managers assumed control over a brand.

Visit the Online Resource Centre and follow the web links to learn more about brand semiotics

Brand Co-creation

The managerial perspective assumes that manufacturers or service providers develop and manage brands, while individual consumers are passive and can only influence brand meaning or perception of a brand. This requires marketers to perform three essential branding activities. Pennington and Ball (2009) suggest these are to enable identification and differentiation, to maintain consistency, and to communicate the existence and attributes to customer and marketing channel audiences.

In recent years this perspective and process has been challenged, as there is increasing evidence that brands can be created by customers. In customer branding, the customer attaches a name, term, or other feature that enables them to identify one seller's good or service as distinct from those of other sellers (AMA, 2012). This is commonly referred to as co-creation and although many indicate that this is not a recent phenomenon, France *et al.* (2015: 6) point out that there is no exact understanding of the co-creation construct, and that there is 'some confusion in the literature, especially in the area of brand co-creation and brand engagement.'

Pennington and Ball (2009: 455) define customer branding as 'a process in which a customer, or customers, define, label, and seek to purchase a subset of an otherwise undifferentiated or unbranded product. The customer can be anywhere along the value chain, including intermediate and end-user customers'.

In conventional branding processes, a business is able to influence external stakeholders and customers through promises of value creation, and internally as means of employee branding and organizational identity. Where there is customer branding, the organization surrenders control of the brand's ability to convey these and other clear messages to customers and employees (Pennington and Ball, 2009).

In conventional branding activities, communication about a brand flows from the marketer to the consumer. In co-creation contexts, it is the customer who knows what they want, badges it, and requests it by the badge they have provided, or by some other characteristic that others will recognize. In other words, in customer branding, the flow is reversed.

Pennington and Ball (2009: 459) identify three key conditions that need to be met for customer branding to occur. First, there must be a variety of offerings in the market, second the delivery and quality of offerings must be acceptable, and third customers must be able to obtain a reliable and satisfactory alternative from within the marketing channel. As the authors state, 'for the customer to expend the effort to take over branding activities that the marketer is not performing, the customer must show certain needs, perceptions and abilities'.

In addition to customer branding, customers can co-create in different ways, but most are rooted in brand value. France *et al.* (2015) refer to co-creation in the context of exchanges with and experiences of a brand, influencing customer perception of a brand, customer-generated advertising, new product development, social media, and word of mouth.

Ideas about brand co-creation are not confined to product or service offerings. For example, Juntunen (2012) found that a range of stakeholders, not just customers, are involved in corporate brand co-creation. These include employees, relatives, friends, university researchers, students, employees and managers of other companies, advertising agencies, financiers, lawyers, graphic designers, and customers. She revealed that stakeholders engage in various sub-processes of corporate brand co-creation, even before a company is formed (Kollmann and Suckow, 2007). These include inventing the corporate name before a company is established, developing a new corporate name, updating the logo and communications material, and developing the proposition and the business after establishment of the company.

Market Insight 13.3
The Mashing of Peppa Pig

Peppa Pig is a popular character in a British-made children's cartoon, the star of a TV series targeted at mixed gender preschool children, aged between 2 and 6 years old. Peppa is a sweet but cheeky anthropomorphic female pig who lives with her little brother George,

Mummy Pig, and Daddy Pig. The gentle narrative revolves around family life and everyday experiences.

Over 200 episodes have been aired and the show is distributed in 180 countries. Significantly, Peppa

Market Insight 13.3
continued

Pig has over 73 licenses and endorses a number of products such as cake mixes, ice lollies, and, more recently, porridge.

The show has spurred the production of character merchandise including playthings and plush collectables, books, DVDs, apps, and clothing. Significantly, in 2010 the show made £200m through merchandising in the UK alone. What is more, in 2012 the brand expanded to major territories, including the USA, Australia, Spain, Russia, and the Benelux countries, and Peppa Pig is set for continued international expansion into Asia and Latin America. Peppa Pig has an enviable presence on Facebook, Twitter, and the wider blogosphere, boasting many unofficial fan-created pages, in addition to the official company ones. The animation company hosts live stage productions where the public can meet Peppa and her posse of family and friends. There is even a theme park in Hampshire which is becoming a popular family destination. It is clear that Peppa Pig can be considered a household name and a brand in its own right.

Peppa Pig has attracted the attention of a range of other content-creating animators. However, these concentrate on making absurd disingenuous mash-ups, combinations of disparate bits of digital video, audio, text, and graphics refashioned into something new and then uploaded to YouTube. Peppa Pig has been mashed up and parodied in a variety of ways, including dancing Gangnam Style, doing the Harlem Shake, or trying her hand as a nightclub disc jockey. At another level she can be seen listening to explicit voice-overs of various episodes, and observe her kill herself and others (Peppa Pig Dies ... haha). The

Peppa Pig is a popular cartoon character, yet is subject to mash-ups and parody in numerous bizarre scenarios
Source: © tanuha2001/Shutterstock.

bizarre scenarios available to view are seemingly endless.

Although these YouTube mash-ups represent a threat, research indicates that they have not tarnished the brand. There is strong disdain for their creators, and most are condemned for exploiting what is widely regarded as an innocent and upstanding brand. The brand is considered a victim—one that had fallen prey to 'pathetic' and 'sad' creators.

Interviews with the mash-up creators revealed that there was no definitive motive behind the creation of these controversial videos. Although the motivations were varied, three broad categories were identified: creativity ('I love making these videos for my own pleasure, it is strangely entertaining, it is fun'), social capital (a genuine sense of gratification out of pleasing others), and aversion (a deep-seated hatred of the brand or pigs).

Source: Wilkinson and Patterson (2013).

Theory into Practice

These mash-ups are amateur productions which present parodies ranging from playful imitations through to clear intentions to criticize a brand. They represent brand co-creation. Mash-up makers construct new narratives around brand mascots in order that their own existence be acknowledged. Thornton (2010) contends that fan videos allow users to produce and distribute 'a packaged self', which is a careful and considered

Market Insight 13.3
continued

construction of the image they wish to portray. YouTube, as the name suggests, says much more about *you*—that is, the content creator—than about the actual content of any videos that mash-up makers upload.

The rise of 'communications anarchy', unleashed by the Internet, has produced an 'architecture of participation' that has led to consumer empowerment on a level previously unimaginable. These co-creators appear to consider themselves to be brand co-owners, rather than passive recipients of company-created brand messages.

Related Topics:
branding; differentiation and positioning; participation.

1 Which other brands might focus on an emotional approach? Are they successful, and why?

2 If customers buy brands with a personality that reflects their own personalities, name three brands that you purchase regularly. How do these reflect your personality?

3 Visit http://www.interbrand.com and find brands where the use of emotion is prominent.

This market insight was kindly contributed by Professor Anthony Patterson, University of Liverpool.

Visit the Online Resource Centre and complete Internet Activity 13.3 to learn more about the Peppa Pig brand.

Research Insight 13.3

To take your learning further, you might wish to read this influential paper.

Muzellec, L., Lynn, T., and Lambkin, M. (2012). Branding in fictional and virtual environments: introducing a new conceptual domain and research agenda. *European Journal of Marketing*, 46(6), 811–26.

Muzellec and colleagues wrote this paper with the aim of introducing and exploring ideas about virtual brands. They argue that the brand concept may now be detached from physical embodiment, and extended to the fictional and computer-synthesized worlds. The paper helps to explain the concepts of proto-brands and reverse product placement.

Visit the Online Resource Centre to read the abstract and access the full paper.

Brand Preference or Relevance

Conventional brand strategies are based on competition for **brand preference**. According to Aaker (2012: 44) this is about 'my brand being better than yours', and this requires making sure customers prefer your brand of fruit juice rather than your competitors' brands. This is achieved by innovations that lead to claims based on 'faster, cheaper, better', resulting in a more attractive, reliable, or less costly brand promise. Inevitably competitors respond very quickly, nullifying any short term gains.

Unfortunately, preference strategies have little impact, as the evidence shows there is little or no shift in sales or market share. This is mainly due to brand and market inertia. Brand preference competition works if the goal is customer retention, but as Aaker (2012: 44) states, 'it can lead to price and margin erosion and a decline into irrelevance'.

An alternative, and little used, strategy is to compete on the basis of being the most relevant brand. The key is to create offerings that have particular characteristics that are so attractive to a segment that any competitive offering that does not have the desirable characteristic will be rejected. Aaker refers to these defining characteristics as 'must haves', and they include 'personality, organizational values, social programs, self-expressive benefits, or community benefits'. Aaker refers to innovations such as SalesForce.com advocating cloud computing, Cirque du Soleil reinventing the circus, and Kevlar, the branded ingredient which created a new subcategory in the body armour market.

Competing through **brand relevance** can generate real growth and is far more effective than the 'faster, cheaper, or better' strategies. It requires innovations which lead to the creation of new categories or subcategories, all of which reflect changes in the market and involve substantial risk and new business models, Aaker claims.

Sector Branding

Brands work in different ways according to the prevailing environment. Here we consider branding within services and in business-to-business, internal, and global contexts.

Service Brands

The development of brand strategies for services is important simply because the intangibility of services requires that customers are helped to understand the value associated with a service offering. Essentially, a brand provides a snapshot of the value and position offered by a service. Brands convey information about the standard of service and, in doing so, seek to achieve two main goals. First, brands can reduce the uncertainty associated with the purchase of services, especially when there are no tangible elements on which to base purchase decisions. Consider the complexity and risk associated with buying financial services, such as insurance, pensions, and savings products. Developing strong brands enables these risks to be rolled up into a single identity that is familiar and trusted. Just think of Virgin Money—a relative newcomer to the financial services market but already well established and growing quickly. The use of sampling and free trials is a popular approach to reducing risk in service-based purchases.

The second goal is to reduce the amount of time people spend searching for a particular service, especially when they are unfamiliar with a particular market or category. When travelling, many visitors to a city will stay at hotels such as Marriott, Travelodge, Holiday Inn, or Hilton because the brands say something about the standard of service that can be expected. Branding shapes customer expectations and can provide a quick answer to a purchase decision. Advertising can also be used to help make the benefits of a service tangible, rather than features that can be limited or boring, or both. Credit cards often promote the feature of a 0% balance transfer, but they also demonstrate the benefits by showing holidays, electrical goods, or fashion items bought as a result of using the credit card.

Good services branding involves the use of logos and symbols plus straplines and slogans. These can also help make the intangible more tangible by relating to some of the core benefits a brand offers. Many service providers use their physical facilities to shape the environment so that customers feel at ease and are attracted into the service process. Booms and Bitner (1981) termed this the **servicescape** and refer to the need to consider customer expectations and their emotional states. Branding the environment using signs, colours, clothing, and other physical items can provide recall of previous use of the service provider and also influence customer expectations. Consider the environment and overall design of fast food restaurants such as McDonald's and Burger King. These servicescapes are designed and replicated in high streets across the globe, are easily recognized, and convey information about the type of food offered and the standard of service. Empirical research by Harris and Ezeh (2008) reinforces the view that restaurant managers should actively manage their servicescapes.

The emotional dimension of service brands has grown in significance as it becomes increasingly difficult to establish and maintain functional differentiation. Through the use of marketing communications, brands seek to develop trust and a positive attachment and identification with a brand's values. This can lead to an emotional preference for a brand and so establish a form of competitive advantage that is difficult to copy. Just as the ownership of prestige brands, such as designer fashion brands, trainers, cars, and watches, can be used to convey status, so ownership (and display) of many prestige service brands can convey similar status and position. Examples of this include travelling first class, use of platinum credit cards, and being a member of certain clubs or societies.

Finally, not all services are able to develop strong brands; they simply do not have the resources, or inclination. However, communications should still be an important part of their marketing. Those delivering services where the credence properties are dominant and customers are unable to distinguish the quality of service can emphasize their professionalism. This can be achieved by displaying certificates and diplomas, having a long list of professional qualifications on their business cards, and referring in their sales literature and websites to the number and types of client they have worked with.

To conclude this section we present a comment made by respondents to a research survey undertaken by Marquardt *et al.* (2011: 54). These services marketing practitioners said that 'the most effective means of building brand meaning for business-to-business services is to promote superior, deeper, and richer customer experiences'. The significance of brand meaning and its link to customer experience is important. We consider customer experience marketing in Chapter 15.

Branding in Business-to-Business Markets

The benefits that can accrue from branding in business-to-business (B2B) marketing are no different from those in consumer markets. Some argue that branding in business markets is not appropriate or necessary, but this view is not widely held any more (Kuhn *et al.*, 2008). However, there are some specific B2B context branding issues that can be distilled into four main dimensions: functional and product use benefits, and emotional, self-expressive, and relational benefits. These are set out in Table 13.1.

Many people assert that business markets have been slow to develop brands and that B2B product-based branding is a relatively underdeveloped area (Mudambi, 2002). In support of this view, Roper and Davies (2010) remark on the scarcity of true business brands. However, many believe that branding in a B2B context is very often corporate rather than product branding and, more importantly, that branding can influence business purchasing decisions.

There could be many reasons for this underdeveloped use of branding, one of which may be the nature of organizational decision-making processes and associated group activities. Mudambi (2002) concludes that branding is not of equal significance to all organizational buyers, nor is it important in all B2B buying situations. Bendixen *et al.* (2004) and Zablah *et al.* (2010) find that delivery, price, and the services offered are consistently more important to buyers than a brand name.

As a counter argument, both Michell *et al.* (2001) and Lennartz *et al.* (2015) suggest that branding is widely used by B2B organizations. This is primarily because product and corporate branding can be important contributors to successful performance. This is, in part, a reflection of the increasing awareness of the importance of relationships within business markets. For example, a partnership might develop whereby the brand, among other things, provides reassurance for a buyer who in turn supports the brand, on a regular or even frequent basis, and pays the brand's price premium. As a result, business brands not only provide solutions on a continuous basis for certain customers but they may also become integral to a long-term relationship. The launch of 'Celanese—The chemistry inside innovation' was made in order to unify the Celanese portfolio, including its associated brands, and was designed to convey their capabilities and diverse product portfolio (Claye *et al.*, 2014).

Lindgreen *et al.* (2010) observe that organizational buyers make decisions using emotional benefits and self-expressive benefits (such as personal and professional satisfaction) in addition to the functional elements. Indeed, work by Roper and Davies (2010: 584) provides timely empirical evidence that B2B brands can have a demonstrable personality and that 'industrial brands can benefit from the concept of brand image and personality'.

Table 13.1 Benefits derived from branding

Brand benefit	B2B example
Functional advantages	Product performance and high quality associations
	Superior service and support associations
	Specific application and/or location advantages
Emotional advantages	Improved confidence and trust through a reduction in uncertainty
Self-expressive advantages	Buyer-related personal and professional satisfaction
Relational advantages	Larger and stronger networks and collaboration opportunities

Market Insight 13.4
B2B Branding...Sintex Is the Name

Sintex Industries is an Indian-based holding company engaged in the manufacture of plastic products and textile manufacturing. The early growth of the company was marked by a series of product failures based around a plastic moulding unit designed to manufacture plastic cans to carry cotton slivers in the textile industry. These were not marketed and further experiments also ended in failure. This forced the owners to consider other possible end-uses which might have substantial market potential. This led to the development of black plastic water tanks in the late 1970s.

At the time there were other very small and geographically fragmented manufacturers of water containers, but it was a commodity market. The owners decided to name their water tanks Sintex, using 'sin' from the plastic sintering process and 'tex' from the word textiles. Most water tanks sit on residential and commercial property roofs in India, and the visual prominence of the word Sintex provides a constant free brand reminder to the community. In addition, Sintex spends 70% of its communication budget on mass media, mainly press and popular magazines. Their involvement in trade fairs and exhibitions, accounts for 7%, outdoor just 3%, and dealers' meetings and other promotional activities account for the remaining 20%. The Sintex website provides company details information about its various products. The website is perceived to be a strong brand building tool. Overall, Sintex spends less than 1.5% of sales on communication.

Part of their success has been attributed to the emphasis placed on innovation. Sintex has developed solutions for the housing sanitation, power, and education sectors, and wishes to be known as a 'thinking company'—one which produces innovative products designed to save the environment, not one that merely produces plastic products.

From a simple beginning, Sintex has become the surrogate brand for all plastic water tanks in India, has approximately 45% of the market, and now operates in nine other countries across four continents.

Source: Sarin (2014); http://www.superbrandsindia.com/; http://in.reuters.com/finance/.

Theory into Practice

Sintex capitalized on a market opportunity within a commodity market. Their subsequent growth and success can be explained in terms of the added value their simple branding activities brought to the different B2B markets in which they chose to operate. However, just developing a brand does not bring long-term success, and it was their development of brand values through innovation that drove both consumer and dealer demand to be associated with Sintex.

Although the market insight does not inform us, it is highly probable that Sintex was able to charge a premium price and hence derive a better margin than its competitors. This resource was invested in innovation of new products and continued the growth of the company.

Related Topics:
brand names; relationships; B2B branding.

1 **To what extent should Sintex's success be accredited to being the first to brand in a commodity market?**

2 **How vulnerable might Sintex be to a global water container brand entering the Indian market?**

3 **How might Sintex's communications evolve as they become increasingly regarded as a 'thinking company'?**

Visit the Online Resource Centre and follow the web links to read the paper by Sarin and learn more about the Structura brand, as well as about Sintex.

To develop business brands three core elements need to be managed. These are symbolic devices, communication, and behaviour. Together these might be considered to be the branding mix. In corporate reputation management, these elements are referred to as the identity mix (Birkigt and Stadler, 1986). All organizations use symbolism to signal who they are and what they stand for. Logos, company names, straplines, colours, architecture, design, workwear, and delivery vehicles are all symbols. Communication can be considered in terms of management communication (internal and external), organization communication (public relations), and marketing communication. These need to be integrated around a central theme or strategic platform. The behaviour of employees and managers, not only with one another but with external stakeholders, is often overlooked in the branding and reputation management process. One of the key tasks is to align the values employees have with the organization's values and this requires training, communication, and attention by management. Some of the issues associated with internal branding are discussed later in this chapter.

Lennartz et al. (2015) found that, to build B2B brands, above all else core brand strength is driven through brand associations, with 'sustainability and corporate governance' as well as 'innovation and expertise' across all countries and industries. In addition, perceptions of product and distribution performance are major factors when building and sustaining B2B brands.

Of importance in B2B markets, but not as critical as in B2C markets, is communications, according to Lennartz and his colleagues. Organizations must develop modern integrated communication programmes with all of their key stakeholder groups. Stakeholders demand transparency, accountability, and instant, often online, access to news, developments, research, and networks. This means that inconsistent or misleading information must be avoided. In addition, the leading contributors to the strength of a corporate brand are seen to be their products and services, followed by a strong management team, internal communications, public relations, social accountability, change management, and the personal reputation of the CEO.

Mudambi (2002) suggests that there are three types, or clusters, of B2B customers based upon the way they each perceive the importance of branding in the organizational purchase decision process. These are set out in Table 13.2

Communications for the low interest cluster need to stimulate interest in the offering and associated purchase decision, perhaps by using testimonials and mini-cases highlighting customers who have experienced similar purchase situations.

Internal Branding

Employees are an integral part of a brand, if only because they interact with customers and other stakeholders. Lennartz et al. (2015: 133) reinforce this when they say that the contact between employees and customers is crucial for driving brand strength. This means that a firm's brand success depends 'significantly on the interactions between firms and customers throughout the selling process'.

They deliver the functional aspects of an organization's offering and they also deliver the emotional dimensions, particularly in service environments. Through interaction with these two elements, long-term relationships between sellers and buyers can develop. Both scholars and practitioners rightly emphasize the need to integrate internal audiences in brand development.

Table 13.2 B2B customer clusters

Cluster name	Characteristics
Highly tangible	Require messages that stress quantifiable and objective benefits of the product and company
Brand receptive	Require messages that emphasize the support of a well-established and highly reputable manufacturer; the emotional and self-expressive benefits should be stressed
Low interest	More likely to respond to brand-based communications that highlight the importance of the purchase decision and which are supported with processes and procedures that assist the ordering systems

Source: Adapted from Mudambi (2002).

This process whereby employees are encouraged to communicate with stakeholders so that organizations ensure that what is promised is realized by customers is referred to as 'living the brand'. Welch and Jackson (2007) considered some of the issues associated with internal communication. They suggest that internal corporate communication refers to communication between an organization's strategic managers and its internal stakeholders, with the purpose of promoting *commitment* to the organization, a sense of *belonging* (to the organization), *awareness* of its changing environment, and *understanding* of its evolving goals, such as that operated by Convergys and White Stuff.

The success of many corporate and service brands is founded on the strength of the internal dimension. The greater the degree to which staff believe and uphold the values, mission, and vision of an organization, the more likely reputation and performance goals will be achieved. Slowly, more energy is being put into the internal aspect of B2B marketing activities.

Global branding

Brands can be considered in terms of the markets they operate in, sometimes referred to as scope. **Brand scope** can involve operating in local and domestic markets, in selected foreign markets, and across a range of international markets. Townsend *et al.* (2010) provided a useful typology of brands (Table 13.3).

The scope or reach of a brand is a result of decisions to enter different geographical regions to achieve particular goals. As organizations extend their scope, so their branding and marketing strategies must adapt to influence local cultures and customer needs. However, global branding is characterized by a consistency of marketing strategies, a transfer of the same strategy across all markets as practised by IBM, AT&T, and China Mobile.

One of the most influential advocates of global branding was Theodore Levitt, whose work on globalization is considered in Chapter 7. Levitt (1983) argued that a global market for uniform products and services requires transnational organizations to standardize their products, packaging, and communications to achieve a common positioning that would be effective

---

Table 13.3 A hierarchy of brand scope

Brand Scope	Criteria and characteristics	Examples
Domestic brand	A brand with a presence only in the home market and managed locally.	White Stuff Timothy Taylor Thornton's William Hill
International brand	Sold across a few country markets and managed largely by the home market, often using local agents in international markets. Positioning, identity, image, and distinguishing characteristics (including attributes, associations, and identifiers of the brand) virtually identical to the home market.	Eddie Stobart Ideal Standard
Multidomestic brand	Sold across multiple country markets, and managed through decentralized management with local control. Positioning, identity, image, and distinguishing characteristics (including attributes, associations, and identifiers of the brand) vary across markets.	Ferrero Samsung Philips Diageo GM Caterpillar
Global brand	Sold across multiple country markets with distribution located in three major developed continents; centralized brand management coordinates local execution. Core essence of the brand remains unchanged; positioning, identity, image, and distinguishing characteristics (including attributes, associations, and identifiers) maintain a high degree of consistency across worldwide markets.	Coca-Cola McDonald's IBM Apple Google

Source: Adapted from Townsend *et al.* (2010).

across cultures. Growth was to be achieved by selling standardized products all over the world (Holt *et al.*, 2004). However, here are few pure examples of this practice, as even 'global' brands such as McDonald's and Coca-Cola adjust their propositions to suit some local market needs.

The way in which an organization manages its brands and associated products with respect to one another is known as a brand portfolio. According to Townsend *et al.* (2009), citing Douglas *et al.* (2001), it seems as if global branding has become more significant, as they observe organizations focusing on core brands and implementing brand portfolio structures to encourage brand consistency across international markets. However, as different brands within a portfolio

Research Insight 13.4

To take your learning further, you might wish to read this influential paper.

Holt, D.B., Quelch, J.A., and Taylor, E.L. (2004). How global brands compete. *Harvard Business Review*, 82(9), 68–81.

This is an important paper that all those interested in global marketing and global brands should read. The authors review the ways global brands compete and reflect on the need for companies to manage their national identities as well as their 'globalness'.

Visit the Online Resource Centre to read the abstract and access the full paper.

are targeted at different market segments, including different geographical markets, it is not unusual for global companies such as Samsung and Toyota to carry international brands within the portfolio.

In addition to the economics of globalization there are prestige and status advantages associated with global brands, which also manifest themselves in terms of improving brand equity (Johansson and Ronkainen, 2005), higher quality, prestige, and intention to purchase (Steenkamp *et al.*, 2003).

Whatever its merits, the purity of the global brand concept has not been entirely realized as issues of adaptation to local market needs, including social and cultural issues, has led to a need to achieve a balance between these two extremes. For example, Coca-Cola adapts the taste to meet the needs of local markets, even across Europe. So, as the consumption of different offerings naturally varies across countries (e.g. chocolate, milk, coffee, cars), it is not surprising that we find manufacturers and producers varying their marketing strategies. What this means is that marketers need to determine which elements can be standardized (e.g. products, name, packaging, service), and which need to be adapted (typically language, communications, and voice-overs) to meet local needs.

Brand Equity

Brand equity is a measure of the value and strength of a brand. It is an assessment of a brand's wealth, sometimes referred to as goodwill. Financially, brands consist of their physical assets plus a sum that represents their reputation or goodwill, with the latter far exceeding the former. So, when Premier Foods, who own Branston sauces and Ambrosia Creamed Rice, paid £1.2bn to buy Rank Hovis McDougall (RHM), who own Oxo, Hovis, and Mr Kipling cakes, they bought the physical assets and the reputation of RHM brands, the sales of which amount to £1.6bn annually (OFT, 2007).

Brand equity is considered important because of the increasing interest in measuring the return on promotional investments and pressure by various stakeholders to value brands for balance sheet purposes. A brand with strong equity is more likely to be able to preserve its customer loyalty and fend off competitor attacks.

There are two main views about how brand equity should be valued—from a financial perspective and from a marketing perspective (Lasser *et al.*, 1995). The financial view is founded on a consideration of a brand's asset value that is based on the net value of all the cash the brand is expected to generate over its lifetime. The marketing perspective is based on the images, beliefs, and core associations consumers have about particular brands, and the degree of loyalty or retention a brand is able to sustain. Measures of market awareness, penetration, involvement, attitudes, and purchase intervals (frequency) are typical. However, Feldwick (1996) suggests that there are three aspects of brand equity:

- brand value, based on a financial and accounting base;
- brand strength, measuring the strength of a consumer's attachment to a brand;
- brand description, represented by the specific attitudes customers have towards a brand.

Brand equity is strongly related to marketing and brand strategy because this type of measurement can help focus management on brand development. However, there is little agreement about what should be measured and how and when it should be measured. Ambler and Vakratsas (1998) argue that organizations should not seek a single set of measures simply because of the varying circumstances and contextual factors that impinge on brand performance. In reality, the measures used by most firms share many common elements.

Stahl *et al.* (2012) researched the relationship between brand equity and customer lifetime value (CLV), which is composed of customer acquisition, retention, and profitability. They found that brand equity has a 'predictable and meaningful impact on CLV'. They conclude that brand equity is a multidimensional concept, because the components of brand equity exert different effects on acquisition, retention, and profit. Most interestingly, they suggest that brand management and customer management should be integrated so that they work together in organizations, and are not separated.

Chapter Summary

To consolidate your learning, the key points from this chapter are summarized here.

- **Explain the characteristics and principal types of brands and branding.**

  Brands are products and services that have added value. Brands help customers to differentiate between the various offerings and to make associations with certain attributes or feelings with a particular brand. There are three main types of brand: manufacturer, distributor, and generic.

- **Discuss ways in which brands work through associations and personalities.**

  Brands are capable of triggering associations in the minds of consumers. These associations may sometimes enable consumers to construe a psychosocial meaning associated with a particular brand. This psychosocial element can be measured in terms of the associations consumers make in terms of five key dimensions: sincerity, excitement, competence, sophistication, and ruggedness. Brand personality provides a form of identity for consumers that expresses symbolic meaning for themselves and for others.

■ **Examine how branding has evolved, utilising relational, and co-creation perspectives.**

Definitions and types of brand (e.g. virtual brands) have evolved and emerged as potentially powerful socio-cultural concepts in which relational and community issues replace the former managerial perspective involving senders and receivers, and the control of one party over another. A co-created brand or customer branding can be seen when a customer attaches a name, term, or other feature that enables them to identify one seller's good or service as distinct from those of other sellers.

■ **Explain how brands can be built.**

Keller's brand pyramid consists of several building blocks, and brands are built through a series of steps. The first enables customers to identify with the brand and help them make associations with a specific product, class, or customer need. The second step establishes what the brand means by linking various tangible and intangible brand associations. The third step encourages customer responses based around brand-related judgement and feelings. The final step is about fostering an active relationship between customers and the brand.

■ **Describe the principal issues associated with branding in services, b2b, internal, and global contexts.**

Branding is important in various sectors. These include services, because the intangibility of services requires that customers are helped to understand the value associated with a service offering. In business markets, branding is increasingly regarded as important because research shows that buyers make decisions based on emotional benefits and self-expressive benefits, not just on utilitarian elements. Employees are an integral part of a customer's brand experience, and the management of global brands requires that there is brand consistency across all markets.

■ **Explore the issues and activities associated with brand equity and demonstrate why branding is important to marketing managers.**

Brand equity is a measure of the value of a brand. It is an assessment of a brand's wealth, sometimes referred to as goodwill. Financially, brands consist of their physical assets plus a sum that represents their reputation or goodwill, with the latter far exceeding the former. There are two main views about how brand equity should be valued, namely the financial and marketing perspectives.

Review Questions

1 How have definitions of brands changed over the past 50 years?
2 What is the difference between intrinsic and extrinsic attributes?
3 Why is branding important to consumers and to organizations?
4 What are the main types of brand?
5 Why is it necessary to consider the broad context of consumers' lives in order to understand the role and relationship that brands play in them?
6 What are Aaker's five dimensions of psychosocial meaning?
7 Explain the phrase coined by Ballantyne and Aitken (2007) that 'brand meanings are socially constructed'.
8 Draw Keller's brand pyramid and name the individual building blocks.
9 What is the difference between preference and relevance brand strategies?
10 Write brief notes explaining the two main views about brand equity.

Worksheet Summary

To apply the knowledge you have gained from this chapter and test your understanding of branding insight visit the **Online Resource Centre** and complete Worksheet 13.1.

Discussion Questions

1. Having read Case Insight 13.1 at the beginning of this chapter, how would you advise Aston Martin to develop brand awareness and brand familiarity in the Chinese market?
2. If brands are capable of having a personality, are they therefore susceptible to personality disorders? Justify your answer.
3. When Ingrid Stevenson was appointed brand manager for a range of well-established fruit juices, one of her first tasks was to understand the market and how consumers related to the brand. How might an understanding of Aaker's Brand Personality Scale help her in this task?
4. To what extent are ideas about co-creation and socially constructed meaning relevant to business-to-business brands?
5. The British celebrity chef Jamie Oliver owns and runs a series of high profile restaurants. He is opening restaurants worldwide, stars in his own ground-breaking chef/food-based TV programmes, and has a number of books and other business interests. Discuss the view that celebrities cannot be brands as they do not meet the common brand criteria.

Visit the **Online Resource Centre** and complete the Multiple Choice Questions to assess your knowledge of Chapter 13.

Glossary

brand multidimensional and emotional constructs which people use to embrace an abstract object or a set of associations in the mind.

brand associations the physical and non-physical product attributes and benefits aligned with attitudes that consumers use to create an image of a brand in their minds.

brand equity a measure of the value and strength of a brand. It is an assessment of a brand's wealth, sometimes referred to as goodwill.

brand extension the use of an established brand name to lever entry into a new market.

brand personalities the associations and images that enable consumers to construe a psychosocial meaning associated with a particular brand.

Brand Personality Scale dimensions used to measure brand personality.

brand positioning a strategic activity used to differentiate and distinguish a brand.

brand preference ensuring customers choose your brand rather than your competitors' brand.

brand relevance the creation of brand characteristics that are so attractive that any competitive brand that does not have the desirable characteristic is rejected.

brand scope the range of international markets in which a brand operates.

customer branding the name, term, or other feature devised by customers that enables them to identify otherwise undifferentiated or unbranded products.

distributor brand brands developed by the wholesalers, distributors, dealers, and retailers who make up the distribution channel. Sometimes referred to as own-label brands.

extrinsic attributes those elements that, if changed, do not alter the material functioning and performance of the product itself.

generic brands brands sold without any promotional materials or any means of identifying the company.

intrinsic attributes the functional characteristics of a product, such as its shape, performance, and physical capacity.

manufacturer brands brands created and sustained by producers in order to encourage consumer awareness, recognition, and purchase.

semiotics the science of signs.

servicescape the stimuli that impact upon customers in a service environment, similar to the atmospherics present in a retail environment.

References

Aaker, D.A. (1991). *Managing Brand Equity*. New York: Free Press.

Aaker, D. (2012). Win the brand relevance battle and then build competitor barriers. *California Management Review*, 54(2), 43–57.

Aaker, D. (2014). *Aaker on Branding*. New York: Morgan James.

Aaker, J. (1997). Dimensions of brand personality. *Journal of Marketing Research*, 34, 347–56.

Achenbaum, A.A. (1993) The mismanagement of brand equity. Presented at ARF Fifth Annual Advertising and Promotion Workshop, 1 February.

Adebayo, D. (2014). Bob Marley's legacy is going up in cannabis smoke. *The Guardian,* 20 November. Retrieve from: http://www.theguardian.com/commentisfree/2014/nov/20/bob-marley-legacy-cannabis-smoke-reggae-dopeheads (accessed 5 March 2015).

Ahmad, A. and Thyagaraj, K.S. (2014). Brand personality and brand equity research: past developments and future directions. *IUP Journal of Brand Management*, 11(3), 19–56.

AMA (2012). Dictionary definition. Retrieve from: http://www.marketingpower.com/_layouts/Dictionary.aspx?dLetter = B (accessed 2 November 2012).

Ambler, T. and Vakratsas, D. (1998). Why not let the agency decide the advertising? *Market Leader*, 1, 32–7.

Anon. (2009). Michael Jackson set to be number one in charts following his death. *The Telegraph,* 27 June. Retrieve from: http://www.telegraph.co.uk/news/worldnews/5662997/Michael-Jackson-set-to-be-number-one-in-charts-following-his-death.html (accessed 1 May 2015).

Anon. (n.d). Elvis in the Guinness World Record Book. Retrieve from: http://www.elvis.net/guinness/guinnessframe.html (accessed 3 November 2015).

Arora, R. and Stoner, C. (2009). A mixed method approach to understanding brand personality. *Journal of Product & Brand Management*, 18(4), 272–83.

Ballantyne, D. and Aitken, R. (2007). Branding in B2B markets: the service-dominant logic. *Journal of Business & Industrial Marketing*, 22(6), 363–71.

Belk, R. (1988). Possessions and the extended self. *Journal of Consumer Research*, 15(2), 139–68.

Bendixen, M., Bukasa, K.A., and Abratt, R. (2004) Brand equity in the business-to-business market. *Industrial Marketing Management*, 33, 371–80.

Bengtsson, A. (2003). Towards a critique of brand relationships. *Advances in Consumer Research,* 30, 154–8.

Birkigt, K. and Stadler, M.M. (1986). *Corporate Identity: Grundlagen, Funktionen, Fallspielen*. Landsberg am Lech: Verlag Moderne Industrie.

Booms, B.H., and Bitner, M.J. (1981). Marketing strategies and organization structure for service firms. In J.H. Donnelly and W.R. George (eds), *The Marketing of Services*. Chicago, IL: American Marketing Association.

Brochado, A., da Silva, R.V., and LaPlaca, P. (2015). Assessing brand personality associations of top-of-mind wine brands. *International Journal of Wine Business Research*, 27(2), 125–42.

Burrows, T. (2014). Mr Kipling will still sell 'exceedingly good cakes' after bosses save famous catchphrase from axe during brand revamp. *Mail Online*, 26 August. Retrieve from: http://www.dailymail.co.uk/news/article-2734466/Mr-Kipling-sell-exceedingly-good-cakes-bosses-save-famous-catchphrase-axe-brand-revamp.html (accessed 11 January 2016).

Caulfield, K. (2012) Amy Winehouse's death led to surge in sales, chart moves. *Billboard*, 23 July. Retrieve from: http://www.billboard.com/articles/news/480976/amy-winehouses-death-led-to-surge-in-sales-chart-moves (accessed 27 September 2015).

Christodoulides, G. (2009) Branding in the post-internet era. *Marketing Theory*, 9(1)141–4.

Claye, A., Myer, T., and Timelin, B. (2014). The brand beyond the brands, McKinsey & Co., May. Retrieve from: www.mckinsey.com (accessed 11 January 2016).

Clayton, M. and Heo, J. (2011). Effects of promotional-based advertising on brand associations. *Journal of Product & Brand Management*, 20(4), 309–15.

Coleman, A. (2015). When branding campaigns go wrong. *The Guardian*, 8 October. Retrieve from: www.theguardian.com/small-business-network/2015/oct/08/when-branding-campaigns-go-wrong (accessed 11 January 2016).

Crawford, M.C. (1985). A new positioning typology. *Journal of Product Innovation Management*, 2(December), 243–53.

Crosby, L.A. (2012). Relational brands. *Marketing Management*, 21(2), 10–11.

de Chernatony, L., and dall'Olmo Riley, F. (1998). Defining a brand: beyond the literature with experts' interpretations. *Journal of Marketing Management*, 14(4/5), 417–43.

de Lencastre, P. and Côrte-Real, A. (2010). One, two, three: a practical brand anatomy. *Brand Management*, 17(6), 399–412.

Douglas, S.P., Craig, C.S., and Nijssen, E.J. (2001). Integrating branding strategy across markets: building international brand architecture. *Journal of International Marketing*, 9(2), 97–114.

Feldwick, P. (1996). What is brand equity anyway, and how do you measure it? *Journal of Marketing Research*, 382, 85–104.

Fournier, S. (1998) Consumers and their brands: developing relationship theory in consumer research. *Journal of Consumer Research*, 24(4), 343–73.

France, C., Merrilees, B., and Miller, D. (2015). Customer brand co-creation: a conceptual model. *Marketing Intelligence & Planning*, 33(6), 848–64.

Harris, L.C. and Ezeh, C. (2008) Servicescape and loyalty intentions: an empirical investigation. *European Journal of Marketing*, 42(3/4), 390–422.

Holt, D.B., Quelch, J.A. and Taylor, E.L. (2004). How global brands compete. *Harvard Business Review*, 82(9), 68–81.

Huggler, J. (2015). German government 'knew VW was rigging emissions test'. *The Telegraph*, 23 September. Retrieved from: http://www.telegraph.co.uk/finance/newsbysector/industry/11884877/German-government-knew-VW-was-rigging-emissions-test.html (1 August 2016).

Jin, S-A. A. and Sung, Y. (2011). The roles of spokes-avatars' personalities in brand communication in 3D virtual environments. *Brand Management*, 17(5), 317–27.

Johansson, J.K. and Ronkainen, I.A. (2005). The esteem of global brands. *Brand Management*, 1(5), 339–54.

Juntunen, M. (2012). Co-creating corporate brands in start-ups. *Marketing Intelligence & Planning*, 30(2), 230–49.

Keller, K.L. (1993). Conceptualizing, measuring, and managing customer-based brand equity. *Journal of Marketing*, 57(January), 1–22.

Keller, K.L. (1998). *Strategic Brand Management: Building, Measuring, and Managing Brand Equity*. Upper Saddle River, NJ: Prentice Hall.

Keller, K.L. (2009). Building strong brands in a modern marketing communications environment. *Journal of Marketing Communications*, 15(2/3), 139–55.

Kollmann, T. and Suckow, C. (2007). The corporate brand naming process in the net economy. *Qualitative Market Research*, 10(4), 349–61.

Kuhn, K-A. L., Alpert, F., and Pope, N.K.Ll. (2008) An application of Keller's brand equity model in a B2B context. *Qualitative Market Research*, 11(1), 40–58.

Lasser, W., Mittal, B., and Sharma, A. (1995). Measuring customer based brand equity. *Journal of Consumer Marketing*, 12(4), 11–19.

Lennartz, E., Fischer, M., Krafft, M., and Peters, K. (2015). Drivers of B2B brand strength—insights from an international study across industries. *Schmalenbach Business Review*, 67(1), 114–37.

Levitt, T. (1983). The globalization of markets. *Harvard Business Review*, May–June, 2–11.

Lindgreen, A., Beverland, M.B., and Farrelly, F. (2010). From strategy to tactics: building, implementing, and managing brand equity in business markets. *Industrial Marketing Management*, 39, 1223–5.

Linville, P. and Carlston, D.E. (1994). Social cognition of the self. In P.G. Devine, D.L. Hamilton, and T.M. Ostrom (eds), *Social Cognition: Impact on Social Psychology*. San Diego, CA: Academic Press, 143–93.

Low, G.S. and Lamb, C.W. (2000). The measurement and dimensionality of brand associations. *Journal of Product and Brand Management*, 9(6), 350–68.

McCracken, G. (1986). Culture and consumption: a theoretical account of the structure and movement of the cultural meaning of consumer goods. *Journal of Consumer Research*, 13, 71–84.

Marquardt, A.J., Golicic, S.L., and Davis, D.F. (2011). B2B services branding in the logistics services industry. *Journal of Services Marketing*, 25(1), 47–57.

Michell, P., King, J., and Reast, J. (2001). Brand values related to industrial products. *Industrial Marketing Management*, 30(5), 415–25.

Mudambi, S. (2002). Branding importance in business-to-business markets: three buyer clusters. *Industrial Marketing Management*, 31(6), 525–33.

Muzellec, L., Lynn, T., and Lambkin, M. (2012). Branding in fictional and virtual environments: introducing a new conceptual domain and research agenda. *European Journal of Marketing*, 46(6), 811–26.

OFT (2007). www.oft.gov.uk/shared_oft/mergers_eaoz/361227/premier.pdf (accessed 2 December 2007).

Pennington, J.R. and Ball, D.A. (2009). Customer branding of commodity products: the customer-developed brand. *Brand Management*, 16(7), 455–67.

Phau, I. and Lau, K.C. (2001). Brand personality and consumer self-expression: single or dual carriageway? *Journal of Brand Management*, 8(6), 428–44.

Ries, A. and Trout, J. (1972). The positioning era cometh. *Advertising Age*, 24 April, 35–8.

Roper, S. and Davies, G. (2010). Business to business branding: external and internal satisfiers and the role of training quality. *European Journal of Marketing*, 44(5), 567–90.

Rossiter, J.R. (2014). Branding explained: defining and measuring brand awareness and brand attitude. *Journal of Brand Management*, 21(7/8), 533–40.

Sarin, S. (2014). Relevance and creation of strong brands for B2B markets. *Vikalpa*, 39(4), 91–100.

Stahl, F., Heitmann, M., Lehmann, D.R., and Neslin, S.A. (2012). The impact of brand equity on customer acquisition, retention and profit margin. *Journal of Marketing*, 76 (July), 44–63.

Steenkamp, J.E., Batra, R., and Alden, D.L. (2003). How perceived brand globalness creates brand value. *Journal of International Business Studies*, 34(1), 53–65.

Thornton, N. (2010). YouTube: transactional fandom and Mexican divas. *Transnational Cinemas*, 1(1), 53–67.

Townsend, J.D., Cavusgil, S.T., and Baba, M.L. (2010). Global integration of brands and new product development at General Motors. *Journal of Product Innovation Management*, 27, 49–65.

Tudor E. and Negricea, I.C. (2012). Brand positioning: a marketing resource and an effective tool for small and medium enterprises. *Journal of Knowledge Management, Economics and Information Technology*, 11(1), 182–90.

Valette-Florence, R. and de Barnier, V. (2013). Towards a micro conception of brand personality: an application for print media brands in a French context. *Journal of Business Research*, 66(7), 897–903.

Welch, M. and Jackson, P.R. (2007). Rethinking internal communication: a stakeholder approach. *Corporate Communications*, 12(2), 177–98.

Wilkinson, C. and Patterson, A. (2014). Peppa Piggy in the middle of marketers and mashup makers: a netnography of absurd animation on YouTube. In S. Brown and S. Ponsonby-McCabe (eds), *Brand Mascots and Other Marketing Animals*. London: Routledge, 123–40.

Zablah, A.R., Brown, B.P., and Donthu, N. (2010). The relative importance of brands in modified rebuy purchase situations. *International Journal of Research in Marketing*, 27(3), 248–60.

Part Four
Principles of Customer Management

Chapter 14
Channels, Supply Chains, and Retailing

Learning Outcomes

After studying this chapter you should be able to:

▶ Describe the nature and characteristics of a marketing channel

▶ Explain the different types of intermediaries and their roles in the marketing channel

▶ Understand the different marketing channel structures and their core characteristics

▶ Explain the factors that influence the design and structure of marketing channels

▶ Describe the main elements that constitute supply chain management

▶ Consider the role and function of retailers in the marketing channel

Case Insight 14.1
Åhléns

Market Insight 14.1
Channelling Motorbikes

Market Insight 14.2
Packaged Goods Companies Look Online

Market Insight 14.3
Getting It There, on Time ... Medicine, IT, and Fashion

Market Insight 14.4
Enhancing Channel Experiences

Market Insight 14.5
Compelling In-store Technologies

Case Insight 14.1
Åhléns

As shopper behaviour is turning increasingly digital, established retailers have to adapt their channel strategies. We talk to Lotta Bjurhult, Business Developer Retail Operations at Sweden's largest department store chain, Åhléns, to find out what it takes to add an online channel to an existing network of department stores.

Åhléns is Sweden's leading department store chain. You could say that we hold a position similar to John Lewis in the UK or Karstadt in Germany. In 2015, we had a turnover of about SEK 5bn, employed 3,000 people, and served a total of 65m visitors in our 70 department stores located throughout Sweden. Our customer base is very loyal with over 2.2m club members who shop on average 8.5 times a year at our stores.

Our mission is to offer carefully selected, priceworthy, and sustainable solutions that we believe can satisfy people's requirements in a simple, inspiring, and accessible way. As with most department stores, we offer a broad assortment of products and provide a wide array of customer service facilities for store customers. In our department stores, customers are offered a carefully considered collection of selected brands and proprietary labels all under one roof. Our customers are able to browse among an inspiring assortment of value-for-money products within home styling and interior design, fashion, beauty, foodstuffs, and entertainment.

Adding an online channel to an existing department store operation is complex. The challenge is to keep the overall experience of Åhléns, which is very much centred on the in-store shopping experience, while simultaneously adapting it to an online setting. Customers consider Åhléns as one department store—they don't care if they buy something offline or online. In developing our online offer we have looked at a range of issues.

In terms of assortment we have used statistics on what customers are already buying online as a starting point.

A key challenge for Åhléns is translating the in store shopping experience online
Source: Courtesy of Åhléns.

We have also considered what products are currently not available in all our local department stores. At the end of 2016, our online channel will hold around 50,000 different products, which means that it will offer a larger assortment than most of our physical department stores, but will be equal in size to our larger department stores in Uppsala and Malmö. Over time, we are aiming to provide the same assortment online as we do in our flagship store Åhléns City Stockholm.

We have also developed a tailor-made IT system to support the online channel. In creating our online store we have gone through and developed all our internal processes—starting with how to relate to suppliers and vendors, on to where to stock and how to deliver products, as well as the role of physical store employees. Going online exposes any weaknesses you might have in your business operations. If something is not really working in a physical store,

Case Insight 14.1
continued

there are store employees who can fix it. Things such as payments and returns, which are quite easily managed in a physical department store, become a lot trickier online.

Another key consideration for us has been how to engage store employees and make them embrace the online channel as part of the overall value proposition of Åhléns. The online channel has profound and long-lasting effects on the role they play in creating a high quality customer experience.

One of my key tasks has been to ensure that in-store employees and customer service embrace the online channel and make it part of the experience offered to our customers every day. This is essential if we are to offer our customers a seamless experience. Key questions for me have been:

What roles should store employees play in integrating the offline and online channels? What activities are needed to ensure their support for a new online channel?

Introduction

Have you ever considered the journey a bottle of water, a computer, or a bag of potatoes might take from its source (manufacturer or producer) in order to be available for you to purchase at the point you prefer? In many cases this journey can be complex, involving transactions between many organizations, countries, and people.

The organizations involved with any one journey are collectively termed a distribution or **marketing channel**. These are chains of organizations that are concerned with the management of the processes and activities involved in creating and moving products from producers and manufacturers to end-user customers. Each organization adds something of value before passing it to the next, and it is this interaction which provides mutual advantage (Kotler and Keller, 2009) and underpins the concept of channel marketing.

Each of the various organizations electing to interact with others performs a specific role in the chain of activities. Some act as manufacturers, some as agents, and others may be distributors, dealers, value-added resellers, wholesalers, or retailers. Whatever the role, it is normally specific and geared to refining, adding value, and moving a product closer to the end-user. This interaction requires coordination if participating organizations are to achieve their goals and make available final products and services that represent superior value to the channel's end-users, especially when there are multichannel activities (Yan *et al.*, 2011).

In this chapter, we consider three main elements. The first concerns the management of the intangible aspects or issues of ownership, control, and flows of communication between the parties responsible for making an offering accessible to target customers, commonly referred to as marketing channel management.

The second element concerns the management of the tangible or physical aspects of moving a product from the producer to the end-user. This must be undertaken so that a customer can freely access an offering and that the final act of the buying process is as convenient and easy as possible. This is part of supply chain management, which includes the logistics associated with moving products closer to end-users. The third and final element is about retailing, a critical element of the way consumers access the products they desire.

Channel Management

Europe's largest clothing maker and retailer, Inditex, has seen its clothing sales rise consistently in recent years because it adds new stock to its fashion stores (e.g. Zara, Pull&Bear, and Massimo) twice a week, keeping the stock fresh and up to date with the latest fashion trends. It achieves this by manufacturing over 50% of its stock in Spain or Portugal; although this is more costly in production, Inditex can get new designs into European and American stores twice as fast than if they have to wait for delivery of stock manufactured in Asia. This shows that by managing their marketing channels Inditex's overall business performance has improved.

If we consider the skills Inditex need to design and assemble a range of garments, to source the materials, and to manufacture, package, and then distribute the final fashion garments to its stores and other customers globally, we can see that a major set of complex operations are required. For many organizations, trying to undertake all these operations is beyond their skill-set or core activity. For all organizations, there is a substantial risk associated with producing too many or too few, too soon or too late for the target market. There are risks associated with changing buyer behaviours, with storage, finance, and competitors' actions to name but a few of the critical variables.

By collaborating with other organizations that have the necessary skills and expertise these uncertainties can be reduced. Working with organizations that can create customer demand or access, and manage specialist financial issues, storage, or transportation, adds value and develops competitive advantage. For example, to reach the 600,000 rural villages in India, Samsung partnered with the Indian Farmers Fertiliser Cooperative Ltd to sell its handsets. With this new marketing channel, Samsung can now reach over 90% of villages in India.

Collectively, organizations that combine to enable offerings to reach end-users quickly and efficiently constitute a marketing channel, sometimes referred to as a **distribution channel**. Organizations that combine together to reduce risk and uncertainty do so by exchanging offerings which are of value to others in the channel. Therefore marketing channels enable organizations to share or reduce uncertainty. By reducing the uncertainty experienced by all members in a channel, each is in a better position to concentrate on other tasks.

How Channels Help to Reduce Uncertainty

Marketing channels enable different types of uncertainty to be decreased in several ways (Fill and McKee, 2012). These include reducing the complexity, increasing value and competitive advantage, routinization, and providing specialization.

Reducing Complexity

The number of transactions and the frequency of contact a producer might have with each individual end-user customer would be so high that the process would be unprofitable. This volume of activity can be seen in Figure 14.1.

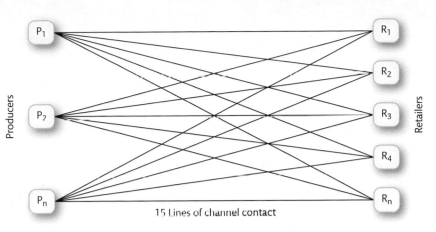

15 Lines of channel contact

Figure 14.1

The complexity of channel exchanges without intermediaries

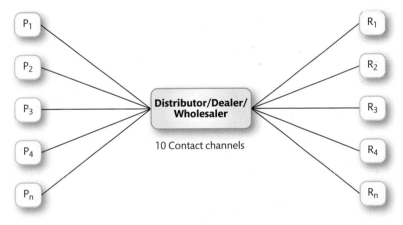

Figure 14.2

The impact of intermediaries on channel exchanges

Now, if an intermediary is introduced into the process the number of transactions falls drastically, as demonstrated in Figure 14.2. The fall in the number of transactions indicates that not only are costs reduced but also that producers are better placed to redirect their attention to the needs of intermediaries. This allows them to focus on their core activities; production or manufacturing. In much the same way end-user customers receive much improved individual support from channel intermediaries than they would probably get from a producer.

Increasing Value and Competitive Advantage

By using intermediaries producers can reduce purchase risk—the uncertainty that customers might reject the offering. Intermediaries rather than producers have the skills and core competences necessary to meet end-user requirements, for example retailing. By improving the overall value that customers perceive in an offering, relative to competing products and customer experience, it is possible to develop competitive advantage.

Routinization

Performance risk can be reduced by improving transaction efficiency. By standardizing or 'routinizing' the transaction process, perhaps by regulating order sizes, automating operations, and managing delivery cycles and payment frequencies, distribution costs can be reduced.

Specialization

By providing specialist training services, maintenance, installation, bespoke deliveries, or credit facilities, intermediaries can develop a service that has real value to other channel members or end-user customers. Value can also be improved for customers by helping them to locate offerings they want. Intermediaries can provide these specialist resources, whereas producers are not normally interested or able to do so. This is because they prefer to produce large quantities of a small range of goods. Unfortunately, end-user customers only want a limited quantity of a wide variety of goods.

Intermediaries provide a solution by bringing together and sorting out all the goods produced by different manufacturers in the category. They then represent these goods in quantities and formats that enable end-user customers to buy the quantities they wish, as frequently as they prefer. This is referred to as sorting and smoothing. Table 14.1 provides an explanation of these forms of specialization.

Intermediaries provide other utility-based benefits. For example, they assist end-users by bringing a product produced a long distance away to a more convenient location for purchase and consumption, i.e. **place utility**. The product might be manufactured during the week, but purchased and consumed at the weekend. Here, manufacturing, purchase, and consumption occur at different points in time, and intermediaries provide **time utility**.

Immediate product availability through retailers enables ownership to pass to the consumer within a short period of time, i.e. **ownership utility**. Finally, intermediaries can also provide information about the product to aid sales and usage. The Internet has led to the development of a new type of intermediary, an information intermediary (e.g. Expedia, Google). Here the key role is to manage information to improve the efficiency and effectiveness of the distribution channel, i.e. **information utility**.

Table 14.1. Aspects of sorting and smoothing

Aspect	Explanation
Sorting out	Grading products into different sizes, qualities, or grades (e.g. potatoes, eggs or fruit)
Accumulation	Bringing together different products from different producers to provide a wider category choice
Allocation	Often referred to as breaking bulk (by wholesalers), this involves disaggregating bulk deliveries into smaller lot sizes that customers are able (and prefer) to buy
Assorting	Assembling different collections of goods/services thought to be of value to the customer (retailers and consumers)

Source: Fill and McKee (2012).

There are some disadvantages to the use of intermediaries. For example, as the number of inter-mediaries in a channel increases, a lack of product control can develop. Some manufacturers are unable to influence intermediaries in terms of in-store merchandising, placement, and even pricing. Furthermore, intermediaries might be susceptible to competitor inducements such as trade promotions. For many manufacturers and producers, intermediaries often become a mar-ket in their own right, requiring considerable time, money, and personnel to support and develop a relationship with them.

 Visit the Online Resource Centre and complete Internet Activity 14.1 to learn more about the role of intermediaries within the film and TV industry.

Types of Intermediary

Having seen that intermediaries play a significant role in marketing channels, we now need to consider the different types that are available. There are, of course, a number of different types of intermediary, each fulfilling different roles and providing various forms of specialization. Some of the more common ones are as follows.

- Agents or brokers—these act as a principal intermediary between the seller of an offering and buyers, bringing them together without taking ownership of the offering. These intermediaries have the legal authority to act on behalf of the manufacturer. For example, universities often use agents to recruit students in overseas markets (e.g. China, India).

- Merchants—a merchant undertakes the same actions as an agent, but takes ownership of a product.

- Distributors or dealers—these distribute the product. They offer value through services asso-ciated with selling inventory, credit, and after-sales service. Often used in B2B markets, they can also be found dealing directly with consumers, e.g. automobile distributors. See Market Insight 14.1 for a view of Honda's dealers and distributors.

- Franchises—a franchisee holds a contract to supply and market an offering to the require-ments or blueprint of the franchisor, the owner of the original offering. The contract might cover many aspects of the design of the offering such as marketing, product assortment, or service delivery. The uniformity of differing branches of McDonald's and KFC is an indication of franchisee contracts; however, franchise agreements are not just used in the fast food or product sectors.

 Visit the Online Resource Centre and follow the web link to the European Franchise Association (EFA) to learn more about business franchise collaboration activities across Europe.

- Wholesalers—a wholesaler stocks goods before the next level of distribution and takes both legal title and physical possession of the goods. In B2C markets, wholesalers do not usually deal with the end consumer but with other intermediaries (e.g. retailers). In B2B markets, sales are made direct to end-customers. Examples include Costco Wholesalers in the USA, and Makro in Europe.

- Retailers—these intermediaries sell directly to end-consumers and may purchase direct from manufacturers or deal with wholesalers. This is dependent on their purchasing power and the volume purchased. Leading retailers include Wal-Mart, Marks & Spencer, Carrefour, and electronics retailers such as Media-Saturn.

Infomediaries are Internet-based organizations designed to provide information to channel members, including end-users.

Managing Marketing Channels

There are two main issues associated with the management of marketing channels. These are the design of the channel, its structure and activities, and secondly the relationships between channel members. These are considered in turn.

Channel Design

The design of an appropriate channel, i.e. its structure, length, and the membership and their roles, vary according to context. For example, the channels necessary to support a new product or organization start-up, are different from those for modifying an existing structure to adapt to

Market Insight 14.1
Channelling Motorbikes

Honda sells over 12m motorcycles each year in the Asia–Oceania region alone, and the management of its distribution networks is a vital element in maintaining customer access and satisfaction. Honda produces a wide range of motorcycles, ranging from the 50cc class to the 1800cc class, and is the largest manufacturer of motorcycles in the world in terms of annual units of production. In the region, Honda's motorcycles are produced at sites in Japan, Indonesia, the Philippines, Pakistan, and India.

In Japan, sales of Honda motorcycles (and automobiles and power products) are made through different distribution networks. Honda's products are sold to consumers primarily through independent retail dealers, and motorcycles are distributed through over 11,500 outlets, including approximately 1,400 authorized dealerships. These authorized dealerships sell all Honda's Japanese motorcycle models, not just selected models.

Most of Honda's overseas sales are made through its main sales subsidiaries, which distribute Honda's products to local wholesalers and retail dealers. In Indonesia, Honda has recently developed its dealer network of 4,000 dealers and service shops to support sales and provide excellent after-sales service. In the USA, Honda's wholly owned subsidiary markets Honda's motorcycle products through a sales network of approximately 1,260 independent local dealers. Many of these motorcycle dealers also sell other Honda products.

In Europe, subsidiaries of the company in the UK, Germany, France, Belgium, the Netherlands, Spain, Switzerland, Austria, Italy, and other European countries distribute Honda's motorcycles through approximately 1,600 independent local dealers.

One core element of Honda's dealer strategy, worldwide, is its comprehensive 4S support system. This covers sales, service, spare parts, and safety.

Market Insight 14.1
continued

For example, Honda provided its dealers in Thailand, Indonesia, Vietnam, and India with an easy-to-use riding simulator, called Riding Trainer, through which riders can get an opportunity to receive risk awareness training and riding practice and, of course, engagement with the Honda brand.

Recently a fifth S has been added, 'second-hand (or used)' business. In Thailand, for example, the second-hand motorcycle business has been deliberately strengthened as a means of developing business. The strategy encourages potential motorcycle owners and those ready for an upgrade to purchase pre-owned Honda models, drawing this segment into the brand.

Sources: http://www.world.honda.com/; http://www.findarticles.com/p/articles/.

Honda use simulators enabling riders to practice riding, receive risk awareness training, and experience the brand

Source: © Bloomberg/Getty.

Theory into Practice

The Honda example demonstrates the variety and complexity of their marketing channels. The design of a marketing channel depends partly on the context, culture, and level of economic development in a country or region. In other words, no one channel design fits every situation.

The level of control and degree to which Honda the manufacturer can control marketing activities associated with its motorbikes varies considerably. Honda's control over the marketing channel is enhanced by the establishment of authorized dealerships and in the USA by wholly owned subsidiaries. At the other end of the spectrum are independent local dealers. Here, Honda have attempted to influence and retain dealers through the use of simulators. This in turn helps attract and retain customers.

Related Topics:

intermediaries; channel structures; channel relationships.

1 Why does Honda set up subsidiary organizations in each overseas region or country?

2 What do you think are the benefits of the 5S support system?

3 What might affect Honda's dealer network (marketing channel) in the future?

changing market conditions. The channel design decision process requires consideration of three main factors.

1 **Distribution intensity decision**: the level of purchase convenience required by the different end-user customer segments to be served.
2 **Channel configuration decision:** the number and type of intermediaries necessary to deliver products to the optimum number of sales outlets.
3 **Multichannel decision**: the number of different types of channels to be used.

This helps us to determine what is the most effective and efficient way to get the offering to the customer.

Key Considerations

When managing distribution channels, we need to consider a variety of factors to ensure that the channel suits the organization's objectives. Three broad elements need to be considered: economics, coverage, and control.

- Economics requires us to recognize where costs are being incurred and profits being made in a channel to maximize our return on investment.
- Coverage is about maximizing the offering's availability in the market for the customer, satisfying the desire to have the offering available to the largest number of customers, in as many locations as possible, at the widest range of times.
- Control refers to achieving the optimum distribution costs without losing decision-making authority over the offering—how it is priced, promoted, and delivered in the distribution channel.

Sometimes, by covering a wide range of delivery times and locations through the use of intermediaries, organizations sacrifice some control in decision-making. Intermediaries start changing the price, image, and display, as they seek to maximize sales of a whole range of products. Think about the positions of HTC, Huawei, Samsung, and Apple. In order to get the maximum number of customers using their mobile phone handsets, they need to have the maximum number of retailers and mobile phone networks promoting and selling their phones. However, the same networks and retailers also sell the handsets of their competitors, such as new entrants Xiaomi and Micromax. As the retailers and networks compete to sign up customers, they push for lower prices, or they demand advertising subsidies to help them sell the phones. So Samsung and LG may discover that their phones are being sold at very low prices, and their brand image being compromised, by retailers and networks who are desperately seeking to maximize their own sales. What happens if LG reduces the number of retailers or networks it deals with in order to increase control over its marketing mix? The danger is, of course, that its competitors will gain market share by continuing to deal with these retailers and networks. In contrast, Apple has specific policies on what distributors can and cannot discount on its products like the iPhone, whereas Google challenged the accepted mobile delivery model by launching its own online storefront for the Google Nexus One handset. All face a trade-off between economics, coverage, and control.

@ **Visit the Online Resource Centre** and follow the web links to the Institute of Supply Chain Management (ISM) and the Chartered Institute of Purchasing and Supply to learn more about the profession and activities of managing the distribution and supply chain.

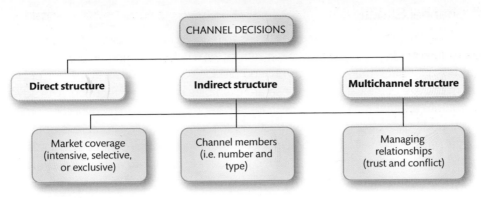

Figure 14.3
Distribution channel strategy decisions

Distribution Channel Strategy

When devising a distribution channel strategy, several key decisions need to be made to serve customers and establish and maintain appropriate buyer–seller relationships. These are summarized in Figure 14.3. The first decision is selecting how the channel will be structured. If the channel requires intermediaries, we need to consider the type of market coverage we want, the number and type of intermediaries to use, and how we should manage the relationships between members in the channel. These choices are important as they can affect the benefits provided to customers.

Channel Structure

Distribution channels can be structured in a number of ways. There are three main configurations involving producers, intermediaries, and customers: 'direct', 'indirect', or 'multi' channel structures. A direct structure involves selling directly to end-user customers with little involvement from other organizations, an indirect structure uses intermediaries, and a multichannel structure combines both. These are presented in Figure 14.4. We now consider the advantages and disadvantages of each of type of channel structure.

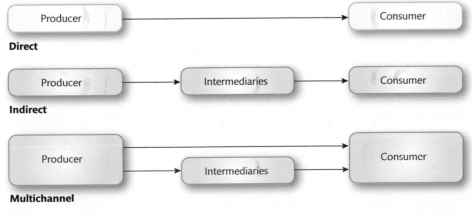

Figure 14.4
Distribution channel structure

Direct Channel Structure

In direct channels, the producer uses strategies to reach end-users directly rather than dealing through an intermediary (an agent, broker, retailer, or wholesaler) (see Figure 14.4). Have you ever been to a farmers' market and purchased produce directly from a farmer, or downloaded music from the site of a local band? These are examples of direct distribution. The advantages of this structure are that the producer or manufacturer maintains control over their product and profitability, and builds strong customer relationships. However, this structure is not suitable for all products. It is ideally suited to those products that require significant customization, technical expertise, or commitment on behalf of the producer to complete a sale (Parker *et al.*, 2006). However, electronic technologies such as the Internet have enabled a greater number of product manufacturers to reach customers directly. Efficiency within the **direct channel structure** can be improved in the following ways.

- Processing orders and distributing the offering electronically directly to customers—Adobe Reader is free universal software manufactured by Adobe Systems Inc. that enables users to read and share electronic documents. To increase cost efficiency of delivery, the organization employs a direct structure via the Internet, providing digital delivery, installation, and customer support.

- Supporting the physical distribution of the product offering directly to customers—one of the best-known examples of this is Dell Computer Corporation's system. Dell sells computer equipment through the organization's website, using telesales for product ordering, and database technology for order processing, tracking, and inventory and delivery management. The organization also distributes its products through its own delivery and installation staff.

The disadvantages of a direct channel structure typically include the large amount of capital and resources required to reach customers. This means that there are virtually no economies of scale. Manufacturers might also suffer from offering a low variety of offerings, which may not meet the needs of buyers. This is especially apparent in B2C markets, such as fast-moving consumer goods (FMCGs). Imagine having to shop for bread, milk, and a soft drink at three differing retail outlets owned by each product manufacturer. Few consumers today would purchase their offerings from individual manufacturers because of the inconvenience and time costs involved. Thus retailers satisfy the needs of end-consumers for variety, something a direct channel of distribution would not necessarily fulfill.

Indirect Channel Structure

Indirect channel structures enable producers to concentrate on the skills and processes necessary to make offerings, and use one or more intermediaries for distribution. For example, Procter & Gamble (P&G) focus their resources and expertise on developing new types of FMCGs, whereas Sainsbury's core retailing activity is to make P&G's products (and others) available to consumers.

Multichannel Structure

An increasing number of organizations adopt a hybrid or **multichannel structure** to distribute goods and services (Park and Keh, 2003). Here, the producer controls some marketing channels and intermediaries control others. For example, many airlines sell their tickets directly to consumers through the Internet, but also rely on travel agents. Music labels also sell their CDs directly, using catalogues and the Internet, as well as independent music retailers such as Rise on the Triangle. Consider the options for the purchase of a mobile device. This could occur directly from the Samsung website, from a service provider such as EE, or perhaps at Tesco while picking up some bread and milk. Samsung, Lenovo, and LG Electronics use service providers, electronic retailers, and wholesale discount clubs alongside their own direct Internet and telesales channels to market and deliver their mobile phone handsets.

The benefits of a multichannel structure include the following:

- Increased reach—by utilizing existing direct networks and the relationships of intermediaries a wider target audience can be reached.

- Producer control—producers have greater control over prices, communication, and can reach customers directly.

- Greater compliance—adherence to channel rules is more likely when producers use multiple intermediaries and are not perceived to be a (direct channel) competitor.

- Optimized margins—producers can improve margins from the direct channel element, and increase their bargaining power as they become less dependent on intermediaries.

- Improved market insight—by developing relationships with their direct customers, producers can derive a better understanding of their needs and markets issues.

The use of multichannel strategies has been encouraged by the growth of the Internet, which has increased the efficiency with which consumers and manufacturers can interact (Park and Keh, 2003). At the same time, technologies are increasing the efficiency of information exchange between producers and intermediaries, for example through electronic data interchange (EDI) and extranets. However, the sharing of profits among channel members can be a source of conflict, especially when intermediaries perceive the producer to be a competitor as well as a supplier. This structure may also confuse and alienate customers who are unsure about which channel they should use.

Research Insight 14.1

To take your learning further, you might wish to read this influential paper.

Rosenbloom, B. (2007). Multi channel strategy in business-to-business markets: prospects and problems. *Industrial Marketing Management*, 36(1), 4–9.

Rosenbloom has written extensively about marketing channels and published several books on the topic. This paper provides an interesting insight into the issues of channel strategy within a business-to-business context.

Visit the Online Resource Centre to read the abstract and access the full paper.

Market Insight 14.2
Packaged Goods Companies Look Online

The impact of e-commerce has been significant in many markets, but the consumer packaged goods (CPG) market has, until recently, avoided any major disruption. Traditionally CPGs have been distributed through independent retailers and supermarkets, using distributors and strategically placed distribution centres. Online sales accounted for less than 1% of total sales in packaged food and approximately 3% in non-food in 2013.

Since then there have been several innovative experiments in e-commerce in the CPG sector. A number of regional grocers have piloted various 'click and collect' operations where products are purchased online and picked up in stores. Perhaps one of the most significant moves has been the trend for major CPG companies to strengthen their digital channel strategies by working with Amazon and other key digital players. One of the primary approaches has been to locate teams of digital and functional specialists at Amazon, and through investment develop co-marketing activities with Amazon.

Amazon has tested Amazon Pantry, which lets its Prime users fill a box with selections of more than 2,000 products and ship them for a small fee. Prime Now offers delivery to the home within one or two hours, and the Dash Button, an Internet-connected device placed anywhere in the home, provides a one-touch way of ordering refills.

Various consumer package goods organizations now work with Amazon in order to strengthen their online offering
Source: © Jeramey Lende/Shutterstock.

In September 2016, Sainsbury's, the supermarket retailer, began the process of integrating Argos, the high street digital retailer, into its business.

Argos was purchased because it enabled Sainsbury's to compete more effectively, and helped it adapt to changes in the retailing environment. It was also felt that there were several synergies between the two organizations that needed developing.

Sources: Alldredge and Ungerman (2015); Alldredge *et al.* (2015); Armstrong (2016); Sheffield (2016).

Theory into Practice

The traditional marketing channels in the packaged goods market are determined largely by market size. Manufacturers distribute their goods direct to large supermarket customers via distribution points and warehouses. Ownership moves from the producer to the retailer. Smaller customers, who buy smaller volumes, buy branded products from distributors such as wholesalers, who then sell them to retailers. In this case ownership moves with the product.

The development of online channels means that manufacturers have direct access to end-user customers, in this case consumers. This lowers many of the supply chain costs, but because of the small number of units involved in any one transaction, distribution costs can raise prices. This can be partially alleviated through click and collect arrangements.

Market Insight 14.2
continued

Related Topics:

co-branding; collaboration; channel intensity.

1 **What might be the forces driving CPG companies to develop e-commerce?**

2 **Outline the advantages and disadvantages of using an online channel for packaged goods.**

3 **Now that Sainsbury's have bought Argos, who might they consider to be their main competitor?**

Channel Intensity

Sometimes referred to as channel coverage, channel intensity refers to the number and dispersion of outlets an end-user customer can use to buy a particular offering. This decision concerns the level of convenience customers expect and suppliers need to provide to be competitive. The wider the coverage, the greater the number of intermediaries, which leads to higher costs associated with the management control of the intermediaries.

A decision to introduce a new channel refers to the addition of a new set of internal or external channel entities to the firm's existing channel system. This could be a decision to establish its own retail stores or provide an online e-commerce shopping facility. For example, Homburg *et al.* (2014) refer to China Unicom who started to sell its telecommunication services in consumer electronics retail stores, such as Suning, in addition to their own specialized telecommunication stores. Although this channel offers a lower level of customer service than China Unicom's own stores, it carries a wider product variety and broader assortment, enabling customers to purchase different kinds of electronic products and related services in one store.

There are three levels of channel intensity: intense, selective, and exclusive (see Figure 14.5).

Intensive	Selective	Exclusive
Distribution through every reasonable outlet in the market	Distribution through multiple, but not all, reasonable outlets in the market	Distribution through a single wholesaling intermediary and/or retailer

Figure 14.5
Intensity of distribution continuum

Intensive distribution involves placing an offering in as many outlets or locations as possible. It is used most commonly for offerings that consumers are unlikely to search for and which they purchase on the basis of convenience or impulse, such as magazines, soft drinks, or confectionery. However, retailers have increased control over the extent to which distribution is intensive. For example, a manufacturer of a new brand of yoghurt might want its new brand put on the shelves of all supermarkets; however, owing to limited shelf space, the retailers might limit their assortment to the leading brands of yoghurt.

Selective distribution occurs when a limited number of outlets are used. This is because when customers are actively involved with a purchase, and experience moderate to high levels of perceived risk, they are prepared to seek out appropriate suppliers. Those that best match their overall requirements are successful. Producers determine and control which intermediaries are to deliver the required products and level of services. Electrical equipment, furniture, clothing, and jewellery are categories where selective distribution is appropriate.

Sometimes, an organization might use an intensive distribution to increase awareness of its brand when entering a new market, but then move to a more selective strategy to improve control over quality and manage costs and price.

Exclusive distribution occurs when intermediaries are given exclusive rights to market an offering within a defined 'territory'. This is useful where significant support is required from the intermediary, and therefore the exclusivity is 'payback' for their investment and support. For example, high prestige goods like Ferrari sports cars and designer fashion apparel like Chanel and Gucci adopt this type of distribution intensity.

If an offering requires complex servicing arrangements or tight control, the exclusive form of distribution may be best. The threat of price competition is also diminished, as it would be inconsistent with the positioning strategy these offerings normally adopt.

Nearly all distribution through the Internet is intensive because of the massive reach of the web. Even the smallest manufacturer can advertise and sell worldwide, using the same courier services as major firms to deliver its offerings.

The decision about the number of intermediaries is often driven by cost considerations. The costs of intensive distribution are higher because of the number of outlets that must be served. The implications of these three distribution strategies are summarized in Table 14.2.

Disintermediation and Reintermediation

Disintermediation concerns the reduction in the number or strength of intermediaries required in a marketing channel. There has been an active debate about whether the rate of disintermediation is increasing (Mills and Camek, 2004; Tay and Chellah, 2011). Ideas about **re-intermediation** are supported by Anderson and Anderson (2002) who argue that the Internet encourages intermediation, and Laffey and Gandy (2009) who believe that new roles have developed through e-commerce for new and existing intermediaries. They refer to eBay and the financial services start-up Zopa as prime examples.

The assumption is that if producers could reach their customers directly they would no longer need intermediaries, or at least they would not need so many of them. Imagine that a music publisher like Sony could reach and sell to every potential customer directly through its website (www.sony.com). Given the state of technology such as PC sound systems, CD burners, or MP3 players, customers could purchase their music directly from Sony and it could be 'distributed' electronically straight to their PC. In such a scenario, Sony would no longer need to deal with high street music

Table 14.2 Intensity of channel coverage

Characteristics	Exclusive	Selective	Intensive
Objectives	Strong image channel control and loyalty, price stability	Moderate market coverage, solid image, some channel control and loyalty	Widespread market coverage, channel acceptance, volume sales
Channel members	Few in number, well-established reputable stores	Moderate in number, well-established better stores	Many in number, all types of outlets
Customers	Few in number, trendsetters, willing to travel to store, brand-loyal	Moderate in number, brand-conscious, somewhat willing to travel to store	Many in number, convenience-oriented
Marketing emphasis	Personal selling, pleasant shopping conditions, good service	Promotional mix, pleasant shopping conditions, good service	Mass advertising, nearby location, items in stock
Examples	Automobiles, designer clothes, caviar	Furniture, clothing, watches	Groceries, household products, magazines

stores, leading to the disintermediation of the distribution channel. Or would this result in a growth in the number of electronic intermediaries such as iTunes for the distribution of music?

The technical possibility of reducing the number of intermediaries doesn't just affect 'bricks-and-mortar' intermediaries, but also electronic intermediaries. In Amazon's case, for example, more consumers could skip the intermediary and buy books online directly from publishers.

Research Insight 14.2

To take your learning further, you might wish to read this influential paper.

Mills, J.F., and Camek, V. (2004). The risks, threats and opportunities of disintermediation: a distributor's view. *International Journal of Physical Distribution and Logistics Management*, **34(9), 714–27.**

This paper discusses the trend in disintermediation observed in many industries. Where many recent papers see disintermediation as a phenomenon related to online transactions, this paper defines it more broadly as the removal or weakening of an intermediary within a supply chain.

@ **Visit the Online Resource Centre to read the abstract and access the full paper.**

Some publishers and printers have been disintermediated, as some authors now sell 'ebooks' directly to the consumer. One such self-publishing author, David Gaughran, refers to the increasing number of book sales and the increasing number of authors who are avoiding traditional publishers (Gaughran, 2013). Where disintermediation does occur, it is strongly dependent on the nature of the offerings distributed. Although there are significant numbers of customers who like buying directly, many customers value and prefer the role of traditional intermediaries such as bricks-and-mortar retailers for certain purchases. In fact, such is the value of some intermediaries to both customers and producers that there has been a trend towards re-intermediation, the introduction of additional intermediaries into the distribution channel.

Managing Relationships in the Channel

An important managerial issue concerns channel relationships. Because channels are open social systems (Katz and Kahn, 1978), some level of conflict between channel members is inevitable. Conflict follows a breakdown in the levels of cooperation between channel partners (Shipley and Egan, 1992) and may well affect channel performance. Gaski (1984: 11) defined channel conflict as 'the perception on the part of a channel member that its goal attainment is being impeded by another, with stress or tension the result'.

Channel conflict may involve intermediaries on the same level (tier), for example between retailers or between agents (**horizontal conflict**). It may also occur between members on different levels (tiers), involving a producer, wholesaler, and a retailer (**vertical conflict**).

If strategies to prevent or avoid conflict have failed, it is necessary to resolve the conflict that erupts. The strategies depicted in Table 14.3 vary from selfishness/stubbornness and a refusal to work with other members, through cooperation and compromise, to one that seeks to

Table 14.3 Conflict resolution strategies

Strategy	Explanation
Accommodation	Modify expectations to incorporate requirements of others
Argument	A considered attempt to convince others of the correctness of your position
Avoidance	Removal from the point of conflict
Compromise	Meet the requirements of others halfway
Cooperation	Mutual reconciliation through cooperation
Instrumentality	Agree minimal requirements to secure short-term agreement
Self-seeking	Seek agreement on own terms or refuse further cooperation

Source: Fill and McKee (2012). Used with kind permission.

Research Insight 14.3

To take your learning further, you might wish to read this influential paper.

Webb, K.L. and Hogan, J.E. (2002). Hybrid channel conflict: causes and effects on channel performance. *Journal of Business and Industrial Marketing*, 17(5), 338–57.

This paper discusses the role of multichannel conflict in not only reducing channel performance but also serving as a mechanism for forcing internal channel coalitions to work harder and smarter to serve their market. The findings indicate that multichannel conflict is an important determinant of both channel performance and satisfaction.

@ Visit the **Online Resource Centre** to read the abstract and access the full paper.

---

accommodate all the views of other parties, even to the extent of jeopardizing one's own position. The prevailing corporate culture, attitude towards risk, and the sense of power that exists within coalitions shapes the chosen strategy.

@ **Visit the Online Resource Centre** and read about the conflict that has arisen in the UK supermarket industry.

Grey Marketing

The unauthorized sale of new branded products diverted from authorized distribution channels, or imported into a country for sale without the consent or knowledge of the manufacturer, is referred to as grey marketing and is a source of channel conflict. Very often this is accompanied by a cut in prices. This activity is not necessarily illegal, but could fall foul of licensing agreements or trade regulations. Sometimes referred to as parallel importation, this can concern the purchase of a product in one country at a considerable discount and its resale in another at a far higher price. Differences in exchange rates can stimulate this activity, as experienced by Chinese shoppers in search of luxury items. As the value of the euro fell in 2015, many Chinese travelled to Europe to buy the same products at a much lower price. This affected the luxury brands who lost out on high margin sales in China and Hong Kong (Stefan, 2015). Webb and Hogan (2002) provide more information about grey marketing.

Supply Chain Management

The second major issue associated with marketing channels concerns the movement of parts, supplies, and finished products. Melnyk *et al.* (2009) believe that **supply chain management** (SCM) is concerned with the value creation chain of all the activities associated with physical distribution. This embraces the chain of suppliers involved in providing raw materials (upstream), through the assembly and manufacturing stages, to distribution to end-user customers (downstream). This linkage is referred to as a supply chain and the process is commonly referred to as supply chain management (SCM). This supersedes the previous terms logistics and, before that, physical distribution.

Integrated SCM refers to the business processes associated with the movement of parts, raw materials, work-in-progress, and finished goods. Unlike marketing channels, which are concerned with the management of customer behaviour, finished goods, and inter-organizational relationships, the goal of SCM is to improve efficiency and effectiveness with regard to the physical movement of products. SCM is essentially about the management of all the business activities necessary to get the right product, in the right place, for the right customer to access in a timely and convenient way (Fill and McKee, 2012).

SCM comprises four main activities. These are **fulfilment**, **transportation**, **stock management**, and **warehousing**. It is argued by Brewer and Speh (2000) that SCM seeks to accomplish four main goals. These are waste reduction, time compression, flexible response, and unit cost reduction. These are explained in Table 14.4.

By achieving these four goals the efficiency of a supply chain is improved and, as a result, end-user customers can experience improved levels of channel performance. Figure 14.6 shows these activities and goals brought together in order to promote superior supply chain performance.

Management of ASDA Wal-Mart's supply chain is based on computerized scanning to inform suppliers very quickly of which products need delivery and in what quantities. More recent developments in electronic technologies, such as RFID tags, are improving the efficiency and effectiveness with which supply chain activities are managed.

Table 14.4 Supply chain management goals

Goal	Explanation
Waste reduction	By reducing the level of duplicated and excess stock in the chain, it becomes possible to harmonize operations between organizations to achieve new levels of uniformity and standardization.
Time compression	Reducing the order-to-delivery cycle time improves efficiency and customer service outputs. A faster cycle indicates a smoother and more efficient operation and associated processes. Faster times mean less stock, faster cash flow, and higher levels of service output.
Flexible response	By managing the order-processing elements (size, time, configuration, handling) specific customer requirements can be met without causing them inconvenience and contributes to efficiency and service delivery.
Unit cost reduction	By understanding the level of service output that is required by the end-user customers it becomes possible to minimize the costs involved in delivering to that required standard.

Source: Fill and McKee (2012). Adapted from Brewer and Speh (2000).

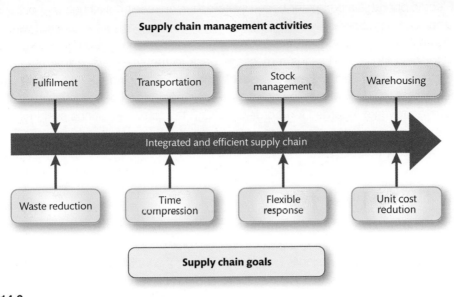

Figure 14.6
Developing high performance supply chains

Cost control is a core SCM activity given that about 15% of an average product's price is accounted for in shipping and transport costs alone. IKEA can sell its furniture 20% cheaper than competitors as it buys it ready for assembly, thereby saving on transport and inventory costs. The Benetton distribution centre in Italy is run largely by robots, delivering numerous goods to 120 countries within 12 days. Benetton also uses just-in-time (JIT) manufacturing, with some garments manufactured in neutral colours and then dyed to order, with very fast turnaround to suit customer requirements. However, beyond lowering costs, many organizations are increasing their focus on managing activities in order to improve customer service, meet the explosion in product variety, and harness the improvements in information and communication technologies.

Fulfilment

Fulfilment or materials handling is about locating and picking stock, and packing and securing it before shipping the selected items or bundle to the next channel member. The increasing use of specialist software, information technology, and equipment helps manage a range of fulfilment activities. Intra-warehouse stock movement needs to be minimized, while inter-warehouse movement is optimized (Fill and McKee, 2012). Automated emails are sent out to customers following online purchase of, for example, music from iTunes, a book from Amazon, or a train ticket. Accuracy and speed of billing and invoicing customers is also vitally important, especially for customer relationships.

In the retailing sector, order-processing technologies provide quick response programmes to help manage a retailer's replenishment of stock from suppliers. Kmart uses this kind of system, with EDI/extranets to transmit daily records of sales to suppliers, who analyse the information, create an order, and send it back to Kmart. Once in Kmart's system, the order is treated as though Kmart created it itself. Many technologies also speed up the billing cycle. For example,

General Electric operates a computer-based system that, on receipt of a customer order, checks the customer's credit rating as well as whether and where the items are in stock. The computer then issues an order to ship, bills the customer, updates the inventory records, sends a production order for new stock, and sends a message back to the salesperson that the customer's order is on the way—all in less than 15 seconds. The hospitality industry also uses order-processing technology to improve service delivery efficiency. Fast food outlets such as McDonald's and KFC have for years recorded food orders through telecommunications systems, transmitting them to food preparation areas, with orders fulfilled within a matter of minutes, improving customer satisfaction in service delivery.

Transportation and Delivery

Transportation is considered to be the most important activity within SCM. Transportation involves the physical movement of products using, for example, road, rail, air, pipeline, and shipping. Sometimes transportation is just seen as a way of supplying tangible goods, but it can also be as relevant to many service organizations, and the delivery of electronic (or digital) products. Consultants, IT companies, and health organizations have to move staff around, incurring transport and accommodation costs. Management of transport usually involves making decisions between usage of one or more transportation methods and ensuring vehicle capacity. Transportation methods also include electronic delivery modes such as electronic vending machines, the telephone, the Internet, or EDI.

Physical Delivery

Information and communication technologies have improved physical product delivery. For example, where freight moves, the size of typical shipments and the time periods within which goods must be delivered has changed with significant economic benefits to all transportation activities. The top of the list of 'must have' systems for transportation are in-vehicle navigation and route guidance solutions to help manage transport fleets, track shipments, and optimize transportation (Dreier, 2003). Amazon's tracking system assigns a tracking number and, using proprietary software, provides information to customers in real time about where the package or shipment is located, improving customer experience.

Electronic Delivery

As early as the introduction of the TV, radio, or even the telephone, electronic technologies have been used to deliver products. Because of product digitization producers of music, games, video, or software are typically unconstrained by the needs of physical distribution; this has increased with the development of the Internet. For example, Wall Street seemed at first to smirk at the E*Trade group's invitation to investors to make their own trades on the Internet. Then the Charles Schwab Corporation jumped at the challenge, and by the late 1990s other brokerages, such as Merrill Lynch and Bank of America Investment Services Inc., were scrambling to catch up. Organizations such as travel agents, banks, and insurance companies which have traditionally relied on customers coming to a branch or agency have quickly moved to using ATMs, mobile telecommunications, and the Internet to reach more customers. The Internet has clearly added to the capacity of these electronic distribution channels, so that huge numbers of customers now bank, trade stocks, and arrange insurance and travel through electronic channels, particularly mobile phones.

Stock Management

Stock or inventory management involves trying to balance responsiveness to customer needs with the resources required to store stock. The management of both finished and unfinished goods can be critical to many organizations. For example, a balance needs to be achieved between the number of finished goods to be available when customers need it (known as speculation) against a store of unfinished goods which can be assembled at a later date or when the stock of finished goods runs low (known as postponement).

Carrying too little stock might jeopardize customer service levels, whilst carrying too much can be expensive and adds to working capital. Imagine the cost of storing all the books Amazon has listed for sale, or the storage of fashion items in the spring ready for summer demand. With JIT systems, producers and retailers carry only small inventories of merchandise, often only enough for a few days' operations. New stock arrives exactly when it is needed, rather than being stored. ASDA Wal-Mart and even Burger King use these systems to track sales to service their outlets worldwide, automatically replenishing their ingredients according to product sales.

Zero-inventory or JIT production is ideal for many organizations as it minimizes the use of resources that are often tied up in stock that doesn't sell. This must be balanced against the risk of not having the products available when customers want them.

Warehousing and Materials Handling

Supply chains involved with the exchange of goods usually require storage facilities for the periods between production, transportation, and purchase/consumption. For example, books, dry goods such as sugar and canned goods, and even clothing require some level of storage between the time they leave the producer/manufacturer and when they are required to be delivered to end-user customers.

Decisions involving the location, size, design, and operating systems used in warehouses are important as they can impact on the performance of others in the supply chain. Producers using distributors will require a relatively small number of warehouses, as the distributors take ownership and physical possession of stock. A higher number of warehouses are required in channels where agents and manufacturers' representatives are preferred, as these intermediaries do not take ownership or physical possession. Organizations must decide on how many and what type of 'warehouses' it needs, and where they should be located. The type of warehouse is dependent on the type of product: tangible, digital, or perishable.

@ **Visit the Online Resource Centre** and use the web link to read about how a major retailer has had to redesign and update its warehousing to cope with online sales.

Warehousing Tangible Goods

For the storage of tangible goods, such as FMCGs, an organization can use either **storage warehouses** or **distribution centres**. Storage warehouses store goods for moderate to long periods (they have a long shelf-life), whereas distribution centres are designed to move goods, rather than just store them. For products that are highly perishable with a short shelf-life, such as fruit and vegetables, distribution centres are more appropriate. Grocery chains such as Woolworths in Australia and Tesco in the UK use large cold-store distribution centres to move perishable items such as fruit and vegetables to their various retail outlets. Storage centres are more appropriate for products with a long shelf-life or which might require stockpiling to meet seasonal demands.

Warehousing Digital 'Products'

Electronic warehousing systems, or database systems, are increasingly being used for the storage of products (or product components) that can be digitized. These systems can be searched or browsed electronically, providing the user with immediate electronic delivery options. For

---

Market Insight 14.3
Getting It There, on Time … Medicine, IT, and Fashion

The distribution of medicines by companies such as bioMérieux, Horiba ABX, and NovoNordisk involves a larger number of issues as human lives are at risk. As a result, logistics providers have to guarantee that products such as insulin are delivered not just securely and on time, but in pristine condition. Warehouses and temperature-controlled trailers use probes and telesurveillance systems to ensure that temperatures are maintained within set parameters during transportation. Speed of delivery is also important, so companies such as XPO Logistics arrange for delivery to be made without breaking the 'cold chain'. The trucks used to transport pharmaceutical products rarely stop, and pallet unloading time is minimized. Systematic controls are carried out each time a driver stops, and deviations in temperature and other problems are detected in real time.

In the IT industry life cycles are only 13 weeks, so yet again on-time delivery is critical. For companies such as ASUS, production and shipments need to be timed precisely to ensure that the transition between old and new products is smooth and results in optimal sales and a minimum of old products still on the shelf. An ASUS notebook made in China takes two and a half weeks to reach North America by ocean freight. In addition, there is a further two weeks to reach customers' stores. So when XPO Logistics improved the ocean schedules using faster vessels, and an evening crew to turn the cargo around on the same day, transit times were slashed. This led to a competitive advantage as ASUS could get new products to market faster than their competitors.

Inditex, whose brands include Zara, Bershka, and Stradivarius, has developed a supply chain built around

The design of the supply chain enables Zara to respond to new fashion trends quickly and efficiently
Source: © Vytautas Kielaitis/Shutterstock.

its customers. The organization can design, produce, and deliver a new garment to its 6,683 stores across 88 countries in just 15 days, and turns orders into delivered items in 24 hours in Europe and 48 hours in America and Asia. This is achieved through a holistic approach to supply chain management, which optimizes the entire chain instead of focusing on individual parts. A single centralized design and production centre consists of three spacious halls, one for women's clothing lines, one for men's, and one for children's. Separate design, sales, and procurement and production planning staff are dedicated to each clothing line. Although it's more expensive to operate three channels, the information flow for each channel is fast, direct, and unencumbered by problems in other channels, making the overall supply chain more responsive.

Sources: Ferdows *et al.* (2004); Hansen (2012); Leob (2015); http://www.inditex.com/documents/; http//www.norbert-dentressangle.co.uk/Client-Success/Case-studies/; http://www.telegraph.co.uk/sponsored/business/.

Market Insight 14.3
continued

Theory into Practice

These examples serve to illustrate the ways in which different parts of the supply chain impact on value creation. The way in which management of each of the supply chain activities (fulfilment, transportation, stock management, and warehousing) can accelerate or impede the development of value. In addition, the goals of supply chain management, waste reduction, time compression, flexible response, and unit cost reduction, can also be observed.

In the literature, SCM, the physical distribution aspect, is clearly separated from activities associated with marketing channel management. Note how in these examples, especially Inditex, SCM is an integral part of the company's marketing channel, and even business model.

Related Topics:

value creation; marketing channel structures, innovation; marketing communications.

1 **Explore the notion that managers of supply chains should have a greater concern for ethical issues than marketing channel managers.**

2 **How might the Norbert Dentressangle Group (and their competitors) encourage potential clients to use their particular services?**

3 **Make a list of the different issues associated with the transportation of dairy products, computers, cars, and medicines.**

---

example, emerald-library.com, ABI-Inform, and ScienceDirect are electronic databases accessible through the web that store a vast array of documents electronically to facilitate customers' search for information. In addition, many organizations use data warehousing facilities where product information, or even actual products, are stored in digital form awaiting distribution. Apple iTunes is the largest music retailer in the world. In 2016, the online store claimed it had categorized over 43m songs, 300,000 TV episodes, 85,000 movies, and thousands of books. This does not include the tens of thousands of games and podcasts stored electronically. Customers can find, download, play, and sync in a fraction of the time it takes to drive to a store.

We will now look more closely at one particular type of intermediary used in B2C markets—the retailer.

Retailing

Retailing encompasses all the activities directly related to the sale of products and services to consumers for personal use. These differ from wholesalers, who distribute the product to businesses, not consumers. Whether they are large retailers, such as Lotte (South Korea), Extra

(Brazil), or Carrefour (France), or one of the thousands of small owner-run retailers in India, they all provide a downstream link between producers and end-consumers.

Retailers help reduce the uncertainty experienced by other intermediaries in the channel, such as wholesalers and manufacturers. This is achieved by taking small quantities of stock on a regular basis, promoting cash flows, and providing demand for their products and services.

Retailers provide consumers with access to products. As such, it is very important to find out what consumers actually want from a retailer in order to deliver value. Convenience and time utility is the primary concern for most consumers, with people increasingly being 'leisure time poor' and keen to trade off shopping time for leisure time (Seiders *et al.*, 2000). Consequently, convenience drives most innovations in retailing, such as supermarkets, department stores, shopping malls, the web, and self-scanning kiosks in pursuit of providing customer convenience. As noted by Seiders *et al.* (2000), from a customer's perspective, convenience means speed and ease in acquiring a product and consists of the following four key elements:

- access—being easy to reach;
- search—enabling customers to be easily able to identify what they want;
- possession—ease of obtaining products;
- transaction—ease of purchase and return of products.

These are outlined in more detail in Table 14.5.

Table 14.5 Retailing convenience: a customer's perspective

Element	Description
Access convenience	■ Accessibility factors include location, availability, hours of operation, parking, proximity to other outlets, as well as telephone, mail, and Internet.
	■ Convenience does not exist without access.
	■ Increasingly, customers want access to products and services to be as fast and direct as possible with very little hassle.
	■ Global trend, e.g. rise of convenience stores in Japan
	■ Direct shopping driven by time and place utility.
Search convenience	■ Identifying and selecting the products wanted is connected to product focus, intelligent outlet design and layout (servicescape), knowledgeable staff, interactive systems, product displays, package and signage, etc.
	■ Solutions can be provided in the form of in-store kiosks, clearly posted prices, and mobile phones linked to knowledge centres for sales staff.
	■ One example of good practice is German discount chain Adler Mode Market GmbH which uses colour-coded tags to help customers quickly spot sizes.
Possession convenience	■ This is about having merchandise in stock and available on a timely basis. For example, Nordstrom clothing store guarantees that advertised products will be in stock. However, possession convenience has limitations for certain channels (e.g. highly customized products).
	■ The Internet scores highly for search convenience, yet is generally low in terms of possession convenience.

Table 14.5 continued	
Element	**Description**
Transaction convenience	■ The speed and ease with which consumers can effect and amend transaction before and after the purchase
	■ A number of innovations exist here—self-scanning in Carrefour, Tesco, and Metro. Well-designed service systems can mitigate the peaks and troughs in store traffic as with the use of in-store traffic counters, as in Sainsbury's, to monitor store traffic.
	■ Even with queue design, single queues in post offices and banks differ from supermarkets because of space and servicescape design.
	■ Transaction convenience is a significant issue on the Internet, with pure Internet retailers having problems with returns and customers not prepared to pay for shipping and handling costs.

Market Insight 14.4
Enhancing Channel Experiences

The rise of digital and mobile marketing and the growth of online shopping has put pressure on retailers to reconsider and improve their in-store customer experience. One of the approaches has been to involve music in retail environments, which has been found to encourage customers to stay longer and spend a little more than when there is no music. Sales can also be improved by matching the music with the products being sold. This is referred to as directional audio. For example, research has shown that sales of French wine increase when French music is played and likewise sales of German wine increase when German music was played. In a similar study in Sweden, shoppers bought 10% more organic products when they could hear the sound of farm animals, with a narrator talking about the various benefits of organic products.

Changes in the luxury retail market have forced retailers to adapt and enhance the in-store experience. Many luxury consumers have been found to be less interested in accumulating possessions and are much more interested in the buying (shopping) experience. One of these involves the use of in-store sales associates to assist luxury customers in their purchase decisions. Whilst the use of personal shoppers in luxury stores is well established, stores such as Bebe, Zara, and Anthropologie now offer personal styling services in-store.

The role of play within retail stores is becoming an important feature in the drive to create meaningful experiences. Hamleys launched their largest European store in Moscow with a central design feature to provide opportunities for customers of all ages to play. Nine different zones, which include an enchanted forest to explore, a motor city with a go-kart track, and a safari section, make the store feel more like a theme park, rather than a pure retail outlet. Each zone is designed to stimulate the senses, and achieves this by mixing interactive attractions and entertainment.

The US clothing and footwear brand Vans opened 'The House of Vans' in the tunnels under Waterloo Station. It offered London's only permanent indoor skate park, art gallery, live music venue, and cinema, with events and exhibitions that are changed regularly. The informality of the environment enables brand relationships to develop through soft interaction.

Market Insight 14.4
continued

Car manufacturer Audi have developed 'Audi City in London'. This environment encourages visitors to explore and configure their ideal car using touchscreens and multi-sensory displays. 'The Lexus Intersect' space focuses on the whole Lexus lifestyle, not just cars. By focusing on a range of topics, from food to fashion, Lexus has positioned itself as a cultural hub more than a showroom.

Sources: Anon. (2014); Regan (2015); Sorin (2015).

The House of Vans is based in the tunnels under Waterloo Station and provides London's only permanent indoor skate park
Source: Courtesy of House of Vans London.

Theory into Practice

What is evident in these retail examples of customer experience is the search for a position that helps a retailer differentiate its brand in such a way that it can provide competitive advantage. What may be an issue, however, is whether these types of experiences provide an advantage that is sustainable. For example, providing touch screens and multisensory displays can easily be replicated by competitors. So, what was once a memorable experience becomes an expectation for all players.

A further issue concerns customer perceived value. A one-off visit may provide a memorable experience, but how many visits need be made before the thrill wears off and the value is negated? How much time can consumers afford to spend experiencing a brand in these ways, and if the answer is 'not very much', then what is the long-term value of providing these experiences? Will customers revert to an online store?

Ideas about experience marketing are considered in Chapter 16.

Related Topics:
purchase decision-making; information processing; branding.

1 **How might a fashion retailer provide memorable in-store experiences?**

2 **Identify those types of retailers who may be more dependent than others on the value-added activities of the marketing channel.**

3 **Go to the websites of a department store (e.g. www.johnlewis.com) and a supermarket. How do they compare? Are there any retailing similarities?**

Research Insight 14.4

To take your learning further, you might wish to read this influential paper.

Glynn, M.S., Brodie, R.J., and Motion, J. (2012). The benefits of manufacturer brands to retailers. *European Journal of Marketing*, 46(9), 1127–49.

In this paper, the authors discuss the key value and benefits consumers derive from retailing. They consider the key benefit of convenience in retailing strategy from a customer's perspective. Convenience means speed and ease, and consists of four key elements—access, search, possession, and transaction.

@ Visit the **Online Resource Centre** to read the abstract and access the full paper.

Types of Retailer

There are numerous types of retailer. These can be classified according to the marketing strategy employed (i.e. product, price, and service) and the store presence (i.e. store or non-store retailing).

Marketing Strategy

Major types of retailer can be classified according to the marketing strategies employed, paying particular attention to three specific elements:

- product assortment
- price level
- customer service.

Table 14.6, although not exhaustive, provides a useful summary of these elements across the differing types of retailing channel.

The types of retailing establishment can be distinguished as follows.

- Department stores—large-scale retailing organizations that offer a very broad and deep assortment of products (both hard and soft goods) and provide a wide array of customer service facilities for store customers. Debenhams has a wide array of products, including home furnishings, foods, cosmetics, clothing, books, and furniture, and also provides variety within each category (e.g. brand, feature variety). Debenhams, like many department stores, provides a wide array of customer service facilities to rationalize higher prices and minimize price competition. Value-added services include wedding registries, clothing alterations, shoe repairs, lay-by facilities, home delivery, and installation.

- Discount retailers—this type of retailer is positioned based on low prices combined with the reduced costs of doing business. The key characteristics here involve a broad but shallow assortment of products, low prices, and very few customer services. For example, Matalan in the UK, Kmart in Australia, and Target in the USA all carry a broad array of soft

Table 14.6 Marketing strategy and retail store classification

Type of retail store	Product assortment	Pricing	Customer service	Example
Department	Very broad and deep, with layout and presentation of products critical	Minimize price competition	Wide array and good quality	David Jones, Debenhams, Harrods
Discount	Broad and shallow	Low price positioning	Few customer service options	Pound Stretcher, Dollar Dazzlers, Poundland
Convenience	Narrow and shallow	High prices	Avoid price competition	Co-op, 7-Eleven
Limited line	Narrow and deep	Traditional—avoids price competition New kinds—low prices	Vary by type	Bicycle stores, sports stores, ladies fashion
Speciality	Very narrow and deep	Avoids price competition	Standard; extensive in some	Running shops, bridal boutiques
Category killer	Narrow, very deep	Low prices	Few to moderate	Staples, Office Works, IKEA
Supermarket	Broad and deep	Some are low price; others avoid price disadvantages	Few and self-service	Tesco plc (UK), Woolworths Ltd (Australia), Carrefour (Europe)
Superstores	Very broad and very deep	Low prices	Few and self-service	Tesco Extra, ASDA Wal-Mart

goods (e.g. apparel) combined with hard goods such as appliances and home furnishings. To keep prices down, the retailers negotiate extensively with suppliers to ensure low merchandise costs.

■ Limited line retailers—this type of retailer has a narrow but deep product assortment and customer services vary from store to store. Clothing retailers, butchers, baked goods, and furniture stores that specialize in a small number of related product categories are all examples. The breadth of product variety differs across limited line stores, and a store may choose to concentrate on several related product lines (e.g. shoes and clothing accessories), a single product line (e.g. shoes), or a specific part of one product line (e.g. sports shoes). Examples include bookstores, jewellers, athletic footwear stores, dress shops, newsagents, etc.

- Category killer stores—as the name suggests these retailers are designed to kill off the competition and are characterized by a narrow but very deep assortment of products, low prices, and few to moderate customer services. Successful examples include IKEA in home furnishings, Staples in office supplies, and B&Q in hardware.

- Supermarkets—founded in the 1930s, these are large self-service retailing environments offering a wide variety of differing merchandise to a large consumer base. Tesco Extra in the UK stocks products ranging from clothing, hardware, music, groceries, and dairy products to soft furnishings. Operating largely on a self-service basis with minimum customer service and centralized register and transactional terminals, supermarkets provide the benefits of a wide product assortment in a single location, offering convenience and variety. Today, supermarkets are the dominant institution for food retailing.

- Convenience stores, or corner shops—these offer a range of grocery and household items that cater for convenience and the last-minute purchase needs of consumers. Key characteristics include long opening times (e.g. 24/7), being family-run, and belonging to a trading group. 7-Eleven, Spar, and the Co-op are all examples. Increasingly, smaller convenience stores are being threatened by large supermarket chains such as ASDA Wal-Mart and Tesco, especially as the laws for longer opening times for larger stores are relaxed (e.g. Sunday trading hours in the UK).

Store Presence

We can further categorize retailers according to their presence, either store or non-store retailing. Most retailing occurs through fixed stores, with existing operators having 'sunk' investment into a physical building and equipment. The physical location of a store is seen as a source of competitive advantage, providing crucial entry barriers to competitors. Several characteristics make store retailing unique from the customer viewpoint. The retail environment provides the sensation of touch, feel, and smell, which is very important for many product categories, such as clothing, books, and perfumes. Furthermore, customers can interact and seek advice with in-store staff. Once a product is selected and a purchase made, customers can walk out of the store with the merchandise in hand.

In contrast, retailing can also involve non-store retailers. These are retail transactions that occur away from a fixed store location. Examples include automatic vending machines, direct selling, and the rise of Internet retailing, or online retailing as it is more commonly known. Direct selling is one of the oldest retailing methods and is the personal contact between a salesperson and a consumer at a location away from a retailing environment. These activities include door-to-door canvassing and party plans, where sales presentations are made within a home to a party of guests. Examples include cosmetics companies such as Avon, Nutri-Metics skincare, and Amway household products. **Telemarketing** or telesales is another form of non-store retailing where purchase occurs over the telephone. During the 1990s, this form of non-store retailing grew extensively due to rapid developments in computer-assisted and TV shopping networks.

Another form of non-store retailing is the **electronic kiosk.** These are placed in shopping malls to assist the retailing experience. These computer-based retailing environments offer increased self-service opportunities, a wide array of products, and a large amount of data and information to help decision-making. Automatic vending machines provide product access 24 hours a day, seven days a week. Products distributed through vending machines are normally convenient and typically low price, and include cigarettes, soft drinks, hot beverages, condoms, newspapers, and magazines. We also see the wide adoption of automatic teller machines (ATMs) to facilitate the delivery of financial retailing services.

Another form of non-store retailing concerns online stores. The key consumer categories on the Internet are travel, clothes, groceries, and consumer electronics. Mallapragada *et al.* (2016) point out that online retailers have a strategic interest in the basket value of an online shopping transaction. This is because the delivery costs associated with an online purchase can amount to 50% of a firm's operating costs, and so impact directly on their profits. This is unlike traditional stores who are only interested in total sales. Thus these researchers suggest that online shopping can be considered as a two-stage process. The first is a browsing stage, which requires consumers to spend time visiting several web pages (page views). This may lead to a purchase decision. The second, purchase, stage, involves the completion of the financial transaction. However, these two stages mask several complexities, involving what it is that is being purchased, the product/service, and where it is being purchased, namely the website. Mallapragada *et al.* (2016: 34) conclude that these factors can influence 'page views and visit duration, which then influence the purchase decision, conditional on which a basket of certain value is realized'.

These two stages should be considered as a **shopper's flow experience**, which needs to be considered when assessing consumer online experiences. This flow impacts on the navigation performance of the website and is something that retailers are urged to constantly monitor and assess (Landers *et al.*, 2015). Optimizing the flow can enhance a consumer's online shopping experience, for example by influencing their sense of control over website interactions, their increased learning, and exploratory and positive search behaviours.

The shopping behaviour of contemporary consumers, however, reflects a mix of online and offline channels, as demonstrated by the growth of 'click and collect' services. This multichannel behaviour is reflected in the increasing array of channels used by organizations to enable consumers to reach their products and services (Rippé *et al.*, 2015). Through social media, mobile devices with location-based applications and reality-based technologies a 'showroom without walls' is created (Brynjolfsson *et al.*, 2013: 24). This enables consumers to collect considerable amounts of information about products which, in turn, changes their level of control in the sales process. This is reflected in the practice of 'showrooming', where consumers use their smartphones in-store to compare prices, get the opinions of family and friends through social media, and then negotiate the purchasing process (MacKenzie *et al.*, 2013). The practice of 'reverse showrooming', or 'webrooming', which occurs when consumers research products online but then complete their purchase in a bricks-and-mortar store, is an attempt by retailers to restore their influence (Adler, 2014).

Visit the Online Resource Centre and complete Internet Activity 14.2 to learn more about the variety of Internet retailing sites and the importance of delivery information for the music sector.

Market Insight 14.5
Compelling In-store Technologies

As customers increasingly expect their in-store experiences to be as convenient and as empowering as online shopping, retailers are striving to offer a seamless shopping experience across multiple channels. Some retailers are looking at improving in-store digital signage so that it interacts with customers in a more personalized and compelling way. Mobiles will be used to control wall-mounted screens and even the whole digital in-store experience and engagement concept.

One approach used by Tesla Motors in Toronto features interactive displays and design studios where customers can configure their own Tesla car on a large touchscreen. They can then review it on an 85-inch video wall at the back of the store.

Some stores owned by Media-Saturn, the European electronics retailer, enable customers to access products via a giant video wall. In Amsterdam, Marks & Spencer use touchscreen technology to produce an endless virtual rail that can hold its full catalogue, rather than a few selections.

Samsung introduced CenterStage, a concept that matches physical products with life-size touch-screen digital displays, helping shoppers to find the right Samsung home appliances for their needs interactively. This process enables customers to better understand product features and benefits through a variety of informational videos, graphics, icons, and multimedia content. It also helps them envisage how an appliance will look in their homes through a 'scene selector' feature. In addition, the information can be saved and shared through mobile devices.

Apple have eliminated cash registers in their stores and instead use salespeople to handle sales transactions with smartphones before sending customers receipts via email. Other options include the use of the Apple Store app, enabling iPhone owners to complete the sales process themselves. This requires customers to scan the barcodes of the products they wish to buy with their iPhone camera, and then pay for the purchases in-store through the EasyPay option in the Apple Store app. Alternatively, click & collect provides convenience and enables customers to save time.

Sources: Kim (2015); Gibson (2015); Nurun Team (2015).

Theory into Practice

Economists might use utility theory to explain the use of online shopping. This theory considers a ranking of consumer preferences, based on both price and income, and the optimal marginal utility that can be achieved. The rationale of this theory holds that online shopping offers convenience, time saving, and potentially lower process involvement.

We know, however, that customers do not make purchases using rational criteria. So, the drive for in-store shopping can be considered in terms of reducing the perceived risk associated with purchasing certain products and services, mainly those where there is no purchase history.

Brand experience (theory), developed by Brakus *et al.* (2009), is thought to be shaped by brand-related stimuli that constitute 'subjective, internal consumer responses', using sensory, affective, behavioural, and intellectual dimensions. Developing online and in-store consistent brand experiences through embedded digital technologies which trigger responses within these four dimensions is one way of interpreting these developments.

The role of in-store experiences might be considered in terms of helping customers perceive consistency in the way a brand is presented in online, mobile, and in-store contexts. This serves to reduce the scope of a pre-purchase search and simplify a customer's shopping experience.

Market Insight 14.5

continued

Related Topics:

branding; services marketing; relationship marketing.

1 Why might some customers not wish to use touchscreen technologies, and what might be a suitable alternative experience for this type of customer?

2 If retailers could collect customer data in-store, how might this information be used to develop the retail experience?

3 Consider your own last significant purchase. Which type of retail channel did you use and why?

Research Insight 14.5

To take your learning further, you might wish to read this influential paper.

Mallapragada, G., Chandukala, S.R., and Liu, Q. (2016). Exploring the effects of 'what' (product) and 'where' (website) characteristics on online shopping behavior. *Journal of Marketing*, 80(2), 21–38.

These researchers explore online shopping behaviour by investigating the impact of various characteristics on an online transaction's basket value, after incorporating the role of other aspects of the browsing process including page views and visit duration. Their results indicate various product and website strategies for online retailers.

Visit the **Online Resource Centre** to read the abstract and access the full paper.

Chapter Summary

To consolidate your learning, the key points from this chapter are summarized here.

■ **Describe the nature and characteristics of a marketing channel.**

Marketing channels are chains of organizations that are concerned with the management of the processes and activities involved in creating and moving particular offerings from producers and manufacturers to end-user customers. Marketing channels enable different types of uncertainty to be lowered by reducing the complexity, increasing value and competitive advantage, routinization, and/or providing specialization.

■ **Explain the different types of intermediaries and their roles in the marketing channel.**

An intermediary is an independent organization that operates as a link between producers and end-user consumers or industrial users. There are several different types of intermediary. These include agents, merchants, distributors, franchises, wholesalers, and retailers. The main role of intermediaries is to reduce uncertainty experienced by producers and manufacturers, and to promote efficiency. The key difference between the various intermediaries is that not all of them take legal title or physical possession of a product.

■ **Understand the different marketing channel structures and their core characteristics.**

There are three main channel structures: 'direct', 'indirect', and 'multichannel'. A direct channel involves selling directly to end-user customers, an indirect channel involves using intermediaries, and a multichannel involves both. At the simplest level, direct channels offer maximum control, but do not always reach all of the target market. Indirect channels can maximize coverage, but often at the expense of control. This is because Intermediaries start adapting the marketing mix and demand a share of the profits in return for their involvement. Multichannel strategies often result in greater channel conflict as intermediaries perceive the manufacturer to be a competitor.

■ **Explain the factors that influence the design and structure of marketing channels.**

When establishing or adapting marketing channels, it is necessary to consider the type of market coverage that is required, the number and type of intermediaries to use, and how the relationships between channel members are to be managed. These choices are important as they can affect the value that is ultimately provided to customers.

■ **Describe the main elements that constitute supply chain management.**

Supply chain management (SCM) concerns the various suppliers involved in providing raw materials (upstream), those that assemble and manufacture products, and those that distribute finished products to end-user customers (downstream). SCM embraces four main activities: fulfilment, transportation, stock management, and warehousing, which also subsume other important activities such as order processing and purchasing. Although these are not traditionally marketing management decisions, it is important to understand that they require a marketing focus and marketing insight.

■ **Consider the role and function of retailers in the marketing channel.**

Retailing concerns all activities directly related to the sale of goods and services to consumers for personal and non-business use. Retailers provide consumers with access to products, and help reduce the uncertainty experienced by other intermediaries in the channel, such as wholesalers and manufacturers. This is achieved by taking small quantities of stock on a regular basis, promoting cash flows, and providing demand for their products and services. The different types of retailing establishment can be classified according to two key characteristics: the marketing strategy (i.e. product, price, and service) and the store presence (i.e. store or non-store retailing).

Review Questions

1 What do we mean by marketing channel management?

2 Why do organizations use intermediaries?

3 Why are economics, coverage, and control important when making marketing channel decisions?

4 What are the key elements of a channel strategy?

5 What are the advantages and disadvantages of the three different channel structures?

6   What are the advantages of using an exclusive rather than an intensive marketing channel strategy?

7   Why is supply chain management of increasing importance to marketers?

8   What are some of the reasons for channel conflict?

9   Identify six types of retailer.

10 What does the term non-store retailing mean? Identify the main types.

Worksheet Summary

@ To apply the knowledge you have gained from this chapter and test your understanding of marketing research and customer insight visit the **Online Resource Centre** and complete Worksheet 14.1.

Discussion Questions

1   Having read Case Insight 14.1, what do you see as the main challenges for Åhléns in developing their online offer? How would you advise Åhléns to deal with them?

2   Discuss the importance of intermediaries. In your discussion, outline the benefits and limitations of three types of intermediary.

3   Select three direct channels and identify two types of product that are best suited to this approach. Identify the benefits of this channel strategy.

4   Convenience has become a critical issue in marketing channel decisions. Assess the arguments for and against focusing on convenience from a customer's perspective.

5   What sort of marketing channels do you believe might be most relevant in the following markets in the year 2020? Identify the three most relevant channels for each of the following product categories:

   A   music and video
   B   home entertainment software (e.g. video games)
   C   business application software
   D   engineering consulting advice (say on mining or construction applications)
   E   financial services
   F   shampoo
   G   personal services (e.g. hairdressing, beauty therapies).

6   Consider how the roles of intermediaries in marketing channels have changed as a result of the introduction of electronic technologies.

 Visit the **Online Resource Centre** and complete the Multiple Choice Questions to assess your knowledge of Chapter 14.

Glossary

direct channel structure where the product goes directly from the producer to the final customer.

disintermediation the reduction in the number or strength of intermediaries that are required in a marketing channel.

distribution centres are designed to move goods, rather than just store them.

distribution channel see marketing channel.

electronic kiosks are being placed in shopping malls to assist the retailing experience. Mediated by hypermedia web-based interfaces, these computer-based retailing environments offer consumers increased self-service opportunity, wide product assortment, and large amounts of data and information aiding decision-making.

exclusive distribution Is where intermediaries are given exclusive rights to market the good or service within a defined 'territory', and thus a limited number of intermediaries are used.

fulfilment activities associated with locating and picking stock, packing, and shipping the selected items to the next channel member.

horizontal conflict may arise between members of a channel on the same level of distribution.

indirect channel structure where the product goes from the producer through an intermediary, or a series of intermediaries such as a wholesaler, retailer, franchisee, agent, or broker, to the final customer.

information utility the provision of information about the product offering before and after sales. It can further provide information about those purchasing it.

intensive distribution means placing your product or service in as many outlets or locations as possible in order to maximize the opportunity for customers to find the good or service.

marketing channel an organized network of agencies and organizations which together perform all the activities required to link producers and manufacturers with consumers, purchasers, and users to distribute product offerings.

multichannel structure the use of multiple sales channels to provide a variety of customer touch points.

ownership utility goods are available immediately from the intermediaries' stocks; thus ownership passes to the purchaser.

place utility the relocation of an offering to enable more convenient purchase and consumption.

re-intermediation the increase in the number or strength of intermediaries that are required in a marketing channel.

retailing all the activities directly related to the sale of goods and services to the ultimate end consumer for personal and non-business use. This is also called the retail trade.

selective distribution where some, but not all, available outlets for the good or service are used.

shopper's flow experience a mental state of complete immersion and absorption within a shopping activity.

stock management managing the balance between the anticipated number of finished goods required by customers, and a sufficient store of unfinished goods which can be assembled at a later date or when the stock of finished goods runs low.

storage warehouses store goods for moderate to long periods.

supply chain management formed when organizations link their individual value chains.

telemarketing or telesales is a form of non-store retailing where purchase occurs over the telephone.

time utility manufacture, purchase, and consumption might occur at differing points in time. Time utility bridges this gap.

transportation the physical movement of products using, for example, road, rail, air, pipeline, and shipping.

vertical conflict conflict between sequential members in a distribution network, such as producers, distributor, and retailers, over such matters as carrying a particular range or price increases.

warehousing facilities used to store tangible goods for the periods between production, transportation, and purchase/consumption.

References

Adler, E. (2014). Reverse showrooming: bricks-and-mortar retailers fight back. *Business Insider UK*, 13 July. Retrieve from: http://uk.businessinsider.com/reverse-showrooming-bricks-and-mortar-retailers-fight-back-2-2014-2?r = US (accessed 13 July 2015).

Alldredge, K. and Ungerman, K. (2015). Cohabiting with your e-commerce partners. *McKinsey Insights*, June. Retrieve from: http://www.mckinsey.com/insights/marketing_sales/cohabiting_with_your_ecommerce_partners (accessed 6 January 2016).

Alldredge, K., Newaskar, P., and Ungerman23 July 2015, K. (2015). The digital future of consumer-packaged-goods companies. *McKinsey Insights*, October. Retrieve from: http://www.mckinsey.com/insights/consumer_and_retail/the_digital_future_of_consumer_packaged_goods_companies (accessed 6 January 2016).

Anderson, E. and Anderson, R. (2002). The new e-commerce intermediaries. *MIT Sloan Management Review*, 43(4), 53–62.

Anon. (2014) How to create immersive in-store experiences with directional audio. *Retail Customer Experience*, 18 September. Retrieve from http://www.retailcustomerexperience.com/articles/how-to-create-immersive-in-store-experiences-with-directional-audio/ (accessed 23 July 2015).

Armstrong, A. (2016). Sainsbury's bid could spell break up of Home Retail. *The Telegraph*, 5 January 2016. Retrieve from: http://www.telegraph.co.uk/finance/12082535/Sainsburys-makes-bid-approach-for-Argos-owner.html (accessed 6 January 2016).

Brakus, J.J., Schmitt, B.H., and Zarantonello, L. (2009) Brand experience: what is it? How is it measured? Does it affect loyalty? *Journal of Marketing*, 73(May), 52–68.

Brewer, P.C. and Speh, T.W. (2000). Using the balanced scorecard to measure supply chain performance. *Journal of Business Logistics*, 21(1), 75–95.

Brynjolfsson, E., Hu, Y.J., and Rahman, M.S. (2013). Competing in the age of omnichannel retailing. *MIT Sloan Management Review*, 54(4), 23–9.

Dreier, G. (2003). Technology that drives transportation. *Transport Technology Today*, 9 July.

Ferdows, K., Lewis, M.A., and Machuca, J.A.D. (2004). Rapid-fire fulfilment. *Harvard Business Review*, 82(11), 104–10.

Fill, C. and McKee, S. (2012). *Business Marketing*. Oxford: Goodfellow.

Gaski, J.F. (1984). The theory of power and conflict in channels of distribution. *Journal of Marketing*, 48, 9–29.

Gaughran, D. (2013). Self-publishing grabs huge market share from traditional publishers, 12 April. Retrieve from: http://davidgaughran.wordpress.com/ (accessed 22 April 2013).

Gibson, R. (2015) Designing digital stores for truly engaging customer experiences. *OnWindows*, 4 March. Retrieve from: http://www.onwindows.com/Article/designing-digital-stores-for-truly-engaging-customer-experiences-44843#.VbSsVrNVhBd (accessed 26 July 2015).

Glynn, M.S., Brodie, R.J., and Motion, J. (2012). The benefits of manufacturer brands to retailers. *European Journal of Marketing*, 46(9), 1127–49.

Hansen, S. (2012). How Zara grew into the world's largest fashion retailer. *New York Times*, 9 November. Retrieve from: http://www.nytimes.com/2012/11/11/magazine/how-zara-grew-into-the-worlds-largest-fashion-retailer.html?pagewanted = all&_r = 0 (accessed 10 January 2013.

Homburg, C., Vollmayr, J., and Hahn, A. (2014) Firm value creation through major channel expansions: evidence from an event study in the United States, Germany, and China. *Journal of Marketing*, 78(May), 38–61.

Katz, D. and Kahn, R.L. (1978). *The Social Psychology of Organisation* (2nd edn). New York: John Wiley.

Kim, S. (2015) The in-store experiences blurring the lines between real and digital. *The Guardian*, 4 March. Retrieve from: http://www.theguardian.com/media-network/marketing-agencies-association-partner-zone/2015/mar/04/instore-experiences-real-digital-samsung (accessed 26 July 2015).

Kotler, P. and Keller, K. (2009). *Marketing Management*. Englewood Cliffs, NJ: Prentice Hall.

Laffey, D. and Gandy, A. (2009). Comparison websites in UK retail financial services. *Journal of Financial Services Marketing*, 14(2), 173–86.

Landers, V.M., Beatty, S., Wang, S., and Mothersbaugh, D.L. (2015). The effect of online versus offline retailer-brand image incongruity on the flow experience. *Journal of Marketing Theory and Practice*, 23(4), 370–87.

Leob, W. (2015) Zara leads in fast fashion. *Forbes*, 30 March, Retrieve from: http://www.forbes.com/sites/walterloeb/2015/03/30/zara-leads-in-fast-fashion/ (accessed 15 July 2015).

MacKenzie, B., Meyer, C., and Noble, S. (2013). How retailers can keep up with consumers. *McKinsey Insights*, October. Retrieve from: http://www.mckinsey.com/insights/consumer_and_retail/how_retailers_can_keep_up_with_consumers?cid = other-eml-alt-mip-mck-oth-2110 (accessed 15 July 2015).

Mallapragada, G., Chandukala, S.R., and Liu, Q. (2016). Exploring the effects of 'what' (product) and 'where' (website) characteristics on online shopping behavior. *Journal of Marketing*, 80(2), 21–38.

Melnyk, S.A., Lummus, R.R., Vokurka, R.J., Burns, L.J., and Sandor, J. (2009). Mapping the future of supply chain management: a Delphi study. *International Journal of Production Research*, 47(16), 4629–53.

Mills, J.F. and Camek, V. (2004). The risks, threats and opportunities of disintermediation: distributor's view. *International Journal of Physical Distribution and Logistics Management*, 34(9), 714–27.

Nurun Team (2015). Building a better shopping experience, *Nurun*. Retrieve from: http://www.nurun.com/en/our-thinking/future-of-retail/building-a-better-shopping-experience/ (accessed 27 July 2015).

Park, S.Y., and Keh, H.T. (2003). Modelling hybrid distribution channels: a game theory analysis. *Journal of Retailing and Consumer Services*, 10, 155–67.

Parker, M., Bridson, K., and Evans, J. (2006). Motivations for developing direct trade relationships. *International Journal of Retail and Distribution Management*, 34(2), 121–34.

Regan, J. (2015). The art of play is becoming serious business for retailers. *The Guardian*, 28 May. Retrieve from: http://www.theguardian.com/media-network/2015/may/28/play-retail-experiences-brands-marketing (accessed 24 July 2015).

Rippé, C.B., Weisfeld-Spolter, S., Yurova, Y., and Sussan, F. (2015). Is there a global multichannel consumer? *International Marketing Review*, 32(3/4), 329–49.

Rosenbloom, B. (2007). Multi channel strategy in business-to-business markets: prospects and problems. *Industrial Marketing Management*, 36(1), 4–9.

Seiders, K., Berry, L.L., and Gresham, L.G. (2000). Attention retailers! How convenient is your convenience strategy? *Sloan Management Review*, Spring, 79–89.

Sheffield, H. (2016). Sainsbury's reveals Argos owner Home Retail Group rejected takeover bid. *The Independent*, 6 January. Retrieve from: http://www.independent.co.uk/news/business/news/sainsburys-reveals-argos-owner-home-retail-group-turned-down-takeover-bid-a6797306.html (accessed 6 January 2016).

Shipley, D. and Egan, C. (1992). Power, conflict and co-operation in brewer–tenant distribution channels. *International Journal of Service Industry Management*, 3(4), 44–62.

Sorin, K. (2015) Evolving retail expectations require enhanced experiences in-store: report. *Luxury Daily*, 2 July. Retrieve from: http://www.luxurydaily.com/evolving-retail-expectations-require-enhanced-experiences-in-store-report/ (accessed 23 July 2015).

Stefan (2015). Why are fashion brands worried about a weak euro and Chinese tourists? *China Ready News*, 30 June. Retrieve from: http://chinareadynews.com/2928/why-are-fashion-brands-worried-about-a-weak-euro-and-chinese-tourists/ (accessed 6 January 2016).

Tay, K.B. and Chelliah, J. (2011). Disintermediation of traditional chemical intermediary roles in the electronic business-to-business (e-B2B) exchange world. *Journal of Strategic Information Systems*, 20(3), 217–31.

Webb, K.L. and Hogan, J.E. (2002). Hybrid channel conflict: causes and effects on channel performance. *Journal of Business and Industrial Marketing*, 17(5), 338–57.

Yan, R., Guo, P., Wang, J., and Amrouche, N. (2011). Product distribution and coordination strategies in a multi-channel context. *Journal of Retailing and Consumer Services*, 18, 19–26.

Chapter 15
Services and Relationship Marketing

Learning Outcomes

After studying this chapter you should be able to:

▶ Explain the nature and characteristics of services

▶ Describe what is meant by the terms service processes, service encounters, and the principles associated with measuring service quality

▶ Outline the principles of relationship marketing and consider the merits of customer retention and loyalty programmes

▶ Understand the concepts of trust, commitment, and customer satisfaction, and explain how they are interlinked

▶ Explain the term 'customer experiences', the dimensions associated with it, how it has evolved, and how it might be measured

Case Insight 15.1
Withers Worldwide

Market Insight 15.1
Purely Products and Purely Services

Market Insight 15.2
Contactless: Speedy and Efficient Service Encounters

Market Insight 15.3
Alliances in the Sky

Market Insight 15.4
No Waiting for Customer Experiences

Case Insight 15.1
Withers Worldwide

Founded in London in 1896, Withers Worldwide has global revenues of over $200m, 163 partners, employs over 1,000 people, has clients in over 80 countries, and has acted for 42% of the top 100 Sunday Times Rich List and 20% of the top 100 of the Forbes Rich List. We speak to Laura Boyle, Head of EU Marketing and Business Development, to explore how Withers works to improve the quality of its client relationships.

Predicting the global nature of private capital, Withers set out over a decade ago from its origins as a London-based firm to do something that law firms had not done before—to develop a genuinely international offering for global wealth. Choosing global centres of private wealth, the firm strives to ensure that we match our clients' evolving needs. We are now the largest law firm focused on the needs of private wealth in the world, with 18 offices across the USA, Europe, Asia Pacific, and the Caribbean. Until recently, other law firms focused on this market have operated from a domestic base.

As a professional services organization, making sure that our employees understand our strategy and brand is paramount, as they liaise with our clients and embody the customer experience. Keeping everyone informed on developments has been challenging, given our rapid expansion. In addition to the usual internal communications, such as newsletters, intranet, and leadership briefings, we have developed 'Withers TV'— TV screens placed in prominent places in our offices. They share daily news updates about clients and our people, so everyone is in the best position to feel part of the Withers Worldwide brand and know how to talk about it externally. This supports more personal communications too—for example, with annual AGM sessions for all staff. We run standardized inductions for new joiners and each team is assigned a business development manager who acts like a key account manager for them as internal clients, connecting them to central strategy, the brand, and our best practice approach.

The variability of our service offering worldwide is a real benefit to our clients; it is how we deliver tailored

services. We need to have lawyers, with associated legal support, operating in different areas of specialism and at differing levels of experience to deliver a comprehensive service, priced in the best way for clients. Any conversation with a prospective client first considers what their needs are, and we calibrate the input of senior partner time required together with the support needed from more junior lawyers and paralegals.

We avoid potential issues around variance in service quality through our marketing function, which incorporates client relationship management specialists. We seek feedback from our clients, but also from those who refer work to us and who recommend us to their clients. Our learning and development team deliver a global employee training programme, ensuring that, as we grow and acquire new teams of lawyers, they are brought into the Withers 'way of working'. We also work hard to ensure that our collective and accumulated knowledge is shared across all offices by running a global precedent system.

The problem we had as an organization focused on the way we sought client feedback. We had always focused on the trusted adviser, client–lawyer, relationship, which involved personal and tailored requests for feedback. But, while we had a good idea where we were doing well and where one-off problems existed, we had no central view of how clients perceived our service quality.

Therefore the following question arose: How should we develop a more comprehensive system to evaluate the quality of how clients experienced our service offering?

Introduction

Services and products are different. One of the distinguishing dimensions of products is that they have a physical presence. Services do not have a physical presence and they cannot be touched. This is because their distinguishing characteristic is that they are an act or a performance (Berry, 1980). A service cannot be put in a bag, taken home, stored in a cupboard, and used at a later date. A service is consumed at the point where it is produced. For example, watching a play in a theatre, learning maths at school, or taking a holiday all involve the simultaneous production and consumption of the play, new knowledge, and leisure.

The service industry sector forms a substantial part of most developed economies. Not surprisingly, the range of services is enormous, and we consume services in nearly all areas of our work, business, home, and leisure activities. Table 15.1 indicates the variety of sectors and some of the areas in which we consume different types of service.

The sheer number of services that are available has grown, partly because it is not always easy to differentiate products just on features, benefits, quality, or price. Competition can be very intense and most product innovations or developments are copied quickly. Services provide an opportunity to add value yet not be copied, as each service is a unique experience.

Most products contain an element of service; there is a product–service combination designed to provide a means of adding value, differentiation, and earning a higher return. The extent to which a service envelops a product varies according to a number of factors. These concern the level of tangibility associated with the type of product, the way in which the service is delivered, variations in supply and demand, the level of customization, the type of relationship between service providers and customers, and the degree of involvement people experience in the service (Lovelock et al., 1999).

Many grocery products have few supporting services, just shelf-stocking and checkout operators. The purchase of new fitted bedroom furniture involves the cupboards, dressers, and wardrobes plus the professional installation service necessary to make the furniture usable. At the other end of the spectrum a visit to the dentist or an evening class entails little physical-product-based support as the personal service is delivered by the service deliverer in the form of the dentist or tutor.

Table 15.1 Service sectors

Sector	Examples
Business	Financial, airlines, hotels, solicitors, lawyers
Manufacturing	Finance and accountants, computer operators, administrators, trainers
Retail	Sales personnel, cashiers, customer support advisers
Institutions	Hospitals, education, museums, charities, churches
Government	Legal system, prisons, military, customs and excise, police

The Nature of Services

In view of these comments about the range and variety of services, and before moving on, it is necessary to define what a service is. As with many topics there is no firm agreement, but for our purposes the following definition, derived from a number of authors, will be used.

> A service is any act or performance offered by one party to another that is essentially intangible. Consumption of the service does not result in any transfer of ownership even though the service process may be attached to a physical product.

Much of this definition is derived from the work of Grönroos (1990), who considered a range of definitions and interpretations. What this definition provides is an indication of the various characteristics and properties that set services apart from products. The two sections that follow examine the key characteristics of services and the way in which the service mix, as opposed to the product mix, is configured.

Distinguishing Characteristics

Services are characterized by five distinct characteristics, as depicted in Figure 15.1. These are **intangibility**, **perishability**, **variability**, **inseparability**, and a lack of **ownership**. These are important aspects that shape the way in which marketers design, deliver, and evaluate the marketing of services.

Intangibility

The purchase of products involves the use of most of our senses. We can touch, see, smell, hear, or even taste products before we buy them, let alone use them. When purchasing a tablet or smartphone it is possible to see the physical product and its various attributes, such as size and colour, to test the functionality, to feel the weight, and touch it. These are important purchasing decision cues, and even if the equipment fails to work properly, it is possible to take it back for a replacement.

Research Insight 15.1

To take your learning further, you might wish to read this influential paper.

Shostack, G.L. (1977). Breaking free from product marketing. *Journal of Marketing,* **41(April), 73–80.**

This passionately written paper seeks to draw a clear and distinct line between the requirements for marketing products and marketing services. Shostack states that a marketing mix that is appropriate for products is not suitable for services. A key thrust of the paper draws on the need for an understanding of the difference between image (for products) and evidence (for services).

Visit the Online Resource Centre to read the abstract and access the full paper.

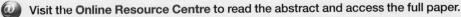

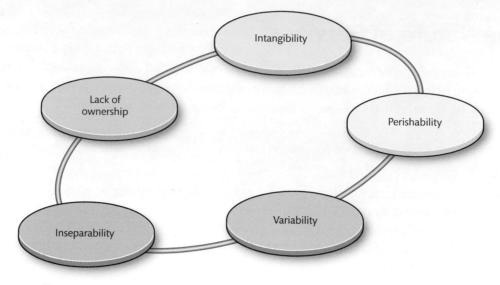

Figure 15.1

The five core characteristics of services

However, if a decision is made to buy additional insurance/support, this will be itemized on the receipt but it is not possible to touch, taste, see, hear, or smell the insurance bought. Services are intangible and they are only delivered and experienced post purchase.

Intangibility does not mean that customers buy services without using their senses. What it does mean is that they use substitute cues to help make these purchasing decisions and to reduce the uncertainty because they cannot touch, see, smell, or hear the service. People make judgements based on a range of quality-related cues. These cues serve to make the intangible service tangible. Two types of cue can be identified: intrinsic and extrinsic cues (Olson and Jacoby, 1972). Intrinsic cues are drawn directly from the 'service product' itself, and are regarded as difficult to change. Extrinsic cues, on the other hand, are said to surround the 'service product' and can be changed relatively easily. Brady *et al.* (2005) found that different types of service brand need different types of cue. Financial and investment-based brands prosper from the use of intrinsic cues, which stress objective information sources, such as a strong reputation, industry rankings, and favourable media reviews. The reverse is true for services that have a more tangible element, such as hotels and transport services. In these circumstances, more subjective communication, such as advertising and referrals through word of mouth are more influential.

Perishability

A bottle of shampoo on a supermarket shelf attracts a number of opportunities to be sold and consumed. When the store closes and opens again the following day, the bottle is still available to be sold, and it remains available until purchased or the expiry date is reached. This is not the case with services. Once a train pulls out of a station, or an aeroplane takes off, or a film starts, those seats are lost and can never be sold. This is referred to as perishability and is an important aspect of services marketing. Services are manufactured and consumed simultaneously; they cannot be stored either prior to or after the service encounter.

The reason why these seats remain empty reflects variations in demand. This may be due to changes in the wider environment and may follow easily predictable patterns of behaviour, for example family holiday travel. One of the tasks of service marketers is to ensure that the number of empty seats and lost forever revenue is minimized. In cases of predictable demand, service managers can vary the level of service capacity—a longer train, a bigger aircraft, or extra screenings of a film (multiplex facilities). However, demand may vary unpredictably, in which case service managers are challenged to provide varying levels of service capacity at short notice.

One of the main ways in which demand patterns can be influenced is through differential pricing. By lowering prices to attract custom during quieter times and raising prices when demand is at its highest, demand can be levelled and marginal revenues increased. Hotel and transport reservation systems have become very sophisticated, making it easier to manage demand and improve efficiency, and, of course, customer service. Some football clubs categorize matches according to the prestige or ranking of the opposition, and adjust prices in order to fill the stadium. In addition to differential pricing, extra services can be introduced to divert demand. Hotels offer specialist breaks, such as golfing or fishing weekends, and mini-vacations to attract retired people outside the holiday season. Leisure parks offer family discounts and bundle free rides into prices to stimulate demand.

Variability

As already stated, an important characteristic of services is that they are produced and consumed by people, simultaneously, as a single event. One of the outcomes of this unique process is that it is exceedingly difficult to standardize the delivery of services around the blueprint model mentioned earlier. It is also difficult to deliver services so that they always meet the brand promise, especially as these promises often serve to frame customer service expectations. If demand increases unexpectedly and there is insufficient capacity to deal with the excess number of customers, service breakdown may occur. A flood of customers at a restaurant may extend the arrival of meals for customers already seated who have ordered their meals. Too many train passengers may mean that there are not enough seats. In both these cases it is not possible to provide a service level that can be consistently reproduced.

A different way of looking at variability is to consider a theatre. The show may be doing well and the lead actors performing to critical acclaim. However, the actual performance that each actor delivers each night will be slightly different. This change may be subtle, such as a change in the tone of voice or an inflexion, and will pass by relatively unnoticed. At the other extreme, some actors go out of their way to make their performance very different. It is alleged that the actor Jane Horrocks once remarked that during the performance of a certain theatre play she deliberately changed each evening's show in order to relieve the boredom.

There has been substantial criticism of some organizations which, in an effort to lower costs, have relocated some or all of their call centre operations offshore. These strategies sometimes fail, as the new provider has insufficient training, insufficient local or product knowledge, or in some cases simply cannot be understood. This type of service experience will vary among customers and for each customer. The resulting fall in customer satisfaction can lead to increased numbers of customers defecting to competitors.

The variability of services does not mean that planning is a worthless activity. By anticipating situations when service breakdown might occur, service managers can provide facilities. For example, entertainment can be provided for queues at cinemas or theme parks in order to change the perception of the length of the time it takes to experience the service (film or ride).

It is difficult to standardize the delivery of services as each 'event' is unique. This variability of service delivery can be observed in theatre performances
Source: © Pavel L Photo and Video/Shutterstock.

Inseparability

As established previously, products can be built, distributed, stored, and eventually consumed at a time specified by the ultimate end-user customer. Services, on the other hand, are consumed at the point they are produced. In other words, service delivery cannot be separated or split out of service provision or service consumption.

This event where delivery coincides with consumption means that not only do customers come into contact with the service providers, but also there must be interaction between the two parties. This interaction is of particular importance, not just to the quality of service production but also to the experience enjoyed by the customer. So, following the earlier example of a theatre play, the show itself may provide suitable entertainment, but the experience may be considerably enhanced if the leading lady, Jane Horrocks, Judi Dench, or Scarlett Johansson, actually performs rather than has the night off because she is unwell. Alternatively, private doctors may develop a strong reputation and, if there is an increase in demand beyond manageable levels, pricing can be used to reduce or reschedule demand for their services.

The service experiences described in the preceding paragraph highlight service delivery as a mass service experience (the play) and as a solo experience (the doctor). The differences impact on the nature of the interaction process. In the mass service experience, the other members of the audience have the opportunity to influence the perceived quality of the experience. Audiences create atmosphere and this may be positively or negatively charged. A good production can involve audiences in a play and keep them focused for the entire performance. However, a poor performance can frustrate audiences, leading to some members walking out and hence influencing the perception others have of the performance and experience of the play.

Interaction within the solo experience (doctor–patient) allows greater control by the service provider, if only because they can manage the immediate context within which the interaction occurs and not be unduly influenced by wider environmental issues. Opportunities exist for flexibility and adaptation as the service delivery unfolds. For example, a check-in operator for an airline operates within a particular context, is not influenced by other major events during the interaction, and can adapt tone of voice, body language, and overall approach to meet the needs of particular travellers.

One final aspect of variability concerns the influence arising from the mixture of customers present during the service delivery. If there is a broad mix of customers, service delivery may be affected as the needs of different groups have to be attended to by the service provider. Such a mixture may dilute the impact of the service actually delivered.

Market Insight 15.1
Purely Products and Purely Services

Sweden's Tetra Pak revolutionized the food packaging industry, Finland's Huhtamäki Oyj is one of the world's leading manufacturers of paper cups and plates, Danish company Schur Technology is a leading North European supplier of total packaging solutions, and the Norwegian company Elopak is a leading global supplier of cartons for liquid food products. Rexam is one of the world's leading consumer packaging groups supporting the beverage, beauty, pharmaceuticals, and food markets.

What is common to all these organizations? Their skill and core competence is in packaging. They make tangible products to which, traditionally, there are few service additions.

Alternatively, Bain, McKinsey, Towers Perrin, and PwC are some of the leading management consulting organizations. Owned by IBM, PwC offers a huge range of services across many industries and sectors. Their approach to work is stated to be through 'connected thinking'. None of these organizations make or sell any products; they provide knowledge and skills, i.e. pure services.

Sources: http://www.schur.com/skabeloner/; http://www.tetrapak.com/; http://www.huhtamaki.com/; http://www.elopak.com/; http://www.rexam.com/; http://www.pwc.com/.

Theory into Practice

The best known and probably the most preferred services theory is called the structural argument. This refers to the differences from products, namely the dimensions of intangibility, perishability, variability, inseparability, and a lack of ownership. An alternative view is called the substitutability argument. This holds that as services are highly differentiated their substitutability is low. Unlike products, whose levels of differentiation are relatively low, their substitutability is high.

This difference in substitutability leads to different competitive conditions for the marketing of products and services. Service providers can act in a similar ways to monopolists. There is a lower need to differentiate and be competitive; indeed, there is an argument that they should not attempt to standardize their offerings.

Packing materials, therefore, are highly substitutable whereas the service providers such as PwC and McKinsey offer individual offerings that are not directly substitutable.

Market Insight 15.1
continued

Related Topics:

service processes; service encounters; service quality measurement; SERVQUAL.

1 **Identify ways in which packaging might influence consumers.**

2 **Think about the role of a marketing consultant and make a list of the different types of**

knowledge that might constitute 'connected thinking'.

3 **Draw the product–service spectrum and place various product–service combinations on it.**

Lack of Ownership

The final characteristic associated with services marketing arises naturally from the other features. Services cannot be owned as nothing is transferred during the interaction or delivery experience. Although a legal transaction often occurs with a service, there is no physical transfer of ownership as there is when a product is purchased. The seat in a theatre, train, plane, or ferry is rented on a temporary basis in exchange for a fee. The terms associated with the rental of the seat determine the time and use or experience to which the seat can be put. However, the seat remains the property of the theatre owner, rail operator, airline, and ferry company, respectively, as it needs to be available for renting to other people for further experiences.

One last point concerns loyalty schemes such as frequent flyer programmes and membership clubs, where the service provider actively promotes a sense of ownership. By creating customer involvement and participation, even though there is nothing to actually own, customers can develop an attitude based around their perceived right to be a part of the service provider.

Visit the Online Resource Centre and follow the web link to the British Bankers Association (BBA) to learn more about financial services.

Service Processes

Services are considered to be processes, and a substantial part of the academic literature on services is based on a process perspective. A process is a series of sequential actions that leads to predetermined outcomes. So, a simple process might be the steps necessary to visit a dentist, whereas a complex process might be the actions necessary to manage passengers on a two-week luxury cruise.

If processes are an integral part of the operations performed by service organizations, in the general sense, what are they processing? Lovelock *et al.* (1999) argue that these processes are directly related to two variables. First, the intensity of the equipment used to deliver a service, and second, the intensity of people involved in the provision of the service. On the one hand, a haircut is people intensive but the failure of a network server is intensely equipment oriented. Lovelock *et al.* present a four-cell categorization of services based on tangible and intangible actions on people's bodies, minds, and physical assets. The categories involve four different processes: people processing, possession processing, mental stimulus processing, and information processing.

People Processing

In this type of processing people have to physically present themselves so that they become immersed within the service process. This involves spending varying amounts of time actively cooperating with the service operation. So, people taking a train have to physically go to the station and get on a train and spend time getting to their destination. People undergoing dentistry work will have made an appointment prior to attending the dentist's surgery, and will sit in the chair, open their mouths, and cooperate with the dentist's various requests. They have physically become involved in the **service process** offered by their dentist.

From a marketing perspective, consideration of the process and the outcomes arising from participation in the service process can lead to ideas about what benefits are being created and what non-financial costs are incurred as a result of the service operation. In the dentistry example, a comfortable chair, background music, non-threatening or neutral to warm decor, and a pleasant manner can be of help.

Possession Processing

Just as people have to go to the service operation for people processing, so objects have to become involved in possession processing. Possessions such as kitchen gadgets, gardens, cars, and computers are liable to break down or need maintenance. Cleaning, storing, repairing, couriering, installation, and removal services are typical possession-processing activities.

In these situations, people will either take an item to the service provider, or invite someone in to undertake the necessary work. In possession processing the level of customer involvement is limited compared with that in people processing. In most cases the sequence of activities is as follows. In order for an object to be attended to a telephone call is often required to fix an appointment. Then the item either needs to be taken to the service provider or the customer must wait for an attendant to visit. A brief to explain the problem/task/solution is given before returning at an agreed time/location to pay and take away the renewed item. This detachment from the service process enables people to focus on other tasks. The key difference here is that the quality of the service is not dependent on the presence of the owner or representative of the possession while the service operation takes place.

Mental Stimulus Processing

These types of service try to shape attitudes or behaviour. In order to achieve this, these services have to be oriented to people's minds—hence the expression mental stimulus processing. So, examples of these types of services include education, entertainment, professional advice, and news. In all of these people have to become involved mentally in the service interaction and give time in order to experience the benefits of this type of service.

Service delivery can be through one of two locations. First, services can be created in a location that is distant from the receiver. In this case media channels are used to deliver the service. Alternatively, services can be delivered and consumed at the point at which they originate, i.e. in a studio, theatre, or hall. One of the key differences here is the form and nature of the audience experience. The theatre experience is likely to be much richer than the distant format. Digital technology has enabled opportunities for increased amounts of interactive communication, even though the experience will be different from the original. In the same way, online or e-learning in its purest form, has not yet become an established format, perhaps because learners need to spend some of their learning time in interaction with their co-learners and in the presence of a tutor, for example the use of summer schools operated by the Open University and the increasing success of blended learning programmes.

Information Processing

The final type of service concerns the huge arena of information processing, the most intangible of all the services. Transformed by advances in technology, and computers in particular, information processing has become quicker, more accurate, and more frequent. The use of technology is important, but we should not exclude people, as individuals have a huge capacity to process information.

One key issue that organizations need to consider concerns the degree to which people should become involved in information processing. They could deliberately route customers away from people processing by reducing the number of clerks and counters, and into information processing by pushing online and ATM operations. easyJet reduces costs by making it difficult for customers to telephone the company and seek advice from expensive staff. Their approach is to drive people to their website and use the FAQs to answer customer queries.

Service Encounters

The development of service marketing strategies involves understanding the frequency and the ways in which customers contact service providers. Once this is understood, strategies can be developed that maintain required levels of service, but the processes and linkages that bring the elements of the services marketing mix and associated systems together can be reformulated. Service marketing strategy, therefore, should be based on insight into the ways in which customers interact or contact a service. The form and nature of the customer encounter is of fundamental importance.

A **service encounter** is best understood as a period of time during which a customer interacts directly with a service (Shostack, 1985). These interactions may be short and encompass all the actions necessary to complete the service experience. Alternatively, they may be protracted, involve several encounters, several representatives of the service provider, and indeed several locations in order for the service experience to be completed. Whatever their length, the quality of a service encounter impacts on perceived service value which, in turn, influences customer satisfaction (Gil *et al.*, 2008).

Originally the term 'encounter' was used to describe the personal interaction between a service provider and customers. A more contemporary interpretation needs to include all those interactions that occur through people and their equipment and machines with the people and

---

Table 15.2 Levels of customer contact

Contact level	Explanation
High contact services	Customers visit the service facility so that they are personally involved throughout the service delivery process, e.g. retail branch banking and higher education.
Medium contact services	Customers visit the service facility but do not remain for the duration of the service delivery, e.g. consulting services and delivering and collecting items to be repaired.
Low contact services	Lillle or no personal contact between customer and service provider. Service is delivered from a remote location, often through electronic means. For example, software repairs and television and radio entertainment.

---

equipment belonging to the service provider (Glyn and Lehtinen, 1995), as set out in Market Insight 15.2. As a result, three levels of customer contact can be observed: high contact services, medium contact services, and low contact services (see Table 15.2).

One of the interesting developments in recent years is the decision by some organizations to move their customers from high contact services to low contact services. Clear examples of this are to be found in the banking sector, with first ATMs, then telephone banking, and now Internet banking, all of which either reduce or remove personal contact with bank employees. Further examples include vending machines, self or rapid check-out facilities in hotels, and online ticket purchases.

Sirianni *et al.* (2013) suggest that by actively branding service encounters organizations can reinforce brand meaning and positioning, whilst influencing customers' responses to brands. They define branded service encounters as 'service interactions in which employee behaviour is strategically aligned with the brand positioning. This strategic alignment may be evident in various elements of the employee's presented behaviour, appearance, and manner that can reinforce brand meaning during service interactions with customers'. This suggests that branded service encounters should be an integral element of any integrated marketing communication activity.

Market Insight 15.2
Contactless: Speedy and Efficient Service Encounters

Whether it is Hong Kong, Auckland, Amsterdam, or London, the huge numbers of people travelling by trains, buses, trams, ferries, and metro systems brings service problems not only in terms of seating capacity and general comfort, but also in terms of the time and queues associated with purchasing travel tickets and enabling people to keep moving. At peak times, queuing for tickets can be frustrating and cause enormous delays.

Ticket offices provide people with an opportunity to discuss their requirements on an interpersonal basis with a member of staff. However, this is an expensive and, at times, time-poor use of resources. There are many people who know what (ticket) they need, and self-service ticket machines are a way of providing a service for people who do not want or need a personal service encounter. An enormous number of people make the

Market Insight 15.2

continued

Oyster cards are prepaid and use wireless technology. This allows customers of the London transport network to get in and out of stations quickly

Source: iStock.com/mikeinlondon.

same journey each day. In much the same way, airlines use e-ticketing and on-airport self check-in solutions, such as **electronic kiosks**, and off-airport self check-in through kiosk, web, and mobile check-in applications.

In London the Oyster card, a pay-as-you-go card, enables travellers to wave the card a few centimetres from a point-of-sale terminal on entry and exit from the transport system tube and the amount for the journey is debited from the card. In 2014 Transport for London introduced contactless payments for journeys on Tube, tram, DLR, London Overground, and National Rail services. Contactless payments work in the same way as Oyster, charging customers an adult-rate pay-as-you-go fare when they touch in and out on readers at the start and end of their journey. The NFC technology spares travellers the time spent topping up Oyster balances, simply because fares are charged directly to

their payment card accounts. The system also calculates the lowest possible fare, ensuring that commuters are charged at the weekly rather than the daily rate.

In Hong Kong the Octopus card is based on a smartcard which incorporates near field communication (NFC). This enables two devices to exchange data when they are adjacent. Here the 'wave and pay' card is used not only for transport and ticketing services, but also for a whole range of purchases including supermarkets, restaurants, gift shops, and even hospitals and cinemas.

The chip technology can be embedded in a variety of products, such as watches, key chains, ornaments, and of course smartphones.

Sources: Oates (2009); Wheatley (2012); Laja (2012); Curtis (2014).

Market Insight 15.2
continued

Theory into Practice

One way of interpreting service encounters is through uncertainty reduction theory. A service provider and user will interact in order to better understand each other, and so reduce the uncertainty that exists between the parties at the outset of their relationship. Through communication, a reduction in uncertainty occurs which drives trust and transaction frequency.

Another interpretation involves role theory. This holds that people are social actors whose behaviour, or performance, has been learned relative to the different positions they occupy.

Related to this interpretation is script theory. This holds that a script contains information about a role that is to be performed. Deviation from the script leads to disorientation.

In these examples the role of the service provider is clear, and the contactless payment system serves to develop the roles so that service receivers are less likely to deviate from their script. This in turn should encourage further interaction and use of the service, with increasingly less uncertainty and disorientation.

Related Topics:

service processes; service quality management; relationship marketing; customer experiences.

1 How would you classify 'wave and pay' as a form of service encounter with transport systems?

2 How might B2B marketers make use of 'wave and pay'?

3 How might a symbol or logo which indicates that a card uses contactless technology assist in the marketing of this service?

Key Dimensions of Services Marketing

The marketing of services can be improved by understanding how customers evaluate service performance. This begs the question: How do customers judge the quality of a bank's services, or those of an airline? This is potentially very difficult, as complex services such as surgery or stockbroking have few tangible clues upon which to make a judgement about whether the service was extremely good, good, satisfactory, poor, or a disgrace. Customers purchasing physical goods can make judgements about the features, style, and colour prior to purchase or during purchase, and even return faulty goods post consumption. This is not possible with some types of services, especially people-processing services.

Service performance is regarded as an important contributor to a firm's financial outcomes. Heskett *et al.* (1994) shows that superior customer service, within a consumer context, leads to increased financial performance. The notion of service time as an indicator of service performance

(Lund and Marinova, 2014) has gained increasing attention as service providers, and retailers in particular, look to gain competitive advantage.

Zeithaml (1981) determined a framework categorizing different services which, in turn, influence the degree to which market offerings can be evaluated. Three main properties were identified.

- Search properties are those elements that help customers to evaluate an offering prior to purchase. As already mentioned, physical products tend to have high search attributes that serve to reduce customer risk and increase purchase confidence.

- Experience properties do not enable evaluation prior to purchase. Sporting events, holidays, and live entertainment can be imagined, they can be explained, and they can be illustrated, but only through the experience of the performance or feel of sitting in an audience of 100,000 people can an evaluation of the service experience be made.

- Credence properties relate to those service characteristics that customers find difficult to evaluate even after purchase and consumption. Zeithaml refers to complex surgery and legal services to demonstrate the point.

As demonstrated earlier, most physical goods are high in search properties. Services, however, reflect the strength of experience and credence characteristics that, in turn, highlight their intangibility and their variability.

This classification has been challenged on the basis that it does not entirely reflect contemporary service markets (Garry and Broderick, 2007). Whereas the original classification vested expertise in the service provider, emerging research recognizes customer expertise and sophistication. With more information, customers have increasing skills and abilities to make judgements about the quality of service offerings, prior to purchase. According to Garry and Broderick, this increased focus on customer attributes should also be matched with a consideration of the attributes we associate with service encounters. Here, they consider issues relating to information accessibility, time and interactivity, and finally the level of customer centricity present within a customer experience.

Many organizations recognize the importance and complexities associated with the marketing of services. As a result they often develop and plan their marketing activities in such a way that they help and reassure their customers prior to, during, and after purchase. This is achieved through the provision of varying levels of information to reduce perceived risk and enhance the service experience. Two techniques, branding and internal marketing, are instrumental in delivering these goals in services marketing.

Understanding service encounters, customer satisfaction, and associated service measurement techniques, however, fails to lead to an understanding beyond the moment of truth, or the point at which the service is actioned. Understanding and measuring the experience that customers take away as a result of an interaction is much more pertinent and insightful.

Measuring Service Quality and Performance

Measuring the quality of a service encounter with financial institutions such as Withers Worldwide and other organizations has become a major factor in the management of service-based organizations. **Service quality** is based on the idea that customer expectations of the service they

Table 15.3 Three approaches to service quality measurement

Contact level	Explanation
Performance measures	Derived from the manufacturing sector, this approach simply asks customers to rate the performance of a service encounter. SERVPERF is the standard measurement technique.
Disconfirmation	This approach is based on the difference between what is expected from a service and what is delivered, as perceived by the customer. SERVQUAL is the standard measurement technique.
Importance–performance	Seeks to compare the performance of the different elements that make up a service with the customer's perception of the relative importance of these elements. IPA (importance–performance analysis) is the standard measurement technique.

will receive shape their perception of the actual service encounter. In essence, therefore, customers compare perceived service with expected service.

So, if the perceived service meets or even exceeds expectations, customers are deemed to be satisfied and are much more likely to return at some point in the future. However, if the perceived service falls below what was expected, they are more likely to feel disappointed and are unlikely to return.

In order to help organizations manage and provide a consistent level of service, various models have been proposed. Primarily these have been based on performance measures, disconfirmation (the gap between expected and perceived service encounter), and importance–performance ideas (Palmer, 2005) (see Table 15.3).

Each of these approaches has strengths and weaknesses, but the one approach that has received most attention is **SERVQUAL** developed by Parasuraman *et al*. (1988). For some it represents the benchmark approach to managing service quality.

SERVQUAL is a disconfirmation model and is based on the difference between the expected services and the actual perceived service. Inherently, this approach assumes that there is a gap between these variables, and five particular types of GAP have been established across service industries.

- **GAP 1—the gap between the customer's expectations and management perception.** By not understanding customer needs correctly, management direct resources into inappropriate areas. For example, train service operators may think that customers want places to store bags, whereas they actually want a seat in a comfortable safe environment.

- **GAP 2—the gap between management perception and service quality specification.** In this case, management perceive customer wants correctly but fail to set a performance standard, fail to clarify it, or set one that is not realistic and hence is unachievable. For example, the train operator understands customers' desire for a comfortable seat, but fails to specify how many should be provided relative to the anticipated number of travellers on each route.

- **GAP 3—the gap between service quality specifications and service delivery.** In this situation the service delivery does not match the specification for the service. This may be due to human error, poor training, or a failure in the technology necessary to deliver parts of a service. For example, the trolley buffet service on a train may be perceived as poor because the trolley operator was impolite because they had not received suitable training or because the supplier had not delivered the sandwiches on time.

- **GAP 4—the gap between service delivery and external communications.** The service promise presented in advertisements, on the website, and in sales literature helps set customer expectations. If these promises are not realized in service delivery practice, customers become dissatisfied. For example, if an advertisement shows the interior of a train with comfortable seats and plenty of space, yet a customer boards a train only to find a lack of space and hard seating, the external communications have misled customers and distorted their view of what might be realistically expected.

- **GAP 5—the gap between perceived service and expected service.** This gap arises because customers misunderstand the service quality relative to what they expect. This may be due to one or more of the previous gaps. For example, a customer might assume that the lack of information when a train comes to a standstill for an unexpectedly long period of time is due to ignorance or a 'they never tell us anything' attitude. In reality, this silence may be due to a failure of the internal communication system.

Using this GAPS approach five different dimensions of service quality have been established.

1 Reliability—the accuracy and dependability of repeated performances of service delivery.

2 Responsiveness—the helpfulness and willingness of staff to provide prompt service.

3 Assurance—the courtesy, confidence, and competence of employees.

4 Empathy—the ease and individualized care shown towards customers.

5 Tangibles—the appearance of employees, the physical location and any facilities and equipment, and the communication materials.

The SERVQUAL model consists of a questionnaire containing 22 items based on these five dimensions. When completed by customers it provides management with opportunities to correct areas where service performance is perceived to be less than satisfactory and learn from and congratulate people about the successful components.

Although SERVQUAL has been used extensively, there are some problems associated with its use. These difficulties concern the different dimensions customers use to assess quality, which varies according to each situation. In addition, there are statistical inconsistencies associated with measuring differences and the scoring techniques, and reliability issues associated with asking customers about their expectations after they have consumed a service (Gabbott and Hogg, 1998). Finally, ideas about measuring satisfaction are being overtaken as understanding about customer experience becomes more widely known. This is explored further at the end of this chapter.

Visit the Online Resource Centre and complete Worksheet 15.1. This will help you learn about the five gaps between actual and expected service quality: reliability, responsiveness, assurance, empathy, and tangibles.

Research Insight 15.2

To take your learning further, you might wish to read this influential paper.

Parasuraman, A., Zeithaml, V., and Berry, L.L. (1988). SERVQUAL: a multiple-item scale for measuring consumer perceptions of service quality. *Journal of Retailing*, **64(1), 5–37.**

This is a classic paper, structured in five sections, which describes the development of SERVQUAL, the multiple-item scale for measuring service quality. It also includes an interesting discussion regarding the scale's properties and its potential applications.

@ Visit the **Online Resource Centre** to read the abstract and access the full paper.

Principles of Relationship Marketing

Our attention now turns to ideas about relationship marketing. First, we look at founding ideas about the exchanges that occur between a pair of buyers and sellers. Two main types can be identified: **market (or discrete) exchanges** and **collaborative exchanges**.

Market (or discrete) exchanges occur where there is no prior history of exchange and no future exchanges are expected between a buyer and a seller. In these transactions the primary focus is on the product and price. Often referred to as 'transactional marketing', the 4Ps approach to the marketing mix variables (the marketing management school of thought) is used to guide and construct transaction behaviour. Buyers are considered to be passive and sellers active in these short-term exchanges.

However, the assumption that buyers are passive was soon challenged by the notion that, in reality, buyers are active problem-solvers and seek solutions that are both efficient and effective. Research into business markets identified that, in practice, purchasing is not about a single discrete event; rather, it is about a stream of activities between two organizations. These activities are sometimes referred to as episodes. Typically, these may be price negotiations, meetings at exhibitions, or a buying decision, but they all take place within the overall context of a relationship. This framed the relationship marketing school of thought, in which the buyer–seller relationship was the central element of analysis. This meant that the focus was no longer the product, or even the individual buying or selling firm, but the relationship and its particular characteristics over time.

Therefore, **relationship marketing** is based on the principle that there is a history of exchanges and an expectation that there will be exchanges in the future. Furthermore, the perspective is long term, envisaging a form of **loyalty** or continued attachment by the buyer to the seller. Price, as the key controlling mechanism, is replaced by customer service and quality of interaction between the two organizations. The exchange is termed collaborative because the focus is on both organizations seeking to achieve their goals in a mutually rewarding way and not at the expense of one another. See Table 15.4 for a more comprehensive list of fundamental differences between transactional and collaborative marketing.

Table 15.4 Characteristics of market and collaborative exchanges		
Attribute	**Market exchange**	**Collaborative exchange**
Length of relationship	Short term Abrupt end	Long term Continuous process
Relational expectations	Conflicts of goals Immediate payment No future problems (there is no future)	Conflicts of interest Deferred payment Future problems expected to be overcome by joint commitment
Communication	Low frequency of communication Formal communication predominates	Frequent communication Informal communication predominates
Cooperation	No joint cooperation	Joint cooperative projects
Responsibilities	Distinct responsibilities Defined obligations	Shared responsibilities Shared obligations

Although market exchanges focus on products and prices, there is still a relational component, if only because interaction requires a basic relationship between parties for the transaction to be completed (Macneil, 1980).

Dwyer *et al*. (1987) refer to relationship marketing as an approach that encompasses a wide range of relationships, not just with customers, but also those that organizations develop with suppliers, regulators, government, competitors, employees, and others. From this, relationship marketing might be regarded as all marketing activities associated with the management of successful relational exchanges.

Theron *et al*. (2013), among others, recognize that the role of collaboration in relationship marketing is important. However, many organizations maintain a variety of relationships with their different customers and suppliers, some highly collaborative and some market oriented, or, as Spekman and Carroway (2005: 1) suggest, 'where they make sense'.

Visit the Online Resource Centre and follow the web link to the Association for the Advancement of Relationship Marketing (AARM) to learn more about continuing professional development in relationship marketing.

The Customer Relationship Lifecycle

Relationship cost theory identified benefits associated with stable and mutually rewarding relationships. Such customers avoided costly switching costs associated with finding new suppliers, whereas suppliers experienced reduced quality costs, incurred when adapting to the needs of new customers.

Research Insight 15.3

To take your learning further, you might wish to read this influential paper.

Reichheld, F.F. and Sasser, E.W. (1990). Zero defections: quality comes to services. *Harvard Business Review*, **September, 105–11.**

Often quoted by other authors and researchers, this paper by Reichheld and Sasser reported that a small increase in the number of retained customers can have a disproportionately large increase in profitability, and this finding has helped propel a wealth of research and interest in relationship marketing. By definition, loyal customers are less likely to switch and therefore incur lower sales and service costs. They also help, through word of mouth, to recruit new customers, so the net result is that they all contribute to higher profits.

Visit the Online Resource Centre to read the abstract and access the full paper.

Reichheld and Sasser (1990) Identified an important association between a small (e.g. 5%) increase in **customer retention** and a large (e.g. 60%) improvement in profitability. So, a long-term relationship leads to lower relationship costs and higher profits. It is on this simple, yet crucial, principle that many organizations develop and run loyalty programmes (see Research Insight 15.3).

By undertaking a customer profitability analysis it is possible to identify those segments that are worth developing. This enables the construction of a portfolio of relationships, from which it is possible to identify relationships that have the potential to provide mutually rewarding benefits. This then provides a third dimension of the customer dynamic, namely **customer development**.

Understanding the economics associated with relationship stability and profitability uncovers three main stages within customer relationships. These are customer acquisition, development, and retention. This suggests similarities to the phases or stages of development associated with the product lifecycle concept.

Taking this idea one step further allows us to develop a **customer relationship lifecycle**. This consists of four main stages, namely **customer acquisition**, **customer development**, **customer retention**, and finally **customer decline** or termination (see Table 15.5).

Just as different strategies can be applied to different phases of the product lifecycle, so it is possible to observe that customers have different requirements as a relationship evolves. These requirements are reflected in the intensity of the relationship, and of course the level of intensity will vary through time. Figure 15.2 gives a visual depiction of the customer relationship lifecycle.

Key to this concept is the differing level of relationship intensity that determines each stage. Bruhn (2003) suggests that there are three primary indicators that make up this intensity dimension. These are the psychological, behavioural, and economic indicators, and are depicted in Figure 15.3.

The psychological intensity indicators are based on a customer's judgement about the quality of the relationship, and the amount of trust in, and commitment to, the seller or supplying organization. These are important foundations for establishing and maintaining ongoing and

Table 15.5 Stages in the customer lifecycle

Lifecycle stage	Explanation
Acquisition	There are three main events. First, both buyers and sellers search for a suitable match. Second, once a suitable partner has been found there is a period of initiation or 'settling in' during which both parties seek out information about the other before any transaction occurs. The third phase is characterized by socialization. Once a transaction occurs the buyer and seller start to become more familiar with each other and gradually begin to reveal more information about themselves.
Development	Sellers encourage buyers to purchase increased quantities, to try other products, to engage with other added value services, and to vary delivery times and quantities. The number and value of transactions increase as both buyer and seller begin to understand each other's requirements and goals in greater detail. During this stage that sellers also develop a better understanding of the wider array of their buyers' stakeholder relationships. This can have a significant influence on the nature of the supplier's relationship with the buyer, often indicating the depth to which the relationship aspires.
Retention	The relationship becomes stabilized, typified by greater levels of trust and commitment between the partners. This allows increased cross-buying and product experimentation, joint projects, and product development. Suppliers often provide customer loyalty schemes in order to increase the volume and value of products and services bought, and to lock in their customers by creating relationship exit barriers.
Decline	Relationships can become destabilized and uncertainty between partners can develop. There are many reasons for this including purchasing agreements and loyalty programmes that are not sufficiently attractive to lock in customers, and changes in the wider environment such as legislative, climatic, or economic developments. Customer recovery strategies are required at the first sign that a relationship is waning.

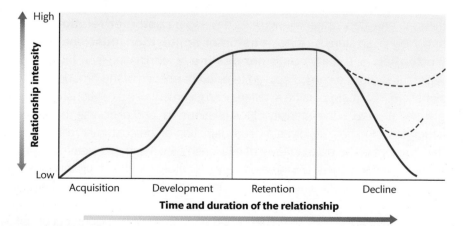

Figure 15.2

The customer relationship lifecycle

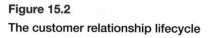

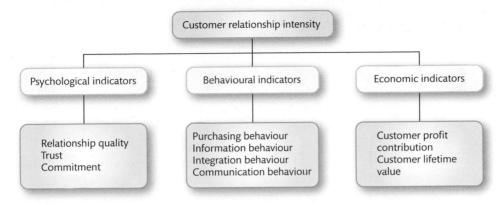

Figure 15.3

Indicators of customer relationship intensity

Source: *Relationship Marketing: Management of Customer Relationships*, Bruhn, M. (2002). Pearson Education Limited.

mutually rewarding two-way relationships. These are explored in more detail later in this chapter. Behavioural intensity indicators refer to the manner and scope of a customer's search for information, including word-of-mouth communication as well as their purchasing behaviour. Economic intensity indicators refer to both the profit contribution and the lifetime value a customer represents.

These three indicators signal the intensity of a relationship. They vary through time and help explain the characteristics associated with each of the relationship stages.

Loyalty, Retention, and Customer Satisfaction

The customer relationship cycle implies that customers who keep coming back to buy from a particular supplier are loyal. One problem with this suggestion is that what is understood to be 'loyalty' may actually be nothing more than pure convenience or habit. A person who regularly attends the same supermarket is not necessarily consciously loyal to the supermarket brand, but is happy with the convenience of the location and the overall quality and value of the products and services offered. Loyalty might be better appreciated in the context of a football supporter who travels to all away and home fixtures (regardless of domestic commitments), is a member of the club, buys into the merchandise and credit card offerings, and defends their club, even when they are relegated at the end of the season.

This cycle of customer attraction (acquisition), development, retention, and eventual decline represents a major difference from the 4Ps approach. The relationship approach is customer-centred, and therefore complements marketing values more effectively than the 4Ps model. However, although the focus has moved from product and prices to relationships, questions remain about whose relationship it is that is being managed. Early interpretations of relationship marketing focused on suppliers' attempts to develop relationships with customers. In other words, they were 'customer relationships' and this meant there was an imbalance or one-sidedness within the relationship. Today, relationship marketing recognizes the need for balanced customer–supplier relationships in which participants share the same level of interest, goodwill, and commitment towards each other.

Types and Levels of Loyalty

The concept of loyalty has attracted much research attention, if only because of the recent and current popularity of this approach. Table 15.6 represents some of the more general types of loyalty that can be observed.

These hierarchical schemes suggest that consumers are capable of varying degrees of loyalty. This type of categorization has been questioned by a number of researchers. Fournier and Yao (1997) doubt the validity of such approaches, and Baldinger and Rubinson (1996) support the idea that consumers work within an evoked set and switch between brands. This view is supported on the grounds that many consumers display elements of curiosity in their purchase habits, enjoy variety, and are happy to switch brands as a result of marketing communication activities and product experiences.

Loyalty at one level can be seen to be about increasing sales volume, i.e. fostering loyal purchase behaviour. However, high levels of repeat purchase are not necessarily an adequate measure of loyalty, as there may be a number of situational factors determining purchase behaviour, such as brand availability (Dick and Basu, 1994). At whichever level of loyalty, customer retention is paramount and neither behavioural nor attitudinal measures alone are adequate indicators of true loyalty. O'Malley (1998) suggests that a combination of the two is of greater use, and that the twin parameters of relative attitudes (to alternatives) and patronage behaviour (the recency, frequency, and monetary model), as suggested by Dick and Basu, offer more accurate indicators of loyalty when used together.

Visit the Online Resource Centre and complete Worksheet 15.2. This will help you learn about the four general types of loyalty—emotional loyalty, price loyalty, incentivised loyalty, and monopoly loyalty—and how these four types of loyalty can exist for one offering across different customers and situations.

This expansion in the number of loyalty programmes led Capizzi et al. (2004) to suggest that five clear trends within the loyalty market can be identified. These are set out in Table 15.7. These trends suggest that successful sales promotions schemes will be those that enable members

Table 15.6 Types of loyalty

Type of loyalty	Explanation
Emotional loyalty	This is a true form of loyalty and is driven by personal identification with real or perceived values and benefits.
Price loyalty	This type of loyalty is driven by rational economic behaviour and the main motivations are cautious management of money or financial necessity.
Incentivized loyalty	This refers to promiscuous buyers with no one favourite brand who demonstrate through repeat experience the value of becoming loyal.
Monopoly loyalty	This class of loyalty arises where a consumer has no purchase choice owing to a national monopoly. This is not a true form of loyalty.

Table 15.7 Five loyalty trends

Trend	Explanation
Ubiquity	The proliferation of loyalty programmes in most mature markets. Many members have little interest in them other than the functionality of points collection.
Coalition	Schemes are run by a number of different organizations in order to share costs, information, and branding (e.g. Nectar) and appear to be the dominant structure industry model.
Imagination	Opportunities to exploit technologies and niche markets will depend on creativity and imagination in order to acquire customer data to feed into the loyalty system.
Wow	To overcome consumer lethargy and boredom with loyalty schemes, many rewards in future will be experiential, emotional, and unique in an attempt to appeal to lifestage and aspirational lifestyle goals—wow them.
Analysis	To be competitive, the use of customer data analytics and business intelligence is becoming critical, if only to feed CRM programmes. Collect and analyse customer information effectively.

Source: Adapted from Capizzi *et al.* (2004).

to perceive significant value linked to their continued association with a scheme. That value will be driven by schemes run by groups of complementary brands, which use technology to understand customer dynamics and communications that complement their preferred values. The medium-term goal might be that these schemes should reflect customers' different relationship needs and recognize the different loyalty levels desired by different people. Market Insight 15.3 describes the main loyalty schemes used by airlines.

Market Insight 15.3
Alliances in the Sky

As costs have increased and competition intensified, airlines around the world have formed strategic alliances. These collaborative schemes require members to share routes, facilities such as executive lounges, and, of course, customers. Three main alliances have emerged.

The Oneworld Alliance consists of 15 airlines, including Qantas, American Airlines, and British Airways, and together they fly to over 150 countries.

The Star Alliance has 26 member airlines, including Air China, Singapore Airlines, and United, and fly to more than 1,269 airports in 193 countries.

Market Insight 15.3
continued

The oneworld® alliance consists of 15 of the world's leading airlines and approximately 30 affiliated carriers. Frequent flyer members within the partner airlines earn and redeem points on eligible Oneworld flights
Source: © EQRoy/Shutterstock.

The SkyTeam has 20 members, including Air France, Delta Airways, and China Airlines, and collectively they serve 1064 destinations.

The use of loyalty schemes in the airline industry is well established. These enable airlines to add value and help to brand their propositions by de-commoditizing their services and offerings. Frequent flier programmes (FFPs) are now regarded as a key part of an alliance's success. Each airline within an alliance has its own loyalty programme, with its own procedures and complexities. In addition to these, alliances offer a single alternative loyalty programme, which is integrated with the home airline's primary loyalty programme. Alliance schemes have several membership tiers, based on usage. The membership tiers in the Oneworld alliance are branded Emerald, Sapphire, and Ruby. In the Star Alliance there are two premium levels, Silver and Gold, whilst SkyTeam offer SkyTeam Elite and Elite Plus.

These schemes offer seamless travel, better usage of amenities at airports, and, through compatible loyalty schemes and code-sharing, the transference of frequent flyer miles from various alliance-based carriers which helps to build customer loyalty to the alliance, not an airline.

Sources: http://www.cheapflights.co.uk/travel-tips/airline-alliances/; http://www.oneworld.com/ffp/my-oneworld-tier-status; http://www.staralliance.com/en/benefits/status-benefits/.

Theory into Practice

Alliances occur when two or more organizations seek mutual collaboration which is deemed beneficial. This means that organizational goals and external opportunities jointly determine the formation of alliances.

Matching theory states that alliances are formed by organizations that seek a mutual fit of resources. Successful matching requires that an organization holding a valued resource must seek something that the approaching organization can provide in return.

Associated with alliances is network theory. Networks are considered as a set of firms that coordinate their activities to fulfil different roles and add different competencies. These are recognized as being important to the strategic success of businesses, especially in B2B markets. Network theory and analysis impacts on relationship marketing, which focuses on the management of customer and other relational exchanges.

Both matching theory and network theory can be used to interpret the formation of alliances in the airline market.

Related Topics:

relationship marketing; trust and commitment; loyalty schemes; customer retention.

> ## Market Insight 15.3
> continued
>
> 1 Do you think that operating both an airline and an alliance loyalty scheme is a good use of resources? Justify your view.
>
> 2 How might smartphone manufacturers retain customers?
>
> 3 Some organizations choose not to offer loyalty schemes, preferring to offer low prices. To what extent does this offer customers better value?

Visit the Online Resource Centre and complete Internet Activity 15.1 to learn more about how to increase customer loyalty.

Relationship Trust, Commitment, and Satisfaction

It is difficult to find agreement about a definition of **trust**, as many authors fail to specify clearly what they mean when using it (Cousins and Stanwix, 2001). However, there is a general consensus that trust is an element associated with personal, intra-organizational, and inter-organizational relationships, and is necessary for their continuation. Gambetta (1988) argues that trust is a means of reducing uncertainty in order for effective relationships to develop.

Cousins and Stanwix also suggest that, although trust is a term used to explain how relationships work, often it actually refers to ideas concerning risk, power, and dependency, and these propositions are used interchangeably. From their research on vehicle manufacturers, it emerges that B2B relationships are about the creation of mutual business advantage and the degree of confidence that one organization has in another.

Trust involves judgements about reliability and integrity and is concerned with the degree of confidence that one party to a relationship has that another will fulfil their obligations and responsibilities. The presence of trust in a relationship is important because it reduces both the threat of opportunism and the possibility of conflict which, in turn, increases the probability of buyer satisfaction. It has been claimed that the three major outcomes from the development of relationship trust are satisfaction, reduced **perceived risk**, and continuity (Pavlou, 2002).

- Perceived risk is concerned with the expectation of loss and therefore is tied closely to organizational performance.
- Trust that a seller will not take advantage of the imbalance of information between buyer and seller effectively reduces risk.
- Continuity is related to business volumes, necessary in online B2B marketplaces, and the development of both on- and offline enduring relationships. Trust is associated with continuity and therefore, when present, is indicative of long-term relationships.

Trust within a consumer context is important as it can reduce uncertainty. Financial institutions such as RBS, UBS, and HSBC have lost considerable amounts of consumer trust as a result of their illegal behaviour, including the Libor rate fixing scandal, cynical charges (PPI), and questionable investments (see Chapter 18). Strong brands provide sufficient information for consumers to make calculated purchase decisions in the absence of full knowledge. In a sense, consumers transfer their responsibility for brand decision-making, and hence brand performance, to the brand itself. Through regular brand purchases, habits or 'routinized response behaviour' develop. This is important not just because complex decision-making is simplified, but because the amount of communication necessary to assist and provoke purchase is considerably reduced.

The presence of trust within a relationship is influenced by four main factors (Young and Wilkinson, 1989): the duration of the relationship, the relative power of the participants, the presence of cooperation, and various environmental factors that may be present at any one moment. Although pertinent, these are quite general factors, and Morgan and Hunt (1994) established what are regarded today as the key underlying dimensions of relationship marketing. In their seminal paper, they argued that it is the presence of both commitment and trust that leads to cooperative behaviour, customer satisfaction, and ultimately successful relationship marketing.

Commitment is important because it implies a desire that a relationship continues and is strengthened because it is of value. Morgan and Hunt proposed that commitment and trust are the **key mediating variables** (KMVs) between five antecedents and five outcomes (see Figure 15.4).

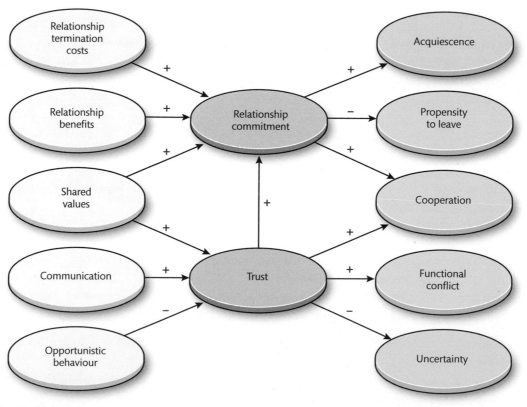

Figure 15.4

The KMV model of relationship marketing

Source: Reprinted with permission from R.M. Morgan and S.D. Hunt (1994), 'The commitment-trust theory of relationship marketing', *Journal of Marketing*, 58(July), 20–38, published by the American Marketing Association.

According to the KMV model, the greater the losses anticipated through the termination of a relationship, the greater the commitment expressed by the exchange partners. When relationship partners share similar values, commitment increases. Morgan and Hunt proposed that building a relationship based on trust and commitment can give rise to a number of benefits. Some of these are developing a set of shared values, reducing costs when the relationship finishes, and increasing profitability as a greater number of end-user customers are retained because of the inherent value and satisfaction they experience. Cooperation arises from a relationship driven by high levels of both trust and commitment (Morgan and Hunt, 1994).

Ryssel *et al.* (2004: 203) recognize that trust (and commitment) has a 'significant impact on the creation of value and conclude that value creation is a function of the atmosphere of a relationship rather than the technology employed'. Trust and commitment are concepts that are central to relationship marketing.

Customer Satisfaction

A natural outcome from building trust and developing commitment is the establishment of customer satisfaction. This is seen as important because satisfaction is thought to be positively related to customer retention, which in turn leads to an improved return on investment and hence profitability. Unsurprisingly, many organizations seek to improve levels of customer satisfaction, with the intention of strengthening customer relationships and driving higher levels of retention and loyalty (Ravald and Grönroos, 1996). So, the simple equation is build trust, drive satisfaction, improve retention, and increase profits.

However, customer satisfaction is not driven by trust alone. Customer expectations play an important role and help shape a customer's perception of product/service performance. Customers compare performance against their expectations and through this process feel a sense of customer satisfaction or dissatisfaction. More recent ideas suggest that the **perceived value** of a relationship can be more important than trust when building customer satisfaction (Ulaga and Eggert, 2005).

Research Insight 15.4

To take your learning further, you might wish to read this influential paper.

Morgan, R.M. and Hunt, S.D. (1994). The commitment–trust theory of relationship marketing. *Journal of Marketing*, 58(July), 20–38.

This well-known paper examines the role of trust and commitment in buyer–supplier relationships. The authors present the KMV model to explain various behavioural and cognitive aspects associated with exchange partnerships. Using social exchange theory, it is argued that, through mutually beneficial exchanges, trust and commitment develop, which in turn leads to longer-lasting relationships.

@ **Visit the Online Resource Centre to read the abstract and access the full paper.**

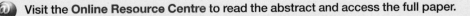

So, if expectations are met, customer satisfaction is achieved. If Withers Worldwide can exceed the expectations of their customers, both parties will be delighted. If expectations are not met, customers will be said to be dissatisfied. This simplistic interpretation can be misleading because satisfaction does not always imply loyalty (Mittal and Lassar, 1998). What may be seen as loyalty may be nothing more than convenience or even inertia, and dissatisfaction need not result in brand desertion (O'Malley, 1998).

Cumby and Barnes (1998) provide a useful insight into what contributes to customer satisfaction.

- Core product/service—the bundle of attributes, features, and benefits that must reach competitive levels if a relationship is to develop.

- Support services and systems—the quality of services and systems used to support the core product/service.

- Technical performance—the synchronization of the core product/services with the support infrastructure to deliver on the promise.

- Elements of customer interaction—the quality of customer care demonstrated through face-to-face and technology-mediated communications.

- Affective dimensions of services—the subtle and non-core interactions that say something about the way the organization feels about the customer.

This is a more useful insight into what it is that drives customer satisfaction, because it incorporates a wide range of factors and recognizes the importance of personal contact. Customer satisfaction and the quality of customer relationships are related, in differing ways, among differing people and contexts. However, one factor that is common to both is the perceived value of the interaction between parties.

Customer Experiences

The path of this chapter began with an exploration of the evolution of marketing practices related to services marketing, which then moved on to consider ideas about customer relationships. This path closes with an exploration of customer experiences (Maklan and Klaus, 2011).

The idea that providing a superior customer service might help in the (repeat) purchase decision process is something that several organizations, including Withers Worldwide, now appreciate. For a long time it was assumed that product quality and pricing were sufficient differentiators. However, product quality is no longer a viable means of establishing competitive advantage, simply because of shortening lifecycles and evolving technologies. Service, although difficult to deliver in a consistent way, is very difficult to replicate and has become an important aspect of customer management.

Although generating customer satisfaction is important, it provides an incomplete picture. Of greater interest is **customer experience**. As Prahalad and Ramaswamy (2004: 137; cited by Iyanna *et al.*, 2012) suggest, the literature on value is no longer embedded in goods and services, or indeed relationships, but 'is now centered in the experiences of consumers'. Customer value is regarded by an increasing number of academics and practitioners as the central marketing activity (Iyanna *et al.*, 2012) and that value is now central to customers' experiences. The implications for marketing are clearly stated by Meyer and Schwager (2007: 118) when they say that 'customer experience encompasses every aspect of a company's offering—the quality of

Research Insight 15.5

To take your learning further, you might wish to read this influential paper.

Meyer, C. and Schwager, A. (2007). Understanding customer experience. *Harvard Business Review*, February, 117–26.

This paper looks at how firms can benefit from adopting a customer experience perspective. It provides a clear understanding of what customer experience is in practice and discusses the managerial issues that can be avoided by utilizing an experience view rather than a relationship only view. It also contains a useful table showing how customer relationship management differs from customer experience management.

@ **Visit the Online Resource Centre to read the abstract and access the full paper.**

customer care, of course, but also advertising, packaging, product and service features, ease of use, and reliability'. For a deeper understanding of the issues arising from the adoption of a customer experience perspective, see Research Insight 15.5.

The importance and significance of customer experience to both individuals and society was first established by Pine and Gilmore (1998) when they referred to the 'experience economy', a term that is frequently used by authors and researchers in this area. Chang and Horng (2010) suggest that themed restaurants, such as Starbucks and the Hard Rock Café, are prime examples of customer experience. These brands are not just about the consumption of coffee, but a situation or environment in which the consumption of services occurs and relationships are developed, which in total provides a meaningful or valuable customer experience. Ismail *et al.* (2011) refer to the trend towards creating unique experiences for customers with a view to developing a competitive advantage, something that is sustainable particularly for those in the service sector, as replication is very difficult.

Before exploring the characteristics and issues associated with customer experience, it is helpful to consider how the concept is defined. Although there have been several attempts to define this concept, there has been little consensus. Some of the more notable definitions are set out in Table 15.8.

There are some similarities between many of these definitions. For example, customer experience is seen to be an individual event, and concerns emotional reactions following direct and indirect interaction with an organization. It is also related to events prior to, during, or after consumption. Perhaps one crucial point is that it is not possible for two people to have or to share the same experience (Pine and Gilmore, 1998). As a result, the task of managing and measuring customer experiences is inherently complex.

To help disentangle some of this complexity Pine and Gilmore derive four distinct realms of experience, based on two dimensions. These dimensions concern a customer's participation in an experience (weak/passive or active/strong), and an individual's connection with the environment of the experience or environmental relationship (from absorption/weak to immersion/strong).

Table 15.8 Definitions of experience

Author	Year	Definitions
Csikszentmihalyi	1977	The individual is experiencing flow when he has 'a unified flowing from one moment to the next, in which he is in control of his actions and in which there is little distinction between self and environment, between stimulus and response, between past, present and future' (p.36).
Holbrook and Hirschman (cited in Carù and Cova, 2003)	1982	Experience is defined as a personal occurrence, often with important emotional significance, founded on the interaction with stimuli which are the products or services consumed.
Carbone and Haeckel	1994	'The take-away impression formed by people's encounters with products, services, and businesses, a perception produced when humans consolidate sensory information' (p.8).
Schmitt	1999	From a customer perspective: 'Experiences involve the entire living being. They often result from direct observation and/or participating in the event—whether they are real, dreamlike or virtual' (p.60).
Shaw and Ivens	2002	'An interaction between an organization and a customer. It is a blend of an organization's physical performance, the senses stimulated and emotions evoked, each intuitively measured against customer experience across all moments of contact' (p.6).
Gentile et al.	2007	'The customer experience originates from a set of interactions between a customer and a product, a company, or part of its organization, which provoke a reaction. This experience is strictly individual and implies the customer's involvement at different levels (rational, emotional, sensorial, physical and spiritual). Its evaluation depends on the comparison between a customer's expectations and the stimuli coming from the interaction with the company and its offering in correspondence of the different moments of contacts or touch-points' (p.397).
Brakus et al.	2009	'… subjective, internal consumer responses (sensations, feelings, and cognitions) and behavioural responses evoked by brand related stimuli that are part of a brand's design and identity, packaging, communications, and environments' (p. 53).
Ismail et al.	2011	'Emotions provoked, sensations felt, knowledge gained and skills acquired through active involvement with the firm before, during, and after consumption.'

Source: Adapted from Ismail *et al.* (2011).

The four realms that emerge from these dimensions are entertainment, educational, aesthetic, and escapist.

- **Educational realm**—occurs when an individual learns and enhances their skills and knowledge as a result of the events unfolding before them (Pine and Gilmore, 1999; Oh *et al.*, 2007).

- **Entertainment realm**—occurs when an individual views a performance, listens to music, or reads for pleasure. The experience is absorbed passively (Pine and Gilmore, 1999).

- **Aesthetic realm**—occurs when an individual passively appreciates an event or environment but leaves without affecting or altering the nature of the environment (Pine and Gilmore, 1999; Oh *et al.*, 2007).

- **Escapist realm**—occurs when individuals become completely immersed in their environment and actively participate so that they affect actual performances or occurrences in the environment (Pine and Gilmore, 1999; Oh *et al.*, 2007).

This approach has subsequently led to research that focuses on the ways in which experiences are produced, narrated, and mediated (Lofgren, 2008).

Various authors have contributed to what might be the key dimensions of customer experience. Of these Nysveen and Pedersen (2014) used the dimensions highlighted by Brakus *et al.* (2009), namely sensory, affective, intellectual and behavioural, and added a further relational dimension, as determined by Nysveen *et al.* (2013).

- The sensory dimension—the extent to which a brand appeals to and makes impressions on consumers' senses.

- The affective dimension—how strongly a brand induces consumer feelings and emotions.

- The intellectual (or cognitive) dimension—how much a brand stimulates a consumer's curiosity, thinking, and problem-solving.

- The behavioural dimension—how strongly a brand engages consumers in physical activities.

- The relational dimension—how well an experience creates value for customers by driving social engagement, providing a social identity and a sense of belonging.

From their research Nysveen and Pedersen (2014) validated the importance of all of these dimensions. However, they stressed the significance of the relational dimension and its strong positive influence on both brand satisfaction and brand loyalty.

Market Insight 15.4
No Waiting for Customer Experiences

When passengers began complaining about the long waiting time at baggage claim, managers at Houston airport increased the number of baggage handlers. The average waiting time fell to eight minutes, but the complaints kept coming even though these figures were good for the industry. The walk from the gate to the baggage claim took a minute ... so seven minutes were spent waiting. Managers then moved the arrival gates away from the main terminal and sent bags to the furthest carousel. Passengers now had a six-minute walk to claim their bags and complaints plummeted to nearly zero.

Part Four > Principles of Customer Management

Market Insight 15.4
continued

Managing the speed at which queues move can impact the customer experience

Source: © SIHA SAKPRACHUM/Shutterstock.

At theme parks around the world, and most notably at Disneyland, queuing times for rides can be excessive. By providing TV screens, films, and music, plus surprise visits from Disney characters and other interactive elements to build anticipation for the ride, customers can be distracted. They even over-estimate the waiting times so guests feel a sense of satisfaction when they have 'beaten the clock' by the time they finally strap in for their ride.

The Nordic Cinema Group (NCG) was formed following the merger of SF Bio, one of the world's oldest film companies, and top Finnish theatre chain Finnkino in May 2013. Since then, admissions, box office, concession sales, and average ticket prices have all increased considerably. Admissions reached 21.5m in 2014, whilst the market share of NCG and its associated companies have also grown, with Sweden at 85%, Finland at 73%, Norway at 24%, Estonia at 47%, Latvia at 45%, and Lithuania at 76%.

One of the reasons for this huge success has been the group's focus not just on 'screening a film' but on offering a 'cinema experience.' This unique experience stimulates people to want to go to the cinema on a regular basis. To create that special experience, the majority of the shows in Sweden and Norway have a presenter who introduces each film, welcomes the audience, and describes the film. In addition, they always try to create some magic in the auditorium, from the moment a ticket is booked. They deliberately create a welcoming atmosphere, with a big screen, the best sound, and very spacious seating.

Sources: Lally (2015); Wylie (2015).

Theory into Practice

The management of waiting times is traditionally considered through queuing theory. This uses mathematical models to examine system performance. However, this approach is production oriented and fails to account for the marketing dimensions.

The customer experience concept is related to the idea of value creation. Indeed, it is the co-creation of value which experiences generate that underpins this topic. The way in which value is created before, during, and after experience events needs to be applied to the different 'experiences' highlighted in this insight. The various experience dimensions referred to in the text—sensory, affective, intellectual, behavioural, and relational—should be applied and considered for their relative worth in helping understand the perceived value customers derive.

Related Topics:

perceived value; co-creation; consumption experiences; service-dominant logic; value in exchange; value in use.

> ## Market Insight 15.4
> continued
>
> 1 To what extent is customer experience capable of being measured?
>
> 2 Explain the key differences between customer satisfaction and experience.
>
> 3 Choose a brand with which you are familiar, and list the different ways in which it might attempt to improve customer experience.

Visit the Online Resource Centre and follow the web links to see how the Customer Experience Professionals Association support the industry.

Experience Quality

In the section on measuring service quality and performance, we considered SERVQUAL, the leading approach to measuring service quality. Although SERVQUAL has many benefits and is used extensively, it is not suitable for measuring experience quality. SERVQUAL does provide a measure of customer satisfaction but, as Maklan and Klaus (2011) argue, it focuses largely upon customers' assessment of the service process and human interactions and is not a suitable vehicle for measuring customer experiences.

Chang and Horng (2010) refer to the study of the quality of life experience by Csikszentmihalyi and LeFevre (1989). They investigated how people evaluate and feel about their own experiences. This led them to define experience quality as 'how customers emotionally evaluate their experiences as they participate in consumption activities'. These authors are keen to point out that the evaluation of experience quality is not just about emotions, but putting more emphasis on the emotional nature of experience quality can 'reveal more of the characteristics of experience that underlie contemporary experience marketing' (Chang and Horng, 2010: 2404).

Therefore, they conceptualize **experience quality** as a customer's emotional judgement about their total experience, and they identify five dimensions for the construct. These are the physical surroundings, the service providers, other customers, customers' companions, and the customers themselves. Chang and Horng (2010) refer to four subdimensions (atmosphere, concentration, imagination, and surprise) of the physical surroundings, and that the dimension of 'customer themselves' has two subdimensions (cognitive learning and having fun). Their study concludes that the development of 'elaborate physical surroundings to elicit positive customers' emotional perceptions of experience quality is significant for experience design. Customers are commonly more impressed with service settings with atmosphere' (Chang and Horng, 2010: 2415). Following their review of the literature, Chahal and Dutta (2014) suggest that there are five dimensions associated with outstanding customer experience. These are sensory experience (sense), affective experience (feel), creative cognitive experience (think), physical experience, behaviours and lifestyles (act), and social identity experience (relate). These are shown in Figure 15.5.

The authors recognize customer experience as a central aspect of contemporary marketing, from both an academic and a practitioner perspective. They also acknowledge the lack of empirical research necessary to consolidate ideas and provide suitable managerial advice. However, their model is useful as it serves to bring together some of the central issues associated with understanding and developing customer experiences.

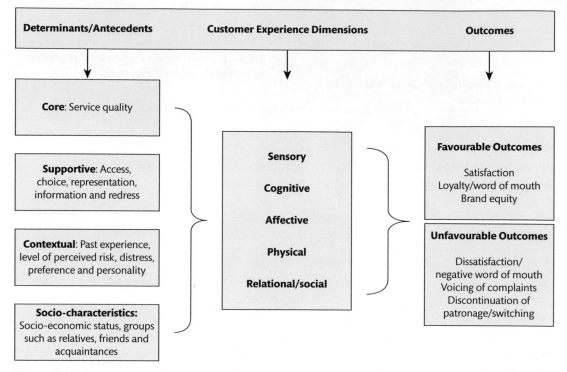

Figure 15.5

A proposed customer experience model

Source: Chahal, H. and Dutta, K. (2014). 'Conceptualising customer experiences: Significant research propositions', *Marketing Review*, 14(4), 361–81. Reproduced by permission of Westburn Publishers Ltd.

Visit the Online Resource Centre and follow the web links to explore more about customer experience.

Chapter Summary

To consolidate your learning, the key points from this chapter are summarized below:

■ **Explain the nature and characteristics of services.**

Unlike products, services are considered to be processes, and products and services have different distinguishing characteristics. These are based around their intangibility (you can touch a product but not a service), perishability (products can be stored but you cannot store a service), variability (each time a service is delivered it is different but products can be identical), inseparability (services are produced and consumed simultaneously), and a lack of ownership (you cannot take legal possession of a service). These are important because they shape the way in which marketers design, develop, deliver, and evaluate the marketing of services.

■ **Describe what is meant by the term service processes, service encounters, and the principles associated with measuring service quality.**

A process is a series of sequential actions that leads to predetermined outcomes. Four main service process categories can be identified: people, possession, mental stimulus, and information processing. A service encounter is best understood as a period of time during which a customer interacts directly with a service (Shostack, 1985). There are three levels of customer contact: high contact services, medium contact services, and low contact services. As more services are introduced, so opportunities for service variability and service failure also develop. Service quality is based on the idea that a customer's expectations of the service they will receive shapes their perception of the actual service encounter. In essence, customers compare perceived service with expected service. SERVQUAL is a major model used to measure service quality. It is a disconfirmation model and is based on the difference between the expected service and the actual perceived service.

■ **Outline the principles of relationship marketing, and consider the merits of customer retention and loyalty programmes.**

Relationship marketing is based on the premise that retained customers are more profitable than transactional marketing-based customers. Loyalty is an important concept within relationship marketing and the loyalty ladder model illustrates the critical point that different customers represent different value to organizations. This suggests that there are many different forms of loyalty, and that different marketing strategies are required to reach each of them.

■ **Understand the concepts of trust, commitment, and customer satisfaction, and explain how they are interlinked.**

There are several key concepts associated with the management of customer relationships. The main ones are trust, commitment, and satisfaction. These are interrelated, and the management of customer relationships should be based on the principles of reducing the influence of power and the incidence of conflict to build customer trust, gain customer commitment, and, through loyalty and retention, generate customer satisfaction. This approach should increase the perceived value of the relationship for all parties.

■ **Explain the term and dimensions of 'customer experiences', how it has evolved, and how it might be measured.**

Customers experience an emotional transition and response through interactions with an organization and its offerings. This individuality of experience implies that there are different types or levels of experience, such as rational, emotional, sensorial, physical, and spiritual. The development of customer experience marketing has been built on evolving ideas concerning service encounters, perceived value, relationship marketing, and customer satisfaction.

? Review Questions

1 Identify the essential characteristics of services and make brief notes explaining how they affect the marketing of services.

2 What are the main types of service processes? Identify their key characteristics?

3 Explain the term 'service encounter'.

4 How does an understanding of the relevant search, experience, and credence properties of a service influence the way they are marketed?

5 Name the five dimensions of service quality and explain their key characteristics.

6 What are the key differences between transactional marketing and relationship marketing?

7 Why is trust an important aspect of relationship marketing?

8 To what extent does the concept of relationship intensity assist our understanding of relationship marketing?

9 Make notes for a short presentation in which you explain the term customer experience, and track its evolution.

10 What dimensions are used by Csikszentmihalyi and LeFevre (1989) to measure experience quality?

Worksheet Summary

To apply the knowledge you have gained from this chapter and test your understanding of services marketing visit the **Online Resource Centre** and complete Worksheet 15.3.

Discussion Questions

1 Having the read Case Insight 15.1, how would you advise Withers Worldwide about how best to evaluate the quality of their service offering?

2 To what extent is the traditional marketing mix a useful basis for developing marketing strategies for service organizations?

3 Westcliffe and Sons make a range of fruit juice drinks. Their business falls into two main segments, consumers and business users, such as local councils and catering companies. Recent sales figures suggest that orders from some catering companies are down on previous years, and some have stopped buying from them altogether. The marketing director of Westcliffe has reported that he cannot understand the reason for the decline in business as product quality and prices are very competitive. Advise the marketing director about the key issues he should consider, and discuss how the company should re-establish itself with the catering companies.

4 Consider the view that loose or arm's length B2B customer relationships can be just as productive as those that are intense and close.

5 Using PowerPoint prepare a short presentation in which you explain the meaning of customer experience.

Visit the **Online Resource Centre** and complete the Multiple Choice Questions to assess your knowledge of Chapter 15.

Glossary

collaborative exchanges a series of transactions between a buyer and seller where the relationship is the main focus.

commitment a desire that a relationship should continue.

customer acquisition the search for and settling in of new customers.

customer decline a stage in a buyer–seller relationship which is stable and holds the strongest levels of trust and commitment.

customer development a period during which buyers and sellers become more familiar with each others' propositions and needs.

customer experience the individual feelings and emotions felt through interactions with an organization and its offerings.

customer relationship lifecycle the four main stages associated with managing customer relationships: customer acquisition, development, retention, and decline or termination.

customer retention a stage in a buyer–seller relationship which is stable and holds the strongest levels of trust and commitment.

electronic kiosk a computer terminal located within a retail environment that provides individuals with information about products and services.

experience quality the emotional evaluation by customers of their experiences as they participate in consumption activities.

inseparability a characteristic of a service, one that refers to its instantaneous production and consumption.

intangibility a characteristic of a service, namely that it does not have physical attributes and so cannot be perceived by the senses—cannot be tasted, seen, touched, smelt, or possessed.

key mediating variables (KMVs) the commitment and trust, used within the Morgan and Hunt model of relationship marketing.

loyalty the extent to which a customer supports, possibly through repeat purchases, a particular brand.

market (or discrete) exchanges a type of transaction between a buyer and seller where the main focus is on the product and price.

ownership goods are available immediately from the intermediaries' stocks, thus ownership passes to the purchaser.

perceived risk the real and imagined uncertainties that customers consider when purchasing products and services.

perceived value the 'net satisfaction' derived from consuming and using a product, not just the costs involved in obtaining it.

perishability a characteristic of a service, one that recognizes that spare or unused capacity cannot be stored for use at some point in the future.

relationship marketing marketing activities associated with the management of successful relational (collaborative) exchanges.

service delivery the means through which services are experienced by customers.

service encounter an event that occurs when a customer interacts directly with a service.

service process a series of sequential actions that lead to the delivery of a predetermined service.

service quality the extent to which customer expectations of a service are met through an actual service encounter.

SERVQUAL a model which measures the difference between the expected service and the actual perceived service.

trust judgements about the reliability, integrity, and the degree of confidence that one party to a relationship has, that another will fulfil their obligations and responsibilities.

variability a characteristic of a service, one that refers to the amount of diversity allowed in each step of service provision.

References

Baldinger, A. and Rubinson, J. (1996). Brand loyalty: the link between attitude and behaviour. *Journal of Advertising Research*, 36(6), 22–34.

Berry, L.L. (1980). Services marketing is different. *Business*, May–June, 24–30.

Brady, M.K., Bourdeau, B.L., and Heskel, J. (2005). The importance of brand cues in intangible service industries: an application to investment services. *Journal of Services Marketing*, 19(6), 401–10.

Brakus, J.J., Schmitt, B.H., and Zarantonello, L. (2009). Brand experience: what is it? How is it measured? Does it affect loyalty? *Journal of Marketing*, 73(May), 52–68.

Bruhn, M. (2003). *Relationship Marketing: Management of Customer Relationships*. Harlow: FT/Prentice Hall.

Carbone, L.P. and Haeckel, S.H. (1994). Engineering customer experiences. *Marketing Management*, 3(3), 8–19

Capizzi, M., Ferguson, R., and Cuthbertson, R. (2004). Loyalty trends for the 21st century. *Journal of Targeting Measurement and Analysis for Marketing*, 12(3), 199–212.

Carù, A. and Cova, B. (2008). Small versus big stories in framing consumption experiences. *Qualitative Market Research*, 11(2), 166–76.

Chahal, H. and Dutta, K. (2014). Conceptualising customer experiences: significant research propositions. *Marketing Review*, 14(4), 361–81.

Chang, T-C. and Horng, S-C. (2010). Conceptualizing and measuring experience quality: the customer's perspective. *Service Industries Journal*, 30(14), 2401–19.

Cousins, P.D. and Stanwix, E. (2001). It's only a matter of confidence! A comparison of relationship management between Japanese and UK non-owned vehicle manufacturers. *International Journal of Operations and Production Management*, 21(9), 1160–80.

Csikszentmihalyi, M. (1977). *Beyond Boredom and Anxiety*. San Francisco, CA: Jossey-Bass.

Csikszentmihalyi, M. and LeFevre, J. (1989). Optimal experience in work and leisure. *Journal of Personality and Social Psychology*, 56(5), 815–22.

Cumby, J.A. and Barnes, J. (1998). How customers are made to feel: the role of affective reactions in driving customer satisfaction. *Customer Relationship Management*, 1(1), 54–63.

Curtis, S. (2014). Transport for London goes contactless. *The Telegraph*, 15 September. Retrieve from: http://www.telegraph.co.uk/technology/news/11096354/Transport-for-London-goes-contactless.html (accessed 25 July 2015).

Dick, A.S. and Basu, K. (1994). Customer loyalty: toward an integrated framework. *Journal of the Academy of Marketing Science*, 22(2), 99–113.

Dwyer, R.F., Schurr, P.H., and Oh, S. (1987). Developing buyer–seller relationships. *Journal of Marketing*, 51(April), 11–27

Fournier, S. and Yao, J.L. (1997). Reviving brand loyalty: a reconceptualisation within the framework of consumer–brand relationships. *International Journal of Research in Marketing*, 14(5), 451–72.

Gabbott, M. and Hogg, G. (1998). *Consumers and Services*. Chichester: John Wiley.

Gambetta, D. (1988). *Trust: Making and Breaking Co-operative Relations*. New York: Blackwell.

Garry, T. and Broderick, A. (2007). Customer attributes or service attributes? Rethinking the search, experience and credence classification basis of services. In *Proceedings of the 21st Service Workshop of the Academy of Marketing*. Helensburgh: Academy of Marketing, 24–39.

Gentile, C., Spiller, N., and Noci, G. (2007). How to sustain the customer experience: an overview of experience components that co-create value with the customer. *European Management Journal*, 25(5), 395–410.

Gil, I., Berenguer, G., and Cervera, A. (2008). The roles of service encounters, service value, and job satisfaction in business relationships. *Industrial Marketing Management*, 37(8), 921–39.

Glyn, W.J. and Lehtinen, U. (1995). The concept of exchange: interactive approaches in services marketing. In W.J. Glyn and J.G. Barnes (eds), *Understanding Services Management*. Chichester: John Wiley, 89–118.

Grönroos, C. (1990), *Service Management and Marketing: Managing the Moment of Truth in Service Competition*. Lexington, MA: Lexington Books.

Heskett, J.L., Jones, T.O., Loveman, G.W. Sasser, S.E., Jr, and Schlesinger, L.A. (1994). Putting the service-profit chain to work. *Harvard Business Review*, 72(2), 164–7.

Ismail, A.R., Melewar, T.C., Lim, L., and Woodside, A. (2011). Customer experiences with brands: literature review and research directions. *Marketing Review*, 11(3), 205–25.

Iyanna, S., Bosangit, C., and Mohd-Any, A.A. (2012). Value evaluation of customer experience using consumer generated content. *International Journal of Management and Marketing Research*, 5(2), 89–102.

Laja, S. (2012). Transport for London's contactless tickets roll out behind schedule. *Government Computing*, 22 May. Retrieve from: http://www.governmentcomputing.com/news/2012/may/22/contactless-tickets-tfl-delay-wave-pay (accessed 16 November 2012).

Lally, K. (2015). Scandinavia success story. *Film Journal International*, 118(7). Retrieve from www.filmjournal.com/features/scandinavia-success-story-cineeurope-hails-jan-bernhardsson-nordic-cinema-group (accessed 10 August 2015).

Lofgren, O. (2008). The secret lives of tourists. Delays, disappointments and daydreams. *Scandinavian Journal of Hospitality and Tourism*, 8(1), 85–101.

Lovelock, C., Vandermerwe, S., and Lewis, B. (1999). *Services Marketing: A European Perspective*. Harlow: FT/Prentice Hall.

Lund, D.J. and Marinova, D. (2014). Managing revenue across retail channels: the interplay of service performance and direct marketing. *Journal of Marketing*, 78(September), 99–118.

Macneil, I.R. (1980). *The New Social Contract*. New Haven, CT: Yale University Press.

Maklan, S. and Klaus, P. (2011) Customer experience: Are we measuring the right things? *International Journal of Market Research*, 53(6), 771–92

Maklan, S., Knox, S., and Peppard, J. (2011). Why CRM fails—and how to fix it. *Sloan Management Review*, 52(4), 77–85.

Meyer, C. and Schwager, A. (2007). Understanding customer experience, *Harvard Business Review*, February, 117–26.

Morgan, R.M. and Hunt, S.D. (1994). The commitment–trust theory of relationship marketing. *Journal of Marketing*, 58(July), 20–38.

Mittal, B. and Lassar, W.M. (1998). Why do consumers switch? The dynamics of satisfaction versus loyalty. *Journal of Services Marketing*, 12(3), 177–94.

Nysveen, H., Pedersen, E.E., and Skard, S. (2013). Brand experiences in service organizations: exploring the individual effects of brand experience dimensions. *Journal of Brand Management*, 20(April/May), 404–23.

Nysveen, H. and Pedersen P.I. (2014). Influences of co-creation on brand experience. *International Journal of Market Research*, 56(6), 807–32.

Oates, J. (2009). Westminster readies 'wave and pay' parking meters. *The Register*, 29 October. Retrieve from: www.theregister.co.uk/2009/10/29/westminster_parking_scheme/ (accessed 14 October 2016).

Oh, H, Fiorie, A.M., and Jeoung, M. (2007). Measuring experience economy concepts: tourism applications. *Journal of Travel Research*, 46, 119–32.

Olson, J.C. and Jacoby, J. (1972). Cue utilization in the quality perception process. In M. Venkatesan (ed.), *Proceedings of the Third Annual Conference of the Association for Consumer Research*. Association for Consumer Research, 167–79.

O'Malley, L. (1998). Can loyalty schemes really build loyalty? *Marketing Intelligence and Planning*, 16(1), 47–55.

Palmer, A. (2005). *Services Marketing*. Maidenhead: McGraw Hill.

Parasuraman, A., Zeithaml, V., and Berry, L.L. (1988). SERVQUAL: a multiple-item scale for measuring consumer perceptions of service quality. *Journal of Retailing*, 64(1), 5–37.

Pavlou, P.A. (2002). Institution-based trust in interorganisational exchange relationships: the role of online B2B marketplaces on trust formation. *Journal of Strategic Information Systems*, 11(3/4), 215–43.

Pine, B. and Gilmore, H. (1999).*The Experience Economy: Work Is Theatre and Every Business a Stage*. Boston: MA: Harvard Business School Press.

Pine, B.J. and Gilmore, J.H. (1998). Welcome to the experience economy. *Harvard Business Review*, July–August, 97–105.

Prahalad, C.K. and Ramaswamy, V. (2004). *The Future of Competition: Co-Creating Unique Value with Customers*. Boston, MA: Harvard Business School Press.

Ravald, A., and Grönroos, C. (1996). The value concept and relationship marketing. *European Journal of Marketing*, 30(2), 19–33.

Reichheld, F.F. and Sasser, E.W. (1990). Zero defections: quality comes to services. *Harvard Business Review*, September, 105–11.

Ryssel, R., Ritter, T., and Gemunden, H.G. (2004). The impact of information technology deployment on trust, commitment and value creation in business relationships. *Journal of Business and Industrial Marketing*, 19(3), 197–207.

Schmitt, B.H. (1999). *Experiential Marketing*. New York: Library of Congress Cataloguing-in-Publication Data.

Shaw, C. and Ivens, J. (2002). *Building Great Customer Experiences*. New York: Palgrave Macmillan.

Shostack, G.L. (1977). Breaking free from product marketing. *Journal of Marketing*, 41(April), 73–80.

Shostack, G.L. (1985). Planning the service encounter. In J.A. Czepiel, M.R. Solomon, and C.F. Surprenant (eds), *The Service Encounter*. Lexington, MA: Lexington Books, 243–54.

Sirianni, N.J., Bitner, M.J., Brown, S.W., and Vlandel, N. (2013). Branded service encounters: strategically aligning employee behavior with the brand positioning. *Journal of Marketing*, 77(November), 108–23.

Spekman, R.E. and Carroway, R. (2005). Making the transition to collaborative buyer–seller relationships: an emerging framework. *Industrial Marketing Management*, 35(1), 10 19.

Theron, E., Terblanche, N.S., and Boshoff, C. (2013). Building long-term marketing relationships: new perspectives on B2B financial services. *South African Journal of Business Management*, 44(4), 33–45.

Ulaga, W. and Eggert, A. (2005). Relationship value in business markets: the construct and its dimensions. *Journal of Business-to-Business Marketing*, 12(1), 73–99.

Wheatley, T. (2012). CNN.com. Retrieve from: http://business.blogs.cnn.com/2011/02/01/excited-about-wave-and-pay-its-old-news-in-hong-kong/ (accessed 16 November 2012).

Wylie, M. (2015). The psychology of queuing, the art of distraction. *NZ Business*, April, 47. Retrieve from: http://nzbusiness.co.nz (accessed 15 August 2015).

Young, L.C. and Wilkinson, I.F. (1989). The role of trust and co-operation in marketing channels: a preliminary study. *European Journal of Marketing*, 23(2), 109–22.

Zeithaml, V.A. (1981).How consumer evaluation processes differ between goods and services. Reprinted in C. Lovelock (ed.), *Services Marketing* (2nd edn). Upper Saddle River, NJ: Prentice Hall, 1991.

Chapter 16
Business-to-Business Marketing

Learning Outcomes

After studying this chapter you should be able to:

▶ Explain the main characteristics of business markets and understand the different types of organizational customer

▶ Describe the different types of offering that are bought and sold in business markets

▶ Set out the main processes and stages associated with organizational buying and purchasing

▶ Explain what business-to-business marketing is and the marketing issues associated with professional service firms

▶ Understand the principles of key account management

Case Insight 16.1
Oxford Instruments

How should organizations develop relationships with business partners in international markets? We speak to Lynn Shepherd, the Group Director of Communications at Oxford Instruments, to find out more.

Oxford Instruments sells a wide range of high technology tools and systems to customers in research and industrial markets all over the world. Its core technologies allow the analysis, manipulation, and fabrication of matter at the atomic and molecular level, so nanotechnology is the prime sector that drives our growth strategy.

We operate in two main markets, the research/academia and industrial markets. In the former we work with highly educated well-informed customers. These include university professors, heads of research labs, and physics-based experts working within niche markets with very specific requirements. Our high-end cutting edge products sell in low volumes and are highly priced. As a result, the buying decisions are usually very complex, and are based around a tender process. These transactions are very relationship dependent, are not cyclic, and on the whole are all in niche markets, where sometimes the buying cycle lasts for five years!

In the industrial market there is little interest in the technology behind the instrument. In addition to a sole trader running a scrap yard, our customers include buyers in multinational companies, government agencies (e.g. NASA), and quality control managers in a range of industrial sectors from food to cement, through automotive and petrochemicals. What is common to them all is that they want to press a switch and get a result quickly. This makes for a less complicated purchase decision process, which involves fewer people and stages, and is often

concluded in a matter of weeks. Although these industrial products sell in higher volumes than those in the research market, they are not mass produced.

In both of these markets it is vital that our sales team establishes a relationship with the customer. For us, relationship marketing is a key ingredient of our marketing activity. Customer relationships must be maintained and nurtured as the reputation of our brand is a key influence on potential purchasers and must be protected.

The growth of our company involves finding and analysing emerging or rapidly growing markets such as Russia, Turkey, and Korea. We identify countries where governments are investing in nanotechnology and industrial growth. Our challenge then involves learning and understanding these new markets, and although the differences in some instances may be small, they are critical. We need to know the potential growth of a target market and determine what might be the optimal method of entering a market. We use a variety of methods including distributor marketing, installing a territory manager, and establishing a wholly owned office.

The essential problem that we faced when we identified India as a potential market was to determine which entry method would be most effective to help establish the credibility of Oxford Instruments and build mutually profitable business relationships.

Introduction

For many of us marketing is concerned with consumer products, those that we buy and consume on a fairly regular basis. There is, however, a colossal market that is often hidden from our daily view of the world. This is referred to as the business market, and **business-to-business marketing** is concerned with the marketing of a huge range of products and services that are bought and sold between organizations.

Some of the characteristics of business-to-business (B2B) marketing are very different from those associated with **consumer marketing**. There are numerous reasons for these differences and the way they impact varies among organizations. In this chapter, we explore the nature and impact of these characteristics. We highlight the main types of business-to-business organizations, learn about the different types of goods and services, and develop an understanding about the way organizations make buying decisions, who makes them and what purchasing strategies can be used.

A traditional perception of business marketing activity is that it concerns salespeople selling products with services attached (Leigh and Marshall, 2001). In many ways this was true, but now that answering most prior-to-purchase questions and much customer order-taking is an online activity, the sales department has shifted its role. Now salespeople focus on managing relationships, increasing customer productivity, and closing deals (Rocco and Bush, 2016).

Citing Vargo and Lusch (2004), Storbacka et al. (2009: 892) state that there 'has been a significant shift from product to service (or solution) selling ("servitization") in many business-to-business interactions'. Research by Storbacka et al. (2009) show that sales is increasingly about process, rather than a series of separate transactions carried out by a specific function. They claim that the sales process is much more relational than it used to be. Second, the sales function now involves close working links between sales and operations, especially as sales becomes increasingly linked with information gathering, processing, and interpretation, resource mobilization, and delivery. This makes sales much more cross-functional than it used to be. Finally, they observe the increasing emphasis on customer issues, and also on sales metrics, suggesting that the sales function has shifted from an operational to a strategic activity.

A key part of B2B marketing is associated with managing the relationships that can develop between organizations and the people who represent them. Therefore managing customers is vitally important, and one task is to identify and manage those customers who are important to the success of the organization. This is referred to as **key account** management, and we examine this topic because it is an important aspect of B2B marketing. Although the chapter focuses on the differences and characteristics of business marketing, we conclude with a reflection of the similarities that exist between business and consumer marketing.

What is Business-to-Business Marketing?

Just imagine the complexity associated with the design and construction of the International Space Station, the Elizabeth Line, London's new underground (Crossrail) link, the King Abdullah Economic City project between Jeddah and Rabigh in Saudi Arabia, or the Hålogaland Bridge in Norway. Specifying, negotiating, buying and selling, building, delivering and storing, and then replacing parts and materials as they become used can involve a vast network of organizations, large and small. The operational task alone is enormous, and the value of the materials, components, labour,

B2B marketing is an important activity in the car manufacturing sector. Managing the relationships among the network of organizations involved in the timely supply of parts and services is critical

Source: © Usoltceva Anastasiia/Shutterstock.

and energy involved far exceeds consumer spending in either the soap, beauty, or confectionery markets. The market for goods and services bought and sold between businesses is simply huge.

To make a car, a manufacturer must try to create value; they do this by buying a range of finished and part-finished items, assembling them, and distributing the completed cars to dealers, who sell them to consumers or businesses (fleet-buyers). The array of parts and finished items that the manufacturer buys involves a huge number of suppliers. This is the business market. The actions undertaken by a supplier of a brake system in order to influence the car manufacturer to select their system rather than a competitor's constitute business-to-business marketing.

Some B2B suppliers seek to manage not only relationships with their direct customers (buyers) but also those relating to their customers' customers. This approach provides valuable market information, creates product preferences among these indirect customers, and drives derived demand. For example, Cisco, the network equipment supplier, supplies systems to service providers, but in addition approaches the service providers' customers to learn about their requirements (Homburg *et al.*, 2014).

In a number of ways, B2B marketing is fundamentally different from consumer goods or services marketing because organizational buyers do not consume the products or services themselves. Unlike consumer markets, where goods and services are consumed individually, invariably by the people who buy them, the essence of business markets is that organizations, not individual people, undertake the act of purchase.

Far larger than the consumer market, the business market comprises many types and sizes of organization. Each organization interacts with a selection of others and forms relationships of varying significance and duration. This web of interaction is referred to as a network. Although organizations are often structurally and legally independent entities, a key characteristic is that they are also interdependent, i.e. they have to work with other organizations, to varying degrees, to achieve their goals.

Characteristics of Business Markets

Business markets are characterized by a number of factors, but the main ones are the nature of demand, the buying processes, international dimensions, and, perhaps most importantly, the relationships that develop between organizations in the process of buying and selling. These are shown in Figure 16.1 and are examined in turn.

The Nature of Demand

There are three key aspects of demand in business markets: derivation, variance, and elasticity. Demand in business markets is ultimately derived from consumers (Gummesson and Polese, 2009). This may seem a little odd, but consider the demand for building trains. When Banverket, the Swedish Railway Administration, and Bombardier Transportation considered developing a 'Green Train', the goal was to develop a new generation of high speed, super-efficient trains to meet the special technical and traffic requirements in the Nordic Countries. Part of the project team's calculation was to estimate the number of people prepared to make train journeys and what they were prepared to pay. Even though each train is the result of hundreds of organizations interacting with one another, it is train passengers (consumers) who actually stimulate demand for the construction of trains.

Demand is variable because consumer preferences and behaviour fluctuate. For example, the demand for rail journeys usually declines following a major train accident or a significant increase in

Figure 16.1

Key characteristics of business markets

fares. It also increases in response to petrol price rises and calls for consumers to be more environmentally aware. The subsequent impact could be felt on rail operators, support services, train manufacturers, and the whole array of suppliers and subcontractors in the market. All of this suggests that organizations should monitor and anticipate demand. See Market Insight 16.1 for an example.

Demand is essentially inelastic. If suppliers raise their prices, most manufacturers will try to absorb the increases into their own cost structures either to avoid letting their customers down in the short term, or because they are tied into fixed price contracts. Incorporating these price increases, at least over the short to medium term, means that there is price inelasticity. In the medium term, manufacturers can eliminate the original parts, redesign the proposition, or search for new suppliers.

The Buying Processes

The buying processes undertaken by organizations differ in a number ways from those used by consumers. These differences are a reflection of the potential high financial value associated with these transactions, product complexity, the relatively large value of individual orders, and the nature of the risk and uncertainty. As a result, organizations have developed particular

Market Insight 16.1
Baltic Baker Predicts and Responds

In many industries demand fluctuates for a number of reasons. These might involve falling prices, rapid technological change, or even volatility where frequent variation in product demand can cause companies to swing between having no stock to periods of overproduction and surplus capacity. This, in turn, can impact on the rate and size of investment made by organizations as they flex themselves in anticipation of 'foreseeable' demand.

For example, the food group VAASAN produces a variety of fresh bakery products and breads for sale in retail chains, restaurants, and hotels. The Northern European group has subsidiaries in Finland, Norway, and Sweden, and is also one of the largest thin crisp and crispbread producers in the world.

One of the critical success factors in the food industry concerns the production of the right products, for the right customers, at the right time—in VAASAN's case, across the Nordic region. The company aims for a minimum on-time delivery rate of 98.5%. Unfortunately, each of the group's subsidiaries had developed different methods to predict customer demand. This represented a business risk, so a standardized process was necessary in order to predict fluctuations in customer demand and adjust production and delivery schedules to meet them.

The solution lay in a demand planning system that gathered and analysed data from multiple sources. These included the company's Enterprise Resource Planning (ERP) system and data warehouse, plus expert opinions from its sales analysts and customers.

This combination of historical sales data and expert prediction allows VAASAN to identify trends in customer demand and generate rolling forecasts. This in turn helps the group to predict its raw materials requirements and to adjust workforce planning and production scheduling to prepare for any anticipated rise in customer orders.

When the Swedish subsidiary won new customers and increased the range of products available to consumers, demand increased by 30%. The demand forecasting solution was used to predict the total sales volumes at each of the new customer's outlets. This in turn gave VAASAN sufficient time to plan and adjust the manufacturing schedule at its bakeries in order to increase the daily production volumes. Not only are customers happy and relationships strengthened, but capacity utilization and plant efficiency is improved significantly, thus minimizing the business risk of over- or underproduction.

Sources: Adapted from: http://www.cafod.org.uk/policy_and_analysis/public_policy_papers; http://www.vaasan.com; http://www.ibm.com/software/success/cssdb.nsf/cs/STRD-8YKKDA?OpenDocument&Site=cognos&cty=en_us.

Market Insight 16.1

continued

Theory into Practice

This example demonstrates the characteristics of business markets. First, the nature of demand in B2B contexts is illustrated.

Demand is variable because consumer preferences and behaviour fluctuate. The various retail and restaurant chains that VAASAN supplies all experience fluctuating daily consumer demand. This in turn is reflected in the range and number of each product ordered by VAASAN's trade customers. By not measuring and predicting demand VAASAN would experience increased costs with unused products, and run an even bigger risk of not meeting their trade customers' orders. Both of these will impact negatively on VAASAN's margins and overall profitability. It will also influence the relationships within VAASAN's marketing channel.

In addition to the nature of demand and the importance of relationships, the international dimensions of business markets can be seen through VAASAN's activities across the Baltic region.

Related Topics:

channel conflict; relationships; supply chains; innovation.

1 From where is the demand for bakery products derived?

2 Do you believe demand for bakery products is elastic or inelastic?

3 How else might a marketing manager overcome this type of volatility?

processes and procedures, which often involve a large number of people. What is central, however, is that the group of people involved in organizational purchasing processes is referred to as a decision-making unit, and that the types of purchase they make are classified as **buyclasses**, all of which are made in various **buyphases**. Details of these processes are outlined later in the section on processes in the decision-making unit.

International Dimensions

In comparison with consumer markets, B2B marketing is much easier to conduct internationally. This is because the needs of businesses around the world are far more similar to one another than the needs of consumers, whose preferences, tastes, and resources vary. As a result, an increasing number of B2B organizations are moving into international markets. This is often enabled by advances in technology, most notably the Internet, which permit organizations enormous geographical coverage.

In comparison with B2C markets, B2B organizations benefit from a lower variety of product functionality and performance. This is partly because the various trading associations across the world have agreed standards relating to content and performance. This means that buying and selling of products and services, wherever located, are relatively simple and the trading environment is reasonably well-regulated and controlled. Many industries(e.g. the steel, plastic, chemicals, and paper industries) have commonly agreed standards, which facilitate inter-organizational exchange processes. In B2C markets there are numerous issues concerning consumer culture and values, and the adaptation of products and promotional activities to meet various colour, ingredient, stylistic, buying processes, packaging, and language requirements.

 Visit the Online Resource Centre and follow the web link to the ABBA, the Association for B2B Agencies to learn more about B2B organizations.

Relationships

If there is one characteristic that separates business marketing from consumer marketing, it is the importance of relationships. In B2C markets, the low **perceived value** of the products and the competitive nature of the market, which makes product substitution relatively easy, makes relationships between manufacturers and consumers relatively more difficult to establish. In business marketing, the interaction between buyers, sellers, and other stakeholders is of major significance. The development and maintenance of relationships between buying and selling organizations is pivotal to success. Interdependence, collaboration, and in some cases partnership over the development, supply, and support of products and services is considered a core element of B2B marketing. Strong inter-organizational relationships are referred to as **embedded ties**. Noordhoff *et al.* (2011) refer to these as a close and reciprocal relationship between a customer firm and a supplier firm. It is accepted that embedded ties improve relational and business performance outcomes because they are understood to facilitate the transfer of complex, sensitive, and even tacit knowledge between partners (Reagans and McEvily, 2003) and improve innovation. In the same way, damage to these ties can become a reason for the termination of a business relationship (Schreiner, 2015).

The importance of relationships in B2B marketing should not be underestimated. More information on relationship issues and concepts can be found in both Chapters 14 and 15.

Research Insight 16.1

To take your learning further, you might wish to read this influential paper.

Dwyer, R.F., Schurr, P.H., and Oh, S. (1987). Developing buyer–seller relationships.
***Journal of Marketing*, 51(April), 11–27.**

This paper is one of the most cited by other researchers in the subject area. Its popularity is based on the critical observation that buyer–seller exchanges are not discrete activities or events, but a part of ongoing relationships. The authors present a framework for developing buyer–seller relationships that links into marketing strategy. See also:

Ha, B-C. and Nam, H. (2016). Ethical judgments in supply chain management: a scenario analysis. *Journal of Business & Industrial Marketing*, 31(1), 59–69.

Visit the Online Resource Centre to read the abstract and access the full paper.

Types of Organizational Customer

Once referred to as industrial marketing, the term B2B marketing has now been adopted because it recognizes the involvement of a range of other, non-industrial, suppliers, agents, and participants. The government, the non-profit sector, and charities and institutions in most countries are responsible for a huge level of B2B activity. Consider the transactions necessary to support various government functions. For example, the huge range of offerings necessary to support the pharmaceutical and medical supplies in the health service, and the products and infrastructure necessary to maintain the prison and military services, all represent a major slice of B2B activity.

It is possible to categorize organizations by their size (revenue or number of employees)—namely large, medium, and small organizations. Macfarlane (2002) refers to global and national organizations, the public sector, small and medium-sized enterprises (SMEs), and small office/home office (SOHOs). However, this approach is too general and fails to accommodate different buyer needs and purchasing procedures. Here, three broad types of B2B organizations are identified: commercial, government, and institutional organizations. See Table 16.1 for a brief outline of their principal characteristics.

Table 16.1 Key types of business organizations

Type of organization		Key characteristics
Commercial	Distributors	Wholesalers, value-added resellers, retailers, and distributors/dealers. Not only do they smooth the progress of products through the marketing channel, but they should also add value to them by providing storage (through distribution centres), services (such as training), or financial support (such as credit facilities). See Market Insight 14.2.
	OEMs	Original equipment manufacturers (OEMs) refers to one company relabelling a product and incorporating it within a different product in order to sell it under their own brand name, and offering its own warranty, support, and licensing. For example, Toyota may have a contract with a headlight manufacturer to supply them with a certain quantity of headlight assemblies. Toyota is the OEM because they build these headlight assemblies into their different cars and sell the car as a Toyota, without identifying the manufacturer of the headlight assembly.
	Users	Users are organizations that purchase goods and services that are then consumed as part of their production and manufacturing processes. Therefore users consume these parts and materials and they do not appear in the final product offering but do contribute to its production. Toyota will purchase many support materials (e.g. machine tools, electrical manufacturing equipment, vending machines, office furniture, and stationery). None of these can be identified within the cars they produce.
	Retailers	Retailers need to purchase goods in order to resell them just as other organizations do. However, the buying processes are not always as complex or as intricate as those normally associated with organizational buying and the group of people who make purchase decisions (the decision-making unit (DMU)). Suppliers need to understand their retailers and their markets.

Table 16.1 continued	
Type of organization	**Key characteristics**
Government	The value of the business undertaken by governments is very high. Health, policing, education, transport, environmental protection, and national defence and security are a few of the areas that require public investment. Many of the larger projects that concern governments and associated ministries are large and complex, and involve a huge number of stakeholders. Although similar in many ways to commercial purchasing procedures and guidelines, those in the government sector are subject to political objectives, budget policies, accountability, and EC Directives (van Weele, 2002).
Institutions	Institutions include not-for-profit organizations such as churches and charities, community-based organizations such as housing associations, and government-related organizations such as hospitals, schools, museums, libraries, and universities. Characteristically, institutions tend to form large buying groups. Through collaboration, the group is able to negotiate greatly reduced prices and much larger discounts, usually related to bulk purchases.

All of these types of B2B organizations—commercial, government, and institutions—buy goods and services on an inter-organizational basis. Consumers are only involved through their interaction with retailers or as end-users of health treatments, education, or policing for which no direct financial exchange occurs. The types of marketing activity used to encourage repeat exchanges between these various types of organization can be considerable. However, one common strategy has been the more overt approach to developing relationships through cooperation and collaboration.

Research Insight 16.2

To take your learning further, you might wish to read this influential paper.

Achrol, R.S. (1997). Changes in the theory of interorganizational relations in marketing: toward a network paradigm. *Journal of the Academy of Marketing Science*, 25(1), 56–71.

Achrol sets out how the then established vertically integrated multidivisional type of organization started to be replaced by new forms of network organization consisting of large numbers of functionally specialized firms tied together in cooperative exchange relationships. He considers four main types, the variables involved, the economic rationale, and the types of coordination and control mechanisms necessary for organizations to adapt to the new environment.

@ Visit the **Online Resource Centre** to read the abstract and access the full paper.

> **Table 16.2 Types of business goods and services**
>
> | Type of goods | Explanation |
> | --- | --- |
> | **Input goods**
Raw materials, semi-manufactured parts, and finished goods. | Input goods have been subjected to different levels of processing (*raw materials*, *semi-manufactured parts*, and *finished* goods), and they lose their individual identities and become part of the finished item. |
> | **Equipment goods**
Otherwise known as capital or investment goods. | These are necessary for manufacturing and operations to take place. Land and buildings, computer systems, and machine tools are all necessary to support the production process, but they cannot be identified in the finished product. |
> | **Supply goods**
Otherwise known as maintenance, repair, and operating materials (MRO) items. | These goods and services are 'consumables' as they are necessary to keep production processes and the organization running.

For example, lubricants, paints, screws, and cleaning materials may all be necessary to maintain a firm's operations. Computer or IT servicing is necessary to maintain operations and to avoid down time, whilst accounting audits are a legal requirement. |

Types of Business Goods and Services

Just as there are a variety of types of organization in the business sector, so the offerings are equally varied and complex. Table 16.2 sets out the three principal business types of goods and services.

Most organizations, at various points in their development, have to decide whether to make/supply their own products and services or buy them in from outsourced providers. This 'make or buy' decision can have far-reaching effects not only on the strategic and operational aspects of an organization, but also on the purchasing function and its role within an organization.

Outsourcing is an increasingly popular activity practised by a wide range of organizations. As a result, purchasing behaviours have had to adapt accordingly, which in turn has impacted on business marketing. The development of 'lean management' techniques has enabled organizations to concentrate on their core processes and outsource all other activities. As organizations become 'leaner', they dramatically reduce their use of resources and the importance of purchasing increases (Durham and Ritchey, 2009).

Visit the Online Resource Centre and complete Internet Activity 16.1 to learn more about how the Internet is used to market computing software to business customers.

Organizational Buyer Behaviour

Only by appreciating the particular behaviour, purchasing systems, people, and policies used by an organization can suitable marketing and selling strategies be implemented. This section builds on the introduction to buyer processes made earlier in this chapter and the information about organizational characteristics introduced in Chapter 6. It considers some of the key issues associated with the way organizations purchase the goods and services necessary to achieve their corporate goals.

Two definitions of **organizational buyer behaviour** reveal important aspects of this subject. First, Webster and Wind (1972: 2) defined organizational buying as 'the decision making process by which formal organizations establish the need for purchased products and services and identify, evaluate and choose among alternative brands and suppliers'. This adopts a buying organization's perspective and highlights the important point that organizational buying behaviour involves processes rather than a single static one-off event. There are a number of stages, or phases, associated with product procurement, each one often requiring a key decision to be made.

A second definition by Parkinson and Baker (1994: 6), cited by Ulkuniemi (2003), states that organizational buying behaviour concerns 'the purchase of a product or service to satisfy organizational rather than individual goals'. This takes a neutral perspective, but makes the point that organizational buyer behaviour is about satisfying organization-wide needs and hence requires marketers to adopt processes that take into account the needs of different people, not a single individual.

Organizational buying behaviour is about three key issues.

- The functions and processes buyers move through when purchasing products for use in business markets.

- Strategy, where purchasing is designed to assist value creation and competitive advantage, and to influence supply chain activities.

- The network of relationships that organizations are part of when purchasing. The placement of orders and contracts between organizations can confirm a current trading relationship, initiate a new set of relationships, or even signal the demise of a relationship.

What should be clear is that organizational buying behaviour is not just about the purchase of goods and services. In addition to this fundamental task, it is concerned with the strategic development of the organization, creating value, and the management of inter-organizational relationships, all key issues in B2B marketing. These issues overlap with each other and are not discrete items.

Hollyoake (2009) argues that business marketing is increasingly about managing buyers' experiences and interactions. This involves creating expectations, often referred to as the brand promise, and then delivering products and services against these promises. It is important that a customer's evaluation of their experience is ahead of what was expected. Hollyoake develops these ideas to consider 'ease of doing business' as a measure of the supplier–customer relationship and to discover the key dimensions of the customer experience. He suggests that experiences are founded on four pillars: trust, interdependence, integrity, and communication. These ideas are also explored in both Chapters 14 and 15.

Grönroos (2009) develops the principles about expectations into a new perspective of (business) marketing, referred to as **promise management**. These ideas are rooted in what Grönroos sees as the purpose of contemporary marketing, namely as a value creation process. Firms are involved in developing and delivering value propositions (promises). These propositions of value can only be realized once an offering is consumed, and that can only be done by customers. Therefore value creation is experienced only by customers as value fulfilment.

Decision-Making Units: Characteristics

Although organizations usually designate a 'buyer' who is responsible for the purchase of a range of offerings, in reality a range of people are involved in the purchasing process. The purchasing process is a means by which an organization creates value. It is, therefore, an integral part of an organization's value at some point in the future. This group of people is referred to as either the **decision-making unit** (DMU) or the **buying centre**. In many circumstances these are informal groupings of people who come together in varying ways to contribute to the decision-making process. Certain projects, usually of major significance or value, require a group of people to be formally constituted who have responsibility to oversee and complete the purchase of a stipulated item or products and services relating to a specific project.

DMUs vary in composition and size according to the nature of each individual purchasing task. Webster and Wind (1972) identified a number of people who undertake different roles within buying centres and these are set out in Figure 16.2.

- **Initiators** start the whole process by requesting the purchase of an item. They may also assume other roles within the DMU or wider organization.

- **Users** literally use the product once it has been acquired, and they will also evaluate its performance. Users may not only initiate the purchase process but are sometimes involved in the specification process. Their role is continuous, although it may vary from the highly involved to the peripheral.

- **Influencers** very often help to set the technical specifications for the proposed purchase and assist the evaluation of alternative offerings by potential suppliers. These may be consultants hired to complete a particular project. For example, an office furniture manufacturer will regard office managers as key decision-makers but understand that specifiers, such as office designers and architects, influence the office manager's decision about furniture. See Market Insight 16.2.

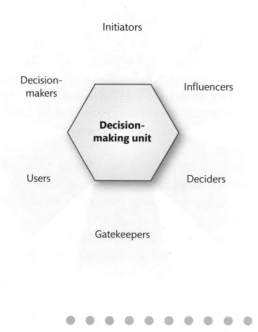

Figure 16.2

Membership of the decision-making unit

Source: Fill and McKee (2012). Reproduced with the kind permission of Goodfellow Publishers.

Market Insight 16.2
The Buyer–Supplier Connection

A B2B online marketplace enables exporters, importers, brokers, and retailers from across the globe to interact with a view to developing buying and selling opportunities. The platform can have a huge influence on purchase decisions.

Alibaba.com is perhaps the world's leading platform for global wholesale trade. The portal brings together sellers, by giving them the tools necessary to reach a global audience for their products, and buyers, by helping them find products and suppliers quickly and efficiently.

Gandys, established in 2011 by brothers Rob and Paul Forkan, is a footwear brand based on stylish and fun

Imprinted into each design is a myriad of their travel experiences combined to express their unique upbringing and adventurous nature
Source: Courtesy of Gandys.

Rob and Paul founded Gandys in order to support their Orphans for Orphans foundation by donating 10% of their profits to helping underprivileged children who are affected by the Tsunami
Source: Courtesy of Gandys.

flipflops. Orphaned by the 2004 tsunami, the brothers decided to set up a social enterprise to make a range of authentic flipflops. To find the right manufacturer they used Alibaba.com. After entering their requirements in the online system they were provided with a list of suitable product manufacturers. Following discussions with several nominated suppliers, a few prototypes were developed. By 2013 over 100 UK boutiques were selling Gandys. In order to grow they needed investment, and they achieved this through a reverse *Dragons' Den* process. This involved inviting several potential wealthy investors to a Brixton pub and asking them to compete for the chance to invest.

The Alibaba.com platform also supplies a range of added-value services designed to support the primary transactional processes. These include training, finance, inspection, and logistics.

Sources: Plummer (2014); Seager (2014); http://www. gandysflipflops.com; http://www.alibaba.com.

Market Insight 16.2
continued

Theory into Practice

The role that influencers such as the Alibaba platform play in B2B marketing is substantial and includes the reduction of uncertainty (risk), in this case institutional risk, and helps to build trust. These are both necessary in order that buyer–seller relationships can develop.

Institutional risk, i.e. trust in organizations rather than individual people or product/service brands, is important in B2B markets where the overall reputation of an organization is crucial when dealing with other organizations. In B2B markets the development of trust to encourage safe purchasing can be vital. To achieve this, organizations use a variety of techniques to lower the uncertainty buyers might experience.

Inter-organizational trust is based on two main dimensions: credibility and benevolence. Credibility concerns the extent to which one organization believes (is confident) that another organization will undertake and complete the agreed roles and tasks. Benevolence is concerned with goodwill, namely that the other organization will not act opportunistically, even if conditions for exploitation arise. In other words, inter-organizational trust involves judgements about another organization's reliability and integrity.

The range of ancillary services provided by Alibaba not only seek to induce trust between buyers and sellers but also encourage commitment and hence forge medium- to longer-term relationships.

Related Topics:

marketing relationships; trust and commitment; relationship lifecycle; KAM.

1 **Make a list of the efficiencies that an online platform can bring to buyer–seller transactions.**

2 **How does this type of platform assist the relationships between buyers and sellers?**

3 **Visit the Alibaba website (http://www.alibaba. com) and list the advantages and disadvantages of using the site from a marketing perspective.**

- **Deciders** are those who make purchasing decisions, and they are the most difficult to identify. This is because they may not have formal authority to make a purchase decision, yet are sufficiently influential internally that their decision carries the most weight. In repeat buying activities, the buyer may also be the decider. However, it is normal practice for a senior manager to authorize expenditure decisions involving sums over a certain financial limit.

- **Buyers** or purchasing managers select suppliers and manage the process whereby the required products are procured. Buyers may not decide which product is to be purchased, but they influence the framework within which the decision is made. They will formally undertake the process whereby products and services are purchased once a decision has been made to procure them. For example, they may be formal buyers and kick-start the purchase of a type of lubricant because the stock figures have fallen to a threshold level that indicates that current supplies will be exhausted within three weeks. They will, therefore, assume the roles of both an initiator and a buyer.

Research Insight 16.3

To take your learning further, you might wish to read this influential paper.

Koh, T.K. and Fichman, M. (2014). Multihoming users' preferences for two-sided exchange networks. *MIS Quarterly*, 38(4), 977–96.

This paper provides some useful background information about online platforms within a B2B context, and multihoming, the concurrent use of competing platforms, in particular. With the proliferation of online B2B exchanges, firms have an increasing number of platforms from which to choose. These researchers examine how selling and buying activities on B2B exchanges affect multihoming buyers' preferences for exchanges.

Ⓐ **Visit the Online Resource Centre to read the abstract and access the full paper.**

- **Gatekeepers** have the potential to control the type and flow of information to the organization and the members of the DMU. These gatekeepers may be assistants, technical personnel, secretaries, or telephone switchboard operators.

The size and form of the buying centre is not static. It can vary according to the complexity of the product being considered and the degree of risk each decision is perceived to carry for the organization. Different roles are required and adopted as the nature of the buying task changes with each new purchase situation (Bonoma, 1982). All of these roles might be subsumed within one individual for certain decisions. It is vital for seller organizations to identify members of the buying centre and to target and refine their messages to meet the needs of each member of the centre.

Membership of the DMU is far from fixed, and this fluidity poses problems for selling organizations simply because it is not always possible to identify key members or shifts in policy or requirements. As Spekman and Gronhaug (1986) point out, the DMU is a 'vague construct that can reach across a number of different functional roles with any number of individuals participating or exerting influence at any one time'. Therefore it is worth noting that, within this context, the behaviour of DMU members is also largely determined by the interpersonal relationships of the members of the centre.

The Decision-Making Unit: Processes

Organizational buying decisions vary in terms of the nature of the offering, the frequency and the relative value of purchases, their strategic impact (if any), and the type of relationship with suppliers. These, and many other factors, are potentially significant to individual buying organizations. However, there are three main types of buying situations. Referred to by Robinson *et al.* (1967) as buyclasses, these are **new task**, **modified rebuy**, and **straight rebuy**. These are summarized in Table 16.3.

Table 16.3	Main characteristics of the buyclasses		
Buyclass	**Degree of familiarity with the problem**	**Information requirements**	**Alternative solutions**
New buy	The problem is fresh to the decision-makers	A great deal of information is required	Alternative solutions are unknown; all are considered new
Modified rebuy	The requirement is not new but is different from previous situations	More information is required but past experience is of use	Buying decision needs new solutions
Rebuy	The problem is identical to previous experiences	Little or no information is required	Alternative solutions not sought or required

Source: *Marketing Communications* (7th edn), Fill, C. and Turnbull, S. (2016). Reproduced with the kind permission of Pearson Education Limited. © Pearson Education Limited (2016).

Buyclasses

New Task

As the name implies, the organization is faced with a first-time buying situation. Risk is inevitably large at this point as there is little collective experience of the product/service or the relevant suppliers. As a result of these factors, there are normally a large number of decision participants. Each participant requires a lot of information, and a relatively long period of time is needed for the information to be assimilated and a decision to be made.

Modified Rebuy

Having purchased a product, uncertainty is reduced but not eliminated, so the organization may request through their buyer(s) that certain modifications be made to future purchases, for example adjustments to the specification of the product, further negotiation on price levels, or perhaps an arrangement for alternative delivery patterns. Fewer people are involved in the decision-making process than in the new task situation.

Straight Rebuy

In this situation, the purchasing department reorders on a routine basis, very often working from an approved list of suppliers. These may be products that an organization consumes in order to keep operating (e.g. office stationery), or may be low value materials used within the operational value-added part of the organization (e.g. the manufacturing processes). No other people are involved with the exercise until different suppliers attempt to change the environment in which the decision is made. For example, a new supplier may interrupt the procedure with a potentially better offer. This may stimulate the emergence of a modified rebuy situation.

Straight rebuy presents classic conditions for the use of automatic reordering systems. Costs can be reduced, managerial time redirected to other projects, and the relationship between buyer and seller embedded within a stronger framework. One possible difficulty is that both parties perceive the system to be a significant exit barrier if conditions change, and this may deter flexibility or restrict opportunities to develop the same or other relationships.

The use of electronic purchasing systems at the straight rebuy stage has enabled organizations to empower employees to make purchases, although control still resides with purchasing managers. Employees can buy direct online from a catalogue list of authorized suppliers. The benefits are that employees are more involved, the purchasing process is speeded up, costs are reduced, and purchasing managers can spend more time with other higher priority activities.

Visit the Online Resource Centre and follow the web link to Electronic Commerce Europe, the biggest online trade network in the world, for more information on the use of electronic B2B purchasing.

Buyphases

Organizational buyer behaviour (OBB) consists of a series of sequential activities through which organizations proceed when making purchasing decisions. Robinson *et al.* (1967) refer to these as buying stages or buyphases. The following sequence of buyphases is particular to the new task situation just described. Many of these buyphases are ignored or compressed according to the complexity of the offering and when either a modified rebuy or straight rebuy situation is encountered.

Need/Problem Recognition

The need/recognition phase is about the identification of a gap. This is the gap between the benefits an organization is experiencing now and the benefits it would like to have. For example, when a new product is to be produced there is an obvious gap between having the necessary materials and components and being out of stock and unable to build. The first decision, therefore, is about how to close this gap. There are two broad options: outsourcing the whole or parts of the production process, or building or making the objects oneself. The need has been recognized and the gap identified. The rest of this section is based on a build decision being taken.

Product Specification

As a result of identifying a problem and the size of the gap, influencers and users can determine the desired characteristics of the product needed to resolve the problem. This may take the form of either a general functional description, or a much more detailed analysis and the creation of a detailed technical specification for a particular product. What sort of photocopier is required? What is it expected to achieve? How many documents should it copy per minute? Is a collator or tray required? This is an important part of the process because if it is executed properly it will narrow the supplier search and save on the costs associated with evaluation prior to a final decision. The results of the functional and detailed specifications are often combined within a purchase order specification.

Supplier and Product Search

At this stage, the buyer actively seeks suppliers who can supply the necessary product(s). There are two main issues at this point. First, will the product match the specification and the required performance standards? Second, will the potential supplier meet the other organizational requirements, such as experience, reputation, accreditation, and credit rating? In most circumstances, organizations review the market and their internal sources of information and arrive at a decision that is based on rational criteria.

Wherever possible, organizations work to reduce uncertainty and risk. By working with others who are known, with whom the organization has direct experience, and who can be trusted, risk and uncertainty can be reduced substantially. This highlights another reason why many organizations prefer to operate within established networks that can provide support and advice when needed.

Evaluation of Proposals

Depending on the complexity and value of the potential order(s), the proposal is a vital part of the process and should be prepared professionally. The proposals from the shortlisted organizations are reviewed in the context of two main criteria: the purchase order specification and the evaluation of the supplying organization. If the potential supplier is already part of the network, little search and review time is needed. If the proposed supplier is not part of the network, a review may be necessary to establish whether it will be appropriate (in terms of price, delivery, and service) and whether there is the potential for a long-term relationship or whether this is a single purchase that is unlikely to be repeated.

Supplier Selection

The DMU will normally undertake a supplier analysis and use a variety of decision criteria, according to the particular type of item sought. A further useful perspective is to view supplier organizations as a continuum, from reliance on a single source to the use of a wide variety of suppliers for the same product. Jackson (1985) proposed that organizations might buy an offering from a range of different suppliers to maintain a range of multiple sources (a practice of many government departments). She labelled this approach 'always a share', as several suppliers are given the opportunity to share the business available to the buying centre. The major disadvantage is that this approach fails to drive cost as low as possible, as the discounts derived from volume sales are not achieved. The advantage to the buying centre is that a relatively small investment is required and little risk is entailed in following such a strategy.

At the other end of the continuum are organizations that only use a single source supplier. All purchases are made from the single source until circumstances change to such a degree that the buyer's needs are no longer being satisfied. Jackson referred to these organizations as 'lost for good', because once a relationship with a new organization has been developed they are lost for good to the original supplier. An increasing number of organizations are choosing to enter alliances with a limited number of suppliers, or even a single source. The objective is to build a long-term relationship, to work together to build quality and help each other achieve their goals. Outsourcing manufacturing activities for non-core activities has increased considerably.

Evaluation

The order is written against the selected supplier, which is then monitored and evaluated against such diverse criteria as responsiveness to enquiries, modifications to the specification, and timing of delivery. When the product is delivered, it may reach the stated specification but fail to satisfy the original need. In this case, the specification needs to be rewritten before any future orders are placed.

Developments in the environment can impact on organizational buyers and change both the nature of decisions and the way they are made. For example, the decision to purchase new plant and machinery requires consideration of the future cash flows generated by the capital item.

Many people will be involved in the decision, and the time necessary for consultation may mean that other parts of the decision-making process are completed simultaneously.

Visit the Online Resource Centre and complete Internet Activity 16.2. This will aid in learning about the seven buying phases that organizations go through when purchasing industrial goods and services.

Buygrids

When the buyphases are linked to the buyclasses, a buygrid is determined. This grid is shown in Table 16.4.

The buygrid serves to illustrate the relationships between buyphases and buyclasses. It is important because it highlights the need to focus on buying situations or contexts, rather than on offerings. Even though this approach was developed over 40 years ago, it is still an important foundation for this topic.

According to the buyphase model, buyers make decisions rationally and sequentially, but this does not entirely match with practical experience. For example, such a long and complex process is not evident in every buying situation and differs according to the kinds of products and services bought, the experience and resources available to organizations, and the prevailing culture. In other words, there are many variables that can influence organizational buying behaviour.

Many of these concepts were developed in the pre-Internet era, and tend to concentrate on dyadic relationships, namely the interchange between buyers and sellers. In many cases this is still true and relevant. However, the development of e-commerce platforms and other digital marketplace exchanges, such as auction sites, introduces a third dimension which suggests

Table 16.4 The buygrid framework

Buyphases	Buyclasses		
	New task	Modified rebuy	Straight rebuy
Problem recognition	Yes	Possibly	No
General need description	Yes	Possibly	No
Product specification	Yes	Yes	Yes
Supplier search	Yes	Possibly	No
Supplier selection	Yes	Possibly	No
Order process specification	Yes	Possibly	No
Performance review	Yes	Yes	Yes

📖 Research Insight 16.4

To take your learning further, you might wish to read this influential paper.

Johnson, W.J. and Lewin, J.E. (1996). Organizational buying behavior: toward an integrative framework. *Journal of Business Research*, 35, 1–15.

Although written in 1996, this paper is important because it includes critical contributions by the leading researchers including the work of Robinson *et al.* (1967), Webster and Wind (1972), and Sheth (1973). It concludes by developing a model of buying behaviour drawing on a number of constructs developed since these three leading models were published.

@ Visit the **Online Resource Centre** to read the abstract and access the full paper.

---

that, in some circumstances, B2B relationships should be considered as a triadic relationship system (seller–platform–buyer). For Chakravarty *et al.* (2014), this means that in some e-commerce settings the platform firm should adopt a customer orientation towards both the seller and buyer firms that they seek to attract and maintain within a relationship.

Purchasing in Organizations

All organizations have to buy a variety of products and services in order to operate normally and achieve their performance targets. What we have set out so far are the general principles, types, and categories associated with organizational buying. However, the way in which organizations buy products and services varies considerably and does not always fit neatly with the categories presented here. For many organizations, professional purchasing is not only an important (if not critical) feature, but is also an integral part of their overall operations and strategic orientation (Ryals and Rogers, 2006; Pressey *et al.*, 2007).

In the past, an organization's purchasing activities could have been characterized as an 'order-delivery response function'. Purchasing departments signed orders and the right deliveries were made at the right place at the right time, and then invoiced correctly. The goal was to play off one supplier against another, and, as a result, reduce costs and improve short-term profits. Purchasing departments used to be regarded as an isolated function within organizations, a necessary but uninteresting aspect of organizational performance.

This perspective changed towards the end of the twentieth century. Now organizations reduce the number of their suppliers, sometimes to just one, and **strategic procurement** (as it is often termed) is used to negotiate with suppliers on a cooperative basis in order to help build long-term relationships. Purchasing has become an integral and strategic part of an organization's operations, and managing a smaller number of suppliers can improve performance considerably. For example, Senn *et al.* (2013: 27) report that Airbus reduced its supplier portfolio by 80%, from 3,000 to 500.

One of the main reasons for this changed approach was research that showed that business performance improves when organizations adopt a collaborative, rather than adversarial, approach to purchasing and account management (Swinder and Seshadri, 2001). Integral to this approach is the use of IT which, according to Rodríguez-Escobar and González-Benito (2015), is an instrument for streamlining and simplifying the way the purchasing task is undertaken. For example, IT can enhance the implementation of various purchasing practices that improve the quality, cost, flexibility, or reliability of supply. This in turn leads to an overall improvement in purchasing performance, which is of benefit to both supplier and buyer.

However, there are several other related issues that have changed the role of purchasing—namely customer sophistication, increasing competition, digital technology, branding, and various strategic issues.

Customer Sophistication

Owing to increasing customer sophistication, organizations are trying to differentiate their offerings and become more specialized. Organizational purchasing has to follow this movement and also become more specialized, otherwise the organization will become increasingly ineffective in meeting customer needs.

Increasing Competition

With increasing competition, margins have been eroded. As a result, more attention has been paid to internal costs and operations. By influencing purchasing costs and managerial costs associated with dealing with multiple suppliers, the profitability of the organization can be directly impacted. Consequently, the importance of purchasing polices, processes, and procedures within organizations has increased.

Digital Technology

The impact of digital technology has been felt across all functions within organizations. Digital marketing refers to the use of all kinds of digital tools, including social media, and encompasses various integrated elements, platforms, and tools that facilitate social interaction. In a B2B context these instruments allow companies to develop interaction and dialogue between businesses and customer networks with a view to securing stronger relationships, increased cooperation, and opportunities for co-creation.

Social media presents a major opportunity for the development of inter-organizational relationships. Research has shown that social media can be used at different stages in the sales process (Schultz et al., 2012). It can be used in the early stages of a customer relationship where awareness, lead building, and prospecting take place, and to maintain business relationships with established customers. Twitter and LinkedIn are used for referral requests to influence potential prospects.

However, the numbers of companies using social media is relatively small, and it is seldom used for business purposes by managers and senior managers (Keinänen and Kuivalainen, 2015). This might be because many senior managers do not use social media within a workplace setting as they do not see it bringing them benefits. It is also because a large number of B2B firms still use linear or one-directional communications, such as email marketing and newsletters (Järvinen et al., 2012). Since the publication of their paper, the use of social media has undoubtedly increased, but it may still be used primarily by younger salespeople who have migrated their personal skills into their work context, rather than having been specifically trained by organizations to use social media within their role (see Market Insight 16.3).

Branding

Despite the view that business brands are important assets that can enhance customer trust, branding remains a greatly under-utilized resource within business marketing. Lennartz *et al.* (2015) and Wiersema (2012) both acknowledge that branding has tremendous potential and is of growing importance within business markets. Indeed, the role of branding within this context appears to be gaining momentum at a time when digital marketing has gained a stronger presence. In a digital interactive environment the brand should be considered as the platform for all of a B2B company's actions. In addition, branding in industrial contexts provides a means of enabling the integration of different functions, an important requirement in B2B organizations (Sisko *et al.*, 2015). For more on branding within business markets see Chapter 13.

Strategic Issues

There are several strategic issues related to the purchasing activities undertaken by organizations. First, there is the 'make or buy' decision. Should organizations make and/or assemble products for resale, or outsource or buy in particular products, parts, services, or sub-assemblies and concentrate on what is referred to as core activities or competences? Second, the benefits that arise through closer cooperation with suppliers and the increasing influence of buyer–seller relationships and 'joint value creation' have inevitably led to a tighter, more professional, and integrated purchasing function. The third strategy-related issue concerns the degree to which the purchasing function is integrated into the organization. New IT systems have raised the level of possible integration of purchasing and operations to the extent that the competitive strength of the organization is enhanced (Hemsworth *et al.*, 2008). As if to highlight the variation in approaches to purchasing behaviour, Svahn and Westerlund (2009) identify six principal purchasing strategies used by organizations.

- The 'price minimizer' purchasing strategy refers to a buyer's efficiency orientation where the main purchasing goal is to seek the lowest price for the offering. To help achieve this, the buyer actively promotes competition among several potential suppliers.

- The 'bargainer' purchasing strategy focuses on a dyadic buyer–seller relationship. Here, the buyer's strategy is to achieve operational efficiency through long-term collaboration with a selected supplier (Håkansson and Snehota, 1995).

- The 'clockwiser' purchasing strategy refers to network relationships that function predictably and precisely, just as a clock works. Again, the goal is strict efficiency, achieved through the vigilant integration of production-based integrated control systems and IT, and the careful coordination of the value activities performed by each supply network partner (Glenn and Wheeler, 2004).

- The 'adaptator' purchasing strategy focuses on adapting the manufacturing processes between the exchange parties. This can arise during the purchase of one major product or service when the seller is required to accommodate its offering to the particular needs of the buyer.

- The 'projector' purchasing strategy occurs between buyers and sellers who are development partners. This can occur during projects when partners develop their offerings in close collaboration, after which the joint development project is completed and the parties continue the development work independently. As an example of this strategy, we could explore the collaboration between Nokia and Skype. These major players in the information and communication technology industry joined their development efforts in order to develop a radically novel type of mobile phone that utilizes the voice-over-Internet service (the free call system created by Skype).

- The 'updater' purchasing strategy is based on collaboration in research and development. Here, collaboration between partners is continuous and the nature of the relationship is not a dyad but a supply network. This collaboration is intentional, as demonstrated by Intel and various PC manufacturers who produce updated versions of personal computers due to constant co-development.

Customer Portfolio Matrix

Companies have an assortment of customers, many of which vary in terms of their values and contribution to the supplier. These customers constitute a portfolio and, although a large portfolio might sound attractive, many organizations have been actively seeking to reduce the numbers of their customers with the goal of increasing efficiency and profitability. For example, Senn *et al.* (2013: 27) refer to 'Tetra Pak, the Swedish–Swiss processing and packaging solutions company, earns roughly half of its revenues from a portfolio of 50 key customers'.

The six core strategies mentioned earlier reflect the complexity and the variety of purchasing activities undertaken by buying organizations. Most supplying organizations have a mixture of different types of customers or accounts. Each account varies in terms of frequency of purchase, types of products and services bought, prices paid, delivery cycles, time taken to pay, the level of support required, purchasing strategies, and many other factors. These variables are partly a reflection of the strength of the relationship between buyer and seller, and they impact on the profitability each account represents to the seller.

It makes sense, therefore, to categorize customers in order to determine their relative profitability. This, in turn, enables sellers to allocate resources to customers according to their potential to deliver profits in the future. One useful approach, called a **customer (or account) portfolio matrix**, brings together the potential attractiveness and the current strength of the relationship between seller and buyer (see Figure 16.3).

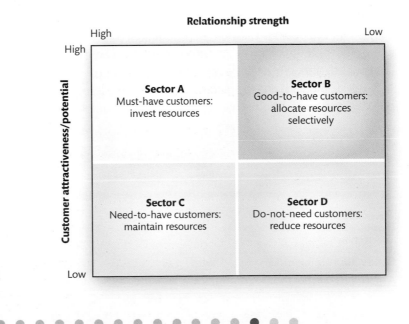

Figure 16.3
Customer portfolio matrix

The relationship dimension incorporates the strengths from a customer's perspective relative to competitors. For example, a strong relationship is indicative of two organizations working closely together, whereas a weak relationship suggests that they have little interest in each other. Customer attractiveness refers to total revenue spend, average rate of growth, and the opportunities a buyer represents to the seller in terms of profit potential. These calculations can be complicated and involve a measure of management judgement. For clarity, these scales are presented as high or low, strong or weak. However, they should be considered as a continuum and accounts can be positioned on the matrix not just in a sector but at a particular position within a sector. As a result strategies can be formulated to move accounts to different positions which, in turn, necessitate the use of different resources.

'Must-have customers' in sector A enjoy a close business relationship and are also attractive in terms of their profit potential. Many of these customers are assigned key account status (see next section in this chapter), but all represent investment opportunities and resources should be allocated to develop them all.

'Good-to-have customers' in sector B are essentially prospects because, although they are highly attractive, their relationship with the seller is currently weak. In this situation, marketing resources should be allocated on a selective basis that is proportional to the value that each prospect represents: high investment for good prospects and low for the others.

Relationships with customers in sector C are strong, but they do not offer strong potential. Therefore, these 'need-to-have customers' are important because they provide steady background business that is marginally profitable, so resources need to be maintained. Where it is identified that some of these customers are supported by a relatively large sales team, significant cost savings can be achieved relatively quickly. There is little reason to invest in the 'do-not-need customers' in sector D. Relationships with these customers are weak, and as they are relatively unattractive in terms of profit potential, many of these customers should be 'let go' and released to competitors. They represent a net drain on the selling organization. Therefore customers in this sector should receive little support and freed-up resources should be directed to customers in sectors A and B.

One of the benefits of developing a customer portfolio matrix is that it becomes easier to allocate sales channels to customers. Multichannel marketing decisions are important and should be rooted within the customer portfolio matrix. A range of channel strategies that relate to the channel needs of business customers and to any end-user target consumer segments can be identified (Payne and Frow, 2004). These can be considered to be part of a spectrum. At one end, channels can consist of a dedicated, personal key account manager (highly personalized sales channel), and at the other end the channel can be purely electronic with no personal contact at all. In the middle, there will be a range of different combinations of personal and electronic channels (see Figure 16.4).

In reality, most business customers will use a mixture of online and offline resources wherever possible and according to their specific needs. Therefore it is important for selling organizations

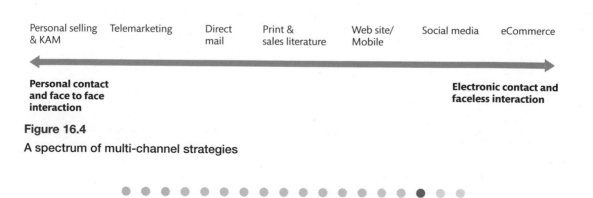

Figure 16.4

A spectrum of multi-channel strategies

to identify and allocate the most appropriate set of channels for their customers, based on the business potential each customer represents. These channels can be changed as the intensity of a customer relationship and their attractiveness develops over time.

Professional Services Marketing

Professional service firms (PSFs) can be distinguished as an independent type of organization. They provide services to all other organizations and can be found in many sectors including engineering, architecture, IT and software, and management consultancy and financial services companies such as PricewaterhouseCoopers (PwC), Deloitte, KPMG, and EY (formerly known as Ernst & Young). They offer extremely complex and customized services that are created and delivered by highly qualified personnel (Reid, 2008). PSFs possess an authority which is granted by the community in which they operate. For example, accounting firms delineate international accounting standards which in turn impact financial markets. They are governed by an ethical code and exhibit a professional culture (Thakor and Kumar, 2000).

According to Gummesson (1978), a professional service is provided by qualified people, is advisory, focuses on problem-solving, and is an assignment from the buyer to the seller. Typical services include management, accounting, law, engineering, surveying, and medicine, and are often referred to as 'knowledge engines for business' (Lorsch and Tierney, 2002: 14).

Greenwood *et al.* (2005: 661) define PSFs as 'those whose primary assets are a highly educated (professional) workforce and whose outputs are intangible services encoded with complex knowledge'. They use this understanding to identify two characteristic dependencies that serve to segregate PSFs from goods-producing organizations. The first concerns a client's dependency on the PSF due to the imbalance of information held by the two parties. The second concerns the dependency on its professional workforce and the high levels of mobility necessary to generate the PSF's output (see Market Insight 16.3).

An important question concerns what is it that characterizes a PSF. Greenwood *et al.* (2005) identify two core characteristics. The first is that the outputs of PSFs are intangible and are

Market Insight 16.3
KPMG Engages Through Social Media

KPMG is one of the world's largest professional services companies, and its High Growth Technology (HGT) Group was established to build strong and meaningful relationships with entrepreneurs and founders of tech start-ups. The goal was to become the 'go-to' professional services provider for the tech sector.

To raise awareness of the HGT Group among relevant companies, and to establish thought leadership and drive traffic, a mobile-optimized microsite and social media strategy, supported by an ongoing programme of content, was activated. It was important to ensure

that the HGT Group's social identity was separate from the corporate KPMG. To that end it was important to grow new follower communities.

New material, including video, blog posts, and infographics, was posted on a weekly basis, which in turn fed the social media strategy, all designed to encourage repeat visits and demonstrate the breadth and credibility of the HGT Group proposition.

Social media was a critical activity as the tech start-up community is active on social media and uses these

Market Insight 16.3
continued

channels to stay informed and connect with like-minded people and companies. Twitter was identified as the main social channel, supported by Instagram. A dedicated Twitter profile was set up for audience acquisition, direct posting, and fostering relationships with media, influencers, and the business community in and around Tech City.

Interestingly, KPMG's agency not only assumed the role of site editor responsible for the creation and

management of the site content, which included editorial, video, blog posts, and infographics, but they also ran social media training workshops for all KPMG HGT Group members. This helped them to get the most from their own use of Twitter and LinkedIn for networking, and to extend the reach of HGT Group content.

Sources: http://www.b2bmarketing.net; http://www.kpmgtechgrowth.co.uk; http://www.thecroc.com/case-study/tech-growth/.

Theory into Practice

KPMG aimed at becoming both a key influencer and valued partner to tech start-ups in this sector. The credentials for a successful influencer involve being credible, being trustworthy, and being seen to behave with integrity.

By linking up through social media KPMG seek to drive word-of-mouth communication and encourage the spread of positive comments about their services. Through time, both forms of dependency can be observed with KPMG. The first dependency concerns a start-up's dependency on KPMG because of the information the PSF holds. The second concerns a start-up's dependency on KPMG in terms of their professional workforce and mobility.

KPMG's attempt to build meaningful long-term relationships with start-ups can be best understood in terms of the ground-changing key mediating variables (KMV) model (Morgan and Hunt, 1994). They demonstrated that it is the presence of both commitment and trust that leads to cooperative behaviour, customer satisfaction, and ultimately successful relationship marketing. They argue that building a relationship based on trust and commitment leads to major benefits: the development of a set of shared values, reduced costs when the relationship finishes, and increased profitability as a greater number of end-user customers are retained because of the inherent value and satisfaction they experience.

Related Topics:
word-of-mouth communication; relationship trust; endorsement; opinion formers and leaders.

1 What value might potential clients perceive, through social media, of working with a large PSF such as KPMG?

2 To what extent do PSFs influence industry standards and regulations? When might there be an ethical issue with PSFs in this role?

3 Find two PSFs in the same industry, and consider their brand identities and their reputation. What are the differences and similarities?

normally applications of complex knowledge. This makes it difficult for customers to compare and evaluate the relative competence of suppliers, and it makes clients dependent on the professionals delivering these services.

The second defining characteristic concerns the engine of this knowledge. This is generated from a highly educated workforce—professionals who are qualified and skilled at customizing complex knowledge to different client situations. PSFs have to attract and retain qualified people who can develop close ties with each client.

These two core characteristics shape the marketing strategies of PSFs. To simplify the outputs into understandable units of information and so convince clients of its superior competence, PSFs strive to develop superior reputations. In order that the workforce continues to deliver complex knowledge and foster the relationships, it is necessary to attract and retain suitable professionals who possess high levels of mobility.

As Greenwood *et al.* (2005) acknowledge, here lies an interesting and self-fulfilling cycle of activities. The quest for suitable professionals is assisted by the development of corporate reputation, as the latter helps attract the best recruits. A strong reputation can lower marketing costs as clients seek out higher status firms (Podolny, 1994). A brand name that carries a high reputation facilitates the charging of premium fees (Krishnan and Schauer, 2000).

PSFs, especially the larger multinational consultancies, invariably adopt relational marketing strategies designed to retain rather than acquire clients. According to Reid (2008), their marketing activities are then geared to generating a financial return and building a business network. However, it is the quality of the client relationship that is critical. This can be both formal (e.g. project briefings) and informal (e.g. social). This in turn requires a range of technical and interpersonal skills, and for the organization to have a clear brand vision and identity, which is internalized by the professional workforce.

For PSFs, the key to successful marketing is the development of a strong reputation, and this involves the creation and maintenance of a corporate brand. Marquardt *et al.* (2011) have developed a service brand process model (see Figure 16.5). This is useful because it identifies three brand management components. The first is the need to develop a compelling brand value proposition, or promise. The second is the use of internal and external communications to inform

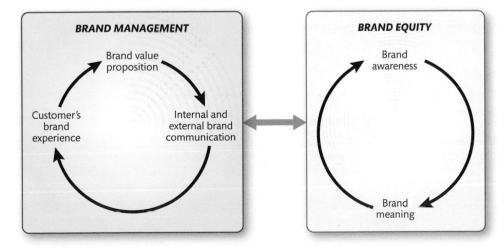

Figure 16.5

B2B service brand process

Source: Marquardt *et al.* (2011).

and influence stakeholders, particularly clients, about the brand. The third and final component concerns customers' experiences with the brand and the realization of the brand promise. These are directly affected by interactions with the professional workforce (Berry, 2000). Indeed, there is general agreement that the development of a strong corporate reputation has to be founded on a workforce that embodies and identifies with the mission and values of the organization (Roper and Davies, 2010). The issue of customer experience is examined in Chapter 15. Collectively, these managerial components impact on the development of brand equity, which Marquardt *et al.* (2011) see as a composite of brand awareness and brand meaning.

Corporate Social Responsibility

Organizations communicate with one another through application of a **corporate communication mix**. The mix provides a series of cues through which stakeholders develop impressions about an organization. It can be considered to be composed of five main elements. These are symbolic, management, marketing, organizational, and behavioural communications (see Table 16.5).

Through the use of the different elements of corporate communication, organizations seek to build strategies that differentiate the firm. Berry (2000: 131) argues that there is 'a conscious effort to be different, a conscious effort to carve out a distinct brand personality'. He also argues that organizations need to represent something that is important to their customers. In the PSF

Table 16.5 The corporate communication mix

Form of corporate communication	Explanation
Symbolic	Communications concerning the visual aspects of an organization. These encompass names, letterheads, logos, signage, emblems, colour schemes, architecture, and the overall appearance of all the design aspects associated with the company.
Management	Communications by managers who have a responsibility for the deployment of resources. These communications may be directed at internal or external audiences.
Marketing	Communications designed to engage customer-oriented audiences with regard to the promotion of an organization's products and services.
Organizational	Communications aimed at a range of stakeholders, not just customers, that are designed to build identification, commitment, and relationships with an organization, and are not sales oriented.
Behavioural	Communications that emanate from the interactions, decisions, tone of voice, and overall empathy between employees and with others outside the organization.

Source: Fill (2013). Based on Birkigt and Stadler (1986) *and* van Riel and Fombrun (2007). Reprinted with the kind permission of Pearson Education.

sector this is represented by superior knowledge, the one critical element that clients want to be associated with and use to compare propositions.

An important use of the mix is the development of corporate social responsibility (CSR), which is considered to be of strategic importance for organizations (Homburg et al., 2013). A key aim of CSR, according to Bhattacharya et al. (2009), is the creation of mutually beneficial relationships with stakeholders over the long term.

Homburg and his colleagues identify two facets of CSR. The first is 'business practice CSR' targeted at the primary stakeholders. These are normally regarded as employees and customers who are involved with a firm's core business operations and with whom there is market exchange. The second facet concerns 'philanthropic CSR' which is targeted at secondary stakeholders, those external to a firm's core business operations. These are essentially community and non-profit organizations, and the goal is to stimulate philanthropic engagement.

Research by Homburg et al. (2013) found that business practice CSR can increase trust in a supplier and philanthropic CSR can improve customer–company identification. Part of their conclusion was that managers should be proactive in their use of CSR issues in their business strategy, that they should engage in CSR continually, and that they should communicate their CSR efforts transparently.

Key Account Management (KAM)

It is common knowledge that not all customers represent the same potential and profitability. However, it is quite common for a small number of customers to contribute a disproportion-ately large part of an organization's income and profitability. As a result, these customers often become essential to the firm's survival, so it is not surprising that, as Sharma and Evanschitzky (2016: 3) report, 'key accounts receive special treatment, with directed additional resources, compared with other sales accounts'.

The term **'key accounts'** has become the established term to refer to those customers who are considered to be strategically important. A key account might offer the supply-side company opportunities to learn about new markets or types of customers. It might provide access to new and valuable resources, offer involvement with other key organizations, or just be symbolically valuable in terms of influence, power, and stature. Size alone is not sufficient for key account status.

The underlying principle of relationship marketing in business markets requires that the focus should shift from short-term transactional exchanges to longer-term and collaborative relation-ships. The fundamental purpose of KAM is to create strategic alliances with key accounts through the development of long-term relationships (Tzempelikosa and Gounaris, 2013). Establishing key accounts and the supporting infrastructure represents a significant investment for organiza-tions and an opportunity cost.

Visit the Online Resource Centre and complete Internet Activity 16.3 to learn more about the use of **sales force automation** (SFA) applications to aid the management of key client accounts.

So, why have so many organizations established and formalized their key account strategies? There are many reasons, some particular to each organization; however, the main ones relate to changes in the competitive environment and in industry structure.

Changes in the Competitive Environment

In an increasingly complex and competitive environment, where product lifecycles appear to be getting shorter and differentiation difficult to sustain, the need to find new ways of enhancing business performance has intensified. One of the ways in which this can be achieved is to provide a range of services that are tailored to the needs of each customer.

Many types of service can be customized, for example customized training, advantageous financial arrangements, extranets, customer-driven delivery routes and timings, product support, and advice facilities. However, it is through the provision of added-value services that relationships are often developed and maintained. Establishing key accounts is a natural extension of providing particular services for key customers. Not only does this enhance the profile of these customers, both internally and externally, but it also helps to focus resources on particular customers and their individual needs.

Changes in Industry Structure

Many organizations have centralized their purchasing activities, a move driven by two main factors. First, the amount of industry consolidation, a process by which a few organizations grow larger by merging or acquiring their competitors so that the industry is concentrated around a small number of large organizations. Industry consolidation has increased substantially in recent years. Second, in industries where consolidation has not been significant, many organizations have moved towards centralizing their purchasing departments, processes, and functions as a means of achieving cost savings, improving effectiveness and efficiencies, and, in doing so, improving profits. ABB Sweden is a global corporation operating in a variety of industry segments, including power generation, pulp and paper, water, and chemicals. Brehmer and Rehme (2009) evaluate the way in which ABB Sweden used three different approaches to key account programmes, recognizing sales opportunities, customer demands, and a need to be more customer-focused.

The result of both of these actions is that there are a smaller number of purchasing units responsible for a larger proportion of business. For business marketers and suppliers generally, these trends towards industrial concentration and purchasing centralization mean that competition is increased and marketing strategies need to be much more customer-specific. Key account programmes are used with the deliberate intention of building relationships, often achieved by influencing levels of trust and commitment in order to generate more business.

However, in relationships between manufacturers and retailers (e.g. the grocery business), the presence of a key account relationship does not appear to have any significant benefit on the amount of resources allocated to the supplier's products (Verbeke *et al.*, 2006).

Key Account Relationship Cycles

Key accounts do not just appear and flourish; they are the result of careful management, nurturing, and time. Key accounts represent a particular strength of relationship and, as with good wine, need time to develop to reach full potential. Consequently, each key account will, at any one moment in time, be at a particular stage of relationship development (Millman and Wilson,

Table 16.6 Key account management development stages	
Development stages within a cycle	**Explanation**
Exploratory	Suppliers identify and isolate those customer accounts that have key account potential.
Basic	In this transactional period exchanges are used by both parties to test each other as potential long-term partners.
Cooperative	An increasing number of people from both parties become involved in the relationship.
Interdependent	Mutual recognition of each other's importance. Very often single-supplier status is conferred.
Integrated	Both parties share sensitive information and undertake joint problem-solving. The relationship is regarded as a single entity.
Disintegrated	The termination or readjustment of the relationship can occur at any time.

1995). Key accounts can be plotted through various stages of a **KAM development cycle**. One such cycle is shown in Table 16.6. The time between stages is not fixed and varies according to the nature and circumstances of the parties involved. The stages can be negotiated quickly in some cases, or negotiations may become protracted. The titles of each of the stages reflect the relationship status of both parties rather than of the selling company (e.g. prospective) or buying company (e.g. preferred supplier).

Managing Key Accounts

Key account managers provide the main link between their employer and their key account customers. They provide a route through which information flows, preferably in both directions. They must be capable of dealing with organizations where buying decisions can be both protracted and delayed (Sharma, 1997), and quick and demanding. However, key account managers do not operate alone and are not the sole point of contact between organizations. Normally, there are a number of levels of interaction between the two organizations, to the extent that there could be 'an entire team dedicated to providing services and support to the key account' (Ojasalo, 2001: 109). Therefore key account managers assume responsibility for all points of contact within the customer organization.

The value that a customer derives from a particular offering will have a significant influence on the level of attention given by the buyer to the supplier's programme. Furthermore, the level to which an organization uses centralized buying procedures will also impact on the effectiveness of a KAM programme. Unsurprisingly, key account sales behaviours cannot be the same as those used in field sales roles. So, as the majority of key account managers are

Market Insight 16.4
Marketing the Big League

The sports industry within which leagues and teams participate is characterized by multiple primary B2B relationships. These occur between the teams and their owners, those who own the league, corporate sponsors, various media groups, and any governing bodies. In addition, there are the business-to-consumer relationships that teams have with their supporters.

In February 2015 the English Premier League governing body awarded the live television broadcast rights for 168 matches, across three football seasons, ending in 2019, to two main media groups, Sky and BT Sport. The sale of these rights raised £5.136bn, to be distributed among the Premier League clubs and also used to support grassroots football.

The sale of broadcast rights is one of several transactions that participant teams benefit from being a member of a league. Indeed, sports leagues such as football's Premier League create value that teams acting individually would not be able to generate. This is because sport leagues drive team cooperation in order to make the league attractive to its various stakeholders. This causes teams to be mutually dependent on each other, yet at the same time they have to be competitive in order to win the league. Team supporters and sports fans, however, have a widening choice of entertainment options, which means that leagues now compete in a broader entertainment market.

The sale of live television broadcast rights by the English Premier League drives substantial income for football clubs.
Source: © Krivosheev Vitaly/Shutterstock.

Professional sports leagues can operate across local, national, and international markets, and the sale of game broadcast rights is a key league activity. At an individual team level, the sale of admissions and concessions at home games, stadium leasing and naming rights, shirt sponsorship, and ancillary merchandise and event sales constitute critical revenue generators. These activities, plus those necessary to sustain a team's operations, all involve a wide range of organizations.

Sources: Mason (1999); Benijts *et al.* (2011); de Menezes (2015).

Theory into Practice

The teams in a league constitute an interactive network, which can be considered using network theory. Participants strive to add value for the league and in doing so create multiple B2B relationships. The Premier League can be interpreted as a marketing channel network. This is a type of marketing channel structure characterized by the performance of the teams and their relationships with intermediaries, in this case the various organizers, such as sponsors and the media, and a focal organization, the league or the sport's governing body.

The interaction and relationships that develop among these teams and in the name of a league enable stability, strong relationships, value creation, and the facilitation of B2B marketing.

Market Insight 16.4
continued

Related Topics:

B2B marketing; transaction and collaborative exchanges; business relationships; channel design and structure; value creation.

1 Think of a sports industry with which you are familiar and make a list of the different stakeholders and the relationships that might exist within it.

2 Identify the ways individual sports teams can create value that benefits their league.

3 How might changes in the environment impact the relationships within sports leagues?

drawn internally from the sales force (Hannah, 1998; cited by Abratt and Kelly, 2002), it is necessary to ensure that they have the correct skills mix or are trained appropriately. Abratt and Kelly (2002) found six factors that were of particular importance when establishing a KAM programme. These were the 'suitability of the key account manager, knowledge and understanding of the key account customer's business, commitment to the KAM partnership, delivering value, the importance of trust and the proper implementation and understanding of the KAM concept'.

In addition to the interpersonal relationships that exist between the customer's contact person and the supplier's key account manager, there are also inter-organizational relationships that may concern system and policy issues. These will vary in strength and some may not be compatible with the tasks facing the key account manager.

Research Insight 16.5

To take your learning further, you might wish to read this influential paper.

Speakman, J.I.F. and Ryals, L. (2012). Key account management: the inside selling job. *Journal of Business & Industrial Marketing*, 27(5), 360–9.

Written by two highly reputable authors, this paper investigates the various roles undertaken by key account managers. In particular, the research shows that key account managers are able to adapt and use a combination of management behaviours, and that these are modified during periods of conflict.

@ Visit the **Online Resource Centre** to read the abstract and access the full paper.

Chapter Summary

To consolidate your learning, the key points from this chapter are summarized here.

■ **Explain the main characteristics of business markets and understand the different types of organizational customer.**

Business markets are characterized by four main factors: the nature of demand, the buying processes, international dimensions, and the relationships that develop between organizations. A range of organizations make up business markets and these are classified as commercial, government, and institutional. These organizations buy products and services to make goods for resale to their customers, but they also consume items that are required to keep their offices and manufacturing units functioning.

■ **Describe the different types of offering that are bought and sold in business markets.**

Products and services bought and sold through business markets are categorized as input goods, equipment goods, and supply goods.

■ **Set out the main processes and stages associated with organizational buying and purchasing.**

Organizational buying behaviour can be understood as a group buying activity in which a number of people with differing roles make purchasing decisions that affect the organization and the achievement of its objectives. Buying decisions can be understood in terms of different types of decisions (buyclasses) and different stages (buyphases).

■ **Explain what business-to-business marketing is and the marketing issues associated with professional service firms.**

B2B marketing is concerned with the identification and satisfaction of business customers' needs. This requires that all stakeholders benefit from the business relationship and associated transactions. Customers derive satisfaction by purchasing offerings that are perceived to provide them and/or their organizations with particular value. Professional service firms focus on developing their reputation as the main means of differentiation.

■ **Understand the principles of key account management.**

Some suppliers refer to some of their strategically important customers as key accounts. Relationships with these customers move through various stages called key account management development cycles. Each stage is marked by particular characteristics, and part of the role of the key account manager is to ensure that all contact between the supplier and the customer builds on strengthening the inter-organizational relationship.

Review Questions

1 In note format and in your own words set out the essential purpose of B2B marketing.
2 What are the key characteristics associated with B2B markets?
3 What are the different types of organizations that make up the business market?
4 Name four of the different types of people that make up a DMU.
5 Distinguish clearly between buyphases and buyclasses.
6 What is the customer portfolio matrix?
7 How are key accounts different from house or major accounts?
8 What are the different phases associated with key account development cycles?

9   How might social media be of help to professional service firms?

10   What are the main characteristics of the B2B marketing mix?

Worksheet Summary

@ To apply the knowledge you have gained from this chapter and test your understanding of B2B marketing, visit the **Online Resource Centre** and complete Worksheet 16.1.

Discussion Questions

1   Having read Case Insight 16.1 what market entry approach and methods do you believe Oxford Instruments should use to enter India in order to build mutually profitable business relationships?

2   Discuss the main characteristics of business marketing and consider whether there is really any major difference when compared with consumer marketing.

3   AstraVera Ltd has been developing a conveyor belt designed to meet new government-driven hygiene standards. The problem in many manufacturing, packaging and assembly plants is that floors underneath conveyor belts can become wet and hence present a danger to people working around the equipment. The new belt has a trough incorporated into it, which runs along its entire length. Spillages feed into the trough where collection sumps and filters remove the excess liquids before they overflow to the floor (developed from Spear, 2006). Make brief notes advising AstraVera's marketing manager about marketing the new conveyor.

4   Working in small groups, select three B2B organizations and identify the main influences on their marketing activities. To what extent is it possible to prioritize these influences and does it matter?

5   Using PowerPoint, prepare a short presentation in which you explain the meaning of buyclasses, buyphases, and buygrids.

@ Visit the **Online Resource Centre** and complete the Multiple Choice Questions to assess your knowledge of Chapter 16.

Glossary

business-to-business marketing the marketing of products and services that are bought and sold between organizations.

buyclasses the different types of buying situations faced by organizations.

buyers also known as purchasing managers, buyers select suppliers and manage the process whereby the required products are procured.

buying centre see decision-making unit.

buyphases the series of sequential activities or stages through which organizations proceed when making purchasing decisions.

consumer marketing the marketing of products and services that are bought by consumers.

corporate communication mix the particular configuration of the symbolic, management, marketing, organizational, and behavioural elements of communication.

customer (or account) portfolio matrix a 2 × 2 grid that is used to reflect the strength of the relationships between a buyer and seller, and the profitability each account represents to the seller.

deciders people who make organizational purchasing decisions; they are often very difficult to identify.

decision-making unit a group of people who make purchasing decisions on behalf of an organization.

embedded ties strong, close and, mutually rewarding relationships between firms.

gatekeepers people who control the type and flow of information into an organization, in particular to members of the DMU.

influencers people who help set the technical specifications for a proposed purchase and assist the evaluation of alternative offerings by potential suppliers.

initiators people who start the organizational buying decision process.

key account a business customer who is strategically significant and with whom a supplier wishes to build a long-lasting relationship.

KAM development cycle the development stages experienced by organizations as relationships with key account customers develop.

modified rebuy the organizational processes associated with the infrequent purchase of products and services.

new task the organizational processes associated with buying a product or service for the first time.

organizational buyer behaviour the characteristics, issues, and processes associated with the behaviour of producers, resellers, government units, and institutions when purchasing goods and services.

perceived value the 'net satisfaction' derived from consuming and using a product, not just the costs involved in obtaining it.

professional service firms organizations that deliver highly complex and customized services, created and delivered by highly qualified personnel

promise management the process of enabling promises to be made to/with customers, making promises to them, and keeping promises by meeting the expectations that have been created by promises.

sales force automation occurs when firms computerize routine tasks or adopt technological tools to improve the efficiency or precision of sales force activities.

straight rebuy the organizational processes associated with the routine reordering of good and services, often undertaken from an approved list of suppliers.

strategic procurement an approach used to negotiate with suppliers on a cooperative basis in order to help build long-term relationships.

users people or groups who use business products and services once they have been acquired and who then evaluate their performance.

References

Abratt, R. and Kelly, P.M. (2002). Perceptions of a successful key account management program. *Industrial Marketing Management*, 31(5), 467–76.

Achrol, R.S. (1997). Changes in the theory of interorganizational relations in marketing: toward a network paradigm. *Journal of the Academy of Marketing Science*, 25(1), 56–71.

Benijts, T., Lagae, W., and Vanclooster, B. (2011). The influence of sport leagues on the business-to-business marketing of teams: the case of professional road cycling. *Journal of Business & Industrial Marketing*, 26(8), 602–13.

Berry, L.L. (2000). Cultivating service brand equity. *Journal of the Academy of Marketing Science*, 28(Winter), 128–37.

Bhattacharya, C.B., Korschun, D., and Sen, S. (2009) Strengthening stakeholder-company relationships through mutually beneficial corporate social responsibility initiatives. *Journal of Business Ethics*, 85(2), 257–72.

Birkigt, K. and Stadler, M.M. (1986). *Corporate Identity, Grundlagen, Funktionen, Fallspielen.* Landsberg am Lech: Verlag Moderne Industrie.

Bonoma, T.V. (1982). Major sales. Who really does the buying? *Harvard Business Review*, 60(3), 111–18.

Brehmer, P-O. and Rehme, J. (2009). Proactive and reactive: drivers for key account management programmes. *European Journal of Marketing*, 43(7/8), 961–84.

Chakravarty, A., Kumar, A., and Grewal, R. (2014) Customer orientation structure for internet-based business-to-business platform firms. *Journal of Marketing*, 78(September), 1–23

de Menezes, J. (2015). Premier League broadcast rights set to be sold for record £4.4bn deal as clubs continue to reap the financial rewards of the top flight. *The Independent*, 10 February. Retrieved from: http://www.independent.co.uk/sport/football/news-and-comment/premier-league-broadcast-rights-set-to-be-sold-for-record-44bn-deal-as-clubs-continue-to-reap-the-financial-rewards-of-the-top-flight-10035695.html (accessed 15 July 2015)

Durham, J. and Ritchey, T. (2009). Leaning forward; removing design inefficiencies and improving quality, 1 July. Retrieve from: http://www.hfmmagazine.com (accessed 5 October 2009).

Fill, C. (2013). *Marketing Communications: Brands, Experiences and Participation* (6th edn). Harlow: FT/Prentice Hall.

Fill, C. and McKee, S. (2012). *Business Marketing*. Oxford: Goodfellow.

Fill, C. and Turnbull, S. (2016). *Marketing Communications: Discovery, Creation, and Conversations* (7th edn). Harlow: FT/Prentice Hall.

Glenn, R.R. and Wheeler, A.R. (2004). A new framework for supply chain manager selection: three hurdles to competitive advantage. *Journal of Marketing Channels*, 11(4), 89–103.

Greenwood, R., Li, S.X., Prakash, R., and Deephouse D.L. (2005) Reputation, diversification, and organizational explanations of performance in professional service firms. *Organization Science*, 16(6), 661–73.

Grönroos, C. (2009). Marketing as promise management: regaining customer management for marketing. *Journal of Business & Industrial Marketing*, 24(5/6), 351–9.

Gummesson, E. (1978). Towards a theory of professional services marketing. *Industrial Marketing Management*, 7(2), 89–95.

Gummesson, E. and Polese, F. (2009). B2B is not an island! *Journal of Business & Industrial Marketing*, 24(5/6), 337–50.

Ha, B-C., and Nam, H. (2016). Ethical judgments in supply chain management: a scenario analysis. *Journal of Business & Industrial Marketing*, 31(1), 59–69.

Håkansson, H. and Snehota, I. (1995) *Developing Relationships in Business Networks*. London: Routledge.

Hannah, G. (1998). From transactions to relationships: challenges for the national account manager. *Journal of Marketing and Sales*, 4(1), 30–3.

Hemsworth, D., Sánchez-Rodríguez, C., and Bidgood, B. (2008). *Total Quality Management & Business Excellence*, 19(1/2), 151–64.

Hollyoake, M. (2009). The four pillars: developing a bonded business-to-business customer experience. *Database Marketing & Customer Strategy Management*, 16(2), 132–58.

Homburg, C., Stierl, M., and Bornemann, T. (2013). Corporate social responsibility in business-to-business markets: how organizational customers account for supplier corporate social responsibility engagement. *Journal of Marketing*, 77(November), 54–72.

Homburg, C., Wilczek, H., and Hahn, A. (2014). Looking beyond the horizon: how to approach the customers' customers in business-to-business markets. *Journal of Marketing*, 78 (September), 58–77.

Jackson, B. (1985). Build customer relationships that last. *Harvard Business Review*, 63(6), 120–8.

Järvinen, J., Tolänen, A., Karjaluoto, H., and Jayawardhena, C. (2012). Digital and social media marketing usage in B2B industrial section. *Marketing Management Journal*, 22(2), 102–17.

Johnson, W.J. and Lewin, J.E. (1996). Organizational buying behavior: toward an integrative framework. *Journal of Business Research*, 35, 1–15.

Keinänen, H. and Kuivalainen, O. (2015). Antecedents of social media B2B use in industrial marketing context: customers' view. *Journal of Business & Industrial Marketing*, 30(6), 711–22.

Koh, T.K. and Fichman, M. (2014). Multihoming users' preferences for two-sided exchange networks. *MIS Quarterly*, 38(4), 977–96.

Krishnan, J. and Schauer, P.C. (2000) The differentiation of quality among auditors: evidence from the not-for-profit sector. *Auditing*, 19(2), 9–25

Leigh, T.W. and Marshall, G.W. (2001). Research priorities in sales strategy and performance. *Journal of Personal Selling and Sales Management*, 21(2), 83–93.

Lennartz, E., Fischer, M., Krafft, M., and Peters, K. (2015). Drivers of B2B brand strength—insights from an international study across industries. *Schmalenbach Business Review*, 67(1), 114–37.

Lorsch, J.W. and Tierney, T.J. (2002). *Aligning the Stars*. Boston, MA: Harvard Business School Press.

Macfarlane, P. (2002). Structuring and measuring the size of business markets. *International Journal of Market Research*, 44(1), 7–31.

Marquardt, A.J., Golicic, S.L., and Davis, D.F. (2011). B2B services branding in the logistics services industry. *Journal of Services Marketing*, 25(1), 47–57.

Mason, D.S. (1999). What is the sports product and who buys it? The marketing of professional sports leagues. *European Journal of Marketing*, 33(3/4), 402–18.

Millman, T., and Wilson, K. (1995). From key account selling to key account management. *Journal of Marketing Practice: Applied Marketing Science*, 1(1), 9–21.

Morgan, R.M. and Hunt, S.D. (1994). The commitment–trust theory of relationship marketing. *Journal of Marketing*, 58(July), 20–38.

Noordhoff, C.S., Kyriakopoulos, K., Moorman, C., Pauwels, P., and Dellaert, B.G.C. (2011). The bright side and dark side of embedded ties in business-to-business innovation. *Journal of Marketing*, 75(September), 34–52.

Ojasalo, J. (2001). Key account management at company and individual levels in business-to-business relationships. *Journal of Business and Industrial Marketing*, 16(3), 199–220.

Parkinson, S.T. and Baker, M.J. (1994). *Organizational Buying Behaviour: Purchasing and Marketing Management Implications*. London: Macmillan.

Payne, A., and Frow, P. (2004). The role of multi-channel integration in customer relationship management. *Industrial Marketing Management*, 33, 527–38.

Plummer, R. (2014). Gandys flip flops: footwear with soul. *BBC Business*, 15 June. Retrieve from: http://www.bbc.co.uk/news/business-27638426 (accessed 22 January 2016).

Podolny, J.M. (1994). Market uncertainty and the social character of economic exchange. *Administrative Science Quarterly,* 39(33), 458–83.

Pressey, A., Tzokas, N., and Winklhofer, H. (2007). Strategic purchasing and the evaluation of 'problem' key supply relationships. What do key suppliers need to know? *Journal of Business & Industrial Marketing*, 22(5), 282–94.

Reagans, R. and McEvily, B. (2003). Network structure and knowledge transfer: the effects of cohesion and range. *Administrative Science Quarterly*, 48(2), 240–67.

Reid, M. (2008). Contemporary marketing in professional services. *Journal of Services Marketing*, 22(5), 374–84.

Robinson, P.J., Faris, C.W., and Wind, Y. (1967). *Industrial Buying and Creative Marketing*, Boston, MA: Allyn & Bacon.

Rocco, R.A. and Bush, A.J. (2016). Exploring buyer–seller dyadic perceptions of technology and relationships: implications for Sales 2.0. *Journal of Research in Interactive Marketing*, 10(1), 1–22.

Rodríguez-Escobar, J.A. and González-Benito, J. (2015). The role of information technology in purchasing function. *Journal of Business & Industrial Marketing*, 30(5), 498–510.

Roper, S. and Davies, G. (2010). Business to business branding: external and internal satisfiers and the role of training quality. *European Journal of Marketing*, 44(5), 567–90.

Ryals, L.J. and Rogers, B. (2006). Holding up the mirror: the impact of strategic procurement practices on account management. *Business Horizons*, 49, 41–50.

Seager, C. (2014). Five minutes with ¼ Gandys flip flops' co-founders, Rob and Paul. *The Guardian*, 9 January. Retrieve from: http://www.theguardian.com/social-enterprise-network/2014/jan/09/gandys-flip-flops-orphans-for-orphans-social-enterprise (accessed 23 January 2016).

Senn, C., Thoma, A., and Yip, G.S. (2013). Customer-centric leadership: how to manage strategic customers as assets in B2B markets. *California Management Review*, 55(3), 27–59.

Schreiner, A. (2015). Triadic analysis of business relationships ending: a case study of a dyad and a third actor. *Journal of Business & Industrial Marketing*, 30(8), 891–905.

Schultz, R., Shwepker, C.H., and Good, D.J. (2012). An exploratory study of social media in business-to-business selling: salesperson characteristics, activities and performance. *Marketing Management Journal*, 22(2), 76–89.

Sharma, A. (1997). Who prefers key account management program? An investigation of business buying behaviour and buying firm characteristics. *Journal of Personal Selling and Sales Management*, 17(4), 27–39.

Sharma, A. and Evanschitzky, H. (2016). Returns on key accounts. Do the results justify the expenditures? *Journal of Business & Industrial Marketing*, 31(2), 174–82.

Sheth, J.N. (1973). A model of industrial buyer behavior. *Journal of Marketing*, 37(October), 50–6.

Sisko, H., Lipiäinen, M., and Karjaluoto, H. (2015) Industrial branding in the digital age. *Journal of Business & Industrial Marketing*, 30(6), 733–41.

Speakman, J.I.F. and Ryals, L. (2012). Key account management: the inside selling job. *Journal of Business & Industrial Marketing*, 27(5), 360–9.

Spear, M. (2006). Smooth movers. Retrieve from www.foodmanufacture.co.uk/news/fullstory.php/aid/3445/Smooth_movers.html (accessed 22 January 2016).

Spekman, R.E. and Gronhaug, K. (1986). Conceptual and methodological issues in buying centre research. *European Journal of Marketing*, 20(7), 50–63.

Storbacka, K., Ryals, L., Davies, I.A., and Nenonen, S. (2009). The changing role of sales: viewing sales as a strategic, cross-functional process. *European Journal of Marketing*, 43(7/8), 890–906.

Svahn, S. and Westerlund, M. (2009). Purchasing strategies in supply relationships. *Journal of Business & Industrial Marketing*, 24(3/4), 173–81.

Swinder, J. and Seshadri, S. (2001). The influence of purchasing strategies on performance. *Journal of Business and Industrial Marketing*, 16(4), 294–306.

Thakor, M.V. and Kumar, A. (2000). What is a professional service? A conceptual review and bi-national investigation. *Journal of Services Marketing*, 14(1), 63–82.

Tzempelikosa, N. and Gounaris, S. (2013). Approaching key account management from a long-term perspective. *Journal of Strategic Marketing*, 21(2), 179–98.

Ulkuniemi, P. (2003). Purchasing software components at the dawn of market. Retrieve from http://herkules.oulu.fi/isbn9514272188/ (accessed 14 October 2016).

van Riel, C.B.M. and Fombrun, C.J. (2007). *Essentials of Corporate Communication*. London: Routledge

van Weele, A.J. (2002). *Purchasing and Supply Chain Management* (3rd edn). London: Thomson.

Vargo, S.L. and Lusch, R.F. (2004). Evolving to a new dominant logic for marketing. *Journal of Marketing*, 68(1), 1–17.

Verbeke, W., Bagozzi, R.P., and Farris, P. (2006). The role of key account programs, trust, and brand strength

on resource allocation in the channel of distribution. *European Journal of Marketing*, 40(5/6), 520–32.

Webster, F.E., and Wind, Y. (1972) *Organizational Buying Behaviour*. Englewood Cliffs, NJ: Prentice Hall.

Wiersema, F. (2012) *The B2B Agenda: The Current State of B2B Marketing and a Look Ahead*. University Park, PA: Institute for the Study of Business Markets.

Part Five

The Social Impacts of Marketing

Chapter 17
Not-For-Profit and Social Marketing

Learning Outcomes

After studying this chapter, you will be able to:

▶ List some key characteristics of not-for-profit organizations

▶ Explain why not-for-profit organizations do not always value their customers

▶ Analyse stakeholders and develop appropriate engagement strategies

▶ Describe and assess cause-related marketing campaigns

▶ Understand how marketing is used in social and political marketing campaigns

Case Insight 17.1
City of London Police

Market Insight 17.1
From Dinners to Ice Buckets

Market Insight 17.2
Kellogg's: The Serial Giver

Market Insight 17.3
Licensing: For a Princely Sum

Market Insight 17.4
Shell Develops Room to Breathe

Market Insight 17.5
No Means No! Get It!

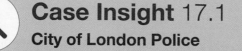

Case Insight 17.1
City of London Police

Founded in 1839, the City of London Police (CoLP) police London's 'Square Mile' financial district, with a national responsibility for fraud and economic crime. Because they also police many high profile public events, they also focus on the prevention of terrorism and crime. We speak to Superintendent Helen Isaac to find out how social marketing is used to support law enforcement.

The force's core mission statement is 'to uphold the law fairly and firmly; preventing crime and anti-social behaviour; keeping the peace; protecting and reassuring the community; investigating crime and bringing offenders to justice.' No other place has the unique blend of tourism, range of businesses, and resident population that the City of London enjoys, where all this diversity is condensed into 1.6km². Our community comprises the 9,000 residents of the City, the 300,000 who travel into the City to work every day, and businesses large and small, in addition to the many famous multinational financial corporations. We also serve the Corporation of London, our local authority (and police authority) for the Square Mile. The Home Office provides us with our 'core grant' and other funding streams for specialist responsibilities, and a number of trade bodies provide extra funding.

The City is a global powerhouse attracting hordes of tourists because of the many iconic locations within the Square Mile. Any act of terrorism here would have a potentially highly damaging impact on the UK economy and on the confidence of our community to keep them safe. To counter this threat, the City introduced the 'ring of steel'—a security and surveillance cordon—in the mid-1990s, following the bombings of Bishopsgate and St Mary Axe by the Provisional Irish Republican Army (IRA), both of which caused severe disruption and damage in the City and resulted in death and injury. This security measure was designed to deter large vehicle borne devices being brought into the City (the main terrorist threat identified), but since the 7/7 bombings the terrorist threat has changed.

One key element of policing is communication with local communities and other stakeholders. Although we use many of the same communication channels that a brand would, our campaigns are rooted in providing a service to the public, not selling. We exist to keep people safe and we measure ourselves accordingly. Our measures of success focus around social considerations including public perceptions of safety and confidence in the CoLP to keep the public safe.

The general public can sometimes see policing as reactive, with police responding after a crime has been committed. But we designed Project Servator as a proactive strategic approach to policing, incorporating unpredictable and highly visible CoLP deployments, involving a wide range of assets including specially trained officers, supported and amplified by community engagement, and media and public relations to help disrupt hostile reconnaissance and wider criminality whilst reassuring and engaging the public. Servator is principally a counter-terrorism operation, but its wider intention is to impress upon terrorists and other criminals that the City's police presence is unpredictable, while simultaneously reassuring the general public around public safety fears. Project Servator is about working with the public as partners in being vigilant and reporting suspicious activity. Our partnership with the community is crucial; they are our eyes and ears.

Given the dual target audience for our communication, we had a seemingly impossible task.

How should we design a social marketing campaign (including message and media mix) which deters terrorists and criminals more generally, but simultaneously reassures the general public and encourages them to report suspicious activity?

Introduction

Over the last 40 years, the role of marketing in not-for-profit organizations has grown substantially as these types of organizations began to realize how marketing helped them develop a strong understanding of customers and other stakeholders. But have you ever wondered whether or not the techniques we use in commercial marketing are relevant in a not-for-profit, where the remit is not to enrich shareholders? Aren't the principles behind marketing incompatible with the mission of a charity? Are there any differences in how we use marketing techniques in a social environment—for example, when governments use marketing to reduce binge drinking, or increase fruit and vegetable consumption to five or six portions a day, or increase voter registration? In this chapter, we answer some of these questions.

So far, our attention has centred on commercial organizations intent on making profits. However, other types of organizations—for example, those that operate in the not-for-profit sector—do not seek to maximize profit. Kotler and Levy (1969) pioneered the ground-breaking application of marketing to not-for-profit enterprises. In the twenty-first century, marketing is readily used by local government, churches, museums, charities, universities, political parties, zoos, public hospitals, and many others, all of which operate without profit as their central goal. However, the view is no longer whether or not marketing should be undertaken by not-for-profits but how it should be applied (Wright *et al.*, 2012). There are also organizations which operate somewhere between being a charity and being a commercial enterprise (e.g. co-operatives). For example, Facebook's CEO Mark Zuckerberg and his wife Priscilla Chan announced in 2015 that they would donate 99% of the Facebook shares they held (worth a cool $45bn) to the Chan Zuckerberg Initiative, a private company, which will itself donate money to various charitable causes (Brandon, 2015).

Despite the similarities between not-for-profit and commercial marketing highlighted by Kotler and Levy (1969), there are some key differences in how marketing is used, particularly in relation to marketing communications. These key differences occur in the following (Rothschild, 1979).

- **Proposition**—with not-for-profit offerings, the unique selling proposition is weaker, i.e. weaker direct benefits. For example, giving to charity provides us with a sense of 'doing good', but this feeling may not be sufficient to induce many people to give. For social marketing, the proposition relates to the audience benefit gained from undertaking a specific desired behaviour (LeFebvre, 2011), e.g. not drinking and driving saves lives.

- **Price**—has different connotations in not-for-profit situations. For example, in a social marketing context, what is the price when **demarketing** (i.e. reducing the demand for) the use of illicit recreational drugs such as cocaine? Is it the potential physical harm that could arise from not stopping using a particular drug, or the damage it could do to the user's relationships with friends and family, for example? In social marketing, therefore, price can be perceived as the incentives and costs of (not) taking up a particular desired behaviour (LeFebvre, 2011). For example, the incentive to stop using cocaine relates to the removal of psychological and physiological problems such as mood swings and the risk of heart-related conditions, whereas the cost might relate to the momentary loss of self-confidence or the feeling of having fun (Jones *et al.*, 2014). In relation to charities, the amount donated is often left to the discretion of the donor (although suggestion of specific amounts tends to be more effective) and is largely determined by the donor, rather than being specified as in a commercial transaction.

- **Involvement**—we speak of high and low involvement in commercial situations regarding how consumers learn more about an offering during the purchasing process. The involvement in not-for-profit situations displays more extreme tendencies. People often either really engage with a charity (e.g. Oxfam, Médecins Sans Frontières) or a political party (e.g. UKIP, England; Feminist Initiative, Sweden) or social cause (PETA, Greenpeace), or show strong reactions against it.

- **Segmentation**—in the not-for-profit environment, it is often important to develop a campaign which drives behaviour in all targets rather than a specific segment, as in commercial markets. For example, a health promotion campaign might wish to encourage all adults to eat five portions of fruit and vegetables a day, although there may well be subgroups who need specific targeted messages (e.g. young children).

Another key difference in the marketing of not-for-profit organizations is the need to check the marketing strategy against the environment, the available resources, and, uniquely, against the organization's social values (Hatten, 1982). In the latter case, the social values of the organization impact not only on why the organization exists but also on how it goes about its marketing activities, including fundraising, promotional programmes, and operational programme developments. In the UK in 2015, major charities such as Oxfam and the British Red Cross came under considerable pressure when it was alleged that they used an outsourced telemarketing firm which employed predatory fundraising techniques, targeting vulnerable people who were confused or even terminally ill. Unsurprisingly, they have dropped these techniques in the wake of the furore (Weaver, 2015).

Table 17.1 outlines the mission statements for various not-for-profit organizations. For commercial organizations, the mission statement usually focuses on being 'best in market' and consequently achieving high levels of profit. In the not-for-profit sector, mission statements focus on causes. The *raison d'être* of a not-for-profit is often to solve a particular societal problem. Of course, if a charity ever truly managed to solve a problem (e.g. cancer charities finding a cure for cancer), would they continue to operate or simply amend their mission? Like any other organization, a charity interacts with its environment and must stay relevant within the context that it operates to attract funding.

Research Insight 17.1

To take your learning further, you might wish to read this influential paper.

Kotler, P. and Levy, S.J. (1969). Broadening the concept of marketing. *Journal of Marketing*, 33(1), 10–15.

In this seminal article, the authors proposed that marketing techniques and concepts, as typified by the 4Ps, could be applied to non-business organizations and therefore could be applied to the marketing of organizations, persons, and ideas. It provoked a considerable debate at the time, with some writers suggesting that the concept of marketing had been broadened too far.

Visit the Online Resource Centre to read the abstract and access the full paper.

> ### Table 17.1 A selection of mission statements from not-for-profit organizations

Organization	Mission statement
Arts Council of England (UK)	The Council's mission is great art and culture for everyone. We work hard to achieve this by championing, developing, and investing in arts and cultural experiences that enrich people's lives. At the heart of this, we have five goals: ■ Excellence is thriving in the arts, museums, and libraries. ■ Everyone has the opportunity to experience, and be inspired by, the arts, museums, and libraries. ■ The arts, museums, and libraries are resilient and environmentally sustainable. ■ The leadership in the arts, museums and libraries are diverse and appropriately skilled. ■ Every child and young person has the opportunity to experience the richness of the arts, museums, and libraries.
Emirates Red Crescent	**Our motto:** Life care. **Our vision:** Leadership and excellence in humanitarian work. **Our mission:** Mobilizing human power to support the vulnerable. **Our role:** Work to support the official authorities in peacetime and wartime, in accordance with the provisions of Article 26 of the First Geneva Convention of 1949. **In peacetime:** Organizing awareness programmes, first aid, protection and control of epidemics, paying attention to the social issues, and providing humanitarian assistance for vulnerable, needy people and victims of accidents and disasters. **In wartime:** Transferring and treating the wounded and assisting prisoners in the scope of the Geneva Conventions. Provide first aid and relief to the victims. Protection of civilians and sheltering the displaced and homeless. Search for missing persons and reunion of separated families.
City of London Police (UK)	**Vision** We are an organization that continually strives to deliver for our community, achieve excellence in everything we do, and in doing so provide a world class service. This is not just in relation to maintaining high performance but also being recognized as a worldwide centre of excellence for our policing services. In order to realize this ambition our vision for the City of London Police is: 'The relentless pursuit of excellence to deliver world class service, staff, performance and reputation' Our core mission is to make the City of London safer by upholding the law fairly and firmly; preventing crime and antisocial behaviour; keeping the peace; protecting and reassuring the community; investigating crime and bringing offenders to justice. Outcome: a City that is safe and secure for all.

Table 17.1 continued	
China Charity Federation (China)	The work of CCF has made a difference in millions of lives by: ■ Delivering much needed assistance at the scene of natural disasters. ■ Equipping the handicapped to better cope with their limitations. ■ Caring for orphans and the aged who would otherwise be neglected. ■ Providing medical equipment and supplies to relieve and prevent illness. ■ Aiding education so that everyone can be well educated. ■ Generally alleviating suffering and helping people to help themselves.
Médecins Sans Frontières (France, International)	We are Médecins Sans Frontières/Doctors Without Borders (MSF). We help people worldwide where the need is greatest, delivering emergency medical aid to people affected by conflict, epidemics, disasters, or exclusion from healthcare.
SIDA (Sweden)	SIDA is a government agency working on behalf of the Swedish Parliament and Government, with the mission to reduce poverty in the world. Through our work and in cooperation with others, we contribute to implementing Sweden's Policy for Global Development (PGU). We work in order to implement Swedish development policy that will enable poor people to improve their lives. Another part of our mission is conducting reform cooperation with Eastern Europe, which is financed through a specific appropriation. The third part of our assignment is to distribute humanitarian aid to people in need of assistance.

Sources: Organizations' websites: http://www.artscouncil.org.uk/what-we-do/mission/; http://www.rcuae.ae/ourPath_en.aspx; https://www.cityoflondon.police.uk/about-us/your-right-to-information/Documents/colp-policing-plan-2015-18.pdf; http://cszh.mca.gov.cn/article/english/; http://www.sida.se/English/About-us/Our-mission/.

NB: In some cases the wording may differ slightly from that on the organization's website. Changes have been made to correct the English and abridge the wording where necessary.

Key Characteristics of Not-for-Profit Organizations

The main characteristics impacting on marketing are the existence of multiple stakeholders, the degree of transparency expected when working to pursue the organization's mission and in dealing with its finances, the presence of multiple objectives in business and social terms, a different orientation compared with commercial organizations, and, finally, different customer perceptions (see Figure 17.1). We consider each of these characteristics below.

Multiple Stakeholders

Although for-profit or private sector organizations interact with a range of stakeholders to achieve their business goals, their focus is on customers and shareholders. What differs about not-for-profit organizations is their concern for a wider group of stakeholders. **Stakeholders** are groups with whom the organization has a relationship, and which impact on the operations

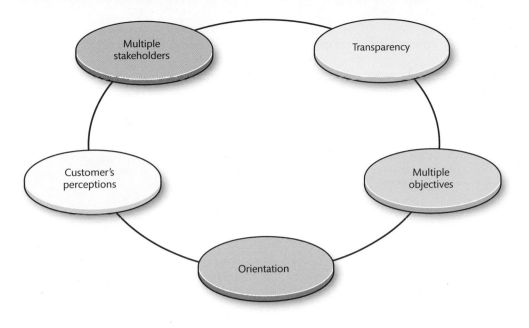

Figure 17.1
Key characteristics of not-for-profit organizations

of the organization. This includes shareholders (or trustees), regulatory bodies, other charity or not-for-profit partners, supply chain partners, employees, and customers. In private companies, revenue is distributed from customers to shareholders; it is initially converted into profits by the organization, and shareholders are rewarded with a dividend as a share of the profits earned. Companies also have stakeholders, but those stakeholders have less influence on how the organization's profits are distributed.

Not-for-profits provide an offering, but their customers or users seldom pay the full costs incurred by the organization to provide them. Many not-for-profits rely on stakeholders to finance the organization's operations. Instead of revenue from customers being used to reward shareholders, there are usually no profits to be redistributed as those who fund the organization do not require a return on their resource provision. For example, central government, local council taxpayers, lottery funding for special projects, and business rate taxes are four of the main sources of income which fund city councils in the UK. Charities are supported by individual and corporate donations. Museums may rely on a mixture of grants, lottery allocations, entrance fees, and individual donations and bequests. Zoos rely on a mixture of grants, entrance fees, and individual donations.

Because they serve multiple stakeholders, not-for-profits do not always value their beneficiary customers (i.e. those who receive their charitable services) as well as they should, and they sometimes fail to explain sufficiently to donors (i.e. supporter customers) how those donations are used. The difficulties arising when seeking to satisfy multiple stakeholder groups are outlined in Table 17.2, which considers beneficiary and supporter customers and explains why charities sometimes fail to satisfy, and undervalue, these groups of customers (Bruce, 1995).

Not-for-profits should determine which of the different stakeholders have the most interest in their activities and the most power to affect their organization's performance. One common method used to distinguish between the interests and power of stakeholders is the stakeholder mapping matrix, outlined in Figure 17.2. The matrix can be used to identify four types of

Table 17.2 Why not-for-profit organizations do not always seem to value their customers

Reasons for not valuing beneficiaries	Reasons for not valuing supporters	Interactive reasons for undervaluing customers
Many not-for-profits exist in a monopolistic situation, which potentially creates an arrogant culture towards beneficiaries.	Donors claim to be approached too often for donations and do not feel sufficiently appreciated.	Dealing with multiple stakeholders can cause inter-group tension as one group's call on resources takes precedence over others. For example, a high value donor for a university might want their donation to be used in a way that is different from that envisaged by the management of the university.
Demand far outstrips supply creating problems in delivering a consistent quality of service.	Volunteer service workers can often feel undervalued and under-supported.	
Lack of market segmentation for beneficiaries undertaken. Research into beneficiary customers' needs is not common because funds available are seen as better used for funding operations.		

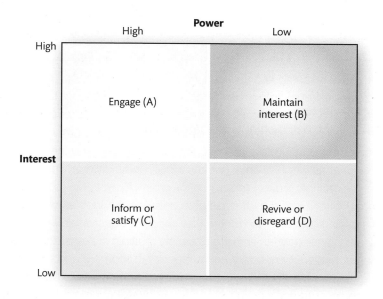

Figure 17.2

The stakeholder mapping matrix

Source: Scholes (2001).

stakeholder, based on the high/low levels of interest that they have in an organization and the level of power they exert over it. Those with high levels of interest and power (group A) are key stakeholders that need to be continuously engaged. They might be funding bodies or powerful regulators, for example. Those with high interest but low levels of power (group B), for example individual donors to charities, should be informed about that charity's activities to maintain their interest. Group C represents those organizations with high power but low interest. It is important for the not-for-profit to increase information flow to these organizations to increase their interest so that they can exert their power in the not-for-profit's favour (as a funding body might), or alternatively to keep them satisfied if they intend to exert their power against the not-for-profit (as a regulator might). Finally, an organization's relationships with those stakeholders who have little power or interest should either be disregarded or revived (group D).

Transparency

The use of public money and donations in not-for-profit organizations requires that their source and allocation is easily understood, audited, and tracked. Such public scrutiny or transparency of funding is a feature that distinguishes these organizations from their private sector counterparts. For donations to continue to flow, not-for-profit organizations should demonstrate trust, integrity, and honesty. For example, UK charities are governed by a set of regulatory requirements which requires them to provide considerably greater information on how they are governed compared with their commercial counterparts. Charities' executive teams are overseen by boards of trustees, often unpaid volunteers who are senior and experienced people who have some interest in running the organization. In parallel, the executive teams of private or public limited companies are overseen by paid executive and non-executive directors.

Private sector organizations declare the minimum financial information required—just enough to comply with government disclosure requirements. Sometimes not-for-profit organizations over-compensate, providing considerable details of their internal procedures and processes. This is because they do not want to be judged as financially incompetent, and they want to avoid adverse media coverage and the negative perceptions that would follow. However, a serious outcome might be that future funding streams are curtailed or even terminated because a charity is seen to have insufficient funds to cover its activities. Equally, providing detailed outlines of organizational structures and plans can also provide competitors with valuable competitive intelligence, which could be detrimental to the organization.

Multiple Objectives

In manufacturing and other sectors, profit is a central overriding goal. Investment decisions are often based on the likely rate of return and resources are allocated according to the contribution (to profit) they will make. Profit provides a relatively easy measure of success. As the name suggests, in the not-for-profit sector, profit is not the central overriding goal. Not-for-profit organizations have a range of goals—a multiple set of tasks that they seek to achieve. These include generating awareness, motivating people to be volunteers, distributing information, contacting customers, raising funds, allocating grants, and **lobbying** Members of Parliament for changes in regulations or legislation (see Chapter 4). Other goals include increasing their geographical spread to reach new people who might benefit from the organization's activities and campaigning to get media attention about a particular issue. In the non-profit sector, performance measurement is challenging, because a wider set of objectives are used.

Orientation

As a general rule, rather than manufacturing, distributing, and selling a physical product, not-for-profit organizations deliver a service. Developing a market orientation (see Chapter 1) is important, because the stronger the market orientation, the stronger the organization's market performance, particularly for smaller charities (Seymour *et al.*, 2006). How the not-for-profit generates income impacts upon the organization's market orientation. In a study of Portuguese not-for-profits, those organizations relying on private funding, as opposed to state funding, were found to be more market oriented and more likely to be successful in fundraising (Macedo and Pinho, 2006).

Not-for-profit organizations need to create positive awareness about their cause or activities. The principal focus of the organization is to motivate and encourage people to become involved and identify with the aims of the organization, which might lead on to financial contributions and/or volunteering support (e.g. by working in a charity's shop, or by contributing financial, marketing, or other professional services expertise).

Raising funds is an ongoing critical activity in the not-for-profit sector. The payment handed over by a customer to a charity does not operate in the same way as the payment by a customer for a banking service at the point of receiving the service. Raising funds for a charity requires people or donors to contribute money, so the expectations of not-for-profit customers are different from those of commercial firms. This leads to a greater focus on engaging supporters to become part of, and identify with, the ethos of the not-for-profit organization rather than simply being a customer.

Customers' Perceptions

Customers of private sector organizations realize that in exchange for an offering they are contributing to the profits of the organization they are dealing with. Customers have a choice, and organizations compete to get their attention and money. In the not-for-profit sector, customers do not always have a choice. Donors are free to give to one charity rather than another, or not to give anything at all. In the public sector, choice is limited, although governments do try to provide some choice (e.g. in school provision or choice of hospital for surgery in many countries). In reality, however, there is little practical opportunity for the public to choose among different public services in the same way as in the private sector. For example, services provided by local councils, such as meal services for the elderly and infirm, magistrates' courts, or building regulations and planning, are effectively single source; there is no choice or alternative supplier. In these cases, pressure to deliver a superior level of service interaction can often be based on an individual's own sense of duty and integrity rather than on any formal organizational service policy and training.

Visit the Online Resource Centre and follow the web link to the National Council of Non-profit Associations (NCNA) to learn more about the challenges and developments facing non-profit organizations.

Types of Not-for-Profit Organization

We can classify four main types of not-for-profit organizations: (1) charities, (2) the **social enterprise** sector, (3) the public sector, and (4) political parties and campaigning organizations. How marketing is used in each of these organizations is considered further in this section.

Charities

The increasing success experienced by many charities has resulted from improved commercial professionalism and the adoption of commercial approaches from the private sector, together with greater collaboration with the private sector through **cause-related marketing** activities. However, there has also been a simultaneous increase in the number of charities in the market-place. This means that there is greater competition as more charities chase a finite number of donor contributions.

The act of making a donation to a charitable organization is the culmination of a decision-making process involving a wide range of variables. Attitude to the cause, personal involve-ment or related experience, and trust in the charity to use the funds appropriately are critical to encouraging donations to be made. Consequently, charities seek to develop empathy with potential donors and build trust from which an initial transaction or donation can be made. Traditionally, the acquisition of a new donor is relatively expensive compared with the low costs associated with the collection of monthly standing orders and direct debits. Costs are minimized when repeat donations occur, so charities, just like private sector organi-zations, practice relationship marketing principles (see Chapter 15). However, charities are recognizing the power of the social media to generate significant increases in fund-raising revenue quickly. Cancer Research UK (CRUK) raised £8m in one week alone in 2014, after the #nomakeupselfie **meme** (where women posted images of themselves without make-up) occurred when a young mother from Staffordshire in England developed a No Make-Up For Cancer Awareness Facebook page, encouraging people to submit a no make-up photo of themselves to #nomakeupselfie and donate £3 to CRUK (Duncan, 2014). Once CRUK real-ized just how many people were taking notice of the campaign, they sent out the following tweet: 'Many are asking—we didn't start #nomakeupselfie #cancerawareness trend. We like the sentiment!' This tweet generated so many retweets that CRUK then generated a text message donation number and tweeted this on Facebook, Twitter, Instagram, and Google + (Eccles, 2014).

The process of giving is based on a strong emotional involvement with the objectives of the charity. This means that charities try to communicate through messages that invoke an emotional response in their target donors. A powerful example of a British charity that has used an emotional appeal in its fundraising to good effect is the National Society for the Prevention of Cruelty to Children (NSPCC). Its Full Stop! campaign, launched between 1999 and 2007 to stop cruelty to children, brought in £250m more than the usual fund-raising initiatives (NSPCC, 2013). Charities need to provide people with a rationale, a reason to give money (see Market Insight 17.1).

Cancer Research UK raised £8m in one week on the back of the #nomakeupselfie meme, a campaign it did not start

Source: © Cancer Research UK (2014).

Market Insight 17.1
From Dinners to Ice Buckets

Not-for-profit marketing is rooted in the tradition of charity, volunteering, and philanthropy, supporting poor or sick people or various good causes—be it education, religion, or art. Giving behaviour has always been associated with the rich and the aristocracy, but it was still common for others to give a pittance to support those in need. During the twentieth century, philanthropy and activities for good causes became more institutionalized and well organized. Increasingly, charities adopt marketing principles when raising funds; they set goals, a mission, and a vision, and segment target audiences. Capable and charismatic leaders run them, and they use various advertising and PR techniques to spread the word.

Market Insight 17.1
continued

Because not-for-profits focus on good causes, they can use creative and controversial forms of communication. One campaign, which totally exceeded expectations and became a global viral hit in 2014, was the 'Ice Bucket Challenge', which gained billions of views on YouTube, raising US$220m in total. The campaign sought to raise funds for research to cure amyotrophic lateral sclerosis (ALS) also known as Lou Gehrig's disease (or motor neuron disease in the UK). The idea was simple: make a video of yourself pouring a bucket full of ice or ice-cold water over your head and donate US$10 to the ALS Association, and nominate others to do the same within 24 hours. Those who declined were encouraged to donate US$100. Various celebrities, including fashion designer Donatella Versace, Microsoft co-founder Bill Gates, and actor Ashton Kutcher, accepted the challenge and nominated others. The ALS Ice Bucket challenge changed the way many people thought about not-for-profit marketing. It showed the importance of creating message content which impacts many people directly via social networking. Today, few not-for-profits have no presence at all on Facebook and most believe that their most important communication tools are email and websites rather than direct mail and street intercepts. Fundraising has also shifted

ALS ice bucket challenge up: and over, down under, in Melbourne
Source: © Scott Barbour/Stringer/Getty.

from gala dinners for a few wealthy donors to cheap viral campaigns for the masses, who each donate smaller sums to influence the world they live in but en masse deliver the income. In August 2014 alone, ALS received an income of US$98.2m compared with $2.7m for the same period in the previous year. The British MND (Motor Neuron Disease) Association typically receives about £200,000 in donations per week but from 22 to 29 August 2014, during the challenge, received £2.7m.

Sources: Dredge (2014); Townsend (2014); McKay (2015).

Theory into Practice

This market insight describes how not-for-profit organizations have made use of the Internet, and specifically social networking sites, to spread a message in order to effect consumer behaviour in a way that they could never previously have achieved before social networking sites existed. By designing content that is more likely to go viral, charities can maximize the number of people who see their message and, by engaging with it, maximize the chance that they will change their behaviour in the direction desired (e.g. donating).

Related Topics:

viral marketing; social media marketing; not-for-profit marketing; social marketing; direct marketing; online engagement.

1 **Why do you think this campaign went viral?**

2 **Do you think any not-for-profit could develop a social media marketing campaign of this type?**

3 **What are the risks for a not-for-profit in developing a campaign which is designed to go viral?**

This market insight was kindly contributed by Dr Denisa Hejlová, Charles University, Prague, Czech Republic.

Charities also try to raise funds by working in partnership with commercial organizations in cause-related marketing campaigns. According to Kotler (2000), companies differentiate themselves by sponsoring popular social causes to win the public's favour. Such an approach, termed cause-related marketing, is a useful way of developing a positive brand image for the private company as it builds not only customer loyalty, but also employee respect. The charity gains vital income from this partnership. The American Marketing Association defines cause-related marketing (also termed cause-marketing) as follows (AMA, 2013):

> Promotional strategy that links a company's sales campaign directly to a non-profit organization. Generally includes an offer by the sponsor to make a donation to the cause with (the) purchase of its product or service. Unlike philanthropy, money spent on cause marketing is a business expense, not a donation, and is expected to show a return on investment.

This type of campaign associates a company's sales with the mission or campaign of a not-for-profit organization and includes a promise to make a donation for each unit bought. However, cooperation between the two organizations can take many forms. Traditionally, these schemes are based on sales promotions, whereby a donation to the charity is made as a percentage of sales. Pampers, the P&G baby and toddler product brand, won the 2015 Business Charity Awards in the UK for its cause-related marketing programme run with UNICEF since 2006 to protect babies from maternal and new-born tetanus. For every Pampers product sold, P&G donate one life-saving tetanus vaccine (worth 4.4p). Over a 10-year period, sufficient funds have been raised to provide 300m vaccines and eliminate tetanus altogether in 15 countries (Anon., 2015a).

Cause-related marketing is an increasingly attractive proposition for organizations, as several reports have found that a very large proportion of consumers (more than 85%) agree that when price and quality are equal, they are more likely to buy an offering associated with a 'cause' or good deed. Therefore companies are increasingly likely to differentiate themselves by co-opting social causes (Kotler, 2000). Other relationships, for example those between pharmaceutical companies and medicine distribution charities, are based on the company providing free product and technical knowledge ('gifts in kind'). A good example of a global cause-related marketing campaign is Kellogg's *Breakfast for Better Days*™ initiative (see Market Insight 17.2).

Market Insight 17.2
Kellogg's: The Serial Giver

Kellogg's is the world's leading manufacturer of breakfast cereals. The company was originally set up in 1906 in Michigan, USA, as the Battle Creek Toasted Corn Flake Company. The company went from strength to strength. In 1930, despite the Great Depression, the company's founder W.K. Kellogg set up the W.K. Kellogg Foundation, investing in particular in children's education. Today, the company operates in 180 countries across the world, and holds well-loved brands such as Corn Flakes, All-Bran, Frosties, Special K, Pop-Tarts, and, after a 2012 acquisition from Procter & Gamble, Pringles. In 2014, the company had net sales of $14.6bn, with an operating profit of $1.02bn, and an employee base of around 30,000 people worldwide. To support the company's global brand positioning, it spent $1.1bn on advertising.

As well as high turnover targets, the Kellogg Company has grand corporate responsibility ambitions. It seeks to provide 1bn cereal and snack servings to

Market Insight 17.2
continued

people in need around the world by 2016 to help alleviate hunger through the global *Breakfast for Better Days*™ initiative. In 2013, Kellogg's provided funding for 98 breakfast projects in 19 countries in Africa, Latin America, Europe, and Asia. By the end of 2014, the company had provided nearly 540,000 breakfasts. Between 2010 and 2014, the company increased its donations in cash and in kind from $31.9m to $53.7m, totalling $237.2m over the five-year period. Since 2011, when the programme was set up, Kellogg's have invested nearly $1m to set up and

support 1100 breakfast clubs in the UK and Ireland through cause-related marketing promotions, using the message 'buy a box, give a bowl'. In an innovative programme, Kellogg's donates its ready-to-eat foods to communities struck by natural disasters, including those hit by a tornado in Moore, Oklahoma, flooded neighbourhoods in Colorado, and parts of the American mid-West also hit by tornadoes.

Sources: Anon. (2013b); Kellogg's (2014, 2015); http://www.kelloggs.com/en_US/our-history.html; http://www.giveachildabreakfast.co.uk/about_breakfast_clubs.aspx.

Theory into Practice

This market insight describes how one of the world's best known fast moving consumer goods companies has developed a global social responsibility programme partly using a cause-related marketing campaign, and partly based on donations of cash and in-kind benefits. It has run this programme in selected country markets worldwide.

Kellogg's®
We don't make cereals for anyone else

Hungry to give: Kellogg's pledged in 2013 to donate 1bn servings of cereal and snacks by the end of 2016
Source: © chrisdorney/Shutterstock.

Related Topics:

cause-related marketing; social responsibility; philanthropy; branding; sales promotion.

1 **How well do you think Kellogg's corporate responsibility initiatives fit its corporate strategy?**

2 **Do you think that Kellogg's spends enough resources on its corporate social responsibility initiatives? Why do you say this?**

3 **How important is it that a company promotes not just a cause-related marketing initiative but the fact that the company is undertaking the initiative in the first place?**

Visit the Online Resource Centre and complete Internet Activity 17.1 to learn more about cause-related marketing.

Cause-related marketing can affect consumers' overall attitude towards the sponsoring company or brand, as well as their cognitive knowledge of the brand (i.e. what they know).

Cause-related marketing campaigns are more effective when they are used over time and there is a strong fit between the brand and the cause (Till and Nowak, 2000). The perceived fit between the company and the cause is important to the effectiveness of the campaign. Nevertheless, there are risks to be considered for the not-for-profit organization. The charitable organization's most important asset is its name, and as cause-related marketing is a business transaction, it is subject to contract and so there is a risk that the charity could suffer reputational damage (Gifford, 1999). Cause-related marketing should be used as part of a wider CSR strategy (Steckstor, 2012). To reduce the risk, charities should not sell their association at less than what it is really worth. They should also obtain the fee up front and control all uses of their name (Gifford, 1999).

Social Enterprises

A new form of organization has begun to emerge, with a format and purpose that has captured the imagination of many different people, including people in commercial business, people working in the social sector, volunteers, academics, and leading political parties. In the UK, the government considers a social enterprise to be an enterprise that 'is a business with primarily social objectives whose surpluses are principally reinvested for that purpose in the business or in the community, rather than being driven by the need to maximize profit for shareholders and owners' (BIS, 2011: 2). Social enterprises blend social objectives with commercial reality. There is a drive to make a profit, but any surplus might be reinvested into the enterprise and not redistributed as a reward to owners. In the UK, Fairtrade schemes, Welsh Water (Glas Cymru), Jamie Oliver's Fifteen, the Co-operative Group, charities, and even farmers' markets are all examples of social enterprise organizations (see Market Insight 17.3). Elsewhere around the world, examples include Groupe SOS in France, which offers products/services to the disadvantaged and socially excluded, and Specialisterne in Denmark, which specializes in software testing and employs

---

📖 Research Insight 17.2

To take your learning further, you might wish to read this influential paper.

Barone, M.J., Miyazaki, A.D., and Taylor, K.A. (2000). The influence of cause-related marketing on consumer choice. Does one good turn deserve another? *Journal of the Academy of Marketing Science*, 28(2), 248–62.

The authors of this article investigate how consumers make choices when offerings are aligned with good causes. The authors find that consumers consider the motivations of the company linking up with a cause before buying. They find that consumer support is based around whether or not the good cause needs to be traded off against a lower performing product or the price. This study indicates that consumers are critical evaluators of cause-related marketing programmes, and managers should take extra note of consumer choice and likely acceptance before launching such programmes.

@ **Visit the Online Resource Centre to read the abstract and access the full paper.**

mainly people with Asperger's syndrome, a form of autism. A very well-known social enterprise is Newman's Own, the food company, set up by the late Hollywood actor Paul Newman in 1982. It gives away all its after-tax profits and, by 2015, the organization had paid over $430m to charitable causes worldwide.

 Visit the Online Resource Centre and follow the web link to the Newman's Own website to learn more about this inspiring social enterprise.

Market Insight 17.3
Licensing: For a Princely Sum

Organic farming has become common in the UK and consumers are concerned not just about what they eat, but about how what they eat is produced. One visionary food brand which has long heralded sustainable farming values is Duchy Originals, launched by HRH The Prince of Wales in 1992 using produce from the Duchy's Home Farm at the Highgrove Estate in Gloucestershire. At the company's ten-year anniversary, the Prince explained the rationale behind the venture: 'I wanted to demonstrate that it was possible to produce food of the highest quality, working in harmony with the environment and nature, using the best ingredients and adding value through expert production'. Importantly, the organization's profits are seeded to the Prince's Charities Foundation. But it hasn't all been plain sailing. The Duchy Originals brand saw a decline during the economic recession of the late 2000s, with losses of around £3.3m in one year.

Since then, the brand has been licensed to Waitrose, the quality multiple retail grocer. This proves to have been a smart move as The Prince of Wales Charitable Foundation received £3.0m from Waitrose in 2014. Duchy Originals from Waitrose now sells around

Milking the (Royal) brand: Duchy Originals milk on sale at Waitrose
Source: © Bloomberg/Getty.

230 products and exports to 30 countries including Belgium, Japan, Australia, and Taiwan. But Prince Charles is not the only one selling royal food. HM King Bhumipol Adulyadej of Thailand's Golden Place brand has been going from strength to strength since 2001. It seems that everyone now wants food fit for royalty, and the fact that profits go to charity makes it even tastier.

Theory into Practice

This market insight outlines how a senior royal figure in the UK, Prince Charles (the heir to the throne), developed an organic produce social enterprise, the profits of which were ploughed back into the Prince's Charities (and how this model has been replicated in another country, Thailand). When sales dropped off during the economic downturn of the late 2000s, after many years of steady growth, the long-term future of

the Duchy Originals brand was secured when it was licensed to upmarket multiple retail grocer Waitrose, bringing in a greater contribution to the Prince's Charities than before the license was granted. The case also highlights how celebrity endorsement can enhance a brand's appeal.

Sources: Anon. (2013c); Rainey (2013); Bridge (2015); http://www.duchyoriginals.com/http://www.goldenplace.co.th/.

Market Insight 17.3
continued

Related Topics:

cause-related marketing; social entrepreneurship; celebrity endorsement; retailing; licensing

1 Do you think that this social enterprise would be able to survive if it did not have the patronage of HRH The Prince of Wales?

2 Do you think it was a good idea to license the Duchy Originals brand to Waitrose? Which other British multiple retailers could the Prince have approached?

3 Take a look at the website of Newman's Own, another social enterprise. How do the business models compare?

However, social enterprises are not restricted in format. The sector is very diverse and includes public limited companies (PLCs), community enterprises, cooperatives, housing associations, charities, and leisure and development trusts, among others. All of these can adopt social enterprise values. Companies, and their wealthy owners, also frequently donate to charitable causes. Examples include Google, Microsoft, Pepsico, and Shell (see Market Insight 17.4). All have active corporate philanthropy programmes with gift matching programmes where the company would match the amounts donated to charity by its employees (Weinger, 2015). Porter has long-argued that companies should be more philanthropic because there is a long-term strategic opportunity in doing so (Porter and Kramer, 2002).

Research Insight 17.3

To take your learning further, you might wish to read this influential paper.

Porter, M.E. and Kramer, M.R. (2002). The competitive advantage of corporate philanthropy. *Harvard Business Review*, 80(12), 56–68.

In this highly cited article, the authors argue that firms must look beyond the public relations value of their social contributions. The key to successful philanthropy is to focus giving on the context in which the firm operates. They explain how Cisco Systems set up the Cisco Networking Academy to train computer network administrators to alleviate a potential constraint on the company's growth, i.e. lack of available trained employees. Interestingly, the authors argue that philanthropy can be the most cost-effective way for a company to improve its competitive context, given that under these circumstances companies can leverage the efforts and resources of not-for-profit organizations and other institutions to make systemic changes.

Ⓐ **Visit the Online Resource Centre to read the abstract and access the full paper.**

Market Insight 17.4
Shell Develops Room to Breathe

A good example of a social marketing campaign is that launched in India by the Shell Foundation (SF), the Anglo-Dutch oil and gas major's charitable foundation. The company has long been trying to develop a market for a more efficient cook stove, which reduces fuel usage, poisonous emissions, and cooking time, but to no, or perhaps, limited avail. Since 2007, SF has partnered with US social enterprise, Envirofit International, to produce a range of clean, efficient, and affordable cook stoves. In late 2008, SF launched the Room To Breathe campaign in Shimoga, Karnataka, India. The aim was to raise awareness of the benefits of the new improved cook stoves, principally because around 70% of residents are impacted by the indoor air pollution caused by existing dirty cook stoves. The campaign's aim was to raise awareness in the local population (of 1.6m), to sell 58,000 cook stoves, and to achieve a metric of campaign spend per additional stove sold of $5.75. It is important to note that all previous attempts by cook stove manufacturers focused around health and environmental benefits of the improved cook stoves had failed. The campaign promoted the cook stoves using billboard and wall paintings, a van campaign, sustained activist householders (typically women operating using a network marketing approach), and using word of mouth amongst Anganwadi workers (government health workers in the villages) and in the latter stages of the campaign through a microfinance initiative (with Grameen Koata) which allowed villagers to buy a stove and repay the cost in instalments (i.e. hire purchase).

Envirofit's cook stoves retailed at ₹1,399 ($28). Other cook stoves promoted through the Room To Breathe programme included Prakti's single pot (₹750 or $15), double pot (₹1,100 or $22), and First Energy's Oarja Plus (₹1,250 or $25). Such prices, whilst competitive, were beyond the affordability of many Indians living in the region.

The campaign enjoyed some success. It ran between October 2009 and July 2012 and hit 300,000 people, raised awareness in the population above the 30% target, but only sold 11,447 improved cook stoves, way below the target of 58,000. The total cost of the campaign was $350,000. Lessons learned by SF and its partners were that having a great product, which was good for the health and made economic sense, was insufficient in itself because people were not aware of the product and its benefits and were suspicious of the new technology. However, the benefits for those who switched were clear. Women perceived that it caused less coughing, meant less cleaning, saved time, was healthier, particularly for children, and kept the husband happy as it did not impact on the taste of the food cooked. Men liked the stove because it saved money and time, the food retained a smoky taste, the cook stove was easier to carry, and the fuel it used was cheaper. However, 55% of people thought the cook stove was too expensive, 21% did not know how to operate it, and 18% did not trust it to deliver the benefits promised.

The campaign achieved the most success in the final phase through the microfinance initiative with Grameen Koata, when stove promotional activities were combined with loans to buy the stoves. This approach ultimately brought the cost of the campaign down to $4 per stove, a level which could then be built into the $30 stove loan.

Source: Bishop *et al.* (2013).

Theory into Practice

This market insight describes how the Foundation of an oil and gas major sought to develop the market, with partners, for a new form of cooker, which would have significant health benefits and cost less in maintenance and running costs. It also demonstrates how difficult it can be to persuade people to adopt new behaviours, and how suspicious people can be with new products/ new suggested behaviours, even when the product

Market Insight 17.4
continued

is a better, less harmful product. The case particularly highlights the importance of developing an appropriate pricing strategy when targeting people on very limited incomes and how important the provision of credit can be in such situations. Finally, the case demonstrates the importance of developing a set of objectives which are carefully measured to evaluate whether or not a social marketing campaign has been successful.

Related Topics:

social marketing; marketing metrics; awareness; advertising.

1 Why do you think it was so difficult to change the behaviour of the target audience, i.e. Indians living in Shimoga in Karnataka, India?

2 Why do you think the Shell Foundation decided to develop this campaign?

3 What are the risks of developing a campaign like this? For stove manufacturers? For the Shell Foundation?

The Public Sector (and Social Marketing Campaigns Supporting Government Objectives)

The term public sector covers a range of activities around the provision of local and central government services, and services provided by government agencies. These services are concerned with satisfying social needs and benefiting society. The public sector in many countries has grown on the back of the ideas embedded within the welfare state, although many of these countries have privatized their telecommunication, water, gas, and electricity provision. The types of services provided are founded on the principle of improving the quality of people's lives.

Public sector organizations operate in industrial, governmental, consumer, and societal markets, and their marketing activities are driven by a complex web of stakeholder relationships. Marketing in the public sector is governed by three main forces: (1) social, (2) economic, and (3) political. The interaction of these forces within an increasingly uncertain and unstable environment makes the provision of customer choice of service more problematic.

Internal marketing is crucial in these organizations. Rather than refer to buyers and sellers, the public sector approach is based around providers and users, where resources and not investment comprise the primary criterion, although this approach is changing. One distinguishing characteristic of the public sector concerns the political tensions that arise between the various stakeholder groups. For example, the conflict between central and local government is crucial, and perceptions of who is responsible for taxation, and why tax rates rise faster than inflation, reflect the power imbalance between the participants.

'Allo 'allo 'allo, what's going on 'ere then? City of London Police use advertising to encourage suspicious activity reporting
Source: Courtesy of the City of London Police.

Governments use marketing for a variety of reasons, including as a complement to law enforcement (as our Case Insight on the City of London Police demonstrates), to help promote services to support companies with their export business as well as using social marketing 'to bring about societal change or improvement, (LeFebvre, 2011:57). Social marketing interventions can be highly effective in achieving behavioural change in target audiences across a variety of social settings (Stead *et al.*, 2007). It is often used to demarket behaviours—for example, not using drugs, or not smoking. For example, a study of French consumers determined that visual messages were more effective than text messages in conveying an anti-smoking message (Gallopel-Morvan *et al.,* 2009). One particularly excellent example is a campaign run by WildAid in California which sought to reduce rhino poaching in Africa (which is illegal) by demarketing the consumption of ground rhino horn as a cure for fever, weak sexual desire, and disease, particularly among Chinese and Vietnamese (WildAid, 2014). One key success factor in social marketing is to have a proper understanding of the causality of the target audience's behaviour, i.e what might cause them to adopt a different behaviour and why they are behaving as they are now (Wymer, 2011).

Social marketing can also be used to promote healthy behaviours; for example, Sport England's award-winning 'This girl can' campaign was designed to improve the participation of women in sport and exercise activities.

The Brazilian Ministry of Health ran a campaign hijacking Tinder and Hornet (two dating apps) to promote a safer sex message by creating a series of fake profiles of people stating a lack of interest in using condoms. Those who swiped right on these profiles were shown a strong warning of the danger of unprotected sex (Toor, 2015).

The idea that marketing techniques could be used in this way was first discussed by Kotler and Zaltman (1971). One example was when the Crown Prince of Thailand, wearing a 'bike for mom' T-shirt, led thousands of cyclists through the streets of Bangkok to celebrate his mother Queen Sirikit's birthday, in a bid to rehabilitate his image (Anon., 2015b).

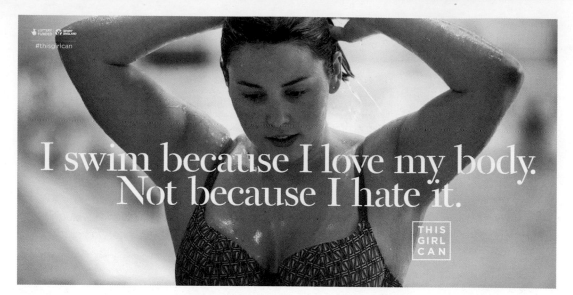

Sport England's 'This girl can' campaign, designed to improve women's self-motivation
Source: Courtesy of Sport England.

There is debate over the extent to which advertising, for example, can really change people's views and behaviour on social issues. A more recent and rather odd example of public sector advertising, was when road signs were installed in Treviso, Italy, in 2010, bearing the words 'Attenzione prostitute' (translating to 'Beware, Prostitutes!'), to warn motorists and pedestrians of their presence. However, such a sign could be entirely counter-productive. By highlighting their presence, such signs might actually encourage the prostitution business—an entirely unwanted side effect (Anon., 2015c).

Nevertheless, most social marketing campaigns are clear-cut, and are designed to advance social causes to the benefit of a particular audience by changing social attitudes and behaviours (see Research Insight 17.4). Social marketing campaigns are typically, but not exclusively, run by public sector organizations. Some examples are as follows.

- Government health departments encouraging healthy eating (e.g. the Danish six-a-day campaign to encourage people to eat more fruit and vegetables), exercising, cessation of smoking and other behaviours, or government departments of transport encouraging road safety.

- The British Heart Foundation ran the 'rock up in red' campaign to raise money to support research into beating heart disease, a campaign previously backed by model and actress Rosie Huntington-Whiteley (Anon., 2013d).

- The police or other emergency services use social marketing campaigns to reduce undesirable behaviour, either as an alternative or a complement to law enforcement. For example, the City of London Police have used handbills and posters to inform the general public about their crime reduction security operations, and social marketing communications including cinema advertising have been used as part of the Wales Arson Reduction Strategy (JAG, 2011).

@ Visit the Online Resource Centre and follow the web link to the Healthcare Communication and Marketing Association Inc. (HCMA) to learn more about marketing communications and the healthcare service profession.

Marketing has the potential to improve mass public communication in terms of ensuring message receipt and positive processing of the message. However, some argue that wholesale application of social marketing principles has considerable ethical implications, and that public oversight bodies should regulate social marketing techniques (Laczniak et al., 1979). A campaign that caused public concern was the US State Department's Shared Values Initiative, after the 11 September 2001 bombing, which spent $5m purchasing airtime on Middle Eastern and Asian TV stations to broadcast adverts designed to convince the Muslim world that America was not waging war on Islam. Eventually, the US State Department canned the ads after serious media criticism, and Al Jazeera and other channels labelled the ads as **propaganda** and refused to air them (Fullerton and Kendrick, 2006).

However, the question then arises as to when is social marketing propagandist? Some argue that social marketing and social propaganda are distinctly different, but related fields (O'Shaughnessy, 1996). A useful distinction is that while social marketing is based on audience wants, identified through audience research, propaganda is a one-way evangelizing communication (i.e. the propagandist is convinced of the message's own rightness, seeks to convince the target, often coercively, and uses research only as a means of increasing the propaganda's effectiveness). Propaganda typically uses language aimed at either uniting or instilling grievances in minority groups.

The idea that marketing can be used to counter negative social ideas, or grievances, has a long pedigree. Edward Bernays, the grandfather of the public relations industry and nephew of Austrian psychoanalyst Sigmund Freud, wrote a far-sighted article on how America should use marketing and public relations techniques to help people 'see' the true alternative between democracy and fascism, and democracy and Nazism, during the Second World War (Bernays, 1942). Governments around the world are increasingly seeking to development public communication programmes to counter the narrative of Islamist groups such as Daesh (also known as 'Islamic State') and Al-Qaeda. These include campaigns to urge law-abiding citizens to report suspicious activity (such as that organized by the City of London Police, outlined in the

Research Insight 17.4

To take your learning further, you might wish to read this influential paper.

Michie, S., van Stralen, M.M., and West, R. (2011). The behaviour change wheel: a new method for characterizing and designing behaviour change interventions. *Implementation Science*, 6(1), 42–53.

In this highly readable article, the authors undertake a systematic literature review to identify frameworks for behaviour change interventions. They synthesize a new framework, based on 19 identified extant behaviour change intervention frameworks, which they call the 'COM-B system'. The COM-B system explains how behavioural change should be analysed from the perspective of the capabilities, opportunities, and motivations that target audiences have to change their behaviour, leading to the design of nine intervention functions: education, persuasion, incentivization, coercion, training, enablement, modelling, environmental restructuring, and restrictions.

Visit the Online Resource Centre to read the abstract and access the full paper.

Case Insight) and the 'If you see something, say something'™ campaign launched by the US Department of Homeland Security in 2010. Others have launched social marketing counter-terrorism campaigns independently of government, such as that produced by a former Islamist extremist who created the Abdullah-X cartoon to stop British Muslims from leaving Britain to join Daesh in Syria (Simpson, 2014).

Visit the Online Resource Centre and follow the web link to the US Department of Homeland Security's website to learn more about how marketing communications are used to counter terrorism.

Political Parties and Campaigning Organizations

The use of marketing by political parties and third-party interest groups has increased since the ubiquitous development of TV and mass media broadcasting worldwide around the 1950s. Scientific methods of assessing market and public opinion have transformed how political campaigns are run. Charities and other campaigning organizations use marketing techniques to influence legislation and public opinion using lobbying techniques. With the development of globalized industries, the interplay between marketing and politics has increased further, and so marketing methods associated with political campaigning are used by companies to influence legislators and regulators (e.g. in the European Parliament, on Capitol Hill in Washington, DC, and at World Trade talks). Regulators seek to influence legislation associated with these markets.

Marketing is used by political parties to exchange political influence (e.g. legislative change/amendments) for political support (e.g. votes, petitions, donations, volunteering). Political marketing can be seen as a marketing–propaganda hybrid, mixing marketing and propaganda. This is particularly the case, but not exclusively so, in America, where **negative campaigning** is rife (O'Shaughnessy, 1990), using 30-second and 15-second advertising spots, including online, to pour out malicious attacks on political opponents. Perhaps the best example of a negative campaign was that aimed at Barack Obama in the 2008 US presidential election, erroneously labelling him a Muslim (when he is in fact a committed Christian) and someone who was not born in the USA (Vaccari and Morini, 2014), and therefore not fit to be President (Harris, 2008). The British Conservative Party also used negative campaigning against the Labour Party in the 1997 British general election, presenting Tony Blair with 'demon eyes' to insinuate that he was the devil. Although the spot was controversial and widely condemned in the media, it actually won an effectiveness award from *Campaign* magazine (Culf, 1997).

Marketing is used by political parties in representative democracies to provide citizens and voters with information on current plans (i.e. manifestos) for running the country. In the process, parties seek to improve social cohesion, democratic participation, and citizen belongingness. The recent use of political marketing in post-war democracies worldwide appears to have co-occurred with a decline in political participation. Whether or not the two effects are related is difficult to determine. Citizens do seem to be increasingly disengaged from political parties. Some argue that marketing in politics has been over-used, thereby damaging public trust; however, the truth is more likely that marketing techniques can be used to promote a poor party or candidate just as much as they can be used to market an excellent party or candidate. In politics, it is difficult to determine between the two until the party enters power. The disaffection and disappointment that citizens and voters then feel can fuel later disengagement. In that sense, politics is a **credence service** (see Chapter 15). In many countries around the world, there are different legal requirements for political advertising compared with commercial advertising. In Britain, political advertising regulations allow comparison of political parties and adverts as long as they are 'decent' and in 'good taste'. In 2001, the BBC refused to air a party election broadcast by the Pro-Life Alliance Party as it contained graphic footage of an abortion (House of Lords, 2003). It is more difficult to determine that a political advert must be truthful, as politics is often a matter of opinion and judgment. In contrast, advertising claims for commercial products must always adhere to the guidelines on taste, decency, and truthfulness (for more on the ethics of political advertising, see Chapter 18).

Most political marketing campaigns (corporate or party political) have historically been undertaken by specialized marketing and PR agencies on an ad hoc basis, although political parties and multinational corporations are increasingly conducting their political marketing activity in-house. In America, political consultants are more specialized, undertaking work in such areas as polling, petition management, fundraising, strategy, media buying, advertising, public affairs, **grassroots lobbying**, law, donor list maintenance, online campaigning, and campaign software consulting. The Internet and social media have become important areas for generating campaign finance and grassroots support, particularly in the USA. The Internet has become the battleground of political campaigning efforts in elections around the world.

As with the use of marketing for social campaigning, its input into politics strikes concern into many who think that politics should not adopt such techniques. Marketing has played a strong role in bringing about revolution against Soviet-allied governments in Serbia, Georgia, and the Ukraine, where American political consultants were advising opposition parties that deployed 'revolutionary symbols and slogans' to encourage activists to take to the streets (Sussman and Krader, 2008). Facebook played an important role in generating support for the 'We are all Khaled Said' campaign, which helped to bring down the Egyptian government in 2011 (Ghonim, 2012) after the government cracked down hard on protesters. Twitter also played a role in generating public support in various revolutions, including in Moldova in 2009 during civil unrest around the election result in which the Communist Party of Moldova (PCRM) allegedly fixed their majority (Mungiu-Pippidi and Munteanu, 2009), and in Iran during student protests in 2009–2010, also over disputed election results (Grossman, 2009). Given marketing's ability to influence the general public, the question arises: What is and what is not a legitimate use of marketing in the political sphere?

Under certain circumstances, it is possible to influence the political environment, and therefore the political agenda (see Chapter 4), in favour of an organization's strategy. Charities and not-for-profit organizations frequently focus on campaigning to change legislation or government policy agendas (a process known as lobbying or public affairs). The organization Purpose.com in the USA has had considerable success working with companies like Google and Audi and organizations like the Bill & Melinda Gates Foundation to build mass movements online to support particular causes. For example, when Audi entered the Indian car market, part of its entry strategy involved designing and promoting clean water machines (Anon., 2013a).

Lobbying or public affairs campaigns often use stunts to obtain media publicity to influence public opinion and, in turn, influence parliamentary opinion in the countries concerned. For example, the global environmental organization Greenpeace campaigns against nuclear policy globally. It is probably best known in this regard for staging a protest against France's nuclear testing in the Pacific in 1985, when its ship *Rainbow Warrior* was bombed in Auckland Harbour, New Zealand, by French secret service agents (BBC, 2006).

Therefore we can see that publicity is important in pressure group campaigning. Typically, pressure groups try to advance policy change despite government opposition. On other occasions, they try to change social behaviour more generally. In Cairo, for example, the Imprint

Movement took out ads in a bid to stop harassment of women on the Metro (Anon., 2015d) (see also Market Insight 17.5). The publicity serves to highlight the cause and to bring supporters from the general public, who can then volunteer their time or support, or provide donations in the same way that they would with a charity.

Market Insight 17.5
No Means No! Get It!

In recent years, Sweden has emerged as a poster-child for progressive values on issues as diverse as social welfare, gender equality, and the environment. Indeed, such values are at the heart of its national identity which influences not only domestic policy but a highly effective form of public diplomacy. After a century of social democracy, there is widespread adherence to the principle of collective action, and high levels of public trust in the institutions of government, which have allowed consecutive administrations to pursue social agendas for a longer term than might otherwise have been the case. And, in those instances where legal compliance might be seen as too 'heavy-handed', they've also allowed state-sponsored social marketing campaigns to successfully steer voluntary behavioural change in areas such as alcohol consumption, smoking, clean energy, and sexual attitudes.

But social marketing isn't solely the preserve of governments. There are a multitude of not-for-profit organizations seeking to influence societal and/or subgroup behaviour and, increasingly, turning to commercial marketing approaches for inspiration. One such organization, FATTA, an advocacy group formed to tackle the issue of sexual violence and demand an amendment to Swedish rape legislation, has—through an approach based on brand co-creation—cultivated a powerful, and growing, political consumer tribe. Formed by two feminist artists and culture and music groups—Crossing Borders and Femtastic—FATTA initially mobilized support from existing memberships. However, the objective from the outset was to reach beyond the traditional audience for such messages (as well as highbrow debate columns of national newspapers) and, utilizing hip-hop music, street art, and culture, directly engage a powerful youth audience across the country.

FATTA's aim of forcing legislative change for a consent law presents numerous difficulties for policy-makers, but should be viewed against a backdrop of powerful social attitudes towards sexual violence, and gender equality more generally, in Sweden. In the period following its launch, FATTA built on its physical community engagement activities with a significant social media presence. Membership numbers grew rapidly and traditional media outlets began to show interest in the organization. Importantly, from the group's perspective, rape cases began to receive more media attention at this time and created many opportunities for discussing the case for a consent law. This, in turn, placed a burden on the target stakeholder group, policy-makers, who were quickly pushed into a defensive position on the issue. FATTA has recently stepped up its efforts to engage more men in the movement with its aptly named FATTA MAN launch and, at the time of writing, there is an ongoing consultation process on the issue.

Sources: Enqvist (2014); http://www.visitsweden.com/sweden/brandguide/The-brand/The-Platform/The-platform-Position/; http://www.fatta.nu.

Theory into Practice

This market insight describes how a pressure group, FATTA, has used social marketing techniques to press the case for a change in Sweden's rape law to require consent between adults indulging in sexual relations. The insight shows how FATTA used marketing techniques to develop a social movement to press for legislative change, effectively developing a grassroots lobbying strategy.

Market Insight 17.5
continued

Related Topics:

social media marketing; stakeholder analysis; grassroots lobbying; public affairs.

1   Do you think social marketing techniques should be used to change rape legislation? Why do you say this?

2   Given the strength of feeling around this issue, does it matter how FATTA use marketing techniques to promote their cause?

3   Should any and all pressure groups be allowed to use social marketing techniques to effect behaviour change? What topics might be 'out of bounds'?

This market insight was kindly contributed by Dr Ian Richardson, Stockholm University with support from Maja Magnusson, Cecilia Granström, and Hanna Kretz.

Chapter Summary

To consolidate your learning, the key points from this chapter are summarized here.

■ **List some of the key characteristics of not-for-profit organizations.**

Not-for-profit organizations are differentiated from their commercial counterparts in numerous ways. Not-for-profit organizations tend to have multiple stakeholders and, because there are no shareholders, any profit earned is reinvested in the organization. Because not-for-profit organizations do not distribute funds to shareholders, and are social enterprises, public sector organizations, or charities, there is a need for transparency in determining how these organizations operate, as they are claiming to act for the common good. Accordingly, they have multiple objectives, rather than a simple profit motivation. Historically, not-for-profit organizations have not been strongly market oriented, but this is changing as they become more experienced in marketing. Customers' perceptions of not-for-profit organizations differ from those of their commercial counterparts because the not-for-profit typically has a unique mission and set of values and a non-financial organizational purpose.

■ **Explain why not-for-profit organizations do not always value their customers.**

Not-for-profit organizations frequently do not value their beneficiary customers because they exist in a monopolistic situation, demand far outstrips supply, a lack of market segmentation activity exists, and research into customer needs is not seen as a priority for expenditure and investment. Not-for-profit organizations frequently also undervalue supporter customers because typically they approach them to solicit funds too often and do not sufficiently appreciate them when they do give. Volunteer service workers who generously give their time can often feel undervalued. Because not-for-profit organizations have multiple stakeholders, problems can arise between these groups, which need resolution but which can often lead to customers feeling undervalued as those tensions are resolved.

■ **Analyse stakeholders and develop appropriate engagement strategies.**

A common way of analysing stakeholders is by mapping them on a power–interest matrix to identify four types based on the level of interest they display in an organization and the level of power they exert. Those with high levels of interest and power (group A) are key stakeholders in need of continuous engagement. Those with high interest but low levels of power (group B) should be informed about the organization's activities to maintain their interest. Group C represents those organizations with high power but low interest. Here, it is important either to increase information flow to these organizations to increase their interest so that they can exert their power in the not-for-profit's favour, or alternatively to keep them satisfied if they intend to exert their power against the not-for-profit. Finally, an organization's relationships with those stakeholders who have little power or interest (Group D) should either be disregarded or revived.

■ **Describe and assess cause-related marketing campaigns.**

A cause-related marketing campaign occurs when companies and non-profit organizations form marketing alliances. Often, these marketing campaigns are focused on sales promotions developed for mutual benefit where the purchase of a commercial offering is linked to donations to a charitable third-party organization. Such campaigns tend to work best where there is a strong strategic fit between the commercial organization and the not-for-profit organization, particularly in relation to the audiences targeted and when the campaign runs over the longer term.

■ **Understand how marketing is used in social and political marketing campaigns.**

Over nearly 50 years, we have embraced the use of marketing for social and political causes. Marketing is commonly used in government social marketing campaigns to drive positive behavioural change and improve citizens' well-being around such causes as encouraging populations to eat healthily, not use drugs or smoke, and not drink and drive, for example. However, we might question whether or not government should have this role and the ethics of using marketing in social and political campaigning. The use of marketing techniques in election campaigns has a long pedigree and is now common in most countries (democratic or otherwise) worldwide. In this scenario, marketing is used to understand the electorate's wants/needs and to provide them with a set of party policies and leaders which suit those needs. In addition to the use of marketing by government to influence society, and by political parties to gain support and votes, marketing is used by third-party organizations (e.g. pressure groups) to drive legislative change in lobbying campaigns, particularly by courting publicity and the media's support more generally.

? Review Questions

1 What key differences exist in marketing communications for not-for-profit versus for-profit organizations?

2 How do not-for-profit organizations differ from commercial organizations in marketing terms?

3 Why don't not-for-profit organizations always value their beneficiaries?

4 Why don't not-for-profit organizations always value their donors?

5 What axes are used on a stakeholder analysis matrix?

6 How is marketing used to raise funds for charitable organizations?

7 What is cause-related marketing?

8 How do we assess cause-related marketing programmes?

9 What is social marketing and what is its purpose?

10 How do public sector organizations use social marketing techniques?

Worksheet Summary

To apply the knowledge you have gained from this chapter and test your understanding of not-for-profit marketing visit the **Online Resource Centre** and complete Worksheet 17.1.

Discussion Questions

1 Having read Case Insight 17.1 on the City of London Police, how would you use marketing and PR techniques for the following purposes?

   A Deter terrorists and criminals more generally.

   B Reassure the general public and encourage them to report suspicious activity.

2 Working in small groups, select three different not-for-profit organizations and consider the following.

   A How do their 'propositions' differ from each other?

   B What is the nature of place (from the 4Ps) for each organization?

   C What is the nature of customer involvement for each proposition?

   D How can the audiences for these not-for-profit offerings be segmented, if at all?

3 Read the section on stakeholder mapping and draw up maps for the following organizations.

   A An international refugee charity undertaking work to alleviate the suffering of refugees from Syria and other middle Eastern countries.

   B The French Republicans as they develop their campaign plan for the presidential election expected in 2017.

   C A Dutch government department developing a road safety awareness campaign to reduce traffic accidents.

   D The UK social enterprise *Big Issue*, set up by John Bird MBE, which works to support the homeless by encouraging them to sell the *Big Issue* magazine and, in 2015, coffee to commuters.

4 Discuss reasons why charitable organizations should, or should not, communicate with donors on details of what the charity has achieved with their donations.

5 Use Google Search to identify how the government in your own country undertakes, if at all, social marketing campaigns in the following areas.

   A The police service.

   B Your government's department of health.

   C Your government's road safety awareness campaigns.

   Visit the **Online Resource Centre** and complete the Multiple Choice Questions to assess your knowledge of Chapter 17.

Glossary

cause-related marketing a campaign where a company is linked to a charity or social cause with the express intention of building its own customer goodwill, providing the charity with an increase in resource and the company with either a concomitant increase in sales of its product/service or a reputational dividend.

credence service a service delivered by professionals which is difficult to evaluate beforehand because of the technical nature of the product/service.

demarketing the use of marketing techniques to discourage, as opposed to encourage, demand for a particular proposition.

grassroots lobbying when the general public is targeted using marketing communications techniques to persuade them to support the case for legislative or regulatory change, often by asking those members of the public to contact Members of Parliament or other political actors directly to press the case.

lobbying the process employed by companies, charities, and third-party interest groups to develop and build relationships with regulatory and political bodies in order to influence legislation in their favour or in order to advance a particular cause.

meme an image, video, or text, containing cultural content, which is passed between users on the Internet.

negative campaigning where marketing communications techniques are used to present opposing candidates or parties in a bad light in order to win electoral advantage.

propaganda a technique used by a communicating party expressing opinions or activities to influence the opinions or activities of a receiving party, to direct them towards a predetermined agenda drawn up by the communicating party, often using psychological and symbolic manipulations.

social enterprise a business whose primary objectives are essentially social and whose surpluses are reinvested for that purpose in the business or in the community, rather than dispersed to the owners.

stakeholders people with an interest, a 'stake', in the levels of profit an organization achieves, its environmental impact, and its ethical conduct in society.

vision how an organization sees its future and what it wants to become.

References

AMA (2013). Dictionary: cause marketing. Retrieve from: http://www.marketingpower.com/_layouts/Dictionary.aspx?dLetter = C (accessed 25 November 2015).

Anon. (2013a). The business of campaigning: profit with purpose. *The Economist*, 26 January, 60.

Anon. (2013b) Kellogg Company launches *Breakfasts for Better Days*™ hunger relief initiative. *PR Newswire*, 25 February. Retrieve from: http://www.prnewswire.com/news-releases-test/kellogg-company-launches-breakfasts-for-better-days-hunger-relief-initiative-193058821.html (accessed 25 November 2015).

Anon. (2013c). Prince Charles's Duchy Originals sees profits jump after bumper sales. *The Telegraph*, 3 January. Retrieve from: http://www.telegraph.co.uk/finance/newsbysector/retailandconsumer/9777533/Prince-Charless-Duchy-Originals-sees-profits-jump-after-bumper-sales.html (accessed 25 November 2015).

Anon. (2013d). Rosie Huntington-Whiteley backs British heart charity's campaign. *Express*, 11 January. Retrieve from: http://www.express.co.uk/celebrity-news/370187/Rosie-Huntington-Whiteley-backs-British-heart-charity-s-campaign (accessed 8 December 2015).

Anon. (2015a). Business Charity Awards. Cause-related marketing—Pampers with UNICEF: 1 pack = 1 vaccine campaign. *Third Sector*, 19 May. Retrieve from: http://www.thirdsector.co.uk/business-charity-awards-2015-cause-related-marketing-pampers-unicef-1-pack-1-vaccine-campaign/communications/article/1347315 (accessed 27 November 2015).

Anon. (2015b). Thailand celebrates queen's birthday with bicycle ride. *The Guardian*, 16 August. Retrieve from: http://www.theguardian.com/world/2015/aug/16/thailand-queens-birthday-bike-for-mom-bangkok-queen-sirikit (accessed 13 October 2015).

Anon. (2015c). Caution! Scantily-clad hazard ahead: Italian prostitutes to get own road sign to warn motorists. *Daily Mail*, 2 April. Retrieve from: http://www.dailymail.co.uk/news/article-1263210/Italian-prostitutes-road-sign-warn-motorists-impending-distraction.html (accessed 13 October 2015).

Anon. (2015d). Slapping back. *The Economist*, 21 November, 57.

Barone, M.J., Miyazaki, A.D., and Taylor, K.A. (2000). The influence of cause-related marketing on consumer choice. Does one good turn deserve another? *Journal of the Academy of Marketing Science*, 28(2), 248–62.

BBC (2006). NZ rules out new Greenpeace probe. *BBC News*, 2 October. Retrieve from: http://news.bbc.co.uk/1/hi/world/asia-pacific/5398170.stm (accessed 25 November 2015).

Bernays. E. (1942). The marketing of national policies: a study of war propaganda. *Journal of Marketing*, 6(3), 236–45.

BIS (2011). *A Guide to Legal Forms for Social Enterprise*. Department of Business Innovation and Skills, November. Retrieve from: http://www.bis.gov.uk/assets/BISCore/business-law/docs/G/11-1400-guide-legal-forms-for-social-enterprise.pdf (accessed 25 November 2015).

Bishop, S., Pursnani, P., and Sumpter, C. (2013). Social marketing in India. *Shell Foundation*, Q1. Retrieve from: http://www.shellfoundation.org/Our-News/Reports-Archive/Latest-Shell-Foundation-Reports/Social-Marketing-in-India (accessed 10 December 2015).

Brandon, R. (2015). Mark Zuckerberg and Priscilla Chan to donate 99 percent of their Facebook fortune. *The Verge*, 1 December. Retrieve from: http://www.theverge.com/2015/12/1/9831554/mark-zuckerberg-charity-45-billion (accessed 10 December 2015).

Bridge, S. (2015). Duchy Originals contributes £3m to the Prince of Wales's Charitable Foundation. *Thisismoney.co.uk*, 10 January. Retrieve from: http://www.thisismoney.co.uk/money/news/article-2904912/Duchy-Originals-contributes-3m-Prince-Wales-s-Charitable-Foundation.html (accessed 25 November 2015).

Bruce, I. (1995). Do not-for-profits value their customers and their needs? *International Marketing Review*, 12(4), 77–84.

Culf, A. (1997). Demon eyes ad wins top award. *The Guardian*, 10 January. Retrieve from: http://www.guardian.co.uk/politics/1997/jan/10/past.andrewculf (accessed 25 November 2015).

Dredge, S. (2014). YouTube videos of the ice bucket challenge pass 1bn views. *The Guardian*, 9 September. Retrieve from: http://www.theguardian.com/technology/2014/sep/08/youtube-ice-bucket-challenge-videos (accessed 25 November 2015).

Duncan, A. (2014). Still wondering who kick-started the #nomakeupselfie craze? Creator revealed to be teenage mum from Stoke-on-Trent. *Metro*, 25 March. Retrieve from: http://metro.co.uk/2014/03/25/still-wondering-who-kick-started-the-nomakeupselfie-craze-creator-revealed-to-be-a-teenage-mum-from-stoke-on-trent-4678163/ (accessed 26 November 2015).

Eccles, A. (2014). How Cancer Research UK raised £8m from a campaign they didn't start. *CharityComms*, 26 March. Retrieve from: http://www.charitycomms.org.uk/articles/how-cancer-research-uk-raised-8m-from-a-campaign-they-didn-t-start (accessed 25 November 2015).

Enqvist, A.F. (2014). FATTA: a campaign that inspires change. *Girl's Globe*, 18 March. Retrieve from: http://girlsglobe.org/2014/03/18/fatta-a-campaign-that-inspires/ (accessed 25 November 2015).

Fullerton, J., and Kendrick, A. (2006). *Advertising's War on Terrorism: The Story of the US State Department's Shared Values Initiative*. Spokane, WA: Marquette Books.

Gallopel-Morvan, K., Gabriel, P., Le Gall-Elly, M., Rieunier, S., and Urien, B. (2009). The use of visual warnings in social marketing: the case of tobacco. *Journal of Business Research*, 64(1), 7–11.

Ghonim, W. (2012). *Revolution 2.0*. London: Fourth Estate.

Gifford, G. (1999). Cause-related marketing: ten rules to protect your non-profit assets. *Nonprofit World*, 17(4), 11–13.

Grossman, L. (2009). Iran protests: Twitter, the medium of the movement. *Time Magazine*, 17.

Harris, P. (2008). US election: It's the most vicious election ever—and here's why. *The Guardian*, 31 August. Retrieve from: http://www.theguardian.com/world/2008/aug/31/uselections2008.barackobama (accessed 25 November 2015).

Hatten, M.L. (1982). Strategic management in not-for-profit organisations. *Strategic Management Journal*, 3, 89–104.

House of Lords (2003). Judgments—Regina v. British Broadcasting Corporation (Appellants) ex parte Pro-Life Alliance (Respondents). Retrieve from: http://www.publications.parliament.uk/pa/ld200203/ldjudgmt/jd030515/bbc-3.htm (accessed September 2016).

JAG (2011). *Wales Arson Reduction Strategy: A Review by the Joint Arson Group*, St. Asaph, Denbighshire, North Wales Fire and Rescue Service, November. Retrieve from: http://www.nwales-fireservice.org.uk/media/64363/wars_review_final_nov_2011.pdf (accessed September 2016).

Jones, N., Baines, P., and Welsh, S. (2014). Counter-marketing in a wicked problem context—the case of cocaine. In N. Bradley and J. Blythe (eds), *Demarketing*. Abingdon: Routledge.

Kellogg's (2014). *Corporate Responsibility Report 2014*. Retrieve from: http://www.kelloggcompany.com/en_US/corporate-responsibility.html (accessed 30 November 2015).

Kellogg's (2015). *2014 Annual Report*. Retrieve from: http://investor.kelloggs.com/investor-relations/annual-reports/default.aspx (accessed 27 November 2015).

Kotler, P. (2000). Future markets. *Executive Excellence*, 17(2), 6.

Kotler, P. and Levy, S.J. (1969). Broadening the concept of marketing. *Journal of Marketing*, 33(1), 10–15.

Kotler, P. and Zaltman, G. (1971). Social marketing: an approach to planned social change. *Journal of Marketing*, 35(3), 3–12.

Laczniak, G.R., Lusch, R.F., and Murphy, P.E. (1979). Social marketing: its ethical dimensions. *Journal of Marketing*, 43(Spring), 29–36.

LeFebvre, R.C. (2011). An integrative model for social marketing. *Journal of Social Marketing*, 1(1), 54–72.

McKay, T. (2015). Remember the ice bucket challenge? Scientists say it worked. *Science.Mic*, 22 August. Retrieve from: http://mic.com/articles/124265/ice-bucket-challenge-did-it-work#.cMtndBoaj (accessed 26 November 2015).

Macedo, I.M. and Pinho, J.C. (2006). The relationship between resource dependence and market orientation: the case of non-profit organisations. *European Journal of Marketing*, 40(5/6), 533–63.

Michie, S., van Stralen, M.M., and West, R. (2011). The behaviour change wheel: a new method for characterizing and designing behaviour change interventions. *Implementation Science*, 6(1), 42–53.

Mungiu-Pippidi, A. and Munteanu, I. (2009). Moldova's 'Twitter Revolution'. *Journal of Democracy*, 20(3), 136–42.

NSPCC (2013). *A Pocket History of the NSPCC*, London: National Society for the Prevention of Cruelty to Children. Retrieve from: http://www.nspcc.org.uk/what-we-do/about-the-nspcc/history-of-NSPCC/history-of-nspcc-booklet_wdf75414.pdf (accessed 21 September 2016).

O'Shaughnessy, N. (1990). *The Phenomenon of Political Marketing*. London: Macmillan.

O'Shaughnessy, N. (1996). Social propaganda and social marketing: a critical difference? *European Journal of Marketing*, 30(10/11), 62–75.

Porter, M.E. and Kramer, M.R. (2002). The competitive advantage of corporate philanthropy. *Harvard Business Review*, 80(12), 56–68.

Rainey, S. (2013). Why Prince Charles's Duchy Originals takes the biscuit. *The Telegraph*, 12 November. Retrieve from: http://www.telegraph.co.uk/news/uknews/prince-charles/10433884/Why-Prince-Charless-Duchy-Originals-takes-the-biscuit.html (accessed 25 November 2015).

Rothschild, M.L. (1979). Marketing communications in non-business situations or why it's so hard to sell brotherhood like soap. *Journal of Marketing*, 43(Spring), 11–20.

Scholes, K. (2001). Stakeholder mapping: a practical tool for public sector managers. In G. Johnson and K. Scholes (eds), *Exploring Public Sector Strategy*. London: FT/Prentice Hall, 165–84.

Seymour, T., Gilbert, D., and Kolsaker, A. (2006). Aspects of market orientation of English and Welsh charities. *Journal of Nonprofit and Public Sector Marketing*, 16(1/2), 151–69.

Simpson, J. (2014). Abdullah-X: The new cartoon made by former extremist aimed at stopping Britain's young Muslims from leaving for Syria. *The Independent*, 14 July. Retrieve from: http://www.independent.co.uk/news/uk/home-news/abdullah-x-the-new-cartoon-made-by-former-extremist-aimed-at-stopping-britain-s-young-muslims-from-9604967.html (accessed 8 December 2015).

Stead, M., Gordon, R., Angus, K., and McDermott, L. (2007). A systematic review of social marketing effectiveness. *Health Education*, 107(2), 126–91.

Steckstor, D. (2012). *The Effects of Cause-Related Marketing on Customers' Attitudes and Buying Behavior*. New York: Gabler Verlag.

Sussman, G. and Krader, S. (2008). Template revolutions: marketing US regime change in Eastern Europe. *Westminster Papers in Communication and Culture*, 5(3), 91–112.

Till, B.D. and Nowak, L.I. (2000). Toward effective use of cause-related marketing alliances. *Journal of Product and Brand Management*, 9(7), 472–84.

Toor, A. (2015). Swipe right on these fake Tinder profiles for a warning about AIDS. *The Verge*, 11 February. Retrieve from: http://www.theverge.com/2015/2/11/8017933/fake-tinder-profiles-aids-awareness-campaign-brazil (accessed 8 December 2015).

Townsend, L. (2014). How much has the ice bucket challenge achieved? *BBC News Magazine*, 2 September. Retrieve from: http://www.bbc.co.uk/news/magazine-29013707 (accessed 25 November 2015).

Vaccari, C. and Morini, M. (2014). The power of smears in two American presidential campaigns. *Journal of Political Marketing*, 13(1–2), 19–45.

Weaver, M. (2015). Watchdog to investigate charities 'boiler room' tactics. *The Guardian*, 7 July. Retrieve from: http://www.theguardian.com/money/2015/jul/07/watchdog-investigate-charities-boiler-room-tactics-pressuring-vulnerable-people (accessed 24 November 2015).

Weinger, A. (2015). Corporate philanthropy. *Triplepundit*, 9 March. Retrieve from: http://www.triplepundit.com/2015/03/5-companies-corporate-philanthropy-right/ (accessed 10 December 2015).

WildAid (2014). Rhino horn demand. Retrieve from: http://www.wildaid.org/sites/default/files/resources/WEBReportRhinoHornDemand2014.pdf (accessed 8 December 2015).

Wright, G., Chew, C., and Hines, A. (2012). The relevance and efficacy of marketing in public and non-profit service management. *Public Management Review*, 14(4), 433–50.

Wymer, W. (2011). Developing more effective social marketing strategies. *Journal of Social Marketing*, 1(1), 17–31.

Chapter 18

Marketing, Society, Sustainability, and Ethics

Learning Outcomes

After studying this chapter, you will be able to:

▶ Assess the negative impact that marketing has on society

▶ Define sustainable marketing and its implications for marketing practice

▶ Define marketing ethics

▶ Explain the common ethical norms applied in marketing

▶ Describe the role of ethics in marketing decision-making

▶ Understand how ethical breaches occur in marketing mix programmes

Case Insight 18.1
innocent

Market Insight 18.1
Unilever's Sustainability Challenge

Market Insight 18.2
Flogging a Dead Horse

Market Insight 18.3
Forex Fixing

Market Insight 18.4
Volkswagen: Up in Smoke?

Market Insight 18.5
Drug Money in China

How do organizations develop and maintain responsible working practices and attitudes towards the environment and at the same time remain compatible with their customers' values? We speak to Tansy Drake, Brand Guardian at innocent, to find out more.

Our purpose at innocent is *to make healthy, natural food and drinks that help people live well and die old*. It's accompanied by five company values which are to be responsible, generous, commercial, entrepreneurial, and natural. They steer our behaviour and how we're going to get there.

Some flinch at a reference to death in a business context, but we believe that it gives us some backbone and something really important to aim for. Both our purpose and values crystallized as the company grew, but doing business responsibly has always been intuitive to innocent's business approach.

It was a central value shared by all three founding members, and subsequently by all employees. So there's never been a decision as such to do business in a particular way. It was just the responsible way. We are a business, so we need to be commercial, and we do that in an entrepreneurial way. But that doesn't exclude being responsible and generous. And we will

always make natural things and be ourselves at work. This explanation hangs in every loo at our offices.

To give substance to our values we have a permanent sustainability team, as well as champions in every part of the business. With that in mind we've tried to make our packaging as low impact as possible.

Our little bottles were our first products, and so in 2002 we started on the journey to have the world's first 100% recycled plastic bottle. We finally achieved it in 2008, but soon found that the quality of the plastic isn't high enough at that level. We dropped back down to 35% and have now edged it up to 50%—but beyond that it isn't good enough for our premium products.

The essential problem we face is that as customers perceive highly recycled bottles to be low quality, how do we stick to our principles and ensure a high level of recyclable content without losing sales?

Introduction

What is critical marketing and what is sustainable marketing? Why are banks reconsidering their ethical policies? When are advertising and marketing communications coercive? When should companies give back to their communities? What is 'good' marketing behaviour and what is 'bad' marketing behaviour? Are corporate social responsibility initiatives a good idea, or are they cynically used to further organizational interests? These are the sorts of question considered in this chapter.

We begin by discussing marketing's shift towards sustainable economic development and the sub-discipline of sustainable marketing, defining and explaining its implications for marketing practice. We look at critical marketing, considering the practices it critiques from the lens of unsustainable marketing. We discuss the topic of ethics, before applying ethical principles to the marketing context. We outline how ethical situations impact on the marketing decision-making process. Four main ethical approaches to marketing decision-making are also considered. Ethical situations arising in product, promotion, price, and distribution programmes are also explained. We consider ethical issues in international marketing, i.e. whether or not different cultures should have different moral rules, and finally we discuss the important topic of bribery as an aberrant element of sales management/lobbying processes.

An understanding of **marketing ethics** is critical to making marketing practice more sustainable. But it is also important, as practitioners, to understand the ethical, legal, and social dimensions of marketing decision-making in order to develop the analytical skills for considering ethical problems when they arise. Otherwise, ethical problems can wreak substantial reputational damage on an organization, threatening its very existence and certainly its leaders' careers.

Sustainable Marketing

Supporters of **sustainable marketing** accept the limitations of marketing philosophy and acknowledge the need to impose regulatory constraints on marketing (van Dam and Apeldoorn, 1996), particularly concerning its impact on the environment. Sustainable economic development, i.e. development that meets the needs of current generations without imposing constraints on the needs of future generations, was first proposed at a United Nations Conference in Stockholm in 1972 (WCED, 1987). To understand why a policy on sustainable development is necessary, consider the following two recent examples of companies causing catastrophic environmental impacts.

- **2010: BP** More than 200m gallons of oil were spilled into the Gulf of Mexico after an oil rig explosion killed 11 people. The oil spill affected 1,000 miles of shoreline, killing thousands of birds, around 153 dolphins, and other local wildlife. The disaster caused BP to initially lose half its share value, and total costs (including fines, compensation, legal fees, and other costs) for the disaster were $53.8bn in 2015 (Bryant, 2011; Anon., 2015a). BP's contractor, Transocean, shared some blame for the incident, receiving a fine of $1.4bn from the US authorities (Anon., 2013a). Another contractor, Halliburton, was also found to be partly liable for some of the damage caused by the incident and reached a $1.1bn settlement in 2014 (Rushe, 2014).

- **2011: Tokyo Electric Power (Tepco)** Three former executives at Tepco were charged with professional negligence contributing to death and injury from the meltdown in 2011 at the Fukushima Daiichi nuclear plant (McCurry, 2016). The meltdown was caused after a magnitude 9 earthquake caused a massive tsunami, flooding the nuclear reactors. The men were charged with failing to take measures to defend the plant, despite knowing the risks of a tsunami. Over 300,000 people were made homeless and 20,000 were killed as a result of the earthquake and the tsunami across Japan (Conca, 2015). In Fukushima Prefecture alone, a further 1,656 people died due to post-disaster health conditions occurring as a result of the government-enforced evacuation of everyone living within 20km of the site, i.e. stress from the evacuation, transfer trauma in relation to the infirm, and those with chronic illnesses unable to access medical treatments (World Nuclear Association, 2016).

Sustainable marketers attempt to broaden sustainable development to the practice of marketing, beyond simple economic development. This introduces the following maxims, known as the three Es of sustainability.

1 Ecological—marketing should not negatively impact upon the environment.

2 Equitable—marketing should not allow or promote inequitable social practices.

3 Economic—marketing should encourage long-term economic development as opposed to short-term economic development.

Sustainable marketing is the 'third age' of green marketing (Peattie, 2001). In the 'first age', ecological green marketing (c.1960s–1970s) was concerned with automobile, oil, and agrichemical companies which encountered environmental problems in the production process. The 'second age', environmental green marketing (c.1980s), saw the development of green consumers, i.e. people who purchased offerings to avoid negative environmental impacts (e.g. cosmetic products that had not been tested on animals). But green marketing was too heavily focused on the purchasing element of consumption (Peattie and Crane, 2005), perhaps because the sustainability debate did not consider the business-to-business dimension sufficiently.

The third age of green marketing is sustainable green marketing. Sustainable marketers should focus on positioning and demand stimulation for recycled and re-manufactured products and build-to-order offerings, as well as considering supply chain management issues such as enabling materials recovery from end-consumers, designing offerings to enable their dismantlement, enabling **reverse logistics** for recycling and re-manufactured offerings, and reducing supply by offering build-to-order offerings (Sharma *et al.*, 2010). In the third age, companies also need to lengthen the time horizons by which they achieve investment returns (e.g. Unilever's CEO Paul Polman scrapped the quarterly shareholder meeting; see Market Insight 18.1) and require emphasis on the full costs of purchase rather than simply the price paid. Proposition development activities should fully consider, equitably, inputs and cooperation from all members of the supply chain. Companies need to adopt environmental auditing methods (e.g. to include costs for disposal as well as development, delivery, and consumption), and organizations may actually discourage consumption in certain cases (Bridges and Wilhelm, 2008), or at least encourage more mindful consumption and temperance rather than acquisitive, repetitive, or aspirational over-consumption behaviour (Sheth *et al.*, 2011). For example, in 2013, Coca-Cola launched a worldwide campaign on obesity (partnering in the UK until 2015 with StreetGames, a sport participation charity) by introducing smaller bottles (375ml) and displaying detailed calorie content on the pack (Mintel, 2013). But Coke has not always been consistent. In 2012, the company was said to have used more water than around a quarter of the world's population, using 79bn gallons to dilute its syrup and an extra 8 trillion gallons in other elements of production (Gwyther, 2015). In 2014, The Body Shop—to maintain its own strict policy against animal testing—removed all products from duty free shelves in airports in China after consumer watchdog Choice revealed that the Chinese Government conducted post-market testing of Body Shop products on animals (Davidson, 2014).

Such longer-term thinking led to the development of the **circular economy**, e.g. Vodafone runs a Red-Hot deal where customers lease a phone and return the old one for an upgrade. Airbnb, founded in 2008 but valued at $25.5bn in 2015, is another example of a company encouraging the sharing, swapping, and renting of possessions (i.e. **collaborative consumption**) in the spare room business (Alba, 2015).

So far, we have considered sustainable marketing, but what happens when marketing activity is unsustainable?

Market Insight 18.1
Unilever's Sustainability Challenge

In 2010, Unilever's CEO Paul Polman launched an ambitious plan called the Sustainable Living Plan. He claimed that Unilever wanted to make a positive societal contribution by helping to solve world environmental and social challenges. Among other targets, the company committed to halving its environmental footprint by 2020 and doubling revenues. Some questioned the feasibility of such a bold plan, warning that if the financial objectives were not met, investors might be less willing to believe in Polman's visionary leadership.

Unilever is an Anglo-Dutch multinational corporation with a turnover of €53.3bn in 2015, manufacturing and marketing many popular brands including Flora, Dove, and Lynx. Around 2bn consumers use Unilever brands every day worldwide, and the company employs 172,000 people. The Sustainable Living Plan seeks to assess the impact that the company's offerings have on society and the environment, setting ambitious targets that go beyond internal operations. To achieve its goals, the company needs to persuade its customers to behave more responsibly and buy ethical alternatives—a challenge because although a majority of consumers express concern about the environment, only a small segment consistently behave according to their attitudes. A year after the launch of the plan, Unilever reported on progress. Although internal operations are more sustainable, chief marketing officer Keith Weed admitted that changing consumer behaviour was more difficult than expected, despite the fact that the Sustainable Living Plan was designed to respond to consumer pressure and social concern for environmental issues. Nearly four years after launch, Unilever's share price had risen 40%, it topped the Globescan/SustainAbility survey for sustainable leadership (by a long way), carbon emissions in its manufacturing operations were a third lower than in 2008, and 48% of its agricultural supplies were sourced sustainably. Five years after launch, halfway into the plan, carbon emissions were down by 37% on 2008 and waste going to landfill down by 85%. But if the company is to achieve a reduction of 50% of emissions, it will not only have to persuade its customers to change the way they live (i.e. by taking shorter showers), but will also require suppliers to become considerably more efficient. There is still a long way to go, but Polman never said that reaching the target would be easy.

Sources: Skapinker (2010); Baker (2012); Polman (2012); Anon. (2015b); Shayon (2015); Unilever (2016).

Theory into Practice

This market insight illustrates how a large multinational company is leading the way in changing customer and supplier behaviour to increase profits whilst simultaneously decreasing environmental impacts. The case also illustrates how a company with a history of pioneering philanthropy can also be highly profitable.

Related Topics:

reverse logistics; recycling; sustainable marketing; theory of planned behaviour.

1 **Why has Unilever launched the Sustainable Living Plan?**

2 **What are the major negative impacts that Unilever's offerings might have on the environment and society?**

3 **Why do you think that some customers are not supporting sustainability initiatives despite stating interest in environmental and social issues?**

This market insight was kindly contributed by Dr Paolo Antonetti, Queen Mary, University of London.

Unsustainable Marketing: The Critical 'Turn'

Some argue that **capitalism** is under siege, given that it is a major cause of social, environmental, and economic problems (Porter and Kramer, 2011). We agree that not all marketing's contributions to society are good. Consequently, there is a need to develop a critical approach to understanding marketing practice. To truly understand the discipline, we need to study both mainstream and critical marketing, given their interdependence (Shankar, 2009). For Gordon et al. (2011) to practice sustainable marketing requires an understanding of green marketing (e.g. energy efficient production, self-regulation), social marketing (e.g. by encouraging ecological lifestyles), and critical marketing (e.g. by changing the marketing system to incentivize sustainable production/consumption). Critical marketing analysis helps in 'problematizing hitherto uncontentious marketing areas to reveal underlying institutional and theoretical dysfunctionalities' (Saren, 2011: 95). A critical approach to marketing suggests that we consider the following (Burton, 2001).

- The need to (re-)evaluate marketing activities, categories, and frameworks, and to improve them so that marketing operates in a desirable manner within society.

- The extent to which marketing knowledge is developed based on our contemporary social world, e.g. much current marketing knowledge encompasses American (and Western) practice and research. What implications does this have for the rest of the world?

- How do the historical and cultural conditions in which we operate, as consumers and as students of marketing, impact on how we see marketing as a discipline?

- How can marketing benefit from other intellectual perspectives, e.g. social anthropology, social psychology, linguistics, philosophy, and sociology?

Some key topics in critical marketing include the notion of marketing as manipulation, commodity fetishism, and the nature of need versus choice (see Tadajewski, 2010). We consider each of these topics next.

Marketing as Manipulation

Since its inception, marketing has been charged with the notion that it serves itself rather than consumers, and that it supports the capitalist rather than the labouring classes. Packard (1960) critiqued marketing by explaining that it beguiled its target audiences, often covertly, and frequently without people even understanding that they were being manipulated.

Marketers and public relations officers certainly do 'frame' their communications to make them more persuasive. **Framing** is the action of presenting persuasive communication and the action of audiences in interpreting that communication to assimilate it into their existing understanding (Scheufele and Tewksbury, 2007). The framing takes place via the framing of situations (e.g. by highlighting sales promotions available for a fixed time only), attributes (e.g. by highlighting usage features of, say, a mobile phone), choices (e.g. by showing a potential car buyer options across the range), actions (e.g. buy now, pay later schemes), issues (e.g. Asda explaining why it boycotted the 2015 UK Black Friday sales promotion), responsibilities (e.g. Save the Children explaining why African children need help in order to elicit donations), and news (e.g. Volkswagen explaining why their chief executive was replaced after the emissions scandal) (Hallahan, 1999; see also Market Insight 18.4).

The problem arises when framing becomes 'spin', as then marketing promotion becomes corporate propaganda. For example, some photographic tricks to make food offerings look great in print adverts include using motor oil as syrup or honey, or glue or shampoo as milk in cereals. For hotels and resorts, photos are frequently doctored to remove unwanted elements or a wide-angle lens is used to make scenes look expansive. In the USA, whilst ads are generally fairly trusted, ads for diet offerings, financial services, and prescription drugs are far less trusted (Anon., 2014a).

Visit the Online Resource Centre and complete Internet Activity 18.1 to learn more about manipulative practices in marketing.

Commodity Fetishism

This critical perspective, derived from Marxist economic theory (Marx, 1867), proposes that society is overly dominated by consumption, and hence fetishizes it (i.e. places supreme importance on it). Marx suggested that, prior to industrialization, goods were produced for their use-value. A producer manufactured a product for a user and exchanged it with the customer. After industrialization, the social relationship between producer and user changed. Marx argued that workers were exploited for their labour, as they became removed from the product they produced and paid on a piece rate rather than on a share of the financial return generated as a result of their labour. In the process, the commodity produced acquired exchange-value, becoming tradable with other commodities within the capitalist market system, benefiting the capitalist (i.e. the investor). Marx felt that the rigid pursuit of capitalism was so doctrinal that it represented a religious ideology. Commodities produced as a result of capitalist endeavour took on a religious aura, worshipped by those seduced by their perceived value (Sherover, 1979). The idea that we are worshipping consumption begs the question of whether marketers meet our wants, our needs, or neither. An unwelcome example of how consumer and worker needs were subverted is that of the horsemeat scandal in 2013 (see Market Insight 18.2); both consumers and workers were duped into respectively eating and processing products that were not what they were supposed to be.

Need and Choice

The received wisdom is that marketing works to meet the needs of customers and consumers. However, Alvesson (1994), coming from outside the marketing discipline, rejects this notion. He argues that people in affluent societies seek more without gaining any further long-term satisfaction from such consumption, because much of the consumption is superficial anyway and because appealing to people's fantasies and highlighting their imperfections (to encourage them to reduce these feelings of inadequacy by buying a particular offering) leads to narcissistic tendencies. Inherently, the notion is that more choice is good, but is that true when more choice can lead to customer confusion and a decline in trust (Newman, 2001). Saren (2007) suggests that, for many people 'to have is to be'—that the meaning of contemporary life is consumption (see Research Insight 18.1). Further, some customers are persuaded and manipulated into purchasing offerings that they do not want or which are unfit for their requirements, for example financial services companies in the UK have been charged with mis-selling payment protection insurance (PPI). By 2015, British banks had had to put aside £27bn for extra administration and to settle customers' compensation claims to cover the claims of 16.5m people, with a further 5.5m still to claim (Treanor, 2015).

Market Insight 18.2
Flogging a Dead Horse

On 16 January 2013, the Food Safety Authority of Ireland reported that traces of equine DNA were found in products labelled 'beef' burgers supplied to Silvercrest Foods in Ireland and Dalepak Hambleton in Britain. As a result, 10m burgers were removed from shelves by supermarket retailers including Aldi, Lidl, Tesco, Iceland, and Dunnes Stores. Frozen meat at Freeza Meats Company in Northern Ireland was found to contain 80% horsemeat, forcing Asda to withdraw its supplies from the shelves. Later, Findus UK 'beef' lasagne, supplied by the French company Comigel, was found to contain 100% horsemeat. Worse, the French company had supplied 28 different companies in 13 European states. Britain and Ireland were not the only countries affected. Swiss food giant Nestlé removed two pasta meals from supermarkets in Italy and Spain. German discount chain Lidl removed ready meals from Finnish, Danish, and Swedish stores after finding that certain meat products were contaminated with horsemeat. Contaminated products were found in other countries including France, Austria, Norway, the Netherlands, and Germany.

Consumers and politicians were shocked. If they were eating horse labelled as beef, what else might they be eating and was it safe? Consumer trust was initially shattered. Kantar Worldpanel, the research firm, reported a 43% drop in British burger sales in the four weeks after the scandal broke and a 13% decline in sales of frozen ready meals over the same period. Key questions arose: Who was at fault? Was it the

'Beef' burgers, but not as we know them, were sold throughout Europe, forcing supermarkets to withdraw millions of packs from their shelves
Source: © papillondream/Shutterstock.

local authorities (who enforce food safety), the retailers (who stock and test the products), the criminals who mislabelled and switched the product, the suppliers (who process and produce the product), the food standards agencies in the countries concerned (who regulate the industry), or even the consumer (for buying ever cheaper products from their supermarkets)? As a consequence, the UK Food Standards Agency set up a National Food Crime Unit (NFCU) and the EU set up the Food Fraud Network. Several slaughterhouse bosses in Britain and a Dutch horsemeat trader in Holland went to jail on various charges relating to the scandal (failing to abide by EU meat traceability regulations and falsifying documents, respectively).

Sources: Anon. (2013b); Lucas (2013); Press Association (2013, 2015); Elder (2015); Hutton (2015).

Theory into Practice

The market insight revealed some shocking facts: no-one (i.e. consumers, retailers, regulators) was sure whether a food product was what it was labelled as or not, and regulation in the European food market was weak. The whole European food industry was highly susceptible to fraud and crime. Whilst consumers lost trust in their suppliers and purchased other food products as substitutes, the criminals (for a time at least) walked off with the extra income generated from selling a meat designated not fit for human consumption (i.e. the meat from a horse carcass), which would therefore have been available cheaply. Criminal meat processors mixed the horsemeat with other meat to dupe retailers and consumers. The lack of empathy for customer and consumer needs is clear for all to see.

Market Insight 18.2
continued

Related Topics:

marketing ethics; crisis management; corporate social responsibility.

1 What marketing factors, if any, do you think led to the scandal arising?

2 Who do you think was at fault? Why do you say this?

3 From a marketing perspective, what do you think would need to be done to rebuild consumer trust?

Although the aggregate marketing system (Wilkie and Moore, 1999; see also Chapter 1) distributes life-saving medicines, food, and important utilities (e.g. heat and light), it distributes anything, including alcohol, tobacco, and gambling products for example. These are products most would regard as dangerous to our health and well-being. Of course, in many cultures around the world, people enjoy drinking, smoking, and gambling. However, if we use these to excess, all three can have addictive properties to varying degrees.

If prostitution and soft drugs, such as cannabis, were made legal in the UK, the aggregate marketing system would distribute them. It already does this in the Netherlands, for instance, where these practices are not illegal. The aggregate marketing system is amoral—not immoral, i.e. designed to harm, but amoral, designed without any care as to whether it harms or not. The system is made moral by the decisions taken by governments and other institutional actors regulating the aggregate marketing system. Illegal offerings can be marketed in almost the same way as legal offerings. For example, this occurs via the 'dark web' (also called **cryptomarkets**)

Research Insight 18.1

To take your learning further, you might wish to read this influential paper.

Saren, M. (2007). To have is to be? A critique of self-creation through consumption. *Marketing Review*, 7(4), 343–54.

This highly readable article critiques the notion that consumers link their identity to their consumption activity to derive satisfaction. Saren argues that the consumption process, seen from the critical theoretical perspective, leads to a never-ending cycle of desire which is never satisfied, and so a consumer's identity can equally never be complete.

Visit the Online Resource Centre to read the abstract and access the full paper.

Paying for products imported from overseas—are you prepared to pay more to give farmers and labourers a fair deal?

Source: © Tracing Tea/Shutterstock.

where illegal offerings, such as drugs, forged passports, guns, stolen credit card details, and other ill-gotten booty, are traded (Franklin, 2013). Previous websites included DarkMarket and Silk Road, both of which were closed by law enforcement officials. Interestingly, whilst previous dark markets worked reasonably well as trading platforms between criminal parties, contemporary cryptomarkets have closed down relatively quickly as site owners have taken customers' money after an initial period of trading. They have therefore been operating more like scam sites (Greenberg, 2016).

Other Controversies

Of particular concern are those situations in which one group is unfairly disadvantaged over another, or where one group exerts its power over another (e.g. the Fairtrade Movement was set up to ensure that in the coffee market, for example, shippers, roasters, and retailers pay fair prices to the supplying farmers, mostly located in developing countries such as Kenya and Colombia). Some controversial issues include the following.

- Is the price paid by companies/organizations in wealthier countries for supplies obtained in poorer countries fair? Major multinational corporations, e.g. Nike and Gap, have been caught exploiting migrant labour in foreign countries to produce expensive branded goods (Ellis *et al*., 2010: 219). The moral dilemma, and the resultant consumer backlash, has in part led to the rise of the Fairtrade Movement.

- To what extent should the propositions and ideas of one country be marketed over the propositions and ideas of another? This is cultural imperialism. What are the cultural implications? For example, China has blocked Twitter, Facebook, and Google from operating, preferring instead to set up its own search engine (Baidu), microblogging site (Weibo), and social networking site (QQ).

- How much should we consume of any one offering? When should governments step in to limit consumption? In Sweden, alcohol retailing is run by the state alcohol monopoly Systembolaget to ensure that public health is not adversely impacted by over-consumption of alcohol. In Britain in 2015, police chiefs urged retailers to abandon the Black Friday sales promotion (an American custom where a sales event is held on the fourth Friday of November, the day after Thanksgiving) after the 2014 flash sale caused 'scenes of chaos' with shoppers literally fighting each other, and to get over each other, to bag the best deals (Clarke-Billings, 2015).

- Are some producers or buyer groups more powerful than others, and what impact, if any, does this have on society? For example, for many years producers have been using intrusive ads (e.g. automatic video, pop-up ads) to raise awareness of their offerings, but ad-blocking software like that from Germany's Eyeo is now commonly available (Anon., 2015c). This makes it difficult for some legitimate organizations, such as publishers (e.g. UK's *The Guardian)*, to make their business models work since they provide free content on the basis that they can raise revenue from advertising to the readership. Therefore should ad-blocking be allowed?

- Does the shift from customer research to customer surveillance benefit customers? For example, retailers are using mannequins integrated with facial recognition software of the type used by law enforcement agencies to track the age, sex, and race of their customers as they pass

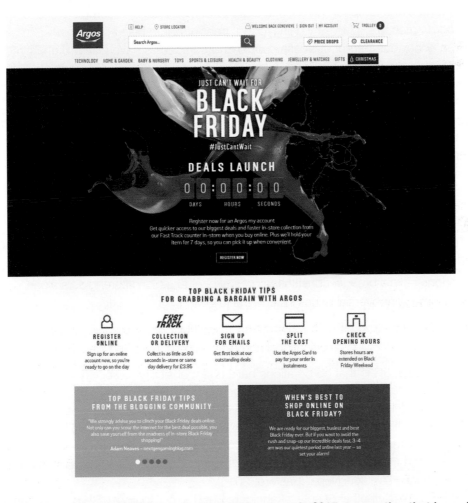

Argos offered many heavily discounted Black Friday deals in 2015, suggesting that bargain hunters browse their website between 3 and 4a.m. to avoid the online queues
Source: Courtesy of Argos.

through or by a store. Depending on whether or not, and how, these data are stored, such an approach has serious ethical implications (Clark, 2012).

These examples illustrate imbalances in power structures between consumers, producers, retailers, and other actors. The question which arises for marketers is: How should these relationships be structured to ensure that they are fair to all concerned?

Although companies are increasingly recognizing the negative impacts they can have on society (**externalities**), many are also increasingly trying to contribute positively to societal development through corporate social responsibility programmes.

Corporate Social Responsibility

Corporate social responsibility (CSR) initiatives are increasingly common. Many companies publish annual CSR or sustainability reports (e.g. BAT, GSK). Governments and supranational organizations actively encourage CSR initiatives (e.g. the UN Global Compact project). CSR practitioners and academics continue to try to demonstrate the commercial effectiveness of CSR programmes to explain why being 'good' translates into being profitable.

Despite any obvious return, business people and companies have given to charity for centuries. Famous cases include the John Paul Getty Foundation in the USA (built on oil industry profits), which funds art and social projects, and Anglo American, the mining conglomerate, which provides welfare support for its employees living with HIV/AIDS in Africa. In 2014, Mars launched a campaign 'Choose (Galaxy®)RED. Make lives better', where donations from special packs of Galaxy® helped to provide more than 3m days worth of life-saving medication to help prevent the transmission of HIV from mothers to their babies in Ghana. The rationale for developing CSR initiatives, irrespective of their financial contribution, is based around the following ideas (Buchholz, 1991: 19):

- Corporations have responsibilities going beyond the production of their offerings at a profit.
- These responsibilities involve helping to solve important social problems, especially those they helped to create.
- Corporations have a broader constituency of stakeholders than shareholders alone.
- The impacts of corporations go beyond simple marketplace transactions.
- Corporations serve a wider range of human values, not captured solely by a focus on economic values.

A central theme of CSR is that corporations have a responsibility to society that goes beyond pursuing profit (Martin, 2002). Intercontinental Hotels Group (IHG) illustrates this by running three core programmes: (1) the IHG Green Engage System, allowing individual hotels to track their carbon footprints; (2) the IHG Academy, where locals from a hotel's community can work in it; (3) IHG Shelter in a Storm, a fundraising programme allowing IHG to come to the aid of employees or guests, e.g. the Crowne Plaza Kathmandu allowed 1,000 people to sleep in the ballroom when an earthquake struck in Nepal (Basford, 2015).

One key problem is whether or not stakeholders view the company's CSR programme as sincere, particularly as customers punish companies they regard as insincere by boycotting them (van de Wen, 2008). For example, Hindustan Unilever's alleged failure to clean up mercury waste

Research Insight 18.2

To take your learning further, you might wish to read this influential paper.

Maignan, I., Ferrell, O.C., and Ferell, L. (2005). A stakeholder model for implementing social responsibility in marketing. *European Journal of Marketing*, 39(9/10), 956–77.

This is a highly cited and readable paper providing a managerial framework to help marketers orient stakeholders' needs when designing corporate responsibility programmes. The authors provide a series of eight steps outlining how to implement CSR: (1) discovering organizational norms and values, (2) identifying stakeholders, (3) identifying stakeholder issues, (4) assessing the meaning of CSR, (5) auditing current practices, (6) implementing CSR initiatives, (7) promoting CSR, and (8) gaining stakeholder feedback.

Visit the Online Resource Centre to read the abstract and access the full paper.

from a former factory in Kodaikanal, Tamil Nadu, has led to calls on social media for a boycott after a 28-year-old Indian rapper launched a critical video on YouTube drawing 2.2m views within two weeks of launch and more than 60,000 signatures on a petition calling for a clean-up and worker compensation (Kazmin, 2015). Incorporating stakeholder feedback into the design of a CSR programme is therefore critical (see Research Insight 18.2).

When CSR is not designed with proper stakeholder feedback, it can be seen as a 'gentle soap for washing dirty hands' (Debeljak *et al.*, 2011: 12). It is often used by companies in industries regarded as unsustainable (e.g. oil and gas, tobacco, and alcohol) because managers believe that it is important (Cai *et al.*, 2011), probably to improve their companies' otherwise poor environmental credentials.

Visit the Online Resource Centre and complete Internet Activity 18.2 to learn more about some of the ethical debates surrounding sportswear manufacture that have occurred over the years.

A counter-argument to developing a corporate responsibility programme might be that we don't usually expect companies to solve the world's social problems at their own cost. For example, we don't expect airlines to offer free seats to the unemployed. This example illustrates the ethical difficulties inherent in marketing decision-making.

Ethics and Marketing

Ethics, a subdiscipline of philosophy, is over 2,000 years old. It is defined as 'moral principles that govern a person's behaviour or the conducting of an activity' and 'the branch of knowledge that deals with moral principles' (Oxford Dictionaries, 2016). Ethics can be divided into the following types.

- **Normative ethics**—concerned with the rational enquiry into standards of right and wrong (i.e. norms), good or bad, with respect to character and conduct, which *ought to be* accepted by a class of individuals.

- **Social or religious ethics**—concerned with what is right and wrong, good and bad, with respect to character and conduct. It does not claim to be established merely on the basis of rational enquiry and makes an implicit claim to general allegiance to something (e.g. God, Allah, the Buddha).

- **Positive morality**—a body of knowledge generally adhered to by a social group of individuals, concerning what is right and wrong, good and bad, with respect to character and conduct.

- **Descriptive ethics**—concerned with the study of the system of beliefs and practices of a social group from the perspective of being outside that group.

- **Meta-ethics**—a form of philosophical enquiry which treats ethical concepts and belief systems as objects of philosophical enquiry in themselves.

Considering morality in marketing gives rise to the question: How should a 'good' marketer behave? To determine how to apply ethics to marketing, we must define what marketing is. The Chartered Institute of Marketing's definition is 'the management process responsible for identifying, anticipating and satisfying customer requirements profitably' (see Chapter 1). Therefore how does ethics relate to marketing? We could suggest that marketing ethics is concerned with how we go about the process of identifying, anticipating, and satisfying customer requirements. The application of ethical principles might consider what meaning is given to the term 'profitable'. Islamic readers, not entirely happy with the objective of a firm being to achieve profit, might feel it more worthy for a firm to aspire to value maximization (Saeed *et al.*, 2001). Because there are both prescriptive and descriptive components of ethics, we define marketing ethics as: 'The analysis and application of moral principles to marketing decision-making and the outcomes of these decisions' (see Research Insight 18.3).

Ethical Norms in Marketing Decision-Making

Norms are suggestions about how we *should* behave. Professional marketing organizations have a code of professional practice that requires members to behave and act in a certain manner, as do many companies and organizations. For example, the American Marketing Association requires its members to (AMA, 2014):

1 Do no harm—by consciously avoiding harmful actions or omissions, embodying high ethical standards, and following applicable laws and regulations in the choices we make.

2 Foster trust in the marketing system—by striving for good faith and fair dealing to contribute toward the efficacy of the exchange process and avoiding deception in product design pricing, communication, and delivery of distribution.

3 Embrace ethical values. By building relationships and enhancing consumer confidence in the integrity of marketing by affirming these core values: honesty (being forthright in dealings with all stakeholders), responsibility (accepting the consequences of the decisions we make), fairness (justifying the needs of the buyers with those of the seller), respect (acknowledging the human dignity of all stakeholders), transparency (being open in all marketing operations), and citizenship (fulfilling economic, legal, philanthropic, and societal responsibilities to our stakeholders).

In ethics, norms typically comprise five general approaches: (1) **deontological ethics**, (2) **teleological ethics**, (3) **managerial egoism**, (4) **utilitarianism**, and (5) **virtue ethics** (see Table 18.1). We outline each approach further in the following sections. Simply read through

Research Insight 18.3

To take your learning further, you might wish to read this influential paper.

Hunt, S.D. and Vitell, S. (2006). The general theory of marketing ethics: a revision and three questions. *Journal of Macromarketing*, 26(2), 143–53.

This article builds upon one of the most highly cited paper in marketing ethics (Hunt and Vitell, 1986), which defined the study of marketing ethics. This paper suggests that the original 1986 theory required revision because the model was applicable in any ethical decision-making situation, not just in business and management contexts, and required empirical testing. The authors argue that ethical judgements lead to intentions and on to behaviour. Our intentions are made on the basis of whether an action is right in itself (i.e. deontological ethics) and whether our intentions are right (i.e. teleological ethics).

Visit the Online Resource Centre to read the abstract and access the full paper.

Table 18.1 The main normative approaches to ethical decision-making

Ethical approach	Explanation
Deontological ethics	An ethical approach where the rightness or wrongness of an action or decision is not judged to be based exclusively on the consequences of that action or decision
Teleological ethics	An ethical approach where the rightness or wrongness of an action is determined by its consequences
Managerial egoism	An ethical approach recognizing that a manager ought to act in his/her own best interests and that an action is right if it benefits the manager undertaking that action
Utilitarianism	An ethical approach developed by English philosopher Jeremy Bentham suggesting that an action is right if, and only if, it conforms to the principle of utility, whereby utility is maximized (i.e. pleasure, happiness, or welfare), and pain or unhappiness minimized, more than any alternative
Virtue ethics	A form of ethical approach associated with Aristotle stressing the importance of developing virtuous principles, 'right' character, and the pursuit of a virtuous life

Research Insight 18.4

To take your learning further, you might wish to read this influential paper.

Laczniak, G.R. and Murphy, P.E. (2006). Normative perspectives for ethical and socially responsible marketing. *Journal of Macromarketing*, 26(2), 154–77.

This paper presents a set of normative ethical perspectives for improving the practice of marketing, including putting people first, achieving a standard in excess of law, being responsible for whatever is intended as the means or ends of a marketing action, cultivating better moral imagination in employees, articulating and embracing a core set of ethical principles, adopting a stakeholder orientation to ethical marketing decisions, and delineating an ethical marketing decision-making protocol.

@ **Visit the Online Resource Centre** to read the abstract and access the full paper.

each section, and the associated examples, to understand the differences. If necessary, read through these sections several times before moving onto the next section to fully understand the concepts (see also Research Insight 18.4).

Deontological Ethics

Deontological ethics proposes that the rightness of an action is not determined by the consequences of that action (Mautner, 1999). Rather, deontological ethics emphasizes the importance of codes of ethics, such as those outlined by the Market Research Society (MRS), governing market research in the UK, or by ESOMAR, the world association for market research. Deontological approaches propose that we have not only a moral duty to ensure customer satisfaction via the finished offering, but also a duty to ensure integrity in how the offering is produced and marketed (see Market Insight 18.3).

Teleological Ethics

Teleological ethics proposes that the rightness of an action depends on the value of the consequences (Mautner, 1999). An organization is acting morally if it does not intend harm to come from its actions but harm is caused by accident anyway, or if its behaviour is 'bad' but 'good' consequences result, for example paying a warlord 'tax' to continue operations in a developing country as Firestone did in Liberia in 1992 (Taddonio, 2014). Utilitarianism and virtue ethics are subsets of teleological ethics.

Managerial Egoism

The rationale for egoism is the pursuit of one's own interests, or self-interest. We assume that the interests of marketing managers align with the interests of owners or directors of the organization (but they might not). The ethical principle of managerial egoism is to maximize shareholder value, or stakeholder value for a non-profit organization. If managers maximize their own self-interest (in a free market), economic welfare is maximized for all, according to Adam Smith (1776). Adopting the managerial egoist principle, we conclude that companies should set their

Market Insight 18.3
Forex Fixing

Between 2009 and 2013 the global banking industry was fined more than £166bn in settlement fees and provisions for bad behaviour including LIBOR (London Interbank Offered Rate) fixing, currency market manipulation, breaching sanctions on Iran, Sudan, and Cuba, money laundering for Mexican drug cartels, abusive mortgage practices in the USA, and mis-selling of payment protection insurance in the UK. That's quite a list of dodgy dealing.

Consider foreign exchange currency market manipulation. This occurred between 2007 and 2013 in a market totalling an estimated £3.3tn a day, 41% of which came through the City of London. Fines imposed by the UK's Financial Conduct Authority (FCA) and numerous regulators in the USA on various international banks, including Barclays and the Royal Bank of Scotland, totalled £6.3bn. Barclays was fined £1.5bn by five regulators, including £284m by the FCA. Barclays, the Royal Bank of Scotland, and HSBC also agreed to pay out £600m to settle a US investor class-action lawsuit related to the fixing of forex markets. Investor claims are also likely to be submitted in London, a much larger market than the USA, meaning that the banks face legal costs running into further billions.

But what did the banks do to deserve these fines and lawsuits? The answer is that their employees rigged the market by colluding with other traders in closed-membership online chatrooms (with names like 'The Bandits Club' and 'The Cartel'), sharing confidential client currency order information which allowed them to submit large currency orders simultaneously during the time that the benchmark price is set. This is the price many customers request to settle deals and it is calculated within the 30 seconds of trading either side of 4p.m. Greenwich Mean Time, the 'fix' time. If just before these big trades occur, the traders also buy some currency on their own trading account using the bank's money (knowing that the currency price will, say, go up because of their client's large currency orders), they can then sell the currency after the large trade has taken place and make a hefty profit (since they bought the currency at a lower exchange rate than the rate at which they later sell it). If several currency traders collude, they are more likely to affect 'the fix' and to a larger degree to their advantage.

Despite the apparent evidence, in 2016 Britain's Serious Fraud Office (SFO) closed the criminal investigation into forex fixing, deciding that there was no serious prospect of getting a conviction under English law. Losers include the banks themselves (because of the fines imposed), the banks' clients because of slight skews in the market, and the financial system itself, as public trust is further undermined.

Sources: Goodley (2014); Kollewe *et al*. (2014); Augar (2015); Treanor and Rushe (2015); Trotman (2015); Treanor (2016).

Theory into Practice

The market insight illustrates the sheer scale of fines and compensation that large global banks have had to pay as a result of their employees' unethical behaviour. Some bank employees, who were sacked for their conduct as part of the regulatory settlements, showed no respect whatsoever for the wider foreign exchange system, acting purely in their own interests (in pursuit of higher profits to the bank and bonuses to themselves). No ethical normative framework (i.e. utilitarian, deontological, teleological, virtue ethics), other than a managerial egoist approach (what is in the trader's interest is in the best interests of everyone) can justify the traders' forex fixing actions. But even the managerial egoist approach, which assumes that managers' interests are linked to shareholders' interests, fails to justify the actions in the longer term, given that the banks eventually received stringent fines (thereby reducing shareholder value).

Market Insight 18.3
continued

Related Topics:
corporate social responsibility; critical marketing.

1 Why do you think global banks have become mired in so many scandals?

2 Barclays has developed an ethical code of conduct—The Barclays Way. Do you think such a policy will help to ensure that a scandal like

forex fixing never happens to them again? Why do you say this?

3 Look up the ethical policies of two other global banks on their websites. How are they similar and how do they differ?

marketing programmes to maximize shareholder or stakeholder value. The celebrated economist Milton Friedman suggested that managers should *only* have responsibility to maximize shareholder returns as they 'lack the wisdom and ability to resolve complex social problems' (Friedman, 1979: 90). However, economists suggest that markets are amoral, and that the free market mechanism does not work to promote ethical decisions; instead it works to supply the optimal amount of offerings in a society. Managerial egoism, because of its focus on the consequences of decisions ('the ends'), is a subset of teleological ethics.

Some say that marketers should not be concerned with ethics as long as they uphold the law and manage their own self-interest, as unethical behaviour is sanctioned in the marketplace anyway (e.g. by boycotts). Firms will therefore pursue their own self-interest by acting ethically anyway (Gaski, 1999). There is evidence to suggest that companies offering services rather than goods require employees to be more ethical, as there is more opportunity for unethical behaviour Because of the greater company–customer interaction and the trust generated accordingly (Rao and Singhapakdi, 1997).

If marketers act only according to the law or a company's self-interest, this can be regarded as a moral minimum. Most societies require companies to go beyond this. With this ethical approach, it is not always possible to determine whether a company is pursuing a managerial egoist approach (i.e. acting in its own self-interest because this benefits others) or only a shareholder value maximization approach. The two appear the same. The cynic wonders whether a company going beyond its legal duties and apparently acting according to higher morals (e.g. Ben & Jerry's, Guaranty Trust Bank) is simply trying to win public support and maximize long-term shareholder value, rather than be ethical.

Utilitarianism

Utilitarianism, developed by the English philosopher Jeremy Bentham, proposes that an action is right if, and only if, its performance is more productive of pleasure or happiness or welfare, or more preventive of pain or unhappiness, than alternatives (Mautner, 1999). Utilitarian arguments are concerned with an action's consequences. Ethical arguments proposed by marketers are typically utilitarian. Marketing itself could be argued to be utilitarian, as it is often concerned with satisfying consumer needs and wants at the market level (Nantel and Weeks, 1996). Utilitarianism is centred around 'producing the greater good for the greatest number of people' (Mautner, 1999). The problem is that the maximization of one group's utility may lead to the minimization of another's. To evaluate the utility associated with a particular decision, we must determine the 'costs' and 'benefits', which are extremely difficult to quantify. For example, where an offering may save lives, such as with life-saving drugs or health treatments, the losers may pay with their lives and the gainers survive, particularly where that offering is in scarce supply. An (extreme) example of utilitarianism is the rationing of supplies, as occurs in wartime, and occurred with electricity supply in Chile in 1999, with petrol in Iran and diesel in China in 2007, and with an extension of rationing to diesel in Iran in 2012. The city of St Petersburg also imposed rationing, but on Metro (underground) travel tokens, when people began panic buying them in very large numbers because the price was due to go up by €0.05 (3 roubles) in 2015 (AFP, 2014).

In his *Theory of Justice*, Rawles argues that in a just society the following two conditions must be met (Rawls, 1972).

1 'Each person is to have an equal right to the most extensive total system of equal basic liberties compatible with a similar system of liberty for all' (Liberty Principle).

2 'Social and economic inequalities are to be arranged so that they are both:

   a) to the greatest benefit of the least advantaged; and

   b) attached to offices and positions open to all under the conditions of fair equality of opportunity' (Difference Principle).

The application of the Difference Principle to marketing situations suggests that vulnerable groups in society should not be disadvantaged further by marketing decisions (which rationing does without an exclusion clause for disadvantaged groups). It is to this principle that the international media implicitly appeal when criticizing international pharmaceutical companies, oil and gas companies, and banks for what they term to be excessive profiteering. This ethical decision-making approach suggests that we have a duty to help the disadvantaged, especially when they are adversely affected by our actions.

Virtue Ethics

Previous normative ethical theories, i.e. managerial egoist, utilitarian, and deontological, provide marketers with decision-making approaches to allow choice between alternative courses of 'right' action. In direct contrast, virtue ethics stresses the development of virtuous principles, with 'right' character, and the pursuit of a virtuous life. This branch of ethics is associated principally with Aristotle (Mautner, 1999). Virtue ethics proposes the development of good character, suggesting that we aim to develop the virtuous organization. But what virtues should organizations develop?

Many organizations claim to be virtuous. The values statements of pharmaceutical and oil and gas companies often emphasize 'integrity'. Tesco, the UK supermarket, artificially inflated its earnings by £250m (by delaying payments to suppliers) which, when exposed, wiped £2bn off its market value and precipitated a Serious Fraud Office investigation (Wearden, 2014; Butler, 2016). But, in its 2013 Tesco and Society Report (Tesco, 2013), Tesco extolled that its plan was to 'use our scale for good' and to 'trade responsibly'.

So, what exactly are virtuous principles and how are they operationalized? Aristotle, in *Nicomachean Ethics*, defines virtue as 'a settled disposition of the mind which determines choice' (Mautner, 1999). He defines 11 virtues: bravery, self-control, generosity, magnificence, self-respect, balanced ambition, gentleness, friendliness, truthfulness, wittiness, and justice. Although a company does not have a character like a person does, its employees do. We can consider how these virtues *might* relate to a company. For example, generosity might relate to the development of CSR or corporate philanthropy programmes, or incentives for employees and channel partners. Table 18.2 outlines each virtue and how it might be applied to organizations.

 Visit the Online Resource Centre and complete Internet Activity 18.3 to learn more about National Australia Bank, which topped Forbes' list of the world's most ethical companies in 2016.

Table 18.2 Moral virtues applied to companies

Moral virtue	Application in business and marketing
Bravery, valour	In relation to innovation/new proposition development and long-term as opposed to short-term goal-setting
Self-control in respect of bodily pleasure	Not given to excessive pricing or profit-taking
Generosity	Development of CSR/philanthropy, or in terms of discounted offerings or other incentives given to employees/others
Magnificence	Aiming to build a large enterprise with a well-defined mission which serves its stakeholders well
Self-respect or pride	Openly communicating to stakeholders the good and bad news associated with a company's operations
Having some ambition but not in excess	Competitive but not at all costs and not combative within an industry
Gentleness or good temper	The use of a balanced approach to dealings with stakeholder relations, e.g. industrial relations, consumer boycotts
Friendliness	The will to join forces with competitors in the same industry where necessary, e.g. for purposes of self-regulation, to develop industry standards, and for an exemplary approach to customer service and satisfaction
Truthfulness	In relation to financial integrity and other stakeholder communications
Wittiness	Taken to mean intelligence and a company's ability to redefine the 'rules of the game' without taking itself too seriously
Justice	The audits of one's own ethical approaches and the initiation of reward/punishment when these are disregarded

The Ethical Decision-Making Process

Having defined five main ways of analysing how organizations should behave, we now consider how they make ethical decisions. Initially, managers must perceive an ethical dilemma as existing before undergoing the ethical decision-making process (Hunt and Vitell, 2006). If no ethical dilemma is perceived, no consideration of alternative action takes place. Further, deciding if a situation has ethical content is culturally specific. Some cultures perceive ethical breaches more easily than others. However, there are also some universal standards. For example, bribery is universally condemned and almost all countries have laws making bribery of public officials illegal, but it still happens in practice (see section on Bribery).

Early attempts to devise frameworks of how to act ethically involved asking a series of reflective questions (Laczniak and Murphy, 1993).

- Does the contemplated action violate the law (legal test)?
- Is this action contrary to widely accepted moral obligations (duties test)?
- Does the proposed action violate any other special obligations that stem from the type of marketing organization in focus (special obligations test)?
- Is the intent of the contemplated action harmful (motives test)?
- Is it likely that any major damage to people or organizations will result from the contemplated action (consequences test)?
- Is there a satisfactory alternative action that produces equal or greater benefits to the parties affected than the proposed action (utilitarian test)?
- Does the contemplated action infringe on property rights, privacy rights, or the inalienable rights of the consumer (rights test)?
- Does the proposed action leave another person or group less well off? Is this person or group already a member of a relatively underprivileged class (justice test)?

An elaborate model of ethical decision-making is shown in Figure 18.1. The authors cite five key issues for ethical consideration; bid rigging, price collusion, bribery, falsifying research data, and advertising deception. In bid rigging, subcontractors might collude to agree in advance who will win a bid, with some submitting bids with overly expensive pricing, to ensure selection of the pre-conceived competitor. Alternatively, companies might not even submit a bid so another company can successfully win the contract. **Collusion** occurs when companies collaborate on submitting bids for some competitions but not others. With price collusion, companies either conspire to set prices or limit production, which has similar effects.

How a person in an organization responds to situations with ethical content depends on their social and cultural environment. Although bribery is illegal worldwide, it remains more prevalent in some countries than others. How an employee makes a decision on an ethical issue is affected by their own knowledge, cultural background, values, and attitudes, and whether or not the company has a corporate ethics policy and guidelines on rewards/punishment for ethical and unethical behaviour.

A person's ethical decision-making depends on how they interact with others (i.e. their reference group). Association with others behaving unethically, combined with the opportunity to be involved in such behaviour oneself, is a major predictor of unethical behaviour (Ferrell and Gresham, 1985). Therefore the behaviour of superiors determines how employees behave and is

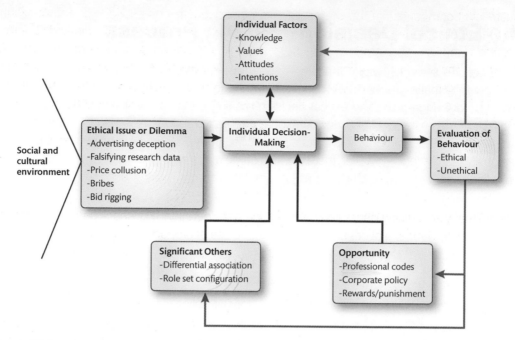

Figure 18.1

A contingency model of ethical decision-making in a marketing organization

Source: Reprinted with permission from *Journal of Marketing*, published by the American Marketing Association, Ferrell and Gresham 1985, 49(3), 87–96.

the most important factor influencing ethical/unethical decisions. Next, we consider how ethics impacts on the marketing mix.

Distribution Management and Ethics

Distribution and production policy can have major ethical dimensions. Ethical breaches in distribution management occur when, for example, companies collude over production quotas, abuse their monopoly status, or overcharge or exploit supply chain partners. The following sections provide examples of companies and situations where ethical breaches have occurred.

- **Collusion**—The best-known and most tolerated global example of production collusion is that which takes place in the oil industry, through OPEC (the Organization of Oil-Exporting Countries) which co-manages oil production quotas in countries such as Nigeria, Saudi Arabia, Iran, Venezuela, and elsewhere.

- **Abuse of monopoly status**—Google abused its monopoly power 'in ways that harmed Internet users and competitors' according to a US Federal Trade Commission (FTC) report in 2012, but the FTC backed off from suing it because they thought it would be a tough case to prosecute (Pagliery, 2015). The European Commission fined Microsoft €561m for failing to adhere to previous EU anti-monopoly judgments regarding Microsoft's dominance of the browser market with Internet Explorer (Halfacree, 2013).

- **Exploitation of supply chain partners**—In France, the Châtel Act stops supermarkets selling at below-cost prices (which damage supply chain partners' margins) and is aimed at increasing competition in the sector. All discounts and services provided by the distributor to the supplier now require stipulation upfront in an annual agreement (Boutin and Guerrero, 2008). In the UK, supermarkets have been shamed into paying dairy farmers a fair price for milk, after the price paid by consumers at supermarket tills dropped below the price of production. One northern England supermarket, Booths, paying 33p a litre against the national average of 24p a litre, saw a 5% increase in sales during the first four weeks after a price increase for its Fair Milk brand (Ruddick, 2015).

Promotion and Ethics

There are many advertising issues prompting ethical consideration, e.g. shock and sexual appeals in advertising, the labelling of consumer products, the use of propaganda and advertising in political campaigns, and marketing to children, each of which is considered in the next sections.

The Use of Sexual and Shock Appeals

Advertisers use emotional appeals to capture attention. We are persuaded by them because we are less likely to consider objections about why we might not agree with the message. For Baudrillard (2005), all advertising has an erotic element to it, because it seduces us into buying something. But the ethical question arises where sexual themes are used explicitly (e.g. naked or semi-naked models) and depending in what circumstances. Diesel, the Italian fashion brand, has also famously used sexual appeals, advertising on the dating apps Tinder and Grindr and on the adult website Pornhub (Allwood, 2016). Pornhub became their top referral website following the advertising deal (Maytom, 2016). A good example of a highly successful and long-running campaign which used sexual appeal in a humorous way in some of its executions was the Got Milk?

The Got Milk? campaign used sex appeal but in a humorous way
Source: Courtesy of MilkPEP and Campbell Ewald.

Campaign run for the California Milk Processor Board by Goodby Silvstein and Partners between 1995 and 2014.

However, advertisers have to be careful that they do not create ads which are easily misinterpreted and cause offence. One example was an advert for a skin-whitening product by Seoul Secret Thailand posted online/YouTube aimed at Thai consumers featuring the blacked-up Thai model/actress, Kirin 'Kris' Horwang and the tagline 'You just need to be white to win', indicating that the model needed to whiten her skin or the blacked-up appearance is how she would look 'if she stopped taking care of herself'. Unsurprisingly, people vented their outrage, labelling the ad racist on social media, because it discriminated against people with darker skin shades. The company was duly forced to remove it and apologize (Anon., 2016a).

Critics argue that sex appeals exploit women, and sometimes men, as sex objects. The fashion industry has decided not to use models aged 16 years or less, but it does use, and encourages, models to become wafer-thin. In 2013, Israel was the world's first country to ban the use of female models whose body mass index (BMI) was less than 18.5 (Bannerman, 2015). Others argue that sexual advertising appeals can be appropriate, depending on the offering (e.g. perfume). For what other offerings is it appropriate, in what countries, to what degree, and targeted at people of what age? Interestingly, a cross-cultural study found that young Chinese consumers hold similar attitudes towards sex advertising appeal use as US consumers and even more favourable attitudes than Australian consumers (Liu *et al*., 2009). Consumers generally prefer mildly erotic ads to non-erotic ads. When erotica is used in cause-related advertising, for example, it is received more favourably if it is congruent with the cause, and more by women than by men (Pope *et al*., 2004).

Shock advertising appeals can also create controversy. Charities often use hard-hitting guilt appeal messages to raise funds for sick children in Africa, for example. Slater and Gordon, a British law firm used a shock appeal with the tagline 'Going through a divorce? Call us, before your ex does', causing upset on social media. But the firm argued that such an approach was necessary to raise awareness of the firm's services in a sector where clients generally have a weak understanding of what solicitors actually offer, including mediation for couples (McAlister, 2015).

Shockingly humorous advert from British law firm created a firestorm on social media, raising awareness of legal services in an area not renowned for advertising—family law.
Source: Courtesy of Slater and Gordon, http://www.slatergordon.co.uk.

Product Labelling

The key ethical issue with product labelling is whether or not labels mislead the buying public. Proper labelling is important in the food, pharmaceutical, and cosmetic industries, because we consume and absorb these offerings into our bodies. Food products, and particularly meat products in Europe and elsewhere, are required to demonstrate their country of origin. For Europe's Muslims, whether or not food products are labelled **halal** is important, as Muslims believe that animals should be slaughtered according to the custom of cutting the animal's throat while it is alive and then draining its blood. Some animal rights groups condemn the practice, and Sweden, Norway, Iceland, Switzerland, and Poland have all banned 'ritual slaughter' despite the fact that it is allowed under EU law (Hasan, 2012).

Unscrupulous companies do circumvent product labelling rules by importing food products from one country, processing them in another, and claiming that they come from the country where they are processed. However, guidelines on label advertising claims in the UK are covered by the Trading Standards Service, which investigates misleading packaging and labelling on behalf of the consumer.

Propaganda and Political Advertising

In many countries, political advertising is exempt from the rules and regulations associated with traditional advertising. As a consequence, it can be highly negative by making vitriolic statements to damage the credibility of other candidates and parties. In the UK, political advertising on billboards, in cinemas, and in magazines is exempt from the advertising rules set by the Advertising Standards Authority (ASA). Unlike their commercial counterparts, political parties are not expected to be truthful, i.e. to validate their claims. For example, the 'No' to Scottish Independence referendum campaign, Better Together, was criticized for an overly negative campaign, labelled Project Fear by some (Pike, 2015), but others argue that the political context often justifies a negative campaign stance when the risks posed to society are great (Morris, 2008). Therefore the ethical question is: Should politicians be exempt from the rules and regulations associated with traditional marketing activity, when many of the adverts used can be so negative?

Visit the Online Resource Centre and follow the web link to the Advertising Standards Authority (ASA) to learn more about advertising rules and regulations.

However, political advertising is not only undertaken by political parties. Other campaigning organizations also use its general approach (see also Chapter 16). For example, marketing tools and techniques are also used by terrorist groups. For example, Al-Qaeda pioneered the use of propaganda videos online to promote the cause of suicide bombing through the Qatari TV station Al Jazeera and on the Internet (O'Shaughnessy and Baines, 2009). More recently, Daesh (also called 'Islamic State') has made extensive use of social media in the West to disseminate violent propaganda, aimed particularly at disaffected Muslims and Muslim converts, to promote their murderous cause and suicide bombing, which they depict as martyrdom (Jones *et al.*, 2015). It is critical to realize that an understanding of marketing and public relations provides users with the means to persuade mass groups of people. The question then arises as to whether it is legitimate for governments and special interest groups (including terrorists) to use these means to persuade citizens and electorates about their causes. The problem, however, is that terrorist groups seldom take notice of any law and their ethical conduct is usually suspect.

Finally, companies also sometimes develop overt political messages and campaign stances (see Chapter 16). Ben & Jerry's, the ice cream brand now owned by Unilever, have also campaigned on socio-political issues, having announced on social media that they are 'open to creating a cannabis-infused ice-cream' and in urging consumers to sign an online petition to tackle climate change at the UN summit in Paris in 2015 (Anon., 2015d).

Marketing to Children

Scholars frequently comment on whether or not children should be targeted for advertising, given their immature views of time, money, and identity. Researchers have found evidence that children are explicitly targeted in promotional campaigns and that parents are concerned by this.

- Children are more exposed to marketing than ever before and parents increasingly feel that they are losing control of the marketing directed at their children.
- Parents are particularly concerned about the marketing channels used (e.g. the Internet, mobile phone, social media, and advergames) which target children directly.
- Inappropriate marketing to children damages the brand, making it less likely that marketers will get past the parent as gatekeeper.
- More appropriate marketing methods are informative and help parents to feel more in control.
- Consumers are willing to support companies that communicate with children in a responsible way.
- Marketers, especially advertisers, should use the means of communication appropriately and educate parents and children alike on newer and less traditional communication media (Daniels and Holmes, 2005).

An example of a company under pressure for its promotion to children is McDonald's, as its offerings appeal particularly to children via the use of licensed characters and celebrity endorsement. Child obesity is regarded as a major problem in many countries (e.g. Australasia, the UK, the EU generally, and the USA). The problem is partly caused by advertising food to children, although inactive lifestyles and lack of exercise also play a part. Fast food retailers are coming under increasing pressure to make their menus healthier.

Products and Ethics

Companies must follow strict guidelines on product quality. Where consumers have concerns about a particular company's product quality, they can inform a government body which will then be charged with looking into the case on the consumer's/customer's behalf. For instance, the UK's Office of Fair Trading, Sweden's Consumer Agency (Konsumentverket), Dubai Central Laboratory, and Ireland's Competition and Consumer Protection Commission all perform this role. Most countries charge organizations with enforcing minimum levels of product quality. The same degree of protection for enforcing service quality does not exist, probably because it is more difficult to monitor service quality, decide on minimum service standards, and determine whether or not breaches have been made. Agencies often provide consumer information. The

UK's Office of Fair Trading provides information on buying warranties for electrical goods, funerals, buying and selling your home, holidays, pawnbroking, ticket agents, and private dentistry—industries where sharp practice frequently occurs.

Visit the Online Resource Centre and follow the web links to the various consumer agencies and government fair trading bodies to learn more about regulations and guidelines that organizations must follow to ensure the health and safety of consumers and the conduct of fair business practice.

Breaches in product quality can be extremely serious, and can lead to loss of life and grave injury, particularly in the food industry. For this reason, countries have separate official bodies charged with enforcing food safety guidelines, e.g. the American Food and Drug Administration, the UK's Food Standards Agency, France's Agence nationale chargée de la sécurité sanitaire de l'alimentation, de l'environnement et du travail (Anses), and the bi-national Food Standards Australia and New Zealand (FSANZ) organization covering both territories.

A recent example of a defective product causing death, injury, and inconvenience occurred when General Motors (GM) failed to promptly recall cars with a faulty ignition switch, causing up to 124 deaths, despite allegedly knowing about the problem up to a decade previously. In 2014, GM paid $900m in criminal damages and eventually recalled 800,000 cars (Smithers, 2016). In 2015, another car manufacturer, Volkswagen, announced a product recall after it was found to have installed software allowing it to falsify emission reports to pass safety tests, affecting up to 11m vehicles (Bryant and Sharman, 2015; see also Market Insight 18.4).

Market Insight 18.4
Volkswagen: Up in Smoke?

On 11 September 2015, the Volkswagen Group announced to the world's media that it was again listed as the most sustainable automaker in the world's leading sustainability rankings. It had even depicted its engineers as angelic in ads aired during the Superbowl in 2014. However, the company's celebrations were short-lived as exactly seven days later, the EPA stunned the global business community by accusing Volkswagen of illegally using 'cheat devices' to evade clean air standards for six years between 2009 and 2014. The scandal affected 11m cars worldwide, 1.2m of which were in the UK. After the accusations were made, Volkswagen CEO Martin Winterkorn resigned as media investigators uncovered systematic abuses within the company taking place over many years, involving managers at all levels of the organization.

Previously, Volkswagen had been viewed as a global leader in corporate social responsibility (CSR). Its annual report was packed full of descriptions of projects it backed and the charities it supported. It was viewed as a 'thought leader' on social issues and a 'change agent' for improving society. Globally, it was ranked as the best company in the world for its CSR work. In the wake of this controversy, critics have begun to question the whole concept of CSR. Some commentators suggested that CSR had become a 'dangerous racket' because it 'allowed companies to parade their virtue and look good while internal standards are allowed to slip'. The scandal has also led many commentators to conclude that Volkswagen was **greenwashing** (i.e. promoting environmental initiatives but actually operating in a way that is damaging to the environment or in an opposite manner to the goal of the announced initiatives) and was more focused on doing the occasional good deed or project, rather than focusing on its core company values.

Market Insight 18.4
continued

Volkswagen has offered to fix the models affected and started the recall in January 2016. Estimated fines could be as much as $45bn in the USA alone, according to the theoretical maximum associated with the civil charges filed by the US Department of Justice, although it is likely to pay only a fraction of that sum. Volkswagen is facing investigations in many countries as well as lawsuits from motorists. Only time will tell if Volkswagen can survive the 'cheating' scandal and the associated loss of customer trust, and whether or not it can bounce back from this devastating blow to its previously 'angelic' brand image.

Sources: Anon. (2015e); Izzo (2015); Kaye (2015); Lynn (2015); Marshall (2015); Paton (2015); Tovey (2016).

After installing 'cheat devices' in their diesel cars, the VW brand is no longer squeaky clean
Source: © villorejo/Shutterstock.

Theory into Practice

This market insight illustrates how employees within Volkswagen, an apparent CSR responsibility leader, displayed shockingly unethical, and illegal, behaviour in engineering 'defeat devices', allowing Volkswagen to cheat stringent emissions tests to gain access to various large automotive markets. Whilst the company did eventually accept responsibility for the cheating, its CEO had to resign as a consequence, and the company is set to pay billions of dollars in fines, lawsuits, and compensation payments. In the UK, the company's share of the overall car market plunged from 9.4% to 7.2% in November 2015, in the months immediately after the emission scandal. The EPA, and other country regulators, will now have to work out what the cost to society is as a result of the higher levels of noxious chemicals that have been released into the atmosphere over a six-year period. As an aside, the case also illustrates the importance of having strong regulatory bodies (e.g. the EPA in the USA) for both the testing of products and the enforcement of punishment for contraventions of the law (e.g. the US Department of Justice).

Related Topics:

corporate deception; product standards.

1 Given the recent scandal, should Volkswagen abandon its CSR efforts?

2 Who is to blame for the emissions scandal at Volkswagen? Is it the CEO, senior engineers who signed off on this, or all the employees who were involved?

3 How have other companies refocused their efforts and recovered from the negative fallout of similar scandals? (Hint: GM and its faulty ignition switches or Toyota's instant acceleration problem).

This market insight was kindly contributed by Marie O'Dwyer, Waterford Institute of Technology, Republic of Ireland.

However, determining when to recall products is a difficult ethical problem. Often, and particularly with food products, the **precautionary principle** operates. For example, the Tulip Food Company, operating in Denmark and Sweden, recalled its Danish deli food products in 2014 despite the fact that the traces of listeria found were miniscule (Herriman, 2014). Where a risk of injury is likely, a product should certainly be recalled. This might occur when:

- a serious consumer illness or injury is caused by product contamination;

- there are similar complaints of illness or injury that apply to a specific product;

- a design or manufacturing failure could result in potential harm to consumers;

- there is defective product labelling that could result in potential harm to consumers, or where a product has been tampered with.

Pricing and Ethics

The main ethical concern in pricing is fairness. Key considerations concern **price gouging**, when prices are set far higher than is considered reasonable, **price discrimination**, where prices are set for different groups of people, and price collusion, when competitors work together to set prices to the detriment of consumers and competitors. Price gouging occurs when companies operate a demand pricing formula (see Chapter 9) where demand is very high, leading to high prices to customers. One example was when Turing Pharmaceuticals raised the price of a life-saving drug from $13.50 to $750, creating a media furore (McCoy and Bomey, 2015).

Price discrimination involves setting different prices for different groups of people. Price discrimination is linked to market segmentation (see Chapter 6). It is not necessarily an unethical practice per se. It is more questionable where there is no difference in the offer, and the price remains the only difference. Price discrimination commonly occurs; for instance, signs at tourist sites in different countries often show the price for foreigners versus the cost for domestic nationals (e.g. at the Taj Mahal in India, the price to visit the monument for international visitors has been 25 times that of the cost for Indian nationals).

Price discrimination occurs on airlines, e.g. easyJet and Ryanair use **yield management** systems to sell airline tickets, with different prices charged by time of booking. Women's haircuts are often more expensive than men's, although it *may* be that the service provided is more attentive and takes longer. Until new EU rules were introduced in 2012, women could obtain up to 40% cheaper car insurance than men in the UK (King, 2012). This is still possible in the USA, where such legislation has not been introduced because, according to esurance (2016), women tend to drive less than men, have fewer accidents, get fewer speeding tickets, and are less likely to be charged with driving under the influence. Price discrimination also occurs when customers haggle (Kimes and Wirtz, 2003). **Haggling** is more common in some markets than others (e.g. house and car buying in Europe), and in some countries than others (e.g. Middle Eastern and Southeast Asian countries). When was the last time you haggled for something? Where were you, what were you buying, and how well did you do?

Another ethical issue in pricing is when companies collude to set prices (see also Market Insight 18.3). Many well-known companies have been fined for this. In 2016, the EU fined Mitsubishi Electric and Hitachi €137.8m for fixing the prices of car alternators and starters between 2004 and 2010. Denso, the world's second-largest car parts maker, avoided a fine by informing on the cartel (Anon., 2016b). Price collusion is regarded as unethical because it results in unfair, and higher, charges to customers, and stifles innovation because competitors do not need to develop better offerings. Consumers also do not then benefit from improvements in quality and performance.

Universalism/Relativism in Marketing Ethics

Some cultures are less likely than others to perceive ethical dilemmas. Ethicists say different groups of people see ethical situations from two perspectives. Under one perspective, universal ethical codes of practice should exist because there are things that are simply 'wrong', no matter what the colour or creed of the people concerned (e.g. murder, bribery, extortion). This is termed universalism. The opposite argument, termed cultural relativism, suggests that different groups consider ethical situations from varied viewpoints and that there is nothing wrong with this (e.g. gifts, corporate entertainment). The debate in international marketing ethics concerns itself with this dichotomy between cultural relativism and ethical universalism.

How should a director of a Western company ensure that local managers do not use bribery to gain access to particular markets? This problem occurred with the French industrial company Alstom when it paid more than $75m to government officials in Indonesia, Saudi Arabia, Egypt, Taiwan, and the Bahamas in bribes, attracting a $773.2m fine from the US Department of Justice in late 2014 (Chon, 2014). The excuse made for bribery is that if managers didn't bribe, competitors would, and they would win the business. From a cultural relativist perspective, such a practice is ethically unacceptable except where bribery might lead to a greater good, say widespread distribution of health-giving pharmaceuticals, whereas the universalist perspective suggests that bribery is a fundamental ethical breach regardless of the circumstances. A study concerning American–Thai differences showed that American marketers were more likely than Thais to perceive unethical marketing behaviours to be serious (Marta and Singhapakdi, 2005). A study of Thai managers suggested that one approach to improve their ethical decision-making would be to encourage idealism, the degree to which individuals 'assume that desirable consequences can, with the "right" action, always be obtained' (Singhapakdi et al., 2000a), rather than relativism, where people reject universal moral rules (Forsyth, 1980). Building on idealism, Singhapakdi et al. (2000b) also found a strong positive relationship between a marketer's religiousness and their degree of idealism, i.e. the more religious someone is, the more likely they are to hold universal ethical principles.

In a study of marketing ethics in Korea, Kim and Chun (2003) found that Koreans perceived the seriousness of ethical problems as follows:

1 bribery;

2 unfair price increases;

3 exaggerated advertising;

4 sexual discrimination.

They found that younger Koreans were less likely to perceive situations as having ethical content, whereas older people perceived less ethical content in bribery situations.

Bribery

Transparency International published a Corrupt Perceptions Index to indicate the perceived level of public sector corruption in different countries. In 2015, Denmark, Finland, Sweden, and New Zealand were the least corrupt governments, whilst the worst perceived offenders were Somalia, North Korea, Afghanistan, and Sudan (Transparency International, 2015). From an analysis of 427 international bribery cases by the **OECD**, the most common offending industries from which bribe payers originate included companies from the extraction (oil and mining), construction, transportation, information/communication, and manufacturing sectors (Kottasova, 2014). Companies in these industries have a greater need for ethical training, confidential helplines, and robust whistle-blowing procedures to allow employees to highlight ethical breaches to senior managers without fear of penalty. Where bribery occurs, it is used either to influence potentially adverse legislative programmes (i.e. for lobbying purposes) or to obtain favourable contracts at another company's expense (i.e. for sales purposes). Many countries' bribery acts are extra-territorial, i.e. personnel can be charged for their activities in other countries. To comply with the UK Bribery Act 2010, for example, British companies must put in place procedures to deter employees from paying bribes (see Market Insight 18.5).

Market Insight 18.5
Drug Money in China

In 2014, GlaxoSmithKline was fined 元3bn (£297m) by Chinese authorities after it was found to have bribed doctors and hospitals to promote its drugs. Numerous GSK senior executives were given suspended jail sentences and deported from the country. GSK was accused of having made $150m in illegal profits as a result of the bribery. The scale and duration of the 15-month investigation at GSK led to a huge increase in whistle-blower reports in China from 48 in 2013 to 652 in 2014 and a considerable drop in Chinese drug sales. In a survey conducted for a white paper by Charney Research, 35% of companies operating in China had paid bribes or given gifts just to stay in business. Bribery also differed by region, being more prevalent in Beijing than Shanghai, and much less prevalent in the north and west of the country. The corruption problem is so bad that nine in ten companies regarded it as a plague on doing business.

GSK Policy Statement on 'Anti-bribery and corruption (ABAC)

■ We do not, directly or through a third party, promise, offer, make, authorize, solicit or accept any financial or other advantage, to or from anyone to obtain or retain business or secure an improper advantage in the conduct of business. This rule applies regardless of whether they are government officials or work in a private sector entity. Financial or other advantage covers anything of value, including cash, gifts, services, job offers, loans, travel expenses, entertainment, or hospitality.

■ We prohibit all facilitation payments as they are bribes. These payments are unofficial, improper, small payments or gifts offered or made to government officials to secure or expedite a routine or necessary action to which we are legally entitled.

■ GSK leadership and managers lead by example, ensuring GSK staff and relevant third parties are aware of the ethical significance and critical role of our ABAC principles and standards.

■ We perform a comprehensive risk assessment to determine the company's exposure to bribery and corruption risk. The risk assessment is reviewed and updated regularly to reflect changes in our risk profile.

Market Insight 18.5
continued

- The ABAC principles and standards established in this Policy are developed and supported by a number of periodically reviewed corporate written standards which constitute our ABAC controls, policies and procedures.

- GSK provides mandatory periodic ABAC training to GSK staff and relevant third parties in accordance with their roles, responsibilities, and the risks they face. It is everyone's responsibility to complete such training in the specified timelines.

- We perform risk-based due diligence prior to engaging any third party or undertaking a business development transaction and ensure appropriate contractual clauses and monitoring controls are put in place as described in the ABAC Third Party and Business Development frameworks.

- Our dedicated ABAC website and regular communications ensure ABAC awareness and support are available across the company.

Sources: Anon. (2014b); Kollewe (2014); GSK (2015); Levick (2015); Roland (2015).

Theory into Practice

The market insight illustrates how senior executives of a major UK multinational pharmaceutical manufacturer were found guilty by public authorities of bribery in China. The case reveals the difficulty of doing business in a country where bribery of public officials is systematic, varied, and expected, but also when the Chinese President has initiated a strong focus on anti-corruption and Western governments are prosecuting companies using extra-territorial laws such as the US Foreign Corrupt Practices Act and the UK Bribery Act.

Related Topics:

guanxi; deontological ethics; ethical codes of conduct.

1 Will the GSK ABAC ethical code stop employees and contractors from offering bribes to public officials in every part of the world including China? Why do you say this?

2 Is it always unethical to pay bribes when doing business? Can you envisage any circumstance where it might be ethical to do so?

3 What other major Western companies are you aware of that have been charged with bribery in China recently? Why do you think bribery is so commonplace in China?

Chapter Summary

To consolidate your learning, the key points from this chapter are summarized here.

■ **Assess the negative impact that marketing has on society.**

The critical marketing perspective suggests that marketing impacts negatively on society. The perspective calls for the (re-)evaluation of marketing activities, categories, and frameworks to improve them, so marketing can operate in a more desirable manner within society. It critiques the nature of marketing knowledge and questions in whose interests existing frameworks, approaches, and techniques operate.

■ **Define sustainable marketing and its implications for marketing practice.**

Sustainable marketing has been termed the third age of green marketing and is concerned with ecological, equitable, and economic impacts of marketing practice. Sustainable marketers seek to meet the needs of existing generations, whilst not compromising on meeting those of future generations. Consequently, companies are re-imagining marketing practices, for example by recovering the costs of investment financing over longer payback periods, by emphasizing the full costs of purchase to customers, by considering all members of the supply chain and ensuring that they are paid equitably, and by demarketing consumption to vulnerable groups or those who are over-consuming.

■ **Define marketing ethics.**

Marketing ethics is concerned with how marketers go about the marketing process. In particular, it is the application of moral principles to decision-making in marketing and the consideration of the outcomes of those decisions.

■ **Explain the common ethical norms applied in marketing.**

Marketing ethics can be divided into normative and descriptive branches, distinguishing between how we *ought* to act and how people *actually behave* when making marketing decisions. The five main normative approaches to marketing decision-making are deontological ethics (doing the *right* thing because it's the *right* thing to do), teleological ethics (the *right* thing to do is the thing with the *right* consequences), managerial egoism (doing the *right* thing because it's the best thing to do for us), utilitarianism (doing the *right* thing for the largest number of people), and virtue ethics (doing the *right* thing for everyone).

■ **Describe the role of ethics in marketing decision-making.**

Models of marketing decision-making outline the importance of the ethical content of a situation, the importance of 'significant others', employees' values, and the ethical training given by a company in line with its own ethical policy. Hunt and Vitell's (2006) model of marketing decision-making stresses the importance of considering what is the *right* thing to do (deontological norms) and what are the *right* intended outcomes for us to follow (teleological norms).

■ **Understand how ethical breaches occur in marketing mix programmes.**

Ethical breaches occur in all aspects of an organization's marketing activity including distribution, pricing, promotion, and product policies. Ethical breaches are often made by employees who may or may not be following company ethical guidelines and codes of conduct appropriately.

? Review Questions

1 Name the key concepts in critical marketing.
2 How will sustainable marketing impact on marketing practice?
3 How do we define marketing ethics?
4 What are the common ethical norms applied in marketing?
5 What role does ethics in marketing play in the marketing decision-making process?
6 What are key ethical considerations when pricing offerings?
7 What are key ethical considerations when promoting offerings?
8 What are key ethical considerations when distributing offerings?
9 What are key ethical concerns when developing the product offering?
10 What is bribery?

✏ Worksheet Summary

 To apply the knowledge you have gained from this chapter and test your understanding of marketing, sustainability, and ethics visit the **Online Resource Centre** and complete Worksheet 18.1.

⚡ Discussion Questions

1 Having read Case Insight 18.1, how should innocent achieve a high level of recyclable content in their bottles without making the offering look less attractive and hence lose sales?

2 Are some offerings more fetishized than others? Identify four offerings where this is the case and discuss the nature of the relationships between manufacturer, retailer, and consumer. Are these relationships exploitative?

3 Go online to find examples of companies with a strong stance on sustainable marketing. Are there any common characteristics across these companies? (Hint: take a look at any of the following companies' websites and search for their sustainability credentials: Britain's Marks & Spencer, Sweden's SCA, France's Danone, Nigeria's Guaranty Trust Bank).

4 Consider Reckitt Benckiser's condom product Durex, designed to reduce the proportion of people sustaining sexually transmitted diseases (STDs) and women having unwanted pregnancies. Would it be appropriate for SSL International to promote condom usage to young children, in (1) Catholic countries and (2) African countries? (Hint: you might need to re-read the section on normative ethics.) Discuss this ethical problem using the following approaches:

A managerial egoism—the principle of managerial self-interest
B utilitarianism—the principle of the greater good for the greater number of people
C deontological ethics—the principle of duty-based ethics.

5 Consider whether or not it is unethical to act in the following ways in the following circumstances.

A You are a salesperson working for a South African construction company trying to secure a road-building contract in Nigeria. You know that if you do not pay a 'commission' to the public official in charge of tendering for the project, you will not win the contract. Should you pay the 'commission' or do you have other choices of action?

B You are a Dubai-based banker. A potential new client in Dubai insists on taking you to a very exclusive restaurant at the Burj al Arab to discuss a loan she requires to purchase a new building for her rapidly expanding business. Should you accept?

C You are a farmer supplying a large chain supermarket in Copenhagen with selected prime cuts of meat products. The supermarket requests an upfront 'listing' fee of 170,000 Danish Krone before they can accept you as a supplier. You can then expect high-value orders of millions of Krone. Should you pay the 'listing fee'? What other courses of action do you have?

Visit the **Online Resource Centre** and complete the Multiple Choice Questions to assess your knowledge of Chapter 18.

Glossary

bid rigging when organizations conspire to determine which company or companies should win a particular contract.

capitalism the political system in which private (as opposed to governmental) capital and wealth is the predominant means of producing and distributing goods.

circular economy a circular economy is an alternative to a traditional linear economy (make, use, dispose) in which we keep resources in use for as long as possible, extract the maximum value from them whilst in use, and then recover and regenerate products and materials at the end of each service life (WRAP, 2016).

collaborative consumption the trend towards the sharing, swapping, and renting of possessions.

collusion when a group of competitor companies conspire to control the market, often at the expense of the consumer/customer, and typically in relation to price fixing.

corporate social responsibility (CSR) typically a programme of social and/or environmental activities undertaken by a company on behalf of one or more of its stakeholders to develop sustainable business operations, foster goodwill, and develop the company's corporate reputation.

cryptomarkets hidden online marketplaces where people go to buy illicit offerings, often using anonymous web browsers and untraceable currency forms for payment.

deontological ethics a form of ethical approach by which the rightness or wrongness of an action or decision is not judged to be exclusively based on the consequences of that action or decision.

externalities negative impacts that arise as a result of economic development, for example on the environment, to society, and so on.

framing the dual action by which communicators present ideas and concepts, and members of an audience interpret those concepts by assimilating them into their pre-existing cognitive schema.

greenwashing occurs when an organization's rhetoric concerning the promotion of its environmental impacts (based on its offering or organizational practices) are not backed up in practice, i.e. it makes misleading claims about how environmentally friendly it is.

guanxi the network of relationships, involving mutual reciprocation of favours, that arises between two or more people when doing business in China.

haggling when a customer argues with a supplier, usually a retailer, over the price to be paid for a good or service and is successful in obtaining a discount.

halal a term referring to what is permissible under sharia law and most typically used in Western societies when referring to permissible foodstuffs. For a food to be halal it must not contain alcohol, blood or its by-products, or the meat of an omnivore or carnivore. In addition, where the food is from an animal, a Muslim must have pronounced the name of Allah before slaughtering the animal.

managerial egoism a form of ethical approach to the effect that a manager ought to act in his/her own best interests and that an action is right if it benefits the manager undertaking that action.

marketing ethics the analysis and application of moral principles to marketing decision-making and the outcomes of these decisions.

OECD Organisation for Economic Co-operation and Development, a grouping of 34 countries which exists to promote the economic and social well-being of people worldwide.

precautionary principle when the risk of a threat to the environment or human health exists, it is better to put in place measures to mitigate that risk than not to do so, even if there is no scientific evidence for a cause–effect relationship for the threat implied by the risk.

price discrimination occurs where the price of a good or service is set differently for certain groups of people.

price gouging occurs when a seller sets the price of a good or service at a level far higher than is considered reasonable.

reverse logistics the process of returning goods in a physical distribution channel. This might be a flow from customer to manufacturer via a retailer (e.g. for repair or replacement).

sustainable marketing marketing activities undertaken to meet the wants/needs of present customers without comprising the wants/needs of future customers, particularly in relation to negative environmental impacts on society.

teleological ethics a form of ethical approach by which the rightness or wrongness of an action or decision is judged primarily on the intentions of the decision-maker.

utilitarianism an ethical approach originally developed by English philosopher and social reformer Jeremy Bentham which postulates that an action is right if, and only if, it conforms to the principle of utility, whereby utility—pleasure, happiness, or welfare—is maximized, or pain or unhappiness minimized, more than any alternative.

virtue ethics principally associated with Aristotle, this branch of ethics stresses the importance of developing virtuous principles, with 'right' character, and the pursuit of a virtuous life.

yield management a system for maximizing the profit generated from activities, which carefully manages price to ensure full utilization of capacity while balancing supply and demand factors.

References

AFP (2014). Russia imposes rationing in token gesture. *Yahoo! News*, 26 December. Retrieve from: http://news.yahoo.com/russia-imposes-rationing-token-gesture-204634332.html (accessed 31 March 2016).

Alba, D. (2015). Airbnb confirms $1.5bn funding round, now valued at $25.5bn. *Wired*, 17 July. Retrieve from: http://www.wired.com/2015/12/airbnb-confirms-1-5-billion-funding-round-now-valued-at-25-5-billion/ (accessed 29 March 2016).

Allwood, E.H. (2016). Why Diesel is about to start advertising on Pornhub. *Dazed*, January. Retrieve from: http://www.dazeddigital.com/fashion/article/29089/1/why-diesel-is-about-to-start-advertising-on-pornhub (accessed 30 April 2016).

Alvesson, M. (1994). Critical theory and consumer marketing. *Scandinavian Journal of Marketing*, 10(3), 291–313.

AMA (2014). *Statement of Ethics*. Retrieve from: https://archive.ama.org/archive/AboutAMA/Pages/Statement%20of%20Ethics.aspx (accessed 29 March 2016).

Anon. (2013a). Transocean agrees to pay $1.4bn oil spill fine. *BBC News*, 3 January. Retrieve from: http://www.bbc.co.uk/news/business-20905472 (accessed 28 March 2016).

Anon. (2013b). Nestlé finds horsemeat in pasta dishes. *Fijilive*, 19 February. Retrieve from: http://fijilive.com/news/2013/02/nestle-finds-horsemeat-in-pasta-dishes/52114.Fijilive (accessed 29 March 2016).

Anon. (2014a). The art of deceptive advertising: from brown shoe polish on burgers to hairspray for brighter ingredients, how commercials trick us into buying their products. *Mail Online*, 11 June. Retrieve from: http://www.dailymail.co.uk/femail/article-2655351/The-art-deceptive-advertising-From-brown-shoe-polish-burgers-hairspray-brighter-ingredients-commercials-trick-buying-products.html (accessed 29 March 2016).

Anon. (2014b). GlaxoSmithKline fined $490m by China for bribery. *BBC News*, 19 September. Retrieve from: http://www.bbc.co.uk/news/business-29271822 (accessed 28 March 2016).

Anon. (2015a). BP and Deepwater Horizon: a costly mistake. *The Economist*, 2 July. Retrieve from: http://www.economist.com/news/business-and-finance/21656847-costly-mistake (accessed 28 March 2016).

Anon. (2015b). In search of the good business. *The Economist*, 9 August. Retrieve from: http://www.economist.com/news/business/21611103-second-time-its-120-year-history-unilever-trying-redefine-what-it-means-be (accessed 29 March 2016).

Anon. (2015c). Online advertising: block shock. *The Economist*, 6 June, 60.

Anon. (2015d). We get the scoop on whether Ben & Jerry's licks rival ice-cream brands on social media. *Marketing*, July, 21.

Anon. (2015e). CSR after the Volkswagen scandal. *Triple Pundit*, 28 October. Retrieve from: http://www.triplepundit.com/2015/10/csr-volkswagen-scandal/ (accessed 29 March 2016).

Anon. (2016a). 'Racist' cosmetic ad comes under fire. *Bangkok Post*, 9 January, 2.

Anon. (2016b). Car parts price-fixing fines for Hitachi and Mitsubishi Electric. *BBC News*, 27 January. Retrieve from: http://www.bbc.co.uk/news/business-35419762 (accessed 1 April 2016).

Augar, P. (2015). How the forex scandal happened. *BBC News*, 20 May. Retrieve from: http://www.bbc.co.uk/news/business-30003693 (accessed 31 March 2016).

Baker, R. (2012). Unilever: Sustainability marketing is biggest challenge. *Marketing Week*, 12 December. Retrieve from: https://www.marketingweek.com/2012/04/24/unilever-sustainability-marketing-is-biggest-challenge/ (accessed 29 March 2016).

Bannerman, L. (2015). I won't lose weight, says angry model. *The Times*, 16 October, 3.

Basford, L. (2015). Corporate responsibility. *The Marketer*, July/August, 30–3.

Baudrillard, J. (2005). *The System of Objects* (trans. James Benedict). London: Verso Books.

Boutin, X. and Guerrero, G. (2008). The 'Loi Galland' and French consumer prices, June. Retrieve from: http://www.insee.fr/en/indicateurs/analys_conj/archives/june2008_d1.pdf (accessed 5 April 2016).

Bridges, C.M. and Wilhelm, W.B. (2008). Going beyond green: the 'why' and 'how' of integrating sustainability into the marketing curriculum. *Journal of Marketing Education*, 30(1), 33–46.

Bryant, B. (2011). Deepwater Horizon and the Gulf oil spill—the key questions answered. *The Guardian*, 20 April. Retrieve from: http://www.theguardian.com/environment/2011/apr/20/deepwater-horizon-key-questions-answered (accessed 5 April 2016).

Bryant, C. and Sharman, A. (2015). Martin Winterkorn resigns as VW boss over emissions scandal. *Financial Times*, 23 September. Retrieve from: http://www.ft.com/cms/s/0/d2288862-61d1-11e5-97e9-7f0bf5e7177b.html#axzz44BoCjw2Z (accessed 28 March 2016).

Buchholz, R.A. (1991). Corporate responsibility and the good society. From economics to ecology: factors which influence corporate policy decisions. *Business Horizons*, 34(4), 19–31.

Burton, D. (2001). Critical marketing theory: the blueprint? *European Journal of Marketing*, 35(5/6), 722–43.

Butler, S. (2016). Tesco delayed payments to suppliers to boost profits, watchdog finds. *The Guardian*, 26 January. Retrieve from: http://www.theguardian.com/business/2016/jan/26/tesco-ordered-change-deal-suppliers (accessed 31 March 2016).

Cai, Y., Jo, H., and Pan, C. (2011). Doing well while doing bad? CSR in controversial industry sectors. *Journal of Business Ethics*, 108(4), 467–80.

Chon, G. (2014). Alstom to pay record $772m for bribery. *Financial Times*, 22 December. Retrieve from: http://www.ft.com/cms/s/0/0a8989c6-8934-11e4-9b7f-00144feabdc0.html#axzz44BoCjw2Z (accessed 28 March 2016).

Clark, L. (2012). Mannequins are spying on shoppers for market analysis. *Wired*, 23 November. Retrieve from: http://www.wired.co.uk/news/archive/2012-11/23/mannequin-spies-on-customers?page = all (accessed 30 September 2016).

Clarke-Billings, L. (2015). Police chiefs urge stores to cancel Black Friday as Asda abandons flash sale. *The Telegraph*, 11 November. Retrieve from: http://www.telegraph.co.uk/news/shopping-and-consumer-news/11985589/Asda-we-will-not-be-part-of-Black-Friday-this-year.html (accessed 29 March 2016).

Conca, J. (2015). The Fukushima disaster wasn't disastrous because of the radiation. *Forbes*, 16 March. Retrieve from: http://www.forbes.com/sites/jamesconca/2015/03/16/the-fukushima-disaster-wasnt-very-disastrous/#4d68476951e7 (accessed 28 March 2016).

Daniels, J. and Holmes, C. (2005). *Responsible Marketing to Children: Exploring the Impact on Adults' Attitudes and Behaviour*. London: Business in the Community.

Davidson, H. (2014). Body Shop removes all its products from Chinese duty free stores. Retrieve from: http://www.theguardian.com/world/2014/mar/12/body-shop-removes-products-from-chinese-duty-free-stores (accessed 28 March 2016).

Debeljak, J., Krkac, K., and Bušljeta Banks, I. (2011). Acquiring CSR practices: from deception to authenticity. *Social Responsibility Journal*, 7(1), 5–22.

Elder, L. (2015). Horse meat scandal: where are we now? *Horse & Hound*, 18 July. Retrieve from: http://www.horseandhound.co.uk/news/horse-meat-scandal-where-are-we-now-502760 (accessed 29 March 2016).

Ellis, N., Fitchett, J., Higgins, M., Jack, G., Lim, M., Saren, M., and Tadajewski, M. (2010). *Marketing: A Critical Textbook*. London: Sage.

esurance (2016). Why women pay less for car insurance. Retrieve from: https://www.esurance.com/info/car/why-women-pay-less-for-car-insurance (accessed 1 April 2016).

Ferrell, O.C. and Gresham, L.G. (1985). A contingency framework for understanding ethical decision making in marketing. *Journal of Marketing*, 49(Summer), 87–96.

Forsyth, D.R. (1980). A taxonomy of ethical ideologies. *Journal of Personality and Social Psychology*, 39(1), 175–84.

Franklin, O. (2013). Unravelling the dark web. *GQ (British)*, February, 184–9.

Friedman, M. (1979). The social responsibility of business is to increase profit. In T. Beauchamp and N. Bowie (eds.), *Ethical Theory and Business*. Englewood Cliffs, NJ: Prentice Hall.

Gaski, J.E. (1999). Does marketing ethics really have anything to say? A critical inventory of the literature. *Journal of Business Ethics*, 18, 315–34.

Goodley, S. (2014). The foreign exchange trader: 'the closer you get to 4pm, the less the risk'. *The Guardian*, 12 March. Retrieve from: http://www.theguardian.com/business/2014/mar/12/forex-trader-closer-4pm-less-risk (accessed 31 March 2016).

Gordon, R.; Carrigan, M., and Hastings, G. (2011). A framework for sustainable marketing. *Marketing Theory*, 11(2), 143–63.

Greenberg, A. (2016). The Silk Road's dark-web dream is dead. *Wired*, 14 January. Retrieve from: http://www.wired.com/2016/01/the-silk-roads-dark-web-dream-is-dead/ (accessed 30 March 2016).

GSK (2015). Anti-bribery and corruption. GlaxoSmithKline Policy Statement 007, 22 December. Retrieve from: http://www.gsk.com/media/930549/anti-bribery-and-corruption-policy-pol-gsk-007-v10.pdf (accessed 5 April 2016).

Gwyther, M. (2015). The real thing: ain't what it used to be. *Management Today*, March, 42–3, 45–6.

Halfacree, G. (2013). Microsoft hit with €561m fine. *Bit-Tech*, 7 March. Retrieve from: http://www.bit-tech.net/news/bits/2013/03/07/microsoft-eu-fine/1 (accessed 29 March 2016).

Hallahan, K. (1999). Seven models of framing: implications for public relations. *Journal of Public Relations Research*, 11(3), 205–42.

Hasan, M. (2012). Mehdi Hasan on the not-so hidden fear behind halal hysteria. *New Statesman*, 9 May. Retrieve from: http://www.newstatesman.com/politics/politics/2012/05/halal-hysteria (accessed 5 April 2016).

Herriman, R. (2014). Deli meat sold in Sweden recalled due to listeria. *Outbreak News Today*, 23 August. Retrieve from: http://outbreaknewstoday.com/deli-meat-sold-in-sweden-recalled-due-to-listeria-36588/ (accessed 31 March 2016).

Hunt, S.D. and Vitell, S. (1986). A general theory of marketing ethics. *Journal of Macromarketing*, 6(1), 5–16.

Hunt, S.D. and Vitell, S.J. (2006). The general theory of marketing ethics: a revision and three questions. *Journal of Macromarketing*, 26(2), 143–53.

Hutton, A. (2015). Dutch trader Willy Selten jailed over horsemeat scandal. *The Times*, 7 April. Retrieve from: http://www.thetimes.co.uk/tto/news/world/europe/article4404198.ece (accessed 29 March 2016).

Izzo, J. (2015). VW scandal a growing-up time for the CSR movement. *Sustainable Brands*, 7 October. Retrieve from: http://www.sustainablebrands.com/news_and_views/marketing_comms/dr_john_izzo/vw_scandal_growing-_time_csr_movement (accessed 28 March 2016).

Jones, N., Baines, P., Craig, R., Tunnicliffe, I., and O'Shaughnessy, N.J. (2015). The Islamist cyberpropaganda threat and its counter-terrorism policy implications. In J.L. Richet (ed.), *Cybersecurity Policies and Strategies for Cyberwarfare Prevention*. Hershey, PA: IGI Global, 341–66.

Kaye, L. (2015). VW scandal exposes what has gone awry with 'CSR'. *Triple Pundit*, 23 February. Retrieve from: http://www.triplepundit.com/2015/09/vw-scandal-exposes-what-is-has-gone-awry-with-csr/ (accessed 29 March 2016).

Kazmin, A. (2015). Social media proves its power as Unilever feels the heat in India. *Financial Times*, 9 August. Retrieve from: http://www.ft.com/cms/s/0/0ec249f6-3ce9-11e5-8613-07d16aad2152.html#axzz44BoCjw2Z (accessed 30 March 2016).

Kim, S.Y. and Chun, S.Y. (2003). A study of marketing ethics in Korea. What do Koreans care about? *International Journal of Management*, 20(3), 377–83.

Kimes, S.E. and Wirtz, J. (2003). Has revenue management become acceptable? Findings from an international study on the perceived fairness of rate fences. *Journal of Service Research*, 6(2), 125–35.

King, M. (2012). Women count cost of car insurance as EU gender rules come into force. *The Guardian*, 21 December. Retrieve from: http://www.guardian.co.uk/money/2012/dec/21/women-car-insurance-eu (accessed 30 March 2016).

Kollewe, J. (2014). GlaxoSmithKline affirms policy of anti-corruption amid 14% profits fall. *The Guardian*, 23 July. Retrieve from: http://www.theguardian.com/business/2014/jul/23/glaxosmithkline-andrew-witty-anti-corruption-profits-fall (accessed 3 April 2016).

Kollewe, J.; Treanor, J., and Hickey, S. (2014). Banks pay out £166bn over six years: a history of banking misdeeds and fines. *The Guardian*, 12 November. Retrieve from: http://www.theguardian.com/business/2014/nov/12/

banks-fined-200bn-six-years-history-banking-penalties-libor-forex (accessed 31 March 2016).

Kottasova, I. (2014). World's most corrupt industries. *CNN Money*, 3 December. Retrieve from: http://money.cnn.com/2014/12/02/news/bribery-foreign-corruption/ (accessed 28 March 2016).

Laczniak, G.R. and Murphy, P.E. (1993). *Ethical Marketing Decisions: The Higher Road.* Englewood Cliffs, NJ: Prentice Hall.

Levick, R. (2015). New data: bribery is often 'an unspoken rule' in China. *Forbes*, 21 January. Retrieve from: http://www.forbes.com/sites/richardlevick/2015/01/21/new-data-bribery-is-often-an-unspoken-rule-in-china/#451e19ec45fc (accessed 1 April 2016).

Liu, F., Cheng, H., and Li, J. (2009). Consumer responses to sex appeal advertising: a cross-cultural study. *International Marketing Review*, 26(4/5), 501–20.

Lucas, L. (2013). Horsemeat scandal sheds light on tastes. *Financial Times*, 14 March. Retrieve from: http://www.ft.com/cms/s/0/7b6700d0-8bfa-11e2-8fcf-00144feabdc0.html#axzz2OsS38aHH (accessed 29 March 2016).

Lynn, M. (2015). Corporate social responsibility has become a racket—and a dangerous one. *The Telegraph*, 28 September. Retrieve from: http://www.telegraph.co.uk/finance/newsbysector/industry/11896546/Corporate-Social-Responsibility-has-become-a-racket-and-a-dangerous-one.html (accessed 28 March 2016).

McAlister, A. (2015). Call us before your ex does…, Slater and Gordon, 19 November. Retrieve from: http://www.slatergordon.co.uk/media-centre/blog/2015/11/call-us-before-your-ex-does-/ (accessed 29 March 2016).

McCoy, K. and Bomey, N. (2015). Shkreli resigns as Turing CEO. *USA Today*, 18 December. Retrieve from: http://www.usatoday.com/story/money/2015/12/18/martin-shkreli-turing-pharmaceuticals/77557514/ (accessed 31 March 2016).

McCurry, J. (2016). Former Tepco bosses charged over Fukushima meltdown. *The Guardian*, 29 February. Retrieve from: http://www.theguardian.com/environment/2016/feb/29/former-tepco-bosses-charged-fukushima (accessed 29 March 2016).

Maignan, I., Ferrell, O.C., and Ferell, L. (2005). A stakeholder model for implementing social responsibility in marketing. *European Journal of Marketing*, 39(9/10), 956–77.

Marshall, J. (2015). The VW scandal: huge consequences, simple ethics lessons, ominous implications. *Ethics Alarms*, 27 September. Retrieve from: http://ethicsalarms.com/2015/09/27/the-vw-scandal-huge-consequences-simple-ethics-lessons-ominous-implications/ (accessed 29 March 2016).

Marta, J.K.M. and Singhapakdi, A. (2005). Comparing Thai and US businesspeople: perceived intensity of unethical marketing practices, corporate ethical values and perceived importance of ethics. *International Marketing Review*, 22(5), 562–77.

Martin, R.L. (2002). The virtue matrix: calculating the return on corporate responsibility. *Harvard Business Review*, 80, 5–11.

Marx, K. (1867). *Capital: Critique of Political Economy*, Vol. 1. London: Penguin, 1990.

Mautner, T. (ed.) (1999). *Penguin Dictionary of Philosophy.* London: Penguin.

Maytom, T. (2016). Pornhub becomes Diesel's top referral website following ad deal. *Mobile Marketing*, 21 March. Retrieve from: http://mobilemarketingmagazine.com/pornhub-becomes-diesels-top-referral-site-following-ad-deal/ (accessed 30 April 2016).

Mintel (2013). Coca-Cola brings anti-obesity push to the UK, 11 April 2013. Retrieve from: http://www.mintel.com (accessed 5 April 2016).

Morris, D. (2008). Negative campaigning is good for America. *US News & World Report*, 6 October. Retrieve from: http://www.usnews.com/opinion/articles/2008/10/06/dick-morris-negative-campaigning-is-good-for-america (accessed 1 April 2016).

Nantel, J. and Weeks, W.A. (1996). Marketing ethics: is there more to it than the utilitarian approach? *European Journal of Marketing*, 30(5), 9–19.

Newman, K. (2001). The sorcerer's apprentice? Alchemy, seduction and confusion in modern marketing. *International Journal of Advertising*, 20, 409–29.

O'Shaughnessy, N.J. and Baines, P. (2009). The selling of terror: the symbolisations and positioning of jihad. *Marketing Theory*, 9(2), 227–41.

Oxford Dictionaries (2016). Ethics definition. Retrieve from: http://oxforddictionaries.com/definition/english/ethics?q = ethics (accessed 30 March 2016).

Packard, V.O. (1960). *The Hidden Persuaders.* Harmondsworth: Penguin Books.

Pagliery, J. (2015). Google abused its monopoly power, FTC experts found. *CNN Money*, 20 March. Retrieve from: http://money.cnn.com/2015/03/19/technology/google-monopoly-ftc/ (accessed 31 March 2016).

Paton, G. (2015). Buyers shun Volkswagen after diesel test scandal. *The Times*, 5 December, 49.

Peattie, K. (2001). Towards sustainability: the third age of green marketing. *Marketing Review*, 2, 129–46.

Peattie, K. and Crane, A. (2005). Green marketing: legend, myth, farce or prophesy? *Qualitative Market Research*, 8(4), 357–70.

Pike, J. (2015). *Project Fear: How an Unlikely Alliance Left a Kingdom United but a Country Divided. London*: Biteback.

Polman, P. (2012). Captain Planet—Interview with Paul Polman. *Harvard Business Review*, June, 112–18.

Pope, N.K.L., Voges, K.E., and Brown, M.R. (2004). The effect of provocation in the form of mild erotica on attitude to the ad and corporate image: differences between cause-related and product-based advertising. *Journal of Advertising*, 33(1), 69–82.

Porter, M.E. and Kramer, M.R. (2011). Creating shared value. *Harvard Business Review*, January-February. Retrieve from: https://hbr.org/2011/01/the-big-idea-creating-shared-value (accessed 3 August 2016).

Press Association (2013). How the horsemeat scandal unfolded—timeline. *The Guardian*, 15 February. Retrieve from: http://www.guardian.co.uk/world/2013/feb/08/how-horsemeat-scandal-unfolded-timeline (accessed 29 March 2016).

Press Association (2015). Slaughterhouse boss admits charges over UK horsemeat scandal. *The Guardian*, 28 January. Retrieve from: http://www.theguardian.com/uk-news/2015/jan/28/horsemeat-charge-peter-boddy-slaughterhouse-admits (accessed 29 March 2016).

Rao, C.P. and Singhapakdi, A. (1997). Marketing ethics: a comparison between services and other marketing professionals. *Journal of Services Marketing*, 11(6), 409–26.

Rawls, J. (1972). *A Theory of Justice*. Cambridge, MA: Harvard University Press.

Roland, D. (2015). GlaxoSmithKline bribery scandal led to 13-fold increase in China whistleblower reports. *The Telegraph*, 26 February. Retrieve from: http://www.telegraph.co.uk/finance/newsbysector/pharmaceuticalsandchemicals/11438063/GlaxoSmithKline-bribery-scandal-led-to-13-fold-increase-in-China-whistleblower-reports.html (accessed 1 April 2016).

Ruddick, G. (2015). Retailer admits 'duty' to farmers. *The Guardian*, 17 August, 21.

Rushe, D. (2014). Halliburton reaches $1.1bn settlement over Deepwater Horizon spill. *The Guardian*, 2 September. Retrieve from: http://www.theguardian.com/environment/2014/sep/02/halliburton-11bn-settlement-deepwater-horizon-spill (accessed 28 March 2016).

Saeed, M., Ahmed, Z.U., and Mukhtar, S-M. (2001). International marketing ethics from an Islamic perspective: a value-maximization approach. *Journal of Business Ethics*, 32, 127–42.

Saren, M. (2007). To have is to be? A critique of self-creation through consumption. *Marketing Review*, 7(4), 343–54.

Saren, M. (2011). Critical marketing: theoretical underpinnings. In G. Hastings, K. Angus, and C. Bryant (eds), *The Sage Handbook of Social Marketing*. London: Sage, 95–107.

Scheufele, D.A. and Tewksbury, D. (2007). Framing, agenda setting and priming: the evolution of three media effects models. *Journal of Communication*, 57, 9–20.

Shankar, A. (2009). Reframing critical marketing. *Journal of Marketing Management*, 25(7–8), 681–96.

Sharma, A., Gopalkrishnan, I.R., Mehotra, A., and Krishnan, R. (2010). Sustainability and business-to-business marketing: a framework and implications. *Industrial Marketing Management*, 39, 330–41.

Shayon, S. (2015). Unilever makes progress on Sustainable Living Plan. *Brandchannel*, 24 November. Retrieve from: http://www.brandchannel.com/2015/11/24/unilever-sustainability-112415/ (accessed 29 March 2016).

Sherover, E. (1979). The virtue of poverty: Marx's transformation of Hegel's concept of the poor. *Canadian Journal of Political and Social Theory*, 3(1), 53–66.

Sheth, J.N., Sethia, N.K., and Srinivas, S. (2011). Mindful consumption: a customer-centric approach to sustainability. *Journal of the Academy of Marketing Science*, 39, 21–39.

Singhapakdi, A., Marta, J.K., Rallapalli, K.C., and Rao, C.P. (2000b). Towards an understanding of religiousness and marketing ethics: an empirical study. *Journal of Business Ethics*, 27, 305–19.

Singhapakdi, A., Salyachivin, S., Virakul, B., and Veerayangkur, V. (2000a). Some important factors underlying ethical decision-making of managers in Thailand. *Journal of Business Ethics*, 27, 271–84.

Skapinker, M. (2010). Long-term corporate plans may be lost in translation. *Financial Times*, 23 November.

Smith, A. (1776). *The Wealth of Nations*. London: Penguin, 1982.

Smithers, R. (2016). Product recalls hit all-time high fuelled by car and food scandals. *The Guardian*, 14 March. Retrieve from: http://www.theguardian.com/money/2016/mar/14/product-recalls-hit-all-time-high-fuelled-by-car-and-food-scandals (accessed 28 March 2016).

Tadajewski, M. (2010). Towards a history of critical marketing studies. *Journal of Marketing Management*, 26(9–10), 773–824.

Taddonio, P. (2014). How we uncovered Firestone's deal with Charles Taylor. *PBS Frontline*, 18 November. Retrieve from: http://www.pbs.org/wgbh/frontline/article/how-we-uncovered-firestones-deal-with-charles-taylor/ (accessed 1 April 2016).

Tesco (2013). *What Matters Now: Using Our Scale for Good. Tesco and Society Report*. Retrieve from: http://www.tescoplc.com/files/pdf/reports/tesco_and_society_2013_ipad.pdf (accessed 31 March 2016).

Tovey, A. (2016). VW accounts delay 'may signal bigger costs from emissions scandal'. *The Telegraph*, 16 February. Retrieve from: http://www.telegraph.co.uk/finance/newsbysector/industry/12160427/VW-accounts-delay-may-signal-bigger-costs-from-emissions-scandal.html (accessed 28 March 2016).

Transparency International (2015). *Corrupt Perceptions Index 2015*. Retrieve from: http://www.transparency.org/cpi2015 (accessed 28 March 2016).

Treanor, J. (2015). FCA unable to estimate future PPI cost to banks. *The Guardian*, 26 November. Retrieve from: http://www.theguardian.com/money/2015/nov/26/fca-unable-to-estimate-future-ppi-cost-to-banks (accessed 30 March 2016).

Treanor, J. (2016). SFO ends foreign exchange fraud inquiry with no charges brought. *The Guardian*, 15 March. Retrieve from: http://www.theguardian.com/law/2016/mar/15/sfo-serious-fraud-office-foreign-exchange-inquiry-forex-rigging (accessed 31 March 2016).

Treanor, J. and Rushe, D. (2015). Banks hit by record fine for rigging forex markets. *The Guardian*, 20 May. Retrieve from: http://www.theguardian.com/business/2015/may/20/banks-hit-by-record-57bn-fine-for-rigging-forex-markets (accessed 31 March 2016).

Trotman, A. (2015). UK investors could start forex lawsuits after banking trio settle for $1bn in US. *The Telegraph*, 22 October. Retrieve from: http://www.telegraph.co.uk/finance/financial-crime/11949515/UK-investors-could-start-forex-lawsuits-after-banking-trio-settle-for-1bn-in-US.html (accessed 31 March 2016).

Unilever (2016). About Unilever. Retrieve from: https://www.unilever.com/about/who-we-are/about-Unilever/ (accessed 29 March 2016).

van Dam, Y.K. and Apeldoorn, P.A.C. (1996). Sustainable marketing. *Journal of Macromarketing*, 16, 45–56.

van de Wen, B. (2008). An ethical framework for the marketing of corporate social responsibility. *Journal of Business Ethics*, 82(2), 339–52.

WCED (World Commission on Environment and Development) (1987). *Our Common Future—The Brundtland Report*. Oxford: Oxford University Press.

Wearden, G. (2014). £2bn wiped off Tesco's value as profit overstating scandal sends shares sliding—as it happened. *The Guardian*, 22 September. Retrieve from: http://www.theguardian.com/business/live/2014/sep/22/tesco-launches-inquiry-after-overstating-profit-forecasts-by-250m-business-live (accessed 31 March 2016).

Wilkie, W.L. and Moore, E.S. (1999). Marketing's contributions to society. *Journal of Marketing*, 63, 198–218.

World Nuclear Association (2016). *Fukushima Incident*. March. Retrieve from: http://www.world-nuclear.org/information-library/safety-and-security/safety-of-plants/fukushima-accident.aspx (accessed 28 March 2016).

WRAP (2016). WRAP and the circular economy. Retrieve from: http://www.wrap.org.uk/content/wrap-and-circular-economy (accessed 28 March 2016).

Index